# A Genealogical and Heraldic History of the Commoners of Great Britain and Ireland, Enjoying Territorial Possessions Or High Official Rank, But Uninvested With Heritable Honours

# HISTORY

OF THE

# COMMONERS OF GREAT BRITAIN

# AND IRELAND.

VOL. III.

# A GENEALOGICAL AND HERALDIC HISTORY OF THE COMMONERS OF GREAT BRITAIN AND IRELAND,

ENJOYING TERRITORIAL POSSESSIONS OR HIGH OFFICIAL RANK;

BUT UNINVESTED WITH HERITABLE HONOURS.

---

BY JOHN BURKE, ESQ.

AUTHOR OF "THE HISTORY OF THE PEERAGE AND BARONETAGE,"

"OF THE EXTINCT AND DORMANT PEERAGE," &c.

---

IN FOUR VOLUMES.

VOL. III.

---

LONDON:

PUBLISHED FOR HENRY COLBURN,

BY R. BENTLEY: BELL AND BRADFUTE, EDINBURGH; J. CUMMING, DUBLIN; AND SOLD BY ALL BOOKSELLERS.

MDCCCXXXVI.

CHARLES WHITTINGHAM, TOOKS COURT, CHANCERY LANE.

TO

GEORGE STANLEY CARY, ESQ.

OF FOLLATON HOUSE, IN THE COUNTY OF DEVON,

OF THE

ANCIENT AND HISTORICAL FAMILY OF THAT NAME,

This Volume,

WITH SENTIMENTS OF SINCERE ESTEEM,

IS

RESPECTFULLY INSCRIBED.

## PREFACE.

In presenting the Third Volume of this Work, nothing remains for the Author beyond again reiterating his acknowledgments of the kind and liberal assistance which he continues to receive from his literary contemporaries, as well as the courtesy universally accorded him by those with whom he finds it necessary to communicate. The Work upon which he is engaged would have been undertaken in vain, by industry no matter how persevering, or exertion however enterprizing, were it not for such important aid; but in this free and flourishing empire, every thing deemed of national usefulness is secure of national protection.

# ALTERATIONS AND ADDITIONS.

DENNE OF KENT AND SUSSEX.

P. 20. Although several writers state WILLIAM DENNE, the first of Denne Hill, to be descended from Ralph de Dene, the father of ELA, who married Sir Jordan Sackville, yet the Dorset Roll calls Ela co-heiress with her sister or niece Sybella, and she is in Collins and elsewhere mentioned as co-heiress of her brother Robert. The Dorset Roll also assigns a different coat of arms to Ralph than that borne by the Dennes of Denne Hill.

P. 21, col. 2, l. 3 from bottom. Sarah Greenland, the wife of Thomas Denne, esq. died at Lydd, and not at Fairfield, as erroneously stated at page 21.

PLUMPTRE OF FREDVILLE.

P. 76, col. 1, l. 22. JOHN PLUMPTRE, esq. of Nottingham, *b.* in 1679, who married Annabella, eldest daughter of Sir Francis Molyneux, bart. had, with other issue,

- JOHN, his heir, of Nottingham, M.P. grandfather of the present JOHN PEMBERTON PLUMPTRE, esq. of Fredville, M.P. for Kent.
- Robert, D.D. master of Queen's College, Cambridge, in 1773, who died in 1788, leaving
  - Joseph, in holy orders, *d. s. p.*
  - James, in holy orders, rector of Great Grandsdon, *d. s. p.*
  - Robert, of Norwich, barrister-at-law, married, and has one daughter.
  - Diana, *m.* 7th April, 1781, to her cousin, the Rev. John Plumptre, and *d.* in 1825.
  - Anne, the authoress, died unmarried.
  - Lydia, } living unmarried
  - Arabella, } in 1836.
  - Jemima, *m.* to Frederick Layton, esq. captain of marines.
- Septimus, who *m.* in 1753, at St. Michael's Royal, College Hill, London, Catharine Young, and left at his decease, 5th February, 1782, aged sixty-four, two surviving sons and one daughter,
  1. John, *b.* 11th March, 1754, baptized at Mansfield 8th April following, vicar of Stone, in the county of Worcester, in 1778, vicar of Stoke Prior in 1788, prebendary of Worcester in 1789, and dean of Gloucester in 1808. He *m.* in 1781, his cousin-german Diana, daughter of the Rev. Robert Plumptre, D.D. and dying in 1825 left issue,
     - John-Francis, *b.* 4th December, 1781, fellow of Eton College, *m.* Caroline, daughter of — Carter, esq. of Foxley, Wilts, and is now (1836) living a widower without issue.
     - Henry-Scawen, M.A, minister of St. Mary's Chapel, Lambeth, and alternate evening preacher at the Foundling Hospital, *b.* 11th December, 1789.
     - Robert-Bathurst, *b.* 27th September, 1791, *m.* Susanna, daughter of the Rev. Iltyd Nicholl, and has issue.
     - Tryphena-Mary.
     - Annabella.
  2. Charles, *b.* 13th February, 1755, rector of Teversal, Notts, and afterwards of Longnewton, in the county of Durham, *m.* 14th January, 1780, Mary, daughter of — Mellar, esq. of Mansfield, and *d.* in May, 1812; he had issue,

Kaye-Francis, *b.* 6th July, 1784, *d.* unmarried in India about the year 1805.

Edward-Hallows, of the Temple, *b.* 27th October, 1785, *m.* in October, 1816, Eliza, dau. of the late Jacob Pitfield, esq. of Symondsbury, Dorset, and has issue.

Frederick-Charles, fellow of University College, Oxford.

Frances, *m.* to George Hodgkinson, of Southwell, Notts, and *d.* in 1833.

Maria, } living unmar-
Dorothy, } ried in 1836.

3. Edward, *d.* young in 1768.

1. Dorothy, *m.* 7th April, 1783, to Francis Evans, esq. of Nottingham, and is now (1836) living a widow.

WENTWORTH OF WOOLLEY.

P. 93. Godfrey Wentworth Wentworth, esq. of Woolley Park, died in 1833, and *not* in 1826.

LUCY OF CHARLECOTE.

P. 97. Martha, third daughter and coheiress of Francis Lucy, esq. (fifth son of Sir Thomas Lucy), by Elizabeth, his wife, daughter and heiress of Bevill Molesworth, esq. of Hoddesdon, Herts, married SIR SAMUEL EYRE, knt. of Newhouse and Chilhampton (see page 291).

P. 99, col. 1, l. 10, for "JUSTICE SLENDER," read "JUSTICE SHALLOW."

WHIELDON OF SPRINGFIELD HOUSE.

P. 116. The subjoined is a more correct engraving of the Whieldon arms than that inserted at page 116:

FERRERS OF BADDESLEY CLINTON.

P. 129, col. 1, l. 14 from bottom, for "GEORGE, VISCOUNT TAMWORTH," read "GEORGE, EARL OF LEICESTER."

D'ARCY OF KILTULLA.

P. 146, col. 1, l. 12. Omit from "and" down to "Firbough."

M'KERRELL OF HILLHOUSE.

P. 173. JOHN M'KERRELL, esq. of Hillhouse, died in 1835.

CORBET OF ELSHAM.

P. 190, col. 2, l. 6 from bottom, for "the second son of Robert (by his wife Dorothy), THOMAS CORBETT acquired the estate of Nash," read "the second son of Robert, THOMAS CORBETT, acquired by his wife, Dorothy, the estate of Nash."

SEYMOUR OF CASTLETOWN.

P. 202. It is there stated that SIR HENRY SEYMOUR married Barbara, daughter of Thomas Morgan, esq. of Tredegar, a fact which admits of doubt, if not of refutation. Collins and Edmonson make Sir Henry to marry Barbara Morgan, and so does an inscription to the memory of Sir John Seymour in Great Bedwin Church, which in enumerating the issue of "the worthie knight," says that his second surviving son, "Sir Henry Seymour, married Barbara, daughter of Thomas Morgan, Esquier." Other authorities, however, of equal credit, call the wife of Sir Henry, "Barbara, daughter of Morgan Wolfe, esq." In a manuscript among the Harleian collections, No. 1529, occurs the following entry: "Henricus Seimor, Miles = Barbara, f. Morgani Wolfe." This assertion is repeated by Sir Richard Hoare, in his History of South Wilts, thus: "Sir Henry Seymour, knighted 1546 =Barbara, dau. to Morgan Wolfe." And in the Herald's College, the following descent of Sir Henry's wife is given: "Sir Henry Seymour, of Marwell, com. Southampton, knight, second son of Sir John Seymour, of Wolfhall, by Margery Wentworth, married Barbara, daughter of Morgan Wolfe, by Gwenllian, daughter and heir of John de Barri. Morgan Wolfe was the son of Howell Wolfe, the son of John Wolfe, esq. the son of Sir William Wolfe, knt. by the daughter and co-heir of Sir Majo Le Sore, of St. Fagans, by the daughter and heir of Huntley."

Besides, in analysing the coat armour of Sir Henry which is set up on the monument of his father in Great

Bedwyn Church, we find it to be as follows: Gu. two wings conjoined and inverted or, with a crescent of the last for the second son of SEYMOUR, impaling quarterly;

1. Arg. a fess between three martlets gu. on a chief sa. three wolves' heads erased arg. for WOLFE of Gwerngotheyn.

2. Per pale sa. and az. three fleurs-de-lys or, for WOLFE-NEWTON.

3. Or, three wolves passant az. for NANFANT.

4. Arg. on a chev. gu. between three stags' heads caboshed sa. three bugle horns arg. stringed or, for LE SORE, of St. Fagans, Glamorganshire.

Thus the arms and the inscription on the same monument disagree. It should be observed that the said monument was erected by Edward, Earl of Hertford, fifty-four years after the death of Sir John, and twelve after that of Sir Henry, on the occasion of Sir John's body being removed to Bedwyn from the ruined church of Easton Priory.

MORRICE OF BETSHANGER.—The following is a more correct account of the early ancestry of this family than that given at pages 232 and 233:

Athelstan or Elystan Glodrydd, Prince of Fferlex, m. Gwladys, daughter of Rhûn ap Ednowain, Prince of Tegengl.

Cadwgan ap Elystan, m. Margaret, daughter of Brochwel ap Aeddan, of Powys.

Hoedliw ap Cadwgan.

Rys ap Hoedliw.

Hoedliw Goch ap Rys.

Gwrgenau ap Hoedliw Goch.

Grono ap Gwrgenau.

Griffith ap Grono.

Madoc ap Griffith.

Howel ap Madoc.

Philip Dorddû ap Howel.

Cadwgan, second son of Philip Dorddû, m. Eva, daughter of Llewelyn Crygeryr.

David ap Cadwgan, m. Tanglwyst, daughter of Griffith ap Ieuan Lloyd, descended from Llowdden.

Philip ap David.

Ieuan ap Philip, of Carm, m. Margaret, daughter of Ieuan ap Meredith.

Rys or Rees ap Ieuan, m. Mallt, daughter and co-heir of Ieuan Gwrgan.

Morgan ap Rees, m. Gwenllian, daughter of David ap Guttin ap Ieuan Ddû.

Morys ap Morgan, m. Ellen, daughter of Ieuan ap Griffith Ddû.

William Morys, &c. as in the body of the work.

BRAY OF SHERE.

P. 244, col. 2, l. 46, for "Mary, m. to — Bluet, esq." read "Mary, m. to Edward Blewitt, esq. of Salford, in Oxfordshire." The issue of this Mary Bray, who married Edward Blewitt, was,

1. EDMUND-REGINALD BLEWITT, whose descendant is residing at Lantarnam.

1. Mary Blewitt, m. to Joseph Newton, esq.
2. Catherine Blewitt, m. to William Durham, esq. and was mother of Catherine Durham, who wedded Colonel Kingsmill Evans (see vol. ii. p. 244).

REES OF KILLYMAENLLWYD.—The following is a more correct account of the descent of this family than that at page 265.

URIEN-RHEGED, Prince of Rheged in Wales, by birth a Cambro-Briton, was fifth in descent from Coel Codevog, King of the Britons. He built the castle of Carrey Cermin, in Carmarthenshire, although the erection of that edifice is ascribed by some to no earlier a date than the time of HENRY I. The style of the architecture and the authority of the Golden Grove MSS. seem, however, to establish its ancient British construction. Urien, who bore for arms arg. a chev. sa. between three ravens ppr. surmounted by a crown, m. the daughter of Gwrlois, Duke of Cornwall, and was direct ancestor of

SIR ELIDIR DDÛ, knight of the Sepulchre, *temp.* RICHARD I. who m. the daughter of Sysyllt, lord of Cantreselyf, and had a son,

PHILIP AP SIR ELIDIR DDÛ, who m. Gwladys, daughter of David Vras (descended from Bledri, son of Cadivor Vawr, lord of Blaencych, who lived *temp.* WILLIAM *the Conqueror*), and was father of

NICHOLAS AP PHILIP, of Newton, in Dynevor, who m. Jenett, daughter of Llewellyn Voethus, descended from Elystan Glodydd,

Prince between Wye and Severn, and had a son and successor,

GRYFFITH AP NICHOLAS, of Newton, who had by his wife, the daughter of Meredith Donne,* of Iscoed, two sons, THOMAS, father of the famed Sir Rhys ap Thomas, K.B. lineal ancestor of the present LORD DYNEVOR, and

OWEN AP GRYFFITH (whom some state to have been the eldest son of Gryffith, *Golden Grove MSS.*) He *m.* Alice, daughter of Henry Malyphant, esq. of Upton, in Pembrokeshire, and had, with other issue, a son and successor,

MORRIS AP OWEN, esq. of Llechdwnny, who *m.* Elizabeth, daughter of Thomas Lewis, esq. of St. Pierre, and had issue,

- JOHN BOWEN, of Bryn y Beirdd, *m.* Margaret, daughter of Howell David ap Einon ap David Vrâs.
- Thomas, from whom descended the Upton family.
- REES, of whom presently.
- Jane, *m.* to Hugh Vaughan, esq. of Mdwelly, the father of John Vaughan, esq. of Golden Grove, whose grandson, John Vaughan was created Earl of Carbery by JAMES I.
- Elizabeth, *m.* to David ap Rhydderch Gwynne, esq. of Glanbran.

The third son,

REES BOWEN, of Llechdwnny, in Kidwelly Land, *m.* Jenet, daughter of Henry ap Owen ap Cadwgan of that place, and had (with two daughters, the elder, Jenet, *m.* to Rees ap Owen, and the younger to John Llwyd Aubrey), a son,

MORRIS BOWEN, esq. of Llechdwnny, who *m.* Catherine, daughter of Thomas ap Rhydderch Gwynne, esq. of Glanbran, and had issue,

- RHYS, his heir.
- Charles.
- Lucy, *m.* to David Read, esq.
- Elizabeth, *m.* to Henry Morgan, esq.

The elder son,

RHYS BOWEN, esq. of Llechdwnny, *m.* Catherine, daughter of John Morgan, of Kidwelly, and had issue,

- MORRIS, of Llechdwnny, high sheriff of Carmarthenshire in 1615. He *m.* Maud, daughter of Sir John Wogan, of Boulston, and had several children, one of whom, Mary, *m.* John Brigstock, esq. to whom Morris, her father, passed the estate for a sum of money. Attached to the ancient property is a chapel on the south side of Kidwelly church, forming a wing to it. On the opposite side is a similar chapel, which belonged to the Mansels of Iscoed.
- JOHN, of whom presently.
- Elizabeth, *m.* to David Lloyd, esq. of Llanstephan.
- Anne.
- Dorothy, *m.* to Thomas Philipps, esq.

The younger son,

JOHN BOWEN, esq. of Carmarthen, living in the early part of the 17th century, *m.* Eva, daughter of David Havard, of the same place, and was father of

WILLIAM BOWEN, esq. whose son,

RHYS WILLIAM AP OWEN, esq. of Kilverry, was father of

JOHN REES AP WILLIAM, esq. who was *s.* by his son,

HECTOR REES, esq. *b.* in 1683, of Killymaenllwyd, from whom the descent down to the present proprietor is correctly given at page 266.

## Family of Hughes,

*Now represented by that of* REES.

GWYNFARDD DYVED, who lived about the year 1038, *temp.* EDWARD the Confessor, was direct ancestor of DANIEL HUGHES, but the intervening line is too extended to be inserted here. We must not, however, omit, that it is mentioned in the Golden Grove MSS. that one of Hughes's ancestors, "Howell *Gawr* was so surnamed for his valour, having overthrown the French king's champion (probably at Chalons, where EDWARD I. held the field at a tournament against all comers), and obtained for his arms gu. a lion rampt. or, in a true love knot arg. inter four delisses, their stalks bending towards the centre of the escocheon of the second." Daniel married, and had a son,

EDWARD HUGHES, esq. of Penymaes,* in Carmarthenshire, who *m.* Mary, daughter of

* This Meredith Donne, or Dwn, was paternally descended from Meiric, king of Dyved, who was one of the four kings that bore the sword before King Arthur at his coronation at Caerlleon upon Usk. His descendant, Gryffith, from some jealousy, so frequent among the Welsh chieftains, and which facilitated the subjugation of the country, took part with Morris de Londres, in his attack on Kidwelly, and was commander of the army in the battle fought near that town against Gwenllian, wife of Griffith ab Rhys, Prince of South Wales, wherein herself and two sons were slain. The place where the battle was fought is called Maes Gwenllian, or Gwenllian's Plain, to this day. Philip, the grandson of Griffith, however, seems to have taken a different course; for he fought a battle against the Anglo-Normans at a place called Cragg-Cyrn, near Kidwelly, in which he defeated them, and burnt that town. From these Donnes was descended Donne of TyGwynne, whose daughter Robert, brother to Hector Rees, married.

* On the Demesne of Penymaes are the remains of a chapel, attached to the family house in Catholic times, and to which an avenue of stately fir trees led from the mansion.

John Bowen, of Kittle Hill, and had three sons, DANIEL, his heir; Rowland, who *m.* the widow of John Mansel, esq. and Samuel. The eldest,

DANIEL HUGHES, esq. of Penymaes, *m.* Mary, daughter of the Rev. James Davies, of Begelly, and was father of

ARTHUR HUGHES, esq. of Penymaes, who *m.* Judith, daughter of the Rev. William George, rector of Stackpool, and left a son and successor,

DANIEL HUGHES, esq. of Penymaes, who *m.* Mary, daughter of Morris Lloyd, esq. and was *s.* by his son,

ARTHUR HUGHES, esq. of Penymaes, who *m.* Esther, daughter of Samuel Thomas, esq. of Pentowyn, and had issue,

I. DANIEL, of Penymaes, high sheriff of Carmarthenshire in 1708. He *m.* Amy, daughter of the Rev. Thomas Powell, rector of Llangunnor, and had an only daughter and heiress,

MARY, *m.* to John Rees esq. of Killymaenllwyd.

II. Lewis, from whom descend the Hugheses, of Treglb, Carmarthenshire.

JONES OF BEALANAMORE.

P. 269, col. 1, l. 3. Admiral Theophilus Jones died in November, 1835.

BURTON OF MOUNT ANVILLE.

P. 271. William Burton, the historian of Leicestershire, was buried in a vault in *Hornbury* Church, not *Tutbury*.

P. 272. Joshua Burton did not die until 4th July, 1829.

P. 273. Charles-James Burton married Eliza, daughter of William *Boteler*, not *Betcher*.

BIDDULPH OF BIDDULPH.

P. 280. JOHN BIDDULPH, esq. of Biddulph, died in 1835.

NICHOLSON OF BALLOW.

P. 357, add after "Robert *b.* 22nd July, 1809," B.A. of Trinity College, Dublin, in February, 1830.

P. 358, col. 1. William Nicholson, *b.* in 1587, who *m.* Janet Brown, and had by her three sons,

1. John, who *d.* before his father, leaving a daughter, Janet, living in 1665.
2. Hugh, who succeeded his father, he was living in 1681, and was *s.* by his brother.
3. William, of Ballow, who *m.* Miss Eleanor Dunlop.

P. 358, col. 1, l. 17, for "Isabella," read "Isabell" (she is so styled in the wills of her father, John Blackwood, of Bangor, her brother, John Blackwood, of Ballyleidy, and her husband, Alexander Hamilton).

P. 358, col. 1, l. 21, for "1797," read "1787."

P. 358, col. 1, l. 40, for "*William* Rose," read "*Richard* Rose."

P. 358, col. 1, l. 43, for "— Wells, of Belfast," read "*George* Wells, of Belfast, merchant."

P. 358, col. 1. John Steele, of Portavoe, was born about the year 1655, and died in 1721.

P. 358, col. 2. John Steele, of Belfast, was born about the year 1689, and died in 1740.

P. 358, col. 2, l. 33, for "*elder*," read "*only*."

O'DONOVAN OF THE COUNTY OF CORK.

P. 399, col. 1, l. 7, for "the *Rev. Morgan Donovan*, A.B. Oxon, born in 1687," read "Morgan Donovan, esq. A.B. Oxon, *b.* in 1687." Mr. Donovan was not in orders nor any other profession, though a graduate of Oxford, and in the commission of the peace from GEORGE II.

CHADWICK OF MAVESYN REDWARE.

P. 438. Add to the issue of the present MR. CHADWICK, a son and heir,

JOHN DE HELBY, *b.* 30th December, 1834, baptized at St. Mary's, Bathwick, near Bath.

P. 443, col. 1, l. 20, for "James Fort*rage*, esq." read "James Fort*rye*, esq."

MACPHERSON OF CLUNY MACPHERSON.

P. 463, col. 1, l. 3 from bottom, for "Ewan, *next brother* of Dougal," read "Ewan, the *uncle* of Dougal."

MACLEOD OF MACLEOD.

P. 484, col. 2, l. 30, for "1831," read "1821."

P. 484, col. 2, l. 39, for "John Leod," read "Harold John Leod."

The late Macleod of Macleod had, besides the issue mentioned at p. 484, a son, Torquil-James, who died 3rd April, 1821, aged seven; and a daughter, Eleanor-Anne, who died 3rd December, 1830, aged thirteen.

PENN OF STOKE PARK.

P. 491, l. 14, for "1104," read "1804."

P. 491, l. 15, for "Sir William Go*mon*, K.C.B." read "Sir William Go*mm*, K.C.B."

P. 494, col. 1. Sophia-Margaret, relict of the Hon. and Most Rev. William Stuart, D.D. Archbishop of Armagh, was daughter of Thomas Penn, esq. of Stoke Pogeis, and *not* of William Baker, esq. of Bayfordbury, as erroneously stated in the body of the work.

DE BURGH OF WEST DRAYTON.

P. 502, col. 2, l. 36, for "armed ar. a bugle horn az." read "stringed as a bugle horn az."

BEDINGFELD OF DITCHINGHAM.

P. 506, col. 2, l. 7 from bottom, for "*O*burgh," read "*Ox*burgh."

TRAPPES OF NIDD.

P. 523. The following is the early descent of the Trappes family.

**Lineage.**

The family of De Trappes, or De Trappé as it is sometimes found written, possessed in the beginning of the 13th century a castle called Delle-Weige, on the borders of Germany, near the Meuse, with a manor and jurisdiction appertaining to the said castle, which is proved by a verdict on the rolls of the said court, anno Domini, 1352.

Severus De Trappé, of Delle Weige, became a carmelite, and gave to his order at his profession a field called to this day "Pié des Carmes," part of the manor of Delle Weige, this Severus died anno 1314.

William De Trappes, knt. called Delle Weige, bore arms, field argent, three caltrops sable (2 and 1), surmounted with a crown, married Gertrude D'Ordingarne, of a noble family, of the county of Cologne, had issue, William de Trappès, Stephen de Trappès, and Severus de Trappès. Stephen de Trappès became a captain in the army of Edward III. by whom he was, after his wars in France, invited to accompany him to England, and from whom he received a grant of lands in or near Theydonbois, in the county of Essex, from whence has descended the family of Trappes.

The original branch of this family was still existent in the county of Liege, in the beginning of the 18th century, and was then allied to the family of Luxembourg.

POYNTZ OF COWDRAY.

P. 537. The present Mr. POYNTZ's two sons, William-Montague-Browne Poyntz, and Courtenay-John-Browne Poyntz, are both deceased.

RHODES OF BELLAIR.

P. 563, col. 2, l. 8 from bottom, for "*L*adsant," read "*C*adsant."

P. 567, col. 2, l. 25 from bottom, for "*T*anger," read "*Z*anger."

P. 568, col. 1, l. 14 from top, for "the *only* son," read "the *eldest* son."

---

VAUGHAN OF BURLTON HALL.

Vol. ii. p. 15, col. 1, lines from foot 24, 30 and 31, for "Newton Chapel," read "Newtown Chapel."

P. 15, col. 2, line 15 from foot, for "1779," read "1773."

P. 239, col. 1, l. 6, for "Ynir ap Cadvioch," read "Ynyr ap Cadviôch."

P. 239, col. 2, l. 27 and 28, for "Gravelkind Tenure," read "Gavelkind Tenure."

P. 240, col. 1, l. 20, for "22nd May," read "2nd May."

P. 240, col. 1, l. 14 from foot, for "Arthur Noneby," read "Arthur Noneley."

P. 241, col. 2, l. 24 from foot, for "Whittal," read "Whettal."

P. 242, col. 1, l. 33, for "1804," read "1803."

CRAWFURDS OF SCOTLAND.

In support of the curious hypothesis respecting the origin of the CRAWFURDS, and their descent from the old EARLS OF RICHMOND, given in vol. ii. p. xiv. we have to add the following remarks; to shew, first, that THEOBALD, the reputed ancestor of the Douglases, and BALDWIN DE BIGGAR, who married the widow of the founder of the Crawfurd family in Scotland, were settlers in Yorkshire under the *Earls of Richmond, previous to their removal to Scotland,* to which country they emigrated by following the fortunes of Reginald, youngest son of their patron Alan, fourth Earl of Richmond, and acquired lands contiguous to his in Strath Clyde and its vicinity: secondly, to adduce the case of the Vaux arms, as illustrative of *the fess being a mark of cadence from the bend:* and thirdly, to confirm the preceding by the recorded relationship of John le Scott (who was nearly allied to the Earl of Richmond) with Galfridus de Crawfurd in a charter quoted by George Crawfurd.

On reference to Clarkson's History of Richmond, compiled chiefly from Gale's Register Honorum Richmondæ, it appears that a charter of Alan, fourth Earl of Richmond, is witnessed in 1145, among others, by THEOBALD and by BALDWIN, and another similar charter in the subsequent year by Baldwin de Multon (Malton), in Richmondshire, the patrimony of the Earls of Richmond. Baldwin would thus appear to have been connected with the Earls of Richmond, as holding lands under them, prior to the appearance of the name in connexion with Scottish record; and, although the occurrence of even one of those uncommon names, THEOBALD or BALDWIN, on record in England, at a period so immediately preceding its first appearance in Scotland, would lead to infer the probable identity of the individual bearing the appellation, that identity may surely be assumed as resting upon sufficient grounds when two individuals of such remarkable cognominals (from the same country) can thus be traced in mutual transactions in both kingdoms. And if the connexion thus apparent between Baldwin and the Earl of Richmond can be shown to have extended itself more intimately on the part of Baldwin with the family of Crawfurd, which, in ignorance of the present adduced facts, we have already traced on

# HISTORY OF THE COMMONERS

OF

# GREAT BRITAIN AND IRELAND.

## ABERCROMBY,

### Speaker of the House of Commons,

ELECTED 19 FEBRUARY, 1835.

ABERCROMBY, *The Right Honourable* JAMES, Speaker of the House of Commons, *b.* 7th November, 1776, *m.* 14th June, 1802, Mary-Anne, daughter of the late Egerton Leigh, esq. of West Hall, in High Legh, and has one son,

RALPH, Secretary of Legation at Berlin, *b.* 6th April, 1803.

Mr. Abercromby, who was formerly Lord Chief Baron of the Court of Exchequer in Scotland, and subsequently Master of the Mint, represents the city of Edinburgh in Parliament, and was elected SPEAKER of the House of Commons in 1835.

### Lineage.

THOMAS ABERCROMBY, of that Ilk, *temp.* JAMES II. of Scotland, who was one of the lords of session, or, as it was then called, of the committee of parliament, left, with a daughter, Margaret, *m.* to Maule, of Panmure, a son,



THOMAS ABERCROMBY, of Abercromby, whose line continued till the reign of CHARLES I. *anno* 1649, when another Thomas Abercromby sold the barony to Sir James Sandilands, who, upon his elevation to the peerage, in 1647, assumed the title of Baron Abercromby. A cadet of the Abercrombys of that Ilk,

HUMPHREY DE ABERCROMBY, obtained, about the year 1315, a charter, from Robert Bruce, of the lands of Harthill and Ardun. He was father of

ALEXANDER DE ABERCROMBY, living in the time of DAVID II. who acquired, from Patrick Hay, a half portion of the lands of Ardhuienyn. To him succeeded another

ALEXANDER DE ABERCROMBY, designed of Pitmithen, father of

ALEXANDER DE ABERCROMBY, of Pitmithen, living in 1454. The next in succession,

JAMES ABERCROMBY, of Pitmithen, Ley, and Birkenbog, *m.* Margaret, daughter of

Sir James Ogilvie, of Findlater, and is supposed to have fallen at Flodden. His son and heir,

GEORGE ABERCROMBY, of Pitmithen, left, by Christian, his wife, daughter of Barclay, of Gartlay, a son,

JAMES ABERCROMBY, of Pitmithen, living in 1527, who *m.* Marjory Hay, said to be a daughter of William, Earl of Errol, and was succeeded by his son,

ALEXANDER ABERCROMBY, of Birkenbog, living in 1550, who *m.* Elizabeth, daughter of Leslie, of Pitcaple, and was father of

ALEXANDER ABERCROMBY, of Birkenbog, who wedded Margaret, daughter of William Leslie, of Balquhain, and had two sons,

- JAMES, his heir.
- Alexander, of Fitterneir, whose son, Alexander, of Fitterneir, married Jean, daughter of John Seaton, of Newark, and had FRANCIS, of Fitterneir, created, by JAMES VII. Lord Glassford for life; and Patrick, M.D. author of the "Martial Achievements of the Scottish Nation."

The elder son,

JAMES ABERCROMBY, of Birkenbog, was father of

ALEXANDER ABERCROMBY, of Birkenbog, falconer to CHARLES I. who *m.* Elizabeth, daughter of Bethune, of Balfour, and had, with a daughter, *m.* to Robert Grant, of Dalvey, three sons,

- I. ALEXANDER, his heir.
- II. John, of Glasshaugh.
- III. Walter, of Braconhills.

The eldest son,

ALEXANDER ABERCROMBY, of Birkenbog, who was created a BARONET in 1636, *m.* first, Jane, daughter of Sir Thomas Urquhart, of Cromarty; secondly, Jane Sutherland, of Kilwinity; and thirdly, Elizabeth, daughter of Sir James Baird, of Auchmedden. By the last lady he had two sons, viz.

- I. JAMES, second baronet, of Birkenbog, great-grandfather of the present SIR ROBERT ABERCROMBY, bart. of Birkenbog.
- II. ALEXANDER, of whose line we have to treat.

Sir Alexander was so zealous a partisan against *King* CHARLES I., that he is styled by an historian of the period "a main covenanter." In May, 1645, he joined Major Urry, and was at the battle of Auldearn; but Montrose retaliated, by quartering himself and some of his troops at Birkenbog. Sir Alexander was *s.* by his elder son, SIR JAMES ABERCROMBY, from whom the present baronet of Birkenbog; while the second son,

ALEXANDER ABERCROMBY, settled at Tullibody, in the county of Clacmannan, having inherited that estate from his cousin, George Abercromby, of Skeith. Alexander was *s.* by his son,

GEORGE ABERCROMBY, esq. of Tullibody, who wedded Mary, daughter of Ralph Dundas, esq. of Manour, and had (with two younger sons, Barnet Abercromby, and General Sir Robert Abercromby, K.B.) his successor,

SIR RALPH ABERCROMBY, of Tullibody, who so gloriously fell at the moment of victory in the chief command of the British forces at the great and decisive battle of Alexandria, 28th March, 1801. This gallant officer *m.* Mary-Anne, dau. of John Menzies, esq. of Fernton, in the county of Perth, which lady, when an official account of the triumph and fate of her lamented husband reached England, was elevated to the peerage as BARONESS ABERCROMBY, with remainder to the male heirs of the deceased general. By Sir Ralph her ladyship had issue,

- GEORGE, present LORD ABERCROMBY. (See BURKE'S *Peerage*.)
- John (Sir), G.C.B. a general officer, who died unmarried in 1817.
- JAMES, SPEAKER OF THE HOUSE OF COMMONS, and, ex-officio, the *first* COMMONER IN THE UNITED KINGDOM.
- Alexander, C.B. a colonel in the army, born 4th March, 1784.
- Anne, married to Donald Cameron, esq. of Lochiel.
- Mary.
- Catherine, *m.* in 1811, to Thomas Buchanan, esq.

*Arms*—Or, a fesse embattled gu. therefrom issuant in chief a dexter arm embowed in armour ppr. garnished or, encircled by a wreath of laurel, the hand supporting the French invincible standard, in bend sinister, also ppr. in base a chev. indented of the second, between three boars' heads erased az.

*Crest*—A bee ppr.

*Motto*—Vive ut vivas.

# GRANVILLE, OF CALWICH ABBEY.

**GRANVILLE, COURT**, esq. of Calwich Abbey, in the county of Stafford, *b.* in 1779, *m.* in 1803, Maria, daughter of Edward Ferrers, esq. of Baddesley Clinton, in Warwickshire, and has issue,

I. BERNARD, *b.* in 1804, who *m.* first, Mathewana-Sarah, second daughter of Captain Onslow, of the Coldstream Guards, eldest son of Admiral Sir Richard Onslow, bart. K. C. B. and has, by her who *d.* in August, 1829, one daughter,

Joan-Frederica-Mathewana.

Mr. Granville wedded, secondly, in 1830, Anne-Catherine, daughter of Admiral Sir Hyde Parker, and has one son and a daughter, viz.

BEVIL, *b.* 20th January, 1834.
Fanny.

II. Granville-John, *b.* in 1807.
III. Court, *b.* in 1808.
IV. Frederic, *b.* in 1810.
I. Harriet-Joan.
II. Mary.
III. Lucy.

This gentleman, whose patronymic is D'EWES, succeeded his father, Bernard D'Ewes, esq. of Wellesbourne, in December, 1822, and assumed in 1827, on inheriting the estates of his uncle, the Rev. John Granville, of Calwich Abbey, the surname and arms of GRANVILLE. Mr. Granville is a magistrate and deputy lieutenant for the counties of Warwick and Stafford.

## Lineage.

"It is a melancholy reflection," says Dr. Borlase, "to look back on so many great families who have formerly adorned the county of Cornwall, and in the male line are now no more; the GRANVILLES, the Carminows, the Champernownes, the Bodrugans, Mohuns, Killegrews, Bevils, Trevanions, which had great sway and possessions in these parts. The most lasting families have only their seasons, more or less, of a certain constitutional strength. They have their spring, and summer sunshine glare, their wane, decline and death." The Granvilles claim descent from ROLLO, the celebrated northern chieftain, who being driven from Norway by the king of Denmark, made a descent upon England, but was repulsed by ALFRED. He was subsequently however more fortunate in a similar attempt upon Normandy. Invading that country in 870, he achieved its complete conquest in 912, and was invested with the ducal dignity. He married Gilbette, daughter of CHARLES the *Simple*, KING OF FRANCE, and had two sons. From the elder, WILLIAM, descended the CONQUEROR, and from ROBERT, the younger, created earl of Corbeil, sprang two brothers, Robert Fitzhamon, who reduced Glamorganshire, (he left an only daughter, Mabel, the wife of Robert de Courcil, natural son to HENRY I.) and

RICHARD, surnamed de GRANVILLE from one of his lordships, who came into England with Duke William, and fought at Hastings. This Richard, who, as heir male, inherited the Norman honours and estates, was earl of Corbeil and baron of Thorigny and Granville. He likewise possessed the castle of Neath, in Glamorganshire. He *m.* Constance, only daughter of Walter Giffard, earl of Buckinghamshire and Longueville, and at his decease, in journeying to the Holy Land, left a son and successor,

RICHARD GRANVILLE, who held, *temp.* HENRY II. the lordship of Bideford by half a knight's fee of the honour of Gloucester. He was direct and lineal ancestor of

SIR THEOBALD GRANVILLE, who *m.* Joice, daughter of Sir Thomas Beaumont, knt. and had a son and successor,

THEOBALD GRANVILLE, who wedded Margaret, daughter of Hugh Courtenay, earl of Devon, and had two sons, JOHN and WILLIAM. The elder,

SIR JOHN GRANVILLE, received the honour of knighthood from RICHARD II. He espoused Margaret, daughter and heiress of Sir John Burghurst, knt. but had no issue. Sir John, who resided at Stow, in Cornwall, and represented the county of Devon in parliament, died *temp.* HENRY IV. and was *s.* by his brother,

WILLIAM GRANVILLE, of Stow, who died about the year 1450, leaving by Philippa, his second wife, daughter of William, Lord Bonville, a son and heir,

SIR THOMAS GRANVILLE, knt. of Stow, high sheriff of Cornwall 21st EDWARD IV. He *m.* Elizabeth, sister of Sir Theobald Gorges, and was *s.* at his decease, in 1483, by his son,

SIR THOMAS GRANVILLE, of Stow, who took part in an insurrection against RICHARD III. but was pardoned. In the 15th of the following reign, we find him an esquire of the body to the same monarch, and the next year he was made a knight of the Bath at the creation of ARTHUR, Prince of Wales. He died about 6th HENRY VIII. and was interred at the east end of the south aisle of Bideford church, where his effigy in armour lies extended under an arch, with the figure of a dog by his side. By Isabel, his first wife, daughter of Sir Oates Gilbert, of Compton, in Devon, he had two sons and six daughters, viz.

- I. ROGER, his heir.
- II. Richard, sheriff of Cornwall 1st and 10th HENRY VIII.
- I. Jane, *m.* first, to John Arundel, of Trerice; and, secondly, to Sir John Charmond.
- II. Philippa, *m.* to Francis Harris, of Hayne.
- III. Anne, *m.* to John Roscarrock.
- IV. Catherine, *m.* to Sir John Arundel, of Lanherne.
- V. Mary, *m.* first, to Richard Bluet; and, secondly, to Thomas St. Aubyn.
- VI. Honor, *m.* first, to John Basset; and, secondly, to Arthur Plantagenet.

Sir Thomas wedded, secondly, Jane, widow of — Hill, and had by her one son, John, and a daughter, Jane, *m.* first, to — Batton; and, secondly, to — Raleigh. His eldest son,

ROGER GRANVILLE, esq. of Stow, called the great housekeeper for his princely hospitality, was sheriff of Cornwall in the reign of HENRY VIII. He *m.* Margaret, daughter and co-heiress of Richard Whitley, of Efford, and had, with seven daughters, three sons, RICHARD, his heir; John; and Digory, of Penheale. He died in 1524, and was *s.* by the eldest,

SIR RICHARD GRANVILLE, knt. of Stow, sheriff of Devon 24th HENRY VIII. and subsequently marshal of Calais. To this Sir Richard, who was of an active and daring spirit, and who served in the wars under the earl of Hertford, the king granted, in the 33rd year of his reign, the manor of Buckland and rectory of Moorwinstow, formerly belonging to the monastery of Bridgewater. He *m.* Matilda, second daughter and co-heir of John Bevil, esq. of Gwarnock, and had, with three daughters, two sons, viz.

- John, who died in his father's lifetime without issue.
- ROGER (Sir), an esquire of the body to HENRY VIII. He *m.* Thomasine, daughter of Thomas Cole, esq. of Slade, in Devon, and had three sons,
  - Charles (Sir), who *d. s. p.*
  - RICHARD (Sir), successor to his grandfather.
  - John, who left no issue.

Sir Richard *d.* in 1552, and was *s.* by his grandson,

SIR RICHARD GRANVILLE, knt. of Stow, a gallant naval commander, who, at the age of sixteen, by permission of *Queen* ELIZABETH, served in the imperial army in Hungary, and attained high reputation for his achievements against the infidels. Returning soon after to his native country, he joined the troops employed for the reduction of Ireland, and, there acquiring the confidence of the Lord Deputy Sydney, was appointed sheriff of the city of Cork. In 1571, he represented the county of Cornwall in Parliament, was subsequently high sheriff of that shire, and complimented with the honour of knighthood, but the bias of his mind, bent chiefly on the plans of foreign discovery, proposed by his relative Sir Walter Raleigh, preferred the enterprize of a naval, to the quiet of a senatorial life. He accordingly, with a squadron fitted out for the purpose, sailed for the coast of Florida in 1585, where he left a colony of one hundred men, and then returned home. Many and successful were his subsequent voyages, and in the memorable year of the Spanish invasion he was entrusted with the care of Cornwall, which prevented, for a while, his distinction in a proper sphere of action. In 1591, however, Sir Richard was dispatched as vice admiral under Lord Thomas Howard, with eight men of war, besides small vessels and tenders, to intercept a rich Spanish fleet from the West Indies. This convoy, protected by a very superior force, unexpectedly appearing, Admiral Howard, considering the great disproportion of the rival squadrons, immediately put to sea, and the rest of his ships, in some confusion, followed his example, except the Revenge, the ship commanded by Granville, who having ninety men sick out of two hundred and fifty, and many others on shore, could not weigh anchor for a considerable time, which prevented him from gaining the wind, and brought the hostile fleet on his weather bow. The Spanish admiral, with four other ships, began a close attack at three in the afternoon: the engagement lasted till break of day next morning, during which the enemy, notwithstanding their vast superiority of force, were driven off fifteen times. At length the greater part of the English crew being either killed or wounded, and the ship reduced to a wreck, no hope of escape remained. Far, however, from thinking of a surrender, Sir Richard exhorted his men rather to yield themselves to the mercy of heaven than to the Spaniards, and to blow the vessel up. But this design was frustrated by the master, who went on board the Spanish Admiral and made known their situation. As soon as the Revenge was in the power of the Spaniards, the admiral gave orders to remove Sir Richard, who was grievously wounded, to his own ship, but the gallant officer survived only three days. John Evelyn, relating this heroic action, exclaims, "Than this what have we more? What can be greater?"

Admiral Granville *m.* Mary, daughter and co-heir of Sir John St. Leger,* of Annery, in Devon, by Catherine, his wife, daughter of George, Lord Abergavenny, and had three sons and three daughters. The eldest son,

SIR BERNARD GRANVILLE, of Bideford, in Devon, and of Stow, in Cornwall, was sheriff of the latter county in the 38th ELIZABETH, served in Parliament for Bodmin in the following year, and subsequently received the honour of knighthood. He *m.* in 1603, Elizabeth, daughter and heiress of Philip Bevil, esq. and niece and heiress of Sir William Bevil, by whom he had issue,

I. BEVIL (Sir), his heir.
II. Richard (Sir), a cavalier commander of great celebrity. This gallant soldier, who learned the rudiments of war under Prince Maurice in Germany, attended *King* CHARLES in his expedition to Scotland, and was subsequently employed in Ireland to quell the rebellion there, having under his orders his near kinsman, the famous George Monk. On the commencement of the civil war, he proceeded to London in order to obtain some arrears due to him by the Parliament, and having effected this, he contrived, by amusing the Commons with the hope that he would accept the command of the horse under Sir William Waller, to join the king at Oxford with his whole regiment, and he thenceforward advanced the royal cause, in an especial degree, by his consummate skill and chivalrous bravery. From Oxford, Sir Richard marched on Saltash, which, with only seven hundred men, he stormed and captured, but some differences having unfortunately arisen between him and Clarendon, he was removed from his command. Retiring to Jersey, he equipped some privateers, and greatly harassed the Republicans by sea. He eventually fixed his residence in France, and dying at Ghent, was interred in the English church, where this simple inscription marks the sacred spot: "Sir Richard Granville, the king's general in the West." Sir Richard married Mary, daughter of Sir John Fitz, of Fitzford, by Gertrude Courtenay, his wife, and had one son, who was put to death by the Parliament, and one daughter, Elizabeth, *m.* to Col. William Lenard.
III. John, of Lincoln's Inn.
IV. Roger, drowned in the king's service.

I. Gertrude, *m.* to Christopher Harris, esq. son and heir of Sir Christopher Harris.

Sir Bernard Granville was *s.* at his decease by his eldest son, the celebrated

SIR BEVIL GRANVILLE, knt. of Stow and Bideford, one of the boldest and most successful of the cavalier leaders. This eminent person was educated at Exeter College, Oxford, and made so rapid a progress in learning, that the degree of bachelor of arts was conferred on him in 1613, when he was but seventeen years of age. In the two last Parliaments of JAMES I. he represented the county of Cornwall, and in all the Parliaments called by CHARLES I. sate either for that shire or for Launceston. In 1638, he raised, at his own expense, a troop of horse, with which he accompanied the king in his first expedition against the Scottish rebels, and on that occasion received the honour of knighthood. In 1642, on the first outbreaking of the civil wars, he joined the royal standard, and marching into Cornwall, rescued that whole county from the Parliament, attacked the partisans of the Commons, who had risen in great numbers in the West, and routed them at Bodmin, Launceston, and Stratton. His last and most brilliant action was at Lansdowne Hill, near Bath, where he fell, in the arms of victory, on the 5th July, 1643.* "On the king's part," says Clarendon, in detailing this engagement, "there were more officers and gentlemen of quality slain than common men, and more hurt than slain. That which would have clouded any victory, and

* Sir John St. Leger was son and heir of Sir Richard St. Leger, whose father was Sir James St. Leger, and whose mother was Anne, eldest daughter and co-heir of Thomas Butler, earl of Ormond, by Eleanor, his wife, daughter of Humphrey de Bohun, earl of Hereford, by the Lady Elizabeth Plantagenet, his wife, daughter of *King* EDWARD I.

* A monument repaired in 1827 by the present Court Granville, esq. still remains at Lansdown to the memory of Sir Bevil.

made the loss of others less spoken of, was the death of Sir Bevil Granville: he was indeed an excellent person, whose activity, interest, and reputation, was the foundation of what had been done in Cornwall; and his temper and affection so public, that no accident which happened could make any impression on him, and his example kept others from taking anything ill, or at least seeming to do so. In a word, a brighter courage and a gentler disposition were never mixed together to make the most cheerful and innocent conversation."

Sir Bevil married Grace, daughter of Sir George Smith, knt. of Exeter, sole heiress to her mother, the daughter and co-heiress of William Vyol, esq. of Trevorder, in Cornwall, and had issue,

- I. Richard, *b.* in 1620, *d.* unm.
- II. JOHN, who was created, in 1661, Viscount Granville, of Lansdowne, and EARL OF BATH. His lordship *m.* Jane, daughter of Sir Peter Wyche, knt. and dying in 1701, left issue,
  1. CHARLES, second earl of Bath, whose son and successor, WILLIAM-HENRY, third earl of Bath, *d.* unm. in 1711.
  2. JOHN, created, in 1702, BARON GRANVILLE, who died without issue in 1707.
  3. Bevil, died unmarried.

  1. Jane. *m.* to Sir William Gower, ancestor of the present DUKE OF SUTHERLAND.
  2. Catherine, *m.* to Craven Payton, esq. of Lancashire.
  3. Grace, *m.* to Sir George Carteret, Lord Carteret, and had issue. Lady Carteret, surviving her husband, was herself elevated to the peerage as COUNTESS GRANVILLE. Her ladyship's granddaughter, the Lady LOUISA CARTERET, married Thomas Thynne, Viscount Weymouth, and was grandmother of Thomas, present marquis of Bath, and of George, Lord Carteret: for a more detailed account of the ennobled branches of the Granville family, refer to BURKE's *Extinct and Dormant Peerage.*
- III. Dennis, living in 1686, dean of Durham, rector of Easington and Elwycke, and chaplain in ordinary to CHARLES II. He *m.* Anne, fourth daughter of John Cosyn, lord bishop of Durham.
- IV. BERNARD, of whom presently.

- I. Elizabeth, *m.* to Sir Peter Prideaux, bart. of Netherton.
- II. Bridget, *m.* to Sir Thomas Higgins, knt.
- III. Johanna, *m.* to Colonel Richard Thornhill.
- IV. Grace, *m.* to Robert Fortescue, esq. of Filley, whose daughter and co-heiress wedded Sir Halsewell Tynte, bart.

Sir Bevil's fourth son,

BERNARD GRANVILLE, esq. was master of the horse and gentleman of the bedchamber to CHARLES II. He wedded Anne, only daughter and heir of Cuthbert Morley, esq. of Haunby, in the county of York, and had issue,

- I. BEVIL (Sir), governor of Barbadoes, *d.* unm. in 1716.
- II. GEORGE, of Stow, in the county of Cornwall, who was elevated to the peerage in 1711, as BARON LANSDOWNE, of Biddeford. His lordship, a poet of considerable reputation, married the Lady Mary Villiers, daughter of Edward, earl of Jersey, and widow of Thomas Thynne, esq. of Old Windsor, in the county of Bucks. By her he had four daughters, his co-heirs, viz.
  - ANNE, *d.* unmarried.
  - MARY, *m.* to William Graham, esq. of Platten, in Ireland.
  - GRACE, *m.* to Thomas Foley, esq. of Whitley, in the county of Hereford, created, in 1776, BARON FOLEY, of Kidderminster. Of this marriage THOMAS, present LORD FOLEY is grandson.
  - ELIZABETH, *d.* unm.
- III. BERNARD, of whom presently.

- I. Anne, *m.* to Sir John Stanley, bart. of Grange Gorman, in Ireland, but *d. s. p.*
- II. Elizabeth, *d.* unm.

Bernard Granville *d.* in 1701, and was buried at Lambeth. His third son,

COLONEL BERNARD GRANVILLE, of Buckland, in the county of Gloucester, *m.* Mary, daughter of Sir Martin Westcomb, bart. consul at Cadiz, and by her (who *d.* in 1747, and was buried in Gloucester cathedral) had two sons and two daughters, viz.

- I. BERNARD, his heir.
- II. Bevil, of Weedon, in Bucks, who *m.* Mary-Anne, daughter of Richard Rose, esq. but *d.* without issue.

- I. Mary, *m.* first, to Alexander Pendarves, esq. of Roscrow, in Cornwall, and, secondly, to the Very Rev. Patrick Delany, dean of Down, but *d.* without issue in 1788. This lady, so justly celebrated for her great literary acquirements, was much esteemed by *King* GEORGE III. and *Queen* CHARLOTTE, and resided constantly with their Majesties both at Kew and Windsor. Her most curious performance was the Hortus Siccus, (now in the possession of her niece, Mrs. Waddington), a work in ten volumes, folio, comprising the most admirable delineations in coloured paper of the different flowers.

Mrs. Delany was the intimate friend of Doctor Burney, the Duchess of Portland, Miss Seward, Swift, Horace Walpole, &c.

II. ANNE, *b.* in 1707, *m.* at Gloucester in 1740, JOHN D'EWES, esq. of Wellesbourne, in the county of Warwick, and died in 1761, leaving issue,

1. Court D'Ewes, died unm.
2. BERNARD D'EWES, of Hagley, in Worcestershire, *b.* in 1743, married, in 1777, Ann, eldest daughter of John Delabere, esq. of Cheltenham, and by her, who *d.* in 1780, had one son and one daughter, viz.
   - COURT, successor to his uncle, the Rev. John Granville, and PRESENT POSSESSOR of Calwich Abbey.
   - Anne, *m.* in January, 1805, to George-Frederick Stratton, esq. of Tew Park, in Oxfordshire, deceased.
3. JOHN D'EWES, successor to his uncle, Bernard Granville, esq. of Calwich Abbey.

1. Mary D'Ewes, *m.* to John Port, esq. of Ilam, in Staffordshire.

Colonel Granville, of Buckland, *d.* in 1733, and was *s.* by his son,

BERNARD GRANVILLE, esq. who purchased from the ancient family of Fleetwood the estate of Calwich Abbey, in the county of Stafford, originally a cell of friars of the order of St. Benedict. Mr. Granville died unmarried in 1775, and bequeathed his estates to his sister Anne's third son,

THE REV. JOHN D'EWES, M.A. vicar of Ilam, in the county of Stafford, and of Norbury, in Derbyshire, *b.* in 1744, who assumed in 1786, upon inheriting Calwich Abbey, the surname and arms of GRANVILLE. He wedded, in 1779, Harriott-Joan, second daughter of John Delabere, esq. of Cheltenham, and had one son, John, and a daughter, Harriet, who both *d.* unmarried. Mr. Granville died in 1826, and was succeeded by his nephew, COURT D'EWES, esq. who assumed the surname of GRANVILLE, and is the present COURT GRANVILLE, esq. of Calwich Abbey.

## Family of D'Ewes.

The D'EWESES of Wellesbourne, who became settled in the counties of Warwick, Gloucester, and Worcester, about the commencement of the seventeenth century, are said to be a branch of the family of D'EWES, originally seated in Suffolk, and of which Sir Simonds D'Ewes was so distinguished a member.

WILLIAM D'EWES, of Coughton, living in 1627, married and had two sons, RICHARD, his heir, and William, of Long Marston, in Gloucestershire, who *d.* 21st November, 1717. The elder son,

RICHARD D'EWES, esq. of Coughton, espoused Mary, daughter and co-heir of Edmund Court, esq. of Maplebury, in the county of Warwick, and by her, who died 20th November, 1683, left at his decease in 1678, (with two daughters, the elder, Elizabeth, who died unmarried 12th July, 1681, and the younger *m.* to — Fortescue, esq.), a son and successor,

COURT D'EWES, esq. of Maplebury, high sheriff of the county of Warwick, in 1714, who *m.* Elizabeth, daughter of Robert Dowley, esq. of Bradley, in Worcestershire, and by her, who died in 1743, had two sons and one daughter, viz.

- COURT, of Maplebury, *b.* in 1693, and died, unm. in July, 1745.
- JOHN, of Wellesbourne, in the county of Warwick, who *m.* as already stated, ANNE, second dau. of BERNARD GRANVILLE, esq. of Buckland, and was grandfather of the present
  - COURT GRANVILLE, esq. of Calwich Abbey.
- Mary, *m.* to John Holyoake, esq. of Morton Bagot, in the county of Warwick. (See vol. ii. p. 598.)

*Arms*—Quarterly, first and fourth, gu. three suffiues or organ rests or, for GRANVILLE; second and third, or, three quaterfoils pierced gu. a chief vair.

*Crest*—On a cap of maintenance a griffin, or.

*Motto*—Deo Patriæ Amicis.

*Estates*—Calwich Abbey, situated on the banks of the river Dove, in the county of Stafford, and Wellesbourne Hall, in Warwickshire.

*Seats*—Calwich Abbey, Staffordshire, and Wellesbourne Hall, Warwickshire. These two seats contain many specimens of the first painters; a splendid landscape by Rembrandt, two by Murillo, by Winants, Wovermans, Teniers, &c. The family portraits are in direct succession, from Sir Richard and Bevil Granville, in 1640, to the present time, comprising paintings of Sir Bevil and Lady Granville, their son, the Earl of Bath, Lord Lansdown, Bernard Granville, Col. Bernard Granville, and his wife, Lady Stanley, by Houseman, Mrs. Delany, by Opie, Bernard D'Ewes, Court D'Ewes, by Opie, John Granville and Harriet his wife, by Barber, and Mrs. Stratton, by Sir Thomas Lawrence, &c. &c.

# GRAY, OF CARNTYNE,

## *Formerly of Dalmarnock.*

GRAY, *The Rev.* JOHN HAMILTON, of Carntyne, in the county of Lanark, *b.* 29th December, 1800, *m.* at Alva House, 23rd June, 1829, Elizabeth-Caroline, eldest daughter of James Raymond Johnstone, esq. of Alva, in Clackmannanshire, (grandson of Sir James Johnstone, bart. of Westerhall, a family which, on the extinction of the male line of the Marquesses of Annandale, became chief of the ancient house of Johnstone,) by Mary his wife, sister of Sir Montague Cholmeley, bart. of Easton, in the county of Lincoln, an ancient branch of the great Cheshire family of Cholmondeley. The issue of this marriage is a dau. born at the baths of Baden-Baden, in Germany, on the 26th June, 1833, and christened there, according to the rites of the Anglican church, on the 14th September, in the same year, by the names of CAROLINE-MARIA-AGNES, to which has since been added the name of ROBINA.

Mr. Hamilton Gray is a magistrate, and, since August, 1824, a deputy lieutenant of the county of Lanark. He was educated at the universities of Göttingen and Oxford, and in the latter he was of Magdalen College, where, in 1823, he took his bachelor's, and, in 1826, his master of arts degree. In 1824, he was called to the Scottish bar; in 1829, he entered into holy orders; and, in 1833, was presented to the livings of Bolsover and Scarcliff, in the county of Derby. He succeeded his father 12th November, 1833.

## Lineage.

This branch of the family of Gray has possessed estates in the county of Lanark for about three hundred years. Its ancestor, who held the lands of Tollcross towards the middle of the sixteenth century, had two sons, JOHN, his heir, and James, who was bred to the law, and is said to have distressed his brother with litigation, which necessitated a sale of the lands of Tollcross. The elder son,

JOHN GRAY, of Tollcross, in Lanarkshire, lived about the close of the sixteenth century, and alienated the property of Tollcross. The name of his wife is unknown. He was father of

WILLIAM GRAY, proprietor of the lands of Carntyne, in the county of Lanark, antecedently to the year 1595, who *m.* first, Margaret Craig, by whom he had a son, ARCHIBALD, his heir. He wedded, secondly, Marion, dau. of Ninian Hill, of Lambhill, in Lanarkshire, and had another son, JOHN, successor to his brother. The Hills were in possession of extensive estates more than two centuries ago, part of which were acquired by marriage with a daughter of the family of Hutchinson.* Several most respectable male descendants of the Hills, of Lambhill, still exist, though what remains of the property has passed, in the female line, to Miss Lilias Graham, the present proprietrix. William Gray was *s.* by his eldest son,

ARCHIBALD GRAY, of Carntyne, who espoused Elizabeth Colquhoun, daughter of Colquhoun of Kenmure, a cadet of Colquhoun of Luss, chief of the name, but having no issue, he resigned, in 1628, the lands of Carntyne to his brother,

JOHN GRAY, who then became of Carntyne. Exactly half a century after, in 1678, he acquired part of the lands of Dalmarnock, another portion continuing in the possession of the family of Woddrop, and thenceforward, for more than a hundred years, Dalmarnock became the principal designation of his descendants. Mr. Gray

* Two members of this (the Hutchinson) family founded a magnificent charity at Glasgow, which still retains their name.

began to work coal on Carntyne, which has supplied a portion of the fuel consumed in the city of Glasgow. He was a zealous covenanter, and his name is held in honour among the favourers of those principles, for having afforded the shelter of his roof to their ministers, and an occasional place of concealment to their proscribed members. He *m.* Janet, daughter of Anderson, of Dovehill, an ancient and opulent family in the neighbourhood of Glasgow, several successive generations of which filled the office of lord provost of the city, from 1654 until 1703. It appears now to be extinct in the direct male line, but among its descendants may be mentioned the lamented Sir John Moore. John Gray was succeeded, in 1687, by his son,

JOHN GRAY, of Dalmarnock and Carntyne, who wedded Anabella, daughter of Walter Gibson,* of Hillhead, in the county of Lanark, and had issue,

- I. JOHN, his heir.
- II. Ninian, who left a son, John, for many years minister of the parish of Camnethan.
- III. Andrew, who had issue,
  1. Margaret, *m.* to James Woddrop, a descendant of the Dalmarnock family.
  2. Anabella, *m.* to Peter Lowe, writer to the signet, in Edinburgh, grandson of Dr. Peter Lowe, physician in ordinary to HENRY IV., King of France, and to Henry, Prince of Wales.
  3. Elizabeth, *m.* to Robert Finlay, merchant, in Glasgow.

John Gray died previous to the year 1715, and was *s.* by his son,

JOHN GRAY, of Dalmarnock and Carntyne. The mind of this gentleman being strongly tinctured with sentiments of loyalty to the exiled royal family, he openly avowed himself a partisan of the Chevalier de St. George, and prepared to join the insurgents in 1715:—the arms which he procured on that occasion are still preserved in the family. He was saved, however, from open rebellion and its probable consequence, forfeiture, by the prudence of his wife, who gave information against him, on account of which he was imprisoned until the restoration of peace. He *m.* Elizabeth, dau. of James Hamilton, of Newton, a scion of the family of Silverton Hill, by Elizabeth, his first wife, daughter of Gabriel Hamilton, of Westburn, cadet of Torrance, and had issue,

- I. JAMES, his heir.
- II. JOHN, *s.* to his father.
- III. Gabriel, of Eastfield, who *m.* Miss Baird, of Muckroft, and had a son, John Gray, esq. now of Eastfield.
- IV. Andrew, who *m.* Miss Cameron, daughter of a cousin of the Locheil family, and had John Gabriel, who *d. s. p.* Janet, and Elizabeth.

- I. Elizabeth, *m.* John Spens, of Stonelaw, in the county of Lanark, descended from Spens, of Kames, in Bute, a scion of Spens, of Wormiston, in Fifeshire, and had two sons, Lieutenant-general John Spens, of Stonelaw, and Capt. George Spens, and two daughters.
- II. Anabella, *m.* Henry Woddrop, of Westhorn, in Lanark, and had a daughter, *m.* to Capt. James Dennistoun, of Westhorn.
- III. Rebecca, *m.* William Ross, son of Professor Ross, of the University of Glasgow, descended from the ennobled house of Ross, but had no issue.
- IV. Jane, *m.* Thomas Buchanan, of Ardoch, in the county of Dumbarton, and had issue, (see vol. ii. p. 337).

John Gray died 27th January, 1742, and was *s.* by his eldest son,

JAMES GRAY, of Dalmarnock and Carntyne, who *m.* first, Elizabeth, daughter of his cousin-german, Elizabeth Hamilton, coheiress of Newton, by William Gray, brother to Gray of Welhouse, and secondly, Jane, daughter of John Corbett, of Tollcross, sister of Colonel James-Corbett-Porterfield, of Porterfield, and grand-niece to William, first Earl of Kilmarnock. Dying, without issue, in 1778, Mr. Gray was *s.* by his next brother,

JOHN GRAY, of Dalmarnock and Carntyne, born in 1715. This gentleman on his accession found the estates heavily encumbered, and had only possessed them four years when he was induced most unfortunately to expose them for sale, in 1784. At that period, the value of land being much reduced, they brought a most inadequate price, and thus the properties of Dalmarnock and Newlands, of yearly increasing value, were lost to the family. Whatever part of his once ample inheritance remained was owing to the judicious management of Mr. Gray's younger son, and ultimate successor, John Gray, who *m.* Isabella, dau. of John Chapman, esq. commissary of Glasgow, by Elizabeth his wife, dau. of Pollock, of

* The family of Gibson, which formerly enjoyed great wealth and influence, still exists in the male line. Walter, one of the younger sons of the family, and brother to Anabella Gray, was the most eminent merchant of his time in Scotland, and greatly contributed to improve the commerce of Glasgow, of which city he was lord provost in 1688. Another younger son was captain of the "Rising Sun," which he commanded in the Darien expedition.

Balgray,* an immediate cadet of Pollock, of Pollock, by a marriage with Marion, daughter of William Stewart, of Castlemick. The Chapmans, originally of English extraction, came, it is said, in the suite of a Duke of Lennox, to Scotland, where, though they never possessed landed property, they held respectable situations in the law. They are now exinct in the male line. Besides their intermarriages with the ancient families of Pollock and Trochrig, they were descended from the Woddrops of Dalmarnock. By Isabella his wife, Mr. Gray had issue,

I. John, died young.

II. James, *b.* in 1754, and *d.* unmarried in 1791.

III. ROBERT, heir to his father.

I. Helen, *m.* William Woddrop, esq. of Dalmarnock, (son of Henry Woddrop, of Dalmarnock, and Lilias his wife, daughter of James Hamilton, of Aitkenhead) and has issue,

1. Henry Woddrop, *d.* unm.
2. John Woddrop, now of Dalmarnock and Garvald, in the county of Peebles, who, on succeeding to the estate of Elsrickle, has assumed the additional surname of ALLAN. He *m.* Miss Hunter, of Kirkland, in Ayrshire, (see vol. ii. p. 502) and has issue.
3. Isabella Waddrop.

II. Margaret, *d.* young.

III. Elizabeth, *d.* unmarried, in 1797.

John Gray *d.* in 1796, and was *s.* in what remained of his property by his only surviving son,

ROBERT GRAY, of Carntyne, *b.* in 1756, who became, in 1823, representative of the ancient family of Hamilton, of Newton, on the decease of its last heiress, Mrs. Montgomery. He *m.* in 1799, Mary-Anne, youngest daughter of Gabriel Hamilton, of Westburn, (representative of Hamilton of Torrance*) by Agnes his wife, daughter, and at length heiress, of George Dundas, esq. of Duddingstoun, in West Lothian, (sprung from Dundas, of Dundas) by Magdalen Lyndsay-Crawford, granddaughter of John, sixteenth Earl of Crawfurd, and first Earl of Lindsay, niece to James and William, first and second Dukes of Hamilton, and sister to John, Viscount Garnock. Mr. Gray had, by Mary-Anne his wife, one son, JOHN, his heir. Mrs. Gray died 6th January, 1809, her husband surviving until the 12th November, 1833, when he died suddenly, in the seventy-eighth year of his age. His whole life was spent in useful exertion, and in acts of disinterested benevolence. He was cool in his judgment, unwearied in his kindness, and viewed with unmoved serenity the events of a life which various causes had saddened. Though laboriously occupied in the attempt to turn to good account the wreck of his family estates, he never refused his time and his exertions to the often ungrateful task of aiding his relations and friends; and when full of years, and of respect, he was removed from this world, the unanimous voice of the poor pronounced upon him the eulogium,—"We have now lost our common good!" He was an active magistrate, and, for nearly forty years, a deputy lieutenant of the county of Lanark. His only son and successor is the present Rev. JOHN HAMILTON GRAY, of Carntyne.

## Family of Hamilton, of Newton.

Now represented by GRAY, OF CARNTYNE.

The family of Silverton Hill, (whence Hamilton of Newton), is a scion of the illustrious house of Hamilton.

SIR WALTER DE HAMILTON, Lord of Cadzow, in Lanark, in 1324, married Mary, daughter of Adam, Lord Gordon, and had two sons, DAVID (Sir) and John (Sir), ancestors of the Hamiltons of Innerwick, and Earls of Haddingtons. The elder

SIR DAVID DE HAMILTON, Lord of Cadzow, *m.* a daughter of William, Earl of Ross, and had (with a younger son, Walter (Sir), ancestor of the Hamiltons of Cambeskeith and Grange) his successor,

---

* By Margaret Boyd his wife, daughter of James Boyd, of Trochrig, in the county of Ayr, descended from Adam Boyd, of Pinkhill, brother of Robert, third Lord Boyd. The most noted of the Trochrig family was JAMES BOYD, Archbishop of Glasgow, who died in 1581. "During the Earl of Marr's regency," says Keith in his Account of Scottish Bishops, "a new kind of episcopacy having been set up, Mr. James Boyd, of Trochrig, a very worthy person, received the title of the see of Glasgow, and he exercised the office of particular pastor at the cathedral church, the barony of Glasgow being then the parish that pertained to that church. When the legality of the episcopal function came to be first called in question by the assembly, in the year 1578, he learnedly and solidly, both from scripture and antiquity, defended the lawfulness of his office; yet, the animosities which he then perceived to be in the hearts of a great many so far impaired his health, that he died in the month of June, 1581.

* The HAMILTONS, of Torrance, descended from Thomas, second son of Thomas Hamilton, of Darngaber, by Helen his wife, daughter of Sir Henry Douglas, of Lochleven, ancestor to the Earl of Morton, which Thomas, of Darngaber, was third son of Sir John Hamilton, Lord of Cadzon, by Janet his wife, daughter of Sir James Douglas, of Dalkeith.

Sir David de Hamilton, Lord of Cadzow, who died before 1392, leaving by Janetta his wife, daughter of Sir William Keith, of Galston, five sons, viz.

John (Sir), his heir.

David, whence the Hamiltons of Bouland.

William, ancestor of the Hamiltons of Brathgate.

Andrew, ancestor of the Hamiltons of Uldston.

John, ancestor of the Hamiltons of Bardowie.

The eldest son,

Sir John Hamilton, Lord of Cadzow, wedded Janet, daughter of Sir James Douglas, of Dalkeith, and had issue,

I. James (Sir), his heir.

II. David, progenitor of the Hamiltons of Dalserf.

III. Thomas, of Darngalier, from whom sprung the Hamiltons of Raplock, Barnes, Torrance, Westburn, Aitkenhead, the Earls of Clanbrassil, &c. &c.

The elder son,

Sir James Hamilton, Lord of Cadzow, wedded Janet, eldest daughter of Sir Alexander Livingston, of Callander, ancestor of the Earls of Linlithgow. Their eldest son, Sir James Hamilton, was created a peer, by the title of Lord Hamilton, and married, in 1474, Princess Mary, eldest daughter of James, second King of Scotland. Their second son,

Sir Alexander Hamilton, of Silverton Hill, became ancestor of the Hamiltons of Silverton Hill, Cubardy, Newton, and Westport. The Hamiltons of Newton were seated on a picturesque estate at the confluence of the Clyde and Calder, in Lanarkshire, which now belongs, in consequence of the will of the last heiress of the family, to Sir James Montgomery, of Stobo Castle. In 1694, the mansion house of Newton, together with the title deeds of the property and family papers, was destroyed by fire, which accident renders it difficult to trace the earlier generations of this branch of the house of Hamilton.

James Hamilton, of Newton, appears to have held his estate under his chief; for, immediately after the fire just alluded to, he obtained a charter of Novodamus of his lands from Anne, Duchess of Hamilton, the then head of the family. He *m.* first, Elizabeth, daughter of Gabriel Hamilton,* of Westburn, by Margaret his wife, daughter of Cunninghame, of Gilbertfield, and had by her a daughter,

Elizabeth, who was educated at Westburn, by her maternal uncle. She *m.* John Gray, of Dalmarnock and Carntyne, and was grandmother of Robert Gray, eventual representative of Hamilton, of Newton.

James Hamilton espoused secondly, Margaret, daughter of Robert Montgomery, of Macbiehill, in the county of Peebles, (descended from Robert, second son of Sir John Montgomery, of Eglinton and Ardrossan, created Lord Montgomery, in 1427,) by Jean his wife, daughter of Sir James Lockhart, of Lee, in the county of Lanark, and had two sons, viz. James and Thomas. The elder,

James Hamilton, of Newton, dying unmarried, the estates and representation of the family devolved on his brother,

Thomas Hamilton, of Newton, who *m.* the sister of Major Clelland, representative of the ancient family of Clelland of Clelland, in Lanarkshire, and by her, who died in 1733, had issue,

I. James, his heir.

II. John, successor to his nephew.

I. Dorothea, *m.* to Andrew Gray, of Wellhouse.

II. Elizabeth, *m.* William Gray, brother of Andrew Gray, of Wellhouse, and had issue,

Elizabeth Gray, married to her mother's cousin-german, James Gray, of Dalmarnock and Carntyne, and *d. s. p.*

Janet Gray, *m.* to Col. Montgomery. Of this lady more hereafter, as heiress of Newton.

Thomas Hamilton was *s.* by his elder son,

James Hamilton, of Newton, who *m.* first, Anabella, third daughter of Sir Robert Pollock, bart. of Pollock, in the county of Renfrew, by Anabella his wife, daughter of Walter Stewart, of Pardovan, and had by her an only son,

James, his heir.

He wedded secondly, a daughter of Buchanan of Drummakill and Ross, in the county of Dumbarton, and had another son,

Thomas, who predeceased his elder brother.

Mr. Hamilton died in 1769, and was *s.* by his son,

James Hamilton, of Newton, at whose demise, unmarried, the estates and representation of the family devolved on his uncle,

John Hamilton, of Newton, who died unmarried, in 1775, and was *s.* by his sisters,

* This gentleman was representative of Hamilton of Torrance, descended from Thomas Hamilton, third son of Sir John Hamilton, Lord of Cadzow, and uncle to Alexander, of Silverton Hill, progenitor of the family of Newton.

DOROTHEA HAMILTON and ELIZABETH HAMILTON, } co-heiresses of Newton. The elder married Andrew Gray, of Wellhouse; the younger, William Gray, and had an only daughter to survive her, namely,

JANET HAMILTON, of Newton, who wedded Col. Richard Montgomery, cousin-german of Sir William Montgomery, bart. of Macbie Hill, and of Sir James Montgomery, bart. lord chief baron of Scotland. By him she had issue,

James-George Hamilton, an officer of dragoons, *d.* unmarried, *v. m.*

Elizabeth, *d.* unmarried, *v. m.*

Mrs. Montgomery survived her children many years, and died in 1823. By a deed of entail, she devised her estate of Newton to her deceased husband's cousin, Sir James Montgomery, bart. of Stobo Castle, in the county of Peebles. The representation, however, of the Hamiltons, of Newton, vested in ROBERT GRAY, of Carntyne, in right of his grandmother, Elizabeth, eldest daughter of James Hamilton, of Newton. Robert Gray, of Carntyne, was father of the present Rev. JOHN HAMILTON GRAY, of Carntyne.

*Arms*—First and fourth, gu. a lion rampant between three cinquefoils, all within a bordure engrailed, arg. for GRAY, of Dalmarnock; second and third, gu. a crescent surmounted of a star, arg. between three cinquefoils, pierced within a bordure ermine, for HAMILTON, of Newton.

*Crests*—An anchor, stuck in the sea, ppr. for GRAY; an oak tree, with a saw issuing out of a ducal coronet for HAMILTON.

*Mottoes*—"Fast," for GRAY; "Through," for HAMILTON.

*Estates*—In Lanarkshire.

*Seat*—Carntyne, in Lanarkshire. The Rev. Mr. Hamilton Gray's present place of residence is Bolsover Castle, a romantic feudal fastness belonging to the Duke of Portland, within the parish of Bolsover, and county of Derby.

## HALE, OF KING'S WALDEN.

HALE, WILLIAM, esq. of King's Walden, in the county of Hertford, *b.* 5th June, 1782; *m.* first, in February, 1815, Elizabeth, only daughter of the Hon. William Leeson, of the Node, son of Joseph, earl of Miltown, and by her, who died in April, 1822, has one son and one daughter, viz.

WILLIAM, *b.* in August, 1816.

Emily-Mary-Brand.

He wedded, secondly, 28th December, 1824, Charlotte, eldest daughter of Sir Richard-Joseph Sullivan, bart. of Thames Ditton, and has by her,

Charles-Cholmeley, *b.* 9th July, 1830.

Charlotte-Eliza.

Mr. Hale succeeded his father 22nd April, 1829.

### Lineage.

The family of HALE has been seated at King's Walden for more than two centuries.

THOMAS HALE, of Codicote, Herts, *m.* Anne, daughter of Edmund Michell, of that place, and had three sons, namely,

RICHARD, his heir.

William, who *m.* Alice, daughter of Thomas Caulfield, of St. Paul's, Walden, and *d.* in 1594.

John, who *m.* the daughter of — Rolt, of Milton, in Bedfordshire.

The eldest son,

RICHARD HALE, purchased the estate of King's Walden, Herts, in the time of ELIZABETH, and became of that place. He *m.* first, Mary Lambert, an heiress, by whom he had a son, WILLIAM, his heir, and secondly, Dyonisia, dau. of — Giffard, of Somersetshire, by whom he had two other sons,

Richard, high sheriff of the county of Hertford in 1632, who *m.* in 1601, Elizabeth, daughter of Sir Thomas Dacres, of Cheshunt, and had issue,

1. Robert, *b.* in 1610, *m.* Anne, daughter and co-heir of Sir Leventhorpe Frank, knt. of Albury.
2. John.

1. Dyonisia, *m.* to Edward Coleman.
2. Mary, *m.* to Thomas Francklyn, esq.
3. Elizabeth, *m.* to George Gent, esq. of Moyns, Essex, (see vol. i. p. 371).
4. Martha.
5. Katharine.

Robert.

Richard Hale, the purchaser of King's Walden and founder of the grammar school at Hertford, *d.* in 1620, and was *s.* by his eldest son,

WILLIAM HALE, esq. of King's Walden, who was high sheriff of Herts in 1621. He *m.* Rose, daughter of Sir George Bond, knt. lord mayor of London in 1587, and died in August, 1634, aged sixty-six, having had issue,

I. Richard, *b.* 13th January, 1596, predeceased his father, in 1623.
II. William, *b.* 12th March, 1597, *d. s. p.* in 1641.
III. ROWLAND, of whom presently.
IV. George, *b.* 30th July, 1601.
V. Thomas, *b.* 1606.
VI. Bernard, *b.* at King's Walden, principal of Peter House, Cambridge, archdeacon of Ely, and D.D. *d.* 29th March, 1663, and was buried in Peter House Chapel, Cambridge.
VII. John (Sir), of Stagenhoe, knighted 25th June, 1660, high sheriff of Herts in 1663, *d.* in 1672, *m.* Rose, daughter of Edmund Bale, esq. of Sadington, in the county of Leicester, and by her, who *d.* 5th August, 1673, aged sixty-three, left, with other issue, who *d. s. p.* a daughter and heiress,
    ROSE, *b.* 24th September, 1645, *m.* to Sir John Austen, bart. of Hall Place, Kent, M.P. for Rye, and conveyed to her husband the estate of Stagenhoe, in Herts.

I. Alicia, *b.* 15th June, 1603, *m.* John, son of Sir John Minne, of Surrey.
II. Winefreda, *b.* 18th February, 1604, *d.* unm. in 1627.
III. Anne, *b.* in 1609, *m.* 14th December, 1626, Charles, son of Sir Thomas Hoskyns, and *d.* in 1651.
IV. Dionisia, *b.* 17th March, 1611, *m.* Sir Thomas Williamson, of Great Markham, Notts, created a baronet in 1642, and *d. s. p.*

The third, but eldest, son to leave issue,

ROWLAND HALE, esq. of King's Walden, *b.* 8th June, 1600, served the office of sheriff of Herts in 1647. He *m.* Elizabeth, daughter of Sir Henry Garwey, knt. alderman of London, and by her, who died 9th January, 1669, in her seventieth year, left at his own demise, 7th April, 1669, a son and successor,

WILLIAM HALE, esq. of King's Walden, who represented the county of Hertford in parliament in the 13th and 31st of CHARLES II. This gentleman *m.* Mary, dau. of Jeremiah Elwes, esq. of Roxby, in the county of Lincoln (see vol. ii. p. 465), by whom, who *d.* 28th July, 1712, at the age of seventy-two, he had ten sons and four daughters, viz.

I. RICHARD, *b.* 4th November, 1659, *m.* 3rd April, 1684, Elizabeth, daughter and heir of Isaac Meynell, esq. of Langley Meynell, in the county of Derby, and by her (who wedded, secondly, the Hon. Robert Cecil, second son of James, third Earl of Salisbury) left at his decease, in 1689, (with a daughter, Mary, maid of honour to *Queen* ANNE, who married Thomas Coke, esq. and was mother of Mary Cooke, the wife of Sir Matthew Lambe, whose son was elevated to the peerage as Viscount Melbourne,) a son and successor,
    WILLIAM HALE, esq. M.P. for Bramber in 1708, and for St. Albans from March, 1715, until his decease, which occurred 2nd October, 1717, at the age of thirty-two. He *m.* Katharine, dau. of Peter Paggen, esq. of Wandsworth, in Surrey, and had two sons,
        WILLIAM, who died unmarried, 16th February, 1741, in his twenty-ninth year.
        PAGGEN, M.P. for Hertfordshire, from 1747 until his death. He *m.* at Whitehall, 20th November, 1742, Elizabeth, third daughter of Humphrey Morice, esq. M.P. of London, sub-governor of the bank, but *d. s. p.* 3rd April, 1755, aged forty.
II. Rowland, *b.* 2nd January, 1661, living in 1669.
III. William, *b.* 17th February, 1663, living in 1669.
IV. John, *b.* 18th January, 1665, living in 1669.
V. Jeremiah, *b.* 10th June, 1668, *d.* 25th January, 1733.
VI. Henry, *b.* 22nd October, 1670, *d.* 10th May, 1735.
VII. Geoffrey, *b.* in 1676.
VIII. BERNARD (Sir), of whom presently.
IX. Thomas, *b.* in 1678.
X. Geoffrey, *b.* in 1680.
I. Mary, *b.* 28th October, 1660, *m.* 27th February, 1678, John Plumer, esq. of Blakeware, in Herts, and *d.* in 1709.

II. Elizabeth, *b.* 5th October, 1670, and died the following year.

III. Katharine, *b.* 15th September, 1673, *m.* 11th December, 1696, to John Hoskyns, esq. of Reigate, in Surrey, a younger son of Charles Hoskyns, esq. of Oxled, in Surrey, and *d.* 5th March, 1704.

IV. Elizabeth, *b.* 14th March, 1682, *m.* to Nicholas Bonfoy, esq. of Abbots Rippon, in the county of Huntingdon, and *d.* in March, 1763.

The eighth son, but in whose descendant the representation of the family is now vested,

SIR BERNARD HALE, baptized at King's Walden, 18th March, 1677, having been called to the bar, and acquiring a high legal character, was constituted, in 1722, chief baron of the Exchequer in Ireland, and subsequently received the honour of knighthood. He *m.* Anne, dau. of — Thursby, esq. of Northamptonshire, and by her, who *d.* at Kensington, 11th April, 1768, had issue,

I. WILLIAM, his heir.

II. Richard, who *d.* in Wimpole Street, London, 14th September, 1812, in his ninety-second year.

III. Bernard, a general officer in the army, colonel of the 20th regiment, appointed lieutenant-governor of Chelsea hospital, 10th May, 1773, and afterwards lieutenant-governor of the Ordnance, *m.* in Sept. 1750, Martha, second daughter of Richard Rigby, esq. of Mistley Hall, Essex, and *d.* 13th March, 1798, leaving a son,

Lieut.-Col. FRANCIS HALE, M.P. who, upon inheriting the estates of his maternal uncle, the Right Hon. Richard Rigby, who died 8th April, 1788, assumed, by sign manual, the surname and arms of Rigby. He *m.* Frances, dau. of Sir Thomas Rumbold, bart. governor of Madras, and had a daughter,

Frances, *m.* in 1808, to William Horace, third Lord Rivers.

IV. John, of Plantation, near Gisborough, in Yorkshire, a general officer in the army, and colonel of the 17th Light Dragoons, which regiment he raised at his own expense; governor of Londonderry and Coolmore-forts in 1781, *m.* Mary, second dau. of William Chaloner, esq. of Gisborough, and *d.* 20th March, 1806, leaving a numerous issue.

I. Catherine, *m.* to Thomas Nugent, esq. common serjeant, of London.

II. Jane, *m.* to the Rev. Martin Madan, eldest son of Col. Madan, by Judith his wife, daughter of Mr. Justice Spencer Cowper.

III. Anne, *d.* unm.

Sir Bernard died in Red Lion Square, London, 7th November, 1729, and was *s.* by his son,

WILLIAM HALE, esq. of King's Walden, who espoused, 23rd December, 1745, Elizabeth, youngest daughter of Sir Charles Farnaby, bart. of Kippington, in Kent, and by her, who *d.* 18th March, 1780, had issue,

I. WILLIAM, his heir.

II. Paggen, a banker, in London, who *m.* at Hatfield, in Herts, 8th February, 1791, Miss Mary Keet, and *d. s. p.* 18th January, 1807.

I. Elizabeth, *m.* to the Rev. Mr. Stillingfleet.

II. Charlotte, *m.* first, to Thomas Duncombe, esq. of Duncombe Park, in the county of York; and secondly, to Thomas Onslow, now Earl Onslow.

III. Sarah, married to the Rev. James Bowles, rector of Burford, in Salop, and *d.* in 1783.

IV. Anne, *m.* 18th April, 1782, to Sir Edward Dering, seventh baronet of Turrenden Dering, in Kent.

Mr. Hale *d.* at Chelsea, the 14th September, 1793, aged seventy-seven, and was buried at King's Walden. His son and successor,

WILLIAM HALE, esq. of King's Walden, wedded 3rd April, 1777, the Hon. Mary Grimston, daughter of James, second Viscount Grimston, and had four sons and two daughters, viz.

WILLIAM, his heir.

Paggen, baptized 17th July, 1784, died at Pimlico, 7th November, 1814.

Cecil-Farnaby-Richard, baptized 1st July, 1786, died at Jamaica, 17th January, 1801, a midshipman in the royal navy.

Henry-Jeremy, baptized 15th January, 1791, curate of King's Walden, *m.* Frances, daughter of John Sowerby, esq. of Putteridgebury, Herts, and died leaving two sons and three daughters.

Charlotte-Bucknall, married her cousin, Cholmely Dering, second son of Sir Edward Dering, bart. of Turrenden Dering, and has issue.

Elizabeth-Mary, *m.* to George Proctor, esq. of Mardocks, Herts.

Mr. Hale died 22nd April, 1829, and was *s.* by his eldest son, the present WILLIAM HALE, esq. of King's Walden.

*Arms*—Az. a chev. embattled, counter embattled or.

*Crest*—A snake ppr. entwined round five arrows or, headed sa. feathered arg. one in pale, four saltier ways.

*Estates*—In Herts.

*Town Residence*—Grosvenor Place.

*Seat*—King's Walden, Herts.

# ETTRICK, OF HIGH BARNES.

ETTRICK, *The Rev.* WILLIAM, of High Barnes, in the county palatine of Durham, *b.* 17th May, 1757, A. M. some time fellow of University College, Oxford, late rector of Toners Piddle, and vicar of Aff-Piddle, in the county of Dorset, *m.* Elizabeth, daughter of William Bishop, esq. of Briants Piddle, in the last mentioned shire, and has had issue,

WILLIAM, *b.* 3rd July, 1801.
Anthony, *b.* 15th September, 1810.
Walter, *b.* 24th February, 1812.
John, *b.* 18th April, 1814.

Elizabeth, *m.* to Lieutenant Novosielski, R.N. of the city of Bath.
Catherine, *m.* to Robert Shank Atcheson, solicitor, of Duke Street, Westminster, and has issue.
Anne, *b.* 22nd July, 1804, *d.* 20th May, 1813.
Isabella, *m.* in 1825 to Robert Horn, esq. of Hunter's Hall, Bishopswearmouth, in the county of Durham.
Hellen.
Mary.

Mr. Ettrick succeeded his father on the 22nd February, 1808.

## Lineage.

The first of this family on record,

ANTHONY ETTERICKE,* was of Barford, or Berford, in the parish of Winborn Minster and county of Dorset. He was born about the year 1504, and was captain of horse at the siege of Boulogne, when that place surrendered in 1544 to HENRY VIII. Although this gallant person is the earliest of his family in Dorsetshire, probably in England; and although of his ancestors or even the place of his birth no memorials remain, yet the station he filled in society and the place of his abode after his return from the French campaign prove that he was a gentleman of consideration. When we recollect the turbulent times which ushered in the sixteenth century, the contemporaneous reigns of the eighth HENRY of England and the fifth JAMES of Scotland, the throes of the nascent reformation in both countries, such an uncertainty regarding a man of rank's origin will not be deemed surprising, nor was it indeed an unusual course to adopt as a matter of precaution, when a man's bitterest foes were often to be found within his own household. The circumstance in the instance before us, however, adds a degree of plausibility to the tradition in the family descended from him, that he was a younger son of the Earl of Dunbarton, in Scotland, whose name was Douglas, and who enjoyed amongst his other dignities the title of LORD ETTRICK, but that being implicated in some of the family feuds, and the exterminating dissensions of his times and country, he was under the necessity of expatriating himself with the greatest secrecy and expedition, unencumbered by aught save his good sword and armorial ensigns. Seeking a secure asylum in the land of his adoption, he selected the most retired and the most remote part of England; and further to remove all identity assumed the name of ETTRICK, somewhat altered too in the mode of spelling. Be the narrative true or false, however, with him commences the family line, as recorded in the books of the Herald's College. He *m.* Lucy, daughter of — Chettle, of Blandford St. Mary's, in Dorsetshire, and dying about 1569, was *s.* by his son,

ANTHONY ETTRICKE, of Berford, who *m.* Maud, daughter of Thomas Squibb, of Shapwick, in Dorsetshire, and dying in 1605, left a son and heir,

* He is called WILLIAM, by SURTEES in his History of Durham, probably on the authority of HUTCHINS.

William Ettricke, of Berford, *b.* in 1590, *m.* Anne, daughter of William Willis, of Pamphill, in the county of Dorset, and had (with two daughters, one *m.* to — Northover, of Somersetshire; the other to Sir William Cowthorp, of Ireland,) three sons, namely,

i. Anthony, of Holt Lodge, in the Forest, county of Dorset, *b.* in 1625, M.P. for Christ Church, Hants, in 1685. This gentleman, who was educated at Trinity College, Oxford, under the worthy, but singular, Dr. Kettle, was esteemed an excellent antiquarian and lawyer, and was the associate of the learned in his time. He contributed the additions to Dorsetshire in Gibson's *Camden*. He died in 1703, and his remains were deposited at Wimborn Minster in a coffin painted with armorial ensigns, clamped with iron, and inclosed within iron railing, being deposited under an arch excavated in the thickness of the wall of the church, under a window in the south aisle. In accounting for this curious selection of the place of his sepulture, Hutchins states, that on some dispute with the authorities of the place, Mr. Ettricke had made a vow that he would not be buried either in their church or churchyard, and the matter was thus compromised. The coffin was made in Mr. Ettricke's lifetime; for the date 1691, though partially erased, is yet visible. He obtained a license in 1692 from the official at Wimborn to make this tomb, for which he conferred upon the church a perpetual rent charge of twenty shillings, which is paid by the corporation of Pool out of the tithes of Parkson, near that place, being part of a fee farm rent charge thereon. He *m.* in 1650, Anne, daughter of the Rev. Edward Davenant, D.D. of Gillingham, in the county of Dorset, and grandniece of John Davenant, Bishop of Salisbury; (this lady was educated by her father, and we are informed that she was "a notable algebraist;") by whom he had issue,

1. William, *b.* about 1652, of the Middle Temple, barrister-at-law, and M.P. for Christ Church from 1688 to 1714. He had previously represented Pool in 1685.* He *m.* first, Elizabeth, daughter of Sir Eden Bacon, bart. of Redgrave, in the county of Suffolk, and had a daughter, Elizabeth, who *m.* Philip Boteler, esq. of Woodhall, in the county of Herts. He wedded, secondly, Frances, daughter of Colonel Thomas Wyndham, of Witham, in the county of Somerset, and had another daughter,

   Rachel, who *d.* unm. leaving the family estate by will to her maid-servant, Anne Powell, from whom the heir-at-law, William Ettricke, recovered £10,000.

   He *d.* 4th December, 1716, and was interred at Wimborn Minster.

2. Edward, *b.* in 1654, citizen and drysalter of London, *d.* in 1718, *m.* Elizabeth, daughter of Thomas Hooper, citizen and grocer, also of London, and had

   Anthony, *b.* 17th November, 1683, who *m.* Anne, daughter of Major Francis Seaton, and had (with a daughter, Elizabeth, who became the wife of a hosier at Bath,) a son,

   William, whose son, another

   William, recovered the £10,000 stated above from Anne Powell. He left issue.

   Edward, *d.* unm. at Oxford.

   William, *d. s. p.*

3. Anthony, *d. s. p.* in 1687.

1. Anne, *m.* to William Player, esq. of Mangleford, in the county of Gloucester. Mr. Player purchased, in 1684, the Poyntz estate of Iron Acton, in Gloucestershire.

2. Lucy, *m.* to John Hoddy, esq. of Northway, in the county of Devon.

ii. Andrew, of Blandford Forum or Sturminster, in the county of Dorset, *m.* Anne, daughter of Robert Barker, of Ashwell, in the same shire, and had two sons,

   Andrew, } both in the royal navy,
   Robert, } and both died issueless.

He died in 1679.

iii. Walter, of whose line we are about to treat.

William Ettricke *d.* in 1666. His youngest son,

Walter Ettricke, esq. of Sunderland, *b.*

* The inscription upon his tomb is said to have been written by Prior.

26th April, 1628, and living in the unhappy times of the civil war and Cromwell's usurpation, distinguished himself amongst the most zealous supporters of the royal cause. While yet a student at Oxford, the troops of the parliament were sent thither to purge the university, when many were imprisoned and some put to death, but Walter Ettricke had the good fortune to effect his escape, and flying into Dorsetshire, his father could only sustain him secretly, not daring to receive openly a person so marked into his family. When the dissensions of the times subsided, he retired into the county palatine of Durham, and settling there became the founder of the third branch of the family. He purchased the estate of High Barnes, a moiety of Barnes, formerly one of the extensive possessions of the family of Bowes,* and he seems also to have been the first of his family who held a valuable leasehold estate under the Bishops of Durham, comprising the ferry boats, meetage, and tolls of Sunderland, for twenty-one years, renewable every seventh year, and which remained in his descendants until an act of parliament was obtained by Rowland Burdon, esq. of Castle Eden, M.P. for the purpose of building a bridge of cast iron over the river Wear. Mr. Surtees makes mention of this leasehold so far back as 1665, and of Walter Ettricke negotiating with Bishop Cosins to change it from years into lives; the bishop, however, declined to agree, apprehending similar applications. Walter Ettricke was some time collector of the customs at Stockton, and afterwards at Sunderland. He was register of the Court of Admiralty in 1661. He *m.* in 1659, Margaret, daughter of William Sedgewick, esq. of Elvet, in the county of Durham, and had six sons and five daughters, viz.

I. William, *b.* 1st June, 1661, collector of the port of Sunderland, *m.* Elizabeth, daughter and co-heir of George Middleton, esq. of Silksworth, in the county of Durham, and became of that place. He *d.* in 1735, and his widow on the 16th February, 1759.

II. Anthony, of whom presently.

III. Walter, IV. William, V. John, VI. Ralph, } all died in infancy, between the years 1666 and 1671.

I. Margaret, bapt. 7th December, 1664, buried 1st September, 1688.

II. Dorothy, bapt. 7th December, 1669, buried 17th July, 1687.

III. Elizabeth, bapt. 2nd June, 1674, buried 24th March, 1690.

IV. Anne, bapt. 28th October, 1677, *m.* 11th September, 1698, to the Rev. Thomas Ogle, M.A. perpetual curate of Bishop Wearmouth, and had a son,

Thomas Ogle, gent. of the city of Durham.

She *d.* in 1751, having been a widow fifty years.

V. Mary, bapt. 28th December, 1680.

Walter Ettricke *d.* at Bath, on the 2nd August, 1700, and was *s.* at High Barnes by his second son,

Anthony Ettricke, esq. of High Barnes,† *b.* 16th August, 1663. This gentleman *m.*

* It appears, by existing deeds, that the whole of the manor of Barnes and Hamelden (now called Hamilton Hill), with Pallion and Clowcroft, as well as the tithe of corn and grain of Ryhope, remained in the family of Bowes until the decease, in 1662, of William Bowes, a minor, and without issue. The estate then descended to his cousin, Mary Bowes, who married William Haddock, which gentleman sold, in 1668, the moiety of Barnes, called Low Barnes, to John Jenkins, subject to a moiety of the tithe, rent, or modus payable to the church of Bishop Wearmouth, with a title to one half of the pews and burying ground within the church, belonging to the whole manor of Barnes. In 1673, William Haddock conveyed the other moiety of Barnes to Walter Ettrick, esq. with the other half of the right of the pews and burying ground belonging to the said manor, subject to a moiety of the modus aforesaid. In these deeds a recital is made of the lease from the Bishop of Durham to Walter Ettrick, of the Ferry over the river Wear, and of the meetage and tolls of Sunderland, dated 1st February, 1694, at a rent of forty shillings a year, for twenty-one years, renewable every seventh year with a fine.

† This gentleman succeeded his father at High Barnes, by a deed of settlement made upon his second marriage in 1700. Owing to the dispersion of the property of the Bowes' family, the payments of the modus for the manor of Barnes and its appurtenances had fallen into confusion, and, in 1702, a suit was instituted in the court of Exchequer by Dr. Robert Grey, the rector of Bishopwearmouth, in which John Jenkins, Anthony Ettrick, and others were made defendants. The aim of the suit was, not to invalidate the antiquity of the modus, but to obtain a higher sum in the payment than had been latterly made by the parties concerned: the dispute was terminated by establishing the ancient amount claimed by Dr. Grey, and a form of receipt to be given by the rectors was dictated by the court in a decree dated 11th December, 1702, of a modus of £14. 13s. 4d. for "*all manner of tithes whatsoever arising from the lands and manor of Barnes, with the appurtenances.*" Notwithstanding this decree of the Exchequer, of *No tithe due of any kind whatsoever*, Dr. Smith, the next rector, set up a demand of "Plow penny, Rook penny, and Peter's pence," on the plea that the modus exempted the inhabitants from tithes arising from

first, Jane, daughter and heiress of Richard Starling, esq. and great niece of Sir Samuel Starling, knt. alderman of London, by whom he had a daughter,

Elizabeth, *m.* first, to Musgrave Davison, esq. and secondly, to Thomas Medlycott, esq. of Venne, in Somersetshire.

He wedded, secondly, Elizabeth, daughter of Henry Coghill, esq. of Aldenham, Herts. By this lady, who wedded after his decease — Wittering, esq. he had two sons and three daughters, viz.

William, his heir.

Henry, a surgeon in the navy, died in the East Indies, aged thirty-one. He *m.* Elizabeth, daughter of Thomas Cartwright, a citizen of London. He left a son,

Walter, who *d.* young.

Sarah, *d.* unm. at the age of sixty.

Elizabeth, living in 1698, unm.

Hellen, lived at St. Albans, *d.* in 1786, unm.

Anthony Ettricke *d.* in 1728, was buried on the 9th December, and *s.* by his elder son,

William Ettrick, esq. of High Barnes, born 22nd December, 1701, in the commission of the peace for the county of Durham, who *m.* in 1722, Isabella, daughter of William Langley, esq. of Elwick, in Norfolk, grandson of Sir Roger Langley, bart. of Sheriff Hutton Park, in the county of York, and had issue,

I. William, his heir.

II. John, *b.* in 1729, died in Jamaica, unmarried.

III. Langley, died in 1735.

IV. Anthony, *b.* in 1734, killed on his passage to Jamaica, unmarried before 1761.

V. Walter, *b.* in 1736, a midshipman in the Royal Navy, died unm. before 1761.

I. Rachel, died unm. in France.

II. Philippa, *b.* in 1738.

III. Judith, *m.* first, to — Woodward, of London, merchant, and, secondly, to Hugh French, M.D. died in 1822.

IV. Anne, *m.* to James Moor, gent. of London, and *d.* 16th September, 1816.

V. Elizabeth, *m.* first, to Edward Weddell, of Yarmouth, in the county of York, and secondly, to John Carter, esq. of the same place. By the latter she had a daughter, Jane Carter, *m.* to William Havelock, esq. of Ingress Park, in Kent, father of Major Havelock, of the 11th Light Dragoons, a knight of the Royal Hanoverian Guelphic order, and aid-de-camp to Baron Alten, at Waterloo (see vol. i. p. 41).

VI. Isabella, died in 1732-3.

William Ettrick acquired, by his marriage, a considerable fortune, but following, with too much zeal, the expensive taste of improvement, became involved in difficulties, and found it necessary to recall from his seafaring life, his eldest William, a gentleman of great prudence and activity, to whom (six months previously to his decease in 1752) he resigned the whole estate, and who thereupon became

William Ettrick, esq. of High Barnes. This gentleman, *b.* 14th May, 1726, passed the early part of his life in the naval service of his country, and, upon his retirement from that profession to take possession of his patrimony, became an active and highly respected magistrate for the county of Durham. He enjoyed the estates for fifty-six years, and, by his excellent management,

---

the land, but not from personal tithes. This demand was of course not admissible, and how the dispute was settled does not further appear, but Dr. Smith died 30th July, 1715, and no such tithe was ever paid, or even demanded by the rectors who followed, Bowes, Laurence, Stillingfleet, Chandler, until the next, Dr. Henry Bland, who entered in 1735, made, in 1767, a vigorous effort to break through by a demand of "Easter offerings, oblations and obventions," yet acknowledging the ancient modus and its validity against prædial tithes, but not to the exclusion of personal. The holy war raged in the courts for two years and upwards, and ended as previously, no such tithe having ever been paid before or since, and a regular receipt for the amount of three years suspended modus in the form prescribed being now found in the bundle of receipts, signed "Henry Bland," rector, 1769.

In the year 1708 Anthony Ettrick entered into an engagement with the persons then entitled to Mr. Jenkins' moiety of Barnes, for the purchase thereof, on behalf of Lancelott Wardell, a quaker; and he therein agreed to convey to Mr. Wardell "the site of the old mansion and other parts of the property adjacent at Low Barnes," which had belonged to his own moiety. By the same agreement Wardell was exempted from his proportion of the modus, which was then laid on High Barnes; and certain lands and the other moiety of the pews and burying ground, with the portion of the modus rent, issuing out of the lands of Pallion, were conveyed to Anthony Ettrick. Notwithstanding all this, when the body of the late owner of High Barnes, thus entitled to the whole space of burying ground appropriated to both moieties of Barnes, was to be buried, there remained barely room for one coffin! the rest having been vaulted, and surreptitiously sold to another family. Thus the splendid monument, destined by the will of Mr. Ettrick, to have been erected on his burial ground, was of necessity withdrawn from the church of Bishopwearmouth.

not only left them unencumbered, but accumulated likewise a large personal property, and erected in 1777-8, a handsome mansion upon the scite of the former family residence.

He wedded, in 1752, Catherine, daughter of Robert Wharton, esq. of Old Park, in the palatinate, and had by her (who died in Nov. 1794) one son and one daughter, viz.

WILLIAM, his heir.

Catherine, *m.* William Budle, of Monkwearmouth, and *d. s. p.* in 1821.

Mr. Ettrick died 22nd February, 1808, aged eighty-two, and was succeeded by his only son, the present Rev. WILLIAM ETTRICK, of High Barnes. By his last will, he left a considerable sum to be expended on a family memorial; and, in consequence, a beautiful cenotaph, which cost upwards of £500, was erected by his son, at High Barnes, with the following inscription, which himself suggested:

To the memory of William Ettrick, esq.
late of High Barnes, in the county of Durham,
and many years an active and upright magistrate
in the said county,
who departed this life on the 22nd February, 1808,
in the eighty-third year of his age:
and by his last will caused this sepulchral
monument to be erected
to perpetuate the memory of his father, William
Ettrick, esq.
and his grandfather, Anthony Ettrick, esq.
and his great-grandfather, Walter Ettrick, esq.
all of High Barnes,
in an humble but grateful acknowledgment of the
kind provision
they have made for their posterity.

*Arms*—Arg. a lion rampant, and a chief gu.

*Crest*—A demi lion rampant gu. holding in the dexter paw a marshal's staff sable, tipped at each end or.

*Estates*—In Durham.

*Seat*—High Barnes.

## DENNE, OF KENT AND SUSSEX.

DENNE, WILLIAM-JOHN, esq. of Winchelsea, in Sussex, *b.* in 1788; *m.* in July, 1817, Mary-Jane, daughter of Major Alexander Orme, of the East India Company's Bengal service, and has an only child,

MARY-JANE.

Mr. Denne succeeded his father in January, 1819.

### Lineage.

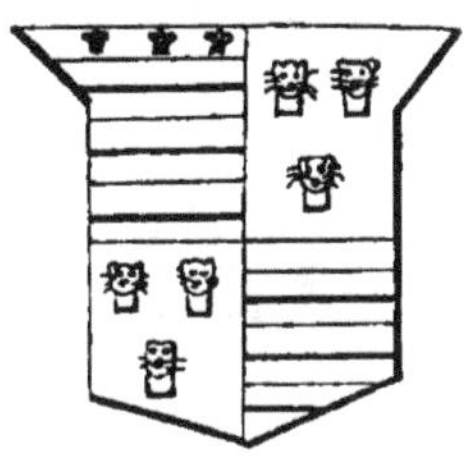

The Dennes were established in Kent, antecedently to the Conquest, by a Norman,

ROBERT DE DENE, who held large estates in Sussex and Kent, as well as in the duchy, and was *Pincerna* or butler to EDWARD the Confessor. His son and heir,

ROBERT DE DENE, was father of

RALPH DE DENE, living in the time of WILLIAM, *the Conqueror*, lord of Buckhurst, in Sussex, who wedded Sybella, sister of Robert de Gatton, and had a son, ROBERT, his heir, and a daughter, ELLA,* *m.* to Sir Jordan Sackville, ancestor of the dukes of Dorset.

This Ralph de Dene, who possessed large estates in Kent and Sussex, founded Otteham Abbey, for monks of the Premonstratensian order. His son and successor,

ROBERT DE DENE, inherited the Kentish

* This Ella, who inherited by will from her father Buckhurst and other estates in Sussex, in her widowhood endowed Bayham Abbey. See charter in the British Museum, by which she gives permission to the abbot and community to remove their establishment from their convent at Otteham, founded by her father Ralph Dene, to Bayham.

estates. He married, and had, with two daughters, Alice, who endowed Bayham Abbey, and Agnes, wife of — De Icklisham, a son,

**William de Denn**, of Denn Hill, in the parish of Kingston on Barham Downs, Kent, who was *s.* by his son,

**Sir Alured de Denn**, of Denn Hill, a person of great learning, seneschal of the priory of Canterbury, and escheator of Kent *anno* 1234, who was appointed by Henry III. to enforce, in conjunction with Sir Henry de Bath, the laws of Romney Marsh. He was *s.* by his son,

**Walter Denne**, of Denne Hill, living in 1256, whose son, another

**Walter Denne**, of Denne Hill, alive in the 9th Edward I. was father of

**John Denne**, of Denne Hill, in 1308, who was *s.* by his son,

**Sir William Denne**, knt. of Denne Hill, who sat in Parliament for the city of Canterbury 19th Edward II. and for the county of Kent in the 14th of the following reign. Sir William espoused Elizabeth, daughter and co-heiress of Hamo de Gatton, of Boughton, and left a son and successor,

**Richard Denne**, of Denne, living in the 16th Richard II. who *m.* Agnes, daughter of — Apuldrefield, of Challock,* and had four sons, Thomas, Michael, John, and Robert; of whom the eldest,

**Thomas Denne**, of Denne Hill, wedded Isabel, daughter and heir of Robert de Earde, and had (with a younger son, Thomas, who died issueless in 1468), his successor,

**John Denne**, of Denne Hill, who *m.* Alice, daughter of Richard Ardren, and had issue,

- Michael, his heir.
- Thomas, of Kingston, who *m.* Agnes, daughter of William Eshehurst, and had an only daughter and heiress, Avis, *m.* to John Crispe, of Quicks, in the Isle of Thanet.
- Parnell, *m.* to William Keale.

The elder son,

**Michael Denne**, esq. of Denne Hill, living in the reigns of Edward IV. and Henry VII. espoused Christiana Coombe, of Lymne, an heiress, and had issue,

- I. Thomas, his heir.
- II. William.
- III. John, of Lymne, Kent, who *m.* and had four sons, viz.
  1. Michael, of Lymne, who *d.* in 1559, leaving issue.
  2. Henry, mentioned in his brother Michael's will.
  3. John, *m.* and had issue.
  4. Peter, *m.* and had issue.
- I. Isabella, *m.* to Simon Quilter.

The eldest son,

**Thomas Denne**, esq. of Denne Hill, left by Alice Eshehurst, his wife, three sons, viz.

- I. Thomas, of Denne Hill, who *m.* Alicia, daughter of Thomas Mett, esq. and had a son and heir,

  **Robert Denne**, esq. of Denne Hill, who *m.* Thomasin, daughter and heir of Thomas Dane, esq. of Herne, and left (with four younger sons and two daughters, Mary, *m.* to Edward Osborne, of Hartlipp, see Tylden, of Milsted and Torré Hill, vol. ii. p. 383, and Silvester, to Thomas Coppin, of Minster, in Thanet) a son and successor,

  **Thomas Denne**, esq. of Denne Hill, recorder of Canterbury, reader of the Inner Temple, and M.P. for Canterbury 21st James I. He *m.* Dorothy, dau. of John Tanfield, esq. of Margareting, in Essex, and dying in 1656, left issue,
  1. Thomas, of Gray's Inn, *d. s. p.*
  2. John, of the Inner Temple, barrister at law, buried in the Temple Church *anno* 1648, *s. p.*
  1. Thomasin, *m.* to Sir Nicholas Crispe, of Quicks.
  2. Bridget, *m.* to Sir John Darell, of Calehill.
  3. Dorothy, *m.* to Roger Lukyn, esq.
  4. Mary, *m.* to Vincent Denne, sergeant at law, recorder of Canterbury, and M.P. for Kent, who became, *jure uxoris*, "of Denne Hill." He *d.* in 1693: she in 1701, leaving four daughters, viz.
     - Dorothy, who had the Wenderton estates, and *m.* Thomas Girder, esq.
     - Mary, *m.* to Stephen Nethersole, esq. of Nethersole.
     - Honeywood, who inherited the Tarmested estate, which was sold by her husband, Gilbert Knowles, esq. to Thomas Harris, of Canterbury.

* "This ancient family," says Philpot, "descended from Henry de Apuldrefield, of Apuldrefield, in Coudham, who was in the catalogue of those eminent Kentish gentlemen who were engaged with Richard I. at the siege of Acre, in Palestine."

BRIDGET, of Denne Hill, *m.* Robert Beake, gent. by whose heirs Denne Hill was sold about 1730. It is now (1834) the seat of General Sir Henry Montresor.

II. WILLIAM, of whom presently.

III. James, of Marley, who *d.* at Kingston in 1574, leaving issue, by Agnes his wife.

The second son of Thomas Denne, of Denne Hill, by Alice Eshehurst his wife,

WILLIAM DENNE, esq. of Kingston, in Kent, proprietor of extensive estates in that county, espoused Agnes, daughter of Nicholas Tufton, esq. of Northiam Place, in Sussex, great grandfather to the first earl of Thanet, and by her, who *d.* in 1588, had issue,

I. VINCENT, of Kingston, LL.D. *m.* Joan Kettell, of London, and dying in 1591, left

1. JOHN, of Gray's Inn, barrister at law, *m.* Lucy, daughter of Walter Aylworth, esq. of St. Stephens, and had, with two sons who *d. s. p.* four daughters, the youngest, Joan, *m.* Henry Johnson, esq.
2. William, of Kingston and Burstead, in Bishopsbourne, ancestor of the DENNES, of Elbridge, now extinct in the male line, but represented through female descent by DENNE DENNE, esq. of Elbridge.
3. Thomas, of Canterbury, *m.* Susan, daughter and co-heir of Arthur Honeywood, esq. of Lenham, and had issue,

   VINCENT, sergeant at law, M.P. who *m.* as above, his relative, Mary Denne, of Denne Hill. He *d.* leaving four daughters, his co-heirs.

   William, } both living in 1663<br>John, }

   Elizabeth, *m.* to her cousin, Vincent Nethersole, esq. of Nethersole House, Kent.
4. Henry, of London, merchant, and of Dane House, Kent, *d.* in 1613.
5. Vincent.

1. Elizabeth, *m.* to Vincent Nethersole, esq. of Nethersole.
2. Jane, *m.* to William Denne, esq. of Bishopsbourne.

II. THOMAS, of whom presently.

I. Mary, *m.* first, to John Coppin, esq.; and, secondly, to Thomas Boys, esq. of Eythorne.

II. Catherine, *m.* to Thomas Gookin, esq. of Ripple Court, Kent.

William Denne (who *m.* Agnes Tufton) *d.* in 1572, and by his will, proved at Canterbury, John Coppyn, esq. and Sir Henry Cripp, knt. trustees, devised property at Adisham, Well, and Beaksbourne, to his second son,

THOMAS DENNE, esq. a bencher of Lincoln's Inn in 1590, who *m.* Jane, daughter of John Swift, esq. of Essex and London, and had (with several younger children, for whom see Visitation)

I. HENRY, of Adisham, a civilian and bencher of Lincoln's Inn, living at the Visitation in 1619. He wedded Mary, daughter of John Hyde, esq. of London, and had an only child, Helen or Elinor, who *d.* unmarried in 1669.

II. JOHN, of whom hereafter.

III. William, of Bishopsbourne, who *m.* his cousin Jane, daughter of Vincent Denne, esq. LL.D. and *d.* in 1616, leaving issue.

The second son,

JOHN DENNE, esq. baptized at Beaksbourne 6th July, 1578, living in 1619 at the visitation of Kent, was of Patricksborne Court Lodge, in that county. He *m.* and left, with a younger son, William, baptized at Adisham, the residence of his grandfather, in 1620, and a daughter, Elizabeth, *b.* in 1624, his successor,

JOHN DENNE, esq. of Patricksbourne Court Lodge, *b.* in 1619, who *d.* in 1690, aged seventy-one, and was buried at Patricksbourne, leaving, by Elizabeth his wife, three sons, viz.

I. DAVID, his heir.

II. Thomas, of Braboren Court, which he purchased in 1700.

III. John, born at Patricksbourne in 1668.

The eldest son,

DAVID DENNE, esq. of Bishopsborne, *b.* at Patricksborne 15th October, 1662; *m.* Sarah, relict of the Rev. Mr. Shipwash, of Wye, and died in 1702, aged thirty-nine, leaving a daughter, Elizabeth, *m.* to Thomas Hogben, and a son,

THOMAS DENNE, esq. of Lydd, *b.* in February, 1701, who *m.* in 1741, Sarah, daughter and co-heir* of Thomas Greenland, esq. of Lydd, and had by her, who *d.* at Fairfield in 1783, five sons and two daughters, viz.

---

* Mary, the other daughter and co-heir *m.* Mark Skinner, esq. of Lydd, and left one daughter, Mary, *m.* first, to Chamberlain Hopkins, esq. and, secondly, to General Thomas Murray, son of Sir David Murray, of Stanhope.

I. JOHN, of Bath, *b.* in 1748, *m.* Miss Anna-Maria Heblewhite, and *d.* in 1828, *s. p.*
II. RICHARD.
III. David, of Lydd, who *m.* Katherine, daughter of Robert Cobb, esq. and *d.* in 1819, leaving issue,
1. David, of Lydd, who *m.* Louisa-Anne, daughter of the late Rev. Thomas Cobb, of Ightham, and has issue.
2. Thomas, of the Temple.
1. Elizabeth, *m.* to the Rev. William Vallance, of Sittingbourne.
2. Cecilia, *m.* to the Rev. Mr. Nares.
3. Katherine.
4. Mary-Julia.
IV. Thomas, who *d.* unmarried in 1783, aged twenty-seven.
V. William, in the army, *d.* unmarried in 1783, aged twenty-one.

I. Sarah, *m.* John Porker, esq. of Muswell Hill, a banker in London, and dying in 1808, left issue,
1. John Porker, of London.
2. Mary Porker, *m.* to Sir John Peter.
3. Elizabeth Porker, *m.* to General George Cookson, R. A.
4. Caroline Porker, *m.* to James Atkinson, esq. of Russell Square, and *d.* in 1810.
5. Emily Porker, *m.* to General Sir Alexander Bryce, R. E.
II. Elizabeth, *m.* to Richard Ruck, esq. of Gravesend, and *d. s. p.*

Mr. Denne *d.* in 1777, possessed of considerable property at Lydd and Romney Marsh, in Kent, and at Winchelsea and in Sussex. His second but eldest son to leave issue,

RICHARD DENNE, esq. of Winchelsea, wedded, in 1783, Mary, daughter of William Steer, esq. of Northampton, by Anne his wife, daughter of the venerable William Rastall, D.D. dean of Southwell, a lineal descendant of Chief Justice Rastall, and had issue,

WILLIAM-JOHN, his heir.
Richard-Greenland, of the Inner Temple, barrister-at-law.
Anna-Maria, of Broadstairs.
Frances, *m.* to Captain Ernest-Christian Welford, of the Royal Engineers.
Mary-Jane, *m.* to Robert-William Newman, esq. of Mamhead, in Devon, late M.P. for Exeter.

Mr. Denne *d.* in January, 1819, and was *s.* by his eldest son, the present WILLIAM-JOHN DENNE, esq.

*Arms*—Quarterly, first and fourth, az. three bars erm. in chief, as many fleurs de lys, or, (coat granted to Thomas Denne, esq. in 1580); second and third, azure, three leopards' heads couped or.

*Crest*—On a chapeau vert, turned up erm. a demi peacock, wings expanded and elevated ppr. This crest was also granted in 1580, but has not been used from time immemorial.

*Estates*—Romney Marsh and Wareham, in Kent; Winchelsea, Icklesham, Rye, &c. &c. in Sussex.

*Town Residence*—Upper Wimpole Street.

## FARQUHAR, OF GILMILNSCROFT.

FARQUHAR-GRAY, JAMES, esq. of Gilmilnscroft, in the county of Ayr, *m.* in 1801, Margaret-Cochrane, eldest daughter of Major James Baillie, of the 7th, or Royal Fusileers, and fort-major of Fort St. George, by Margaret Ross, his wife, eldest daughter of Lord Anchorville, late one of the senators of the College of Justice, and has issue,

JOHN.
Margaret.
Jane.

Mr. Gray-Farquhar, who is lieutenant-colonel of the Royal Ayrshire Militia, succeeded to Gilmilnscroft upon the demise of his mother in 1809. He had inherited, in 1801, a considerable property in Northumberland on the death of Robert Farquhar, of Rothburry, lieutenant-colonel of the 81st regiment.

## Lineage.

The family of FARQUHAR has enjoyed its present possessions, in Kyle Stewart, for many generations. The first proprietor on record,

ROBERT FARQUHAR, must have been laird of Gilmilnscroft, in the latter end of the fourteenth century, for, in the commencement of the fifteenth, *anno* 1407, an infeftment was granted by Agnes Wallace, gudewife of Gilmilnscroft, and relict of Robert Farquhar, to her son,

ALEXANDER FARQUHAR, of Gilmilnscroft, who was *s.* by

THOMAS FARQUHAR, of Gilmilnscroft, who had a charter from JAMES I. king of Scotland, in which he is styled son of Alexander Farquhar. He appears to have been father of

JOHN FARQUHAR, of Gilmilnscroft, who had a charter in 1445, from the commendator of the abbey of Melrose, of the lands of Castle Cavil. He wedded Margaret, dau. of the laird of Barquharrie, and was progenitor of

ALEXANDER FARQUHAR, of Gilmilnscroft, who married and had, with a daughter Catherine, *m.* about the year 1546, to John Hamilton, of Camskeith, a son and successor,

ANDREW FARQUHAR, of Gilmilnscroft, who died in 1556. He was father of

ALEXANDER FARQUHAR, of Gilmilnscroft, who wedded, in 1586, a daughter of Charles Campbell, of Glaisnock (of the Loudoun family, in the deed of entail of Hugh, the first Lord Loudoun, dated in 1613), by whom he left at his decease, in 1625, a son and successor,

ROBERT FARQUHAR, of Gilmilnscroft. In 1641 Robert Farquhar of Gilmilnscroft, and George Reid, of Daldilling, had a ratification in parliament of the lands of Kylesmure, to themselves and remanent vassals; and in 1643 Farquhar was nominated by parliament among the commissioners of the county of Air, who "shall convein at the burgh of Ayr, with the wholl heritoures, lyferenteres, tacksmen, titulares, propper wad-setteres, pensiouneres, conjunctfieres, ladyterceres, and uthers, in order to assess themselves towards a loan of the general sum of 1,200,000 marks Scot; together with 100,000 marks of like money, for collecting the same over the kingdom at large, for defraying the expense that had been incurred by the sending of an army of 10,000 soldiers to Ireland to suppress the rebellion there. Such have been the greate necessities and wants of that airmie, als weill officeres as souldieres, not only through default of their ordinarie pay, but also of victual in the spairest measure." The sum ordered thus to be lent, for Ayrshire, was £49,480. Scots; also £7,068. for the more immediate use of the army within the kingdom. The first assessment or loan to be repaid by the parliament of England.* Robert Farquhar appears to have died some time in the year 1646, and was *s.* by his son,

ROBERT FARQUHAR, of Gilmilnscroft, who under the designation of GUILDMIDSCROFT, *Younger*, was appointed one of the committee of war for Ayrshire, for the furthering of the service of the kingdom, on the 11th February, 1646. He espoused, 22nd September, 1651, Elizabeth, daughter of James Ross, of Ballneill, in the county of Wigton, and with her received 8000 marks of tocher. The subscribing witnesses to the marriage contract were Mr. James Dalrymple, of Stair; John Macdowall, brother to Sir James Macdowall, of Garthland; and Alexander Baillie, son to John Baillie. The Mr. James Dalrymple† here mentioned was subsequently raised to the peerage by the title of Viscount Stair.

Gilmilnscroft appears to have died without issue, for, in 1670,

ROBERT FARQUHAR, of Lightshaw (son of Mungo Farquhar, and grandson of Farquhar of Gilmilnscroft) succeeded his cousin

---

* Robertson's Ayrshire.

† James Dalrymple (Lord Stair), wedded Margaret, the eldest daughter of Ross, of Ballneil, and was thus brother-in-law to Gilmilnscroft. Of this Margaret, who was a most extraordinary woman, many singular tales are told, amongst others, the following is to be found in LAW's *Memorial*, "She lived to a great age, and at her death desired that she might not be put under ground, but that her coffin should stand upright on one end of it, promising that while she remained in that situation the Dalrymples should continue to flourish. It is certain her coffin stands upright in the aisle of the church of Kirkleston, the burial-place belonging to the family; and it is probable that this odd position of her corpse, and the sudden rise of so many of that name, without any very visible reason, might have given occasion to the vulgar conjecture that she was a witch." She is also thought to have been the prototype of Lady Ashton, in the Bride of Lammermoor,—" *Oer true a tale.*"

Robert Farquhar, the preceding laird. This gentleman, who lived in the reigns of CHARLES II. and his brother JAMES, adhered steadfastly to the principles of the covenanters, yet conducted himself with so much prudence as to avoid the resentment of the court, while he preserved the confidence of his own party. The colours which were borne by the Dalgain division at their different rencounters with their opponents, were entrusted to his care in the intervals of repose, and remained concealed in the mansion of Gilmilnscroft until the revolution in 1688, when they were publicly exhibited. At that time a new device was added: a Scots thistle, surmounted with an imperial crown, splendidly emblazoned in blue, scarlet and gold, under which was written in large golden letters, "For God, the Covenant, Presbyterianism, Reformation, Crown, and Country. 1689." The flag remains in good preservation.

Gilmilnscroft *m.* Julian, daughter of Nisbet, of Greenholme, and had three sons and two daughters, viz.

JAMES, his heir.
Hugh, a colonel in the army.
George.

Sarah, *m.* to John Reid, of Ballochmyle.
Barbara.

The eldest son,

JAMES FARQUHAR, esq. of Gilmilnscroft, succeeded his father in 1698. He wedded, in 1700, Jean, daughter of William Porterfield, of that Ilk, by Annabella, his wife, daughter of Steward, of Blackhall, and had issue,

I. Robert, who predeceased his father.
II. ALEXANDER.

I. Annabella, *m.* to Andrew Brown, esq. of Water Head.
II. Margaret, *m.* to Duncan Campbell, of Barbieston.
III. Ann.
IV. Jean, *m.* to John Whyte, of Neuk.
V. Mary, *m.* to Charles Campbell, esq. brother of Barbieston.

Mr. Farquhar was succeeded by his only son,

ALEXANDER FARQUHAR, esq. of Gilmilnscroft, who *m.* first, Agnes, eldest daughter of John Campbell, of Whitehaugh, by Catherine Ferguson, his wife, a daughter of Auchenblain, but by her had no child. He wedded, secondly, Elizabeth, daughter of Joseph Wilson, of Barmuir, provost of Ayr, by Isabella, daughter of Muir, of Blairstoun, and had a daughter,

JANE, his heiress.

He espoused, thirdly, Jean, daughter of Alexander Cunninghame, of Polquharne, which lady died without issue. Gilmilnscroft was succeeded by his only child,

JANE FARQUHAR, of Gilmilnscroft, who wedded, in 1777, JOHN GRAY, esq. of Kilmerdenny (see family of GRAY, at foot), and had issue,

I. JAMES, her heir.
II. Alexander, formerly in the army.
III. John, lieutenant, 40th regiment, who died in consequence of wounds received at Salamanca.
IV. William, a merchant in Glasgow.
V. Andrew, comptroller of the customs at Irvine, who *m.* in 1820, Margaret, daughter of the late Benjamin Barton, esq. late commissary-clerk of Glasgow, and has a son John, and other issue.
VI. Robert, who died in 1807.

I. Eliza, *m.* to John Ashburnham, M.D. of London.

The heiress of Gilmilnscroft died in 1809, and was succeeded by her eldest son, the present JAMES GRAY-FARQUHAR, esq. of Gilmilnscroft.

### Family of Gray.

This family derives from a common progenitor with the extinct ducal houses of Suffolk and Kent,* the baronial houses of Gray and Warwick, and the existing houses of Tankerville and Stamford, namely, from Anschetel de Croy, one of the companions in arms of the Conqueror. The Scottish barons sprung immediately from the Greys of Chillingham, in Northumberland. Of those,

ANDREW, THIRD LORD GRAY, living in 1564, married, for his second wife, the Lady Elizabeth Stewart, sister, by the mother's side, of JAMES II. and had several sons. The third,

ANDREW GRAY, of Muirton, was grandfather of

THOMAS GRAY, of Brighouse, whose son,

SIR WILLIAM GRAY, of Pittendrum, was one of the greatest merchants of his time in Scotland. Adhering to the royal cause in the civil wars, he was fined by the parliament of St. Andrews, for corresponding with Montrose, in the sum of 100,000 marks, and was imprisoned in Edinburgh Castle until the penalty was modified to 35,000, which he instantly paid. A loan of £10,000. was subsequently extorted from him, but never returned. Sir William did not long survive these hardships, but died

* For a full account of the early Greys, see BURKE's *Extinct Peerage*.

in 1648. He married Egidia, sister of Sir John Smith, of Grotbill and King's Cramond, lord provost of Edinburgh, by whom he had six sons and twelve daughters. Of these ten formed honourable alliances, especially Agnes, who wedded, first, Sir John Dundas, of New Liston, by whom she had an only daughter and heiress, Elizabeth Dundas, who espoused John, first Earl of Stair. Lady. Dundas married, secondly, Sir Archibald Primrose, lord register, ancestor of the noble family of Roseberry.

Of the sons of Sir William Gray,

I. WILLIAM, the eldest, *m.* ANNE, MISTRESS OF GRAY, and on his marriage had 232,000 marks from his father. He was killed in a duel with the Earl of Southesk in 1660, leaving a son,

PATRICK, who succeeded his maternal grandfather as ninth BARON GRAY. His lordship *m.* Barbara Murray, daughter of Andrew, Lord Balvaid, and had an only daughter,

MARJORY, Mistress of Gray, who *m.* her cousin, John Gray.

II. Robert, the second son, was killed at Inverkeithing, leaving a son,

JOHN, of Crichie, who married his cousin, Marjory, Mistress of Gray, and, by a peculiarity in a new patent of peerage, became, after her death, tenth LORD GRAY, even in the lifetime of his father-in-law Patrick, the ninth lord, and as such took the oaths in parliament in 1707. He was direct ancestor of FRANCIS, present LORD GRAY.

III. David, the third son, was slain at Tangier with the Earl of Teviot.

IV. Andrew, the fourth son, minister of Glasgow, was ordained when only nineteen years of age, and died before attaining his twenty-second, in 1696.

V. JOHN, the fifth son, of whose line we are about to treat.

The youngest,

JOHN GRAY, was father of

ANDREW GRAY, whose only son,

JOHN GRAY, was minister of the High Church of Glasgow. He *m.* first, Margaret, daughter of the Rev. Mr. Morton, minister of Bothwell, by his wife, a daughter of Porter, of Livlland, and had a son, ANDREW, who for many years was minister of New Kilpatrick, in Dumbartonshire, in which parish he acquired the lands and mansion of Kilmardenny, about five miles north-west of Glasgow. Mr. Gray wedded, secondly, Mary, daughter of Aird, of Miltown, by Elizabeth, his wife, daughter of Nisbet, of Greenholme, and by her had a son,

JAMES GRAY, minister of Strathblane, the adjoining parish to that in which his half-brother Andrew was settled. He *m.* in 1769, Agnes, daughter of William Fogo, of Killorn, in Perthshire, by his first wife, Agnes, daughter of Campbell, of Ederline, in Argyleshire, (whose mother was a daughter of Graham, of Killearn). By this lady he had two sons and five daughters,

JOHN, his heir.
William, who died unmarried.

Agnes.
Mary, died unmarried.
Elizabeth, *m.* to John Longmuir, esq. of Glasgow, and *d.* in 1809, *s. p.*
Margaret, died unmarried.
Jean, *m.* to William Mayne, esq. of Glasgow, and died in 1810, leaving issue,

Mr. Gray's eldest son,

JOHN GRAY, married, as already stated, JANE, heiress of Gilmilnscroft, assumed the surname of FARQUHAR, and *d.* in 1823, leaving, inter alios, a son and successor, the present Lieutenant-colonel GRAY-FARQUHAR, of Gilmilnscroft.

*Arms*—Arg. a lion rampant sa. armed and langued or, between three sinister hands, two and one, couped paleways gu.

*Crest*—A dexter hand, couped as in the arms.

*Supporters*—Two greyhounds, ppr.

*Motto*—Sto, cado, fide et armis.

*Estates*—In Ayrshire.

*Seat*—Gilmilnscroft, in Kyle Stewart.

# HAY NEWTON, OF NEWTON.

**NEWTON-HAY, RICHARD,** esq. of Newton Hall, in the county of Haddington, succeeded his father in February, 1829.

Mr. Hay Newton is a deputy lieutenant for Haddingtonshire.

## Lineage.

This is a branch of the noble house of TWEEDDALE.

LORD WILLIAM HAY, of Newhall, third son of John, second marquess of Tweeddale, *m.* Margaret, only child of John Hay, esq. of Limplum, and *d.* in 1723, leaving, *inter alios*,

- I. JOHN, from whom descend GEORGE, the present MARQUESS OF TWEEDDALE, and the HAYS, of Newhall, who have assumed the additional surname of MACKENZIE.
- II. James, who *d.* in 1779, leaving issue.
- III. RICHARD, of whom presently.

The third son,

RICHARD HAY, esq. assumed the surname of NEWTON, on inheriting the estates of that family. He *m.* Anne, only daughter of John Stuart,* esq. of Kincardine, by Christiana Macleod, his second wife, and by her, who *d.* in 1777, had issue,

- I. RICHARD, died unm.
- II. WILLIAM, his father's heir.
- III. John, an officer in the Royal Marines, drowned in the Pomona frigate, which foundered in the West Indies in 1789.
- I. Frances, *m.* to — Anderson, and had no issue.
- II. Ann, died unm.
- III. Jane, who *m.* James Walker, esq. of Dalry, and was mother of the present Sir Francis-Walker Drummond, bart. of Hawthornden.
- IV. Grace, died unm.

Mr. Hay-Newton *d.* 29th June, 1776, and was *s.* by his son,

WILLIAM HAY-NEWTON, esq. of Newton, *b.* in 1747, who wedded Alicia, daughter of Anthony Forster, esq. of Jardinefield, in the county of Berwick, and had issue,

- I. RICHARD, his heir.
- II. William-Waring, of Blackburn, in the county of Berwick, *m.* Jane-Frances, daughter of the late Thomas Gregson, esq.
- III. George-Forster.
- IV. John-Stuart, *m.* 4th August, 1829, Margaret-Eliza, daughter of the late William Fairlie, esq. of London, and has issue,
  1. William-Drummond-Ogilvy, *b.* in 1832.
  2. Margaret Fairlie, *b.* in 1830.
- V. Anthony-James.

Mr. Hay-Newton *d.* in 1829, and was *s.* by his eldest son, the present RICHARD HAY-NEWTON, esq. of Newton.

### Family of Newton, of Newton.

It does not appear, from any records now extant, at what period this ancient family and chief of the name first acquired property in Scotland. They were in possession of the estate previous to the year 1377, as shewn by a charter granted by ROBERT II. of Scotland, at Methven, in favour of William de Newton, and his heirs, which proceeds on resignation made in his majesty's hands as superior by Robert de Swinton, a cadet of the ancient house of Swinton, of Swinton, with consent of Margaret Newton his spouse, who was heiress of Newton. How long William remained in possession, or by whom succeeded, is not distinctly ascertained. During the re-

* Sir John Stuart, count of Maida, who commanded the British army, when they gained the great and decisive victory over the French at Maida, in Calabria, was nephew to Anne Stuart, who *m.* Richard Hay-Newton, esq.

gency of Robert, duke of Albany, there is an Alexander de Newton named as witness to a charter granted by that nobleman.

In 1450, on the 24th September, William de Newton granted a charter of Mortification of the annual rents of Artam, subjects belonging to him situated within the burgh of Haddington, in favour of the collegiate church of Bothans, now Yester, "which for the salvation of his own soul, and the soul of Marian his spouse, his ancestors and successors, and all faithful deceased persons, he gave, granted, and confirmed to God, and the Blessed Virgin Mary, and to Cuthbert provost of the collegiate church of Bothans, and to the prebendaries of the same, the most celebrated and for ever to be celebrated for their divinity." By acceptance of this deed, the members of the said collegiate church bound themselves to say a certain number of masses annually for the souls of the said William and Marian, according to the tenure of such grants. The next proprietor of whom the records make mention is John de Newton, who was succeeded by his grandson William, who had a brother, Archibald, and one sister, married to Borthwick of Gamelston, besides a son named John, who predeceased his father, and whose widow, Janett Wolf, succeeded in life rent to the lands of Kidlaw. William, the third proprietor, was succeeded by his grandson,

William Newton, of Newton, a bold and faithful adherent of the ill-fated Mary Stuart. This laird had the misfortune to kill, in a duel, his friend Hamilton, of Redhouse, under the following singular circumstances: during the invasion of Scotland by the duke of Somerset, the castle of Yester, formerly called Bothans, sustained a severe siege, and it was only by reducing the garrison to extremities that the besiegers forced it to surrender. Newton, of Newton, and the then Hamilton, of Redhouse, both officers in the garrison, while on guard, having openly expressed their sentiments on the conduct of the duke, in not the most courtly terms, his grace determined that on the capture of the castle, the blood of one of them should be shed by the hand of the other, as an atonement for the crime of disrespect they had committed. Accordingly both gentlemen, who were intimate friends, were conveyed by the duke's order to Haddington, and in his grace's presence compelled to fight a duel at the Water Haugh there, when Mr. Hamilton was killed. William Newton married, first, a daughter of Fentoun, of that ilk; and, secondly, Marion Home, relict of James Lawson. By the latter he appears to have had three sons and two daughters, viz.

I. John, who predeceased his father, leaving two daughters,
   Barbara, } who, for a certain
   Elizabeth, } sum of money, renounced to their uncle, Patrick, all right to the estate.

II. Patrick, successor to his father.

III. Thomas.

I. Janet.

II. Margaret.

In 1559, Newton was employed as a deputy for the ambitious James, earl of Bothwell, then high admiral of Scotland, as appears by an obligation granted by Bothwell to him of this date; and, in 1568, we find him devotedly attached to the cause of Mary Stuart, fighting under her banner at Langside. This procedure, incurring the pain of forfeiture, a gift of escheat of his heritable and moveable estate was issued under the privy seal, in favour of his youngest son, Thomas. The deed runs in the king's name, with consent of the regent Murray, and describes the cause of forfeiture. Whether he accompanied the queen is doubtful, but if not he went immediately afterwards, as there is a curious account of furnishings made to him and his household at the period in question: his active and heroic exploits seem to have reduced the Newton family to great emergencies. However, under a general act of pacification, granted by the king's friends in favour of those of the queen, Newton was restored to his estate, but not without certain sureties being taken for his good behaviour. Henry Ogle, of Hartramwood, and David Livingston, burgess of Edinburgh, became bound as pledges to present him before the regent and the lords of secret council upon ten days warning, and that he should remain a faithful and obedient subject to his majesty, under the pain of one thousand pounds: the regent and council shortly after, either from suspicion or actual proof of his interference in behalf of his royal mistress, charged Henry Ogle to present Newton before them, and neither making their appearance, the regent decreed that Henry Ogle had incurred the penalty, and ordained letters of "horning and poynding of his lands and goodes to be decreet for uptaking the sazyn;" but Newton's son, Patrick, becoming surety for Ogle, the penalty was not exacted; and finally, James, earl of Morton, obtaining the regency, Patrick was entirely relieved from responsibility on account of his father, by a discharge granted to him in 1587, at Holyrood House, by Morton. The laird of Newton lived to a great age, and, after settling the fee of his possessions on his sons, seems to have devolved the management of his worldly matters on his son, Patrick, from whom he received an annuity. He died about the year 1590, and was succeeded by his said son,

PATRICK NEWTON, of Newton, who *m.* first, Margaret, daughter of James Hamilton; and, secondly, Christian Wallace; but had issue only by the former, viz. two sons and four daughters; Archibald, William, Margaret, Sibella, Jane, and another. In 1568, a grant was made to Patrick, (previously to his succession), executed by Queen Mary subsequently to her majesty's escape from Lochleven Castle, and prior to the battle of Langside; by which certain duties which had become due and payable to the crown on the death of John, Patrick's elder brother, as well as the casualties due for the marriages of Barbara and Elizabeth, were conveyed to Patrick in these terms: "ordains aine letter to be made, under her privy seall in due form, to loved Patrick Newton, son to William Newton, of that ilk, his aires and assignes." This document is without date, and appears to have been executed in great haste. The grant seems to have been redeemed by the crown shortly after the defeat of the queen's party, and conveyed to secretary Maitland, who again reconveyed it to Patrick, on account of friendship as he expresses himself. Although Patrick's constitution was ill fitted for such exploits as those of his father, he nevertheless neglected not his parliamentary duties, and we find his own, and his ancestors' services acknowledged by the crown in a curious letter addressed to him by Adam Newton, advocate and tutor to Prince Henry. In this, Adam states, that his own and his ancestors' services to the crown of Scotland were duly appreciated by *King* JAMES, is testified by a charter of confirmation and Novodamus under the great seal, dated 26th January, 1598, in favour of Patrick, of the barony of Newton, on resignation made in his majesty's hands as superior, and there is likewise a writ of exemption, under the privy seal, from future services. Patrick *d.* in August, 1602, and was *s.* by his son,

ARCHIBALD NEWTON, of Newton, then in minority, who at the instance of his brother-in-law, James, Lord Hay, of Yester, and Sir Robert Kerr, settled his estate on his wife Christian, third daughter of William, sixth Lord Hay, in life rent; but this settlement being subsequently renounced, another was made reserving the lands of Newton to himself in life rent and to his eldest son Patrick in fee, on which the said Patrick obtained a charter of confirmation and novodamus from the crown, under reservation of his father's life rent. Archibald and his wife lived to a good old age, and left two sons and two daughters, viz. PATRICK, JOHN, Margaret, and Mary. The elder son,

PATRICK NEWTON, of Newton, executed two several bonds of taillie in 1635 and 1641, which are remarkable on account of naming as a substitute one Peter Newton, who is there designed as servitor to his majesty *King* CHARLES I.* Patrick wedded Janet, daughter of Sir James Bannatyne, of Newhall, and left an only child,

THOMAS NEWTON, of Newton, who being in minority, his uncle, John, then in the Dutch service, obtained from the crown a gift of tutory, as guardian to his nephew, but as his profession obliged him to reside in Holland, he appointed Alexander Hay,

---

* That the family of the great Sir ISAAC NEWTON was a branch of this Scottish house, appears more than probable. The proprietor of the Newton estate, at the period of King James's accession to the English crown, was (as above stated) Patrick Newton, son of William, a zealous supporter of the cause of the unfortunate Queen Mary. Patrick is supposed to have accompanied the king to England, for he was a favourite of the ruling power, and a great friend of Maitland. In 1594 he applied to his majesty for an exemption in future from all personal services, on account of his divers infirmities, which request was accordingly granted by a special writ under the privy seal, dated at Holyrood House the 5th July, and produced before the sheriff of Edinburgh in the September of the same year; if he went to England, he returned again, as he died at Newton Hall.

According to Dr. Reid, there is little doubt that one of the family settled in England, either at this period or shortly afterwards, as by a bond of taillie executed by Patrick, son of Archibald, in 1635, in favour of his brother John and his heirs male, the next person called to them is designed PETER NEWTON, (servitor to his Majesty Charles I.), whom failing, to his heirs male. There can be no question about this person's being a cadet of the family, and if what is said of Sir Isaac's descent be true, undoubtedly the situation which this Peter seems to have held, corresponds with the account given of Sir Isaac's ancestor. He is also designed in a second bond of taillie, executed by Patrick in the same manner, in 1641. The proprietor contemporary with Sir Isaac was Sir Richard: it has been currently said that Sir Isaac and Sir Richard were not only related but corresponded; and it is easily accounted for how no documents to this effect are to be found in the charter chest at Newton. Dame Helen Livingstone survived Sir Richard her husband, and being naturally disappointed that she had no son to succeed, she carefully destroyed all the correspondence of her husband's and her own time, besides dispersing a library and all the plate. This appears the more striking as the whole correspondence, for many generations previous to this period, had been carefully preserved. Lady Newton repaired to West Quarter soon after Sir Richard's death, carrying every moveable with her, as it is said, rather than it should become the property of the heir, who seems to have incurred her displeasure by uniformly refusing to accompany her to the parish church.

of Barra, factor and chamberlain for the management of the estate, subject to the control of Lord Hay, of Yester, and Sir James Bannatyne (see a curious memorandum of the 21st September, 1649, given by John on his leaving Scotland). At this period civil commotions distracted Scotland, and the contributions levied for the numerous garrisons were severely felt by the then Newton; who was subjected to the payment of sums of money for the garrisons of Leith and Tamptatton, and obliged to supply that of the castle of Bothans with money, bread, drink, and mutton, and also hay, corn, and straw, for the horses, beside having a number of troops quartered on the barony. This laird dying without issue, was buried by torch-light within the old church of Bothans, and succeeded by his uncle,

John Newton, of Newton, who married a Dutch lady named Cecilia Vandertail, by whom he acquired a considerable fortune, and had two sons and two daughters, viz. Richard, James, Margaret, and Cornelia. After John's succession he remained in the Dutch service, and seldom visited Scotland. He did not neglect his interests at home, for shortly after his nephew's death, he appointed Alexander Ogilvy his factor, with the most particular orders, and maintained a regular correspondence with Ogilvy in his absence, who appears, in all matters of importance, to be instructed to obtain the counsel and advice of Lord Humbie. In this correspondence there is much curious matter, shewing the customs of the age. John Newton built large additions to the house and all the garden walls. At this time the ward or prison was so crowded with culprits, that on an application from Lord Hay of Yester's tenants for liberty to work limestone, Ogilvy thus recommends the mode of giving them a supply by a letter to the laird of Newton: "I hear great murmurings amongst the Lord Hay's tenants for lymestone, and yor own complaines sare for them also, if ye pleas let the prisone dor be opened, and let them have some of the prisoners for a ransom, ye may do as ye think gude." In 1656, Newton came over to Scotland for the purpose of settling divers matters with Ogilvy, and he procured a passport, dated 21st August in the same year, from the famous General Monk. He *d.* in 1658, and was *s.* by his son,

Richard Newton, of Newton, who being educated under the eye of his father, inherited his feelings and prejudices, particularly in regard to a due observance of the rights of his barony (see Minutes of the Baron Court, which are truly ridiculous and very curious). This court had been held from time immemorial within the town of Newton, called Long-Newton, (from the straggling length and appearance of the village), on a green mount which lay in the middle of the village, and had a circle cut out at the top of it. Its proceedings were conducted with the greatest solemnity, under the superintendance of three different officers, with regular salaries, a baron baillie, procurator fiscal, and clerk. Gentlemen were empowered to hold a court whenever in their opinion the refractory state of the barony required it, and the decrees were generally to the discomfiture of the unfortunate culprits. This laird, who succeeded to a good deal of property in Holland, went thither with his sister Cornelia, as appears by a passport signed by Charles II. and remained abroad until the year 1667, when he returned and was employed to raise the troops required in East Lothian for the king's service. He *m.* in 1668, the famous Lady Julian Home, sister to Sir Patrick Home of Polwarth, created by William III. earl of Marchmont,* but survived his marriage little more than a year, when he was *s.* by his only son,

Richard Newton, of Newton, whose affairs were conducted, during his minority,

* Sir Patrick Home, of Polwarth, first Earl of Marchmont, early distinguished himself in the cause of liberty. When the privy council passed an order, compelling the counties to pay the expense of the garrisons arbitrarily placed in them, he refused to pay his quota, and by a bill of suspension presented to the court of session, endeavoured to procure redress. The council ordered him to be imprisoned for no other crime, as it would appear, than that of having attempted to procure by a *legal* process, a *legal* decision on a point of law. After having remained in close confinement in Stirling Castle for nearly *four* years, he was set at liberty through the favour and interest of the duke of Monmouth. Having afterwards engaged in schemes connected with those imputed to Sidney and Russel, orders were issued for seizing him at his house of Marchmont, but having had timely notice of his danger from his relation Home, of Nine Wells, a gentleman attached to the royal cause, but whom party spirit had not rendered insensible to the ties of friendship. He found means to conceal himself for a time, and shortly after to escape beyond sea. His concealment was in the family burying place, where the means of sustaining life were brought to him by his daughter, a girl of fifteen years of age, whose duty and affection furnished her with courage to brave the terrors, to which she was exposed by any intercourse with her father. Sir Patrick returned with the earl of Argyle's expedition in favour of Monmouth, but after the result of that unfortunate invasion, he was obliged again to seek security by concealing himself some time in the house, under the protection of Lady Eleanor Dunbar, sister to the earl of Eglintoun, after which he found means to escape to Holland, from whence he returned and was created, first, Lord Home, of Polwarth, and then earl of Marchmont.

with great judgment by his mother, Lady Julian Newton, who died in 1692, leaving her son in full possession of his paternal estate, which had accumulated, under her guardianship, to a considerable amount. Early instructed in the principles to which his uncle was attached. This laird naturally espoused the cause of *King* WILLIAM, and was created by that monarch a baronet, at the same time that Sir Patrick Home was raised to the peerage. Sir Richard is designed knight baronet in numerous documents, and a receipt is extant for the fees payable at his creation. He *m.* a daughter of Sir William Livingstone, of West Quarter, but having no issue, settled, under reservation of Lady Newton's life rent, the estate of Newton, by entail dated 18th June, 1724, on RICHARD HAY, esq. fourth son of Lord William Hay, and grandfather of RICHARD HAY-NEWTON, esq. present possessor of Newton.

*Arms*—Quarterly, first and fourth, vert a lion rampant or, on a chief of the second three roses gu. for NEWTON; second and third, quarterly, first and fourth arg. three escutcheons gu.; second, az. three cinquefoils arg.; third, gu. three bars erm. for HAY.

*Crests*—A demi lion rampant holding in his dexter paw a naked sword, ppr. for NEWTON. A goat's head erased arg. armed or, for HAY.

*Mottoes*—For NEWTON, Pro patria: for HAY, Spare nought.

*Supporters*—Two lions guardant gu, each gorged with a collar or.

*Estates*—In Haddingtonshire.

*Seat*—Newton Hall, North Britain.

## PENNANT, OF DOWNING AND BYCHTON.

PENNANT, DAVID, esq. of Downing and Bychton, in the county of Flint, *b.* 8th November, 1763; *m.* 12th December, 1793, Louisa, second daughter of Sir Henry Peyton, bart. and niece of John, earl of Stradbroke, and has one son,

DAVID, *b.* 22nd January, 1796, who *m.* first, the Lady Caroline Spencer-Churchill, only daughter of George, duke of Marlborough, and by her, who died in 1824, had an only child, Caroline, *b.* 8th December, 1823, who *d.* 22nd January, 1832. He wedded, secondly, the Lady Emma Brudenell, daughter of Robert, earl of Cardigan, and had by her a daughter, Louisa. Mr. Pennant died 15th February, 1836.

Mr. Pennant, who succeeded his father in 1798, served the office of high sheriff of Flintshire the following year.

### Lineage.

This is another branch of the descendants of TUDOR TREVOR, to whom so many of the principal families of North Wales and the Marches trace their origin (see vol. ii. p. 329). Tudur Trevor was father of LLUDDOCCA, father of LLOWARCH GAM, father of EDNYVED, whose son, RYS SAIS, so called because he could speak the Saxon, or English language, possessed great estates in North Wales and Shropshire at the period of the Norman conquest, which he divided among his sons in the year 1070. The eldest, TUDUR, was father of BLEDDYN, the father of OWEN, the father of THOMAS, whose son,

MEILIR, was seated at Bryn, in the township of Halghton, and parish of Hanmer, Flintshire. He was father of

MADOC AP MEILIR, who acquired the estate of Bychton, in the parish of Whiteford, Flintshire, by marriage with Alice, the daughter and heir of Philip o Ffhychdyn, (that is, in English, Philip of Bychton), son of Philip y Swydden Wyddel, or Philip, the Irish officer, one of the cavaliers who accompanied Gruffydd ap Cynan, Prince of Wales, from Ireland, to assist him in recovering his dominions, then usurped by Trahacarn ap Caradog. The great and decisive victory obtained by Gruffydd over the usurper, (and in which Trahaiarn was slain), on the mountains of Carno, in the county of Montgomery, *anno* 1077, the valour of Philip mainly achieved, and Gruffydd, thus reinstated in his principality, was not unmindful of his Milesian general, for he bestowed upon him great possessions, of which Bychton, in the parish of Whitford, formed a part. The arms, borne by his son Philip, who was seated at Bychton, were "Ar. three bars wavy az. the centre bar charged with three sheldrakes of the first." These ensigns, acquired with the Bychton estate, the descendants of Madoc and Alice have quartered down to the present day. Ierwerth (or Edward), the son of Madoc and Alice, was father of Kenrick, the father of Ithel, the father of Tudur, whose son,

David ap Tudur, first adopted the cognomen of Pennant, and from him all of the name derive their descent. This surname is truly British, derived from *Pen*, a head, and *Nant*, a dingle, the ancient mansion of Bychton being seated at the head of a very considerable dingle on the old family estate. David *m.* first, Janet, daughter of David, of Trefcastle, in Tegengl, and had by her a son and two daughters, viz.

Rees, his heir.

Jane, *m.* to John David, of Bachcurig.

Anne, *m.* to Griffith ap Lln ap Blethyn, of Panty Llongdy.

David Pennant wedded, secondly, Anne, daughter of John Done, of Utkington, in Cheshire, by Anne his wife, daughter of Richard Heaton, of Heaton, and had

Thomas, abbot of Basingwerk, Flintshire, celebrated by Guttyn Owain, a Welsh bard of the year 1480, who records the hospitality of the abbot in a poem printed in the collection of Mr. Rhys Jones. The poet is so liberal of his praise as to say, "that he gave twice the treasure of a king in wine." Guttyn Owain and Tudor Aled, another noted bard, speak not only of the abbot's works of utility; of the water and windmills he erected; of his having enlarged and beautified the abbey; but also compliment him on his prowess in battle. Thomas Pennant, quitting his profession, became, in the law term, a monk *deraigne*, and *m.* Angharad, daughter of Gwilim ap Griffith, of the great house of Penrhyn, in Carnarvonshire, by whom he had issue,

1. Edward, of Holywell, who *m.* Catharine, daughter of John ap Davydd ap Ithel Vychan, and was ancestor of the Pennants of Bagillt. (See the end of this article).
2. Thomas, vicar of Holywell.
3. Nicholas, abbot of Basingwerk, who married and had a son,

   Edward, of Holywell, who *m.* Jane, daughter and heiress of Thomas ap Howel, of Calived, and was father of

   John, of Holywell, who *m.* Margaret, daughter of Hugh Mostyn, of the Grange, and had, with other issue, a daughter, Lucy, wife of Peter Ellis, of Cairns, and a son and heir,

   John, of Holywell, who *m.* Mary, daughter and heir of Thomas ap Thomas, of Mertyn, in the parish of Whitford, and had an only daughter and heiress,

   Margaret, *m.* to David Pennant, esq. of Bychton.

1. Agnes, *m.* to John Griffith, esq. of Twna.
2. Margaret, *m.* to Griffith Lloyd ap John ap Griffith ap David.

Roger.

Hugh, offeiriad or priest, a distinguished poet of the reign of Henry VIII. In 1575, at an Eisteddfod at Caerwis, he was secondary student in vocal song.

David Pennant's eldest son,

Rees Pennant, of Bychton, espoused Margaret, daughter of Rees ap Reinallt, of Pentre Hobbyn, and was father of

Hugh Pennant, of Bychton, who *m.* Janet, daughter of Richard ap Howel ap Ievan Vychan, of Mostyn, sister to Thomas Mostyn, of Mostyn, and Pyers Mostyn, of Talacre. By this lady he had issue,

Thomas, his heir.

Richard.

William, an eminent goldsmith of London, who lived at the Queen's Head, in Smithfield, and by the sign of his shop, and by several bequests he made to persons about the court, he probably was goldsmith and jeweller to the royal family. He purchased considerable estates, and at his demise left a large fortune to his nephew Hugh, together with a considerable sum in charity to Whitford parish, which still enjoys the same.

John.

Pyers, one of the four gentlemen ushers to *Queen* Elizabeth. He obtained for himself and other members of his family a grant of the crest now borne by the Pennants, together with a confirmation of their arms on the 2nd of

May, 1580, from Robert Cooke, clarencieux king of arms.

Nicholas, who *m.* Catharine, daughter of Griffith ap John ap Robert, of Whitford, and had a son,

JOHN PENNANT, esq. who wedded Jane, daughter and heiress of John Lloyd ap Llewellyn ap Rees, of DOWNING, by whom he acquired that estate, whereon he erected a mansion in 1627. The materials were brought from Nant y bi, a dingle opposite to the house. There is a tradition that the stones were rolled along a platform from the top of the quarry, raised on an inclined plane, till they reached the building, and there were elevated as the work increased in height, till the whole was completed. The house is in the form of a Roman H, a mode of architecture very common in Wales at that period. On the front is the pious motto, *Heb Dduw heb ddim, a Duw a digon:* that is, "Without God there is nothing, with God enough." John Pennant had, by the heiress of Downing, with two daughters, Margaret, *m.* to Thomas Parry, and Catharine, *m.* to Robert ap Edward, a son and successor,

HUGH PENNANT, esq. of Downing, who *m.* Mary, daughter of John Humphreys, esq. of Plas Belyn, and relict of Edward Jones, esq. of Ial, and was *s.* by his son,

ROBERT PENNANT, esq. of Downing, who *m.* Mary, daughter and co-heiress of Harry Conway, esq. of Nant, and had issue,

1. Hugh, who *d. s. p.* in 1675.
2. John, who *d. s. p.* in 1691.
3. THOMAS, who *d.* issueless in 1724, and bequeathed Downing to DAVID PENNANT, esq. of Bychton.

1. Lucy, *d.* in 1703.
2. Jane.
3. Catharine, *d.* in 1701.

Catharine, *m.* to Thomas Parry, esq. of Morland.

Janet, *m.* to John ap Rees, of Tur Abbot.

Grace.

Jane.

Mary.

Eleanor.

Hugh Pennant was *s.* by his eldest son,

THOMAS PENNANT, esq. of Bychton, who wedded Catharine, daughter of David Llwyd ap David of Glanyllyn, near Bala, and widow of Roger Middleton, esq. of Gwaenynog. By her he had, with two daughters, Jane, wife of Thomas ap Thomas, of Meliden, and Catharine, wife of Richard Sneyd, esq. a son and successor,

HUGH PENNANT, esq. of Bychton, who *m.* Lucy, daughter of Henry Conway, esq. of Bodshyddan, and by her, who died in February, 1611, had issue,

I. PYERS, his heir.
II. Thomas.
III. Hugh, *m.* a daughter of Edward Owen, esq.

I. Grace, *m.* to Gronwy Griffith, esq.
II. Catharine, *m.* to Edward Meredith, esq. of Chester.
III. Elinor, *d.* unm.

The eldest son,

PYERS PENNANT, esq. of Bychton, was high sheriff of Flintshire in 1611. He *m.* Jane, daughter of Morris Kyffin, esq. of Maenan, by Margaret, daughter of Thomas Mostyn, esq. of Mostyn, and had issue,

I. THOMAS, his heir.
II. DAVID, successor to his brother.
III. HUGH, of Bryn Shone, major in the service of CHARLES I. who greatly distinguished himself in the Isle of Anglesey against General Mytton, *m.* first, Margaret,* baroness Longford, daughter of Sir Thomas Cave, knt.; and, secondly, Elizabeth, dau. of John Eyton, esq. of Leeswood. He died in 1669.

I. Elizabeth, *m.* to Peter Griffith, esq. of Caerwys Hall.
II. Lucy, *m.* to Harry Conway, esq. of Nant.
III. Grace, *m.* to Thomas Matthews, esq. of Denbigh.
IV. Margaret, *m.* to John Vaughan, esq. of Bronhinlog.
V. Jane, *m.* to John Humphreys, esq. of the Wern.

Pyers Pennant *d.* in 1623, and was *s.* by his eldest son,

THOMAS PENNANT, esq. of Bychton, high sheriff of Flintshire in 1633, who *m.* Margaret, daughter of Edward Wynne, esq. of Ystrad, son of Morris Wynne, esq. of Gwe-

* This lady had four husbands; she paid our country the compliment of beginning and ending with a Welshman: her first was Sir John Wynne, of Gwedir, junior; they lived unhappily together, which sent him on his travels to Italy, where he died at Luçca. She then took one of the Milesian race, for she married Sir Francis Aungier, Master of the Rolls in Ireland, afterwards created Baron Longford. Thirdly, she gave her hand to an Englishman, Sir Thomas Wenman, of Oxfordshire; and, finally, she resigned her antiquated charms to our gallant major, who in the year 1656 deposited her with his ancestors, in the church of Whitford.—*Thomas Pennant.*

dir, but having no issue, he was *s.* at his decease, in 1634, by his brother,

DAVID PENNANT, esq. of Bychton, sheriff of Flintshire in 1642. This gentleman, during the civil wars, adhered to the royal cause, and held a major's commission in that service. "He was," says his descendant, Thomas Pennant the historian, "an officer in the garrison of Denbigh when it was besieged and taken by my maternal great great grandfather, General Mytton. My loyal ancestor suffered there a long imprisonment. Bychton was plundered, and the distress of the family so great, that he was kept from starving by force of conjugal affection, for his wife often walked with a bag of oatmeal from the parish of Whiteford to Denbigh to relieve his wants." * He *m.* Margaret, daughter and heiress of John Pennant, esq. of Holywell, and by her, who *d.* in 1700, had issue,

- PYERS, his heir.
- John, who *m.* Sarah, daughter of — Parry, esq. of Merton, and *d.* in 1709, aged sixty-nine. He was buried at Chelsea, "where," says Thomas Pennant, "he had resided, and where my father often visited him during the boyish holydays. My father told me he was frequently taken by him to the Don Saltero Coffee House, where he used to see poor Richard Cromwell, a little and very neat old man, with a most placid countenance, the effect of his innocent and unambitious life."
- Mary, *m.* to John Salusbury, esq. of Bachegraig.

Major Pennant *d.* in 1666, and was *s.* by his son,

PYERS PENNANT, esq. of Bychton, vice admiral of North Wales, who *m.* Catharine,† daughter of Robert Davies, esq. of Gwasaney, by Ann his wife, daughter and heiress of Sir Peter Mutton, knt. of Llannerch, chief justice of North Wales, (see vol. ii. pages 277 and 521), and had issue,

- PETER, his heir.
- Robert, *b.* in 1664, buried ‡ at Pancras in 1689. He was attended to his grave, as was then the custom, by a most numerous set of friends, among whom were two bishops and the first gentry of North Wales, who happened then to be in town.
- Eliza, died in infancy.
- Mary, *m.* to Simon Thelwall, esq. of Llanbedr.
- Catherine, died in 1740.

Pyers Pennant *d.* in 1690, and was *s.* by his elder son,

PETER PENNANT, esq. of Bychton, who *m.* first, Catharine, second daughter of Owen Wynne, esq. of Glynn, sheriff of Merionethshire in 1674, of Flintshire in 1675, and of Carnarvonshire in 1676, by Elizabeth his wife, daughter and heiress of Robert Mostyn, esq. of Nant, and had issue,

- I. DAVID, his heir.
- II. John, A.M. rector of Hadley, and chaplain to the Princess Dowager of Wales, *d.* in 1770, aged seventy.
- III. Robert, } both died *s. p.*
- IV. Peter, }

- I. Elizabeth, *b.* in 1687, *d.* in 1775.
- II. Catharine, *b.* in 1688, *d.* in 1754.
- III. Margaret, *b.* in 1690, *d.* in 1775.

Mr. Pennant, on the demise of his first wife, went into the army *temp. Queen* ANNE, and served at the siege of Brussels. Disgusted however with his colonel, Sir Thomas Prendergast, after demanding satisfaction, which Sir Henry declined, he resigned, and passed the remainder of his days at Bychton. He wedded, secondly, the widow of Robert Davies, esq. of Gwasaney and Llannerch, and daughter of — Vaughan, esq. of Trawsgoed, but had no other issue. He *d.* in 1736, and was *s.* by his son,

DAVID PENNANT, esq. of Bychton, who inherited Downing from his kinsman, Thomas Pennant, esq. He *m.* Arabella, third daughter of Richard Mytton, esq. of Halston, in Shropshire, by Sarah his wife, daughter of Sir John Houblon, knt. lord mayor of London, and had issue,

* Notwithstanding the zeal of his house for the royal cause, it suffered very little in respect to the general composition of delinquents; the Bychton estate only paid 42*l.* 14*s.* whereas Robert Pennant, of Downing, paid not less than 298*l.* for his estate, which was very far inferior to the other. The occasion was this: Robert Pennant had the misfortune to have a hot headed young fellow in his house, when a small detachment of the adverse party, with a cornet at the head approached the place. He persuaded the family to resist; the doors were barricadoed, a musket fired, and the cornet wounded. The house was soon forced, and of course plundered; but such was the moderation of the party, no carnage ensued, and the only revenge seems to have been the disproportionate fine afterwards levied.

† Was one of the celebrated seven sisters of the house of Gwysaney, who were all married about the same time, and all became widows.

‡ With this inscription:

Gentilibus suis compositus
Robertus Pennant
Filius secundus Pyercei Pennant, de Bychton,
In com. Flint. arm.
Et Katherinæ, sororis Roberti Davies,
Hic reconditus.
Qui cum omnia obiisset munera.
Juvenem quæ suis charum reddere poterant
Febre Londini correptus,
Desideratus æque ac notus decessit
Ætatis Ao. 24,
MDC.XXXIX.

I. THOMAS, his heir.
II. John, *d.* young in 1728.

I. Sarah, / II. Catharine, { twins, born in 1729, both died unmarried; the former in 1780, the latter in 1797.

Mr. Pennant, who was high sheriff of Flintshire in 1739, *d.* in January, 1763, aged seventy-eight, and was *s.* by his son,

THOMAS PENNANT, esq. of Downing and Bychton, the celebrated naturalist and traveller. This distinguished person, who was born at Downing 14th June, 1726, studied at Queen's College, Oxford, and afterwards removed to Oriel College, in the same university, where he took the degree of D.C.L. in 1771. At twelve years of age he was inspired with a passion for natural history by a present of Willughby's "Ornithology," from Mrs. Piozzi's father; and for minerals and fossils by a visit to Doctor Borlase in 1747 His first production was an account of an earthquake, felt in Flintshire, 2nd April, 1750, which appeared in the Philosophical Transactions in 1756; and the following year he was chosen a member of the Royal Society of Upsal, through the influence of the great Linnæus, with whom he corresponded. In 1761, he commenced the folio edition of "the British Zoology," which was afterwards republished in quarto and octavo, and translated into German by C. Theop. Murr. This work was followed by his "Indian Zoology," 1769, "Synopsis of Quadrupeds," 1771, "Genera of Birds." "History of Quadrupeds," 1781, "Arctic Zoology," 1786, and "Index to Buffon's Natural History of Birds," 1787; which are his principal works relative to the department of science, which he chiefly cultivated; but he also published a number of detached essays and papers in the Philosophical Transactions on similar subjects. In 1765, Mr. Pennant travelled to the continent and visited Buffon, Haller, Pallas, and other eminent foreigners. He was admitted into the Royal Society in 1767. In 1769 he undertook a journey into Scotland, of which he published an account in 1771; and another volume appeared in 1776, relating to a second tour in the same country, and a voyage to the Hebrides. In 1778, he published a tour in Wales; to which was afterwards added, in a subsequent volume, a journey to Snowdon. He produced, in 1782, a narrative of a "Journey from Chester to London;" and, in 1790, his popular "Account of London." In 1793, he professedly took leave of the public, in a piece of autobiography, which he entitled "The literary Life of the late Thomas Pennant;" but this did not prove to be his latest production, as he afterwards committed to the press a "History of the Parishes of Whiteford and Holywell." He died 16th December, 1798, at his seat in Flintshire. After his death appeared "Outlines of the Globe;" his "Journey from London to the Isle of Wight," 1801; his "Tour from Downing to Alston Moor;" and his "Tour from Alston Moor to Harrowgate." Mr. Pennant married first, in 1759, Elizabeth, daughter of James Falconer, esq. of Chester, and by her, who *d.* in June, 1764, had two sons and one daughter, viz.

Thomas, *d.* an infant in 1760.
DAVID, successor to his father.

Arabella, *m.* to Edward, son of Sir Walden Hanmer, bart. and died in 1828.

He wedded, secondly, in 1777, Anne, daughter of Sir Thomas Mostyn, bart. of Mostyn, by whom, who *d.* in 1802, he had

Thomas, rector of Weston Turville, Bucks, *b.* in 1780, who *m.* Caroline, daughter of Thomas Griffith, esq. of Rhual.

Sarah, *b.* in 1779, and *d.* in 1794.

Mr. Pennant, who served the office of high sheriff of Flintshire in 1761, *d.* 16th December, 1798, and was *s.* by his son, the present DAVID PENNANT, esq. of Downing and Bychton.

*Arms*—First, party per bend sinister, ermine and ermines, a lion rampt. or, langued and armed gu.; second, arg. three bars wavy az. in the centre bar three sheldrakes of the first; third, az. three boars in pale arg.; fourth, arg. on a bend az. three fleurs de lys of the field.

*Crest*—Out of a ducal coronet, an heraldic antelope's head arg. horned and maned or.

*Estates*—In Flintshire.

*Seats*—Downing and Bychton, both in Flintshire.

### Family of Pennant, of Bagillt.

EDWARD PENNANT, eldest son of Thomas Pennant, abbot of Basingwerk, second son of David ap Tudur Pennant, of Bychton, was seated at Holywell, in Flintshire. He *m.* Catharine, daughter of John ap Davydd ap Ithel Vychan, and had, with other issue,

HENRY, his heir.

David, of Hendre Figillt, who *m.* Deili, daughter and heir of John ap Ievan, of Halton.

Jane, *m.* to Thomas Conway, esq. of Nant.

The elder son,

HENRY PENNANT, esq. of Holywell and Bagillt, by Margaret his wife, daughter of John ap Griffith Vychan, of Pant y Llongdy, had one son and six daughters, viz.

NICHOLAS, his heir.

Jane, *m.* to John Dicas, of Kinnerton.
Alice, *m.* to Henry ap Hugh, of Holywell.
Anne, *m.* to Thomas ap Thomas, of Whitford.
Margaret, *m.* to Hugh Thomas, of Llanasaph.
Ellen, died unm.
Catharine.

The son and heir,

NICHOLAS PENNANT, esq. of Holywell and Bagillt, espoused Jane, daughter of William Mostyn, esq. of Basinwerke, and had, *inter alios*, a daughter, Elizabeth, wife of Robert Woolmer, and a son and successor,

EDWARD PENNANT, esq. of Bagillt, who *m.* Eliza, daughter of Edward Giffard, esq. of White Ladies, county of Stafford, and had issue,

I. EDWARD, his heir.
II. Gifford, a military officer, who went to Jamaica in 1655. He *m.* 7th September, 1669, Elizabeth Aldwinkle, and *d.* in 1676, leaving, with a daughter, Elizabeth, *m.* to — Lewis, esq. a son,
   EDWARD PENNANT, esq. *b.* 1672, of Clarendon, in Jamaica, chief justice of the island, who *m.* Elizabeth, daughter of Col. John Moore, and aunt of Sir Henry Moore, bart. Lieut. Governor of Jamaica, by whom he had issue,
   1. Edward.
   2. John, who *m.* Bonella, dau. of — Hodges, esq. and had two sons, one of whom was John, who *d. s. p.*; the other,
      RICHARD, of Winnington and Penrhyn Castle, was created BARON PENRHYN, of the kingdom of Ireland. His lordship *m.* Anne-Susannah, daughter and heir of General Hugh Warburton, but died without issue.
   3. Samuel (Sir), knt. lord mayor of London in 1749. He died the following year.
   4. Gifford.
   5. Henry.
   1. Judith, *m.* to John Lewis, esq.
   2. Smart, *m.* to Rev. William May, rector of Kingston, killed in the storm of 1722.
   3. Elizabeth, *m.* to Henry Dawkins, esq. of Jamaica, and had two sons,
      HENRY DAWKINS, esq. who *m.* the Lady Julia Colyer, daughter of the earl of Portmore, and had issue,
         James Dawkins.
         Henry Dawkins.
         GEORGE-HAY DAWKINS, now PENNANT, esq. of Penrhyn Castle.
         Richard Dawkins.
         Edward Dawkins.
         John Dawkins.
      James Dawkins, the oriental traveller.
   4. Sarah, *m.* to Col. Thomas Rowden.
   5. Mary, *m.* to John Morant, esq.
III. George.
I. Frances, *m.* to Robert Owen, bishop of St. Asaph.
II. Elizabeth, *m.* to Philip Longton, esq.
III. Anne, *m.* to Edward Parry, esq.
IV. Jane.
V. Mary, *m.* to John Mostyn, esq. of Brynford.
VI. Winefred.
VII. Agnes.
VIII. Mildred.

The eldest son,

EDWARD PENNANT, esq. of Bagillt, wedded Catharine, daughter of Edward Kynaston, esq. of Oteley, and by her, who *d.* in 1726, had, with three younger sons and two daughters, Trevor, the wife of John Lloyd, esq. of Pentre Hobbyn, and Catherine, wife of John Wynne, esq. of Tower, a son and successor,

ROGER PENNANT, esq. of Bagillt, who *m.* Elizabeth, daughter of — Mostyn, esq. of Rhyd, and had two sons and five daughters, viz. EDWARD, his heir; John; Dorothy; Elizabeth; Anne; Catharine; and Margaret, the wife of Thomas Crichley, esq. she *d.* in 1762. Mr. Pennant *d.* in 1735, and was *s.* by his elder son,

EDWARD PENNANT, esq. of Bagillt, who espoused Mary, daughter of George Waterman, esq. of Barbadoes, and had two sons, EDWARD, his heir, and William, who *d.* unmarried in 1753. Mr. Pennant was *s.* at his demise in 1741, by the elder,

EDWARD PENNANT, esq. of Bagillt, high sheriff of Flintshire in 1753, who *d.* unm. at Marseilles in 1778, having previously (in 1776) sold Bagillt Hall, and all his estates in Holywell township, to THOMAS PENNANT, esq. of Downing.

# EGERTON, OF TATTON PARK.

**EGERTON, WILBRAHAM,** esq. of Tatton Park, in the county of Chester, *b.* 1st September, 1781; *m.* 11th January, 1806, his first cousin, Elizabeth, second daughter of Sir Christopher Sykes, bart. of Sledmere House, Yorkshire, and has had issue,

I. WILLIAM-TATTON, M. P. for Cheshire, *b.* 30th December, 1806; *m.* 18th December, 1830, the Lady Charlotte-Elizabeth Loftus, eldest daughter of the Marquess of Ely, and has had two sons, Wilbraham, *b.* 17th January, 1832, and Loftus-Edward, *b.* 25th July, 1833, (who died an infant,) with a daughter, *b.* in November, 1834.
II. Wilbraham, captain 43rd light infantry, *b.* 31st May, 1808.
III. Thomas, *b.* 16th November, 1809.
IV. George, *b.* in May, 1813, and *d.* in August, 1814.
V. Mark, *b.* 27th January, 1815, and *d.* 28th December, 1831.
VI. Edward-Christopher, *b.* 27th July, 1816.
VII. Charles-Randle, *b.* 12th May, 1818.

I. Elizabeth-Beatrix, died an infant in 1811.
II. Elizabeth-Mary-Charlotte, died an infant in 1821.
III. Charlotte-Lucy-Beatrix.

This gentleman, who succeeded his father 17th April, 1806, represented the county of Chester for nineteen years in parliament, and served the office of sheriff in 1808. He is lieutenant-colonel of the Yeomanry Cavalry, lieutenant-colonel of the Local Militia, and a magistrate and deputy lieutenant for Cheshire.

## Lineage.

This branch of the Egerton family has enjoyed, for a long series of years, extensive estates and leading influence in the palatinate of Chester.

SIR THOMAS EGERTON, (son of Sir Richard Egerton, of Ridley), the celebrated LORD CHANCELLOR, was born in Cheshire about the year 1540, and admitted of Brazennose College, Oxford, in 1556. The Athenæ Oxonienses give an account of his early pursuits, and state his having "applied his muse to severe study in this university, where, continuing about three years, he laid a foundation whereon to build profounder learning. Afterwards, going to Lincoln's Inn, he made a most happy progress in the municipal laws, and at length was a counsellor of note." In 1581, Mr. Egerton's eminent abilities were rewarded with the office of solicitor-general, and in 1592 with the attorney-generalship. In 1594, he was raised to the Rolls bench, having previously received the honour of knighthood; and, in 1596, obtained the custody of the great seal, as the title of lord keeper. To this high station he was elevated by the especial favour of his royal mistress, and the universal wish of the country, "every one," as Camden says, "having conceived mighty hopes and expectations of his lordship." After retaining this office during the reign of ELIZABETH, he was created, by her successor, on the 21st July, 1603, BARON ELLESMERE, and constituted LORD HIGH CHANCELLOR of ENGLAND. To attempt even the most abridged epitome of the affairs in which Lord Ellesmere appears a principal actor, during his eventful and splendid career, would far exceed our limits. Among those, however, may be especially noted the treaties with the Dutch and the Danes, 40th and 42nd ELIZABETH; his exertions in behalf of the ill-fated Essex; the trials of Lords Cobham and Grey de Wilton in 1603; the negotiations respecting the proposed union of the crowns of England and Scotland in 1604; the struggle with Lord Chief Justice Coke, in reference to the jurisdiction of the Court of Chancery in 1615; and the trial of the earl and countess of Somerset, in the following year, for the murder of Sir Thomas Overbury. The lord chancellor, now more than seventy-six years of age, feeling both the powers of his mind and body shrink under the pressure of age and infirmity, entreated from the king, in two pathetic letters, a discharge from his high office which he had held nearly twenty-two years. His majesty complied, and after advancing the chancellor to the dignity of VISCOUNT BRACKLEY, received the seals in person from his lordship, on his death bed, with tears of respect and gratitude, and expressed the intention of adding the earldom of Bridgewater to his previous honours. His lordship died 15th March, 1617, "in a good old age, and full of virtuous fame;" and, in the words of Camden, "forte quanto propius Reipublicæ mala viderat, ut integer honestum finem voluit." Hacket, in his life of Archbishop Williams, says he was one "qui nihil in vita nisi laudandum aut fecit, aut dixit, aut sensit." His apprehension was keen and ready; his judgment deep and sound; his elocution elegant and easy. As a lawyer, he was prudent in counsel, extensive in information, and just in principle; so that while he lived he was excelled by none; and when he died he was lamented by all. In a word, as a statesman, he was faithful and patriotic; and as a judge, impartial and incorrupt.* His lordship *m.* first, Elizabeth, daughter of Thomas Ravenscroft, esq. of Bretton, in Flintshire; secondly, Elizabeth, Lady Wolley, sister of Sir George More, knt. of Losely, in Surrey, lieutenant of the Tower; and, thirdly, Alice, dowager countess of Derby, daughter of Sir John Spencer, of Althorp. By the first lady only, who *d.* in 1588, he had issue, viz. two sons and one daughter,

I. THOMAS (Sir), knt. who died in Ireland *v. p.* 23rd August, 1599, aged twenty-five, leaving by Elizabeth his wife, daughter of Thomas Venables, baron of Kinderton, three daughters,

- Elizabeth, *m.* to John Dutton, eldest son of Thomas Dutton, esq. of Dutton, in Cheshire, and died in 1611.
- Mary, *m.* to Sir Thomas Leigh, knt. afterwards Lord Leigh, of Stoneleigh.
- Vere, *m.* to William Booth, esq. of Dunham Massey.

II. JOHN, successor to his father.

I. Mary, who *m.* Sir Francis Leigh, K.B. of Newnham Regis, in the county of Warwick, father of Francis, earl of Chichester.

Lord Brackley was *s.* at his decease by his only surviving son,

JOHN EGERTON, second viscount, who was advanced to the EARLDOM of BRIDGEWATER on the 27th May, 1617. This nobleman, distinguishing himself in Ireland under the earl of Essex in 1599, received the honour of knighthood, and, at the coronation of JAMES I. was made a knight of the Bath. His lordship's appointment, in 1633, to the lord presidency of Wales and the Marches, gave rise to Milton's immortal *Comus*, and is thus recorded by Warton: "I have been informed," says that writer, "from a manuscript of Oldys, that Lord Bridgewater, being appointed lord president of Wales, entered upon his official residence at Ludlow Castle with great solemnity. Upon this occasion, he was attended by a large concourse of the neighbouring nobility and gentry. Among the rest came his children; in particular Lord Brackley, Mr. Thomas Egerton, and Lady Alice, .

> —— to attend their father's state
> And new entrusted sceptre.

They had been on a visit at a house of the Egerton family in Herefordshire; and in passing through Haywood forest were benighted; and the Lady Alice was even lost for a short time. This accident, which in the end was attended with no bad consequences, furnished the subject for a mask for a Michaelmas festivity, and produced *Comus*." The earl wedded the Lady Frances Stanley,* second daughter and co-heir of Ferdinando, earl of Derby, and by her,

* Ben Jonson has addressed several epigrams to Chancellor Egerton: one of which we subjoin;

*To Thomas Lord Chancellor.*

Whilst thy weigh'd judgments, Egerton, I hear,
And know thee then a judge not of one year;
Whilst I behold thee live with purest hands,
That no affection in thy voice commands;
That still thou 'rt present in the better cause;
And no less wise than skilful in the laws;
Whilst thou art certain to thy words once gone,
As is thy conscience, which is always one:
The virgin long since fled from earth I see,
T' our times return'd, hath made her heaven in thee.

* Lady Frances Stanley's grandmother, the Lady Margaret Clifford, was only child of Henry earl of Cumberland, and of Eleanor his countess, younger daughter and co-heir of Charles Brandon, duke of Suffolk, by Mary his wife, queen dowager of France, youngest sister of *King* HENRY VIII.

who *d.* 11th March, 1635, had four sons and eleven daughters, namely,

I. James, } who both *d.* young.
II. Charles, }
III. JOHN, his father's heir.
IV. Thomas, *d.* unm.

I. Frances, *m.* to Sir John Hobart, bart. of Blickling, and *d. s. p.*
II. Arabella, *m.* to Oliver, Lord St. John, son of Oliver, earl of Bolingbroke.
III. Elizabeth, *m.* to David Cecil, esq. afterwards earl of Exeter.
IV. Mary, *m.* to Richard, Lord Herbert, of Cherbury.
V. Cecilia, *d.* unm.
VI. Alice, *d.* unm.
VII. Anne, *d.* unm.
VIII. Penelope, *m.* to Sir Robert Napier, bart. of Luton Hoo, in Bedfordshire.
IX. Catharine, *m.* to William Courteen, esq. son and heir of Sir William Courteen, bart. of London.
X. Magdalen, *m.* to Sir Gervase Cutler, of Stainburgh, in Yorkshire.
XI. Alice, *m.* to Richard, earl of Carberry.

Lord Bridgewater *d.* 4th December, 1649, and was *s.* by his son,

JOHN EGERTON, second earl of Bridgewater, who espoused, in the nineteenth year of his age, the Lady Elizabeth Cavendish, daughter of William, duke of Newcastle, and had issue,

I. JOHN, K.B. third earl of Bridgewater, ancestor of the EARLS and DUKES of BRIDGEWATER.
II. William (Sir), K.B. of Worsley, in Lancashire, M.P. for Aylesbury, who *m.* Honora, sister of Thomas, Lord Leigh, of Stoneleigh, and *d.* in December, 1691, leaving four daughters, who all *d.* unmarried, except the youngest,
    Honora, *b.* in 1685, *m.* to Thomas-Arden Bagot, esq. of Pipe Hall, in Staffordshire.
III. THOMAS, of whom presently, as progenitor of the EGERTONS, of TATTON.
IV. Charles, of Newborough, in Staffordshire, M.P. *b.* in 1654, who *m.* Elizabeth, widow of Randolph Egerton, esq. of Betley, and daughter and heir of Henry Murray, and *d.* in 1717, leaving a son of his own name.
V. Steward, *b.* in 1660, *d.* unm.

I. Frances, died in infancy.
II. Elizabeth, *m.* to Robert Sidney, earl of Leicester.
III. Catharine, died an infant.

The earl *d.* 26th October, 1686, when the manor of Tatton, and the other Cheshire estates of the family, passed to his third son,

THE HON. THOMAS EGERTON, of Tatton Park, *b.* 16th March, 1651, who *m.* Hesther, only daughter of Sir John Busby,* knt. of Addington, in Bucks, by Judith his first wife, daughter and co-heir of Sir William Manwaring, knt. of West Chester, and by her, who died in 1724, had four sons and one daughter, viz.

I. JOHN, his heir.
II. Thomas, *b.* in 1680, *d.* unm.
III. William, LL.D. chancellor and prebendary of Hereford, prebendary of Canterbury, rector of Penshurst, &c. *b.* 6th July, 1682; *m.* Anne, dau. of Sir Francis Head, bart. of Rochester, and *d.* 26th February, 1737, leaving issue,
    John, who *d.* in November, 1740, aged seventeen.
    Charlotte, co-heiress, who *m.* William Hammond, esq. of St. Alban's Court, in Kent, and *d.* in 1770, leaving issue (see vol. i. p. 132.)
    Jemima, co-heiress, who *m.* in 1747, Edward Brydges, esq. of Wootton Court, in Kent, and had, with other issue, the present SIR SAMUEL EGERTON BRYDGES, bart. of Denton Court.
IV. Mainwaring, *b.* in 1683, *d.* in 1686.

I. Elizabeth, *m.* to the Rev. Peter Leigh, of the West Hall, in High Leigh.

Mr. Egerton *d.* 29th October, 1685, was buried at Little Gaddesden, in Herts, and *s.* by his eldest son,

JOHN EGERTON, esq. of Tatton Park, *b.* 12th February, 1679, who wedded Elizabeth, daughter of Samuel Barbour, esq. sister and heiress of Samuel Hill, esq. of Shenstone Park, in the county of Stafford, and by her, who died in 1743, had issue,

I. JOHN, his heir.
II. SAMUEL, successor to his brother.
I. HESTER, eventually sole heiress.
II. Elizabeth, *d.* unm. 1763.

Mr. Egerton *d.* in 1724, was interred at Rosthorne, and *s.* by his elder son,

JOHN EGERTON, esq. of Tatton Park, *b.* 14th October, 1710, who *m.* in April, 1735,

* This gentleman, who died in 1700, was son of Robert Busby, esq. of Addington, by his wife, a daughter of Sir John Gore, knt. of New Place, in Herts. Sir John Gore had married Bridget, daughter of Sir Edward Harington, bart. grandson of Sir James Harington and Lucy his wife, sister to Sir Henry Sidney, of Penshurst.

Christian, daughter of John Ward, esq. of Capesthorne, but dying in 1738, without male issue, the estates and representation of this branch of the family devolved on his brother,

SAMUEL EGERTON, esq. of Tatton Park, *b.* 28th December, 1711, who wedded Beatrix, youngest daughter and co-heir of the Rev. John Copley, of Battly, rector of Elmley, in Yorkshire, and by her, who *d.* in April, 1755, had an only daughter, Beatrix, who *m.* Daniel Wilson, esq. of Dalham Tower, in Westmoreland, but predeceased her father, without surviving issue. Mr. Egerton died himself 10th February, 1780, advanced in years, being one of the representatives in that and the three preceding parliaments for the county of Chester. He devised his great estates, with divers remainders, in tail to his only sister,

HESTER EGERTON, who had *m.* in May, 1747, WILLIAM TATTON, esq. of Withenshaw, but who, upon inheriting her brother's possessions, resumed, by sign manual, 8th May, 1780, her maiden name. She *d.* the 9th of the following July, leaving a daughter, Elizabeth Tatton, the wife of Sir Christopher Sykes, bart. of Sledmere, M.P. and a son and successor,

WILLIAM-TATTON EGERTON, esq. of Tatton and Withenshaw, *b.* 9th May, 1749. This gentleman, who, from his extensive landed possessions and great personal influence, was esteemed one of the leading commoners in the kingdom, represented the county of Chester in parliament. He *m.* thrice (see *family of Tatton*, p. 41), and dying in 1806, was *s.* in the Egerton estates by his eldest surviving son, the present WILBRAHAM EGERTON, esq. of Tatton.

*Arms*—Arg. a lion rampant gu. between three pheons sa.

*Crest*—On a chapeau gu. turned up erm. a lion rampant gu. supporting a dart argent.

*Motto*—Sic donec.

*Estates*—Tatton, Rosthern, Ollerton, &c. were possessed by Sir Alen de Tatton, ancestor of the present proprietor in the earliest period of authentic history. The elder branch became extinct after a few descents: the heiress married William Massey, fourth son of Hamon de Massey, baron of Dunham Massey, whose descendants retained possession of the Tatton property without intermission until the reign of EDWARD IV. From the Tattons, of Tatton, the family of Withenshaw are undoubtedly a branch: it is a curious fact, that the estates should again return into the possession of the Tatton family, after so long an alienation.

*Town Residence*—St. James's Square.

*Seat*—Tatton Park, near Knutsford.

## TATTON, OF WITHENSHAW.

TATTON, THOMAS-WILLIAM, esq. of Withenshaw, in the county of Chester, *b.* 2nd June, 1816, *s.* his father in 1827.

### Lineage.

The Tattons, of Kenworthy, from whom the family before us derives, were a branch of the ancient house of Tatton, of Tatton, which was allied to the barons of Dunham Massey.

ROBERT TATTON, of Kenworthy, by his marriage with Alice, daughter and heiress of William de Massey, of Withenshaw, in Cheshire, acquired that estate, and was direct ancestor of

ROBERT TATTON, of Withenshaw, who *m.* Alice, sister of William Massie, of Coddington, living in the 3rd of EDWARD IV., and daughter of Hugh Massie, by Agnes his wife, daughter and heiress of Nicholas Bold, great great grandson of Sir Richard Bold, of Bold. By Alice Massie, Robert left four sons, viz.

I. WILLIAM, who *m.* a daughter of William Davenport, of Bramall, but *d. s. p.*
II. Robert, a priest, who of course died unmarried.
III. JOHN, of whom presently.
IV. Bartholomew.

The third son,

JOHN TATTON, wedded Margaret, daughter of Ralph Davenport, of Chester, a younger son of Ralph Davenport, of Henbury, and left (with a daughter, Elizabeth, *m.* first, to — Bradborne; and, secondly, to Thomas Ashley, of Shepley), a son and successor,

ROBERT TATTON, of Withenshaw, who *m.* Dorothy, fourth daughter of George Booth, esq. of Dunham, and by her, who died in 1608, had issue,

I. WILLIAM, his heir.
II. John.
III. Robert, of the Parsonage at Northenden, died in 1610.
IV. Edward, of Etchells, *m.* Margaret Corke, and died in 1632.
V. Nicholas, *m.* in 1596, Dorothy Linney.

I. Elizabeth, *m.* in 1570, to John Ward, of Capesthorne.
II. Dorothy, *m.* in 1582, to James Bradshawe, esq. of the Haugh, in the county of Chester.

Robert Tatton *d.* in June, 1579, and was *s.* by his eldest son,

WILLIAM TATTON, esq. of Withenshaw, who *m.* Mary, daughter of Sir Edward Fitton, knt. of Gawsworth, and by her, who died in 1614, left at his decease, 19th May, 1611, a son and successor,

ROBERT TATTON, esq. of Withenshaw, who espoused Eleanor, third daughter of John Warren, esq. of Poynton, and had issue,

I WILLIAM, his heir.
II. Robert, living 14th January, 9th JAMES I.
III. George, died an infant in 1590.
IV. Philip.
V. George, *b.* in 1612.

I. Elizabeth, *b.* in 1587; *m.* first, to John Latham, esq. of Wilmslow; and, secondly, to George Mainwaring, esq. second son of Sir Randal Mainwaring, of Peover.
II. Margaret, died unm. in 1609.
III. Mary.

Robert Tatton *d.* at Southwark, near London, in 1623, and was *s.* by his son,

WILLIAM TATTON, esq. of Withenshaw, *b.* in 1581, who *m.* in 1602, Katherine, eldest daughter of Sir George Leycester, bart. of Toft, and by her, who wedded, secondly, the Rev. W. Nicolls, D. D and *d.* in 1665, left at his demise in 1616, with three daughters, Anne, who *d.* in infancy, Margaret, the wife of Richard Twyford, esq. of Diddesbury, and Eleanor, *b.* in 1612, a son and successor,

ROBERT TATTON, esq. of Withenshaw, *b.* 14th May, 1606, who served the office of sheriff for Cheshire in 1645. During the civil wars, this gentleman was a staunch supporter of the royal cause, and sustained a siege at Withenshaw against the parliamentary forces. It is thus noticed in Burghall's diary: "February 25, 1643-4, Mr. Tatton's house at Withenshaw was taken by the parliament, who had laid a long siege to it. There were in it only Mr. Tatton, some gentlemen, and but a few soldiers, who had quarter for life. The ammunition was but little." Col. Duckenfield conducted the attack, and finally effected the reduction of the mansion by bringing two pieces of ordnance from Manchester. In the last century, six skeletons were found in the garden at Withenshaw lying close together, who were supposed to be soldiers buried during the siege in the house, which was then much larger than it is at present. There is a tradition that one of the parliament officers exposed himself by sitting on a wall, and that a female domestic begged for a musket to try if "she could bring him down," and succeeded. Mr. Watson supposes this officer to have been "Captayne Adams, slayne at Withenshawe," on Sunday the 25th, who was buried at Stockport 25th February, 1643-4. Mr. Tatton compounded for his estate at £707. 13*s.* 4*d.* and appears to have been oppressed by other vexatious charges, in consequence of which he appealed against his portion of subsequent parliament levies. These disastrous consequences of loyalty must have been severely felt, as Webb, writing in 1622, speaks of the Tattons as being "much eclipsed," and "by troubles and encumbrances, whereunto greatest estates are oft subject, obscured," and "places the chiefest hope of raising the house on that grandchild," upon whom these calamities subsequently fell. Mr. Tatton *m.* in 1628, Anne, third daughter and co-heiress of William Brereton, esq. of Ashley, and by her, who died in 1670, had four sons and two daughters, viz.

I. WILLIAM, his heir.
II. Robert, of Stockport, *b.* in 1639, who *m.* Anne, daughter of William Davenport, esq. of Bramall, and *d.* in 1685, leaving issue,

WILLIAM, successor to his cousin Robert.

Thomas, of Stockport, living in

1689, when he was made heir in remainder to the Withenshaw estate by will of his cousin Robert Tatton. He *m.* Mary, only daughter and heir of Charles Poole, esq. of Marley, in Cheshire, and had two sons and one daughter,

Robert, of Stockport, who *m.* Frances Shepley, and died *s. p.* in 1743.

Edward, died unm. in 1783.

Mary, died young.

Anne.

III. Richard.

IV. Thomas, of Peel, in the county of Chester, *m.* Mary, daughter of Edward Pegge, esq. of Beauchief, and had two daughters, Anne and Eleanor.

I. Mary, *b.* in 1629.

II. Anne, *b.* in 1632, *m.* in 1664, to Sir Amos Meredith, bart.

Robert Tatton *d.* in 1669, was buried at Northenden, and *s.* by his son,

WILLIAM TATTON, esq. of Withenshaw, *b.* in 1636, who espoused Anne, only surviving child of Rowland Eyre, esq. of Bradway, in the county of Derby, and by her (who *m.* secondly, Robert Radcliffe, esq. second son of Sir Alexander Radcliffe, of Ordeshall) had a daughter, Anne, *m.* to John Greenhalgh, esq. of Brandlesome, and a son,

ROBERT TATTON, esq. of Withenshaw, *b.* in 1668, who *m.* Frances, daughter of Peter Legh, esq. of Lyme, but by her (who wedded, secondly, Sir Gilbert Clarke; and, thirdly, Dr. Shippen) having no issue, was *s.* at his decease by his cousin,

WILLIAM TATTON, esq. of Withenshaw, *b.* at Bramall 5th August, 1674, who *m.* in 1698, Hannah, daughter and heiress of Peter Wright, esq. of Macclesfield, and had

I. WILLIAM, his heir.

II. Thomas, of Heaton Norris, who *m.* first, Penelope, youngest daughter of Matthew, Lord Ducie; and, secondly, Catherine, daughter of Hugh Foulkes, esq. of Polesbey, in Denbighshire, but *d. s. p.* in 1775.

I. Anne, *b.* in 1702, *m.* Samuel Kirke, esq. of Whitehough, and had a dau. Catherine Kirke, the wife of the Rev. William Plumbe (see vol. i. page 292).

II. Frances, died unm. in 1776, aged seventy.

III. Barbara, of Macclesfield, also died unm. in 1776.

IV. Mary, *d.* unm.

V. Lucy, *m.* to John Stafford, esq.

VI. Margaret, *d.* unm.

VII. Catherine, *d.* unm.

Mr. Tatton died in 1732, and was *s.* by his son,

WILLIAM TATTON, esq. of Withenshaw, *b.* in 1703. This gentleman *m.* first, Catherine, eldest daughter of Edward Warren, esq. of Poynton, who dying without issue in 1742, he wedded, secondly, in 1747, Hester, daughter of John Egerton, esq. of Tatton, and eventually heiress of her brother Samuel Egerton, esq. By this lady, who *d.* 9th July, 1780, having previously resumed the name of EGERTON, he had one son and one daughter, viz.

WILLIAM, his heir.

Elizabeth, *m.* to Sir Christopher Sykes, bart.

Mr. Tatton *d.* in 1776, and was *s.* by his son,

WILLIAM TATTON, esq. of Withenshaw, who assumed, upon inheriting the great estates of his mother's family, the surname and arms of EGERTON, of Tatton. This gentleman, who was born in 1749, and who represented the county of Chester in parliament, *m.* first, in 1773, Frances-Maria,* eldest daughter of the Very Rev. Dean Fountayne (see vol. ii. p. 269), and by her (who *d.* in 1777) had two sons and a daughter, viz.

WILLIAM, of Withenshaw, *b.* in 1774, M.P. for Beverley in 1796; *d.* unm. in 1799.

Thomas, *d.* in 1778, aged four.

Frances-Maria, *d.* young in 1781.

He wedded, secondly, in 1780, Mary, second daughter of Richard-Wilbraham Bootle, esq. of Rode and Lathom, and by her, who *d.* in 1784, had issue,

WILBRAHAM, of Tatton. See family of EGERTON, of TATTON.

THOMAS-WILLIAM, of Withenshaw.

John, *b.* in 1784, and *d.* in 1786.

Mary-Elizabeth, *m.* to Sir Mark Masterman Sykes, bart. of Sledmere.

---

* On this lady's monument, in the church of Northenden, are the following lines:

If e'er on earth true happiness were found,
'Twas thine, blest shade, that happiness to prove;
A father's fondest wish thy duty crown'd,
Thy softer virtues fix'd a husband's love.
Ah! when he led thee to the nuptial fane,
How smiled the morning with auspicious rays!
How triumphed youth and beauty in thy train,
And flattering health that promised length of days!
Heav'n join'd your hearts; three pledges of your joy
Were given in thrice the years revolving round;
Here, reader, pause; and own, with pitying eye,
That not on earth true happiness is found.

She died January 9th, 1777, aged twenty-six.

Mr. Egerton espoused, thirdly, Anna-Maria, eldest daughter of Sir George Armytage, bart. of Kirklees, by whom he had no surviving issue; and, fourthly, in 1803, Charlotte-Clara, daughter of Thomas-Watkinson Payler, esq. of Kent, which lady died *s. p.* in 1804. Mr. Egerton died himself in 1806, and was *s.* in the Egerton estates by his eldest surviving son, WILBRAHAM EGERTON, esq. while the Withenshaw property passed, under his will, to

THOMAS-WILLIAM EGERTON, esq. *b.* 29th October, 1783, who assumed in consequence the surname and arms of TATTON. He *m.* in 1807, Emma, daughter of the Hon. John Grey, third son of Harry, fourth earl of Stamford, and had issue,

- I. THOMAS-WILLIAM, his heir.
- I. Emma, *m.* in February, 1832, to Harry Mainwaring, esq. son of Sir Thomas Mainwaring, bart.
- II. Mary-Elizabeth, died in 1821.
- III. Henrietta.
- IV. Frances.
- V. Louisa.
- VI. Sophia.
- VII. Susanna-Theodosia.
- VIII. Anna-Maria.

Mr. Tatton, who was sheriff of Cheshire in 1809, died in London 2nd March, 1827, and a cenotaph is erected to his memory by his widow, in the parish church of Northenden, in the form of a simple and elegant sarcophagus. His son and successor is the present THOMAS-WILLIAM TATTON, esq. of Withenshaw.

*Arms*—Quarterly, arg. and gu.; in the first and fourth quarter a crescent sa., in the second and third another of the first.

*Crest*—A greyhound sejant arg. collared and tied to a tree ppr.

*Estates*—In Cheshire.

*Seat*—Withenshaw, in that county.

## CHUTE, OF CHUTE HALL.

CHUTE, RICHARD, esq. of Chute Hall, in the county of Kerry, *b.* in October, 1763; *m.* first, in 1785, Agnes, daughter of Rowland Bateman, esq. of Oak Park, and has issue,

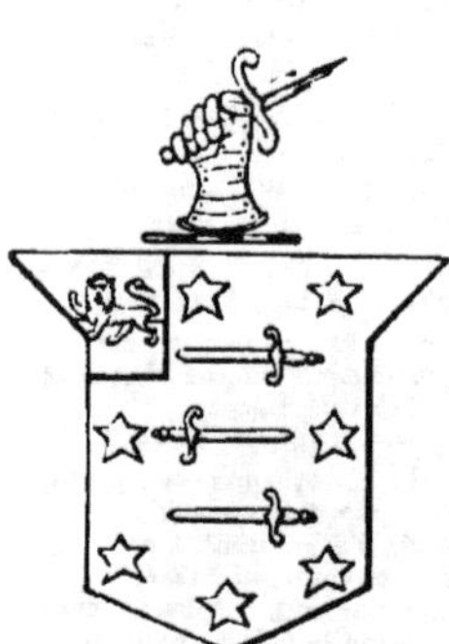

- I. FRANCIS, of Spring Hill, captain in the Kerry militia, who *m.* first, Mary-Anne, daughter of Trevor Bomford, esq. of Dublin, and has three sons and one daughter, viz.

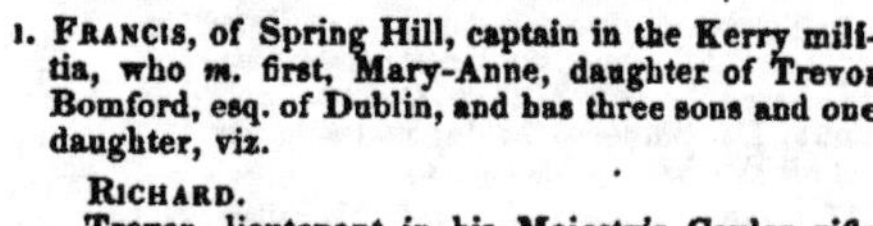

  RICHARD.
  Trevor, lieutenant in his Majesty's Ceylon rifle regiment.
  Rowland.
  Mary.

  Capt. Chute wedded, secondly, Arabella, daughter of the Rev. Maynard Denny, of Churchill, brother of Sir Barry Denny, first bart. of Tralee, M.P. for the county of Kerry, and that lady has two sons and two daughters.

- II. Rowland, who served many years in the army during the late war, and retired a captain in the 58th regiment. He *m.* Frances, daughter of James Crosbie, esq. of Ballyheig Castle, formerly M.P. and governor of the county of Kerry, and present colonel commandant of its militia. By this lady Capt. Rowland Chute has two sons and two daughters.

- I. Lætitia, *m.* to William Raymond, esq. of Dromin, in the county of Kerry.
- II. Ruth.
- III. Agnes, *m.* to Richard Mason, esq. of Cappanahane, in the county of Limerick.

Mr. Chute espoused, secondly, in 1798, Elizabeth, daughter of the Rev. Dr. William Maunsell, D.D. of the city of Limerick, and by her has two sons and three daughters,

- I. William-Maunsell.
- II. Richard, M.D. member of the college of surgeons, resident in Tralee.
- I. Elizabeth.
- II. Dorothea, *m.* to William Neligan, esq. of Tralee.
- III. Margaret.

Mr. Chute, who succeeded his father in March, 1782, acted for many years as a magistrate of the county of Kerry until, from declining health, he was compelled to retire from the bench. He served the office of high sheriff, shortly after his attaining majority, in 1786.

## Lineage.

The Chutes, of Chute Hall, derive from that branch of the ancient family of Chute, which was seated in the county of Kent. The Hampshire and Norfolk lines are now represented by William-Lyde-Wiggett Chute, esq. of the Vine and of Pickenham Hall. (See vol. i. p. 632.)

The first who settled in Ireland,

George Chute, a military officer, went into that kingdom during the rebellion of Desmond, and obtained grants of land near Dingle, and in the county of Limerick, which were soon however alienated. He *m.* an Evans, of the county of Cork, and had a son,

Daniel Chute, who acquired, in marriage with a daughter of Mc Elligott, the lands of Tulligaron or Chute Hall, which were afterwards (with others since disposed of) confirmed by patent, in 1630, under which they are now held. He left (with a daughter, *m.* to — Crosbie, esq.) a son and successor,

Richard Chute, esq. of Tulligaron, in the county of Kerry, who wedded a daughter of Crosbie, of Tubrid, and had issue. At the restoration, in 1660, Mr. Crosbie, of Tubrid, being high sheriff of Kerry, returned Chute to parliament as member for that county, in opposition to Blennerhasset, of Ballyseedy, who petitioned against the return and succeeded. Some curious particulars connected with this contest are set forth in the first volume of the Irish Commons' Journals, and it was probably owing to the expenses then incurred that the alienation of the grants above alluded to took place. Richard Chute was *s.* by his son,

Eusebius Chute, esq. of Tulligaron, who *m.* Mary, sister of Mr. Justice Bernard, of the court of Common Pleas in Ireland, (raised to the bench in 1726,) ancestor of the earls of Bandon. By this lady he had issue,

- I. Richard, his heir.
- II. Francis, who died collector of Tralee, leaving no issue.
- III. Pierce, ancestor of the Chutes, of Tralee.
- IV. Arthur, in holy orders, who died unmarried.

The eldest son,

Richard Chute, esq. of Tulligaron, wedded Charity, daughter of John Herbert, esq. of Castle Island, in the county of Kerry, and had issue,

- I. Francis, his heir.
- II. Richard, of Roxboro, in Kerry, who *m.* Jane, daughter of — Austen, esq. of Waterfall, in the same county, and left one son and two daughters, viz.
  - Richard, who *m.* Miss Morris, of Ballybeggin, in Kerry, and has one son, George, and three daughters.
  - Mary, *m.* to Hugh Jamison, esq. of Cork.
  - Charity, *m.* to Robert Torrens, esq. M.P. for Bolton.
- I. Margaret, *m.* to George Rowan, esq. of Rahtarmy, in the county of Kerry, and had issue.
- II. Agnes, *m.* to John Sealy, esq. of Maglass, in Kerry, and had issue.
- III. Catherine, *m.* to Cornelius M'Gillicuddy, (M'Gillicuddy, of the Reeks), and had issue.

Mr. Chute was *s.* at his decease by his eldest son,

Francis Chute, esq. of Tulligaron, or Chute Hall, who *m.* in 1761, Ruth, daughter of Sir Riggs Falkiner, bart. of Anne Mount, in the county of Cork, and had issue,

- I. Richard, his heir.
- II. Falkiner, captain in the 22nd regiment of light dragoons, who *m.* Anne, daughter of Captain Goddard, of the Queen's County, and left at his decease an only daughter,
  - Catherine, *m.* to William Cooke, esq. of Retreat, near Athlone.
- III. Caleb, captain in the 69th foot, who *m.* Elizabeth, daughter of Theophilus

Yielding, esq. of Caher Anne, in the county of Kerry.

IV. Francis-Bernard, who *m.* Jane, daughter of John Rowan, esq. of Castle Gregory, and has issue,
   1. Francis-Bernard.
   2. Elizabeth.

V. Arthur, who *m.* Frances, daughter of John Lindsay, esq. of Lindville, in the south liberties of the city of Cork, and has issue,
   1. Francis, in holy orders.
   2. John, also in orders.
   1. Frances.
   2. Ruth.
   3. Anne.

I. Margaret, *m.* to Thomas-William Sandes, esq. of Sallowglin, in the county of Kerry.

II. Ruth, *m.* to the late Thomas Elliott, esq. of Garrynthenavally, in Kerry.

Mr. Chute *d.* in 1782, and was *s.* by his eldest son, the present RICHARD CHUTE, esq. of Chute Hall.

*Arms*—Gu. semee of mullets or, three swords barways, ppr. the middlemost encountering the other two; a canton per fesse arg. and vert, thereon a lion passant.

*Crest*—A dexter cubit arm in armour, the hand on a gauntlet grasping a broken sword, in bend sinister ppr. pommel and hilt or.

*Motto*—Fortune de guerre.

*Estates*—Tulligaron, near Tralee, acquired by marriage, and one-sixth part of the seignorial grant of Mount Eagle Royal, (or Castle Island), in the county of Kerry, held by fee-farm lease jointly with five other gentlemen, under the representatives of Herbert, earl of Powis.

*Seat*—Chute Hall, situated about two miles and a half eastward from Tralee.

## MASSIE, OF CODDINGTON.

MASSIE, THE REV. RICHARD, of Coddington, in the county of Chester, *b.* in 1771; *m.* Hester-Lee, eldest daughter of Edward Townshend, esq. of Wincham, in the same shire, and has had issue,

I. RICHARD, *m.* 7th January, 1834, Mary-Anne, eldest daughter of H. R. Hughes, esq. of Bache Hall, Cheshire.
II. Thomas-Leche.
III. Edward.
IV. William-Henry.
V. Townshend.
VI. John-Bevis.
VII. Watkin.
VIII. Charles.
IX. George, died an infant.
X. Robert-George.
XI. Hugh-Hamon.
XII. Henry, deceased.

I. Eliza-Anne, *m.* in 1823, to William T. Buchanan, esq. of Ravenscroft.
II. Hester-Susannah, *m.* in 1828, to Rev. John Armistead, vicar of Sandbach.
III. Frances-Maria, *m.* in 1827, to Rev. G. B. Blomfield, prebendary of Chester and rector of Stevenage, Herts, brother to the bishop of London.
IV. Sidney.
V. Barbara-Henrietta.
VI. Cornelea-Lee, deceased.
VII. Harriet-Vyse, *m.* in 1829, to Laurence Armistead, esq. of Cranage Hall, in Cheshire.
VIII. Anna-Maria.
IX. Charlotte.
X. Mary-Mackenzie.

Mr. Massie, who is rector of Eccleston, succeeded his father in 1802.

## Lineage.

The early descent of the MASSIES, of Coddington, has long been a matter of dispute, some of the pedigrees deriving them from a younger son of Sir John Massie, of Tatton, supposed to have been slain at Shrewsbury, whose eldest son *d.* 8th HENRY V.; and others from Hamon, son of Sir John Massey, of Puddington, who also fell at the battle of Shrewsbury. "The probabilities," says Ormerod, "are in favour of the Tatton branch, as far as can be argued from correspondence of dates, and no stress can be laid on a subsequent settlement made by John Massie in the sixteenth century, whereby he settled Coddington in remainder on the Puddington family, in the event of his issue failing, as this settlement overlooked acknowledged nearer relations, the Massies of Broxton and the Massies of Eggerley."

HUGH MASSIE settled at Coddington in consequence of his marriage with Agnes, daughter and heiress of Nicholas Bold, of Coddington, great grandson of John, third son of Sir John Bold, of Bold, in Lancashire. Hugh had (with four daughters, Anne, *m.* to David Dod, esq. of Edge; Alice, *m.* to Robert Tatton, esq. of Withenshaw; Maud, the wife of Thomas Cottingham, esq. of Wirral; and Margaret, of Philip Aldersey, esq. of Middle Aldersey) several sons, of whom the third,

WILLIAM MASSIE, esq. purchased, in the 18th of HENRY VI. from Sir Philip Boteler, the manors of Coddington, Bechin, Eggerley, &c. subject to a rent charge of twenty-five marks per annum, which, by a deed, 8th HENRY VIII. was fixed at forty marks. He wedded Alice, daughter and heiress of Adam Woton, of Edgerley and Chester, and by her, who *m.* secondly, Hugh Ball, of Coddington, had two sons, namely,

I. MORGAN, of Eggerley, on whom his mother's lands were entailed. He *m.* Margery, daughter of John Davenport, esq. of Davenport, by Maud his wife, daughter of Sir Andrew Brereton, knt. of Brereton, and had an only son and heir,

ROBERT, ancestor of the MASSIES, of Eggerley, in whom that manor remained vested until the time of CHARLES II., when it was purchased from them by Samuel Smallwood, whose lineal descendant, Thomas Smallwood, esq. was proprietor in 1759. It was shortly after sold to the Rev. Thomas Ince.

II. JOHN.

The second son,

JOHN MASSIE, esq. inherited, under his father's deed of partition, 3rd EDWARD IV. the lands of Coddington. He *m.* Margaret, daughter and heiress of Holme, of Coddington, and had a son and successor,

ROBERT MASSIE, esq. of Coddington, who died before 23rd HENRY VII. as appears by an award of the said manor, leaving a daughter, Anne, the wife of William Massey, of Grafton, and a son,

WILLIAM MASSIE, esq. of Coddington, living 23rd HENRY VII. who *m.* Alice, dau. of Edward de Crew, and had issue,

I. ROBERT, his heir.

II. John, of Broxton, living *temp.* HENRY VIII. who *m.* Margaret, daughter and heiress of Richard Larton, esq. of Larton, and had, with a daughter, Johanna, *m.* to John Aldersey, of Middle Aldersey, a son,

EDWARD MASSIE, esq. of Larton, ancestor of the MASSIES of BROXTON, who continued there seated to the commencement of the eighteenth century, when the estate was sold by HUGH MASSIE to John Dod, esq. a descendant of the Dods, of Edge. This branch of the Massie family enjoyed great respectability and extensive possessions, holding estates in eleven townships of Cheshire, and the manors of Halghton and Yale, in the county of Denbigh.

The elder son,

ROBERT MASSIE, esq. of Coddington, living *temp.* HENRY VIII. espoused Dorothy, daughter of Sir Hugh Calveley, knt. of Lea, by Christiana his wife, daughter of Thomas Cottingham, esq. and had, with two daughters, Elizabeth, wife of Henry Holme, and Jane, of Thomas Salisbury, several sons, the eldest of whom,

ROGER MASSIE, esq. of Coddington, held that manor, and lands in Bechin from the Lord Dacre as of his manor of Wemme, by fealty, and the render of a rose yearly. He wedded Elizabeth, daughter of Randle Brereton, esq. of Eccleston and Wettenhall, and had issue,

JOHN, his heir.

Jane.

Elizabeth, who *m.* William Barnston, esq. of Churton, in Cheshire, and *d.* 13th January, 1606, leaving issue.

Roger Massie *d.* 20th April, 24th HENRY VIII. and was *s.* by his son,

JOHN MASSIE, esq. of Coddington, who made, *temp.* EDWARD VI. the settlement we have alluded to in the commencement of this narrative, by which his estates were entailed on the male issue of his two sons, with remainder to the Masseys, of Puddington. He *m.* first, Ellen, daughter of Thomas Daniel, of Tabley, by whom he had one son, Thomas, who died *s. p.*; secondly, Margaret, daughter of Randle Bamvile, esq. of Chester; thirdly, Grace, daughter of Sir Thomas Grosvenor, of Eaton; and, fourthly, Mary, daughter and heiress of Edward Hughes, esq. of Holt, in the county of Denbigh, receiver to Queen Elizabeth for Cheshire and Flintshire. By his second and third wives John Massie had no child, but by his third he had issue two sons and four daughters, viz.

JOHN, his heir.

William, of London.

Mary, *m.* to Lawrence Starkey, esq. of Wrenbury.

Jane, *m.* to Richard Philips, esq. of Stockton.

Margaret.

Anne, *m.* to Edward Johnes, esq. of Grosvelt.

The elder son,

JOHN MASSIE, esq. of Coddington, wedded Anne, eldest daughter of Richard Grosvenor, esq. of Eaton, high sheriff of Cheshire in 1602, by Christiana his wife, daughter of Sir Richard Brooke, bart. of Norton, and had issue,

I. John, *b.* in 1601, *d. s. p.*

II. ROGER, his father's heir.

III. Richard, died issueless.

IV. George, also died without issue.

V. EDWARD, one of the most distinguished military leaders during the civil wars of the reign of CHARLES I. This gallant person, who held a commission in the royal army in the expedition against Scotland, attended, on the commencement of the troubles, at York, with the intention of serving the king: but "finding himself," says Clarendon, "not enough known there, and that there would be little gotten but in the comfort of a good conscience, he went to London, where there was more money and fewer officers," and on his arrival was made lieutenant-colonel to the earl of Stamford, and appointed governor of the city of Gloucester. The same historian details, at greater length than our limits will permit, the device by which Colonel Massie inveigled the king to undertake in person the siege of Gloucester, and commemorates also the determined defence of the besieged, a defence to which, as it gave the parliament time to recover their broken spirits and forces, may be attributed "the greatness to which they afterwards aspired." In 1645, Massie obtained the rank of major-general, and in the same year his name twice occurs in official contemporary publications, the first of which is an account of his engagement with Prince Rupert's forces at Ledbury, where Massie uniformly charged in person at the head of his troops. "Prince Rupert," says Massie, in a letter descriptive of the engagement, "sent me word by my trumpeter that I sent, that in the fight he sought me, but knew me not till after, no more than I knew him. But it seems we charged each other, and he shot my horse under me, and I did as much for him. At that charge many commanders of theirs fell." The success at Ledbury was followed by the capture of Evesham, which was stormed with great gallantry in five places at once by the parliament forces under General Massie. In 1647, he was one of the officers employed by the city to enlist new forces during the differences between the army and parliament, after the seizure of the king's person. In these discussions he took an active part, and opposing the intentions now plainly manifested by Cromwell, he was, with other officers of the presbyterian party, committed to prison. Massie, however, effected his escape, fled to Holland, and had the boldness to present himself to Prince Charles as a sufferer for the king. Massie's abilities and bravery were not to be neglected, and retaining his rank, he obtained the command of a regiment of horse under the duke of Buckingham; and in the king's march to Worcester was dispatched, on account of his connexion with the presbyterians, one day's march in advance of the royal army, to give notice of his majesty's coming, and to draw the gentry to attend upon him. In this new cause Massie displayed his wonted activity and skill; but, having secured a pass in the neighbourhood of Worcester, he attempted to follow up an advantage of little importance, and received a dangerous wound, which prevented him from exerting his services in a moment of the greatest need to the king. In the flight from Worcester, General Massie rode six miles with his majesty, but not being able to keep pace any longer, the king took his leave of him, with tears trickling down his cheeks, saying, "Farewell, my dear and faithful friend, the Lord bless and preserve us both;" and so they parted. The major-general wheeled off by way of Bromsgrove, but being unable from the anguish of his wounds to journey further, he threw himself on the mercy of the countess of Stamford, and was received as a prisoner at Broadgate manor. The last effort of Massie was an unsuccessful endeavour to seize Gloucester for the king. Clarendon attributes the failure, in some degree, to the errors caused by a stormy and tempestuous night in which the attempt was made, to which circumstance however Massie was indebted for his personal safety. He had been seized by a troop of horse, and was conveyed by them towards his prison, being bound on his horse before a trooper. In the darkest part of the night, in a woody and hilly defile, he contrived to throw the soldier, and disentangling himself from his hold by means of his great strength and agility, he secured his retreat into the woods.*

General Massie, of whom a fine portrait is still preserved at Pool Hall, the seat of his collateral descendant, died in Ireland, without issue, and was interred at Abbey Leix.

vi. William, who *m.* in London.

vii. Richard, *d. s. p.* in Ireland.

viii. Robert, citizen of London, *m.* Jane Massey, of Hoggesdon, in Middlesex, and died in 1670, leaving a son, Edward.

ix. Hugh, of London, merchant, who *d.* about the year 1659, leaving issue, Hugh, Mabel, and Elizabeth, all minors in 1670.

x. George.

xi. Hamon.

i. Grace.

ii. Christiana, died young.

iii. Grace.

iv. Margaret, *m.* to Hugh Williamson, esq. of Chowley.

v. Christiana.

vi. Anne, *m.* to Edward Owen, esq. of Shrewsbury.

vii. Mary.

The eldest surviving son and heir,

Roger Massie, esq. of Coddington, aged fifty-nine in 1663, *m.* in 1649, Mary, daughter of Roger Middleton, esq. of Cadwgan, in Denbighshire, and had issue,

i. John, his heir.

ii. Roger, ancestor of the Masseys, of Pool Hall. (See *that family*).

iii. Edward, of Rosthorne, who died in 1730, leaving, *inter alios*, a son, Richard-Middleton Massey, M. D. F.R.S. and Sec. S. A. who, by his second wife, Sarah, daughter of John Marshall, gent. of Wisbech, had five sons and one daughter. The direct male line of the Massies, of Rosthorne, terminated in the youngest of Dr. Massey's sons,

James Massey, esq. who had, by his second wife, Martha, daughter of Thomas Ravald, of Manchester, one son and three daughters, viz.

John, who predeceased his father *s. p.*

Elizabeth, *m.* to the Rev. Robert Wright, D.D. rector of Whitechapel.

Martha-Maria.

---

* See Clarendon, Ormerod, and several rare pamphlets preserved in the British Museum.

The following abstract of the entire series of the military services of General Massie up to 1646, is taken from 'Ricraft's Survey of England's Champions:' "Served under the earl of Essex at Worcester, Sept. 12, 1642: at Edgehill, Oct. 22, 1642: appointed governor of Gloucester; defeated Lord Herbert's forces, March 30, 1643: relieved (after the defence of Gloucester) by Essex, Sept. 5, 1643: defeated Col. Vavasor from Tewkesbury, Dec. 6, 1643: defeated Sir John Winter from Newnham, and dismantled the garrison of Wotton, Dec. 4, 1643: defeated scattered forces from Gloucester, March 20, 1644: defeated Sir John Winter and took the town of Little Dean, May 7, 1644: stormed Beverstone Castle, May 27, 1644: took Malmesbury, May 30, 1644: and subsequently Chippenham: defeated and killed General Mynne, near Kidmally, Aug. 12, 1644: took Monmouth Castle, Sept. 26, 1644: gained a victory at Betsly Sconce, in Dean forest, Sept. 30, 1644: defeated Sir John Winter near Beechly shortly afterwards: secured the frontier garrisons in the district under his command: again defeated Sir John Winter, Feb. 26, 1645: routed Prince Maurice coming from Bristol, March 24, 1645: stormed Evesham, May 27, 1645: and subsequently 'led brave Fairfax the way into the West;' witness the daily skirmishes he was in for five or six weeks together, beating the enemy to retreats at least 120 miles, taking and killing many, notwithstanding the enemy was four to one."

To these achievements, Vicars, in 'England's Worthies,' adds the capture of Tewkesbury (1644): a second defeat of Bristol royalists: "the first conquering blow at that brave fight and famous victory at Langport:" and "the most furious and successful onset at Tiverton, in Cornwall."

Sarah, *m.* to Domville Poole, esq. of Dane Bank, and had issue.

I. Anne, *b.* in 1659, *m.* to Trafford Barnston, esq. of Churton, in Cheshire.

Roger Massie was *s.* by his eldest son,

JOHN MASSIE, esq. of Coddington, *b.* in 1651, who *m.* first, in 1674, Elizabeth, dau. and heiress of William Wilson, esq. of Chester and Terne, registrar of Chester, and by her had issue,

John, *d. s. p.*

William, who *m.* in 1712, Anne, daughter of Sir John Williams, bart. of Pengethley, but died *s. p.* in 1729.

Anne, died unm. in 1727.

Margaret.

Elizabeth, *m.* to Francis Elcock, esq. of Pool.

Mr. Massie married, secondly, in 1693, Dorothy, daughter of Peter Dutton, esq. of Hatton, and widow of John Walthall, esq. by whom he had no issue; and, thirdly, in 1711, Elizabeth, daughter of John Puleston, esq. of Pickhill, by Anne his wife, daughter of Richard Alport, esq. of Overton. By the last lady he left, at his decease in 1730, a daughter, Mary, *m.* to Eubule Roberts, esq. of Llanprydd, in Denbighshire, and a son,

RICHARD MASSIE, esq. of Coddington, who wedded, 17th April, 1735, Charlotte, daughter of the Rev. Thomas Lloyd, of Plas Power, in Denbighshire, and by her, who died in 1783, had issue,

I. JOHN, his heir.

II. THOMAS, successor to his brother.

III. William, of Chester, *b.* in 1740, *d. s. p.* in 1806.

IV. Richard-Myddelton, *b.* in 1743, *d.* an infant.

V. Edward, *b.* in 1747, *m.* and left a son, Watkin.

VI. Robert, *b.* in 1748, died *s. p.*

VII. Charles, *b.* in 1750, *m.* Benedicta, daughter of Robert Lloyd, esq. a younger brother of the family of Maesmynan, and left issue, William, Thomas, Maria, and Emma.

I. Maria-Sobieski, died unm.

II. Elizabeth, *m.* to William Lloyd, esq. of Plas Power, and *d. s. p.*

III. Ann, *d.* unm.

IV. Frances, died young.

Mr. Massie was *s.* at his decease, in March, 1770, by his eldest son,

JOHN MASSIE, esq. of Coddington, *b.* in 1736, at whose decease *s. p.* in 1773, the estates devolved on his brother,

THOMAS MASSIE, esq. of Coddington, *b.* in 1738, who *m.* Elizabeth, daughter of Nathaniel Marriot, esq. of Cheshunt, Herts, and dying in 1802, left an only child, the present REV. RICHARD MASSIE, of Coddington.

*Arms*—Quarterly gu. and or; in first and fourth quarters, three fleurs de lys arg. for difference a canton arg.

*Crest*—A demi pegasus with wings displayed, quarterly or and gu.

*Estates*—In Cheshire.

*Residence*—Eccleston rectory. The family seat, Coddington Hall, an ancient timber edifice, has been entirely taken down.

## MASSEY, OF POOL HALL.

MASSEY, WILLIAM, esq. of Pool Hall, in the county of Chester, *m.* in 1817, Mary, only daughter of John Goodman, esq. of Porthamel, in Anglesea, and has issue,

I. FRANCIS-ELCOCK.

II. William-Glynne.

I. Margaret-Henrietta-Maria.

Mr. Massey inherited the estates, upon the demise of his mother, in 1825.

## Lineage.

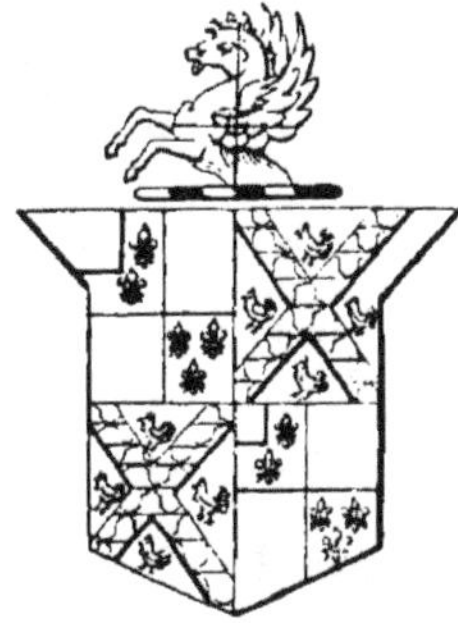

This is a branch of the ancient family of Massie, of Coddington.

ROGER MASSEY, esq. second son of Roger Massie, esq. of Coddington, who was born in 1604, by Mary his wife, daughter of Roger Middleton, esq. of Cadwgan, in the county of Denbigh, and nephew of the celebrated General Massey, espoused Mary, daughter of — Edwards, esq. of Chester, and had two sons,

- JOHN, father of John (who had a son, Robert, vicar of Eccleston) and of Roger, who *d. s. p.*
- ROGER, of whom immediately.

The second son,

ROGER MASSEY, esq. married and had two sons and two daughters, viz. Thomas, of Chester;* WILLIAM, of whom presently; Grace and Mary, who both *d.* unm.

The second son,

THE REV. WILLIAM MASSEY, rector of Ditchingham, in Norfolk, wedded Elizabeth, second daughter and eventual heiress of Francis Elcocke, esq. of White Pool, in the county of Chester, and by her had issue,

- ROGER, in holy orders, archdeacon of Barnstaple and rector of Cheriton Bishop, in Devon, and of Lawhitton, in Cornwall, *m.* Miss Anne Arnold, and had issue one son, John, and four daughters.
- WILLIAM, who inherited his mother's estates.
- Elizabeth.
- Sarah.

Mrs. Massey, the heiress of Pool, died in 1825, and was *s.* by her son, the present WILLIAM MASSEY, esq. of Poole Hall.

* Thomas Massey, of Chester, left three sons, William, (father of Thomas and James St. John Massey), Cholmondeley, and Henry.

### Family of Elcocke.

ALEXANDER ELCOCKE, of Stockport, (son of Nicholas Elcocke, and grandson of Thomas Elcocke, of the same place, living *temp.* HENRY VII.) wedded Elizabeth, daughter and heiress of Thomas Cranage, of Poole, and had by her three daughters, (Jane, *m.* to — Kaye, esq. of Yorkshire; Margaret, to Henry Wright, esq. of Nantwich; and Katherine, to William Hyde, esq. of Denton) and several sons, of whom the eldest was FRANCIS. Alexander Elcocke *d.* 15th November, 3rd EDWARD VI. and appears, by inquisition taken the following year, to have held lands in Whitepoole, Horpoole, Worleston, Cranage, and Wich Malbank, from Sir Thomas Grosvenor, knt. and Richard Leigh, esq. of Baguley, in socage, by fealty; also lands in Wincham, Stockport, and Wimbalds Trafford. His son and heir,

FRANCIS ELCOCKE, esq. of Poole and Stockport, died 24th October, 33rd ELIZABETH, (inquisition *post mortem* dated the same year), leaving, by Dorothy, his first wife, daughter of John Waring, esq. of Nantwich, a son and successor,

ALEXANDER ELCOCKE, esq. of Poole, aged fourteen at his father's death. This gentleman *m.* first, Margaret, daughter of William Bromley, esq. of Dorfold, and had, with other issue, a son and heir, FRANCIS. He wedded, secondly, Elizabeth, daughter and co-heiress of Robert Sparke, esq. of Nantwich, and had further issue, Alexander, who entered his descent at the visitation of 1613. He (the elder Alexander) was *s.* at his decease by his son,

FRANCIS ELCOCKE, esq. of Poole, *b.* in 1596, who *m.* first, Elizabeth Doleman, of Pocklington, in the county of York, and by her had one son, ALEXANDER, his heir. He espoused, secondly, a daughter of Urian Gaskell, of Adlington, and was by her father of Anthony, dean of York and minister of Taxal. His elder son,

ALEXANDER ELCOCKE, esq. of Poole, left at his demise by his wife, a daughter of the family of Windsor, of Beam Bridge, a son and successor,

FRANCIS ELCOCKE, esq. of Poole, who *m.* Elizabeth, daughter of John Massie, esq. of Coddington, who died in 1730, by Elizabeth his wife, daughter and heiress of William Wilson, esq. of Terne, and had issue,

- FRANCIS, his heir.
- Alexander, who *m.* Miss Hughson, of Chester, and had issue.
- John, who *m.* Miss Wilbraham, daugh-

ter of — Wilbraham, esq. of Dorfold, and had issue.

William, *d. s. p.*

Elizabeth, *m.* to — Salmon, of Nantwich.

Mr. Elcock was *s.* at his decease by his eldest son,

FRANCIS ELCOCKE, esq. of Poole, living in 1740, who *m.* a daughter of — Newton, esq. of Carrickfergus, and had two daughters, ANN, who died unmarried in 1812, aged eighty, and ELIZABETH, eventually sole heiress, who wedded, as already stated, the REV. WILLIAM MASSEY, and was mother of the present WILLIAM MASSEY, esq. of Pool Hall.

*Arms*—First and fourth, quarterly, gu. and or; in first and fourth quarters, three fleurs de lys arg.: for difference a canton arg. for MASSEY; second and third, gu. a saltier varry between four cocks statant arg.

*Crest*—A demi pegasus with wings displayed; quarterly, or and gu.

*Estates*—In Cheshire.

*Seat*—Pool Hall, near Nantwich.

# HAWKER, OF LONGPARISH HOUSE.

HAWKER, PETER, esq. of Longparish House, in the county of Hants, *b.* 24th December, 1786; *m.* 19th March, 1811, Julia, only child of Hooker Barttelot, esq. late major in the South Hants militia, (see vol. ii. page 629), and has issue,

PETER-WILLIAM LANOE, *b.* 19th January, 1812, lieutenant in the 74th regiment.

Mary-Laurie.

Sophia-Sidney.

This gentleman, who retired, with a temporary pension, from the 14th light dragoons, when senior captain, in consequence of a severe wound received in the Peninsula, was appointed, by the earl of Malmsbury, in 1815, major, and by the duke of Wellington, in 1821, lieutenant-colonel, of the North Hants militia, at the special desire of his present majesty, then duke of Clarence. Colonel Hawker succeeded his father, 6th February, 1790, and is a deputy-lieutenant for Hants. Col. Hawker's celebrated work on Sporting has become one of the standard publications of England.

## Lineage.

The representatives of this family have, without the omission of a single generation, served as officers in the army since the reign of ELIZABETH, but the early commissions, prior to the year 1694, which are stated to have borne date so far back as the year 1558, having been lost by the neglect of a person to whom they were confided, the regular pedigree can be traced no higher than the time of WILLIAM and MARY.

PETER HAWKER, esq. captain of *Queen* MARY's dragoons in 1694, was father of

PETER HAWKER, esq. who obtained his commission as major in *Queen* ANNE's dragoons in 1703, his lieutenant-colonelcy in 1707, was appointed general by brevet and colonel of a regiment of dragoons in 1712. General Hawker was *s.* at his decease by his son,

PETER HAWKER, esq. of Longparish, in the county of Hants, made lieutenant-colonel of dragoons in 1715, and governor of Portsmouth in 1717. This gentleman, who was interred in the governor's chapel of that garrison, left by his wife, Elizabeth Hyde, an only son,

PETER HAWKER, esq. of Longparish, ensign of foot in 1726, cornet of horse guards in 1727, lieutenant in 1734, and captain in 1740. Captain Hawker espoused Arethusa, only daughter and heiress of George Ryves, esq. of Ranston, in the county of Dorset, and had issue,

1. PETER-RYVES, his heir.

II. George, in holy orders, rector of Wareham, Dorset, who *m.* Mary, sister of the Rev. William Butler, and had issue,

1. Peter-Ryves, who died half pay major 30th foot, leaving George, and other children.
2. Edmund, lieutenant of artillery, killed at the siege of Badajos.
1. Mary-Erle, } both
2. Arethusa-Ellen, } deceased.

III. Edmund, captain royal navy, who *m.* Miss Poles, and had two daughters,

1. Sarah, *m.* to the Rev. David Williams, of Overton, Hants.
2. Mary-Anne, *m.* to Parry, esq. barrister-at-law.

IV. Erle, major of the 62nd regiment, died unm.

I. Arethusa, who died unm.

Captain Hawker died before his wife, who wedded, secondly, Thomas Sidney, son of the earl of Leicester, and had one daughter, Letitia-Ann-Hawker Sidney. Captain Hawker was *s.* by his eldest son,

PETER-RYVES HAWKER, esq. of Longparish, lieutenant-colonel of the 1st regiment of horse guards in 1777, who inherited estates in Middlesex under the will of Major Charles Lanoe, of the same regiment. Colonel Hawker *m.* at Marylebone church, London, about the year 1780, Mary-Wilson Yonge, an Irish lady; he died the 6th of February, 1790, and was *s.* by his only son, the present Lieutenant-colonel HAWKER, of Longparish House.

*Arms*—Sa. a hawk arg. beaked and membered or, on a perch of the last, quartering the ensigns of RYVES.

*Crest*—A hawk's head erased or.

*Motto*—Accipiter prædam sequitur, nos, gloriam.

*Estates*—The chief landed possessions of the family were, above a century ago, in Wiltshire: but the present estates are in Middlesex, inherited from Major Lanoe; and at LONGPARISH, in Hants, enjoyed for more than a hundred years. Colonel Hawker has also a small property and a (dilapidated old) manor house in the parish of Ballington, of which place he is lord of the manor.

*Town Residence*—3, Bentinck Street, (Col. Hawker's *own* house, now let); 2, Dorset Place, his present residence.

*Seat*—Longparish House, near Andover.

### Family of Ryves, of Ranston.

The family of Ryves, of Ranston, was a junior branch of the ancient and influential house seated at Damory Court, in the county of Dorset.

JOHN RYVES, esq. of Damory Court, living in the early part of the sixteenth century, *m.* Amye, daughter of — Harvey, esq. of Lawnson, in Dorsetshire, and had issue,

I. JOHN, of Damory Court, who *m.* Elizabeth, daughter of John Merven, esq. and died in 1587, leaving eight sons, namely,

1. JOHN (Sir), of Damory Court, who *m.* first, Anne, daughter of Sir Robert Naper, of Dorsetshire; and, secondly, Dorothy, daughter of Henry Hastings, esq. of Woodlands. The latter survived her husband, and wedded, secondly, Thomas Tregonwell, esq.
2. George.
3. Charles, D.D. member of New College, Oxford, in 1602.
4. Henry, whose grandson, John, was the last of the Damory line.
5. James.
6. William (Sir), who settled in Ireland, where he filled several high official appointments and purchased extensive estates, including Rathsallow, Crunmore, Cayanmoie, in the county of Down, Ballyferinott, near Dublin, and the rectory of Naas. He *m.* first, a daughter of — Latham, esq. of Latham Hall, in Lancashire; and, secondly, a daughter of John Waldram; by the former of whom he had (with four daughters, one *m.* to Sir John Stanley, another to Sir Arthur Lee, and a third, Elizabeth, to Edward Berkeley, esq. of Pylle), four sons, viz.

William, who *m.* Elizabeth, daughter of Sir Edward Bagshaw, of Finglass, and had issue, William, Thomas, (*m.* Jane, dau. of Capt. Burrows) Bagshaw, and Frank.

Charles, a master in Chancery, who *m.* Jane Ogden, and had two sons, viz.

Sir Richard Ryves, knt. a judge and recorder of Dublin and Kilkenny, who *m.* Miss Savage, and had issue.

Jeremiah Ryves, who *m.* Ann Maude, niece of the bishop of Ossory.

George, who *m.* Ann, second daughter of Sir Edward Bagshaw.

John, who *m.* Mrs. Plunkett.
7. Valentine.
8. Thomas (Sir), an eminent advocate, master in Chancery, and judge of the faculty and prerogative court in Ireland. He was knighted by CHARLES I. and stoutly fought on the royal side during the civil wars. Sir Thomas *d.* 2nd January, 1651, and was buried in St. Clement Danes, London.

II. HENRY, of whom presently.
III. Valentine.
IV. Richard.
V. Thomas.

I. Mary, *m.* to William Adeyn, alias Barbett, of Dorset.
II. Margaret, *m.* to Richard Lawrence, esq. of Stepleton, in Dorset.
III. Jane, *m.* to Thomas Sydenham, esq. of Winfrith.

The second son of John Ryves, of Damory Court,

HENRY RYVES, esq. was father of

JOHN RYVES, esq. of Ranston, whose son,

ROBERT RYVES, esq. died in 1551, leaving a son and successor,

ROBERT RYVES, esq. of Ranston, who left five sons, viz. JOHN, his heir; Robert, of Randleston, in Dorset, who *m.* Margaret, dau. and co-heir of William Gillett, esq. of the Isle of Purbeck; James; Richard, who *m.* Editha, daughter of John Seymer, esq. of Hanford; and Matthew. The eldest son,

JOHN RYVES, esq. of Ranston, *m.* Ann, daughter of George Burley, esq. of Longparish, in Dorsetshire, and had issue,

I. GEORGE, his heir.
II. John, who *m.* Mary, daughter of Thomas Hussey, esq. of Dorset, and had John and Elizabeth.
III. Richard.
IV. Robert.

I. Margaret.
II. Mellet.
III. Ann, *m.* to Ralph Stawel, esq. who, in consideration of his eminent services in the royal cause, was elevated to the peerage, in 1683, as BARON STAWEL, of Somerton. (See BURKE's *Extinct Peerage.*)

The eldest son and heir,

GEORGE RYVES, esq. of Ranston, espoused, early in the seventeenth century, Elizabeth, daughter of Henry Ryves, esq. younger brother of Sir John Ryves, of Damory Court, and had issue,

I. GEORGE, *b.* in 1627, served the office of high sheriff for Dorsetshire, *m.* Mary, dau. of Thomas Chafin, esq. of Chettle, and dying in 1689, left two daughters, Elizabeth and Mary.
II. Charles.
III. Henry.
IV. Thomas.
V. RICHARD, of whom presently.
VI. Robert.

I. Elizabeth, *m.* to Henry Rose, esq.

The third son,

RICHARD RYVES, esq. wedded a sister of Sir Edward Northey, attorney-general, and was father of

THOMAS RYVES, esq. comptroller of the prize office, who *m.* Anne, daughter of — Cochin, esq. and had two sons and four daughters, namely,

I. GEORGE, his heir.
II. Thomas, who died at Bombay in 1723, leaving, by Elizabeth his wife, relict of William Kyffin, esq. governor of Anjango, (with two daughters, Elizabeth, *m.* to Colonel Skipton, of the guards, and Susannah, to Mr. Serjeant William Girdler), a son and heir,

THOMAS RYVES, esq. who sold the last of the Dorset property in 1781. He *m.* first, Elizabeth, daughter and co-heir of Sir Anthony-Thomas Abdy, bart. of Felix Hall, Essex, and had by her two sons and two daughters, viz.

Thomas, a military officer, who married in America.
John, lost in the East Indies in 1768.
Elizabeth.
Charlotte, *m.* to James Williams, esq. of Spetisbury, in Dorsetshire.

Mr. Ryves wedded, secondly, Anna-Maria, daughter of Daniel Graham, esq. and dying in 1788, left by this lady two sons and one daughter, viz.

George-Frederick, a rear-admiral in the royal navy, *b.* 1758, *m.* first, 1792, Catharine-Elizabeth, daughter of the Hon. James-Everard Arundell, of Ashcombe, in Wilts; and, secondly, in 1806, Emma, daughter of Richard - Robert Graham, esq. Admiral Ryves died 20th May, 1826, leaving issue, by his first wife, two sons and a daughter, viz. George - Frederick, R. N. Henry - Wyndham, R. A. and Catherine - Elizabeth; and by his second wife, four sons and one daughter, viz. Charles - Graham, Walter-Robert, Edward-Augustus,

Herbert-Thomas, and Mary-Emma.

Henry, who *m.* Sarah, daughter of Thomas Hall, esq. of Golbury, Herts.

Maria-Georgiana, *m.* to William Leigh Symes, esq. of Esher, in Surrey.

I. Elizabeth.

II. Mary.

III. Ann, *m.* to Edward Berkeley, son of William Portman, esq. of Bryanston.

IV. Dorothy.

V. Arundell.

Mr. Ryves *d.* in 1704, and was *s.* by his son,

George Ryves esq. of Ranston, who *m.* Arethusia, daughter of Edmund Pleydell, esq. M.P. who *d.* in 1726, by Anne his wife, only daughter and heir of Sir John Morton, of Melborne, St. Giles, in the county of Dorset, and had an only daughter,

Arethusa, who *m.* first, as already stated, Peter Hawker, esq. of Longparish House, in the county of Hants, and was by him grandmother of the present Lieutenant-colonel Hawker, of Longparish. She espoused secondly, Thomas Sidney, son of the Earl of Leicester, and had one dau. Letitia-Ann-Hawker Sidney.

## LYSTER, OF ROWTON CASTLE.

LYSTER, HENRY, Esq. of Rowton Castle, in the county of Salop, *b.* 18th October, 1798, *m.* at St. George's, Hanover Square, 13th October, 1824, the Lady Charlotte-Barbara Ashley Cooper, youngest dau. of Cropley, fifth Earl of Shaftesbury.

Mr. Lyster, who is in the commission of the peace for Shropshire, *s.* his father 3rd May, 1819, and is the fourteenth possessor of Rowton Castle, from his first Shropshire ancestor, William Lyster.

### Lineage.

The family of Lyster, of Rowton, is considered to have sprung from the same stock as the Lysters of Gisborne, in Craven, which house has lately been ennobled by the title of Ribblesdale.

William Lyster, of Shrewsbury, the first name in the Heraldic Visitation for Salop, is found to have purchased Rowton Castle, and to have been seated there in the year 1451. He *m.* first, Elizabeth, daughter of Edward Leighton, of Leighton and Church Stretton, and secondly, Jane, daughter of Sir Ralph Wotton, knt. by the former of whom he had, with a daughter, Isabella, the wife of John Forester, esq. of Watling Street, ancestor of the Lords Foresters, a son and successor,

Richard Lyster, esq. of Rowton, in the county of Salop, *b.* in 1451, who *m.* Agnes, daughter of Ralph Fitzherbert, esq. of Norbury, in Derbyshire, (see vol. i. p. 79) and was father of

John Lyster, esq. of Rowton, who wedded first, Christabella, daughter of John Gattacre, of Gattacre, and had by her two sons, Richard, his heir, and William. He espoused secondly, Katherine, daughter of Roger Bromley, and had a numerous issue, but which does not appear to have been commemorated beyond the second generation. John Lyster's eldest son,

Richard Lyster, esq. of Rowton, *m.* Jane, daughter of Thomas Jennyngs, of Walleborne, in Salop, and had three sons and one daughter, namely, Michael, his heir, John, Gabriel, and Christabella, the wife of Thomas Wells. He was *s.* by the eldest son,

Michael Lyster, esq. of Rowton, who

wedded Elizabeth, daughter of Richard Lee, esq. of Langley, in Shropshire, and had one son and two daughters, viz.

RICHARD, his heir.

Margaret, *m.* to Richard Acton, esq. of Dunwall, second son of Robert Acton, esq. of Aldenham.

Elizabeth, *d.* unm.

Michael Lyster *d.* in 1598, was buried at Broughton, Salop, and succeeded by his son,

RICHARD LYSTER, esq. of Rowton, who *m.* Mary, daughter of Michael Chambers, of Shrewsbury, and had issue,

I. THOMAS (Sir), his heir.
II. Francis, } twins.
III. Thomas, }

I. Sarah, *m.* to Francis Harries, esq. of Bishop's Castle.
II. Ann, *m.* first, to Henry Brabason, esq. of the county of Hereford, and secondly to Charles Kynaston.
III. Elizabeth, *m.* to — Lutwyche.
IV. Maria, *d.* unm.
V. Martha, *m.* to Edward Powell, esq.

Richard Lyster was *s.* at his decease, in October, 1635, by his eldest son,

SIR THOMAS LYSTER, of Rowton, who, according to the visitations, was eleven years of age in 1623. This gentleman was a devoted adherent of *King* CHARLES I., and on the appearance of that monarch at Shrewsbury, in the first campaign of the civil wars, he waited on the king, then residing in the council house, the family residence of the Lysters, and recruited the empty coffers of his majesty by the welcome present of five hundred pieces of gold. He was knighted on this occasion, and afterwards held a high command in the garrison established in Shrewsbury; on the fall of the town he was taken prisoner, but his lady gallantly held out the castle at Rowton for nearly a fortnight against all the efforts of the republican officer, Col. Mytton, nor did she surrender her post till she had obtained good terms from that commander. Sir Thomas espoused, first, Elizabeth, dau. of John Adye, of the county of Kent, and had by her one son, RICHARD, his heir, and one daughter, Elizabeth, the wife of — Draycott, of Ireland. He *m.* secondly, Mary, daughter of Sir John Hanmer, bart. of Hanmer, by whom he had a son, Thomas, barrister-at-law, who *d.* unmarried, and two daughters, Dorothy, the wife of William Jordan, esq. and Mary, who *d.* unmarried. Sir Thomas *d.* in 1655, was buried 17th March in that year, at St. Chads, Shrewsbury, and was *s.* by his son,

RICHARD LYSTER, esq. of Rowton Castle, who served the office of high sheriff for Shropshire in 1684. He *m.* first, Elizabeth, daughter of Sir Thomas Eyton, of Eyton, and by her had one son and one daughter,

THOMAS, his heir.

Margaret, *m.* to William Beaw, son of the Bishop of Llandaff.

He wedded secondly, Sarah, only child and sole heir of Thomas Hughes, esq. of Moynes Court, in the county of Monmouth, and had issue,

Richard, of Moynes Court, who *m.* Elizabeth, eldest daughter and co-heir of Hugh Derwas, esq. of Penhrôs, in Montgomeryshire, and had a daughter and heiress,

ELIZABETH, who wedded the Rev. Lewis Owen, D.D. youngest son of Sir Robert Owen, of Porkington, and uncle of Margaret Owen, who *m.* Owen Ormsby, esq. and was mother of Mrs. Ormsby Gore. By Dr. Owen the heiress of Moynes Court left, with a daughter, Margaret, who *d.* unmarried, in 1816, a son,

JOHN OWEN, esq. of Penhrôs, in the county of Montgomery, and of Moynes Court, in Monmouthshire, who died, at an advanced age, unmarried, 16th December, 1823, when he devised the Penhrôs and his other Montgomeryshire estates to Mrs. Ormsby Gore,* and the Moynes Court estates to Lieut.-colonel John Lyster, brother of the present Henry Lyster, esq. of Rowton Castle.

John, who *d. s. p.*

Sarah.

Mary.

Elizabeth.

Mr. Lyster *d.* in 1698, and was *s.* by his son,

THOMAS LYSTER, esq. of Rowton Castle, who *m.* Elizabeth, daughter of Dr. Beaw, Bishop of Llandaff, by Cecilia his wife, daughter of Charles, eighth Lord de la War, descended from Archbishop Chichele, founder of All Souls College, Oxford, and from two stocks of the royal line of Plantagenet. This union produced three sons and three daughters, namely,

I. RICHARD, his heir.
II. Francis, *d.* unm.
III. Thomas, in holy orders, rector of the first portion of Westbury, and of Neenton, in Salop, who *m.* Anne,

---

* For an account of the ORMSBY GORE family see vol. i. p. 85.

daughter of the Rev. George Fisher, and died in 1772, aged seventy-three, having had issue,

1. RICHARD, who inherited the Rowton estate on the decease of Anne, relict of his uncle, Richard.
2. Corbet Watkin, *d.* unm.
3. Edward, *d.* unm.

I. Jane, *m.* to John Powys, esq. of Berwick.
II. Dorothea.
III. Ann.

Mr. Lyster *d.* 7th March, 1701-2, and was *s.* by his eldest son,

RICHARD LYSTER, esq. of Rowton Castle, who represented the county of Salop for the unusual period of thirty years. The great hospitality and universal popularity of this gentleman are still very freshly remembered; he was a firm supporter of the exiled royal house, and constantly opposed the whig administrations of his day. It is related of him, that his first return to parliament was for the borough of Shrewsbury, for which place, after a strenuous contest, he was elected by a considerable majority. His opponent, however, disputed the return, and endeavoured to destroy the majority by disfranchising an extensive suburb, which, till that period, had always enjoyed the elective franchise, and as he was a supporter of the government, the whole whig party joined in the attempt, and succeeded in throwing out the successful candidate. Upon the decision being announced in the commons, Mr. Lyster, feeling very keenly the injustice of the proceeding, put on his hat, and with his back to the speaker, walked down the house; when his manner being remarked, he was called to order, and pointed out to the chair. Turning abruptly round he instantly said, "When you learn justice I will learn manners." This drew down upon him the increased wrath of the house, and probably he would have been compelled to ask pardon on his knees, or to visit the Tower, had not Sir Robert Walpole, who on all occasions knew how to throw the grace of good temper over his corruptions and tyranny, exclaimed, with a smile, "Let him go, we have served him bad enough already." The indignation which this ill treatment occasioned mainly contributed to securing the representation of his native county for the remainder of his life. In illustration of the manners of his day, we may add, that on his departure from Rowton to take his seat, his tenants annually escorted him the first two stages on his journey, while his London tradespeople, duly apprized of his approach, with the same punctilio, advanced two stages from town to bring him into London.

He wedded Anne, daughter of Robert Pigott, esq. of Chetwynd, and had three children, Thomas, Richard, and Anne, who all *d.* young. Mr. Lyster *d.* in 1766, aged seventy-five, and was *s.* in the Rowton estate by his widow, Anne, at whose demise in 1781, it passed to her husband's nephew,

RICHARD LYSTER, esq. of Rowton Castle, who *m.* Mary, daughter of Moses Smith, esq. and had two sons, viz.

RICHARD, his heir.
Thomas-Moses, rector of Oldbury, Salop.

Mr. Lyster *d.* 14th April, 1794, and was *s.* by his elder son,

RICHARD LYSTER, esq. of Rowton Castle, who espoused Mary, daughter of the Rev. John Rodd, of Barton-on-the-Heath, in the county of Oxford, and dying 23rd May, 1807, left a son and successor,

RICHARD LYSTER, esq. of Rowton Castle, lieut.-col. of the 22nd Light Dragoons, who served the office of high sheriff for Shropshire in 1812. He *m.* 10th December, 1794, Penelope-Anne, daughter of Henry Price, esq. of Knighton, in the county of Radnor, and by her, who *d.* in January, 1829, had issue,

Richard, *b.* 12th December, 1797, and *d.* in March, 1806.
HENRY, heir to his father.
John, lieut.-colonel in the Grenadier Guards, to whom the late John Owen, esq. of Penhrôs, left the Moynes Court estate.
Thomas-Price, *b.* 19th July, 1802, in the royal navy, died in January, 1820.
Mary, *m.* 1830, to the Rev. Richard Webster Huntley, A.M. of Boxwell Court, in the county of Gloucester, (see vol. ii. p. 468).
Georgiana.

Col. Lyster, who represented Shrewsbury in three parliaments, and until his death, *d.* in St. James's Place, London, 3rd May, 1819, was buried at Alberbury, the 13th of that month, and was *s.* by his eldest surviving son, the present HENRY LYSTER, esq. of Rowton Castle.

*Arms*—Ermine, on a fess sa. three mullets, arg.

*Crest*—A stag's head erased ppr.

*Motto*—Loyal au mort.

*Estates*—Rowton Castle, &c., Writton Castle, and Kinnerton, in the Stiperstone mountains; Neenton, near Bridgnorth, Edenhope, and Aldon, all in the county of Salop.

*Seat*—Rowton Castle, Salop.

# MURRAY, OF PHILIPHAUGH.

MURRAY, JAMES, esq. of Philiphaugh, in the county of Selkirk, *m.* Mary Dale, daughter of Henry Hughes, esq. and has issue,

I. JOHN. II. James. III. Basil. I. Jessy.

Mr. Murray *s.* his brother, in 1830, and is the seventeenth generation of this family, in a direct male line.

## Lineage.

The first of this family on record

ARCHIBALD DE MORAVIA, mentioned in the chartulary of Newbottle, in 1280, was descended (the author of the critical remarks upon Ragman's Roll presumes) from the Morays, lords of Bothwel, who, by marriage of a daughter of Sir David Olifard, got considerable possessions in the county of Selkirk. In 1296, he subscribed the oath of fealty to EDWARD I., and *d.* in the reign of ROBERT BRUCE, leaving a son and successor,

ROGER DE MORAVIA, who obtained, in 1321, from James, Lord Douglas, superior of his lands, a charter "terrarum de Fala," which estate, subsequently designated Falahill, continued for many years to be the chief title of the family. Roger *d.* at an advanced age, in 1380, and was *s.* by his son,

ALEXANDER DE MORAVIA, mentioned in a charter under the great seal, from ROBERT II. before the year 1380. He was father of

PATRICK MURRAY, of Falahill, living in 1413, who *d. temp.* JAMES II. and was *s.* by his son,

JOHN MURRAY, of Falahill, who, upon the resignation of Thomas Hop Pringle, got a charter from *King* JAMES III. *Johanni de Moravia de Falahill*, of part of the lands of Philiphaugh, dated 20th July, 1461. His son,

PATRICK MURRAY, of Falahill, acquiring from Robert Watson several acres of land about Philiphaugh, had a charter from the said Robert, dated 20th February, 1477. He subsequently obtained charters of lands in 1480 and 1492. He *m.* and had one son and a daughter, namely,

JOHN, his heir.

Margaret, who wedded James, Earl of Buchan, and had a son,

James Stewart, Lord Traquair, ancestor of the Earls of Traquair.

Patrick Murray *d.* at the close of the fifteenth century, and was succeeded by his son,

JOHN MURRAY, of Falahill, who upon his father's resignation, got a charter under the great seal from JAMES IV., "Johanni Murray filio et hæredi apparenti Patricii Murray de Falahill terrarum de Gervastoun," in 1489; afterwards, in 1497, another charter dated 5th November, in that year, of the lands of Cranston, Riddel, &c. and eventually, on his own resignation, a charter, dated 10th October, 1508, of half of the lands of Philiphaugh.

This chieftain, the celebrated "Outlaw Murray," who, with five hundred of his men, bid defiance to the king of Scotland, JAMES IV., is immortalized by the beautiful ballad,* preserved in the Minstrelsy of the Scottish Border, and for ages a popular song in Selkirkshire. "The

* "There (i. e. Ettrick Forest) an outlaw keeps
five hundred men;
He keepis a royalle companie!
His merrymen are a' in ae liverye clad,
O' the Lincome greene saye gaye to see;
He and his ladye in purple clad,
O! gin they lived not royallie.
Word is gane to our noble king,
In Edinburgh, where that he lay,

tradition of Ettrick Forest," says Sir Walter Scott, "bears, that the outlaw was a man of prodigious strength, possessing a batton or club, with which he laid *lee* (i. e. waste) the country for many miles round; and that he was at length slain by Buccleugh, or some of his clan, at a little mount, covered with fir trees, adjoining to Newark Castle, and said to have been a part of the garden; a varying tradition bears the place of his death to have been near to the house of the Duke of Buccleugh's gamekeeper, beneath the castle, and that the fatal arrow was shot by Scott, of Haining, from the ruins of a cottage on the opposite side of the Yarrow. There was extant, within these twenty years, some verses of a song on his death. The feud between the outlaw and the Scotts may serve to explain the asperity with which the chieftain of that clan is handled in the ballad."*

The song relates the departure of JAMES IV. with "full five thousand men" to suppress the insurrection of the outlaw, and subsequently the humiliating necessity to which the king of Scotland was reduced to compromise with his rebellious subject, by granting† to him the heritable sheriffship of the shire of Selkirk.‡

Murray espoused the Lady Margaret Hepburn, daughter of Patrick, first Earl of Bothwell, and had two sons and three daughters, viz.

I. JAMES, his heir.

II. William, who *m.* Janet, daughter and heiress of William Romanno, of that Ilk, and had a son and successor,

WILLIAM MURRAY, of Romanno, living in 1531, who *m.* Margaret, daughter of Tweedie, of Drumelzier, and dying in the reign of *Queen* MARY, was succeeded by his son,

JOHN MURRAY, of Romanno, living in 1587, who *m.* Agnes, daughter of Nisbet, of Nisbet, and was father of

WILLIAM MURRAY, of Romanno, in 1612, who *m.* first, Susan, daughter of John Hamilton, of Broomhill, and had by her one son, DAVID, his heir. He *m.* secondly, Elizabeth Howieson, a daughter of the ancient family of Braehead, and had by her three sons and one daughter, namely, ADAM, progenitor of the MURRAYS, of CARDON; Gideon, who *d.* in Ireland; William; and Margaret, second wife of Sir Alexander Murray, of Blackbarony. The laird of Romanno *d. temp.* JAMES VI. and was *s.* by his eldest son,

SIR DAVID MURRAY, knt. who acquired the lands and barony of Stanhope, in Peeblesshire. He *m.* the Lady Lilias Fleming, daughter of John, Earl of Wigton, and had a son and successor,

SIR WILLIAM MURRAY, of Stanhope, created a baronet of Nova Scotia in 1664. From this gentleman lineally derives the present

SIR JOHN MURRAY, bart. of Stanhope. (See BURKE's *Peerage and Baronetage.*)

I. Elizabeth, *m.* to James Douglas, of Cavers, heritable sheriff of the county of Roxburgh.

II. Isabel, *m.* to Robert Scot, of Hoppeslie.

III. Janet, *m.* to Sir Robert Stewart, of Minto, and had issue.

John Murray, the outlaw, *d.* in the early part of JAMES V.'s reign, and was *s.* by his elder son,

JAMES MURRAY, of Falahill, who had one charter under the great seal, dated 9th November, 1526, "Jacobo Murray de Falahill terrarum de Kirkurd, Mounthouses," &c., in the shire of Peebles, and in two years after another, of several lands near the burgh of Selkirk, to himself in liferent and to Patrick his son and heir apparent in fee. He *m.* a daughter of Sir John Cranston, of that Ilk, and dying about the year 1529, was *s.* by his son,

PATRICK MURRAY, of Falahill, who obtained under the great seal a charter, dated 28th January, 1528, "Patricio Murray filio

---

That there was an outlaw in Ettricke Foreste
Counted him nought, nor a' his countrie gay.
'I make a vowe,' then the gude king said,
'Unto the man that deir bought me,
I'se either be king of Ettricke Foreste,
Or king of Scotlande that outlaw shall be.'"
&c. &c. &c.
*The Sang of the Outlaw Murray.*

* "Then out and spak the nobel king,
And round him cast a wilie e'e—
Now ha'd thy tongue, Sir Walter Scott,
Nor speik of reif nor felonie;
For, had everye honeste man his awin kye,
A right pure clan thy name wad be."

† Wha ever heard, in ony times,
Sicken an outlaw in his degré,
Sic favor get before a king
As did the OUTLAW MURRAY of the foreste frie?"
*Old Ballad.*

‡ This office continued with his descendants until the government acquired all the Scot's heritable jurisdictions in 1748.

et hæredi Jacobi Murray de Falahill, terrarum de PHILIPHAUGH," and in 1529 a charter of the lands and barony of Cranston, Riddel, &c. He subsequently, in 1540, had the customs of the burgh of Selkirk and the heritable sheriffship of that county, which had been granted by *King* JAMES IV. to his grandfather, confirmed, and ratified to himself and his heirs. Patrick Murray wedded a daughter of John, Lord Fleming, and *d.* in the reign of *Queen* MARY, leaving a daughter, *m.* to Somerville, of Cambusnethan, and a son, his successor,

PATRICK MURRAY, of Falahill, who acquired, in 1588, a charter of the lands of Hany, Lewinshope, and Hairhead. He *m.* Agnes, daughter of Sir Andrew Murray, of Blackbarony, and had issue,

- I. JOHN (Sir), his heir.
- II. Patrick, who got a charter under the great seal, dated 10th August, 1613, of the lands of Winterhopehead, &c. in Annandale.
- III. James, who was bred a merchant, in Edinburgh. He *m.* Bethia Maule, descended from the Panmure family, and had three sons, viz.
  1. James (Sir), of Skirling.
  2. Robert (Sir), of Priestfield or Melgrim.
  3. Patrick, of Deuchar.
- I. Isabel, *m.* to John Abernethy, Bishop of Caithness.
- II. ——, *m.* to Kerr, of Greenhead.
- III. Elizabeth, *m.* to Robert Scott, of Haining.
- IV. ——, *m.* to John Scott, of Tushelaw.

The laird *d.* in the commencement of the reign of JAMES VI. and was succeeded by his son,

SIR JOHN MURRAY, knt. the first of the family, designed "of Philiphaugh." This gentleman had four charters under the great seal, one dated 22nd August, 1584, "Johanni Murray de Falahill, at Philiphaugh, filio et hæredi Patricii Murray de Falahill, octodecim terras husbandrias jacen. infra dominium de Selkirk;" the second, dated 1st May, 1603, "Domino Johanni Murray de Philiphaugh, vicecom. de Selkirk terrarum de Hangingshaw," &c.; the third, dated 20th March, 1604, "Terrarum ecclesiasticarum de Traquair in vicecom. de Peebles;" and the fourth, in 1624, "Quarundem aliarum terrarum Baroniæ de Buckcleugh." He espoused first, Janet, daughter of Scot, of Ardross, and had by her two sons and three daughters, viz.

- I. JAMES (Sir), knighted by CHARLES I., who obtained by charter the lands and barony of Balincrief, &c. in the shires of Edinburgh and Haddington, and the lands of Quhytburn, Daviestoun, &c. in 1633. He *m.* Anne, daughter of Sir Thomas Craig, of Riccartoun, and dying before his father, left two sons and four daughters, namely,
  1. JOHN (Sir), successor to his grandfather.
  2. James, a colonel in the army and deputy governor of Edinburgh Castle.
  1. Janet, *m.* to James Scott, of Gallashiels, and had issue.
  2. Elizabeth, *m.* to Cranston, of Glen.
  3. Margaret, *m.* first, to Dr. Burnet, and secondly to Colonel Douglas.
  4. Isabel, *m.* to James Naesmyth, of Posso.
- II. Gideon, aide-de-camp to *King* CHARLES I. in whose service he lost his life.
- I. ——, *m.* to Kerr, of Chatto.
- II. Anne, *m.* to John Shaw, of the Sauchie family.
- III. Gresel, *d.* unm.

He wedded secondly, Helen, daughter of Sir James Pringle, of Gallashiels, and had further issue,

- I. John, of Ashiesteel.
- II. William, } who both fell fighting
- III. David, } under the royal banner. They died issueless.
- I. Helen, married to Scot, of Breadmeadows.
- II. Elizabeth, *m.* to Mr. Knox.
- III. Isabel.

Sir John Murray was a person of much ability, and distinguished in his generation. He sate in parliament in 1621, and survived till about the year 1640, when he died, at a very advanced age, and was succeeded by his grandson,

SIR JOHN MURRAY, knt. of Philiphaugh, who was appointed by parliament one of the judges for trying those of the counties of Roxburgh and Selkirk, who had joined the gallant Graham's standard in 1646. He subsequently, in 1649, claimed £12,014. for the damages he had sustained from Montrose. Sir John wedded first, Anne, daughter of Sir Archibald Douglas, of Cavers, heritable sheriff of the county of Roxburgh, and had six sons and four daughters, viz.

- I. JAMES (Sir), his heir.
- II. John, of Bowhill, one of the senators of the college of justice.
- III. William, a colonel in the army.
- IV. Archibald, }
- V. Thomas, } all *d.* young.
- VI. Lewis, }
- I. Anne, *m.* first, to Alexander Pringle, of Whitebank; and, secondly, to Robert Rutherford, of Bowland.

II. Janet.
III. Rachel.
IV. Elizabeth.

Sir John Murray *m.* secondly, Margaret, daughter of Sir John Scott, of Scotstarvet, and widow of John Trotter, of Charterhall, and had by her an only daughter, Jean, who died young. He *d.* in 1676, and was *s.* by his eldest son,

SIR JAMES MURRAY, of Philiphaugh, *b.* in 1655, who was appointed one of the senators of the college of justice in 1689, and lord register in 1705. This learned person *m.* first, Anne, daughter of Hepburn, of Blackcastle, who *d.* issueless; and, secondly, Margaret, daughter of Sir Alexander Don, of Newton, by whom he had three sons and five daughters, viz.

I. JOHN, his heir.
II. James, } both *d.* unm.
III. Alexander, }

I. Rachel, *d.* unm.
II. Anne, *m.* to Pringle, of Haining.
III. Elizabeth.
IV. Jane.
V. Margaret.

Sir James *d.* in 1708, and was *s.* by his eldest son,

JOHN MURRAY, esq. of Philiphaugh, heritable sheriff of the county of Selkirk, (which office had been more than two hundred and fifty years in the family,) and a member of the British parliament from 1725 until his death. He wedded Eleanora, daughter of Lord Basil Hamilton, son of William, duke of Hamilton, and had by her four sons and two daughters, viz.

I. Basil, a youth of great promise, who *d.* in the flower of his age unm.
II. JOHN, heir to his father.
III. David.
IV. Charles.

I. Mary, *m.* to Sir Alexander Don, bart. of Newton, and had issue.
II. Margaret.

The laird of Philiphaugh *d.* in 1753, and was *s.* by his eldest son,

JOHN MURRAY. esq. of Philiphaugh, who espoused Miss Thomson, and had three sons and four daughters, viz.

I. JOHN, his heir.
II. Charles, *d.* unm.
III. JAMES, successor to his brother.

I. Janet, *m.* to — Dennis, esq. of the island of Jamaica.
II. Eleanora, *m.* to Sir James Nasmyth, bart. of Posso.
III. Mary, *m.* to John Macqueen, esq. of Jamaica.
IV. Margaret, *m.* to Capt. Baugh, of the 58th regiment.

Mr. Murray *d.* in 1800, and was *s.* by his eldest son,

JOHN MURRAY, esq. of Philiphaugh, at whose decease unmarried, in 1830, the estates and representation of this great and ancient family devolved on his only surviving brother, the present JAMES MURRAY, esq. of Philiphaugh.

*Arms*—Arg. a hunting horn sa, stringed and garnished gu.; on a chief az. three stars of the first.

*Crest*—A demi naked man winding his horn, ppr.

*Motto*—Hinc usque superna venabor.

*Estates*—In Selkirkshire.

*Seat*—Philiphaugh, in that county. At Philiphaugh the gallant marquess of Montrose was defeated by General Leslie: the remains of the entrenchments are still visible on the field where the battle was fought, and a few years since several implements of war and a small culverin were dug up.

## CROMPTON-STANSFIELD, OF ESHOLT HALL.

STANSFIELD-CROMPTON, WILLIAM-ROOKES, esq. of Esholt Hall, in the West Riding of Yorkshire, *b.* 3rd August, 1790; *m.* 17th June, 1824, Emma, eldest daughter of William Markham, esq. of Becca Hall, son of Archbishop Markham. (See vol. ii. p. 207.)

This gentleman, whose patronymic is CROMPTON, inheriting, 13th February, 1832, upon the demise of his father, Joshua Crompton, esq., his mother's estates, assumed, in compliance with her testamentary injunction, the additional surname and arms of STANSFIELD.

Mr. Crompton Stansfield is a master of arts of Jesus College, Cambridge, and a magistrate and deputy-lieutenant for the North and West Ridings of Yorkshire.

## Lineage.

The family of Stansfield, or Stansfeld as anciently written, trace their descent from one of the companions-in-arms of WILLIAM THE CONQUEROR, who obtained the grant of the lordship of Stansfeld. His descendants have remained ever since enjoying high respectability in the county of York, and their ancient residence, Stansfield Hall, is still to be seen in the once beautiful valley of Todmorden.

JORDAN DE STANSFELD, son of Wyons Maryons, lord of Stansfeld at the Conquest, *m.* a daughter of Sir John Towneley, of Towneley, and had, with three younger sons, (Thomas, Robert, and Oliver, constable of Pontefract Castle), a successor,

JOHN STANSFELD, of Stansfeld, father, by Elizabeth his wife, daughter of Thomas Entwistle, of a daughter, Jane, the wife of Rafe Copley, of Copley, and of a son,

RICHARD STANSFELD, of Stansfeld, living *temp.* HENRY I. who espoused Alice, daughter of Sir Thomas Tonstal, knt. of Thurland Castle, and had four sons, Edmund, Robert, Hugh, and Roger. The eldest,

EDMUND STANSFELD, of Stansfeld, *m.* Agnes, daughter of Thomas de Midgley, and was father of

RALPH STANSFELD, of Stansfeld, who *m.* Jane, daughter of Thomas Copley, of Copley, and had three sons, HENRY, Ralph, and William, and a daughter, Joan. The eldest son and heir,

HENRY STANSFELD, of Stansfeld, wedded Dionis, daughter of Bryan Thornhill, of Thornhill, in Yorkshire, and was *s.* by his son,

WILLIAM STANSFELD, of Stansfeld, who *m.* Joane, daughter of Sir John Burton, knt. of Kinslow, in Yorkshire, and was father of

THOMAS STANSFELD, of Stansfeld, living at the close of the fourteenth century, who is supposed, from the circumstance of the arms over the mantelpiece being placed along with those of Lascells, to have built the old mansion of Stansfeld Hall, situated in a very beautiful part of the valley of Todmorden: it is within the parish of Halifax and township of Stansfeld, or, as it is now spelt, Stansfield. He *m.* Barbara, daughter of John Lascells, of Lascells Hall, in the county of York, and had a son and successor,

JOHN STANSFELD, esq. of Stansfeld Hall, who *m.* in 1410, Mary, daughter of John Fleming, esq. of Wathe, lineally descended from Sir Michael le Fleming, (kinsman to WILLIAM THE CONQUEROR, and one of his commanders,) and had issue,

- I. THOMAS, his heir.
- II. Henry.
- I. Ann, *m.* Thomas Savile, second son of Henry Savile, by Ellen his wife, daughter of Thomas Copley, of Copley, and had four sons, viz.
  - John Savile, of Hullenedge.
  - Thomas Savile, who *m.* Elizabeth, Lady Waterton, of Walton.
  - Henry Savile.
  - Nicholas Savile, of Newhall, ancestor of the Savilles, earls of Mexborough.
- II. Isabel.
- III. Jane.
- IV. Elizabeth.
- V. Mary.

The elder son,

THOMAS STANSFELD, esq. of Stansfeld Hall, by Alice his wife, daughter of John Savile, was father of

WILLIAM STANSFELD, esq. of Stansfeld Hall, who *m.* Elizabeth, daughter of John Duckenfield, esq. of Duckenfield, in the county of Chester, and had two sons,

- JAMES, of Stansfeld Hall, living in 1536, in which year he removed to Hurtshead.
- THOMAS, whose line we have to detail.

The second son,

THOMAS STANSFELD, of Heptonstall, in Stansfeld, whose will was proved in 1508, married a lady named Blanche, but of what family is not recorded, and had two sons, LAWRENCE, his heir, and Thomas, of Sowerby, who died about the year 1537, leaving a silver chalice to Crosstone Chapel. The elder,

LAWRENCE STANSFELD, of Stansfeld, wedded Isabell Horsfall, and dying about 1534, (his will was proved in that year), was buried in Heptonstall Church, and *s.* by his son,

THOMAS STANSFELD, of Sowerby, who *m.* Alice, daughter of — Mitchell, of Heptonstall, and had three sons, Thomas, who appears to have died unmarried, LAWRENCE, successor to his father, and Nicholas, of Wadsworth Royd, whose will was proved in 1587. Thomas Stansfeld died possessed of lands in Stansfeld and Langfield in 1564, and was *s.* by his son,

LAWRENCE STANSFELD, of Sowerby, who died about the year 1591, leaving by Elizabeth, whose maiden surname is unknown, a son and heir,

NICHOLAS STANSFELD, esq. of Norland, who *m.* at Halifax, in 1591, Susan Hopkinson, and left at his decease, in 1599, a son,

JOHN STANSFELD, esq. of Sowerby, *b.* in 1592, who *m.* at Halifax in 1612, Martha, daughter of — Bentley, and had four sons and one daughter, of whom the second son, Joshua, commanded a company of militia during the civil wars, and fought in 1642 at Atherton Moor, where Lord Fairfax was defeated by the marquis of Newcastle. The eldest son,

JOSIAS STANSFELD, esq. of Breck, in Sowerby, *b.* in 1619, *d.* in 1702, having had issue seven sons, viz.

I. TIMOTHY, of Pond, (a house which tradition affirms the Stansfields to have possessed since the Conquest), who was ancestor of Timothy Stansfeld, esq. of Newcross, Surrey, and of Robert Stansfeld, esq. of Field House, near Sowerby.
II. Joshua, of Horton, near Bradford, died in 1732, leaving issue.
III. SAMUEL, of whom hereafter.
IV. James, of Bowood, in Sowerby, who died in 1730. His daughter, Martha, *m.* Joshua Tillotson, esq. nephew to the archbishop.
V. Ely, M. A. vicar of Newark, who *d.* in 1719, leaving one son, who *d. s. p.*
VI. Josias, of Haugh End, in which house Archbishop Tillotson was born. Josias had one son, John, who *d. s. p.* and one daughter, Sarah, *m.* to Martin Hotham, esq. of York.
VII. John, of Sowerby, *b.* in 1657, who *m.* in 1681, Elizabeth, daughter of — Hirst, esq. of Adswood Hall, in Cheshire, and *d.* in 1737, leaving a son,

ELY STANSFELD, esq. of Sowerby, *b.* in 1683, *m.* in 1713, Mary, daughter of John Farrar, esq. of Cliff Hill, and had one son, DAVID, and two daughters, Elizabeth, the wife of Joseph Moore, of Halifax, (and mother of an only daughter, Mary, *m.* to William Threlkeld, esq.), and Mary, who *d.* unmarried in 1778. Mr. Stansfeld *d.* in 1734, and was *s.* by his son,

DAVID STANSFELD, esq. of Hope House, Halifax, *b.* in 1720, who *m.* in 1748, Ellen, daughter of the Rev. Timothy Alred, of Morley, and *d.* in 1769, leaving a daughter, Nelly, *m.* to John Rawson, esq. of Stony Royd, near Halifax, and a son and successor,

DAVID STANSFELD, esq. of Leeds, *b.* 13th February, 1755, who *m.* in 1776, Sarah, daughter and heiress of Thomas Wolrich, esq. of Armley House, in Yorkshire, and had issue,

1. THOMAS-WOLRICH, *b.* in 1779.
2. George, *b.* in 1784, *m.* in 1814, Anna, daughter of Richard Micklethwaite, esq. of New Laiths Grange, and has issue.
3. William, *b.* in 1785, *m.* in 1815, Margaret, daughter and co-heir of James Milnes, esq. of Manor House, Flockton, in Yorkshire, and has issue.
4. David, *b.* in 1788, lost on his passage from South America in 1810.
5. Josias, *b.* in 1790.
6. James, *b.* in 1792.
7. Hatton-Hamer, *b.* in 1793.
8. Henry, *b.* in 1795.
9. Hamer, *b.* in 1797.

1. Peggy, *m.* in 1802, to James Bischoff, esq. and has issue.
2. Eleanor.
3. Mary.
4. Sarah.

The third son,

SAMUEL STANSFIELD, esq. of Bradford, wedded, 12th April, 1675, Mary Clarkson, of Bradford, and *d.* in September, 1727, aged seventy-nine, leaving a son and successor,

ROBERT STANSFIELD, esq. of Bradford, *b.* in 1676, who *m.* first, in 1703, Elizabeth, daughter of the Rev. Thomas Sharp, M. A. of Little Horton, and by her, who died in 1722, had to survive youth an only daughter,

Faith, *m.* to Richard-Gilpin Sawry, esq.

Mr. Stansfield wedded, secondly, in 1723, Anne, daughter of William Busfield, esq. of Rishworth, and had, with other issue who died unmarried, one son and one daughter, viz.

ROBERT, his heir.
ANN, successor to her brother.

The only son and heir,

ROBERT STANSFIELD, esq. of Bradford, *b.* in 1727, who purchased, in 1755, ESHOLT Hall or Priory, in Yorkshire, espoused Jane, eldest daughter of Richard Ferrand, esq. of Harden Hall, by Mary his wife, daughter of William Busfield, esq. of Rishworth, but dying without issue, 14th September, 1772, was *s.* by his sister,

ANN STANSFIELD, of Esholt Hall, *b.* 27th August, 1729, who *m.* 27th August, 1756, WILLIAM ROOKES, esq. of Roydes Hall, senior bencher of Gray's Inn, and dying 12th February, 1798, was *s.* by her daughter,

ANNA-MARIA ROOKES, of Esholt Hall, who wedded, 28th February, 1786, JOSHUA CROMPTON, esq. of York, third son of Samuel Crompton,* esq. of Derby and of Beal, in Yorkshire, and had issue,

I. WILLIAM-ROOKES CROMPTON, her heir.

II. Joshua-Samuel Crompton, of Sion Hill, *b.* 17th September, 1799, M. A. of Jesus College, Cambridge, a magistrate of the North and West Ridings of Yorkshire, and late M.P. for Ripon. This gentleman inherited, by will, his father's property in the North Riding.

III. Robert-Edward Crompton, of Azerley Hall, *b.* 8th August, 1804, B. A. of Trinity College, Cambridge, subsequently an officer in the 15th Hussars. He succeeded, by his father's will, to the estates of Azerley and Sutton, near Ripon, in Yorkshire.

I. Maria-Anne Crompton, *m.* 4th July, 1814, to Henry Preston, esq. of Moreby Hall, high sheriff of Yorkshire in 1834, and has one son and one daughter, Thomas-Henry Preston and Anna-Maria Preston.

II. Mary-Frances Crompton, *m.* 4th December, 1828, to Lieut.-col. Sir William-Lewis Herries, K. G. H. brother to the Rt. Hon. John Charles Herries, and has two sons, Herbert-Crompton Herries and Frederick-Stansfield Herries.

III. Elizabeth-Jane Crompton.

IV. Henrietta-Matilda Crompton.

V. Margaret-Sarah Crompton.

VI. Caroline-Rachel Crompton.

The heiress of Esholt died 5th June, 1819, and devised by will to her eldest son, the present WILLIAM-ROOKES CROMPTON-STANSFIELD, esq. of Esholt Hall, (on the death of his father), the property bequeathed to her by her mother.

*Arms*—Quarterly, first and fourth, sa. three goats passant arg. for STANSFIELD; second, vert, on a bend arg. double cotised erm. a lion passant gu. between two covered cups or, on a chief az. three pheons gold, for CROMPTON; third, arg. a fess sa. between three rooks ppr. for ROOKES.

*Crests*—First, for STANSFIELD, a lion's head erased, encircled by a wreath; second, for CROMPTON, a demi horse sa. vulned in the chest with an arrow ppr.

*Motto*—Nosce teipsum, for STANSFIELD: love and loyalty, for CROMPTON.

*Estates*—In Yorkshire.

*Seat*—Esholt Hall, or Priory, in the West Riding of Yorkshire. The priory of Essheholt was founded by Simon de Ward, in the middle of the twelfth century, and dedicated to God, St. Mary, and St. Leonard; a proof of the sincere and profuse devotion of that period, for while Simon freely bestowed the fairest and most fruitful portion of his estates on strangers, he was content to reserve for himself and his posterity a mansion and domain at Guiseley, which no modern landholder, who had been possessed of both, would have been content to inhabit for twelve months. Esholt Priory fell of course with the smaller foundations, and remained vested in the crown until granted, nine years after his dissolution to Henry Thompson, one of the king's gens-d'armes at Boulogne. In this family it continued somewhat more than a century, when it was transferred to the neighbouring and more distinguished house of Calverley by the marriage of Frances, daughter and heiress of Henry Thompson, esq. with Sir Walter Calverley. His son, Sir Walter Calverley, bart. built on the site of the priory, in the earliest part of the last century, a magnificent house, and planted a fine avenue of elms from Apperley Bridge, which, notwithstanding the change of taste, from the noble growth to which they have attained, reconcile the most fastidious eye to their rectilinear disposition. Along this approach the house is seen to great advantage, with two fronts of handsome white stone, beautifully backed by native oak woods, with the more distant hills of Upper Aresale beyond. It is not improbable that till the great de-

* This gentleman, SAMUEL CROMPTON, esq. who was eldest son of Samuel Crompton, esq. of Derby, and Ann his wife, (baptized in 1688), daughter of William Rodes, esq. of Great Houghton, wedded Elizabeth, daughter of Samuel Fox, esq. of Derby, and had four sons and one daughter, viz.

I. SAMUEL CROMPTON, esq. of Wood End and Beal, in Yorkshire, *b.* in 1750, *m.* Sarah, daughter of Samuel Fox, esq. and *d.* in 1810, leaving one son and one daughter.

II. JOHN CROMPTON, esq. of The Lilies, *b.* in 1753, mayor of the town and high sheriff for the county of Derby in 1810. He *m.* Elizabeth, daughter of Archibald Bell, esq. and *d.* in 1834, leaving two sons and two daughters.

III. JOSHUA CROMPTON, esq. of York, who *m.* as in the text, the heiress of Esholt Hall.

IV. GILBERT CROMPTON, esq. of York, *b.* in 1755, *m.* Eliza, daughter of the Rev. George Johnson, rector of Loftus, in the North Riding of Yorkshire, and vicar of Norton, in the county of Durham, and has issue.

I. ELIZABETH CROMPTON, *b.* in 1745, residing in Derby.

molition of the buildings by Sir Walter Calverley, much of the priory continued in its original state; now a few pointed arches in some of the offices alone remain to attest that a religious house once occupied the site. The builder of the present mansion died in 1749, and his son, of the same name, sold the manor house of Esholt to Robert Stansfield, esq. of Bradford, great uncle of the present proprietor.

### Family of Rookes.

RICHARD ROOKES, esq. living in the reign of HENRY VII. son of William Rookes, of Roydes Hall, in the West Riding of Yorkshire, espoused Mary, daughter of John Rawden, esq. of Rawden, and was *s.* by his son,

RICHARD ROOKES, esq. of Roydes Hall, *temp.* HENRY VIII. father, by Elizabeth his wife, daughter of Robert Waterhouse, esq. of Halifax, of

JOHN ROOKES, esq. of Roydes Hall, who *m.* Jennet, daughter and co-heir of Richard Watson, of Lofthouse, near Wakefield, and by her, who wedded, secondly, Stephen Latton, gent. left a son and successor,

WILLIAM ROOKES, esq. of Roydes Hall, who *m.* Elizabeth, daughter of Richard Wilkinson, of Bradford, and had issue,

- I. WILLIAM, his heir.
- II. James, fellow and bursar of University College, Oxford.
- III. Richard, } both left issue.
- IV. Robert, } both left issue.
- V. Tempest.
- VI. Maximilian, left issue.
- VII. John.

- I. Bridget, *m.* to Mark Hoppey, of Esholt.
- II. Barbara, *m.* to Richard Pearson.
- III. Grace, *m.* to Richard Rawlinson.
- IV. Susan, *m.* to Michael Holdsworth.
- V. Prudence, *m.* to John Ramsden.

The eldest son,

WILLIAM ROOKES, esq. of Roydes Hall, living 20th CHARLES I. *m.* first, Jane, daughter of John Thornhill, esq. of Fixby, in the county of York, by whom he had a son, WILLIAM, his heir; and, secondly, Susan, daughter of Mr. Rosethorn, and widow of Mr. Radcliffe, of Lancashire, by whom he had another son. He was *s.* by the elder,

WILLIAM ROOKES, esq. of Roydes Hall, who espoused Mary, daughter of George Hopkinson, esq. of Lofthouse, and sister of the well known antiquary, and had issue,

- William, who died while a student at University College, Oxford.
- GEORGE, heir.
- JOHN, successor to his brother.
- Jane, who *m.* Robert Parker, esq. second son of Edward Parker, esq. of Browsholme, and *d. s. p.* in 1712. Mr. Parker was a great antiquary and collector of MSS., coins, &c.
- Mary, died young.

The eldest surviving son,

GEORGE ROOKES, esq. of Roydes Hall, living in 1677, *m.* Jane, daughter of Capt. Henry Crossland, of Helmsley, in the North Riding of Yorkshire, but dying without surviving issue, (his only daughter, Katharine, having predeceased him in 1682, aged four years), he was *s.* by his brother,

JOHN ROOKES, esq. of Roydes Hall, who espoused, first, Anne, daughter and heir of George Hopkinson, esq. of Lofthouse, and had two sons, WILLIAM and George. He *m.* secondly, Elizabeth, daughter of the Rev. Marmaduke Cooke, D.D. vicar of Leeds and prebendary of York, by whom (who died 17th December, 1695), he had issue,

- I. John, *d.* in 1700, and was buried at Bradford.
- II. Marmaduke, who died 27th April, 1724, leaving by Jane his wife, daughter of William Turner, esq. of Wakefield, an only daughter and heiress,
  - Elizabeth, who *m.* Christopher Hodgson, M.D. of Wakefield, but dying *s. p.* 15th March, 1789, aged seventy-three, left her estate at Barrowby to her cousin, William Rookes, esq. of Esholt.

- I. Elizabeth.
- II. Mary.
- III. Jane.
- IV. Anne.

Mr. Rookes *d.* 30th May, 1713, and was *s.* by his son,

WILLIAM ROOKES, esq. of Roydes Hall, (of Jesus College, Cambridge,) who *m.* Mary, daughter of William Rodes, esq. of Great Houghton, by Mary his wife, dau. of Richard Wilson, esq. of Leeds, and had issue,

- I. EDWARD, of Roydes Hall, *b.* in 1713, *m.* first, in 1740, Mary, daughter and heir of Robert Leeds, esq. of Milford, and assumed in consequence the surname of LEEDS. He wedded, secondly, Henrietta, daughter of Sandford Hardcastle, esq. of Wakefield, and sister of Thomas Arthington, esq. of Arthington. This lady died *s. p.* in 1803. By his first wife, Mr. Rookes Leeds, who *d.* in 1788, had four daughters, viz.
  - Mary Leeds, who *m.* George Walker, esq. of Middlewood Hall, and *d. s. p.* in 1803.
  - Jane Leeds, who *m.* William Serjeantson, esq. of Wakefield, and had a son,
    - William-Rookes-Leeds Serjeantson, esq. of Camphill,

*b.* in 1766, *m.* 2nd June, 1795, Elizabeth, daughter of Henry Dawkins, esq. of Standlinch, by the Lady Juliana Colyeare his wife, dau. of the Earl of Portmore.

Elizabeth Leeds, *d.* unmarried, in 1763.

Anne Leeds, *m.* to the Rev. Jeremiah Smith, of Woodside, in Sussex.

II. WILLIAM, *b.* 27th August, 1719, at Roydes Hall, *m.* at Otley, on his own and his wife's birthday, 27th August, 1758, Ann, sister and heiress of ROBERT STANSFIELD, esq. of Esholt Hall, and was grandfather of the present

WILLIAM - ROOKES CROMPTON - STANSFIELD, esq. of Esholt Hall.

III. John, *d.* young.

I. Mary, *d.* unm. 1793.

II. Ann, *d.* in infancy.

III. Elizabeth, *d.* unm. in 1770.

## LAWRENCE, OF SEVENHAMPTON.

LAWRENCE, WALTER-LAWRENCE, esq. of Sandywell Park, in the county of Gloucester, *b.* 21st May, 1799, *m.* 24th July, 1824, Mary, only daughter of Christian Speldt, esq. of Stratford, in Essex, and has three daughters, viz.

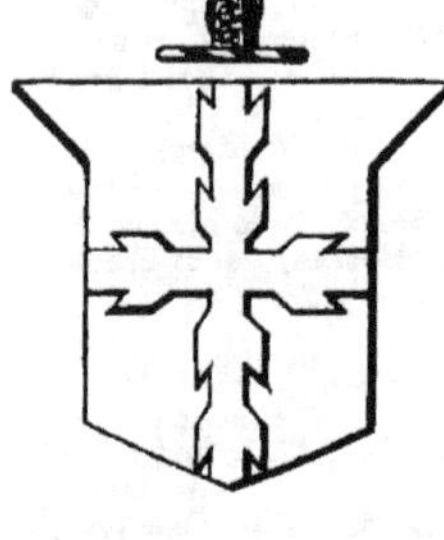

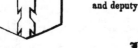

Mary-Elizabeth.
Alice.
Agatha.

This gentleman, whose patronymic is MORRIS, assumed in its stead the surname and arms of LAWRENCE, by the desire of his maternal grandfather, Walter Lawrence, esq. He succeeded to the Sandiwell estate in 1823, under the will of Mr. Lightbourn, and is a magistrate and deputy lieutenant for the county of Gloucester.

### Lineage.

The family of LAWRENCE was originally seated in the county of Lancaster.

SIR ROBERT LAWRENCE, of Ashton Hall, in that shire, accompanied the lion-hearted RICHARD to Palestine, and distinguishing himself at the siege of Acre, in 1191, was made a knight-banneret, and obtained for his arms "Arg. a cross raguly gu." He was father of

SIR ROBERT LAWRENCE, who wedded a daughter of James Trafford, esq. of Trafford, in Lancashire, and had a son and successor,

JAMES LAWRENCE, living in the 37th of HENRY III. who *m.* in 1252, Matilda, only dau. and heiress of John Washington, of Washington, in Lancashire, and acquired by his marriage the manors of Washington, Sedgwick, &c. in that county. His son and successor,

JOHN LAWRENCE, levied a fine of Washington and Sedgwick, in 1283. He *m.* Margaret, daughter of Walter Chesford, and was father of

JOHN LAWRENCE, who presented to the church of Washington, in 1326, and died about the year 1360, leaving, by Elizabeth his wife, daughter of — Holt, of Stably, in Lancashire, a son and heir,

SIR ROBERT LAWRENCE, knt. who *m.* Margaret Holden, of Lancashire, and had four sons, namely,

I. ROBERT (Sir), his heir.

II. Thomas, whose son, Arthur, seated at Prior's Court, in the county of Gloucester, was ancestor of SIR JOHN LAWRENCE, of Chelsea, who was created a BARONET in 1628. This branch of the family is now EXTINCT.

III. William, *b.* in 1395, who served in France, and subsequently joining Lionel, Lord Welles, fought under the Lancastrian banner at St. Albans, in 1455, where he was slain, and buried in the abbey church.

IV. Edmund.

The eldest son,

Sir Robert Lawrence, living in 1454, espoused Amphilbis, daughter of Edward Longford, esq. of Longford, in the county of Lancaster, and had three sons, namely,

i. James (Sir), knt. styled "of Standish," to distinguish him from another Sir James Lawrence then living. He *m.* Cecily, daughter and heiress of — Boteler, esq. of Lancashire, and had two sons and one daughter,

1. Thomas (Sir), knt. who *m.* Eleanor, dau. of Lionel, Lord Welles, K.G., by Joan, his wife, dau. and heir of Sir Robert Waterton, knt. (See Burke's *Extinct Peerage.*) By this alliance Sir Thomas acquired several manors in the counties of Lincoln, Nottingham, and York, as appears by a deed of partition, dated 6th April, 2nd Henry VII. and had two sons, viz.

Sir John Lawrence, the seventh knight in a direct line, who enjoyed thirty-four manors, amounting, in 1591, to £6,000. per annum, but being outlawed, for having killed a gentleman usher of *King* Henry VII. he died an exile in France, issueless, when Ashton Hall, and his other estates passed, by royal permission, to his relatives, Lords Monteagle and Gerard. Many of the Lawrences were at this time seated at Withington, Canbury, and Priors Court, in the county of Gloucester; at Fisbury, in Wilts, at Crich Grange, in the Isle of Purbeck,* and at St. James's Park, in Suffolk.

Thomas Lawrence, died *s. p.*

2. Robert, *d.* without issue.

1. Cecily, *m.* to William Gerard, esq. ancestor of the Lords Gerard, of Bromley.

ii. Robert, of whom presently.

iii. Nicholas, from whom descended

Littleton Lawrence, esq. of Cricklade, who inherited the mansion and estates of Shurdington, under the will of William Lawrence, esq. and his descendants still possess them.

The second son,

Robert Lawrence, esq. *m.* Margaret, daughter of John Lawrence, esq. of Rixton, in Lancashire, by Mary his wife, daughter of Eudo, eldest son of Richard, Lord Welles, and had issue,

i. Robert (Sir), who *m.* the daughter of Thomas Stanley, esq. and *d. s. p.* in 1511.

ii. John, who, with Sir Edmund Howard, commanded a wing of the English army at Flodden. He *d.* without issue, aged thirty-eight.

iii. William.

The third son,

William Lawrence, esq. living in 1509, purchased landed property to the amount of £2,000. per annum, including Sevenhampton, &c. in the county of Gloucester, the manor of Sea House, in Somerset, Blackley Park and Norton, in Worcestershire, Staple Farm and Newhouse, subsequently possessed by Dr. Robert Fielding, in right of his wife, Upcot Farm, and many other estates. He wedded Isabel, daughter and coheir of John Molyneux, esq. of Chorley, in Lancashire, and had issue,

i. John, LL.D. archdeacon of Worcester, parson of Withington, who *d. s. p.*

ii. Robert, of whom presently.

iii. William.

iv. Edmund, of Withington.

v. Thomas, of Compton, in the parish of Withington.

The second son,

Robert Lawrence, esq. *b.* at Withington, in 1521, had by his first wife three daughters, the wives of Truman, Hodgkins, and Rogers; and by his second,

---

* Sir Oliver Laurence, living *temp.* Henry VIII., founder of the Crich Grange branch, was seventh son of Nicholas Lawrence, esq. of Agercroft, third son of Sir Giles Laurence, of Standish. He *m.* the Lady Anne Wriothesley, dau. of Thomas, the first and celebrated Earl of Southampton, and had a son and successor,

Edward Laurence, esq. who died 28th August, 1601, leaving by Alice his wife, daughter of Thomas Trenchard, esq. of Lichet, a son,

Sir Edward Laurence, of Crich Grange, in Dorset, who was knighted in 1619. He died in 1629, and was *s.* by his son,

Sir Edward Laurence, of Crich Grange, knighted at Oxford in 1643, who *m.* in 1623, Grace, daughter of Henry Bruen, esq. and dying in 1647, left, with two daughters, Elizabeth, *m.* to Robert Culliford, esq. of Encombe, and Margaret, to William Floyer, esq. of Hayes, (see vol. i. p. 606.) a son,

Sir Robert Laurence, knt. of Crich Grange, who wedded Jane, daughter and heir of John Williams, esq. of Tynham, and was *s.* in 1666, by his son,

John Laurence, esq. of Crich Grange, who *d. s. p.* having sold all his estates to Nathaniel Bond, esq.

Eleanor, daughter of John Stratford, of Farncot, three sons, viz.

I. WILLIAM, to whom his father gave the Shurdington estates, &c. This William was father of

ANTHONY, of Shurdington, whose son and heir,

WILLIAM, died without issue, leaving his estates at Shurdington to his widow, Dulcibella, for life, remainder to divers distant relations, excluding, through some pique, the descendants of Anthony, of Sevenhampton, his heirs at law. Littleton Lawrence, of Cricklade, descendant of a younger branch, took the Shurdington estates under this will, and his heirs still enjoy them.

II. Robert, who had the manor of Sevenhampton, but dying issueless, he devised Oldeswell to William, the son of his elder brother, and the manor of Sevenhampton, Andoversford, &c. to the grandsons of his younger brother, Anthony.

III. ANTHONY.

Robert Lawrence died in 1585. His third son,

ANTHONY LAWRENCE, esq. in whose descendants the representation of the senior branch of this ancient family is now vested, wedded a daughter of William Gradwell, esq. of Gray's Inn, and had issue,

I. ANTHONY, his heir.

II. Francis.

III. William, *d. s. p.*

I. Elizabeth, *m.* to William Rogers, esq. of Sandiwell.

Anthony was *s.* at his decease by his eldest son,

ANTHONY LAWRENCE, esq. who *m.* Mary, daughter of Giles Broadway, esq. of Portlip, and had two sons and three daughters, namely, ROBERT, his heir, Anthony, of Dowdeswell, Ann, *m.* to Giles Roberts, esq. of Oudswell, Mary, *m.* to John Dowle, esq. of Badginton, and Elizabeth, *m.* to John Freme, esq. The elder son,

ROBERT LAWRENCE, esq. of Sevenhampton, wedded Mary, daughter of John Rogers, esq. of Hasleton, and had issue,

I. ANTHONY, M.D. whose line ended in his three daughters and co-heirs viz.

ELIZABETH, *m.* to — Moore, esq.

CULPEPPER, *m.* to — Pembruge, esq.

MARY, *d.* unm.

II. Robert, *d.* aged twenty.

III. WALTER, of whom presently.

I. Elizabeth, *m.* to William Norden, esq.

II. Mary, *m.* to Carew Williams, esq. of Corndale.

III. Ann, *m.* to Thomas Ludlow, esq.

The third son,

WALTER LAWRENCE, esq. of Painswick, espoused Anne, daughter of Edmund Webb, esq. and had, with several other children, who all *d.* unmarried, a daughter, Joanna, wife of Ethell Perks, esq. and a son his successor,

WALTER LAWRENCE, esq. of Sevenhampton, who *m.* Mary, daughter of John Cocks, esq. of Woodmancote, in the county of Gloucester, a branch of the family of Cocks, of Dumbleton, progenitors of the ennobled house of Somers, and had issue,

Robert, in holy orders, *d.* unmarried.

WALTER, heir to his father.

John, in holy orders, rector of Sevenhampton, living unmarried in 1806, aged seventy-three.

Mr. Lawrence was *s.* at his decease by his elder surviving son,

WALTER LAWRENCE, esq. of Sevenhampton, who wedded Mary, only surviving child of Thomas Hayward, esq. by Dorothy his wife, another daughter of the said John Cocks, esq. of Woodmancote, and left at his decease an only surviving child,

MARY LAWRENCE, of Sevenhampton, representative, through her two grandmothers, of the family of Cocks, of Woodmancote, whose estate she holds, and whose arms she quarters. The heiress of Sevenhampton *m.* in 1797, William Morris, esq. brother of Robert Morris, esq. M.P. for Gloucester, and has an only surviving child, the present WALTER-LAWRENCE LAWRENCE, esq. of Sandywell Park.

*Arms*—Arg. a cross raguly gu.

*Crest*—The tail and lower part of a fish, erect and couped ppr.

*Estates*—In Gloucestershire.

*Seat*—Sandywell Park.

# MURRAY, OF TOUCHADAM AND POLMAISE.

**MURRAY, WILLIAM,** esq. of Touchadam and Polmaise, both in the county of Stirling, *b.* 6th July, 1773; *m.* 11th June, 1799, Anne, daughter of Sir William Maxwell, bart. of Monreith.

This gentleman, who is vice-lieutenant of the county of Stirling, and lieutenant-colonel of the Yeomanry of that shire, succeeded his father in 1814.

## Lineage.

This family has been seated for centuries in the county of Stirling, and is supposed to derive from the noble house of Bothwel. Its patriarch,

SIR WILLIAM DE MORAVIA, designed of Sanford, joined ROBERT BRUCE in defence of the liberties of his country, but, being taken prisoner by the English, was sent to London in 1306, and remained in captivity there until exchanged after the battle of Bannockburn. Sir William's son and successor,

SIR ANDREW DE MORAVIA, obtained from King David Bruce two charters; the first, granting the lands of Kepmad, dated in 1365; and the second, bestowing Tulchadam, Tulchmallar, &c. in 1369. Sir William died *temp.* ROBERT II. and was *s.* by his son,

WILLIAM DE MORAVIA, of Touchadam, living in 1392, in which year he had a charter from *King* ROBERT III. He wedded Christian Cunninghame, and was father of

ALEXANDER DE MORAVIA, of Touchadam, who, in 1455, upon the resignation of his father, got a charter, from JAMES II. of the lands of Weigateschaw, in the county of Lanark; and Touchadam, Newark, &c. in the shire of Stirling; all erected into a barony. He *m.* — Sutherland, and had a son and successor,

WILLIAM MURRAY, of Touchadam, constable of the castle of Stirling in the reign of JAMES III. This laird acquired, in 1459, the lands of Buchadrock, in Stirlingshire, and in 1462, in a baron court held at Dunipace concerning part of the lands of Herbertshire, of which William, earl of Orkney, was superior, William Murray, of Touchadam was, by his lordship, appointed judge.

Touchadam married a lady named Christian, and had four sons,

I. DAVID, his heir.
II. John, father of JOHN, of Gawamore, successor to his uncle.
III. Herbert.
IV. Patrick.

The eldest son,

DAVID MURRAY, of Touchadam, having no issue, made a resignation of his whole estate to his nephew,

JOHN MURRAY, of Gawamore, captain of the king's guards and lord provost of Edinburgh, who, upon the demise of his uncle about the year 1474, became "of Touchadam," and got a confirmation thereof under the great seal. This John Murray was a firm and devoted adherent of *King* JAMES III. After the battle of Stirling, he was deprived of a considerable portion of his estate, and a great number of the old family writs were embezzled and lost. He espoused a daughter of — Seaton, of Winton, and had a son and heir,

WILLIAM MURRAY, of Touchadam, living in 1507, who *m.* Agnes, daughter of John Cockburn, of Ormiston, and was *s.* at his decease, in 1514, by his son,

JOHN MURRAY, of Touchadam, who had a charter under the great seal, dated 9th June, 1541, of the lands of Sandieholmes, in Lanarkshire. He wedded the Lady Janet Erskine, daughter of Robert, fourth earl of Marr, and had two sons, William and James, by the elder of whom,

WILLIAM MURRAY, of Touchadam, he was succeeded. This laird married Agnes, dau. and co-heir of James Cunninghame, of Polmais, in the county of Stirling, and dying in 1569, left, with a daughter, Agnes, a son and successor,

SIR JOHN MURRAY, of Touchadam and Polmais, who got a charter, dated 26th December, 1602, to himself and Jaen Cockburn his wife, of several lands in Stirlingshire, containing a new erection, in consideration of the many good services he had himself rendered to the king, as well as of the loyalty so frequently displayed by his great-great-grandfather, John Murray, of Touchadam. Sir John *m.* Jean, daughter of John Cockburn, of Ormiston, and was *s.* by his son,

SIR WILLIAM MURRAY, of Touchadam and Polmais, who obtained from CHARLES I. a charter of the lands of Cowie in 1636. During the conflicts which harassed the reign of that ill-fated prince, Sir William strained every nerve in defence of the royal cause, and, in consequence, suffered severely from the enactments of the adverse party. He was in the engagement of the duke of Hamilton, and in 1654, was emerced by Cromwell in the sum of fifteen hundred pounds. He died shortly after, and left, by Elizabeth his wife, daughter of Sir Alexander Gibson, of Durie, a son and successor,

JOHN MURRAY, of Polmais and Touchadam, served heir to his father in January, 1655. He *m.* Janet, daughter of Sir John Nisbet, of Dean, lord provost of Edinburgh, and was *s.* by his son,

JOHN MURRAY, of Touchadam and Polmais, who wedded Anne, daughter of Sir Alexander Gibson, of Durie, one of the senators of the college of justice, and had five sons, viz.

I. JOHN, his heir.
II. WILLIAM, eventual inheritor.
III. George, who married and had issue.
IV. Adam, M. D. *d. s. p.*
V. Mungo, who married and had issue.

The eldest son,

JOHN MURRAY, of Touchadam and Polmais, infeft in his father's lifetime, married Lilias, daughter of Stirling, of Keir, and dying in 1716, was *s.* by the elder of two sons,

JOHN MURRAY, of Touchadam and Polmais, who dying unm. was *s.* by his brother,

WILLIAM MURRAY, of Touchadam and Polmais, at whose decease likewise unm. the estates reverted to his uncle,

WILLIAM MURRAY, of Touchadam and Polmais, who was served heir to the whole estate in 1729. He *m.* first, Cecilia, dau. of Gibson, of Durie, by whom he had a son and daughter, who both *d.* in infancy. He wedded secondly, Elizabeth, daughter of Sir Alexander Gibson, bart. of Pentland, and had three sons and one daughter, viz.

I. WILLIAM, his heir.
II. Alexander, who *d.* unm.
III. John, who *m.* Isabella, daughter of PROFESSOR Hercules Lindsay, and had issue,
   1. John, merchant, of Liverpool, *m.* Elizabeth, daughter of James Bryce, esq. and has two sons and one daughter.
   2. Cecilia, *m.* to John Russell, esq.

I. Margaret, *m.* to the Marchese Accrambonie.

William Murray *d.* in 1758, and was *s.* by his son,

WILLIAM MURRAY, of Touchadam and Polmais, who *m.* first, Margaret, daughter of John Callander, esq. of Craigforth, and by her had a son, WILLIAM, his heir. He wedded, secondly, Anne, daughter of Lawrence Campbell, esq. of Clathick and Kilermont, by whom he had,

John, capt. R. N. deceased.
Archibald, East India company's service, deceased.
Alexander, an advocate, who *m.* Miss Johnina Wilkinson, of the county of Denbigh.
Anne, *m.* to Robert Bruce, esq. of Kennet. (See vol. ii. page 485).

Mr. Murray espoused, thirdly, Grace, daughter of Alexander Speirs, esq. of Elderslie, and by this lady had one son and three daughters, viz.

Peter, died in infancy.
Mary, *m.* to Alexander Speirs, esq. of Culvrench, in Stirlingshire.
Grace.
Elizabeth, died an infant.

Polmaise *d.* in 1814, and was *s.* by his eldest son, the present WILLIAM MURRAY, esq. of Polmaise and Touchadam.

*Arms*—Az. three stars within a double tressure, flory counterflory or.

*Crest*—A mermaid, holding in her dexter hand a mirror, in her sinister a comb.

*Motto*—Tout prest.

*Estates*—In Stirlingshire, acquired in the fourteenth century.

*Seat*—Polmaise.

# GRIMSTON, OF GRIMSTON GARTH.

GRIMSTON, CHARLES, esq. of Grimston Garth and Kilnwick, both in the East Riding of the county of York, *b.* 2nd July, 1791; *m.* 10th November, 1823, Jane, third surviving daughter of the Very Rev. Thomas Trench, dean of Kildare, and niece of Frederick, present Lord Ashtown, by whom he has issue,

MARMADUKE-JERARD, *b.* 27th November, 1826.
Walter-John, *b.* 9th February, 1828.
William-Henry, *b.* 1st November, 1830.
Daniel-Thomas, *b.* 8th July, 1832.
Roger, *b.* 5th March, 1834.
Maria-Emma.
Frances-Dorothy.
Jane.
Catherine.

This gentleman, who succeeded his father in 1821, is colonel of the East York militia, and a magistrate and deputy-lieutenant for the same Riding.

## Lineage.

SYLVESTER DE GRYMESTONE came over from Normandy as standard-bearer in the army of WILLIAM, *the Conqueror*, to whom he did homage for Grymestone and Holmpton, and his lands elsewhere, to hold of the Lord Rosse as of his seigniorie and manor of Rosse in Holdernesse, which Lord Rosse was lord chamberlain of the king's household in 1066. Sylvester married, it is supposed, in Normandy, and had a son and successor,

DANIEL DE GRYMESTONE, who wedded the daughter of Sir Adam Surmvall, or Somerville, of Brent Hall, near Pattrington, and had three sons,

I. THOMAS (Sir), his heir.
II. Daniel, who *m.* the daughter of Rolland Sherwarde, and had a son, Rolland, who died young.
III. Oswald, who *m.* the daughter of John Mussard, of Leawde Burton, and had a son, John.

The eldest son,

SIR THOMAS DE GRYMESTONE, knt. of Grymestone, living *temp.* STEPHEN, wedded the daughter of Sir John Bosville, of Awdesley, and had a son and successor,

SIR JOHN DE GRYMESTONE, of Grymestone, who received the honour of knighthood from HENRY II. He *m.* the daughter and heiress of Sir John Goodmanham, knt. of Goodmanham, in whose right he became lord of the manor of Goodmanham, holden under Henry Piercy, earl of Northumberland, and left by her, at his decease, 12th October, 1165, (buried at Goodmanham,) a son,

SIR MARTIN DE GRYMESTONE, of Grymestone, knt. living *temp.* HENRY III. who espoused the daughter and co-heiress of Sir John Collam, knt. of Collam, and had two sons, viz.

ROGER, his heir.
Alexander, *m.* the daughter of Sir John Frowiske, of the county of Middlesex, and had a son, Martin, lord of Edmonton.

Sir Martin was *s.* by his elder son,

SIR ROGER DE GRYMESTONE, knt. of Grymestone, lord of the manors of Grymestone, Tunstall, Holmpton, Goodmanham, and Collam, who *m.* the daughter of Sir Fowke Constable, lord of Frishmarshe, and was *s.* by his elder son,

SIR JERARD DE GRYMESTONE, knt. of Grymestone, who sold, in 1353, fifty-three oxgangs of land in the manor and lordship of Risby, some land in Cottingham, half the moietie of Holmpton in Holdernesse, and certain lands in Bewlake and Moscrofte. Sir Jerard wedded the daughter of Sir John Baskerville, knt. but having no issue, was *s.* by his brother,

WALTER DE GRYMESTONE, of Grymestone, who *m.* the daughter and co-heir of Harbarde Flinton, of Flinton, and had three sons,

WILLIAM, his heir.
Jerard, *m.* the daughter of William Asheton, and was father of Anthony Grimston, of Nidd, in Nitherdaile.
John, who was made dean of Dorchester in the 12th year of RICHARD II. and in the 15th of the same reign ABBOT OF SELBY. He *d.* in 1398, and was solemnly interred in the monastery of Selby.

Walter de Grymestone enjoyed, in right of his wife, the lordships of Flinton, in Holderness, and Laresby, in the county of Lincoln, which lands were formerly possessed by Sir John de la Lyne. The manor of Flinton was holden upon the manor of Humbleton, lately belonging to the dissolved monastery of Thornton Cunliffe, in Lincolnshire. Laresby was holden under Ralph Neville, earl of Westmoreland, upon his manor of Grimsby, paying a pair of white gloves and one penny for all service.

Walter's eldest son and successor,

WILLIAM DE GRYMESTONE, of Grymestone, wedded Armatrude, daughter of Sir John Rysam, knt. of Rysam, in Holderness, and had three sons, viz.

I. THOMAS, his heir.
II. Robert, who, marrying the daughter of Sir Anthony Spelman, removed to the estates obtained through his wife in Suffolk, and was *s.* by his son,
  EDWARD DE GRYMESTONE, from whom descended the Grimstons of Suffolk, who were raised to the rank of BARONET in 1612. The male line of this branch, of which SIR HARBOTTLE GRIMSTON was a distinguished member, expired in 1700, when the estates were inherited by the last baronet's grand-nephew,
    WILLIAM LUCKYN, esq. M. P. for St. Albans, (grandson of Sir Capel Luckyn by MARY GRIMSTON), who assumed the surname of GRIMSTON, and was elevated to the peerage of Ireland by the titles of Baron Dunboyne and VISCOUNT GRIMSTON in 1719. His lordship's great grandson is the present EARL OF VERULAM. (See BURKE'S *Peerage*).
III. John, made second dean of Windsor in 1416.

The eldest son,

THOMAS GRIMSTON, of Grimston, living in the reign of HENRY V. wedded Dioness, daughter of —— de Sutton, lord of Sutton, Southcotes, and Stone Ferry, and was *s.* at his decease by his eldest son,

SIR ROGER GRIMSTON, knt. of Grimston, who left no issue by his wife, the daughter of Sir John Antwisle, of Lancashire, and was accordingly *s.* by his brother,

THOMAS GRIMSTON, of Grimston, living in 1436, who wedded the daughter of Sir William Fitzwilliam, knt. of Aldwark, near Rotherham, and had issue,

I. William, who *d. s. p.*
II. WALTER, successor to his father.
I. Margaret, *m.* to Robert Stowthingham, of Sentriforthing, in Holdernesse, and had issue.
II. Ann, *m.* to William Vavasour, esq. (See vol. i. p. 52.)

The only surviving son and his father's successor,

WALTER GRIMSTON, esq. of Grimston, espoused the daughter and co-heiress of Sir John Portington, knt. appointed judge of the court of Common Pleas in 1444, and was father of

THOMAS GRIMSTON, esq. of Grimston, who was living *temp.* HENRY VII. He *m.* an heiress named Newark, and had, with two daughters, (the elder *m.* to George Brigham, of Brigham, and the younger *d.* unm.) six sons, viz. William, who died young; WALTER, successor to his father; John, who wedded the daughter and heiress of — Ewry; Henry, rector of Collam, Goodmanham, and Laresbie; with two other sons, who died without issue. The eldest son and heir,

WALTER GRIMSTON, esq. of Grimston, *m.* the daughter of John Dakins, of Brandesburton, and had, with a daughter, (Elizabeth, the wife of Marmaduke Constable, son and heir of Sir William Constable, knt. of Hatfield), an only son,

THOMAS GRIMSTON, esq. of Grimston, who wedded the daughter of Nicholas Girlington, of Harkfurth, and had seventeen children, of whom

THOMAS, succeeded his father.
Francis, *m.* Susannah, daughter of William Wensley, esq. of Brandesburton.
John, *m.* Grace, daughter of William Strickland, esq. of Boynton, and had three sons, viz.
  Marmaduke.
  Francis.
  Henry, of Fraisthorpe, who *m.* the daughter of William Strickland, esq. of Eston, and had a son,
    John Grimston, of Dring or Dringhoe, in Holdernesse, ancestor of the GRIMSTONS, of Neswick.
Marmaduke, *m.* the daughter of John

Starley, gent. and had issue, John, Robert, Thomas, and Dorothy.

Edward, *m.* the daughter of Ralph Pollard, of Brompton, and had a daughter, Catherine.

Ann, *m.* to Robert Wright, esq. of Plowland, in the county of York.

Maud, *m.* to John Thwenge, esq. of Upper Helmesley, and had a son, Marmaduke Thwenge, esq. of Upper Helmesley, *b.* in 1560, whose only daughter, Margery, espoused George Wilmer, esq. (See vol. ii. p. 148).

Thomas Grimston was *s.* by his eldest son,

THOMAS GRIMSTON, esq. of Grimston, living in 1540, who *m.* the daughter and heiress of Marmaduke Thwaites, esq. of Little Smeaton, and had issue,

MARMADUKE (Sir), his heir.

Thomas, who *m.* the daughter of John Strelly, esq. of Lamblery, Notts, but *d. s. p.*

John, who *m.* a lady named Owen, of the county of Oxford, and had (with two daughters, Frances and Dorothy) one son,

MARMADUKE (Sir), eventual inheritor of the estates and representation of the family.

Thwaites, who *m.* a daughter of Henry Mainwaring, esq. of Cheshire.

Walter, who *m.* the daughter and coheir of Marmaduke Thurkell, esq.

Christopher, who *m.* a daughter of Francis Barnye, esq. of Gunton, in Norfolk.

——, *m.* to William Thornton, esq.

Catherine, *m.* to John Eastoft, esq. of Eastoft.

Joan, *m.* to John Hopton, esq.

Dorothy, *m.* to Henry Holme, esq. of Paul Holme.

Cicell, *m.* to Robert Saltmarshe, esq. of Saltmarshe.

Thomas Grimston, who, in right of his wife, became lord of the manors of Little Smeaton, Berkby, Southmoors, and Little Danby, was *s.* by his son,

SIR MARMADUKE GRIMSTON, knt. of Grimston, *temp. Queen* ELIZABETH, who *m.* the daughter of George Gill, esq. of the county of Hertford, and had by her one son, Thomas, who *d. s. p.* It appears by some marriage articles of later date, made between William Grimston, esq. of Grimston Garth, and Dorothy, daughter of Sir Thomas Norcliffe, bart. of Langton, that Sir Marmaduke married Dame Elizabeth Brown, who survived him, but this was most probably a second marriage, as nothing has arisen to contradict the first. Sir Marmaduke's nephew (the only son of his brother John) another

SIR MARMADUKE GRIMSTON, of Grimston, knighted by *King* JAMES I. in 1603, eventually inherited the estates and continued the line of the family. This gentleman served the office of high sheriff for Yorkshire in 1598, and Drake, in his Eboracum, mentions his being one of the learned council at York to JAMES I. in the first year of his reign. He *m.* the daughter of Sir William Dalton, of Hawkeswell, in Yorkshire, (see vol. i. p. 529) and had one son and one daughter, viz.

WILLIAM, his heir.

Theophania, *m.* to Leonard Beckwith, esq. of Handale Abbey, in Cleveland.

Sir Marmaduke Grimston was *s.* by his only son,

WILLIAM GRIMSTON, esq. of Grimston, who adhered, during the civil wars, with unshaken loyalty to CHARLES I. suffered much by sequestration, and for redemption of an estate for support sold Flinton, Wanholme, and part of Grimston. He also settled the lordships of Goodmanham and Little Smeaton on John, his son, who gave them, after the death of his own son, to his sisters, who sold Goodmanham to the earl of Burlington. William Grimston *m.* first, a daughter of Christopher Byerley, esq. of Midridge Grange, in the county of Durham, and had by her three sons and one daughter, viz.

WILLIAM, his heir.

Marmaduke, } *d.* young.
Henry, }

Dorothy, *d.* young.

He wedded, secondly, a daughter of Sir Robert Strickland, of Thornton Briggs, in Yorkshire, and had to survive youth,

John, *m.* Miss Lockwood, of Sewerby, and had a son, Thomas, who died young.

Charles, who had one son and one daughter, Peter and Frances.

Margaret, *m.* to — Maskall, esq. of London.

Mary, *m.* to Thomas Mosley, esq. of York.

Elizabeth, *m.* to Philip Langdale, esq. of Houghton.

Dorothy, *m.* to Robert Medley, esq. civilian of York.

Mr. Grimston espoused, thirdly, the widow of Mr. Laiton, and daughter of Lord Evers, but by this lady had no issue. He was *s.* by his eldest son,

WILLIAM GRIMSTON, esq. of Grimston, *b.* 16th August, 1640, who sold part of Garton and the advowson of Goodmanham. During the life of this proprietor, the old family mansion at Grimston Garth was burnt down.

He espoused Dorothy, daughter of Sir Thomas Norcliffe, knt. of Langton, by Dorothy his wife, daughter of Thomas, Viscount Fairfax, of Emely, and had three sons and three daughters, viz.

William, who died before his father, aged nineteen.
THOMAS, heir.
Marmaduke, died an ensign in Colonel Wharton's regiment in the fatal camp at Dundalk.

Dorothy, *m.* to Nathaniel Gooche, gent. of Hull.
Ann, *m.* to Thomas Rider, esq. and had a son, Grimston Rider.
Alathea, *m.* to Benjamin Laughton, esq. of Newhill, Yorkshire.

Mr. Grimston *d.* 5th August, 1711, and was *s.* by his son,

THOMAS GRIMSTON, esq. of Grimston Garth, *b.* 8th October, 1664, who *m.* Dorothy, daughter of Sir John Legard, bart. of Ganton, by Frances, his second wife, eldest daughter and co-heir of Sir Thomas Widdrington,* sergeant at law, and left at his decease, 13th April, 1729, an only surviving son and successor,

THOMAS GRIMSTON, esq. of Grimston Garth, *b.* 26th September, 1702, who *m.* 16th October, 1722, Jane, daughter and coheir of John Close, esq. of Richmond, in Yorkshire, by Jane his wife, sister and heir of Charles Estouteville, esq. of Hunmanby, and had, to survive youth, an only son, JOHN, his heir. Mr. Grimston inherited, in right of his wife, from the Estouteville family, lands in Hunmanby, Fordon, and Ergham, together with the right of presentation to the rectory of Ergham. He also acquired under the will of his distant relative Admiral Medley, the estate of Kilnwick, purchased by the admiral from Col. Condon, as well as the property of Little Smeaton, which had formerly belonged to his own ancestors. Mr. Grimston *d.* 22nd October, 1751, was buried at Kilnwick, and *s.* by his son,

JOHN GRIMSTON, esq. of Grimston Garth and Kilnwick, *b.* 17th February, 1724, who wedded, 12th March, 1753, Jane, youngest daughter of Sir Thomas Legard, bart. of Ganton, by Frances his wife, sister and coheir of John Digby, esq. of Mansfield Woodhouse, and by her, who *d.* 11th November, 1758, had issue,

I. THOMAS, his heir.
II. John, died young.
III. Henry, died unm. 23rd October, 1820, and was buried at Kensington.

I. Jane, *m.* to Lieut. Col. George Legard, of the 69th regiment, third son of Sir Digby Legard, bart. of Ganton.
II. Frances, died unm. 10th October, 1833, and buried at Kilnwick.

Mr. Grimston *d.* 21st June, 1780, was buried at Kilnwick, and *s.* by his son,

THOMAS GRIMSTON, esq. of Grimston Garth and Kilnwick, *b.* 29th December, 1753, who espoused, 19th February, 1780, Frances, second daughter of Sir Digby Legard, bart. of Ganton, and by her, who *d.* in 1827, had issue,

I. Medley-Sylvester, *b.* 14th May, 1781, *d. v. p.* 30th August, 1801, unmarried, and was buried at Bowness, in Westmoreland.
II. Walter, *b.* 7th July, 1782, and died unm. 6th September, 1801, at Rosetta, in Egypt, where he was then serving as ensign in the 58th regiment.
III. William-John, *b.* 24th June, 1783, and died 16th April, 1784.
IV. CHARLES, heir to his father.
V. Edward, *b.* 13th August, 1793, died an infant.
VI. Oswald, *b.* 22nd October, 1794, who *m.* 16th September, 1830, Ernle-Mary, eldest daughter of the Rev. Mr. Money, of Marcle, in Herefordshire, and has one son and two daughters.
VII. Henry-Estouteville.

I. Emma.

Mr. Grimston died 2nd May, 1821, was buried at Kilnwick, and succeeded by his son, the present CHARLES GRIMSTON, esq. of Grimston Garth and Kilnwick.

*Arms*—Arg. on a fess sa. three mullets of six points or, pierced gu. Mr. Grimston bears forty quarterings: the principal are Goodmanham, Collam, Flinton, De Laland, Portington, Thwaites, Acklom, Danby, Middleton, Conyers, Close, Estouteville, Fitzwilliam, Lacy, Cromwell, Dabignie, Hugh Lupus, &c.

*Crest*—A stag's head, with a ring round the neck, arg.

*Motto*—Faitz proverount.

*Estates*—In the county of York.

*Seats*—Grimston Garth and Kilnwick, near Beverley.

* By Frances his wife, daughter of Ferdinando, Lord Fairfax, and of Mary, daughter of Edmund Sheffield, first earl of Mulgrave, K. G.

# PLUMPTRE, OF FREDVILLE.

**PLUMPTRE, JOHN-PEMBERTON**, esq. of Fredville, in the county of Kent, *b.* 3rd May, 1791; *m.* 2nd April, 1818, Catharine-Matilda, fourth daughter of the late Paul-Cobb Methuen, esq. of Corsham House, Wilts, (see vol. i. p. 394), and has three daughters, viz.

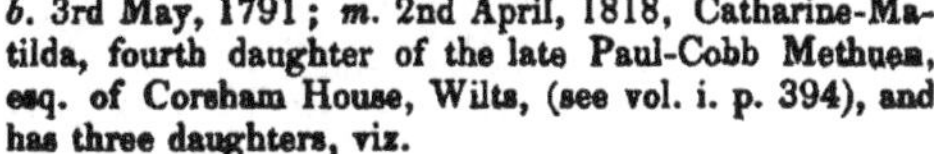

Catharine-Emma.
Cecilia-Matilda.
Matilda-Charlotte-Louisa.

Mr. Plumptre, who is a magistrate and deputy-lieutenant for Kent, represents the Eastern Division of that county in parliament. He succeeded his father 7th November, 1827.

## Lineage.

The family of PLUMPTRE, settled for centuries in the town of Nottingham, represented that borough in parliament from the time of the Plantagenets. In the 15th of EDWARD I. PAUL DE PLUMPTRE, surnamed *the Clerk*, son of William, son of THOMAS DE PLUMPTRE, living tempore *King* JOHN, claimed from Thomas, son of William de Plumptre, a yearly rent of ten merks sterling in Plumptre, with divers portions of lands, but failed in the attempt. He was father of

HENRY DE PLUMPTRE, whose son,

WILLIAM DE PLUMPTRE, living in the 3rd and 18th of EDWARD III. married and had issue,

I. HENRY, his heir.

II. John, M.P. for Nottingham, in the last parliament of RICHARD II. He *m.* a lady named Emma, and dying in 1415, was buried at St. Peter's, Nottingham. "This John," says Thoroton, "had licence 16th RICHARD II. to found a certain hospital or house of God, for two chaplains, whereof one should be master; and for thirteen widows broken with old age and depressed with poverty, in a certain messuage in Nottingham, and to give the said messuage and ten other messuages, and two tofts, with the appurtenances to the said master or warden, and his successors, viz. the one messuage for the habitation of the said chaplains and widows, and the rest for their sustentation, to pray for the wholesome estate of the said John, and Emma his wife, whilst they should live, and for their souls afterwards. In the year 1400, July 12, seeing that God had vouchsafed him to build a certain hospital at the Bridge End of Nottingham, in honour of God, and the annuntiation of his mother, the blessed Virgin, for the sustenance of thirteen poor women, he proposed to ordain a chantry, and willed that it should be at the altar of the annuntiation of the blessed Virgin Mary, in the chapel built beneath the said hospital, and should be of two chaplains perpetually to pray for the state of the king, of him the said John de Plumptre, and Emma, his wife, and of the whole community of Nottingham, who, with the prior of Lenton, after the death of John, the founder, were to present to it, and each of the two chaplains were, for their stipends, to have one hundred shillings yearly, paid in money, out of the said ten tenements and two tofts in Nottingham."

III. John, mentioned in the wills of his two elder brothers.

I. Elisota, also named in her brother's wills.

The eldest son,

HENRY DE PLUMPTRE, of Nottingham, who flourished in the reign of RICHARD II. wedded a lady named Margaret, but of what family is not recorded, and by her, who died in 1421, had a son, JOHN, his heir. Henry de Plumptre died in 1408, (having in that year made his will, in which he gave a legacy to his sister, Elisota, and another to John, his younger brother, beside very many other) and was *s.* by his son,

JOHN DE PLUMPTRE, of Nottingham, who *m.* Helen Strelley, of Woodborough, and died in April, 1471, being buried at St. Peter's, Nottingham, and leaving, with a younger son, Thomas, a priest, his successor,

HENRY DE PLUMPTRE, of Nottingham, who espoused Matilda, daughter and heir of Robert Medocroft, by Joan, his wife, daughter and heir of John Knaresborough, of Kyme, in the county of Lincoln, and had two sons and two daughters; HENRY, his heir; and John, living 2nd HENRY VII. who died *s. p.* Margaret, wife of George Baxter, and Joan, wife of John Burton. To the elder son,

HENRY PLUMPTRE, esq. of Nottingham, "Thomas Poge, of Mislerton, gent. conveyed in 23rd of HENRY VII. one messuage and thirteen cottages, whereof the messuage and nine cottages lay together on the north side of the church-yard of St. Mary, in Nottingham, where *now* (Thoroton, from whom this conveyance is extracted, wrote in 1677) is situated the chief mansion-house of Henry Plumptre, esq." This Henry wedded, 18th HENRY VIII. Elizabeth, daughter of Maurice Orrell, and dying in June, 1508, was interred at St. Nicholas, and succeeded by his son,

JOHN PLUMPTRE, esq. of Nottingham, born 5th January, 1504. This gentleman *m.* first, Katherine, daughter of John Kyme, of Styckford, in Lincolnshire, and by her had two sons, NICHOLAS, his heir, and William, and one daughter, Beatrix, the wife of Adley Clay, esq. He espoused secondly, a lady named Agnes, by whom he had two more sons, and one daughter, namely,

George, who *m.* Cassandra, relict of William Reason, and had two daughters, Anne, *m.* to Roger Smith, and Catharine, the wife of the Rev. Isaac Sharpe, of Thorpe, near Newark.

Leonellus.

Agnes.

John Plumptre died in July, 1552, and was buried in the north choir of St. Mary's, Nottingham. His eldest son and successor,

NICHOLAS PLUMPTRE, esq. of Nottingham, represented that town in parliament, 13th ELIZABETH. He *m.* first, 15th December, 1572, Anne, eldest daughter of John Sharpe, esq. of Wickham, and subsequently of Frisby, in the county of Leicester, by Mary, his wife, daughter of William Saunders, esq. of Welford, Northamptonshire. By her, who died in April, 1580, he had one son and one daughter, namely, HENRY, his heir; and Mary, bapt. 9th May, 1577. Mr. Plumptre married secondly a lady named Eleanor, who survived until 1602. He *d.* in September, 1579, was buried at St. Mary's, Nottingham, and succeeded by his son,

HENRY PLUMPTRE, esq. of Nottingham, bapt. 19th September, 1579, who *m.* 25th August, 1597, Ann, second daughter of Richard Parkyns, esq. of Boney, Notts, (an ancient and influential family,* raised to the Irish peerage in 1795, as Baron Rancliffe), and by her, who died 22nd April, 1639, had four sons and four daughters, viz.

I. NICHOLAS, bapt. 21st November, 1598, his heir.

II. Richard, bapt. 30th October, 1599, died *s. p.* in America.

III. John, slain near Ashby-de-la-Zouch, in 1644, fighting under the royal banner.

IV. HUNTINGDON, successor to his brother.

I. Elizabeth, bapt. 1st January, 1600, and *d.* 23rd January, 1603.

II. Anne, bapt. 4th April, 1603, *m.* to the Rev. Ralph Hansby, vicar of St. Mary's, Nottingham, and of Barton, in Fabis, in the same shire.

III. Catharine, bapt. 28th February, 1607, died unm. 15th April, 1629.

IV. Elizabeth, bapt. 31st May, 1611, *m.* to William West, esq. of Beston, Notts.

This Henry Plumptre, and Nicholas and Huntingdon, his sons, obtained in 1632, a confirmation from Richard, archbishop of York, of a certain chapel or oratory, with a choir adjoining it, in the north side of St. Mary's church, called the chapel of All Saints, "to hear divine service, pray, and bury in." He died 26th July, 1642, was

* The family of Parkyns came originally from Upton and Mattisfield, in the county of Berks. Richard Parkyns, esq. (great grandson of Thomas Parkyns, esq. of Upton), in the commission of the peace and recorder of the towns of Nottingham and Leicester, died in 1603, leaving, by Elizabeth, his wife, daughter of Aden Beresford, esq. of Fenny Bentley, in Derbyshire, and relict of Humphrey Barlow, esq. of Stoke, inter alios, a son and heir, Sir George Parkyns, of Bunney, direct ancestor of the present Lord Rancliffe, and a daughter. ANN, *m.* as in the text, to Henry Plumptre, esq. of Nottingham.

there interred, and succeeded by his eldest son,

NICHOLAS PLUMPTRE, esq. of Nottingham, at whose decease, unmarried, 3rd April, 1644, the estates and representation of the family vested in his brother,

HUNTINGDON PLUMPTRE, M.D. of Nottingham, bapt. 5th February, 1601, a gentleman of great professional reputation, who is recorded in Gervase Holles's Memoirs of the Earls of Clare, as attending the first earl in his last illness, being "accounted the best physician at Nottingham." He was likewise noted for his wit and learning, and when a young master of arts at Cambridge, published "Epigrammatum Opusculum, duobis libellis distinctum, Lond. 1629, 8vo." and subsequently "Homeri Batrachomyomachia Latino carmine redditа, variisque in locis aucta et illustrata." In 1650 he pulled down the hospital erected by his ancestor, rebuilt it as it now appears, and so advanced the rents that the monthly allowance to the poor became double what it was previous. Of the decay and eventual renewal of the Plumptre Hospital, Thoroton gives the following account: "After the dissolution of the monasteries in the 2nd EDWARD VI. Sir Gervase Clifton, Sir John Hersey, Sir Anthony Neville, knights, and William Bolles, esq. commissioners for the survey of colleges, chapels, &c. certified that no poor were then to be found in this hospital, and that the lands were then wholly employed to the benefit of one Sir Piers Bursdale, priest, master thereof. Afterwards both the hospital and chapel became ruinous and demolished, and the very materials embezelled, till after divers patents of the said mastership, Nicholas Plumptre, of Nottingham, 24th ELIZABETH, obtained one, and with the fines he received made some reparations, and brought in some poor, but, after his decease, during the mastership of Richard Parkyns, of Boney, and Sir George, his son, who, it seems, were trusted successively, for Henry Plumptre, son and heir of the said Nicholas, in his nonage, both the hospital and tenements belonging to it grew into great decay, until after Sir George's death, that Nicholas Plumptre, son and heir of Henry, last named, became master by a patent, 5th CHARLES I. and made some repairs and amendments, which yet were not judged sufficient by his brother and heir, Huntingdon Plumptre, doctor of physick, who succeeded him in the mastership, which he obtained in 1645."

Dr. Plumptre m. first, 18th July, 1638, Jane, youngest daughter of Richard Scott, esq. of Byshopdicke Hall, in the county of York, but that lady dying s. p. 5th June, 1641, he espoused secondly, 14th August, 1642, Christian, third daughter of Sir Richard Brooke, of Norton, in Cheshire, by Catherine,* his wife, daughter of Sir Henry Neville, M.P. of Billingbere, in Berks, and had issue,

I. HENRY, his heir.
II. John, b. 20th November, 1649.
III. Richard, who married twice, but died without surviving issue, 24th February, 1699.
I. Amanda, b. 1647, died young.
II. Faustina, m. to the Rev. Drue Cressener, D.D. rector of Soham, in Cambridgeshire.
III. Arabella, d. unm. 15th August, 1693.
IV. Amanda, m. to William Orde, esq. of Beale.

Dr. Plumptre died in June, 1660, and was s. by his eldest son,

HENRY PLUMPTRE, esq. of Nottingham, b. 19th September, 1644, who wedded first, Mary, daughter of Thomas Blayney, esq. of Herefordshire, and by her, who died in 1673, had one daughter, Christina, who died unm. in 1693. He m. secondly, Joyce, daughter of Henry Sacheverell, esq. of Barton, and widow of John Milward, esq. of Snitterton, in Derbyshire, by whom, who died in 1708, he had three sons, viz.

I. JOHN, his heir.
II. Henry, b. 15th February, 1680, m. Dorothy, daughter of — Wigsall, esq. of Derbyshire, and relict of Mr. Stanley, a younger son of the Hampshire family of that name, and by her, who died in 1760, aged seventy-nine, he left at his decease, in November, 1746, one son and one daughter, viz.

Russell, b. 4th January, 1709,

* Descent of Catherine Neville from

EDWARD III. King of England.
|
Edmund, duke of York.
|
Constance, of York, m. Thomas, Earl of Gloucester.
|
Isabella le Despencer, m. Richard Beauchamp, earl of Worcester.
|
Elizabeth Beauchamp, m. Sir Edward Neville.
|
George, Lord Abergavenny.
|
Sir Edward Neville, beheaded.
|
Sir Henry Neville, of Billingbere.
|
Sir Henry Neville, of Billingbere, m. Anne, daughter of Sir Henry Killigrewe.
|
Catharine Neville, who m. Sir Richard Brooke, and was mother of Christian, wife of Dr. Plumptree.

D.M. regius professor of physic in the University of Cambridge, and for several years father of the university. He was of Queen's College, where he proceeded M.B. 1733, M.D. 1738, and was appointed regius professor of physic in 1741. He *m.* and had one daughter, who *m.* — Ward, esq. of Wilbraham, in the county of Cambridge. Dr. Plumptre died in October, 1793.

Amanda, *b.* 29th November, 1711, and *d.* 26th June, 1766.

III. Fitzwilliam, *b.* 24th October, 1686, *m.* Jane, widow of Commodore Owen, and *d.* 3rd December, 1749.

Mr. Plumptre died 29th December, 1693, was interred at St. Mary's,* and succeeded by his son,

JOHN PLUMPTRE, esq. of Nottingham, born 1679, who *m.* Annabella, eldest daughter of Sir Francis Molyneux,† bart. of Teversall, M.P. for Nottinghamshire, by Diana, his wife, sister of Seroop, Lord Viscount How, and by her, who died 27th June, 1745, had issue,

I. Henry, *b.* in 1708, and *d.* in 1718.
II. JOHN, heir.
III. Charles, *b.* 16th July, 1712, D.D. archdeacon of Ely, and rector of St. Mary Woolnoth, London, and of Orpington, Kent. Dr. Plumptre *d.* 14th September, 1779.
IV. Francis, who married on the 7th April, 1755.
V. Polydore, *b.* 1st November, 1714, *m.* 11th December, 1760, Elizabeth Eyre, and *d.* 15th April, 1777.
VI. Septimus, *m.* Miss Catherine Younge.
VII. Robert, D.D. master of Queen's College, Cambridge, 1760, casuistical professor of that university on the resignation of Bishop Law, 1769, vice chancellor 1761, 1777, prebendary of Norwich, rector of Wimple, and vicar of Whadden, in Cambridge. He *d.* 29th October, 1788, having married 7th September, 1756, Anne Newcome.

I. Maria, *m.* 1752, to Dr. Thomas Wilbraham.
II. Annabella.

Mr. Plumptre *d.* 29th September, 1751, and was *s.* by his son,

JOHN PLUMPTRE, esq. of Nottingham, *b.* 10th February, 1710, who represented the town of Nottingham for many years in parliament. He *m.* first, in 1750, Margaretta, daughter of Sir Brook Bridges, bart. of Goodnestone, but had no issue. He wedded secondly, in 1758, Mary, daughter of Philips Glover, esq. of Wispington, in Lincolnshire, cousin to the author of *Leonidas*, by whom (who died in 1782) he left at his decease, a daughter, Mary, who *m.* in 1785, Sir Richard-Carr Glynn, bart. of Gaunts, and a son and successor,

JOHN PLUMPTRE, esq. of Fredville, in Kent, and of Nottingham, who served the office of sheriff for the former in 1798, when Arthur O'Connor and others were tried under a special commission, at Maidstone, for high treason. Mr. Plumptre *m.* in 1788, Charlotte, daughter of the Rev. Jeremy Pemberton, of Trumpington, near Cambridge, and had issue,

JOHN-PEMBERTON, his heir.

* At the west end of Plumptre Chapel is a beautiful monument of marble, with the following elegant epitaph over this gentleman:

Hic infra requescit pars terrena
Henrici Plumptre Armig.
Mortui 29 Decembris 1693 ætatis 49
Qualis vir fuerit scire aves.
Ab antiqua stripe in oppido Nottinghamiæ ortus
Omnigenam eruditionem honestis moribus adjunxit
Eruditionis finem duxit esse regimen vitæ
Hinc factâ sibi morum suprema lege
Benevolentia universali
Pietatis haud fucatæ evasit exemplar singulare
Amicus, civis, maritus, Pater, miserorum Patronus
Qualem jam exoptare licet vix reperire.
Viduam reliquit ejus amantissimam
Jocosam Henrici Sacheverel Armigeri
De Morley in agro Derbiensi filiam natu secundam
Quæ cum tres filios vivo peperisset
Johannem, Henricum et Fitzwilliams,
Optimi Patris monumenta
Hunc etiam lapidem in perpetuam memoriam
Mortuo cum lachrymis poni curavit.
Hic quoq. demum letho
Consortionem redintegravit interruptam.
Illa Jocosa
Verbo omnes complectar Laudes
Conjux illo digna viro
Functa fato 8 die Novembris
1708 ætatis 69.

† The Molyneuxs of Teversall were a branch of the family seated at Sefton, in Lancashire, founded in England, by William de Moulines, one of the Norman nobles in the train of the Conqueror, whose name stands in the eighteenth order upon the Roll of Battel Abbey.

SIR RICHARD MOLYNEUX, of Sefton, one of the heroes of AGINCOURT, married Joan, daughter and heir of Sir Gilbert Haydock, and relict of Sir Peter Legh, of Lyme, and had, with other issue, two sons, SIR RICHARD MOLYNEUX, ancestor of the ennobled house of SEFTON; and SIR THOMAS MOLYNEUX, knight banneret, progenitor of the MOLYNEUX's of Teversal,—a family which maintained for a lengthened series of years the first rank among the landed proprietors of Nottinghamshire, and allied with the most distinguished houses in England.

Charles-Thomas, rector of Claypole, in Lincolnshire, *m.* in 1825, Caroline, second daughter of John Calcraft, esq. of Ancaster, in the same county, and by her (who *d.* 12th June, 1833) has one daughter, Fanny-Sophia.

Henry-Western, rector of Eastwood, Notts, *m.* in April, 1828, Eleanor, only daughter of the late Sir Brook-William Bridges, bart. of Goodnestone Park, Kent, and has one son and three daughters.

Charlotte-Sophia, *d.* unm. 22nd August, 1809.

Emma-Maria, *m.* to Henry Gipps, esq. who afterwards took holy orders.

Mary-Louisa, *m.* to John Smyth, esq. captain royal engineers, and died in Demerara 21st January, 1833.

Frances-Matilda, *m.* to Robert Ramsden, esq. of Carlton Hall, Notts.

Annabella-Helen.

Augusta-Catherine.

Emilia-Septima.

Octavia-Anne.

Mr. Plumptre died 7th November, 1827, and was *s.* by his eldest son, the present John-Pemberton Plumptre, esq. M.P. of Fredville.

*Arms*—Arg. a chev. between two mullets pierced in chief and an annulet in base sa.

*Crest*—A phœnix or, out of flames ppr.

*Motto*—Sufficit meruisse.

*Estates*—Principally in Kent and in the town and county of Nottingham. There is also some property in London.

*Town Residence*—No. 3, Great George Street, Westminster.

*Seat*—Fredville, Kent.

## BADCOCK, OF LINCOLNSHIRE AND BUCKS.

### Representing Lovell, of Harleston.

BADCOCK, LOVELL-BENJAMIN, esq. lieutenant-colonel commanding the 15th, or King's hussars.

Colonel Badcock served, with distinction, in the 14th dragoons, in France, Spain, and Portugal. He succeeded his father 13th April, 1821.

### Lineage.

The Rev. Benjamin Lovell, who appears, from strong presumptive evidence, to have been descended from the baronial house of Tichmersh,* was born about the year 1600, and appointed in 1639, Parson of Preston Bagot, in the county of Warwick. He married and had three sons, viz.

I. Salathiel, named after the puritans of those days.

II. Robert, buried at Coventry.

III. John, buried at Preston Bagot.

(These two were evidently named after the eldest and third sons of William Lord Lovell.)

In 1658, the Rev. Benjamin Lovell buried his wife at Leckhampsted, Bucks, from which rectory he was driven, as a Roundhead, during the troubled times in which he lived:—what subsequently became of him has not been ascertained, but his eldest son,

Sir Salathiel Lovell, who entered Gray's Inn, in 1649, became eminent at the bar, and was made a sergeant at law in 1692, receiving at the same time the honor of knighthood. He was afterwards appointed recorder of London, deputy recorder of Northampton, and eventually in 1708, one of the barons of the Exchequer. Sir Salathiel, who purchased the manor of Harleston, in Northamptonshire, where himself, his

* For an account of the Lovells, Barons Lovell, of Tichmersh, see Burke's *Extinct Peerage*.

wife, and most of his children are buried, wedded about the year 1660, a lady named Mary, and by her, who died 9th December, 1719, had, with other issue,

SAMUEL, his heir.

Henry, who *m.* Mary, daughter and coheir of Thomas Cole, esq. of London, and left, at his decease in 1724, an only daughter,

MARY, who *m.* first, the Hon. Samuel Grimston; and secondly, in 1740, William-Wildman, second Viscount Barrington.

Maria, *m.* to Joseph Townshend, esq. of London, and died in London, 8th August, 1743, aged eighty-three, being at her own request buried at Harleston. By her will she bequeaths the reversion of £2000, together with all her diamonds, pearls, plate, &c. to her "dear niece, Mary Badcock, the daughter of my nephew, Captain Samuel Lovell, and the wife of my nephew, Richard Lovell Badcock, esq. of Twickenham.

Penelope, bapt. in September, 1667, *m.* to the Rev. Michael Stanhope, D.D. canon of Windsor, and died 8th July, 1738, leaving, with other issue, a son, ARTHUR CHARLES STANHOPE, esq. father of Philip Stanhope, who succeeding to the honors of his family in 1773, became fifth EARL of CHESTERFIELD.

Jane, bapt. 5th June, 1687, who *m.* about the year 1713, Richard Badcock, of London, merchant, and by him, who died 12th August, 1722, left a son,

RICHARD LOVELL BADCOCK, esq. of Twickenham, of whom presently.

Sir Salathiel lived to an advanced age, and so long survived his memory, that he was called the *Obliviscor* of London. He died 3rd May, 1713, aged eighty-one, and was *s.* by his son,

SAMUEL LOVELL, esq. a Welsh judge, bapt. 18th September, 1665, who *m.* in 1692, Miss Sergeant, and by her, who died in London, April, 1736, had one son and one daughter, namely,

SAMUEL, his heir.

Rachel-Jane, *m.* in 1732, to Richard Edgeworth, esq. of Edgeworthstown, in the county of Longford, and *d.* in 1764, leaving issue.

Mr. Lovell was *s.* at his decease by his only son,

SAMUEL LOVELL, esq. of Kensington, *b.* in 1690, a captain in the Guards, who died 24th April, 1751, leaving an only daughter and heiress,

MARY LOVELL, who wedded in 1742, her cousin, Richard Lovell Badcock, esq. of Twickenham, in Middlesex, and of Maplethorpe Hall, in the county of Lincoln, son of Richard Badcock, of London, by Mary, his wife, daughter of Sir Salathiel Lovel. Of this marriage there were,

LOVELL BADCOCK, the heir.

THOMAS-STANHOPE BADCOCK, successor to his brother.

Mary Badcock, *m.* to the Rev. Richard Gardner.

Mr. Badcock died at the Hotwells, Bristol, 7th September, 1749, was buried in the cathedral there, and succeeded by his elder son,

LOVELL BADCOCK, esq. of Little Missenden Abbey, in the county of Bucks, and of Maplethorpe Hall, in Lincolnshire, *b.* in 1744, who was lieutenant-colonel of the Buckinghamshire militia, and a magistrate and deputy-lieutenant for that county. He likewise served the office of sheriff. He died unm. in 1797, aged fifty-three, and was buried in the church of Little Missenden. His estates devolved on his brother,

THOMAS STANHOPE BADCOCK, esq. of Little Missenden Abbey, and Maplethorpe Hall, a magistrate and deputy-lieutenant for the county of Buckingham, who was high-sheriff thereof in 1808. He *m.* at Tewkesbury, 17th February, 1782, Anne, daughter of William Buckle, esq. of the Mythe House, and Chasely, in Gloucestershire, by Anne, his wife, daughter of George Turberville, esq. and had issue,

I. LOVELL-BENJAMIN, his heir.

II. William-Stanhope, capt. R.N. who served under Lord Nelson, at Trafalgar, in 1805, and was present at the capture of Washington in 1814. He *m.* 2nd January, 1822, Selina, youngest daughter of the late Sir Henry Harpur-Crewe, bart. of Calke Abbey, and sister of the present baronet, by whom he has issue,

Lovell-Stanhope-Richard, *b.* at Terret House, Bucks, 4th December, 1826.

Selina-Frances.

Georgiana-Jane.

Matilda-Sophia.

I. Anne, *m.* 21st September, 1809, to Major-General Sir Jasper Nicolls, K.C.B. and has one son, Francis-Hastings-Gustavus Nicolls, and eight daughters.

II. Sophia, *m.* 9th June, 1814, to the Rev. James Duke Coleridge, eldest son of Colonel Coleridge, of Heaths Court, Ottery St. Mary's, Devon, and has two daughters, Sophia Coleridge, and Frances Anne Lovell Coleridge.

Mr. Badcock died 13th April, 1821, was buried in the Abbey Church, Bath, and succeeded by his elder son, the present Lieutenant-Colonel LOVELL BENJAMIN BADCOCK.

*Arms*—Barry nebuly of six or, and gules.

*Crest*—A talbot passant arg.

*Motto*—Tempus omnia monstrat.

*Estates*—In Lincolnshire. Little Messenden Abbey, the family seat and property in Bucks, has been sold to Captain Arnold. Maplethorp Hall, in Lincolnshire, has also passed from the family, having been purchased by Colonel Sibthorpe.

## WILSON PATTEN, OF BANK HALL.

PATTEN-WILSON, JOHN, esq. of Bank Hall, in the county of Lancaster, *b.* 26th April, 1802; *m.* in April, 1828, his cousin, Anna-Maria, daughter and co-heiress of the late Peter Patten-Bold, esq. of Bold, in the same shire, and has two daughters, viz.

ANNA-MARIA.
ELLINOR.

This gentleman, who succeeded his father in 1827, is a deputy-lieutenant for Lancashire, and major in the militia. He formerly represented that whole county in parliament, and now sits for the Northern Division.

### Lineage.

The family of PATTEN claims an ancestry coeval with the Conquest, but was not settled in Lancashire until the reign of HENRY VIII.

RICHARD PATTEN, living in 1119, son and heir of Richard Patten, or Patine, of Patten House, near Chelmsford, in the county of Essex, *m.* a daughter of the ancient Derbyshire family of Eyre, and had a son and successor,

RICHARD PATTEN, Lord of Dagenham Court and Patten House, both in the county of Essex, who espoused Mary, daughter and co-heir of Ralph Dagenham of Dagenham Court, and had three sons, Richard, Robert, and John, of whom the eldest,

RICHARD PATTEN, living in the 5th HENRY III, was father of

JOHN PATTEN, who *m.* a Derbyshire lady, named Revyle, and had, with a daughter, Agnes, the wife of John Segar, a son and successor,

JOHN PATTEN, who wedded — Poole, of the county of Derby, and had two sons, JOHN, his heir, and William of Wheldryk, in Yorkshire, who *m.* Emma Everingham, and had a son, Thomas, of Wheldryk, living in 1429, who left two daughters and co-heirs, named Agnes and Idonea. John Patten's elder son and successor,

JOHN PATTEN, of Dagenham Court, in Essex, and of Waynflete, in Lincolnshire, flourished in the reign of EDWARD III. and was alive in 1376. He espoused the daughter and heiress of Sir Oswald Westingcroft, of Westingcroft, in Lancashire, and had a son,

NICHOLAS PATTEN, of Waynflete, in the county of Lincoln, who had three sons, namely,

I. JOHN, of Waynflete, who left an illegitimate daughter, Joan, wife of — Valence, of Kent.
II. NICHOLAS, Lord of Dagenham, who left a daughter, Margaret, *m.* to — Bostock, of Cheshire, and a son,
    ROBERT, of Dagenham, living *temp.* HENRY IV. who married and had daughters only. Juliana, one of these co-heirs, marrying Richard Churchstyle, of Essex, conveyed to him the manor of Dagenham.
III. RICHARD.

The third son,

RICHARD PATTEN, *alias* WAYNFLETE, of Waynflete, sometime in the reigns of the fifth or sixth HENRIES, wedded Margery, daughter of Sir William Brereton, knt. of Brereton, in Cheshire, (who *d.* 4th HENRY VI., by Anylla, his wife, daughter of Hugh Venables), and had issue,

I. WILLIAM PATTEN, *alias* WAYNFLETE, the illustrious founder of Magdalen College, Oxford, who was born at Waynflete, (whence, as was the custom of those times, he derived his surname,) but the exact period of his birth has never yet been ascertained. He was educated at Winchester school, and studied afterwards at Oxford, but in what college is uncertain. The historian of Winchester is inclined to prefer New College, which is most consistent with the progress of education at Wykeham's school. Wood acknowledges that although his name does not occur among the fellows of New College, nor among those of Merton, where Holinshed places him, unless he was a chaplain or postmaster, yet "the general vogue is for the college of William of Wykeham." Wherever he studied, his proficiency in the literature of the times, and in philosophy and divinity, in which last he took the degree of bachelor, is said to have been great, and the fame he acquired as schoolmaster, at Winchester, with the classical library he formed, is a proof that he surpassed in such learning as was then attainable.

Of his preferments in the church we have no account that can be relied upon. Wood says he was rector of Wraxall in 1433, which is barely possible, and that he was rector of Chedsey in 1469, which is highly improbable, for he had then been twenty years Bishop of Winchester. It is, however, more clearly ascertained that, about 1429, he was appointed head master of Winchester school. In 1438 he was master of St. Mary Magdalen Hospital, near Winchester, which is supposed to have suggested to him the name and patroness of his foundation at Oxford. In 1440, when HENRY VI. visited Winchester, for the purpose of inspecting the discipline, constitution, and progress of Wykeham's school, on the model of which he had begun to found one at Eton, he procured the consent of Waynflete to remove thither with thirty-five of his scholars and five fellows, whose education Waynflete superintended until 1442, when he was appointed provost of that celebrated seminary. On the demise of Cardinal Beaufort, in 1447, he was advanced to the see of Winchester, which he held for the long space of thirty-nine years, during which he amply justified the recommendation of the king, being distinguished for "piety, learning, and prudence." His acknowledged talents and political sagacity procured him the unreserved confidence of his royal master, who appears to have treated him with condescending familiarity, employed him in affairs of critical importance, and received throughout the whole of his turbulent reign abundant proofs of his invariable loyalty and attachment. In October, 1456, he was constituted LORD HIGH CHANCELLOR in the room of Bourchier, Archbishop of Canterbury, and held the seals of office nearly four years, resigning in the month of July, 1460, about which time he accompanied the king to Northampton, and was with him a few days before the fatal battle near that place, in which the Lancastrians were defeated. Waynflete's attachment to HENRY's cause had been uniform and decided, yet his high character appears to have protected him. EDWARD IV. treated him not only with respect, but with some degree of magnanimity, as he twice issued a special pardon in his favour, and condescended to visit his newly founded college at Oxford. The evening of the bishop's life was passed free from political strife and danger, and he lived to witness the quiet union of the rival roses, in the nuptials of Henry of Richmond and Elizabeth of York. This learned prelate, celebrated by historians for piety, temper, and humanity, died 11th August, 1486, and was interred, with great funeral pomp, in Winchester cathedral, in a magnificent sepulchral chapel, which is kept in the finest preservation by the society of Magdalen College. (See *Chalmers*, *Chandler*, &c. &c.)

II. John Patten, *alias* Waynflete, dean of Chichester, there buried.

III. RICHARD PATTEN, founder of the Lancastrian family before us.

The third son of Richard Patten, and brother of Bishop Waynflete,

RICHARD PATTEN, of Boslow, in the county of Derby, living in the reign of HENRY VI. *m.* and had two sons and one daughter, viz.

I. **Richard**, of London, who *m.* Grace, daughter of John Baskerville, by the daughter and heiress of — Godard, of Herefordshire, and dying in 1536, left one son and four daughters, viz.

1. **William**, sometime lord of the manor of Stoke Newington, *m.* Anne, daughter and co-heiress of Richard Johnson, of Boston, in Lincolnshire, and had issue,

Mercury, living 9th October, 1603, who was Bluemantle pursuivant in the college of arms from 1527 to 1611.

Richard.

Thomas.

Gratian, of St. Andrews, Holborn, *d.* in October, 1603, leaving by his wife, Elizabeth Collis, who married secondly, Mr. Trussel, of Winchester, a son, William.

Elizabeth, *m.* to Sir Thomas Cony, knight, of Basing Thorpe, in the county of Lincoln.

Pallas.

Anne.

1. Joan, *m.* first to William Streete, of Islington, living in 1536, and secondly, to Thomas Percy, of Stanwell, Middlesex.
2. Lettice, *m.* to Richard Staverton, of Bray, in Berks.
3. Mary, *m.* to Christopher Marton, of Ashton.
4. Alice, *m.* first to Thomas Searle, of Essex, living in 1536, and secondly, to Armigel Wade, of Hampstead.

II. Humphrey, of whom presently.

I. Helen, *m.* to John Robynson, named in the will of her brother, Richard, which bears date 29th April, 1536.

The younger son,

Humphrey Patten, who became seated at Warrington, in the county of Lancaster, *temp.* Henry VIII., wedded Jane, daughter of Thomas Rixtone, gent. of Great Sankey, in the same shire, and was *s.* at his decease (being buried at Warrington) by his son,

Thomas Patten, of Warrington, who espoused, in 1560, Julian, daughter of John Marshall, gent. of the same place, and had, with five daughters, Ellen, Alice, Elizabeth, Dorcas, and Margaret, two sons, Thomas, his heir, and John, *b.* in 1565, who died and was buried at Lancaster. The elder son,

Thomas Patten, of Patten Lane, Warrington, *b.* in 1561, *m.* Ellen, daughter of George Diggles, and by her, who was interred at Warrington, had issue,

I. Thomas, his heir.

II. John, *b.* in 1598, who *m.* first, Margaret, daughter of Richard Mather, and had a daughter, Ellen, and secondly, Anne, daughter of Nicholas Croft, of Sutton, in Lancashire, by whom he had a son, Thomas, who wedded Ellen, daughter of John Middleton, and had three sons. John Patten *d.* in 1676.

III. Anthony, of the Isle of Man, *b.* in 1601, and *d.* in 1641, leaving a son, Cæsar.

IV. William, of Preston, *b.* 4th September, 1604, alderman and register of the Court of Chancery, at Lancaster, who *m.* first, Margery, dau. of Thomas Banyster, of Preston, and by her had three daughters, Ellen, *m.* to John Anderson, citizen of London, Jennet, *m.* to Thomas Cooper, of Preston, and Elizabeth, *m.* to John Ryley, of the same town. Mr. Alderman Patten wedded secondly, Mary, daughter of James Archer, of Preston, and dying in 1660, left by her several children, of whom all *d.* unmarried excepting three, that follow:

1. William, of Preston, baptized 10th May, 1646, who *m.* a daughter of — Bellingham, of Bellingham, in Northumberland, and had three sons and four daughters.
2. Thomas, of Preston, lord of Thornley, barrister-at-law, and M.P. for Preston in 1688, who *d.* in 1697, leaving by his wife, the daughter and heiress of — Doughty, esq. of Coln Hall, in Lancashire, an only child,

Elizabeth, who *m.* Sir Thomas Stanley, bart. of Bickerstaff, and was mother of Sir Edward Stanley, bart. afterwards eleventh Earl of Derby.

3. Henry, of Elverton, Hants, in holy orders, *m.* and had issue,

Thomas Patten *d.* in 1639, was buried at Warrington, and *s.* by his eldest son,

Thomas Patten, esq. of Patten Lane, *b.* in 1595, who wedded first, Alice, daughter of Thomas Taylor, esq. of Preston-on-the-Hill, in the county of Chester, and by her had an only child, Thomas, who appears to have died unmarried. He espoused secondly, Susan, daughter and heir of Robert Drinkwater, esq. and by her, who *d.* in 1688, had (with other issue, all of whom *d. s. p.*)

I. Thomas, his heir.

II. William, of Warrington, merchant, *b.* in 1640, *m.* in 1668, Rachel, daughter of the Rev. Hugh Barrow, A.M.

vicar of Lancaster, and *d.* in 1698, leaving issue to survive youth,

1. Thomas, *b.* in 1662, who *m.* Sarah, dau. of Thomas Shaw, gent. of Manchester, and dying in 1733, left issue,
   - William, of London, *b.* 9th June, 1700, *m.* Mary, daughter of Edward Farnworth, esq. of Runshaw, and had one son, Thomas, a Roman Catholic clergyman, with two daughters, Margaret and Elizabeth.
   - Robert, of Warrington, *b.* in 1707, who *m.* in 1734, Bridget, daughter of Thomas Patten, esq. of Patten Lane, and *d.* in 1772, leaving an only surviving child,
     - Robert Patten, esq. who wedded, in 1765, Hannah, daughter of George Leigh, esq. of Ouhtrington, sheriff of Cheshire in 1749, and *d.* in 1779, leaving one son, Thomas-Leigh, born in 1766, who *d. s. p.* and two daughters, Margaret, the wife of — Bower, esq. and Sarah, the wife of Owen Jones, esq. of Liverpool.
   - Thomas, D.D. rector of Childrey, in Berkshire, *b.* in 1714, *m.* in 1765, Elizabeth, dau. of Peter Brooke, esq. of Mere, high sheriff of Cheshire in 1728, by Frances his wife, only daughter and heiress of Francis Hollinshead, esq. of Wheelock, in the palatinate. Dr. Patten, the respected author of several religious works, died 28th February, 1790.
   - Sarah, *b.* in 1691, *m.* to Thomas Newton, esq. of Manchester.
   - Rachel, *d.* in 1755, unm.
   - Mary, *m.* to John Nichols, of Liverpool, merchant.
   - Lydia, *m.* to Walter Noble, esq. of Chorley Hall, Staffordshire, and *d.* in 1752.
   - Dorothy, *d.* unm.
   - Elizabeth, *d.* unmarried, in 1772.
2. Hugh, of Liverpool, *b.* in 1675, *m.* Sarah Tarleton, widow of — Dudley, esq. and *d.* in 1736.

1. Mary, } *d.* unm.
2. Rachel, }
3. Susannah, *b.* in 1682, *m.* to John Murray, esq. of the Isle of Man, and was mother of John Murray, esq. ambassador to Constantinople in 1768.
4. Dorcas, *m.* to the Rev. John Worsley, A.M. minister of Trinity Chapel, Warrington, and *d.* in 1753, aged sixty-nine.

III. Peter, A.M. Fellow of New College, Oxford, *b.* in 1644, *d.* in 1673.

IV. John, *b.* in 1647.

V. Robert, *b.* in 1648, *m.* Dorcas, dau. of the Rev. Dr. Byfield, and *d.* in 1720.

I. Susan, *m.* to John Barrow, esq. of Sankey, in Lancashire.

II. Ellen, *m.* to John Cottam, esq. of Preston.

Thomas Patten *d.* in 1663, and was *s.* by his eldest son,

Thomas Patten, esq. of Patten Lane, *b.* in 1638, who wedded, 4th December, 1660, Mary, daughter of John Leigh, esq. of Ouhtrington, in Cheshire, son of John Leigh, esq. of the same place, by Alice his wife, daughter of William Massey, esq. of Massey Green, and by her, who *d.* 19th April, 1720, had issue,

I. Thomas, his heir.

II. John, *b.* in 1664, *d.* in 1688.

III. William, of London, *b.* in 1668, *m.* in 1692, Miss Elizabeth Jackson, and *d.* in 1740, leaving an only daughter and heiress,
   - Mary, who *m.* her cousin, the Rev. Thomas Wilson, D.D. prebendary of Westminster.

IV. George, *b.* in 1672, *m.* Miss Sutton, of Gropenhall, Cheshire, and *d.* in 1729, without surviving issue.

I. Elizabeth, *b.* in 1666, *m.* to John Golbourne, esq. of Warrington.

II. Mary, who *m.* in 1698, the Right Rev. Thomas Wilson, D. D. bishop of Sodor and Man,* and had one son,

* Thomas Wilson, the pious and venerable bishop of Sodor and Man, was born at Burton, in Cheshire, *anno* 1663, and was fifth son of Nathaniel Wilson, of Burton, by Alice his wife, sister of Dr. Sherlock. His education was completed at Trinity College, Dublin, on leaving which, in 1686, he was licensed to the curacy of New Church, in Winwick parish, of which his uncle, Dr. Sherlock, was rector. To this circumstance he was indebted for his introduction to the Stanley family, from whom, in 1697, he received the bishopric of Sodor and Man. The annual receipts of his new preferment did not exceed £300. in money, out of which small stipend and the produce of his demesnes he contrived to maintain his house, to relieve distressed mariners, and feed and clothe the poor of the island. His life was, in fact, one uniform display of the most genuine and active benevolence, considering him-

The Rev. THOMAS WILSON, D.D. prebendary of Westminster, chaplain and sub-almoner to *King* GEORGE II., *b.* 24th August, 1703, married at Whitehall chapel, 4th February, 1733, his cousin-german, Mary, only dau. and heiress of William Patten, esq. of London, but having no issue, he devised the Wilson estates to his maternal family, the PATTENS, with the injunction that the inheritor should assume the additional surname and arms of Wilson. He died at Alfred House, Bath, 15th April, 1784, aged eighty.

Mr. Patten *d.* in 1684, was buried at Warrington, and *s.* by his son,

THOMAS PATTEN, esq. of Patten Lane, baptized 2nd August, 1662, who *m.* 20th July, 1686, Margaret, eldest daughter of Jonathan Blackburne, esq. of Orford, in the county of Lancaster, and *d.* in 1726, leaving

I. THOMAS, his heir.

II. Jonathan, of Manchester, *b.* 13th April, 1695, who *m.* first, 3rd July, 1716, Catharine, daughter of Randal Feilden, esq. of Blackburne, (see vol. ii. p. 445) and had by her, who *d.* in 1731, with two daughters, both of whom *d.* unmarried, a son and heir,

Jonathan, of Manchester, born in 1734, *m.* in 1762, Anne, daughter of Robert Feilden, esq. and *d.* in 1792, leaving two sons and a daughter, viz. Jonathan, Thomas, and Elizabeth.

He wedded secondly, in 1732, Jane, daughter of John Sydall, esq. and relict of John Green, esq. of Holcome, in Lancashire, by whom, who *d.* in 1743, he had three daughters, Jane and Anne, who *d.* young, and Lettice, wife of Joseph Rose, of London, merchant. Mr. Patten married thirdly, in 1746, Sarah, daughter of John Cheshire, of Manchester, merchant.

I. Bridget, *m.* in 1734, to Robert Patten, esq. of Warrington.

The elder son,

THOMAS PATTEN, esq. lord of Winmarleigh, in the county of Lancaster, a deputy lieutenant of that shire, *b.* in 1690, erected, from a design of the architect Gibbs, the mansion of Bank Hall, near Warrington. He *m.* 16th June, 1728, Lettice, second dau. and co-heir of the Rev. James Peake, M.A. and by her, who *d.* in 1735, left at his decease, 21st February, 1772, a daughter, Frances, *b.* in 1730, *m.* in 1752, to Sir Richard Brooke, bart. and a son and successor,

THOMAS PATTEN, esq. of Bank Hall, a magistrate and deputy lieutenant for the county of Lancaster, and lieutenant-colonel of the royal Lancashire militia, who served the office of high sheriff for that shire in 1773, and for Cheshire in 1775. He *m.* 17th January, 1757, Dorothea, second dau. of Peter Bold, esq. of Bold, M.P. for Lan-

---

self as the steward, not the proprietor, of the revenues of the bishopric, he devoted his income to what he esteemed its proper use. The poor who could spin or weave found the best market at Bishop's Court, where they bartered the produce of their labour for corn. Tailors and shoemakers were kept in the house constantly employed, to make into garments or shoes the cloth or leather which his corn had purchased; and the aged and infirm were supplied according to their several wants. At the same time he kept an open, hospitable table, covered with the produce of his own demesnes, and to which all sects and parties were alike welcome. To the duties of his sacred function he applied himself with the utmost zeal, and endeavoured by his exhortations and example to animate the clergy of the island to a regular and faithful discharge of their pastoral office. So great indeed was his perseverance, and so successful his endeavours, that Lord Chancellor King used to declare that, "if the ancient discipline of the church were elsewhere lost, it might still be found in all its purity in the Isle of Man." In 1707, the degree of D.D. was conferred upon him by the universities of Oxford and Cambridge; and in the same year he printed the church catechism in Manks and English, for the use of the schools which he had established in various parts of his diocese, and which he superintended with the greatest care. About the year 1722, the orthodoxy of his spirit seems to have involved him in altercations and difficulties. Mrs. Horne, the wife of the governor of the island, had defamed Mrs. Puller and Sir Robert Pool, and in consequence being contumacious, and refusing to ask pardon of the persons injured, was interdicted by the bishop from the holy communion. But his archdeacon, Mr. Horribin, who was chaplain to Captain Horne, received the lady, and incurred suspension in consequence at the hands of his lordship. The governor conceiving this to be a stretch of power beyond the law fined the bishop in the sum of £50. and his two vicars-general in that of £20. each; and on their refusing to discharge those arbitrary penalties, committed them all to Castle Rushin, a damp and gloomy prison, where Dr. Wilson was treated with the utmost rigour. The bishop appealed to the lords justices, when the proceedings of the governor were declared extrajudicial and irregular, and the fines were ordered to be restored. His lordship survived until his ninety-third year, when he expired on the 7th March, 1755, universally esteemed and lamented. His attachment to his flock had been so sincere, that no temptation (he had been offered the valuable see of Exeter) could seduce him from the services of his little diocese.

His works, consisting of religious tracts and sermons, were collected by his son, and published in 1780.

cashire, and had six daughters, Anna-Maria, Lettice, Dorothea, Frances, Mary, and Everilda, and four sons, viz.

I. Thomas, who *d.* young.
II. PETER, his heir.
III. THOMAS, *s.* to his brother.
IV. Richard, *d.* young, in 1774.

Col. Patten was *s.* at his decease, 19th March, 1806, aged eighty-six, by his son,

PETER PATTEN, esq. of Bank Hall, M.P. for Newton from 1797 to 1806, and for Malmesbury from 1813 to 1818, colonel of the royal Lancashire militia, &c. who assumed, upon inheriting the Bold estates, at the decease of his aunt, Anna-Maria Bold, of Bold, the additional surname and arms of BOLD. He *m.* Mary, youngest daughter of the Rev. John Parker, of Astle, in Cheshire, and of Brightmet, in the county of Lancaster, by whom he had four daughters, viz.

I. MARY, who *s.* her father at Bold Hall, and married Prince Sapieha, a Polish nobleman, but *d. s. p.* in 1824, when the estates passed to her next sister,
II DOROTHEA, inheritrix of Bold Hall, *m.* 23rd May, 1820, Henry Hoghton, esq. (only son of Sir Henry Philip Hoghton, bart. of Hoghton Tower) who has assumed the surname of BOLD, and has issue.
III. FRANCES.
IV. ANNA-MARIA, *m.* to her cousin, JOHN WILSON PATTEN, esq. of Bank Hall, M.P.

Col. Patten Bold, *d.* 17th October, 1819,* aged fifty-five, and was *s.* in the representation of the family by his brother,

THOMAS WILSON-PATTEN, esq. M.P. of Bank Hall, lieutenant-colonel of the 5th royal Lancashire militia, *b.* 22nd February, 1770, who had assumed the additional surname of WILSON, at the request of the Bishop of Sodor and Man, and by the testamentary injunction of his lordship's son, from whom the Patten family inherited the Cheshire, and a portion of their Lancashire estates. Col. Wilson-Patten wedded, in 1800, Elizabeth, eldest daughter of Nathan Hyde, esq. of Ardwick, and left at his decease, in 1826, a daughter, Elizabeth, *m.* to Sir John Buller Yarde Buller, bart. of Lupton House, Devonshire, and a son his successor, the present JOHN WILSON-PATTEN, esq. of Bank Hall, M.P.

* In the chapel at Bold there is a monument by Chantry, erected to PETER PATTEN-BOLD, esq. with this inscription:—

"In memory of Peter Patten-Bold, esq. colonel of the 1st regiment of royal Lancashire militia, and during twenty-one years a member of the British parliament; animated by a steady loyalty, and consistent love of freedom, his public life was distinguished by an impartial adherence to the dictates of his conscience and to the principles of the British constitution."

He died 17th October, 1819, aged fifty-five, leaving a widow and four daughters.

*Arms of Bold*—Arg. a griffin segreant sa.

*Crest*—Out of a ducal coronet gu. a demi-griffin issuant sa. with wings expanded or, beaked and taloned gu.

*Arms*—Quarterly, first and fourth, fusilly erm. and sa. a canton gu. for PATTEN; second and third, sa. a wolf rampt. or, in chief three estoiles of the second, for WILSON.

*Crests*—First, a griffin's head erased, for PATTEN; second, a demi-wolf rampt. for WILSON.

*Mottoes*—For PATTEN, Nullâ pallescere culpâ. For WILSON, Virtus ad sidera tollit.

*Estates*—In Lancashire, Cheshire, and Staffordshire.

*Seats*—Bank Hall, near Warrington, and Light Oaks, near Cheadle.

### Family of Bold.

The BOLDS were seated, it is affirmed, before the Conquest at Bold, in the county of Lancaster; and in the reign of HENRY III. we find in *Testa de Nevil* that MATTHEW DE BOLDE, the grandson of WILLIAM DE BOLDE, of BOLDE, was employed on an inquisition to make a return of the "Nomina villarum, serjeantes and knights fees," in the hundred of West Derby. They have ever since maintained the highest place among the great landed proprietors of the north of England, have constantly received the honour of knighthood, have represented their native shire in parliament, and have allied with its most distinguished families.

SIR RICHARD BOLD, knt. of Bold, living in the time of RICHARD II. (great-great grandson of the said Matthew) had three sons, JOHN, his heir; BALDWIN, who became seated at UPTON, in Cheshire; and John, whose great grand-daughter, Agnes, married Hugh Massey, son of Hugh Massey, of Tatton. From Sir Richard's eldest son,

JOHN BOLD, of Bold, who had a grant from HENRY IV. of free warren, in Prescot, under the forest of Symondswood, lineally descended, (his great-great grandson)

SIR RICHARD BOLD, knt. of Bold, *temp.* HENRY VIII. who *m.* Margaret, daughter of Sir Thomas Butler, knt. of Bewsey, and had issue,

I. RICHARD, his heir.
II. Francis, of Cranshaw, who married

Catherine Barnes, sister of the Bishop of Durham.

III. John, who *m.* Anne, daughter of Sir Thomas Laughton, of Walton, and had a son, Henry, whose daughter, Elizabeth, married to — Mussel, of London. John Bold wedded secondly, the dau. of Richard Atherton, of North Moels, and had by her a son, John, father of Anne, wife of Sir Alexander Holland, of Sutton.

I. Margaret, *m.* to Thomas Ireland, of the Hutt.

II. Elizabeth, *m.* to Henry Byrom, of Byrom.

III. Anne, *m.* to Richard Butler, of Rawcliffe.

IV. Dorothy, *m.* to Sir John Holcroft, of Holcroft.

V. Maud, *m.* to Sir Richard Sherburne, of Stonyhurst.

The eldest son,

RICHARD BOLD, esq. of Bold, *m.* first, Elizabeth, daughter of Sir Thomas Gerard, of Bryn, and had one son, Richard, whose line failed, and a daughter, Anne, *m.* to Francis Tunstall, esq. of Thurland. Richard Bold wedded secondly, Margaret, dau. of William Wooful, and by her was father of

WILLIAM BOLD, esq. whose son, by Prudence his wife, daughter of William Brooke, of Norton,

RICHARD BOLD, esq. of Bold, living in 1613, espoused Ann, daughter of Sir Peter Leigh, knt. of Lyme, and had issue. He *d.* in 1635, and was direct ancestor* of

* Of the intermediate line, RICHARD BOLD, esq. *m.* Elizabeth, daughter of Thomas Norton, esq. of Barkisland, and died M.P. for Lancashire in 1704. His father was Peter Bold, esq. of Bold.

PETER BOLD, esq. of Bold Hall, M.P. for Lancashire in 1736, 1750, and 1754, who *m.* Anna-Maria, daughter of Godfrey Wentworth, esq. of Woolley, (see page 93) and had six daughters, viz.

ANNA-MARIA, his sole heiress.

DOROTHEA, *m.* to Thomas Patten, esq. of Bank Hall, and was mother of PETER PATTEN, esq. who succeeded his aunt at BOLD.

FRANCES, *m.* 13th September, 1759, to Fleetwood Hesketh, esq. of Rossall, and was grandmother of the present PETER HESKETH-FLEETWOOD, esq. of Rossall, M.P. for Preston.

MARY, *m.* to Thomas Hunt, esq. of Mollington.

GOVERILDA.

ELENOR.

He *d.* 12th September, 1762, aged fifty-nine, and was succeeded by his eldest daughter,

ANNA-MARIA BOLD, of Bold, at whose decease, unmarried, 25th November, 1813, aged eighty-one, the estates of the Bold family passed to her nephew, PETER PATTEN, esq. as already stated.

*** Among the Bradshaw papers, at Marple, is a letter, dated December, 1649, addressed to Peter Bold, esq. of Bold. It is from Henry Bradshawe, the elder brother of the president, congratulating the Commonwealth on the acquisition of Mr. Bold for a friend, and Mr. Bold on the comfort and honour which he and his family would reap thereby, though the daily trouble thereof might be more than his tender years might admit of.

## D'AETH, OF KNOWLTON COURT.

D'AETH-HUGHES, GEORGE-WILLIAM, esq. of Knowlton Court, in Kent, a captain in the royal navy, *m.* 20th July, 1816, Harriet, daughter of the late Sir Edward Knatchbull, bart. of Mersham Hatch, and has issue,

I. NARBOROUGH.
II. Edward-Henry.
III. George-Wyndham.
IV. Charles.

I. Harriet.
II. Frances.
III. Elizabeth.

This gentleman, whose patronymic is HUGHES, assumed by sign manual, 30th May, 1808, the additional surname and arms of D'AETH, in consequence of inheriting the estates of his grand-uncle, Sir Narborough D'Aeth, bart.

## Lineage.

This family, which derives its surname from Aeth, in Flanders, is of ancient standing in the county of Kent.

WILLIAM D'AETH, of Dartford, espoused *temp.* EDWARD VI. Anne, daughter and heir of — Vaughan, esq. of Erith, and by her had nine children, as appears recorded on his tombstone still remaining in Dartford church. His eldest son,

THOMAS D'AETH, living in 1615, married Joan, daughter of William Head, and had a son and successor,

THOMAS D'AETH, esq. who wedded Mary, daughter of Mr. Serjeant Barton, and had, with two elder sons, Adrian and Abel, who both died without issue,

THOMAS D'AETH, esq. an eminent merchant of the city of London. This gentleman wedded Elhanna, daughter of Sir John Rolt, knt. of Milton Earnest, in the county of Bedford, and left at his decease, an only surviving son,

SIR THOMAS D'AETH, created a BARONET, 16th July, 1716, who married first, Elizabeth, daughter of Admiral Sir John Narborough, knt. one of the commissioners of the navy to *King* CHARLES II. and sole heiress of her brother, Sir John Narborough, of Knowlton Court, bart. Sir John Narborough, and his only brother, James Narborough, esq. were unfortunately cast away, with their father-in-law, Sir Cloudesley Shovel, on the rocks of Scilly, 22nd October, 1707. By the heiress of Knowlton, Sir Thomas D'Aeth had

I. NARBOROUGH, his heir.
II. Thomas.
I. Elizabeth, who *m.* in 1740, the Hon. and Rev. Godfrey Dawney, one of the prebendaries of Canterbury, son of Henry, second Viscount Downe, and *d. s. p.*
II. Elhanna, *m.* to Captain Fitzgerald, of the French service, and *d. s. p.*
III. Sophia, *m.* in 1749, William Champneys, esq. of Vintners, in Kent, but died without issue, in 1772. Mr. Champneys left by a former wife an only surviving daughter and heiress, Harriet Champneys, *m.* to John Byrte, or Burt, esq. of Boley Hill.
IV. Bethia, *m.* first, to Herbert Palmer, esq. of Wingham, in Kent, and secondly, to John Cosnan, esq. She *d. s. p.*
V. HARRIET, under age in 1735, *m.* Josiah Hardy, esq. consul at Cadiz, and had five daughters, namely,
 1. HARRIET HARDY, who became the second wife of William Hughes, esq. of Betshanger, in Kent, and by him, who died in April, 1786, had one son and three daughters, viz.
  GEORGE-WILLIAM HUGHES, who succeeded to Knowlton on the demise of Sir Narborough D'Aeth, in 1808, and is the present proprietor.
  Harriet Hughes, *m.* to George Leonard Austen, esq. of Sevenoaks, in Kent.
  Louisa Hughes.
  Charlotte Hughes, died unmarried.
 2. Elizabeth-Sophia Hardy, *m.* to Edward Markland, esq. of Leeds.
 3. Priscella Hardy, *m.* to John Godby, esq. of Greenwich.
 4. Louisa Hardy, *m.* to John Cooke, esq. captain of the Bellerophon, killed at Trafalgar.
 5. Charlotte Hardy, *m.* to Lieutenant Colonel George John Hamilton, R.A.

Sir Thomas D'Aeth married secondly, Jane, daughter of Walter Williams, esq. of Dingeston, in the county of Monmouth, and had by her one son,

Francis, in holy orders, rector of Knowlton, who died unm. in 1784.

Sir Thomas was chosen member of parliament for Canterbury in 1708, and for Sandwich in 1714. He died 4th January, 1745, and was succeeded by his son,

SIR NARBOROUGH D'AETH, second bart. of Knowlton Court, who *m.* Anne, daughter and heir of John Clarke, esq. of Blake Hall, in Essex, and dying in 1773 (his will, dated 15th February, 1771, was proved 24th Jasuary, 1774), was succeeded by his only child,

SIR NARBOROUGH D'AETH, third bart. of Knowlton Court, who died unm. in April, 1808, was buried at Knowlton, and succeeded in his estates by (the grandson of his aunt, HARRIET) his cousin, the present GEORGE WILLIAM HUGHES-D'AETH, esq. of Knowlton Court.

### Family of Hughes.

JOHN HUGHES, esq. of Newbery, in Berkshire, son of Thomas Hughes, esq. of the same place, by Elizabeth Hodges, his wife, died about the year 1710, leaving a daughter, Hannah, m. to Thomas Cowslad, esq. and a son,

THOMAS HUGHES, M.D. of Oxford, who espoused in 1743, Mary, only surviving child and heiress of William Smith, esq. of Eltham, one of the six clerks in Chancery, by Sarah, his wife, daughter of Sir John Shaw, bart. and had one son and one daughter, viz.

WILLIAM, his heir.

Mary, who m. Lieut.-colonel Timms, and was mother of John Timms, esq. who assumed the surname and arms of ELWES, (see vol. ii. p. 466).

Dr. Hughes, whose will bears date in 1760, was s. by his son,

WILLIAM HUGHES, esq. of Betshanger, in Kent, who wedded first, Mary, eldest daughter of John Hallett, esq. son of James Hallett, esq. of Dunmow Priory, in Essex, by Mary, his wife, daughter of Sir Ambrose Crowley, knt. of Greenwich, and grandson of Sir James Hallett, knt. and Mary, his wife, dau. of Thomas Duncombe, esq. of Broughton, in Bucks. By this lady, who died in 1780, and was buried at Little Dunmow, Mr. Hughes had four sons and three daughters, viz.

I. William, } who both died in infancy.
II. Thomas, }

III. CHARLES, in holy orders, rector of Gestingthorpe, in Essex, and of Wixoe, in Suffolk, and vicar of Patrixburn, in Kent, who assumed by sign manual in May, 1823, the additional surname and arms of HALLETT. He m. in May, 1806, Frances-Anne, daughter of the late Sir Edward Knatchbull, bart. of Mersham Hatch, and has issue,

1. JAMES, b. in 1807.
2. Edward Knatchbull, b. in 1808.
3. Charles, b. in 1809.
4. William, b. in 1812.
5. Henry, b. in 1814.
6. John-Henry, b. in 1818.
7. George-Wyndham, b. in 1819.
8. Abraham-Vernon, b. in 1821.
9. Frederick, b. in 1825.
1. Frances.
2. Mary.
3. Anna-Maria.

IV. Henry, of Albany Chambers, London.

I. Mary, m. to William Wells, esq. of Redleafe, in Kent, and dying in June, 1818, was buried at Penshurst.
II. Elizabeth.
III. Anne.

Mr. Hughes married secondly, Harriet, eldest daughter and co-heir of Josiah Hardy, esq. by Harriet, his wife, daughter of Sir THOMAS D'AETH, bart. and by her had three daughters, as already stated, with one son, the present GEORGE WILLIAM HUGHES-D'AETH, esq. of Knowlton Court.

*Arms*—Quarterly; first and fourth, sa. a griffin passant or, between three crescents arg.; second and third, sa. a chev. between three fleur delys arg.

*Crest*—A griffin's head erased or, in the mouth a trefoil slipped vert.

*Estates*—In Kent.

*Seat*—Knowlton Court, in that county.

## DYMOCK, OF PENLEY HALL AND ELLESMERE.

DYMOCK, EDWARD, esq. of Penley Hall, in the county of Flint, and of Ellesmere, in Shropshire, b. 16th December, 1774; m. in 1804, Mary, daughter of John Jones, esq. of Coed-y-Glynn, in the county of Denbigh, and has issue,

EDWARD-HUMPHREY, in holy orders, b. in 1809.
John, b. in 1816.
Robert-Myddelton, b. in 1817.
Thomas-Biddulph, b. in 1823.
Mary-Anne, m. in 1825, to Robert-Darwin Vaughton, esq. of Whitchurch, in the county of Salop.

This gentleman, a magistrate and deputy-lieutenant for the county of Flint, and formerly major in the West Shropshire local militia, succeeded his father in 1784.

Here we have another branch of the numerous descendants of TUDUR TREVOR, (see family of VAUGHAN, of Burlton Hall, p. 239), to whom so many of the principal families of North Wales, and the marches thereof, trace their origin.

RYS SAIS, so called because he could speak the Saxon or English language, possessed great estates in North Wales and Shropshire at the period of the Norman conquest, which he divided among his sons in the year 1070. His eldest son, TUDUR, was father of BLEDDYN, the father of OWEN, who had several children: one of these, THOMAS, was father of MEILIR, who resided at Bryn, in Halghton, in the parish of Hanmer, and was ancestor of the PENNANTS, of Downing, Bichton, &c. Another son of OWEN AP BLEDDYN was OWEN VYCHAN, father of CADWYAN, the father of RIRID, whose son,

MADOC AP RIRID, espoused Margaret, daughter of Ithel Anwyl, a chieftain of Têgengl, (as most of Flintshire was at that period called by the Welsh), and had a son and successor,

DAVID AP MADOC, who, according to the mode of address then used in Wales, was called "DAI MADOC;" for David ap Madoc would thus be spoken, *Dai* being the diminutive of David. He *m.* Margaret, daughter and heir of Tudur ap Ririd, of Penley, by whom he acquired that estate, and had a son and heir,

DAVID AP DAI MADOC, whose name, by mutation of address, was David *Dai Madoc*, that is David, the son of Dai (David) Madoc, and from the mode of expression then customary *David Dai Madoc* became DAVID DAMOC, or DYMOCK, for it is written both ways in ancient manuscripts. Henceforward Damoc or Dymock became the adopted surname of the family. David Dai Madoc, who lived at Willington, in the county of Flint, wedded Margaret, daughter of David Voel, of Hanmer, (son of David, one of the sons of Sir John Hopton, or Upton, of Bettisfield, in Hanmer, lineal male ancestor of the Hanmers, of Hanmer, now represented by Sir John Hanmer, bart.), and had a son,

IEUAN DYMOCK, of Penley and Willington, in the county of Flint, father, by Lucy his wife, daughter of Richard ap Madoc ap Llewelyn, of Halghton, in the same shire, of

THOMAS DYMOCK, *hên*,* esq. of Penley and Willington. This gentleman *m.* Margaret, daughter and heir of Griffith ap Morgan Goch, of Willington Hall, by whom he acquired that estate, and had issue. He *d.* 6th December, 1487, and was *s.* by his son,

THOMAS DYMOCK, esq. of Willington Hall and Penley, who *m.* Margaret, daughter of Sir Randle Brereton, knt. of Malpas, in the county of Chester, and dying ten days after his father, 16th December, 1487, was *s.* by his eldest son,

RANDLE DYMOCK, esq. of Willington and Penley, who wedded Elizabeth, daughter of Griffith Hanmer, esq. of Fens, and had two sons, viz.

> HUMPHREY, *m.* to Elen, daughter of William Davies, esq. and had one son, Randle, who *d. s. p.* and four daughters.
>
> EDWARD.

The second son,

EDWARD DYMOCK, esq. married four times, and by three of his wives had issue. By the first, Catherine, daughter of Richard Conway, esq. he had two sons, Humphrey and Randle, who both died *s. p.* and five daughters. By the second, Magdalen, dau. of Roger Puleston, esq. as appears by a deed dated in 1622, he had another son, WILLIAM, who succeeded to the estates. The third wife, Catherine, daughter of William Mostyn, esq. died without issue; and the fourth, Margaret, daughter of Thomas Kynaston, esq. left one son, Thomas, and a daughter, Anne. He was *s.* by his elder surviving son,

WILLIAM DYMOCK, esq. of Willington Hall and Penley, living in the reign of ELIZABETH, who *m.* Margaret, daughter of William Hanmer, esq. of Fens, and had two sons and four daughters, viz.

> I. HUMPHREY, of Willington, who *m.* Anne, daughter of Sir Thomas Hanmer, knt. and by her (who died in

---

* The term *hên* in Welsh is applied to persons who attain a very great age.

1667) left at his decease in 1650, four sons and five daughters, viz.

1. THOMAS, 2. William, 3. Charles, 4. Humphrey, } The eldest son, Thomas Dymock, esq. of Willington, inherited. He and his brother Humphrey were the last survivors, and after their decease the Willington estate was sold to Sir John Trevor, of Brynkinalt, Speaker of the House of Commons, who died in 1696. The four brothers died *s. p.*

1. Mary.
2. Margaret.
3. Dorothy.
4. Catherine.
5. Ursula.

II. EDWARD, of whom presently.

I. Ellen.
II. Mary.
III. Magdalen.
IV. Elizabeth.

The younger son,

EDWARD DYMOCK, esq. of Penley, wedded Mary, daughter of John Davenport, esq. and was father of

EDWARD DYMOCK, esq. of Penley, who espoused Mary, daughter of David Jones, esq. of Oakenholt, and had three sons and one daughter, viz.

I. EDWARD, his heir.
II. John, who *d. s. p.*
III. William, who married and had a son,
John, of Whitchurch, in Salop, father, by Elizabeth his wife, of
EDWARD DYMOCK, esq. of whom hereafter as successor to his great uncle, in the Penley estate.

I. Elizabeth, *m.* to Edward Morrall, esq. of Plas Yolyn. (See vol. ii. page 596).

Mr. Dymock died in 1705, was buried at Hanmer, and *s.* by his eldest son,

EDWARD DYMOCK, esq. of Penley, who died unmarried, and left the Penley estate to his grand-nephew,

EDWARD DYMOCK, esq. *b.* in 1730, who wedded Elizabeth, daughter of Humphrey Brown, esq. and had three sons, (EDWARD, John, and William), by the eldest of whom,

EDWARD DYMOCK, esq. of Penley, *b.* in 1752, he was succeeded in 1760. This gentleman espoused, 8th January, 1774, Mary, daughter of Edward Edwards, esq. of Pentre Heylin, in the county of Salop, and had issue,

EDWARD, his heir.
John, William, Thomas, } who all died *s. p.*
Mary, *d.* unm.
Christian, Elizabeth, Frances, Anne, } now resident at Whitchurch, in Salop.

Mr. Dymock *d.* in 1784, and was *s.* by his eldest son, the present EDWARD DYMOCK, esq. of Penley Hall.

*Arms*—Per bend sinister ermine and ermines, a lion rampant langued and armed gu.

*Crest*—An arm in armour, ppr. holding in the hand a spear sa.

*Motto*—Pro rege et lege dimico.

*Estate*—Penley, in that part of the parish of Ellesmere which is situated in Flintshire.

*Seat*—Penley Hall.

## WENTWORTH, OF WOOLLEY.

WENTWORTH, GODFREY, esq. of Woolley Park, in the county of York, *b.* 14th September, 1797; *m.* 20th June, 1822, Anne, fourth daughter of Walter Fawkes, esq. of Farnley Hall, in the same shire, and has issue,

GODFREY-HAWKSWORTH.
George-Edward.

Anne.
Rosamond-Frances.
Catharine-Mary.

Mr. Wentworth, who succeeded his father in 1826, is a magistrate and deputy-lieutenant for Yorkshire.

## Lineage.

This is a distinguished and powerful branch of the ancient stock of Wentworth Woodhouse, in the county of York, a family which has been rooted there from the earliest period to which the genealogist can usually ascend in his investigations. Of the orthography of the lands, whence originated the name, Domesday Book, and all the old charters have it *Winteworth*, and such is still the pronunciation of the common people, who do not easily fall into new modes of speech. As to its derivation, Mr. Hunter, "in his History of Doncaster," makes the following remarks: "The latter half of the name *(worth)*, is one of the most frequent local terminals, and appears to denote some degree of cultivation. The former half affords room for conjecture. It has been suggested that it may be the word *gwint*, preserved in the Breton language, which is a dialect of the Celtic, where it denotes *elevation*. This sense would undoubtedly apply well to Wentworth, which stands high, as does also another place of the same name, in the isle of Ely, relatively to the fens around it. Celtic etymologies are, however, to be admitted with great caution in investigating the names of places cultivated or populated; and perhaps the scribe of Domesday, who, in one of the five instances in which the word occurs, has written it thus, *Wintrerworde*, may have presented us with an ancient and expiring orthography from whence we may conclude that the name of Wentworth is to be classed with Wintrerton, Winterburn, Winteredge, and other places which have obtained those names from their high exposed or cold situations."

While the lands of Wentworth Woodhouse continued to be the seat of the chiefs, and descended from sire to son, in an unbroken series, till the succession of male heirs failed with William, the second earl of Strafford, the junior scions of the family founded, in several instances, houses of rank and influence, the WENTWORTHS of WOOLLEY, of North and South Elmsal,* of Bretton,† of Wentworth Castle,‡ of Nettlested,§ &c.

THOMAS WENTWORTH, of Wentworth Woodhouse, son of William Wentworth, by Isabel, his wife, daughter of Sir Richard Fitzwilliam, of Aldwark, succeeded to the estates and representation of the family, in the 23rd of HENRY VII. He wedded Beatrix, daughter of Sir Richard Woodruffe, knt. of Woolley, whose house was then in the plenitude of its prosperity, and had issue,

I. WILLIAM, of Wentworth Woodhouse, who enjoyed the estates only a few months, dying 4th July, 1549. He *m.* Catherine, daughter of Ralph Beeston, of Beeston, and was *s.* by his son,

THOMAS WENTWORTH, esq. of Wentworth Woodhouse, high

---

* The WENTWORTHS of North ELMSAL acquired that estate temp. EDWARD III. in marriage with Alice, daughter and heiress of John Bissett, and continued there for several centuries, until the year 1741, when their male line expired with Sir Butler Cavendish Wentworth, bart. the estates devolving on that gentleman's half sister, CATHERINE WENTWORTH, who wedded HUGH CHOLMLEY, esq. of Whitby, in the county of York, M.P. for Hedon, and sheriff of that shire in 1724. The WENTWORTHS of SOUTH ELMSAL sprung from a younger son of Thomas Wentworth, of North Elmsal, are also now extinct.

† The WENTWORTHS of BRETTON, deriving from Richard Wentworth, of Everton, in the county of Nottingham, third son of John Wentworth, of Elmsal, by Agnes, his wife, sister and co-heir of Sir William Dronsfield, of Bretton, became extinct in the male line upon the demise of Sir Thomas Wentworth Blackett, bart. 9th July, 1792. The estates of Bretton, &c. are now enjoyed by the BEAUMONT family, (see vol. ii. p. 523).

‡ The WENTWORTHS of WENTWORTH CASTLE were founded by Sir William Wentworth, of Ashby, in Lincolnshire, slain at Marston Moor, who was a younger son of Sir William Wentworth, bart. of Wentworth Woodhouse, and brother to Thomas, first earl of Strafford. They became extinct in the male line in 1799. The estates are now possessed by Frederic Thomas William Vernon Wentworth, esq. of Wentworth Castle, (see vol. ii. p. 81).

§ For an account of the WENTWORTHS of NETTLESTED, earls of Cleveland, and barons Wentworth, now represented by Anna Isabella, Dowager Lady Byron, and the Hon. Nathaniel Curzon, between whom the barony of Wentworth is in abeyance, refer to BURKE'S *Extinct and Dormant Peerage*.

sheriff for Yorkshire in the 24th ELIZABETH. This gentleman augmented in a great degree his inheritance by his marriage with Margaret, daughter of William Gascoigne, esq. of Gawthorpe, long one of the principal families of the West Riding, and whose pedigree boasted of the name of chief justice Gascoigne. By this lady, Mr. Wentworth left at his decease, in 1587, one son and four daughters, namely,

1. WILLIAM (Sir), of Wentworth Woodhouse, created a BARONET in 1611, father of Thomas Wentworth, the ill-fated EARL OF STRAFFORD, and grandfather of the LADY ANNE WENTWORTH, who wedded Edward Watson, second LORD ROCKINGHAM. The great grand-daughter and eventual heiress of this marriage,
   - LADY ANNE WENTWORTH, espoused in 1744, William, third EARL FITZWILLIAM, and was grandmother of CHARLES-WILLIAM, present EARL FITZWILLIAM. See BURKE's *Peerage*.

1. Elizabeth, *m.* in 1577, to Thomas Danby, esq. of Farnley.
2. Barbara, died unmarried.
3. Margaret, *m.* first, to Michael, son and heir of John Lord D'Arcy; and secondly, to Jasper Blitheman, esq. of New Latres.
4. Catherine, *m.* in 1596, to the unfortunate Thomas Gargrave,* esq. of Nostel.

II. MICHAEL, of whom presently.
III. Thomas, who *m.* Grace, daughter of John Gascoigne, esq. of Lasingcroft, in Yorkshire, and had, with three daughters, Mary, Grace, and Elizabeth, an only son, Thomas.
IV. Bryan.

I. Elizabeth, *m.* to Ralph Denam.
II. Isabella, *m.* to Nicholas Wombwell, esq. of Greesbrook, in Yorkshire.
III. Beatrix, *m.* to Thomas Worrall, esq. of Loversall, in Yorkshire.

Thomas Wentworth *d.* 5th December, 1548, and was buried at Wentworth. His second son,

MICHAEL WENTWORTH, esq. of Mendam Priory, in the county of Suffolk, living in the 39th of HENRY VIII. was cofferer to the king and comptroller to the queen. He *m.* Isabel, daughter and heir of Percival Whitley, esq. of Whitley, in Yorkshire, and had by her, who died in 1560, three sons and three daughters. He died 13th October, 1558, and in the inquisition taken the 30th of the following April, it is found that his son and heir,

THOMAS WENTWORTH, esq. of Mendam Priory, in Suffolk, and of Whitley, in the county of York, was then aged seventeen years and two months. This gentleman espoused Susan, dau. of Christopher Hopton, esq. of Armley Hall, in the latter shire, and had (with two daughters, Beatrix, *m.* to John Green, esq. of Dean Grange, in Horsforth, and Mary, the wife of Robert Con-

* Few names are of more frequent occurrence in the affairs of the West Riding of Yorkshire, than that of GARGRAVE, derived, it is presumed, from a village so called, in Craven. The first recorded ancestor of the family of SIR JOHN GARGRAVE, who was tutor to Richard, duke of York, and a warrior as well as scholar, served under HENRY V. as master of the ordnance in France. He was direct progenitor of Sir Thomas Gargrave, speaker of the house of Commons, who purchasing in the 9th ELIZABETH, NOSTEL, with other estates in the county of York, established his family there. His son and heir,

SIR COTTON GARGRAVE, knt. of Nostel, wedded first, Bridget, daughter of Sir William Fairfax, of Steeton, and by her had to survive himself, an only son, THOMAS, of Nostel, who married, as in the text, Catherine, daughter of Thomas Wentworth, and was executed for murder at York. Sir Cotton espoused secondly, Agnes, daughter of Thomas Waterton, esq. of Walton, and had (with other issue, of whom one daughter, Elizabeth, *m.* William Fenwick, esq. of Stanton, and another, Frances, *m.* Stephen Tempest, esq. of Broughton), a son,

SIR RICHARD GARGRAVE, knt. of Kinsley and Nostel, sheriff of Yorkshire, 3rd JAMES I. who, by a course of extravagant and wanton expenditure, was forced to sell his estates, and became so reduced in circumstances, that Dodsworth, writing in 1634, speaking of him says, "that he now lyeth in the Temple for Sanctuary, having consumed his whole estate, to the value of £3500 per annum, at the least, and hath not a penny to maintain himself, but what the purchasers of some part of his lands, in reversion after his mother's death, allow him, in hope he will survive his mother, who hath not consented to the sale."

Beyond this (says Mr. Hunter) I have not been able to trace him. The memory of his extravagance and his vices yet lingers about Kinsley. The rustic moralist still points his counsel with the story of Sir Richard Gargrave, who could once ride on his own land from Wakefield to Doncaster, and had horses innumerable at his command, but was at last reduced to travel with the pack-horses to London, and was found dead in an old ostelry with his head upon a pack-saddle.

ingby, esq. of Herefordshire) a son and successor,

MICHAEL WENTWORTH, esq. who purchased WOOLLEY, and other lands in the county of York, *anno* 1599, from Francis Woodruffe, esq. He wedded Frances, daughter and sole heir of George Downes, esq. of Paunton, in Herefordshire, and had issue,

- I. Thomas, *b.* in 1595, who predeceased him, unmarried.
- II. MICHAEL, heir to his father.
- III. GEORGE (Sir), successor to his brother.
- IV. Matthew, capt. of a troop of horse, died *s. p.* will dated 1646, proved 1651.
- V. JOHN, successor to his brother, Sir George.
- I. Dorothy, *m.* to John Wood, esq. of Copmanthorpe.
- II. Elizabeth, *m.* first, to Thomas Oldfield, esq. of Wadlands; and secondly, to Richard Beaumont, esq. of Mirfield.
- III. Alice, *d.* unm.
- IV. Mary, *m.* to Richard Langley, esq. of Millington, in Yorkshire.
- V. Rosamond, *m.* first, to Bertram Reveley, esq. of Throple; and secondly, to Robert Widdrington, esq. of Carlington, both in Northumberland.
- VI. Margaret, *m.* 11th February, 1628, to William Wombwell, esq. of Wombwell.

Michael Wentworth, who enjoyed his purchase of Woolley more than forty years, died just at the commencement of the civil wars, and by the inquisition taken 9th September, 1642, it was found that he had died seized of the manors of Woolley, Notton, Kirshell, Pool, and Brackenholm, the manor or grange of Owston, alias Wolston, in the county of the city of York, and half the tithe of garbs in Notton and Chevet. He was *s.* by his eldest son,

MICHAEL WENTWORTH, esq. of Woolley, aged forty-five in 1642, who died unm. and was succeeded by his next brother,

SIR GEORGE WENTWORTH, knt. of Woolley, who, on the breaking out of the civil war, zealously followed the example of the whole race of Wentworth, espoused the cause of the king. Amongst other acts of devotion he raised for his majesty a regiment of foot, at his own expense, and as colonel, commanded it himself. He *m.* first, Anne, daughter of Thomas, Lord Fairfax, of Denton, by whom he had two sons, namely,

MICHAEL, *b.* in 1622, who *m.* Catherine, daughter of Sir William St. Quintin, bart. but predeceased his father without issue in 1658. His widow wedded secondly, Sir John Kaye, bart. of Woodsom; thirdly, Henry Sandys, esq. of Down, in Kent; and fourthly, Alexander, earl of Eglintoun.

William, *b.* 1624, and *d.* in 1625.

Sir Godfrey espoused secondly, Everild, second daughter and co-heir of Christopher Maltby, esq. of Maltby, and by her had issue,

George, } both died young.
Christopher, }

Everild, *m.* to John Thornhill, esq. of Fixby.

Frances, *m.* 12th January, 1657, Thomas Grantham, esq.

Anne, *m.* to William Osbaldeston, esq. of Hunmanby.

Sir Godfrey Wentworth died 18th October, 1660, aged sixty, and was *s.* by his brother,

JOHN WENTWORTH, esq. of Woolley, *b.* in 1607, who wedded Elizabeth, daughter of Arthur Aldburgh, esq. of Aldburgh, in Yorkshire, and by her (who died in 1675), left at his decease, 22nd February, 1682, a son and successor,

SIR MICHAEL WENTWORTH, of Woolley, *b.* in 1654, knighted at Windsor, 5th July, 1681, who *m.* 18th November, 1673, Dorothy, daughter of Sir Godfrey Copley, bart. of Sprotborough, by Elizabeth, his second wife, daughter of William Stanhope, esq. of Linley, Notts, and had issue,

- I. WILLIAM, his heir.
- II. John, *d.* unm. 1700, aged twenty-three.
- III. GODFREY, *b.* in 1678, *m.* Anna-Maria, daughter of Giles Clarke, esq. of the Temple, and had, with other issue, who died unmarried,
  - GODFREY, successor to his uncle.
  - Anna-Maria, *m.* first, 21st November, 1726, to the Rev. Edward Sylvester, and secondly, to Peter Bold, esq. of Bold Hall.
- IV. Michael, *d.* unm. in 1724.
- V. Thomas, of Horbury, who *m.* Margaret, daughter of — Webster, and relict first, of Francis Nevile, esq. of Chevet; and secondly, of George Empson, of Gowle, and had an only son,
  - William, of Horbury, who *m.* Catherine, daughter of Sir Lyon Pilkington, bart. and widow of the Rev. Cavendish Nevile, of Chevet, and died without surviving issue, in 1785.
- VI. George, } died young.
- VII. James, }
- VIII. Matthew, of Wakefield, *b.* 13th April, 1689, *m.* in 1721, Anne, daughter of James Sill, of Wakefield, and relict of John Nevile, esq. of Chevet, and died in 1749, leaving issue,

1. Peregrine, of Tolston Lodge, Bramham Moor, registrar of the West Riding, *b.* 1722, *m.* first, Mary, dau. of Beilby Thompson, esq. of Escrick, and secondly, Mary, eldest daughter of Ralph Ashton, esq. of Cuerdale, in Lancashire, widow of the Rev. John Witton, of Lupset Hall, but died *s. p.* in 1809.
2. Michael, of Little Harbour, near Portsmouth, *m.* Miss Wentworth, and *d.* in 1792, leaving issue.

1. Dorothy, *m.* Peter Serle, esq. of Testwood, in Hants, and had issue.

I. Elizabeth, *b.* in 1677, *m.* in 1696, to William Wombwell, esq. of Wombwell.
II. Dorothy.
III. Frances, *m.* in 1716, to Thomas Hinchliffe, esq. of London.
IV. Anne, *m.* first, in 1705, to Sir Lion Pilkington, bart. of Chevet; secondly, to Sir Charles Dalston, bart. of Heath Hall, and thirdly, in 1730, to John Maude, esq. of Alverthorpe Hall, (see vol. ii. p. 86) all in the county of York.
V. Rosamond, died young.
VI. Catherine.
VII. Margaret.

Sir Michael died in 1696, and was *s.* by his eldest son,

William Wentworth, esq. of Woolley, *b.* in 1675, who wedded Catherine, daughter of Charles Turner, esq. of Kirk Leatham, in Yorkshire, but dying *s. p.* at Bath, 3rd June, 1729, was *s.* by his nephew,

Godfrey Wentworth, esq. of Woolley and Hickleton, who represented the city of York in parliament. He *m.* in 1727, his cousin, Dorothy, eldest surviving daughter of Sir Lion Pilkington, bart. and had issue,

I. William, died unm. in 1746.
II. Godfrey, died unm. in 1757.
III. John, died in infancy.

I. Anna-Maria, *b.* 9th June, 1736, *m.* in 1760, Sir George Armytage, bart. of Kirklees, M.P. and dying in 1788, left issue,

George Armytage, who succeeded his father, and is the present baronet of Kirkless.

John Armytage, who *m.* Anne, daughter of John Harvey Thursby, esq. of Abington Abbey, (see vol. i. p. 320).

Godfrey - Wentworth Armytage, successor to his maternal grandfather.

Anna-Maria Armytage, *m.* to William Egerton, esq. of Tatton.

Henrietta Armytage, *m.* first, to James Grady, esq. of Harley-street, and secondly, to Jacob Bosanquet, esq.

Charlotte Armytage, *m.* to the Venerable John Eyre, archdeacon of York.

II. Dorothy, died in infancy.
III. Catherine, *d.* unm. in 1821.

Mr. Wentworth died 18th January, 1789, aged eighty-four, and was *s.* by (the third son of his eldest daughter), his grandson,

Godfrey Wentworth Armytage, esq. *b.* 9th May, 1778, who then became "of Woolley," and assumed the surname and arms of Wentworth. He *m.* in 1794, Amelia, daughter of Walter Ramsden Hawksworth, esq. of Hawksworth Hall, near Otley, who afterwards took the name of Fawkes, and had issue,

I. Godfrey, his heir.
II. John, *b.* in 1789, who *m.* Henrietta, daughter of Jacob Bosanquet, esq.
III. William, *b.* in 1807.

I. Amelia.
II. Anna-Maria. *d.* young.
III. Catherine.
IV. Frances, *m.* to — Clements, esq.
V. Charlotte, *m.* 15th November, 1834, to William Arch Campbell, esq. of Wilton-place, Middlesex.
VI. Dorothea.
VII. Mary-Elizabeth.

Mr. Wentworth represented Tregoney in parliament, was a magistrate and deputy-lieutenant for the West Riding of Yorkshire, and served the office of high-sheriff in 1796. He died in 1826, and was succeeded by his eldest son, the present Godfrey Wentworth, esq. of Woolley.

*Arms*—Sa. a chev. between three leopards' heads or.

*Crest*—A griffin passant.

*Estates*—In the West Riding of the county of York, in the parish of Royston, comprising the separate townships of Woolley, which came into the family in 1559; and of Notton, Staircross, Cold Hiendley, acquired subsequently.

*Seat*—Woolley Park, near Wakefield.

# CURRER, OF CLIFTON HOUSE.

CURRER, *The Rev.* DANSON-RICHARDSON, of Clifton House, in the county of York, *b.* 3rd April, 1784; *m.* 28th November, 1815, Hannah, elder daughter of the late Sir William Foulis, bart. of Ingleby Manor, in Cleveland, and has issue,

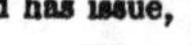

I. WILLIAM.
II. Richard-Roundell.
III. John Richardson.
IV. Henry-George.
V. Charles-Savile.

I. Mary-Anne.
II. Eleanor-Hannah Richardson.

This gentleman, whose patronymic is ROUNDELL, assumed by sign manual, in 1801, upon the demise of his brother, the surname of CURRER only, in pursuance of the testamentary injunction of his maternal grand-uncle. John Currer, esq. of Kildwick Hall. Mr. Currer is a master of arts, of Christchurch, Oxford, a magistrate for the three Ridings of the county of York, as well as for the liberty of St. Peter's, York, a deputy lieutenant for the West and East Ridings, and a commissioner of assessed taxes for the West and North Ridings.

## Lineage.

The CURRERS have been seated at Kildwick, in Yorkshire, for nearly three centuries.

HUGH CURRER, of Kildwick, in Craven, *m.* Anne, daughter of — Knowles, of Riding, and had two sons, William Currer, of Marley, who wedded Isabel, daughter of Christopher Maude, esq. of Holling Hall, (see vol. ii. page 85), and

HENRY CURRER, of Kildwick, who *m.* Ann, daughter of Christopher Wade, of Plumtree Banks, and by her (who espoused. secondly, the Rev. Edward Horrocks), left at his decease, 19th August, 1568, four sons and nine daughters, viz.

I. WILLIAM, who removed to Stainton Cotes, in the parish of Gargrave, and died 22nd June, 20th JAMES I.
II. HUGH, of whom presently.
III. Henry, who resided at Middleton, in the parish of Ilkley.
IV. Christopher, who died young.

I. Margaret, *m.* in 1576, to Hugh Bawdwine.
II. Agnes, *m.* in 1576, to William Bawdwine.
III. Anne, *m.* in 1582, to Rev. Alexander Horrocks.
IV. Isabel, *m.* in 1583, to John Emmot.
V. Jane, *m.* in 1584, to Stephen Dixon.
VI. Lucy, *m.* in 1584, to Miles Gill.
VII. Sybella, *m.* in 1592, to Edmund Hirde.
VIII. Mary, *m.* in 1593, to Edmund Bawdwine.
IX. Agnetta, *m.* in 1580, to Rowland Watson.

The second son,

HUGH CURRER, esq. who purchased the manor of Kildwick, in Craven, wedded Helena, daughter of John Halstead, esq. of Rowley, in Lancashire, and had issue,

I. HENRY, his heir.
II. Hugh, who lived at Steeton, died in 1636, aged forty-eight.
III. Christopher, *b.* in 1590, *d.* in 1611.
IV. William, } twins, *b.* in 1592. The
V. Samuel, } younger died an infant; the elder resided at Kildwick Grange, Craven.

Hugh Currer *d.* in 1617, was buried at Kildwick on 27th February, and succeeded by his son,

HENRY CURRER, esq. of Kildwick, bapt. 4th June, 1587, who *m.* first, Anne, daughter and sole heir of John Harrison, esq. of

Flasby, and had by her four sons and six daughters, viz.

I. HUGH, his heir.

II. Henry, *d.* unm. in London in 1654.

III. John, of Bradley.

IV. William, died young in 1624.

I. Helena, *m.* to Roger Whaley, of Winterburn.

II. Mary, *m.* to Thomas Hammond, of Threshfield Hall.

III. Ann, *m.* to William Watson, of Silsden Moor.

IV. Sarah, } twins, both *d.* young.
V. Susan, }

VI. Martha, *m.* to Edmund Bawdwen, of Stone Gap, in the parish of Kilnwick.

Mr. Currer wedded, secondly, Eleanor, dau. of William Lowther, esq. of Ingleton, and widow of William Newby, of Barwick, but had no issue. He *d.* 1st April, 1653, and was *s.* by his son,

HUGH CURRER, esq. of Kildwick, *b.* in 1608, who *m.* first, Blanch, daughter of Thomas Ferrand, esq. of Carleton, by Blanch his wife, daughter of Edmund Towneley, esq. of Royle, and had one son, Henry, who died an infant. He espoused, secondly, Anne, daughter of Peter Haworth, esq. of Thurcroft, in the county of Lancaster, and widow of Robert Winckley, esq. of Winckley. By this lady, who *d.* in 1656, he had one son and five daughters, viz.

I. HENRY, his heir.

I. Ann, *m.* first, to William Busfield, merchant, of Leeds; and, secondly, to Robert Ferrand, esq. of Harden Grange.

II. Eleanor, *m.* in 1685, to Richard Entwistle, esq. of Foxholes, in Lancashire.

III. Grace, *m.* in 1674, to John Leche, esq. of Carden, in the county of Chester (see vol. ii. p. 367).

IV. Mary, *m.* in 1677, to the Rev. Robert Pickering, rector of Eccleston, son of Robert Pickering, esq. of Thelwall.

V. Elizabeth, *m.* in 1676, to Ellis Meredith, esq. of Pentrybychan, in Denbighshire.

Mr. Currer *d.* in 1690, and was *s.* by his son,

HENRY CURRER, esq. of Kildwick, *b.* 25th July, 1651, who *m.* first, Margaret, daughter of Abraham Fothergill, esq. of London, and by her, who *d.* in 1697, had issue,

I. HAWORTH, his heir.

I. Ann, *m.* Benjamin Ferrand, esq. of St. Ives, and died *s. p.*

II. DOROTHY, *b.* in 1687, who *m.* RICHARD RICHARDSON, M.D. of Bierley, (see family of RICHARDSON), and *d.* in 1763, leaving issue,

1. RICHARD RICHARDSON, esq. of Bierley, lord of the manor of Okenshaw and Cleck Heaton, a magistrate and deputy lieutenant for the West Riding, *b.* in 1708, who married in 1750, Dorothy, only daughter and heir of William Smallshaw, esq. of Bolton in the Moors, by Mary his wife, daughter of John Starkie, esq. of Huntroyde, but died *s. p.* in 1781.

2. William Richardson, M.D. of Ripon, *b.* in 1709, and *d.* unm. in 1783.

3. Henry Richardson, A. M. rector of Thornton, in Craven, *b.* in 1710, *m.* in 1747, Mary, dau. of Benjamin Dawson, esq. of Oldham, merchant, and died in 1778, leaving two sons and two daughters, viz.

Richard Richardson, esq. *b.* 19th January, 1755, a captain in Sir Thomas Egerton's regiment of royal Lancashire volunteers, *d.* unm. at Lisbon 24th May, 1782, whither he had gone for the recovery of his health, and was buried there.

HENRY RICHARDSON, in holy orders, of whom hereafter as successor to his uncle, John, in the CURRER estates.

Dorothy Richardson, of Gargrave.

Mary Richardson, *b.* in 1752, who *m.* in 1775, the Rev. William Roundell, of Gledstone, a magistrate and deputy-lieutenant for the West Riding, and had issue,

RICHARD-HENRY ROUNDELL, esq. now of Gledstone. (For an account of the ROUNDELL family see vol. i. p. 342).

WILLIAM-HARTLEY ROUNDELL, of whom presently as successor to his grand-uncle.

DANSON - RICHARDSON ROUNDELL, in holy orders, successor to his brother William, and PRESENT PROPRIETOR.

Henry-Dawson Roundell, *b.* in 1785, M.A. rector of Fringford, Oxon.

Savile-Richardson Roundell.

Septimus-Warde Roundell.
Eleanor Roundell.
Mary-Anne Roundell.
Dorothea - Richardson Roundell, *m.* to Rev. William J. Palmer, M. A. rector of Mixbury, Oxon.

4. JOHN RICHARDSON, of whom presently as successor to his cousin, SARAH CURRER.
5. Thomas Richardson, *b.* in 1724, *d.* unm. in 1763.
1. Dorothy Richardson, *b.* in 1712, *m.* in 1730, Sir John-Lister Kaye, bart. of Denby Grange, in the county of York, and *d.* in 1772, leaving issue.
2. Margaret Richardson, *d.* unm. in 1764.

III. Elizabeth, *d.* unm. in 1704.
IV. Margaret, *d.* unm. at York.
V. Henrietta-Maria, also *d.* unm.

Henry Currer, of Kildwick, wedded, secondly, Mary, daughter of Edmund Watson, esq. of East Hage, in the county of York, and widow of Thomas Yarborough, esq. of Campsall, but had no issue. He died 19th January, 1723, and lies interred at Kildwick. "He was," says his monumental inscription, "a great proficient in the study of the law; but, allured by the charms of a private life, retired to the place of his birth, where he chose rather to employ the skill he had acquired therein to the benefit of his country, in the dispensation of justice on the bench, than to the improvement of his own fortune, in attendance at the bar. He excelled in all the relations of life, in discharging the several obligations of a loving husband and affectionate father, of a sincere friend and obliging neighbour, tenderly, discreetly, faithfully, and conscientiously." He was *s.* by his only son,

HAWORTH CURRER, esq. of Kildwick, *b.* 26th January, 1690, who *m.* 5th July, 1722, Sarah, fourth daughter of Tobias Harvey, esq. of Womersley, and by her, who died in 1766, had one son and one daughter, HENRY and SARAH. He *d.* 13th April, 1744, and was *s.* by his son,

HENRY CURRER, esq. of Kildwick, *b.* in 1728, who espoused, in 1756, Mary, daughter and co-heir of Richardson Ferrand, esq. of Harden, but *d. s. p.* on the 10th March, in the same year, and was buried at Kildwick, where a monument is erected to his memory. His widow *m.* secondly, Peter Bell, esq. second son of Ralph Bell, esq. of Thirsk. Mr. Currer was succeeded in his estates by his sister,

SARAH CURRER, of Kildwick, *b.* in 1729, who *d.* unm. at Widcombe, near Bath, in 1759, and was interred in the abbey church in that city, where her monument still remains. She was succeeded by (the fourth son of her aunt, Dorothy Currer, by her husband, Richard Richardson, esq. of Bierley), her first cousin,

JOHN RICHARDSON, esq. a magistrate and deputy-lieutenant for the West Riding, who then became "of Kildwick," and assumed the surname and arms of CURRER. He *d.* unmarried, 22nd June, 1784, and was *s.* by his nephew,

THE REV. HENRY RICHARDSON, A.M. *b.* 9th December, 1758, rector of Thornton, in Craven, who assumed a short time before his death, on inheriting the Kildwick estates, the surname and arms of CURRER. He *m.* at Gargrave, in 1783, Margaret-Clive, only daughter of Matthew Wilson, esq. of Eshton, by Frances his wife, daughter of Richard Clive, esq. of Stych, in Shropshire, and by her (who wedded, secondly, her cousin, Matthew Wilson, esq. second son of the Rev. Henry Wilson), had an only daughter and heiress,

FRANCES-MARY.

Mr. Richardson Currer *d.* 10th November, 1784, when the acquired estates of his uncle and predecessor, John Currer, esq. passed under the will of that gentleman to (the son of his the Rev. Mr. Richardson Currer's sister Mary) his nephew,

WILLIAM-HARTLEY ROUNDELL, esq. *b.* in 1780, who assumed in consequence the surname and arms of CURRER. This gentleman died unmarried, 12th February, 1801, and was *s.* by his brother, the Rev. Danson-Richardson Roundell, who, having changed his name for that of CURRER, is the present Rev. DANSON-RICHARDSON CURRER, of Clifton House.

*Arms*—Quarterly, first and fourth, erm. three bars gemelles sa. on a chief az. a lion passant guardant arg. for CURRER; second and third, or, a fesse gu. between three laurel branches ppr. for ROUNDELL.

*Crests*—First, a lion's head erased arg. collared sa. pierced arg. for CURRER; second, a short sword in pale arg. hilt and pommel or, gripe gu.

*Motto*—Merere.

*Estates*—In the parish of Kildwick, Gisburn, and Kirkby Malzeard, in the West Riding, and Pickering, in the North Riding of Yorkshire.

*Seat*—Clifton House, North Riding of Yorkshire.

# LUCY, OF CHARLECOTE.

**LUCY, GEORGE,** esq. of Charlecote, in the county of Warwick, *b.* 8th June, 1789, *m.* 2nd December, 1823, Mary-Elizabeth, daughter of Sir John Williams, bart. of Bodelwydden, in Flintshire, and has issue,

WILLIAM-FULK, *b.* 10th September, 1824.
Henry-Spenser, *b.* 28th November, 1830.
Mary-Emily, *b.* 2nd February, 1826.
Caroline, *b.* 13th January, 1828.

Mr. Lucy succeeded his father on the 12th January, 1823. He was M.P. for the borough of Fowey, Cornwall, from 1820 to 1830, and sheriff of the county of Warwick in 1831.

## Lineage.

THURSTANE DE CHARLECOTE, supposed to have been a younger son of Thurstane de Montfort,* of Beldesert, in the county of Warwick, *temp.* RICHARD I. was father of

SIR WALTER DE CHARLECOTE, upon whom Henry de Montfort conferred the village of Charlecote, and the grant was confirmed by RICHARD I. who added divers immunities and privileges, which were all ratified by *King* JOHN in the fifth year of that monarch's reign (1203). Sir Walter left a son,

SIR WILLIAM DE LUCY, the first of the Charlecotes who bore that surname, and Sir William Dugdale surmises that he did so because his mother *might* have been the heir of some branch of the great baronial family of LUCY, which had derived its designation from a place in Normandy. Of this house was HENRY DE LUCY, governor of Falais, so distinguished during the conflict between *King* STEPHEN and the *Empress* MAUD, who was afterwards, in the time of HENRY II. justiciary of England; and at one period, in the temporary absence of the king beyond sea, lieutenant of the kingdom.

Sir William de Lucy had a confirmation of the lordship of Charlecote from Thurston de Montfort, son and successor of the Thurstane de Montfort above specified. He took up arms with the barons against *King* JOHN, when his lands were all seized by the crown; but returning to his allegiance, he had a full restoration in the first year of the ensuing monarch. In the 20th of HENRY III. Sir William had the custody of the counties of Warwick and Leicester, with the castle of Kenilworth. He married, first, Isabel, daughter of Absalom de Aldermonstone; and secondly, Maud, sister and one of the co-heirs of John Cotele. He founded the monastery of Thelesford, and dying about the 32nd HENRY III. (1247) was succeeded by the son of his second marriage,

SIR WILLIAM LUCY, knt. of Charlecote, who wedded Amicia, daughter and heiress of William de Furches, and heiress likewise of William Fitz-Warine, by whom he had a son and heir,

FOUK DE LUCY, of Charlecote (in the immediate retinue of the celebrated PETER DE MONTFORT), who, after the battle of Lewes, *temp.* HENRY III. was constituted one of the *nine* governors of the kingdom. De Lucy acquired so much reputation by his gallantry in the Baron's war, that being indebted to one Elyas de Blund, a Jew, of London, in a large amount, he obtained a special mandate, dated 49th HENRY III. (1264) and directed to the commissioners in whose hands the estates of the Jews then seized upon were entrusted, to deliver up to him all his bonds, and to cancel the debt. Subsequently, however, the royal cause having attained the ascendancy by the victorious arms of *Prince* EDWARD, De Lucy and his

* For the MONTFORTS see *Burke's Extinct and Dormant Peerage.*

associates were glad to compromise for their estates under the *Dictum de Kenilworth.* "This Fouk," says Dugdale, "was a special lover of good horses, as it would seem, for in the 11th of EDWARD I. he gave forty marks to two Londoners that were merchants of horses, for a black charger, about which time a fat ox was sold for sixteen shillings." He died in the 31st of EDWARD I. (1302) and was *s.* by his son,

SIR WILLIAM LUCY, of Charlecote, a person of celebrity in his generation, and representative in several parliaments for the county of Warwick. He was succeeded by his son,

SIR WILLIAM LUCY, of Charlecote, who received a military summons in the 19th of EDWARD III. to attend the king into France, but being then joined in commission with the sheriff to array one hundred and sixty archers in Warwickshire for the king's service, his attendance was dispensed with, and he was thereby deprived of sharing in the glory of Cressy. He died in three years afterwards (22nd EDWARD III. 1348) and was *s.* by his son,

THOMAS LUCY, of Charlecote, who was *s.* at his decease by his son,

SIR WILLIAM LUCY, of Charlecote, who being a knight was retained in the 5th RICHARD II. (1381) to serve JOHN OF GAUNT, Duke of Lancaster and KING OF CASTILE, for life, with one esquire, in times of war and peace. In the first year of the next king he represented the county of Warwick in parliament. His son and successor,

SIR THOMAS LUCY, of Charlecote, was also in the retinue of JOHN OF GAUNT. In the 7th of HENRY IV. (1405) he was member of parliament for Warwickshire, and the next year sheriff for the counties of Warwick and Leicester. He wedded Alice, daughter, and eventually heiress, of Sir William Hugford, and acquired by that lady a fair inheritance in the counties of Bedford and Salop. He died 28th July, 3rd HENRY V. (1415), leaving by the said Alice (who married, in eight weeks after his decease, Richard Archer, of Tamworth) a son and successor,

WILLIAM LUCY, of Charlecote, who during his minority was in ward to John Boteler, of Warrington. Upon the decease of Elizabeth Lady Clinton, in the 2nd of HENRY VI. (1423) he was found to be her cousin and next heir. In the war of the Roses, William Lucy arrayed himself under the banner of the house of York. He wedded Elizabeth, daughter of Reginald, Lord Grey de Ruthyn, and dying in the 6th EDWARD IV. (1466) was succeeded by his son,

SIR WILLIAM LUCY, of Charlecote, created a knight of the Bath at the coronation of HENRY the Seventh's queen. He espoused, first, Margaret, daughter of John Brecknock, treasurer to *King* HENRY VI.; and secondly, Alice, daughter of William Hanbury. He died in 1492, and was succeeded by his eldest son by his first wife,

EDMUND LUCY, esq. of Charlecote, born in 1464, who appears to have been a soldier of high repute in the reign of HENRY VII. for we find him in command of a division of the royal army at the battle of Stoke, and afterwards retained to serve the king in his French wars, with two men at arms. He was summoned, 10th HENRY VII. (1494), with other persons of rank, to attend at the creation of the king's son, the Duke of York, to be made a knight of the Bath; but it seems he did not appear, for in the April following (1495) 11th HENRY VII. his testament bears date, and in *that* he is styled esquire. He wedded Elizabeth, daughter and heiress of Walter Tramsington, by whom he had no issue; and secondly, Jane, daughter of Richard Ludlow, and was succeeded at his decease (the probate of his testament being 19th May, 1498, 14th HENRY VII.) by his eldest son,

SIR THOMAS LUCY, knt. of Charlecote, one of the servers to *King* HENRY VIII. who wedded Elizabeth, relict of George Catesby, esq. of Ashby-Legers, in the county of Northampton, and daughter of Sir Richard Empson, knt. by whom he had issue,

- WILLIAM, his heir.
- Thomas, upon whom his father settled the manor of Cleybrooke, in Leicestershire.
- Edmund, who inherited the manors of Beckering and Sharpenho.

- Anne, *m.* to Thomas Herbert, esq.
- Radigund, *m.* to — Betts, esq.
- Barbara, *m.* to Richard Tracy, esq. of Stanway, in Gloucestershire.

Sir Thomas Lucy died in 1525, and was *s.* by his eldest son,

WILLIAM LUCY, esq. of Charlecote, who *m.* Anne, daughter of Richard Fermer, esq. of East Neston, in Northamptonshire, and was succeeded, in the 5th of EDWARD VI. 1551, by his eldest son,

SIR THOMAS LUCY, of Charlecote, who, in the 1st of *Queen* ELIZABETH, rebuilt the manor-house with brick, as it now stands. He was knighted a few years afterwards, and he subsequently represented the county of Warwick in parliament. His remarkable prosecution of SHAKSPEARE, for deer-stealing, in Fulbroke-park, has attached, however, more celebrity to his name than any of the honours which he had enjoyed. This prosecution was conducted with much bitterness, in consequence of a lampoon, written by the poet on Sir Thomas, who at length compelled him, about the year 1585-6, to fly from his native place. The great dramatist subsequently avenged himself, by delineating his prosecutor under the character of JUSTICE SLENDER. Sir Thomas Lucy wedded Joice, daughter and heiress of Thomas Acton, esq. of Sutton, in Worcestershire, and had a daughter, Anne, married to Sir Edward Aston, knt. of Tixhall, and dying in 1600, was *s.* by his only son,

SIR THOMAS LUCY, of Charlecote, who wedded, first, Dorothy, daughter of Nicholas Arnold, esq. by whom he had a son, Thomas, who died young: and a daughter, Joyce, the wife of Sir William Cook, knt. of Highnam. Sir Thomas *m.* secondly, Constance, daughter and heir of Sir Richard Kingsmill, of High Clere, Hants, and had by that lady six sons and several daughters, viz.

- I. THOMAS, his heir.
- II. RICHARD, who received the honour of knighthood 8th January, 1617, and was created a BARONET 11th March following. He *m.* first, Elizabeth, daughter and co-heiress of Sir Henry Cock, of Broxburn, in Herts, and relict of the Hon. Robert West, by whom he had (with a daughter, Constantia, *m.* to Henry, Lord Colerain) an only son and successor,
    - SIR KINGSMILL LUCY, second baronet of Facombe, in Hampshire, who *m.* Lady Theophila Berkeley, and left a son and two daughters, viz.
        1. BERKELEY (Sir), third baronet, who wedded Catherine, daughter of Charles Cotton, esq. of Beresford, and left at his decease an only daughter and heiress,
            - MARY, *m.* to the Hon. Charles Compton.

            Sir Berkeley, dying without male issue, the BARONETCY EXPIRED at his decease.
        2. Theophila, married to Sir William Ingoldsby, bart.
        3. Mary, *d.* unm.
- III. George, slain in France.
- IV. WILLIAM, in holy orders, D.D. rector of Burgh-Clere and High-Clere, in Hampshire, *m.* Martha, daughter of William Angell, of London, esq. Dr. Lucy was an eminent divine, and a staunch supporter of the royal cause. Having suffered great persecution, he survived to witness the restoration of the monarchy, and was consecrated bishop of St. David's in 1660, wherein he continued until his decease. "He was a person," says Wood, in the *Athenæ Oxonienses*, "of signal candour and virtues requisite in a clergyman, which in the very worst of times gained him great esteem from the very enemies of his cause and faction." His lordship *d.* 4th October, 1677, and was buried in the collegiate church of Brecknock, in Wales. He was grandfather of WILLIAM LUCY, esq. of Castle Carey, in Somersetshire, and of GEORGE LUCY, esq. of Pembroke.
- V. Robert, died in France, 1615, *s. p.*
- VI. Francis, of the city of Westminster, living 1682, married and had a son,
    - Richard, who *m.* Rebecca, daughter and heiress of Thomas Chapman, esq. of Wormley, and relict of Sir Thomas Playters.

- I. Elizabeth, first wife of Sir Anthony Hungerford, of Down-Ampney, county of Gloucester.
- II. Anne.
- III. Bridget.

Sir Thomas Lucy died in 1605, and lies buried in a chapel on the north side of the church of Charlecote, where a splendid monument has been erected to his memory by Dame Constance, his widow. He was *s.* by his eldest son,

SIR THOMAS LUCY, of Charlecote, member for Warwickshire in six successive parliaments, who espoused Alice, daughter and heiress of Thomas Spencer, esq. of Claverden, in Warwickshire, and had issue,

- SPENCER, ROBERT, RICHARD, } successively of Charlecote.
- Thomas.
- William.
- FOULK (Sir), *m.* Isabella, daughter and sole heiress of John Davenport, esq. of Henbury, in Cheshire, and had with other issue,
    - DAVENPORT, who eventually inherited CHARLECOTE.
    - GEORGE, WILLIAM, } who both became of Charlecote.
    - Fulke, *m.* to Elizabeth Mason, of London, and was father of THOMAS LUCY, who succeeded his uncle, the Rev. William Lucy, D.D. at Charlecote in February, 1723-4, and of GEORGE LUCY, who inherited from his brother.

Lucy, *m.* to the Rev. John Hammond. The grandson of this lady,

The Rev. JOHN HAMMOND, occurs in the sequel as eventual inheritor of CHARLECOTE and the estates of the Lucy family.

Constance, *m.* first, to Sir William Spencer, bart.; and secondly, to Sir Edward Smith.

Margaret, *d.* unm.

Bridget, *m.* to Sir Bryan Broughton.

Alice, *m.* to Sir William Underhill.

Mary, *m.* to Sir Matthew Herbert.

Elizabeth, *m.* to Sir John Walcot.

Sir Thomas Lucy *d.* in December, 1640, and his virtues are set forth in a Latin inscription upon a noble and curious monument at Charlecote. Of Sir Thomas it was said, that "his tables were ever open to the learned, and his gates never fast to the poor." He was *s.* by his eldest son,

SPENCER LUCY, esq. of Charlecote, a colonel in the royal army. This gentleman took the degree of doctor of physic at Oxford in 1643. He married Mary, daughter of Henry Brett, of Down Hatherley, in the county of Gloucester, but dying without issue in 1648, the estates devolved upon his brother,

ROBERT LUCY, esq. of Charlecote, who wedded Margaret, daughter of Thomas Spencer, esq. of Upton, by whom (who *m.* after his decease, Thomas, Lord Arundel, of Wardour) he had an only daughter, BRIDGET, *m.* to William, Viscount Molyneux. He died in 1658, without male issue, and was *s.* by his next brother,

RICHARD LUCY, esq. of Charlecote, who *m.* Elizabeth, daughter of Thomas Urry, esq. of Thorley, in the Isle of Wight, by whom he had Thomas, his son and heir, and Richard, who died young; with a daughter, Constance, the wife of Sir John Burgoyne, bart. of Sutton. He died in 1677, and was succeeded by

THOMAS LUCY, esq. of Charlecote, who wedded Catherine, daughter of Robert Wheatley, esq. of Brecknol, in Bucks, by whom (who *m.* after his decease, George, Duke of Northumberland) he had an only daughter, ELIZABETH, *m.* to Clement Throgmorton, esq. of Haseley. This Thomas *d.* in 1684, leaving no male issue, and was *s.* by (the eldest son of Sir Fulk Lucy, sixth son of the last Sir Thomas Lucy aforesaid and Isabella Davenport) his first cousin,

DAVENPORT LUCY, esq. of Charlecote, at whose decease, unm. in 1690, the estates devolved upon his brother,

GEORGE LUCY, esq. of Charlecote, who wedded, first, Mary, daughter and heiress of John Broun, esq. of Finham, and secondly, Jane, daughter and co-heir of George Broun, esq. of Coundon. He *d. s. p.* in 1721, and was *s.* by his brother,

THE REV. WILLIAM LUCY, D.D. of Charlecote, who *m.* Frances, eldest daughter of Henry Balguy, esq. of Hope, in the county of Derby, but had no issue. He was rector of Hampton Lucy, and a prebendary of the cathedral church of Wells, and dying in February, 1723-4, was *s.* by (the elder son of his brother Fulke, by his wife, Elizabeth Mason, of London,) his nephew,

THOMAS LUCY, esq. of Charlecote, who died unmarried 26th December, 1744, and was *s.* by his only brother,

GEORGE LUCY, esq. of Charlecote, who was sheriff of the county of Warwick in 1769. This gentleman died unmarried 1st December, 1786, and was *s.* by his kinsman,

THE REV. JOHN HAMMOND, being described, in his predecessor's will, as the next person in remainder, to whom stood limited after his decease, without issue male, the family estates, and grandson of the Rev. John Hammond and Alice Lucy, second daughter of Sir Fulke Lucy and Isabella Davenport. He assumed the surname and arms of Lucy only, by sign manual, dated 9th February, 1787. He *m.* in May, 1788, Maria, daughter of John Lane, esq. of Bentley Hall, in the county of Stafford, and *d.* 12th January, 1823, leaving issue two sons, namely, John (the younger), in holy orders, *b.* 19th August, 1790, and his heir, the present GEORGE LUCY, esq. of Charlecote.

*Arms*—Gules, three luces or pikes, hauriant, between nine cross crosslets, arg.

*Crest*—In a ducal coronet gules a boar's head couped ermine between two wings displayed, tusked and crined or, tongue of the first.

*Motto*—With truth and diligence.

*Estates*—In Warwickshire, held since the Conquest; in the counties of Gloucester and Cornwall, acquired by purchase.

*Seat*—CHARLECOTE, in Warwickshire.

# IRWIN, OF TANRAGOE.

IRWIN, JOHN, esq. of Tanragoe, in the county of Sligo, colonel of the Sligo militia, *b.* 17th April, 1770.

Colonel Irwin is in the commission of the peace since 1793, was formerly a governor of the county, and served the office of high sheriff in 1822.

## Lineage.

The Irwins of Tanragoe have maintained a position of great respectability amongst the gentry of the county of Sligo, since their settlement in Ireland, but from which branch of the Scottish Irvines or Irvings, they descend has not been ascertained. The peculiar name of *Crinus*, borne by members of the family, is traditionally derived from *Krynin* Abethnae, the second husband of the mother of Duncan, king of Scotland, to whom and his descendants that monarch granted the privilege of bearing *the thistle* as a crest.

John Irwin, esq. who wedded a daughter of Colonel Lewis Jones, of Ardnaglass, held a command in the parliamentary army, in which his father-in-law also served, and accompanying Cromwell into Ireland, settled in the county of Sligo. He was father of

Alexander Irwin, esq. of the county of Sligo, who married the sister of — Griffith, esq. of Ballincar, and aunt of Colonel Griffith, father of Anne, countess of Harrington, and of Lady Rich. By this lady Mr. Irwin had six sons, who all died without issue, excepting the eldest,

John Irwin, esq. of Tanragoe, born in 1680, a colonel in the army. He *m.* first, Lady Mary Dilkes, widow of — Dilkes, esq. of the county of Cork, but had no issue; and secondly, Susanna Cadden, of an ancient Cavan family, by whom he had one son and two daughters, viz.

Lewis-Francis, his heir.

Letitia, *m.* to Captain Thomas Webber, of the 4th Horse, and had one son and a daughter.

Margaret, who *m.* Robert Browne, esq. of Fortland, in the county of Sligo.

Col. Irwin died in 1752, and was *s.* by his son,

Lewis-Francis Irwin, esq. of Tanragoe, *b.* in 1728, who *m.* in 1766, Elizabeth, only sister of the late John Harrison, esq. of Norton Place, in the county of Lincoln, and by her, who died in 1815, aged eighty-two, had issue,

- I. John, his heir.
- II. Crinus, in holy orders, archdeacon of Ossory, who *m.* in 1807, Amy, eldest daughter of the late Mr. Justice Chamberlain, judge of the King's Bench, in Ireland, and has, with four daughters, two sons,
  1. John-Lewis.
  2. Lewis-Chamberlain.
- I. Elizabeth, *m.* to Robert Jones, esq. of Fortland, in the county of Sligo, and died in 1822, leaving two sons, Robert Jones, and Lewis George Jones, and seven daughters.
- II. Margaret, *m.* the late Rev. Shuckburgh Upton, of the Templeton family, and has two sons and one daughter, namely,
  1. Lewis Upton.
  2. Arthur Upton.
  1. Elizabeth Upton, *m.* to Theophilus Lucas Clements, esq. of Rakenny, in the county of Cavan.
- III. Beatrice-Susanna, *m.* to Benjamin Agar, esq. of Brockfield, in the county of York, and has issue,
  1. John Agar.
  2. Benjamin Agar.
  1. Elizabeth Agar.

Mr. Irwin died in 1785, and was *s.* by his elder son, the present Col. Irwin, of Tanragoe.

*Arms*—Arg. three holly leaves ppr.

*Crest*—A hand issuing out of a cloud, grasping a branch of thistle, ppr.

*Motto*—Nemo me impune lacessit.

*Estates*—In the county of Sligo.

*Seat*—Tanragoe, Collooney.

# MOORE, OF CORSWALL.

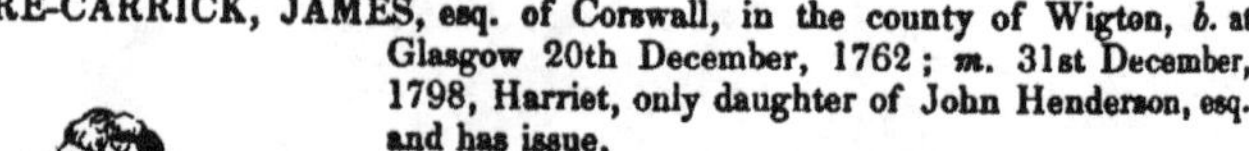

MOORE-CARRICK, JAMES, esq. of Corswall, in the county of Wigton, *b.* at Glasgow 20th December, 1762; *m.* 31st December, 1798, Harriet, only daughter of John Henderson, esq. and has issue,

JOHN-CARRICK, *b.* 13th February, 1805; *m.* in 1835.
Graham-Francis, *b.* 18th September, 1807.
Harriet-Jane.
Louisa.
Julia.

This gentleman, who succeeded to the representation of his family, upon the demise of his brother, the gallant and lamented Sir John Moore, assumed the additional surname of CARRICK, in compliance with the testamentary injunction of his relative, Robert Carrick, late a banker at Glasgow, who bequeathed to him estates in the counties of Wigton, Kirkcudbright, and Ayr.

## Lineage.

This family claims to be descended from the Moores, or Mures, of Rowallan, but tradition alone confirms the assumption.

CHARLES MOORE, esq. a captain in the army, who served in the wars of WILLIAM III. espoused Miss Hay, of the family of the earls of Kinnoul, and was father of

THE REV. CHARLES MOORE, minister of Stirling, who *m.* Marion, daughter of John Anderson, esq. of Dovehill, an old and respected family, and was *s.* by his only surviving son,

JOHN MOORE, M.D. of Dovehill, who was born at Stirling in 1730. This eminent person maintained for many years a distinguished place in the literary world, and his works have been universally read and admired. The principal are "ZELUCO," "Edward," and "Mordaunt." Dr. Moore wedded Jane, youngest daughter of the Rev. John Simson,* professor of divinity in the university of Glasgow, and had issue,

I. JOHN (Sir), his heir.
II. JAMES, present representative of the family.
III. GRAHAM (Sir), K.C.B. vice admiral in the royal navy.
IV. Charles, of Lincoln's Inn, barrister-at-law, died unm.
V. Francis, formerly under secretary of war.

I. Jane.

Dr. Moore was *s.* at his decease by his eldest son, the celebrated

SIR JOHN MOORE, born at Glasgow, 13th November, 1761. This gallant officer embraced from his youth the profession of arms, with the feelings and sentiments of a soldier; he felt that a perfect knowledge and an exact performance of the humble but important duties of a subaltern are the best foundations for subsequent military fame, and his ardent mind, while it looked forward to those brilliant achievements, for which it was formed, applied itself with

---

* PROFESSOR SIMSON's half sister, (the daughter of his father by a former marriage), Agnes Simson, *m.* John Simson, of Kirktownhall, and had seventeen sons, six of whom only attained manhood, viz.

I. ROBERT SIMSON, M.D. the celebrated professor of mathematics in the university of Glasgow, who died in 1768 unmarried.
II. Patrick Simson, in holy orders, minister of the gospel at Coventry, who left a daughter, Anne, *m.* to her cousin, Dr. Robert Simson.
III. Thomas Simson, M.D. professor of medicine in the college of St. Andrews, who *m.* the daughter of Sir John Preston, of Preston Hall, and had four sons and two daughters, viz.
    1. John, who *d.* unm.

energy and exemplary assiduity to the duties of that station. Having risen to command, he early signalized his name in the West Indies, in Holland, and in Egypt. The unremitting attention, with which he devoted himself to the duties of every branch of his profession, obtained him the confidence, and he became the companion in arms of that illustrious officer, Sir Ralph Abercromby, who fell at the head of his victorious troops in an action which maintained our national superiority over the arms of France. In that engagement General Moore was wounded, when leading on the reserve with his usual gallantry; and on his return his majesty conferred upon him the honour of knighthood, and the order of the Bath. His subsequent career, the battle of Corunna, and the death of the gallant commander, in the arms of victory, are too well known to require more than the bare mention here." "Like the immortal Wolfe," says Sir John Hope, in his dispatch to government, "he was snatched from his country at an early period of a life spent in her service; like Wolfe, his last moments were gilded by the prospect of success, and cheered by the acclamations of victory; like Wolfe, also his memory will for ever remain sacred in that country which he sincerely loved, and which he had so faithfully served." The interment of Sir John Moore took place early on the morning succeeding his death. A grave only three feet deep was dug by his officers on the bastion of Corunna, and there were deposited, uncoffined, the mortal remains of the lamented hero.* In the cathedral church of St. Paul, however, a grateful nation has reared a monument to his memory. Sir John, who at the period of his decease in 1809, was commander in chief of the British forces in Spain, a lieutenant-general in the army, and colonel of the 52nd regiment of foot, being unmarried, was succeeded in the representation of the family by his next brother, the present JAMES CARRICK-MOORE, esq. of Corswall.

*Arms*—Arg. on a fesse az. three mullets pierced of the field, within a bordure, invected gu.

*Crest*—A moor's head in profile, couped at the shoulders, ppr.

*Motto*—Duris non pangor.

*Estates*—In the counties of Wigton, Kirkcudbright, and Ayr.

*Seat*—Corswall, Wigtonshire, North Britain.

---

2. Robert, a physician at Coventry, who m. his cousin, Anne, daughter of the Rev. Patrick Simson, and had three sons: Robert, in holy orders; Thomas, of Coventry; Patrick, of Fillongley; and two daughters, Agnes, m. to the Rev. Mr. Hewet, rector of Fillongley, and Preston, *d.* unm.
3. Patrick, a clergyman in the church of Scotland, *d.* unm.
4. James, M. D. professor of medicine at St. Andrews, *d.* unm.

1. Agnes, m. to Professor Wilson, and has, with other issue, a daughter, m. to the Right Hon. Francis Jeffery, one of the lords of session, under the title of Lord Jeffery.
2. Preston, m. to Professor Craigie, of St. Andrews.

IV. John Simson, who m. Agnes, second daughter of John Prentice, merchant in Glasgow, and was father of John Simson, esq. of Hill, in Dumbartonshire.

V. Matthew Simson, a merchant in Glasgow, whose line is extinct.

VI. William Simson, *d.* unm.

---

* Epitaph on Sir John Moore, by the Rev. Dr. Parr, inscribed on a marble monument erected at Corunna.

H. S. E.<br>
JOHANNES MOORE,<br>
Allectus in equestrem ordinem Balnei<br>
A Georgio tertio Britanniarum rege;<br>
Ortu Scotus,<br>
Imperator fortis idemque innocens,<br>
Et rei militaris peritissimus<br>
Scientia et usu:<br>
Qui<br>
In Batavia, Corsica, Ægypto, India Occidentali,<br>
Hostes fugatos vidit;<br>
Hispanorum tetra et detestabili tyrannide oppressorum<br>
Jura leges aras et focos,<br>
Summo quo potuit studio tutatus est;<br>
Et post varios belli casus<br>
Cum ad Corunnam ægre accessisset<br>
Milites suos,<br>
Longo itinere, fame, frigore enectos,<br>
Ad subeundam prælii dimicationem<br>
Hortando erexit,<br>
Audendo confirmavit;<br>
Et Gallis numero copiarum fretis<br>
Et felicitate ducis pæne perpetua superbientibus<br>
Victoriam e manibus eripuit,<br>
Legioni quadragesimæ secundæ,<br>
Societate periculorum diu secum conjunctissæ<br>
Et memori rerum in Ægypto prospere gestarum,<br>
De virtute digna commilitionibus suis<br>
Gratulatus est;<br>
Et vulnere pro patria sociisque ejus accepto<br>
Vitam, uti multum et sæpe optaverat.<br>
Bene consummavit<br>
XVII Kal. Februar. Anno Sacro MDCCCIX.

---

GEORGIUS, Georgii Tertii filius,<br>
Brittaniarum regnum unitum regens,<br>
Et qui Regiæ Majestati a sanctoribus consiliis sunt,<br>
Hoc monumentum<br>
Ponemdum curaverunt.<br>
Anno Sacro<br>
MDCCCXIII.

# MASSINGBERD, OF GUNBY.

**MASSINGBERD, PEREGRINE,** esq. of Gunby, in the county of Lincoln, *b.* 29th January, 1780; *m.* 18th August, 1802, Elizabeth-Mary-Anne, daughter and heiress of Henry Massingberd, esq. and has had issue,

- Henry-Langton, *b.* 29th May, 1803; *d.* in 1810.
- ALGERNON LANGTON, *b.* 23rd May, 1804; *m.* Caroline-Georgina, daughter of William Pearce, esq. residing at Weasenham, in Norfolk, and has one child,
  - ALGERNON, *b.* in September, 1828.
- Samuel-Langton, *b.* in 1805; *d.* in 1814.
- Bennet-Langton, *b.* in 1813; *d.* in 1814.
- Charles-Langton, *b.* 23rd April, 1815.
- Elizabeth-Langton, *d.* in 1818.
- Mary-Langton, *m.* first, January, 1813, to William-Hastings Neville, esq. youngest son of General Neville, and has issue, Staphanie-Langton Neville, *b.* in 1831, and Rothes-Hastings Neville, *b.* in 1832.
- Margaret-Clarissa.

This gentleman, who is second son of Bennet Langton,* esq. of Langton, by his wife, the Lady Mary Leslie, dowager countess of Rothes, assumed the surname and arms of Massingberd, on inheriting, in right of his wife, the Gunby estates.

## Lineage.

The ancient and eminent family of Massingberd has been seated in the county of Lincoln for many centuries. (For the early descents refer to the account of the Massingberds of Ormsby, vol. i. p. 663.)

SIR THOMAS MASSINGBERD, knt. representative of the family in the sixteenth century, wedded Joan, younger daughter and heir (her elder sister, Agnes, was prioress of the nunnery of Crabhouse, in Norfolk) of John Braytoft, of Braytoft Hall, and, receiving with her a considerable estate, made that seat his chief place of residence. Surviving his wife, Sir Thomas became, in the reign of HENRY VIII. a knight of St. John of Jerusalem, and added the second escutcheon to the family arms. He had issue,

1. AUGUSTINE, who purchased, in 1538, the manors belonging to Sir John Markham, in Bratoft and elsewhere.

* GEORGE LANGTON, esq. eldest son and heir of George Langton, by his wife Miss Fern, wedded Diana, daughter of Edmund Turnor, esq. of Stoke Rochfort, in the county of Lincoln, and had issue,

I. BENNET, who *m.* in 1770, Mary, dowager countess of Rothes, daughter of Gresham Lloyd, esq. by Mary Holt, his wife, great niece of the Lord Chief Justice Holt, and had issue,

1. GEORGE LANGTON, esq. of Langton, in the county of Lincoln.
2. PEREGRINE LANGTON, esq. now MASSINGBERD, of Gunby.
3. Algernon Langton, *b.* in 1781, originally a military officer, but subsequently in holy orders, *m.* Mary-Anne, sister of Edward Drewe, esq. of Grange, in the county of Devon, and *d.* in 1829, leaving one child, Bennet.
4. Charles Langton, a naval officer, *d.* in 1810.

1. Mary, } both *d.* unm.
2. Diana, }
3. Jane.
4. Elizabeth, }
5. Isabella, } *d.* unm.
6. Margaret, }

II. Fern, died young.

I. Diana, *m.* to the Rev. Dr. Uvedale.

II. Juliet, *m.* to the Rev. William Brackenbury.

He *m.* Margaret, daughter of Robert Elrington, esq. of Hoxton, in Middlesex, and dying in the lifetime of his father, 7th February, 1549, left four sons and five daughters, namely,

1. THOMAS, successor to his grandfather.
2. William, who was interred at Saltfleetby, St. Peters, in 1572. He *m.* a daughter of Richard Clayton, of London, and had a son and heir,
   Oswald, a goldsmith, in London, who resided at Farnham, in Surrey. He wedded Mary Slighwright, daughter of a barrister of Gray's Inn, and had a son,
      John, an eminent merchant of London, and treasurer of the East India Company, who *m.* Cecilia, daughter of Thomas Pellit, merchant, of London, and dying in 1653, left issue,
         ELIZABETH, married to George, first Lord Berkeley.
         MARY, *m.* to Robert, third Earl of Lindsey.
3. Christopher, who was appointed, 1st August, 1548, clerk of the council within the town of Calais, for life.
4. John, who *m.* Dorothy, relict of Ralph Quadring, esq. and eldest daughter of Sir Robert Hussey, knt. of Linwood, by Margaret his wife, daughter and co-heir of Sir Thomas Say, knt. of Liston, in Essex, and *d.* in 1580, leaving, with two daughters, Edith, *m.* first, to Mr. Baker, and secondly, to Mr. Nicholls, and Ann, the wife of John Booth, of Kyme, a son, Augustin, who resided at Sutterton, and *d. s. p.* in 1614.

1. Grace, *m.* to Stephen Spackman.
2. Anne, *m.* first, to Christopher Forcet, of Billesby, and secondly, to Christopher Somercotes, of Somercotes.
3. Ursula, *m.* to John Davy.
4. Edith, *m.* to Augustin Caundish, and *d.* in 1590.
5. Elizabeth, buried at Braytoft, 18th October, 1588.

II. Oswald, confrere of St. John's, who had a yearly pension of ten pounds assigned to him on the first suppression of the order, in 1540. In five years after, he obtained license, under the king's sign manual, to travel beyond sea, with one servant and two horses, by the appellation of Sir Oswald Massingberd, knight of the order of St. John of Jerusalem. At the final dissolution of the order, in 1559, he was prior of Kilmainham, in Ireland.

III. Alan, who *d.* unm.

IV. Martin, who *m.* Ursula Elrington, and had three sons, and one daughter.

I. Edith, married to Richard Lytler, of Tathwell.

II. Cecily, *m.* to Thomas Moore.

III. Dorothy,
IV. Grace,
V. Christian, } all *d.* unmarried.

Sir Thomas Massingberd died 25th May, 1552, and was interred at Gunby, under a large marble tombstone, with his portraiture in complete armour, (a lion at his feet) and his lady's inlaid in brass thereon, having a large shield, a little above, between their heads, and four small shields on each side. The following mutilated inscription still remains: " S[r] Thomas Massyngberde, knt. and dame Johan his wyfe, specyale desyers all resnabull creatures of your charyte to gyfe lawde and prays unto ——— queen of everlasting life with ———." Sir Thomas was *s.* by his grandson,

THOMAS MASSINGBERD, esq. of Braytoft Hall, M.P. for Calais in 1552, who *m.* first, Alice, daughter and heir of Richard Bevercoats, esq. of Newark, and had issue,

I. THOMAS, his heir.

II. George, who *m.* Alice Milles, of Abingdon, in the county of Berks, and left at his decease an only surviving child, Edward, baptized in June, 1589, who wedded Judith, dau. of Armigill Sharples, of Louth, in Lincolnshire, and had two sons, Abraham, of the same place, who died before the year 1649, leaving issue, and Charles.

III. Augustin, died at Gunby, in 1580, unmarried.

I. Katharine, *m.* to Thomas Cole.

II. Margaret, *d.* unmarried.

III. Grace, *m.* to Alan Raithy.

He wedded secondly, Dorothy, daughter and heir of Richard Ballard, gent. of Orby, and had further issue,

I. William, of Bratoft, who *m.* Helen Quadring, of Burgh, and had issue.

I. Frances, *m.* to Samuel Newcomen, of Low Toynton.

II. Jane, married to Robert Dighton, of Bramston.

III. Dorothy.

Thomas Massingberd *d.* in 1584, and was *s.* by his eldest son,

THOMAS MASSINGBERD, esq. who resided, during his father's lifetime, at Saltfleetby St. Peter's. He *m.* Frances, daughter of Sir George Fitz Williams, knt. of Maplethorpe, and had, with other children, who all died unmarried,

I. THOMAS, his heir.
II. Henry, who *m.* Alice Busshey, and had, *inter alios*, a son, Nathaniel, upon whom his grandfather settled the estate at Croft, which he purchased from Mr. John Brown, and likewise the lands in Thorpe, formerly in the possession of Robert Hill and John Greene.
I. Frances, *m.* to Francis Cave, esq. of Ingerby, in Leicestershire.
II. Jane, *m.* to Francis Gyrnwick.
III. Mary, *m.* to Edward Pigot, gent.
IV. Susanna, *m.* to Robert Hastings, of Bilsby.
V. Bridget, *m.* to William Thory, of Winthorpe.
VI. Alice, *m.* first to Robert Stevenson, and secondly to — Lowndes, esq.

Mr. Massingberd died at Gunby, 11th September, 1620, and was succeeded by his eldest son,

THOMAS MASSINGBERD, esq. of Gunby, barrister-at-law, who resided for some time at Louth. He espoused Frances, daughter of Robert Halton, esq. of Clee, serjeant-at-law, by Joan his wife, daughter of John Draner, or Drayner, esq. of Hoxton, and had (with other children, who *d. s. p.*),

I. HENRY, his heir.
II. DRAYNER (Sir), *b.* 11th December, 1615, and ancestor of the MASSINGBERDS, of South Ormsby, (see vol. i. p. 661).
I. Frances, *m.* first, to John Day, of Sausethorp, and secondly, to Thomas Pitcher, esq. of Trumpington, in the county of Cambridge.
II. Elizabeth, *m.* to John Booth, esq.
III. Susanna, married first, in 1625, to Richard Cater, esq. who was killed by a fall from his horse, 10th July, 1631, and secondly, in 1635, to Richard Godney, esq. of Swaby.
IV. Alice, *m.* to Thomas Day, esq. of Sausethorp.
V. Margaret, *m.* to Leonard Purley, gent. of Farlsthorp.

Mr. Massingberd, who *d.* suddenly on his way to church, 5th November, 1636, was buried at Gunby, and *s.* by his son,

HENRY MASSINGBERD, esq. of Gunby, admitted of Christ College, Cambridge, 18th April, 1627, as fellow commoner, whence he removed to the Inner Temple, of which he was entered a student 7th June, 1629, and remained there to the following April only. During the civil war of the reign of CHARLES I. he took an active part, and raised a troop of horse for the service of the parliament. In the constable's accounts for the parish of Friskney, one shilling is charged as given to Captain Massingberd's cornet, towards his colours. Another item is, "spent by two soldiers, sent to the town by Mr. Mashenberd and Mr. Misserdine, two shillings." Another, "for a horse from John Cotes, of Boston, being sent to Captain Massingberd from the committee at Boston, one shilling."* So warmly did he espouse the parliamentary cause that both his brother, Sir Drayner, and himself were indicted at Grantham for high treason. In 1658, the protector, CROMWELL, created him a BARONET, and the preamble in the patent states the honour to be conferred "as well for his faithfulness and good affection to us and his countrey, as for his descent, patrimony, ample estate, and ingenious education, every way answerable, who out of a liberal mind hath undertaken to maintain thirty foot souldiers in our dominion of Ireland, for three whole years." The original patent, which was renewed at the restoration, the family still preserve. It bears the initials of Oliver's Christian name, encircling a good likeness of him, in a robe of ermine.

Sir Henry wedded first, Elizabeth, youngest daughter of William Lyster, esq. of Rippingale and Colby, and had to survive infancy,

Henry, who died unmarried, at his chambers in the Inner Temple, in 1666, aged twenty-five.
John, who died unmarried, at Barnet, in 1671.
Frances, *m.* first, to George Saunderson, esq. of Thoresby, and secondly, to Timothy Hildyard, esq.
Elizabeth, *m.* to Sir Nicholas Stoughton, bart. of Stoke, in Surrey.

The baronet espoused secondly, Anne, relict of Nicholas Stoughton, esq. of Stoke, and daughter and sole heir of William Evans, esq. of London. By her he had one son to survive, WILLIAM, his heir. He *m.* thirdly, 27th November, 1679, Elizabeth, dau. of — Rayner, esq. of Yorkshire, but by that lady had no child. He died in September, 1680, aged seventy-one, and was *s.* by his son,

SIR WILLIAM MASSINGBERD, second bart. of Gunby, who *m.* 11th July, 1673, Elizabeth, daughter of Richard Wynn, esq. of London, and had one son and one daughter, viz.

WILLIAM, his heir.
ELIZABETH, successor to her brother.

Sir William was *s.* by his son,

SIR WILLIAM MASSINGBERD, third bart. of Gunby, M.P. for Lincolnshire, *b.* in 1677, at whose decease, unmarried, the baronetcy

* Oldfield's History of Wainfleet.

expired, while the estates devolved on his sister,

ELIZABETH MASSINGBERD, of Gunby, who wedded Thomas Meux, esq. and had a son,

WILLIAM MEUX, esq. of Gunby, who assumed the surname and arms of MASSINGBERD only. He *m.* first, Miss Thornborough, by whom he had,

THOMAS, who *m.* Miss Elizabeth Emerson, sister to Sir Walter Amcotts, bart. and predeceasing his father, in 1777, left issue,

HENRY, successor to his grandfather.

Thomas, capt. R. N. of Candlesby House, in the county of Lincoln, and of Beckingham House, near Bawtry, Yorkshire, *b.* in 1763, *m.* 12th February, 1794, Elizabeth Hawksmore Waterhouse, and had two sons, Thomas Massingberd, esq. and the Rev. H. Massingberd, besides three daughters, Christiana, Louisa, Ellen, and Mary-Jane.

Charles.

Emily.

Mr. (Meux) Massingberd wedded secondly, Miss Drake, and had,

William, *m.* Miss Pastern.
Samuel, died unm.
George, living in America.
Francis, *d.* unm.
Caroline, } both *d.* unm.
Margaret, }

Ann, *m.* to John Pyke, esq.
Katherine, *m.* to the Rev. Francis Wilson.
Mary-Joice, *m.* to the Rev. Edward Brackenbury.
Sarah-Elizabeth, *m.* to Radcliffe Pearl Todd, esq.

He died in 1780, and was *s.* by his grandson,

HENRY MASSINGBERD, esq. of Gunby, who espoused Miss Elizabeth Hoare, and died about the year 1787, leaving an only daughter and heiress, ELIZABETH MARY-ANNE MASSINGBERD, who wedded, as already stated, Peregrine Langton, esq. who assumed in consequence the surname and arms of MASSINGBERD, and is the present PEREGRINE MASSINGBERD, of Gunby.

*Arms*—Quarterly, first and fourth, az. three quatrefoils, (two and one,) and in chief a boar passant or, charged on the shoulder with a cross patée gu.; second and third, quarterly, or and arg. on a cross humettee gu. between four lions rampant sa. two escallops of the first.

*Crests*—First, a dragon's head erased, quarterly, or and gu. between two wings az. Second, a lion's head erased, charged with two broad arrows in saltire, arg. barbed or, between four gouttes d'eau.

*Motto*—Est meruisse satis.

*Estates*—In the county of Lincoln, including the manors of Gunby, Bratoft, and Markby.

*Seat*—Gunby Hall, built in 1700, by Sir William Massingberd, bart.

## TAYLOR, OF BIFRONS.

TAYLOR, EDWARD, esq. of Bifrons, in Kent, *b.* 24th June, 1774; *m.* 6th September, 1802, Louisa, only child of the Rev. J. C. Beckingham, of Bourn House, in the same county, the last representative of the ancient family of Aucher, and has issue,

HERBERT-EDWARD, captain 85th regiment.
Brook-John, lieutenant 81st regiment.
Aucher-Beckingham.
Bridges, in the office for foreign affairs.
Wilbraham.

Mary-Louisa, *m.* in 1824, to the Hon. James Knox, M.P. for Dungannon, and has a daughter.
Louisa-Charlotte, *m.* in 1828, to George-Cornwall Legh, esq. of High Legh, in Cheshire.
Emily-Octavia, *m.* in 1833, to William Deedes, esq. of Sandling, in Kent, and has one son.

Mr. Taylor represented the city of Canterbury in parliament from 1807 to 1812.

## Lineage.

This family, originally from Whitchurch, in Shropshire, spelt their name, in 1500, Taylour.

Nathaniel Taylour, esq. represented the county of Bedford in parliament, and was also recorder of Colchester, in Essex, during the usurpation of Cromwell. He *m.* the daughter of Colonel Bridges, of Wallingford, in Essex, ancestor of Sir Brook Bridges, bart. of Goodnestone, Kent, and had eighteen children, most of whom were born in Brook House, Holborn, and several died young. His son,

John Taylor, esq. born 7th December, 1655, purchased Bifrons, and other estates, situated in Kent, A.D. 1694. He wedded Olivia, daughter of Sir Nicholas Tempest, bart. of Durham, and by her, who died in 1716, and was buried at Patrixbourn, had issue,

Brook, his heir.
Herbert, successor to his brother.
Upton, James, Nathaniel, John, Hannah, — all died young, and were buried at Patrixbourn.

John Taylor died 4th April, 1729, was buried at Patrixbourn, and succeeded by his eldest son,

Brook Taylor, esq. of Bifrons, D.C.L. born at Edmonton, 18th August, 1685. This gentleman, distinguished as a mathematician, and as the author of a learned treatise on Linear Perspective, was chosen fellow of the Royal Society in 1712, and elected secretary in 1714, in which year he took his degree, at Cambridge, of doctor of civil law. He espoused Elizabeth, daughter of John Sawbridge, esq. of Olantigh, in Kent, and by her, who died in 1729, and was buried at Patrixbourn, had an only daughter,

Elizabeth, baptized 25th March, 1730, *m.* to Sir William Young, bart.

Brook Taylor died in London, in 1731, was interred at St. Anne's, and succeeded by his brother,

The Rev. Herbert Taylor, of Bifrons, rector of Hunton, and vicar of Patrixbourn, baptized 15th May, 1698. This gentleman *m.* Mary, daughter of Dr. Wake, prebendary of Canterbury, and nephew of Archbishop Wake, ancestor of Sir William Wake, bart. of Courteen, and had issue,

Herbert, his heir.
Edward, successor to his brother.

The Rev. Herbert Taylor died 29th September, 1763, was buried in the family vault at Patrixbourn, and succeeded by his elder son,

Herbert Taylor, esq. of Bifrons, at whose decease, unmarried, in London, 19th November, 1767, aged thirty-six, the estates devolved on his brother,

The Rev. Edward Taylor, born 26th August, 1734, who *m.* in 1769, Margaret, sister of Thomas Watkinson Payler,* esq. of the county of Kent, (whose family first bore the name of Turner, and descended from William Turner, esq. of Sutton Valence, an officer of *King* Henry VIII.'s household,) and by her, who died at Brussels, 27th April, 1780, aged thirty-six, had five sons and three daughters, viz.

Edward, his heir.

Herbert (Sir), born 29th September, 1779, a lieut.-general in the army, colonel of the 85th Regiment, first aid-de-camp to the king, and his majesty's private secretary, also master of St. Katherine's, and knight grand cross of the orders of the Bath and Guelph. Sir Herbert wedded Charlotte Albinia, daughter of Edward Desbrowe, esq. (vice chamberlain to *Queen* Charlotte) by Charlotte his wife, daughter of George, third Earl of Buckinghamshire, and has one dau. Charlotte. He sat in parliament for Windsor from 1820 to 1823, when he resigned his seat.

Brook (Sir), *b.* 30th December, 1776, knight grand cross of the Hanoverian Guelphic order, one of his majesty's most honourable privy council, and, at various times, envoy-extraordinary and minister plenipotentiary to the courts of Hesse

* This gentleman, who died about the year 1816, married three wives, first, Charlotte, second daughter of William Hammond, esq. of St. Alban's Court; secondly, Miss Wynn, sister of Sir Edmund Wynn, bart.; and thirdly, Mrs. O'Callaghan, of Limerick. By the first only he had issue, viz. Thomas, major of dragoons, William, in holy orders, James, lieutenant-colonel in the army, John, Henry, Anthony, in holy orders, another son, and Charlotte, the wife of William Egerton, esq. of Tatton. Mrs. O'Callaghan (his last wife) was the widow of Edmund O'Callaghan, esq. of Kilgory, in the county of Limerick, who fell in a duel with Mr. M'Namara, and by whom she had four daughters, the co-heirs of their father,

1. Bridged, married to the late Thomas O'Reilly, esq.
2. Catherine, married to the Hon. Thomas Browne, brother and heir presumptive to the Earl of Kenmare.
3. Ellen, married to James Bagot, esq. of Castle Bagot, in the county of Dublin.
4. Elizabeth, married to Gerald Dease, esq. of Turbotstown, nephew to Lord Fingal.

Cassel, Wirtemburg, Bavaria, and Prussia.

William, twin brother with Brook, formerly in the office for foreign affairs, who was unfortunately drowned in the Thames, 16th July, 1797, buried at Patrixbourn.

Bridges-Watkinson, *b.* in 1778, captain in the royal navy, who was accidentally drowned in the Adriatic, off Brindisi, 24th February, 1814, when in command of his majesty's frigate, Apollo. He had served with great zeal and distinction during the whole of the war, participated in the actions of the 1st of June with Earl Howe, and at the Nile under Lord Nelson, with whom he was at the attack upon Teneriffe, and was wounded in the Leander when she fought the Genereux. Monuments were erected to his memory at Brindisi by the inhabitants, at Portsmouth by the officers of the Apollo, and at Patrixbourn by his own family. It is remarkable that he saved the lives of three individuals, at different times, *when drowning*, at the risk of his own.

Mary-Elizabeth, *m.* 19th April, 1796, Edward Wilbraham Bootle, esq. of Lathom House, Lancashire, since created Lord Skelmersdale, and has issue,

Hon. Richard Bootle Wilbraham, who *m.* Jessy, third daughter of Sir Richard Brooke, bart. of Norton Priory, and has one daughter.

Hon. Edward Bootle-Wilbraham, in the guards.

Hon. Mary Bootle-Wilbraham.

Hon. Emma-Caroline Bootle-Wilbraham, married to Edward Lord Stanley.

Charlotte, *m.* 3rd March, 1794, the Rev. Edward Northey, canon of Windsor, and by him (who *d.* in February, 1828), has issue,

1. Edward Northey, who married Charlotte, daughter of Lieutenant-general Sir George Anson, G.C.B. uncle to the Earl of Lichfield.
2. William Northey, in the army, who married Agnes, daughter of General Bouel, and niece of Baron Fagel, in Holland.

1. Charlotte Northey.
2. Lucy Northey.
3. Mary Northey.

Margaret, died unmarried, at Lathom House, 24th October, 1809, and is buried at Melling, in Lancashire.

*Arms*—Gu. three roses arg. barbed vert; a chief vair.

*Crest*—A lion's head erased arg. collared gu. charged with three roses of the first.

*Estates*—In Kent.

*Seat*—Bifrons.

## O'BRIEN, OF BLATHERWYCKE.

O'BRIEN, STAFFORD, esq. of Blatherwycke Park, in the county of Northampton, *b.* 29th October, 1783; *m.* 7th June, 1808, the Honourable Emma Noel, daughter of Sir Gerard-Noel Noel, bart. M.P. by Diana his wife, Baroness Barham, and has issue,

I. AUGUSTUS.
II. Henry.
III. Algernon.

I. Emma, died unmarried.
II. Angelina, *m.* to the Hon. A. Fitzroy.
III. Fanny, died unmarried.
IV. Lilly.

Mr. O'Brien, who succeeded his father, Henry O'Brien, esq. is in the commission of the peace, and was high sheriff of the county of Rutland in 1809.

## Lineage.

This is a branch of the ancient stem of Dromoland. (See BURKE'S *Peerage and Baronetage.*)

SIR DONATUS O'BRIEN, of Dromoland (son of Cornelius O'Brien, esq. of Leamanagh, and lineally descended from the kings of Thomond), was born in 1642, and educated in London, as appears by a decree in Chancery, dated 1st February, 1680. He had two grants of land under the acts of settlement; and, by privy seal, dated at Whitehall 16th October, and by patent at Dublin, 9th November, 1686, was created a BARONET. He *m.* first, Lucia, second daughter of Sir George Hamilton, and had by her a son,

LUCIUS, ancestor of the present SIR EDWARD O'BRIEN, bart. of Dromoland, in the county of Clare.

Sir Donatus espoused, secondly, in July, 1677, Elizabeth, daughter of Joseph Deane, esq. of Cromlin (see vol. ii. p. 690), and widow of Henry Grey, esq. of Dublin, by whom, who *d.* in 1683, he had, with two daughters, Honora and Elizabeth, one son,

HENRY O'BRIEN, esq. who became seated at Stonehall, in the county of Clare. This gentleman wedded, in 1699, Susanna, dau. and co-heiress of WILLIAM STAFFORD, esq. of Blatherwycke,* in Northamptonshire, and had issue,

I. Stafford, who *d.* young.
II. HENRY, his heir.
III. DONATUS, of whom presently.
IV. William, in holy orders, died unm. 1751.

I. Elizabeth, *m.* to John Rice, esq. of the county of Kildare.
II. Anne, *m.* to Edward Butler, esq.
III. Susannah, *m.* first, in 1722, to James Rice, esq. of Mount Rice, in the county of Kildare; and secondly, Augustine Levers, esq.
IV. Catherine, *m.* in 1727, to Patrick French, esq. barrister-at-law.
V. Margaret, who *d.* unm.
VI. Frances, *m.* to Hyacinth D'Arcy, esq. of Ballycursane, in the county of Galway.

Mr. O'Brien *d.* 15th January, 1723 (his widow married, in 1728, Arthur Geoghegan, esq. of Castletown, in Westmeath, who assumed the surname of STAFFORD), and was *s.* by his son,

HENRY O'BRIEN, esq. of Stonehall, in the county of Clare, and of Blatherwycke Park, Northamptonshire, *b.* 1st March, 1708, who *m.* in November, 1730, Margaret, daughter of William Stammer, esq. of Carnelly, in the county of Galway, and had an only surviving daughter, Susannah, *m.* to Edward O'Brien, esq. of Inistimon, in Clare. Mr. O'Brien *d.* 17th March, 1757 (his widow surviving, *m.* secondly, Alexander Shearer, esq. of Limerick), and was *s.* by his brother,

DONATUS O'BRIEN, esq. who settled in the county of York, where he married Miss Mary Becket, of Barnesley, aunt to the late Sir John Becket, bart. and had six sons and three daughters, viz.

I. Donatus, who *d.* unm.
II. HENRY, eventual heir.
III. Lucius.
IV. Stafford.
V. William, } who both died unm.
VI. Spersto, }

I. Susanna, *m.* to the Rev. Bacon Bedingfeld, of Ditchingham Hall, Norfolk, and had one son and five daughters, viz.
   John-James Bedingfeld, esq. now of Ditchingham. *(See family of Bedingfeld.)*
   Susanna-Harriet Bedingfeld, married, first, to John Talbot, esq. only brother of the late Earl of Shrewsbury: and secondly, to the Hon. Henry Roper Curzon, eldest son of Lord Teynham.
   Lucy-Eleanor Bedingfeld.
   Caroline Bedingfeld, *m.* to Joseph Mortimer, esq.
   Matilda-Stafford-Sophia Bedingfeld, *m.* to her cousin, Donatus O'Brien, esq. of Tixover.
II. Mary, *m.* to Smith Kirkham, esq. of Luffenham, in Rutlandshire, and had one daughter, *m.* the late Rev. Charles Burton.
III. Eleanor, *m.* Colonel James Tufton Phelp, of Coston House, in the county of Leicester, and has issue,
   Edward-Tufton Phelp, esq. now of Coston House, who *m.* Ellen, only sister of William-Edward Powell, esq. of Nanteos, M.P. and lord lieutenant for the county of Cardigan (see vol. i. p. 230).
   Cecil-Tufton Phelp, who *m.* Miss Knight.

* The manor of Blatherwycke was acquired by SIR HUMPHREY STAFFORD, sprung from the old baronial house of Stafford, in the time of HENRY VI. by marriage with Alianore, daughter and co-heir of Sir Thomas Aylesbury, and continued with his descendants, who allied with the ancient families of Fray, Tame, Cave, Clopton, Fermor, Seymour, &c. until conveyed by the sisters and co-heirs of the last male heir, WILLIAM STAFFORD, esq. to their husbands; the elder, Susanna, marrying HENRY O'BRIEN, esq. as in the text; and the younger, Anne, becoming the wife of George, Lord Carbery.

Laura-Edwyna Phelp, *m.* to William Edward Powell, esq. of Nanteos, M.P.
Julia-Phelp.
Fanny-Phelp.
Octavia-Phelp, *m.* to Major Archibald Crawfurd, of the Hon. East India Company's Artillery, brother to the present Robert Crawfurd, esq. of Newfield (see vol. i. p. 554).
Eleanor-Phelp, *m.* to Capt. Cherry, late of the Royal Horse Guards.

Mr. O'Brien's eldest surviving son,

HENRY O'BRIEN, esq. of Stone Hall and Blatherwycke Park, who inherited the estates of his paternal family in Ireland, as well as the Stafford possessions in England, *d.* in 1811, leaving, by Margaret Flenary, two sons and five daughters, namely,

I. STAFFORD, his heir, and PRESENT PROPRIETOR.
II. Donatus, who *m.* his first cousin, Matilda Stafford Sophia, daughter of the Rev. Bacon Bedingfeld, of Ditchingham, and has issue.

I. Mary-Anne, *m.* Thomas Hotchkin, esq. of South Luffenham, and has issue.
II. Margaret, *m.* to John Slater Wilkinson, esq. of Hilcot House, in the county of Derby, and has issue.
III. Letitia, *m.* to the Hon. Thomas Orde Pawlett, second son of the late Lord Bolton, and has issue.
IV. Frances, *m.* to Robert Crawfurd, esq. of Newfield, in Ayrshire, and has issue (see vol. i. p. 551).
V. Eleanor, *m.* to Arthur Annesley, esq. of Bletchingdon Park, in the county of Oxford, (see vol. i. p. 7), and has issue.

*Arms*—Quarterly; 1st and 4th, per pale gu. and or, three lions counterchanged. 2nd, arg. three piles gu. 3rd, arg. a pheon.

*Crest*—Issuing out of clouds a naked arm embowed, the hand grasping a sword, all ppr.

*Motto*—Vigeur de dessus.

*Estates*—In Ireland, acquired in 1600; and in Northamptonshire, England, in 1708.

*Seat*—Blatherwycke Park, near Wansford.

# RICHARDSON, OF FINDEN PLACE.

RICHARDSON, WILLIAM-WESTBROOK, esq. of Finden Place, in Sussex, *b.* 18th August, 1788, a magistrate and deputy lieutenant for that county, succeeded his cousin, William Richardson, esq. in 1801.

## Lineage.

This is a branch of the Northern House of Richardson, of Bierley.

NICHOLAS RICHARDSON, of the county of Durham, came into Yorkshire in 1561, and purchased estates at Tong, North Bierley, and Woodhall, all in the West Riding. He married, first, Margaret, daughter of John Midgley, of Clayton, in Bradforddale, and by her had one son and two daughters, viz. RICHARD, his heir; Helena, *b.* in 1573, *m.* to Richard Cordingley, of Holm; and Margaret, *b.* in 1574, the wife of Michael Jenkinson, of Pudsey. Nicholas Richardson wedded secondly, Ann, daughter of Lionel Goodall, and had several other sons, who all died young, and one daughter, Ann, *m.* in 1605, to Christopher Cave, of Otley. He died in 1616, and was *s.* by his son,

RICHARD RICHARDSON, esq. of North Bierley, *b.* in 1576, who married first, in 1599, Ann, daughter and heiress of William Pollard, and had,

I. WILLIAM, his heir.
II. RICHARD, successor to his brother.
III. Thomas, a merchant, *b.* in 1609.
IV. Nicholas, *d.* in infancy.

I. Ann, *m.* to Thomas Langley, of Horbury.

II. Alice, *b.* in 1614, *m.* to Thomas Senior, of Hopton, within Merfield.

III. Sarah, *b.* in 1616, *m.* first, to Richard Jenkinson, of Pudsey; and secondly, to Robert Milner, esq. of the same place.

IV. Beatrice, *b.* in 1622, *m.* James Sayle, of Pudsey, esq. and had two daughters, viz.

Beatrice Sayle, *m.* to Richard Hutton, esq. of Pudsey, great grandson of Archbishop Hutton.

Faith Sayle, *m.* to Thomas Sharpe, of Horton, (eldest brother of Mr. Abraham Sharpe, the mathematician), and had an only daughter and heiress,

Elizabeth Sharpe, *m.* to Robert Stansfield, esq. of Bradford.

Richard Richardson, who *m.* secondly, Mrs. Susannah Swaine, but had no other issue, died in 1634, and was *s.* by his eldest son,

William Richardson, esq. of Bierley, *b.* in 1602, who *m.* Elizabeth, eldest daughter of George Hopkinson, esq. of Loft House, and sister to the learned antiquary, John Hopkinson, whose MS. collections relating to the antiquities of the county of York, in forty volumes, are preserved in the family library of the Richardsons. Mr. Richardson died issueless, in 1648, was buried at Bradford, 22nd February, in that year, and succeeded by his brother,

Richard Richardson, esq. of Bradford, who became "of Bierley." This gentleman (*b.* in 1604), paid a fine of £40. for declining the honor of knighthood from Charles I. as appears by the receipt dated 5th October, 1630, signed "Wentworth," and still in the possession of the family. He wedded Jane, second daughter of George Hopkinson, esq. of Loft House, and by her, who died in 1662, had issue,

I. William, of Bierley, *b.* in 1629, *m.* in 1659, Susannah, daughter of Gilbert Savile, esq. of Greetland, in Yorkshire, and had two sons and one daughter, viz.

1. Richard, of Bierley, M.D. in the commission of the peace for the West Riding, born in 1663, who married, first, in 1699, Sarah, only daughter and heiress of John Crossley, esq. of Kirkshaw House, Halifax, by whom he had an only child, Richard, who died young. He wedded secondly, Dorothy, daughter of Henry Currer, esq. of Kildwick, and had issue, (see family of Currer, of Kildwick).

2. William, of High Fearnley, in Yorkshire, *b.* in 1666, who *m.* Mary daughter and heir of John Kirshaw, of Hoyle House, Halifax, merchant, and had, with other issue, who died unm. a daughter,

Martha, *m.* to Edward Iveson, esq. son of Henry Iveson, esq. of Black Bank, high sheriff of Yorkshire in 1708.

1. Jane, *m.* to Edward Ferrand, esq. of Harden.

II. Richard, of Newall, *b.* in 1635, who died in 1699, leaving an only son, William, who *d. s. p.* in 1711.

III. John, of Birks, one of the lords of the manor of Bradford, *b.* in 1636, precentor and canon residentiary of York, and archdeacon of Cleveland. His first wife, Ann Kent, died *s. p.* He *m.* secondly, in 1672, Hannah, sister of Dr. John Sharp, archbishop of York, and had issue.

IV. George, of Woodhall, *b.* in 1644, *m.* Sarah, daughter of Richard Langley, esq. of Priestly Green, Halifax. This gentleman's male line ceased with his grandson, George, who died in 1748.

V. Samuel, in holy orders, rector of Burnham Sutton, Norfolk, *b.* in 1647, who *m.* Frances, daughter of the Rev. Philip Cornwallis. His male line ceased with his grandson, Joseph, who died in 1763, leaving two daughters, his co-heirs.

VI. Joseph, of whom presently.

I. Elizabeth, *m.* to William Pollard, gent. of Bierley.

II. Ann, *m.* to William Brook, gent. of Lum.

III. Judith, *m.* to John Thornton, of Tyersall, in the parish of Calverley, and from this marriage the Smyths of Heath derive.

Richard Richardson died in 1656, and by his will, which bears date 14th February, 1655, it appears that he was seized of the manor of Okenshaw and Heaton, and one fourth part of the manor of Bradford, with considerable estates in the county of York. His youngest son,

The Rev. Joseph Richardson, rector of Dunsfold and Hambledon, in Surrey, *b.* in 1648, wedded in 1683, Elizabeth, daughter and co-heir of John Peebles, esq. of Dewsbury, by whom, who died in 1726, he acquired that manor, and had issue,

I. Joseph, his heir.

I. Jane, *m.* to the Rev. Edward Eliot, rector of Buttermere, in Wilts, only son of Sir William Eliot, knt. of Busbridge.

II. Elizabeth, who *m.* the Rev. Thomas Warton, B.D. vicar of Basingstoke,

Hants, and of Cobham, in Surrey, sometime fellow of Magdalen College, Oxford, and professor of poetry in that university, and had two sons,

Joseph Warton, B.D. late master of Winchester School.

THOMAS WARTON, B.D. late fellow of Trinity College, and professor of poetry at Oxford, Poet Laureate, and author of the History of English Poetry.

III. Mary, *m.* to John Churchar, gent. of Midhurst, and *d.* aged ninety-five, without issue.

IV. Ann, *m.* to John Payne, esq. of Melford, in Surrey, and *d.* aged ninety, *s. p.*

Mr. Richardson died 18th June, 1742, and was *s.* by his only son,

JOSEPH RICHARDSON, esq. of Gray's Inn, barrister-at-law, *b.* 14th July, 1689, who *m.* in 1723, Elizabeth, second daughter and co-heir of John Minshull, esq. of Portslade, in Sussex, by Barbara, his wife, daughter, and eventual heiress of William Westbrooke, esq. of East Ferring. By this lady, who *d.* in 1752, he acquired considerable estates in the county of Sussex, and had issue,

I. WILLIAM-WESTBROOKE, his heir.

II. John, fellow of King's College, Cambridge, rector of Winterbourne, Strickland, and Witherston, and vicar of Hermitage, in Dorset, *b.* in 1727, died unm. 28th November, 1795.

III. Laurence, of London, *b.* in 1729, died unm. in 1772.

IV. Thomas, of Warminghurst Park, *b.* in 1732, who *m.* 26th March, 1787, Frances, second daughter of John Margesson, esq. of Offington, in Sussex, and dying in 1797, left issue,

WILLIAM-WESTBROOKE, successor to his cousin.

John, *b.* 10th March, 1790, *d.* 20th July, 1825, unm.

Thomas, *b.* 27th December, 1791, a captain of Dragoons, and deputy lieutenant for Sussex.

Mr. Richardson died 2nd January, 1734, and was *s.* by his eldest son,

WILLIAM WESTBROOKE RICHARDSON, esq. lord of the manors of Goring and East Ferring, in Sussex, and of Dewsbury, in Yorkshire, *b.* 16th November, 1725, who *m.* in 1758, Barbara, daughter and co-heir of Richard Johnson, esq. of London, merchant, and had issue,

WILLIAM, his heir.

Joseph, a cornet of dragoons, *b.* in 1757, died unm. in 1797.

Richard, *b.* in 1758, died 28th December, 1759.

Barbara Elizabeth, died unm. in 1770.

Mr. Richardson, who served the office of sheriff for Sussex in 1770, died in 1771, and was *s.* by his son,

WILLIAM RICHARDSON, esq. of Finden Place, in the county of Sussex, *b.* in 1754, wedded in 1779, Mary, eldest daughter of John Margesson, esq. of Offington, (see vol. i. p. 296), but by her, who died 10th April, 1828, leaving no issue, he was *s.* at his decease, 16th June, 1801, by his cousin, the present WILLIAM WESTBROOKE RICHARDSON, esq. of Finden Place.

*Arms*—Sa. on a chief arg. three lions' heads erased of the field.

*Crest*—Out of a mural crown or, a dexter arm in armour couped at the elbow, brandishing a falchion arg. the gripe vert, pomel and hilt or.

*Estates*—In Sussex.

*Seat*—Finden Place, Sussex.

## DUNDAS, OF BARTON COURT.

DUNDAS-DEANS-WHITLEY, JAMES, esq. of Barton Court, in the county of Berks, a post captain in the royal navy, and naval aid-de-camp to the king, *b.* 4th December, 1785; *m.* 28th April, 1808, his first cousin, Janet, only daughter of the late Charles Dundas, Lord Amesbury, by Ann his wife, daughter and sole heiress of Ralph Whitley, esq. of Aston Hall, Flintshire, and has issue,

CHARLES, of the Coldstream guards.

James, M.A. of Magdalen College, Cambridge.

Ann, *m.* to John-Archer Houblon, esq. of Great Hallingbury, Essex.

Janet.

Sophia.

This gentleman, whose patronymic is DEANS, assuming by sign manual the surnames of Whitley and Dundas, is now Captain Whitley-Deans-Dundas. He is a magistrate and deputy lieutenant for Berkshire, and represented Greenwich in the last parliament.

## Lineage.

DUNDAS, of FINGASK, eldest son of James Dundas, of Dundas, by Christian, his second wife, daughter of John, Lord Innermeath, and Lorn, was returned heir to his father in divers lands *anno* 1431 (see vol. i. p. 642). He *m.* Eupham, daughter of Sir Alexander Livingston, of Callender, and had one son and two daughters, viz.

ALEXANDER, his heir.

Elizabeth, *m.* to Sir David Guthrie.

Margaret, *m.* to Alexander Cockburn, of Langton.

Fingask died in 1451, during his confinement in Dumbarton Castle, wherein he had been imprisoned, through the hostility of William, earl of Douglas, and was *s.* by his son,

ALEXANDER DUNDAS, of Fingask, who married Isabel, daughter of Lawrence, Lord Oliphant, and had several sons, with one daughter, the wife of Law, of Lawbridge. He fell at Flodden, in 1513, together with four of his sons, and was *s.* by his eldest son,

ALEXANDER DUNDAS, of Fingask, who procured from JAMES V. a charter of confirmation of the lands of Coates, in the lordship of Elcho. He *m.* Elizabeth, daughter of Sir David Bruce, of Clackmannan, and had issue,

I. ARCHIBALD, his heir.

II. Robert.

III. Thomas, of Findhorn.

I. Margaret, *m.* first, to William Kerr, of Ancram, ancestor of the Marquises of Lothian; and secondly, to Sir George Douglas, of Mordington.

II. Nicholas, *m.* to Alexander Corville, commendator of Culross. Their eldest daughter, Grizel Colville, became the wife of Sir John Preston, of Valleyfield; and their second daughter, Jean Colville, of Robert Bruce, of Blair Hall.

Alexander Dundas was slain at Pinkie, and succeeded by his eldest son,

ARCHIBALD DUNDAS, of Fingask, served heir to his father in 1548, William Lord Ruthven being then sheriff. This Archibald was a man of much influence in the time of JAMES VI. as appears by a letter of that monarch, dated in 1579, to Alexander Blair, of Balthyock, relative to the affairs of the county of Perth, he recommending him to consult with Archibald Dundas, of Fingask, as a person in whom he (the king) placed the greatest confidence. He was succeeded at his decease by his son,

WILLIAM DUNDAS, of Fingask, who wedded, in 1582, Margaret, eldest daughter and heir of Sir David Carnegie, of Clouthie, but having no issue, was succeeded by his brother,

ARCHIBALD DUNDAS, who, upon his own resignation, got a charter of confirmation of the lands and barony of Fingask, in favour of himself and his heirs male, *anno* 1609. He married first, Jane, daughter of Sir David Carnegie, by Eupham, his second wife, daughter of Sir David Wemyss, of Wemyss, and had a son, JOHN, his heir; and a daughter, Nicholas, *m.* to Fairlie, of Braid. Archibald wedded secondly, Giles, daughter of Lawrence Mercer, of Aldie, and had a son, Lawrence, professor of humanity at Edinburgh. The eldest son,

SIR JOHN DUNDAS, of Fingask, returned heir to his father in 1624, received the honour of knighthood from CHARLES I. at Dunfermline in 1633. Enthusiastically attached to the unfortunate monarch, and nearly related by his mother to the great and gallant marquis of Montrose, he devoted his energies and fortune to the royal cause, and ruined his estate,—the transmitted inheritance of so long a line of ancestry. He espoused first, Anne, daughter of Sir William Moncrief, of that Ilk, but had no issue; and secondly, Margaret, daughter of George Dundas, of Dundas, by whom he had an only son, his successor in 1670,

JOHN DUNDAS, of Fingask, who *m.* Magdalen, daughter of Thomas Allardyce, son of Allardyce, of that Ilk, and was succeeded in 1724, by his son,

THOMAS DUNDAS, of Fingask, who acquired a considerable estate in the county Stirling, and got a charter under the great seal *anno* 1739, for erecting his lands into a barony, under the designation of the barony of Fingask. He *m.* Berthea, daughter of John Baillie, of Castlecarry, and had two sons, namely,

I. THOMAS, his heir.

II. Lawrence, of Kerse, M.P. for Edinburgh 1768, created a baronet of

Great Britain, with remainder to his brother, Thomas. He *m.* Margaret, daughter of Alexander Bruce, of Kennet, and dying in 1781, was succeeded by his son,

Sir Thomas Dundas, second bart. of Kerse, who was elevated to the peerage as Baron Dundas, of Aske, in Yorkshire.

The elder son,

Thomas Dundas, esq. of Fingask, was M.P. for the stewartry of Orkney and Shetland. This gentleman *m.* first, Anne, daughter of James Graham, of Airth, judge of the high court of Admiralty for Scotland, but had no issue; and secondly, in 1744, Lady Janet Maitland, daughter of Charles, sixth earl of Lauderdale, by whom he had, with four daughters,

I. Thomas, a general officer of distinction, who *m.* Eleanor Elizabeth, daughter of Alexander, earl of Home, and died at Guadaloupe, 3rd June, 1794, leaving issue.

II. Charles, of whom presently.

I. Margaret, *m.* to A. Gibson, esq.

II. Berthia, *m.* to George Haldane, esq.

III. Mary, *m.* to James Bruce, esq. of Kinnaird.

IV. Janet, *m.* James Deans, esq. M.D. of Calcutta, by whom she had James Deans, esq. who assumed the surname of Dundas, and is the present Captain Dundas, of Barton Place.

Mr. Dundas died in 1786. His second son,

Charles Dundas, esq. of Barton Court, in the county of Berks, for many years representative in parliament for that shire, was elevated to the peerage 10th May, 1832, as Baron Amesbury, of Kentbury Amesbury, but enjoyed the honour for two months only, dying 30th June, 1832. He espoused first, Ann, daughter and sole heiress of Ralph Whitley, esq. of Aston Hall, in Flintshire, and had by her an only daughter,

Janet, who wedded her cousin, Capt. James Deans, which gentleman having taken the surname and inherited the estates of the family of Dundas, is the present James Whitley-Deans-Dundas, esq. of Barton Court.

Lord Amesbury wedded secondly, his cousin, Margaret, third daughter of the late Hon. Charles Barclay, and widow first, of Charles Ogilvy, esq. and secondly, of Major Archibald Erskine.

## Family of Whitley.

Adam de Aston possessed, *temp.* Edward III. the Aston estate, in the parish of Hawarden, and the county of Flint, which was conveyed by the heiress of his son, Richard, to Henry de Messam. William, great grandson of Henry de Messam, had an only daughter and heir, Margaret, who wedded Richard Whitley, and from this marriage the estate has descended to its present proprietor. Fifth in descent from Richard Whitley, and Margaret, his wife, was

Thomas Whitley, esq. who served the office of sheriff for Flintshire in 1638. He was one of the most devoted adherents of *King* Charles I. and was fined £125. by the parliament for his exertions in the royal cause. He was twice married, by his first wife, Dorothy, daughter of Thomas Ravenscroft, esq. he had one son, Robert Whitley, esq. afterwards of Aston, and two daughters. By the second wife, Elizabeth, daughter of Roger Brereton, of Stoke, he had five sons and five daughters. Roger Whitley, the eldest son of the second marriage, was a colonel in the service of Charles I. and governor of Aberystwith Castle; Thomas Whitley, the second son, was slain in the defence of Hawarden Castle, for the same monarch; John Whitley, the third son, was a colonel of Foot in the royal army, and fell in defending Conway against the parliamentary forces; Ralph Whitley, the fourth son, survived the disastrous period of the Commonwealth, and was made receiver of North Wales, by *King* Charles II.; and Peter Whitley, the fifth son, was also an active royalist, and an attendant upon Prince Rupert.

The descendant of Thomas Whitley, high sheriff in 1638, another

Thomas Whitley, esq. of Aston Hall, wedded Anne, daughter of Thomas Loder, esq. of Balsdon Park, (by Elizabeth, his wife, daughter of Sir Jonathan Raymond, of Barton Court, Berks, who had obtained that estate in marriage with the daughter of Philip Jemmet, esq. alderman of London), and had a son and successor,

Ralph Whitley, esq. of Aston Hall, in Flintshire, and of Barton Court, in the county of Berks, whose only daughter and heiress, by Margaret, his wife,

Janet Whitley, of Aston Hall, espoused Charles Dundas, esq. M.P. for Berkshire, and left, at her decease, an only daughter, Janet Whitley-Dundas, who *m.* 28th April, 1808, as already stated, James Deans, esq. the present Captain Whitley-Deans Dundas, of Barton Court.

*Arms*—Quarterly; first and fourth, arg. a lion rampant gu. within a bordure flory counterflory; second, arg. on a chief gu. three garbs or, for Whitley; third, az. a cross moline arg. for Deans.

*Crests*—First, for Dundas, a lion's head

full faced, looking through a bush of oak, ppr.; second, for WHITLEY, a stag's head, arg. attired or, holding in its mouth the end of a scroll bearing the motto, "Live to live."

*Mottoes*—Essayez, for DUNDAS. Arte vel marte, for DEANS.

*Estates*—In Berkshire, Flintshire, &c.

*Town Residence.*—Baker-street, Portman-square.

*Seats*—Barton Court, near Hungerford Berks; and Aston Hall, Flintshire.

## WHIELDON, OF SPRINGFIELD HOUSE.

WHIELDON, GEORGE, esq. of Springfield House, in the county of Warwick, and of Welton Place, Northamptonshire, *b.* 27th March, 1786, *m.* first, 9th November, 1809, Saba, second dau. of the late Josiah Spode, esq. of The Mount, in Staffordshire, but by that lady had no issue. He wedded, secondly, 19th February, 1817, Mary, third daughter of the late Richard Brettell, esq. of Finstall House, and of Stourbridge, in the county of Worcester, and has

I. GEORGE, *b.* 1818.
II. Arthur-Edward.
III. Harry-Thomas-Turner.
I. Georgina-Elizabeth.
II. Katherine-Mary.

Mr. Whieldon, who is in the commission of the peace and deputy lieutenancy of the county of Stafford, had the gratification of receiving from his friends and neighbours, in 1826, an elegant silver candelabrum, value one hundred guineas, "as a small tribute expressive of their sense of his able and upright discharge of the responsible duties of the magistracy."

### Lineage.

THOMAS WHIELDON, esq. of Fenton Hall, in the county of Stafford, who was high sheriff of that shire in 1787, espoused 13th September, 1776, Sarah, daughter of John Turner, esq. of Cumberland Place, London, and left at his decease, in 1794, three surviving sons, GEORGE WHIELDON, esq. now of Springfield House; Thomas Whieldon, esq. resident at Rome; and the Rev. Edward Whieldon, of Wood House, in Staffordshire, rector of Burslem, and perpetual curate of Bradley, with a dau. Charlotte, wife of Daniel Bird Baddeley, esq. of Ivy House.

*Arms*—Gu. on a chev. arg. between three pears stalked and leaved or, as many crosses sa. a chief ermine thereon a lion passant of the fourth.

*Crest*—Upon a mount vert between two branches of oak ppr. a fer de moline fess ways sa. thereon perched a parrot vert collared gu. holding in the dexter claw a pear stalked and leaved.

*Motto*—Virtus præstantior auro.

*Estates*—At Fenton, in the parish of Stoke-upon-Trent, Staffordshire; and Springfield, &c. in the parishes of Bedworth, Exhall, and Foleshill, in Warwickshire, whereon there is a valuable mine of coal and an extensive colliery established, called the Hawkesbury Colliery, giving employment to upwards of two hundred workmen.

*Seats*—Welton Place, Northamptonshire; and Springfield House, Warwickshire.

## WESTBY, OF THORNHILL.

WESTBY, WILLIAM, esq. of Thornhill, in the county of Dublin, *b.* 18th June, 1753; *m.* first, in Tottenham church, Middlesex, 18th April, 1781, Mary, daughter of George Fletcher, esq. of Tottenham, and had issue (Mrs. Westby died on the 17th May, 1797),

I. William, who died young.

II. NICHOLAS, *b.* 28th October, 1787; *m.* 25th August, 1815, the Hon. Emily-Susannah-Laura Waldegrave, eldest daughter of William, late Lord Radstock, and has had,
   1. William-Waldegrave, } *d.* young.
   2. Nicholas-Granville, } *d.* young.
   3. Edward-Perceval, *b.* 11th July, 1828.
   1. Emily-Elizabeth.
   2. Erina-Laura, *d.* 1st March, 1834.
   3. Caroline-Mary.
   4. Louisa-Isabella.
   5. Horatia-Caroline.

III. George, lieutenant in the 95th, or rifle regiment, *b.* 2nd June, 1790; killed 5th May, 1811, at Fuentes D'Onore, in Spain; *d.* unm.

IV. Edward, cornet in the 2nd North British dragoons, *b.* 25th August, 1794; killed at Waterloo, 18th June, 1815; *d.* unm.

I. Mary.

II. Louisa.

III. Wilhelmina, *m.* to Richard Moore, esq. of the county of Tipperary, barrister-at-law, and has issue.

Mr. Westby wedded, secondly, 28th August, 1809, Elizabeth, daughter of George-Boleyn Whitney, esq. of Newpass, in the county of Westmeath, but has not increased his family by other issue. He is the eldest son and representative of the late William Westby, esq. of High Park, in the county of Wicklow.

### Lineage.

Owing, it is stated, to the destruction of the parish registry of Ennis, in the county of Clare, there is no possibility of now ascertaining the actual founder of this family in Ireland. He is presumed to have been a THOMAS WESTBY, son of Major Westby, of Rawcliffe, in the county of Lancaster, who settled at Clonmel. (See vol. i. page 589.) Of this Thomas little is known, neither the name of his wife nor the time of his death: he is supposed, however, to have left the following issue,

NICHOLAS, of Ennis, in the county of Clare.

James, who had a son and daughter, namely,
   Nicholas, who died unm. in 1729.
   Mary, died unm. in 1775.

Humberston, of Strokestown, in the county of Roscommon, *m.* first, in 1684, Rhodia, daughter of Colonel Perceval; and secondly, a Miss Mahon, and had,
   Edward, who *d.* unm. 9th November, 1732.

George.

The eldest son (and first authenticated ancestor of the family),

NICHOLAS WESTBY, esq. of Ennis, in the county of Clare, collector of the customs of that port, *m.* in 1698, Frances, daughter of John Stepney, esq. of Durrow, in the Queen's county, and acquired, as the marriage portion of his wife, the estate of High

Park, in the county of Wicklow. By this lady (who died 29th March, 1732, proof of her will bears date in 1734) he had one son and two daughters, viz.

WILLIAM, his heir.

Jane, born at Ennis, 12th September, 1699, *m.* 13th June, 1717, to Robert Perceval, esq. of Knightsbrooke, in the county of Meath.

Frances, born at Ennis, 10th October, 1701, died on the 13th of the same month.

Nicholas Westby *d.* 19th October, 1716, (his will was proved in the Court of Prerogative of Dublin in the same year), and was *s.* by his son,

WILLIAM WESTBY, esq. of High Park, in the county of Wicklow, born 3rd November, 1702, *m.* in 1743, Mary, daughter of Brigadier-general Jones, by Mary, daughter and sole heiress of Richard Neville,* esq. of Furnace, in the county of Kildare, and had issue,

I. WILLIAM, *b.* 19th November, 1745, *d.* young.

II. NICHOLAS, heir to his father.

III. Edward, *b.* 5th May, 1752, *d.* young.

IV. WILLIAM, OF THORNHILL, representative now of the family.

V. EDWARD, who inherited High Park under the will of his eldest brother, and is the present EDWARD WESTBY, esq. of High Park. See WESTBY, of *High Park*.

VI. George, *b.* 20th October, 1756, died in January, 1763.

I. Mary, *b.* 8th July, 1744, *m.* to Thomas Brown, esq. of New Grove, in the county of Clare, and died in February, 1776, leaving issue.

II. Frances, *b.* 28th February, 1747, *d.* unm. 6th July, 1808, and was buried in St. Peter's, Dublin. Will proved in 1809.

III. Jane, *b.* 5th October, 1748, died unm. 11th March, 1825. Will proved in that year.

IV. Martha, *b.* 29th November, 1749, died unm. 13th December, 1779, at the Hot Wells, near Bristol, and was buried in St. Peter's, Dublin.

Mr. Westby, who served the office of sheriff for the county of Wicklow in 1733, died 12th October, 1757. His lady, surviving him above thirty years, died on the 3rd October, 1794. Their wills were proved in Dublin the respective years of their decease, and they were both interred in St. Peter's, in that city. He was *s.* by his eldest surviving son,

NICHOLAS WESTBY, esq. of High Park, *b.* 26th March, 1751, old style. This gentleman, who represented the borough of Tulsk, as well as the county of Wicklow, in several parliaments, rejected with a scorn a peerage offered by the government to influence his vote on the important question of union, and patriotically opposed that measure to the last. He served the office of sheriff for the county of Wicklow, and died unmarried 30th November, 1800. His will was proved in 1801, under which the mansion and estate of High Park passed to the younger of his two surviving brothers, EDWARD WESTBY, esq. while the representation of the family, &c. devolved upon the elder, WILLIAM WESTBY, esq. of Thornhill.

*Arms*—Quarterly, first and fourth arg. on a chev. az. three cinquefoils pierced of the first; second, arg. on a chief indented gu. three crosses pattee fitchee; third, or, three garbs sa.

*Crest*—A martlet sa. in the mouth a sprig or.

*Motto*—Nec volenti nec volanti.

*Estates*—In the county of Clare.

*Town Residence*—6, Merrion Square.

*Seat*—Thornhill, near Bray.

* By Mary, his wife, daughter of Richard Barry, esq. of The Rock, in the county of Cork, and sister of James Barry, whose daughter and heiress, Judith, married, 8th June, 1719, John, first Lord Farnham, and brought him Newtown-Barry, and all the estates of that branch of the Barrymore family. Brigadier-General Jones, Mrs. Westby's father, who represented for many years the borough of Wexford in parliament, and once the county, was appointed colonel of the 38th regiment of foot, the 25th December, 1729. His son, ARTHUR JONES, assumed the name and arms of Neville on inheriting the Furnace estates. He was great-grandfather of HENRIETTA NEVILLE, who married, first, Edward, eldest son of Sir Edward Dering, of Surrenden, in Kent; and secondly, Sir William Geary, of Oxenheath.

## WESTBY, OF HIGH PARK.

**WESTBY, EDWARD,** esq. of High Park, in the county of Wicklow, *b.* 11th September, 1755, called to the bar of Ireland in Hilary term, 1779, made a bencher of King's Inn, Dublin, Trinity term, 1789, and was one of the masters in Chancery from 1788 to 1814; *m.* first, in 1787, Anne, daughter of Richard Palmer, esq. of Glannacurragh Castle, in the King's County, and by her, who died 22nd June, 1791, had issue,

Frances, *m.* 18th October, 1816, to Richard Donovan, esq. of Ballymore, in the county of Wexford, and has issue.

Mary, *m.* in 1817, to Joshua Nunn, esq. of St. Margaret's, in the county of Wexford, and has issue.

Mr. Westby wedded, secondly, Phœbie, third daughter of Richard Palmer, esq. of Glannacurragh Castle, and has three sons, with three other daughters, namely,

William-Jones, *b.* 23rd November, 1802, a magistrate and deputy lieutenant for Wicklow, and high sheriff in 1827; *m.* 9th June, 1828, Catharine, daughter of Colonel Grogan, of Seafield, in the county of Dublin, and has issue,

1. William-Henry-Jones, *b.* 23rd July, 1831; bapt. at Kiltegan, 23rd August following.
2. George-Jones, *b.* in York Street, Dublin, 3rd January, 1834; baptized at Kiltegan.

1. Maria-Palmer.

Nicholas-Henry-Jones, *b.* 13th July, 1805, formerly a lieutenant in the 2nd regiment of foot, and subsequently in the 1st royal dragoons, married and has issue.

Henry-Humberston-Jones, *b.* 9th July, 1809, in holy orders, presented to the rectory of Oldcastle, in Meath, in 1834.

Martha-Jones.

Anne-Palmer, *m.* in St. Peter's, Dublin, 2nd August, 1831, to Parsons, fifth son of Sir Hugh Crofton, bart. of Mohill House, in the county of Leitrim, and has issue.

Jane-Jones, *m.* at Kiltegan church, Wicklow, 17th December, 1831, to James Perceval, esq. of Barntown House, in the county of Wexford, a major in the army, formerly a captain in the 95th regiment, now the rifle brigade, and has issue.

Mr. Westby having, in 1814, disposed of his mastership in Chancery, which obliged him to reside in Dublin, retired to High Park, a mansion and extensive demesne devised him by his eldest brother, and having rebuilt the house, which was destroyed by fire in the rebellion of 1798, has continued since to reside there. He was high sheriff for Wicklow in 1807.

### Lineage.

For descent and arms, see Westby, of Thornhill.

*Estates* — Killamoat, Ballykillmurry, Rathdaffbegg, Killcarney, Carrigbrack, Knocknagilky, and High Park, all in the county of Wicklow.

*Town Residence*—29, York Street, Dublin.

*Seat*—High Park, near Baltinglas.

# GRAHAM, OF FINTRY.

GRAHAM, ROBERT, esq. of Fintry, *b.* 16th January, 1816, succeeded to the representation of this branch of the ancient family of Graham, upon the demise of his father, 17th March, 1822.

## Lineage.

SIR WILLIAM GRAHAM, lord of Kincardine, chief of the name, and ancestor of the Dukes of Montrose, *m.* in 1406, for his second wife, the Lady Mary Stuart,* daughter of ROBERT III. king of Scotland, and widow of George, Earl of Angus, and of Sir James Kennedy, of Dunure, progenitor of the Marquis of Ailsa. Of this marriage the sons were

- ROBERT (Sir), who became "of Fintry."
- PATRICK, first archbishop of St. Andrews, who obtained, with the primacy, a legatine commission to reform the abuses of the church, and is described as "a singular good man, and of great virtue." He *s.* his half brother, Bishop James Kennedy in the see of Saint Andrews.
- WILLIAM, ancestor of the GRAHAMS, of Garvock.
- Harry.
- Walter, from whom descended the GRAHAMS, of Knockdolian, in Carrick, and of Wallacetown, in Dumbarton.

The eldest son,

SIR ROBERT GRAHAM, was styled of Fintry, from part of his possessions in Stirlingshire, but although these lands were afterwards exchanged, in the seventeenth century, with the family of Montrose, for others in Angus, Fintry has always continued to be the designation of his descendants, and their usual place of residence in Angusshire was so named. Sir Robert, sometimes styled of Ewsdall, from having succeeded his father and mother in the barony of Malanork, in Dumfries, was, in conjunction with Sir James Scrymgeour, of Dudhope, appointed justiciary of all Scotland, benorth the Forth. He *m.* Janet, dau. and heiress of Sir Richard Lovell, of Balumbie, (a branch of the extinct Earls of Egmont) by Elizabeth,* his wife, dau. of Sir Henry Douglas, of Lochleven, and had issue,

- ROBERT, his heir.
- JOHN, ancestor of GRAHAM, of CLAVERHOUSE, (*see conclusion of this article*).
- Margaret, *m.* to John Erskine, of Dun.
- Elizabeth, *m.* to Andrew Halliburton, of Pitcur.

Sir Robert Graham, who exchanged, in 1480, the lands of Ewsdall with Archibald, Earl of Angus for those of Balargus, in Angus, which he bestowed on his second son, was succeeded at his decease by his eldest son,

ROBERT GRAHAM, of Fintry, who wedded† the Lady Elizabeth Douglas, daughter of John, Earl of Angus, and was succeeded by his son,

SIR DAVID GRAHAM, third laird of Fintry, who *m.* a daughter of William, first Earl of Montrose, by Annabella his wife, daughter of John, first Lord Drummond, and left a son and successor,

* The Lady Mary wedded, fourthly, Sir William Edmonstone.

* "This lady, maid of honour to Joanna queen of JAMES I. of Scotland, was in the royal apartment when it was attacked by the assassins of that king, in 1437; on the first alarm she went to secure the door, but the bar having been removed she thrust her arm into its place, in the hopes of keeping them out; they broke her arm in forcing open the door and finished their bloody tragedy."—*Douglas.*

† In the marriage contract, dated 1476, failing Elizabeth, her sisters, Margaret, Lilias, and Elyson, are successively betrothed to the said Robert Graham.

WILLIAM GRAHAM, fourth of Fintry, who obtained, in 1529 and 1541, charters from JAMES V. constituting his extensive lands in Forfarshire, Stirlingshire, and Perthshire, into "two free baronries, to be held blench of the crown, to be called the baronries of Strathdichty, Comitis, in Forfarshire, and Buchlivy Graham, in Monteith." He appears to have been a man of literature, and a Latin poem by him is printed on the reverse of the title page of the second edition of a very rare book, "Bepartitum in Morali Philosophia Opusculum: ex variis auctoribus per Magistrum Guilielmum Manderston Scotum nuperrime Collectum. Parhisiis, 1523." FINTRY married Catharine, daughter of John Beaton, of Balfour, and sister of Cardinal Beaton, Archbishop of St. Andrews and Chancellor of Scotland, and was succeeded by his son,

SIR DAVID GRAHAM, fifth of Fintry, who received the honour of knighthood from JAMES VI. He *m.* Margaret, daughter of James, Lord Ogilvy, ancestor of the Earls of Airlie, and had three sons and one daughter, Alyson, *m.* to John Creighton, of Innermylie. His eldest son and successor,

DAVID GRAHAM, sixth of Fintry, married Barbara, daughter of Sir James Scott, of Balwearie, (lineal descendant of the celebrated Sir Michael Scott) and had two sons, viz.

DAVID, his heir.

James, who possessed the lands of Monorgan and Craigo.

Fintry was beheaded at Edinburgh, in 1592, for his participation with the Earls of Huntley and Errol in the popish plot, and was *s.* by his son,

DAVID GRAHAM, seventh of Fintry, who wedded Mary, daughter of Sir James Halliburton, of Pitcur, by Margaret his wife, daughter of Sir James Scrymgeour, of Dudhope, first Viscount Dudhope, and left two sons and one daughter, *m.* to Mackintosh, of Mackintosh.

This laird spent a great portion of the family estates in the royal cause during the civil wars, and his second son, James, left the college of Saint Andrews to join the standard of their chief, the gallant Marquis of Montrose; in the account of whose public funeral, A.D. 1661, by Bishop Wishart, the father and son are thus mentioned:—"The purse carried by David Graham, of Fentrie; this noble gentleman's predecessor was the son of the Lord Graham, then head of the house of Montrose, who, upon a second marriage on King James the First his sister, begot the first baron of Fentry, which, in a direct male line, hath continued to this baron; and as their birth was high, so their qualifications have in every respect been great, for in all ages since their rise, nothing unbecoming loyal subjects or persons of honour could be laid to their charge, and he who possesseth it now can claim as large a share as any of his ancestors.

"The arms of the defunct in mourning, by James Graham, of Bucklevy, son to the Baron of Fentry, a gentleman which nothing could ever startle from his majesty's service, and that he was a favourite of the deceased, and accompanied his son in the late Highland war, is sufficient to speak his praises." David Graham was succeeded by his son,

JOHN GRAHAM, eighth of Fintry, who espoused the Lady Margaret Scrymgeour, only child of James, Earl of Dundee, by the Lady Margaret Ramsey his wife, daughter of the Earl of Dalhousie, and had one son, who died young. He was *s.* at his decease by his brother,

JAMES GRAHAM, ninth of Fintry, who had previously inherited from his uncle the estates of Manorgan, Craigo, and Bucklevy, which lands he entirely expended in the service of his royal master. In 1679 he was lieut.-colonel of the Angus regiment, and had the offer of a baronetcy from CHARLES II. but declined the proffered honour. He *m.* Ann, daughter of Col. Hay, of Killour,* by the daughter and heiress of Whitelaw, of Whitson and Whitelaw. The issue of this marriage were,

I. DAVID, his heir.
II. William, colonel in the army, *m.* in 1691, Agnes, daughter of Sir William Foulis, bart. of Ingleby, in Yorkshire, and had several children, but the male line of his descendants is now extinct.
I. Isabella, *m.* to Mylne, of Mylnefield.
II. Jean, *m.* to Fletcher, of Balinshoe.
III. Margaret, *m.* first, to Sir James Kinlock, bart. of that Ilk, and secondly, to Ogilvie, of Balfour.

The elder son,

DAVID GRAHAM, tenth laird of Fintry, *m.* Anna, eldest daughter of Robert Moray, of Abercairny, by Anna his wife, daughter of Patrick Græme, of Inchbrakie, and had to survive youth one son and ten daughters, viz.

I. ROBERT, his heir.
I. Anna, *m.* to Gardyne, of Middleton and Laton.
II. Margaret, *m.* to Carnegy, of Balnamoon.
III. Emily, *m.* first, to Hunter, of Burn-

* Of the noble house of ERROL, the KILLOUR branch of the HAYS inherited the honours of the family, and became Earls of Errol, on the decease of George, the tenth earl, *s. p.* in 1674.—BURKE's *Peerage and Baronetage.*

side, and secondly, to Sir William Nairne, bart. of Dunsinnane.

IV. Isabella, married to Duncan, of Ardownie.

V. Agnes, *m.* to Robertson, of Carnonstie.

VI. Jane, *m.* to — Rutheford, esq.'

VII. Grizel, *m.* to — Graham, esq.

VIII. Mary, *m.* to Guthrie, of Clepping-ton.

IX. Elizabeth, *m.* to — Stewart, esq.

X. Lilias, *m.* to — Wallace, esq.

David Graham, was succeeded by his only son,

ROBERT GRAHAM, eleventh of Fintry, who espoused, in 1735, Margaret, daughter of Sir William Murray, of Ochtertyre, by Catherine his wife, daughter of Hugh, tenth Lord Lovat,* and had issue,

I. ROBERT, his heir.

II. James, captain in the 1st regiment, or Royals, *d.* unmarried, at Naples, in 1779.

III. David, East India Company's civil service, died unmarried, at Vellore, in 1789.

I. Catharine, } both *d.* unm.
II. Helen, }

III. Ann, *m.* to Robert Fletcher, esq. of Balinshoe.

IV. Margaret, *m.* to Alexander Bower, esq. of Kincaldrum.

V. Elizabeth, *m.* to William Douglas, esq. of Brigton.

Fintry was *s.* by his eldest son,

ROBERT GRAHAM, 12th of Fintry, born 17th January, 1749, who married Margaret-Elizabeth, daughter of Thomas Mylne, esq. of Mylnefield, (by Isabella his wife, only daughter of Dr. George Gray, of Huntington, younger son of Gray, of Hackerton, a scion of the ennobled house of Gray) and had issue,

I. Robert, who was assassinated at Benares, by the treachery of a native chief, in 1799, aged twenty-four.

II. JOHN, heir to his father.

III. Thomas, captain R. N. *m.* Maria, daughter of Admiral George Dundas, and died at Valparaiso, while in command of the Doris frigate, 9th April, 1822.

IV. David, *b.* 28th January, 1785, died unmarried, 11th September, 1824.

V. James-Scott, *b.* in October, 1796, *d.* in 1804.

I. Isabella-Gray, *d.* in infancy.

II. Isabella.

III. Margaret, died unmarried, aged eighteen.

IV. Anne, *m.* to General the Hon. John Brodrick, youngest son of George, fourth Viscount Middleton, and has issue.

V. Elizabeth-Kinlock, died an infant.

VI. Elizabeth, *m.* to James Keay, esq. of Snaigon, Perthshire.

VII. Helen-Christian, married to Henry Cloete, esq. eldest son of Laurence Cloete, esq. of Zamdvleete, C. B. S. and has issue.

VIII. Mary-Cathcart.

IX. Jemima-Agnes, *m.* to Major William Belden-Dundas, eldest son of Admiral George Dundas, (of the family of Dundas, of Manor).

X. Emily-Georgina.

XI. Catherine-Margaret.

XII. Roberta.

XIII. Caroline-A.-Mackay, *m.* 12th July, 1830, to A. Morton Carr, esq. solicitor of excise, in Scotland, (of the family of Carr, of Esholt and Helton Hall, in Northumberland).

The twelfth laird of Fintry died 10th January, 1815, and was *s.* by his son,

JOHN GRAHAM, esq. thirteenth of Fintry, *b.* 24th April, 1778, who entering the army, at the age of sixteen, accompanied his regiment (the 90th) in the expedition to Isle Dieu in 1795. In 1797 he joined Lord Lynedock, then Col. Graham, at that period with the Austrian army. Returning from that service, he received the appointment of aid-de-camp to the Earl of Chatham, and proceeded with his lordship, in 1799, to the Helder. Subsequently, having raised one hundred men for the 93rd Highlanders, he obtained a majority in the regiment, and acted with it at the capture of the Cape of Good Hope in 1806, where he remained in command of the rifle corps until 1812, when he returned to England on leave of absence, and went with Lord Lynedock to Holland, in 1813, as aid-de-camp and private military secretary. In 1815, he resumed his command at the Cape, and was commandant of Simon's Town at the time of his decease, 17th March, 1822. He *m.* 24th July, 1812, Johanna-Catharine, daughter of Rodolph Cloete, esq. of Westerford, Cape of Good Hope, and by her (who wedded secondly, in November, 1826, Capt. Edward Danford, 49th regiment) had one son and three daughters, viz.

ROBERT, his heir.
Johanna-Catharina.
Elizabeth-Margaret.
Isabella-Anne.

Col. Graham was *s.* at his decease by his son, ROBERT GRAHAM, esq. now of Fintry.

* By Amelia his wife, daughter of the Marquess of Athol, and grand-daughter of Charlotte de la Tremouille, the celebrated Countess of Derby, who so gallantly defended the Isle of Man against Cromwell. Her ladyship was grand-daughter of William, first Prince of Orange.

*Arms*—Or, on a chief sa. three escallops of the first, surrounded by a double tressure to mark the royal descent. Three piles sa. as representing the family of Lovel of Balumbie.

*Crest*—A phœnix in flames.

*Motto*—Bon fin.

### Graham, of Claverhouse.

JOHN GRAHAM, second son of Sir Robert Graham, the first of Fintry, obtained from Archibald, earl of Angus, a charter of the lands of Balargus, in Forfarshire. He *m.* Matilda, daughter of Sir James Scrimgeour, constable of Dundee, and was succeeded by his son,

JOHN GRAHAM, of Balargus, who acquired in 1530, the lands of Kirkton, and subsequently those of Claverhouse. He wedded Margaret, daughter of John Bethune, of Balfour, and had a son and successor,

JOHN GRAHAM, of Claverhouse, living in 1541, who *m.* Anne, daughter of Robert Lundin, of Balgony, in Fife, and was *s.* at his decease, about 1580, by his elder son,

SIR WILLIAM GRAHAM, of Claverhouse, who, by Marian, his wife, daughter of Thomas Fotheringhame, of Powie, had two sons,

- GEORGE, his heir.
- Walter, ancestor of the Grahams of Duntroon.

Sir William died in October, 1642, and was *s.* by his son,

GEORGE GRAHAM, of Claverhouse, who died in April, 1645, leaving two sons, by the elder,

SIR WILLIAM GRAHAM, of Claverhouse, he was succeeded. This laird augmented considerably the family estates, and obtained by charter, under the great seal, the lands and barony of Ogilvie. He *m.* the Lady Jean Carnegie, fourth daughter of John, first earl of Northesk, and had two sons, JOHN and DAVID; and two daughters, Margaret, *m.* to Sir Robert Graham, of Morphy; and Anne, *m.* to Robert Young, of Auldbar. Sir William was succeeded by his elder son,

JOHN GRAHAM, of Claverhouse, a distinguished, perhaps the most distinguished soldier of the era in which he lived. Animated from his earliest years by the study of the poets and orators of antiquity, as well as by the traditionary songs of the highland bards, Claverhouse entered, at a very youthful age, on a military life, and served in the low countries against the French in the war of 1672, eminently signalizing himself at the battle of Seneff. Shortly afterward he returned home, and obtained a regiment from CHARLES II. for the especial purpose of forcing the non-conformists into communion with the established church. During the progress of the war which ensued, his success was varied. In 1679, he attacked a conventicle on Loudoun Hill, in Ayrshire, and after a close and furious engagement at Drumclog, suffered defeat, but retrieved his fortune in the well known action of Bothwell Bridge: the acts of cruelty, however, which followed, and which procured for Graham the appellation of *Bloody Clavers*, have indelibly tarnished his gallantry and reputation. In palliation, he justified the course he had adopted by the allegation that "terror was true mercy, if it put an end to, or prevented war." After the flight of JAMES II. by whom he had been created VISCOUNT DUNDEE, and during the consequent proceedings in Scotland, Claverhouse became chiefly conspicuous. When the ill-fated king withdrew to Rochester, he endeavoured to dissuade his departure from the kingdom: "Give me your majesty's commission to raise ten thousand of the disbanded soldiers," said the gallant and sanguine Dundee, "and marching through England with the royal standard at our head, we will drive the Dutch invader at the point of the sword into the sea."* This counsel proving ineffective, Graham proceeded with his dragoons to Stirling, and there called a parliament of the friends of the abdicated monarch. The convention sent a party to apprehend him; but he retired into Lockabar, and summoning a general rendezvous of the clans, raised upwards of two thousand men. With these he marched to Blair, in Atholl, and Mackay, King William's general, advancing with four thousand foot and two troops of horse, they met at the pass of Killicranky, on the 17th June, 1689. Mackay drew up his men in order of battle, and wished to bring on the engagement without delay; but the Scottish commander well knowing that night would be of advantage to the highlanders, whether successful or defeated, delayed the attack until half an hour before sunset; at that moment he ordered his troops to rush down from their station and begin the conflict in a series of small columns on the wings of the enemy, calculating that this onset was most likely to bring on an action hand to hand, in which he was certain of the superiority of his clansmen. Such had been the disposition of Dundee's kinsman and model, the gallant Marquis of Montrose, at the battle of Alderne. The enthusiastic and impetuous charge of the

* At a subsequent period, Dundee unsuccessfully conjured his royal master, who was wasting time and means in Ireland, to embark, with a part of his army for Scotland, where his presence would fix the wavering, and intimidate the timid, and where hosts of shepherds would start up warriors at the first wave of his banner on their mountains.

Scotch proved irresistible; Mackay fled, defeated with the loss of two thousand men, and escaped to Stirling, apprehensive of the pursuit of Dundee. But the gallant Graham was no more. After a desperate conflict with the enemy's artillery, he returned to cut off the retreat, but at the moment that his arm was extended to his troops, he received a shot through an opening in his armour,* and dropped from horseback as he attempted to ride off the field. He survived, however, to write a concise and dignified account of his success to James.† Had he lived to improve this important victory, little doubt can be entertained that he would have recovered the whole of Scotland beyond the Forth. But his death was fatal to his party, by whom his memory has been cherished, almost to adoration, and a poet thus pathetically addresses his shade, and bewails the loss sustained by Scotland;

Ultime Scotorum, potuit quo sospite solo
  Libertas patriæ salva fuisse tuæ
Te moriente novos accepit Scotia cives
  Accepitque novos te moriente Deos.
Illa tibi superesse negat, tu non potes illi,
  Ergo Caledonia, nomen inane, vale
Tuque vale gentis priscæ fortissime ductor,
  Optime Scotorum, atque ultime, Grame, vale.

"Graham of Claverhouse," says Sir Walter Scott, "was low of stature, and slightly, though elegantly formed, his gesture, language, and manners were those of one whose life had been spent among the noble and the gay. His features exhibited even feminine regularity, an oval face, a straight and well formed nose, dark hazel eyes, a complexion just sufficiently tinged with brown to save it from the charge of effeminacy, a short upper lip curved like that of a Grecian statue, and slightly shaded by small mustachios of light brown, joined to a profusion of long curled locks of the same colour which fell down on each side of his face, contributed to form such a countenance as limners like to paint, and ladies to look upon. The severity of his character, as well as the higher attributes of undaunted and enterprising valour which even his enemies were compelled to admit, lay concealed under an exterior which seemed adapted to the court or the saloon, rather than to the field. The same gentleness and gaiety of expression which reigned in his features seemed to inspire his actions and gestures; and, on the whole he was generally esteemed, at first sight, rather qualified to the votary of pleasure than ambition. But under this soft exterior was hidden a spirit unbounded in daring, and in aspiring, yet cautious and prudent as that of Machiavel himself. Profound in politics, and imbued of course with that disregard for individual rights which its intrigues usually generate, this leader was cool and collected in danger, fierce and ardent in pursuing success, careless of death himself, and ruthless in inflicting it upon others.* Such are the characters formed in times of civil discord, when the highest qualities, perverted by party spirit, and inflamed by habitual opposition, are too often combined with vices and excesses which deprive them at once of their merit and of their lustre."

Lord Dundee m. Jean, youngest daughter of William Lord Cochrane, and by her (who wedded secondly), William, third Lord Kilsyth, had a son,

James, second Viscount Dundee, who died young, in December, 1689, and was succeeded by his uncle,

David, third Viscount Dundee, who fought at Killicranky, and was outlawed. He died without issue in 1700.

* The buff coat Dundee wore at Killicranky is still preserved at Pennycuick House, the seat of Sir George Clerk, bart. and the fatal shot hole is under the arm pit.—*Minstrelsy of the Border.*

† King William hearing that the express dispatched to Edinburgh with the account of the defeat had been detained a day on the road, exclaimed, "Dundee must certainly have fallen, otherwise he would have been there before it could have arrived." At a later period, William being urged to reinforce the troops in Scotland, replied, "It is needless: the war died with Dundee."

* All other punishments save death disgraced, he said, a gentleman, and all who were with him were of that rank, but that death was a relief from the consciousness of crime. It is reported, that having seen a youth fly in his first action, Dundee pretended he had sent him to the rear on a message; the youth fled a second time;—he brought him to the front of the army, and declaring that "a gentleman's son ought not to fall by the hands of a common executioner," shot him with his own pistol.

# GRÆME, OF GARVOCK.

GRÆME, ROBERT, esq. of Garvock, in the county of Perth, *b.* 4th September, 1766; *m.* 1st September, 1802, Jane-Anne, only daughter of William Aytoun, esq. second son of Roger Aytoun, seventh laird of Inchdarnie, and chief of the family of Aytoun, by whom he has had issue,

JAMES, *b.* 23rd July, 1803.
William, *b.* 30th December, 1806; *d.* 14th March, 1820.
Robert, *b.* 13th June, 1811.

Isabella-Edmondstoun.
Mary.
Jane-Anne.
Janet-Rollo.
Katharine-Oliphant.

This gentleman, who is in the commission of the peace and a deputy lieutenant for Perthshire, succeeded his father in 1812.

## Lineage.

This family is directly descended from Sir William Graham, of Kincardine, ancestor of the ducal house of Montrose, through a princess of the royal line of Scotland.

The first who appears on record is

WILLIAM DE GRAHAM, who settled in Scotland under *King* DAVID I. He obtained from that monarch a grant of the lands of Abercorn and Dalkeith, and witnessed the charter to the monks of Holyroodhouse in 1128. Directly descended from him was

SIR WILLIAM GRAHAM, of Kincardine, styled in the charters, "Willielmus dominus de Grame de Kincardin." He was commissioner to treat with the English, 11th December, 1406; had a safe conduct into England, 15th May, 1412, and another from thence to Scotland about the release of JAMES I., 16th April, 1413. A charter was granted 4th August, 1420, "Willielmo Domino de Grame militi et Mariotæ Stewart, *Sorori* Roberti Ducis Albaniæ Sponsæ dicti Willielmi," of the lands of Auld Montrose, Kinnaber, and Charleton, in the county of Forfar.

By his first marriage Sir William Graham had two sons, from the elder of whom descends the family of Montrose. He *m.* secondly, the Lady Mary Stuart, second daughter of *King* ROBERT III., relict of George, Earl of Angus, and Sir James Kennedy, of Dunmure, and subsequently the wife of Sir Archibald Edmonstone, of Duntreith, and by her he had several sons, of whom,

I. SIR ROBERT GRAHAM, of Strathcarron, was ancestor of Grahams, of Fintry, of Claverhouse, Viscounts of Dundee, and the Grahams of Duntroon (see p. 120).
II. Patrick, was consecrated Bishop of Brechin, 1463, translated to the episcopal see of St. Andrews, 1466.
III. WILLIAM, was the

GRÆME, of Garvock, and direct ancestor of the present family. He was a soldier, and for his faithful services to *King* JAMES I. his uncle, obtained, in early life, a grant of the lands and barony of Garvock, which was afterwards confirmed in 1473, and from him the estate has descended in the direct line, from father to son, to the present time, as appears from documents in the family charter chest. He lived to an advanced age, and left a son,

MATTHEW LE GRÆME, of Garvock, who succeeded to William in 1502, but died soon afterwards, being advanced in years before his father's death. He was succeeded by his son,

ARCHIBALD GRÆME, who fell at the disasterous battle of Flodden, on 9th September, 1513, leaving a son and successor,

JOHN GRÆME, of Garvock, who married first, Mirabell Whyte, daughter of John Whyte, of Lumbany, and secondly, Katharine Arnot, daughter of Walter Arnot, of that Ilk, in 1545. He left two sons,

I. JAMES, who succeeded him.

II. John, of Balgowan, ancestor of the Grahams, of Balgowan, and of the gallant Lord Lyndock, the hero of Barrosa. Among the sheriff records at Perth, *anno* 1586, there exist several contracts entered into betwixt "John Graham, of Garvock, and John Graham, of Balgourre his sone." In the same record and year, there is also mention made of "John Graham, of Balgourre, and Marjorie Rollock his spouse," designed "Lady Inchbraikie." She was eldest daughter of Andrew Rollo, of Duncrub, and widow of George Græme, of Inchbraco.

JAMES GRÆME, of Garvock, succeeded to his father, John, and married Janet Bonar, daughter of Bonar, of Kelty, in 1571, by whom he had issue. He was succeeded by his eldest son,

NINIAN GRÆME, who *m.* Elizabeth Oliphant, daughter of Laurence Oliphant, of Fergandenny, in 1606, and by her he was father of

JOHN GRÆME, of Garvock, who *m.* Agnes Drummond, daughter of George Drummond, of Balloch, in 1638. This lady had only one brother, who was of weak intellect, and sold the estate of Ballock to the Earl of Perth, for the trifling sum of a bodle (a small Scotch coin) per day during his lifetime. Her son, James Græme, of Garvock, afterwards disputed the validity of the sale, claiming the estate through his mother, but the cause was tried before the earl himself, who was then chancellor of Scotland, and he decided in his own favour.

JAMES GRÆME, of Garvock, succeeded to his father, John, and on the 14th December, 1677, he was served heir-in-general of John Graham, of Balgowan, (the second of that family) by a retour of that date upon record, wherein the *latter* is designed the son of the brother of his great grandfather, "Jacobus Grahame de Garvock hæres Joannis Grahame de Balgown *filii fratis proavi.*" He purchased from Haldane, of Gleneagles, the lands of Kippen, a property in Strathern, about two miles distant from Garvock, which is still in the family. He married Anne Stewart, daughter of John Stewart, of Arntullie and Cardneys, in 1678, and was *s.* by his eldest son,

JAMES GRÆME, who married, first, Amelia, daughter of Sir Robert Moray, of Abercairney, by whom he had three sons, James, John, and ROBERT, and two daughters, Anna and Elizabeth. He married, secondly, in 1720, Bettie Bell, sister of Charles Bell, of Craigfovelie, but by her he had no issue. He was *s.* by his youngest and only surviving son,

ROBERT GRÆME, who married, in 1736, Katherine, daughter of James Oliphant, esq. of Gask, by whom he had four sons, James, Lawrence, Charles-James-Stewart, and Robert, with two daughters, Amelia-Anna-Sophia and Margaret. This laird was involved in the rising of 1745, after which he escaped to France, and entered into the French service, where he remained for several years, leaving his estate to his eldest son. He returned, however, afterwards, and died in his native country. He was *s.* by his son,

JAMES GRÆME, of Garvock, who married, first, in 1764, Mary, daughter of the Rev. Henry Nisbet, of the family of Dean, by Miss Graham, of Duchray; and secondly, Mary, daughter of Captain Robertson, of the British army. By his first wife he had five sons and three daughters, viz.

ROBERT, his heir.

James, Henry, Moray, Lawrence, } all of whom died abroad without issue.

Janet, *m.* to Captain Rollo, grandson of Robert, fourth Lord Rollo, and has issue.

Katherine, Elizabeth, } both died unm.

GARVOCK *d.* in 1812, and was *s.* by his only surviving son, the present ROBERT GRÆME, esq.

*Arms*—Or, three piles, gu. issuing from a chief, sa. charged with as many escallops of the first.

*Crest*—A lion rampant gu.

*Motto*—Noli me tangere.

*Estates*—Garvock and Kippen, both in Perthshire.

*Seat*—Garvock.

# FERRERS, OF BADDESLEY CLINTON.

FERRERS, MARMION-EDWARD, esq. of Baddesley Clinton, in the county of Warwick, *b.* 13th October, 1813, inherited the estates and representation of this, the only remaining branch of the once potent name of Ferrers, upon the demise of his father, 10th August, 1830.

## Lineage.

This ancient family, than which few can claim a higher or more illustrious descent, derives from Walchelin, a Norman, whose son,

HENRY FERRERS, assumed the name from Ferriers, a small town of Gastinois, in France, otherwise called Ferrieres from the iron mines, with which that country abounded, and in allusion to the circumstance, he bore for his arms "six horses' shoes," either from the similitude of his cognomen to the French Ferrier, or because the seigneurie produced iron, so essential to the soldier and cavalier in those rude times, when war was esteemed the chief business of life, and the adroit management of the steed, even amongst the nobility, the first of accomplishments. Henry de Ferrers came into England with THE CONQUEROR, and obtained a grant of Tutbury Castle, in the county of Stafford. He *m.* Bertha ——, and had issue,

ROBERT, his heir.

Eugenulph, who *d. s. p.*

Walkelin, of Radbourne, whose grandson, Robert, living *temp.* HENRY II. left two daughters, his co-heirs, viz.

MARGERY, who wedded Sir John Chandos, and from this marriage lineally descends the present EDWARD-SACHEVERELL-CHANDOS POLE, esq. of Radbourn Hall, in the county of Derby. *(See that family.)*

ERMITRUDE, *m.* to Sir William de Stafford.

The eldest son,

ROBERT DE FERRARS, having contributed, at the head of the Derbyshire men, to *King* STEPHEN's victory over David of Scotland at Northallerton, was created by that monarch EARL OF DERBY. He was lineal ancestor of

WILLIAM DE FERRERS, seventh earl of Derby, who married, for his second wife, Margaret, daughter and co-heir of Roger de Quinci, earl of Winchester, and had two sons,

1. ROBERT, eighth earl of Derby, (for detail, see BURKE's *Extinct and Dormant Peerage*), whose eldest son,

JOHN DE FERRERS, inherited Chartley Castle, and was summoned to parliament 27th EDWARD I. as BARON FERRERS, of Chartley. His last male descendant,

WILLIAM DE FERRERS, sixth Baron Ferrers, of Chartley, left at his decease, 28th HENRY VI. an only son,

ANNE FERRERS, who wedded Walter Devereux, who was summoned to parliament, *jure uxoris*, as seventh Baron Ferrers, of Chartley. His lordship fell at Bosworth, adhering to the side of RICHARD, and was *s.* by his son,

SIR JOHN DEVEREUX, eighth Baron Ferrers, of Chartley, who *m.* Cicely, sister and sole heiress of Henry Bourchier, earl of Ewe and Essex, and Baroness Bourchier in her own right, (maternally descended from Thomas Plantagenet, son of EDWARD III.), and had a son and successor,

WALTER DEVEREUX, ninth Baron Ferrers, of Chartley, and first Viscount Hereford. His lordship was *s.* by his grandson,

WALTER DEVEREUX, tenth Baron Ferrers, of Chartley, and first earl of Essex, whose son and successor,

ROBERT DEVEREUX, eleventh Baron Ferrers, of Chartley, and the second and celebrated earl of Essex, *m.* Frances, daughter and heiress of Sir Francis Walsingham, and relict of Sir Philip Sidney, by whom he left (with a son, ROBERT, third earl of Essex, and twelfth Baron Ferrers, who died issueless), two daughters, co-heirs to their brother,

Frances, *m.* to William, duke of Somerset, whose male line failed in 1675,

and

DOROTHY DEVEREUX, who wedded Sir Henry Shirley, bart. of Stanton, and their grandson,

SIR ROBERT SHIRLEY, on the failure of the male line of the elder coheir, having the abeyance terminated in his favour by CHARLES II. in 1677, was summoned as thirteenth BARON FERRERS, of Chartley. His lordship, who was created EARL FERRERS and Viscount Tamworth in 1711, was father of

THE HON. ROBERT SHIRLEY, who *m.* Anne, grand-daughter and sole heiress of John Ferrers, esq. of Tamworth Castle, and hence lineally descends George, Marquis Townshend, present Lord Ferrers, of Chartley.

II. WILLIAM, of whom immediately.

The second son,

WILLIAM FERRERS, obtained, by gift of Margaret his mother, the co-heir of the earl of Winchester, the manor of Groby, in the county of Leicester, and assumed, thereupon, the arms of De Quinci, "gu. seven mascles or." He *m.* Eleanor, daughter of Matthew, Lord Lovaine, and, dying in 1287, was *s.* by his son,

WILLIAM FERRERS, who was summoned to parliament as BARON FERRERS, of Groby. His lordship's direct descendant, (for the intermediate line refer to BURKE's *Extinct and Dormant Peerage*),

WILLIAM FERRERS, fifth Baron Ferrers, of Groby, wedded Philippa, daughter of Roger, Lord Clifford, and dying 23rd HENRY VI. left three sons, viz.

I. HENRY, who died during his father's lifetime, leaving by Isabel, second daughter and co-heir of Thomas Mowbray, duke of Norfolk, an only daughter,

ELIZABETH, who *m.* Sir Edward Grey, and carried the barony of Groby into the Grey family.

II. THOMAS (Sir), of whom presently.

III. John, whence the Ferrers, of Mercute, now extinct.

The second son,

SIR THOMAS FERRERS, knt. espoused Elizabeth, eldest sister and co-heir of Sir Baldwin Frevile, and inherited, in her right, Tamworth Castle. Sir Thomas died 37th HENRY VI. leaving issue,

I. THOMAS (Sir), second lord of Tamworth Castle, who *m.* Anne, sister of William, Lord Hastings, and was *s.* at his decease, 22nd August, 14th HENRY VII. by his grandson,

SIR JOHN FERRERS, knt. of Tamworth Castle, who wedded Dorothy, daughter of William Harper, esq. of Rushall, in Staffordshire, and was father of

SIR HUMPHREY FERRERS, of Tamworth Castle, who *m.* first, Margaret, daughter of Mr. Sergeant Thomas Pigot; and, secondly, Dorothy, dau. and co-heir of Thomas Marrow, esq. widow of Francis Cockain, of Pooley, and niece of Constantia Brome, wife of Sir Edward Ferrers, of Baddesley Clinton. Sir Humphrey died 1st MARY, leaving, by his first wife, a son and successor,

JOHN FERRERS, esq. of Tamworth Castle, who *m.* Barbara, daughter of Francis Cockain, esq. by Dorothy Marrow, and had, with other issue, a daughter, Dorothy, *m.* to Edward Holte, esq. and a son,

SIR HUMPHREY FERRERS, knt. of Tamworth Castle, who *m.* 5th ELIZABETH, Anne, dau. of Humphrey Bradburne, of Lee, in Derbyshire, and left at his decease, 5th JAMES I. a numerous progeny, of whom Susanna, the youngest daughter, wedded Sir George Gresley, bart. of Drakelow, and

SIR JOHN FERRERS, knt. of Tamworth Castle, the eldest son, succeeded his father. He *m.* Dorothy, daughter of Sir John Puckeringe, keeper of the great seal, and had (with three daughters, Frances, *m.* to Sir John Packington, of Westwood; Anne, *m.* to Sir Simon Archer, of Umberslade; and Jane, *m.* to Sir Thomas Rous), a son and successor,

SIR HUMPHREY FERRERS, knt. of Tamworth Castle, who inherited and died in 1633. He wedded Anne, daughter of Sir John Packington, and had by her (who *m.* secondly, Philip, earl of Chesterfield), an only son,

JOHN FERRERS, esq. of Tamworth Castle, *b.* in 1629, M.P. for Derbyshire at the restoration of CHARLES II. *m.* Anne, dau. of Sir Dudley Carleton, and had a daughter, Dorothy, the wife of Richard, earl of Arran, and a son,

HUMPHREY (SIR), knt. who died in 1678, two years previously to his father, leaving, by Elizabeth his wife, dau. of Gervase Pigott, esq. of Thrumpton, Notts, an only dau. and heiress,

ANNE FERRERS, who espoused (as already stated) the Hon. Robert Shirley, eldest son of Robert, first Earl Ferrers, and thirteenth Lord Ferrers, of Chartley, and had an only daughter and heiress,

ELIZABETH SHIRLEY, who *m.* James Compton, earl of Northampton. Their only daughter and heiress,

LADY CHARLOTTE COMPTON, Baroness Ferrers and Compton, *m.* George, first MARQUESS TOWNSHEND, and had a son and successor,

GEORGE, VISCOUNT TAMWORTH, who then became sixteenth Baron Ferrers, of Chartley. His lordship was created earl of Leicester in 1784, and inherited the MARQUISATE OF TOWNSHEND at the decease of his father, as second marquess. He *m.* Charlotte, dau. of Eaton-Mainwaring Ellerker, esq. of Risby Park, and had George, present Marquis Townshend, and seventeenth Baron Ferrers, of Chartley, with several other children, one of whom, the Lady Harriet Anne Townshend, espoused EDWARD FERRERS, esq. of Baddesley Clinton.

II. HENRY (Sir), of whom we are more immediately about to treat.

The second son,

SIR HENRY FERRERS, knt. of Hambleton, in the county of Rutland, wedded Margaret, daughter and co-heir of William Hikstall, esq. of East Peckham, in Kent, and had (with a daughter, Elizabeth) a son and successor,

SIR EDWARD FERRERS, *b.* in 1470; who *m.* in 1497, Constance, daughter of Nicholas Brome, esq. of Baddesley Clinton, in the county of Warwick, by whom, who died 30th September, 1551, he acquired that estate, and had issue,

I. HENRY, who *m.* in 1524, Catherine, daughter and co-heir of Sir John Hampden, knt. of Hampden, and predeceasing his father, in 1526, left an only child,

EDWARD, successor to his grandfather.

II. Edward, who *m.* Elizabeth, daughter and heir of William Grey, esq. of Wood Bevington, in Warwickshire, and had three daughters, of whom the eldest, Elizabeth, married Thomas Randolph, esq. who purchased the interest of the other sisters, and became sole lord of the manor.

III. George.

IV. Nicholas.

I. Jane, *m.* to William Finden.

II. Ursula, *m.* to — Beaufoy.

III. Anne, *m.* to — Knightley.

IV. Margaret, *m.* to Thomas Froggenall.

V. Elizabeth, *m.* to — Hampden.

VI. Alice.

Sir Edward Ferrers served the office of high sheriff for Warwickshire in the 5th and 10th of HENRY VIII.; he was *s.* by his grandson,

EDWARD FERRERS, esq. of Baddesley Clinton, *b.* in 1526, who, in the 1st of *Queen* MARY, represented the borough of Warwick in parliament. He *m.* in 1548, Bridget, daughter of William, second Lord Windsor, and dying 10th August, 1564, (his widow survived until 1582), was *s.* by his eldest son,

HENRY FERRERS, esq. of Baddesley Clinton, *b.* 26th January, 1549, whom Dugdale styles an eminent antiquarian, and describes as "a man of distinguished worth, reflecting lustre on the ancient and noble family to which he belonged." Camden, likewise, bears testimony to his exalted character, and to the extent of his knowledge, particularly in antiquities. He *m.* in October, 1582, Jane, dau. and co-heir of Henry White, esq. of South Warnborn, in Hampshire, son of Sir Thomas White, knt. and by her, who died 7th September, 1586, aged twenty-three, left at his decease, 10th October, 1633, a daughter, Mary, and a son and successor,

EDWARD FERRERS, esq. of Baddesley Clinton, *b.* 1st November, 1585, sheriff of Warwickshire in the 17th CHARLES I. This gentleman espoused, 24th February, 1611, Anne, eldest dau. of William Peyto, esq. of Chesterton, and by that lady, who *d.* 12th September, 1618, aged thirty-three, had one son, and two daughters, namely, HENRY, his heir, Eleanor, and Catharine. Mr. Ferrers *d.* 22nd March, 1650-1, and was *s.* by his son,

HENRY FERRERS, esq. of Baddesley Clinton, *b.* 6th December, 1616, sheriff of Warwickshire 16th CHARLES II. who, upon the death of John Ferrers, of Tamworth Castle, in 1680, became heir male of the family. He *m.* in April, 1638, Bridget, daughter of Edward Willoughby, esq. of Causell, Notts, and had a numerous family. He *d.* in 1698, (his wife had predeceased him in the preceding year), and was *s.* by his eldest son,

GEORGE FERRERS, esq. of Baddesley Clinton, *b.* in 1639, who *d.* 11th August, 1712, leaving by Elizabeth his wife, only daughter of William Kempson, esq. of Ardens Grafton, in Warwickshire, a daughter, Mary Magdalen, and a son,

EDWARD FERRERS, esq. of Baddesley Clinton, *b.* 5th January, 1658-9. This gentleman wedded, 26th February, 1712, Teresa, daughter of Sir Isaac Gibson, of Worcester, and by her, who *d.* in 1734, had one son and one daughter, viz.

THOMAS, his heir.

Mary, *m.* to — Berkeley, esq.

Mr. Ferrers was *s.* at his decease, in 1729, by his son,

THOMAS FERRERS, esq. of Baddesley Clinton, *b.* 4th April, 1713, who *m.* 10th June, 1737, Margaret, daughter of John Kimpson, esq. of Henley in Arden, and had two sons and five daughters, viz.

I. EDWARD, his heir.
II. Henry.

I. Mary.
II. Teresa.
III. Frances.
IV. Anne.
V. Elizabeth.

The elder son,

EDWARD FERRERS, esq. of Baddesley Clinton, inherited the estates upon the demise of his father in 1760. He *m.* in 1763, Hester, daughter of Christopher Bird, esq. of London, and by her, who *d.* in 1822, had two sons and seven daughters, viz.

I. EDWARD, his heir.
II. Thomas, a major in the army, who served during the whole of the peninsular war, and was killed by a fall from the ramparts of a fortress in France.

I. Hester, died unm.
II. Lucy, was the third wife of Robert Willoughby, esq. of Cliff, and left a daughter, *m.* to — Bateman, esq.
III. Frances, died unm.
IV. Maria, *m.* to Court Granville, esq. of Calwich Abbey, in the county of Stafford.
V. Catherine, *m.* to — Edwards, esq.
VI. Elizabeth, *m.* in 1803, to John Gerard, esq. of Windle Hall, in Lancashire, and was mother of the present Sir John Gerard, bart. of Bryn.
VII. Anne-Teresa, *m.* first, to Henry Clifford, esq. barrister-at-law, brother to Sir Thomas-Hugh Clifford Constable, baronet, and grandson of Hugh, fourth Lord Clifford; and, secondly, to Edward Hebden, esq.

Mr. Ferrers *d.* 25th February, 1794, and was *s.* by his son,

EDWARD FERRERS, esq. of Baddesley Clinton, *b.* 17th April, 1765, who *m.* 18th August, 1788, Helena, daughter and heiress of George Alexander, esq. of Stirtlec, in the county of Huntingdon, and had issue,

I. EDWARD, his heir.
II. George-Thomas, *b.* 21st December, 1791, who *m.* 8th September, 1817, Mary, eldest daughter of George Gillow, esq. of Hammersmith, Middlesex, and had five sons and two daughters, viz.
    1. George-Joseph, *b.* 18th March, 1819.
    2. Thomas-John, *b.* in 1821.
    3. Richard-Vincent, *b.* 12th April, 1823.
    4. Edmund, *b.* 1824.
    5. Bernard, *b.* 1829.

    1. Mary.
    2. Sarah.

I. Mary, *m.* to John-Bruno Bowdon, esq. of Southgate House, in the county of Derby.
II. Magdalen, *m.* to George Pickering, esq.
III. Caroline.

Mr. Ferrers *d.* 25th September, 1795, and was *s.* by his son,

EDWARD FERRERS, esq. of Baddesley Clinton, *b.* 31st January, 1790, a magistrate and deputy lieutenant for the county of Warwick, who *m.* 11th March, 1813, the Lady Harriet-Anne-Ferrers Townshend, second daughter of George, Marquis Townshend, and sixteenth Baron Ferrers, of Chartley, and had issue,

I. MARMION-EDWARD, his heir.
II. Charles, *b.* 2nd September, 1814.
III. Groby-Thomas, *b.* 19th July, 1816; died 23rd September, 1831.
IV. Compton-Gerard, *b.* 12th May, 1818.
V. Tamworth-George, *b.* 22nd September, 1827.
I. Henrietta-Elizabeth.
II. Margaret-Anne.
III. Constance-Charlotte.

Mr. Ferrers died 10th August, 1830, and was succeeded by his eldest son, the present MARMION-EDWARD FERRERS, esq. of Baddesley Clinton.

*Arms*—Quarterly, first and fourth, vair or and gu. (ensigns of the feudal earls of Derby after the match of the third earl with Peverill); second, sa. six horse shoes arg. three, two, and one, FERRERS ancient; third, gu. seven mascles or, a canton erm. FERRERS of Groby.

*Crest*—A unicorn passant erm.

*** Prior to the extinction of the senior branch of the family seated at Tamworth Castle, the line of Baddesley Clinton bore "gu. seven mascles or, a canton erm; but having now become sole surviving male heirs of this ancient house, the Ferrerses of Baddesley have resumed the old arms.

*Motto*—Splendio tritus.

*Estate*—Baddesley Clinton, in the Hemlingford Hundred of the county of Warwick.

*Seat*—Baddesley Clinton Hall, eight miles from Warwick. This ancient mansion received its first name from Bade, a Saxon, who held it in the time of EDWARD the Confessor, and its second from Sir Thomas de Clinton, of Coshill, who obtained the estate *temp.* HENRY III. in right of his wife Margery, daughter and heiress of James de Besiege, whence, after various transmissions, it passed by purchase, in the reign of HENRY IV. to John Brome, a wealthy lawyer of Warwick, who resided in a house at the north end of the bridge, which long retained the name of Brome Place: at his decease, in consequence of a wound received in a dispute with one John Hearthill, the manor of Baddesley devolved on his son, Nicholas Brome, and subsequently by the marriage of his daughter, Constance, on Sir Edward Ferrers, grandson of Sir Thomas Ferrers, of Tamworth Castle. The hall is a structure of very ancient date, though the time of its erection is not exactly known; it is a stone building of low elevation, but of considerable extent; forming three sides of a square, of which the fourth, if it ever existed, has long since disappeared: a moat surrounds the mansion, and a bridge conducts to the entrance, leading through the lofty arch of an embattled gateway into the inner court.

THE HISTORY OF BADDESLEY CLINTON,
By Henry Ferrers, esq. the Antiquary,
*temp.* ELIZABETH.

This seate and soyle from Saxon, Bade, a man of honest fame,
Who held it in the Saxon's tyme, of Baddesley took the name,
When Edward King the Confessor did weare the English crown,
The same was then possest by —— a man of some renowne;
And England being conquer'd in lot it did alyghte
To Giffry Wirie, of noble birth, an Andegavian knight,
A member Hamlet all this whyle, of Hampton here at hand,
With Hampton so to Moulbray went as all the wive's land
To Bisege, in that name it runs awhyle, and then is gone
To Clinton as his heyre who leaves it to a younger son,
And in that time the name of Baddesley Clinton was begun.
From them agayne by wedding of their heyre at first it came
To Conisby, and after him to Foukes, who weds the same.
From Foukes to Dudley by a Sales, and so to Burdet past,
To Mitley Neat, by Mitley's will it came to Brome at last,
Brome honours much the place, and after some descents of Bromes,
To Ferrers for a daughter's part of heyres in match it comes.
In this last name it lasteth still, and so long—longer shall
As God shall please who is the Lord and King and God of all.

# REVELEY, OF BRYN Y GWIN.

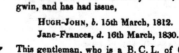

REVELEY, HUGH, esq. of Bryn y gwin, in the county of Merioneth, *b.* 15th July, 1772; *m.* 11th January, 1803, Jane, only daughter and heiress of Robert-Hartley Owen, esq. of Bryn y gwin, and has had issue,

HUGH-JOHN, *b.* 15th March, 1812.

Jane-Frances, *d.* 16th March, 1830.

This gentleman, who is a B. C. L. of Christ Church, Oxford, was secretary to Sir John Mitford while Speaker of the House of Commons, and afterwards, when that learned person was constituted LORD CHANCELLOR of Ireland, and created BARON REDESDALE, filled the office of purse bearer to his lordship.

Mr. Reveley is a magistrate and deputy lieutenant for the county of Merioneth, and was high sheriff in 1811.

## Lineage.

The REVELEYS, who trace their descent to the reign of EDWARD II. were originally seated in the manor house of Reveley, on the northern bank of the river Breamish, at the south eastern foot of Cheviot, and subsequently at Ancroft, in Northumberland, (for a detailed account, see vol. ii. p. 287). Their possessions, it would appear, were at one time considerable. In the reign of JAMES I. GEORGE REVELEY, of Ancroft, purchased from the last Lord Eure, the manors of Newton, Underwood, and Throphill, which Sir Simon Eure had acquired, *temp.* HENRY III. from Lord Bertram, of Mitford. During the civil wars, WILLIAM REVELEY, of Ancroft (who had married a niece of the earl of Stafford), with a body of troops raised by himself, fought for *King* CHARLES, at the fatal field of Marston Moor; and was slain, having attained the rank of major, at the decisive battle of Naseby.

The father of this stout cavalier lies interred in the chancel of Mitford church, were a large mural monument, decorated with arms, bears the following inscription:

" Here lyeth interred, with,
in, this, mold, a, generous, and,
Virtuous, Wight, whose,
due, deserte, cannot, be, tolde,
from, slender, skill, unto,
his, right: He, was, descended,
from, a, race, of, worshipfull,
Antiquities, loved, he, was,
in, his, life, space, of, high,
eke, of, low, degree, rest,
Bartram, in, this, house, of, clay,
Reveley, unto, the, latter, day;

Underneath is his effigy cut in relief on the stone cover of his tomb, his hands lifted up as in the act of prayer: on the edge in capital letters appear these lines:

Bartram to us so dutiful a son,
if more were fit it should for thee be done,
who deceased the 7th October, anno domini 1622.

On the marriage of

WILLIAM REVELEY, esq. of Newton Underwood, (who was born in 1662,) with Margery, daughter and heiress of Robert Willey, esq. of Newby Wiske, the seat of the family was removed from Northumberland to Yorkshire, and the Hall House of Newby Wiske erected. By the heiress of Willey, Mr. Reveley had issue,

WILLEY, who succeeded to the estates of Newton Underwood and Newby Wiske. He *m.* in 1717, Rachel, daughter of Henry Neale, esq. of London, and was father of

ELIZABETH, who *m.* JOHN MITFORD, esq. of Exbury, and was great grandmother of

HENRY REVELEY MITFORD, esq. of Exbury, who inherits the estates of the Reveley family, (see vol. ii. p. 285).

GEORGE, of whom presently.

Philadelphia, *b.* in 1688, who wedded

Langdale Smithson, esq. second son of Sir Hugh Smithson, bart, and had an only son,

SIR HUGH SMITHSON, *b.* at Newby Wiske, who was created DUKE of NORTHUMBERLAND.

Margery, *b.* in 1689, *m.* to — Crohair.

Barbara, died unmarried.

Mr. Reveley died 24th February, 1725. His second son,

GEORGE REVELEY, esq. born in 1699, married Miss Elizabeth Tucker, and by her, who died in London, in July, 1747, had two sons, HENRY, his heir; and Hugh, who died unmarried, 2nd May, 1762. Mr. Reveley *d.* himself at Alicante, in Spain, in 1760, and was *s.* by his son,

HENRY REVELEY, esq. born at Alicante, in 1737, for many years a commissioner of the Excise. This gentleman, an excellent musician and connoisseur in the fine arts, formed a choice collection of the old masters' drawings and etchings now at Bryn y gwin. He was the author himself of a volume entitled "Notices of the drawings of the most distinguished masters," edited by his son, in 1826. Mr. Reveley wedded in 1771, Jane, sister of Sir Claude Champion de Crespigny, bart. and daughter of Philip Champion de Crespigny, esq. of Camberwell, by Miss Fonnereau, his wife, and by her, who died 4th February, 1829, aged eighty-six, had issue,

HUGH, his heir.

Algernon, *b.* 27th December, 1786, entered the India civil service as a writer in 1803, and, after remaining several years at Calcutta, returned and settled in England.

Elizabeth-Anne, who *m.* in 1796, Cadwallader Blayney Trevor Roper, esq. of Plas Têg, in Flintshire, son of the Hon. and Rev. Mr. Roper, (son of Lord Teynham), and cousin to Lord Dacre, from whom he inherited his estates in the counties of Flint and Kent. Mrs. Trevor Roper died 14th June, 1816.

Henrietta, *m.* to Matthew Buckle, esq. capt. R.N. son of Admiral Buckle, of Nork, in Surrey, (see vol. i. p. 575).

Mr. Reveley died in 1798, and was *s.* by his elder son, the present HUGH REVELEY, esq. of Bryn-y-gwin.

*Arms*—Arg. a chev. engrailed gu. between three stars of twelve points az.

*Crest*—An estoile as in the arms.

*Motto*—Optima revelatio stella.

*Estates*—In the county of Merioneth.

*Seat*—Bryn-y-gwin, near Dolgellan.

## BALFOUR, OF TRENABY.

BALFOUR, JOHN, esq. of Trenaby, in the county of Orkney, *b.* 6th November, 1750; *m.* 10th November, 1783, Henrietta, sister of Sir Benjamin Sullivan, and of the Right Hon. John Sullivan, of Richings Park, but has no issue.

Mr. Balfour, who represented, for twelve years, his native county, Orkney, in parliament, succeeded his father in 1786, and his mother in 1796.

### Lineage.

The family of Balfour, which derived its name from its patrimony of Balor, or Balfour, in Fifeshire, long enjoyed the hereditary office of sheriff of that county, in which there were more freeholders of the name than of any other, even so late as the reign of CHARLES II. Besides many illustrious descendants in the female line, it has been ennobled by three peerages, viz. Burleigh and Kilwinning, in Scotland, and Balfour of Clonawley, in Ireland. Although the pedigree goes back to the time of DUNCAN I. (1033—1039), the first mentioned in the public records is

SIR MICHAEL DE BALFOUR, who obtained a charter from WILLIAM *the Lion*, dated at Forfar, about the year 1196. His son,

SIR INGELRAM DE BALFOUR, was sheriff of Fife in 1229, and *d.* in 1239, leaving a son and successor,

HENRY BALFOUR, father of

JOHN BALFOUR, who fell among the flower of the barons of Fifeshire at the sack of Berwick by EDWARD I. 30th March, 1296, and was *s.* by his son,

SIR DUNCAN BALFOUR, sheriff of Fife, one of the patriotic few who adhered to the fortunes of the renowned Sir William Wallace. He was slain 12th June, 1298, at the battle of Blackironside, where the Scottish hero defeated, with great slaughter, the English under Aymer de Valence, Earl of Pembroke. Sir Duncan's son,

SIR JOHN BALFOUR, who succeeded to his father's estates and office, that of sheriff of Fife. Sir John participated in the victory obtained at Dillecarew, in 1300, by Sir John Fraser and Sir William Wallace, but received a severe wound in the conflict. His son and successor,

SIR MICHAEL BALFOUR, sheriff of Fife in 1314, died in 1344, leaving two sons, viz.

I. JOHN (Sir), who succeeded to the estates of Balfour, and to the office of sheriff of Fife. He *d.* in 1375, and left an only daughter and heiress,

 MARGARET, who wedded Sir Robert Bethune, and hence descend the Bethunes of Balfour.

II. ADAM, of whose line we have to treat.

Sir Michael's second son,

ADAM BALFOUR, who married the granddaughter of Macduff, brother of Colbane, Earl of Fife, acquired the lands of Pittencrieff in dowry. He died of wounds received at the battle of Durham, and was buried in Melrose Abbey, *anno* 1346. His son,

SIR MICHAEL BALFOUR, was brought up by his kinsman, Duncan, twelfth Earl of Fife, who gave, in 1353, "consanguineo suo Michaeli de Balfour," in exchange for Pittencrieff, the much more valuable lands of Mount Whanny. The Countess Isabella, daughter of Earl Duncan, also bestowed many grants upon her "cousin" Sir Michael, who, at her death, without issue, should have succeeded as her nearest heir, all the descendants of Earl Colbane failing in her; but the Regent Albany, who claimed the earldom, was a competitor too powerful to be lightly opposed, and Sir Michael seems to have waved his rights. He *d.* about 1385, and was succeeded by his eldest son,

MICHAEL BALFOUR, of Mountwhanny, who *m.* and had three sons, namely,

I. GEORGE, his heir.

II. John, of Balquevy, progenitor of the Balfours of Drumyler, Forret, Runderston, Torry and Boghall, Kinloch, &c.

III. David, of Carroldstone.

The eldest son,

GEORGE BALFOUR, of Munquhanny, had two sons, JOHN (Sir), his heir, and James, of Ballo. The elder

SIR JOHN BALFOUR, sheriff of Fife in 1449, predeceased his father, being killed at the siege of Roxburgh, 1460, leaving three sons,

MICHAEL.

John, bishop of Brechin, lord chancellor of Scotland.

James, sub-dean of Brechin.

The eldest son,

MICHAEL BALFOUR, of Munquhanny, succeeded his grandfather, and wedded Janet, daughter of Sir Andrew Ogilvy, of Inchmartin, by whom he had two sons and one daughter,

MICHAEL (Sir), his heir.

John, of Baledimond.

Margaret, *m.* to William, third Earl of Rothes.

Michael was succeeded by his elder son,

SIR MICHAEL BALFOUR, of Munquhanny, an especial favourite of JAMES IV. who, in 1493, "pro singulari favori quem habuit erga dictum Michaelem," erected his lands into a barony, to be called the Barony of Munquhanny. He *m.* Marjory, daughter of Andrew Dury, of that Ilk, and had issue,

ANDREW, his heir.

Margaret, *m.* to Patrick Wemyss, of Pittencrieff, master of the household to JAMES V.

Janet, *m.* to Patrick Kircaldy, uncle of the celebrated Sir William Kircaldy, of Grange.

Sir Michael fell at Flodden, where his brother-in-law, the Earl of Rothes, was also slain, and was *s.* by his son,

ANDREW BALFOUR, of Mountwhany, who wedded Janet, third daughter of Sir Alexander Bruce, of Earlshall, and had issue,

I. MICHAEL, his heir.

II. Gilbert (Sir), of Westray, master of *Queen* MARY's household, sheriff of Orkney, fowd of Zetland, and captain of Kirkwall Castle.

III. JAMES (Sir), of Pittendriech, a distinguished actor in the turbulent times of the unhappy MARY and her son, JAMES V. He was successively commendator of Pittenween, lord clerk register, lord president of the Court of Session, and governor of Edinburgh Castle. Sir James *m.* Margaret, daughter and heiress of Michael Balfour, of Burlie, and had, with three daughters, the eldest *m.* to Sir Michael Arnot, of Arnot; the second, to Sir John Henderson, of Fordel: and the third, to Barclay of Collairny: six sons, viz.

1. MICHAEL (Sir), of Burleigh, who was elevated to the peerage 7th August, 1606, as LORD BALFOUR, of Burleigh. His lordship married twice, and left, by his second wife, Margaret, dau. of Lundie, of that Ilk, an only daughter and heiress,
   - MARGARET, Baroness Balfour, of Burleigh. Her ladyship wedded Robert (son of Sir Robert Arnot, of Ferny), who assumed the name of Balfour, and had the title of Lord Burleigh, in virtue of the royal mandate. His lordship died 10th August, 1663, leaving one son and four daughters, viz.
     - JOHN, Lord Balfour, of Burleigh, ancestor of the Lords Burleigh,* and of the BALFOURS OF FERNY AND DUNBOG.
     - Jean, *m.* in 1628, to David, second Earl of Wemyss.
     - Margaret, *m.* to Sir James Crawford, of Kilbirny.
     - Isabel, *m.* to Thomas, first Lord Ruthven.
     - ——, *m.* to Arnot, of Ferny.
2. JAMES (Sir), created by JAMES I. a peer of Ireland, by the title of BARON CLONAWLEY. His lordship appears to have died issueless.
3. Alexander, of Balgarvie, ancestor of many families of the name.
4. Henry (Sir), a general in the army of the States of Holland.
5. William, who went to Ireland.
6. David, died at sea, on his voyage to Holland.

IV. David, of Balbutheis.

V. George, prior of the Charterhouse.

VI. Robert, of Grange, provost of St. Mary's.

VII. John, of Rothlees.

Andrew Balfour was succeeded by his eldest son,

MICHAEL BALFOUR, of Mountwhany, commendator of Melrose, who espoused Janet, daughter of David Boswell, of Auchinlek, by the Lady Janet Hamilton, sister of the Regent Arran, and dying in 1570, was *s.* by his son,

SIR MICHAEL BALFOUR, of Mounwhannie, who removed his residence, in 1588, to Noltland Castle, in the Island of Westray, in Orkney, which he inherited from his cousin-german, Archibald Balfour, of Westray. Sir Michael wedded Mariota Adamson, daughter of Patrick, archbishop of St. Andrews, and had two sons,

I. ANDREW (Sir), of Strathore and Mounwhannie, who *m.* Mary, daughter of Sir James Melville, of Halhill, and was ancestor of the BALFOURS of Grange, who became EXTINCT in the beginning of the last century.

II. MICHAEL.

The second son,

MICHAEL BALFOUR, of Garth, wedded Margaret, daughter of Malcolm Sinclair, of Quendal, in Zetland, great-grandson of William, the last Sinclair, Earl of Orkney, and had five sons and two daughters,

I. PATRICK, his heir.

II. Robert, of Trenaby.

III. John, of Garth.

IV. George.

V. Michael, ancestor of the Balfours of Langskail.

I. Ursula, *m.* to James Fea, of Clestran.

II. Elizabeth, *m.* to James Sinclair, of Golt.

The eldest son,

PATRICK BALFOUR, of Pharay, was a staunch royalist, and though his age and infirmities prevented his accompanying Montrose in the ill-fated expedition of 1650, his assistance in levying troops for the king's service, and the hospitable shelter afforded to the fugitives at Noltland Castle, when the cause was ruined by the defeat at Kirbuster, drew on him the wrath of the Scottish parliament, by which he was heavily fined, and put out of the commission of war for Orkney. He *m.* Barbara, daughter of Francis Mudie, of Breckness, and had two sons, GEORGE and Robert, by the elder of whom,

---

* ROBERT, fifth Lord Balfour, of Burleigh, being attached, when young, to a person of very inferior rank, was sent abroad, in the hope that the sentiment would be obliterated. Before his departure, however, he declared that if the girl married in his absence he would, on his return, put her husband to death. He did return, and, true to his purpose, finding that she had wedded one Henry Stenhouse, a schoolmaster, at Inverkeithing, repaired directly to the schoolhouse, and inflicted a mortal wound on the unfortunate dominie, in the midst of his scholars; for this cold-blooded murder he was tried, convicted, and sentenced to decapitation, but found means to escape in the clothes of his sister. Taking part afterwards in the rising of 1715, he was attainted. He died issueless in 1757.

George Balfour, of Pharay, he was succeeded in 1664. This laird married, first, Marjory, dau. of James Barkie, esq. of Tankerness, and had two sons and one daughter,

Patrick, who died an infant.

William, of Pharay, whose only child, Isabel, *m.* Archibald Stuart, of Brugh.

Barbara, *m.* to William Traill, esq. of Westness.

He *m.* secondly, Lady Mary Mackenzie, only daughter of Murdoch, bishop of Orkney, and, dying in 1706, left, *inter alios*, a son,

John Balfour, of Trenaby, who *s.* to a portion of his father's estate. He married Elizabeth, daughter of Thomas Traill, of Skaill, and had five sons and one daughter: William, his heir; Thomas, of Huip; John, M.D.; Robert; Archibald; and Mary, *m.* to John Traill, of Westness. He died in 1742, and was *s.* by his eldest son,

William Balfour, of Trenaby, born in 1719, who married, 9th February, 1744, Elizabeth Coventrie,* heiress of Newark, daughter of the Rev. Thomas Coventrie, and had issue,

I. John, his heir.

II. Thomas, of Elwick, a colonel in the army, born 3rd February, 1752, and died, at Bath, in 1799. He *m.* in 1776, Frances Ligonier, niece of Field-marshal John, Earl Ligonier, commander-in-chief of the British forces, and only sister of Edward, second Earl Ligonier, by whom he had,

John-Edward-Ligonier, captain in the 9th Foot, *b.* 11th January, 1780, killed at Alkmaar, 19th September, 1799.

William, of Elwick, commander in the Royal Navy, born 8th December, 1781, married, first, Mary Balfour Manson, dau. of William Manson, esq. comptroller of the Customs, at Kirkwall; and secondly, Mary Margaret, daughter of Andrew Barkie, esq. and has issue by both ladies.

Mary, *m.* to the Rev. Alexander Brunton, D.D. Professor of Oriental Languages in the University of Edinburgh, but died 19th December, 1818, without issue.

III. David, writer to the Signet, born 28th October, 1754, *m.* Marion, dau. of George M'Intosh, esq. of Dunchatton, and died 25th May, 1813, leaving issue,

William, late lieutenant-colonel of the 82nd regiment, married and has issue.

Mary, *m.* to Godfrey Meynell, esq. of Langley Meynell, in Derbyshire, and has issue.

I. Elizabeth, *m.* William Manson, esq. and had one child, Mary Balfour Manson, *m.* to her cousin, Captain William Balfour, of Elwick.

II. Margaret, *b.* 27th January, 1747, *d.* unmarried.

III. Catherine, *b.* 3rd March, 1749, *d.* an infant.

IV. Mary, *b.* 29th May, 1757, *m.* to Captain George Craigie, of Saviskaill, and died without issue 6th December, 1818.

Mr. Balfour died in October, 1786, and was *s.* by his eldest son, the present John Balfour, esq. of Trenaby.

*Arms*—Arg. a cheveron sa. charged with an otter's head erased of the first, in base a saltier couped of the second: quartering Macduff, Ogilvy, Dury, Bruce, Boswell, Adamson, Sinclair, Mudy, Mackenzie, Traill, and Coventry.

*Crest*—A right arm, couped at the elbow, holding a baton.

*Motto*—Forward.

*Estates*—In Orkney. Noltland and Trenaby form part of a large grant by Mary, Queen of Scots, to Sir Gilbert Balfour, of Westray, master of her household. Besides his valuable maternal estate of Newark, Mr. Balfour inherited the property of his uncle, Thomas Balfour, of Huip, and has lately purchased the Græmsay, Stenness and Gaersay estates from the representatives of the late Sir William Honyman, bart.

*Town Residence*—18, Curzon Street, Mayfair.

*Seats*—Charleton Grove, Kent; Noltland Castle and Trenaby House, Orkney.

* Her progenitor, William Covingtrie, settled in the Orkneys in 1613, and *m.* Jane Taylour. Their eldest son, John, *m.* Jane Kirkness, and had an only son, David Covingtree, of Enhallow, who by his wife, Nicola Traill, daughter of James Traill, of Westive, had two sons, John Covingtrie, of Newark, who died unmarried, and the Rev. Thomas Coventry, who succeeded his brother, and *m.* Elizabeth, daughter of Thomas Loutit, of Lykin, by whom he had David Covengtry, of Newark, who died without issue, and a daughter Elizabeth, *m.* to William Balfour, of Trenaby.

# WOOD, OF SWANWICK.

WOOD, THE REV. JOHN, of Swanwick Hall, in the county of Derby, rector of Kingsley, in Staffordshire, and vicar of Pentridge, born 25th November, 1776; married, at Uffington, 22nd September, 1803, Emily-Susanna, eldest daughter of Abel-Walford Bellairs, esq. of Stamford, and has issue,

I. HUGH, in holy orders, *b.* 16th August, 1804.
II. John, *b.* 16th May, 1807.
III. Edward, *b.* 23rd June, 1811.
IV. William, *b.* 30th December, 1812.

I. Emilia-Jane.
II. Frances-Mary.
III. Susanna.
IV. Ellen.
V. Catherine.
VI. Rose-Emma.

Mr. Wood inherited the estates upon the demise of his father.

## Lineage.

From old deeds and papers, it appears that this family possessed property at Swanwick, in the early part of the 16th century, and that the same was settled in the third year of PHILIP and MARY, by Christopher Wood, upon a Hugh Wood, who resided thereon; this, together, with portions of other ancient estates acquired by subsequent marriages, is now enjoyed by the Rev. John Wood.

ROBERT WOOD, of Swanwick, married Anne, daughter and co-heir of John Rowbotham, of Farley, and had, with a daughter, Anne, the wife of Bernard Lucas, esq. of Hasland (see vol. ii. p. 172), a son,

JOHN WOOD, gentleman, of Swanwick, who married in 1722, Martha, daughter and co-heir of John Wilson, esq. of Heanor, by Mary Richardson, of Smalley, his wife, and had, with other issue, a son and successor,

THE REV. JOHN WOOD, of Swanwick, *b.* 30th December, 1723, who *d.* without issue, in June, 1786, at Edensor, in the county of Derby. His youngest brother,

HUGH WOOD, esq. of Swanwick, eventually inherited the family estates. This gentleman wedded first, 28th December, 1769, Sarah, daughter of Clement Rossington, esq. of Scropton, in Derbyshire, but had no issue. He *m.* secondly, 14th March, 1775, the cousin of his first wife, Mary, daughter of the Rev. Jonathan Peake, vicar of Dronfield, by Sarah, his wife, daughter of the said Clement Rossington, esq.* and had two sons and one daughter, viz.

JOHN, his heir.
Robert, of Ripley, *b.* 7th March, 1781.
Mary.

Mr. Wood was succeeded at his decease by his elder son, the present Rev. JOHN WOOD, of Swanwick.

*Arms*—Az. three naked savages ppr. in their dexter hands a shield arg. charged with a cross gu. in their sinister a club resting on their shoulders, also ppr.

*Crest*—An oak tree ppr. charged with acorns or.

*Estates*—In Derbyshire, a portion possessed since the reign of EDWARD VI.

*Seat*—Swanwick Hall, Derbyshire.

* By Sarah, his wife, daughter of Francis Burton, esq. lord of the manor of Dronfield, and Helena, his wife, daughter and heir of Cassibelan Burton, esq. only son of WILLIAM BURTON, esq. of Lindley, author of the History of Leicestershire.

## WOOD, OF SINGLETON LODGE.

WOOD, GEORGE-WILLIAM, esq. of Singleton Lodge, in the county of Lancaster, *b.* at Leeds 26th July, 1781; *m.* there the 22nd November, 1810, Sarah, daughter of Joseph Oates, esq. of Weetwood Hall, in Yorkshire, by Elizabeth his wife, eldest daughter of Joshua Rayner, esq. of Leeds, merchant,* and eventually coheir, with her sister Sarah, the wife of William Smithson, esq. of Heath, of their brother Milnes Rayner, esq. By this lady he has an only child,

WILLIAM-RAYNER, *b.* 26th August, 1811.

Mr. Wood, who succeeded his father in 1808, was one of the representatives in the last parliament for the southern division of the county of Lancaster.

### Lineage.

BENJAMIN WOOD, gent. of Northampton, born 16th March, 1718, married, at Collingtree, 21st May, 1744, Elizabeth, daughter of Robert Wingreave, of Collingtree, near Northampton, and by her, who died 8th December, 1748, had a son, WILLIAM. Mr. Wood died in September, 1783, was buried at Castle Hill Chapel, and succeeded by his son,

THE REV. WILLIAM WOOD, of Leeds, in the county of York, F.L.S. minister of Mill Hill Chapel, there, born at Collingtree, 29th May, 1745. This gentleman wedded 29th September, 1780, Louisa Anne, daughter of George Oates, esq. of Newton Hall, by Sarah, his wife, only surviving daughter and heir of Joseph Jolley, of Manchester, merchant, (descended from John Jolley, of Leek, in the county of Stafford, ancestor of Hylton Jolliffe, esq. member in the present parliament for the borough of Petersfield, whose progenitor, Thomas Jolley, esq. of Cofton Hall, in the county of Worcester, assumed the surname of Joliffee). Of this marriage there were issue,

- GEORGE WILLIAM, heir to his father.
- William, born at Leeds, 4th August, 1782, died unmarried in London, April, 1811, and was buried at Islington.
- Frederick, born 3rd June, 1784, died 22nd June, 1796.
- Louisa-Anne, *m.* at Leeds, 26th November, 1823, to the Rev. Samuel Crawford, of that borough, minister of Call Lane Chapel, and has surviving issue, two sons and one daughter, viz.
  - William Crawford, born 8th November, 1824.
  - Alexander Crawford, born 6th March, 1832.
  - Jane Crawford, born 7th June, 1828.

Mr. Wood died at Leeds, 1st April, 1808, (Mrs. Wood, 24th September, 1800), was buried at Mill Hill Chapel, and succeeded by his son, the present GEORGE WILLIAM WOOD, esq. late M.P. for South Lancashire.

*Arms*—On a chief, sa. an open Bible, ppr. clasped gold, between two mill rinds of the first.

*Crest*—A boar passant reguardant sa. collared, chained and hoofed or, before a tree, ppr.

*Motto*—Civil and religious liberty.

*Seat*—Singleton Lodge, Lancashire.

* By Sarah, daughter of William Milnes, of Chesterfield, in the county of Derby.

# BRAILSFORD, OF BARKWITH HOUSE.

BRAILSFORD, THOMAS, esq. of Barkwith House, in the county of Lincoln, lord of the manor of Toft Hill and Toft Grange, in that shire, *b.* 10th October, 1787; *m.* 14th January, 1815, Anne, daughter of James Shipley, esq. by Elizabeth his wife, one of the co-heiresses of the late William Heathcote, esq. of the colony of Demerara, and of Stancliffe Hall, in the county of Derby, and has issue,

I. THOMAS, *b.* 2nd November, 1816.
II. Samuel, *b.* 1st May, 1819.
III. John-Arthur-Heathcote, *b.* 18th April, 1822.
IV. William, *b.* 2nd June, 1825.

I. Eliza. II. Ellen.
III. Alsina. IV. Emma-Dorothea.

Mr. Brailsford, who is a deputy lieutenant of the county of Lincoln, inherited a portion of his estates upon the demise of his great-uncle in 1808, and the remainder at the death of his uncle in 1820.

## Lineage.

"The ancient family of Brailsford," says Lysons in his Magna Britannia, "was of Brailsford, in the county of Derby, *temp.* HENRY II. Nicholas, the first who assumed the name, was son of Elsinus, who lived in the reign of WILLIAM the Conqueror. In the time of RICHARD II. the heiress of the elder branch married Bassett of Chedle. John Brailsford, the representative of a younger branch, settled at Senior, in Hucknall, in the reign of EDWARD VI. was servant to Sir John Harpur, in 1662; his father had sold the family estate, but Senior was then possessed by a cousin, as appears by Dugdale's Visitation of Derbyshire."

THOMAS BRAILSFORD, of South Normanton, descended from the Brailsfords of Senior, married sometime before the year 1680, Elizabeth Smyth, of Bolsover, an heiress, and had a son and successor,

THOMAS BRAILSFORD, of Bolsover and South Normanton, father, by Frances Machon, of Mansfield, his wife, whom he wedded, 30th September, 1713, of Samuel Brailsford, of Rowthorne, who died in 1808, and of

THOMAS BRAILSFORD, of Bolsover and South Normanton, in the county of Derby, who espoused in 1740, Ellen Newbould, of Mansfield Woodhouse, Notts, and had two sons and one daughter, viz.

THOMAS, his heir.
Samuel, born in April, 1745, *m.* in August, 1786, Mary, daughter of Nicholas Christian, esq. of Castleton, in the Isle of Man, and died in 1798, leaving two sons,
THOMAS, successor to his uncle.
Samuel, army surgeon, who died at Pendennis Castle, Cornwall, in 1809.
Elizabeth, *d.* an infant.

Mr. Brailsford was succeeded by his elder son,

THOMAS BRAILSFORD, esq. of South Normanton, born in 1742, at whose decease, without issue, in 1820, the estates and representation of the family devolved on his nephew, the present THOMAS BRAILSFORD, esq. of Barkwith House.

*Arms*—Or, a cinquefoil sa. on a chief indented ermine, two pommes each charged with a cross arg.

*Crest*—A unicorn's head arg. erased gu. armed and maned or, entwined by a serpent ppr. and charged on the neck with a pomme and thereon a cross, as in the arms.

*Motto*—In Jehovah, fides mea.

*Estates*—Messuages and lands at South Normanton, conveyed by deed by Anne Brailsford to her nephew, Thomas Brailsford, grandfather of the Thomas Brailsford who married Elizabeth Smyth, in December, 1627. Messuages and lands in Bolsover, at Chesterfield, and at Mansfield Woodhouse. Mansion and lands at East Barkwith, in Lincolnshire, purchased by the present proprietor's great uncle, Samuel Brailsford, in 1770. Manor of Toft Hill and Toft Grange, in the same county, bought from Lady Banks, in 1820.

*Seat*—Barkwith House, Lincolnshire.

# LOWRY, OF POMEROY HOUSE.

LOWRY, ROBERT-WILLIAM, esq. of Pomeroy House, in the county of Tyrone, *m.* 6th February, 1815, Anna, only daughter of Admiral Graves, of the ennobled family of the same name, and has issue,

ROBERT-WILLIAM.
John-Fetherstone.
Hester.
Elizabeth.
Anna.

Mr. Lowry, a magistrate and deputy lieutenant for the county of Tyrone, succeeded his brother in 1807. He was sheriff in 1812.

## Lineage.

JOHN LOWRY, esq. sprung from an ancient Scottish family, migrated to Ireland, and settled at Ahenis, in the county of Tyrone. He *m.* first, a daughter of Hamilton, of Ballyfallow, and by her, who died at Londonderry, during its celebrated siege in 1689, left one son and three daughters, viz.

I. William, who went to the East Indies, and died unm.

I. Elizabeth, *m.* to Francis Perry, esq. of Tathyreagh, in Tyrone.

II. Margaret, *m.* to John Keys, esq. of Cavancurr, in the county of Donegall.

III. Mary, *m.* to Archibald Woods, esq. of Trinsallah, in the same shire.

Mr. Lowry wedded secondly, Miss Mary Buchanan, a Scottish lady, and had

II. John, who died unm.

III. ROBERT, successor to his father.

IV. Catharine, *m.* to Samuel Perry, esq. of Moylaghmore.

V. Rebecca, *m.* to William Moore, esq. of Drumond.

VI. Anne, *m.* to Robert M'Clintock, esq. of Castrues.

VII. Jane, *m.* to John M'Clintock, esq. of Trintaugh.

The only surviving son,

ROBERT LOWRY, esq. of Ahenis, espoused Anne, daughter of the Rev. James Sinclair, of Hollyhill, rector of the parish of Loch Patrick (second son of Sir James Sinclair, of Caithness, by Anne, his wife, daughter of James Galbraith, esq. M. P. for John's Town in 1661), and had issue,

I. Robert, of Melbury, in the county of Donegall, M.P. who *m.* Margaret, daughter of the venerable Archdeacon Hamilton, but *d. s. p.*

II. GALBRAITH, of Ahenis, thrice elected knight of the shire for Tyrone. He *m.* Sarah, second daughter and coheir of John Corry, esq. and had, with a daughter, Anne, the wife of William Willoughby Cole, Lord Enniskillen, a son and heir,

ARMAR LOWRY, esq. of Ahenis, who assumed the additional surname of CORRY, and was raised to the peerage, as EARL of BELMORE. His son is the present earl. (See BURKE'S *Peerage and Baronetage.*)

III. JAMES, of whom presently.

Mr. Lowry, of Ahenis, was succeeded in his principal estates by his elder surviving son, while the younger,

THE REV. JAMES LOWRY, rector of Clogheny, founded the branch seated at Pomeroy House. This gentleman *m.* Hester, dau. of William Richardson, esq. of Richhill, M.P. for the county of Armagh, and had issue,

I. ROBERT, his heir.
II. John, in holy orders, rector of Sommerset.
III. James, in holy orders, of Rockdale House.
I. Hester, *m.* to Major Thomas Dickson, M.P. of Woodville, in the county of Leitrim.

The eldest son,

ROBERT LOWRY, esq. of Pomeroy House, wedded Eliza, daughter of Major Tighe, a cavalry officer, resident at Ballyshannon, a scion of the Tighes of Michelstown, in Westmeath, and had issue,

I. JAMES, his heir.
II. ROBERT-WILLIAM, successor to his brother.
III. John, late an officer in the 8th regiment. } both now on half-pay.
IV. Armer, late an officer in the 45th regiment. }
V. William, late lieutenant of H. M. King George IV. yatch.
I. Hester.
II. Elizabeth.

Mr. Lowry was succeeded by his eldest son,

JAMES LOWRY, esq. of Pomeroy House, an officer in the 14th light dragoons, at whose decease, without issue, in 1807, the estates and representation of this branch of the Lowry family passed to his brother, the present ROBERT-WILLIAM LOWRY, of Pomeroy House.

*Arms*—Sa. a cup arg. with a garland between two laurel branches, all issuing out of the same vert.

*Crest*—A garland of laurel between two branches of the same ppr.

*Mottoes*—Virtus semper viridis, and Floreant lauri.

*Estates*—The manor of Chichester and Leggin, including the town of Pomeroy, in the barony of Dungannon, and county of Tyrone, possessed about one hundred and fifty years; and property at Baskine, in Westmeath, acquired in marriage, by the present proprietor.

*Seat*—Pomeroy House, near Dungannon.

## BAGWELL, OF MARLFIELD.

BAGWELL, JOHN, esq. of Marlfield and Oaklands House, in the county of Tipperary, and of East Grove, in the Cove of Cork, *b.* 3rd April, 1810, inherited the estates upon the demise of his uncle, the Right Hon. William Bagwell, M.P. in 1826. Mr. Bagwell is in the commission of the peace for the counties of Tipperary and Waterford, and in the deputy lieutenancy of the former, of which shire he was high sheriff in 1834.

### Lineage.

JOHN BACKWEL, OR BAGWELL, (brother of Backwell, the original proprietor of the Bank, in London, now the firm of Child and Co. and also of William Backwel, the author of "The Mystery of Astronomy made easy to the meanest capacity," published in 1655, in eight volumes), a captain in Cromwell's army, settled in Ireland, where he married, and had a son,

WILLIAM BAGWELL, esq. of Ballyloughane, in the county of Tipperary, where he was possessed of twelve hundred acres, having bought the fee in 1707, and in 1712, he purchased the lands of Gormanstown, in the same shire. He was *s.* by his only son,

JOHN BAGWELL, esq. who became an eminent banker at Clonmell, and purchased the Burgagery, and other estates, producing the annual income of twenty thousand pounds. He married the daughter of the Rev. Mr. Shaw, of Dublin, a presbyterian clergyman, and *d.* in 1754, leaving two sons and three daughters. His second son,

WILLIAM BAGWELL, esq. was elected in

1756, for the borough of Clonmell, and his return being subsequently petitioned against, was established by a majority of one only. He *m.* in 1749, the daughter of John Harper, esq. and thus acquired the estates now held by the Bagwell family, in the county of Cork. He died in 1756, and left, with three daughters, a son and heir,

JOHN BAGWELL, esq. who purchased Marlfield, in the county of Tipperary, and the patronage of the borough of Clonmell, the member for which borough the Bagwells returned until the passing of the reform bill. In 1775, Mr. Bagwell contested unsuccessfully the representation of the city of Cork; in 1790, he was declared, by a committee of the House of Commons, member for the county of Tipperary, Mr. Matthew, the late earl of Landaff, being unseated; and in 1793, he raised the Tipperary regiment of militia, to which he was appointed colonel. He wedded in 1774, Miss Hare, daughter of Richard Hare, esq. of Ennismore, and sister of William, present earl of Listowell, by whom he had issue,

- WILLIAM, his heir.
- Richard, who *m.* in 1808, Margaret, eldest daughter of Edward Croker, esq. of Ballinaguard, in the county of Limerick, and had issue,
  - JOHN, successor to his uncle.
  - Edward.
  - Margaret.
  - Mary.
  - Jane.
- John, Benjamin, } who both died unmarried.
- Margaret, *m.* to John Keily, esq. of Strangally Castle.
- Jane, *m.* to Lieutenant General Sir Eyre Coote, of West Park, Hants.
- Catherine, *m.* to John Croker, esq. of Ballinaguard.
- Mary, *m.* to Henry Langley, esq. of Brittas Castle.

Colonel Bagwell was succeeded at his decease, by his eldest son,

THE RIGHT HON. COLONEL WILLIAM BAGWELL, of Marlfield, M.P. a privy counsellor and muster master general for Ireland, at whose decease, unmarried, in 1826, the estates devolved on his nephew, the present JOHN BAGWELL, esq. of Marlfield.

*Arms*—Paly of six arg. and az. on a chief gu. a lion passant arg.

*Crest*—Out of a mural crown a demi bull, all ppr.

*Motto*—In fide et in bello fortis.

*Estates*—In the counties of Tipperary, Cork, &c.

*Seat*—Marlfield, and Oaklands House, near Clonmell; and East Grove, cove of Cork.

## D'ARCY, OF KILTULLA.

D'ARCY, JOHN, esq. of Kiltulla House and of Clifden Castle, both in the county of Galway, *b.* 26th November, 1785; *m.* first, on the 4th June, 1804, Frances, daughter of Andrew Blake, esq. of Castle Grove, and niece of the late Viscount Netterville, by whom (who died 15th April, 1815) he has issue,

- I. HYACINTH-JOHN.
- II. Patrick.
- III. James.
- I. Isabella.
- II. Julia, *m.* to Richard Levingston, esq.

He wedded, secondly, 3rd March, 1821, Louisa-Bagot, daughter of the late Walter Sneyd, esq. of Keele Hall, in Staffordshire, and his wife, the Hon. Louisa Bagot, sister of the present Lord Bagot, and has five other sons and two daughters, viz.

- I. Edmund.
- II. Henry.
- III. Richard.
- IV. William.
- V. Norman.
- I. Elizabeth.
- II. Louisa.

Mr. D'Arcy, who has been for the last twenty-five years in the commission of the peace, served the office of high sheriff for the county of Galway in 1811. He is the founder of the beautiful town of Clifden, on the Bay of Anber, now in the most flourishing condition.

## Lineage.

The family of DE ARCY ranks with the most eminent established in England by the NORMAN CONQUEST, and amongst the peerages of past times, there are two BARONIES in *abeyance*, one *forfeited* BARONY, and three EXTINCT BARONIES, all of which had been conferred upon members of the house of D'ARCY, beside the *extinct* EARLDOM OF HOLDERNESS. When the general survey was made,

NORMAN DE ARCI enjoyed not fewer than thirty-three lordships in the county of Lincoln, which he derived directly from the CONQUEROR, and of which NOCTON became the chief residence of himself and his descendants for several generations. He was *s.* by his son,

ROBERT D'ARCY, who founded a priory of Augustin monks at Nocton, and was otherwise a bountiful benefactor to the church. He was *s.* by his son,

THOMAS D'ARCY, who, in the 12th of HENRY II., on the assessment in aid of marrying that king's daughter, certified that he then held twenty knights' fees *de veteri feoffemento*, with half a knight's fee, and a fourth part *de novo*, for which he paid £13. 6*s.* 8*d.* He *d.* in 1180, and was *s.* by his son,

THOMAS D'ARCY, whose son and heir,

NORMAN D'ARCY, joining the baronial standard, in the time of *King* JOHN, had his lands seized by the crown, and retained until the general pacification in the beginning of HENRY III.'s reign. He died soon after, and was *s.* by his son,

PHILIP D'ARCY, of Nocton, a distinguished soldier in the reigns of JOHN and HENRY III. He *m.* Isabel, daughter and co-heir of Roger Bertram, of Mitford, (see vol. ii. page 282) and dying in 1263, was *s.* by his son,

NORMAN D'ARCY, of Nocton, who *m.* in the 43rd HENRY III. Elizabeth, daughter of John Delafeld, and had issue,

- PHILIP, who inherited Nocton, and was summoned to parliament, as a BARON, from 29th December, 1299, to 20th October, 1332. He died in the latter year, and was *s.* by his son,
  - NORMAN, second baron, who *d.* in 1340, and was succeeded by his son,
  - PHILIP, third baron, at whose decease issueless, this BARONY OF D'ARCY fell into abeyance, between his next heirs, namely,
    - SIR PHILIP DE LIMBURG, knt. son of Julian, eldest sister of the first baron, and
    - AGNES, wife of SIR ROGER DE PEDWARDINE, younger sister of the same nobleman.
- JOHN, of whom presently.
- Robert, of Stailingburgh, in the county of Lincoln, who left an only daughter and heiress, Margaret, the wife of John Argentine.

The second son,

JOHN D'ARCY, an eminent soldier and statesman in the reigns of the first, second, and third EDWARDS, filled some of the highest offices of the government, and was eventually summoned to parliament in the 6th year of EDWARD III. In the time of EDWARD II. he was governor of Norham Castle, sheriff of the counties of Nottingham, Derby, and Lancaster, and JUSTICE OF IRELAND. On the accession of EDWARD III. he was made sheriff of Yorkshire and governor of York Castle, and re-constituted JUSTICE OF IRELAND, to which high office and the government of the country he was re-appointed in the next year. While in Ireland, Lord D'Arcy at the head of an army marched into the province of Ulster to avenge the death of his wife's nephew, William de Burgh,* Earl of Ulster, but before his arrival the country people had already taken ample revenge, by destroying no less than three hundred persons in one day. The lord justice thereupon changed his course, and leaving Thomas Burke, his lieutenant, in Ireland, joined the king in Scotland, who was then pursuing the vic-

* WILLIAM DE BURGH, third EARL OF ULSTER, was murdered in the twenty-third year of his age, *anno* 1333, by Robert Fitz-Richard Mandeville and his servants, near the Fords, in his way to Carrickfergus. His wife, the Lady Maud Plantagenet, daughter of Henry, Earl of Lancaster, and granddaughter of *King* HENRY III., with her daughter, the sole heiress of her deceased lord, returned immediately to England, and the assassination causing a prodigious outcry, the Lord Justice D'Arcy called a parliament, by whose advice he sailed for Carrickfergus, but before his arrival the country people had destroyed the murderers, with their abettors, killing, in one day, more than three hundred persons.—BURKE's *Peerage and Baronetage.*

torious career which placed EDWARD BALIOL on the Scottish throne. Lord D'Arcy was subsequently constable of the Tower of London, and ambassador at the courts of France and Scotland. He finally shared in the glory of CRESSY, and was constituted JUSTICE OF IRELAND and CONSTABLE OF THE TOWER for life. He married first, Emeline, daughter and co-heir of Walter Heron, of Hedleston, in the county of Northumberland, by whom he had

JOHN, his successor, second LORD D'ARCY, for whose line, see BURKE'S *Extinct and Dormant Peerage*.

Roger, from whom the D'Arcys of Essex sprang.

Adomar.

His lordship wedded secondly, 2nd July 1329, the Lady Joane de Burgh, daughter of Richard de Burgh, Earl of Ulster, and his wife, Maud, daughter and heir of Hugh de Lacie, the younger, Earl of Ulster, by this lady he had another son and daughter, viz.

WILLIAM.

Elizabeth, *m.* to James Butler, second EARL OF ORMONDE.

Lord D'Arcy died 30th May, 1347, and was *s.* in his title by the eldest son of his first marriage, JOHN, second lord. The only son of his second marriage,

WILLIAM D'ARCY, born at Maynooth, in the county of Kildare, in 1330, having had divers lands assigned to him in consideration of his father's great public services, settled at Platten, in the county of Meath. He *m.* Catharine, daughter of Sir Robert Fitzgerald, of Alloone, in Kildare, and was *s.* by his son,

JOHN D'ARCY, of Platten, who married a daughter of Pettyt, baron of Mullingar, and left a son and successor,

WILLIAM D'ARCY, of Platten, who *m.* Anne, daughter of — Barnewall, of Crickstown, and was father of

JOHN D'ARCY, of Platten. This gentleman wedded the Hon. Margaret Fleming, elder daughter of David, Lord Slane, who died in 1463, and co-heir of her brother, Thomas, Lord Slane, who died issueless, in 1471. He was *s.* by his son,

JOHN D'ARCY, of Platten, who had two sons,

I. JOHN, of Platten, who was succeeded by his son,

WILLIAM (Sir), of Platten. This gentleman was constituted, in 1523, vice-treasurer of Ireland. He was the author of a work, entitled "The Decay of Ireland, and the Causes of it," and was "a man," says Harris, in his Writers of Ireland, "of wisdom and learning, and one who, for his good services to the English interest in that country, had great merit." He died far advanced in years, in 1540, and left, with other issue, a daughter, Eleanor, *m.* to Robert Plunket, fifth Lord Dunsaney, and a son and successor,

CHRISTOPHER, of Platten, who *m.* first, Elizabeth Draicott, and secondly, Mary, dau. of Sir Nicholas Whyte, of Leixlip, master of the Rolls, by whom (who *m.* secondly, Robert Browne, of Mulrankan, and thirdly, Sir Nicholas St. Lawrence, twenty-first Lord Howth) he had three sons. His eldest son,

GEORGE D'ARCY, of Platten was slain in the service of *Queen* ELIZABETH, leaving by Cicelia his wife, daughter of Christopher Ffagan, an alderman of Dublin, a daughter, Bridget, the wife of John Fitzpatrick, esq. of Castletown, ancestor of the Earls of Upper Ossory, and a son,

NICHOLAS D'ARCY, of Platten, a minor in 1617, who forfeited the estates in 1641.

II. NICHOLAS.

The younger son,

NICHOLAS D'ARCY, was a captain of horse, and being quartered in Mayo, *m.* Jane, daughter and heir of O'Duraghy, of Partry, in that county, and was succeeded by his son,

THOMAS D'ARCY, father of

CONYERS D'ARCY, who was succeeded by his son,

NICHOLAS D'ARCY, of Kiltulla, in the county of Galway, who had two sons,

JAMES, his heir.

Richard, whose only daughter married Robert Blake, of Ardfry, and was mother of the *Right Hon.* SIR RICHARD BLAKE, of Ardfry, of the privy council in the time of CHARLES I. M.P. for Galway in 1639, and speaker of the supreme council of confederated catholics, at Kilkenny, in 1648. From Sir Richard lineally descends the noble house of WALLSCOURT.

The elder son,

JAMES D'ARCY, of Kiltulla, surnamed

*Riveagh*, or the *Swarthy*, was a person of great influence and power in the province of Connaught, of which he was made VICE PRESIDENT by *Queen* ELIZABETH. He was likewise chief magistrate of the town of Galway, where there is a monument to his memory, in the Franciscan Abbey. He *d.* in 1603, leaving seven sons and a daughter, viz.

I. NICHOLAS, whose two sons, James and Dominick, both *d. s. p.* The elder, who was a barrister-at-law, settled his large estates in the counties of Galway, Mayo, Roscommon, and Clare, on his first cousin, JAMES D'ARCY, of Kiltulla.

II. Martin, ancestor of the D'ARCYS of Clunuane, in the county of Clare.

III. James, from whom the families of Ballybocock, Gorteen, Hounswood, and Tuam.

IV. Anthony, who, beside sons, from whom sprung the D'ARCIES of Brest, in France, had two daughters,

  Catherine, *m.* to Marcus French, esq. ancestor of the Frenches of Rahasane.

  Anastace, *m.* to James Daly, esq. of Carrownekelly, in the county of Galway, and was mother of DENNIS DALY, who was a justice of the common pleas and a privy counsellor in the time of JAMES II.

V. Mark.

VI. Andrew, whose daughter wedded Richard Martin, esq. barrister-at-law, ancestor of the Martins of Tullyra, in the county of Galway.

VII. PATRICK.

I. Anastace, *m.* to Sir Dominick Brown, knt. and was mother of Geoffrey Brown, (from whom the BROWNS of Castlemagarret), and four daughters.

The youngest son,

PATRICK D'ARCY, esq. of Kiltulla, *b.* in 1598, is described by Harris as "a gentleman educated in the profession of the common law, who was an active member of the house of commons, in the parliament assembled at Dublin, in 1640, when the papists had a share in the legislature as well as the protestants." By an order of the house, a speech of his was subsequently published, under the title of "An Argument, delivered by Patrick D'Arcy, esq. in the parliament of Ireland, the 9th of June, 1641." This argument was made at a conference of the house of commons with a committee of the lords, in the castle of Dublin, upon certain questions propounded to the judges of Ireland, in full parliament, and upon the answers of the judges to the said interrogatories. Himself and his nephew, Geoffrey Browne, were amongst the commissioners appointed by the general assembly of confederate catholics, held at Kilkenny in the time of the grand rebellion, to conclude a peace with the Marquess of Ormonde, the king's lieutenant; and "the drawing up of the articles was left to the said Mr. Patrick D'Arcy and Mr. Geoffrey Browne, and by them performed according to the sense of the assembly." These articles were signed and sealed 28th March, 1646, by the lord lieutenant, on the king's behalf; and by the Lord Muskery, Sir Robert Talbot, John Dillon, Patrick D'Arcy, and Geoffry Browne, on the part of the confederates, in the presence of the marquess of Clanricarde, the Lord Digby, Sir Maurice Eustace, and Doctor Gerald Tennell." D'Arcy was hereupon constituted by the assembly one of the commissioners to raise an army of ten thousand men, and to tax the kingdom for their pay, in support of the royal cause. He died in Dublin, *anno* 1668, and was interred at Kilconnel, in the county of Galway, leaving by his wife, Elizabeth, daughter of Sir Peter French, an only son,

JAMES D'ARCY, esq. of Kiltulla, who *m.* Frances Trusnot, a lady of Britanny, whose father was captain of a man of war, in the service of LOUIS XIII. and her mother, Anne Keating (his wife), was maid of honor to HENRIETTA-MARIA, QUEEN *Consort* of CHARLES I. By this lady, Mr. D'Arcy, who *d.* in 1692, had issue,

HYACINTH, his heir.

Anne.
Frances.
Bridget.
Clare.

The son and heir,

HYACINTH D'ARCY, of Kiltulla, a captain in the army, *b.* in 1665, *m.* Catherine, daughter of John D'Arcy, esq. of Gorteen, in the county of Mayo, and had issue,

I. PATRICK, who *m.* Anne, only daughter of Walter Blake, esq. of Oranmore, in the county of Galway, but died *s. p.*

II. JOHN.

III. James, who *m.* first, Jane, daughter of Richard Martyn, esq. of Dangan, in the county of Galway, and had a son, Richard, who married in December, 1751, at Bourdeaux, a rich American widow, the daughter of — Kirwan, esq. James wedded, secondly, Mary, daughter of Matthew Shee, of Nantz, and had other issue.

IV. Martin, *m.* in 1752, Mary, daughter of Thomas D'Arcy, of Brest.

V. Hyacinth, died unm.

VI. Stephen, who *m.* Miss Anne French,

of the Rahasane family, and had several sons and daughters.

VII. Francis.

VIII. Walter, *m.* Anastasia, daughter of John D'Arcy, esq. of Gorteen.

IX. Sylvester, *d.* unm.

I. Anastasia, *m.* to Denis Daly, esq. of Raford, in the county of Galway, and had a son and heir,

Denis Daly, esq. of Raford, who *m.* the Lady Anne Burke, elder daughter of Michael, earl of Clanrickarde, and had daughters only, his co-heirs, one of whom married, in 1832, Andrew Blake, esq. son of Colonel Blake, of Firbough.

II. Frances, *m.* to R. French, esq. of Duran, in the county of Galway.

III. Catharine.

Capt. Hyacinth D'Arcy's second son,

JOHN D'ARCY, esq. espoused Jane, daughter of Sir Robert Lynch, bart. of Castle Cara, and had issue,

I. HYACINTH, *m.* Frances, youngest daughter of Henry O'Brien, esq. of Stone Hall, in the county of Clare, (see p. 110), but died *s. p.*

II. JOHN, of whom presently.

III. Patrick, member of the Royal Academy of Science at Paris, *d. s. p.*

The second son,

JOHN D'ARCY, esq. married in 1752, Catharine, daughter of Col. Isidore Lynch, of Drincong Castle, and had one son and one daughter, viz.

HYACINTH, his heir.

Jane, *m.* first, to her kinsman, M. Le Comte D'Arcy, lieutenant-general of the armies of the king of France, grand cordon of St. Louis, first aide-camp to LOUIS XVI. and member of the Academie of Science. The count died of the cholera morbus, in 1780, on his route to assume the command of the troops in Flanders. The countess wedded secondly, Matthew Talbot, esq. of Castle Talbot, in the county of Wexford.

Mr. D'Arcy was *s.* by his son,

HYACINTH D'ARCY, esq. This gentleman *m.* first, Mary, dau. of F. Blake, esq. of Rahara, in the county of Roscommon, by whom he had no issue; and secondly, in 1784, Julia, daughter of Mark Lynch, esq. of Barna, in the county of Galway, by whom he had one daughter, who died unmarried, and two sons,

JOHN, his heir, the present JOHN D'ARCY, esq. of Kiltulla and Clifden Castle.

Mark.

*Arms*---Az. semée of cross crosslets and three cinquefoils, arg.

*Crest*---A spear broken in three pieces or, headed arg. and banded together in the middle by a riband, gu.

*Motto*---Un dieu, un roi.

*Estates*---The family estates in the counties of Mayo, Roscommon, Sligo, Galway, and Clare, now all forfeited, with the exception of the lands of Kiltulla, Longford, and Clifden, which were given as compensation, at the restoration of CHARLES II.

*Seats*---Kiltulla House, and Clifden Castle.

## GOODFORD, OF CHILTON CANTELO.

GOODFORD, JOHN, esq. of Chilton Cantelo, in the county of Somerset, *b.* 27th December, 1784; *m.* 4th January, 1810, Charlotte, fourth daughter of Montague Cholmeley, esq. of Easton, in Lincolnshire, and sister of the late Sir Montague Cholmeley, bart. by whom he has had issue,

HENRY, *b.* 2nd April, 1811.

Charles-Old, *b.* 15th July, 1812.

Montague-John, *b.* 20th November, 1822.

Mary-Ann, *d.* 5th February, 1833.

Maria.

Penelope.

Mr. Goodford succeeded his father 14th August, 1787. He is an active magistrate for the counties of Somerset and Dorset, and a deputy lieutenant and chairman of the Quarter Sessions in the former, of which he served the office of sheriff in 1816.

## Lineage.

SAMUEL GOODFORD, of Yeovil, *m.* first, in May, 1716, Ann, daughter of Philip Taylor, of Weymouth, and had by her,

- SAMUEL, his heir.
- Ann.
- Elizabeth, *m.* in February, 1747, to John Daniel, of Yeovil.

Mr. Goodford wedded, secondly, in July, 1731, Elizabeth, relict of John Old, of Yeovil, and daughter of Jeremiah Hayne, but had no other issue. His only son,

SAMUEL GOODFORD, esq. of the Inner Temple, and of Trent, in the county of Somerset, who *m.* in October, 1739, Mary, only surviving child of John and Elizabeth Old, and had by her, who died in 1767, one daughter, Mary, *m.* in July, 1767, to Thomas Blakemore, esq. of Briggins Park, Herts, and a son and successor,

JOHN-OLD GOODFORD, esq. of Yeovil, who served the office of sheriff for Somersetshire in 1774. He *m.* in October, 1776, Maria, second daughter of Edward Phelips, esq. of Montacute House, and had issue,

- JOHN, his heir.
- Maria, who *d.* 6th April, 1816.
- Elizabeth, *m.* in 1812, to James-Paul Bridger, esq. of Buckingham, in Sussex, lieutenant-colonel 12th light dragoons, and *d.* 26th May, 1828.
- Harriett, *d.* unm.
- Mary-Ann, *d.* young.

Mr. Goodford *d.* 14th August, 1787, and was *s.* by his son, the present JOHN GOODFORD, esq. of Chilton Cantelo.

*Arms*—Az. on a chev. between three boars' heads arg. langued and couped gu. as many pellets.

*Crest*—A boar's head arg. langued gu. charged on the neck with a pellet.

*Estates*—Manors of Chilton Cantelo, Old Sock, and Mudford, with lands in Yeovil, Preston Bermondsey, Ashington, Mudford and Chilton Cantelo, in the county of Somerset, acquired in 1715, and subsequently.

*Seat*—Chilton Cantelo, near Yeovil.

# DAYRELL, OF LILLINGSTON DAYRELL.

DAYRELL, RICHARD, esq. of Lillingston Dayrell, in the county of Buckingham, *b.* 1st April, 1779; *m.* first, in 1802, Ann, only child of Gabriel Parker, gent. and had one son, Richard Meyrick, *b.* in 1806, who died in 1810. He wedded, secondly, in 1807, Frances-Elizabeth, eldest daughter of John Dax, esq. master of the Exchequer Office of Pleas. Mr. Dayrell was formerly a captain in the 85th regiment, but was obliged to retire from the service at the early age of nineteen, owing to the loss of a leg. He is a magistrate and deputy lieutenant for the county of Bucks, and was high sheriff in 1808. Captain Dayrell succeeded his uncle in 1803.

## Lineage.

The family of Dayrell or Darell was established in England by one of the companions in arms of the CONQUEROR, and the name of its founder appears on the roll of Battel Abbey. Numerous divergent branches were planted in various counties, and for centuries flourished in all; the principal were those of CALEHILL and SCOTNEY * in Kent; of SESAY † in Yorkshire; of LITTLECOTE ‡ in Wilts; of PAGEHAM in Sussex;

* See vol. i. p. 133.

† The last male heir of SESAY, SIR GEORGE DARELL, died in 1466, leaving a daughter and heiress, Joan, who married SIR GUY DAWNEY, of Cowick, in the county of York.

‡ The LITTLECOTE line was founded by WIL-

and of TREWORNAN§ in Cornwall. The Dayrells of Lillingston Dayrell derive from a common ancestor with the Calehill family, and have possessed the broad lands which they now hold ever since the CONQUEST.

RICHARD DAYRELL, brother of Elias Dayrell, was seised in fee of a messuage in Lillingston Dayrell, in the county of Buckingham, *temp.* RICHARD I. or JOHN, and was father of a daughter, Alice, the wife of Peter Crendon. The next possessor on record,

— DAIRELL, of Lillingston Dairell, in Bucks, and of Hanworth, in Middlesex, had two sons, RALPH, his heir; and Lawrence, the first rector of Lillingston, living in 1255, who had a son, Richard. The elder son,

RALPH DAIRELL, of Lillingston Dairell and Hanworth, living in 10th HENRY III. married, it is supposed, an heiress named Juliana de Barré, and had three sons, viz.

HENRY, his heir.

Richard, who gave donations to Suffield Abbey in 1253.

Robert, also a benefactor to the same abbey, as was his son, Ralph.

The eldest son and heir,

HENRY DAIRELL, of Hanworth and Lillingston, who flourished in the reigns of HENRY III. and EDWARD I. wedded twice. By his second wife, Alicia, whose mother, Christian, was daughter and heiress of Alexander Hampden, he appears to have had no issue. By his first, Johanna, daughter and co-heir of Roger de Samford, and first cousin to Alicia de Samford, wife of

---

iam DARELL, sub-treasurer of England, *temp* RICHARD II. who married Elizabeth, daughter and heiress of Thomas Calston, esq. lord of Littlecote, in Wiltshire, and acquired with her that estate. He had issue,

I. GEORGE, his heir.

II. Richard (Sir), also sub-treasurer of England, who *m.* Margaret, daughter and coheir of Edmund Beaufort, Duke of Somerset, and relict of Humphrey Stafford, Earl of Buckingham. By this lady, a direct descendant of the royal line of Plantagenet, Sir Richard left an only daughter and heiress,

MARGARET, *m.* to James Touchet, Lord Audley.

III. Constantine, of Collingborne, *m.* Julia, daughter of Robert Collingborne, and had a son,

WILLIAM, who acquired the lands of PAGEHAM, in Sussex, by marriage with Joan, daughter and heiress of William Knottesworth. He was father of

MARMADUKE, of Pageham, whose will, dated 17th June, 1558, was proved the following July. He *m.* Anne, daughter of Richard Scott, esq. brother of Sir Reginald Scott, of Scotts Hall, Kent, and left an only daughter and heiress,

MARY, who wedded the Rev. EDWARD DARELL, third son of Thomas Darell, esq. of Scotney, and had issue,

1. THOMAS (Sir), of Pageham.
2. Philip.
3. John.
4. Marmaduke (Sir), knt. of Fulmere, Bucks (cofferer to JAMES I. and CHARLES I.), who *m.* Anne, daughter of John Lennard, esq. of Knoll, in Kent, and had two sons, SAMPSON (Sir), of Fulmere; and Marmaduke, of Horstow, in Lincolnshire.
5. Christopher.
6. Henry.
7. George, D. D. prebendary of Westminster, who *m.* Anne, daughter of John Darell, esq. of Calehill, and died in 1631.
1. Elizabeth, *m.* to George Shakerley, gent. of Ottam.

William Darell, of Littlecote, was succeeded by his eldest son,

SIR GEORGE DARELL, knt. of Littlecote, who married, first, Margaret, daughter of John, Lord Stourton, and had an only daughter, Elizabeth, *m.* to Sir Henry Seymour, who died 7th HENRY VII. He wedded, secondly, Jane, daughter of Sir William Hawke, knt. by Margaret, his wife, daughter of Sir Richard Widvile, and left a son and successor,

SIR EDWARD DARELL, knt. of Littlecote, who *m.* first, Jane, daughter of Sir Richard Croft, knight banneret; secondly, Mary, daughter of Sir John Radcliffe, Lord Fitzwalter; and thirdly, Alice, relict of Sir Edward Stanhope. By his first wife, Sir Edward had two daughters, one of whom, Anne, wedded Sir John Hungerford, and one son,

JOHN DARELL, esq. who was slain at Arde, in Picardy, during the lifetime of his father. He *m.* Jane, daughter of John Fettyplace, esq. of Shifford, and was father of

EDWARD DARELL, esq. of Littlecote, living *temp.* EDWARD VI. who *m.* Elizabeth, daughter of Sir Thomas Essex, knt. and had, with a daughter, Eleanor, the wife of Egremund Ratcliffe, a son and successor,

WILLIAM DARELL, esq. of Littlecote, living in 1587, who alienated to Sir John Popham the estate of Littlecote. For the curious tradition of the supposed murder at Littlecote House, and of the consequent ruin of this branch of the family, refer to vol. ii. p. xii.

§ See vol. i. p. 368.

Robert de Vere, Earl of Oxford, he had a daughter, Emma, *m.* to Richard de Grusset, and a son,

Sir Ralph Dairell, of Lillingston Dairell, alive in 1282, who married and had one son, Henry, and a daughter, the wife of John de Beckhampton. Sir Ralph was *s.* by his son,

Henry Dairell, of Lillingston, in 1309, who married a lady named Emma, but of what family is not recorded. He was succeeded by

John Dairell, Lord of Lillingston Dairell, in 1338, who is presumed to have been son of his predecessor. This John was father of

Roger Dairell, of Lillingston Dairell, who represented Buckinghamshire in several parliaments during the reigns of Richard II. and Henry IV. and presented to Hanworth rectory in 1362. He *m.* Joan, daughter and heiress of Thomas Agmondesham, and had, with Thomas, Nicholas, and Roger, an elder son, his successor,

John Dairell, of Lillingston Dairell, alive in the 3rd of Henry V. He married Eleanor, daughter and co-heir (with her sisters, the wives of Chetwood and Ingoldesby,) of Thomas Langport, of Bifield and Foxcote, and had two sons, viz.

Paul, his heir.

Thomas, to whom his mother granted, 39th Henry VI. lands in Dodford and Foxcote.

John Dairell died in 1417, and was *s.* by his son,

Paul Dairell, of Lillingston Dairell, who wedded Margaret, sister of Sir John Prisot, chief justice of the Court of Common Pleas, and dying 29th March, 1491, left, with a daughter, Isabel, *m.* to Richard Pigott, esq. of Rippon, in Yorkshire, and of Beckampton, Bucks, a son and successor,

Thomas Dairell, of Lillingston Dairell, who served the office of sheriff for the counties of Bedford and Buckingham in the 11th and 20th of Henry VII. He *m.* Dorothy, daughter of Henry Danvers, of London, third son of John Danvers, of Colthorpe, and had issue,

I. Paul, his heir.
II. Henry.
III. Richard, who, it appears, applied to the Heralds' College for a renewal of the family arms.
IV. George, who occurs as rector of Lillingston in 1556.

Thomas Dairell was succeeded by his eldest son,

Paul Dairell, esq. of Lillingston Dairell, who married, first, *temp.* Henry VIII. Margaret, daughter of John Cheney, of Cheshambrys, in Buckinghamshire; secondly, Susannah, daughter of — Crewe, esq.; and thirdly, Dorothy,* daughter of John Young, esq. of Crome Dabitot, in Worcestershire. By the first he had,

I. Paul, his heir.
II. Francis, who married Anne, daughter of Thomas Woodford, and was father of

Edmund Dayrell, esq. of Lamport, who *m.* the daughter and heiress of — Isham, esq. of Northamptonshire, and was succeeded by his son,

Abel Dayrell, esq. of Lamport, who *m.* Elizabeth, dau. of J. Miller, esq. of Draughton, Northants, and had five sons and four daughters, viz. John, Edmund, Paul, Abel, William, Mary, Elizabeth, Dorothy, and Anne.

I. Dorothy, *m.* first, to Walter Young, of London, merchant; and secondly, to John Quarles, also a London merchant.
II. Anne, *m.* to Edward Leighton, esq. of Watlesborough, in Shropshire.

Paul Dayrell died 25th May, 1556, seised of the manor, 1 messuage, 5 cottages, and 1000 acres of land, in Lillingston Dayrell; 1 messuage, 80 acres of land, and a water-mill, in Twyford and Charendon; 1 messuage, 2 crofts, 20 acres, and a dove-house, in Lechampstead; 1 messuage and 85 acres of land, in Foxcote. His elder son and successor,

Paul Dayrell, esq. of Lillingston Dayrell, sheriff of Buckinghamshire in the 5th and 22nd of Elizabeth, married Frances, daughter of William Saunders, esq. of Welford, and had issue,

I. Thomas, his heir.
II. Francis, ancestor of the Dayrells of Shudy Camps, in Cambridgeshire (*See that family*).
III. William.
IV. Walter, some time reader of Gray's Inn, who died 21st June, 1623, and was buried in the church of St. Nicholas, at Abingdon, in Berkshire, where a marble fixed on the north wall bears the following inscription: "A memorial of Walter Dairell, esq. (who) deceased June 21, MDCXXIII, in the LXII year of his age, at Graies Inn, where he was some tyme an approved reader; and here interred, where he was the careful recorder of the toune (Abingdon); Lillingstone

* This lady had been married twice previously; first to William Haddon, father of Walter Haddon, a famous reformer, and secondly to William Saunders, esq. of Welford, Northamptonshire.

(the seat of the ancient family De Hairell, vulgarly Dairell,) was honoured with his birth, but this toun is trusted with the treasure of his bones. His worth claimes Fame for his trumpet, and Memory itself for his monument. In the famous university of Oxford he was hopeful,—in the Innes of Court compleat,—the barr found him not merely tongue-deep, or a verbal lawyer, for he was eminent, as well for soundness of judgement as flourish of speech. His law was not opposite to the Gospel; the advancement of the clergy being his joy, and the beauty of God's House his delight. He was a man of an even temper, abhorring the licentious libertine, and yet not encouraging the undisciplined disciplinarian. His wife was Alice, the daughter of Thomas Mayot, gent. of Abingdon, with whom he perfected the circle of 26 yeares marriage so happily, that no division was known betwixt them but his death. The issue he had by her was three sons and three daughters, the lively modells of himself, in whom he yet outlives mortality. Ad victorem ne quærent tumuli fastum nam memphida vincet, Marmor quod Dairell indicit hic situs est. Posterity doth owe the memorial to the Piety of Alice, his loving wife." Walter Dayrell's issue were,

1. Paul, living in 1695, who married Barbara, daughter of Sir John Sidney, fourth son of Sir Henry Sidney, and dying in 1698, left one son and two daughters, viz.
   - Pembroke, living unmarried in 1699.
   - Mary, *m.* to John Pierce, grandson to the Bishop of Bath and Wells.
   - Alice.
2. Thomas, who died without issue.
3. Walter, archdeacon of Winchester, *d. s. p.*

1. Frances, *m.* first, to Robert Hovendon, esq. of Stanton-Harcourt, in Oxfordshire; and secondly, to Thomas Gorges, of the family of the Lord Gorges of Ridgley.
2. Alice, *m.* to Charles Halloway, of Oxford, serjeant-at-law, who died in 1679, aged eighty-four.
3. Mary, *m.* to Thomas Kyte, esq. uncle to Sir William Kyte, of Ebberington, in Gloucestershire.

Paul Dayrell died in 1606, and was succeeded by his son,

Sir Thomas Dayrell, knt. of Lillingston Dayrell, who married Margery, daughter and co-heiress of Robert Horne, Bishop of Winchester, and had issue,

- I. Thomas, his heir.
- II. Peter, successor to his brother.
- III. Henry, *d.* in 1585.
- IV. John.
- V. Paul.

- I. Anne, *m.* to Timothy Egerton, esq. of Walgrange and Leek, in the county of Stafford, son and heir of Thomas Egerton, master of the mint to *Queen* Mary.
- II. Mary, *m.* 15th May, 1614, to Sir Henry St. George, knt. garter king of arms, and had issue,
  1. Sir Thomas St. George, garter king of arms, who *m.* Clara, daughter of the Rev. John Pymlow, rector of Cliffe, and had a daughter, Eleanor, the second wife of Thomas Coote, esq. of Coote Hill, one of the justices of the Court of King's Bench in Ireland.
  2. William St. George, a colonel of foot in the service of Charles I. slain at the storming of Leicester in 1645.
  3. Henry St. George, garter king of arms.
  4. Richard St. George, ulster king of arms.

  1. Elizabeth St. George, *m.* Col. Richard Bourke.
  2. Mary St. George, *m.* to Ferdinando Hastings, esq. of Braunston, in Leicestershire, fifth son of Sir Henry Hastings.
  3. Frances St. George, *m.* to George Tucker, esq. of Milton and Crayford, in the county of Kent, and had issue,
     - John Tucker, under secretary to *Queen* Anne and keeper of the state papers, died unmarried.
     - Frances Tucker, *m.* to Richard Dayrell, esq. of Lillingston.
- III. Rebecca, *m.* to George Owen, esq.

Sir Thomas, whose portrait is at Stowe, painted at the age of fifty-four, in 1607, and bearing the quartered arms of Dayrell and Hampden, died in 1617, and was *s.* by his son,

Thomas Dayrell, esq. of Lillingston Dayrell, high sheriff for Bucks 3rd Charles I. who died without issue 11th May, 1628, and was *s.* by his brother,

Peter Dayrell, esq. of Lillingston Dayrell, a devoted royalist, who attended *King* CHARLES I. to Oxford, and was included in the list of gentlemen intended to have been honoured with the knighthood of the royal oak. (See Appendix to vol. i.) He *m.* first, Catherine, daughter of Edward Cuthbert, of London; secondly, Elizabeth, daughter of Anthony Pratt, esq. of Weldon, in Northamptonshire; and thirdly, Elizabeth, daughter of John Wickstead, esq. of Cambridge. By Elizabeth Pratt, his second wife, who died 11th October, 1686, aged ninety-nine, Captain Dayrell had issue,

- I. THOMAS, died unm. in 1669.
- II. Peter, died 23rd February, 1670, leaving no issue by Elizabeth Pollard, his wife.
- III. ANTHONY, heir to his father.
- IV. PAUL, successor to his nephew.
- V. RICHARD, who inherited from his brother Paul.

- I. Frances, *m.* to Matthew Wilkes, esq. of Leighton Buzzard.
- II. Anne, died unmarried.
- III. Maria, supposed to have married — Wheeler, esq.
- IV. Eleanora, wife of — Reed, of Olney.

Capt. Dayrell's third son and eventual successor,

THE REV. ANTHONY DAYRELL, rector of Lillingston, married Miss Anne Perkins, and died 30th November, 1676, aged fifty-six, leaving a son and heir,

THOMAS DAYRELL, esq. of Lillingston Dayrell, at whose decease unmarried the estates and representation of the family reverted on his uncle,

PAUL DAYRELL, esq. of Lillingston Dayrell, who married first, Elizabeth, daughter of Anthony Pecket, citizen of London, and had a daughter, Frances, the wife of Henry Goldsmith, gent. He wedded secondly, Margery, daughter of — Palmer, esq. but by her, who married secondly, — Disney, esq. had no issue. Dying in 1690, he was succeeded by his brother,

RICHARD DAYRELL, esq. of Lillingston Dayrell, who *m.* Frances, daughter of George Tucker, esq. of Crayford, in Kent, and had issue,

- I. PETER, his heir.
- II. THOMAS, successor to his brother.
- III. John, died unm.
- IV. Paul, died unm. 1755.

- I. Frances, *b.* 1703-4, *m.* William Darell, esq. of St. Mary-le-Strand, London, (son of Thomas Darell, esq. of Chacroft, Hants, and grandson of Thomas Darell, esq. of Treworman, in Cornwall, sprung from a scion of the Pageham line), and had a son,

  HENRY ST. GEORGE DARELL, who inherited the estate of Coldrinick, under the will of his first cousin, Charles Trelawny, esq. and assumed the surname and arms of TRELAWNY. (See vol. i. p. 369).
- II. Elizabeth, } who died unmarried.
- III. Catharine, } who died unmarried.

Mr. Dayrell died in 1704, and was succeeded by his eldest son,

PETER DAYRELL, esq. of Lillingston Dayrell, who died cœlebs in 1725, and was succeeded by his brother,

THOMAS DAYRELL, esq. of Lillingston Dayrell, who *m.* Mary, daughter of the Rev. Stephen Townshend, rector of Preston Bissett, Bucks, and dying in 1729, left a son and successor,

THE REV. RICHARD DAYRELL, D. D. rector and lord of the manor of Lillingston Dayrell, *b.* in 1720, at Preston Bissett. This gentleman wedded Anne, daughter of Sir John Langham, bart. of Cottesbrooke, in Northamptonshire, and niece to Richard Viscount Cobham, and had by her, who *d.* in 1730,

- I. RICHARD, his heir.
- II. PAUL, successor to his brother.
- III. Henry, capt. R.N. *b.* in June, 1746, *m.* in 1776, Mary Martha Penelope, eldest daughter of John Miller, gent. of Buckingham, and had one son and three daughters, viz.
  - RICHARD, successor to his uncle, Paul, and PRESENT PROPRIETOR.
  - Anna-Maria, who *m.* the Rev. John Theodore Archibald Reed, rector of Leckhampsted, Bucks, and had issue.
  - Frances-Langham, who *m.* William Read, gent.
  - Phillis-Elizabeth-Georgiana, who died in infancy.
- IV. John-Langham, *b.* 2nd July, 1756, in holy orders, rector of Lillingston Dayrell, who *m.* first, Mary, daughter of William Wilson, gent. and secondly, Frances, only child and heiress of the Rev. Mr. Knight, rector of Lillingston Lovel, Oxon.

Dr. Dayrell died 14th April, 1767, aged forty-seven, and was succeeded by his son,

RICHARD DAYRELL, esq. of Lillingston Dayrell, a captain in the 10th dragoons, who entailed the family estates on his brothers and their heirs *male*, with remainder, in default of such issue, on the Dayrells of Lamport. Captain Dayrell, who was in the commission of the peace and lieutenancy for Bucks, and had served the office of sheriff, died in 1800, unmarried, and was succeeded by his brother,

Paul Dayrell, esq. of Lillingston Dayrell, *b.* in June, 1746, a captain in the 52nd regiment, who resided in America, where he married, and died without issue, in 1803, when the estates and representation of the family devolved on his nephew, the present Richard Dayrell, esq. of Lillingston Dayrell.

*Arms*—Quarterly; first and fourth, az. a lion rampant or, crowned arg. Second and third, arg. three bars sa. charged with six cinquefoils of the first.

*Crest*—A goat's head erased ppr.

*Motto*—Secure vivere mors est.

*Estates*—In Buckinghamshire. The manor and estate and presentation to the rectory of Lillingston Dayrell has been held by the family from the Conquest.

*Seat*—Lillingston Dayrell, four miles from Buckingham. The family now resides at Padbury Lodge.

⁂ The present Captain Dayrell possesses a purlieu-horn which shews the right his family enjoys of hunting the outlying deer of the king's forest of Whittlebury, and other adjacent confines. An anecdote is told of one of his ancestors, who while hunting the purlieus drove a deer to a boundary, and the animal endeavouring to leap fell backwards across the ditch, and the forest keepers, who were on the alert, attempting to sieze him, Dayrell drew his hanger and cut the deer in two, exclaiming "I have the haunches, you may have the rest."

## DAYRELL, OF SHUDY CAMPS.

DAYRELL, FRANCIS, esq. of Shudy Camps Park, in the county of Cambridge, *b.* 18th July, 1798, a captain in the army, inherited the estates, upon the demise of his father, in August, 1821.

Captain Dayrell is in the commission of the peace for Cambridgeshire.

### Lineage.

This is a branch of the eminent and ancient stock of Dayrell, of Lillingston Dayrell, in the county of Buckingham, (see p. 147.)

Francis Dayrell, esq. second son of Paul Dayrell, esq. of Lillingston, high sheriff for Buckinghamshire in 1579, married Barbara, daughter of Anthony Powell, esq. of the county of Gloucester, and had one son and three daughters, viz.

- Thomas (Sir), his heir.
- Bridget, } both died unm.
- Frances, }
- Susan, *m.* to Thomas Winne, clerk of the checque to the band of gentlemen pensioners *temp.* Charles I.

Francis Dayrell died 29th January, 1614, was interred in Bittlesden Chapel, under the following inscription:

Hic jacet Franciscus Dayrell, filius Pauli Dayrell de Lillingston
qui obiit 29 Januarii 1614.
Quid tua vita, Dolor, quid mors, tibi meta dolorum;
Mors vitam sequitur, vita beata necem:
Ergone defunctum vita lacrymabimur abait,
Præstat abesse viris possit ut esse Deo.

and succeeded by his son,

Sir Thomas Dayrell, knt. who seated himself at Shudy Camps, in the county of Cambridge. Of this gentleman it is recorded in his monumental inscription, that "he was eminent for his loyalty and services to their majesties Charles I. and II. in the civil wars, was universally esteemed for his great learning, and beloved of all who knew him, and particularly by the county of Cambridge, where in his old age he served in the quality of deputy lieutenant and justice of the peace to the time of his death. In his younger years, he was of Lincoln's Inn, where from the comelyness of his person, he was chosen, by the consent of the four inns of court, to command that grand masque (in which many gentlemen of eminent note and quality in the succeeding times had their several parts), that was represented before their majesties, the king and queen, in the banqueting house, at Whitehall, on Candlemas night, in the year 1633, and a second time by special direction from their majesties to Sir Ralph Freman, then lord mayor of London, at Merchant Taylor's Hall, when his majesty, as a mark of his royal favour, was pleased to confer on him the honour of knighthood."

Sir Thomas *m.* Sarah, daughter and co-heir of Sir Hugh Windham, bart. of Pilsden Court, in the county of Dorset, and had issue,

- Thomas, died unm.
- FRANCIS (Sir), his father's heir.
- MARMADUKE (Sir), successor to his brother.
- Wyndham, died unm.

- Mary, died unm.
- Sarah, *m.* to Francis Windham, esq. only son of Sir George Windham, and was ancestor of the WINDHAMS of Cromer, (see vol. ii. page 244).

He died in 1669, and was succeeded by his son,

SIR FRANCIS DAYRELL, knt. of Shudy Camps, who *m.* Elizabeth, daughter and co-heir of Edward Lewis, esq. of the Van, in the county of Glamorgan, but dying without issue, in 1675, the estates devolved on his brother,

SIR MARMADUKE DAYRELL, of Shudy Camps. This gentleman wedded first, Mary, only daughter of Sir Justinian Isham, bart. of Lamport, in Northamptonshire, but had no issue; and secondly, Mary, daughter and heiress of William Glasscock, esq. of Farnham, in Essex, by whom he left, at his decease in 1712, a son and successor,

FRANCIS DAYRELL, esq. of Shudy Camps, who *m.* Elizabeth, daughter of Peter Witchcomb, esq. of Braxted Lodge, Essex, and one of the co-heiresses of Sir Brownlow Sherrard, bart. of Lobthorp, in Lincolnshire, and had a son,

MARMADUKE DAYRELL, esq. of Shudy Camps, living in 1784, who espoused Henrietta, daughter of Warner Tempest, esq. of the Island of Antigua, and had, with three daughters, all now deceased, except the youngest, Maria, two sons,

- MARMADUKE, his heir.
- Francis-Valentine, deceased.

Mr. Dayrell was succeeded at his decease by his elder son,

MARMADUKE DAYRELL, esq. of Shudy Camps, who *m.* in 1797, Mildred-Rebecca, daughter of the late Sir Robert Lawley, bart. and sister to Lord Wenlock, by whom he had issue,

- FRANCIS, his heir.
- Thomas, in holy orders, rector of Marston, Yorkshire, *b.* in 1802, *m.* Maria, daughter of the late Rev. Mr. Hawksworth, and has one son and one daughter.
- Christopher-Jeaffreson, *b.* in 1808.
- Robert-William, *b.* in 1812.

- Jane-Elizabeth, *m.* to the Rev. Fitzgerald Wintour, of Barton, in the county of Nottingham, and has two sons and two daughters.

Mr. Dayrell died in August, 1821, and was *s.* by his eldest son, the present FRANCIS DAYRELL, esq. of Shudy Camps.

*Arms*---Az. a lion rampant or, crowned arg. armed and langued gu.

*Crest*---Out of a ducal coronet a goat's head erased ppr.

*Motto*---Virtus mille scuta.

*Estates*---In Cambridgeshire.

*Seat*---Shudy Camps Park, Cambridgeshire.

## COSBY, OF STRADBALLY.

COSBY, THOMAS-PHILLIPS, esq. of Stradbally Hall, in the Queen's County, *b.* 20th September, 1803; inherited, on the demise of his father, on the 22nd January, 1832.

This gentleman was sheriff of his native county in 1834, and one of the governors thereof prior to the alteration recently made by parliament in the local jurisdiction of Ireland. He continues in the commission of the peace, and is beside a deputy lieutenant.

## Lineage.

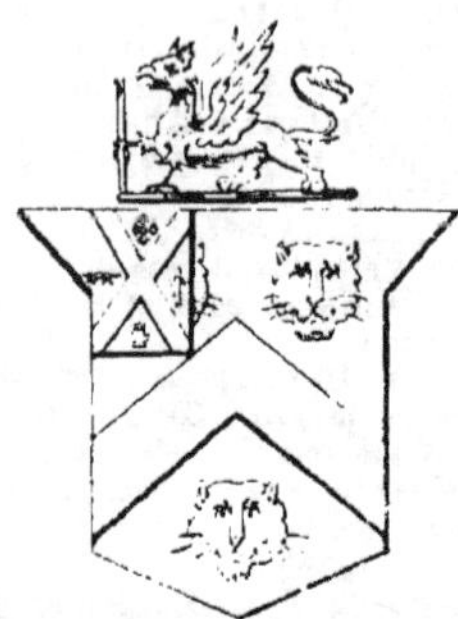

In the time of *Queen* MARY, this family, originally of the counties of Leicester and Lincoln, settled in Ireland, and it has since moved in the first grade of country gentlemen.

ROBERT COSSBYE,* of Hermaston, in Lincolnshire, living in 1516, *m.* Isabel, dau. and heiress of Ralph Pare, esq. of Great Leak, Notts. (by Isabel, his wife, daughter and heiress of John Blake, of Hermaston), and had a son and heir,

JOHN COSBIE, who wedded Mable, daughter of — Agard, of Foston, in Nottinghamshire, and had two sons, namely, Richard Cosby, of Great Leake (whose only daughter and heiress, Bridget, became the wife of William Towers, gent. of Thunnocke), and

FRANCIS COSBIE, the patriarch of the family in Ireland, a man famed for personal courage, as well as civil and military talents. When young he served in the wars of HENRY VIII. in the Low Countries, and was not undistinguished. His abandonment of his native soil arose from the downfall of the Protector SOMERSET, whose daughter Mary, widow of Sir Henry Payton, knt. he had married. Deeming the disgrace and death of that once potent nobleman a sentence of exclusion from place and preferment in England, against his immediate connections at least, Cosbie, Mary Seymour, his first wife, being then dead, emigrated to Ireland, taking with him his second wife, Elizabeth Paulmes, and the two surviving sons of the first. Here, in the land of his adoption, he soon found the opportunity of establishing a reputation, which he despaired of effecting in the land of his birth. He became an active defender of the Pale against the inroads of the Irish; and his vigilance, zeal and success attracting the observation of government, he was appointed by *Queen* MARY, under her majesty's sign manual, dated 14th February, 1558, GENERAL OF THE KERN, a post of great trust and importance in those times. In 1559 he represented the borough of Thomastown in parliament, when he was constituted by *Queen* ELIZABETH sheriff of the county of Kildare, being denominated in his patent, (dated 24th January, in the first year of her majesty's reign), "OF EVAN," now "MUNSTER EVAN," which place he held under an old grant from the crown, and was invested at the same time with the extraordinary and unenviable privilege of exercising martial law under his own authority solely, and of dealing out such punishments, even the most penal, as he should deem meet. Arbitrary power has rarely consorted with justice or mercy, and few have passed through the fiery ordeal of its unhallowed possession with reputation unscathed, for few have been found virtuous or firm enough to withstand the temptation of persecuting their fellows. Unhappily for the memory of Francis Cosbie, his name may not be written down amongst the merciful; but in his day, and in the wretched land over which he became a ruler, oppression and cruelty were of such frequent occurrence as to become familiar to men's minds, and to be stripped of more than a moiety of the horror that tyranny usually inspires. Cosbie, in furtherance of his commission, caused a gallows to be erected in the immediate vicinity of his own residence, on a spot still bearing the name of Gallows-hill, and there he is accused of having committed the most atrocious excesses. One practice is recorded, that of hanging his victim *alive* in chains, and placing within view a loaf of bread, in order to aggravate the excruciating tortures of hunger; his conduct, however, received the high commendation of the lord-deputy, Sidney, who, in the state papers, represents the district over which General Cosbie so ruthlessly presided to be in such profound tranquillity, under that officer's government, that it was almost useless to make the country shire ground. Cosbie eventually fell at the battle of Glandillough, at the head of the Kern which he valiantly led to the charge, although then seventy years of age. Of this action, and the general's death, Camden gives the following

* Son of JOHN COSSEBYE, grandson of WILLIAM COSSEBYE, and great-grandson of ROBERT COSSEBY, of COSSEBYE, in the county of Leicester.

narrative: "When Arthur, LORD GREY, landed in Ireland to assume the lieutenancy, before he had been invested with the sword and the other insignia of office, learning that some rebels, under the command of Fitz-Eustace, and Phelim M'Hugh, a chief of the numerous sept of the O'Byrnes, who had their retreat in Glandillough, twenty-five miles south of Dublin, were devastating the adjacent country, commanded the leaders of the band, assembled from all quarters to welcome his arrival, to take the field with himself against the insurgents, who, upon being apprised of the movement, retreated into the valley of Glandillough, a grassy spot, fit for feeding sheep, but so full of marshy ground, rocky precipices, and thick shrubby woods, by which the vale was entirely encompassed, that the paths and passes were hardly known to its own inhabitants. On the army's reaching this place, COSBY, general of the light Irish foot, denominated Kerns, aware of the many advantages it afforded the enemy, described to the other leaders the danger to be encountered in attacking him there, but at the same time exhorted them with the utmost intrepidity to brave all peril; and putting himself at once, although seventy years of age, at the head of his men, led them to the charge. The instant, however, the royal army had entered the valley, it was overwhelmed with a shower of arrows like hailstones from the rebels, who lay concealed on every side amongst the bushes and underwood, so that they could not even be discovered. The greater part of the invaders fell, and the remainder, struggling through the most perilous passes amongst the precipices, escaped with difficulty to the lord-lieutenant, who awaited the event on the brow of the hill, with the Earl of Kildare, and James Wingfield, engineer-general, who well knowing the risk encountered, kept one of his nephews, George Carew, jun. with him against his will. There were lost in this attack Peter Carew the younger, George Moore Audley, and COSBY himself, a man flourishing in military glory."

By his first wife, Mary, the Duke of Somerset's daughter, and Sir Henry Peyton's widow, Francis Cosbie had three sons, viz.

- ALEXANDER, inheritor of the estates.
- Henry, who died before his father settled in Ireland.
- Arnold, who served under Robert, Earl of Leicester, with great reputation in the Low Countries, *anno* 1686, with the celebrated Sir Philip Sidney, and was at the battle of Zupton, where Sir Philip received his mortal wound. Captain Cosbie remained after the Earl of Leicester's return to England, and obtained from *Queen* ELIZABETH,* in consideration of his good services, a pension of three shillings per day on the Irish establishment, until he should be otherwise provided for in the army of that kingdom. Notwithstanding this apparent protection of the court, he suffered, in two years afterwards, the utmost penalty of the criminal law, for killing the Lord Bourke, of Castle Connel, in a duel on Finchley Common, the queen peremptorily refusing to extend to him her royal mercy.

By his second wife, Elizabeth Paulmes, General Cosbie had an only child,

- Catherine, *m.* to Archibald Moor, esq. but *d.* issueless.

Although the active service in which General Cosbie was constantly engaged seldom permitted him to have a fixed place of abode, he seems to have considered and used the Abbey of Stradbally as the seat of his family: it was then, evidently from the ruins which remained until the year 1722, an extensive and handsome pile of building; but Colonel Cosbie having let the ground in that year to Colonel Nathaniel Mitchel, he pulled down the greater part of those venerable remains of antiquity for materials to build his mansion-house, leaving nothing standing but part of an old chapel, which is still visible. Francis Cosbie was *s.* by his eldest son,

ALEXANDER COSBIE, esq. of Stradbally Abbey, who seems to have been engaged during the whole of his time in warfare with the O'Moores. CAMDEN, in his life of ELIZABETH, recounts his being once taken by treachery during a conference with Rory, *Oge*, near Leighlin, and that he was rescued when bound to a tree, by Harpole, but not before he had received a wound from a knife, inflicted by Rory. This Francis possessed the same arbitrary power over the lives and limbs of his countrymen that was conferred upon his father, and seems to have abused it quite as barbarously. The tradition of the country records, that he was wont to hang multitudes of his enemies upon a sallow tree near the abbey; and he was accustomed to remark, that his sallow looked melancholy and denuded, whenever he observed it without the appendage of one or two of his foemen dangling from its branches: hence the soubriquet of SILLAGE, or the "*Sallow*," conferred upon the family. His excesses were, however, so unjustifiable, notwithstanding the latitude of his commission, that he found it necessary to solicit

* By her majesty's letter to the Lord-deputy Fitzwilliams, dated at Greenwich, 27th April, 1588.

and obtain a patent of indemnity from the queen, which her majesty styles "her pardon to Alexander Cosbie for the cruelties that happened during his wars with the O'Moores." This instrument is dated 6th December, 1593.

He married DORCAS, daughter of WILLIAM SYDNEY,* esq. of Orford, in Kent, and had fifteen children. This lady, who had been one of the maids of honour to *Queen* ELIZABETH, obtained, through her influential connexions at court, grants in Ireland (in Leix) so extensive, that at one period the family were the territorial lords of more than a moiety of the Queen's County. Amongst other estates thus acquired, the towns of Ballynakil, Ballyroan, and Mountrath, with a considerable portion of Maryborough, beside the lordships of Gallin, Rushball, and Trimahoe may be enumerated; but of that splendid inheritance all that now remains to the Cosbys is Trimahoe.† The grantee, herself, alienated the town of Ballynakil and the lordship of Gallin for one hundred pounds, which she received in silver shillings—of so little value did she regard the possession of lands which her husband and sons were so frequently obliged to defend with their swords. It is worthy of remark that in all grants, and even in private writings, Dorcas continued to use the name of Sydney, and never assumed that of her husband. With the exception of intervals passed at Penshurst in visiting their distinguished relatives there, Alexander Cosbie and his wife resided entirely at the Abbey of Stradbally, and enjoyed high reputation amongst the English settlers. The feud with the O'Moores, enduring however in all its lawless violence, came at length to issue, in 1596, and proved fatal to Cosbie and his eldest son. In that year ANTHONY O'MOORE, the chief of the insurgent clans, bearing his name, sent to demand a passage over Stradbally bridge, but the requisition being deemed by Cosby a challenge, was promptly and peremptorily denied, and preparations were commenced without loss of time to defend the pass, should the enemy attempt to force it. That attempt being made by O'MOORE, on the 19th of May, the Lord of Stradbally, at the head of his Kern, accompanied by his son and heir, FRANCIS, who had married, about a year previously, Hellen, daughter of Thomas Harpole, esq. of Shrule, and had born to him a son, William, but nine weeks before, met his foe in deadly combat on the bridge, while the conflict was witnessed from a window in the abbey by Dorcas Sydney and her daughter-in-law. For some time the valour of the Cosbies was irresistible, and the fortune of the day appeared to be theirs. Alexander, however, pursuing his advantage with extraordinary impetuosity, received a wound which proved at once mortal, and instantly turned the tide of battle. The Kern, with melancholy howling for the fate of their leader, began to give way, when Francis Cosby, fearing that he should be entirely abandoned, leaped over the bridge in the hope of making good his retreat to the abbey; but the instant that he had cleared the battlements, he was mortally wounded, and fell dead into the river. These scenes, one should have imagined, would have appalled the *now* widowed ladies who had witnessed them; yet it is recorded that Hellen Harpole, with the coolest presence of mind, cautioned her mother-in-law to retain in her recollection how the elder Cosbie fell before his son, her husband, who had, by thus inheriting the estates even for a few minutes, entitled her to her thirds, or dowry. It is not known how the ladies eventually escaped; but the infant, WILLIAM COSBY, was carried off and preserved by his nurse. O'Moore, pursuing his victory, took possession of the abbey, and, after sacking, committed it to the flames, when many of the patents, and other valuable documents of the family, were destroyed in the conflagration.

The issue of Alexander Cosby and Dorcas Sidney, were

I. FRANCIS, *b.* 1st January, 1571, and baptized with much ceremony in St. Patrick's Church, Dublin, the lord deputy standing god-father. He was captain of the Kern, and fell, as already stated, immediately AFTER his father, at the battle of Stradbally Bridge, on the 19th of May, 1590, leaving by his wife, Hellen Harpole, (who wedded secondly, Sir Thomas Loftus, of Killian, in the King's County), an infant child, WILLIAM, *b.* in 1596, who succeeded him.

II. William, *b.* in 1573, } both died young.

III. John, *b.* in 1574. } both died young.

IV. RICHARD, successor to his nephew.

V. Humphrey, *b.* 20th September, 1581, *d.* young.

VI. Charles, *b.* 12th September, 1585, *m.* a daughter of the Loftus family.

VII. John, *b.* 4th August, 1589, *d.* young.

VIII. ——, a son, *d.* in infancy.

IX. Arnold, *b.* 20th June, 1591, settled

* Grand-nephew of William Sydney, Lord of Cranleigh.

† The inheritance of this estate from DORCAS SYDNEY entitles the COSBYS to quarter the SYDNEY arms; and the frequent occurrence of SYDNEY as a Christian name in the family, may be traced to the connexion formed through that lady.

in the county of Cavan, and planted a branch of the family there.

I. Mable, *b.* 12th August, 1598, *m.* to George Harpole, esq. of Shrule, in the Queen's County, and *d.* in 1632, leaving issue.

II. Rose, *b.* in the queen's house, at Otford, in Kent, 20th November, 1582, said to have wedded a Lord Howth.

III. Elizabeth, *b.* 8th September, 1584.
IV. Edith, *b.* 11th August, 1588.
V. Mary, *b.* 16th July, 1590.
VI. Anne.
} These ladies all died young.

The melancholy catastrophy of Alexander Cosby and his son appears to have created a strong public feeling at the time, and the queen taking the state of the family into her gracious consideration, was pleased to grant, by letters patent, in which the circumstances of the battle of the bridge are recited, to DORCAS SYDNEY and HELLEN HARPOLE, the wardship of the infant, WILLIAM COSBY, besides conferring upon them pensions, in considerations of the many essential services rendered by their husbands to the crown. Alexander Cosby was succeeded, although for a few minutes only, by his eldest son,

FRANCIS COSBY, esq. of Stradbally Abbey, who being slain, as stated above, never enjoyed the inheritance, but left it to his infant child,

WILLIAM COSBY, esq. of Stradbally Abbey, who died young, when the estates reverted to his uncle,

RICHARD COSBY, esq. who thus became "of Stradbally Abbey," and in order to repair the loss occasioned by the destruction of the family records, at the time of the burning of the abbey, obtained under the commission of *King* JAMES I. for the remedy of defective titles, a new patent, of the same import as the old one, which is still extant. This Richard, who was captain of the Kerne, and esteemed of great martial courage and ability, eagerly solicitous on becoming chief of his line, to avenge the death of his father and brother, dared the O'MOORES to a pitched battle, and the challenge being accepted, the contending clans met once more (A.D. 1606), in the glyn of Augnabily, under the rock of Dunnamace, when a most bloody conflict ensued, terminating in the triumph of Cosby, and the total defeat of his foes, who were never afterwards able to make head against him. Capt. Cosby himself displayed great personal boldness, and received so many dangerous wounds in the action, that he could not be removed from the field to Stradbally, but was carried to Dysert House, then the seat of Sir Robert Pigot, where he remained a considerable time before he was so far recovered as to be enabled to return home. During his confinement, Elizabeth Pigot, one of the daughters of his hospitable host, attended him with so much kindness and care, that he subsequently solicited her hand, and she became his wife soon after his re-establishment at Stradbally. This union, although in every other point unexceptionable, proved in a high degree prejudicial to the fortunes of the family, for his mother, Dorcas Sydney,* who entertained a deep rooted antipathy to the Pigots, taking offence at the alliance, immediately went over to England, where she married a second husband, Sir Thomas Zouch, and left all her estates in Ireland, excepting Timahoe, to the Zouches, while she leased that for a long term to Sir Thomas Loftus, who had become, in 1615, the second husband of her daughter-in-law, Hellen, the widow of Francis Cosby. Richard Cosby had, by Elizabeth Pigot, who died in 1669, four sons and a daughter, viz.

I. ALEXANDER, his heir.

II. Francis, *b.* 5th July, 1612, member of parliament for Carisford, *m.* Anne, daughter of Sir Thomas Loftus, of Killian, by whom (who *d.* in 1673), he had issue,

1. ALEXANDER, successor of his uncle.

2. Thomas, of Vicarstown, *m.* Anne, daughter of Sir William Smith, and dying in 1713, left a son,

Francis, of Vicarstown, who wedded Anne, daughter of --- Pigot, esq. and by her, who *d.* 30th March, 1783, had, with two daughters, Frances and Anne, two sons, viz.

Thomas, of Vicarstown, an officer in the army, *b.* in 1742, who left at his decease, 10th December, 1788, a son,

THOMAS COSBY, of Vicarstown, who inherited the Stradbally estates on the decease of ADMIRAL COSBY.

---

* Dorcas survived Sir Thomas Zouch, who died in 1625. There is in the Sydney papers a letter from the earl of Pembroke to his uncle, Robert, earl of Leicester, promising to support her in a difference which she had with Sir Edward Zouch, her husband's son and heir, at the same time assuring him that Sir Edward would not wrong her.

Francis, who *d.* at the Cape of Good Hope, in 1776.

3. Sydney, of Ballymanus, who *m.* Sarah, daughter of — Harding, esq. and *d.* in 1716, leaving,

Francis, of Polesbridge, *m.* to Judith, daughter of — Pigot, esq. and dying in 1763, left a son, Sydney, who wedded Henrietta, daughter of Henry Hughes, esq. of the barony of Forte.

Arthur, of Rathcrea, *b.* in 1705, *m.* Anne, daughter of — Bowen, esq. and had a daughter, Anne, the wife of — Clarke, esq.

Anne, *m.* to Colclough Fitzgerald, esq. of Ballyrider.

III. Sydney, *b.* 2nd October, 1613, *m.* a daughter of — Seger, esq.

IV. William, captain in the army, wedded Jane, daughter of — Stafford, esq. and *d.* 13th September, 1663, leaving a son,

Richard, who *m.* Thomasine, daughter of Francis Brereton, esq. and had a son, Captain William Cosby. He (Richard) died in 1730.

I. Dorcas, *m.* to William Loftus, esq. of Ballymann, (see vol. i. p. 210).

Richard Cosby* was *s.* by his eldest son,

Alexander Cosby, esq. of Stradbally, *b.* 8th February, 1610, who espoused Anne, daughter of Sir Francis Slingsby, knt. of Kilmore, in the county of Cork, but dying without issue, was *s.* by his nephew,

Alexander Cosby, esq. of Stradbally Hall, who wedded Elizabeth, daughter of Henry L'Estrange, esq. of Moystown, in the King's County, by whom (who *d.* in 1692), he had eleven sons and five daughters, namely,

I. Dudley, his heir.

II. Francis, *d.* young.

III. Henry, captain of foot, *d.* in Spain, in 1715. He had *m.* a Miss Higgins.

IV. Thomas, major of foot, *m.* Jane, daughter of Henry Loftus, esq. and sister of Nicholas, Viscount Loftus, of Ely, by whom he had two daughters,

Anne, *m.* to Charles Davis, esq.

Jane.

V. Loftus, captain of foot, *d.* at Marseilles, 3rd January, 1726.

VI. Seymer, VII. Sydney, VIII. Harpole, — all died young.

IX. Alexander, lieut.-col. in the army, and lieutenant-governor of Nova Scotia, where he died 26th December, 1743, leaving by Anne his wife, daughter of Alexander Winnard, esq. of Annapolis, two sons and two daughters, viz.

William, a captain in the army, died of the small pox, at Windsor, in 1748.

Phillips, who eventually inherited Stradbally.

Elizabeth, *m.* to Capt. Foye.

Mary, *m.* to Capt. Charles Cotterel.

X. William, a brigadier general in the army, colonel of the Royal Irish, governor of New York and the Jerseys, equerry to the queen, &c., married Grace, sister of George Montague, Earl of Halifax, K. B. and left by that lady (who died 25th December, 1767) at his decease, 10th March, 1736, the following issue,

William, an officer in the army.

Henry, R.N. *d.* in 1753.

Elizabeth, *m.* to Lord Augustus Fitzroy, second son of Charles, Duke of Grafton.

Grace, *m.* to — Murray, esq. of New York.

XI. Arnold, *d.* young.

I. Anne, *m.* to William Wall, esq. of Coolnamuck, in the county of Waterford.

II. Elizabeth, *m.* to Lieutenant-general Richard Phillips, colonel of a regiment of horse, and governor of Nova Scotia, and died 24th January, 1739. The general died in 1752, aged 101.

III. Jane, *b.* in 1661.

IV. Dorcas, *m.* to — Forbes, esq.

V. Celia, *m.* to William Weldon, esq. of Rosscumro, in the King's County.

Alexander Cosby died in 1694, and was *s.* by his eldest son,

Dudley Cosby, esq. of Stradbally Hall, lieut.-colonel in the army, and M.P. for the Queen's County. This gentleman married Sarah, daughter of Periam Pole, esq.† of Ballyfin, in that shire, and had

Poole, his heir.

Sarah, *m.* to Robert Meredith, esq. of Shrowland, in Kildare.

Col. Cosby died 24th May, 1729, and was *s.* by his son,

* On gaining the victory of Dunnamace, Richard Cosby, to distinguish himself from the rest of his family, obtained a new grant of arms, viz. three leopards' heads, with a chevron table, retaining the canton, with some alterations.

† By Anne his wife, daughter of Henry Colley, esq. of Castle Carbery, in Kildare.

POLE COSBY, esq. of Stradbally Hall, who wedded Mary, daughter and co-heir of Henry Dodwell, esq. of Manor Dodwell, in the county of Roscommon, and left by her, who died 9th January, 1742, at his decease, 20th May, 1766, a daughter, Sarah, born in 1730, married first, to the Right Hon. Arthur Upton, of Castle Upton, and secondly, to Robert, Earl of Farnham, (his lordship's second wife, see BURKE's *Peerage and Baronetage*,) with a son, his successor,

DUDLEY-ALEXANDER-SYDNEY COSBY, esq. of Stradbally Hall, who was created, in 1768, a peer of Ireland, under the title of BARON SYDNEY, of Leix, in the Queen's County. His lordship held no military employment, but was minister plenipotentiary to the court of Denmark. He espoused, in December, 1773, the Lady Isabella St. Lawrence, dau. of Thomas, first Earl of Howth, and aunt of the present earl, but died in the ensuing month, 17th January, 1774, without issue, leaving the estate burdened with the enormous debt of £36,000. arising from his own imprudent expenditure. His peerage became of course extinct, while the inheritance reverted to (the only surviving son of LIEUT.-COLONEL ALEXANDER COSBY, governor of Nova Scotia, by his wife, Anne Winned, of Annapolis, and grandson of Alexander Cosby, of Stradbally Hall, and his wife, Elizabeth L'Estrange) his lordship's cousin,

PHILLIPS COSBY, esq. then a captain in the royal navy. This gentleman, to relieve himself from the encumbrance left by his predecessor, was obliged to alienate a moiety of the Stradbally estate, but he had previously to establish his right by the issue of a suit at law of four years' endurance against the claim of the Earl of Farnham, founded upon the alledged heirship of Sarah, Lord Sydney's sister, and his lordship's second countess; but Lord Sydney, having made a will in his (Cosby's) favour, and republished it when his lordship married Lady Isabella St. Lawrence, the jury, without leaving the box, decided that the property was Captain Cosby's. In his professional career Captain Cosby, before and after his accession to the family estates, was actively engaged, and established the reputation of a gallant and experienced officer. In 1760, he was appointed commander of his majesty's sloop, the Laurel. In 1761, he was made a post captain; the next year he commanded the Isis, of fifty guns and three hundred and fifty men, in the Mediterranean, under the flag of Vice-admiral Sir Charles Saunders. From 1765 to 1770 (years of peace) he was captain of the Montreal frigate, of thirty-two guns and two hundred and forty men, in the same sea. In 1769 he brought home the remains of his Royal Highness the Duke of York, brother of *King* GEORGE III. who had died abroad, and having docked his ship, sailed back to his station in the Mediterranean, where he soon after had the honour of entertaining on board his Imperial Majesty, JOSEPH II. EMPEROR OF GERMANY, and a numerous train of nobility, the emperor presenting him with a gold enamelled snuff box, of great value, in acknowledgment of his politeness and hospitality. He had afterwards the honour to receive, as a passenger, his *Serene Highness*, the hereditary PRINCE OF BRUNSWICK, (brother-in-law to his own illustrious sovereign, GEORGE III.) and landed the prince at the Gulph of Frejus, on his way to Persia, who rewarded him with a splendid diamond ring. In 1770, he was called home, and reached Spithead in July, when he was appointed, within a brief interval, collector of Basséterra, in the Island of St. Christopher's, to which post he immediately repaired, but did not remain long abroad. In January, 1774, he came, as already stated, into the possession of the family estate, and resided at Stradbally Hall for the next four years, but the war then breaking out, he resumed his professional duties, and being appointed to the command of the Centaur, of seventy-four guns and six hundred and fifty men, was second in the van division in the action of the 27th July, 1778, off Ushant, under Admiral Kepple, (afterwards Lord Kepple,) against the French fleet. From that period, until nearly the close of the American war, Captain Cosby was constantly employed in the Altantic, in command of the ROBUST, of seventy-four guns and six hundred men, and on the 16th March, 1781, led the English fleet, on both tacks, against the French off the Cape of Virginia. In this action the Robust sustained the fire of three ships, until she became a complete wreck, and was taken in tow by the America of sixty-four guns. The vice-admiral, (Arbuthnot) in his communication with the admiralty, bore honourable testimony to Cosby's gallant conduct, as well as in a letter*

* Copy of a letter from Vice-admiral Arbuthnot to Captain Cosby.

"Sir,

"You have, during the time that we left Gardners' Bay, conducted yourself like an experienced diligent officer, particularly on the 16th instant, in which you have approved yourself a gallant naval commander, that has done honour to yourself and country; and both yourself, officers, and ship's company have my warmest thanks for your spirited conduct.

"I have ordered the America to assist you with twenty men, and so soon as we get to anchor you shall have every assistance that is in the power of Sir, &c.

"M. ARBUTHNOT.

"Royal Oak, off Cape Charles,
16th March, 1781."

addressed to the captain himself, immediately after the engagement. In 1782, the Robust, from her dismantled condition, on returning to England was put out of commission, and Captain Cosby repaired to Stradbally Hall. In the year 1785 he was again called out, and then constituted commodore, and commander-in-chief of all his majesty's ships and vessels in the Mediterranean, when he sailed from Spithead in the TRUSTY of fifty guns, three hundred and thirty-seven men, having previously hoisted the broad pendant. He remained on his station until 1789. In 1790, on the expectation of a war with Spain, Captain Cosby was appointed commander-in-chief of his majesty's ships employed at Cork, in the service of raising men for the fleet, with power to hoist a broad pendant on board any of the ships wherever he might happen to be, and to have a captain under him: in the September of the same year, he attained the rank of rear-admiral of the White, but peace being preserved by the submission of Spain, he returned to Stradbally, at the close of the year. In 1792, being again in active service, he was appointed commander-in-chief at the port of Plymouth, and promoted soon after to vice-admiral of the Blue; being subsequently engaged, at the commencement of the war, with republican France, he attained, in succession, the gradations of vice-admiral of the Red, of admiral of the Blue, and of admiral of the White. He finally returned to Stradbally Hall to reside, on the 27th April, 1799. Admiral Cosby *m.* in August, 1792, Eliza, daughter of W. Gunthorpe, esq. and sister of W. Gunthorpe, esq. of Southampton, but having no issue, was *s.* at his decease by (the great-great grandson of Francis Cosby, M.P. for Carisford, and Anne his wife, daughter of Sir Thomas Loftus, of Killian, which Francis was second son of Richard Cosby, of Stradbally, and Elizabeth Pigot) his kinsman,

THOMAS COSBY, esq. of Vicarstown, who *m.* Miss Johnstone, an heiress, of the Annandale family, and had three sons, viz.

- Dudley-Sydney, drowned, 3rd July, 1787.
- Francis, drowned, at Cork, 25th August, 1791.
- THOMAS, successor to the estates.

Mr. Cosby *d.* 10th December, 1788, and was *s.* by his only surviving child,

THOMAS COSBY, esq. of Stradbally Hall, governor of the Queen's County, who *m.* in 1802, Charlotte-Elizabeth, daughter of the Right Hon. Thomas Kelly, lord chief-justice of the court of Common Pleas, in Ireland, and had issue,

- I. THOMAS-PHILLIPS, his heir.
- II. William, in holy orders, *m.* Miss Jephson, niece of Lord Dunnally, and has one son, Thomas.
- III. Sydney.
- IV. Wellesley-Pole.

- I. Frances-Elizabeth.
- II. Harriett, *m.* to Frederick Trench, esq. of Sopwell Hall, nephew and heir presumptive of Lord Ashtown.

Mr. Cosby, who served the office of sheriff for the Queen's County, died 22nd January, 1832, and was *s.* by his eldest son, the present THOMAS-PHILLIPS COSBY, esq. of Stradbally Hall.

*Arms*—Arg. a chevron between three leopards' faces sa. on a canton of the first, a saltier vert between a cross crosslet in chief, and a dexter hand couped at the wrist in base gu., in the dexter side a lizard, and in the sinister a lucy haurient vert.

*Crest*—A griffin, his wings erect, gu. supporting a standard, the head broken off, or.

*Motto*—Audaces fortuna juvat.

*Estates*—In the Queen's County.

*Seat*—Stradbally Hall.

## LAMPLUGH, OF LAMPLUGH.

(Now Lamplugh-Raper, of Lamplugh.)

RAPER-LAMPLUGH, JOHN-LAMPLUGH, esq. of Lamplugh, in the county of Cumberland, and of Lotherton, in Yorkshire, *b.* at Abberford 19th July, 1790; *m.* 25th October, 1813, Jane, second daughter of Benjamin Brooksbank, esq. of Healaugh Hall, in the West Riding of York.

This gentleman, whose patronymic is RAPER, assumed by sign manual, 10th March, 1825, the additional surname and arms of LAMPLUGH.

## Lineage.

"Lamplugh, in the fells," says Denton, "is that manor-house and seignory in the barony of Egremont, which gave name to the ancient family of Lamplughs, a race of valourous gentlemen successively, for their worthyness knyghted in the field, all or most of them."

ADAM DE LAMPLUGH (son of Sir Robert de Lamplugh, lord of Lamplugh, in Cumberland, and of Hailkord, in Lancashire, *temp.* HENRY II. and RICHARD I.), had a confirmation, with many privileges, from Richard de Lucy, lord of Coupland. His son,

SIR ROBERT DE LAMPLUGH, of Lamplugh, knighted 43rd HENRY III. wedded a lady, named Meliora, who paid a relief to HENRY III. on her marriage, and was succeeded by his son,

RALPH DE LAMPLUGH, living 7th EDWARD III., who married Margaret* —, and had a son,

SIR ROBERT DE LAMPLUGH, knt. of Lamplugh, who, by Constance his wife, had three sons, William, who *d. s. p.*; John, heir to his father; Ralph, with a daughter, Christian. The eldest surviving son,

SIR JOHN DE LAMPLUGH, knt. 9th EDWARD I. was great grandfather of

SIR THOMAS DE LAMPLUGH, knt. who represented the shire of Cumberland 8th RICHARD II. Sir Thomas was succeeded by his son,

JOHN DE LAMPLUGH, father of

HUGH DE LAMPLUGH, living 13th HENRY IV. who espoused Margaret, daughter of Thomas Pickering, and had a son and successor,

SIR JOHN DE LAMPLUGH, high sheriff of Cumberland in the 8th of HENRY V. and 11th HENRY VI. who *m.* Margaret, daughter of John Eglesfield, and had a son,

SIR THOMAS DE LAMPLUGH, knt. 7th EDWARD IV. who *m.* Eleanor, daughter and co-heir of Sir Henry Fenwick, of Fenwick, in the county of Northumberland, and was father of

JOHN DE LAMPLUGH, living 19th EDWARD IV. whose son,

JOHN DE LAMPLUGH, living 1st HENRY VII. *m.* Isabell, daughter of Sir John de Pennington, knt. and had issue,

- JOHN, his heir.
- Thomas, of Skellsmore, in Cumberland, whose son,
  - Adam Lamplugh, marrying Agnes, daughter of Robert Ben, of Cumberland, had, with two daughters, Jane and Mary, a son,
    - Thomas Lamplugh, of Little Riston, in Yorkshire, *anno* 1584, who *m.* Jane, daughter of Robert Fairfax, esq. of Pockthorpe, and had issue,
      1. CHRISTOPHER, of Riston, in 1612, who married Anne, daughter and co-heir of Thomas Roper, of Octon.
      2. THOMAS, who purchased the manor of Ribton, in Cumberland, and died in 1670, aged eighty-three, leaving, by Agnes his wife, (with another son, Richard,* who *m.* Frances, dau. of Sir Christopher Lowther, bart. of Whitehaven).
         - THOMAS LAMPLUGH, D. D. archbishop of York,† who *m.*

* This lady was impleaded by Cospatrick, son of Orme, and Lord of Workington, for the wardship of Robert, her son, and lost the tuition of him.

* This Richard de Lamplugh left a daughter, Jane, *m.* first, to John Senhouse, esq. of Netherhall; and secondly, to Charles Orfeur, esq. of Plumland, in Cumberland.

† DR. LAMPLUGH, sometime fellow of Queen's College, Oxford, was successively rector of Binfield, in Berkshire, of Charlton-on-Ottmore, in Oxfordshire, principal of St. Alban's Hall, Oxford, archdeacon of London, prebendary of Worcester, vicar of St. Martin's in the Fields, dean of Rochester, bishop of Exeter, and ARCHBISHOP OF YORK, in which see he was enthronized by proxy, 19th December, 1688. He died at Bishopthorpe, 5th May, 1691, aged seventy-six, and was buried in York Minster, where his monument bears the following inscription: "Hic in spe resurgendi depositum jacet quod mortale fuit Reverendissimi in Christo Patris Thomæ Lamplugh, archiepiscopi Eboracensis, S. T. P, ex antiquâ et generosâ

Catherine, daughter of Edward Davenant, D. D. nephew of John Davenant, Bishop of Salisbury, and had a son and successor,

THOMAS LAMPLUGH, D. D. archdeacon of Richmond, *b.* in 1661, who married a lady named Margaret, and had, with other issue, a son and heir,

THOMAS LAMPLUGH, rector of Bolton Percy, and canon residentiary of York, of whom hereafter, as INHERITOR of LAMPLUGH, upon the demise and under the devise of THOMAS LAMPLUGH, esq.

John de Lamplugh, was *s.* by his son,

SIR JOHN DE LAMPLUGH, knt. of Lamplugh, sheriff of Cumberland 29th HENRY VIII. who *m.* first, Isabella, daughter of Sir Christopher Curwen, of Workington, (see vol. i. p. 578) and had by her a son,

JOHN, his heir.

He *m.* secondly, Catherine, daughter and co-heir of Guy Foster, of Howsam, and had three daughters, viz.

Mary, *m.* to Thomas Skelton.
Mable.
Frances, *m.* to David Fleming, third son of Hugh Fleming.

Sir John was *s.* by his son,

JOHN LAMPLUGH, of Lamplugh, who *m.* two wives, by the first, Jane Blennerhasset, he had one son, Edward, who died issueless, and by the second, Isabel, daughter of Christopher Stapleton, of Wighill, another son, his successor,

RICHARD LAMPLUGH, esq. of Lamplugh, father, by Alice Warde his wife, of

JOHN LAMPLUGH, esq. of Lamplugh, who *m.* Elizabeth, dau. of Sir Edward Musgrave, knt. and dying in 1636, was *s.* by his son,

JOHN LAMPLUGH, esq. of Lamplugh, *b.* in 1619. This gentleman, devoted to the royal cause during the civil war, was colonel of a regiment of foot under Prince Rupert, and fought at Marston Moor, in 1644, where, commanding the Yellow Colours, he received several wounds, and was taken prisoner. He *m.* first, Jane, daughter of Roger Kirby, esq. of the county of Lancaster; secondly, Frances, Lady Lowther, daughter of Christopher Lancaster, esq. of Stockbridge, in Cumberland, and thirdly, Frances, daughter of Thomas Lamplugh, esq. of Ribton. By the last only he had issue, viz.

I. THOMAS, his heir.
II. Edward, *d.* unm.
III. John, *d. s. p.*
I. Elizabeth, second wife of Henry Brougham, esq. of Scales, in Cumberland. Upon the demise of Elizabeth, daughter of Thomas Lamplugh, in 1773, the male line failing, this Elizabeth became heir general of the senior branch of the house of Lamplugh, of Lamplugh, which is now represented by her eldest male descendant, HENRY, LORD BROUGHAM AND VAUX. (See BURKE'S *Peerage*).
II. Phœbe, appears to have died unm.

Col. Lamplugh was succeeded at his decease by his eldest son,

THOMAS LAMPLUGH, esq. of Lamplugh, *b.* in 1657, who served the office of sheriff for Cumberland in the 13th WILLIAM III. His son and successor,

THOMAS LAMPLUGH, esq. of Lamplugh, by Frances his wife, had an only dau. and heiress,

ELIZABETH, *m.* to George Irton, esq. of Irton, but died *s. p.* devising by will, dated 6th November, 1773, her estate at Dovenby, to the Rev. Thomas Lamplugh, of Copgrove, in the county of York, for life, with remainder, in default of male issue, to Peter Brougham, descended from Elizabeth Lamplugh, of Lamplugh. He succeeded in 1783, and died in 1791 *s. p.* when Dovenby passed to his niece and heiress, Mary Dykes (see vol. i. p. 265).

Mr. Lamplugh *d.* in 1737, and bequeathed, by will dated 1734, "the capital messuage of Lamplugh Hall, and the demesne lands of Lamplugh, &c. to his, the testator's, cousin,"

THE REV. THOMAS LAMPLUGH, rector of Bolton Percy, and canon residentiary of York Minster, grandson of the archbishop of York. This gentleman *m.* 17th April, 1721, Honor, daughter of William Chaloner, esq. of Guisborough, in the county of York, and had issue,

I. THOMAS, his heir.
I. Honor, *d.* unm. 2nd January, 1795.
II. Mary, died unm. before 1783.
III. Katherine, co-heir to her brother Thomas, *m.* the Rev. Godfrey Wolley, rector of Thurnscoe, and of Warmsworth, and, dying in 1804, left issue,

Lamplughorum de Lamplugh, in agro Cumbriensi Familiâ oriundi." There is no positive proof that his Grace was exactly descended as stated in the text, though the presumptive evidence of the fact is strong.

Edward Wolley, of Fulford Grange, and Nether Hall, in the county of York, who assumed the surname and arms of COPLEY in 1810. He *d.* in 1813.

Thomas Wolley, vice-admiral of the White, married, and has issue.

Godfrey Wolley, in holy orders, rector of Hutton Bushel, died in 1822.

Isaac Wolley, captain R.N. *m.* and had issue.

Honor Wolley, *m.* to the Rev. Anthony Fountayne Eyre.

Cordelia Wolley, *m.* to George Bower, esq. of Sheffield.

Katherine Wolley, *m.* to John Raper, esq. of Lotherton, and was mother of the present JOHN LAMPLUGH LAMPLUGH RAPER, esq. of Lamplugh.

Mary Wolley.

IV. ANNE, co-heir to her brother, who *m.* 8th October, 1750, John Raper, esq. of Abberford, in the county of York, and dying in July, 1783, left a son,

JOHN RAPER, of Abberford and Lotherton, who *s.* his uncle, Thomas Lamplugh, at LAMPLUGH.

V. Jane, *m.* to Samuel Pawson, of York, merchant.

VI. Sarah, *d.* young.

The Rev. Thomas Lamplugh was *s.* by his only son,

THE REV. THOMAS LAMPLUGH, of Lamplugh, rector of Copgrove and Goldesborough, and prebendary of Wistow, who *m.* Mary, daughter of James Collins, gent. of Knaresborough and Foleyfote, but, dying without issue in 1783, was *s.* by (the son of his sister Anne) his nephew,

JOHN RAPER, esq. of Abberford and Lotherton, who then became also "of Lamplugh." He *m.* at Fulford, 16th October, 1789, Katherine, third daughter of the Rev. Godfrey Wolley, by Katherine, his wife, daughter of the Rev. Thomas Lamplugh, of Lamplugh, and had two sons and one daughter, viz.

JOHN-LAMPLUGH RAPER, his heir.

Henry Raper, of Lincoln's Inn, barrister-at-law, *b.* 12th February, 1795, *m.* 16th December, 1824, Georgiana third daughter of John Moore, esq. captain in the 5th regiment of Dragoon Guards.

Ann Raper, *m.* to James Brooksbank, merchant, of London, second son of Benjamin Brooksbank, esq. of Healaugh Hall, in the West Riding of York.

Mr. Raper *d.* the 3rd of July, 1824, and was *s.* by his elder son, the present JOHN LAMPLUGH LAMPLUGH-RAPER, esq. of Lamplugh.

*Arms*—Or, a cross fleury sa.

*Crest*—A goat's head arg. attired and bearded or.

*Estates*—In Yorkshire and Cumberland.

*Seats*—Lamplugh Hall, Cumberland; Lotherton, in Yorkshire.

## BLOUNT, OF MAPLE-DURHAM.

BLOUNT, MICHAEL-HENRY-MARY, esq. of Maple-Durham, in the county of Oxford, *b.* 8th August, 1789; *m.* 15th May, 1817, the Honorable Elizabeth Petre, fourth daughter of Robert-Edward, tenth Lord Petre, and has surviving issue,

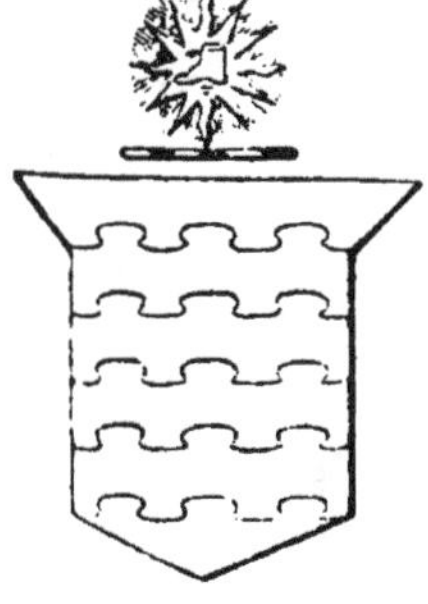

MICHAEL CHARLES, *b.* 19th April, 1819.
Edmund-Walter.
Charles-John.
Arthur-William.
John.

Mary-Catharine.
Charlotte-Elizabeth.
Georgiana-Frances.
Henrietta-Matilda.

Mr. Blount is a magistrate and deputy lieutenant for Oxfordshire, and served the office of sheriff in 1832. He inherited the estates at the decease of his father, 29th October, 1821.

## Lineage.

The origin and history of this most ancient and distinguished family has been elaborately investigated by SIR ALEXANDER CROKE, knt. LL.D. of Studley Priory, in Oxfordshire, (see vol. i. p. 354,) who traces it from the COUNTS OF GUISNES, in Picardy, a race of nobles, descended themselves from the Scandinavian rulers of Denmark. RODOLPH, third count of Guisnes, had three sons, by his wife, Rosetta, daughter of the COUNT DE ST. POL, all of whom accompanied the NORMAN in his expedition against England, in 1066, and contributing to the triumph of their chief, shared amply in the spoils of conquest. One of the brothers returned to his native country; the other two adopted that which they had so gallantly helped to win, and abided there; of these, SIR WILLIAM LE BLOUNT, the younger, was a general of foot, at Hastings, and was rewarded by grants of seven lordships in Lincolnshire; his son was seated at Saxlingham, in Norfolk, and the great-granddaughter of that gentleman, sole heiress of her line, MARIA LE BLOUNT, marrying in the next century, SIR STEPHEN LE BLOUNT, the descendant and representative of her great-great-great uncle, SIR ROBERT LE BLOUNT, united the families of the two brothers.

The elder brother,

SIR ROBERT LE BLOUNT, had the command of the CONQUEROR'S ships of war, and is styled "DUX NAVIUM MILITARIUM." His portion of the *Spolia opima* embraced thirteen manors in Suffolk, in which county he was the first feudal BARON OF IXWORTH, (the place of his residence), and lord of Orford Castle. He *m.* Gundreda, youngest daughter of Henry, Earl Ferrers, and had a son and heir,

GILBERT LE BLOUNT, second baron of Ixworth, who came into England with his father. This feudal lord founded a priory of black canons, at Ixworth, and marrying Alicia de Colekirke, was *s.* by his son,

WILLIAM LE BLOUNT, third lord of Ixworth, *temp.* HENRY II. who rebuilt the priory of Ixworth, which had been destroyed during the contest between the *Empress* MAUD and *King* STEPHEN. By his wife, Sarah, daughter of Hubert de Monchensi, he was father of

GILBERT OR HUBERT LE BLOUNT, fourth baron, living 20th HENRY II. 1173, who wedded Agnes de L'Isle (de Insulâ), who was alive 10th RICHARD I. (1198), he had two sons, namely,

WILLIAM, *b.* in 1153, who inherited as fifth LORD OF IXWORTH, and marrying Cecilia de Vere, had issue,

WILLIAM, his successor.

AGNES, *m.* to SIR WILLIAM DE CRIKETOT.
* ROISIA, *m.* to ROBERT DE VALOINGS, lord of Orford, in Suffolk.
} co-heirs to their brother.

This baron *d.* at the age of thirty-two, in 1185, and was *s.* by his son,

WILLIAM LE BLOUNT, sixth lord of Ixworth, who was standard bearer to Simon de Montford, earl of Leicester, and fell at LEWES, on the 14th May, 1264. He was afterwards attainted in parliament, when the barony of Ixworth became forfeited. He had married Alicia de Capella, (who lived to the 10th EDWARD I. *anno* 1281), but having no issue, his sisters became his heirs.

STEPHEN (Sir).

The chief branch of the family, the barons of Ixworth having, as above stated, expired with the sixth feudal lord, at the battle of Lewes, the representation devolved upon the line of the younger son of Gilbert, by Agnes de L'Isle.

SIR STEPHEN LE BLOUNT, who was living in the 10th RICHARD I. *anno* 1198. He espoused his kinswoman, MARIA LE BLOUNT, sole daughter and heiress of SIR WILLIAM LE BLOUNT, the descendant and representative of SIR WILLIAM LE BLOUNT, of Saxlingham, in Suffolk, one of the brothers who came over with the CONQUEROR, and thus the lines of the two brothers merging formed the parent stock, whence have since sprang the different families of the name. Of this marriage there were two sons, Sir John Blount (the younger, who *m.* Constance, one of the sisters and co-heirs of Sir Richard de Wrotham, justice of the common pleas), and the son and heir,

SIR ROBERT LE BLOUNT, who was a witness to the charter of Hilton Abbey, in Staffordshire, in the 8th HENRY III. *anno* 1223. He wedded Isabel, daughter and co-heir of the feudal lord of Odinsels, and acquired the manor of Belton, in the county of Rutland, as a part of the lady's portion. He died in the 17th EDWARD I. *anno* 1288, leaving two sons, viz.

I. RALPH (Sir), lord of Belton, who recovered lands, 14th EDWARD I. *anno* 1285, in Saxlingham, which had been his grandfather's. He *m.* Cecilia, or Alicia, daughter and coheir of Sir John Lovet, of Hampton

* g.g. of Willoughby

Lovet, in the county of Worcester, and was grandfather of SIR JOHN BLOUNT, summoned to parliament as BARON BLOUNT, of Belton, in the 1st EDWARD III. *anno* 1327; and of NICHOLAS DE BLOUNT, who adopted the surname of CROKE, and was ancestor of the CROKES, of Studley Priory, (see vol. i. p. 354.)

II. WILLIAM (Sir).

Upon the extinction of the noble house of BLOUNT OF BELTON, the representation devolved on the descendant of Nicholas le Blount, and now vests *de jure* in SIR ALEXANDER CROKE; but the name surviving in the descendants of the younger son,

SIR WILLIAM LE BLOUNT, they may certainly claim, without urging any unwarrantable pretension, to be *de facto* chiefs. Sir William espoused the Lady Isabel de Beauchamp, daughter of William, first Earl of Warwick, and widow of Henry Lovet, of Elmley Lovet, in the county of Worcester. He *d.* in the 9th or 10th of EDWARD II. (1315 or 1316), having had issue,

PETER, one of the chamberlains in 1313 to *King* EDWARD II. died issueless.

WALTER.

The second son,

SIR WALTER LE BLOUNT, of the Rock, in the county of Worcester, married JOHANNA, third sister and co-heir of SIR WILLIAM DE SODINGTON (who died 30th EDWARD I. *anno* 1301), and thus became proprietor of the manor of Sodington, in the county of Worcester. He *d.* in 1322, and was *s.* by his son,

SIR WILLIAM LE BLOUNT, who had a command in Scotland in 1335. He *m.* Margaret, third daughter and co-heir of Theobald de Verdon, Lord of Alton Castle, in the county of Stafford, lord justice of Ireland.. The lady was born in 1310; there were no issue of the marriage, and Sir William dying 11th EDWARD III. *anno* 1337, seised of the Castle of Weobly, in Herefordshire; Batterby, and lands in Fenton, Romesore, and Biddulph, in the county of Stafford; Sodington and Timberlake, in Worcestershire, was *s.* by his brother,

SIR JOHN LE BLOUNT, then thirty-nine years of age, who was in the service of the Earl of Lancaster, and had obtained from that nobleman a grant for life of the manor of Passingham, in the county of Northampton; he had also lands from the earl in Holland and Duffield, in the county of Derby, and at Tiberton, in Gloucestershire. He *m.* two wives; first, ISOLDA, daughter and heir of SIR THOMAS DE MOUNTJOY, by whom he acquired a large accession of estates, and had issue,

JOHN (Sir), who wedded twice; first, Juliana, daughter of — Foulhurst; and secondly, Isabella, daughter and heir of Sir Bryan Cornwall, of Kinlet. By the second he was ancestor of the Blounts of Kinlet, now represented by William Lacon Childe, esq. By the first he had a son,

JOHN BLOUNT, of Sodington, aged fourteen at the decease of his grandfather in 1358. From this gentleman we pass to his lineal descendant,

SIR WALTER BLOUNT, knt. of Sodington, who was created a BARONET, 5th October, 1642 (see BURKE'S *Peerage and Baronetage*). The fifth in succession from this gentleman,

SIR WILLIAM BLOUNT, sixth baronet, *m.* in 1766, Mary, elder daughter and co-heir of James, Lord Aston, of Forfar, and one of the representatives of the elder branch of the family of SIR RALPH SADLIER (see vol. ii. p. 562). The present SIR EDWARD BLOUNT, bart. of Sodington, only son of the late Sir Walter Blount, and nephew of Edward Blount, esq. of Bryanstone-square, member in the late parliament for Horsham, is grandson of this marriage.

Walter, who *d. s. p.*

His second wife was Eleanor, second daughter of John Beauchamp, of Hache, in the county of Somerset, and widow of John Meriet, of Meriet, in the same shire; by this lady he left at his decease in the 32nd of EDWARD III. *anno* 1358,* a son, the heroic

SIR WALTER BLOUNT, so celebrated for his martial prowess in the warlike times of EDWARD III. RICHARD II. and HENRY IV. and immortalized by the muse of SHAKSPEARE for his devotion, even unto death, to *King* HENRY. Sir Walter fell at the battle of Shrewsbury on the 22nd June, 1403, wherein, being standard-bearer, he was arrayed in the same armour as his royal master, and was slain, according to the poet, in single combat by the Earl of Douglas, who had supposed he was contending with the king himself.

*Blunt.* What is thy name, that in the battle thus
Thou crossest me? what honour dost thou seek
Upon my head?

*Doug.* Know then, my name is Douglas;
And I do haunt thee in battle thus,
Because some tell me thou art a king.

*Blunt.* They tell thee true.

---

* About this time the family began to omit the prefix LE to their name, calling themselves BLOUNT only.

*Doug*. The Lord Stafford dear to-day hath bought
Thy likeness; for, instead of thee, King Harry,
The sword hath ended him: so shall it thee,
Unless thou yield thee as my prisoner.
*Blunt*. I was not born a yielder, thou proud Scot;
And thou shalt find a king that will revenge
Lord Stafford's death.
[*they fight, and* BLUNT *is slain*.
*Enter* HOTSPUR.
*Hot*. O Douglas, hadst thou fought at Holmedon thus,
I never had triumph'd upon Scot.
*Doug*. All's done, all's won, here breathless lies the king.
*Hot*. Where?
*Doug*. Here.
*Hot*. This, Douglas; no, I know full well:
A GALLANT KNIGHT he was, his name was BLUNT,
Semblably furnished like the king himself.

In this battle the impetuous HOTSPUR, the renowned PERCY, likewise met his doom. Having thus rehearsed the dramatic version of the valiant soldier's death, we retrace our course, to detail some passages in his eventful life. In 1367, we find Sir Walter accompanying the BLACK PRINCE, and his brother the DUKE OF LANCASTER (John of Gaunt), upon the expedition into Spain, to aid PETER *the Cruel*, KING OF CASTILLE, and assisting on the 3rd of April in that year at the battle of Najara, which restored Peter to his throne. Thenceforward for a series of years, indeed until the prince's decease, he appears to have been immediately and confidentially attached to the Duke, having chosen his wife, whom he married about the year 1372, from amongst the ladies in the suite of CONSTANTIA OF CASTILLE (eldest daughter of PETER, and his successor on the throne, who became the royal consort of JOHN OF GAUNT), when the princess visited England in 1369. In 1398, the duke granted one hundred marks a-year to Sir Walter for the good services which had been rendered to him by the knight and his wife, the Lady Sancia. The Lady Sancia's maiden designation was DONNA SANCHA DE AYALA. She was the daughter of DON DIEGO GOMEZ DE TOLEDO, alcalde mayor, and chief justice of Toledo, and notario mayor, or principal secretary of the kingdom of Castille, by his wife, Inez Alfon de Ayala, one of the most ancient and illustrious houses in Spain. JOHN OF GAUNT at his decease appointed Sir Walter one of his executors, and bequeathed him a legacy of one hundred marks, £66. 6*s*. 8*d*.

In 1374, Sir Walter's half brother, Sir John Blount, of Sodington, conveyed to him numerous manors, which he had inherited from his mother, Isolda, heiress of the Mountjoy family. In 1381 he became proprietor, by purchase, of the large estates of the BAKEPUIZ family, in the counties of Derby, Stafford, Leicester, and Hertford. In 1385 he obtained a charter for a fair and free warren in his demesne lands at Barton, and other manors in Derbyshire. In 1399 he was ranger of Needwood forest, and knight of the shire for the county of Derby. By his wife, Donna Sancha, who survived him, and lived until 1418, he left issue,

I. JOHN (Sir), his heir, one of the great warriors who have immortalized the reign and times of HENRY V.
II. THOMAS (Sir), successor to his brother.
III. James (Sir), who *m*. Anne, daughter of Roger Parker, esq. of Lellinghall, and was father of ROGER BLOUNT,*

* This ROGER BLOUNT, of Grendon, in the county of Hereford, wedded Elizabeth, daughter of Sir Robert Whitney, of Whitney, and had two sons, viz.

THOMAS, his heir.
Walter, of Eldersfield, ancestor of the Blounts of Eldersfield, Churchtown, Mintie, and Bristol.

The elder son,

THOMAS BLOUNT, of Bromyard, *m*. the daughter of Sir Richard Bridges, and was father of

WALTER BLOUNT, of Grendon, who left, by Peryn, daughter of Thomas Barton, of Barton Hall, three sons, namely,

I. JOHN, who *m*. Joan, daughter of Sir Richard Bodenham, and had one son, James, who *m*. a daughter of Sir Edward Mervin, and had two daughters, Anne, the wife of R. Berrington, of Stoke Lucy, and Elizabeth, of Myntridge of Bosbury.
II. THOMAS.
III. Richard, of Monkland, who died *s. p.*

The second son,

THOMAS BLOUNT, esq. of Hereford, who served as captain under Lord Mountjoy at Tournay, *m*. Maria, daughter of David Lloyd, esq. and had two sons, Edmund of Pembridge, sheriff, 8th HENRY VII. and

ROGER BLOUNT, esq. of Grendon, who espoused Maria, daughter of W. Berington, esq. of Winsley, and had issue,

I. RICHARD, barrister-at-law, married Rachel Smith, and had two daughters, Anne, the wife of Wallop Brabazon, esq. brother to the Earl of Meath, and Elizabeth, of — Clarke of Wellington.
II. Thomas, who died *s. p.*
III. John, lieutenant-colonel in the army of St. Macor, Flanders.
IV. Edmund, who died *s. p.*
V. James (Sir), standard-bearer to Lord Mountjoy, died *s. p.*
VI. MYLES, of Orlton, of whom presently.
I. Jane, *m*. to James Bridges, esq. of the Ley, Herefordshire.
II. Elizabeth, *m*. to — Vaughan, esq.

The sixth son of Roger Blount, of Grendon,

MYLES BLOUNT, esq. of Orlton, died in 1663, leaving, by Anne Bustard, of Addlebury, *inter alios*, two sons, Thomas the Lawyer, an antiquary and writer of celebrity, and

MYLES BLOUNT, esq. father of

of Grendon, ancestor of the BLOUNTS of Grendon, Eldersfield, Orleton, &c.

IV. Peter, *d. s. p.*

I. Constantia, *m.* to John Sutton, Lord Dudley.

II. Anne, *m.* to Thomas Griffith, of Whichnor, in the county of Salop, living in 1415.

Sir Walter was succeeded by his eldest son,

SIR JOHN BLOUNT, K. G. who was governor of Calais, and defeated in Aquitaine, in 1412, a French army commanded by a marshal of France, for which achievement he was created a knight of the garter the next year. In 1418, when Rouen was besieged by *King* HENRY V. Sir John Blount assisted at the siege. He died without issue, and was *s.* by his brother,

SIR THOMAS BLOUNT, treasurer of Normandy, who was then seated at Elwaston, in Derbyshire, and to whom the Duke of Exeter gave one thousand marks (£666. 6*s.* 8*d.*) to found a charity at Leicester. Sir Thomas *m.* first, Margaret, daughter of Sir Thomas Greseley, knt. of Greseley, in the county of Derby, and dying in 1456, left two sons and three daughters, viz.

I. WALTER (Sir), lord high treasurer of England, created, in 1464, by patent, BARON MOUNTJOY, a dignity which expired with his descendant, Charles Blount, Earl of Devonshire, in 1606. (*See* BURKE'S *Extinct and Dormant Peerage.*)

II. THOMAS (Sir), of whom presently.

I. Elizabeth, *m.* to Ralph Shirley, of West Neston, in Sussex.

II. Sanchia, *m.* to Edward Langford.

III. Agnes, *m.* to — Wolseley.

Upon the extinction of the Lords Mountjoy, the representation of the family devolved upon the descendant of the second son, the above named

SIR THOMAS BLOUNT: proceed we therefore with his line. In 1462, *King* EDWARD IV. granted him the manor of Milton Ross, and other estates in the counties of Leicester and Lincoln, and appointed him, in the same year, treasurer of Calais. He married, first, Agnes, daughter and heir of Sir John Hawley, knt. of Canons Utterby, in Lincolnshire, and had issue,

I. ROBERT, born in 1459, who died in 1514.

II. Elizabeth, *m.* to Richard Hansard.

Sir Thomas espoused, secondly, Catharine, daughter of Sir Gervase Clifton, of Clifton, Notts. and left by that lady, at his decease, 8th EDWARD IV. 1468, an only son,

RICHARD BLOUNT, who *m.* ELIZABETH, only daughter and heir of WILLIAM DE LA FORD, of Iver, in the county of Buckingham, by whom he acquired the estate in that place, and purchasing the manor of MAPLE DURHAM GURNEY, in the county of Oxford, on the 1st February, 1489, fixed his permanent abode there. He served the office of sheriff for Bucks and Bedfordshire in the 18th HENRY VII. A. D. 1502. He *d.* on the 31st November, 1508 (buried at Iver, Bucks), leaving one son and two daughters, viz.

RICHARD (Sir), his successor.

Anne, *m.* to Francis Conyers, of Wakerley, in Northamptonshire.

Elizabeth, *m.* to Thomas Woodford, of Burnham, in the county of Bucks.

The son and heir,

SIR RICHARD BLOUNT, of Maple Durham Gurney, was one of the gentlemen of the chamber to *King* HENRY VIII. of the Privy chamber to EDWARD VI. and held various offices of trust under ELIZABETH, amongst others that of lieutenant of the Tower. He *m.* Elizabeth, daughter of Sir Richard Lister, chief-justice of England, and sister of Sir Michael Lister,* knight of the Bath, by which lady he had issue,

MICHAEL (Sir), his successor.

Richard (Sir), who resided at Dodsham or Dysham, in Sussex. He *m.* the Hon. Elizabeth West, second daughter of William, first Lord De la Warre, by whom (who *d.* in 1595) he had a son, William.

Elizabeth, *m.* to Nicholas St. John, of Lidiard Tregoze, ancestor of the Viscounts Bolingbroke.

Barbara, *m.* to Francis Shirley, of East Grinstead, in Sussex.

Sir Richard *d.* 11th August, 1564, was bu-

---

THOMAS BLOUNT, esq. who *m.* Miss Mary Mostyn, and dying in 1731, left a son,

EDWARD BLOUNT, esq. who *m.* Miss Cotham, and had issue,

I. Thomas, M. D.

II. Edward, died in 1805.

III. Roland, *m.* Elizabeth, daughter of John Davies, esq. of Henfryn, and *d.* in 1812, leaving a daughter,

Elizabeth-Helen, *m.* first, to John Browne, esq. of Belfast, and secondly to Jonadab William Hunt, esq. of Northwich.

IV. William, M. D. of Hereford, *b.* in 1760, *m.* Mary, daughter of Lacon Lambe, esq. of Bedney, Herefordshire, and had issue,

1. William, of Cumberland Street, married a daughter of the late Thomas Wright, esq. of Fitzwalters, in Essex, and by her (who is deceased) has one son.

1. Elizabeth, } one of whom married
2. Catherine, } Dr. Matthews.

* From this gentleman, the Christian name of "Michael" came into the family.

ried under a splendid monument in the church of St. Peter in Vinculis, in the Tower, erected by his widow (whose will was proved 26th June, 1582), and *s.* by his elder son,

SIR MICHAEL BLOUNT, of Maple Durham, born in 1529. This gentleman succeeded Sir Owen Hopton as lieutenant of the Tower;* and in the list of prisoners delivered to him on assuming office, 6th July, 1590, we find Philip, Earl of Arundel, and Sir Thomas Fitzherbert, of Norbury, beside twenty-nine others, in all thirty-one. On the 1st of April, 1570 *Queen* ELIZABETH sent her letter of trust to Sir Michael to receive the loan money. In 1581 (4th February) he purchased the manor of MAPLE DURHAM CHAWSEY, for £900, and soon after erected the fine mansion of Maple Durham, still existing in the most perfect state. He was sheriff of Oxfordshire in 1586 and 1597. On the death of Charles Blount, Earl of Devonshire, 3rd April, 1606, Sir Michael Blount claimed the BARONY OF MOUNTJOY, one of the honours of that nobleman, as his next heir, but unsuccessfully. He *m.* MARY, sister and co-heir of THOMAS MOORE, esq. of Bicester, in Oxfordshire, by whom (who *d.* 23rd December, 1592) he had five sons and six daughters, namely,

- I. RICHARD (Sir), his successor.
- II. Thomas, *b.* 2nd April, 1567, *m.* ——, daughter and co-heir of John Brocket.
- III. Charles (Sir), *b.* 5th November, 1568, knighted at Cadiz, in 1596, supposed to have been drowned at sea in 1598, on his passage to Ireland.
- IV. Henry, *b.* 17th August, 1571, *d. s. p.*
- V. Robert, *b.* 3rd February, 1573.

- I. Catharine, *b.* 11th April, 1563, *m.* to Sir John Blount, *alias* Croke, of Chilton Bucks and Studley Priory, one of the justices of the king's bench, ancestor of Sir Alexander Croke, historian of the Blount family.
- II. Mary, *b.* 15th November, 1565.
- III. Anne, } both died young.
- IV. Elizabeth, } both died young.
- V. Frances, *b.* 23rd February, 1569.
- VI. Elizabeth, *b.* 28th July, 1574.

The date of the decease of Sir Michael Blount is not upon record. He was buried under a sumptuous monument near his father, in St. Peter's Church, in the Tower, and *s.* by his eldest son,

SIR RICHARD BLOUNT, knt. of Maple Durham, *b.* 28th June, 1564, *m.* first, Cicily, daughter of Sir Richard Baker, of Sisinghurst, in Kent, and had issue,

- I. CHARLES (Sir), his heir.
- II. Walter, *b.* in 1600, *d.* 26th April, 1619.
- III. Richard, born about 1601, a commissioner for the loan money in 1626, sheriff for Oxfordshire in the same year, *m.* Frances, dau. of Sir John Burroughs, garter king of arms.
- IV. Lister, of Bicester, in the county of Oxford, called after his godfather, Charles Lister, esq. of New Windsor, *m.* Joyce, daughter of Sir Allen Apsley, lieutenant of the Tower.

- I. Mary.
- II. Elizabeth, *m.* to George Browne, of Caversham, son and heir of Sir George Browne, second son of Sir Anthony Browne, Viscount Montague.
- III. Frances, *m.* to Sir William Dormer, third son of Sir John Dormer, of Dorton, Bucks.

Sir Richard wedded secondly, Elizabeth, daughter of Sir Francis Moore, knt. of Fawley, in Berkshire, and increased his family by the three following children,

- V. WILLIAM, of Kidmore End, who *m.* Elizabeth, daughter of Sir Ralph De la Vale, of Seton, in Northumberland, by whom (who *d.* 22nd March, 1706), he had,
  - LISTER, of whom hereafter, as inheritor of Maple Durham, under the settlement of his cousin, WALTER BLOUNT, who *d.* in 1671.
  - Walter, } both *d. s. p.*
  - Charles, } both *d. s. p.*
- VI. Henry, *d.* in 1622.
- IV. Jane, *m.* to Sir William Moore, of Fawley, in the county of Berks.

This proprietor of Maple Durham, *d.* 22nd November, 1619, and was *s.* by his eldest son,

SIR CHARLES BLOUNT, knt. of Maple Durham, who built the almshouses there in 1598. This gentleman, a zealous supporter of the royal cause, had his house plundered by the parliamentary army, in 1642-3, and was slain himself fighting under the royal banner, at Oxford, on the 1st June, 1644. His estates were ordered to be sold by parliament, 18th November, 1652. He *m.* DOROTHY, daughter and sole heir of SIR FRANCIS CLERKE, knt. of Houghton Conquest, in Bedfordshire, and by her (who was buried at Maple Durham, 19th October, 1646, will proved 18th March, 1647), had two sons and two daughters, viz.

- I. MICHAEL, who succeeded his father.
- II. WALTER, heir to his brother.

- I. Anne, *m.* first, to John Swinburne, esq. of Capheaton, in Northumber-

* In *Queen* ELIZABETH's time there was no constable of the Tower.

land; and secondly, to Francis Godfrey, esq.

II. Elizabeth.

The elder son,

MICHAEL BLOUNT, esq. of Maple Durham, succeeded his father, but was killed by a footman at Charing Cross, 25th April, 1649, when about twenty years of age; dying unm. he was *s.* by his brother,

WALTER BLOUNT, esq. of Maple Durham, who *m.* first, Philippa, daughter of — Benlowes, esq. of Essex. That lady dying in 1667 (issueless), he wedded secondly, Dorothy, daughter of Edmund Plowden, esq. of Plowden, in the county of Salop, by whom he had a daughter, Elizabeth, who died an infant. He died himself in May, 1671, having by deed, of the 5th February, in the previous year, settled the estates of Maple Durham on his cousin, (refer to Sir Richard Blount, who married, for his second wife, Elizabeth, daughter of Sir Francis Moore, and died 22nd November, 1619),

LISTER BLOUNT, esq. *b.* in 1654, who thus became of "Maple Durham." This gentleman *m.* in 1683, Mary, daughter of Anthony Englefield, esq. of White Knights, and had surviving issue,

MICHAEL, his successor.

Teresa, *b.* at Paris, 15th October, 1688.
Martha, *b.* 15th June, 1690.
} These two ladies were the intimate friends of Pope, and their friendship is frequently reverted to in his works. They first became acquainted with the poet at White Knights, near Reading, the house of their grandfather, a great lover of poetry and admirer of Pope. The close vicinity of White Knights, Maple Durham, and Binfield, and the marked attention paid to the author's rising reputation, created an intimacy between the families, which was cemented by the conformity of their religious and political sentiments. "Their acquaintance," says Dr. Johnson, "began early, the life of each was pictured on the other's mind, their conversation was therefore endearing, for when they met there was an immediate coalition of congenial notions." When Pope needed more than the common offices of friendship, and when the gentle attentions of female kindness could alone soothe his continued infirmities, those consoling services in his hour of weakness and pain he experienced from the Misses Blount. He and they were constantly together, and if at any time absent they carried on a continued correspondence. By his will, dated a few months before his death, the poet bequeathed to the younger Miss Blount £100, the furniture of the grotto, the urns in his garden, and the interest of his whole property for her life. Miss Martha Blount, the Parthenia of Pope, died in 1763. Miss Teresa Blount (who assumed the name of Zephilinda in her correspondence with Mr. Moore, who styled himself Alexis,) died in 1759.

Mr. Blount died 25th June, 1710, and was *s.* by his son,

MICHAEL BLOUNT, esq. of Maple Durham, *b.* 26th March, 1693, *m.* in 1715, MARY-AGNES, daughter and co-heir of SIR JOSEPH TICHBORNE, of Tichborne, in the county of Hants, (and his wife, Mary, daughter of Anthony Kempe, esq. of Slindon, in Sussex,) by which lady (who was born in 1695, and died 19th May, 1777, aged eighty-two) he had three sons and two daughters, namely,

I. MICHAEL, his heir.
II. Henry-Tichborne, *b.* 6th December, 1723, ordained a catholic priest, at Arras, 30th March, 1748, appointed PRESIDENT OF DOUAY COLLEGE in 1770, and resided there until 1780. He subsequently took up his abode in the convent of English nuns at Louvain, and accompanied those ladies to England in 1794. He died at Maple Durham, 29th May, 1810, in his eighty-seventh year.
III. Walter, *b.* 13th December, 1727, *d.* a Benedictine monk, at Douay, 14th October, 1746.
I. Mary, *b.* 19th November, 1716, *m.* to Sir Henry Tichborne, bart. and died 10th February, 1799, in her eighty-third year.
II. Frances, born 1st October, 1717, a Benedictine nun, at Brussels, died there in 1740.

He died on the 2nd November, 1739, and was *s.* by his eldest son,

MICHAEL BLOUNT, esq. of Maple Durham, born 14th April, 1719, *m.* 16th August, 1742, Mary-Eugenia, eldest daughter of Mannock Strickland, esq. of Lincoln's Inn, by whom (who was born 10th July, 1723, and died 12th December, 1762) he had issue,

I. MICHAEL, his heir.
II. Joseph, *b.* 15th July, 1752, married Mary, daughter of Francis Canning, esq. of Foxcote, in the county of Warwick, (the lady was born in 1752, and was living in March, 1835,) by whom he left at his decease (he died at St. Cyr, near Lyons, and is interred there)
   1. Joseph, born in 1779, *m.* first, Jane, daughter of John Sater-

thwaite, esq. of Mansergh Hall, Westmoreland, but there was no issue of that marriage. He wedded, secondly, 19th February, 1816, Anne, only daughter of Mr. Richard Martin, of Hurstborne Tarrant, in Hampshire, and by this lady had an only daughter.

2. Michael, *m.* Catharine, daughter and co-heir of Francis Wright, esq. of Bedford Square, London, (by his wife, Catharine Petre, who wedded, after the death of Mr. Wright, Michael Blount, esq. of Maple Durham,) and has issue.

 1. Elizabeth, *m.* in July, 1802, to Ralph Riddell, esq. of Felton Park, in Northumberland.
 2. Frances.

I. Mary-Eugenia, born 14th February, 1745, *m.* first, 15th November, 1765, to Charles Stonor, esq. of Stonor, (see vol. ii. p. 444,) and secondly, in 1783, to Thomas Canning, second son of Thomas Canning, esq. of Foxcote, in Warwickshire.

II. Martha, born in 1762, *d.* unmarried, 5th February, 1780.

Mr. Blount died 5th February, 1792, and was *s.* by his eldest son,

MICHAEL BLOUNT, esq. of Maple Durham, *b.* 4th July, 1743, *m.* first, at Bristol, 15th April, 1781, Eleanora, second daughter of Maurice Fitzgerald, esq. of Punchers' Grange, in the county of Kildare. By this lady, who died on the 12th May, in the next year, and was buried at Maple Durham, he had a daughter, Maria-Eugenia, *b.* in January, 1782, *d.* 2nd August, 1791. He wedded, secondly, 27th August, 1787, Catharine, daughter and sole heir of John Petre, esq. of Belhouse, in the parish of Stanford Rivers, Essex, and widow of Francis Wright, esq. of Bedford Square, by whom he had two sons and two daughters, namely,

MICHAEL-HENRY-MARY, his successor.
Walter-Thomas-Mary.

Henrietta, *m.* 16th September, 1811, to John Wright, esq. of Bellsize Park, Hampstead.
Juliana-Mary, *m.* to — Nolan.

Mr. Blount died 29th October, 1821, and was *s.* by his son, the present MICHAEL-HENRY-MARY BLOUNT, esq. of Maple Durham.

*Arms*—Barry, nebulé or and sa.; quartering AYALA, CASTILLE, and BEAUCHAMP.

*Crest*—A wolf passant sa. between two cornets, out of a ducal coronet or: also, a foot in the sun, with the motto, "Lux tua, via mea." The latter is the crest now generally adopted.

*Estates*—In Oxfordshire.

*Seat*—Maple Durham.

## SCOTT, OF MALLENY.

SCOTT, THOMAS, esq. of Malleny, in the shire of Midlothian, *b.* 25th December, 1745, a deputy lieutenant for that county.

This gentleman, a general in the army, and, with one exception, the oldest officer in the British service, obtained an ensigncy in the 24th regiment 20th May, 1761, and his career has since been highly distinguished. He served under Prince Ferdinand during the whole of the campaign of 1762, and carried the colours of his regiment at the battle of Wellemstall, and at the attack of the British picquets on the Fulda. In 1763, returning home, he was stationed in Ireland, and obtained his lieutenancy in 1765. In 1776, he accompanied his regiment to America, served two campaigns under General Burgoyne, with a company of marksmen attached to a large body of Indians, and acquitted himself so much to the satisfaction of his commanding officer, Brigadier Fraser, that he twice received thanks in public orders. After the battle of the 19th September, 1777, the critical situation of Burgoyne rendering it indispensably necessary to communicate with Sir Henry Clinton, the commander-in-chief, two officers were selected, who should take different routes, to apprise Sir Henry of the perilous position of the British forces. Captain Scott, who was well known as an excellent pedestrian, was chosen as one of the envoys, and accomplished his journey with great address and courage. In 1788, he returned to Europe; in 1791, served, during the Spanish armament, with a detachment of the 53rd regiment, for six months on board his majesty's ship Hannibal, commanded by Sir John Colpoys, and proceeding, in 1793, to the continent with Sir Ralph Abercromby, assisted at the sieges of Valenciennes and Dunkirk, and in the attack in which the Austrian General D'Alton was killed. He was also at the siege of Niewport, and received the commission of major for his exertions in its defence.

During the three days that Prince William of Gloucester commanded the brigade, which consisted of the 14th, 37th, and 53rd regiments, Major Scott was attached to the staff of his royal highness, was present at the attack of the village of Premont, and participated in the action of the 24th May, being wounded that day in the inside of the right thigh by a musket ball. In 1794, he was appointed lieutenant-colonel of one of the battalions of the 94th, and in the following year proceeded with it to Gibraltar, and in 1796 to the Cape of Good Hope. He served the whole of the campaign of 1799, in the Mysore country, and was at the capture of Seringapatam. In 1800, Colonel Scott, in consequence of ill health, deemed it expedient to return to Europe, and left Hindostan. The Indiaman, however, in which he was a passenger, being boarded and taken by a French privateer, in the British Channel, close to the Isle of Wight, Colonel Scott was detained some weeks at Cherbourg until exchanged, in consequence of an application to the French government by the desire of the Duke of York. In 1801, he was appointed colonel by brevet; in 1802, inspecting field officer of the Edinburgh recruiting district; in 1803, deputy inspector-general of the recruiting service in North Britain; in 1804, brigadier-general; in 1808, major-general on the staff; and, in 1813, lieutenant-general. It is a remarkable circumstance in the history of General Scott's life, that from the time he was appointed ensign to his promotion to the rank of general, a period of no less than fifty-two years, he had served without ever being on half pay or unemployed. Since his retirement from his staff appointment, the general has chiefly resided at Malleny, where, after a long and severe military career, he enjoys a well-earned repose, alike distinguished for his benevolence, hospitality, and kindness to his tenants.

## Lineage.

The Scotts of Malleny, an ancient branch of Buccleugh, appears to have separated from the parent stock during its residence in Lanarkshire. The first of the family that settled in Midlothean was

James Scott, of Scotsloch, who lived in the reigns of *Queen* Mary and James VI. He was father of

Laurence Scott, of Clerkington, a distinguished person in the time of Charles I. who was appointed clerk to the privy council, and one of the principal clerks of session. From several charters under the great seal, it appears that his possessions were extensive in Edinburghshire. He *m.* Elizabeth, daughter of Hop Pringle, of Torsance, and had, with two daughters, one *m.* to Lauder, of Hatton, and the other to Houstoun, three sons, viz.

William, his heir.

James, who received from his father the lands of Bonnytoun, in West Lothian.

Laurence, ancestor of the Scotts of Bavelaw.

The eldest son,

Sir William Scott, of Clerkington, received the honor of knighthood from Charles I. and was appointed in 1642, one of the senators of the college of justice. He married first, a daughter of Morrison, of Preston Grange, and had a son, Laurence, his heir. He married secondly, Barbara, daughter of Sir John Dalmahoy, of that Ilk, and had by her, three sons and three daughters, viz.

I. John, successor to his brother.

II. James, of Scotsloch.

III. Robert, dean of Hamilton.

I. Barbara, *m.* first, to a son of Stewart, of Blackhall; and secondly, to Sir William Drummond, of Hathornden.

II. Agnes, *m.* to Sir John Home, of Renton.

III. ——, *m.* to Ogilvie, of Muckle, in Angus.

Sir William Scott was succeeded by his son,

LAURENCE SCOTT, esq. of Clerkington, who married a daughter of Sir John Dalmahoy, and had two daughters only, the elder, the wife of George Winram, esq. of Egemouth, and the younger, of Robert Kennedy, esq. comptroller of the customs, at Borrowstones. Dying thus without male issue, he was succeeded by his brother,

JOHN SCOTT, esq. who received from his father in patrimony, the lands and barony of Malleny, in Midlothian, which has ever since been the chief title of the family. He *m.* Anne, daughter of Sir Thomas Nicolson, of Cockburnspath, and had, with two daughters, the elder *m.* to Sir William Calderwood, of Polton, one of the senators of the college of justice; and the younger, to her cousin, Laurence Scott, of Bevelaw, two sons, viz.

I. THOMAS, his heir.

II. William, an advocate at the Scottish bar, who married, first, Magdalen, daughter and heiress of William Blair, esq. of Blair, and had one son,

1. WILLIAM, who inherited the estate and assumed the surname of BLAIR. He died without issue, in 1732, when he settled his lands upon the children of his father's second marriage.

William Scott (the elder), wedded secondly, Catherine, only daughter of Alexander Tait, merchant, in Edinburgh, and had five sons and six daughters, who all assumed the surname of BLAIR, viz.

2. HAMILTON BLAIR, esq. of Blair, major in the Scots Greys, who *m.* Jane, youngest daughter of Sydenham Williams, esq. of Herringston, in the county of Dorset (see vol. i. p. 617), and dying in 1782, left, with two daughters, Agatha, *m.* to Lieutenant-General Avarne; and Jane, to Robert Williams, esq. of Cerne Abbas, in Dorsetshire, a son and successor,

WILLIAM BLAIR, esq. of Blair, colonel of the Ayrshire regiment of Fencible Cavalry, who *m.* Magdalen, eldest daughter of the late John Fordyce, esq. of Ayton, in Berwickshire, and had five sons, and seven daughters. Of the latter, the eldest, Catherine, married Matthew Fortescue, esq. of Stephenstown, in the county of Louth; and the third, Jane Louisa, was wife of Colonel Jackson, of Enniscoe, in the county of Mayo.

3. Alexander Blair, surveyor of the customs, at Port Glasgow, who *m.* Elizabeth, only daughter of John Hamilton, esq. of Grange, in Ayrshire, and had issue.

4. John Blair, captain of foot, who fell at Minden, in 1759.

5. Thomas Blair, a cornet in the Scots Greys, killed at the battle of Vald, in 1747.

6. William Blair, a lieutenant of foot, killed at Oswego, in India, in 1756.

1. Anne Blair, *m.* to David Blair, esq. of Adamton, and had a daughter, Catherine, the wife of Sir William Maxwell, bart. of Monreith.

2. Magdalen Blair, *m.* to Sir William Maxwell, bart. of Monreith, and had, with other issue, a daughter, Jane, wife of Alexander, duke of Gordon.

3. Janet Blair, *m.* to Alexander Tait, esq. one of the principal clerks of session, and had issue.

4. Barbara Blair, *m.* to William Fullarton, esq. of that Ilk, and had issue.

5. Catherine Blair, died unm.

6. Mary Blair, *m.* to Sir John Sinclair, bart. of Stevenston, and had issue.

John Scott died in 1709, and was succeeded by his son,

THOMAS SCOTT, esq. of Malleny, who *m.* Isabel, daughter of Sir John Lauder, bart. of Fountain Hall, one of the senators of the college of justice, and had four sons and six daughters, viz.

I. JOHN, who entered the Portugese military service, wherein he remained several years, and having returned to Scotland, died at Malleny, 20th September, 1791.

II. THOMAS, the present General SCOTT, of Malleny.

III. James, who commanded a ship in India, and died there.

IV. Alexander, who served in the Scots Brigade, in Holland, and attained the rank of major in the British army. He now resides at Lymphoy, on the estate of Malleny.

V. Archibald, who was in the military service of the East India Company, and fell in action.

VI. Francis Carteret, who went in 1774, collector of customs, to Montego Bay, in Jamaica, and returned in 1800. He *m.* in 1801, Charlotte-

Elizabeth, eldest daughter of the late Major General George Cunningham, of the Scots Brigade and had six sons and five daughters, viz.

1. Thomas, *b.* at Ravelrig, in the county of Midlothian, in 1802, and died in 1832.
2. Carteret-George, captain in the hon. East India company's service *m.* first, in 1830, Charlotte, daughter of the late Colonel M'Dougal, and grandniece of George, marquis of Tweeddale. This lady died in 1831, and Capt. Scott wedded secondly, in 1833, Emily, daughter of Capt. Frederick Holmes Coffin, R.N.
3. George, in the island of Jamaica.
4. Alexander, captain in the 53rd regiment.
5. John, lieutenant in the same regiment.
6. Stair-Primrose, bred to the law.

1. Isabella-Frances, *m.* in 1824, to George More Nisbett, esq. of Cairnhill, in the county of Lanark, and has two sons and three daughters.
2. Charlotte, died in 1814.
3. Jane.
4. Charlotte-Elizabeth.
5. Lavinia-Cockburn.

VII. Hamilton, in the military service of the East India company, killed in action.

VIII. George, who after serving in the West Indies, and attaining the rank of lieutenant-colonel in the British army, retired from the line, and is now lieutenant-colonel of the Edinburgh regiment of North British Militia.

I. Margaret.
II. Jane.
III. Susan.
IV. Molly.

The second but eldest surviving son of Thomas Scott, is the present General SCOTT, of Malleny.

*Arms*—Or, on a bend az. a star between two crescents of the first, for SCOTT, of Buccleugh, and, for difference, in base an arrow bendways, ppr. feathered and barbed arg.

*Crest*—A stag lodged, ppr.

*Motto*—Amo probos.

*Estates*—In Midlothian.

*Seat*—Malleny House, by Currie.

## M'KERRELL, OF HILLHOUSE.

M'KERRELL, JOHN, esq. of Hillhouse, in the county of Ayr, late master of the Mint at Madras, succeeded his father in 1820.

### Lineage.

The M'KERRELLS have flourished, from a remote period, in the shire of Ayr, but, with many other Caledonian families, have to deplore, that by the spoliation of the *first* EDWARD, in the thirteenth century, and the destruction by fire of the herald's archives at Edinburgh, in the seventeenth, they are deprived of direct evidence in tracing their origin, and can now deduce it on presumptive proof alone. The tradition from sire to son bears that they came out of Ireland, and it carries back the possession of the estate of Hillhouse full five hundred years, to the glorious era of ROBERT THE BRUCE, a period when vast changes occurred in the proprietary of the soil, and when the chiefs of numerous houses, still in a high state of prosperity, were endowed by that illustrious prince.

The name KIRIELL appears on the roll of Battle Abbey; hence the family is presumed to be of Norman descent, its advent from Ireland rather upholding than upsetting the presumption, if the swarm of Anglo-Norman adventurers who joined the banner of EARL STRONGBOW, and invaded that country in 1170, be taken into consideration. "Of the Norman barons," says Sir Walter Scott, "Scotland received from time to time such numerous accessions, that they may be said, with few exceptions, to form the ancestors of the Scottish nobility, and of many of the most distinguished families amongst the gentry; a fact so well known, that it were useless to bring proof of it here."

KIRIELL, KIREL, KIRREL, or KERRELL, (as at various times spelt), is a surname now very rarely to be met with. It is said to exist in Sweden, another proof of Normanic origin: in Scotland, the family of Hillhouse alone bears it.

The first of the name, and the most remote now on Scottish record, SIR JOHN M'KIREL,* distinguished himself at the celebrated battle of OTTERBURN, 19th August, 1388, by wounding and capturing ROUEL DE PERCIE, who held the second command in the English host, and whose brother, the renowned HOTSPUR, was made prisoner by SIR JOHN MONTGOMERIE,† (from whom spring the earls of Eglinton), in the same sanguinary conflict. That this Sir John M'Kirel was an ancestor of the Hillhouse family, the circumstance of the latter bearing the arms‡ which he acquired by his prowess in that celebrated battle appears conclusive, although a chasm of nearly two centuries occurs in the pedigree.

The following is Froissart's account of the battle of Otterbourn, and the mention of M'Kirel:

"De touts les besognes, batailles et rencontres qui sont cy dessous en ceste histoire (dont ie traitte et ay traittè) grandes, moyennes et petites, ceste cy, dont ie parle pour le present, en fut l'une des plus dures, et des mieux combattues sans feintise, car il n'y auoit homme, chevalier, n'escuyer qui ne s'acquittast et fit son devoir, et tout main a main. Cette battaille fut quasi pareille a la bataille de Becherel: car aussi elle fut moult bien combattue e longuement. Les enfants au Compte de Northomberllande, Messire Henry et Messire Raeul de Persy (qui là estoient soueraines capitaines) s'acquitterent loyaument par bien combattre: et quasi pareil party, que celui, par qui le Comte de Douglas fut arrestè, auint et cheut a Messire Raoul de Persy; car il se bouta si auant entre ses ennemis, qu'il fut enclos, et durement naurè, mis a la grosse haleine, pris et fiancè d'un *Chevalier*, lequel estoit de la charge et du meme hostel de Moray, et l'appeloit on *Jehan Makirel*. En le prenant et fiançant, le Cheualier Escoçois demanda a Messire Raoul de Persy, qui l'estoit, (car il estoit si muiet que point ne le cognoissoit) et Messire Raoul (qui estoit si outrè que plus ne pouuait, et luy couloit le sang tout aual, qui l'affoiblissoit) luy dit; je suis Messire Raoul de Persy. Adonc dit l'Escoçois, Messire Raoul rècoux ou non rècoux, ie vous fiance mon prisonnier. Je suis *Makirel*. Bien dit Messire Raoul, je le veieil, mais entendez a mois, car ie suis trop durement naurè, et mes chausses et mes greues sont là toutes emplies de sang. A ces mots estoit le cheualiere Escoçois ententif, quand delez luy il ouyt crier Moray et au compte: et recit le compte et sa banniere droit deiez a luy. Si luy dit Messire Jehan Makirel, Monseigneur, tenez. Je vous baille Messire Raoul de Persy pour prisonnier; mais faites entendre a luy, car il est durement naurè. Le Comte de Moray de ceste parole fut rèiouy moult grandement: et dit, Makirel, tu as bien gagnè les esperons. Adonc fit il venir ses gens, et leua charger Messire Raoul de Persy: lesquels luy banderent et etancherent ces playes. Si se tanoit la bataille fort et dure et ne sauoit on encores lesquels en auroient le meilleur; car ie vous dy qu'il y eut là plusieurs prises et rècousses faites, qui toutes ne vindrent pas a cognaissance."

The next of the name, although probably there were six intermediate links at least, from whom the chain continues unbroken,

WILLIAM M'KERREL, of Hillhouse, *m.* in 1577, Elizabeth, daughter of John Fuller-

* MAC, or "SON OF," was a common prefixture in both Scotland and Ireland.

† The death of Sir John Montgomerie's son, Hugh, in this bloody raid has been commemorated in the old and popular ballad of Chevy Chace:

> Against SIR HUGH MONTGOMERIE
> So straight his shaft he set,
> The grey goose wing that was thereon,
> In his heart's blood was wet.

‡ If heraldry may be trusted, and for long after its institution its purity as a science, and its utility still in restoring the severed links of affinity when broken asunder, through loss of documentary evidence, are manifest, the arms of this family must have been those of Sir John M'Kerel, for they are founded on the Percie coat, which was az. five fusils in fess or. The arms of M'Kerrel being az. three fusils gu, on a fess or, within a bordure engrailed for distinction, leaving no question but that in consequence of the capture of Percie, this formed one of those cases described by heralds of arms by conquest: for as M'Kerrel was then a knight, (chevalier, in Froissart), and no other honour or reward being recorded of him, it follows that this augmentation to, or grant of arms, was his reward; and their inheritage, coupled with Froissart's record, is the best of all proofs of the descent of the present family of Hillhouse from Sir John, and also of the correctness of one part of the tradition above.

ton, of Dregham, by Helen, daughter of Sir J. Chalmers, of Gadgirth, and was *s.* by his son,

William M'Kerrel, of Hillhouse, whose name is among the witnesses to the marriage of James Fullarton, of that Ilk, in 1624. His son,

Magister William M'Kerrel, of Hillhouse, appears in the retour, dated 1630, as proprietor of several lands in the parish of Dundonald, and of Knock Gall, in the parish of Ochiltree. In 1636 he is retoured heir to his father in the fifty-shilling lands of Godring,* and of the Kemmoch land, and was succeeded himself at his decease by his son,

William M'Kerrell, of Hillhouse, whose retour is dated in 1643, and who was *s.* by his brother,

John M'Kerrell, of Hillhouse, who *m.* about the year 1670, Elizabeth Wallace, daughter of the Bishop of the Isles, and was father of

John M'Kerrell, of Hillhouse, who wedded Elizabeth, daughter of William Fairlie, of Fairlie, by his wife, Jane, only daughter of the *last* Sir William Mure, of Rowallan,† and had issue,

William.
John.
Jean.
Elizabeth.

He was *s.* by his eldest son,

William M'Kerrell, of Hillhouse. This laird *m.* Mary Vaux, of French extraction, whose family sought refuge in this country from the persecution which followed the revocation of the edict of Nantz. Her father was in holy orders, and one of the canons of St. Paul's cathedral. By this lady he had William and John, with a daughter Elizabeth. He was *s.* by his elder son,

William M'Kerrel, esq. of Hillhouse, at whose decease, unmarried, the estates devolved on his brother,

John M'Kerrel, esq. of Hillhouse, who married Margaret, sister of the late William Fulton, esq. of Park, in the county of Renfrew, and had issue,

I. William, his heir.
II. John, married first, Miss Hervey, of Edinburgh, and had John, Alexander, and William. He wedded secondly, Helen Stuart, niece of Robert Marice, esq. of Craig, and had a fourth son, Archibald.
III. Robert, who *m.* Miss Shultz, of Frankfort, and had one son and two daughters, viz.
    Robert.
    Margaret.
    Augusta-Jane, *m.* to Count Segure, the French chargé d'affaires at Palermo.
IV. Fulton, married first, to his cousin-german, Elizabeth, daughter of Fulton, of Hartfield, but had no issue. He wedded secondly, Mary, daughter of James M'Call, esq. of Breahead, and had three daughters, Sarah, Margaret, and Mary.

I. Margaret, married to the late Moses Crawfurd, esq. of Newfield, and had issue. (See vol. i. p. 554.)
II. Mary.
III. Elizabeth, *m.* to Col. John Reid, of the Hon. East Ind. service, and died, leaving a dau. Elizabeth M'Kerrell Reid, who wedded James Cambell, esq. of Treesbanks, (refer to vol. ii. p. 359).
IV. Jane, *m.* to her cousin, Robert Fulton, of Hartfield, late lieut.-colonel of the 79th Foot, with which regiment he served in Egypt and the Peninsula; she has issue,
    Robert Fulton, captain in the 79th regiment.
    John Fulton, lieutenant in the East India Company's service.
    William Fulton.
    Jane Fulton.
V. Marion, *m.* to the late James Kibble, esq. of Whittford and Greenlaw House, in the county of Renfrew, and had one son, Robert Kibble, who died young.
VI. Agnes, *m.* to John-Edward Wright, esq. of Bolton-on-Swale, (see vol. ii. p. 678).

Mr. M'Kerrell died in 1811, aged seventy-nine, and was *s.* by his eldest son,

William Mc Kerrell, esq. of Hillhouse, who *m.* first, Miss Reid, sister of the late Robert Reid, esq. of Adamton, but had no issue. He wedded secondly, Miss Gowan, by whom he had five sons and four daughters, viz.

John, his heir.
Robert, died in India.

* Now Rosemount, the property and seat of Lord James Stuart, M.P. for the Ayr district of boroughs.

† The Mures of Rowallan were of great antiquity and consideration in the shire of Ayr, and were distinguished by their alliance with the royal family of Scotland, through the marriage of King Robert II. (the first of the Stuart dynasty) with Elizabeth, daughter of Sir Adam Mure, of Rowallan, when residing at his castle of Dundonald, in Kyle Stuart. From that union *lineally* descended James VI. of Scotland, and first of England. The present marchioness dowager of Hastings is now the representative of the family of Rowallan, and possesses the estate (see vol. i. p. 453).

William, *d.* young.
Henry.
James, *d.* in 1833.
Janet.
Margaret.
Anne, *m.* to James Brown, esq. and has issue.
Mary.

This gentleman, who had the honour of raising, at Paisley, the first volunteer corps embodied in Scotland during the French revolutionary war, died in 1821, and was *s.* by his eldest son, JOHN M'KERREL, esq. now of Hillhouse.

*Arms*—Az. three fusils gu. on a fess or, within a bordure engrailed.

*Crest*—An ancient warrior in armour, with a shield and spear, a star over the latter's point.

*Motto*—Dulcis pro patriâ labor.

*Estates*—In Ayrshire.

*Seat*—Hillhouse, four miles south of Irvine.

# PRICE, OF CASTLE MADOC.

## Representing Powell, of Castle Madoc.

PRICE, HUGH, esq. of Castle Madoc, in the county of Brecknock, *b.* 29th March, 1786; *m.* 30th September, 1818, Sophia-Juliana-Bulama, daughter of the late Francis Brodie, esq. barrister-at-law, and has had issue,

Charles-Powell, *b.* 10th September, 1821, now deceased.
HUGH-POWELL, *b.* 16th November, 1822.
Grace-Powell.
Eleanor-Powell.

Mr. Price succeeded his father 13th June, 1803. He is in the commission of the peace for the county of Brecon, and served the office of sheriff in 1815.

## Lineage.

The PRICES deriving their estates from the POWELLS of Castle Madoc, we shall commence with the descent of that ancient family until it merges in that of PRICE.

CARADOG *Vreichvras*, or Caradog with the brawny arm, a prince of the Cornish Britons at the close of the fifth and in the early part of the sixth centuries, one of the knights of *King* ARTHUR's Round Table, and in the Welsh Triads styled one of the three celebrated commanders of cavalry, was direct ancestor of

MAENYRCH, Lord of Brecon, whose son,

BLEDDYN AP MAENYRCH, was Lord of Brecon in the reign of WILLIAM *Rufus* of England, at which period the lordship was invaded by Bernard Newmarch, a Norman adventurer, who, with his followers, defeated the forces of Bleddyn. The unfortunate chieftain being slain in the battle, was by his sons conveyed to the abbey of Strata Florida, in Cardiganshire, and there buried. His extensive domains were, however, seized upon by Newmarch, and for the most part divided between himself and his Norman followers. Nevertheless, Bleddyn's sons still retained a portion of their father's patrimony, and from one of them, named BLEGWRYD, descended, in the fifth degree,

EINION, who dwelt in Llywel, in the county of Brecon, and was called EINION *Sais*, because he could speak the English language. Third in descent from Einion was

LLEWELYN, who wedded Matilda, daughter of Ieuan ap Rys ap Ivor, of Elvel, and had two sons, HOWEL, ancestor of the

POWELLS of Castle Madoc, and DAVID GAM, so celebrated in history as the enemy of Owain Glyndwr, and supporter of the English interest; but more renowned by his prowess on the field of AZINCOURT, in coming to the rescue of *King* HENRY when the gallant monarch was placed in a situation of imminent peril. Here David Gam received a mortal wound, but, before he breathed his last, had the honour of knighthood conferred upon him by his royal master. Llewelyn's elder son,

HOWEL, espoused Margaret, daughter of Gwilim Philip Thomas ap Elydr, and had two sons and two daughters, viz.

GWILYM DEW, his heir.

Thomas, who *m.* first, a daughter of John Mear, of Brecon, and had two sons, Owen and Rees, who married in Yorkshire. Thomas wedded, secondly, Margaret Winstone, of Willersley, and had a daughter, Alice, the wife of Thomas Havardhir.

Maud, *m.* to Morgan David Powel Vychan.

Margaret, *m.* to Gwilim Thomas Griffith ap Owen Gethin.

The elder son,

GWILYM DEW, married Mary, daughter of Jenkin Richard Jenkin, of Aberyscir, and was *s.* by his son,

HOWEL DEW, father, by Maud, his wife, daughter of Roger Madoc Rich David, of

GWILYM, who *m.* Catherine, daughter of John Rees Jenkin, of Glynnedd, and had a son,

HOWEL, of Argoed, who wedded, first, Margaret, dau. of William John Havard, and had one son, THOMAS, his heir, and one daughter, Maud, the wife of John Meredith Watkin Morgan. He married, secondly, Elinor, daughter of Roger Vaughan, and by her was father of William of Buallt, ancestor of the Powells of Cilmeri. Howel's elder son,

THOMAS POWELL, esq. married Sibil, daughter of Sir William Vaughan, knt. and was *s.* by his son,

WILLIAM POWELL, esq. of Castle Madoc, who wedded Matilda, daughter of Griffith Jeffrey, of Glyntawe, and left a son and successor,

HUGH POWELL, esq. of Castle Madoc, living in 1600, who *m.* Elizabeth, daughter of Thomas Gwyn, of Trecastle, and had three sons with one daughter, namely,

I. WILLIAM, his heir.

II. Another son.

III. Thomas, who *m.* Anne, daughter of Howel Gwyn, of Trecastle, and left a daughter, Mary, the wife of Capt. Thomas Price, of Devynock.

I. Jennet, *m.* to Watkin Pritchard.

Hugh Powell died in 1624, and was *s.* by his son,

WILLIAM POWELL, esq. of Castle Madoc, who died in 1637, leaving by Anne, his wife, daughter of Rees Kemeys, esq. of Llanvair ys coed, with five daughters, three sons, namely, HUGH, his heir; Thomas, who *m.* the daughter and co-heir of Lewis Gwyn, esq. of Bishop's Castle, but died without issue; and Griffith. The eldest son,

HUGH POWELL, esq. of Castle Madoc, wedded Catherine, daughter of Roger Vaughan, of Merthyr, and had, with two daughters, Margaret, the wife of Geffrey Williams, esq., and ———, *m.* to Rees Penryn, esq., two sons, CHARLES, his heir, and George, who espoused Anne, daughter of John Herbert, esq. of Court Henry. Mr. Powell died in 1686, and was *s.* by his son,

CHARLES POWELL, esq. of Castle Madoc. This gentleman married Elizabeth, daughter of George Gwyn, of Llanelwedd, and sister to Sir Rowland Gwyn, by whom he left at his decease in 1729, with younger children, a son and successor,

HUGH HOWELL POWELL, esq. of Castle Madoc, *b.* in 1683, who *m.* Margaret, dau. and heir of Walter Thomas, esq. of Talwenfawr, and had two sons and five daughters, viz.

I. CHARLES, his heir.

II. Hugh, colonel in the army, *d. s. p.*

I. Elizabeth.

II. PENELOPE, who wedded ROGER PRICE, esq. of Maes-yr-Onn, son of Roger Price, esq. and had several sons and daughters, who all died issueless, excepting the second son, the Rev.

HUGH PRICE, of whom hereafter as INHERITOR of the CASTLE MADOC estate.

III. Dorothy.

IV. Margaret.

V. Catharine.

Mr. Powell died in 1749, and was *s.* by his son,

CHARLES POWELL, esq. of Castle Madoc, who married Catherine, daughter of Hugh Penny, esq. of Cefn, and had two daughters, CATHERINE, his heir; and Margaret, who died unmarried in her father's lifetime. Mr. Powell died in 1796, and was *s.* by his only surviving child,

CATHERINE POWELL, of Castle Madoc, at whose decease unmarried in September, 1798, the estates passed to (the son of her aunt Penelope) her cousin,

THE REV. HUGH PRICE, M.A. rector of Rettendon and Little Ilford, in the county of Essex, who then became of "Castle Madoc." He *m.* Sarah, daughter of John Turner, esq. of King's Stanley, and had issue,

Charles, who died young.

Hugh, heir to his father.

Anne.

Sarah.

Mr. Price died 13th June, 1803, and was succeeded by his only surviving son, the present Hugh Price, esq. of Castle Madoc.

*Estates*—In Breconshire.

*Seat*—Castle Madoc. The present edifice was erected by one of the Powells in the year 1588, according to the inscription on an iron plate over the entrance, which bears the three spears' heads and chevron: before its erection, there stood a castellated mansion with a keep, over which was an artificial mound, still in existence, on which stood the Welsh tower.

## DUNDAS, OF DUDDINGSTOUN.

DUNDAS-HAMILTON, GABRIEL, esq. of Duddingstoun, in West Lothian, succeeded his father in 1820, *m.* Isabella, eldest daughter of James Dennistoun, esq. of Dennistoun* and Colgrain, in Dumbartonshire, by Miss Dreghorn his wife, heiress of Ruchill, and had issue,

I. John, *b.* in 1805, captain of the 1st foot.
II. James.
III. David, *d.* in 1833.
IV. Gabriel.
V. Robert.
VI. George.

I. Margaret.
II. Grace.
III. Jessie.
IV. Marion.
V. Elizabeth.

Mr. Hamilton-Dundas was formerly an officer in the 3rd foot guards, and served with his regiment in Egypt. He is major commandant of the West Lothian yeomanry, deputy lieutenant for Haddingtonshire, and in the commission of the peace for the counties of Haddington and Lanark.

### Lineage.

This is a branch of the ancient stock of Dundas of Dundas (see vol i. p. 643).

Sir William Dundas, of that Ilk, who was served heir to his father in 1494, married Margaret, daughter of Archibald Wauchope, of Niddery, an ancient and still distinguished family, and had two sons,

I. James (Sir), ancestor of the Dundases of Dundas, Arniston, &c.
II. William, progenitor of Duddingstoun.

The second son,

William Dundas, espoused Marjory Lindsay, heiress of Duddingstoun, and with her acquired that estate. He was succeeded by his elder son,

William Dundas, of Duddingstoun, who resided for many years in Sweden, and married a lady of that country. He left no male issue, and was succeeded by his brother,

David Dundas, of Duddingstoun, who

* For an account of the ancient family of Dennistoun, and their alliance with the royal family of Scotland through Isabella Dennistoun, grandmother of *King* Robert III. see Wood's *Douglas.*

married Marjory, daughter of John Hamilton, of Orbiston, great-grandson of Gavin Hamilton, fourth son of Sir James Hamilton, Lord of Cadzow. By her he had two sons,

I. JAMES.

II. George, ancestor of the family of DUNDAS of Manor.

The elder son,

JAMES DUNDAS, of Duddingstoun, married Isabella, daughter of William Maule, son of Thomas Maule, of Panmure, and uncle of Patrick, first Earl of Panmure, by Bethia Guthrie, daughter of Alexander Guthrie, of the family of Guthrie of Guthrie, by Janet, daughter of Henderson of Fordel. By her he had,

I. GEORGE, *b.* in 1612.

II. William.

I. Bethia, *b.* in 1614, wife of James Home, brother of Home of St. Leonards.

Duddingstoun was *s.* by his son,

GEORGE DUNDAS, of Duddingstoun, a parliamentarian in the civil wars *temp.* CHARLES I. and one of the committee of estates in 1649. In 1636, he married Catherine Moneypenny,* daughter of John Moneypenny, of Pitmilly, an ancient family still existing in great respectability, which had for its cadets the Lords Moneypenny, and the Seigneurs de Concressault in France. Catherine's mother was Susannah Colville, daughter of Sir A. Colville, commendator of Culross, by Nicolas, daughter of Dundas of Fingask, by a daughter of Bruce of Clackmannan. George Dundas died in 1684, and his wife, Catherine Moneypenny, in 1694. They had twelve children, of whom, John, the eldest surviving son, born in 1641, succeeded his father, and became

JOHN DUNDAS, of Duddingstoun. He married, in 1670, Anne, daughter of Sir David Carmichael, of Balmedie, descended from the ancient family of Carmichael of Carmichael, by the Hon. Anne Carmichael, daughter to James, first Lord Carmichael, and aunt to the first Earl of Hyndford. By her, who died in 1711, he had eight sons and four daughters, of whom

I. GEORGE, succeeded him.

II. David, *b.* in 1673, was called to the bar; he died unm.

III. John, of Newhalls, *b.* in 1682, *m.* Christian, daughter of David Mure, of Blackhorn, and had a son, DAVID, of Newhalls.

I. Anna, *b.* in 1677, *m.* to Moncrieff of Rhynd, and *d.* in 1728.

II. Isabella, *b.* in 1680, *m.* to Binning of Wallingford, and *d.* in 1724.

The eldest son,

GEORGE DUNDAS, of Duddingstoun, married Magdalen Lindsay-Craufurd, daughter of Patrick Lindsay-Craufurd, of Kilbirney, granddaughter of John Lindsay, fifteenth Earl Craufurd and first Earl of Lindsay, niece to James and William, Dukes of Hamilton, sister to John Lindsay-Craufurd, Viscount Garnock, and to Margaret, Countess of Glasgow. By this lady he had, among other children, who left no issue,

JOHN, his heir.

AGNES, wife of Gabriel Hamilton, of Westburn, a cadet of Hamilton of Torrance, and eventual inheritor of the estates.

The son and successor,

JOHN DUNDAS, of Duddingstoun, married Lady Margaret Hope, daughter to Charles, Earl of Hopetoun, by Lady Henrietta Johnstone, daughter of William, Marquis of Annandale. They had no issue; and on the death of John Dundas, the Duddingstoun estates passed for a few years to the heir male, David Dundas, of Newhalls, son of John, younger son of John Dundas, of Duddingstoun; but on his death they reverted to the daughter of George Dundas and Magdalen Lindsay-Craufurd,

AGNES DUNDAS, of Duddingstoun, who *m.* Gabriel Hamilton,† of Westburn, and had issue,

* Catherine Moneypenny's paternal grandmother was Euphemia Colville, daughter of Sir James Colville, of Easter Wemyss (father of the first Lord Colville), by Janet Douglas, of Lochleven, niece of William, Earl of Morton.

† SIR JOHN DE HAMILTON, Lord of Cadzow, married Janet, daughter of Sir James Douglas, of Dalkeith, and had three sons, viz.

I. JAMES (Sir), of Cadzow, ancestor to the ducal house of Hamilton.

II. David, ancestor of the Hamiltons of Dalserf.

III. THOMAS, of Darngaber.

The third son,

THOMAS HAMILTON, of Darngaber, married Helen, daughter of Sir Henry Douglas, of Lochleven, and had JAMES, ancestor of the Hamiltons of Raploch, represented by Hamilton of Barns, and

THOMAS HAMILTON, who *m.* the heiress of Torrance of Torrance, and was ancestor of the Hamiltons of Torrance, Westburn, Aitkenhead, and various other families. A cadet of the family of Torrance,

ANDREW HAMILTON, of Westburn, whose name occurs in a deed under the privy seal in 1604, was father of

GABRIEL HAMILTON, of Westburn, who lived during the protectorate of CROMWELL and the reign of CHARLES II. In 1646, he was one of the committee of war for the county of Lanark, and joining, after the restoration, the covenanters, had to endure severe pecuniary penalties. He *m.* Margaret, daughter of Cunninghame of Gilbert-

I. GABRIEL HAMILTON, of Westburn, *b.* in 1736, a captain in the army, died immediately after he had been amongst the first to enter the Moro Castle, at the Havannah.
II. Archibald Hamilton.
III. Hope-Archibald Hamilton.
IV. George Hamilton.
V. —— Hamilton.
VI. JOHN HAMILTON, *b.* in 1745, his father and mother's sole surviving son and heir.
VII. David Hamilton.

I. Margaret Hamilton, wife of Captain Nasmyth, R.N. and had no issue.
II. Graham-Christian Hamilton.
III. Agnes Hamilton.
IV. Agnes Hamilton.
V. Magdalen-Elizabeth Hamilton.
VI. Christian Hamilton, wife of the Hon. Charles Napier, of Merchiston Hall, second son of Francis, fifth Lord Napier, by Lady Henrietta Hope, daughter of Charles, Earl of Hopetoun, and was mother of

1. Francis Napier.
2. Hamilton Napier.
3. CHARLES NAPIER, of the royal navy, *recently* so celebrated by the victory he achieved as admiral of the fleet of DONNA MARIA, Queen of Portugal, by whom he has been created Count Cape St. Vincent. He is married and has issue.
4. Thomas-Erskine Napier, of Woodcote, a colonel in the army, who married Miss Margaret Falconner, and has one daughter.

1. Harriet Napier, wife of George Gordon, of Hallhead, nephew to the Earl of Aberdeen and the Duchess of Gordon, and has issue.
2. Agnes-Dundas Napier, died in 1816 unmarried.
3. Christian-Graham Napier, who died in 1811, *m.* Charles Campbell, of Combie, and had issue.

VII. Mary-Anne Hamilton, *m.* to Robert Gray, of Carntyne, representative of the families of Gray of Dalmarnock, and Hamilton of Newton, and had an only son,

John-Hamilton Gray, of Carntyne, born in December, 1800, in holy orders, vicar of Bolsover and Scarcliff, in the county of Derby, who married Miss Johnstone, of Alva, and has one daughter.

Gabriel Hamilton, of Westburn, died many years before his wife, Agnes Dundas, who lived to a very advanced age, dying about the year 1798. During a long widowhood she achieved the difficult task of restoring the dilapidated estates of her husband's family, and at the close of her life found herself seated with augmented wealth in the ancient halls of her youth, in which she was succeeded by her eldest surviving son,

JOHN HAMILTON-DUNDAS, of Duddingstoun and Westburn, who inherited all the family estates. He married Grizzel, daughter of John Hamilton, of Barns, representative of the great Raploch branch of the house of Hamilton, descended from John, Lord of Cadzow. By her he had

GABRIEL, his heir.
John, David, James, George, — who died before their father, all officers in the army, navy, or the East India Company's service.
Marion.
Agnes.
Margaret.
Magdalen-Elizabeth.
Eleanor.

Mr. Hamilton-Dundas died in 1820, and was succeeded by his only surviving son, the present GABRIEL HAMILTON-DUNDAS, esq. of Duddingstoun.

---

field, by a daughter of Cunninghame of Craigends, a cadet of Glencairne, and had issue,

I. GABRIEL, his heir.
II. ARCHIBALD, successor to his brother.
III. James.

I. Elizabeth, *m.* to James Hamilton, of Newton, cadet of Silverton Hill, and had a daughter, Elizabeth, wife of John Gray, of Dalmarnock.
II. ——, wife of A. Lang, esq. of Overton, in Dumbartonshire.
III. ——, *m.* to Buchanan of Achintoshaw, in Dumbartonshire.

Gabriel Hamilton died in 1669, and was *s.* by his son,

GABRIEL HAMILTON, of Westburn, who died without issue, and was succeeded by his brother,

ARCHIBALD HAMILTON, of Westburn, who *m.* first, a daughter of Hay of Craignethan, but had no issue; and secondly, Margaret, daughter of Claud Hamilton, of Barns, representative of the family of Raploch, by Anne, daughter of Sir Walter Stewart, of Allanton, and had,

I. GABRIEL, his heir.
II. Robert, died without issue.

I. Anne, *m.* to the Rev. Mr. Millar, of Millheugh, minister of Hamilton, and was mother of John Millar, the celebrated lawyer, and author of "Essays on the British Constitution and the Origin of Ranks."

He was succeeded by his son,

GABRIEL HAMILTON, of Westburn, who married, as stated in the text, AGNES DUNDAS, heiress of Duddingstoun.

### Families of Lindsay and Crawfurd.

On the death of Lady Mary Lindsay Crawfurd, in 1833, the representation of these distinguished families devolved on her nearest relatives the Earl of Glasgow and Mr. Hamilton Dundas.

#### Family of Lindsay.

William de Lindsay, lived in the reign of David I. of Scotland. He is mentioned in 1145. His descendant,

David de Lindsay, who died 1230, *m.* the daughter and co-heir of John de Craufurd, and with her acquired the barony of Craufurd. His descendant,

Sir David Lindsay, of Craufurd, married, in 1325, Mary, daughter and co-heir of the great house of Abernethy, and had three sons, founders of the great branches of the family of Lindsay,

- I. Sir James Lindsay, of Craufurd, ancestor to the first branch, the Earls of Craufurd.
- II. Sir Alexander Lindsay, of Glenesk, ancestor to the Earls of Balcarras.
- III. Sir William Lindsay, of Byres, ancestor to the Lords Lindsay, of the Byers who became Earls of Craufurd, of the second branch, the second subdivision of which branch is represented by Mr. Hamilton Dundas conjointly with the Earl of Glasgow.

The last descendant of the elder brother, (Sir James Lindsay, of Craufurd), was Ludovic, fourteenth Earl of Craufurd, who died about 1646. He resigned his titles to the crown, and obtained a new patent in favour of John, Lord Lindsay, of the Byres.

This John, Lord Lindsay, was the representative of the third of the above mentioned brothers. He was lord high treasurer of Scotland, and had been created, 1641, Earl of Lindsay, and on the death of Earl Ludovic became fifteenth Earl of Crawford. He married Lady Margaret Hamilton, daughter to James, second marquis, and sister to James and William, first and second Dukes of Hamilton. By her he had,

- I. William, his heir.
- II. Patrick, of whom hereafter.
- I. Anne, wife of John, Duke of Rothes.
- II. Christian, wife of John, Earl of Haddington.
- III. Helen, wife of Sir Robert Sinclair, of Hevenson, bart.
- IV. Elizabeth, wife of David, Earl of Northesk.

The eldest son,

William, sixteenth Earl of Craufurd and second Earl of Lindsay, was ancestor of the first subdivision of the second branch of the Earls of Craufurd, which failed in the person of General John Craufurd, eighteenth earl, in 1749, when the titles and estates devolved on the descendants of Patrick, second son of the fifteenth earl, and nephew of the Duke of Hamilton; which

Patrick Lindsay, married, in 1664, Margaret Craufurd, daughter and heiress of Sir John Craufurd, of Kilbirney, and assumed the surname and arms of Craufurd. By her he had,

- I. John.
- I. Margaret, wife of David, Earl of Glasgow, great grandmother of the present earl.
- II. Anne, wife of Hon. Henry Maule, son of the Earl of Panmure. Her son, Lord Maule, *d.* without issue.
- III. Magdalen, wife of George Dundas, of Duddingstoun, great grandmother of Mr. Hamilton Dundas.

The Hon. P. Lindsay Craufurd was *s.* by his son,

John Lindsay Craufurd, who was created, in 1703, Viscount of Garnock. His grandson,

George, fourth Viscount Garnock, succeeded to the earldoms of Crawford and Lindsay on the death of General John Craufurd, the eighteenth earl, in 1749, and became nineteenth earl of the second subdivision of the second branch. His son,

George Lindsay Crauford, twentieth earl, died without issue, in 1808, when the honours of the family became dormant, as they continue. His lordship's sister,

Lady Mary Lindsay Crawfurd, *d.* unm. in 1833, and was succeeded in the estates, both of the Crauford and Garnock families, by the Earl of Glasgow, as heir of entail, while the honour of representing these two distinguished families is divided between his lordship and Mr. Hamilton Dundas, as the descendants of two sisters, co-heiresses of line.

#### Family of Craufurd, of Kilbirney.

Galfridus de Crawfurd lived in the reign of *King* William *the Lion*, in the latter part of the twelfth century; and is supposed (from strong presumptive evidence, see vol. ii. p. xiv.) to have sprung from a younger son of the old Earls of Richmond.

Sir John Crawfurd, of Crawfurd, his successor, *d.* in 1248, in the reign of Alexander II., and left two daughters, his coheirs, the elder was wife of Hugh de Douglas, progenitor of the family of Douglas, and the younger was wife of David de Lindsay, ancestor of the first and second branches of the Earls of Crawford, and of the Earls of Balcarras.

But besides this family, which was accounted the chief of the name, another branch of the Crawfurds was settled in Ayrshire. Sir Reginald Crawfurd lived about the year 1220, and married Margaret, heiress of James, Lord of Loudon; their descendants were the powerful family of CRAWFURD, OF LOUDON, which ended in an heiress, Susannah, married to Sir Duncan Campbell, and hence sprang the Earls of Loudon. (See vol. i. p. 551.)

MALCOLM CRAWFURD, of the Loudon family, married the dau. and co-heiress of Galbraith, Lord of Greenock, by whom he had

MALCOLM CRAWFURD, who in the reign of JAMES III. married Marjory, daughter and heiress of John Barclay, of Kilbirney, the last of the male line of the distinguished race of Barclay, Lords of Ardrossan. By her he had

MALCOLM CRAUFURD, of Kilbirney, who obtained a charter of the lands of Kilbirney, in 1499. He married Marion Crighton, daughter to Robert, Lord Sanquhar, and dying in 1500, was *s.* by

ROBERT CRAWFURD, of Kilbirney, who *m.* Margaret, sister to the first Lord Semple, and had a son,

LAWRENCE CRAWFURD, of Kilbirney. It appears that a portion of the ancient lordship of Crawfurd, in Lanarkshire, (the greater part of which had passed to the Lindsays, Earls of Crawfurd, by marriage,) still continued in the possession of the house of Kilbirney, as descended from this ancient stock. These remnants of the barony of Crawfurd, this Lawrence exchanged with Sir James Hamilton, of Finnart, for the lands of Drumray, in Dumbartonshire. He also made a pious and charitable donation in 1547, the year of his death. He *m.* Helen Campbell, daughter of Sir Hugh Campbell, of Loudon, by whom he had,

- I. HUGH.
- II. John, of Easter Greenock.
- III. Thomas, ancestor to the Crawfurds, barts. of Jordanhill, and the Crawfurds, of Cartsburn.

The eldest son and heir,

HUGH CRAWFURD, of Kilbirney, a zealous adherent of *Queen* MARY, had by Margaret his wife, daughter of Sir John Colquhoun, of Seep, a son and successor,

MALCOLM CRAWFURD, of Kilbirney, who *m.* Margaret, daughter of John Cuningham, of Glengarnock, by whom he left at his decease, in 1595, a son and heir,

JOHN CRAWFURD, of Kilbirney, who *m.* Margaret, daughter of John Blair, of Blair, and dying in 1622, was succeeded by his son,

JOHN CRAWFURD, of Kilbirney. He *m.* Mary, daughter of James, Earl of Glencairn, and died in 1629. His son,

SIR JOHN CRAWFURD, of Kilbirney, created a BARONET in 1642, died in 1661. He *m.* first, Margaret Balfour, daughter of Robert Lord Burleigh, and secondly, Magdalen, daughter of David, Lord Carnegie, son and heir of David, first Earl of Southesk, by the latter he left at his decease, in 1661, two daughters,

- I. ANNE, wife of Sir Archibald Stewart, bart. of Blackhall and Ardgowan.
- II. MARGARET, on whom her father settled his estate, obliging her heirs to bear the name of Craufurd. This lady,

MARGARET CRAUFURD, of Kilbirney, *m.* Patrick Lindsay, second son of John, fifteenth Earl of Crawford and first Earl of Lindsay. The issue of this marriage were only three,

- I. JOHN, great grandfather of the late and twentieth Earl of Craufurd, and of Lady Mary Lindsay Craufurd.
- I. MARGARET, wife of David, Earl of Glasgow. Her ladyship was great-grandmother to the present Earl of Glasgow.
- II. MAGDALEN, *m.* to GEORGE DUNDAS, of Duddingstoun, and was great-grandmother of GABRIEL HAMILTON DUNDAS, esq. of Duddingstoun.

*Arms*—Quarterly, first and fourth, arg. a lion rampant gu. langued az. holding within his paws a man's heart, ppr. for DUNDAS, of Duddingstoun; second and third, gu. three cinquefoils pierced ermine, within a bordure potent and counterpotent of the second and the first, for HAMILTON, of WESTBURN. Quartering Lyndesay, Crawfurd, Dreghorn, &c.

*Crests*—First, a hand, holding a star az. for DUNDAS; second, a hand, holding a spear ppr., for HAMILTON.

*Mottoes*—Essayez, for DUNDAS. Et arma et Virtus, for HAMILTON.

*Estates*—In West Lothian and Lanarkshire.

*Seats*—Duddingstoun, in West Lothian, and Ruchill, in Lanarkshire; Westburn and Gilbertfield Tower, the old seats of the Hamiltons and Cunninghames, were sold ten years ago.

## WILSON, OF ESHTON HALL.

WILSON, MATTHEW, esq. of Eshton Hall, in the county of York, *b.* 10th August, 1772; *m.* at Gargrave 24th November, 1800, his first cousin, Mary-Clive, only surviving daughter and heiress of Matthew Wilson, esq. of Eshton Hall, and widow of the Rev. Henry Richardson-Currer; by this lady he has issue,

I. MATTHEW, a magistrate for the West Riding, and for the county of Lancaster, baptized at Gargrave 26th October, 1802; educated at Harrow School; gentleman commoner and B. A. of Brazennose, Oxford; married 15th June, 1826, at St. James's, Westminster, Sophia-Louisa-Emerson, only daughter and heiress of Sir Wharton Amcotts, bart. of Kettlethorpe, in the county of Lincoln, twenty years M.P. for East Retford, (by Amelia-Teresa Campbell, his second wife,) and by her, who died at Kildwick Hall 29th September, 1833, and was buried at Gargrave, has one surviving son,

MATTHEW-WHARTON, *b.* at Bierley Hall 20th March, 1827, baptized at Gargrave.

II. Henry-Currer, in holy orders, *b.* 8th October, 1803, registered at Gargrave 2nd April, 1806, A. M. of Lincoln College, Oxford, rector of Marton and vicar of Tunstal.

I. Margaret-Frances-Anne-Clive, baptized at Gargrave.

II. Frances-Mary, baptized at Gargrave.

III. Henrietta-Fourness, baptized at Gargrave, *m.* there 10th November, 1829, Charles Hampden, only son of Charles-Hampden Turner, esq. of Rook's Nest, near Godstone, Surrey, by Mary Rhode his wife, and has one son, Charles Hampden, *b.* 27th January, 1832, and two daughters, Henrietta-Margaret-Mary and Frances-Sarah Hampden.

Mr. Wilson is a magistrate and deputy lieutenant for the West Riding and for the county of Lancaster. He rebuilt Eshton Hall in the years 1825 and 1826.

### Lineage.

MATTHEW WILSON, esq. a merchant, of London, son of Robert and Alice Wilson, of Brigsteare, in the parish of Haversham, in Westmoreland, settled this family at Eshton, by purchasing the hall, estate, and manor, together with the lands of Nether Heselden, in the parish of Arnecliffe, from Sir Robert Bindloss, bart. of Borwick Hall, in the county of Lancaster. The conveyance bears date 21st January, 1646, and he came to reside at Eshton Hall, 30th May, 1648. He died in London, November, 1656, and was buried in St. Mary's, Abchurch. His successor,

JOHN WILSON, esq. of Eshton Hall, during whose minority Captain John Backhouse, of Yellands, and his wife, Agnes, sister of the said Matthew, resided at Eshton Hall, (afterwards at Nether Heselden, devised them by his will), inherited in 1684 from Thomas Hammond, of Thresfield Hall, all that gentleman's estates. In 1700, he resigned Eshton to his eldest son, Matthew, and passed the remainder of his life at Threshfield Hall, where he died 7th May, 1706, intestate, and was buried at Gargrave. At his death his property was valued at £500 per annum in land and £5000 money. His younger children received £1250 each. By Dorothy, his wife, who was buried at Gargrave, 9th October, 1684, he had issue,

I. MATTHEW, his heir.

II. John, baptized at Gargrave in 1678, *d.* in 1705.

III. Francis, baptized at Gargrave, 27th February, 1681, who resided many years at Threshfield Hall, but he afterwards purchased and settled at

Crownest, near Settle. He *m.* Margaret, daughter of Anthony Sparke, esq. of Bishop Auckland, and had an only daughter and heiress,

DOROTHY, *m.* to — Bowser, esq. of Bishop Auckland.

I. Dorothy, baptized at Gargrave in 1682, *m.* there, 17th May, 1701, to Henry Coulthurst, esq. of Gargrave, and died in 1708. She had six sons, who all died without issue.

II. Anne, baptized at Gargrave, 18th April, 1683, *m.* at Linton, 9th April, 1706, John Tennant, gent. of Chapel House, in the parish of Burnsal, and by him (who wedded, secondly, Jane Serjeantson, maternal aunt of the late Lord Grantley,) had issue, who all died young excepting Dorothy, the wife of Samuel Dunn, esq. of Howden.

John Wilson was *s.* at his decease by his eldest son,

MATTHEW WILSON, esq. of Eshton Hall, educated at Trinity College, Cambridge, who *m.* Anne, daughter of Francis Blackbourne, esq. of Marrick Abbey, in Swaledale, and by her, who was buried at Gargrave, 13th March, 1723, had five sons and four daughters, viz.

I. John, died an infant in 1705.

II. MATTHEW, heir to his father.

III. Timothy, died an infant in 1711-12.

IV. Roger, LL.B. baptized at Gargrave, 20th October, 1711, of Emanuel College, Cambridge, vicar of Wiggenhall, St. Magdalen, Norfolk, and incumbent curate of the parochial chapel of Colne, in Lancashire. He *m.* Thomasine, daughter of Thomas Bate, esq. of Garbaldisham, in Norfolk, and died in 1789 (he was buried at Otley), having had a daughter, Elizabeth, who died young, and a son,

Matthew, of Manor House, Otley, deputy-lieutenant for Lancashire, and for the North Riding of the county of York, late captain in the 4th regiment of Royal Lancashire Militia, *m.* Martha, daughter and co-heiress of William Barcroft, esq. of Foulridge Hall and Moyna, and died 28th February, 1826.

V. William, died young.

I. Catherine, *m.* to Mr. Thomas Swainson, of Stockport.

II. Dorothy, baptized at Gargrave, 7th January, 1701-2, *m.* to Hugh Tillotson, esq. of Skipton, and had a son, Matthew Tillotson, who died 8th March, 1815, leaving all his estates to Matthew Wilson, esq. of Eshton Hall.

III. Anne, baptized in 1703, *m.* first, to Mr. John Swainson, of Skipton; and secondly, to James Morley, esq. of Scale House. The ancestor of the latter gentleman, Francis Morley, esq. of Winnington, married Cassandra Lambert, sister of the celebrated parliamentary general.

IV. Elizabeth, *m.* to Mr. Samuel John Swire, of Swadford, of the Cononley family (see vol. ii. p. 342).

Matthew Wilson died in 1717, was interred at Gargrave 12th November, and succeeded by his son,

MATTHEW WILSON, esq. of Eshton Hall, baptized at Gargrave 14th October, 1706, of Trinity College, Cambridge, who married Margaret, daughter of Henry Wiglesworth, esq. of Staidburn, by Anne, his first wife, daughter and co-heiress of John Cromack, esq. of Wiswall, near Whalley,* and had issue,

I. MATTHEW, his heir.

II. Henry, A.M. of St. John's College, Cambridge, rector of Staidburn and vicar of Otley, baptized at Gargrave, 23rd January, 1723, *m.* Anne, daughter and heiress of Thomas Fourness, esq. of Otley, and left at his decease, 13th December, 1781 (he was buried at Otley, where a monument is erected to his memory), two sons and one daughter, viz.

1. Thomas-Fourness, in holy orders, B.A. of Trinity College, Cambridge, *b.* 22nd July, 1769, now of Burley Hall, near Otley, perpetual curate of Silsden and White Chapels, a magistrate for the liberties of Cawood, Wistow, and Otley, *m.* at York, 1st March, 1813, Eleanor, daughter of Sir Robert Eden, bart. of Windlestone House, in Durham, and niece of the Lords Auckland and Henley. By her he has issue,

   1. John-Eden, *b.* 30th November, 1813.
   2. Morton-Eden, *b.* 30th June, 1817.
   3. Thomas-Fourness, *b.* 17th May, 1819.
   4. Robert, *b.* 6th May, 1822.

   1. Eleanor-Anne.
   2. Maria-Frances.

2. MATTHEW, now of Eshton Hall.

* By Anne, his wife, daughter and heiress of John Brigges, esq. of Sawley. The other daughter and co-heiress of Cromack was second wife of John Bradyll, esq. of Portfield.

I. Rebecca, *m.* at Otley, 27th August, 1811, to John Tennant Stansfield Tennant, esq. of Chapel House, late in the commission of the peace, and captain in the 3rd West York Militia. By him, who died 14th August, 1830, and was buried in Otley Church, she left at her decease, 8th December, 1819, being interred at Coniston Chapel, one son, John-Robert, *b.* 17th January, 1815, and Margaret-Anne-Wilson.

I. Anne, died an infant.

II. Margaret, baptized at Gargrave, 10th September, 1734, *m.* at Skipton, 15th August, 1763, the Rev. Thomas Butler, rector of Bentham and Whittington, and archdeacon of the diocese of Chester, youngest son of Edmund Butler, esq. of Kirkland Hall, in Lancashire. She died 24th March, 1818, and was buried at Bentham, having had three sons and four daughters, all now deceased except Jane, relict of E. Thornton, esq. of Whittington Hall, Westmoreland.

Mr. Wilson died 27th March, 1769, was buried at Gargrave, and succeeded by his son,

MATTHEW WILSON, esq. of Eshton Hall, of St. John's College, Cambridge, barrister-at-law, *b.* 12th February, 1730, and registered at Gargrave. He *m.* 7th July, 1759, Frances,* daughter of Richard Clive, esq. of Styche, in the county of Salop, member for Montgomeryshire in several successive parliaments, and sister of Robert, first Lord Clive. By this lady, who was born 12th February, 1734, and died 3rd October, 1798, he left at his decease, 16th April, 1802, (being buried at Gargrave, where a monument is erected to himself and his wife,) an only daughter and heiress,

MARGARET-CLIVE WILSON, of Eshton Hall, *b.* 22nd April, 1764, who wedded, first, at Gargrave, 3rd February, 1783, the Rev. Henry Richardson, A.M. rector of Thornton, who assumed shortly before his death the surname and arms of CURRER, upon inheriting the estates of Sarah Currer (see p. 94), and had by him, who died 10th November, 1784, and was buried at Thornton, where a monument is erected to his memory, an only daughter,

FRANCES-MARY RICHARDSON-CURRER, heiress to her father and representative of the ancient families of Richardson of Bierley and Currer of Kildwick (see p. 111).

The heiress of Eshton married, secondly, at Gargrave, 24th November, 1800, her first cousin, MATTHEW WILSON, esq. now of Eshton Hall.

*Arms*—Sa. a wolf rampant or, in chief three estoiles of the last.

*Crest*—A demi-wolf or.

*Motto*—Res non verba.

*Estates*—In the parishes and townships of Eshton, Gargrave, Sawley, Skipton, Carlton, Threshfield, Linton, Hebden, Arncliffe, Otley, Cowling, Winterburn cum Flasby, and Bank Newton, all in Yorkshire.

*Seat*—Eshton Hall, Gargrave, Craven.

---

* This lady lineally derived from the royal line of Plantagenet.

EDWARD I.=Eleanor of Castile

Lady Elizabeth Plantagenet=Humphrey de Bohun, Earl of Hereford

William de Bohun, Earl of Northampton=Elizabeth de Badlesmere

Elizabeth de Bohun=Richard Fitzalan, Earl of Arundel

Elizabeth Fitzalan, Duchess of Norfolk=Sir Robert Gousell, knt.

Joan Gousell=Thomas Stanley, baron and K.G.

Catherine Stanley=John Savage, of Clifton

John Savage=Dorothy Vernon

Alice Savage=William Brereton, of Brereton

William Brereton=Anne Booth

JANE BRERETON, who *m.* RICHARD CLIVE, esq., and from this marriage lineally descended FRANCES CLIVE, who wedded MATTHEW WILSON, esq. of Eshton.

# CLERK-RATTRAY, OF CRAIGHALL RATTRAY.

RATTRAY-CLERK, ROBERT, esq. of Craighall Rattray, in the shire of Perth, *b.* in December, 1796; *m.* in February, 1824, Christina, daughter of the late J. Richardson, esq. of Pitfour, and has issue,

JAMES, *b.* in October, 1832.
Adam, *b.* in December, 1833.
Elizabeth-Susan.
Jane.
Charlotte-Mary.
Helen-Christina.

Mr. Clerk-Rattray, who is a magistrate and deputy lieutenant for Perthshire, *s.* his father, the late James Clerk-Rattray, one of the barons of the Exchequer in Scotland, 29th August, 1831.

## Lineage.

The surname of Rattray is derived from the barony of the same name in the county of Perth, and was assumed at a very remote era. The first of the family upon record,

ALANUS DE RATHERIFF, who lived in the reigns of WILLIAM the Lion and ALEXANDER II. was father of

SIR THOMAS DE RATTRAY, who received the honour of knighthood from ALEXANDER III. By Christian his wife, he acquired part of the lands of Glencaveryn and Kincaldrum, in Forfarshire, as appears from an agreement, "super controversia inter dominum Thomam de Ratrey militem, actorem nomine Christinæ uxoris suæ, ex parte unâ, et viros religiosos abbat. et convent. de Aberbrothick ex altera; super limitibus terrarum de Glencaveryn et Kyncaldrum; &c." This deed, to which the seals of the earl of Buchan, the bishops of St. Andrews and Brechin, the earl of Marr, Sir Thomas Rattray and his spouse, are appended, bears date in 1253. In 1267, Sir Thomas witnessed a donation to the priory of St. Andrew, and in 1272 obtained from Simon, abbot of Dunfermline, the lands of Bendathen. He died shortly after, leaving EUSTATIUS his heir, and John, witness to a deed in the time of ALEXANDER III.

The elder,

EUSTATIUS DE RATREFF, designed "Dominus de eodem," *temp.* ALEXANDER III. was father of

SIR ADAM RATREFF, of Ratreff, who is styled in Prynne's Collections, "Nobilis vir dominus de Ratreff, anno 1291," and in Rymer's Fœd. Angl. when Sir Adam, with many others, was compelled to submit to *King* EDWARD I. it is stated, "Nobiles viri Adam de Retrefe et Willielmus de Maule fecerunt fidelitatem dicto regi, anno 1292." He testified a charter in Macfalane's Collections, wherein he is designed, "Dominus Adam de Retrefe *miles*," 4th October, 1294, and in 1296 was again compelled to swear allegiance to EDWARD of England. Sir Adam died before the year 1315, and was *s.* by his son,

ALEXANDER DE RATRIE, of that Ilk, one of the barons of the parliament held at Ayr in 1315 by Robert Bruce, to arrange the deed of succession to the crown. He died *s. p.* and was *s.* by his brother,

EUSTATIUS DE RATRIE, of that Ilk, who was tried for a conspiracy against ROBERT I. in August, 1320, but acquitted. His son and successor,

JOHN DE RATTRIE, of that Ilk, living in the reign of DAVID BRUCE, had, with a daughter, Margaret, wife of John de Meghill, of Meghill, a son and successor,

JOHN DE RATTRIE, of that Ilk, who is witness in a confirmation granted by Sir William Scot, of Balweary, "dilecto consanguineo suo Johanni de Lindsay, filio Alexandri Lindsay de Cavill en Fife," dated at Balweary, "in festo sanctæ Margaretæ Reginæ," 10th June, 1399. He died at the close of the reign of JAMES I. and was *s.* by his son,

PATRICK RATTRAY, of that Ilk, mentioned in a charter of Sir Walter Haliburton, 24th July, 1453, and in one to the monastery of Aberbrothick in 1456. He was father of

SIR SILVESTER RATTRAY, of that Ilk, who was appointed one of the ambassadors extraordinary to treat with the court of England, for which he obtained a safe conduct, dated 12th June, 1463, and is then designed "Dominus Silvester de Rattray miles." He was a person of great influence at the Scottish court, possessed an ample inheritance, and sat in the parliament of 1481. He *m.* Alison Hepburn, and had a son and successor,

SIR JOHN RATTRAY, of that Ilk, who was knighted by JAMES IV. He *m.* Elizabeth, daughter of James, second Lord Kennedy, and had three sons and one daughter, viz.

- I. JOHN, a military officer, who wedded Margaret Abercrombie, but died in Holland before his father, without issue.
- II. PATRICK, } successively heirs.
- III. SILVESTER, }
- I. Grizel, *m.* to John Stewart, third earl of Athol.

After the decease of Sir John, a calamitous and almost ruinous contest arose between his younger sons, and their brother-in-law the earl of Athol. Tradition affirms that the earl, having married Sir John's only daughter, deemed himself entitled to a portion at least of the Rattray estate, and being a person of great power and authority, came, with a considerable body of men, took possession of the castle of Rattray, and carried off the family writs; while Patrick Rattray, the second son, totally unable to resist so potent a nobleman, retired to the castle of Craighall, which he gallantly defended, and succeeded in holding together with the lands of Craighall and Kinballoch; the Athol family continuing to possess the greater part of the lands of Rattray, until they were evicted from them by an appraising at the instance of Sir Robert Crichton, of Clunie, about the beginning of the seventeenth century. The said

PATRICK RATTRAY, dying unmarried, the representation of the family devolved upon his brother,

SILVESTER RATTRAY, who endeavoured to serve himself heir to his father and brothers at Perth, in which county his lands lay, but found it impossible, because (as the writ bears) the earl of Athol and his friends are "magnæ potestatis et fortitudinis" in that town. Rattray applied in consequence to *King* JAMES V. and obtained from his majesty a commission under the great seal to have service done at Dundee. In this commission it is narrated that Patrick, his brother, had been "postpositus et impeditus" for the space of twelve years by the said earl, from getting himself served in the lands that fell to him by the death of his father and brother John; and that, post lites magnasque expensas per dictum Patricium in præfata materia, præfatus comes misit Walterum Leslie, Johannem Stewart, alias John of Lorn, Thomas Laing, David Stewart, suos servitores, et eorum complices, et dictum Patricium in sua capella ipsius loci de Kynballoch interficere causavit: et idem Silvester informatur, quod dictus comes, et sui complices, sibi similiter facere intendunt, si sua brevia de hujusmodi terris prosequi volet." This extraordinary commission is dated at Edinburgh 17th October, 1533, to which the great seal is appended, and in consequence Silvester Rattray was served heir to his father Sir John, and to his brothers John and Patrick, in the barony of Craighall and Kynballoch, and infeft therein at Dundee in 1534. He *m.* Marjory, daughter of Andrew, third Lord Gray, (relict of Kennenmouth, of that Ilk,) and had, with a daughter, Elizabeth, *m.* to John Blair, of Ardblair, a son and successor,

DAVID RATTRAY, of Craighall and Kynballoch, who was served heir to his father before the sheriff of Perth, in the lands of Kynballoch, and certain others lying within the barony of Rattray, *anno* 1554. He wedded Isabel, daughter of Alexander Ramsay, of Banff, and had two sons,

- GEORGE, his heir.
- Silvester, minister at Auchtergevan, ancestor of Rattray, of Dalnoon.

David Rattray, who got a charter in 1566, from Richard Livingstone and John Spens, the commissioners for receiving resignations and granting new infeftments of church-lands, of the estate of Chapletoun, died in the commencement of the reign of JAMES VI. and was succeeded by his eldest son,

GEORGE RATTRAY, of Craighall, served heir to his father before the sheriff of Perth, 6th August, 1586. He *m.* Janet, daughter of George Drummond, of Blair, and had a son and successor,

SILVESTER RATTRAY, of Craighall, infeft in all his father's lands by a charter under the great seal, dated 26th October, 1604. He *m.* Agnes, daughter of Lambie, of Dunkenie, and had two sons, viz.

- DAVID, his heir.
- Silvester, bred to the church, progenitors of the RATTRAYS of Persie.

The elder son,

DAVID RATTRAY, of Craighall, served heir to his father 22nd June, 1613, obtained from CHARLES I. a charter of the lands and barony of Myretown, Herries, the four merk land of Skeith, the forty shilling land of Meltone, Kirkinner, &c. in the shire of Wigton, dated 2nd February, 1629, and subsequently (in 1640) from the same monarch, of the lands and barony of Saltoun, in the counties of East and Midlothian. He died soon after, and by Agnes Hay, his wife, left a son,

PATRICK RATTRAY, of Craighall, who, upon his own resignation, got a charter under the great seal from CHARLES I. dated 28th February, 1648, of the lands of Craighall, Kynballock, &c. containing a *Novodamus*, and erecting them into a free barony, to be called Craighall Rattray, in all time coming. He *m.* Anne Drummond, daughter of John, second Lord Maderty, and had, with a daughter, *m.* to Ogilvie, of Balfour, a son and successor,

JAMES RATTRAY, of Craighall, who had a charter under the great seal, dated 30th April, 1672, of the lands of Chapletoun, &c. containing a *Novodamus*. He was afterwards served heir in general before the sheriff of Perth, to Sir John Rattray, of that Ilk, who was "tritavus patris Jacobi Rattray, de Craighall, latoris praesentium;" and at the same time, heir in special to Patrick, his father. He wedded Elizabeth, daughter of Sir George Hay, of Meginch, and had a son,

DR. THOMAS RATTRAY, of Craighall, a man of singular piety and learning, who was served heir to his father before the sheriff of Perth, on the 13th July, 1692. He espoused Margaret Galloway, daughter of Thomas, Lord Dunkeld, and had two sons and three daughters, viz.

- I. JAMES, of Craighall, who *m.* Marjory, daughter of John Graham, esq. of Balgowan, and had issue.
- II. John, an eminent surgeon in Edinburgh, who *m.* first, Christian, daughter of George Main, esq. of that city; and secondly, Mary, daughter of George Lockhart, esq. of Carnwath. By both wives he had issue.

- I. MARGARET, *m.* to Dr. Clerk, sprung from a scion of Pennywick; of this lady hereafter.
- II. Jean, *m.* first, to Sir James Elphinstone, bart. and secondly, to Colonel George Mure, a brother of Caldwell.
- III. Grisel, *m.* to William Macewen, esq. writer to the signet.

Dr. Rattray died in 1743, and was *s.* by his elder son, James. His eldest daughter, (by whose descendant Craighall Rattray is now possessed),

MARGARET RATTRAY, wedded in 1720, the celebrated Dr. John Clerk, president of the Royal College of Physicians, at Edinburgh, and for more than thirty years the first medical practitioner in Scotland. He purchased the lands of Listonshiels and Spittal, in Midlothian, and got a charter under the great seal. By Margaret, his wife, Dr. Clerk had five sons and one daughter, viz.

- I. THOMAS CLERK, of Listonshiels.
- II. Robert Clerk, a colonel in the army.
- III. DAVID CLERK, of whom presently.
- IV. Hugh Clerk, in the East India Company's service, died unm.
- V. Duncan Clerk, a Lisbon merchant.

- I. Margaret Clerk, died unm.

Dr. Clerk's third son,

DAVID CLERK, M.D. of Edinburgh, physician to the royal infirmary, married Helen, daughter of James Duff, esq. of Craigston, in the county of Aberdeen, and dying in 1768, left two sons, JAMES and Robert, by whom the elder,

JAMES CLERK, esq. became of "Craighall Rattray," and assumed the surname of RATTRAY. This gentleman distinguished himself at the Scottish bar, and was constituted a baron of the Exchequer. He *m.* in January, 1791, Jane, daughter of Admiral Duff, of Fetteresso, and dying in 1831, left, with one daughter, Jane, a son and successor, the present ROBERT CLERK-RATTRAY, esq. of Craighall Rattray.

*Arms*—Az. three cross crosslets fitchee or.

*Crest*—On a mullet, a flaming heart ppr.

*Supporters*—Two serpents.

*Motto*—Super sidera votum.

*Estates*—Craighall Rattray, in Perthshire, traced in the family to the eleventh century; Bonnington, in Midlothian, acquired in 1774.

*Seats*—Craighall Rattray.

## CORBETT, OF ELSHAM AND DARNHALL.

CORBETT, THOMAS-GEORGE, esq. of Elsham, in the county of Lincoln, and of Darnhall, in Cheshire, succeeded his father 8th February, 1832. Mr. Corbett represents the Northern Division of Lincolnshire in parliament.

## Lineage.

This is a junior branch of one of the most noble and ancient families, whose descent can be traced, by authentic records, to a period preceding the Norman Conquest.

CORBET (to whom Le Carpentier, in his *Histoire du Cambray*, gives the surname of Hugh), was a man of considerable importance in the Pais de Caux, in Normandy. He had four sons, Hugh, Roger, Renaud, and Robert. Hugh, the eldest son, was like his father, a knight, and from him descended the Corbets of France. Renaud, the third son, was the ancestor of the Corbets of Flanders. Roger and Robert, the second and fourth sons, accompanied their father in the expedition of the CONQUEROR, and obtained from that monarch large possessions, chiefly in Shropshire, where their relation, Roger de Montgomery, earl of Shrewsbury, was their patron and lord paramount.

ROBERT CORBET, the fourth son, and younger of the two brothers who came with their father to England, held fifteen manors in Shropshire, under Earl Roger de Montgomery; his male line ended with his son, Robert Corbet, lord of Alcester, who left no issue, though many genealogists (See BURKE's *Extinct Peerage*, &c.) have erroneously described him as the ancestor of the Barons Corbet, of Caus, of whom hereafter.

ROGER CORBET, the second son of Corbet, and elder of the two brothers who served under the NORMAN, held twenty-four manors in Shropshire, and one in Montgomeryshire, from his kinsman, Earl Roger de Montgomery, and was also highly in the confidence of Robert de Belesme, the third Earl of Shrewsbury. This Roger Corbet, the progenitor of all the Shropshire Corbets and their various branches, had three sons, William, Ebraid, and Simon.

WILLIAM CORBET, the eldest son, was seated at Wattlesborough, in the county of Salop, and had three sons, viz.

I. THOMAS.
II. ROBERT (Sir), of Caus, knt. whose younger son, Richard, accompanied *King* RICHARD I. to the siege of Acon. The eldest son, Sir Robert Corbet, was lord of Caus, in the 22nd HENRY II. and was ancestor of the Barons Corbet, of Caus, now extinct, (see BURKE's *Extinct Peerage*), and of the Corbets, formerly of Leigh, but now of Sundorne Castle, near Shrewsbury.
III. Philip.

The eldest son,

THOMAS CORBET, succeeded his father, at Wattlesborough, and had two sons,

I. ROGER, his heir.
II. Thomas, ancestor of the Corbets of Hadley, and King's Bromley, which line ended in an heiress, married to John Grevile, in the reign of HENRY V.

The elder son,

ROGER CORBET, succeeded at Wettlesborough, and was father of

SIR RICHARD CORBET, knt. who married Joan, daughter and heiress of Bartholomew Thoret, of Moreton, otherwise Moreton Thoret, in the county of Salop, now called Moreton Corbet, and still in the possession of the lineal descendants of this marriage. Sir Richard removed from Wattlesborough to Moreton, where he was succeeded by his son,

RICHARD CORBET, father of

SIR ROBERT CORBET, knt. of Moreton Corbet, sheriff of Shropshire in 1288, who, by his wife, Matilda, was father of

SIR THOMAS CORBET, knt. of Moreton Corbet, whose son,

SIR ROBERT CORBET, knt. of Moreton Corbet, died in the 49th EDWARD III. and was succeeded by his son,

SIR ROGER CORBET, knt. of Moreton Corbet, who acquired the estate of Shawbury, in the county of Salop, (now the property of his descendant, Sir Andrew Corbet, bart.) by marriage with Margaret de Erdington, the heiress of that place. Their son,

ROBERT CORBET, of Moreton Corbet, was sheriff of Shropshire in 1419, and married Margaret, daughter of Sir William Mallory, knt. Their son,

SIR ROGER CORBET, knt. of Moreton Corbet, married Elizabeth, daughter and sole heir of Thomas Hopton, of Hopton

Castle, in the county of Salop, by whom he was father of

SIR RICHARD CORBET, knt. of Moreton Corbet, who married Elizabeth, daughter of Walter, Lord Ferrers, of Chartley; and their son,

SIR ROBERT CORBET, knt. of Moreton Corbet, sheriff of Shropshire in 1507, married Elizabeth, daughter of Sir Henry Vernon, knt. of Nether Haddon. She survived her husband fifty years, and was called "the old Lady Corbet, of Shawbury." She had by Sir Robert Corbet, with three daughters, three sons, viz.

- I. ROGER (Sir), his heir.
- II. Richard, sheriff of Shropshire in 1561.
- III. Reginald, who married Alice, sister and co-heir of William Gratewood, of Adderley and Stoke-upon-Tern, in the county of Salop, whose father, John Gratewood, became possessed of those estates by marriage with Jane, sister and co-heir of Sir Rowland Hill, knt. lord mayor of London. This Reginald Corbet was a judge in the North Wales circuit, and a justice of the queen's bench, and was ancestor of the line of Corbet, of Stoke and Adderley, baronets, now extinct.

The eldest son,

SIR ROGER CORBET, succeeded his father at Moreton Corbet. He was sheriff of Shropshire in 1530, and married Ann, daughter of Andrew Lord Windsor, by which lady he had issue,

- I. ANDREW (Sir), his heir.
- II. Walter.
- III. Robert.
- IV. Jerome.

Sir Roger was *s.* by his son,

Sir ANDREW CORBET, knt. of Moreton Corbet, who was sheriff of Shropshire in 1551. By his wife, Jane, daughter of Sir Robert Needham, knt. he had seven sons and three daughters, viz.

- I. ROBERT, his heir.
- II. Richard (Sir), knt. of whom hereafter.
- III. Reginald, } who all *d. s. p.*
- IV. Roger, }
- V. Francis, }
- VI. Vincent (Sir), knt. of whom hereafter, as ancestor of the Corbets, now of Moreton Corbet, and Corbetts of Elsham and Darnhall.
- VII. Arthur, *d. s. p.*

- I. Anne, married Sir Walter Leveson, knt. of Lilleshall.
- II. Margaret, married Thomas Harley, esq. of Brampton Bryan.
- III. Mary.

The eldest son,

ROBERT CORBET, succeeded his father in 1578, and received the honour of knighthood. He married Ann, daughter of Oliver, Lord St. John, of Bletsoe, by whom he had two daughters, who conveyed large estates to their husbands, viz. Elizabeth, wife of Sir Henry Wallop, knt. (ancestor of the Earl of Portsmouth), and Anne, wife of Sir Adolphus Carey, knt. In the Moreton Corbet estates, however, he was succeeded by his brother,

SIR RICHARD CORBET, knight of the Bath, who died without issue, in 1606, and was succeeded by his eldest surviving brother,

SIR VINCENT CORBET, knt. of Moreton Corbet, who married Frances, daughter and heir of William Humfreston, esq. of Humfreston, in the county of Salop, and had issue,

- I. SIR ANDREW CORBET, knt. of Moreton Corbet, who married Elizabeth, daughter of William Boothby, esq. and was ancestor of the present SIR ANDREW CORBET, bart. of Moreton Corbet, (See BURKE'S *Peerage and Baronetage*), and of SIR VINCENT CORBET, bart. whose widow, Dame Sarah Corbet, was created VISCOUNTESS CORBET, of Linslade, for life, (See BURKE'S *Extinct Peerage*).
- II. ROBERT, of whom hereafter.

- I. Margaret, married first, to Thomas Corbet, esq. of Stanwardine, in the county of Salop; and secondly, to Sir Thomas Scriven, knt. of Frodesley, in the county of Salop.
- II. Mary, married Sir Richard Hussey, knt. of Albright Hussey, in the county of Salop.

Sir Vincent's second son,

ROBERT CORBET, esq. succeeded to the Humfreston estate. He married Bridget, eldest daughter and heiress of Sir James Pryse, knt. of Ynysymaengwyn, in the county of Merioneth, (which lady re-married to Sir Walter Lloyd, knt.) and by her had issue,

- I. VINCENT, of Ynysymaengwyn, ancestor of the CORBETS of that place. (See vol. ii. p. 91.)
- II. THOMAS, of whom presently.
- III. James.

- I. Elizabeth.
- II. Bridget.
- III. Jane.
- IV. Mary.

The second son of Robert, (by his wife Dorothy),

THOMAS CORBET, acquired the estate of Nash, in the county of Pembroke, and had, with other issue, a son,

WILLIAM CORBETT, (who adopted the mode of writing his name with two *t's*).

He was secretary to the Admiralty, and married Eleanor, one of the three daughters and co-heirs of Colonel John Jones, of Nantoes, in the county of Cardigan, by whom he had three sons, viz.

I. Thomas, who married, and had an only child, Elizabeth.
II. Vincent, who died unm.
III. WILLIAM.

The youngest,

WILLIAM CORBETT, was cashier of his majesty's navy, and married first, Mary, daughter of Thomas Staniford, esq. serjeant-at-law, by whom he had a son,

I. THOMAS, born in 1730, of whom presently.

William Corbett, esq. married secondly, Sarah Dighton, and by her had issue, viz.

II. Andrew, married to Augusta, fourth daughter of John, earl of Bute, and sister of John, marquis of Bute.
I. Charlotte, married to John Philipps Adams, esq. of the county of Pembroke.

The eldest son of William Corbett, by his first wife, Mary,

THOMAS CORBETT, esq. was of Darnhall, in the county of Chester, married Elizabeth, only child and heir of Humphrey Edwin, esq. of St. Albans, in the county of Herts, by Mary, his wife, daughter of William Thompson, of Elsham, in the county of Lincoln, esq. and by the death of her maternal uncle, Robert Thompson, esq. without issue, in 1788, she became sole heir of her said grandfather, and entitled to quarter the arms of Thompson. By this lady Thomas Corbett had issue,

I. WILLIAM, his heir.
II. Edwin, who married Ann, daughter of the late John Blackburne, esq. of Hale, M.P. for the county of Lancaster, and has issue, Edwin, and several other children.

Mr. Corbett *d.* 18th December, 1808, and was *s.* by his son,

WILLIAM CORBETT, esq. of Darnhall, who in accordance with the will of his maternal great uncle, Robert Thompson, esq. of Elsham, took the name and arms of THOMPSON, in addition to those of CORBETT, by royal licence, dated 20th July, 1810; he married in 1794, Jane Eleanor, eldest daughter of General Ainslie, and niece of the late Sir Robert Ainslie, bart. ambassador to the Ottoman Porte, and by her had (with several other children), the present THOMAS GEORGE CORBETT, esq. of Elsham, who succeeded his father in the family estates, 3rd February, 1832, and is one of the representatives of the northern division of the county of Lincoln, in the present parliament.

*Arms*—Or, a raven, ppr.

*Crest*—An elephant and castle, ppr.

*Motto*—Deus pascit corvos.

*Estates*—Darnhall, in the county palatine of Chester, purchased by William Corbett, secretary to the Admiralty, but which had formerly belonged to another branch of the family. See *Ormerod's History of the County Palatine.* Elsham, in the county of Lincoln; and Ryther, in the county of York, derived from the Thompson family, a branch of which was elevated to the peerage, by the title of Baron Haversham. (See BURKE's *Extinct Peerage.*)

*Seats*—Elsham, in the county of Lincoln; and Darnhall, in the county of Chester.

## PIGOTT, OF EDGMOND.

PIGOTT, *The Rev.* JOHN-DRYDEN, of Edgmond, in the county of Salop, rector of the same place and Habberley, *m.* 3rd February, 1806, Frances, second daughter and co-heir of Henry Bevan, esq. of Shrewsbury, by whom he has issue,

I. John-Dryden, in holy orders, *b.* 18th April, 1808, B.A. of Christ Church, Oxford.
II. William-Henry.
III. Arthur-James.
IV. Leighton-Price.
V. Francis.
VI. Frederick.
VII. George-William.

I. Louisa-Harriott.
II. Frances-Sarah.
III. Augusta-Honora.
IV. Arabella.
V. Rosamond-Dorothy-Henrietta-Ord.

Mr. Pigott *s.* his father in 1811.

## Lineage.

In an elaborate MS. compiled and emblazoned in the College of Arms, containing "Sundrie Ancient Remembrances of Arms, Genealogies, and other Notes of Gentillity belonging to the Worshipfull Name and Families of Pigot or Picot," it is stated that "In the first reign of the Normans there flourished in this land two noble familys of the surname of Pigot; and that they were of the like noble linage or offspring in the Dutchy of Normandy before the Norman conquest of England, appeareth by the reverend testimonies of our ancient Heralds books and chronicles: the first whereof being named otherwiles Pigot and Picot, was Viscount Hereditary of Cambridge Sheer or Grantbridge, and Baron of Boorne or Brune in the said County in the reign of King William the Conqueror. After his death, Robert Pigot, his sonn, succeeded in the Baronie, and he forfeited the same by takeing part with Robert, Duke of Normandy, against William Rufus; and King Henry the First gave the same to Payne Peverell. This Peverell married the sister of the said Lord Robert Pigot, as Mr. Cambden noteth in his description of Cambridgeshire."

"The other family of the Pigots that is said to have been of noble title about the Conqueror's time, did flourish in the west parts of the realm, namely, in Wales, on the Marches thereof, as it seemeth. For Humphrey Lloyd and Doctor Powell in their Chronicles of Wales, p. 167, affirm that in the reign of King Henry the First, anno 1109, Cadocan ap Blethin, Lord of Powes, married the daughter of the Lord Pigot, of Say, a nobleman of Normandie, and had divers townes and lordships in that countrie by gift of the said Pigot, and a son also, by his daughter, named Henry, to whom the King gave a portion of his uncle Jerworth's ransome, which Jerworth ap Blethin was the said King's prisoner.

"It is supposed from a branch of this Pigot are lineally descended those Pigotts, which have many ages since continued at *Chetwin, in Shropshire*, their arms being 3 fuzills or millpecks as aforesaid, likewise in Flintshire, Cheshire, Herefordshire, &c. whereof there are many gentlemen remaining in Wales to this day, as is reported and known."

Of the Cheshire branch of Pigot, it is known by authentic records that Gilbert Pigot or Pichot, was mesne lord of Broxton, at a period approximating to the Norman conquest. Robert Pigot, and William, his son, by charter, granted to the monks of St. Werberg, in Chester, the town of Chelleford; and another, Gilbert Pigot, was a benefactor to the abbey of Pulton, in that county, in the year 1210.

Richard Pigot, "*of Cheshire*," presumed to have been of the family of Pigot, of Butley, in that county, and to have been descended from Gilbert, lord of Broxton, before mentioned, married the daughter and co-heiress of Sir Richard de Peshale, of Chetwynd, in the county of Salop, and with her obtained that fine estate. His grandson,

Robert Pigott, of Chetwynd, was sheriff of Shropshire in 1517, and he (as also did several of his descendants) bore for arms, *azure, a chevron between three mullets or, on a chief ermine, three fusils sable.* The chevron and mullets were borne by the Peshales of Chetwynd, in consequence of the marriage of Sir Richard de Peshale, sheriff of Shropshire in 1333, with Joan, daughter and heir of Reginald, son of Sir John de Chetwynd, by which marriage the Chetwynd estate was obtained by the Peshale family. Robert Pigott, esq.[1] married Margaret, daughter of Sir John Blunt, knt. of Kinlet, by whom he had issue,

Thomas Pigott, esq. of Chetwynd, whose son,

Robert Pigott, esq. of Chetwynd, was sheriff of Shropshire in 1574. By Elizabeth, his wife, daughter of William Gatacre, esq. of Gatacre, in the county of Salop, he had numerous issue, and was succeeded by his eldest son,

Thomas Pigott, esq. of Chetwynd, sheriff of Shropshire in 1615, he married Dorothy, daughter of Thomas Eyton, esq. of Eyton, in the county of Salop, and dying in 1620, was succeeded in his estates by his son,

WALTER PIGOTT, esq. of Chetwynd, sheriff of Shropshire in 1624, who married Katharine, daughter of Sir Richard Leveson, knt. and had a son,

THOMAS PIGOTT, esq. of Chetwynd, who married Anne, daughter of Ralph Sneyd, esq. of Keele, in the county of Stafford, and dying in 1665, was succeeded by his son,

WALTER PIGOTT, esq. of Chetwynd, who married Anne, daughter of Sir John Dryden, bart. of Canons Ashby, in the county of Northampton, and had issue,

- I. ROBERT, his heir.
- II. Dryden, rector of Edgmond, in the county of Salop.

- I. Mary.

Walter Pigott died in 1669, and was succeeded by his eldest son,

ROBERT Pigott, esq. of Chetwynd, sheriff of Shropshire in 1697, who married Frances, daughter of William Ward, esq. of Willingsworth, in the county of Stafford, (brother of Edward, Lord Dudley and Ward), by whom he had issue,

- I. ROBERT, his heir, born 21st November, 1699.
- II. John.
- III. Thomas.
- IV. William, rector of Edgmond and Chetwynd, in the county of Salop, ancestor of Colonel Pigott, of Doddershall Park. (See that family.)
- V. Benjamin.
- VI. Francis.

- I. Honor, married to John Harvey, esq.
- II. Ann, married to Richard Lyster, esq. of Rowton, in the county of Salop.

Mr. Pigott was succeeded in his extensive estates by his eldest son,

ROBERT PIGOTT, esq. of Chetwynd Park, in the county of Salop, and of Chesterton Hall, in the county of Huntingdon. This gentleman married, first, Diana, dau. and co-heir of Richard Rocke, esq. of Shrewsbury, but had no issue. He married, secondly, Anne, daughter of — Peers, esq. of Criggion, in the county of Montgomery, by whom he had

- I. ROBERT, his heir.
- II. Thomas.
- III. WILLIAM, rector of Chetwynd and Edgmond, of whom hereafter.

- I. Frances.
- II. Honor.
- III. Ann.
- IV. Rebecca, married John Mytton, esq. of Halston.

The date of Mr. Pigott's death is known by the remarkable wager recorded in Burrows' Reports, under the title of "The Earl of March *versus* Pigott," in which Lord Mansfield decided, that the impossibility of a contingency is no bar to its becoming the subject of a wager, provided the impossibility is unknown to both the parties at the time of laying it. The case was this: Mr. R. Pigott and Mr. Codrington agreed to *run their fathers' lives* one against the other. Sir William Codrington being a little turned of fifty; Mr. Pigott, senior, upwards of seventy; but the latter was *already* dead. He died in Shropshire, (150 miles from London), at two o'clock in the morning of the day on which the bet was made at Newmarket, after dinner. This circumstance was at the time unknown to, and not even suspected by either party; but hence Mr. Pigott was induced to resist payment of the five hundred guineas, for which the wager was laid; and Lord March, afterwards the well-known Duke of Queensberry, who had taken Mr. Codrington's bet, was compelled to bring his action, in which he succeeded. Dying thus, in May, 1770, Mr. Pigott was succeeded at Chetwynd, by his eldest son,

ROBERT PIGOTT, esq. who served the office of sheriff for Shropshire, in 1774, soon after which, becoming alarmed (as it is said) at the gloomy aspect of affairs in this country, consequent upon the commencement of the American war, he sold the ancient inheritance of Chetwynd, which had been in his name for twelve generations, and hastened to rescue seventy thousand pounds, the inadequate consideration which he had received for it, from his anticipated wreck of the kingdom, by retiring to the continent, and there lost a considerable part of this property, on the failure of those to whom he had entrusted it. He lived for some time at Geneva, married abroad, and had a son, who died before him. His own death happened at Toulouse, on the 7th July, 1794.

Thus terminated the principal line of the family of Pigott, of Chetwynd, but the family itself was continued by

THE REV. WILLIAM PIGOTT, rector of Chetwynd and Edgmond, brother of the last Robert Pigott, of Chetwynd. He married Arabella, daughter of John Mytton, esq. of Halston, in the county of Salop, by whom he had issue,

- I. William, who was a captain in the 82nd regiment of Foot, and died at Gibraltar, in 1795.
- II. JOHN-DRYDEN, his successor in the Edgmond estate.

- I. Arabella.
- II. Anne, married John Corbet, esq. of Sundorne Castle, in the county of Salop.
- III. Mary.
- IV. Harriott.

The Rev. William Pigott died 9th March, 1811, in his seventieth year, and was succeeded in his estates by his son, the present Rev. JOHN-DRYDEN PIGOTT, rector of Edgmond and Habberley, in the county of Salop.

*Arms*—Ermine, three fusils (conjoined in fess) sable.

*Crest*—A wolf's head erased arg. langued gules.

*Estates*—The manor, estate, and advowson of the rectory, of Edgmond, in the county of Salop, with other lands in the counties of Salop and Montgomery.

*Seat*—Edgmond, Shropshire.

## HARLAND, OF SUTTON HALL.

HARLAND, WILLIAM-CHARLES, esq. of Sutton Hall, in the county of York, *b.* 25th January, 1804, *m.* 17th May, 1827, Catherine, only daughter of Robert Eden Duncombe Shafto, esq. of Whitworth Park, in the palatinate of Durham, by Catherine, third daughter of Sir John Eden, bart. of Windlestone Hall.

This gentleman, who succeeded his aunt, Lady Hoar Harland, in 1826, is a deputy lieutenant for the county, and member of parliament for the city of Durham.

### Lineage

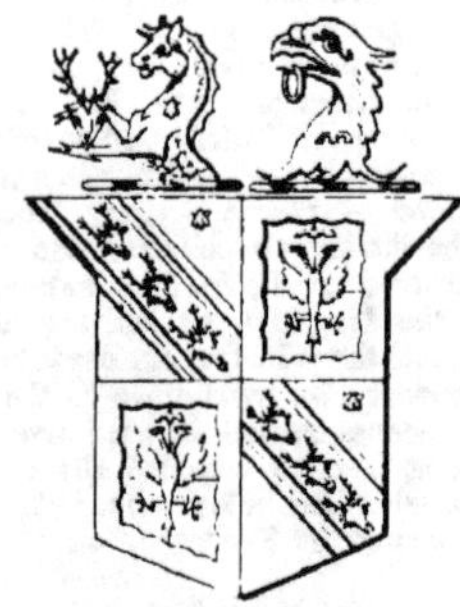

The original surname of this family, indiscriminately spelt Hoar, Hoare, Hoore, and Hoor, but most anciently Hore, is of great antiquity in Middlesex, Surrey, and the adjoining counties. Alardus le Hore paid fines to *King* JOHN in 1208 for lands in Muriel, Bucks;* Walterus le Hore held lands, in the year 1235, of HENRY III., in Leatherhead, in the county of Surrey, for the service of finding a house to contain prisoners; † and Robertus le Hore was living in London in 1331. Another Walterus le Hore, accompanying the Earl of Northampton, with numerous nobles, knights, and other gentlemen, into "parts beyond the sea," on the king's service, had letters of protection and attorney from EDWARD III. *anno* 1337. John Hoor had similar letters from HENRY IV. in 1405, to accompany the king's son, Thomas, Duke of Lancaster.‡ John Hore was at the siege of Rouen in the train of HENRY V.; and Thomas Hoore or Hore was justice of the peace for Southwark in 1496. We find the name in London and its vicinity during the succeeding reigns till that of JAMES I. The connected pedigree in the Herald's College commences with

WILLIAM HOAR, born about the year 1680, who inherited a small estate in Middlesex. He *m.* Miss Martha Baker, and dying in 1739, was buried at Stepney, leaving one son and two daughters, viz.

GEORGE, his heir.

Martha, *m.* to Thomas Davison, esq. of Blakiston, in Durham, and was mother of Thomas Davison, who inherited the estate of Kippax Park, in Yorkshire, and assumed the surname of BLAND. (See BLAND, OF KIPPAX PARK.)

Susanna, *m.* to the Rev. Joseph Butler, rector of Shadwell and prebendary of St. Paul's.

The only son,

GEORGE HOAR, esq. of Middleton St. George, in the county of Durham, born at Limehouse, was keeper of the regalia of England in the Tower of London. He wedded, at Redmarshall, 1st January, 1750, Frances, daughter of William Sleigh, esq. of Stockton-upon-Tees, by Mary, his wife, daughter of Charles Bathurst, esq. of Clints

* Cap. Dom. Westm.

† Manning's Hist. of Surrey and Placita Coronæ, 19th HEN. III.

‡ Rymer's Fœdera.

and Arkendale, M. P. for Richmond (see vol. ii. p. 63), and had issue,

WILLIAM, his heir.

George, of Twyford Lodge, Hants, who m. Miss Elizabeth Cooke, but was divorced.

Charles, who assumed the surname and arms of HARLAND, 26th May, 1802, having married, at Easingwood, during that year, Anne, only daughter and heiress of PHILIP HARLAND, esq. of SUTTON HALL, and widow of the Rev. Henry Goodrick. He was subsequently created a BARONET, but dying without issue, the title expired. His widow, the heiress of Sutton Hall, survived until the 24th June, 1826, when she was succeeded by the nephew of her husband, the present WILLIAM-CHARLES HARLAND, esq. of Sutton Hall.

Thomas, an admiral in the royal navy, m. at Marylebone, 20th May, 1788, Katherine-Dorothy, daughter of Peregrine Bertie, esq. of Low Layton, Essex, and assumed the surname and arms of BERTIE.

Ralph, of Bath, m. 21st June, 1788, Elizabeth, daughter of Peregrine Bertie, esq. and sister of his brother's wife.

Mary, m. at St. James's, Westminster, 8th January, 1785, to Richard Mark Dickens, esq. colonel of the 34th regiment, and had issue.

Frances.

George Hoar's eldest son,

WILLIAM HOAR, esq. barrister-at-law, wedded 30th November, 1780, Anne, daughter of John Wilkinson, esq. of Stockton-upon-Tees, and had issue,

WILLIAM-CHARLES, his heir.

Anne.

Mr. Hoar, who assumed the surname of HARLAND, died in December, 1834, and was succeeded by his son, the present WILLIAM-CHARLES HARLAND, esq. of Sutton Hall.

*Arms*—Quarterly; 1st and 4th, ar. on a bend between two cottizes three stags' heads caboshed az. for HARLAND. 2nd and 3rd, quarterly, sa. and gu. over all an eagle displayed, with two heads arg. within a bordure invecked, counterchanged, for HOAR.

*Crests*—1st. A sea horse ppr. holding between his hoofs a stag's head caboshed az. charged with an escallop, for HARLAND. 2nd. An eagle's head erased arg. charged with a label of three points, pendant from the beak an annulet, for HOAR.

*Estates*—Sutton Hall and Huby, in the North Riding of Yorkshire: a portion of the property was in the family before the Restoration, and another granted to Captain Richard Harland for his services in the royalist army at the battle of Marston Moor. Also the Middleton estate near Darlington, in the county of Durham, which has been possessed for some time by the family.

*Seat*—Sutton Hall, Yorkshire.

## CHILDE, OF KINLET.

CHILDE, WILLIAM-LACON, esq. of Kinlet, in the county of Salop, *b.* 3rd January, 1786; *m.* 13th August, 1807, Harriet, second daughter of the late William Cludde, esq. of Orleton, (see vol. i p. 483,) and has issue,

I. WILLIAM-LACON, *b.* 6th June, 1810.
II. Jonathan, *b.* 8th October, 1811.
III. Charles-Orlando, *b.* 27th December, 1812.
IV. Edward-George, *b.* 23rd December, 1818.
V. Arthur, *b.* 2nd April, 1820.

I. Harriet.
II. Anna-Maria.
III. Catherine.
IV. Lucy, } twins.
V. Mary, }

Mr. Lacon Childe, who is a magistrate for the counties of Salop and Worcester, and a deputy lieutenant for the former shire, succeeded his father 3rd February, 1824. He served the office of sheriff for Shropshire in 1828, and represented the borough of Wenlock in the first parliament of GEORGE IV.

## Lineage.

The patronymic of this ancient family was BALDWYN; and the unwearied research of the late Rev. John-Brickdale Blakeway, of Shrewsbury, as evinced, in his account of the "Sheriffs of Shropshire," has proved, almost beyond a doubt, that these Baldwyns derive their descent from BAWDEWYN, who occurs in the roll of Battel Abbey, as one of the companions of WILLIAM *the Conqueror*, who was afterwards castellan of Montgomery under that monarch, and from whom that town acquires its Welsh appellation *Tre-Faldwin*, or *The Town of Baldwin*. That this family of BAWDEWIN, Baldwyn, or Baldwin, for the name has been written in these and many other ways, was seated at Dodelebury, or Diddlebury, (more recently denominated Delbury), in Corvedale, in Shropshire, from a very remote period, is beyond all question. A pedigree, drawn up with great care, commences with an undoubted progenitor, BAWDEWIN de Brugge, (i. e. Bawdewin of Bridgenorth), whose son,

GEORGE FITZ BAWDEWIN, had the manor of Kingsmeade, in Yorkshire, the stewardship of Montgomery Castle, and lands in Hope Bowdler and Smethcote, in the county of Salop. The fact of George Fitz Bawdewin holding the stewardship of Montgomery Castle, strongly indicates a connexion between him and Bawdewin, the Norman castellan, of the same fortress. Two centuries, however, must have elapsed between any contemporary of the Conqueror and Baldwin de Brugge: for ROGER BALDWYN, grandson of the aforesaid George, is known to have died in, or not long before, the year 1398. This Roger is presumed to be the first of the family who obtained Dodelebury, for his wife Jane was daughter and heiress of William de Wigley, by Alice le Childe, whose great grandfather, John L'Enfant, or the Child, is stated to have married Emblema, the daughter and co-heir of Richard Acheley, the younger, of that place, a descendant of William Achilles, as the name is there written, who is found in the *Testa de Nevill* of the reign of HENRY III. to hold the tenth part of a knight's fee in Dodelebur, of the barony of Walter de Clifford.

WILLIAM BALDWIN, of Diddlebury, grandson of Roger, had passed the middle age of life in 1468, for he then bestowed his lands in Manslow upon his son,

JOHN BALDWIN, and Elizabeth his wife. Their son,

JOHN BAWDWYN, yeoman of the crown, occurs in the roll for the collection of a benevolence (as it was called) in Shropshire, in the year 1491. This gentleman, by his situation about the royal person, had the opportunity of introducing at court his eldest son,

WILLIAM BAWDEWYN, who during the reign of *Queen* MARY, enjoyed the confidential office of cupbearer to her majesty, and was still living in 1576, when Sir Henry Compton, knt. Lord Compton, granted to him, by the name of William Baldwyne, of Diddlebury, gentleman, the manor and advowson of Kyre Wyard, in Worcestershire. He *d.* without issue, and was *s.* in estate by his brother,

RICHARD BALDWYN, who married at Shipton, in the county of Salop, on the 7th November, 1545, Margery, daughter of Lawrence Ludlow, of Moore House, in Corvedale, and was *s.* by his eldest son,

THOMAS BALDWYN, *b.* in 1546, who, like his grandfather and uncle, spent many of his years within the circuit of a court, as agent to the Earl of Shrewsbury, then engaged in the dangerous office of guarding the Scottish queen. In LODGE'S *Illustrations*, vol. ii. p. 234, is a letter signed "T. Bawdewyn," and directed to the earl of Shrewsbury, 1st July, 1580. It informs his lordship that ELIZABETH is resolute against his going to Chatsworth with *Queen* MARY. A letter of the earl's to Mr. Baldwyn (ib. 257) proves the great confidence that nobleman placed in him, and expresses an anxiety to be permitted to resign his burdensome charge of guarding the queen, adding, "I have too many spyes in my house already, and mind to make choice of others I may trust." Hunter's History of Hallamshire contains a letter directed to Mr. Baldwyn, by the name of "my loving friend Mr. Thomas Bawdewine, at Could Harbar in London," dated April, 1581, and proving that he was not unknown to the ministers of ELIZABETH; and in the same work "one Baldwin" is mentioned as a confidential agent of the earl of Shrewsbury. In a room in Beauchamp's Tower, in the Tower of London, anciently the place of confinement for state prisoners, were discovered, some years ago, a number of inscriptions, chiefly made with nails, and all of them the autographs of the unfortunate individuals who thus endeavoured to beguile for a time the tedious hours of confinement. They have been published in the thirteenth volume of the Archæologia, and since, in Mr. Brayley's history of that fortress. Among them is one which runs thus:

1585. THOMAS BAWDEWIN. JULI.
AS VERTUE MAKETH LIFE
SO SIN CAWSETH DEATH.

To which is added a representation of a pair of scales, evidently intimating the writer's confidence in his own integrity, and desire to obtain justice. Mr. Brand, who has written an elaborate dissertation on these inscriptions, not finding, as he says, either in "the State Papers, Rymer's Fœdera, Strype, Dod, nor Howe," any mention of this person, "suspects he had been imprisoned here for counterfeiting the queen's coin." But there is not a shadow of doubt that he was the Thomas Baldwyn above-mentioned, and the suspicion of the learned commentator is, consequently, unjust to his memory. His epitaph, still remaining at Diddlebury, records his escape from the *sea, the sword, and the cruel tower.*

"Qui mare, qui ferrum, duræ qui vincula turris
Quondam transivit;"

which, of course, it would not have done if the allusion had been calculated to awaken so disgraceful a recollection: but his imprisonment had a higher and more honourable origin. The trembling anxiety of ELIZABETH and her ministers, respecting the safe custody of their most important captive, the queen of Scots, and the ungrateful and harassing task imposed upon the earl of Shrewsbury, as her keeper, are alike matter of history. Perhaps, when ELIZABETH'S illegitimacy in the eyes of the other sovereigns of Europe, and MARY'S pertinacious claim to her crown, supported, as it was ready to be, by every state and almost every individual of the Catholic faith, be taken into fair consideration, the vexatious treatment of that illustrious prisoner will lose somewhat of the character of tyranny and cruelty ascribed to it; but, in the mean time, it is notorious that every avenue of escape, possible or impossible, was guarded with the narrowest scrutiny, and every precaution adopted which the most experienced gaoler could suggest. It has been shewn that Thomas Bawdewin was connected with the earl of Shrewsbury, and in the *State Papers* of Sir Ralph Sadlier is a letter from Curle, the Scottish queen's secretary, to the same gentleman; much cannot be collected from it, for it is written in a kind of cypher; but this, under the circumstances, would make it more alarming and of greater apparent importance; it evidently relates to some business of the royal captive, and, from the repository in which it was found, it must have reached the hands of government. All this was quite sufficient in those days to warrant the apprehension of any one to whom so suspicious a paper was addressed; it bears date September, 1584, the year preceding the inscription that has been quoted, and must inspire a wish to learn the issue of its author's confinement; and this is supplied by a passage in the pedigree already mentioned; but whether Mr. Bawdewin was re-appointed, after his release, to his former official station, and thus obtained an entire vindication of his character, or whether the appointment preceded his imprisonment, is not stated in this document, the passage from which is as follows:—"Thomas Bawdewin,* esq. of Diddlebury, by the privie counsell of *Queen* ELIZABETH, appoynted as . . . . (here is a blank) for the affayres of Mary, queen of Scots, and George, earl of Salop, after three years imprisonment in the Tower, married Bertran, (this should be Gertrude), daughter of Robert Corbett, esq. of Stanwardine." After this liberation, he adopted a motto from the psalmist, piously ascribing the event to a merciful Providence: *Per Deum meum transilio murum.* He had reason, indeed, to congratulate himself upon his escape; for it was seldom, in those *golden* days, that any one could do so, who had once attracted the sinister notice of the state. Upon the whole it seems most probable, that, when released, he quitted the dangerous vortex of a court, and retired to his paternal estate in Corvedale, where he died at a good old age, in October, 1614, and where his posterity continued, for five generations, until Richard Bawdewin sold the Diddlebury estate to Frederick Cornewall, esq. captain R. N. father of the late Bishop Worcester, whose son is the present proprietor.

WILLIAM BALDWIN, second brother of Thomas Bawdewin, the prisoner, was of Elsich, in the chapelry of Cerfton and parish of Diddlebury. The family name had been hitherto written indiscriminately; but from this point of divergence, the two branches chose to distinguish themselves by a different mode of spelling. William's son,

CHARLES BALDWYN, esq. was born in

* JOHN BAWDEWIN, second son of this Thomas, was servant, in 1616, to Edward Talbot, soon afterwards Earl of Shrewsbury, and son to Earl George, in whose service Mr. Bawdewin, the father, was so long continued. In those days, a gentleman's son was not considered as submitting to any degradation by serving a nobleman, or even a knight, in a menial capacity. Mr. Talbot, in a letter published in the *Strafford Letters*, (page 3), uses the phrase "John Bawdewin, my man;" and so in some curious depositions preserved in the History of Whalley, p. 228, touching a right of pews in the parish church, Sir John Towneley is represented as saying (it was in the reign of HENRY VIII.) "my man, Shuttleworth, made this form, and here will I sit when I come." The gentleman whom the knight bluffly calls "*my man*," was, however, (says Dr. Whitaker,) a person of property, and was probably his principal agent, or perhaps one of his esquires.

1593, and in the troubles which marked the earlier part of the ensuing century, strenuously supported the royal cause. He represented the town of Ludlow, in the long parliament, until he was disabled, (February 5, 1643,) for deserting (as the term was) the service of the house, being in the king's quarters, and adhering to that party. He married, in 1617, one of the daughters and co-heirs of Francis Holland, of Burwarton, in Shropshire, and either his estate or delinquency was greater than those of his cousin, Edward Bawdewin, of Diddlebury, for while the latter was admitted to compound for £245. Mr. Baldwin was obliged to pay nearly double that sum. He had two sons, who both rose to the honour of knighthood, and to great eminence in different departments of the law,

SAMUEL (Sir), his heir.

Timothy (Sir), who was admitted of Baliol College, Oxford, in 1634, (being then fifteen years of age,) of the Inner Temple in the following year, became a fellow of All Souls, and had obtained so high a character for knowledge, intrepidity, and loyalty, as to be selected by the university to be one of its council on the occasion of the parliamentary visitation. He was ejected from his fellowship, but was afterwards restored, and enjoyed it in 1663, when, by the name of Dr. Timothy Baldwyn, he published *Zouch's Tract on the Admiralty*. He became also a master in Chancery, and chancellor of the diocese of Chester. In "Wood's Athenæ" a more extensive account of his history may be found. He *m.* first, Ellen, daughter of Sir William Owen, knt. of Condover, and relict of Sir George Norton, knt. of Abbots Leigh, near Bristol, and secondly, Mary, daughter of Gerard Skrymshire, esq. of Aqualate, a very distinguished royalist, relict of Nicholas Acton, esq. of Brockleton, in the county of Worcester, but left no issue.

The elder son,

SIR SAMUEL BALDWYN, born in 1618, pursued the study of the common law, was admitted of Baliol College and of the Inner Temple, at the same time, with his brother, was made a serjeant in 1669, king's serjeant in 1672, and deceasing in 1683, was buried in the Temple church, being styled on his monument, "of Stoke Castle," an estate which he rented, on a long lease, from the Earl of Craven, and of which place his brother, Sir Timothy was sometimes called. Sir Samuel married the daughter of Richard Walcot, esq. of London, merchant, and was succeeded at his decease in 1683, by his eldest surviving son,

CHARLES BALDWYN, esq. of Elsich and Stoke Castle, who *m.* Elizabeth, daughter and heir of Nicholas Acton, esq. by Mary, his wife, sister and co-heir of Edwin Skrymsher, esq. of Aqualate, and had issue,

I. Edwin, died unm.
II. Acton, who *m.* Elinor, daughter of Sir Charles Skrymsher, knt. of Norbury, but *d. s. p.*
III. CHARLES, heir.
IV. Samuel, who *m.* Katherine, daughter of Thomas Lamplugh, D. D.

I. Elizabeth.

Mr. Baldwin *d.* 4th January, 1706, aged fifty-five, and was *s.* by his son,

CHARLES BALDWIN, esq. who *m.* first, Elizabeth, daughter of John Allgood, esq. of Newcastle, and widow of Sir Patrick Strahan, of Glenkindy, Aberdeenshire, and had two sons and two daughters, CHARLES, his heir, Samuel, who *d. s. p.*, Elizabeth, and Barbara. He wedded, secondly, Anne, daughter of Robert Gayer, esq. of Stoke, Bucks, and widow of Francis Annesley, LL.D. but by her had no issue. His son and successor,

CHARLES BALDWYN, esq. of Aqualate, represented the county of Salop for many years in parliament. He wedded Catherine, elder daughter and co-heir of William Lacon Childe, esq. of KINLET, by Catherine his wife, daughter of Samuel Pytts, esq. of Kyre, and had issue,

I. WILLIAM, his heir.
II. Charles, *b.* 26th February, 1758, and *d.* 18th September, 1811.

I. Catherine.

Mr. Baldwyn was *s.* at his decease by his elder son,

WILLIAM BALDWYN, esq. who, inheriting the estates of his maternal ancestors, assumed the surname and arms of CHILDE only. He espoused, 20th November, 1775, Annabella, second daughter of Sir Charlton Leighton, bart. and by her, who died 21st January, 1816, had one son and one daughter, viz.

WILLIAM-LACON, his heir.

Annabella, who *m.* Samuel-Richard Alleyne, esq. and has three daughters, viz. Annabella-Matilda, Caroline-Charity, and Harriet.

Mr. (Baldwyn) Childe died 3rd February, 1824, and was *s.* by his son, the present WILLIAM-LACON CHILDE, esq. of Kinlet.

### Families of Lacon and Childe.

The very ancient family of LACON, whose name has at various periods been written Laken, Lakyn, Lakin, and Lacon, was seated at Lacon, in the county of Salop, at a remote era. Fourth in descent from John

Laken, lord of the manor of Laken, or Lacon, in the 21st year of EDWARD III., who was fifth in descent from Sir Robert de Lakyn, also lord of the same manor, was

SIR RICHARD LAKYN, knt. sheriff of Salop, in 1415, who witnessed the Earl of Arundel's charter to Oswestry, 8th HENRY IV., married Elizabeth, heiress of Sir Hamond Peshale, of Willey, knt. and was father of

SIR WILLIAM LAKEN, knt. of Willey, sheriff of Salop, in 1452, whose son,

RICHARD LAKEN, of Willey, served the same office in 1477. He was father, by Joan his wife, daughter of Thomas Hoorde, of

SIR THOMAS LAKEN, of Willey, who received the honour of knighthood, and was sheriff in 1510. He *m.* Mary, daughter of Sir Richard Corbet, of Morton Corbett, and had four sons and five daughters, viz.

I. RICHARD (Sir), his heir.
II. Edward, *d. s. p.*
III. William, *s. p.*
IV. Launcelot, *m.* Elizabeth Gray, and was father of Christopher Lacon, of Kenley.

I. Alice, *m.* to John Corbett.
II. Agnes, *m.* to Robert Berington, of Salop.
III. Dorothy, *m.* to Sir Richard Walwyn, knt.
IV. Mary, married to Thomas Acton, of Sutton.
V. Jane, *m.* first, to George Bromley, and secondly, to William Egerton.

The eldest son and successor,

RICHARD LAKEN, esq. of Willey, sheriff in 1540, wedded Agnes, daughter of Sir John Blount,* of Kinlet, and was *s.* by his son,

ROWLAND LACON, esq. of Willey, high sheriff in 1571, who obtained the KINLET estate by the devise of his uncle, Sir George Blount, and was father, by Ellen his wife, daughter of William Brigges, of

SIR FRANCIS LACON, knt. of Willey and Kinlet, high sheriff in 1612. This gentleman, who sold considerable portions of the family property, *m.* Jane, youngest daughter of Anthony Browne, first Viscount Montagu (by his second wife, Magdalen, daughter of William, Lord Dacre, of Gillesland), and was *s.* by his son,

ROWLAND LACON, esq. of Kinlet, whose devotion and services to *King* CHARLES I. caused a further dismemberment of the estates: the remnant fell, at his decease, to his only daughter,

---

* The Blounts of Kinlet were a junior branch of the ancient family seated at Sodington, in the county of Worcester.

SIR JOHN BLOUNT, knt. of Sodington, descended from the Lords of Guisnes (refer to family of BLOUNT of *Maple Durham*) *m.* first, Juliana Foulhurst, by whom he had a son, JOHN, progenitor of the present Sodington family, and secondly, Isabella, daughter and heir of Sir Bryan Cornwall, of Kinlet, son of Sir Edmund Cornwall, by Elizabeth his wife, daughter and co-heir of Sir Bryan Brampton, of Kinlet. By his second wife, Sir John Blount left at his decease, in 1424, a son,

JOHN BLOUNT, of Dodington, who *m.* Alice, daughter of Kynard Delabere, of Herefordshire, and was *s.* at his demise in 1442, by his son,

HUMPHREY BLOUNT, of Dodington, who inherited, from his maternal ancestors, the estate of KINLET, in the county of Salop, and served the office of sheriff for that shire in 1461. He wedded Elizabeth, daughter of Sir Robert Winnington, knt. and widow of John Delves, esq. of Delves Hall, and had a son and successor,

SIR THOMAS BLOUNT, of Kinlet, aged twenty-one years, at his father's decease, in 1477. This gentleman was high sheriff of Salop in 1480, and received the honour of knighthood. He *m.* Anne, daughter of Sir Richard Croft, of Croft Castle, and had no fewer than twenty children. The eldest,

SIR JOHN BLOUNT, of Kinlet, *b.* in 1484, succeeded his father in the 16th of HENRY VIII. He *m.* Catherine, daughter and heir of Sir Hugh Pershall, of Knightly, in Staffordshire, and had issue,

I. GEORGE (Sir), his heir.
II. Henry, of Bewdley.
III. William.

I. Elizabeth, mother, by HENRY VIII., of Henry Fitzroy, Duke of Richmond. This lady, "who was thought," says Lord Herbert, of Cherbury, "for her rare ornaments of nature and education, to be the beauty and mistress-piece of her time," wedded first, Sir Gilbert Talboys, Lord Talboys, and secondly, Edward, Lord Clinton.
II. Rosa, *m.* to William Grisling, of Lincolnshire.
III. Albora.
IV. AGNES, *m.* as in the text, to Richard Laken, esq. of Willey.
V. Isabella, *m.* to William Read.

Sir John Blount was succeeded by his eldest son,

SIR GEORGE BLOUNT, knt. of Kinlet, who, according to the fashion of the day, served while a youth with distinction in the French and Scottish campaigns of HENRY VIII. and EDWARD VI., and was high in favour at the court of the former monarch. He served the office of high sheriff for Shropshire in 1564, and, marrying Christiana, or Constance, daughter of Sir John Talbot, of Grafton, had an only daughter, Dorothy, *m.* first, to John Purslow, esq. of Sidbury, and secondly, to Edward Bullock, esq. of Bradeley. Sir George Blount died in 1582, and, for some cause unknown, devised his estates to his nephew, Roland Laken, esq. of Willey, "whom," says Mr. Blakensay, "he probably selected as being equally with himself descended from the Bramptons, the ancient Lords of Kinlet."

* qd. by Peckham of Denham — Blount, Cornwall, Brampton . [illegible]

ANNE LACON, of Kinlet, who espoused Sir William Childe, knt. LL.D. a master in Chancery. "My hopes," says Fuller, in his Worthies of Shropshire, 1662, speaking of the Lacons, "are according to my desires, that this ancient family is still extant in this county; though, I suspect, shrewdly shattered in estate." Sir William Childe was a younger son of the old stock of Childe, of Northwick, in Worcestershire, a family seated for ages in that shire. His second son,

THOMAS CHILDE, esq. of the Birch, in the parish of Kinlet, was high sheriff of Shropshire in 1795. He left a son and successor,

WILLIAM LACON CHILDE, esq. M.P. for the county of Salop, who wedded Catherine, daughter of Samuel Pytts, esq. of Kyre, in Worcestershire, and *d.* in 1756, leaving two daughters, the younger married — Woodroffe, esq. but *d. s. p.*, while the elder,

CATHERINE CHILDE, who inherited her father's estates, married, as already stated, CHARLES BALDWYN, esq. of Aqualate, and was grandmother of the present WILLIAM LACON CHILDE, esq. of Kinlet and Kyre.

*Arms*—Quarterly, first and fourth, gu. a chev. ermine, between three eagles close arg., for CHILDE; second, quarterly, per fesse, indented erm. and az., for LACON; third, arg. a saltier sa., for BALDWYN.

*Crest*—An eagle, with wings expanded, argent, enveloped round the neck with a snake ppr.

*Estates*—At Kinlet, in Shropshire, and Kyre, in the counties of Worcester and Hereford.

*Seats*—Kinlet Hall, Shropshire, and Kyre House, Worcestershire.

## SEYMOUR, OF CASTLETOWN.

SEYMOUR, AARON-CROSSLEY, esq. of Castletown House, in the Queen's County, *b.* 19th December, 1789, *m.* at Cheltenham, 3rd April, 1818, Anne, only daughter and heiress of John Geale, esq.* of Mount Geale, in the county of Kilkenny, by whom (who *d.* 28th February, 1825) he had issue,

JOHN-CROSSLEY-GEALE, *b.* 11th Nov. 1819.
Catherine-Elizabeth-Frances.
Emilia-Olivia-Anne, } both died young.
Letitia-Anne-Adelaide, }

Mr. Seymour inherited from his father on the 19th of May, 1831.

---

* By Anne, his wife, daughter of C. Jackson, esq. of Nottinghamshire, Mr. Geale was her second husband; her first, Mr. Kelly, an eminent barrister, fell in a duel with Col. Whaley, and left, (by the said Anne Jackson) an only daughter and heiress, Frances Kelly, who married Richard Drought, esq. of the Queen's County, and had several children.

The family of GEALE originally came from Lancashire, and settled in Ireland some considerable number of years back. JOHN GEALE, esq. of Mount Geale, in the county of Kilkenny, is the first we have any account of; and he appears to have made a slight alteration in the spelling of the name, which is usually written *Gale* by the Lancashire, and all other branches of the family. He had several sons, one of whom emigrated to America, and was grandfather of Susanna Geale, who married Alan, first Lord Gardner, by whom she had a numerous issue.

BENJAMIN GEALE succeeded at Mount Geale. He was alderman and lord mayor of Dublin; and was twice the unsuccessful candidate in two sharply contested elections for the representation of that city. He married Anne, eldest daughter of Frederick Falkiner, esq. of Abbot's-town, county of Dublin, by Elizabeth, daughter of James Hamilton, esq. of Bailiborough, in the county of Cavan, by whom he had three sons and two daughters, viz.

I. JOHN GEALE, who succeeded at Mount Geale, and whose only daughter and heir, Anne, married AARON CROSSLEY-SEYMOUR, esq. He died July 25, 1820.

II. Frederick, deceased, who married Letitia, daughter of P. Brady, esq. and had five sons and three daughters, viz.

1. Benjamin, married Catherine, daughter of Charles Wild, esq. (by Mary, daughter of Thomas Tipping, of Beaulieu, esq. and sister of Sophia, who married Charles, eighth Lord Blayney) and by her, who died in 1819, left issue.
2. Frederick, died unmarried.
3. John, died in 1815.
4. Daniel, married Anne, daughter of Benjamin Bickley, esq., of Bristol.
5. Henry, died in 1818.

## Lineage.

This family, now settled for nearly three hundred years in Ireland, *claims* to be a branch of the great house of SEYMOUR,* so memorable in the eventful times of HENRY VIII. and Edward VI., for the rapidity of its rise, the vastness of its power, and the depth of its fall.

SIR JOHN SEYMOUR, eldest son and heir of Sir Henry Seymour, by his first wife, Elizabeth, daughter of Sir George Darell, of Littlecote in Wilts, married Margery, second daughter of Sir Henry Wentworth, K.B., of Nettlested, in the county of Suffolk, and dying in 1536,† left issue,

I. John, who died unm. 15th July, 1520.
II. EDWARD, DUKE OF SOMERSET, one day the proud and potent PROTECTOR, ruling without rivalry, and without control, the next a convicted and decapitated traitor, despoiled and attainted. From this unfortunate nobleman the *extant* ducal family of Somerset, and the Marquesses of Hertford, directly derive.
III. HENRY, (Sir) of whom presently.
IV. THOMAS, Lord High Admiral of England, who became the second husband of the QUEEN *Dowager*, KATHARINE PARR, and was raised to the peerage as Baron Seymour, of Sudley. This nobleman was beheaded on Tower Hill, 10th March, 1548-9, under the authority of his brother, the *Protector* SOMERSET, (*refer to* BURKE's *Extinct and Dormant Peerage*).
V. John, } *d.* young.
VI. Anthony, }

I. JANE, the third QUEEN *Consort* of HENRY VIII, and mother of *King* EDWARD VI.‡
II. Elizabeth, *m.* first, to Sir Anthony Oughtred, knt. and, secondly, to Gregory, Lord Cromwell.
III. Margaret, died young.
IV. Dorothy, the wife, first, of Sir Clement Smith, knt. of Little Baddow, in Essex, and after his decease, of Thomas Leventhorpe, esq. of Shingey Hall, in Hertfordshire.

Lady Seymour survived her husband, and died in the year 1560. By her last will she bequeathed divers legacies of plate, jewels, &c. to her relations, and mentions Edward and Henry Seymour, sons of the Duke of Somerset, as her godsons. The sole executorship she confers on her second son,

SIR HENRY SEYMOUR, who received the honor of knighthood at the coronation of his nephew, *King* EDWARD VI., being one of the forty in substitution of knights of the Bath, who were not created for want of time to perform the ceremony. In 1551, then in the king's service, he obtained a grant of lands; amongst which were the

---

1. Letitia, married the Rev. William Bushe, rector of St. George's, Dublin, and of Templepont, in the county of Cavan (son of Jervis Parker Bushe, esq. of Kilfane, by Miss Grattan, sister of the Right Hon. Henry Grattan, of Tinnyhinch, in the county of Wicklow) younger brother of Jervis Bushe, who married Miss Latham, sister to the Countess of Listowel and daughter of John Latham, esq. of Meldrum, county of Tipperary; and by her, who died at Clifton, in 1819, left issue two daughters, Isabella, and Letitia.
2. Isabella, married, 1819, to James Thorpe, esq. of Dublin, brother of the Rev. Dr. Thorpe, who married, May, 1834, Anabel-Elizabeth, Countess of Pomfret, eldest daughter of Sir Richard Borough, bart.
3. Elizabeth, married to her cousin, William Richardson, esq. an officer in the Horse Guards, and died in 1820, without surviving issue.

III. Daniel, who left a numerous issue, of whom Piers Geale, esq. the eldest son, married Miss Crofton, cousin to Sir Edward Crofton, bart. of Moate, in the county of Roscommon, and had issue Elizabeth, married to Sir Marcus Somerville, bart. of Somerville, county of Meath.

I. Anne, died at Montaban, in France, unm.
II. Elizabeth, *d.* unmarried.

* For the early descent of the SEYMOURS, refer to *Burke's Extinct and Dormant Peerage*, under the Duke of Somerset.

† The remains of Sir John Seymour were interred in the church of Easton Priory, but that building falling into ruin, they were removed to the church of Great Bedwin, in Wiltshire, where a monument stands erected to his memory by his grandson, Edward, Earl of Hertford.

large manors of Marvell and Twyford, in the county of Southampton, with the parks and house of Marvell, which had constituted a portion of the estates of the bishopric of Winchester; and the next year he had a further mark of royal favor, in the acquisition for life, through the generosity of the crown, of the manors of Somerford and Hurn, in the same county, with other lands, to the yearly value of £202. 6*s.* 9*d.* Sir Henry represented the county of Wilts in the parliament called by his nephew, and served the office of sheriff for the county of Southampton in 1568. Leading the retired life of a country gentleman, far removed from the turmoils of the court, and not taking any part in the politics of the period, these grants alone appear to be the extent of Sir Henry's participation in the fortunes of his family. He *m.* Barbara, daughter of Thomas Morgan, esq. of Tredegar, and left one son, JOHN (Sir), with several daughters.* Speaking of Sir Henry Seymour, in his History of the Reformation, HEYLIN has the following singular narrative: "There goes a story that the priest officiating at Ouslebury (of which parish Marvelle was a part) after the mass had been abolished by the king's authority, was violently dragged thence by this Sir Henry, beaten and most reproachfully handled by him, his servants universally refusing to serve him as the instruments of his rage and fury; and that the poor priest, having after an opportunity to get into the church, did openly curse the said Sir Henry and his posterity, with bell, book, and candle, according to the use observed in the church of Rome, which, whether it was so, or that the main foundation of their estate being laid on sacrilege, could promise no long blessing to it, certain it is, that his posterity was brought beneath a degree of poverty." Sir Henry dying in 1578, was *s.* by his son,

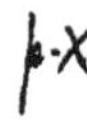

SIR JOHN SEYMOUR, knt. of Marvell, who had served the office of sheriff for Southampton, in 1568. This gentleman *m.* Susan, youngest daughter of Lord Chidiock Powlett, third son of William, Marquess of Winchester, (by his first wife, Elizabeth, daughter of Sir William Capel, progenitor of the *extant* Earls of Essex) and left at his decease three sons,

EDWARD, Henry, Thomas, } upon whom the downfall of their family appears to have entailed the most woeful consequences, lowering the unfortunate brothers not only from their grade in society, but reducing them to actual poverty, until, to quote HEYLIN again, "There remained not to any one of them one foot of land, or so much as a penny of money to supply their necessities, but what they have from the charity of the Marquis of Hertford, and the charity of the well disposed people which have affection or relation to them." Having alienated their paternal property, the three brothers emigrated to Ireland, and established themselves at Limerick, then much frequented by settlers from England: the two younger, Henry and Thomas, dying without issue, the line of EDWARD, therefore, alone remains.

EDWARD SEYMOUR, the eldest son of Sir John Seymour and Susan Powlett, representative of the Seymours of Marvell, espoused, prior to his settlement in Ireland, a daughter of Edward Onley, esq. of Catesby, in Northamptonshire, and having several children, was *s.* at his decease by his eldest son,

EDWARD SEYMOUR, who wedded a daughter of William Hartwell, esq. an alderman of Limerick, and Mayor in 1659, and left an only son,

JOHN SEYMOUR, an alderman of the city of Limerick, who was chosen sheriff in 1708, and served the office of Mayor in 1720. This worthy citizen *m.* Jane, daughter of Seymour Wroughton, esq. of Heskett, in Wiltshire, and had issue,

I. JOHN, his heir.
II. William, *m.* Jane, second daughter of Mr. Alderman Edward Wight, of Limerick, (by his second wife Miss Hawkesworth) and left a son,
   John, in holy orders, Rector of Palace, in the county of Limerick. This gentleman, *m.* Grizzle, youngest daughter and co-

* Of whom JANE became the wife of Sir Edward Rodney, of Stoke Rodney, and Pelton, in Somersetshire, the heiress of which family married Sir Thomas Bridges, of Keinsham, a younger branch of the Bridgeses, Dukes of Chandos. Lady Rodney had seventeen children, but her sons having no issue male, the honors in this branch became extinct. It was this Lady Rodney who, in conjunction with her son-in-law, Sir Theodore Newton, of Bilton, in the county of Gloucester, bestowed the choir organ (which now stands on the north side) upon the abbey church at Bath. Her eldest son married a daughter of Sir Robert Southwell, of Woodrising, in Norfolk. George Rodney, the second son, wedded Anne, daughter of Sir Thomas Lake, of Cannons, in Middlesex. She was widow of William Cecil, Lord Ros, who *d. s. p.* in 1618, and was involved with her mother, Lady Lake, (daughter of Sir William Ryther, lord mayor of London) in fomenting disputes between his lordship and his grandmother, the old Countess of Exeter, which eventually became so serious as to deprive Sir Thomas Lake, then Secretary of State, of the king's favor, and of all his offices of emolument and honor. (For this extraordinary affair, see BURKE's *Extinct Peerage*.)

heir of Willian Hobart, esq. of High Mount, in the county of Cork, and great grand-daughter of Sir Miles Hobart, of Wiltshire, by whom he* had,

1. William Hobart,† an officer in the 60th regiment, who died unm. in the West Indies, in 1797.
2. MICHAEL,‡ *b.* 8th November, 1768, an admiral of the royal navy, and a knight grand cross of the Bath, who for his gallant services was created a baronet, 31st May, 1809. *See* BURKE'S *Peerage and Baronetage.*
3. John, in holy orders, Rector of Ulloa, in the Diocese of Cashell, *m.* Catherine, daughter of — Millett, esq. of Fethard, in the county of Tipperary, and relict of James Jacob, esq. of Mowbarnham, in the same county, by whom he left John, in holy orders, with Frances, the wife of the Rev. Mr. Foster, nephew to Sir Thomas Foster, bart. and Wilhelmina.
4. Richard of the R. N. killed at the close of the action between the Amazon Frigate, Captain Parker, of which he was first lieutenant, and the Belle Poule, French Frigate.
5. Frances, *m.* to Robert Ormsby, esq. Captain Sligo Militia, and died in 1805, leaving an only son, Robert Ormsby, who is married, and has issue.

III. James, sheriff of Limerick, in 1728, *m.* ——, daughter of Hezekial Holland, esq. mayor of that city in 1713, but had no surviving issue.

IV. Richard, sheriff of Limerick in 1730.

V. Walter, sheriff of Limerick in 1742, *m.* Miss Binden, daughter of David Binden, esq. sheriff of Limerick in 1716. Without issue.

Alderman John Seymour died in 1735, and was *s.* by his eldest son,

JOHN SEYMOUR, esq. who resided in Dublin, and *m.* Frances, eldest daughter and co-heir of Aaron Crossley, esq.* by Madamoiselle Peracheau, daughter of Pierre André Peracheau,† of Saumur, and (by her who died in April, 1760) left at his decease in 1754, an only son, his successor,

AARON CROSSLEY SEYMOUR, esq. of Castletown House, in the Queen's County, who *m.* Margaret, second daughter of Matthew Cassan, esq. of Sheffield in the same shire, by his first wife, Anne, daughter of Jonathan

* The Rev. John Seymour was a man of exemplary piety, of most amiable disposition, and of great learning. He was one of the domestic chaplains of Dr. Michial Cox, Archbishop of Cashell, and at the time of his decease, July, 1795, held the rectory of Abington, with the chancellorship of Emly.

† Two years before his death, Captain Seymour made an extraordinary escape from the French prison ship, at Point à Petre, in Guadaloupe, by swimming from her in the evening, in company with the master of a Bermuda vessel. Having reached the beach, and finding a canoe, they pushed off, and were taken up the next day at noon, off the Saints Isles, by the Bellona, Man-of-War.

‡ Of High Mount, in the county of Cork, and Friery Park in Devonshire.

* Mr. Crossley was the son of Abraham Crossley, esq. a younger son of John Crossley, esq. of Scaytcliffe, near Todmorden, in Lancashire. He published "a Peerage," in folio, above one hundred and twenty years ago, which is now so scarce, that a copy is rarely to be met with. It was printed in Dublin in 1710, at which period the author held a situation of some importance in the Herald's office there, and was esteemed learned in antiquities. In the preface, he has preserved much of the history of the Irish branch of the Seymours, to whose representative his eldest daughter was then united, and upon HIS AUTHORITY their descent from the family of the PROTECTOR, as we have now detailed, is chiefly founded. Mr. Crossley further mentions, that Mrs. Seymour, the great grandmother of his son-in-law, was then very far advanced in life, having endured all the horrors of the siege of Limerick, and that from her he ascertained that her husband had come from "Marvell," in Hampshire, with many of the other particulars which he had embodied in his work.

Susanna, the other daughter and co-heir of Aaron Crossley, married Chetwood Eustace, who succeeded to the dignity of Lord Portlester, of Harristoun, in the county of Kildare, and left, with two daughters, Elizabeth and Abigail, who both died unm. a son, William Eustace, successor to his father in the barony of Portlester, who *m.* Elizabeth, daughter of — Dalton, esq. but leaving no issue, the peerage at his decease became extinct.

† By his wife, Madamoiselle Gabrielle Fonnereau, of the city of La Rochelle, sister of Zacharie Fonnereau, who fled on the revocation of the Edict of Nants, and settling in London, became the founder of the family of Fonnereau of Christ-Church Park, in Suffolk. Madamoiselle Gabrielle abandoned La Belle France for a similar cause, and sought an asylum in Ireland, at the time that the La Touche's and other families of respectability took refuge in that country. She was naturalized at the Court of Queen's Bench in Dublin, on the 10th February, 1710, upon taking the necessary oaths.

Baldwin, esq. of Coolkerry, and Summerhill, both also in the Queen's County, by which lady, who died, aged 81, on the 25th January, 1812, he had four sons, viz.

I. JOHN-CROSSLEY, in holy orders, his heir.

II. Matthew-Cassan, of Lodge, near Drogheda, *m.* first, Frances Smith, niece of Graves Cholmley, esq. of Platten, by whom (who *d.* in 1811) he had

Aaron-Crossley, in the service of the East India Company, died in India, unm.

Graves-Cholmley, also in the East India Company service, and now deceased.

Matthew, } both dead.
John, }

He wedded, secondly, Maria, daughter of the Rev. Roger Curtis, of Mount Hanover, in the county of Meath, but left no other issue.

III. Aaron-Crossley, in the East India Company civil service, register to the secretary of the revenue and judicial departments at Bengal, *m.* first, Maria, daughter and sole heir of Dr. Hogarth, and left by her, who *d.* 31st July, 1816, an only daughter, Frances-Maria, who *m.* her cousin, John Crossley Seymour, esq. of Coolnagower. Mr. Aaron Seymour wedded secondly, Mrs. Browne, and has left issue by that lady.

IV. Stephen, Captain of the Pegasus frigate, R. N. signalized himself under Lord Howe, on the 1st of June, 1794, and was lost at sea a few years after, aged 28.

Mr. Seymour *d.* in 1787, and was *s.* by his eldest son,

The Rev. JOHN CROSSLEY SEYMOUR, vicar of Cahirelley, in the diocese of Cashell. This gentleman, *m.* in January, 1789, Catherine, eldest daughter and co-heir (with her sister Frances, living unmarried) of the Rev. Edward Wight, Rector of Meelick, in the county, and of St. Munchins, in the city of Limerick,* by whom he had a numerous progeny (twenty four children) of which lived to maturity the following eight sons and seven daughters.

I. AARON CROSSLEY, his successor.

II. Edward Wight, *b.* in January, 1791, *m.* in 1821, Margaret, daughter of Peter Roe, esq. of Rockville, in the county of Dublin, and has John-Wight-Edward, and other issue.

III. John-Crossley, of Coolnagower, in the Queen's County, *m.* his cousin, Frances-Maria, only daughter of Aaron Crossley Seymour, esq. of the East India Company's service, and has issue.

IV. Matthew-Cassan.

V. Stephen-Sheffield, *m.* Selina, daughter of Dr. Hart, of Durrow, and is now deceased.

VI. William-Hobart, deceased.

VII. Michael, in holy orders.

VIII. Richard Hobart.

I. Frances, *m.* 28th November, 1816, to Joseph Thomas Keane, esq. and has issue.

II. Jane, deceased.

III. Margaretta-Eliza, *d.* aged twenty, 19th June, 1819.

IV. Catherine.

V. Eliza.

VI. Mary-Anne, *m.* in 1822, to Robert Guinness, esq. of Stillorgan park, in the county of Dublin.

VII. Charlotte-Alicia, *d.* 19th April, 1819.

The Rev. John-Crossley Seymour, who was a man of high and much respected character, died on the 19th May, 1831, and was *s.* by his eldest son, the present AARON-CROSSLEY SEYMOUR, esq. of Castletown.

*Arms*—Quarterly; 1st, gu. two wings conjoined in lure, the tips downwards or, for SEYMOUR. 2nd, per chev. or and vert, in chief a tau between two crosses patonce fitchee gu. in base a hind trippant arg. charged on the neck with a tau of the third, for CROSSLEY. 3rd, gu. a chev. between three boars' heads couped or, for WIGHT. 4th, sa. an estoile of eight points or, between two flanches erm. for HOBART.

*Crest*—Out of a ducal coronet or, a phœnix in flames, ppr. with wings expanded or.

*Motto*—Foy pour devoir.

*Estates*—In the counties of Cork, Limerick, Dublin, and Queen's County.

*Seat*—Castletown House, Queen's County.

## Family of Wight, of Wightfield.

EDWARD WIGHT, who accompanied General Ireton to Ireland, and settled in Limerick, was elected sheriff of that city in 1676, became subsequently an alderman, and served the office of mayor in 1694 and 1711. During his occupancy of the civic chair, money became very scarce in Limerick, and an act was passed authorizing him to have coin struck at the Limerick mint. Some years after he returned to England, and brought back with him to Ireland *eleven* sisters, all of whom married into the most respectable families amongst the English settlers in Limerick, and in the records that remain, we find the names of Tierney, Pike, Piggot, Hobart, Nicholson, Stevens, Daxon,

* By Frances, his wife, elder daughter and co-heir of Willian Hobart, esq. of High Mount, in the county of Cork, grandson of Sir Miles Hobart, of Wiltshire.

Hickman, Hartwell, Holland,* and Odell. Alderman Edward Wight *m.* first, Miss Hoare,† of a highly respectable family, long seated in Limerick, and had two sons, viz.

I. Rice, who died in 1737, leaving a son, John Wight, and a daughter, Sarah, *m.* to Mr. Dupont, of Cork. The descendants of John Wight emigrated to the West Indies, where this branch has become extinct in the male line.

II. RICHARD, in holy orders, rector of Rathronan, and archdeacon of Limerick. He died in 1762, leaving one son, and two daughters, viz.

1. EDWARD, also rector of Rathronan, and archdeacon of Limerick. He *m.* Miss Burgh, relict of Michael Cox, esq. nephew of Dr. Michael Cox, archbishop of Cashell, and grandson of Sir Richard Cox, bart. Lord Chancellor of Ireland. He left issue,

EDWARD WIGHT, in holy orders, rector of Rathronan, who *m.* his cousin Mary, daughter of the Rev. William John Bowen, of Bowen's Court, and had one son, Edward, and a daughter, Catherine, both died unm.

Catherine Wight, married to Thomas Spring, esq. of Castlemain, only son of Thomas Spring, esq. by Hannah, his wife, youngest daughter of Francis Annesley, esq. of Ballysonan, in the county of Kildare, and had an only child,

CATHERINE SPRING, who wedded in 1785, Stephen Edward Rice, esq. of Mount Trenchard, in the county of Limerick, and left issue, the Right Hon. THOMAS SPRING RICE, M. P. for Cambridge, and Mary Rice, *m.* to Sir Aubrey de Vere, bart. of Currah.

Elizabeth, *m.* to Molesworth Greene, esq. of Mountpelier, near Dublin, but *d. s. p.*

1. Elizabeth, *m.* to Bartholomew Gibbins, esq. of Gibbins Grove, in the county of Cork, and had five sons and four daughters, viz.

Richard Gibbins, in holy orders, who *m.* first, Miss Hyde, dau. of Arthur Hyde, esq. of Castle Hyde, M. P. for the county of Cork, and secondly, Catherine, sister to William Odell, esq. of the Grove, M. P. for the county of Limerick. By the latter he had a daughter, Jane, the wife of Thomas Odell, esq. and two sons, Bartholomew (who *m.* Miss Smith) and Thomas, in holy orders, (who *m.* Miss Roberts,‡ of Charleville).

Bartholomew Gibbins, who *m.* Miss Armstead, of Cork, but died issueless. His widow espoused George Wade, esq.

Edward Gibbins, colonel in the Hon. East India Company service, died unm.

---

* Miss Wight, who *m.* — Holland, esq. of Limerick, left, with two daughters, a son, Alderman Holland, whose grand-daughter, Elizabeth Holland, wedded Ralph Ouseley, esq. and was mother of the present Sir Gore Ouseley, bart.

† From a brother of this lady descended the Rev. DEANE HOARE, a gentleman of great benevolence and philanthropy, under whose superintendance the cathedral of Limerick was much improved and beautified in 1752. Mr. Hoare was one of the original founders of the county hospital, and the house of industry. He *m.* Miss Ingram, eldest daughter of aldermen John Ingram, of Limerick, and sister of the Rev. Jacob Ingram, chancellor of St. Mary's Catherine, grandaughter of Dr. Thomas Smyth, Bishop of Limerick, and niece of Dr. Arthur Smyth, Archbishop of Dublin. The Rev. Deane Hoare left two sons, viz.

I. JOHN HOARE, in holy orders, rector of Rath Keale, chancellor of St. Mary's, and vicar general of the diocese of Limerick. He *m.* Rachel, daughter of Sir Edward Newenham, bart. and died in 1813, aged forty-seven, leaving issue.

II. WILLIAM HOARE, in holy orders, minister of St. George's, and vicar general of the diocese of Limerick, *b.* 31st October, 1773, who *m.* Miss Guinness, sister of Arthur Guinness, esq. of Beaumont, in the county of Dublin.

‡ J. B. Roberts, esq. of Charleville, in the county of Cork, left five daughters, viz.

1. Catherine Roberts.
2. Sarah Roberts, *m.* to Charles Dudley Oliver, esq. (son of John Oliver, D. D. Archdeacon of Ardagh, by Miss Ryder, daughter of the Archbishop of Tuam) nephew of the Right Hon. Silver Oliver, of Castle Oliver, in the county of Limerick, and brother to Alicia, Viscountess Lifford, and Robert Dudley Oliver, Admiral of the Royal Navy.
3. Charlotte Roberts, *m.* to the Rev. Dr. Townley, of Margate.
4. Mary Roberts, *m.* to Bowles Reeves, esq.
5. Agnes Roberts, *m.* to the Rev Thomas Gibbins.

Arthur Gibbins, also colonel in the Hon. East India Company service, who *m.* in 1802, Catherine, daughter of John Cuthbert, esq. of Cork, and has a daughter, Mary.

Thomas Gibbins, an eminent physician, who *d.* unm.

Mary Gibbins, *m.* to William Yielding, esq. of the county of Kerry, nephew of William Yielding, esq. of Bellvue, in the county of Limerick, whose daughter, Millicent Agnes, *m.* Sir Rowland Blennerhasset, bt. of Blennerville, in Kerry.

Catherine, *m.* to William Crofts, and left four daughters.

Jane.

Elizabeth, married to colonel Roberts.

2. Catherine, *m.* to the Rev. William John Bowen, of Bowens Ford, in the county of Cork, and had three daughters, viz.

Mary Bowen, *m.* to her cousin, the Rev. Edward Wight, rector of Rathronan.

Elizabeth Bowen, *m.* to Lullum Batwell, esq. of the county of Cork, and left issue, Andrew Batwell, *m.* Miss Galway, daughter of John Galway, esq. of Mallow; and Jane Batwell, the wife of Edward Massey, esq. of Glenville.

Jane Bowen, *m.* to John Fitzmaurice, esq. of Lixnaw, in Kerry, grandson of the Hon. James Fitzmaurice, brother of Thomas, first Earl of Kerry.

Mr. Alderman Wight, married secondly, Miss Bindon, daughter of Alderman Henry Bindon, by whom he had no issue; and thirdly, Miss Hawkesworth, and had four other sons and three daughters, viz.

JOHN, of whom presently.

Thomas, died unm.

Williamson, in holy orders, who *m.* first, Miss Dupont; and secondly, Barbara, daughter of Sir George Mitchell, and left issue, Edward, John, Elizabeth, *m.* to William Galway, esq. and Philicia, to Dr. Aikenhead, of Cork.

George, married, and left issue, Picmar Wight, who *m.* his cousin Mary, daughter of Alderman John Wight.

Frances, *m.* to William Hobart, esq. eldest son of William Hobart, esq. of Dunmore, in the county of Waterford, by his wife, Miss Hawkesworth, and left issue.

Jane, *m.* to William Seymour, esq. and had a son, the Rev. John Seymour, father of the Admiral Sir Michael Seymour, bart.

Judith, *m.* to William M'Cormack, esq. but *d. s. p.*

The alderman died in 1723. His eldest son, by his third marriage,

JOHN WIGHT, esq. seated at Wightfield, near Limerick, was sheriff of Limerick in 1729, and filled the civic chair in 1741. He *m.* his cousin, Frances, daughter of William Hobart,* esq. of Dunmore, in the county of Waterford, and had issue,

EDWARD, in holy orders, rector of Melick, and St. Munchins, in Limerick, *m.* his cousin Frances, daughter of William Hobart, esq. of High Mount, in the county of Cork, and of Mount Melick, in the King's County, by whom he left at his demise, *vita patris*, in 1775, two sons and two daughters,

HOBART, died unm.

John, also died unm.

CATHERINE, *m.* (as already stated) to the Rev. JOHN CROSSLEY SEYMOUR.

Frances.

Eliza, *m.* to Sexten Baylee, esq. alderman and mayor of Limerick in 1758, uncle of the late Henry Baylee, esq. of Loughgur, and had issue,

Sexten Baylee, who *m.* Miss Anne

---

* EDWARD HOBART, esq. the first of the family who settled in Ireland, was seated at Dunmore, in the county of Waterford. He married, and left two sons,

WILLIAM, his heir.

Andrew, of Lackensillage, in the county of Waterford, *m.* Sarah Alice, daughter of William Usher, esq. of the county of Waterford (son of Arthur Usher, esq. by Judith, his wife, daughter of Sir Robert Newcomen, bart. of Mosstoum, in Longford) and had one son and one daughter, who both died unmarried. He died in 1765.

The elder son,

WILLIAM HOBART, esq. of Dunmore, *m.* Miss Hawkesworth (whose sister wedded Alderman Edward Wight) and left at his decease, in 1720, a daughter, Frances, *m.* to her cousin, Alderman John Wight, of Wightfield, and a son in minority,

WILLIAM HOBART, esq. of Mount Melick, in the King's County, and of High Mount, in the county of Cork, who espoused his cousin, Frances, daughter of Mr. Alderman Wight, and left two daughters, his co-heirs, FRANCES, *m.* to her cousin, Rev. Edward Wight, and Grizzle, *m.* to her cousin, the Rev. John Seymour: in the descendants of these marriages, the representation of the Hobart family now rests, viz. in Aaron Crossley Seymour, esq. and Sir Michael Seymour, bart. to whom also the estate descends.

Taverner; and secondly, Eliza, relict of Walter Widenham, esq. By the latter he has issue, John, Pery, Edmund, and Jane.
Pery Baylee, died unm.
Eliza Baylee, *m.* first, to captain Matthew Plaince, and secondly, to W. H. Baylee, esq. She died *s. p.* in 1833.
Jane, died unm.

Mary, *m.* to her cousin, Pickmar Wight, esq. and died at an advanced age, in 1830, having had issue,
George Wight, died unm.
John Wight, who *m.* Catherine, daughter of Henry Bowen, esq. of Bowen's Court.
Grizzel Wight, *m.* to the Rev. Thomas Jones, and has issue.
Alderman John Wight died in 1782.

## RIDDELL, OF FELTON PARK.

RIDDELL, THOMAS, esq. of Felton Park and Swinburne Castle, both in the county of Northumberland, *b.* 18th May, 1802, *m.* 15th October, 1827. Mary, daughter of the late William Throckmorton, esq. of Lincoln's Inn, and has f sons, viz.

THOMAS-WILLIAM, *b.* 14th October, 1828.
John-Giffard, *b.* 10th January, 1830.
Walter, *b.* 17th July, 1831.
Robert, *b.* 24th August, 1832.

Mr. Riddell succeeded his father on the 9th March, 1833. He is in the commission of the peace for Northumberland.

### Lineage.

The ancient family of Riddell derives from

SIR JORDAN DE RIDEL, (brother of Galfred de Ridel, Baron of Blaye) who held a moiety of the lordship of Tilmouth, in Northumberland, in the 17th of EDWARD I. In the next reign (8th of EDWARD II.),

SIR WILLIAM DE RIDELL filled the important office of sheriff for the county of Northumberland, and was appointed by patent, dated 5th June, 1314, from Bishop Kellaw, Constable of Norham castle. He *m.* Emma, and had two sons, namely,

I. WILLIAM, who held the manor of Tilmouth. He *d.* 4th EDWARD III. leaving three daughters, his coheirs,
ISABELLA, *b.* in 1299, *m.* to Alan Claverynge.
CONSTANTIA, *b.* in 1303, *m.* to Sir John Kyngeston, knt.
JOAN, *b.* in 1307, *m.* to Gerard Widdrington.
II. HUGH.

The younger,

HUGH DE RIDEL, living in the 4th EDWARD III., 1329, was father of

THOMAS DE RIDEL, who made his will in 1358, and left a son,

THOMAS RIDELL, father of

THOMAS RIDELL, who wedded one of the daughters and coheirs of Harbotel, of Northumberland, and left a son and heir,

JOHN RIDELL, who was sheriff of Newcastle upon Tyne, in 1478. He *m.* —, and had issue,

THOMAS, his heir.
Peter.
William, sheriff of Newcastle in 1500.

The eldest son,

THOMAS RIDELL, was thrice mayor of

Newcastle in the years 1510, 1521, and 1526. He wedded Eleanor, daughter of Ralph Claxton, esq., and sister of William Claxton, of Wynyard, and by her (who *m.* for her second husband Edward Swinburne) had a son and successor,

PETER RIDELL, living a merchant at Newcastle in 1549, who *m.* Dorothy, eldest daughter of John Brandling, mayor of the same borough in 1509, and sister of Sir Ralph Brandling, knt., (*see* vol. ii, p. 39) and had issue,

- I. THOMAS, his heir, who *d. s. p.*
- II. Peter, of Newcastle, wedded Eleanor, daughter of John Swinburne, of the same place, and had
  - William, *b.* in 1581.
  - Peter, *b.* in 1591.
  - Thomas, *b.* in 1599.
  - Barbara, *b.* in 1584, *m.* first, in 1608, to John Sotheron, and secondly, to Anthony Theobald.
- III. WILLIAM, of whom presently.

- I. Eleanor, *m.* to Henry Lawe.
- II. Katherine, *m.* in 1580 to Anthony Lawe.

The youngest son,

WILLIAM RIDEL, of Newcastle, merchant adventurer, sheriff of that borough in 1575, and mayor in 1582, 1590, and 1595. This worshipful citizen married twice; by his first wife, Anne, daughter and heir of William Lawson, he had an only son, THOMAS, (Sir) his heir. By the second, Barbara, daughter of Alderman Bertram Anderson, (who *d.* in 1627, and was buried on the 11th November, her will bears date 30th October, 3rd CHARLES I.) he had eight other sons and a daughter, viz.

- Peter (Sir), sheriff of Newcastle in 1604, mayor in 1619 and 1635. Member of parliament for the borough in 1623, 1626, 1628, and 1640, *m.* first, Isabel,* daughter of Mr. Alderman Atkinson, of Newcastle, and had by that lady, who *d.* in 1614, four sons and four daughters. Sir Peter wedded, secondly, Mary, second daughter and coheir of Thomas Surtees, esq. (heir male of the Dinsdale family) and had two more daughters, Anne, *m.* in 1638, to Cuthbert Carr, esq. of St. Helen Auckland, in Durham, and Isabel, *b.* in 1618.
- Henry, *b.* in 1574, *d.* at Elbinge, in Germany, issueless.
- William, *b.* in 1578, married, and had five sons and as many daughters.
- George, *b.* in 1580.
- Robert, *b.* in 1582, *d.* young.
- Michael, *b.* in 1583, *d.* in 1613, probably *s. p.*
- John, *b.* in 1585.
- Robert, *b.* in 1590, of Newcastle, died in 1635 without issue, seised of certain lands in Lanchester, leaving his brother, Sir Peter, his heir. He had married, in 1621, Jane Cole, who survived his widow until 1651.
- Alice, *b.* in 1587.

The only son of the first marriage,

SIR THOMAS RIDEL, knight of Gateshead, in the Palatinate of Durham, was sheriff of Newcastle in 1601, mayor in 1604 and 1616, and member of parliament for the borough in 1620, and again with his brother, Sir Peter Ridel in 1628. He *m.* Elizabeth, daughter of Sir John Conyers, knight of Sockburn, and had issue,

- I. WILLIAM (Sir), his heir, who in the *time* of ELIZABETH, was one of the grand lessees in trust for the corporation of Newcastle, of the lordships of Gateshead, and Whickham. He *m.* first, Katherine, daughter of Sir Henry Widdrington, of Widdrington, and had an only surviving child,
  - WILLIAM, of Gateshead, who died 1698, leaving by Isabel, his first wife, a daughter,
    - JANE, the wife of Mark Ridell, esq.
  - and by Margaret, his second wife, a son, and another daughter, viz.
    - WILLIAM, of Gateshead, who *d. s. p.* in 1710.
    - Catherine, who died unm. in 1750.
- II. THOMAS (Sir).
- III. Peter, *d. s. p.*
- IV. George, *b.* in 1602. D. C. L. Judge Advocate in the Army of the Marquess of Newcastle, and during the siege of Hull in 1645, *m.* Jane, dau. and co-heir of — Eysdale, chancellor of the diocese of York, and had a son, Thomas, and a daughter, Margaret.
- V. Robert, *b.* in 1612, *m.* a French lady, named Magdalen.
- VI. Ephraim, *b.* in 1615.

- I. Anne, *m.* to Sir John Clavering, knt. of Callaly (see vol. i. p. 239).
- II. Elizabeth, *d.* in 1606.
- III. Mary, *m.* to Sir Francis Radcliffe, bart. of Dilston.
- IV. Eleanor, *b.* in 1610.
- V. Jane, *m.* to John Forcer, esq. of Harber House, in the county of Durham.

The second son, (in whose descendant the representation eventually centred),

SIR THOMAS RIDELL, knight of Fenham,

* Her sister married the Right Rev. William James, Bishop of Durham.

was recorder of Newcastle, and representative of the borough in parliament, in the 18th of James I. During the troubles of the ensuing reign, Sir Thomas espoused, with extraordinary zeal, the royal cause. He commanded a regiment of foot in the service of the king, was governor of Tynemouth Castle, and so distinguished, that a reward of one thousand pounds was offered for his apprehension. He effected his escape, however, in a small fishing smack from Berwick, and died at Antwerp in 1652, "a banished man," his lordship of Tunstal having been previously sold to satisfy his composition. He *m.* in 1629, Barbara, dau. of Sir Alexander Davison, knight of Blakiston, and widow of Ralph Calverley, by whom he had issue,

- Thomas, his heir, baptized 17th June, 1632.
- Ralph, *b.* in 1636.
- Barbara, *b.* in 1630.
- Anne, *b.* in 1632, *m.* to Francis, second son of Marmaduke Tunstal, esq. of Wycliffe, in the county of York.
- Elizabeth, *b.* in 1634, *m.* to Ralph Wilson, esq. of Field House, near Gateshead.
- Margery, *b.* in 1639, living in 1661 a nun at Pointoise in France.
- Jane, *b.* in 1641.
- Eleanor, *b.* in 1643.

Sir Thomas was *s.* by his eldest son,

Thomas Riddell, esq. of Fenham, in the county of Northumberland, which estate he sold in the year 1695, under an act of parliament, to John Orde, esq. of Newcastle, and purchasing Swinburne, settled there. He *m.* Mary, eldest daughter of Edward Grey, esq. of Bichfield, in Northumberland, and had (with other daughters, who all died unm.) the following issue,

- I. Thomas, *b.* in 1656, } both *d.* young.
- II. William, *b.* in 1658, } both *d.* young.
- III. Edward, *the heir.*
- IV. Alexander, *b.* in 1663.
- V. Mark, a physician, sometime of Hunton, and afterwards of Morpeth, *b.* in 1665, *m.* Jane, daughter of William Ridell, esq. of Gateshead, and had one son, Edward of Morpeth, living in 1731, when his (the Doctor's) will, which bears date in 1721, was proved.
- VI. John, *d.* in 1672.
- VII. Thomas.
- VIII. William.
- I. Elizabeth, *m.* to William Shaftoe, esq. of Bavington.

Mr. Riddell *d.* about the year 1704, and was *s.* by his eldest surviving son,

Edward Riddell, esq. of Swinburne Castle, *b.* in 1669, who wedded Dorothy, daughter of Robert Dalton, esq. of Thurnham, in Lancashire, and dying in 1731, was *s.* by his only son,

Thomas Riddell, esq. of Swinburne Castle. This gentleman, who was involved in the rising of 1715, saved himself by escaping from Lancaster Castle, but not being excepted from the general pardon, he was allowed to return to his estate, and reside there unmolested. He *m.* in 1726, Mary, daughter of William Widdrington, esq. of Cheesburn Grange, and sister and co-heir of Ralph Widdrington, by whom he had issue,

- Thomas, his successor.
- Ralph, who inheriting the estates of his uncle, Ralph Widdrington, esq. became "of Cheesburn Grange." (See Riddell of Cheesburn Grange.)
- Dorothy, *d.* unm.
- Barbara, *m.* to — Nelson, esq. of Lancashire.
- ——, *m.* to —Maxwell, esq. of Kirkoswald, N. B.

He was *s.* at his decease by his elder son,

Thomas Riddell, esq. of Swinburne Castle, who had been engaged with his father in the insurrection of 1715, and was carried up to London, where being with several others arraigned for high treason in 1716, he pleaded guilty, but experienced the royal mercy. He espoused Elizabeth, only dau. and heiress of Edward Horsley Widdrington, esq. of Felton, in Northumberland, by whom he acquired that estate, with Longhorsley, in the same county, and had issue,

- I. Thomas, heir to Swinburne.
- II. Edward, who inherited the estates of the Widdringtons, through his mother, and became "of Felton and Horsley." He *m.* 5th July, 1792, Isabella, daughter of William Salvin, esq. of Croxdale, but died *s. p.* on the 26th January, in the next year, at Stella Hall, Durham. His widow married in 1803, Ralph Riddell, esq. of Cheesburn Grange.
- III. Ralph, heir to his elder brother, Thomas.
- I. Mary.
- II. Dorothy, *d.* unm.
- III. Elizabeth, *m.* to John Clifton, esq. of Lytham.
- IV. Anne, *m.* to Sir Walter Blount, bart. of Sodington.

This Thomas Riddell sold Fenham Colliery to the Ord family, who had already purchased the feesimple of the land. He died in 1777, and was *s.* by his eldest son,

Thomas Riddell, esq. of Swinburne Castle, who *m.* 19th April, 1790, Margaret, dau. of William Salvin, esq. of Croxdale, and had an only child, Thomas, who predeceased him. He died himself in 1798, and was *s.* by his youngest and only surviving brother,

RALPH RIDDELL, esq. of Felton and Horsley, which estates he had inherited at the decease of his brother EDWARD, issueless, in 1793. He *m.* 23rd July, 1801, Elizabeth, daughter of Joseph Blount, esq. second son of Michael Blount, esq. of Maple Durham, (see page 170), and had issue,

- THOMAS, his heir.
- Edward Widdrington, *b.* 4th September, 1803, *m.* 1st July 1830, Catherine, daughter of Thomas Stapleton, esq. of Richmond, in the county of York.
- William, *b.* 5th February, 1807, in holy orders of the church of Rome.
- Henry, *b.* 24th February, 1815.
- Charles-Francis, *b.* 1st October, 1817.
- Elizabeth-Anne.

Mr. Riddell died on the 9th March, 1833, and was succeeded by his eldest son, the present THOMAS RIDDELL, esq. of Felton Park, and Swinburne Castle, both in the county of Northumberland.

### Family of Horsley.

The old and knightly race of HORSLEY, from which the estates of Felton and Horsley have come, through the Widdringtons, to the Riddells, were land owners in Northumberland* at a very remote period, probably preceding the time of HENRY III. for Roger de Horsley occurs as a witness to a deed without a date, by which Roger de Merlay conveyed five bovates of land, situated in Horsley, Sheles, and Todburn, to Adam de Plesseto and his heirs.

The name of

SIR JOHN DE HORSLEY, Knight Banneret, appears in a document written about 1522, as John Horsley, and as then dwelling in a place belonging to his father, over whose lands, to the value of fifty marks yearly he had the whole rule; beside which, he himself had lands, out of which he could dispend £40 a year, and serve the king with thirty horsemen. In 1547, he fought at Musselburgh, and was made a BANNERET on the field of battle. In 1552, he was a commissioner of enclosures, in the East Marches, at which time he was Captain of Bamborough Castle, and he and Sir John Foster had the appointment of the watch in that year, from Warnmouth to Doxford Burn. He left, with a daughter, ISABELLA, of whom presently, an only son,

CUTHBERT, of Horsley, member of parliament for Northumberland in the 7th of EDWARD VI. and 1st of *Queen* MARY, whose name is to be found in a list of gentlemen, of the Middle Marches, made in 1550, and in 1552, amongst the Commissioners of Enclosures, in the same district. In 1568, he was proprietor of Scranwood, a moiety of the ville and manor of Horsley, Brinkheugh, &c. he had a daughter, Elizabeth, the wife of John Bell, of Bellasis, and a son and heir,

JOHN HORSLEY, esq. of Horsley, who *m.* Eleanor, daughter of William Hilton, esq. of Hilton Castle, in Durham, and dying about 1605, left

- GEORGE, of Horsley, who wedded Catherine, daughter of — Grey, of Chillingham, but died *s. p.* about 1615.
- Anne, *m.* to Robert Horsley, of Brinkheugh.

The only daughter of Sir John de Horsley,

ISABELLA HORSLEY, espoused Thomas Horsley, esq. of Brinkheugh, (whose arms were three horses' heads), and was mother of

LANCELOT HORSLEY, esq. of Brinkheugh, who *m.* Elizabeth, dau. of John Widdrington, esq. of Hauxley, and had two sons and three daughters, viz.

- THOMAS (Sir) his heir.
- Robert, of Brinkheugh, who *m.* Anne, daughter of John Horsley, esq.
- Catherine, *m.* to — Fulwood, esq.
- Margaret.
- Florentina.

He died in 1609, and was *s.* by his elder son,

SIR THOMAS HORSLEY, knt. of Horsley, *b.* 25th August, 1612, who *m.* Eleanor, dau. of William Calverley, esq. of Calverley, and had issue,

- WILLIAM, who wedded Rebecca, dau. of Robert Salvin esq. of Durham, but died without issue, in his (Sir Thomas's) life time.
- DOROTHY, of whom presently.
- MARY.

Amongst the guests at Horsley, Kenet mentions the reception of General Monk by Sir Thomas, in the following words—"General Monk was at Wooler, 1st January, 1601; at Whittingham the next day, and in his way to Morpeth, on the 3rd he was entertained, with his whole train, by this honest old knight at his house, very kindly and nobly," and again he says, "the night before we came to Morpeth, we had good quarters, and were contented with what the house afforded. The gentleman was of the Romish religion, and informed us that Lambert's forces had quartered there, and told us plainly, he had rather they should have prevailed. We had so much of good manners as not to be angry with him in his

* At Long Horsley.

own house, or for his private opinion." Sir Thomas served the office of sheriff for Northumberland, about the year 1664. His will bears date in 1685. His eldest daughter,

DOROTHY HORSLEY, m. first, about 1655, Robert L'Isle, esq. but by him, who died in 1657, had no issue. She wedded secondly, the Hon. Edward Widdrington, son of Sir William Widdrington, of Widdrington, Lord Widdrington, (see BURKE's *Extinct Peerage*) and by that gentleman, who fell at the Battle of the Boyne, left, with three daughters, a son and successor,

EDWARD WIDDRINGTON, esq. of Felton, *b.* in 1658, who *m.* Elizabeth,* daughter of Caryl, third Viscount Molyneux, and left at his decease, in 1705, with two daughters, Theresa, *m.* to Sir William Wheeler, bart. of Leamington, Hastaug, in the county of Warwick, and Bridget, a son and successor,

EDWARD HORSLEY WIDDRINGTON, esq. of Felton, whose will was proved in 1763. He *m.* Elizabeth, daughter of Humphrey Weld, esq. of Lulworth Castle, in the county of Dorset, and left an only daughter and heiress,

ELIZABETH WIDDRINGTON, who married THOMAS RIDDELL, esq. as stated under Riddell.

* Sister of Anne, wife of William Widdrington, esq. of Cheesburn Grange.

*Arms*—Arg. a fess between three Rye sheaves, az.

*Crest*—A demi-lion couped or, holding a rye sheaf.

*Motto*—Deus solus auget aristas.

*Estates*—Felton and Long Horsley, in Northumberland, acquired by the marriage of the present proprietor's grandfather, with Elizabeth, daughter and heiress of Edward Horsley Widdrington, esq. Swinburne, purchased in 1695, by T. Riddell, esq. of Fenham, and Little Swinburne, purchased by the late R. Riddell, esq.

*Seats*—Felton Park, and Swinburne Castle, Northumberland.

## LONG-WELLESLEY, OF DRAYCOT CERNE.

WELLESLEY-LONG-TYLNEY, WILLIAM-RICHARD-ARTHUR, esq. of Draycot, in the county of Wilts, *b.* October, 1813, inherited the estates from his mother, Catherine, sister and heiress of Sir James Tilney-Long, bart.

### Lineage.

The ancient family of Long, now represented through his mother by Mr. Wellesley (for whose paternal descent refer to BURKE's *Peerage*) flourished in the county of Wilts, for many generations, 'knyghtes,' as Camden says, 'and men of greate worship.' We find them first established at South Wraxall, in that county, but whether by grant, by purchase, or by marriage, does not distinctly appear.* The tradition men-

* We shall give the account of their supposed origin in the words of Leland and Camden, premising, however, that persons styled le Long and Longus, are to be met with in deeds considerably anterior to the time stated, as for example, Sir William le Long, a knight of Gloucestershire, temp. HENRY III. bearing for his arms, gules a saltire engrailed, or. Aylmer Long stated to have held one knight's fee, in Wilts, in the 15th of HENRY II. Robert Long, who held land at Langley Burrell, in the same county, about the time of HENRY III. Gilbert and John Long, sons of Walter Long, said to have founded the hospital of St. John, at Exeter, in the 23rd of HENRY III. Leland writes as follows:

tioned by that author, of their alliance to the Preux family, is in some degree supported by the close resemblance of the coat of arms (the coate of Preux being sa. semée of cross crosslets, or, 3 lioncels rampant argent) while the descents bear out the statement of Leland. However this may be, it is clear that they were of some repute as early as the time of Henry IV. and a monument of about that date in the church of Wraxall, sufficiently attests the respectability of one of their first alliances, the bearings on it being Long, impaling Berkley, quartering Seymour. Tradition begins the pedigree with a Long, married to a Stourton, to whom succeeded his son, married to a Berkley, of Beverstone, who was again succeeded by his son, Roger Long, or le Long, married to a Seymour, or St. Maur. Without dismissing these personages as altogether fabulous, (for there really are some grounds for a portion at least of the theory), we shall begin with the first known possessor of Wraxall, namely

ROBERT LONG, or LONGE, who was in the commission of the peace in 1426, and was M. P. for Wiltshire in 1433. He m. Alice, daughter and heiress of Reginald Popham,* of North Bradley, in the county of Wilts, and had issue,

I. HENRY, his heir.
II. John, m. Margaret, daughter of Edward Wayte, by the heiress of Draycot Cerne,† and sister and co-heir of Thomas Wayte, of the Temple, and of Draycot, and had issue,
  1. THOMAS, afterwards SIR THOMAS.
  2. Richard, (Sir).
  3. William.
III. Reginald, died before 1490.

Robert Long died subsequently to 1459, (when we find him mentioned in the will of Robert, Lord Hungerford, son of the Lord Treasurer) and was succeeded by his son,

HENRY LONG, of Wraxall, who was sheriff of Wilts in 1457, 1476 and 1483. He m. first, Joan, daughter of — Ernleigh, but by her, who died 1468, had no issue; secondly, Margaret daughter of John Newburgh, of Lullworth, in the county of Dorset, by whom also he had no issue, and thirdly, another Joan, who survived him, and had likewise no issue. We find him mentioned in the will of Margaret Lady Hungerford, the relict of Robert before mentioned, in 1479. He died October 20, 1490, and was buried in the chancel of the Church of Wraxall, being succeeded in his estates by his nephew,

SIR THOMAS LONG, of Wraxall and Draycot, knt. Sheriff of Wilts in 1501, who was among the "great compaignye of noble men," who served under Edward, Duke of Buckingham, against Perkin Warbeck (see Hardyng's Chronicles). He received the honour of knighthood at the marriage of Prince Arthur, and married Mary, daughter of Sir George Darell, of Littlecote,‡ in the county of Wilts, and had issue,

---

"The original setting up of the House of the Longes, came (as I learned from Mr. Boneham) by these means. One Long Thomas, a stoute felaw, was sette up by one of the old Lordes Hungerfordes; and after by cause this Thomas was caullid long Thomas, Long after was usurped for the name of the family. This Long Thomas master had sum lande by Hungreford's procuration. Then succeeded hym Robert and Henry. Then came one Thomas Long, descending of a younger brother, and good skille of the lawe, and had the inheritances of the aforesaid Longes. Syr Henry and Syr Richard Longe, were sunnes to this Thomas."

Camden, in his Remains, says:

"In respect of stature, I could recite to you other examples; but I will only add this, which I have read, that a young gentleman of the house of Preux, being of tall stature, attending on the Lord Hungerford, Lord Treasurer of England, was among his fellows called Long H., who after preferred to a good marriage by his Lord, was called H. Long, that name continued to his posterity, knights and men of greate worship."

The name of Preux occurs in the roll of Battle Abbey, and the family was seated at Gidley Castle, in Devonshire, soon after the conquest. William le Preux was member for Wilton, in Wiltshire, 28th of EDWARD I.

* The connection of this family of Popham, with that of the Judge, does not distinctly appear. There is, however, but little doubt of the affinity. A moiety of the manor of Barton Stacey, in Hants, was held by Robert Long, in the 25th of HENRY VI. and by his son, John, in the 18th of EDWARD IV. which manor was held by Sir Philip Popham, and Elizabeth, his wife, in the 21st of RICHARD II.

† The Cernes were Lords of Melcombe, in the county of Dorset, in the time of RICHARD I. and Galfridus de Cerne was Lord of Draycot, in the time of HENRY III. The property, and with it the advowson, has descended, therefore, without alienation to the present possessor through six centuries, of which it was in the Long family for nearly four. The last of the Cernes, Lords of Draycot, (Richard de Cerne) died in the 8th of HENRY VI. and was succeeded by John de Herringe, from whom the property passed, through the Waytes, to the Longs; but by what intermarriage is not exactly known. The other sister and co-heiress of Thomas Wayte, married Sir John Chalers, knt. who was sheriff of Berks in 1449. Draycot was held by the service of being marshal at the coronation.

‡ The Darells were settled in Wiltshire, by the marriage of William Darell, a younger son of Darell, of Sessay, in Yorkshire, with Elizabeth Calston, the heiress of Littlecote. The Calstons had previously intermarried with a co-heiress of St. Martin. One of the daughters of Sir George

I. Henry, his heir.

II. Richard, (Sir) knight* of Shengay and Hardwick, in the county of Cambridge, gentleman of the privy chamber, captain of Guernsey, and master of the hawks and buckhounds, *m.* Margaret, daughter and heir of John Donnington, esq. and relict of Sir Thomas Kitson, of Hengrave, in the county of Suffolk, knt. She died in 1561, æt. 52, having remarried John Bourchier, Earl of Bath. Sir Richard had issue,

Henry, *b.* March 22, 1534.

Catharine, *m.* Edward Fisher, esq. of Ickington, in the county of Warwick.

Jane.

Mary.

Sir Richard died 1545, and was succeeded by his son,

Henry Long, esq.† of Shengay, M. P. for the county of Cambridge 1571, married Dorothy, daughter of Nicholas Clarke, of North Weston, in the county of Oxon, who remarried Sir Charles Morrison, of Cashiobury. Mr. Long died in 1573, and was *s.* by his only surviving daughter and heir,

Elizabeth, *m.* to William, Lord Russell, of Thornhaugh, ancestor to the Duke of Bedford. She died in 1611, and was buried at Watford.

III. Thomas.

IV. Robert, of Mawditt, parish of Somerford, Wilts.

V. John.

VI. William.

VII. Edward.

I. Joan, *m.* Edward Mylle, esq. grandson of Sir William Mylle, of Tre-Mylle, in the county of Gloucester.

Sir Thomas *d.* in 1510, and was succeeded by his son,

Sir Henry Long, knt. of Wraxall and Draycot, Sheriff of Wilts in 1512-26-37-42, and for Somerset in 1538, member for Wilts in 1552-3. Sir Henry was one of the attendants of Henry VIII. at the field of the Cloth of Gold, and was knighted for making a gallant charge at Therouenne in Picardy, in the sight of Henry, when he received the grant of a new crest, viz. the lion's head with the hand in its mouth. His banner bears the motto, "Fortune soies eureux." He *m.* first, Frideswide, dau. of Sir John Hungerford, of Down Ampney, great-grandson of the Lord Treasurer, and had issue,

I. Thomas, *d. s. p.*

II. John, *d.* in infancy.

I. Elizabeth, *m.* Michael Quinton, of Bubton, Wilts, and had issue.

II. Jane, *m.* Thomas Leversedge, of Frome Selwood, in the county of Somerset.

He *m.* secondly, Eleanor, daughter of Richard Wrottesley, of Wrottesley, in the county of Stafford, and relict of Edmund Leversedge, of Frome Selwood, by her, who *d.* in 1543, he had issue,

I. Robert, his heir.

II. Benedict.

III. Edmund, of Kelwayes, or Titherton Calloway, in the county of Wilts, *m.* Susan, daughter of Nicholas Snell, of Kington St. Michael, in the same county, M. P. for Wilts, and who remarried Hugh Barret, of Titherton. He had issue,

Henry.

Cicely.

Alice.

IV. Anthony, of Ashley, in the parish of Box, in the county of Wilts, *m.* Alice, daughter of William Butler,

---

Darell married Sir John Seymour, grandfather to the Protector. The last of the Darells of Littlecote, William Darell, died *s. p.* in 1590, aged about 51. His next heir was Thomas, his brother, who was of Hungerford, and was father to Sir John Darell, of West Woodhay, Berks, created a baronet, 13th of June, 1622.

* Sir Richard bore the canopy over Edward VI. at his baptism, and received large grants of Abbey lands at the dissolution of monasteries, viz. the hospital of St. Nicholas at Salisbury, Reading Place, in London, the manors of East Greenwich, in Kent, Filolshall and Coggeshall, in Essex, and great Saxham, in Suffolk, &c. &c.

† Henry VIII. was his godfather (see Gage's Hengrave). He was buried in the church of St. Andrew's Wardrobe, under a "comely monument," as Stowe informs us, "at the East end of the chancel," on which was the following inscription:

Marmoreum decus hoc consortis munere grato,
Non vitâ, verùm nomine, *Longus* habet.

Here lieth Henry Long, esq. of Shingay, son and heir of Sir Richard Long, knt. gentleman of the privy chamber to *King* Henry VIII. the third son of Sir Thomas Long, knight, of Wiltshire, who married Dorothy, the daughter of Nicholas Clarke, esq. of Weston, and Elizabeth Ramsay, his wife, sole heir of Thomas Ramsay, esq. of Hicham, her father, by whom he had issue, one son and three daughters. He died the 15th day of April, anno Domini 1573, leaving alive, at that time of his death, Elizabeth, his sole daughter and heir.

Dorothea uxor, conjugis amore posuit.
Nomine *Longus*, vitâ brevis, inclitus ortu,
Ingenio præstans, et pietatis amans.

This conjugal memorial, of which the versification is in part defective, perished in the great fire.

of Badminton, in the county of Gloucester, by Margaret, daughter of — Pierce, by Elizabeth, sister and heir of Thomas Mountford, of Ashley. He had issue,

1. William, *s. p.*
2. Thomas, *s. p.*
3. HENRY, his heir.
4. Francis, *s. p.*
5. Silvester, *s. p.*
6. Robert, *s. p.*

1. Thomazine.
2. Margaret.
3. Jane.
4. Eleanor.
5. Elizabeth.
6. Dorothy.
7. Edith.

Anthony Long, died May, 1578, and was buried at Box, under a monument yet existing, and having a shield bearing Long, Popham, Seymour and Long, impaling his wife's arms. He was *s.* by his son,

Henry Long, of Ashley, *m.* first, Mary, daughter of Richard Paulett, of Minety (son of Sir Hugh and brother of Sir Amias Paulett, the keeper of Mary Queen of Scots), by Mary, sister of Anthony Hungerford, of Lea, near Malmesbury, and had issue,

Henry, who accompanied CHARLES II. in 1660.

Mary, *s. p.*
Elizabeth, *s. p.*

He *m.* secondly, Israel, daughter of Anthony Hungerford, of Lea,* and had issue,

Anthony, of Walcot near Bath.
Alice, *m.* John Bonny, of Bath.
Anne, *m.* George Long, of Bath.

Anthony Long, of Walcot, *m.* Anne, daughter of Richard Long, of Avening, in the county of Gloucester, and had issue,

NATHANIEL.
Richard, *d. s. p.*; buried at Hampton Rode, in the county of Gloucester.
Timothy.
Josias.

NATHANIEL LONG,† of London, merchant, *m.* Sarah, daughter of Giles Lytcott, comptroller general of the customs, son of Sir John Lytcott, of Moulsey, Surrey, by Mary, sister of Sir Thomas Overbury. She *d.* in 1731, aged 63, and he died in 1714; aged 63, having had issue,

Richard, *d.* in infancy.
Lytcott, *b.* in 1675.
Nathaniel, *b.* in 1677.
George, *b.* in 1690.
John.

Anne, *d.* in infancy.
Lucy.
Sarah, *b.* in 1678, *m.* to — Knight.
Alice, *m.* to — Greene.

v. Richard, of Lineham in the county of Wilts, *m.* ——, sister of Thomas Browne, of Winterbourne Basset, in the county of Wilts, and dying in 1558, was *s.* by his son,

EDMUND, of Lineham, *b.* in 1555, *m.* Rachael, daughter of John Coxwell, of Ablington, in the county of Gloucester, and had issue,

1. HENRY, (died *vitâ patris*) *m.* Margaret, daughter of Leonard Duckett, and had issue,
   Catharine, *b.* in 1612, *m.* Leonard Atkins, of Sutton Benger.
2. RICHARD, his heir male.
3. Walter, *b.* 1595, *m.* Maria ——, and dying in 1630, had issue,
   Walter, *b.* 1628, *d.* in 1700, *s. p.*
   Rachael.
4. John.

1. Eleanor, *m.* — Willes, of Somerset.
2. Mary, *m.* — Bishop, of Montgomery.
3. Norton, *b.* 1606, *m.* — Smith.
4. Anne.
5. Elizabeth.
6. Jane.
7. Frances.

Edmund Long, of Lineham, died in 1635, and was succeeded by his son,

RICHARD LONG, of Lineham, *m.* first, Mary, daughter of William Miles, of Glos-

* He was grandson of Sir Anthony Hungerford, of Down Ampney, who was great-great-grandson of the Lord Treasurer. There is now not a vestige of the mansion of these Hungerfords at Lea. It existed in Aubrey's time.

† He is called on his monument at Allhallows, Barking, "Colonel" Nathaniel Long. John is the only son mentioned in the wills of Nathaniel and his wife, in 1714, and 1731. It is therefore probable that the other sons died *s. p.* Thurloe, Cromwell's Secretary, married the sister of Giles Lytcott.

cester, and had issue by her, who *d.* in 1665,

EDMUND, his heir.

Richard, *d.* in 1655.

He *m.* secondly, Susanna, daughter of — Clarke, and had issue,

Humphry, *d.* in 1679, *s. p.*

Susanna, married Robert Compton, living in 1680.

Richard Long, of Lineham, *d.* 1639, and was succeeded by his son,

EDMUND LONG, of Lineham, *b.* 1621, *m.* Barbara, daughter of Sir George Ayliffe, knt. of Rabson, in the county of Wilts, and had issue,

EDMUND, *m.* Mary ——, *d.* 1681, *s. p.* and sold Lineham.

William, *b.* in 1655.

Richard, *b.* in 1660, died in 1662.

Oliver, *d.* in Ireland, in 1716.

George.

Lucy.

Deborah.

Martha, *m.* — Danvers.

Barbara.

Mary.

Elizabeth, *m.* Christopher Guise, third son of Henry Guise, of Winterbourne, in the county of Gloucester, brother of the first baronet.

I. Margery, *m.* Robert Hungerford, of Cadenham, great-grandson of Sir Edward Hungerford, of Down Ampney, son of the treasurer.

II. Thomazine.

III. Cicely, *m.* Francis Stradling, of Somersetshire.

Sir Henry Long *d.* in 1556, and was *s.* by his son,

SIR ROBERT LONG, knt. of Wraxall and Draycot, *b.* in 1517, sheriff of Wilts in 1575, who served at the siege of Boulogne. He *m.* Barbara, daughter of Sir Edward Carne, knt. of Wenny, in the county of Glamorgan, and by her, who *d.* in 1606, had issue,

I. WALTER, his heir.

II. Robert.

III. Henry, slain by Charles and Henry Danvers.*

IV. Jewell, so named after Jewell, Bishop of Sarum, *d.* in 1647, buried at Box.*

I. Anne, *m.* Sir Thomas Snell, of Kingston St. Michael, and had issue.

Sir Robert *d.* in 1581, and was succeeded by his son,

SIR WALTER LONG, knt.† of Wraxall and Draycot, sheriff in 1602, M. P. for Wilts in 1592, *m.* first, Mary,‡ daughter of Sir William Packington, of Westwood, in the county of Worcester, and had issue,

I. JOHN, his heir, of Wraxall, *m.* Anne, daughter of Sir William Eyre, of Chaldfield, Wilts, and had issue,

WILLIAM, *b.* in 1615, who *m.* Mary, daughter of Robert Shaa, son of Thomas Shaa,§ by Mary, dau.

---

* This was the celebrated Earl of Danby, stated on his monument at Dauntsey to have died "full of *honour*, woundes, and dayes!!" This murder took place at Somerford. "The assassination," says Aubrey, "of Harry Long, was contrived in the parlour of the parsonage here. Mr. Attwood was then parson; he was drowned coming home."

* His monument, recorded in Aubrey, has a scriptural pun in the form of a quotation from Malachi: "And they shall be mine in the day when I shall gather my jewels."

† He was in friendship with Sir Walter Raleigh, and like his great prototype, was the first to introduce the fashion of smoking amongst the Wiltshire gentry. "They had first," says Aubrey, "silver pipes." The intercourse between the two Sir Walters arose, according to Aubrey, thus: "Sir Walter Long of Draycot, (grandfather to this Sir James Long) married a daughter of Sir John Thynne, by which means," Sir Carey Raleigh, the elder brother of Sir Walter, having married Sir John Thynne's widow, "and their consimility of disposition, there was a very conjunct friendship between the two brothers and him; and old John Long, who then waited on Sir Walter Long, being one time in the privy gardens with his master, saw the Earl of Nottingham wipe the dust from Sir Walter R.'s shoes with his cloak, in compliment." The ostentatious style of living in those days was fully supported by the owner of Draycot. "Old Sir Walter Long, of Draycot, kept a trumpeter, rode with thirty servants and retainers. Hence the sheriff's trumpets at this day. No younger brothers were to betake themselves to trade, but were churchmen or retainers to great men."

‡ It was probably this Lady Long who made the usual exchange of new years gifts with the Queen (Elizabeth) in 1588-9, and 1599-1600. On the first occasion she gave "a skrimskyer of cloth of silver, embroidered all over with beasts and flowers, and a woman in the middest, lyned with carnation flush." The queen in return gave her fifteen ounces of gilt plate. On the second occasion, she gave her majesty "one smocke of fine holland, the sleeves wrought with black silke," and got in exchange eighteen ounces of gilt plate.

§ He was grandson of Sir Edmund Shaa, Lord Mayor. Walter Lord Hungerford was beheaded in 1541. He was son of Sir Edward Hungerford, of Heytesbury, by Jane, daughter of John, Lord Zouche.

of Walter Lord Hungerford, and *d. s. p.* in 1647.

JOHN, eventual heir.

Walter, of Bristol, *b.* in 1623; *d.* 11th October, 1669. His son, by Barbara his wife,

Walter, of Wraxall, died in 1731, aged 84, bequeathing the estate of Wraxall, &c. to the son of his cousin, Catharine, the wife of John Long, of Monkton.

Edward, of Trowbridge, *b.* in 1626, *m.* Elizabeth, daughter of the Rev. Thomas Twist, and *d. s. p.* in 1650.

Hesther, *m.* to John Aubrey, of Netherham, and had issue.

The eldest surviving son,

JOHN LONG, esq. of Wraxall, who died 23rd February, 1652, *m.* twice; by the first wife he had a daughter, Mary, *m.* to John Aubrey, and by the second, Catharine, dau. of John Paynter, who wedded secondly, Edward Aubrey, of Wraxall, one son and three daughters, viz.

HOPE LONG, esq. of Wraxall, who *m.* first, Mary, dau. of John Long, of Monkton, and grand-daughter of Edward Long, and had issue,

John, born in 1672, *d. s. p.*

Catharine, *b.* in 1674, *m.* to Michael Tidcombe, esq. and had issue.*

He wedded secondly, Grace, relict of — Blanchard, of Preston, in the county of Somerset, but by her had no issue. Mr. Hope Long died in 1715, when the estates passed to his cousin, Walter Long, esq. son of Walter, of Bristol.

Catharine, *m.* to John Long, esq. grandson of Edward Long, of Monkton,† and had issue.

Elizabeth.

Anne, *m.* to Henry Long, esq. of Melksham, son of Richard Long, of Collingbourne, Wilts, and had issue.*

II. Thomas, who *d. s. p.*

I. Barbara, *m.* to Morice Berkeley, of Beverstone Castle, Gloucestershire, and had issue.

Sir Walter wedded, secondly, Catharine,† daughter of Sir John Thynne, of Longleat, and by her, who *m.* for her second husband, Sir Edward Fox, of Gwernoga, in Montgomeryshire, had issue,

I. WALTER, of whom presently, as ancestor to the DRAYCOT line.

II. Thomas, who had an only son slain at Tangiers.

III. Charles, died an infant.

IV. Henry, slain at the Isle of Rhé, in 1672.

V. Robert, (Sir) secretary of state, auditor of the Exchequer, and a privy councillor, created a BARONET, 1st September, 1662, M. P. for Tewkesbury in 1658, died unm. 13th July, 1673. Sir Robert was a great favourite of the Queen, and is frequently mentioned, but in no friendly terms, by Clarendon. His arms may be seen in glass in the hall at Lincoln's Inn.

I. Anne, *m.* to Somerset Fox, esq. of Kaynham, in Shropshire, son of Sir Edward Fox, of Gwernoga, by Elizabeth, his wife, daughter of Sir Charles Somerset.

II. Olivia, *m.* to colonel Fowler, of the county of Stafford.

* The representation of the elder branch of the Longs is in the descendants of this marriage, if any exist. If not, it vests in the present Sir Bourchier Wrey, the issue of Catharine, wife of John Long, being now extinct.

† This family is alluded to in a note (vol. ii, p. 165). Its most distinguished members were Sir Walter Long, bart. of Whaddon, the celebrated parliamentarian, and Sir Lislebone Long, knt. of Stratton in Somersetshire, speaker of the House of Commons on Chute's illness, in 1658.

* Richard Long, of Collingbourne, was the direct ancestor of R. G. Long, esq. of Rowd Ashton, late M. P. for Wilts. Sir Bourchier Wrey is the representative of Henry Long of Melksham, and Walter Long, esq. now M. P. for Wilts (the son of Mr. R. G. Long) is therefore (through his mother, who is Sir Bourchier Wrey's sister) descended from John Long, of Wraxall, who died in 1652. Mr. Long of Rowd Ashton is the present possessor of Wraxall, which he inherited under the will of Walter Long, grandson of Catharine, sister of Hope Long.

† The story of the separation of the two properties of Wraxall and Draycot, by the machinations of this lady, who had endeavoured to secure both for her son Walter, is thus related by Aubrey in his miscellanies:

" Sir Walter Long, of Draycot, (grandfather of Sir James Long) had two wives; the first a dau. of Sir — Packington, in Worcestershire, by whom he had a son. His second wife was a daughter of Sir John Thynne, of Long-Leat, by whom he had several sons and daughters. The second wife did use much artifice to render the son by the first wife (who had not much Promethean fire) odious to his father; she would get her acquaintance to make him drunk, and then expose him in that condition to his father; in fine she never left off her attempts, till she got Sir Walter to disin-

III. Frances.

IV. Jane, *m.* to William Jordan, of Whitley, in Wilts.

V. Elizabeth, *m.* to William Wisdom, of Oxfordshire.

VI. Dorothy, *m.* to Ralph Goodwin, of Ludlow, a learned author, and, according to Aubrey, an excellent poet.

Sir Walter Long died in 1610, and was *s.* at Wraxall by his son John before mentioned. His eldest son by his second marriage,

SIR WALTER LONG, knt. succeeded to Draycot. He was M.P. for Wilts, and for Westbury in 1625; *m.* first, Anne, daughter of James Ley, Earl of Marlborough, Lord High Treasurer of England, and had issue,

JAMES, his heir.

He *m.* secondly, Elizabeth, daughter of George Master, esq. of Cirencester, and by her (who remarried Edward Oldisworth, of Bradley, county of Gloucester, and died 1658, aged 58, being buried at Wotton-under-edge,) had issue,

Walter, of Marlborough, a captain in the army of Charles I. *d.* 1673, *s. p.*

Sir Walter *d.* 1637, and was succeeded by his son,

SIR JAMES LONG, bart.* of Draycot, *b.* 1617, succeeded to the baronetcy on the death of his uncle Sir Robert, agreeably to the limitation, *m.* Dorothy, daughter of Sir Edward Leech, knt. of Shipley, county of Derby, and by her, who *d.* 1710, had issue,

JAMES, who predeceased his father, leaving by his first wife, Susan, daughter of Colonel Giles Strangwayes, of Melbury, several children,† who all *d. s. p.* excepting JAMES, (successor to his grandfather; and

herit him. She laid the scene for the doing this at Bath, at the assizes, where was her brother, Sir Egrimond Thynne, an eminent Serjeant-at-law, who drew up the writing; and his clerk was to sit up all night to engross it; as he was writing, he perceived a shadow on the parchment from the candle; he looked up, and there appeared a hand, which immediately vanished; he was startled at it, but thought it might be only his fancy, being sleepy, so he writ on; by and by a fine white hand interposed between the writing and the candle (he could discern it was a woman's hand) but vanished as before; I have forgot, it appeared a third time. But with that the clerk threw down his pen, and would engross no more, but goes and tells his master of it, and absolutely refused to do it. But it was done by somebody, and Sir Walter Long was prevailed with to seal and sign it. He lived not long after; and his body did not go quiet to the grave, it being arrested at the church porch by the trustees of the first lady. The heir's relations took his part, and commenced a suit against Sir Walter (the second son) and compelled him to accept of a moiety of the estate; so the eldest son kept south Wraxall, and Sir Walter, the second son, Draycot Cernes, &c. This was about the middle of the reign of *King* JAMES I."

Sir Walter's will was proved in 1610, and bears out this statement. Supernatural agencies were very active against this lady. "Sir Walter Long's (of Draycott, in Wilts) widow," says Aubrey, "did make a solemn promise to him, on his death bed, that she would not marry after his decease. But not long after, one Sir — Fox, a very beautiful young gentleman, did win her love; so that notwithstanding her promise aforesaid, she married him. She married at South Wraxall, where the picture of Sir Walter hung over the parlour door, as it doth now at Draycot. As Sir — Fox led his bride by the hand from the church (which is near to the house) into the parlour, the string of the picture broke, and the picture fell on her shoulder, and cracked in the fall: (it was painted on wood as was the fashion in those days). This made her ladyship reflect on her promise, and drew some tears from her eyes."

* He was the friend of Aubrey, who writes, 'I should be both orator and soldier to give this honoured friend of mine, a gentleman absolute in all numbers, his due character.' He says that he was of Westminster School, and afterwards of Magdalen College, Oxford, that his wife was a "most elegant beautie and wit," and that he commanded a regiment of horse during the civil wars. In this character, although the worthy antiquary would have him dedicated "tam marti quam mercurio," he does not appear to have been fortunate, his whole regiment having been captured by Waller and Cromwell, near Devizes, in 1645. Clarendon says, "by reason of his great defect of courage and conduct," but Clarendon had a quarrel with his uncle the secretary, as appears in various parts of his history, and other accounts exonerate Sir James from blame.

Aubrey continues the summing up of his friend's character as follows. "Good sword-man; admirable extempore orator; great memorie; great historian and romanceer; great falconer and for horsemanship. For insects exceedingly curious, and searching long since in natural things. Oliver, Protector, hawking at Hounslowe heath, discoursing with him, fell in love with his company, and commanded him to weare his sword, and to meet him hawking, which made the strict cavaliers look on him with an evil eye."

His love of 'natural things' seems to have been inherited from his grandfather, who, "about the beginning of King James, digged for silver," at Draycot, "through blue clay, and got £20 worth, but at £60 charge or better!!"

† His daughter Anne, who died unmarried 22nd December, 1711, was a distinguished person in the fashionable world, both for her beauty and her accomplishments. She figures in "The British Court," a poem published in 1707. Lord Wharton wrote the following verses round one of the glasses at the Kit-cat club in compliment to her:

"Fill the glass; let the haut-boys sound
While bright Longy's health goes round,
With eternal beauty blest,
Drink your glass, and think the rest."

by his second wife, Mary, relict of — Kightley, of Ireland, a daughter, Mary, m. to Colonel Butler of that kingdom) his heir.

Jane, d. 1651, æt. 11.

Jane, d. 1692, s. p.

Margaret, m. Sir Richard Mason, of Bishop's Castle, county of Salop.

Dorothy, m. Sir Henry Heron, K.B. of Cressy Hall, county of Lincoln, and had issue.

Deborah, d. s. p.

Sir James Long died February, 1691-2, and was s. by his grandson,

SIR JAMES LONG, bart. of Draycot, M.P. for Chippenham in 1705, 7, 8, and 10, and for Wootton Basset in 1714, b. 1681, m. Henrietta, daughter of Fulke, Lord Brooke, and by her, who died in 1765, had issue,

James, d. 1708, s. p.

ROBERT, his heir.

Susan.

Rachael.

Jane, d. 1708.

Dorothy, d. 1757.

Sir James d. March 16, 1729, and was succeeded by his son,

SIR ROBERT LONG, bart. of Draycot, M.P. for Wootton Basset, 1734, and for Wilts, b. 1705, m. Emma, daughter and heir of Richard Child, Earl of Tylney, of Wanstead, county of Essex, and Tylney Hall, county of Hants, and by her, who died 8th March, 1758, had issue,

I. JAMES, his heir.
II. Robert, d. 1739.
III. Richard, d. young.
IV. Charles, of Grittleton, county of Wilts, m. Hannah, daughter of Thomas Phipps, esq. of Heywood, Wilts, who remarried James Dawkins, esq. eldest son of Henry Dawkins, esq. of Standlynch, county of Wilts. He died 1783, and had issue,

Emma, m. William Scrope, esq. of Castle Combe, county of Wilts, and has issue an only daughter, married to George Poulett Thomson, esq. M.P. for Stroud, who assumed the name of Scrope on his marriage.

I. Dorothy.
II. Emma.

Sir Robert d. Feb. 10, 1767, was buried at Draycot, and succeeded by his son,

SIR JAMES LONG, bart. of Draycot, who assumed the additional name of Tylney, M.P. for Wilts, b. 1736, m. first Harriett, fourth daughter of Jacob Bouverie, Viscount Folkestone, and by her, who d. 13th Nov. 1777, had no issue. He m. secondly, Catharine, daughter of Other Windsor, fourth earl of Plymouth, and by her, who d. 1823, had issue,

JAMES TYLNEY, his heir.

CATHARINE, successor to her brother.

Dorothy, living in 1835.

Emma, living in 1835.

Sir James Tylney Long died 28th November, 1794, aged fifty-eight, and was succeeded by his son,

SIR JAMES TYLNEY LONG, bart of Draycot, who died September 14th, 1805, aged eleven, being the last known male descendant of the Longs of Wraxall and Draycot. He was buried at Draycot. His extensive estates devolved on his eldest sister,

CATHARINE LONG, of Draycot, Wanstead, &c. b. in 1789, who m. the Hon. William Wellesley-Pole, only son of William, Lord Maryborough, and had issue,

WILLIAM-RICHARD-ARTHUR, her heir.

James-Fitzroy-Henry, b. August, 1815.

Victoria-Catharine-Mary, b. May 6th 1818.

Mrs. Long-Wellesley died in 1826, and was s. by her son, the present WILLIAM-RICHARD-ARTHUR TYLNEY-LONG-WELLESLEY, esq. of Draycot.

*Arms*—Quarterly, first and fourth, gu. a cross arg. between five plates in each quarter, for WELLESLEY. Second and third, quarterly, first, sable semée of cross-crosslets, a lion rampant, argent (Long); second, argent, on a chief, gules, a bezant between two bucks' heads, cabossed, or, (Popham); third, gules, a pair of wings, or, (Seymour); fourth, gules, a chevron engrailed, ermine, between three eagles close, argent, (Child, Earl Tylney).

*Crest*—For WELLESLEY, out of a ducal coronet, or, a demi-lion rampant gu. holding a forked pennon. For LONG, out of a ducal coronet, or, a demi-lion rampant, argent. Another, granted to Sir Henry Long, by Henry VIII. for his services in a gallant charge at Therouenne, in Picardy, viz. on a wreath a lion's head, argent, in its mouth a hand erased, gules.

*Estates*—Draycot, in the county of Wilts, Tylney Hall, in the county of Hants, and Wanstead, in the county of Essex.

---

The 'British Court' commemorates her in the following rather lame lines:

" Long is discovered by her sweet regard,
With the same pleasure seen that she is heard,
Modest, but not precise, free, but not wild,
Neither affected, too reserved, nor mild.

She corresponded with Swift from her place of retirement at Lynn, where she had gone in consequence of pecuniary distresses. Her last letter to him is dated November 18th, 1711, and it appears that she had assumed the name of Smyth. The Dean laments her death with great feeling. He severely censures " her brute of a brother, Sir James Long," and says that he had ordered a paragraph to be put in the Post Boy, giving an account of her death, and making honourable mention of her. She is frequently noticed in his works.

# BETTON, OF GREAT BERWICK.

BETTON, RICHARD, esq. *b.* 3rd October, 1808; *m.* on the 13th October, 1831, Charlotte-Margaretta, youngest daughter of the late Richard Salwey, esq. of Moor Park, near Ludlow, county of Salop.

## Lineage.

This family is one of the most ancient in the county of Salop, and is presumed to have been originally seated at Betton Strange, near Shrewsbury.

By deed, dated the 2nd of RICHARD II. (1378), we learn that John de Betton was then dead, having left Margaret, his widow, and Richard de Betton, his son and heir. This Richard was father of

WILLIAM BETTON, of Great Berwick, near Shrewsbury, whose residence there in the year 1403 is proved by the records in the Exchequer of the town of Shrewsbury. The celebrated battle of Shrewsbury was fought close to his estate on the 20th of July in that year; and on the evening preceding the battle, the renowned Henry Hotspur took possession of the house of William Betton, and made it his head quarters, to the great loss and annoyance of the proprietor, who suffered much by the contributions levied upon him by that impetuous young nobleman and his followers. An anecdote in accordance with the superstition of that period is connected with Hotspur's sojourn here. In the morning previous to the battle, his forces having moved about a mile from Great Berwick towards the scene of action, and Hotspur having placed himself at their head, he perceived that an engagement was unavoidable, on which he called for his favourite sword. His attendants informed him that it was left behind at Berwick, of which village it does not appear that he had till then learned the name. At these words he turned pale, and said, "I perceive that my plough is drawing to its last furrow; for a wizard told me in Northumberland, that I should perish at Berwick, which I vainly interpreted of that town in the north." The result of the battle is matter of history, and universally known. William Betton was succeeded at Great Berwick by his son, also named

WILLIAM BETTON, who was living there in 1470, and was succeeded by his son,

RICHARD BETTON, who was of Great Berwick in 1494. He was father of

THOMAS BETTON, of Great Berwick, living in 1543, whose son and heir,

RICHARD BETTON, of Great Berwick, *m.* Eleanor Jackes, and was bailiff of Shrewsbury in 1613, in which year he died. His eldest son,

RICHARD BETTON, esq. of Great Berwick, had a numerous issue, of which the eldest son,

RICHARD BETTON, esq. of Great Berwick, married Eleanor, daughter of Edward Purcell, esq. of Onslow, in the county of Salop, and had, with other issue, a son and heir,

RICHARD BETTON, esq. baptized at St. Mary's, Shrewsbury, 6th February, 1614-15, who by his wife, Elizabeth, had issue,

- I. RICHARD, his heir.
- II. John, whose son, James Betton, was father of John Betton, the father of Sir John Betton, knt. late of Shrewsbury.
- III. Nathaniel, whose son, John, was father of
  - Nathaniel Betton, esq. late of Shrewsbury, who by Mary, his wife, had issue,
    - 1. John Betton, who entered the army, and was a captain in the 3rd Dragoon Guards, in which regiment he served in the Peninsula, and died at Merida in Spain, on the

20th November, 1809, aged thirty-one.
2. Richard Betton, of Shrewsbury, who died unmarried in 1825.
3. Nathaniel Betton, now of Shrewsbury.

1. Mary, married Thomas G. Gwyn, esq. of Shrewsbury.

Mr. Betton was succeeded at Great Berwick by his eldest son,

RICHARD BETTON, esq. who died in 1726, and was succeeded by his only surviving son,

RICHARD BETTON, esq. of Great Berwick, born in 1684, *m.* 20th February, 1706-7, Dorothy, daughter of Edward Lloyd, esq. of Leaton, in the county of Salop, by whom he had issue,

RICHARD, his heir, born in 1710.

Elizabeth, married John Watkins, esq. of Shotton.

Dying in 1764, Mr. Betton was succeeded by his only son,

RICHARD BETTON, esq. of Great Berwick, who married Mary, daughter of Charles Maddox, esq. of Whitcott, in the county of Salop, and had issue,

I. RICHARD, his heir.
II. Charles, of Whitchurch, near Ross, in the county of Hereford, who married Miss Mary Young, by whom he had, with daughters, an only son,
   Charles Betton, who married, first, Miss Mary Anne Bird, secondly, Miss Mary Butcher, and had issue,
      Joseph.
      Mary.

I. Anne, who married Thomas Bayley, esq. of Preston Brockhurst.

Mr. Betton died in 1767, and was succeeded by his eldest son,

RICHARD BETTON, esq. of Great Berwick, *b.* in 1744, who married Priscilla, daughter and eventually sole heir of John Bright, esq. of Totterton House, in the county of Salop, by whom he had issue,

I. RICHARD, his heir.
II. John Bright Betton, M.A. vicar of Lydbury North, born in 1773, who, in succeeding to the Totterton, &c. estates, took by royal sign manual, dated 12th October, 1807, the name of BRIGHT, and used the arms of BRIGHT only. He married, on the 22nd January, 1806, Mary, eldest daughter of Thomas Beale, esq. of Heath House, and dying on the 22nd December, 1833, left issue,
   1. John Bright, born 10th November, 1811, his only son and heir.

   1. Eliza.
   2. Mary.
   3. Frances.
   4. Amelia.
   5. Louisa.

Mr. Betton died on the 7th February, 1790, and was succeeded in the Great Berwick and other estates by his eldest son,

RICHARD BETTON, esq. *b.* 16th Nov. 1768, major in the Shropshire regiment of militia, who married, on the 17th February, 1795, Mary-Anne, daughter of the Rev. Aaron Foster, of Wells, in the county of Somerset, by whom he had issue,

I. RICHARD, his heir.

I. Mary-Anne, married, 8th December, 1825, her first cousin, Thomas Foster, esq. (son of the Rev. R. Foster, of Wells, in the county of Somerset), lieutenant of the Royal Engineers, and has issue,
   1. Arabella-Lætitia Foster, born 29th August, 1827.
   2. Geraldine-Harriett Foster, born 4th October, 1832.
II. Harriett, married, 18th March, 1829, Thomas H. Rimington, esq. lieutenant of the Royal Engineers, only son of General Rimington, of the Artillery, by whom she has a daughter,
   Charlotte-Mary-Anne Rimington, born 2nd October, 1833.

Major Betton died on the 15th June, 1819, and was succeeded by his only son, RICHARD BETTON, esq. the present representative of the family, who, in 1831, sold the Great Berwick estate to the Hon. Henry Wentworth Powys, of Berwick Leyborne, brother of the present Earl of Denbigh.

*Arms*—Arg. two pales sa. each charged with three crosslets fitchee or.

*Crest*—A demi-lion rampant.

*Motto*—Nunquam non paratus.

*Estates*—Newton, Bromlow, Aston Pigott, all in Shropshire.

*Seat*—Overton, near Ludlow, in the county of Salop.

# LYSONS, OF HEMPSTED.

LYSONS, *The Reverend* SAMUEL, of Hempsted Court, in the county of Gloucester, *b.* 17th March, 1806, *m.* 1st January, 1834, Eliza-Sophia-Theresa-Henrietta, eldest daughter of Major-general Sir Lorenzo Moore, K.C.H. and C.B. and has a daughter.

ALICE-ELIZABETH.

Mr. Lysons succeeded his father 3rd January, 1834. He is rector of Rodmarton, and in the commission of the peace for Gloucestershire.

## Lineage.

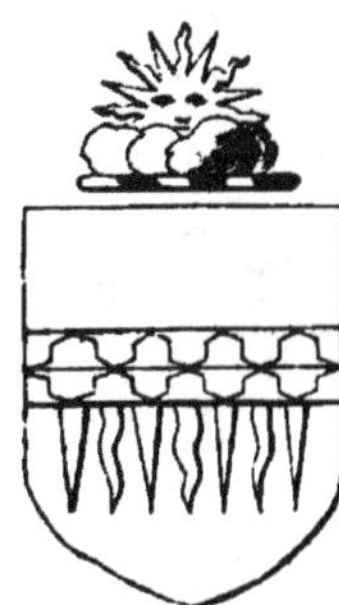

This family, which has been established for nearly three centuries in the county of Gloucester, is traditionally said to have migrated thither from Wales. Leland, in his Itinerary, makes mention of the Lysans as inhabiting the town of Neath, in Glamorganshire, *temp.* HENRY VIII. then in reduced circumstances. "One Lysan, a gentilman of auncient stok but mene landes about XL li by the yere dwellith in the towne of Nethe. The Lysans say that theire familie was there in fame before the conquest of the Normans." And in the cathedral church of Llandaff one of the stalls is entitled Sancti Dulbritii sive Doctoris Lysons, founded *temp.* HENRY VIII. Lewis Leysaunce, or Lysons, was sheriff of Gloucester 4th EDWARD VI. and master of Margaret's Hospital in that city, 2nd and 3rd MARY.

In the register of burials for Westbury upon Severn, where the family settled about the year 1550, occur the names of John Lysons, interred 3rd January, 1587, and Alice, his wife, buried 2nd May, 1598.

WILLIAM LEYSON, LISON, or LYSONS (for the name is written in several different ways in the registers), supposed to have been a son of John and Alice, bought an estate called Netherlay, or the Lower Lay, in the parish of Westbury on Severn, in the year 1606. He *m.* a lady named Anne, and had issue,

I. JOHN, his heir.
II. Arthur, of Hempsted, in the county of Gloucester.
III. Thomas, of Worcester, mayor of that city in 1651, who proclaimed, in conjunction with Mr. James Bridges, the sheriff, on the 23rd August, 1651, CHARLES the Second, king of Great Britain, for which he was prosecuted by the parliament,* and confined in Warwick Castle, whence he was sent, with Major-general Massey, the Earl of Traquair, and other prisoners, to London to take his trial. On the restoration, *King* CHARLES II. granted, by letters patent, to Thomas Lysons, second son of this loyal citizen, certain customs arising out of the port of Kingston upon Hull.
IV. DANIEL, of whom presently.

The fourth son,

DANIEL LYSONS, esq. born in November, 1604, *m.* Sarah, daughter of — Clutterbuck, esq. of King's Stanley, and died in 1674, leaving a son and successor,

DANIEL LYSONS, esq. born in 1643, who wedded Anne, daughter of Nicholas Webb, esq. and was succeeded at his decease, in 1681, by his son,

DANIEL LYSONS, esq. of Hempsted, born in 1672, who rebuilt the manor-house there. He *m.* in 1693, Elizabeth, daughter and co-heir of Thomas Ridler, esq. and left, with seven other children, who died *s. p.*

DANIEL, his heir.
John, LL.D. fellow of Magdalen college, Oxford.

* *Vide* Boscobel.

The eldest son,

DANIEL LYSONS, esq. of Hempsted, born 1st December, 1697, m. 20th February, 1725, Elizabeth, daughter of Samuel Mee, esq. of Gloucester, and had issue,

DANIEL, his heir.
SAMUEL, successor to his brother.

Elizabeth, m. to John Reeve, esq.
Mary, m. to Stephen Woodifield, esq.
Anne, Hester, Priscilla, } who died unmarried.

The elder son and successor,

DANIEL LYSONS, M.D. of Hempsted Court, fellow of All Souls college, Oxford, born 21st March, 1727, m. 6th December, 1768, Mary, daughter of Richard Rogers, esq. of Dowdeswell, in the county of Gloucester, but dying without issue was succeeded by his brother,

THE REV. SAMUEL LYSONS, M.A. born 28th December, 1730, rector of Rodmarton and Cherington, who m. Mary, daughter of Samuel Peach, esq. of Chalford, in Gloucestershire, and had issue,

I. DANIEL, his heir.

II. Samuel, born 17th May, 1763, the eminent writer on British topography and antiquities. In 1784, having previously become a member of the Inner Temple, Mr. Lysons came to London, and there practised as a special pleader until 1798, when he was called to the bar. In 1786 he was elected a member of the Society of Antiquaries, and it may be justly said that no individual ever more zealously or more successfully supported its character and usefulness. During eleven years he held the honorary office of director, and was eventually appointed one of its vice-presidents. In 1797 he became a member of the Royal Society; and in 1810 was selected for its vice-president and director. "Till the beginning of the year 1804," says Mr. Jerdan, in his interesting account of this distinguished antiquary, "Mr. Lysons continued to practise with considerable success at the bar, and went the Oxford circuit, notwithstanding his increasing distaste to what he often forcibly termed, 'brawling in a court of justice.' At that period, however, an event occurred which led him to the uninterrupted pursuit of those objects for which his mind was so peculiarly framed. At the close of the preceding year, the office of keeper of the records in the Tower had become vacant, and was conferred upon him." This appointment he held until his death, in 1819. The works of Mr. Lysons relate principally to the Roman antiquities of Britain, including "Reliquiæ Brittanico-Romanæ;" "Roman Remains discovered at Woodchester," &c. He also published a volume of Miscellaneous Antiquities of Gloucestershire; and, in conjunction with his brother, the Rev. Daniel Lysons, the earlier volumes of that great topographical work, the "MAGNA BRITANNIA." There were but few eminent men of his day, either as literary characters or patrons of literature, that Mr. Lysons did not number among his friends and acquaintance. On a short visit to London in the summer of 1784, to enter at the Temple, he was the bearer of an introductory letter from Mrs. Thrale to Dr. Johnson, who in his reply, dated the 26th June, says, "this morning I saw Mr. Lysons; he is an agreeable young man, and likely enough to do all he designs. I received him as one sent by you ought to be received, and I hope he will tell you he was satisfied." In the first week that he came to settle in London he was introduced to Sir Joseph Banks, with whom he continued on terms of intimate friendship till his death. His introduction to Horace Walpole occurred about the same time, and with Sir Thomas Lawrence he continued ever in cordial friendship. To his profound knowledge of history and antiquities Mr. Lysons united great classical learning; and the comprehensive powers of his memory assisted him in his labours, and gave peculiar charms to his conversation. He died unmarried in 1819, esteemed and respected as a son, a brother, and a friend.

I. Mary, born in 1675, m. to Charles Brandon Trye, esq. F.R.S. of Leckhampton Court, in the county of Gloucester. (See vol. i. p. 604.)

II. Elizabeth, born in 1772, m. to John Marshall Collard, esq.

Mr. Lysons died in 1804, and was s. in the family estates and in the rectory of Rodmarton by his son,

THE REV. DANIEL LYSONS, M.A., F.R.S., F.A.S., H.S. and L.S. of Hempsted Court, a celebrated topographer and antiquary, author of the "Environs of London," and several other works, and joint author with his brother of the "Magna Britannia," b. 28th April, 1762, m. first, in 1801, Sarah, eldest daughter of Lieutenant-colonel Thomas Carteret Hardy, of the York Fusileers, and by her, who died in 1808, had two sons and two daughters, viz.

Daniel, died in 1814, aged ten years.
SAMUEL, heir.

Sarah, m. 5th October, 1831, to the Rev. John Haygarth, rector of Upham, Hants, and died 18th May, 1833, leaving one daughter.
Charlotte, m. at Naples, 14th November, 1825, to Sir James Carnegie, bart. of Southesk, N. B. and has three sons.

He wedded, secondly, Josepha-Catherine-Susanna, daughter of John Gilbert-Cooper, esq. of Thurgarton Priory, Notts. and had by her,

Daniel, born 1st August, 1816, ensign in the 1st, or Royal Regiment of Infantry.
Catherine-Susanna.

Mr. Lysons died 3rd January, 1834, and was succeeded by his eldest son, the present REV. SAMUEL LYSONS, of Hempsted Court.

*Arms*—Gu. on a chief az. a bend nebulé, from which issue the rays of the sun ppr.

*Crest*—No crest is assigned to this family in the herald's visitation in 1672, but they have borne for nearly three centuries, The sun rising out of a bank of clouds ppr.

*Motto*—Valebit.

*Estates*—Hempsted and Longney, together with the rectory of Rodmarton, in the county of Gloucester.

*Seat*—Hempsted Court, near Gloucester.

## LEIGH, OF STONELEIGH.

LEIGH, CHANDOS, esq. of Stoneleigh Abbey, in the county of Warwick, and of Adlestrop, in Gloucestershire, *b.* 27th June, 1791; *m.* 8th June, 1819, Margarette, daughter of the Rev. William-Shippen Willes,* of Astrop House, in the county of Northampton, and has issue,

WILLIAM-HENRY, *b.* 17th January, 1824.
Edward-Chandos, *b.* at Stoneleigh Abbey, 22nd December, 1832.

Julia-Anna-Eliza.
Emma-Margarette.
Caroline-Eliza, } twins.
Augusta, }
Mary.
Louisa-Georgina.

Mr. Leigh succeeded his father on the 27th October, 1823. In the literary world Mr. Chandos Leigh is known as the author of some popular poetic works.

### Lineage.

This is a branch of the great Cheshire family of Leigh, founded by

SIR THOMAS LEIGH, knt.† lord mayor of London in 1558, who was brought up by Sir Rowland Hill, a merchant and alderman of the same city, and obtained the hand of that opulent citizen's favourite niece, Alice, daughter of John Barker, otherwise Covedale, of Wolverton, and with her the greater part of his wealth.‡ Sir Thomas was knighted during his mayoralty, and dying 17th November, 1571, (will proved 14th December following; inquisition 24th October, 1572), was buried in Mercer's Chapel,§ London. His widow survived him

* Son of Judge Willes, and grandson of the chief justice.

† Great-great-grandson of Sir Peter Leigh, knight-banneret, who fell at AGINCOURT in 1415.

‡ The chief part of Sir Rowland's estate was entailed upon the issue of the marriage.

§ Upon his tomb is the following epitaph:

Sir Thomas Leigh bi civil life,
All offices did beare,
Which in this city worshipfull
Or honorable were:

two and thirty years; she resided at Stoneleigh, and lived to see her children's children to the fourth generation. She was buried in 1603 at that place, where she had founded an hospital for five poor men and five poor women, all of them to be unmarried persons, and to be nominated after her decease by her third son, and his heirs for ever. Sir Thomas Leigh had issue,

I. ROWLAND, his heir.

II. Richard, living in 1568; *d.* in 1570, *s.p.*

III. THOMAS, of Stoneleigh, who was knighted by *Queen* ELIZABETH, and created a baronet on the institution of the order in 1611. He *d.* 1st February, 1625, (will proved 24th May, 1626), and was *s.* by his grandson,

SIR THOMAS LEIGH, the second baronet, who was elevated to the peerage by *King* CHARLES I. (patent dated at Oxford 1st July, 1643), as BARON LEIGH, of Stoneleigh. He *m.* Mary, one of the daughters and co-heirs of Sir Thomas Egerton, niece of John, first earl of Bridgewater, and grand-daughter of Lord Chancellor Egerton, Viscount Brackley, and dying 22nd February, 1672, was *s.* by his grandson,

THOMAS, second Lord Leigh, of Stoneleigh,* who *m.* first, Elizabeth, dau. of Richard Brown, esq. of Shingleton, in the county of Kent, but by that lady had no issue. He espoused, secondly, the Hon. Eleanor Watson, eldest daughter of Edward, second Lord Rockingham, by the Lady Anne Wentworth, dau. of the celebrated earl of Strafford, and had (with daughters) two surviving sons, namely,

EDWARD, his successor.

Charles, who inherited the estates of his uncle, the Hon. Charles Leigh, of Leighton Buzzard. He *m.* the Lady Barbara Lumley, daughter of Richard, earl of Scarborough, but died 28th July, 1749, without issue (will dated 30th July, 1748; proved 7th Sept. 1749).

His lordship *d.* in November, 1710, and was *s.* by his elder son,

EDWARD, third Lord Leigh, *b.* 13th January, 1684, who *m.* Mary, daughter and heir of Thomas Holbech, esq. of Fillongley, in Warwickshire, (see vol. i. p. 660) and dying 16th March, 1737-8, was *s.* by his only surviving son,

THOMAS, fourth Lord Leigh. This nobleman *m.* first, Maria-Rebecca, daughter of John Craven, esq. and sister of William, fifth Lord Craven, by whom he had (with three sons, all named Thomas, who died young)

EDWARD, his successor.

MARY, who inherited Stoneleigh, at the decease of her brother *s. p.* in 1786, which property came to the *Rev.* THOMAS LEIGH at her decease 2nd July, 1806.

His lordship wedded, secondly, Catherine, daughter of Rowland Berkeley, esq. of Cotheridge, in Worcestershire, and had another daughter, Anne, *m.* to Andrew Hacket, esq. She died of the small pox *s. p.* Lord Leigh *d.* 30th November, 1749, (will dated 23rd June, 1748; codicil 2nd November, 1749; proved 7th April, 1750), and was *s.* by his only surviving son,

EDWARD, fifth Lord Leigh, *b.* 1st March, 1742, and *d.* at Stoneleigh unmarried, 26th March, 1786, when the BARONY OF LEIGH became extinct.

IV. WILLIAM (Sir), of Newnham Regis, in the county of Warwick, who *m.* Catherine, daughter of Sir James Harrington, knt. of Exton, in Rutlandshire, and was *s.* by his son,

SIR FRANCIS LEIGH, K. B. who *m.* Margaret, or Mary, daughter of the Lord Chancellor Egerton, Baron Ellesmere and Viscount Brackley, and had issue,

FRANCIS, created a baronet in 1618, BARON DUNSMORE in 1628, and EARL OF CHICHESTER in 1644, (refer to BURKE's *Extinct and Dormant Peerage*).

---

Whom as God blessed with great wealth,
So losses did he feele;
Yet never changed he constant minde,
Tho' fortune turn'd her wheele.
  Learning he lov'd and helpt the poore
  To them that knew him deere;
For whom his lady and loving wife
This tomb hath builded here.

* His Lordship had three sisters;

I. Honora, *m.* first, to Sir William Egerton, and secondly, to Hugh, Lord Willoughby, of Parham.

II. Mary, *m.* to Arden Bagot, esq. of Pipe Hall, Warwickshire.

III. Jane, *m.* to William, Viscount Tracey.

Robert, *d. s. p.* aged sixty-three in 1663; will proved 23rd November, 1672.

Alice, *m.* to John Scrimshire, esq.

Julian, *m.* to Sir Richard Newdigate, bart.

I. Mary, *m.* first, to Richard Cobbe, and secondly to Robert Andrews, of London.

II. Alice, *m.* to Thomas Connye, of Basingthorpe, in Lincolnshire.

III. Katherine, *m.* to Edward Barber, sergeant-at-law, of the county of Somerset.

IV. Winifred, *m.* to Sir George Bond, knt. of London.

The eldest son and heir (of Sir Thomas Leigh and Alice Barber),

ROWLAND LEIGH, esq. of Longborough, in the county of Warwick, (living 30th September, 1596), *m.* first, Margery, daughter of Thomas Lowe, citizen and vintner of London, and had an only daughter, Elizabeth, who wedded, first, — Hanmer, and secondly, — Broughton. He espoused, secondly, Catherine, daughter of Sir Richard Berkeley, knt. of Stoke Giffard, in Gloucestershire, and had two sons and two daughters, viz.

WILLIAM, his heir.

Thomas, baptized at Tirley, in the county of Gloucester, 13th September, 1579; married, but died issueless; administration granted 27th October, 1599, to Frances, his widow.

——, *m.* to William Deane, esq. of Nethercote, in Oxfordshire; their daughter and heir,

Dorothy Deane, *m.* Sir Richard Harrison, of Hurst, in Berkshire.

——, *m.* to — Bolton, and *d. s. p.*

Rowland Leigh was *s.* by his only surviving son,

WILLIAM LEIGH, esq. of Longborough, who *m.* Elizabeth, daughter of Sir William Whorwood, knt. of Sandwell Castle, in the county of Stafford, and by her (who *d.* 23rd March, 1664-5, aged eighty-three) had issue,

I. WILLIAM, his successor.

II. Thomas, buried at Adlestrop, 1st August, 1612.

III. George, a captain in the service of *King* CHARLES I. in 1632, *m.* the relict of — Harrison, of Hurst.

I. Catherine, baptized at Adlestrop, 22nd July, 1610.

II. Isabella, baptized 4th August, 1612, *m.* first, to Gerrvase Warmshey, of Worcester, gent.; and, secondly, to Sir John Covert, bart. of Haugham, in Sussex.

III. Elizabeth, baptized 22nd May, 1615, *m.* to John Chamberlain, esq. of Maugersbury, near Stowe, in Gloucestershire.

IV. Anne, baptized 29th February, 1619, *m.* first, to William Hodges, gent. of Brodwell, in the county of Gloucester; secondly, to — Waterwick; and, thirdly, to John Croft.

Mr. Leigh *d.* at the age of forty-six, in 1632, (will proved 14th October in that year), was buried at Longborough, and *s.* by his eldest son,

WILLIAM LEIGH, esq. of Adlestrop, in the county of Gloucester, who *m.* first, Margaret, daughter of Sir William Guise, knt. of Elmore, in Gloucestershire, and had four sons and a daughter, viz.

WILLIAM, who *m.* a lady named Bird, and had (with a daughter, who died young) a son, William.

Thomas, died unmarried in 1660, aged about twenty-two.

George, } both *d.* unm.
John, }

Elizabeth, baptized 21st July, 1636, *m.* to Gideon Harvey, M.D. and had issue; she *d.* in 1694.

He wedded, secondly, a daughter of — Sanders, gent. of Warwick, but by her had no issue; and, thirdly, Joan, daughter of Thomas Perry, esq. of the city of Gloucester, and had

THEOPHILUS, of whom presently.

Joseph,
Benjamin,
Perry, } all died unm.
William,
Thomas,

Thomas, of University College, Cambridge, *b.* 23rd December, 1674, *d.* unm. 1st March, 1688.

Sarah, *b.* 14th September, 1656, *m.* to Henry Wright, esq. and had a son,

Thomas Wright, who wedded his cousin Cassandra, daughter of Theophilus Leigh, esq. of Adlestrop.

Martha, *b.* at Adlestrop 24th October, 1660.

Anne, *b.* 16th February, 1661.

William Leigh *d.* on the 17th June, 1690, aged eighty-six, at Adlestrop, and was buried there on the 21st of the same month. The eldest son of his third marriage,

THEOPHILUS LEIGH, esq. of Adlestrop, *m.* first, Elizabeth, daughter and sole heir of Sir William Craven, knt. of Lenchwick, in the county of Worcester, (license for marriage dated 16th December, 1673, the lady aged twenty-one), and had, with several other children, all of whom died in infancy, Typhena, *b.* in 1678, living unmarried in 1722. He wedded, secondly, (by license dated 26th November, 1689), the Honourable Mary Brydges, daughter of James, eighth Lord Chandos, of Sudeley, and by that lady (who *d.* 13th June, 1703, aged thirty-eight) had

I. WILLIAM, his heir.

II. James, colonel of a regiment, *b.* 17th and baptized at Adlestrop 18th September, 1692, *d.* unm. 16th January, 1713-14.

III. Theophilus, in holy orders, D. D. Master of Baliol College, Oxford, *b.* 28th, and bapt. 29th October, 1693, *m.* Anne, only daughter of Edward Bee, esq. of Beckley, in Oxfordshire, and had issue,

James, *b.* in 1733, *d.* in 1736.
Edward, *b.* 4th December, 1738.

Mary, *b.* 20th July, and bapt. at Adlestrop 20th August, 1731, *m.* at Oxford 3rd November, 1762, to her first cousin, the Rev. Thomas Leigh, LL.B. rector of Broadwell and Adlestrop, and *d. s. p.* 2nd February, 1797.
Anne, buried 8th March, 1736.
Cassandra, buried 30th April, 1740.
Cassandra, *b.* 27th January, 1742-3, *m.* to the Rev. Samuel Cooke, M.A. vicar of Little Bookham, Surrey.

IV. Thomas, in holy orders, D.D. rector of Harden, in the county of Oxford, *b.* 16th, and bapt. at Adlestrop 21st December, 1696, *m.* Jane, dau. of Doctor Walker, (a physician), of Oxford, and had two sons and three daughters, namely,

James, who took the surname of Perrott, *m.* Jane Cholmondeley, and *d. s. p.*
Thomas.
Jane, *m.* to — Cooper.
Cassandra, *m.* to — Austin.

Doctor Thomas Leigh *d.* in February, 1764.

V. Henry, *b.* 2nd, and bapt. at Adlestrop 4th January, 1697, *d.* unm.

VI. Charles, in holy orders, rector of Lanwarne, in Herefordshire, *b.* 23rd, and bapt. 28th November, 1700, *m.* Anne, daughter of — Rosse, of Ross, in that county, and dying in May, 1766, was buried at Rosse.

I. Emma, *b.* in the parish of St. Margaret's, Westminster, 5th October, 1690, baptized there, *m.* Peter Waldo, D. D.

II. Elizabeth, *b.* 29th November, 1694.

III. Cassandra, *b.* 28th, and bapt. 29th November, 1695, *m.* to her cousin-german, Thomas Wright, esq.

IV. Maria, *b.* 2nd, and bapt. 4th April, 1699, *m.* to Sir Hungerford Hoskyns, bart.

V. Catherine, *b.* 19th, bapt. 34th March, 1701-2.

VI. Anne, *b.* 13th, and bapt. 14th June, 1703, *m.* to the Rev. John Hoskyns.

Theophilus Leigh *d.* 10th February, 1724-5, was buried at Adlestrop 19th of the same month, (will proved 3rd July, 1725), and *s.* by his eldest son,

WILLIAM LEIGH, esq. of Adlestrop, *b.* at St. Margaret's, Westminster, 3rd November, 1691, who *m.* Mary, daughter of Robert Lord, esq. of York Buildings, and by her (who *d.* 10th July, 1756, aged sixty-one) had issue,

I. JAMES, his heir.

II. William, rector of Little Ilford, Essex, *b.* in the parish of St. George, Westminster, 1st April, 1732, *d.* unm. 2nd April, 1764, buried at Adlestrop.

III. Thomas, LL.B. rector of Broadwell and Adlestrop, and fellow of Magdalen College, Oxford, *b.* and bapt. at Adlestrop 22nd July, 1734, *m.* at Oxford 3rd November, 1762, Mary, eldest daughter of Dr. Theophilus Leigh, but *d. s. p.*

I. Cassandra, born in the parish of St. Martin in the Fields 11th April, 1723, *m.* 8th September, 1739, to Sir Edward Turner, bart. of Ambrosden, in the county of Oxford.

II. Mary, *d.* unm. in February, and buried 3rd March, 1768.

III. Elizabeth, bapt. 6th December, 1735, *d.* unm. in April, 1818, and buried at Adlestrop.

Mr. Leigh *d.* 9th December, 1757, aged sixty-six, was buried at Adlestrop, and *s.* by his son,

JAMES LEIGH, esq. of Adlestrop, bapt. at Longborough 7th July, 1724, who *m.* at Luggershall, Wilts, 10th March, 1755, the Lady Caroline Bridges, eldest daughter of Henry, duke of Chandos, by Mary his first wife, eldest daughter and co-heir of Charles, earl of Aylesbury, and left at his decease, 31st March, 1774, (he was buried at Adlestrop), an only child and successor,

JAMES HENRY LEIGH, esq. of Adlestrop, *b.* 8th February, 1765, who inherited the Stoneleigh estates in 1806. He *m.* 8th December, 1786, at Broughton, in Oxfordshire, the Hon. Julia-Judith Twisleton, eldest dau. of Thomas, Lord Saye and Sele, and had issue,

I. CHANDOS, his heir.

I. Julia.

II. Caroline-Eliza, m. to James-Buller East, esq.
III. Mary, m. to Frederick-Acton Colville, esq.
IV. Augusta, m. to Charles-Lennox-Grenville Berkeley, esq. and second son of Admiral the Hon. Sir George Berkeley, by Lady Emily Lenox.

Mr. Leigh died at Stoneleigh Abbey 27th October, 1823, was buried at Adlestrop, and succeeded by his son, the present CHANDOS LEIGH, esq. of Stoneleigh Abbey and Adlestrop.

*Arms*—Gu. a cross eng. arg. in the dexter canton a lozenge of the second.

*Crest*—A unicorn's head erased argent, armed and crined or.

*Estates*—In the counties of Warwick, Stafford, Bedford, Chester and Gloucester.

*Seats*—Stoneleigh Abbey, Warwickshire; Adlestrop, Gloucestershire.

## BAGGE, OF STRADSETT.

BAGGE, WILLIAM, esq. of Stradsett, in the county of Norfolk, *b.* 17th June, 1810; *m.* 11th July, 1833, Frances, fourth daughter of the late Sir Thomas Preston, bart. of Beeston Hall, and has a daughter,

FRANCES-HENRIETTA.

Mr. Bagge succeeded his father, 3rd June, 1827.

### Lineage.

The family of BAGGE is of Northern extraction, and a branch of the old Swedish stock of the same name which still continues in that kingdom. It was established in England about three hundred years ago, and has held lands in Norfolk since 1560. The first recorded ancestor,

SIMON BAGGE, married and had two sons, Simon, M.A. of Caius College, Cambridge, who died unm. and

JOHN BAGGE, of Cockley Cley, *b.* in 1561, who married a lady named Susannah, and dying in 1625, was *s.* by his son,

JOHN BAGGE, esq. of Stradsett, who was father, by Mary his wife, of another

JOHN BAGGE, esq. of Stradsett, who wedded Sarah, daughter of — Gynn, esq. and had issue,

I. WILLIAM, his heir.
II. Charles, m. Barbara, daughter of E. Elsden, esq. and had a son, Charles, D.D. who espoused Anne, daughter of Thomas Warner, esq. of Walsingham, and had issue.
I. Sarah, m. to Maxey Allen, esq. and had issue.

The elder son,

WILLIAM BAGGE, esq. of Stradsett, *b.* in 1700, married Jane, only child and heiress of Peter Dixon, esq. of Islington Hall, in Norfolk, and had issue,

I. William, who *d.* unm. in 1801.
II. THOMAS, heir.
I. Jane, *d.* unm. in 1791.
II. Susan, *d.* unm. in 1800.
III. Elizabeth, m. to the Rev. Richard Hamond, second son of A. Hamond, esq. of High House, Norfolk.

The second son,

THOMAS BAGGE, esq. of Stradsett Hall, *b.* in 1740, *m.* first, Pleasance, daughter and co-heiress (with her sisters, the wives of Anthony Hamond, esq. of High House, and of Samuel Browne, esq.*) of Philip Case,

---

* This gentleman had, by Miss Case, two daughters,

Hester Browne, m. to Sir Jacob Astley, bart. of Melton Constable.

Pleasance Browne, m. to Edward-Roger Pratt, esq. of Ryston. (See vol. i. p. 231).

esq. and had two sons and two daughters, viz.

I. THOMAS-PHILIP, his heir.
II. William.
I. Pleasance, *m.* to the Rev. Dr. Hutton, rector of Gaywood, and *d.* in 1830, leaving issue.
II. Jane, *m.* to Sir Thomas Preston, bart. of Beeston Hall, and has issue.

Mr. Bagge wedded, secondly, Anne, daughter of Thomas-Lee Warner, esq. of Walsingham, and widow of Dr. Charles Bagge, by whom he had another daughter,

III. Anne, *m.* in July, 1829, to Capt. William Fitzroy, eldest son of Lieut. Gen. the Hon. William Fitzroy, and grandson of the first Lord Southampton.

He *d.* in August, in 1807, and was *s.* by his son,

THOMAS-PHILIP BAGGE, esq. of Stradsett, who *m.* in April, 1808, Grace, youngest daughter of Richard Salisbury, esq. of Lancaster, and by her (who *d.* 27th January, 1834) had issue,

Thomas-Philip, *b.* 29th January, 1809, *d.* in February, 1816.
WILLIAM, successor to his father.
Richard, twin with William, *b.* in 1810.
Edward, twin with Pleasance, *b.* 2nd December, 1812.
Henry-Case, in the Hon. East India Company's civil service, *b.* 22nd November, 1814.
Arthur, died young, in 1828.
Philip-Salisbury, *b.* 18th October, 1817.
Maria, *m.* 17th June, 1831, to Henry Villebois, esq. eldest son of H. Villebois, esq. of Marham House, Norfolk.
Pleasance.

Mr. Bagge died 3rd June, 1827, and was succeeded by his eldest surviving son, the present WILLIAM BAGGE, esq. of Stradsett Hall.

*Arms*—Lozengy, gu. and arg. on a chief or, three cinquefoils az.

*Crest*—Two wings.

*Motto*—Spes est in Deo.

*Estates*—All in Norfolk, comprising Stradsett, Islington, Gaywood, and Mint-lynn.

*Seat*—Stradsett Hall, Norfolk.

## WALMESLEY, OF SHOLLEY.

WALMESLEY, THOMAS-GEORGE, esq. of Sholley, in the county of Lancaster, *b.* 16th August, 1795, *m.* 4th May, 1824, Miss Susan-Elizabeth Trusler, of Slindon, in Sussex, and has surviving issue,

ANTHONY, *b.* 25th November, 1826.
John, *b.* 26th January, 1830.

Mr. Walmesley succeeded his father.

### Lineage.

The following extract from an old parchment, dated in 1640, exhibits the source whence the family, of which we are about to treat, derived a portion of its early inheritance:

"It doth appear by a deed, maid in the 4th year of Richard ye first, the land now in our possession in Bicarsteth and Houghton, wear given in free mariage by WILLIAM, son of William, son of SIMON DE BICARSTETH, of Bicarsteth, with Ann, his daughter, who did marrie RALPH, son of HENRY MOSSOCKE, wch messuage was called Tenescohenet, and by some old deeds Heathen Head; and the crest then belonging to Mossocke was an oake wth achornes growing upon ye moss, in the form of a barrel: sprung out of the mouth."

"The next marriage we find any mention of is Henry, the son of Thomas Mossocke, who did marry Johan, the first daughter of Alen Norres, in the reign of HENRY ye first, wth whom he had severall lands in Wolfall, Walton, Speake, Ditton and Hipton."

"The next to this we find anything of, is HENRY, son of Thomas Mossocke, who did marry one of the daughters of Philip Wettvall, of Choaviston, in Cheshire, knt. by whom he had land there to the value of forty pounds p: an: which was by his son sould to the Lord Chancellor Egerton: this marriage was solemnized in the reign of Philip and Mary."

"Then THOMAS, son of ys Henry, did marrie with Margrett, daughter of Laurance Ireland, of Lidiatt, esq. and Ann, one of the daughters of Mollinux of the Wood, esq. in the begining of Queen Elizabeth's raign, by whom he was to haue the reversion of a lease wthout impeachment of waste of Conschoe for thirty and one years, but he dieing before it fell, his heir being an infant was defeated of it."

"HENRY MOSSOCK, son of Thomas, did marrie Jane, the daughter of John More, of Bankhall, esq. Her mother being the daughter of Edward Scasbrick, of Scasbrick, esq. in the reign of K. James ye st: by whom he had in portion 400 and 50 pounds."

"THOMAS, son of Henry, did marrie the youngest daughter of Thomas Berrington, of Molte Hall, in ye county of Salope, esq. in ye raign of our soveraign Lord Charles ye st: an: 1638. And to a second wife he married, Ann Urmestone, the daughter of Richard Urmestone, ye year 1650 being of West Leight, and having no heirs it fell to his brother Henry, who never marriing, it came to RICHARD WALMESLEY, of Showley, his father, THOMAS WALMESLEY, haveing married y^e sister of y^e said Thomas and Henry Mossocke."

THOMAS WALMESLEY, living in the twenty-second of HENRY VII. *m.* Elizabeth, daughter of William Travers, of Neathby, in the county of Lancaster, and was father of another

THOMAS WALMESLEY, living in the twenty-eighth of HENRY VIII. who wedded Margaret, daughter of --- Livesay, of Livesay, in Lancashire, and died on the 17th of April, 1584, having had eight sons and two daughters, viz.

I. THOMAS (Sir), an eminent lawyer and serjeant-at-law in ELIZABETH'S reign, and one of the judges of the court of Common Pleas in that of *King* JAMES I. Sir Thomas founded the family of DUNKENHALGH, now extinct, for which see conclusion.

II. RICHARD, of Sholay.

III. Robert, of Coldecots, in the county of Lancaster. This gentleman *m.* Isabell, daughter of Ralph Parkinson, of Chiping, in the same shire, and had two sons,
  1. Thomas, who inherited Coldecotes, *b.* in 1661, *m.* first, Elizabeth, daughter and sole heir of Richard Grimshaw, of Newhouse; and secondly, Katharine, daughter of --- Hall, of Blandford, in Cheshire. By the former he had issue,
     Robert, of Oldcots, thirty-five years of age 13th September, 1664, *m.* Anne, daughter of --- Thornton, of Thornton, in Yorkshire.
     Richard.
     Charles.

     Isabell.
     Anne, *m.* to William Cromback, of Clerk Hill, Lancashire.
  2. Richard, of Holcroft, in Lancashire, who had a son,
     Thomas, *b.* in 1651.

IV. Edward, of Banister Hall, in the county of Lancaster, *m.* Anne, daughter of Hawkesworth, of Hawkesworth, in Yorkshire, and died about the year 1601. He had issue,
  1. Thomas, who *m.* Frances, daughter of Edward Stanley, of Moor Hall, in the county of Lancaster.
  2. Edward, of Banister Hall, living in 1664, then seventy-one years of age. He *m.* Dorothy, daughter of Christopher Anderton, of Horwich, in Lancashire, and widow of William Walton, of Walton in the Dale.
  3. Richard, *d.* young.

  1. Rosamund, *m.* to Thomas Winkley, of Bellington, Lancashire.
  2. Jane, *m.* to Richard Craven, of Dinkley, Lancashire.
  3. Elizabeth, *m.* to Robert Hopkinson, of Preston.

V. William, merchant, of London, died without issue.

VI. Nicholas, merchant, of London, *m.* Sarah, daughter of Sir Thomas Kemble, who served the office of lord mayor, and left a son, Thomas, of Chafout St. Peter's, Bucks, who *m.*

Elizabeth, daughter of — Ellis, of London.

VII. Henry, a priest.

VIII. John, of Gray's Inn, barrister-at-law.

I. Alice, *m.* to --- Hothersall, of Hothersall, in Lancashire.

II. Elizabeth, *m.* to --- Nowell, of Measley, in the same county, gent.

The second son,

RICHARD WALMESLEY, esq. of Sholay, or Sholley, marrying Margaret, daughter of William Walmesley, esq. of Fishwick, in Lancashire, had two sons, Thomas, who *d.* unmarried, and his successor at his decease, about the year 1609,

RICHARD WALMESLEY, esq. of Sholley, *b.* in 1598, who wedded Ellen, daughter of William Gerrard, esq. of Radborne, and had issue,

I. RICHARD, who died in his father's lifetime, leaving by his wife, Elizabeth, daughter of Thomas Southworth, of Samsbury, in Lancashire, an only child,

ELIZABETH, the wife of Thomas Cottam, of Dilworth.

II. Gerard, *d.* young.

III. THOMAS, who inherited Sholley.

IV. John, *m.* first, Anne, dau. of Laur. Bryers, of Buckshaw, and had an only dau. *m.* to Rich. Chorley, of Hartwood Green, whose descendants are now all extinct. He wedded, secondly, Margaret Plesington, and from that marriage the Walmesleys of Westwood House. (See vol. i. p. 278.)

V. William, } both *d.* young.
VI. George, }

I. Margaret, this lady lived to an advanced age.

II. Janet, *m.* to John Sherborne, esq. of Balyhall, in Lancashire, and *d.* without surviving issue.

He was *s.* at his decease by his third, but eldest surviving son,

THOMAS WALMESLEY, esq. of Sholley, living in 1664, who *m.* ELIZABETH, the heiress of the MOSSOCKES, as mentioned in the introduction. She was the daughter of Henry Mossocke, of Cunscough, near Ormskirk, and brought that estate into the family of her husband. They had a daughter, Anne, who died a nun, in Flanders, and a son and heir,

RICHARD WALMESLEY, esq. of Sholley, *b.* in 1656, living in 1733, who wedded Jane Houghton, of Park Hall, sister of William Houghton, esq. and by her (who *d.* 13th November, 1722) had issue,

I. THOMAS, his successor.

II. William, *d. s. p.* 16th March, 1752.

III. John, living in 1733, died without issue.

IV. Edward, killed at sea.

V. Richard, living in 1733, in holy orders, *d.* at Ormskirk, 5th May, 1735.

VI. Robert, lost at sea.

VII. Charles, died a prisoner at Liverpool in 1716.

VIII. Henry, *d.* in 1734, without issue.

IX. James, *d.* 7th April, 1777.

X. Francis, died in returning from India, in April, 1760, left no issue.

I. Elizabeth, *d.* unm. in 1733.

II. Anne, *d.* unm. in 1732.

III. Margaret, *b.* 7th January, 1700, *m.* to William Colgrave, esq. and *d.* in 1768.

IV. Dorothy, *d.* young.

He was *s.* by his eldest son,

THOMAS WALMESLEY, esq. of Sholley, *b.* 21st October, 1685, who *m.* (in London) Mary, daughter of William Colgrave, esq. and had issue,

Richard, *b.* 14th December, 1709, living in 1733, but *d.* unm. in the lifetime of his father.

THOMAS-COLGRAVE, his father's heir.

Joseph, *b.* 7th October, 1715, died at Liverpool in April, 1759, *s. p.*

Francis, *b.* 11th April, 1758, died at Dollwort, in Lorrain, being subprior of the monastery.

Mary, *d.* unm.

Mr. Walmesley *d.* 20th April, 1756, and was *s.* by his eldest surviving son,

THOMAS-COLGRAVE WALMESLEY, esq. of Sholley, *b.* 28th August, 1713. This gentleman *m.* 10th April, 1758, Miss Elizabeth Turner, of Hampstead Heath, and left at his decease, 12th May, 1775,

I. RICHARD-JOSEPH, his heir.

II. Thomas-William, *b.* 10th September, 1767, died at Richmond, in Surrey, 5th January, 1825, and buried in the vault at Moorfields chapel, London.

III. Robert, a monk of La Trappe, *b.* 12th February, 1770.

I. Catherine, *b.* 17th April, 1759, died 7th January, 1785, unm.

II. Elizabeth-Mercy-Magdalen, *b.* 22nd July, 1760, *d.* 26th August, 1787, never having enjoyed health or happiness after the death of her elder sister. Both were interred in the vault of the Turners, at Hampstead.

III. Mercy, *b.* 17th October, 1761, died 23rd March, 1807, unm.

IV. Anne, *b.* 7th February, 1763, died unm. 26th October, 1814.

V. Frances, *b.* 16th February, 1772, *m.* at Hammersmith church, to Nicholas Selby, esq.

VI. Ellen-Monica.

He *d.* 12th May, 1775, was buried at Ingatestone church, and *s.* by his eldest son,

RICHARD JOSEPH WALMESLEY, esq. of Sholley, *b.* 22nd August, 1764, who wedded, 25th August, 1794, at Hammersmith church, Miss Manby, and had four sons and a daughter, viz.

THOMAS-GEORGE, his heir.

Richard, *b.* 25th November, 1796, *m.* Miss Marianne Lescher, of Hampstead.

Henry, *b.* 1st November, 1799, *m.* 1st May, 1832, Miss Mary Havers, of Beacons.

Michael, *b.* 5th April, 1800.

Frances.

Mr. Walmesley was *s.* by his eldest son, the present THOMAS-GEORGE WALMESLEY, esq. of Sholley.

## Walmesley, of Dunkenhalgh.

EXTINCT IN THE MALE LINE.

This, the elder branch of the family, sprang from

SIR THOMAS WALMESLEY, knt. of Dunkenhalgh, in the county of Lancaster, an eminent lawyer in the reigns of ELIZABETH and JAMES I. In the former, *anno* 1580, he was called by writ to the degree of serjeant-at-law, and in the latter, 10th May, 1589, made one of the judges of the court of Common Pleas. Sir Thomas *m.* Anne, only daughter and heiress of Robert Shuttelworth, esq. of Hackinge, in Lancashire, by Jane, his wife, the sister and heir of Richard Browne, gent. of Ribleton Hall, in the same county, and by her (who died at Dunkenhalgh, 19th April, 1635) left at his decease, in the 10th of JAMES I. (he was buried at Blackburn, "under a fair monument," which was demolished by the parliamentary army about 1644) an only son and heir,

THOMAS WALMESLEY, esq. of Dunkenhalgh, living in 1614, who *m.* first, Eleanor, daughter of Sir John Danvers,* knt. by his wife, Elizabeth, youngest of the four daughters and co-heirs of John Nevil, Lord Latimer, and by her, who died in September, 1601, had two sons and two daughters, viz.

I. John, *d.* in April, 1600, and was buried at Cowthorp 25th of that month.

II. THOMAS (Sir), knighted 11th August, 1617, who *m.* Juliana, daughter of Sir Richard Molyneux, bart. of Septon, in Lancashire, and sister of the first Viscount Molyneux, by whom (who died in October, 1668) he had issue, viz.

1. RICHARD, successor to his grandfather.
2. Thomas, } *d.* young.
3. John, }
4. William, of Lowerhall, who had three wives, but died *s.p.*

1. Anne, *d.* unm. in 1644.
2. Juliana, *m.* to Francis Viscount Canington, and *d.* without issue.
3. Eleanor, *m.* to Sir Godfrey Copley, bart.

I. Elizabeth, *m.* to Richard Sherborn, esq. of Stonyhurst, in Lancashire, but *d.* 12th December, 1666, without issue.

II. ANNE, *m.* first, to William Middleton, esq. of Stockeld, in the county of York; and secondly, to Sir Edward Osborne, bart. of Kiveton, in the same county. By the latter she left an only son,

SIR THOMAS OSBORNE, bart. who was advanced to the peerage as Viscount Latimer, Earl of Danby, Marquess of Carmarthen, and DUKE OF LEEDS (see BURKE's *Peerage and Baronetage*).

He wedded, secondly, Mary Houghton, sister of Sir Richard Houghton, bart. of Houghton Tower, and had another son,

III. Charles, of Selby, in Yorkshire, who had two wives: first, Mary, daughter, of Thomas Chernock, esq. of Astley; and second, Anne, daughter of — Clerk, esq. of Yorkshire (she re-married Charles Fairfax, of York), but had no issue. He *d.* in 1672.

Mr. Walmesley died 12th March, 1641, was buried in the parish church of Blackburn, and *s.* by his grandson,

RICHARD WALMESLEY, esq. of Dunkenhalgh, who wedded Mary, daughter and coheir of Bartholomew Fromonds, esq. of Cheame. By this lady (who died in 1687, and was buried at Paris) he acquired an estate of four hundred pounds per annum, and had issue,

* His second son, SIR HENRY DANVERS, was created Baron Danvers, and EARL OF DANBY, but dying unm. 20th January, 1643, those honours expired. (BURKE's *Extinct and Dormant Peerage*.)

I. Thomas, who died at Paris 26th August, 1677, in the lifetime of his father.

II. Richard, died at Rome, *s. p.* 23rd November, 1680.

III. Charles, died at St. Omers, 2nd June, 1680, *s. p.*

IV. BARTHOLOMEW, eventual heir.

I. Mary, a nun at Paris, living in 1708.

II. Juliana, *m.* to William Diccenson, esq. of Wrightington, in Lancashire.

III. Anne, a nun at Paris.

IV. Elianora-Mathea, living in 1708, *m.* to Thomas Clifton, esq. of Clifton and Lytham.

He died 26th April, 1679, was buried at Blackburn, and succeeded by his son,

BARTHOLOMEW WALMESLEY, esq. of Dunkenhalgh. This gentleman *m.* Dorothy, daughter and co-heir of John Smith, esq. and by her (who died 1st November, 1689, and was interred at Bezeres, in Provence) had surviving issue,

FRANCIS, his heir.

CATHERINE, *m.* first, 1st March, 1711-12, to Robert Lord Petre, and secondly, to Charles Lord Stourton. By the former she had an only son, Robert-James, eighth Lord Petre; by the latter no issue.

Mr. Walmesley died 29th December, 1701, and was *s.* by his son,

FRANCIS WALMESLEY, esq. of Dunkenhalgh, *b.* 13th October, 1696, who died without issue, when the male line of this elder branch of the Walmesleys EXPIRED, and Catherine, his sister, became sole heir to the real and personal fortune. The former, comprising the great estates in Yorkshire and Lancashire, passed into the family of PETRE, and the latter, consisting of an enormous funded property, devolved on that of STOURTON.

*Arms*—Gu. on a chief erm. two hurts.

*Crest*—A lion statant guardant, ducally crowned gu. granted 20th August, 1560, in the reign of Elizabeth. The Walmesleys were long in possession of the arms prior to the grant of this crest, which was given to them, having lost their former one.

*Estates*—In Lancashire.

*Seat*—Sholley.

# MORRICE, OF BETSHANGER.

MORRICE, FREDERICK-EDWARD, esq. of Betshanger House, in the county of Kent, *b.* 8th December, 1778, *m.* 6th June, 1816, Elizabeth, daughter of the late Henry Ellison, esq. of Hebburn Hall, in the palatinate of Durham, and has one son,

FREDERICK-FRANCIS-JAMES, *b.* 12th March, 1820.

Mr. Morrice, who succeeded his father 9th January, 1815, is a magistrate, and deputy-lieutenant for the county of Kent.

## Lineage.

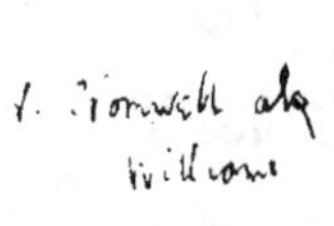

The family of Morrice is of great antiquity, and can be traced in lineal descent from ATHELSTAN GLODRYDD,* prince of Ferlys, betwixt Wye and Severn, who sprung from the old princes of Powys, and who, through his mother, Rheingar, daughter and heir of Grono ap Tudor Trevor, was eighth in a direct line from Caradoc Vriechfras, lord of Hereford, one of the knights of King Arthur's Round Table. Athelstan wedded Gwladys, daughter and heir of Ryn, lord of Pegain, and was father of

* Athelstan Glodrydd was godson of Athelstan, king of England, and founded the fourth royal tribe of Wales.

**Kydwgan ap Elystan**,* prince of Ferlys, who *m.* Elen, daughter of — Brockwel, lord of Powis, and had a son,

**Idnerth ap Kydwgan**, lord of Radnor, prince of Ferlys, who was father, by Gwenllian, daughter of Foreth ap Owen, lord of Keveliog, of

**Gwrgenay ap Idnerth**, lord of Radnor, prince of Ferlys, who *m.* Elen, daughter and heir of Rhys ap Aron, lord of Langathen, and from this marriage lineally descended †

**Morys ap Morgan**, who wedded Ellen, daughter of Ievan ap Guffddoy, sprung from a common ancestor with himself, and had issue,

I. **William**, his heir.
II. Gruffyth, *d. s. p.*
III. Philip, *d. s. p.*
IV. Ievan, from whom derived the Morices of Werrington. (See conclusion.)

The eldest son,

**William Morys**, captain in the royal navy, married a lady, presumed, from the arms upon the plate in the possession of the present Mr. Morrice, to have been of the Devonshire family of Martyn, and had a son and successor,

**William Morrice**, esq. who wedded Jane, daughter of John Castell, esq. of Ashbury, Devon, and had three sons and one daughter, viz.

**William**, *b.* in 1670, captain in the army, *d. s. p.*

**Salmon**, of whom presently.

Bezabiel, living in 1740, who died without issue. His widow survived until 1790.

Jane, *m.* to Captain Martyn, R.N. and died without issue.

Captain Morrice died in 1680. His second son,

**Salmon Morrice**, esq. entering the royal navy, distinguished himself in various commands, and attained the rank of admiral of the White. He *m.* Elizabeth, daughter and sole heir of William Wright, esq. a naval commissioner, and by her, who died in 1733, had issue,

Wright, born at Betshanger, *m.* Sarah, daughter of Thomas Peke, esq. of Hills Court, in Ash, but died issueless in the lifetime of his father.

**William**, heir to his father.

Sarah.

Elizabeth, *m.* to Thomas Boteler, esq.

Jane.

Maria-Susanna.

Admiral Morrice, who purchased the estate of Betshanger, in the county of Kent, in 1712, died in 1740, was buried at Betshanger, and succeeded by his only surviving son,

**William Morrice**, esq. of Betshanger, who *m.* Mary, daughter and heir of Robert Chadwick, esq. captain R. N. of Northfleet, (see family of *Chadwick of Healey*), and had three sons, **William**, his heir; **James**, successor to his brother; and Thomas, lieutenant R.N. died unmarried. Mr. Morrice died in 1758 (his widow surviving until 1803), and was succeeded by his son,

**William Morrice**, esq. of Betshanger, born 24th May, 1733, lieutenant-colonel of the 10th Dragoons, at whose decease, unm. in 1787, the estates devolved on his brother,

**The Rev. James Morrice**, M. A. rector of Betshanger, and vicar of Flower, in Northamptonshire, born in July, 1739. This gentleman espoused Maria Coltee Ducarel, daughter of the late Adrian Coltee Ducarel, esq. and niece of Andrew Coltee Ducarel, LL.D. of Doctors Commons. By her, who died 12th September, 1834, he had two sons and three daughters, viz.

**Frederick-Edward**, his heir.

Andrew-Ducarel, rector of Betshanger, married, and has a son, William, born 9th February, 1815, and other issue.

Charlotte-Elizabeth, *m.* to Henry Bon-

---

* The Earl of Cadogan also derives from Kydwgan ap Elystan.

† The intermediate descent was as follows:

Gwrgenay ap Idnerth = Ellen, daughter of Rhys ap Aron
|
Howell ap Madoc = Elinor, dau. of Warren ap David Voel
|
Philip dorddy of Llinwent, in Radnorshire = Eva, daughter of Kin Crygdryer, lord of Harpton
|
David, second son of Philip dorddy = Joan, dau. and heir of Owen ap Kinrychan ap Llawddon
|
Ievan Phellip, of Caron = Margaret, daughter of Ievan ap Meredyth
|
Rees ap Ievan = Mallt, daughter and coheir of Ievan Gwrgan
|
Morgan ap Rees = Gwellian, dau. of David ap Gttun ap Ievanddy
|
Morys ap Morgan.

ham, esq. of Portland-place, M.P. for Sandwich, and has issue.

Maria-Margaret, *m.* to Thomas Halliday, esq. of Wimpole-street, and has issue.

Theodosia-Frances, *m.* to Edward Vernon, esq. of Cheshire, and has issue.

Mr. Morrice died 9th January, 1815, and was succeeded by his son, the present FREDERICK EDWARD MORRICE, esq. of Betshanger, the direct descendant of Vreichfras, lord of Hereford, one of the knights of King Arthur's Round Table.

*Arms*—Quarterly: first, gu. a lion rampant, reguardant or, for Morrice; second, per bend ermine, and ermine all over a lion rampant or, for Tudor Trevor; third, arg. three boars' heads couped sable, two and one, for Cadogan; fourth, gu. an escutcheon within an orle of martlets, arg. Chadwick, quartering the ensigns of forty-six families, including Okeden, Healey, Carwarden, Mavesyn, Westcote Lyttelton, Quatermain, Grey of Rotherfield, Fitz-Osborn, Yvery, Vernon, Venables, Avenel, Baliol, Camville, Marmion, Tuberville, Meyric, Morgan Gam, Pembridge, Bagot, and Malory.

*Crest*—On a rest a falcon proper, beaked and belled, or.

*Estates*—In Kent.

*Seat*—Betshanger, near Sandwich.

## Morice, of Werrington.

IEVAN MORICE, youngest son of Morys ap Morgan, and brother to William Morys, the progenitor of the Kentish family, was fellow of All Souls, Oxford, doctor of laws, and chancellor of Exeter, in 1594. He *m.* Mary, daughter of John Castle, esq. of Ashbury, in Devon, and by her (who wedded, secondly, Sir Nicholas Prideaux, knt. of Souldon) left at his decease, in 1605, a son,

SIR WILLIAM MORICE, born in the parish of St. Martin, Exeter, 6th November, 1602, who was left under the guardianship of his mother. At the age of eighteen, he was entered a fellow commoner of Exeter College, Oxford, and there pursued his studies with such diligence and success, that Dr. Prideaux, at that time rector of Exeter, would frequently say that though Morice was but little in stature, yet in time he would come to be great in the state. "Sir William," says an almost contemporaneous writer,* "having proceeded bachelor of arts, retired into his county, and lived with his mother at Chuston, in West Putford, a small parish, six miles to the west of Bytheford, where he most sedulously followed his studies; and his mother, till her decease, which was in October, 1647, managing all his concerns, he had leisure to furnish himself with all sorts of good literature. Soon after his return home, he was married to one of the grand-daughters of Sir Nicholas Prideaux; and in the year 1640 his name was inserted in the commission of the peace for Devon. In 1645, he was chosen knight of the shire for Devon, to serve in the long parliament, but did not take his seat until General Monk restored the secluded members. In 1651, he was made high sheriff, having, during the previous year, settled his family at Werrington, on the borders of Cornwall, which estate he had purchased from Sir Francis Drake, bart. of Buckland. In 1658, he was chosen a burgess for Newport, in Cornwall, and being related, by his wife, to General Monk, he contracted an acquaintance with him, and so far recommended himself to the general's esteem, that, on his coming to England, he made choice of him for his chief, if not only, confidant in the management of the great affair of the king's restoration, wherefore, in February, 1659, Morice received from his majesty, by the hands of Sir John Granville, the signet of secretary of state; and, in 1660, on the king's landing, was honoured with knighthood. In 1661, Sir William became M.P. for Plymouth; and, in 1668, having continued in the no less laborious than honourable office of principal secretary of state, for more than seven years, being also well stricken in years, and knowing, that between the bustles of life and the business of death there ought to be allowed a certain space of time, fully satiated with the delights and glories of the court, prudently craved his majesty's leave that he might withdraw from thence: and so, with the king's gracious consent, he resigned his secretaryship, and was succeeded therein by Sir John Trevor. Which done, Sir William retreated into his own country, and passed the remainder of his days in a quiet retirement, at his house at Werrington, where he erected a fair library, valued at £1200: nor was he wanting in works of charity, for he built and endowed an almshouse for six poor people, in the parish of Sutcombe, near Holdsworthy, where each of the occupants hath two fair rooms, and two shillings a week duly paid them. There was one thing singular in this honourable

* Prince.

gentleman, that although he kept a domestic chaplain in his family, yet (when present) he was always his own chaplain at his table, notwithstanding several divines were there; and if a clergyman pretended to say grace, Sir William used to say, 'Hold, man, I am king, priest, and prophet, in my own house.'"

Sir William *m.* as already stated, Elizabeth, daughter of Humphrey Prideaux, esq. of Souldon, and had issue,

I. WILLIAM, his heir.

II. John, a Turkey merchant, who *m.* Miss Lowther, and was father of
  John Morice, M.P. for Newport, *temp.* GEORGE I. who *m.* Elizabeth, daughter of Sir Jeffrey Jeffreys, alderman of London, and dying in 1734-5, left a daughter, his eventual heiress, *m.* in 1740, to Jeffrey Jeffreys, esq. of the Priory, Brecon.

III. Humphrey, a Hamburgh merchant, who *m.* a daughter of the Lincolnshire family of Trollope, and had a son, Humphrey, sub-governor of the Bank, and M.P. for Grampound.

IV. Nicholas, died unm.

I. Thomasine, *m.* to Sir Walter Moyle, of Bake, in Cornwall.

II. Gertrude, *m.* to Sir Robert Cotton, knt. of Hatley St. George.

III. Elizabeth, died unm.

IV. Anne, *m.* to Sir John Pole, bart. of Shute.

Sir William *d.* 12th December, 1676, and was *s.* by his son,

WILLIAM MORICE, of Werrington, who was created a BARONET 13th CHARLES II. He *m.* first, Gertrude, daughter of Sir John Bampfylde, bart. of Poltimore, and had by her one son and two daughters, namely,

I. William, who *m.* Anne, daughter and co-heir of Richard Lower, M.D. but predeceased his father *s. p.*

I. Mary, *m.* to Sir John Carew, of Anthony.

II. Gertrude, *m.* to Sir Walter Young, bart.

Sir William wedded, secondly, a daughter of Richard Reynell, esq. of Ogwell, in Devon, and by her had an only son,

SIR NICHOLAS MORICE, second Baronet of Werrington, M.P. for Newport in the reigns of *Queen* ANNE, and her two immediate successors. This gentleman espoused the Lady Catherine Herbert, eldest daughter of Thomas, Earl of Pembroke, and by her (who died in 1716) had one son and two daughters, namely,

I. WILLIAM, his heir.

I. Catherine, *m.* to Sir John St. Aubin, bart. of Clowanee, in Cornwall.

II. Barbara, *m.* in 1728, to Sir John Molesworth, bart. of Pencarrow, in Cornwall.

Sir Nicholas *d.* in 1726, and was *s.* by his only son,

SIR WILLIAM MORICE, third Baronet of Werrington, M.P. successively for Newport and Launceston, who *m.* first, 1731, Lady Lucy Wharton, daughter of Thomas, Marquis of Wharton; and, secondly, Anne, daughter of Thomas Bury, esq. of Bury Narber, in Devonshire, but dying without issue the baronetcy expired, while his great estates were inherited by the families of St. Aubin and Molesworth. Werrington is now the property of the Duke of Northumberland.

## BRISCO, OF COGHURST.

BRISCO, MUSGRAVE, esq. of Coghurst, in the county of Sussex, *b.* 15th April, 1791; *m.* 8th October, 1828, Frances, daughter of the late Henry Woodgate, esq. of Spring Grove, Pembury, Kent, by the Honorable Georgina Hamilton, his wife, sister to the present Viscount Boyne.

Mr. Brisco, who is a magistrate and deputy-lieutenant for the counties of Sussex and York, succeeded his father 25th January, 1834.

## Lineage.

This is a junior branch of the house of Crofton Hall, in Cumberland, now represented by Sir Wastell Briscoe, bart. The surname was originally DE BIRKSKEUGH, from the family's dwelling at Birkskeugh, or Birkswood, near Newbiggin, in a lordship belonging to the priory of Carlisle, which lands, or a great portion of them, remain in the chief's possession.

ROBERT BRISCO, great grandson of Robert Brisco, of Brisco, was living in the reign of EDWARD I. His younger son,

ISOLD BRISCO, wedded Margaret, daughter and heiress of Sir John Crofton, and thus acquired the manors of Crofton, Winhow, and Dundraw. He was father of

CHRISTOPHER BRISCO, of Crofton. It appears by an arbitrament between the prior of Carlisle and this Christopher, concerning the manor of Brisco, that the said manor should remain to the prior and his successors, paying to the said Christopher one hundred merks; and the capital messuage, with the woods for building, should continue with the said Christopher and his heirs. This Christopher kept fourteen soldiers at Briscothorn upon Esk. He was taken prisoner at the burning of Wigton; and upon that and similar occasions was compelled to mortgage a considerable part of his estate. His son and successor,

ROBERT BRISCO, of Crofton, *m.* Isabel, daughter of William Dykes, of Warthole, and had five sons and two daughters, viz.

I. Thomas, a priest.
II. ROBERT, successor to his father.
III. Isold, who served against the Saracens, and died a hermit.
IV. Edward, ancestor of the families of Westward and Aldenham, Herts.
V. Alexander, progenitor of the Briscoes of Yarwell, Northamptonshire.

I. Syth, *m.* to Richard Brown.
II. Susan, *m.* to Robert Ellis, of Bothill.

The second son and heir,

ROBERT BRISCO, of Crofton, *m.* Catharine, daughter of Clement Skelton, of Petrel Wray, and had a son,

JOHN BRISCO, of Crofton, who wedded Janet, daughter of Thomas Salkeld, of Corby, and was father of

RICHARD BRISCO, of Crofton, who had, by his wife, a daughter, of Leigh, of Frisengton, and had two sons, ROBERT, his heir, and Leonard, whose son, Robert, marrying the heiress of Coldhall, founded that branch, now extinct. The elder,

ROBERT BRISCO, of Crofton, who was slain at the battle of Soltoun Moss, *temp.* HENRY VIII. left a son and successor,

JOHN BRISCO, esq. of Crofton, who espoused Anne, daughter of William Musgrave, esq. of Hayton Castle, in Cumberland, a branch of the ancient Northern family seated at Hartley Castle, which acquired the lordship and estate of Hayton in the reign of HENRY VI. by marriage with the daughter and heiress of William Covel. John Brisco purchased Leigh's part of the manor of Orton, in Cumberland, from Sir Wilfrid Lawson, and Maud his wife, widow of Thomas Leigh, of Isell; and another third portion from Thomas Blennerhassett, of Carlisle. He was *s.* by his son,

WILLIAM BRISCO, esq. of Crofton, who completed the purchase of the manor of Orton. He wedded Jane, daughter of William Orfeur, esq. of Highclose, and was father of

JOHN BRISCO, esq. of Crofton. This gentleman *m.* Mary, daughter of Sir John Braithwaite, of Burneshead, and had, with other children, who died unmarried,

I. WILLIAM, his heir.
II. John, who *m.* Judith Bewley.
III. Edward, a merchant in London, who *m.* Miss Tolson, of the ancient family of Tolson, of Bridekirke.

I. Dorothy, *m.* to Sir John Ponsonby, knt. of Haugh Heale, who settled in Ireland, during the protectorate of Cromwell, and acquired great estates in that kingdom. His son, William Ponsonby, esq. of Besborough, M.P. for the county of Kilkenny, was elevated to the peerage of Ireland as BARON BESBOROUGH in 1721.
II. Grace, *m.* to Clement Skelton, esq. of Petrel Wray.
III. Mary, *m.* to the Rev. Joseph Nicholson.

IV. Agnes, m. to William Rayson, of Dalston.

The eldest son,

WILLIAM BRISCO, esq. of Crofton, m. first, Susanna, daughter of Sir Randal Cranfield, by whom he had one son, who died young; and, secondly, Susanna, daughter of Francis Brown, alderman of London, and had issue,

I. JOHN, his heir.
II. William, a merchant in London, *d. s. p.*
III. Thomas, who m. Jane, daughter of Lancelot Fletcher, esq. of Tallantere, and widow of Major Crisp, and had issue.

William Brisco was *s.* by his son,

JOHN BRISCO, esq. of Crofton, who m. Mercy, daughter of Mr. Alderman William Johnson, of Newcastle on Tyne and Kibblesworth, and had six sons and four daughters, viz.

I. William, died unm.
II. JOHN, heir.
III. Thomas, died unm.
IV. Nathaniel, died unm.
V. Richard.
VI. Henry.

I. Margaret, m. to George Langstaff, gent.
II. Susanna, m. to the Rev. David Bell, rector of Aspatric.
III. Abigail, m. to Henry Brisco, esq. of Backborough, in Ireland.
IV. Mary.

Mr. Brisco was *s.* at his decease by his eldest son,

JOHN BRISCO, esq. of Crofton, living towards the close of the seventeenth century, who wedded Catharine, second daughter of Sir Richard Musgrave, bart. of Hayton Castle, by Dorothy his wife, daughter and co-heir of William James, esq. of Washington, in Durham, grandson of Bishop James, and had issue,

I. Richard, who m. Miss Lamplugh, but predeceased his father without issue.
II. JOHN, D.D. of Crofton Hall, rector of Orton and vicar of Aspatrie, m. Catharine, daughter of John Hylton, esq. of Hylton Castle, and was father of JOHN BRISCO, esq. of Crofton Hall, created a BARONET in 1782. (See BURKE's *Peerage and Baronetage.*)
III. William, rector of Dessington.
IV. MUSGRAVE, of whom presently.
V. James, of Beaumaris.
VI. Wastell, who went to Jamaica, and married Mrs. Campbell.
VII. Ralph, m. Dorothy, daughter of the Rev. Jonathan Rowland.

I. Dorothy, m. to Richard Lamplugh, esq. of Ribton.
II. Catherine, m. to John Holme, gent. of Carlisle.

The fourth son,

MUSGRAVE BRISCO, esq. captain in the army, m. Mary, only daughter and heiress of Edward Dyne,* esq. of Coghurst and Lankhurst, in Sussex, by whom he had issue,

I. Richard, in holy orders, *d. s. p.*
II. John, in the East India Company's service, died unm.
III. Edward-Dyne, captain in the provincial cavalry, a deputy lieutenant for the West Riding of Yorkshire, died unm.
IV. WASTELL, of whom presently.

The fourth but only son to leave issue,

WASTEL BRISCO, esq. of Coghurst, in Sussex, was captain in the Coldstream guards, a deputy lieutenant for the counties

---

* The family of Dyne was one of respectability in Sussex.

JAMES DYNE, seated in that county, married, and had two sons, viz.

JOHN, his heir.
Thomas, of East Grinstead, in Sussex, whose daughter, Timothea, m. her cousin, John Dyne, esq. and died in 1682.

The elder son,

JOHN DYNE, gent. of Ashettesford, in Kent, m. Margaret, daughter of — Baker, of Westwell, in the same county, and dying in 1646, (he was buried at Bethersden), was *s.* by his son,

JOHN DYNE, esq. of Westfield, Sussex, who wedded his cousin-german, Timothea, daughter and co-heir of Thomas Dyne, esq. of East Grinstead, and had issue,

I. EDWARD, his heir.
II. THOMAS, successor to his brother.
III. John.
IV. James, baptized at Westfield 20th February, 1653, who married and had issue.
V. William, buried at Westfield in 1666.
VI. Henry, bapt. 2nd July, 1668.

I. Timothea, baptized 8th June, 1658.
II. Margaret, bapt. 20th October, 1661, and died 1663.

John Dyne dying in 1678, was buried at Westfield, and *s.* by his son,

EDWARD DYNE, esq. of Westfield, aged fourteen in 1662, at whose decease, unmarried, the estates devolved on his brother,

THOMAS DYNE, esq. of Westfield and Lankhurst, baptized April, 1651, at Westfield, who *m.* Joanna, daughter of — Elkin, and dying in 1723, was *s.* by his son,

EDWARD DYNE, esq. of Lankhurst, jurat of Hastings, who *m.* Mary, daughter of William Fletcher, esq. of Conghurst or Coghurst, in Sussex, and left at his decease, in 1732, an only daughter and heiress,

MARY-FLETCHER DYNE, *b.* in 1714; *m.* as in the text, to MUSGRAVE BRISCO, esq.

of Sussex and York, and in the commission of the peace for the former. He *m.* 24th October, 1785, Sarah, daughter of — Goulbourn, esq. and had issue,

I. MUSGRAVE, his heir.

II. Wastel, of Bohemia House, near Hastings, *b.* 16th November, 1792; *m.* in June 1822, Maria, daughter of John Lade, esq. of Boughton House, Kent, and has surviving issue,

1. Wastel, *b.* 29th July, 1824.
2. Arthur.
3. Musgrave-Dyne.

1. Maria.
2. Eliza.
3. Sarah.

Mr. Wastel Brisco, who is a magistrate and deputy-lieutenant for Sussex, possesses an estate in Lincolnshire, as well as in that county.

I. Sarah, *m.* 7th June, 1810, to William Camac, esq. of Mansfield Street and of Hastings.

Mr. Brisco *d.* 25th January, 1834, and was *s.* by his eldest son, the present MUSGRAVE BRISCO, esq. of Coghurst.

*Arms*—Arg. three greyhounds courant in pale sa. Quartering the ensigns of Crofton, Whinnos, Skelton, Dyne, and Fletcher.

*Crest*—A greyhound courant, in pursuit of a hare.

*Motto*—Grata sume manu.

*Estates*—In Sussex and Yorkshire.

*Town Residence*—38, Devonshire Place.

*Seat*—Coghurst, near Hastings.

# BIGLAND, OF BIGLAND.

BIGLAND, GEORGE, esq. of Bigland Hall, in the county of Lancaster, *b.* 6th April, 1782, succeeded his father. Mr. Bigland is a deputy-lieutenant for Lancashire.

## Lineage.

The Biglands, one of the most ancient families in Lancashire, tradition affirms to have been seated at Bigland* so early as the Norman conquest; and their crest, "a lion, holding in his paw an ear of Big-wheat," may possibly allude to the acquisition of the estate by grant from one of the feudal lords of that period, who is said to have carried a similar bearing. It was not unusual in those times to permit a follower to assume part of his chieftain's arms. From the remains still existing of many old towers on the coast of Lancashire, it may be inferred that the county was subject to incursions from the northern powers, and thence a satisfactory reason may be derived why the family documents of the Biglands do not ascend to an earlier era than to the date when the attested pedigree commences. Besides, it does not appear that the herald's visitations went north of the sands, beyond which Bigland Hall is situated; and West, the historian of many neighbouring families, strictly confined himself to those who either lived, or enjoyed considerable property in the district of Furness. That the family, how-

* In front of the kitchen chimney at Bigland Hall, the only very ancient part of the house, is an old oak beam, with rude carved work upon it, and in very peculiar characters, the initials, I.B.M.B. 1167. At Arundel Castle is now preserved a piece of an old carved coat of arms in stone, with some characters very similar, in the peculiar formation, to those at Bigland. It was discovered among some ruins near the castle, and is supposed to be above seven hundred years old.

ever, was of rank and influence in the part of the country where it resided, its intermarriages with the Prestons of Holker, the Sandys of Furness, the Bellinghams of Fearns, the Thornboroughs of Hampsfield, the Daltons of Thurnham, the Wilsons of Dalham Tower, the Huddlestons of Millum Castle, the Braddylls of Coneshead Priory, &c. sufficiently attest. The first recorded ancestor,

EDWARD BYGLANDE, of Byglande, in the parish of Cartmel, Lancashire, living about the time of HENRY VII. married, and had issue,

I. HENRY, his heir.

II. Edward, of Cartmel, who married and had two sons, Edward and John. The latter,

JOHN BIGLAND, settled in the county of Essex, and died at Chelmsford in October, 1559, leaving a daughter, Thomasin, the wife of Charles Dubbes, and a son,

EDWARD BIGLAND, who *m.* at Chelmsford, in Essex, 8th August, 1575, Margaret Neale, and was succeeded by his son,

THE REV. EDWARD BIGLAND, M.A. rector of Leake, in the county of Nottingham, who *m.* Mary, daughter and heir of — Bendish, esq. and died in 1650, leaving, with other issue, a daughter, Anne, *m.* in 1639, to John Barwell, esq. of Garradon, in Leicestershire, and a son,

EDWARD BIGLAND, esq. of Grays Inn, in Middlesex, and of Long Whatton, in Leicestershire, sergeant at law, and M.P. for Nottingham. He *m.* Anne, only dau. and eventual heiress of Peter Richier, M.D. and *d.* in 1704, leaving (with two daughters, Mary, *m.* to Robert Wilmot, esq. of Duffield, grandson of Sir Nicholas Wilmot, bart. of Osmaston, and Anna-Berthia, the wife of John Arden, esq. of Arden, in Cheshire) a son and successor,

HENRY BIGLAND, esq. of Long Whatton and Frolesworth, in the county of Leicester, who *m.* Orme, daughter of Charles Whinyates, esq. of Peterborough, and had issue,

1. EDWARD, his heir.

2. Henry, died at Bermudas, unmarried.

1. Orme, born in 1708, *m.* first, 4th April, 1732, to Isaac Bayley, esq. of Chesterton, in the county of Huntingdon; and secondly, to Cooper Thornhill, esq. of Stilton. She died in 1767, leaving by her first husband two sons,

JOHN BAYLEY, of Peterborough, who *m.* Sarah, daughter of White Kennet, esq. and grand-daughter of Dr. Kennet, bishop of Peterborough, and had a son, the present

SIR JOHN BAYLEY, bart. late one of the barons of the Court of Exchequer, born 1763.

Isaac Bayley, who *m.* Mary, daughter of Edward Bigland, esq. of Long Whatton.

2. Anne - Bethia, died young.

Henry Bigland was interred at Clerkenwell, and succeeded by his son,

EDWARD BIGLAND, esq. of Long Whatton and Peterborough, born in 1710, who *m.* first, Elizabeth, daughter of Charles Pitfield, esq. of Hoxton, but by her, who died in 1738, had no issue; and secondly, Mary, daughter of Robert Depupe, of Dogsthorpe, and relict of White Kennet, by whom he had one son and three daughters, viz.

Edward, of Frolesworth and Peterborough, born in 1745, died unm.

Mary, born at Peterborough, 26th March, 1744, *m.* in 1772 to Isaac Bayley, esq.

Orme, born at Peterborough, 9th March, 1747, *m.* in 1772, to Roger Darvall, esq.

Lucy-Eliza, born at Peterborough, 5th October, 1754, *m.* in 1778, to Wright Thomas Squire, esq. of Peterborough.

The elder son and successor of Edward Byglande, of Byglande,

HENRY BIGLAND, of Bigland, espoused Jenett, daughter of George Preston, living in 1560, and died before 24th November, 15th HENRY VIII. leaving a son and successor,

EDWARD BIGLAND, of Bigland, who wedded a daughter of the ancient family of Sandys, of Furness Fell, and had three sons and two daughters, viz.

I. HENRY, his heir.
II. George, of Cartmel, married Agnes, daughter of George Denton, of Cumberland, and was father of
   James, of Cartmel, *m.* 2nd September, 1621, Elizabeth, daughter of Backhouse of Eversham, in Westmoreland, and hence derives, in the female line, the present SIR RALPH BIGLAND, Garter King of Arms.
III. James.

I. Janet.
II. Margaret.

Edward Bigland died in 1563, was interred at Cartmel, and succeeded by his eldest son,

HENRY BIGLAND, esq. of Bigland, who *m.* Isabel, daughter of --- Bellingham, esq. of Westmoreland, and by her, who died in 1622, had issue,

I. GEORGE, his heir.
II. James, of Grange, in the parish of Cartmel, *m.* there, 2nd June, 1600, Jennet, daughter of Harrison, esq. of Cartmel, and dying 27th November, 1623, left, with five daughters, a son,
   Henry, of Grange, born in 1607, who *m.* Anne daughter of Rowland Thornborough, esq. of Hampsfield, in Lancashire, by Jane, his wife, daughter of Thomas Dalton, esq. of Thurnham, and had issue,
      1. Henry, a legatee in the will of Henry Bigland, of Bigland, for £100, on condition that he did not go with his father to Ireland.
      2. James.
      3. George.

      1. Jane.
III. Henry, of Cartmel.

Henry Bigland died in 1616, and was *s.* by his son,

GEORGE BIGLAND, esq. of Bigland, who *m.* 15th October, 1608, Isabel, daughter of John Myers, of Cartmel, and had issue,

I. JAMES, his heir.
II. JOHN, successor to his brother.
III. Thomas, *d.* unm. 1646.
IV. Henry, baptized 1621, *d.* unm. in 1646.
V. George, baptized 2nd September, 1630, *d.* unm. 1685.
VI. Edward, *d.* unm.

I. Anne, baptized 2nd March, 1612, *m.* to Edward Robinson, esq. of Newby Bridge.
II. Sarah, baptized 26th February, 1615, *m.* to --- Atkinson, esq. of Westmoreland.
III. Isabel, baptized 15th February, 1618, *m.* to --- Battersby, esq.
IV. Bridget, baptized 5th August, 1627, *m.* to William Kilner, esq.

George Bigland died in 1644, and was buried at Cartmel, 29th October. His will bears date 1st June, 1643, and was proved at Richmond 1st February in the following year. His widow survived until April, 1645, when she was buried at Cartmel, leaving many legacies, and among others a bequest to the grammar-school in that town. The eldest son and successor,

JAMES BIGLAND, esq. of Bigland, Burnbarrow, and Ellerside, died unmarried in 1645, and was *s.* by his brother,

JOHN BIGLAND, esq. of Bigland, Burnbarrow, and Ellerside, baptized at Cartmel, 17th June, 1610. This gentleman wedded Jane, daughter of Thomas Fletcher, esq. of Winander, by Mary, his wife, daughter of William Knipe, esq. of Broughton Hall, and had issue,

I. GEORGE, his heir.
II. THOMAS, successor to his brother.
III. Henry, a merchant at Hamburgh, born in 1651, died unmarried.
IV. James.
V. John.
VI. Edward, living in 1693.
VII. William, *d. v. p.* unm.

I. Mary, died during her father's lifetime, unm.
II. Anne, born in 1660, *m.* to Edward Kellet, esq. of Mireside.
III. Isabel, *d.* unm.
IV. Sarah, *d.* unm.

Mr. Bigland's will bears date 6th April, 1670, and devises all his estates in Lancashire and Westmoreland, chargeable with certain legacies, to his eldest son,

GEORGE BIGLAND, esq. of Bigland, baptized at Cartmel, 30th October, 1647, who erected and endowed the free-school at Browedge, near Bigland. He died unm. in 1685 (his will bears date 18th May in that year), and was *s.* by his brother,

THOMAS BIGLAND, esq. of Bigland, baptized at Cartmel 22nd April, 1649, who *m.* in 1687, Elizabeth, daughter and heiress of the Rev. William Wilson, rector of Winander, a scion of the Wilsons of Dalham Tower, and had issue,

I. JOHN, his heir.
II. Henry, born in 1693, died unm. buried at Kendal.
III. Thomas, born in 1698, died unm. buried at Kendal.
IV. GEORGE, successor to his brother John.

I. Jane, born in 1688, died unmarried in 1712, buried in Kendal church, where a monument is erected to her memory. She left a legacy to Cartmel school, to which foundation the Bigland family were considerable contributors.
II. Sarah, died unm. in October, 1767.
III. Elizabeth, *m.* to — Stedman, of Richmond-on-Swale.
IV. Dorothy, *m.* Robert Thornton, merchant, of Lancaster.

Mr. Bigland was *s.* by his eldest son,

JOHN BIGLAND, esq. of Bigland, baptized 22nd February, 1690, who espoused Dorothy, daughter and heir of the Rev. William Wells, by Elizabeth, his wife, daughter of Thomas Huddleston, esq. of Millum Castle, but dying issueless, in 1747, the estates devolved on his only surviving brother,

GEORGE BIGLAND, esq. of Bigland, baptized 30th November, 1701. This gentleman *m.* at Desington, 7th April, 1749, Mary,* daughter of John Fox, gent. of Whitehaven, by Mary, his wife, daughter and coheir of Edward Towerson, and had two sons, viz.

I. GEORGE, his heir.
II. Thomas, born in 1751, died in November, 1829.

Mr. Bigland died suddenly at Wheatenhurst, in Gloucestershire, upon his return from Bristol, where he had been for the benefit of his health, on the 20th September, 1752, and was *s.* by his son,

* This lady married, after Mr. Bigland's decease, Thomas Sunderland, esq.

GEORGE BIGLAND, esq. of Bigland, born at Bigland, 5th May, 1750, who *m.* first, in 1781, Anne, second dau. and co-heir of Robert Watters, esq. of Whitehaven, high-sheriff for Cumberland, and had by her, who *d.* in 1783, one son,

I. GEORGE, his heir.

He *m.* secondly, at Ulverstone, 23rd November, 1784, Sarah, daughter of John Gale, esq. of Whitehaven, high-sheriff for Cumberland, and sister of the late Wilson Braddyll, esq. of Conishead Priory, and by her, who died in 1830, had two sons and four daughters, namely,

II. John, captain in the Royal Lancashire Militia, *m.* in 1828.
III. Wilson-Braddyll, captain R. N. *m.* 8th January, 1822, Emily, second daughter of the late Samuel Leeke, esq. a magistrate and deputy-lieutenant for Hants, and sister of Captain Sir Henry Leeke, R. N. By this lady he has issue,
    1. George-Selsey, born 27th September, 1822.
    2. Wilson-Henry-John, born 7th January, 1824.
    1. Sophia-Georgiana.

I. Sarah, *m.* to Pudsey Dawson, esq. of Lancliff Hall, Yorkshire, and died at Bigland, 26th December, 1816.
II. Georgina, died in 1820, and was buried at York, unm.
III. Mary, died at Bigland, in 1812, unmarried.
IV. Dorothy, died at Bigland, unm.

Mr. Bigland died in January, 1831, was interred at York, and succeeded by his eldest son, the present GEORGE BIGLAND, esq. of Bigland.

*Arms*—Az. two ears of Big-wheat or, quartering arg. three wolves' heads sa. for WILSON.

*Crest*—A lion passant, reguardant, gu. holding in his fore-paw an ear of Big-wheat, as in the arms.

*Mottoes*—Above the crest, Gratitudo: below the shield, Spes labor levis.

*Estates*—In Lancashire.

*Seat*—Bigland Hall, near Cartmel.

## BRAY, OF SHERE.

BRAY, EDWARD, esq. of Shere, in the county of Surrey, *b.* 20th July, 1793, succeeded his grandfather, WILLIAM BRAY, the county historian, at the decease of that gentleman in 1812.

## Lineage.

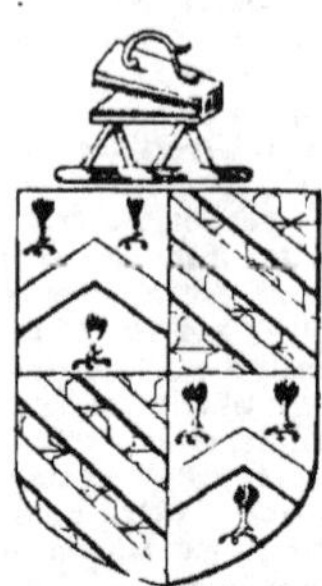

The name of the SIEUR DE BRAY occurs in the Roll of Battle Abbey, amongst the associates in arms of the CONQUEROR, and although the authenticity of that celebrated record has in many instances been questioned, in this the statement is confirmed by the fact of WILLIAM DE BRAY being one of the subscribing witnesses to the charter of the year 1088, conferred by the NORMAN on the Abbey he had founded in commemoration of his triumph at Hastings. No grant of lands appears however in Domesday Book to the Brays; but that the family supplied sheriffs * to Northamptonshire, Bedfordshire, Bucks, and some other counties between 1202 and 1273, is fully established.

WILLIAM DE BRAY witnessed the charter to Battle Abbey in 1088.

RALPH DE BRAY was sheriff of the counties of Northampton, Southampton, Somerset, Dorset, Oxford, Leicester, Bedford, and Bucks, in the reigns of the *Kings* JOHN and HENRY III. that is between the years 1202 and 1234. In the 17th of the latter monarch, in the great quarrel between the King and Hubert de Burgh, Earl of Kent, Hubert having taken sanctuary † in the chapel of Brentwood, in Essex, belonging to the Abbot of Waltham, HENRY appointed Ralph de Bray and Ralph de Norwich *(justiciarios nostros)* to receive from the earl an abjuration of the king's realm, if he would not go out of sanctuary, and appear in the king's courts and abide the judgment there; or to do him justice in the king's court if he would quit sanctuary, and appear therein according to the agreement between the king and him.

In the 44th of HENRY III. 1260,

WILLIAM DE BRAY was possessed of two knights' fees in Wollaston, and obtained a weekly market on Thursday at his manor there, and a fair every year on the eve of the invention of the Holy Cross and two days following. He was succeeded by

SIR ROBERT DE BRAY, one of the knights returned as having £40 a year in land, in the county of Northampton, summoned to attend *King* EDWARD I. in his wars in Scotland, and again by *King* EDWARD II. This Sir Robert, under the designation of Sir Robert de Bray, of Wollaston, attended the sheriff of Northampton, in 1304, to arrest Nicholas, Lord Seagrave, on his lordship's return from the Continent, he having left England without the king's license, to settle a dispute in the court of the King of France between himself and John de Cornwell. Sir Robert de Bray, amongst his other trusts, was ranger of Sancy Forest, in Northamptonshire. He was *s.* by his son,

SIR JAMES DE BRAY, living *temp.* RICHARD I. and of *King* JOHN, whose son,

ANSELM DE BRAY, was *s.* by his son,

---

* The sheriff of a county is an officer of high rank and importance in the present day, but was of still higher at the time when much of the revenues of the Crown arose from escheats, the levy of which required the assistance of the sheriff, who was responsible to the king for the produce.

† From the time of the Saxon kings, churches and churchyards, under certain modifications, afforded sanctuary to offenders, with the exception of those guilty of sacrilege or treason. The criminal within forty days was obliged to cloathe himself in sackcloth, confess his crime before the coroner, solemnly abjure the realm, and taking a cross in his hand repair to an appointed port, embark and depart the country. If apprehended, or brought back in his way thither within forty days, he had a right to plead privilege of sanctuary, and to demand a free passage. Should the offender neglect this appeal to the coroner, and remained in the sanctuary, when the forty days limited had expired, it became an act of felony in any one to afford him sustenance. The coroner was to take the abjuration of the criminal at the church in the following form:

"This hear then, Sir Coroner, that I am a murderer of one or more, a stealer of sheep, (or any thing else), and because I have done many such evils and robberies in this land, I do abjure the realm of our Edward, King of England, and I shall hasten me towards the port of which thou hast given me; and that I shall not go out of the highway, and if I do I will that I be taken as a robber and a felon of our lord the king, and that at such place I will diligently seek for passage, and that I will tarry there but one flood or ebb, if I can have passage; and unless I can have it in such a place I will go every day into the sea up to my knees assaying to pass over; and unless I can do this, within forty days, I will put myself again into the church, as a robber and felon of our lord the king, so God me help and his holy judgment".

WILLIAM DE BRAY, whose son,

THOMAS DE BRAY, married for his second wife the daughter of — Braxby, and left a son,

WILLIAM BRAY, father of

EDMUND BRAY, whose son,

SIR RICHARD BRAY, is said by some to have been of the privy council to HENRY VI.; by others he is called the King's Physician; the former is the more probable, as he was buried in Worcester cathedral. He had two wives; by the first, Margaret, dau. of John Sandes, esq. of Furnes Felles, in Lancashire, he had an only son,

JOHN (Sir), whose only daughter and heir,

MARGARET BRAY, espoused Sir William Sandys, summoned to parliament in 1529, as BARON SANDYS, *of the Vine*, and conveyed to his lordship a considerable estate.* The barony of Sandys fell into *abeyance*, on the decease of the eighth lord, about the year 1700, and it so continues. (See BURKE's *Extinct Peerage*).

By the second, Joan, Sir Richard had two other sons, namely,

I. REGINALD (Sir), who being in the service of Margaret, Countess of Richmond, ‡ was confidentially employed in the negotiations preceding the enterprize of her son, the earl, which placed that prince on the throne as HENRY VII. Sir Reginald was made a knight banneret at Bosworth, and afterwards one of the knights of the body to the new king, who further rewarded his fidelity and zeal by large grants§ of land, and by conferring upon him the order of the Bath, and finally that of the GARTER. He was also of the privy council, and held for one year the office of Lord Treasurer.|| He *m.* Catherine, daughter of Nicholas Hussey; but dying without issue, devised the principal part of his landed estate between his nephew, Edmund Bray, and his niece, MARGARET, the wife of Lord Sandys. Sir Reginald laid the first stone of HENRY *the Seventh's* CHAPEL, at Westminster, on the 24th January, 1502-3, and died on the 5th August, in the same year. By his will he directed that his body should be buried in the chapel, on the south side of the church of Our Ladie and St. George, in the castle

* There is an old room at the Vine wainscotted, on which MARGARET BRAY's arms with those of SANDYS appear carved in several places; they remain also on some stones of the now ruined chapel of the Holy Ghost, near Basingstoke, and on a wall in Basingstoke church. On the subject of Lord Sandys' alliance with the heiress of Bray, tradition preserves the following distich:

My Lord Sandys, my Lord Sandys,  
Lift up both your hands,  
And down on your knees and pray,  
That when you come from France,  
You may lead up the dance,  
With good Mistress Margery Bray.

‡ Reginald Bray was receiver-general to Sir Henry Stafford, the second husband of the Countess, (see Tudor, Earl of Richmond, BURKE's Extinct Peerage), who by his will bequeathed to him (Reginald) his grissel courser. Bray continued after the death of Sir Henry, in the service of the noble widow, and on her subsequent marriage with Lord Stanley, was put in trust for her dower of five hundred marks per annum.

§ The manor of SHERE, Vachery, and Cranley, in Surrey, had long been in possession of the earls of Ormonde, but reverting to the Crown on the attainder of James the fifth earl, who was likewise Earl of Wiltshire, in 1461, EDWARD IV. granted this manor to John Touchet, Lord Audley, who died 26th November, 1491, and was buried in the chancel of the church at Shere. Notwithstanding the attainder of the Earl of Ormonde and Wilts, and the grant of the manor to Lord Audley, the earl's brother attempted at least to recover the estate; for by his deed dated 28th January, in the 1st of HENRY VII. he granted to Sir Reginald Bray, knt. the MANOR OF SHERE, and the manor and lordship of Vachery, in Cranley, reserving the liberty of hunting, and taking beasts of chase in the park of Vachery, at his pleasure; also liberty of lodging in the manor-house of Shere, for himself, servants, and horses, whenever he pleased. To hold to Sir Reginald and his assigns for life, he finding a chaplain, and a chantry priest yearly to celebrate divine service in the chapel of the manor of Vachery, and not cutting any great timber except for building repairs. Sir Reginald does not however appear at any time to have had the actual possession of the manor, as we find Lord Audley enjoying it after the attainder of Ormonde, and his son James, Lord Audley inheriting those lands with his title. This James was the Lord Audley so notorious as the leader of the Cornish rebels, defeated by *King* HENRY at Blackheath, and subsequently beheaded and attainted. We further find his son, by his second wife, Sir James Audley, suffering a recovery in the Hilary Term next following the attainder of his father, and selling the estate to Sir Reginald Bray.

|| Sir Reginald "bore in his arms (says BRYDGES in the History of Northamptonshire) a Thorn, with a Crown in the middle, in memory, it is supposed, of his finding the crown (of *King* RICHARD) in a bush in Bosworth field." Of this device there was, in the last century, when Brydges wrote (he died in 1724), a representation in the hall window of STENE, one of the manors, part of the forfeited estates of the Lord Lovel, granted to Sir Reginald Bray.

of Windsor, which he had new made with that intent, and also in honour of Almighty God.*

II. JOHN.

The younger son,

JOHN BRAY, esq. who was buried in the chancel of the church at Chelsea, *m.* ——, and had, with a daughter, the wife of Sir John Norris, three sons,

I. EDMUND (Sir), who inherited a large portion of his uncle Sir Reginald Bray's property, which was confirmed under a deed of settlement, made between himself and Sir William Sandys and his wife Dame Margery Sandys, in adjustment of a dispute between the parties regarding the lands of the deceased. This Edmund was about the age of eighteen at the death of Sir Reginald, who had acted as his guardian and took care of his education. He *m.* Jane,† daughter and heir of Richard Halywell, esq. and had JOHN, his heir, with several daughters. In the 6th of HENRY VIII. (1515) he was sheriff of the county of Bedford, and was summoned to parliament as BARON BRAY, of Eaton-Bray, in that county, on the 3rd November, 21st of the same monarch. (See BURKE'S *Extinct and Dormant Peerage.*)

II. EDWARD (Sir), of whom presently.

III. REGINALD, who *m.* Anne, daughter and heiress of Richard Monington, esq. of Barrington, in Gloucestershire, and had, with four other sons,*

EDMOND BRAY, of Barrington, who wedded Agnes, daughter and heir of Edmond Harman, of Taynton, and had, with four daughters, three sons, viz.

1. EDMOND, his heir.
2. Silvester, who was settled at Fifield.
3. John, who purchased Fifield from his brother Silvester.

The eldest son,

EDMOND BRAY, of Barrington, *m.* Dorothy, daughter of Sir John Tracy, of Todington, and had, with a daughter, one son, his successor,

SIR GILES BRAY, of Barrington, who received the honour of knighthood. He married Anne, daughter of Richard Chetwood, and was succeeded by his son,

SIR EDMOND BRAY, knt. of Barrington, father of

REGINALD BRAY, esq. of Barrington, who left four sons, and was succeeded by the eldest,

EDMOND BRAY, esq. of Barrington, who *m.* Frances, daughter and co-heir of Sir John Morgan, of Llantarnam, in Monmouthshire, and had two sons and three daughters, viz.

1. Reginald-Morgan, born in 1705, who sold the Barrington estate in 1740 to Lord Chancellor Talbot, from whom it descended to Lord Dynevor.
2. Edmond, died an infant.
1. Mary, *m.* — Bluet, esq. and had issue.
2. Frances, *m.* to — Bushell,

* That the chapel of St. George, at Windsor, owes much to the skill as well as to the liberality and magnificence of Sir Reginald there can be little doubt. His arms, sometimes singly, sometimes impaling those of Hussey (the family of his wife), his device of a flax or hemp breaker, the initials of his name, and those of his wife, in so many parts of the ceiling and windows, could not have been so placed without a more than ordinary claim to the distinction. His will that his executors should finish the chapel, according to the form and intention of the foundation, would seem to refer to a planned drawing in his possession, and shows that the work had been carried on at his own expense.

† Sir Reginald Bray purchased the wardship of this young lady, that she might become the wife of his nephew, as appears by deed dated 12th February, 1497, made between the said Sir Reginald and Sir John Norbury, her grandfather, in contemplation of "a marriage to be had between Edmund Bray, son of John Bray, brother of the same Sir Reginald, and Jane Halywell, daughter and heir presumptive of Richard Halywell, esq. cousin and heir apparent of Sir John Norbury, (that is to say), daughter of Anne, who was the daughter of the said Sir John Norbury." In consideration of three hundred marks paid by Sir Reginald, Sir John settled immense estates upon his said heir, in the counties of Warwick, Worcester, Surrey, and Hants.

* The three eldest sons died without issue. The fifth and youngest, Reginald Bray, had the estate at Steyne and Hinton settled on him. He wedded Ann, daughter of Thomas, Lord Vaux, and left six daughters, his co-heirs, of whom the fourth, Temperance, wedded Sir Thomas Crewe, serjeant-at-law, and had a son, John Crewe, created Lord Crewe, who purchasing the shares of the other co-heirs, obtained the whole of the estate at Stene and Hinton, which passed with his lordship's grand-daughter, in marriage, to Henry Grey, duke of Kent, and was eventually sold to Sarah, Duchess of Marlborough, by whose descendant, the present Earl of Spencer, it is now enjoyed.

esq. who assumed the surname of Fettiplace, and had two sons and three daughters,
Robert, *d.* in 1799.
Charles, *d.* in 1805.
Frances, *m.* to Richard Gorges, esq. and had two sons and six daughters.*
Mary, *m.* first, to — Blandyshaw, esq. and secondly, to William Kemeys, esq.
Arabella, *m.* to John Webb, esq.
3. Jane, *m.* to V. Cornwall, esq.

The second son of John Bray,

SIR EDWARD BRAY, knt. of Vachery Park, in Cranley, Surrey, was sheriff of Surrey and Sussex in the 30th of HENRY VIII. and represented the former county in the two parliaments of *Queen* MARY. Sir Edward, who appears to have been bred a soldier, was one of the knights appointed to accompany *King* HENRY to Calais to meet the French monarch; and he is stated to have been Master of the Ordnance in the time of *Queen* MARY, and to have marched at the head of some troops to Charing-cross to attack Wyatt in the insurrection which he had fomented against her majesty. He *m.* first, Elizabeth, daughter and co-heir of Henry Lovell, esq. of Sussex, but by that lady, from whom he was divorced, and who espoused, secondly, Sir Anthony Windsor, he had no issue. He wedded, secondly, Beatrice, daughter of R. Shirley, esq. of Wiston, in Sussex, and had two sons and one daughter, viz.

I. EDWARD (Sir), his heir.
II. Owen, of Chobham, in Surrey, who *m.* Ann, daughter and heir of John Danister, esq. one of the Barons of the Exchequer, and had issue,
John, who *d. s. p.*
Edward, of Chobham, who married Susan, daughter and co-heir of John Doyley, esq. of Merton, in Oxfordshire, and had a son Owen, who married and had several children, and four daughters, Susan, *m.* first to Hum. Laward, and secondly to — Melton, esq.; Ann, the wife of Edmund Percy, of Cowes Castle; Frances and Dorothy.
Jane, *m.* to — Hudson.
Mary, *m.* to Wharton, of Yorkshire.
Dorothy, *m.* to Thomas Stamp, of Berkshire.
Frances, *m.* to Captain John Lattin.
Ann, *m.* to Thomas Dolman, of Shaw, Berks.
I. Beatrice, *m.* to Thomas Elrington, esq.

Sir Edward survived his second wife, and married, thirdly, Jane, daughter of Sir Matthew Browne, of Betchworth Castle, in the parish of Dorking, but had no more issue. He died in 1558, and by his will, dated in that year, directed that his body should be buried in the parish church of Cranley, and that all the poor folks for whom he had made houses should carry his body to the church, and have for their reward twelvepence each. The will then proceeds, after some minor legacies, to affirm the settlement of divers manors and lands for his wife's jointure, and to state that "she should quietly enjoy the same without interruption of his son Edward." It further provides, in case the said Edward, or his heirs, should attempt to disturb the quiet possession of his step-mother, that that lady should have all the testator's fee-simple lands, tenements, rents, reversions, and hereditaments whatsoever. Lady Bray survived for several years, and resided at the mansion-house at Vachery, where she carried on the iron forge which had been established there, and soon took occasion to quarrel with Sir Edward, her step-son. Amongst other things, she wrote to William More, of Loseley, that he, Sir Edward, had summoned her workmen there to her great damage, and she desired Mr. More's favour. At another period she complained that he had broken down the head of her pond, and at other times had been guilty of such like disturbances; under cover of which she availed herself of the power so improperly given by her husband's will, and sold great part of the estate in Cranley and Ewhurst for little more than nominal considerations, as appears by several deeds, in many of which were conveyances to her own relatives and dependents. What remained of Sir Edward Bray's great estates at the decease of his widow, devolved on his son,

SIR EDWARD BRAY, knt. M.P. for Helston in the 13th ELIZABETH, who *m.* first, Mary, daughter of Simon Elrington, esq. of Northampton, and had by her an only son, Reginald, described as heir-apparent, and of the Inner Temple in 1557, being then of age, who appears to have died issueless. Sir Edward wedded, secondly, Elizabeth, daughter of William Roper, esq. of Eltham, in Kent, by Margaret, his wife, daughter of

* Of the daughters of Richard Gorges, esq.
Meliora Gorges, *m.* D. Dacre, esq.
Mary Gorges, *m.* Thynne Howe Gwynne, esq.
Elizabeth Gorges, *m.* Henry Sheldon, esq.

Sir Thomas More, and had another son, also named REGINALD. He *m.* thirdly, Magdalene, daughter of Sir Thomas Cotton, of Kent, by whom, who died in 1563, he had no issue: and fourthly, a lady named Mary, by whom (who wedded, secondly, Sir Edmund Tylney, master of the revels to *Queen* ELIZABETH) he had three daughters,

- I. Mary, baptized at Shere, 8th October, 1564, *m.* to Sir George Chowne, knt. of Wrotham, Kent.
- II. Magdalen, baptized at Shere, 2nd April, 1566, *m.* to George Bowes, esq. of Durham.
- III. Frances, baptized at Shere, 22nd July, 1568, *m.* to George Gastrell, esq.

Sir Edward, who sold a great part of his possessions, including the manor of Hawnes, Houghton Regis, Kempson, and Eaton Bray, in the counties of Berks and Buckingham, died in 1581, was buried at Shere, and *s.* by his son,

REGINALD BRAY, esq. of Shere, baptized there 1st May, 1555, who *m.* Elizabeth, daughter of Richard Covert, esq. of Hascomb, in Surrey, an ancient family, possessing the manor of Hascomb, and left a son and successor,

EDWARD BRAY, esq. of Shere, born in 1577, who made Tower-hill the place of his residence. He *m.* first, Jane, daughter of Edward Covert, esq. of Tuynham, in Sussex, and by her, who *d.* in 1618, had issue,

- I. EDWARD, his heir.
- I. Elizabeth, buried at Shere in 1610.
- II. Timothea, *m.* to John Harmer, esq. of Weston, Herts.
- III. Magdalen, buried in 1623.
- IV. Jane, baptized in 1616, *m.* to Anthony Duncomb, esq.

Edward Bray wedded, secondly, Miss Comber, of Shermanbury, and had by her a daughter, Grace, *m.* to — Goodwin. He was *s.* by his son,

EDWARD BRAY, esq. of Shere, baptized 10th September, 1609, who, like his father, resided at Tower-hill. He *m.* Susanna, daughter of William Heath, esq. of Pedinghoe, in Sussex, and had a son and successor,

EDWARD BRAY, esq. of Shere, baptized 18th October, 1640, who espoused Frances, daughter of Vincent Randyll, esq. of Chilworth, the proprietor of a large estate in that village, who was engaged in the making of gunpowder, the manufactory of which had been established there by the Evelyn family. The issue of this marriage were,

- I. Randyll, who entered the navy, and was a lieutenant in the Dreadnought man-of-war at the attack on Gibraltar in 1704, under the command of Sir George Rooke. It is not known where he died.
- II. EDWARD, heir to his father.
- III. Benjamin, baptized 19th September, 1693, *d.* unm. 29th August, 1772.
- I. Frances, *d.* in 1704.
- II. Jane.

Mr. Bray died in 1714, and was succeeded by his son,

EDWARD BRAY, esq. of Shere, baptized 4th January, 1687, who *m.* in 1727, Ann, daughter of the Rev. George Duncumb, rector of Shere,* (which living Mr. Duncumb's father had purchased of Mr. Bray's grandfather), and had issue,

- I. GEORGE, his heir.
- II. Edward, surgeon in the 35th regiment of foot, baptized 9th February, 1730, died unmarried in Ireland 19th November, 1773.
- III. Charles, baptized 19th September, 1733, *d.* 1735.
- IV. WILLIAM, successor to his brother.

Mr. Bray died at Greenwich, in 1740, and was *s.* by his eldest son,

THE REV. GEORGE BRAY, of Shere, educated at Lincoln college, Oxford, who died unm. 1st March, 1803, and was succeeded by his brother,

WILLIAM BRAY, esq. of Shere, the learned antiquary and historian of Surrey, baptized 7th November, 1736. This gentleman *m.* Mary, daughter of Henry Stevens, gent. and had issue,

- I. William, born in 1759, buried at Shere in 1767.
- II. Thomas, born and died in 1762.
- III. John, born in 1765, and died in 1767.
- IV. EDWARD, born 31st January, 1768, who *m.* Mary-Ann-Catherine, daughter of Daniel Malthus, esq. of Albury, in Surrey, and sister of the celebrated writer on population, and pre-deceasing his father, in 1814, left issue,
  1. EDWARD, successor to his grandfather.
  2. Reginald, *b.* in 1797.
  3. William, in holy orders.
  1. Henrietta-Mary, *m.* to Augustus Warren, esq.
  2. Louisa.
  3. Catherine.
- V. George, *b.* in 1770, and *d.* in 1772.
- I. Mary.
- II. Catherine.
- III. Amelia-Caroline, *d.* unm. 1789.

Mr. Bray, who was treasurer to the Society of Antiquaries, and editor of the Evelyn

* By his wife, a daughter of Sir Richard Heath, baron of the Exchequer.

Memoirs, died in 1832, and was succeeded by his grandson, the present EDWARD BRAY, esq. of Shere.

*Arms*—Quarterly, first and fourth arg. a chev. between three eagles' legs, sa. erased à la cuisse, their talons gu.; second and third vairy, arg. and az. three bends gu.

*Crest*—A flax breaker or.

*Estates*—The manor of Shere, Vachery, and Cranley, (besides other property in Shere and Cranley), which was granted to Sir Reginald Bray by HENRY VII.

*Seat*—Shere.

## CLOSE, OF ELM PARK, NOW OF DRUMBANAGHER.

CLOSE, MAXWELL, esq. of Drumbanagher, in the county of Armagh, a lieutenant-colonel in the army, *b.* in March, 1783, *m.* in 1820, Anna-Elizabeth, second daughter of Charles Brownlow, esq. of Lurgan, son of the Right Honourable William Brownlow, and has issue,

MAXWELL, *b.* 25th June, 1827.
Barry, *b.* 22nd June, 1833.

Colonel Close, who is a magistrate and deputy lieutenant for the county of Armagh, succeeded his father, the Rev. Samuel Close, in 1817, and served the office of sheriff during the following year.

### Lineage.

RICHARD CLOSE, the first of the family who settled in Ireland, was the younger son of a respectable house in Yorkshire, and held a commission in the army, sent from England, in the reign of CHARLES I. into that kingdom, where he remained after the termination of the civil wars, and became one of the lords of the soil, as we find him seised of four tates, or townlands, in the county of Monaghan, *temp.* CHARLES II. After the restoration he fixed himself at Lisnegarvey, (now Lisburn), in the county of Antrim, where a Protestant colony had been located under the protection of the then Lord Conway. There he lived and died, leaving a son and heir,

RICHARD CLOSE, esq. who inherited the Monaghan estates. He married the sister of Samuel Waring, esq. of Waringstown, in the county of Down, M.P. for Hillsborough, and received from that gentleman a grant of lands contiguous to Waringstown, on which he built a good house and resided. He considerably enlarged the family estate by purchasing a tract of land on the river Ban, between Rathfriland and Castlewellan, in Downshire, and after the disturbances in 1688, which obliged him to leave his home and join the Protestants, then united at Lisburn, under the Lord Conway and Sir Arthur Rawdon, he returned (subsequently to the battle of Boyne), having suffered great losses during the harassing conflicts of the times. He left at his decease (with three daughters, the eldest *m.* to the Rev. Dean Welch, the second to — Jones, esq. and the third to John Peirse, esq.) five sons, viz.

I. RICHARD, who succeeded to the estates in Down and Monaghan. This gentleman *m.* the dau. of Toby Hall, esq. of Narrow-water, and dying about the year 1720, at Waringstown, where he was buried, left a dau. *m.* to Davys Wilson, esq. of Carrickfergus, and two sons, viz.

1. SAMUEL, who inherited his fa-

ther's landed property in Monaghan and Down, and served the office of sheriff for both those counties on attaining majority. He wedded the daughter of — Stewart, esq. of Ballintoy, in Antrim, and had one son, Samuel, who was drowned, when a schoolboy, at Ringsend, near Dublin, by venturing upon ice not sufficiently strong to bear him. His death was an unfortunate event to the family, for it enabled his father to levy fines and dock the estates, which he did, and having sold all his landed possessions, he retired to England, where he resided for several years, and died in or about 1781, leaving no issue.

2. Toby, a captain in the corps of invalids in England, died unm.

II. SAMUEL, of whom presently.

III. Henry, who resided at Waringstown, and married the daughter of Meredyth Workman, esq. of Mahon, in the county of Armagh, by whom he left issue, Meredyth, Mary, and Rachael, who all died unmarried.

IV. John, a captain in the army, who was killed at the siege of Gibraltar.

V. William, who *m.* the daughter of — Tuberg, esq. and left a son, Samuel, who died unmarried.

The second son, (in whose descendant the representation of the Close family is now vested),

THE REV. SAMUEL CLOSE, who was presented to the rectory of Donaghhenry, or Stewardstown, in the county of Tyrone, *anno* 1721, married Catharine, daughter of Captain James Butler, of Ringhaddy, in Downshire, by Dame Margaret Maxwell, of Mullatinny, (now Elm Park), in the county of Armagh, relict of Sir Robert Maxwell, bart. of Ballycastle, in the county of Derry. This Dame Margaret Maxwell was the daughter and heiress of Henry Maxwell, esq. of Mullatinny, who was the son of James Maxwell, the third son of Robert Maxwell, Dean of Armagh, (a younger son of the house of Calderwood, in Scotland), who, after building the house of Mullatinny in 1626, was murdered in 1641, by Sir Phelim O'Neill, at College Hall, the seat of his elder brother, Dr. Robert Maxwell, afterwards Bishop of Kilmore, and founder of the Farnham family. Captain James Butler, who was of the Ormonde branch of the Butlers, resided with the Lady Maxwell his wife, at Mullatinny, and died there, having first bequeathed, by his will, made in 1713, his own estates, Cloghabeg and Knockabultoge, in the parish of Gowran, in the city of Kilkenny; with all his freehold estates in that county and lease of Bramblestown, and all his personal estate there and arrears due out of the house in Patrick Street, city of Kilkenny, and inhabited by Mr. Edward Butler, treasurer to the Duke of Ormonde, to his eldest son, James Butler, esq. by a former wife; and the estate of Ballycastle, in the county of Derry, which he enjoyed in right of Lady Maxwell his wife, to whom it had been bequeathed by her first husband, Sir Robert Maxwell, to his daughter Catharine, after the death of her mother, by whom it was afterwards settled on the Rev. Samuel Close and his issue, on the marriage of that gentleman with Catharine Butler, her daughter; but they both died before her at Mullatinny, leaving one son and four daughters, namely,

I. MAXWELL.

I. Margaret, *m.* to Captain Charles Woolly, and had a daughter, Mary-Anne, the wife of Captain Amos Vereker, of the county of Limerick.

II. Mary, died unm.

III. Catharine, died unm.

IV. Elizabeth, *m.* to Peter Gervais, esq. and had one son, the Rev. Francis Gervais, of Cecil, in the county of Tyrone, rector of Carlingford, and two daughters, Mary-Anne Gervais, *m.* to the Rev. Daniel Kelly, rector of Killeshel, and Elizabeth Gervais, *m.* to John Windsor, esq. capt. R. A.

The son and successor,

MAXWELL CLOSE, esq. succeeded his grandmother, Lady Maxwell, who *d.* in 1758, in the possession of Elm Park, and the lands settled upon him. He *m.* in 1748, Mary, eldest dau. of Captain Robert Maxwell, of Fellows Hall, in the county of Armagh, brother of John, Lord Farnham, and had issue,

I. SAMUEL, his heir.

II. Robert, died unm.

III. Barry, *b.* in December, 1756, a major-general in the army,* who was

* Barry Close entered into the military service of the East India Company, and soon attracted by his great talents the notice of his superior officers. After serving at Tanjore, Pondicherry, &c. he had the honour to act in staff situations at the two memorable sieges of Seringapatam, in the Mysore, the first under Marquis Cornwallis, and the second under General Lord Harris, when by the capture of that city, and the fall of Tippoo Saib, a very considerable addition was made to the territorial possessions of the Company, and the interests of the British nation in India.

On this occasion his merits were acknowledged in a letter, dated Seringapatam, 13th May, 1799, from General Lord Harris to the Governor-general, published by his direction in general orders, at Madras, on the 24th of May, 1799, of which

created a baronet in 1812. He died in April, 1813, when the title expired.

IV. Farnham, died in the island of Guadaloupe in 1794, lieutenant-colonel of the 65th regiment, unm.

I. Grace, *b.* in January, 1750, *m.* to the Rev. Dr. St. John Blacker.

II. Catharine, *b.* in November, 1753, *m.* to Arthur Noble, esq.

III. Margaret.

IV. Mary.

V. Elizabeth.

Mr. Close died in 1793, was buried at Tynan, near the remains of his father and

---

the following is an extract:—"In every point of view I must call your Lordship's particular attention to the adjutant-general of the army. His general character as an officer is too well established by a long and distinguished course of the most meritorious service to require my testimony. But the particular exertions of his talents on the present service, in directing, regulating, and assisting the progress of our departments, when embarrassed by all the difficulties attending a deficiency of conveyance for an uncommonly extensive equipment, during the advance of the army, and the ability and zeal displayed by him in superintending the various operations of an arduous siege, where he was ever present, stimulating the exertions of others, or assisting their judgment and labour by his own, claim from me to be stated to your Lordship in the most forcible terms. It is my earnest wish that my sentiments on this subject may be publicly recorded, and it is my firm opinion that if the success of this army has been of importance to the British interests, that success is to be attributed in a very considerable degree to Lieutenant-colonel Close."

Soon after this he received from the honourable committee of the board of directors a present of a sword set with diamonds, value three hundred pounds sterling, as a mark of their approbation of his conduct, and was appointed a commissioner with others to view and report upon the state of the district then ceded to the Company. He was subsequently selected by Marquis Wellesley, the then governor-general, to fill the important station of resident at Poona, the court of the Peshwa, the chief of the Mahratta princes, who all seemed at that time not very favourably disposed to the interests of the company. In this arduous and difficult situation, which required all his address and management, he had the good fortune, under the guidance of the marquis and his own sound judgment, to succeed in conciliating the peshwa and his ministers, and of preserving that government in friendship with the Company, during the war with Scindia, Holcar, and other Eastern princes; of which ample testimony has been given by the marquis in his letter to the honourable committee of the directors, dated 20th June, 1803, laid, with other papers, before the House of Commons pending the parliamentary inquiry into the conduct of the Mahratta war. He says, "It would be injustice to Lieutenant-colonel Close to suffer this dispatch to depart without adding my earnest request that your honourable committee may be pleased to direct your particular attention to the zeal, ability and industry which have distinguished the eminent services of that valuable public officer during the late important crisis in the Mahratta empire. In adverting to the conduct of Lieutenant-colonel Close, at the peshwa's court, your honourable committee will remark with satisfaction the unabated continuance of those able, honest, and indefatigable exertions which furnished the most effectual aid in the conquest and settlement of the Mysore, and which have since contributed to establish through the rajah's government a system of internal administration calculated to augment and secure the happiness and prosperity of that flourishing country."

After Marquess Wellesley returned to Europe, Colonel Close remained at Poona, until summoned by the government of Madras to afford his assistance in reconciling some unhappy disputes and jealousies which had taken place among the military on the Madras establishment, and which threatened serious consequences. In this difficult situation of affairs, (says the writer of an account of that transaction, published in London in 1810) "the government thought proper to call into action the service of Colonel Close, an officer of the greatest talents, and possessing a mind distinguished by vigour and enterprise, and whose whole life had been devoted to the service of his country." "They knew him (said another writer in the *Quarterly Review*) to be of a skill equally approved and a courage equally clear in action and in council. They knew that by a native elevation of mind and intellect he had risen above the prejudices natural to the members of a numerous provincial army. They knew that a long residence amidst the effeminacy of Eastern courts, and the chicanery of Eastern cabinets, while it had inured him to a perfect acquaintance with their native character, had yet left unimpaired the purity of his patriotic ardour and the correctness of his military principles. They knew that his high qualifications and eminent services, political and warlike, had rendered his name not more respectable in the eyes of his countrymen than venerable to the native soldiery. And they were not disappointed in the use he made of such influence, which was proved by his exertions to restore peace and harmony among his brother officers and the troops they commanded, which however required all his prudence and courage when attended with no inconsiderable share of personal danger, and in the end were not without effect, as appeared by the account of that affair, published in London (as before mentioned)."

He was soon afterwards sent with the subsidiary force of 12,000 men to repress the depredations of Meer Khan, an Indian chief, who had made incursions into the territories of the Company; and having succeeded in that affair, he resumed his station at Poona. But having now resided in India nearly thirty-five years, and his health requiring a change of climate, he applied for permission to return to

grandmother, Lady Maxwell, and *s.* by his eldest son,

THE REV. SAMUEL CLOSE, of Elm Park, rector of Keady, in the county of Armagh, and of Drakestown, in Meath. He espoused Deborah, third daughter of the Rev. Arthur Champagné, dean of Clonmacnoise, son of Major Josias Champagné, by the Lady Jane Forbes his wife, daughter of Arthur, Earl of Granard, and had four sons and three daughters, viz.

I. MAXWELL, his heir.

II. Robert, a major in the East India Company's service, who *m.* Caroline, sister of the late Sir Thomas Palmer, bart. of Northamptonshire, and has issue.

III. Henry-Samuel, *m.* Jane, daughter of the Rev. Holt Waring, of Waringstown, in the county of Down, and has issue.

IV. John-Forbes, in holy orders, rector of Kilkeel, in Downshire, who *m.* Mary, youngest daughter of Charles Brownlow, esq. of Lurgan, and has issue.

I. Mary, *m.* to Sir Justinian Isham, bart. of Lamport, in the county of Northampton, and has issue.

II. Jane, *m.* to Captain Chidley Coote, brother of Sir Charles-Henry Coote, bart. of Ballyfin, in the Queen's County, and has issue.

III. Harriet, *m.* to the Rev. Ralph Coote, youngest brother of Sir C. H. Coote, bart.

Mr. Close died in 1817, and was succeeded by his son, the present MAXWELL CLOSE, esq. of Drumbanagher.

*Arms*—Az. on a chev. arg. between three mullets or, two bugle horns ppr. stringed gu. with a stirrup-iron in the centre ppr.: quartering Maxwell and Butler.

*Crest*—A demi lion vert, holding a battle-axe or, headed arg.

*Mottoes*—Fortis et fidelis for CLOSE. Sine cruce, sine luce for MAXWELL.

*Estates*—In the county of Armagh.

*Seat*—Drumbanagher, near Newry.

---

England, which was granted, and declared by the Governor of Madras in general orders, published on the 15th September, 1810, in the following terms: "Colonel Close is permitted to proceed to Europe on furlough. The important services rendered by Colonel Close in the high and confidential situation which he has held under the government of this presidency have so frequently received the testimony of public approbation, that it would be superfluous to recapitulate them. The governor in council, however, cannot allow that officer to depart, without again expressing the high sense which this government must ever entertain of services so eminent and distinguished, which have contributed so essentially to the prosperity of the British interests in the Deccan, and which so justly entitle him to the strongest expressions of public gratitude and applause."

At this time he returned to England, having succeeded to the rank of major-general; and shortly afterwards his royal highness the Prince Regent, in the name and behalf of His Majesty, was graciously pleased to confer on him the dignity of a baronet of the United Kingdom of Great Britain and Ireland, by letters patent, dated the 12th day of December, 1812.

# PLOWDEN, OF PLOWDEN.

PLOWDEN, EDMUND, esq. of Plowden, in the county of Salop, and of Aston, in Northamptonshire, *m.* Anna-Maria, daughter of Robert Burton, esq. of Logner, in Salop, and had an only child,

MARIA, *m.* to the Rev. John Eyton, vicar of Willington, and rector of Eyton, by whom, who died 10th January, 1823, she left at her decease, in October, 1825, several sons and daughters.

Mr. Plowden succeeded his father in 1766.

## Lineage.

The family of PLOWDEN has been seated at Plowden, in Salop, from a period anteceding the earliest records extant in the vicinity.

ROGER PLOWDEN, of Plowden, who was a crusader under CŒUR DE LION, is stated to have been present at the siege of Acre in 1194, and to have received for his gallant services there the augmentation of the *fleurs de lys* borne ever since by his descendants. He was father of

PHILIP PLOWDEN, of Plowden, whose son,

JOHN PLOWDEN, of Plowden, was father of another

JOHN PLOWDEN, of Plowden, who was *s.* by his son,

JOHN PLOWDEN, of Plowden, who *m.* Joan, daughter of John Salter, by Anne his wife, daughter of Sir Adam de Montgomery, knt. and was father of

JOHN PLOWDEN, of Plowden, who left by his wife Maud, one of the daughters of Sir John Barley, knt. a son and heir,

EDMUND PLOWDEN, of Plowden. This gentleman *m.* Jane, daughter of Edmund Cloebury, esq. and was *s.* by his son,

JOHN PLOWDEN, of Plowden, who wedded Margaret, daughter of John Blayney, esq. and had a son and successor,

HUMPHREY PLOWDEN, esq. of Plowden, who *m.* Elizabeth, daughter of John Sturry, esq. of Rossall, near Shrewsbury, and relict of William Wollascott, esq. and had issue,

- EDMUND, his heir.
- Edward, *m.* Mary, daughter of Thomas Lee, esq. of Langley, in Salop, and had a son, Humphrey.
- Mary, *m.* to Thomas Lee, esq. of Langley.
- Anchoret, *m.* to Rowland Eyton, esq. of Eyton, in Salop.
- Margaret, *m.* to Richard Sandford, esq. of the Isle, Salop. (See vol. ii. p. 671.)
- Jane, *m.* to Richard Blunden, esq. of Burghfield, Berks.

He *d.* 21st March, 1557, and was *s.* by his elder son,

EDMUND PLOWDEN, esq. of Plowden, sergeant-at-law, one of the most eminent lawyers of his day, whom WOOD, in the *Athenæ*, says, "was accounted the oracle of the law," and that "his commentaries or reports of divers law cases in the reigns of EDWARD VI., *Queen* MARY, and *Queen* ELIZABETH, were highly esteemed." To the early and active patronage however (added to his own abilities and learning) of Sir Francis Englefield, he was indebted chiefly for his advancement in life. Of that statesman's Shropshire estates he was entrusted with the administration, and there is a curious detail connected with a promise he had obtained, from Sir Francis's nephew and heir, of a lease of the Isle of Up Rossal, one of those whereon he had placed his brother-in-law, Richard Sandford, to his nephew, Humphrey Sandford, and which Englefield most ungratefully violated. This, considering the great services he had rendered the family, was no very extraordinary favour; for independently of adhering to Sir Francis when, on the demise of MARY, he sought voluntary exile on account of his religion, Plowden, who had acquired the wardship of the young Englefield, instead of disposing of his ward either by marrying him to one of his own daughters, or selling the trust, as he was fully empowered to do, and as others did every day under the feudal system, made a free gift of his authority to the ward himself. As the particulars of this transaction tend to illustrate the state of society and manners at the period, the following extracts from a manuscript written by Mr. Andrew Plowden, of Burghfield, Berks, nephew of Sergeant Plowden, may not prove uninteresting:—"Mr. John Englefield (brother to Sir Francis) died, [April 1, 1567] Francis Englefield, his son and heir, being a child of the age of about v or vi yeares, and fell in ward, by reason of a tenure in capite, to the Queene. Mr. Plowden then being at London, having intelligence thereof in a morninge very early, upon the newes, presently rose out of bed, and went to the court, he then being of counsell with William, the Earle of Pembroke, one of her Majesties privie counsell: which earle had often times before praide Mr. Plowden to espie out some suit to the Queene worth five hundred pounds, and promised he would obtain it, saiuge he was indepted to Mr. Plowden in soe much. He came to the earle, told him of the death of Mr. John Englefield, and of the wardship of his sonne; put him in mind of his promise; praid the earle to get the wardship for him, in lieu and recompence of his lordship's promise, and Mr. Plowden's service to his lordship. The earle being, although unlearned, an excellent wise man, and knowinge the good will Mr. Plowden bore to the house of Englefield, answered, 'True Mr. Plowden my promise is so, but I meant it for your owne good, and not for the good and comodity of any other. If I obtain this suit for you, you will not benefitt yourselfe thereby; but you will bestow it upon the widowe, or at Sir Francis's direction; and therefore I pray you, (said he) seeke out some other thinge: this will not be for your profitt, and I am therefore loath to deale therein.' 'Sir,' said Mr. Plowden, 'I beseech you leave that to my discression; I will accept it at your handes insted of any good turne, and as a gift to me by your honour of five hundred pounds. The earle seeinge Mr. Plowden thus earnest, beinge a bedd, rose, went to hir Majestie, and afterward to the Master of the Wardes, and fully obtained it for Mr. Plowden, and caused the same to be entred accordingly. Within halfe an hower after, and before Mr. Plowden departed the court, the Lord Hunsden came to have optained it; but it was in vaine, for it was gone before, as aforesaid."

Mr. Plowden's gift of the wardship to Mr. Englefield, and his request in behalf of his nephew, are thus related by Mr. Blunden: "Aboute the pointe of young Englefield's ayge of xxi yeres, Mrs. Englefield, Mr. Francis Fytten [her brother], and young Englefield, were att Shiplake. After dynner Mr. Plowden went into his newe parlor, called them unto him; called also Mr. Perkyns, who then before had married his eldest daughter, ould Mr. Wollascott, younge Edmund Plowden, my cozen Humffrey Sandford, and myselfe, and I know not whether any others. There beinge, torned his talke to yonge Mr. Englefield, and sayd thus in effecte: 'Mr. Englefield you are my warde, and now come to your full adge; what saye you and your friendes to me for it? I did gett your wardshippe of my selfe, without the helpe of any of your friendes. My old Lord Pembroke did it att my request' . . . and told in substance that which I have before rehearsed . . . and added furthere 'that he was not in any case soe beholding or bound to Sir Francis, or any of his friendes, that should move him to bestowe soe greate a benifitt uppon any of them; for,' sayd he, 'Mr. Englefield, your expectation is greate, and accordinge to that I may now have for your wardship and marriage, and my ould Lord Montague hath offered for you two thousand pounds: and as for Sir Francis Englefield, he is farre more bounde and beholdinge to me than I to him: and there is noe privye or secrett matter but I may make my best of you.'" The Englefields acknowledge his goodness, and Mr. Plowden gives the heir his marriage; "and take it (says he) for a gift of two thousand pounds, and in recompence of it I crave noe benifitt for myselfe or my owne children. But here I have in my house my *cozen*,* Humffrey Sandford, my sister's sonne, and his wife, and some of theire children. He hath served your uncle, Sir Francis, in the partes beyond the seas many yeres att my charge; for I gave him every yere xxtie markes standing to serve Sir Francis, besydes many other wantes I supplied to him; and his fathere alsoe gave him some what; all of which he spent in your uncle's service. . . . In consyderacon of this service done to your uncle, and for this my liberality towards you, I only praye you, when such things as be in his fatheres hands shall come to your disposition, that you will make a lease thereof to him, his wife, and sonne, for theire three lives, att the old rente; and this I do not accompte past two hundred pounds." The promise was of course made, but after Mr. Plowden's death forgotten, and Mr. Englefield not only refused to fulfil his engagement to the son, but even proceeded to dispossess the father. The whole of this curious affair is too long for transcription, but the fatal effect upon the elder Mr. Sandford is related with much feeling by Mr. Blunden: "When all would not serve, he presently fell sicke, called his wife and family to him, and thus complayned: 'Howe I bestowed my sonne's service to my intollerable charges soe many yeres uppon his uncle beyond the seas? Have I adventured my sonne and heyre upon him soe longe, alwayes in hazzard of the Queene's displeasure, and reddy alwayes to be attainted, my bloud and house to be corrupted for doing his uncle service? And is this the reward I have? Wife! carry me to Plowden. He hath killed me, he hath killed me! Lett me not dye on his grounde. I will not dye on his grounde.' And with all speede caused himselfe to be carried to Plowden, where, with these continuall wordes in his mouth, 'he hath killed me, he hath killed me!' he languished about a moneth, and then, of very sorrowe and conceyte, died." †

* It was formerly usual to call nephews and nieces by the name of cousin: and this is not yet quite worn out among old people in the country.

† The old gentleman's son, Humphrey Sand-

Mr. Sergeant Plowden *m.* Katherine, daughter of William Sheldon, esq. of Beeley, in the county of Oxford, and had issue,

EDMUND, his heir.

FRANCIS, successor to his brother.

Mary, *m.* to Richard White, esq. of Hutton, in Essex.

Anne, *m.* to Edmund Perkins, esq. of Upton, Berks.

Margaret, *m.* to John Walcot, esq.

This eminent person, again to quote Wood, "died in 1584, aged sixty-seven, and left behind him a fair estate in lands at Plowden, in the county of Salop; at Shiplake, in Oxfordshire; and at Burfield, in Berks; as also a son of both his names to enjoy;" which son,

EDMUND PLOWDEN, esq. of Plowden, dying two years after his father, (1586), was interred "in the chapel built and erected by his ancestors, wherein some of them were buried, adjoining to the chapel of North Lidbury, in the county of Salop, near to which place the village and estate of Plowden is situate." Never having married, he was *s.* by his brother,

FRANCIS PLOWDEN, esq. of Plowden, who *m.* Mary, daughter of Thomas Fermor, esq. of Somerton, in Oxfordshire, and had issue,

I. FRANCIS, his heir.

II. Edmund, of Wansted, in Hampshire, styled in his will, 29th July, 1655, "Sir Edmund Plowden, lord earl palatine, governor, and captain general of the province of New Albion, in America." He *m.* Mabel, daughter of Peter Mariner, and grand-child and heir of John Chatterton, esq. of Chatterton, in Lancashire, and hence the Plowdens of Lassam, Hants.

III. Thomas.

I. Mary.

II. Catherine.

III. Anne.

Mr. Plowden *d.* 11th December, 1652, aged ninety, was buried at Shiplake, in Oxfordshire, and *s.* by his eldest son,

FRANCIS PLOWDEN, esq. of Plowden, who wedded Elizabeth, daughter and heiress of Alban Butler, esq.* of Aston le Walls, in Northamptonshire, and had

EDMUND, his successor,

Mary, *m.* to Edward Massey, esq. of Puddington.

---

ford, the nephew of Mr. Sergeant Plowden, eventually became the purchaser of the Isle Estate (from which his father was thus driven); the purchase was made by Mr. Sandford from the vendee of the Queen, after it became forfeited to the Crown by the voluntary exile of Sir Francis Englefield, and this estate is now in the possession of Mr. Sandford's lineal descendant. (See vol. ii. page 671.)

* The manor of Aston le Walls was acquired by JOHN BUTLER, esq. second son of Ralph Butler, of Sawbridgeworth, in marriage with Margaret, daughter and heiress of Sir John De Sutton, alias Dudley, younger brother of the Lord Sutton. He died in 1563, leaving a son and successor,

ALBAN BUTLER, esq. of Aston le Walls, who married twice, but had male issue by his first wife, Sibil, daughter of Simon Raleigh, esq. of Farnborough, only, viz.

I. GEORGE, his heir.

II. Simon, bapt. 6th May, 1549, who *m.* Barbara, daughter of Lawrence Washington, esq. of Sulgrave, and settled at Appletree, in Northamptonshire. He died in 1628, and was great grandfather of

THE REV. JOHN BUTLER, B. D. of Appletree, *b.* in 1626, who *m.* Martha, daughter of the Rev. Isaac Perkins, of Catesby, and dying in 1698, was succeeded by his son,

SIMON BUTLER, esq. of Appletree, *b.* in 1662, who *m.* Anne, daughter of Henry Birch, esq. of Goscot, in Staffordshire, and left issue,

Charles, who died in 1768, aged sixty-one.

ALBAN, in holy orders, author of "The Lives of the Saints," &c. *b.* in 1710; *d.* at St. Omers, 15th May, 1773, aged sixty-three.

James, of Pall Mall, Westminster, *b.* at Appletree 8th September, 1711; *m.* 6th January, 1741, Mary, daughter of John Grano, of Ambleteuse, in Picardy, and dying in 1792, left a son,

CHARLES BUTLER, an eminent lawyer and king's counsel, author of "Horæ Biblicæ," and editor of "Coke on Littleton," &c. who *m.* in 1776, Mary, daughter of Thomas-John Eyston, esq. of East Hendred, Berks, (see vol. i. p. 38), and died in 1832, leaving two daughters, his co-heirs, viz.

MARY, *m.* to Lieut. Col. Stonor.

THERESA, *m.* to Andrew H. Lynch, esq. M. P. for Galway.

III. Thomas, *b.* 1555.

The eldest son,

GEORGE BUTLER, esq. of Aston le Walls, bapt. 12th October, 1540; *m.* 1563, Elizabeth, daughter of Edmund Odingsell, esq. and had a son and successor,

ALBAN BUTLER, esq. of Aston le Walls, who *m.* Anne, daughter of Ferdinand Pulton, esq. of Bourton, Bucks, and by her, who died in 1631, left at his decease, in 1617, an only surviving child and heiress, ELIZABETH, *m.* as in the text, to FRANCIS PLOWDEN, esq. of Plowden.

Elizabeth, died unm.

Katherine, *m.* to Sir Daniel Rothwell, bart.

He *d.* 18th January, 1661, and was *s.* by his son,

EDMUND PLOWDEN, esq. of Plowden, and Aston le Walls, *b.* 6th February, 1716; *m.* Elizabeth, daughter of Richard Cotton, esq. of Bedhampton, in Sussex, and had (with four other sons, who all *d. s. p.*)

EDMUND, his heir.

Francis, comptroller of the household to *King* JAMES II. *m.* Mary, daughter of the Hon. John-Stafford Howard, and grand-daughter of Sir William Howard, Viscount Stafford, so unjustly brought to the block and attainted in 1678.* Mr. Francis Plowden died at St. Germains, in France, leaving (with a son, FRANCIS, a celebrated Catholic divine, and controversial writer) an only daughter and eventual heiress,

MARY PLOWDEN, who wedded Sir George Jerningham, bart. of Cossy Hall, in Norfolk, and was mother of

SIR WILLIAM JERNINGHAM, whose son and heir,

SIR GEORGE JERNINGHAM, the attainder of Viscount Stafford being reversed in 1824, was restored to the BARONY of STAFFORD, and is the present lord.

Elizabeth, *m.* to Walter Blount, esq. of Maple Durham.

Mr. Plowden *d.* 20th May, 1666, and was *s.* by his elder son,

EDMUND PLOWDEN, esq. of Plowden and Aston, who *m.* Penelope, daughter and coheir of Sir Maurice Drummond, bart. and had (with several other sons, who all died issueless) WILLIAM, his heir, and Dorothy, married, first, to Philip Draycot, esq. and, secondly, to Sir William Goring. He died 27th November, 1677, and was *s.* by his son,

WILLIAM PLOWDEN, esq. of Plowden and Aston, *b.* in 1666. This gentleman, who held the rank of colonel in the life-guards of *King* JAMES II., adhered to the fortunes of that prince both in Ireland and France; but after a short residence at the court of St. Germains, obtained, through the interest of his wife's uncle the Duke of Shrewsbury, and the Countess of Sunderland, permission to return to England, and to take possession of the family estates, his three elder brothers having died issueless. From his presumed attachment to the countess originated the song of Plowden, of Plowden Hall, by the comic poet Wycherley. He rebuilt the manor house at Aston, and lived there a few years, but being a Catholic, he became obnoxious to the violent Whigs of the neighbourhood; and not having taken the oath of allegiance to *King* WILLIAM, his six coach horses, by virtue of an act recently passed against non-jurors, were seized on entering Banbury and impounded by a magistrate, being worth above five pounds each. He immediately quitted Aston in disgust, and it has since been deserted by the family. Colonel Plowden married thrice: of the first marriage, with Mary, daughter of — Morley, esq. there was no issue; of the second, with Mary, daughter of John Stonor, esq. of Stonor, there was one son and two daughters, viz.

WILLIAM, his heir.

Penelope, *m.* first, to Thomas Foley, esq. of Stourbridge; and, secondly, to Richard Whitworth, esq.

Frances, *m.* in 1723, to Robert Aglionby Slaney, esq. of Halton Grange, in the county of Salop.

Mr. Plowden's third wife was Maria, dau. of Sir C. Lyttleton, and by her he had three sons who died *s. p.* and two daughters,

Mary, *m.* to Anthony Wright, esq. of Wealside, in Essex.

Barbara-Anne, *m.* to Thomas Cameron, M.D. of Cameron.

He *d.* 5th March, 1740-1, and was *s.* by his son,

WILLIAM PLOWDEN, esq. of Plowden and Aston, *b.* 27th August, 1754; *m.* in 1726, Frances, daughter of Sir Charles Dormer, and had issue,

EDMUND, his successor.

Frances, *m.* to Robert Taaffe, esq. of Ireland.

---

* SIR WILLIAM HOWARD, was the younger son of Thomas, Earl of Arundel, who was created Earl of Norfolk and Earl Marshal. He married the Honourable Mary Stafford, sister and heiress of Henry Stafford, Baron Stafford, and great-great-great-grand-daughter of EDWARD DE STAFFORD, DUKE OF BUCKINGHAM, beheaded and attainted in 1521, through the machination of Wolsey: (the fate of his grace drew from the Emperor Charles V. the exclamation, "A butcher's dog has killed the finest buck in England!") Subsequently to his marriage, Sir William Howard and his wife were both raised to the peerage, 12th September, 1640, as BARON and BARONESS STAFFORD, with remainder to their heirs male, and general. His lordship was created VISCOUNT STAFFORD, 11th November, 1640. He fell a victim eventually to the perjury of the infamous Titus Oats, and was attainted and beheaded in 1678. For a detail of the great house of Stafford, refer to BURKE'S *Extinct and Dormant Peerage.*

Anne-Mary, *m.* to Edward Haggerston, esq.

Mary, *m.* to Robert Garvey, esq. of Rouen.

Mr. Plowden *d.* 27th August, 1754, and was *s.* by his son,

EDMUND PLOWDEN, esq. of Plowden and Aston, who wedded, 20th July, 1755, Elizabeth, daughter and co-heir of Sir Berkeley Lucy, bart. of Netley Abbey, Hants, and had two sons and four daughters, viz.

EDMUND, his successor.

William, *m.* 13th November, 1797, Mary, daughter of Simon Winter, esq. and died in November, 1824. He had issue,

William-Henry-Francis, *b.* in 1802.

Charles-Joseph, *b.* in 1805.

Anna-Maria.

Elizabeth-Lucy, *m.* in 1777, to Sir Henry Tichborne, bart. and dying 24th January, 1829, left, with three younger sons and a daughter, the present

SIR HENRY TICHBORNE.

Lucy-Mary, *m.* to Anthony Wright, esq. of Wealside, in Essex.

Frances-Xaveria, *m.* to Francis Constable, esq. of Burton Constable, and *d. s. p.*

Mary-Margaretta, *m.* in 1787, to Charles Throckmorton, esq. and *d. s. p.*

Mr. Plowden *d.* in 1766, and was *s.* by his elder son, the present EDMUND PLOWDEN, esq. of Plowden.

*Arms*—Az. a fess dancette, the two upper points terminating in fleur-de-lys or.

*Crest*—On a mount vert, a buck passant sa. attired or.

*Estates*—In Northamptonshire, Shropshire, &c.

*Seat*—Plowden Hall, Salop.

*** A descendant of the Plowden family has of late years highly distinguished himself in the literary world, FRANCIS PLOWDEN, the eminent Chancery barrister, and author of a History of Ireland, who died in 1829, having had one son, Captain Plowden, shot in a duel, and two daughters, Anna-Maria, the late Countess of Dundonald, and Mary, *m.* to John Murrough, esq. of Cork.

## JENKINS, OF BICTON HALL.

JENKINS, RICHARD, esq. of Bicton Hall, and Abbey House, both in the county of Salop, *b.* at Cruckton, 18th February, 1785; *m.* 31st March, 1824, Elizabeth-Helen, daughter of Hugh Spottiswoode, esq. of the East India Company's Civil Service, and has issue,

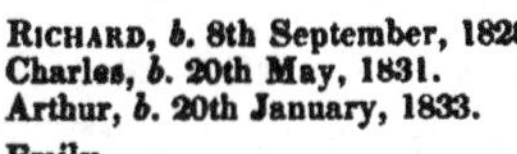

RICHARD, *b.* 8th September, 1828.
Charles, *b.* 20th May, 1831.
Arthur, *b.* 20th January, 1833.

Emily.
Cecilia-Harriot-Theophila.

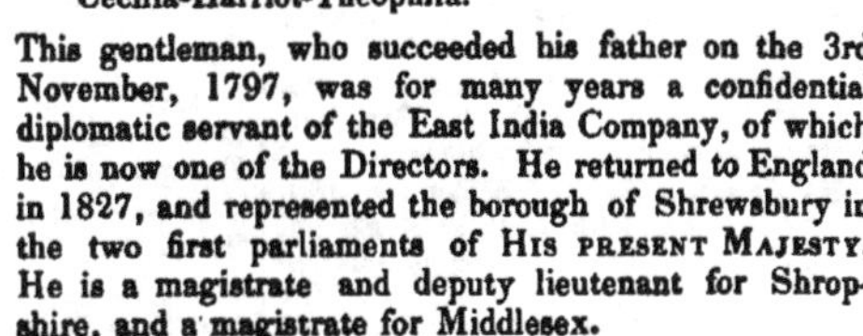

This gentleman, who succeeded his father on the 3rd November, 1797, was for many years a confidential diplomatic servant of the East India Company, of which he is now one of the Directors. He returned to England in 1827, and represented the borough of Shrewsbury in the two first parliaments of HIS PRESENT MAJESTY. He is a magistrate and deputy lieutenant for Shropshire, and a magistrate for Middlesex.

### Lineage.

RICHARD JENKINS, *b.* in 1621, of Blandford, in the county of Dorset, sprung from a family anciently settled in Yorkshire, attaching himself to the celebrated royalist, Lord Colepeper, was with that nobleman at St. Germains in 1649, and subsequently accompanied him when ambassador extraordinary to the Emperor of Russia and the United Provinces. "All the time," as stated in a document in possession of his representatives, "employed in business of trust and importance, in all which he demeaned himself faithfully, diligently, and discreetly." In 1651, he returned to England, and settled at Charlton Hill, near Worcester, holding several employments under Lord Newport, lord lieutenant of the county. He *m.* in 1668, Mary, daughter and co-heir of Richard Bagot, esq. of Hargrave, in Shropshire, and with her acquired *that* and other estates in the parish of Alberbury. He *d.* in 1697, and was *s.* by his son,

THOMAS JENKINS, esq. of the Abbey Foregate, Shrewsbury, who wedded 7th February, 1708, Gertrude, daughter of Captain Richard Wingfield, second son of Samuel Wingfield, esq. of Preston Brockhurst, Salop, and had issue,

RICHARD, his heir.
Thomas, *m.* Rachael, daughter of Sir Edward Leighton, bart. and had
Edward, of Charlton Hill.
Emma, *m.* to John Jenkins, esq. of Bicton.

Mr. Jenkins, who was high sheriff for Salop in 1729, died 29th December, 1730, and he is described in the London Evening Post, January 14, 1731, "to have been a gentleman of great reading and good judgment, affectionate in the relations of husband and brother, whose life and conversation were so peaceable and inoffensive that he gained many friends and had not a known enemy in the world." His son and successor,

RICHARD JENKINS, esq. *b.* 28th August, 1709, married first, Letitia, daughter and heiress of John Muckleston, esq. of Bicton, and by her, who *d.* 16th July, 1740, had two sons, Richard, who died unmarried, and JOHN, his heir. He wedded, secondly, Emma, daughter of Sir Francis Charlton, of Ludford, and relict of John Lloyd, esq. of Aston Hall, Salop, by whom he had a daughter, Mary-Gertrude, *m.* to the Venerable Edward Browne, Archdeacon of Ross, son of the Archbishop of Tuam. Mr. Jenkins was *s.* at his decease by his son,

JOHN JENKINS, esq. of Bicton, *b.* 16th July, 1740, who *m.* 16th April, 1759, Emma, daughter of Thomas Jenkins, esq. of Shrewsbury, by Rachel his wife, daughter of Sir Edward Leighton, bart. of Loton Park, and had by her, who died in 1764, four sons, viz.

I. RICHARD, his heir.
II. William, died unmarried.
III. Edward, who *m.* Elizabeth, eldest daughter of George Ravenscroft, esq. of Wrexham, and had issue.
IV. Thomas, who *m.* Mary Hale, of Macclesfield, and left no issue.

Mr. Jenkins *d.* 28th June, 1771, and was *s.* by his son,

RICHARD JENKINS, esq. of Bicton, born there 6th March, 1760, who *m.* in October, 1781, Harriet-Constantia, dau. of George Ravenscroft, esq. of Wrexham, in Denbighshire, and by her, who died at Bicton 19th April, 1832, had issue,

I. RICHARD, his heir.
II. Charles-Edward-Orlando, *b.* 19th January, 1789, who died unmarried, 16th July, 1823, in India, a captain of artillery in the Company's service.
I. Harriett-Constantia, *m.* to Edward Gatacre, esq. of Gatacre Hall.
II. Elizabeth, *m.* to Robert Jenkins, esq. of Charlton Hill, Salop.
III. Frances-Mary-Gertrude.
IV. Letitia-Emma-Sally, *m.* to the Rev. Charles Wingfield, of the Gro, in the county of Montgomery.

Mr. Jenkins died at Bicton, 3rd November, 1797, and was *s.* by his son, RICHARD JENKINS, esq. now of Bicton.

*Arms*—Or, a lion rampant reguardant sa. Quartering Bagot and Muckleston.

*Crest*—On a mural crown sa. a lion passant reguardant or.

*Motto*—Perge sed caute.

*Estates*—In Shropshire, Bicton and Rosshall, near Shrewsbury, with Penylaw, near Oswestry, which came by Letitia Muckleston. Hargrave, with other estates in the parish of Alberbury, by Mary Bagot, besides property acquired by purchase in the same neighbourhood, and in the Abbey Foregate, Shrewsbury.

*Town Residence*—19, Upper Harley Street.

*Seats*—Bicton Hall, and Abbey House, both near Shrewsbury.

# SMITH, OF TOGSTON.

SMITH, THOMAS-GEORGE, esq. of Togston, in Northumberland, succeeded his father in March 1812.

## Lineage.

This family of Smith, long resident in Northumberland, purchased the property at Amble in the reign of CHARLES I. and it is still in their possession. The lands were originally held by the family under the monastery of Tynemouth before the suppression of religious houses. About the year 1660,

WILLIAM SMITH, esq. son of Thomas Smith, esq. of Amble, *m.* a daughter of John Patterson, esq. of Togston, by whom he acquired that estate, and had a son and successor,

THOMAS SMITH, esq. of Togston, who wedded Elizabeth, daughter of John Davison, esq. and dying the year after his marriage, was succeeded by his only child,

THOMAS SMITH, esq. of Togston, who *m.* Frances, daughter of John Cook, esq. and had two sons and eight daughters, viz.

I. WILLIAM, his heir.
II. Thomas, an alderman of Newcastle-upon-Tyne, *m.* Miss Pearson.

I. Mary, *m.* to Mr. Walker, a merchant in Newcastle.
II. Elizabeth, died unmarried.
III. Jane, *m.* to William, second son of William Lawson, esq. of Longhirst.
IV. Frances, *m.* to Edward, second son of G. Wilson, esq. of Hepscot Hall.
V. Dorothy, *m.* to Thomas Bell, esq. of Shortridge.
VI. Margaret, *m.* to Ralph Fenwick, esq. of Shortridge.
VII. Anne, *m.* to Richard, second son of William Brown, esq. of Willington.
VIII. Sarah, died unmarried.

Mr. Smith *d.* in 1772, and was *s.* by his elder son,

WILLIAM SMITH, esq. of Togston, a deputy lieutenant and deputy vice-admiral for Northumberland. This gentleman *m.* in 1778, Elizabeth, daughter of George Ditchburn, esq. of Preston, and had issue,

I. THOMAS-GEORGE, his heir.

I. Elizabeth, *m.* in 1816, to Dixon Dixon, esq. of Benton.
II. Frances.
III. Anne.
IV. Isabella.

Mr. Smith *d.* 22nd March, 1812, and was *s.* by his son, the present THOMAS-GEORGE SMITH, esq. of Togston.

*Arms*—Az. a castle arg. on a chief or three storks' heads erased gu.

*Crest*—A stork arg. in his beak a serpent ppr.

*Estates*—Togston and Amble, in Northumberland: and Togston Barns, recently (in 1812) purchased.

*Seat*—Togston.

# LOWNDES-STONE, OF BRIGHTWELL PARK.

**LOWNDES-STONE, WILLIAM-FRANCIS,** esq. of Brightwell Park, in the county of Oxford, *m.* 3rd October, 1811, Caroline, second daughter of Sir William Strickland, bart. of Boynton, in Yorkshire, and has issue,

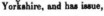

WILLIAM-CHARLES, *b.* 7th August, 1812.
Caroline-Isabella, *m.* 24th July, 1832, to James More Molyneux, esq. of Loseley Park, in Surrey, and has issue.
Isabella-Anne.
Emma.

Mr. Lowndes succeeded his father, the late William Lowndes-Stone, esq. in May, 1830, and assumed the additional surname of "Stone." He was sheriff of Oxfordshire in 1834, and had the honorary degree of D.C.L. conferred upon him by the university at the installation of the Duke of Wellington. He is a magistrate and deputy lieutenant.

## Lineage.

The existing house of LOWNDES-STONE inheriting the principal part of its possessions from the families of Carleton, Stone, and Lowe, it will be necessary, after deducing the paternal descent, to detail each of those lines.

### Family of Lowndes.

ROBERT LOWNDES, of Cheshire, a scion of the Lowndeses of Leigh Hall, in that county, married, in 1576, Jane Cocke, and had (with an elder son, Robert, who wedded Alice Spooner, and died in his father's lifetime issueless,) his successor,

WILLIAM LOWNDES, esq. *b.* in 1585, *m.* Frances Wendover, and was *s.* by his son,

ROBERT LOWNDES, esq. who wedded Elizabeth, daughter of Peter Fitzjames, and left a son and heir,

WILLIAM LOWNDES, esq. who was secretary to the Treasury in 1652. He *m.* first, in 1679, Elizabeth, daughter of Sir Roger Harsnett, knt. and by her (who died in 1680) had a son,

ROBERT, ancestor of the present WILLIAM SELBY LOWNDES, esq. of Winslow and Whaddon, formerly M.P. for Bucks.

He wedded, secondly, in 1683, Jane Hopper, by whom (who died in 1685) he had a daughter, Anne, *b.* in 1684, who married; and thirdly, Elizabeth, daughter of Richard Martyn, D.D. by whom (who died in 1689) he had one son and one daughter, namely,

WILLIAM, of whom presently.
Elizabeth, *b.* in 1688, *m.* to Thomas Duncombe, esq. and died in 1712.

Mr. Lowndes espoused, fourthly, in 1691, Rebecca, daughter of John Shales, esq. and had, with six other sons and seven daughters,

CHARLES, of Chesham, in the county of Bucks, ancestor of the family of Lowndes seated there.

*Queen* ANNE, in consideration of his eminent services, conferred upon Mr. Lowndes, who was many years a member of the House of Commons, and chairman of Ways and Means, and to whom the nation is indebted for originating the funding system, the office of auditor of the land revenue, *for life*, in reversion to his sons, with an augmentation to his coat of arms. His second son,

WILLIAM LOWNDES, esq. of Astwood Bury, in the county of Buckingham, married, in 1711, Margaret, daughter and heir of — Layton, esq. and had issue,

1. WILLIAM, *b.* in 1712, *m.* in 1744, Catharine, eldest daughter of Francis Lowe, esq. of BALDWYN BRIGHTWELL, in the county of Oxford, and assumed, in pursuance of the testamentary injunction of Mr. Lowe, the surname of STONE and had issue,

WILLIAM, successor to his grandfather.

Catharine, *b.* in 1747.

Mr. William Lowndes-Stone died, before his father, in 1773, and was buried at Brightwell. His widow survived until 1789, and was interred near her husband, where a monument is erected to their memory.

II. Layton, died unm. in 1747.
III. John, died unm. in 1756.
IV. Robert, } both died unm.
V. Charles, }
VI. Richard, a lieutenant in the royal navy, who married, in 1751, Bridget, daughter of William Dalston, esq. of Great Salkeld, in Cumberland, and had, with two daughters, who died in infancy, two sons,

1. William, *b.* in May, 1752, who was bred to the bar, and was for more than twenty years one of the commissioners of the Board of Taxes. He died unmarried in 1828.
2. Richard, of Rose Hill, Dorking, Surrey, *b.* 4th October, 1756, who *m.* 12th April, 1787, Rebecca, younger daughter of Henry Brougham, esq. of Brougham Hall, Westmoreland, and aunt to the present Lord Brougham, and has issue,

Henry-Dalston, *b.* in 1789, *m.* Sarah, daughter of William Lowe, esq. and has issue.

William-Loftus, *b.* in April, 1793, *m.* 28th February, 1818, Eliza, daughter of Samuel Crompton Cox, esq. one of the masters of the Court of Chancery, and has issue.

Rebecca, *m.* to James Randall, esq. barrister-at-law.

VII. Henry, *b.* in 1723, *m.* in 1751, Mary-Magdalen, only daughter of Edward Arnold, esq. but *d. s. p.*
VIII. Thomas, in holy orders, rector of North Crawley, Bucks, died unmarried.
IX. Edward, died in infancy.

I. Margaret, died unmarried in 1747.

Mr. Lowndes died in 1775, and was buried at Astwood Church, where a monument is erected to his memory. He was *s.* by his grandson,

WILLIAM LOWNDES, esq. of Astwood and North Crawley, Bucks, and of Baldwyn Brightwell, in the county of Oxford, *b.* in 1750, who assumed, upon the demise of his mother in 1789, the surname and arms of STONE. He wedded, in 1775, his cousin Elizabeth, second daughter and co-heir of Richard Garth, esq. of Morden, in Surrey, and had issue,

I. WILLIAM-FRANCIS, his heir.
II. Richard, in holy orders, *b.* in 1790, *m.* Mary, daughter of — Douglas, esq. of Worcester, and has issue.
III. Henry-Owen, *b.* in 1795, settled in America.

I. Elizabeth, *m.* in 1799, to John Fane, esq. of Wormsley, Oxon, and has several children.
II. Catharine, *m.* in 1812, to the Rev. J. Holland, of Aston, in Oxfordshire, and has a daughter, Catharine Holland.
III. Clara, died, under age, unm.
IV. Anne, *m.* in 1822, to William H. Sharpe, esq. of London, and has issue.
V. Mary, *m.* in 1812, to Edward Jodrell, esq. second son of Richard Paul Jodrell, esq. of Nethercot, Oxfordshire, and has two sons and one daughter.

Mr. Lowndes-Stone, who built the present mansion at Brightwell, the ancient residence of the Carleton and Stone families having been destroyed by fire in 1787, died in 1830, was buried at Brightwell, where a monument is erected to him, and succeeded by his son, the present WILLIAM-FRANCIS LOWNDES-STONE, esq. of Brightwell Park.

### Family of Carleton.

The Carletons came originally from Lincolnshire, and were settled there about the time of EDWARD I.

JOHN CARLETON, eldest son of John Carleton, esq. of Walton-upon-Thames, appears to have inherited the estates of Brightwell and Holcombe, in Oxfordshire, from John Cottesmore about the year 1500. He *m.* Joyce, daughter of John Welbroke, esq. of Oxenheath, in Kent, by Margaret, his wife, daughter and co-heir of Richard Culpeper, and had issue,

I. ANTHONY, his heir.
II. George, who *m.* Elizabeth, daughter of Walter Mohun, esq. of Woolaston, in the county of Northampton, and relict of Edward Cope, esq. of Hanwell, Oxon.
III. John, died unm.

I. Anne, *m.* Rowland Lytton, esq. of Knebworth, governor of Boulogne (see vol. i. p. 447).

John Carleton died in 1547, was buried in Brightwell Chancel, where a monument remains to his memory, and *s.* by his son,

ANTHONY CARLETON, esq. of Brightwell, who *m.* first, Anne, daughter and co-heir of

Thomas Pecent, esq. of Diggonswell, Herts, and had by her, who died in 1562, John, who died unmarried, and Joyce, the wife of Thomas Denton, esq. of Ambrosden, in Oxfordshire. He wedded, secondly, Joyce, sixth daughter of Sir John Goodwin, of Winchendon, in Buckinghamshire, and had

I. GEORGE, his heir.

II. Dudley, who received the honor of knighthood from *King* JAMES at Windsor in 1610, and afterwards being vice-chamberlain to CHARLES I. was employed as ambassador, first to Venice, and subsequently to Savoy. He was created in 1628 Baron Carleton and Viscount Dorchester. He wedded, first, Anne, daughter and co-heir of George, second son of Sir William Garrard, of Dorney, Bucks (refer to vol. i. page 591), and by her, who died in 1627, and was buried in Westminster Abbey, had one son, Henry, who died in infancy. He *m.* secondly, Anne, daughter of Sir William Glemham, of Glemham, Suffolk, and relict of Paul, Viscount Bayning, by whom he had a posthumous daughter, who died young. Lord Dorchester died himself in 1632, and was interred in St. Paul's Chapel, Westminster Abbey, where a monument was raised to his memory. *See* BURKE'S *Extinct Peerage.*

I. Elizabeth, *m.* to Alexander Williams.

II. Bridget, *m.* to Sir Hercules Underhill.

III. Anne, *m.* to John Dove, D.D.

IV. Alice, died unm. in 1640.

Anthony Carleton died in 1575, was buried at Brightwell, and succeeded by his eldest son,

GEORGE CARLETON, esq. who *m.* first, Elizabeth, daughter and co-heir of Sir John Brockett, of Brockett Hall, Herts, and had by her, who died in 1595, a son, JOHN, his heir. He *m.* secondly, Catharine, daughter of — Harrison, esquire of the stable to *Queen* ELIZABETH, and had further issue,

George.

Dudley, appointed in 1630 his majesty's resident in Holland, and in 1637 clerk of the council, who by his first wife had one daughter, and by his second, Lucy, daughter of Sir Herbert Croft, four daughters, namely,

Dorothy, *m.* to William Vamburg, of London, merchant.

Lucy, living in 1634.

Mary, *m.* to Edward Pearce, gent. of Parson's Green.

Elisabeth, *m.* to Giles Vamburg, esq.

Joyce.

Elizabeth, *m.* to John Harrison, esq. of Brickhill, Bucks.

Bridget, *m.* to John Chambers, M.D.

George Carleton died in 1627, and was succeeded by his son,

JOHN CARLETON, esq. who succeeded also to the estates of his uncle, Lord Dorchester, and was created a baronet in 1627. He *m.* in that year, Anne, eldest daughter of Sir R. Houghton, knt. of Houghton Tower, in Lancashire, and relict of Sir John Cotton, of Langwade, in Cambridgeshire, by whom he had one son and two daughters, viz.

GEORGE (Sir), second baronet, who died unmarried.

ANNE, *m.* to George Garth, esq. of Morden, in Surrey.

CATHARINE, *m.* to JOHN STONE, esq.

Sir John Carleton died in 1637, and was buried at Brightwell. His estates eventually passed to his two daughters and coheirs.

### Family of Stone.

JOHN STONE, esq. of London, sergeant-at-law, second son of William Stone, of Segenhoe, descended from an ancient Bedfordshire family, married a daughter of — Cornwall, and had issue,

I. RICHARD, his heir.

II. William, died unm.

I. Catharine, *m.* to Sir R. Chester.

Mr. Sergeant Stone died in 1640, was buried in London, and succeeded by his son,

SIR RICHARD STONE, knighted by *King* CHARLES in 1651, who *m.* first, Elizabeth, daughter of Thomas Bennett, a merchant in London, and had issue,

I. JOHN, his heir.

II. Edward, died unm. and was buried at Brightwell.

I. Anne, *m.* first, to Anthony Goldsborough, esq. by whom she had two daughters; and secondly, to William Colvill, esq. of Newton, Isle of Ely, by whom she had three other daughters.

II. DOROTHY, *m.* to FRANCIS LOWE, esq. of Gray's Inn, London, and had a son,

JOHN LOWE, who was father, by Frances, his wife, daughter of Sir Henry Stapylton, bart. of Myton, of

FRANCIS LOWE, who succeeded his cousin, John Stone, esq. of Brightwell.

III. Cicely, *m.* to Christopher Lowe, esq.

IV. Jane, died unm.

Sir Richard wedded, secondly, Elizabeth, daughter of Richard Gery, esq. of Bushmead, in Bedfordshire, and had another son and daughter,

III. Thomas, of Rushden, Herts, who *m*. Penelope, second daughter of Sir Stephen Soames, of Thurlow, Suffolk, and had three daughters, Penelope, Catharine, and Beata.

v. Catharine, *m*. to Sir John Lawrence, knt. of London.

Sir Richard Stone died in 1661, was buried in London, and succeeded by his eldest son,

JOHN STONE, esq. who married, first, Catharine, second daughter and eventual co-heir of Sir John Carleton, bart. of Brightwell and Holcombe, in Oxfordshire, and had by her, who died in 1668, and was buried at Brightwell, six sons and one daughter, viz.

I. CARLETON, his heir.
II. Edward, died young.
III. JOHN, successor to his brother.
IV. Dudley, died unm.
V. Henry, died in infancy.
VI. Richard, died unm.

I. Catharine, *m*. to — Dorrill, and *d. s. p.* a widow, and was buried at Brightwell in 1713.

Mr. Stone *m*. secondly, in 1681, Frances, relict of William Glanville, esq. of Broad Hinton, Wilts, but by her, who survived him, had no issue. He died in 1704, was buried at Brightwell, and succeeded by his son,

CARLETON STONE, esq. of Brightwell, who married Winifred, daughter and co-heir of William Glanville, esq. of Broadhinton, but dying *s. p.* in 1708, the estates passed to his brother,

JOHN STONE, esq. of Brightwell, who espoused Mary,* second daughter and co-heir of Henry Pascall, esq. of Great Baddow Hall, Essex, by Catharine, his wife, daughter of Sir Henry Appleton, bart. but dying without issue in 1732, the last of his family and name, he bequeathed his estates to Mary Stone, his widow, for life, with remainder to his cousin and heir,

FRANCIS LOWE, esq. who accordingly inherited Brightwell at the decease of Mrs. Stone in 1639. The family of Lowe, originally De Loup, came into England at the Conquest, and settled in Bedfordshire in the reign of HENRY VII. Francis Lowe *m*. Elizabeth or Frances, daughter of John Corrance, esq. of Parham, and sister of Clemence Corrance, esq. M.P. for Oxford, by whom he had issue,

John, who died unmarried, and was buried in the chancel at Brightwell, where a monument is erected to him.

CATHARINE, who *m*. in 1747, WILLIAM LOWNDES, esq. as already stated, and was grandmother of the present WILLIAM-FRANCIS LOWNDES-STONE, esq. of Brightwell.

Anne, *m*. to Thomas Polter, esq. and had two daughters, who died unmarried.

Mr. Lowe dying in June, 1754, devised his estates, which he inherited from John Stone, to his daughter Catharine, with remainder to the issue male, with divers other remainders, directing that all the plate marked with the arms of his cousin, John Stone, esq. should remain as heir-looms in the mansion-house at Brightwell, and further directing that the person or persons entitled to the said estates, and the husband and husbands of such persons, so soon as they or she shall come into actual possession thereof, shall immediately take upon him, her, or them, the surname of STONE, and procure an act of parliament to continue the premises in the name and family of Stone, and sign his, her, or their name Stone, and bear the arms which were borne by his cousin, John Stone. Whereupon an act of parliament was obtained the 28th GEORGE II. and William Lowndes, esq. and Catherine, his wife, immediately took the name of STONE, as their successors have done since.

*Arms*—Quarterly; 1st and 4th, arg. three cinquefoils sa. a chief of the second, for STONE; 2nd and 3rd, fretty arg. and sa. on a canton gu. a leopard's head erased or, wreathed vert, for LOWNDES.

*Crests*—1st. Out of a ducal coronet or, a griffin's head erm. for STONE. 2nd. A leopard's head erased or, with a chaplet vert.

*Motto*—Mediocria firma.

*Estates*—In the counties of Buckingham and Oxford.

*Seat*—Brightwell Park.

* Her sister, the other co-heir, was Catherine Verney, Viscountess Fermanagh. Mary Pascall is erroneously stated in vol. i. p. 341, to have married Admiral Wilson. She is interred at Brightwell.

# CANNING, OF FOXCOTE.

CANNING, ROBERT, esq. of Foxcote, in the county of Warwick, *b.* in 1773, *m.* first, Catherine, daughter of John Berkeley, esq. of Spetchley, by his second wife, Jane, daughter and co-heir of Sir William Compton, bart. (see vol. i. p. 471), which lady died without issue in February, 1823. He married, secondly, Maria, second daughter and co-heir of the Rev. Joseph Bonnor Cherton, of Longford House, Gloucestershire, and has had issue,

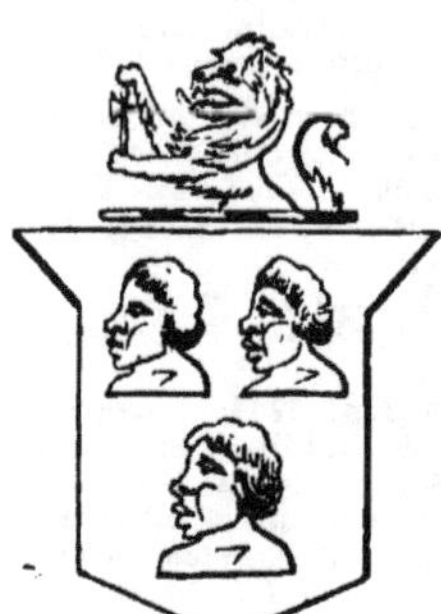

Francis-Robert, *b.* 10th August, 1829, *d.* December following.

Robert-Francis, *b.* 23rd January, 1831, *d.* January following.

Maria.

Mr. Canning succeeded to Foxcote upon the demise of his brother in 1831. He is a magistrate and deputy lieutenant for the county of Gloucester, and served the office of high sheriff for that shire in 1832.

## Lineage.

The lands of FOXCOTE have been in the family of CANNING now more than four centuries: they came with an heir-female in the time of HENRY VI. and have descended since uninterruptedly through heirs-male.*

John Le Marshall, of Foxcote, was father of Jeffrey Le Marshall, who married Mary, daughter and heir of John Bridport, of Bridport, in the county of Dorset, and had Gilbert Le Marshall, whose only daughter and heir, Eustatia Le Marshall, wedded John Salmon, son and heir of Thomas Salmon, of Chedle, and left two daughters, co-heirs, viz. AGNES SALMON, who became the wife of THOMAS CANNINGE, esq. and MATILDA SALMON, married to Edmund Dalby, esq.

In the partition of the property of Salmon, Foxcote became the sole inheritance of Agnes. Thomas Canninge, her husband, was the son of John, the son of another John Canninge, brother to Jeffrey Canynge, the father of Sir Thomas Caninge, lord mayor of London in 1456, and of William Canynge, whom HENRY VI. in a letter to the magistrate of Dantzic, calls "his beloved and eminent merchant of Bristol," celebrated also for re-edifying and repairing the church of St. Mary Redcliff, in that city, (see Rymer's Fœdera, p. 226.)

THOMAS CANINGE and Agnes, his wife, were succeeded by their son,

* This is fully established in a pedigree drawn up and approved by Sir William Segur, principal King of Arms, under his seal of office, dated 10th August, 1622.

RICHARD CANINGE, of Foxcote, who married Mary, daughter of Humphrey Campton, and had two sons,

I. THOMAS, his heir.
II. John, of Todenham, who married ——, daughter of — Savadge, of Bengworth, in Worcestershire, and founded the branch of the family which continued at Todenham for several generations.

The elder son,

THOMAS CANNINGE, of Foxcote, married Jane, daughter of Richard Boughton, of Cundecot, in the county of Gloucester, and had issue,

I. RICHARD, his heir.
II. George, *m.* Sybil, dau. of Reeve James, of Broxley, in Worcestershire.
III. William.
IV. Henry.
V. Thomas.
I. Jane.
II. Mary.

The eldest son and successor,

RICHARD CANNINGE, esq. of Foxcote, *m.* Elizabeth, daughter of Richard Petty, of Ilmington, and had

I. RICHARD, his heir.
II. Thomas, merchant at Bristol.
III. William, of the city of London.
IV. Isaac, Turkey merchant, died at Constantinople.
V. Edward.
VI. Robert.
VII. Paul, ambassador to the Great Mogul, died at Agra.

VIII. George, of Barton-on-the-Heath, married Anne, daughter of Gilbert Walker, of Walford, in the county of Worcester, and had issue. This George Canning went to Ireland early in the seventeenth century, and settled at Garvagh, in the county of Londonderry, of which manor he had a grant from *Queen* ELIZABETH. He died in 1646. His son, William Canning, esq. of Garvagh, was father of George Canning, esq. whose son,

GEORGE CANNING, esq. of Garvagh, lieutenant-colonel of the Londonderry Militia, wedded Abigail, fourth daughter of Robert Stratford, esq. of Baltinglass, M.P. for the county of Wicklow in 1662 (she was aunt of John, first Earl of Aldborough), by whom he left a son and successor,

STRATFORD CANNING, esq. of Garvagh, who *m.* Letitia, daughter and heir of Obadiah Newburgh, esq. of the county of Cavan, and died in 1775, having had issue,

1. GEORGE, of the Middle Temple. This gentleman died in 1771, (having incurred the displeasure of his father, and the penalty of disinheritance by an improvident marriage,) leaving one infant child, the afterwards celebrated GEORGE CANNING, who died in 1827, holding the great office of FIRST MINISTER OF THE CROWN, lamented, in the strict sense of the word, by the people, over whose destinies it was his fortune to be called upon to preside.
2. PAUL, who *s.* his father at Garvagh, and was father of
   GEORGE, elevated to the peerage of Ireland as BARON GARVAGH in 1818 (see BURKE'S *Peerage*).
3. Stratford, a merchant in London, father of the Right Hon. SIR STRATFORD CANNING, M.P. and other issue.

1. Mary, *m.* to the Rev. Henry Bernard,* son of William, Bishop of Londonderry.
2. Elizabeth, *m.* to Westby Perceval, esq.

* This was, we believe, Dr. Bernard, the well known dean of Derry, commemorated by Goldsmith in Retaliation,—

"Our Dean shall be venison, just fresh from the plains!"

Richard Canninge was *s.* by his eldest son,

RICHARD CANNINGE, esq. of Foxcote, who married, first, Mary, daughter of William Sambache, of Broadway, in the county of Worcester; and secondly, Jane, daughter of Edward Porter, of Aston, in the county of Gloucester. He had by his first wife two sons and two daughters,

I. WILLIAM, who succeeded him.
II. Richard, who married Jane, daughter of Stafford, of the county of Stafford, and was father of Richard Canning, living in 1622.

I. Ann, wife of Thomas Jacobs.
II. Eleanor, wife of John Wakerley, esq. of Sudbury, in the county of Suffolk.

The elder son,

WILLIAM CANNINGE, esq. of Foxcote, *m.* first, Anne, daughter and heir of Thomas Haywoode, of Bradforton; and secondly, Mary, daughter of Edward Porter, of Acton, in the county of Gloucester, and sister of Sir Endymion Porter. By the former he left

I. RICHARD, his heir.
II. Thomas.
III. William.

He was *s.* by his eldest son,

RICHARD CANNING, esq. of Foxcote, who married Grace, daughter of Edward Fowler, esq. of St. Thomas, in the county of Stafford, and had five sons,

I. William, } who both *d. s. p.*
II. Nicholas, }
III. RICHARD, who succeeded his father.
IV. John.
V. Thomas.

The third but eldest surviving son,

RICHARD CANNING, esq. of Foxcote, living *temp.* CHARLES II. married Jane, daughter of Charles Busby, brother of Sir John Busby, knt. of Addington, Bucks, 1683, and was *s.* by his son,

FRANCIS CANNING, esq. of Foxcote, living in 1720, who married Apolonia, daughter and at length sole heir of Robert Barker,* esq. of Montewecke, in the county of Essex, and had issue,

I. FRANCIS, his heir.
II. Richard.

* By his wife, Catherine, dau. and (after the decease of her brother Henry, *s. p.*) sole heir of Sir Henry Audley, knt. of Beerchurch, and heir likewise of her mother, Anne, dau. and co-heir of Humphrey Packington, of Chadsley-Corbet, Worcestershire. Sir Henry Audley was son of Robert Audley, of Beerchurch (the great-grandson of Robert Audley, brother of Lord Chancellor Audley, *temp.* HENRY VIII.) by Katherine, second dau. of Edward, third Lord Windsor, by the Lady Katherine De Vere, only child of John, sixteenth Earl of Oxford, by his first countess, the Lady Dorothy Nevill, dau. of Ralph, fourth Earl of Westmoreland, and his wife, the Lady Katherine Stafford, dau. of Edward, Duke of Buckingham.

Brize I. Anne, wife of — Greenward, esq. of Bruers Norton, in Oxfordshire.

The son and heir,

FRANCIS CANNING, esq. of Foxcote, *m.* Mary, dau. and (by the death of her brothers *s. p.*) sole heir. Mr. Petre was fourth in descent from John, fourth son of William, second Lord Petre, of Writtle, by Catherine, dau. of Edward, Earl of Worcester. By this marriage the Cannings of Foxcote eventually became the representatives of several ancient families (see termination). The issue were five sons and two daughters,

I. FRANCIS, heir to his father.
II. Robert, *d. s. p.* in 1769.
III. John, *d. s. p.* in 1751.
IV. Edward, *d. s. p.*
V. Thomas, married Mary, daughter of Michael Blount, esq. of Maple Durham, and widow of Charles Stonor, esq. of Stonor, and had issue,
  1. Thomas, who *d. s. p.* in 1824.
  2. Edward, *m.* Louisa, daughter of William Spencer, second son of Lord Charles Spencer.

I. Ann, born in 1748, superior of the English Augustin nuns at Paris during the French revolution. Owing to her unparalleled fortitude, and the profound respect she was held in, even by some of the chief actors during the reign of terror, she was able to preserve her convent (the only one not suppressed in France) from confiscation, and her nuns from the guillotine. Many of the families of the first nobility of France were indebted to her for essential services rendered to them during and after the revolution. She *d.* 9th March, 1820, universally beloved and regretted.
II. Mary, *m.* to Joseph Blount, esq. of Chaldgrave, in Oxfordshire.

Mr. Canning's son and heir,

FRANCIS CANNING, esq. of Foxcote, *m.* Catherine, dau. of Thomas Giffard, esq. of Chillington (see vol. i. p. 208), and had issue,

I. FRANCIS, his heir.
II. ROBERT, successor to his brother.
III. John, major in the Native Bengal Infantry, died 1st September, 1824, leaving by Mary-Anne, his wife, daughter of Sir John Randall Meridyth, bart. of Newtown, in the county of Meath, two daughters, namely,
  1. Eliza-Minto.
  2. Julia-Matilda.

Mr. Canning was succeeded at his decease by his eldest son,

FRANCIS CANNING, esq. of Foxcote, who *m.* Jane, daughter of Ferdinand Huddleston, esq. of Sawston, in the county of Cambridge, but dying *s. p.* in 1831, was succeeded by his brother, the present ROBERT CANNING, esq. of Foxcote.

### Family of Petre of Fidlers.

SIR WILLIAM PETRE, of Tor Brian, Devonshire, secretary of state to HENRY VIII. married, for his second wife, Anne, daughter of Sir William Browne, lord mayor of London in 1514, and was father of

SIR JOHN PETRE, who was elevated to the peerage as Lord Petre, Baron of Writtle, in 1603. His lordship married Mary, daughter of Sir Edward Waldegrave, knt. of Barclay, in Essex, and was *s.* at his decease in 1637 by his son,

WILLIAM, second Lord Petre, of Writtle, who married Catherine, second daughter of Edward, fourth Earl of Worcester, and had

I. ROBERT, third Lord Petre.
II. William, ancestor of the Petres of Bellhouse.
III. Thomas.
IV. JOHN, of whom presently.
V. Henry.
VI. George.

I. Elizabeth, *m.* to William Sheldon, esq. of Beoley, in Worcestershire.
II. Mary, *m.* to John, Lord Teynham.
III. Catherine, *m.* to John Carrel, of Harting, in Sussex.

The fourth son,

THE HON. JOHN PETRE, was of Fidlers, in Essex. He married thrice. By his first wife, Elizabeth (who *d.* in 1658), daughter of Thomas Pordage, esq. of Radmersham, he left, at his decease in 1696, a son and successor,

JOHN PETRE, esq. of Fidlers, who married Mary, daughter of Sir Francis Mannock, bart. of Gifford's Hall, and was father of

JOSEPH PETRE, esq. of Fidlers, who *m.* Catherine, daughter of Sir William Andrews, bart. of Hildersham, in the county of Cambridge, and left at his decease, in 1721, a son and heir,

JOHN PETRE, esq. of Fidlers, who *m.* Anne, daughter of Sir Robert Throckmorton, bart. of Weston, and had (with other issue, who *d. s. p.*) a daughter, MARY, who married FRANCIS CANNING, esq. of Foxcote, and was ultimately sole heir to the family of Petre of Fidlers.

*Arms*—Arg. three Moors' heads couped in profile, ppr.

*Crest*—A demi-lion arg. holding in dexter paw a battle-axe.

*Estates*—Foxcote and Stoke, with the manor of Ilmington, Warwickshire; Prior's Ditton and Middleton, in the county of Salop; Hartpury, Gloucestershire.

*Seat*—Foxcote, Warwickshire; Hartpury, Gloucestershire.

# REES, OF KILLYMAENLLWYD.

REES, JOHN, esq. of Killymaenllwyd, in the county of Carmarthen, *b.* 4th September, 1781, *m.* 19th May, 1803, Anne-Catherine, third daughter of the late Elias VanderHorst,* esq. American consul at Bristol, and has issue,

I. JOHN-HUGHES, a magistrate for Carmarthenshire, *b.* 3rd November, 1806, *m.* 15th October, 1832, Isabella, only dau. of the late Thomas Rutson, esq. of Colham Green House, in the county of Middlesex, and has one son,

Myson-John VanderHorst, *b.* 5th May, 1834.

II. Charles-Courtenay, *m.* in 1832, Rosa, second daughter of Henry Llewen, esq. commander R.N. of Thistleboon, in the county of Glamorgan.

III. Arthur-Augustus.

I. Harriot-Cooper, *d.* unm.

II. Anna-Mansel, *m.* in 1834, to Charles David Williams, esq. commander R.N. of Stamford Hill, only son of the late Colonel Sir Daniel Williams.

III. Frances-Mansel, *m.* in 1833, to Miles Smith, esq. second son of the late --- Smith, esq. of Gwernllwynweth, in Glamorganshire.

IV. Helen.

Mr. Rees, who succeeded his father 14th December, 1802, is a magistrate and deputy-lieutenant for the county of Carmarthen, and was formerly lieutenant-colonel of the local militia. He served nearly six years in the navy as midshipman, and was discharged at the peace of Amiens, when he married, and did not re-enter the service. He was present at the capture of the Dutch fleet in the Helder, and participated in the battles of Camperdown and Copenhagen, serving, during the latter engagement, in the Ardent, the second ship that led into action.

---

* ELIAS VANDERHORST was maternally descended from a noble French family, named "Toisson," which fled, on the revocation of the edict of Nantes, from their native land to South Carolina, as an asylum, leaving very considerable property, with a chateau in the country, and the mansion in Paris, now well known as *Meurice's Hotel*, in the Rue St. Honoré, to their Catholic relatives, who enjoyed it until the French revolution, when all property underwent a change. The last direct descendant, Madame de Sangeant, when at a very advanced age, sought in vain (unfortunately for the family) for that Protestant branch which had emigrated to North America, and of which Elias VanderHorst was then the representative. He did not, however, hear of the enquiry, until too late to profit by it, though a more distant relative, the late Lord Lyttleton, did to a very considerable amount. Paternally, Elias VanderHorst was the immediate lineal descendant of Baron VanderHorst, of Holland, (whose portrait by Sir Peter Lely is now in the possession of Elias's daughter, Miss VanderHorst, of Royal York Crescent, Clifton). The VanderHorsts accompanied the Prince of Orange when he was called to the English throne, and the then chief of the family received from the hand of that monarch a medal in commemoration of the event, together with an autograph letter from his majesty. Subsequently they emigrated to America, and acquired considerable property there. Elias VanderHorst was born in that part of the world, and commanded a company in the British army at the age of nineteen; but, coming to England for change of climate, the war with America broke out, which cut off, for the time, the resources from his transatlantic property. He was offered a pension as a refugee, by his connexion George Lord Lyttleton, then one of the treasury lords, but declined it, preferring to embark the capital he had brought with him in trade (by entering into partnership with some merchants at Bristol), for the maintenance of his family whilst his pecuniary resources were locked up by the war, to becoming a burden on his country. His only son, Thomas Cooper VanderHorst, has succeeded in recovering most of the property thus left. In America, the adopted country of the VanderHorsts, one nephew of Elias VanderHorst, filled the office of Governor of South Carolina, another that of Secretary of State, and a third that of General.

## Lineage.

This family, long resident in the county of Carmarthen, claims descent from a common ancestor with the noble house of Dynevor. Urien Reged, so styled from his having large possessions in the district of Reged, South Wales, which comprised a portion of the present counties of Carmarthen, Glamorgan, and Pembroke, was ancestor of SIR ELIDIR DDU (or Sir Elidir *the Black*, from the darkness of his complexion) a crusader, who received the honour of knighthood, as a Knight of the Sepulchre, at the shrine of our Saviour, in the Holy City. The seventh son of Sir Elidir,

PHILIP, had himself many children, of whom

NICHOLAS, the eldest son, was grandfather of Thomas, whose son, Sir Rhys ap Thomas, was created a knight of the garter by HENRY VII. and obtained from that monarch other proofs of the king's recollection of his efforts to place him on the throne. Sir Griffith Rhys, eldest son of Sir Rhys ap Thomas, was the lineal ancestor of George, present LORD DYNEVOR.

GWILYM, founded the Killymaenllwyd family.

The second son,

GWILYM AP PHILIP, was of Llandilo Vawr, in the county of Carmarthen, and his son, Rys, was father of Meredith, who seated himself at Cilymaenllwyd, which appears to have remained with his descendants for several generations, but was for a short time alienated, though subsequently regained by marriage. Meredyth was direct ancestor of *

EVAN LLOYD AP RYDDERCH, who married Gwenllian, daughter of John ap Harry, living in 1595, and had four sons, viz.

JOHN, of Tre Castell, in Llandilo Vawr. He *m.* Jane, daughter of David Lloyd ap Morgan, but was living without issue in 1595.

WILLIAM, of whom presently.

Thomas, } both living unmarried
Morgan, } in 1595.

The second son,

WILLIAM AP EVAN LLOYD, was of Cilymaenlwyd in 1595. He did not marry until after that year. His son and successor,

PHILIP AP WILLIAM, of Cilymaenllwyd, *temp.* CHARLES I. was father of

JOHN AP PHILIP, of Cilymaenllwyd, who is supposed, from strong presumptive evidence, to have been brother or father of †

RHYS, who lived on his own estate at Kilverry, in the parish of Llanelly, Carmarthenshire. He married, and had one son,

JOHN REES, who also resided at Kilverry. This gentleman appears to have been the first of the family who spelt the name as it is now written. His eldest ‡ son and successor,

HECTOR REES, esq. born in 1683, a magistrate for the county of Carmarthen, served the office of sheriff for that shire in 1745, the year of Prince Charles's insurrection, and was offered knighthood for his conduct during that eventful period, but declined the honour. He *m.* in 1719, Jane, daughter of Evan Price, esq. of Penyfan, grandson of Price of Penllergare, and had issue,

I. JOHN, his heir.
II. Edward, who *d.* unm. leaving the Penyfan estate away from the heir-at-law to the Johneses of Dolecothy.
I. Jane, *m.* to John Johnes, esq. of Dolecothy, in Carmarthenshire.
II. Margaret, *m.* to Evan Griffiths, esq. of Llangorman, Pembrokeshire.

Hector Rees was *s.* by his eldest son,

JOHN REES, esq. born in 1724, a magistrate for Carmarthenshire, who *m.* Mary, only child and heiress of Daniel Hughes, esq. of Penymaes, and had issue,

I. JOHN, his heir.
II. Arthur, lieutenant R.N. *d.* unm.
I. Hester, }
II. Mary, } who all died
III. Jane, } unmarried.
IV. Eliza, }

Mr. Rees *d.* in 1760, and was *s.* by his son,

JOHN REES, esq. of Killymaenllwyd, *b.* in 1749, a magistrate and high-sheriff for Carmarthenshire, who *m.* in 1775, Amy, second daughter of Sir William Mansel, bart. of Iscoed, and had issue,

---

* The intervening descent was as follows:

Meredith ap Rys
|
Gruffith ap Meredith
|
John Lloyd ap Gruffith
|
Rydderch ap John Lloyd
|
Evan Lloyd ap Rydderch.

† Another account says that HECTOR REES was sixth in descent from Rhys ap Owen, of Llechdwnny, in the parish of Llangendeirne, Carmarthenshire, from whom also descended Morris Bowen, of Llechdwnny, high sheriff in 1615. It appears by this statement that one branch took the name of Bowen, from Ap Owen, and the other, retaining the Welsh custom for some years, ultimately continued that of REES or RHYS.

‡ His younger son, Robert Rees, married the daughter of Robert Donne, of Ty Gwyn, in the parish of Pembrey, Carmarthenshire.

I. JOHN, his heir.
II. Charles, of Portland-place, Bath, captain in the 53rd foot, *m.* in May, 1813, Harriet, only child of the late Sir Watts Horton, bart. of Chadderton Hall, Lancashire, by the Hon. Harriet Stanley, his wife, aunt of the present Earl of Derby.
III. Richard, of Carmarthen.

I. Rebecca.
II. Jane, *m.* 5th February, 1809, to Alexander, eldest son of Alexander Raby, esq. of Cobham, Surrey.
III. Eliza.
IV. Frances, who *d.* unm.

Mr. Rees died 14th December, 1802, and was succeeded by his son, the present JOHN REES, esq. of Killymaenllwyd.

*Arms*—Those of Hughes of Penymaes, borne in consequence of the marriage with the heiress of that family.

*Crest*—A talbot.

*Motto*—Spes melioris ævi.

*Estate*—The PENYMAES estate, situated in the parishes of Llangendeirne and Llandeveilog, in Carmarthenshire, acquired with the heiress of Hughes; and the KILLYMAENLWYD, situated in the parishes of Pembrey Llanelly and Llangendeirne, also in Carmarthen.

*Seat*—Killymaenllwyd, near Llanelly. This residence takes its name from a solitary ridge of rock which projects from the sands under the house, "cily," signifying in Welsh a retreat, and "maenllwyd," a grey stone, or rock.

## JONES, OF BEALANAMORE AND HEADFORT.

JONES, WALTER, esq. of Bealanamore, in the county of Dublin, of Headfort, in Leitrim, and of Hayle Place, in Kent, colonel of the Leitrim militia, *b.* in Dublin 29th December, 1754; *m.* at Curzon Street Chapel, Middlesex, 8th October, 1805, Catherine-Penelope, daughter and co-heir of the Rev. Lascelles Iremonger, vicar of Chatford, Hants, by Catharine his wife, daughter of Chidley Morgan, esq. and has five daughters, (all baptized in the parish of St. George, Hanover Square),

I. Maria-Sophia.
II. Catherine-Penelope.
III. Elizabeth-Martia, *m.* to the Rev. George Marsham, (son of the Hon. Dr. Marsham, uncle to the Earl of Romney), rector of Allington and Halden, in Kent.
IV. Sophia.
V. Anne.

Colonel Jones, who succeeded his father, the Right Hon. Theophilus Jones, 8th December, 1811, was formerly representative in parliament for Coleraine, and one of the governors of the county of Leitrim.

### Lineage.

BRYAN JONES, esq. of the city of Dublin, auditor of war, descended from an ancient family in Wales, had a grant of lands from King JAMES I. in 1622, of which he made a settlement by indenture, dated 11th September, 1660, wherein he names his wife, his eldest son and heir apparent Walter, his second son Nicholas, and his daughter Mary. He *m.* Elizabeth, daughter of Walter White, esq. of Pitchers Town, in the county of Kildare, and by her (who died 19th, and was buried in St. John's Church, Dublin, 22nd August, 1681) had issue,

I. WALTER, his heir.
II. Nicholas, of the city of Dublin, whose will, dated 12th December, 1695, was proved the 3rd of January following. He *m.* before 1673, Elizabeth, daughter of John Sargeant, of Dublin, merchant, and had issue,
   1. John, who died without male issue 29th April, 1697.
   2. Thomas, a minor 12th December, 1695, who wedded (settlement before marriage dated 12th February, 1701) Jane, second

daughter of Elnathan Lumme, esq. of Dublin, but died without male issue 26th December, 1720.

3. Walter, born before 12th March, 1688, died without male issue in the lifetime of his brother, Thomas.

1. Catherine, unmarried in 1688, afterwards became the wife of Benjamin Chetwode, esq. She died before 12th December, 1695, leaving one daughter, Elizabeth, who was married to Christopher Usher, esq. and was living in 1754.
2. Elizabeth, *m.* to Major Richard Carthy, and had an only child, Thomas Carthy, who died in Dublin unmarried before 1754.
3. Jane, *m.* first, to the Rev. Ralph Vizier; and secondly, before 1705, to William Wilson, of Dublin. She died before her brother, Thomas, leaving a son, Thomas, living in 1754.

I. Mary, called one of the daughters of Bryan Jones, in her father's settlement of 1660. The only daughter named in his will 1671, and then wife of Robert Aickin.

Bryan Jones *d.* 7th, and was buried in St. John's Church, Dublin, 9th November, 1671. He was *s.* by his elder son,

WALTER JONES, esq. of Dublin, who *m.* 13th January, 1661, Elizabeth, second dau. and eventually only surviving child and heir of the Rev. William Howard, alias Hayward, alias Hayworth, of Dublin, (descended from a family of Hayworth, seated at Fazakerley and Burscough, in Lancashire), by Sarah his wife, daughter of the Very Rev. John Parker, dean of Killaloe, and prebendary of St. Michael's, Dublin, and had issue,

I. Thomas, died an infant in 1663, and was interred in the burial place of his great grandfather, Walter White, in St. John's, Dublin.
II. THEOPHILUS, heir to his father.
III. Bryan, *b.* 7th October, 1667, named in his mother's will.
IV. William, *b.* 25th October, 1668; living in 1688, but not named in his mother's will.
V. John, *b.* 15th April, 1670, died in infancy.

I. Sarah, *b.* 25th April, 1671, executrix of her mother's will 11th November, 1695, living unm. in 1790.
II. Elizabeth, *b.* in 1673, died an infant.
III. Mary, *b.* in 1674, died an infant.
IV. Anne, *b.* 23rd April, 1680, } both
V. Jane, *b.* 15th January, 1681, } named in their mother's will.

Walter Jones died intestate 17th February, 1687, and was buried in St. Werburgh's Church, Dublin, 20th of the same month. His widow survived until the year 1695. He was *s.* by his eldest surviving son,

THEOPHILUS JONES, esq. *b.* 2nd September, 1666, sometime of Bealanamore, in the county of Dublin, and afterwards of Headfort, in the county of Leitrim. This gentleman espoused (marriage settlement dated 24th January, 1692) Margaret, daughter of Nicholas Bolton, esq. of Brazeel, in the former shire, and widow of John Edkins, esq. of Roper's Rest, and had two sons, viz.

I. WALTER, his heir.
II. Bolton, of Dromard, in the county of Leitrim, whose will, dated 4th April, 1779, was proved 28th February, 1782.

Theophilus Jones *d.* 15th April, 1736, and was *s.* by his son,

WALTER JONES, esq. of Headfort, and of the city of Dublin, living 15th June, 1753, who *m.* (articles before marriage dated 31st August, 1722) Olivia, elder daughter and co-heir of the Hon. Chidley Coote,* of Coote Hall, in the county of Roscommon, by Mary his wife, eldest daughter of Sir Robert King, bart. of Rockingham, in the same shire, and had one son and four daughters, namely,

I. THEOPHILUS, his heir.

I. Margaret, *b.* 21st March, 1724; *m.* 22nd March, 1754, to Chidley Morgan, esq. second son of Mark-Anthony Morgan, esq. M.P. and had one son, Chidley, and two daughters, Olivia and Catherine.
II. Catherine, *m.* 3rd January, 1758, to Sir Nicholas Barry, bart.
III. Elizabeth, *m.* to Edward Crofton, esq.
IV. Frances, *m.* in October, 1760, to Lieut.-Gen. Thomas Bligh, brother to John Bligh, first Earl of Darnley.

The only son and successor,

THE RIGHT HON. THEOPHILUS JONES, of Headfort, a privy counsellor in Ireland, represented the county of Leitrim, and subsequently the borough of Coleraine in parliament. He *m.* first, 29th March, 1754, the Lady Catherine Beresford, daughter of Marcus, Earl of Tyrone, and widow of Thomas Christmas, esq. by whom (who *d.*

* The Hon. Chidley Coote was the third son of Richard Coote, esq. created, in 1660, BARON COOTE, of Coloony, in the county of Sligo, who was third son of Sir Charles Coote, bart. Mr. Chidley Coote's second daughter and co-heir was CATHERINE, who *m.* Mark-Anthony Morgan, esq. of Castletown, in Sligo, M.P. for Athy, and had two sons and three daughters, viz. Hugh; Chidley, whose daughter, Catherine, wedded the Rev. Lascelles Iremonger; Mary, *m.* in 1741, to Sir Henry Tuite, bart.; Penelope and Martha.

28th March, 1763, and was buried in Dublin) he had issue,

I. WALTER, his heir.

II. Theophilus, of Bolton Row, London, b. in September, 1760, appointed post-captain R.N. 1782, rear-admiral of the Blue in 1804, of the White in 1805, of the Red in 1808, vice-admiral of the Blue in 1809, of the White in 1810, and of the Red in 1814; living unm. in 1835.

III. James, of Merrion Square, Dublin, in holy orders, rector of Urney, in the diocese of Derry, m. first, Lydia, daughter of Theobald Wolfe, and had by her (who d. in 1793) four sons and two daughters, namely,

1. Theophilus, of Dublin, barrister-at-law.
2. Theobald, a post-captain in the R. N. M. P. for the county of Londonderry.
3. James, in holy orders.
4. Walter, of Dublin, married and has issue.

1. Elizabeth.
2. Catherine, d. unm.

The Rev. James Jones wedded, secondly, 1st October, 1796, Anne, daughter of Sir Robert Blackwood, bart. (by Dorcas his wife, Baroness Dufferin and Clanboyne), and relict of the Very Rev. John Ryder, dean of Lismore, son of John, archbishop of Tuam. Mr. Jones d. in 1835, and was buried at Urney.

The Right Hon. Theophilus Jones m. secondly, in 1768, Anne, daughter of Colonel John Murray,* some time M. P. for Monaghan, (by Mary his wife, daughter of Sir Alexander Cairnes, bart. and widow of Cadwallader, Lord Blayney), and had by her one son, Henry, who died young, and two daughters, Maria, d. unmarried, and Anne, died in infancy. Mr. Jones died in Conduit Street, Hanover Square, 8th December, 1811, was buried in Dublin, and succeeded by his eldest son, the present WALTER JONES, esq. of Headfort, &c.

*Arms*—Gu. two lyoncells ramp. guardant or, armed and langued az. on a quarter of the second a fret of the first, quartering Hayward, Coote, and Cuffe.

*Crest*—A Talbot's head couped arg. langued and chained gu.

*Motto*—Deus fortitudo mea.

*Estates*—In the counties of Leitrim, Dublin, &c. in Ireland; and in Kent, England.

*Town Residence*—Bolton Row, Piccadilly.

*Seats*—Headfort, county of Leitrim, and Hayle Place, near Maidstone, Kent.

* Colonel Murray had three daughters, who were co-heirs of their mother, Mary, Dowager Lady Blayney, namely,

ELIZABETH, m. to Gen. Robert Cuninghame.
ANNE, m. to the Right Hon. Theophilus Jones.
HARRIET, m. to Henry Westenra, esq.

The husband of the eldest sister (we presume *eldest*), General Cuninghame, was created in 1796 BARON ROSSMORE of the kingdom of Ireland, and having no children himself, the patent was made in remainder to the male issue of Mrs. Jones and Mrs. Westenra; the son of the former dying young, the title, on the decease of the first lord, devolved upon Warner William Westenra, the present LORD ROSSMORE, Mrs. Westenra's eldest son. *See* BURKE's *Peerage and Baronetage.*

## BURTON,

### One of the Judges of the Court of King's Bench in Ireland.

BURTON, *The Honorable* CHARLES, of Mount Anville, in the county of Dublin, and of Eyre Court Castle, in the county of Galway, b. 14th October, 1760, m. in 1787, Anna, daughter of — Andrews, esq. by whom, who d. 10th March, 1822, he has an only daughter,

ELIZA-FELICIA, who wedded, at St. Peter's church, Dublin, 8th November, 1819, John Beatty West, esq. barrister-at-law, and King's counsel, in Ireland, recently a candidate for the representation of the city of Dublin, and has (with several daughters) an only son,

CHARLES-BURTON WEST.

Mr. Justice Burton was made King's counsel in 1806, appointed King's serjeant in 1817, and elevated to the Bench in January, 1821.

## Lineage.

This is a junior branch of the Burtons of Higham and Lindley, in the county of Leicester.

From

INGENULFE DE BURTON, who came to England with the CONQUEROR, descended

ROBERT DE BURTON, who gave the village of Great Hodenhall, in Warwickshire, to the nuns of Eaton. He was living in the time of HENRY II. and was father of three sons, viz.

- I. Henry, lord of Ibstock in 1204, who left three daughters,
  1. Ada, *m.* to Robert de Garshall. Her descendant, the eventual heiress of the Garshalls,
     Elizabeth de Garshall, *m.* Sir Robert de Burdett, knt. of Huncote.
  2. Maud, *m.* and had issue.
  3. Joan, *m.* to Sir Robert de Vernon.
- II. William, of whom presently.
- III. Robert, from whom descended
  Sir William de Burton, chief justice of the Common Pleas in Ireland *temp.* EDWARD III.

The second son,

WILLIAM DE BURTON, was father of

SIR JAMES DE BURTON, esquire of the body to RICHARD I. by whom he was knighted. He accompanied his heroic master to the Holy Land, and was present at the siege of Cyprus, for which services he appears to have obtained a grant of arms: az. semee of estoiles, a crescent arg. with a winged serpent for his crest. His son,

OLIVER DE BURTON, was father of

RICHARD DE BURTON, living in 1251, whose son,

ADAM DE BURTON, of Tutbury, living in 1274 and 1321, *m.* Jane, daughter and heiress of Richard de Mortimer, and was *s.* by his son,

NICHOLAS DE BURTON, living in 1321 and 1329, who *m.* Agnes, sister and heir of John Curzon, of Falde, in Staffordshire, and was *s.* by his son,

WILLIAM DE BURTON, of Falde, who died in 1382. He married twice: by his second wife, Joan Creveques, he had no issue, but by the first, Maud, daughter of William Curteis, and sister and heir of Thomas Curteis, he was father of three sons, namely,

- I. Oliver, steward of the honour of Tutbury under John of Gaunt.
- II. RICHARD.
- III. William, abbot of Rowcester, in the county of Stafford.

The second son,

RICHARD DE BURTON, *m.* Maud, sister of Robert Gibbon, of Tutbury, and had two sons,

- WILLIAM (Sir), his successor.
- Richard, of Chesterfield, ancestor of Thomas Burton, esq. high sheriff of the county of Derby in 1628, and of FRANCIS BURTON, esq. sheriff of the same in 1666, of whom in the sequel.

He died 9th May, 1420, and was *s.* by his elder son,

SIR WILLIAM BURTON, knt. standard-bearer to *King* HENRY VI. and lieutenant of Needwood Forest, who was slain in the seventieth year of his age at the battle of Towton, 29th March, 1461. This gallant person *m.* Elizabeth, daughter and co-heir of William Coton, esq. of Coton-under-Needwood, in the county of Stafford, and was *s.* by his son,

RALPH BURTON, esq. of Mayfield and Falde, both in the county of Stafford, who wedded, in 1478, Elizabeth, daughter of Philip Okehover, esq. of Okehover, in the county of Stafford, by whom (who *d.* 10th February, 1532, aged eighty) he had issue,

- JAMES, his heir.
- William, *d. s. p.*
- Modevina, *m.* in 1519, to William Crewker, of Twiford, in the county of Derby.
- Dorothy, *m.* to John Wilnes, of Melburne, in the county of Derby.

Ralph died in 1511, at the age of sixty-eight, and was *s.* by his elder son,

JAMES BURTON, esq. of Falde. This gentleman *m.* in 1512, Elizabeth, eldest daughter and co-heir of John Hardwick,* esq. of Lindley, in Leicestershire, and had six sons and three daughters, viz.

- ROBERT, his successor.
- Thomas.
- Ralph.
- Richard, of London, buried at Stepney.
- James.
- Margaret, *d.* unm.
- Catherine, *m.* to — Miller, esq. of Lee, in Wilts.
- Mary, *m.* to John Wakefield, of Castle Gresley, in the county of Derby.

He *d.* in 1544, aged sixty-three, was buried at Higham, and *s.* by his eldest son,

ROBERT BURTON, esq. *b.* in 1512, who wedded, in 1543, Catherine, daughter of

* Of this John de Hardwick, it is said that he conducted the Earl of Richmond to the field of Bosworth, and that by his skill and conduct the earl obtained the advantage of ground, wind, and sun.

William Repington, esq. of Amington, and dying 16th August, 1558 (buried at Higham) left, with other issue, his successor,

RALPH BURTON, esq. of Lindley, *b.* 14th August, 1547, who *m.* Dorothy, daughter of William Faunt, esq. of Foston, by whom (who *d.* in 1571) he left at his decease, in 1619, four sons and five daughters, viz.

I. WILLIAM, the historian of Leicestershire, *b.* 24th August, 1575, of the Inner Temple, barrister-at-law, inheritor of Lindley at the decease of his father, *m.* in 1607, Jane, daughter of Humphrey Adderley, esq. of Weddington, in the county of Warwick, and dying 6th April, 1645 (buried at Tutbury), was *s.* by his son,

CASSIBELAN BURTON, esq. of Lindley, a justice of the peace, *b.* in 1609, *m.* in 1639, Helen, daughter and co-heir of Sir Nicholas Trott, of Quickswood, Herts, and had issue,

Constantine, *d.* unm.

Cassibelan, *b.* in 1643, page to James, Duke of York, *d.* in London, *anno* 1677.

James, } twins, *d.* unm.
John, }

HELEN.

He *d.* in 1681. His only daughter and eventual heiress,

HELEN BURTON, *b.* in 1647, *m.* FRANCIS BURTON, esq. lord of Dronfield, who was sheriff of Derbyshire in 1666, and conveyed to her husband the remnant of the estate at Falde, in Staffordshire, and those at Higham and Lindley. She had two sons and three daughters, viz.

RALPH BURTON, of Dronfield, killed by a fall from his horse in 1714, and *d.* unm.

Constantine Burton, *d. s. p.* in 1707, having been cast away in Ostend Bay.

Frances, *d.* unm.

Helen, *m.* to Godfrey Froggatt, esq. of Whittington, in the county of Derby.

Sarah, *m.* to Clement Rossington, esq. and their daughter, Sarah, wedding the Rev. Jonathan Peake, vicar of Dronfield, was mother of Mary Peake, the wife of Hugh Wood, esq. of Swanwick. (See page 137.)

II. ROBERT, *b.* 8th February, 1576, the celebrated author of the ***Anatomy of Melancholy***. This learned and eminent person was educated at Oxford, and there took the degree of bachelor in divinity. He embraced subsequently the ecclesiastical profession, and became rector of Legram, in Leicestershire. His literary acquirements, which were various and diffuse, are fully displayed in the remarkable work which he wrote, entitled "The Anatomy of Melancholy, by Democritus, junior." This treatise, which was published in 1621, has been repeatedly reprinted. Burton died in January, 1639-40, at Oxford, and was buried at Christchurch.

The personal character of Robert Burton was very peculiar. He was a man of integrity and benevolence, but subject to strange fits of hypochondriac melancholy, which rendered his conduct flighty and inconsistent. Sometimes he was an agreeable and lively companion, delighting those around him with perpetual sallies of wit and humour; while at other times he would be devoured with spleen and ennui, from which he sought relief and diversion by the composition of his Anatomy of Melancholy. Whatever effect, however, the work may have had on its author, it seems to have been most beneficial to others, for we are informed by Anthony Wood that the bookseller who first published it acquired an estate by the speculation. As to its literary merits, Archbishop Herring describes "Burton upon Melancholy" as an author the pleasantest, the most learned, and most full of sterling sense. He adds, that "the wits of *Queen* ANNE's reign, and the beginning of GEORGE I. were not a little beholden to him." In recent times Lord Byron contributes his high opinion to Burton's reputation.

III. GEORGE, of whom presently.

IV. Ralph.

I. Elizabeth, *m.* to Michael, son of George Purefoy, esq. of Langley.

II. Anne, *m.* in 1596, to George Bradshawe, esq. of Morebarne.

III. Mary, *m.* to Ralph Grey, esq.

IV. Jane, *m.* to Henry Bannister, esq. of Upton.

V. Catherine, *m.* in 1584, to E. Jackson esq.

The line of William Burton terminated, as recounted, with HELEN, his grand-daughter, and his next brother, ROBERT, author of the "Anatomy of Melancholy," dying unmarried, the continuation of the family rested with the descendants of a younger brother,

GEORGE BURTON, esq. lord of a moiety of the manor of Bedworth, in the parish of Higham, and county of Leicester, who was born on the 28th August, 1579, and died 18th May, 1642, leaving a son and heir,

JOHN BURTON, esq. of Bedworth, who *m.* about the year 1657, Winifred, eldest dau. and co-heir of Ralph and Mabell Wright, of Tissington, in the county of Derby, and had four sons, namely,

I. George, baptized at Tissington, 25th November, 1658, *m.* in 1715, Elizabeth, daughter of Mr. Denton, of Croxton, in the county of Leicester, and died issueless in 1733. His widow died 20th November, 1756, both interred in the parish church of Bakewell, in Derbyshire.

II. JOSHUA, of whom immediately.

III. Jonathan, baptized at Tissington, 5th November, 1663.

IV. Benjamin, *b.* at Bakewell, and baptized there 1st May, 1669, married and had a large family. This gentleman, who was in the army, emigrated to Ireland.

The second son, and continuator of the family,

JOSHUA BURTON, esq. baptized at Bakewell, 7th February, 1660, *m.* in 1703, at Soulden, in the county of Oxford, Elizabeth, eldest daughter of John Pruce, of Aynho, gent. and died 13th December, 1741. His widow died 29th October, 1763, both interred at Aynho. They had issue,

I. JOHN, *b.* 24th May, 1706, *m.* Sarah, daughter and co-heir of — Bever, of Putney, in Surrey, and dying 18th June, 1758, was buried at Barnes, in the same county, and *s.* by his son,

JOSHUA BURTON, *b.* 14th November, 1747, baptized at Putney, 4th December following, *m.* 20th July, 1775, at St. Martin's in the Fields, Mary, his cousin-german, daughter of Edmond Burton. He *d.* 4th July, 1820 (buried at All Saints, Poplar), having had four sons and two daughters, viz.

Joshua, *d.* an infant.

Charles, died at thirteen years of age, and was buried at Newington Butts.

Edmund, *b.* 17th December, 1783, died unmarried at sea, being wrecked in the ship Memphis in the year 1808.

Henry, *b.* 27th October, 1785, died unmarried at St. Domingo in January, 1811.

Sarah-Johanna, *d.* in infancy.

Maria-Frances.

II. George, *b.* 22nd December, 1707, *d.* unm. 22nd April, 1732, buried at Barnes.

III. FRANCIS, through whom the family is continued.

IV. Edmund.

V. William.

The third son,

FRANCIS BURTON, esq. *m.* on the 6th February, 1743, at the parish church of St. Anne's, Blackfriars, London, Anne, youngest daughter of James Singer, esq. of Barn Elms, in the county of Surrey, and sister and heiress of the Rev. Westbrooke Singer, by whom (who *d.* at Bath in April, 1792, and was buried at Aynho, in Northamptonshire) he had twelve children, of whom survived infancy,

I. JAMES, *b.* 1st May, 1745, in holy orders, chaplain in ordinary to *Kings* GEORGE III. and GEORGE IV. senior canon of Christchurch, rector of Over Warton, in the county of Oxford, vicar of Little Berkhampstead, Herts, incumbent of first portion of Waddesdon rectory, Bucks, and for many years a magistrate of the county of Oxford. This venerable and well known divine was educated at Magdalen college, Oxford, where he proceeded M.A. in 1768, B.D. in 1788, D.D. in 1789, and became a fellow. He *m.* in 1744, Mary-Anne, only daughter of Robert Jenner, D.C.L. regius professor of civil law, by whom (who *d.* 5th December, 1788, and was buried in the family vault of her father at Fetcham, in Surrey), he had five sons and four daughters, namely,

1. ARTHUR-FRANCIS-THOMAS, in holy orders, A. M. rector of Hampstead Norris, born at Reading, 16th June, 1777, *m.* 21st February, 1802, at St. Andrew's, Holborn, Mary, daughter of --- Cole, esq. by whom he left at his decease, 9th April, 1819, an only child,

ELIZA BURTON.

2. James-Singer, born at Carrington, in Bedfordshire, 15th April, 1778, A.M. gentleman usher to *King* GEORGE III. died unmarried in London, 27th September, 1818, and was interred at Iffley, in Oxfordshire.

3. Charles-William, baptized 23rd April, 1780, major in the 8th Native Infantry on the Bengal establishment, died in September 1816, at Mizapore, where a tomb has been erected to his memory. He *m.* Mary-Anne, daughter of J. Borthwick Gilchrist, LL.D. professor of Oriental languages in the college of Fort William, by whom he left at his decease,

Charles-Æneas, *now* head of the family, born at Balasore, 15th February, 1812, an officer in the 40th Native Infantry, *m.* 1st March, 1832, in London, Elizabeth-Jane, relict of H. Bradley, esq. and has one child,

Charles-William, born 18th November, 1833.

Arthur-Robert, *b.* at Jampore, 11th April, 1815, in the Royal Navy.

Cecilia-Somerville, *m.* in 1833, to Gilchrist Wycher, esq.

4. Robert, baptized 12th May, 1779, A.B. of Worcester college, Oxford, *d.* unm. 14th August, 1801, and was buried at Iffley.
5. Cecil-Hill, baptized 4th December, 1788, captain in the 54th Foot, died at Hydradad, in the East Indies, in June, 1813, and was buried there.
1. Rachel.
2. Mary-Anne, *m.* in November, 1814, to the Rev. Edward Marshall, A.M. fellow of Oriel college, Oxford, son of — Marshall, esq. of Enstone, in Oxfordshire, and has issue. Mr. Marshall assumed the surname of Hacker, on succeeding to an estate bequeathed to his only brother, who *d. s. p.*
3. Elizabeth, } *d.* infants.
4. Martha, }

II. Charles, one of the judges of the King's Bench in Ireland.

III. Edmund, *b.* 14th October, 1760, twin with his brother Charles, an attorney-at-law, and town clerk of the borough of Daventry, in Northamptonshire, *d.* 19th February, 1820. He *m.* at Wolfhamcote, in Warwickshire, 17th December, 1784, Elizabeth, only daughter of the Rev. John Mather, of Chorley, in Lancashire, by Bridget, eldest daughter of Robert Clerke, esq. of Wolfhamcote, and left eight sons and two daughters, viz.

1. Francis, resident at Unsworth Lodge, in the county of Lancaster, *b.* 16th February, 1788, *m.* 13th July, 1826, Sophia-Alethea, youngest daughter of William Norris, M.D. of Springfield, in the county of York, and of Kingston upon Hull.
2. Edmund-Singer, *b.* 13th July, 1789, attorney-at-law, and town clerk of the borough of Daventry, *m.* 28th October, 1824, Anna-Maria, eldest daughter of Clarke Watkins, esq. of that place, and has three sons and five daughters.
3. Clerke, *b.* 15th December, 1790, appointed master of the Supreme Court at the Cape of Good Hope, 1st January, 1828.
4. Charles-James, *b.* 29th March, 1792, in holy orders, fellow of Queen's college, vicar of Lydd, in Kent, *m.* 5th July, 1819, Eliza, second daughter of William Belcher, esq. of Canterbury, and has issue.
5. William-Westbrooke, *b.* 31st January, 1794, an officer in the royal navy during the late war, but afterwards studying law, was called to the bar in 1824. He is now one of the judges at Sydney, New South Wales. He *m.* 5th April, 1827, Margaret, daughter of L. Smith, esq.
6. Henry, barrister-at-law, *b.* 28th June, 1797, *m.* 24th September, 1822, Elizabeth, eldest daughter of R. W. Clarkson, gent. and has issue.
7. Thomas-Clerke, *b.* 20th November, 1798, midshipman R.N. *d.* 26th August, 1816.
8. Robert-Clerke, *b.* 5th September, 1802, M.A. in holy orders.
1. Anne-Singer, *m.* 5th October, 1813, to Henry, only son of Henry Bradley, esq. of Hertford, by whom she left, at her decease, 17th September, 1818, a son and daughter.
2. Elizabeth-Jane, *m.* in August, 1823, to H. Bradley, esq. of London, and has issue.

I. Anne, *b.* 12th August, 1747, *m.* in December, 1778, to John Hayley, esq. of Chesterton, by whom (who *d.* 12th August, 1834) she had one son, who died in infancy. She died in June, 1803.

II. Elizabeth-Felicia, *b.* 27th April, 1750.

III. Sibilla, *b.* 18th January, 1752, new style, deceased.

The second surviving son, but eleventh child, is the present MR. JUSTICE BURTON, of the Court of King's Bench, in Ireland.

*Arms*—Az. a fesse between three talbots' heads erased or, having thirty-two quarterings, of which the principal are Curzon, Rolleston, Curteis, Cotton, Ridware, Hastings, Odingsell, Bracebridge, Arden, Singer and Westbrooke.

*Crests*—First, a beacon arg. burning ppr. standing upon a mount, vert; second, a cypress tree ppr. on a ducal coronet or; third, a serpent winged, with legs az. scaled arg. standing on a ducal crown.

*Motto*—Lux vitæ.

*Town Residence*—Stephen's Green, Dublin.

*Seats*—Mount Anville, county of Dublin; Eyre Court Castle, in the county of Galway.

# WALLACE, OF KELLY.

WALLACE, ROBERT, esq. of Kelly, in the county of Ayr, M.P. for Greenock, *m.* Margaret, second daughter of Sir William Forbes, bart. of Craigievar, and granddaughter (maternally) of Robert, twelfth Lord Sempill. Mr. Wallace succeeded his father in 1805, and became representative of the ancient house of ELLERSLIE.

## Lineage.

This family claims, rightfully it is believed, the representation of *that* from which sprang the renowned Scottish hero, WILLIAM WALLACE,* one of the most illustrious characters in the pages of history, ancient or modern, whether regarded as a patriot, rousing the dormant energies of his country—a statesman, concentrating those energies for action—or a soldier, directing them to victory. "When the nobility," says Buchanan, "had neither strength or courage to undertake great matters, there presently started up one William Wallace, a man of an ancient and noble race, but having himself little or no estate, yet this man performed in this war not only beyond expectation, but almost beyond belief." Wallace hurled defiance at the royal agressor, braved the tyrant's power, baffled it, and would have saved his country, but for the treachery of a base, rude, and jealous aristocracy; he did not however fight and fall in vain—

> For Freedom's battle once begun,
> Bequeathed by bleeding sire to son,
> Tho' baffled oft is ever won.

—in after ages his reputation again nerved

* WALLACE's person is thus described by HENRY, *the Minstrel*, generally called *Blind Harry*, his metrycal historian.

> "Wallace statur off gretnes and of hycht,
> Was jugyt thus, be discretion off rycht,
> That saw him, both in dissembil* and weid;†
> Nyne quarters large‡ he was, in length, indeid:
> Thryd part in schuldrys braid was he,
> Rycht sembly, strong, and lusty, for to see:
> Bow and§ bron haryt, on brou and breis lycht;
> Clear aspre‖ eyne, like to the diamonds brycht;
> Under the chin, on the left side was seyne
> Be hurt a wain; his colour was sanguine;
> Wounds he had in many divers place;
> But fair, and well kepyt was his face.

* Undress. † Dressed. ‡ Six feet nine inches. § Curled. ‖ Sharp.

This is corroborated by his other historians; all representing him of extraordinary height, and great bodily strength. *Hollinshed* says, he was "a young gentleman of so large a stature, and notable strength of bodie, with such skill and knowledge in warlike enterprises, and of such hardiness in attempting all manner of exploits, that his match was not anywhere lightlie to be found." "There is an anecdote," says Robertson, (Ayrshire Families) "in confirmation of the uncommon strength ascribed to Wallace, related by *Hector Boeis*, which, in another respect, is curious, as it affords an example of longevity, not unsimilar to that of the Irish Countess of Desmond, who attained to a still more advanced age. The date is the year 1430. At that time JAMES I. was in Perth, and perhaps having heard *Henry, the Minstrel*, recite some of Wallace's ex-the right arm of his country, and served as a talisman to burst the shackles with which another despot sought to bind her: it now shines the brightest luminary in her national glory.

SIR MALCOLM WALLACE, of Ellerslie, second son of Adam Wallace, of Riccardton, and younger brother of Adam, progenitor of the Wallaces of Craigie, appears to have been married twice. By his first wife, whose name is not mentioned, he had a son, MALCOLM, who along with himself was killed by the English in 1295, as thus recorded by *Blind* HARRY, the *Minstrel*.

"The knycht Fenwick, that cruel was and keyne;
He had at dede of Wallace fadyr beyne:
And his brodyr, that doughty was and der."

He is said also to have had two daughters: the elder married to the father of Thomas Halliday, a celebrated patriot, who had considerable property in Annandale; the younger, to the father of Edward Little, another of the band of patriots. Sir Malcolm wedded, secondly, MARGARET CRAUFURD, daughter of Hugh Craufurd, of Loudoun, and by that lady became father of SIR WILLIAM WALLACE in the year 1276. "It is also said (we quote from ROBERTSON'S *Ayrshire Families*) that he had a son by this lady elder than Sir William, called Andrew, the inheritor of Ellerslie, who died without issue. The grounds of this conjecture, however, do not seem so strong as to entitle it to implicit belief." The representation of the family devolved, on the death of Sir Malcolm and his son Malcolm, upon

SIR WILLIAM WALLACE, who is designed of Ellerslie, although there is some doubt that he was ever proprietor of the estate. One of the earliest exploits of Wallace was to avenge the death of his father and brother. Collecting a body of fifty resolute men, in the July of 1296, he met Fenwick, at Loudoun Hill, the spot where Sir Malcolm Wallace fell the preceding year, and there, after putting a hundred horsemen to the sword, compelled the rest, amounting to fourscore, to

---

ploits, found his curiosity excited to visit a noble lady, of great age, who was able to inform him of many ancient matters. She lived in the castle of Kinnoul, on the opposite side of the river, and was probably a widow of one of the Lords of Erskine, a branch of whose family continued to be denominated from the barony of Kimnoul, till about the year 1440. It was *Bosis'* way to relate an event as circumstantially as if he had been one of the parties present, and engaged in it. I shall therefore give the anecdote in his own manner, by translating his own words:—

"In consequence of her extreme old age, she had lost her sight; but all her other senses were entire, and her body was yet firm, and lively. She had seen William Wallace and Robert Bruce, and frequently told particulars concerning them. The king, who entertained a love and veneration for greatness, resolved to visit the old lady, that he might hear her describe the manners and strength of the two heroes, who were admired in his time, as they now are in ours. He therefore sent a message, acquainting her that he was to come to her next day.

"She received the message gratefully, and gave immediate orders to her handmaids to prepare every thing for his reception, in the best manner; particularly that they should display her pieces of tapestry, some of which were uncommonly rich and beautiful.

"All her servants became busily employed, for their work was in some degree unusual, as she had not of a long time been accustomed to receive princely visitors.

"The next day, when told the king was approaching, she went down into the hall of her castle, dressed with as much elegance and finery, as her old age and the fashion of the time would permit, attended by a train of matrons, many of whom were her own descendants, of which number some appeared much more altered and disfigured by age than she herself was.

"One of her matrons having informed her that the king was entering the hall, she arose from her seat and advanced to meet him, so easily and gracefully, that he doubted of her being wholly blind. At his desire she embraced and kissed him.

"Her attendant assured him that she was wholly blind, but that, from long custom, she had acquired these easy movements.

"He took her by the hand, and sat down, desiring her to sit on the seat next to him; and then, in long conference, he interrogated her about ancient matters.

"He was much delighted with her conversation. Among other things, he asked her to tell him what sort of a man William Wallace was; what his personal figure; what his courage; and with what degree of strength he was endowed. He put the same questions to her concerning Robert Bruce.

"'Robert,' said she, 'was a man beautiful, and of a fine appearance. His strength was so great, that he could easily have overcome any mortal man of his time; but in so far as he excelled other men, he was excelled by Wallace, both in stature and bodily strength; for in wrestling, Wallace could have overcome two such men as Robert was.'

"The king made some inquiries concerning his own immediate parents, and his other ancestors; and, having heard her relate many things, returned to Perth, well pleased with the visit he had made. This lady could not have been less than 130 years old. The Countess of Desmond alluded to was 140 at her death."

Sir Walter Scott, in his History of Scotland, after describing the natural construction of the Scottish nobility, and accounting thus for their base submission to a foreign conqueror, proceeds —"If the Scoto-nobles had lightly transferred their allegiance to Edward, it was otherwise with the middle and lower proprietors. . . . . . As soon as Edward with his army had crossed the frontiers, they broke out into a number of petty

fly, leaving a considerable booty in the hands of the victor. The subsequent glorious career of the patriot has been so frequently recorded by historian, bard, and minstrel, that it were vain to enlarge upon it here. Of the fatal battle that terminated it, Lord Hailes gives the following account. "He (King Edward) established his head quarters at Temple Liston, between Edinburgh and Linlithgow . . . at that moment intelligence arrived, that the Scots were at Falkirk. Edward instantly marched against them. His army lay that night in the fields. At break of day the Scottish army was descried forming on a stony plain, at the side of a small eminence in the neighbourhood of Falkirk. Wallace ranged his infantry in four bodies of a circular form. The archers, commanded by Sir John Stewart, were placed in the intervals. The horse, amounting to no more than one thousand, were at some distance in the rear; on the front of the Scots lay a morass. Having drawn up his troops in this order, Wallace pleasantly said, 'Now I have brought you to *the ring*, dance according to your skill.' Edward placed his chief confidence in the numerous and formidable body of horsemen, whom he had selected for the Scottish expedition. He ranged them in three lines. (No mention is made of the disposition of the infantry.) The shock of the English cavalry on each side was violent, and gallantly withstood by the Scottish infantry. But the Scottish cavalry, dismayed at the number and force of the English men at arms, immediately quitted the field. Steward, while giving orders to his archers, was thrown from his horse and slain. His archers crowded round his body and perished with him. Often did the English strive to force the Scottish circle: 'they could not penetrate into that wood of spears,' as one of their historians speaks. By repeated charges the outermost ranks were brought to the ground. The English infantry incessantly galled the Scots with showers of stones and arrows. Macduff

---

insurrections, unconnected indeed, but sufficiently numerous to indicate a disposition for hostilities, which wanted but a leader to render it general. They found one in Sir William Wallace. This champion of his country was of Anglo-Norman descent, but not so distinguished by birth and fortune as to enjoy high rank, great wealth, or participate in that chilling indifference to the public honour and interest which these advantages were apt to create in their possessor. He was born in Renfrewshire, a district of the ancient kingdom of Strath-Clyde, and his nurse may have soothed him with tales and songs of the Welch bards, as there is room to suppose that the British language was still lingering in remote corners of the country, where it had been once universal. At any rate, Wallace was bred up free from the egotistic and selfish principles which are but too natural to the air of a court, and peculiarly unfavourable to the character of a patriot. Popular Scottish tradition, which delights to dwell upon the beloved champion of the people, describes William Wallace as of dignified stature, unequalled strength and dexterity, and so brave, that only on one occasion, and that under the influence of a supernatural power, is he allowed by tradition to have experienced the sensation of fear. . . . . The nature of Wallace was fierce, but not inaccessible to pity or remorse. As his unruly soldiers pillaged the church of Hexham, he took the canons under his immediate protection. 'Abide with me,' he said, 'holy men; for my people are evil doers, and I may not correct them.'" . . . . . Sir Walter's account of the fatal battle of Falkirk is substantially the same as that of Lord Hailes, but in a more spirited and chivalrous strain. "The Scottish archers, under command of Sir John Stewart, brother of the steward of Scotland, were drawn up in the intervals between the masses of infantry. They were chiefly brought from the wooded districts of Selkirk. We hear of no Highland bowman amongst them. . . . . The English cavalry began the action. The marshal of England led half of the men-at-arms straight upon the Scottish front, but, in doing so, involved them in the morass. The bishop of Durham, who commanded the other division of the English cavalry, was wheeling round the morass on the east, and, perceiving this misfortune, became disposed to wait for support. 'To mass, Bishop!' said Ralph Basset, of Drayton, and charged with the whole body. The Scottish men-at-arms went off without couching their lances; but the infantry stood their ground firmly. In the turmoil that followed, Sir John Stewart fell from his horse, and was slain among the archers of Ettricke, who died in defending or avenging him. . . . . But what Edward prized more than the surrender of the last fortress which resisted his arms in Scotland, was the captivity of her last patriot. He had found in a Scottish nobleman, Sir John Monteith, a person willing to become his agent in searching for Wallace among the wilds, where he was driven to find refuge. Wallace was finally betrayed to the English by his unworthy and apostate countryman, who obtained an opportunity of seizing him at Robroyston, near Glasgow, by the treachery of a servant. Sir William Wallace was instantly transferred to London, where he was brought to trial in Westminster Hall, with as much apparatus of infamy as the ingenuity of his enemies could devise. He was crowned with a garland of oak, to intimate that he had been king of outlaws. The arraignment charged him with high treason, in respect that he had stormed and taken towns and castles, and shed much blood. 'Traitor,' said Wallace, 'was I never.' The rest of the charges he confessed, and proceeded to justify them. He was condemned and executed by decapitation. His head was placed on a pinacle on London Bridge, and his quarters were distributed over the kingdom. Thus died the courageous patriot, leaving a remembrance which will be immortal in the hearts of his countrymen."

and Sir John Graham fell. At length the Scots were broken by the number and weight of the English cavalry, and the rout became universal.—22nd July, 1298." In the course of a few years the whole country, with the exception of Stirling Castle, was re-subdued by the English. This was in 1303. Lord Hailes continues—"Amid this wreck of the national liberties, Wallace despaired not: he had lived a *freeman*—a *freeman* he resolved to die. Frazer, who had too oft complied with the times, now caught the same heroic sentiments. But their endeavours to arouse their countrymen were in vain. The season of resistance was past. Wallace perceived that there remained no more hope, and sought out a place of concealment, where, eluding the vengeance of Edward, he might silently lament over his fallen country." According to HENRY, the *Minstrel*, Wallace subsequently retired into France, whence he had only a short time returned before he was betrayed into the hands of his foes, in the July of 1305; most accounts say by Sir John Monteith: but Lord Hailes vindicates the knight from so infamous an act of treachery to his friend. Wallace was immediately conveyed to London, and there suffered a cruel death in the September following, by the command of Edward, who had his limbs, as *Buchanan* expresses it, "for the terror of others, hanged up in the most noted places of London and of Scotland." There are contending opinions regarding the marriage of Wallace. The *Minstrel* and *Blair* declare for it. The following passage from the latter is given by *Nisbet*, in his account of the family of Baillie of Lamingtoun:*—"So far as the history of Sir William Wallace can be depended on, it vouches this marriage and alliance; for the author, *Mr. Blair*, tells us expressly, that Sir William's daughter was married to a squire of the Baliol blood, and that way got the barony of Lamingtoun, which had formerly belonged to those of the surname of Braidfoot, whose heir-female of that name was married to Sir William Wallace." While Dr. Chalmers, commenting on this statement, says, that "it is unsupported by any recorded authority, and is certainly erroneous. Sir William had no legitimate issue, but he left a natural daughter, who is said to have married Sir William Baillie, of Stoprig, the progenitor of the Baillies of Lamingtoun.

Here there is a chasm in the line of Ellerlie. Craufurd says, "the lands of Ellerly returned to the family of Craigie, and a younger son of that ancient family obtained them in patrimony about the beginning of the reign of ROBERT the Third, anno 1390." In the account of the family of Cragie, by Robertson, it is stated that this younger son obtained these lands by marrying *the heiress of Wallace of Ellerslie*, about the same period. Both statements evidently refer to one individual.

JAMES WALLACE, third son of John Wallace, of Riccardton, by the heiress of Lindsay, of Craigie, who married the heiress of Wallace, of Ellerslie, and by her he acquired that property, in the county of Renfrew, which had for more than a century preceding been held by a younger branch of the Riccardton or Craigie family. According to Craufurd he had two sons,

JOHN.

Thomas, to whom his father, in 1398, resigned the lands of Auchinbothy, in the barony parish of Paisley. From him, in after times, descended the Wallaces of Johnston by mar-

---

* Through this family the MARQUESS OF ANGLESEY, the Duchess of Portland, Lord Doune, Lady Canning, Farquharson of Invercauld, and others, boast of the blood of Baliol and Wallace.

SIR ALEXANDER BALIOL, of Cavers, uncle to JOHN BALIOL, KING OF SCOTS, was great chamberlane of Scotland in 1298. He married Isabel, daughter and heiress of Richard de Chellam, and widow of David de Strathbogie, Earl of Athol, and had two sons, Andrew, his successor, and

WILLIAM DE BALIOL, who had the lands of Penstoun and Stoprig, in East Lothian and Carnbrue, in Clydesdale. This William, it would appear, is the same who married the heiress of Lamingtoun (mentioned by *Blair*) and his son,

SIR WILLIAM BAILLIE, of Lamingtoun, (living in 1308) was the husband of Sir William Wallace's daughter, and by her, father of

WILLIAM BAILLIE, of Lamingtoun, who was *s.* by his son and heir,

SIR WILLIAM BAILLIE, of Lamingtoun and Stoprig, of which latter he is designed at the time he became a hostage in England for the ransom of JAMES the First, in 1432, when he was exchanged for David Leslie of that ilk. He was *s.* by his son,

SIR WILLIAM BAILLIE, of Lamingtoun, whose son and successor,

SIR WILLIAM BAILLIE, of Lamingtoun, was father of

WILLIAM BAILLIE, of Lamingtoun, who married his cousin Elizabeth, daughter of Robert Douglas, of Lochleven, and was *s.* by his son,

SIR WILLIAM BAILLIE, of Lamingtoun, who was appointed principal Master of the Wardrobe to *Queen* MARY in 1542. He married Lady Janet Hamilton, daughter of James, Earl of Arran, and widow of David Boswell, of Auchinleck, and by her he had two sons, viz.

1. WILLIAM (Sir), who inherited Lamingtoun, and fought on the side of MARY, at Langside, which caused his estates to undergo a temporary sequestration. The male line of this Laird terminated with WILLIAM

riage of an heiress of the name of Nisbet, and which family failed in the person of William Wallace, of Johnston, in the reign of CHARLES I., and the lands were then acquired by Sir Ludovick Howston of that Ilk, and still remain with his descendants.

The next that is mentioned by Craufurd is

JOHN WALLACE, of Ellerslie, who is to be found in the chartury of Paisley, in 1432. Probably the son of the preceding, though Craufurd does not mention the affinity, neither does he state the connexion of the next on his list,

GEORGE WALLACE, of Ellerslie, living in 1468, who is said to have been father of

PATRICK WALLACE, of Ellerslie, a person of consideration in the time of JAMES IV., between the years 1488 and 1513, who was *s.* by his son,

WILLIAM WALLACE, of Ellerslie, father of

JOHN WALLACE, of Ellerslie, who wedded a daughter of Cunninghame, of Craigends. He acquired the lands of Ellenton, of which himself and his wife obtained a charter in 1530. His son and heir,

WILLIAM WALLACE, of Ellerslie, *m.* Catherine, daughter of Hugh Craufurd, of Kilbirnie, and had a son, WILLIAM, his successor. He obtained a charter of his lands in 1554, and was *s.* by his son,

WILLIAM WALLACE, of Ellerslie, who, in 1556, obtained a precept of Clare Constat from his superior, William of Craigie, as heir to his father William. In 1583 he had a charter of confirmation of the lands to Helinton, or Elienton, and, in 1597, the lands of Ryreswraeths and Windyhill. He *m.* Jean, daughter of James Chalmers, of Gardgirth, and had three sons,

I. WILLIAM, his successor.

II. JOHN, who *m.* Margaret, daughter and heiress of John Hamilton, of Ferguslee, of the family of Orbiestoun, and thereby acquired that property in the vicinity of Paisley. This marriage must have taken place before the 27th July, 1624, as under that date there is mention made, in the index to the records, of a charter "to John Wallace, of Ferguslee," although the charter itself is not to be found. But there is a charter on record, dated 9th July, 1647, granted by the crown, in favour of John Wallace, who married Margaret Hamilton, bearing to be an implement of their contract of marriage, and referring to a former charter granted to him by Lord Aberdeen, of which the date is not legible. This John Wallace had issue,

JAMES, designed of Lora Bank,* who died unm.

WILLIAM.

Allan, *d.* without issue.

The second son,

WILLIAM WALLACE, *m.* Margaret, daughter and sole heir of Hugh Stewart, of Neilstoun-side, and by her acquired the lands of Neilstounside and Drumgrain, and had two sons,

JOHN, who succeeded to the representation of the ELLERSLIE FAMILY.

WILLIAM, merchant at Glasgow.

III. James, who acquired, in 1605 and 1612, the lands of Muirhead and Limpatestone, parish of Paisley.

Ellerslie was *s.* by his eldest son,

WILLIAM WALLACE, of Ellerslie, whose

---

BAILLIE, of Lamingtoun, whose daughter and heiress,

MARGARET BAILLIE, *m.* Sir James Carmichael, of Bonnytoun, and left at her decease, in 1759, an only dau. and eventual heiress,

HENRIETTA BAILLIE, of Lamingtoun, who *m.* in 1741, Robert Dundas, of Arniston, Lord President of the Court of Session, and had issue,

WILLIAM, of Lamingtoun, died unmarried.

ELIZABETH, heiress to her brother, *m.* Admiral Sir John Lockhart Ross, of Balnagowan.

Henrietta, *m.* to Visc. Duncan.

Margaret, *m.* to General John Scott, and was mother of the Duchess of Portland, Lady Doun, and Lady Canning.

Anne, *m.* to George Buchan, of Kello.

II. ———.

From the second son, ———, sprang

The Rev. LEWIS BAILY, who accompanied JAMES the (Sixth) First, into England in 1603, as chaplain to Henry Prince of Wales, and preceptor to Prince Charles, afterwards CHARLES the First. He *m.* Anne, daughter of Sir Henry Bagenal, of Newry Castle, in Ireland, and was *s.* by his elder son,

NICHOLAS BAYLY, who was father of

SIR EDWARD BAYLY, created a baronet of Ireland in 1730, and *s.* by his eldest son,

SIR NICHOLAS BAILY, second baronet, who *m.* Caroline, daughter and sole heiress of the Hon. Thomas Paget, and was *s.* by his second son,

HENRY BAYLY, who assumed the surname of PAGET alone, was created Earl of Uxbridge, and was father of the present Marquis of Anglesey.

* Fegualee was alienated about this time to Col. Hugh Cochrane, brother of the Earl of Dundonald.

retour is dated 3rd May, 1627. He was father of

HUGH WALLACE, of Ellerslie, who, in 1637, was served heir to his grandfather in the lands of Windyhill, and other estates. This laird, in 1678, alienated Ellerslie to Sir Thomas Wallace, of Craigie, who conveyed it to his own second son, Thomas, afterwards Sir Thomas Wallace, of Craigie, which latter, in 1700, transferred the estate to John Wallace, eldest son of William Wallace, merchant in Glasgow, brother of John Wallace, of Neilstounside. Hugh Wallace m. the Hon. Isabel Sandilands, sister of James, second Lord Torphichen, but leaving no surviving issue at his decease, the representation of the family devolved upon his kinsman,

JOHN WALLACE, of Neilstounside* (refer to John, second son of William Wallace and Jean Chalmers), who left three daughters, his co-heirs, who sold Neilstoun, in 1713, to Alexander Finlayson. At his decease the representation fell to his brother,

WILLIAM WALLACE, of Glasgow, who had acquired the lands of Overkirtoun and others, in the parish of Neilstoun. He had two sons, JOHN and THOMAS. The elder,

JOHN WALLACE, having purchased the estate of Ellerslie from Sir Thomas Wallace, of Craigie, became "of Ellerslie." He m. Jean, daughter of Dr. Thomas Kennedy, a physician in Glasgow, and had an only daughter and heiress,

HELEN, who m. Archibald Campbell, of Succoth, and was mother of

SIR ILAY CAMPBELL, bart. lord president of the Court of Session in Scotland, as LORD SUCCOTH.

At his decease, the old family estate of Ellerslie passed to his daughter, who, with the consent of her husband, alienated it to — Spiers. The male representation then devolved upon his brother,

THOMAS WALLACE, of Cairnhill, in Kyle Stewart, near Kilmarnock, which property he acquired from a family of the same name, that had been in possession of it for more than two centuries. He m. in 1710, Lilias, daughter of William Cunninghame, of Craigends, and had three sons and a daughter, namely,

WILLIAM, who succeeded to Cairnhill. He m. a daughter of Archibald Campbell, of Succoth, by whom he had three sons, who all died issueless, and a daughter,

LILIAS, who inherited Cairnhill.

JOHN, of whom presently.

Hugh, married, and left Hugh, with other issue.

Margaret, m. to John Nelson, merchant in Glasgow.

The second son,

JOHN WALLACE, became, on the failure of the male issue of his brother William, representative of the family. This gentleman acquired the estate of Cessnock, which he subsequently sold, and purchased, in 1792, the lands of Kelly from the representative of the old family of Bannatyne, which had enjoyed it for ages. He m. Janet, daughter of Robert Colquhoun, esq. and left two sons and three daughters, viz.

ROBERT, his successor.

James.

Mary, m. to Capt. Archibald Cunninghame, brother of Thornton.

Jessie, m. to John Cunninghame, esq. brother of Sir William Cunninghame-Fairlie, bart.

Christian, m. to Thomas King, esq. of Drums, in Renfrewshire, who died in 1802, leaving two sons and a daughter, viz.

James King.

John-Wallace King.

Jessie King.

Mr. Wallace died in 1805, and was s. by his elder son, the present ROBERT WALLACE, esq. of Kelly, "who (says Robertson) is the undoubted male representative of the family of Wallace, of Ellerslie, as descended from a younger son of Craige-Wallace, in the reign of ROBERT III. there can be no question; and this, whether that son obtained these lands, according to Craufurd, as a patrimony from the Craigie family, or whether he obtained them through marriage with the heiress of Wallace of Ellerslie, according to the annals of the Craigie family, as otherwise stated. That this latter house too of Ellerslie, was of the same family as SIR WILLIAM WALLACE, there is every reason to believe, but how nearly connected, does not precisely appear."

*Arms*—Gu. a lion rampant or.

*Crest*—Two eagles' necks and heads conjoined.

*Estates*—In Ayrshire.

*Seat*—Kelly House.

* We presume that we are right in fixing this gentleman as the immediate continuator of the line after the decease of Hugh; if not, his brother William, of Glasgow, or that gentleman's son and heir, John, who eventually inherited, was.

# BIDDULPH, OF BIDDULPH.

BIDDULPH, JOHN, esq. of Biddulph, in the county of Stafford, and of Burton Park, in the county of Sussex, succeeded his father May, 1784.

This gentleman is the head of the ancient family of Biddulph, and in uninterrupted lineal male descent of the elder branch, to which all others are traced.

## Lineage.

This name and family claims a Saxon origin and derivation such as few now extant in England can boast.

BIDDULPH, variously written Bydulf, Bradulf, &c. is a word purely Saxon, compounded of Bid, Biedw, and ulf, or wulf, literally the *wolf-killer*. The latter entered into the composition of a vast number of names during the Heptarch, as *Ethelwulf*, *Ceolwulf*, *&c.* when skill and courage in the chase of the hordes of this ferocious animal must have been held in high estimation.*

That a family of this name existed in the Saxon times in the northern parts, we have evidence in the early chronicles, in which we find "A. D. 790, Beadulfus, or Baldulf, consecrated Bishop of Whitern, on the 16th day before the Calends of August, by Archbishop Eanbald, of York, and Bishop Ethelbert. Whitern was the capital of the kingdom of Galloway, on the other side of the Solway Frith, then recently subdued from the Strath-cluyd Britons, under Walwein, nephew of the great Arthur, and becoming a province of the potent Northumbrian kingdom of the Heptarchy, received both its civil and spiritual governors from York.

The date of Bishop Beadulf's death is not recorded, but it appears that he visited his native province on solemn occasions, as we find him on the death of *Ethelred*, assisting Archbishop Eanbald, and other bishops, by whom *Erdulf*, the successor in the Northumbrian kingdom, "was consecrated and raised to his throne at York, on the seventh day before the Calends of June, A. D. 796."

Biddulph (Bidulf, or Beadulf according to the old Saxon orthography) is a village and lordship in the north part of the county of Stafford, or "the Moorlands," on the very borders of Cheshire, which either acquired its name from its possessors, or conferred it on them. It had fallen to the crown by their resistance to the Norman invasion, like the greater part of the lands in England, and, not having been granted out, was recorded among the "Terra regis," in the Domesday Survey, and unlike the most part of it, appears to have been restored, through a female representative, to the line of its ancient owners.

"The BIDDULPHS do derive themselves (says Erdeswick) from one Ormus le Guidon, the son of RICARDUS FORESTARIUS" of Norman race, who held, as appears by Domesday, ten lordships in the county of Stafford, which were conferred upon him in reward of his services. Biddulph, and other large possessions were not included in these.

The tradition is that RICHARD THE FORESTER was only sixteen years of age when he came in, and that subsequently, having the Saxon heiress given to him in marriage, these latter were restored either to him or to his son, in whose possession we find them in the succeeding reign. A great part of these estates lay in a wild country bordered by the river Trent, and much covered with wood,—he thence probably derived the designation of FORESTARIUS, for, he may

* A different origin of the name is suggested in our Baronetage, but as *this* is confirmed by the arms, and was adopted by the late learned antiquary, the Rev. John Whitaker, a connexion of the family, it is probably correct. We trace the same in other languages, as Hugh Lupus, Canteloupe, &c. and even in the heroic ages we have 'αντίθεον Λυκοφόντην, in the Catalogue of Homer's Chieftains.

have held such an appointment under his Sovereign.—Surnames had not been generally adopted, but men were distinguished by their birth as Fitz—; by personal or mental qualities, as *Rufus*, *Beauclerc;* or by their office or employment, as *Forestarius*, and his neighbour *de Ferrarius*, or *Ferrers*. Thus Ormus "le Guidon" must have been a Standard-bearer to the king, or to one of the great barons de Toni, (Stafford) Ferrers, Chester, or Shrewsbury, whose territories lay in the same neighbourhood as his own, and with whom it seems Richard and his son were joined, when the chivalry of Cheshire and Stafford were led against the Welch in the reigns of William the First, and William Rufus, to the end of which latter, the Forrester, having survived his master the Conqueror, seems to have lived.

Ormus le Guidon, his only son, succeeded him in all his possessions. He was also called de Darleston, from a Lordship near Stone, the seat of his principal residence. He wedded . . . . the daughter of Nicolas de Beauchamp,* Vice Com. de Stafford, by Emmeline, daughter and heir of Urso de Abitot, both great and powerful nobles. Ormus, it should seem, lived through the reigns of the William II. Henry I. and Stephen. What part he took in the affairs of those stirring times is not precisely stated, nor under whose banner he acquired his honourable cognomen. As large possessions were conferred upon him, in addition to those which he inherited from his father Richard the Forester, and those he held as predatory to the church of Burton,† there seems no doubt but he served his sovereigns with valour and fidelity.

There is documentary evidence of connection with Ranulph, Earl of Chester, one of the most accomplished nobles of his time, and son-in-law to Robert Earl of Gloucester, which probably determined the line which Ormus and his son Robert took in the contest for the succession between Stephen and the Empress Maud, and her son Henry II. into whose reign a comparison of the dates in the Burton Abbey Register, leads us to suppose that he lived to see the establishment of the line of Plantagenet on the throne.

Ormus had four sons by the daughter of Nicholas Beauchamp, Vice com. de Stafford; Robert, Edward, Thomas, and Alured. His eldest son, Robert, succeeded him at Darleston, as predatory to the Abbey of Burton, as well as to the greater part of his lay possessions.

Robert's son, Ralph de Darleston, dying *s. p.* his sister Alina, *m.* to Ingenulfus de Gresley, was his heir. She divided the family possessions as follows:—

Darleston, Fenton, and part of Biddulph, to Avisia, her daughter, the wife of Henry de Verdon, which, after three descents came to Alicia de Verdon, who *m.* Edward Manwaring, third brother of Sir Ranulf Manwaring, knt. of Pever, in Cheshire, in which family part of Biddulph remains to this day. Tunstall, Chattersly, and Chell, to her other daughter Petronella, *m.* to Henry de Audeley (Aldithelegh) founder of the ancient and noble line of Audley. To Roger, the son of Edward, her uncle, *Middle-Biddulph*. To Thomas, her other uncle, she gave *Over-Biddulph*, and *Normanscote*. And to Alured, her third uncle, Kniperslу; his descendants taking their name from the place from *temp.* Hen. III. till 2nd Rich. II. when Katherine, the heiress of Knipperaly, carried the estate into the family of Bowyer, in which a Baronetcy (since extinct) was created in

* In a later age, there has been another intermarriage between one branch of the Biddulphs, and the female representative of one line of the Beauchamps.

† A series of documents is extant, taken from the Registers of Burton Abbey, exhibiting the nature of the connexion between the convent, and successive heads of this powerful family, and not only establishing several points of its history, but curious, as throwing light upon the manners and habits of the age.

The first of these is a "Convention" made between Godfrey Abbot, of Burton, and Ormus de Darlaveston (as he is called) done in a chapter held of the monks, who were assenting to the grant. "The abbot granted Darlweston to Ormus, himself, and to his son Robert, born of the dau. of Nicholas, the Viscount, for ninepence yearly rent. The said Ormus, and his son, on their part, were to entertain hospitably the abbot, whenever he would, and to aid and assist him, with his followers and vassals, whenever he had need; and, upon their death, their bodies were to be carried to Burton, to be buried, where they were to be very honorably received by the monks. And, with them was to be brought *the whole* of their chattels, whatever they had in all places. In like manner concerning the wife of Ormus, when she died; her body was to be received with great honour, and buried at Burton." Other similar "conventions" with their descendants appear.

Such was the nature of the relations established in those times between the church and the great land-owners, involving on the part of the latter, protection and aid of the strong arm, for the weaker party, whose lands they held at an easy rate; hospitality and mutual good offices on the part of both; and, on that of the church, what might best tend to soften the rude habits and dispositions of these military tenants, and their followers—a kindly provision of the offices of religion, following them, as we have seen, to the last solemn rites of the tomb.

1660. The male line of the Bowyers, however, failed, and the representation passed, through female heirs, to Sir Nigel Bowyer Gresley, bart. and Charles Bowyer Adderly, esq. of Hams, in the county of Warwick.

Of the descendants of Ormus, the descent is thus shortly traced, of the female *elder* branch, through the VERDONS, MANWARINGS, and AUDLEYS, and of his *fourth* son, Alured, to the BOWYERS, &c.

The descendants of THOMAS, the *third* son, took the name of OVERTON, from inheriting Over-Biddulph, and after five descents merged in the second branch, by the marriage of Cicily, the daughter and heir of Thomas Overton, with John de Biddulph.

But the lineal male representative of ORMUS le GUIDON (on failure of the male line of Robert de Darleston, his eldest son) and the direct line of Biddulph come from EDWARD, his *second* son, who first took the name of Biddulph from that part of the family possessions, which has continued in the same line in direct uninterrupted dedescent for twenty generations, during a period of more than seven hundred years.

The seat of their residence was on or near the same scite on which the noble edifice, now in ruins, was afterwards erected; but, like the Norman buildings in general, of far different character, rude and massive, affording little accommodation but a strong hold, such as the times required, and to which its situation, placed high, and on the very verge of the Moorlands, must have greatly contributed.

Edward's son, ROGER de BIDDULPH, succeeded to these possessions in the division made of the great estates of his grandfather Ormus, between his male representatives and the *Audleys* and *Verdons*, in right of the female branches.

It should seem that the whole kindred adhered to King John, being of the number of "those Lords who (as the Chronicle says) were constant to him with all his faults."

17 Henry III., A.D. 1223, Henry de Audley, founded HILTON ABBEY, near his Castle of Helegh, and endowed it with lands in puram. et perpet. eleemosynam. Of these, Normanscote was derived from the gift or confirmation of his cousin, Sir HENRY BIDDULPH, knt., son of Thomas de Overton, or Over-Biddulph, it having been part of the family possessions from the Conquest. It appears that other parts of the territories of the Barons of Audley were derived from the same stock, as in the Charter of Confirmation of *King* HENRY III. in addition to those by grant from the great Ranulf, Earl of Chester, and Hugh de Lacy, Constable of Chester (with both of whom all this Staffordshire kindred seem to have been strictly allied) there are comprised,

"Ex dono *Nic. de Verdon*. Aldithlegh cum omnibus pertinent, et libert. suis." "Ex. dono *Engenulfi de Gresley*, et Alivæ ux. ejus Tunstall, &c." And lands "Ex dono Margaretæ de extraneo, filiæ Guidonis extranei;" a dau. it is presumed of Ormus.

HILTON Abbey was, according to the custom of those times, the burial-place of the founders and their kindred, but its ruins afford no trace of their tombs.

The family which had been thus "constant to the father, were more tender of the son," and continued their devotion to the race of Plantagenet, in the person of HENRY III. They were particularly attached to his brother Richard, Earl of Cornwall, whom James de Audley attended when he was crowned King of the Romans, at Aix la Chapelle, in 1257.

In the great Barons' wars, headed by the powerful Simon de Montfort, the Earl of Leicester, they were loyal to their king, (the Earl of Cornwall, and many of the northern lords, being drawn over to his side,) and aided *Prince* EDWARD in the battle of Evesham, where the defeat and death of Mountfort ultimately broke the power of the confederate Barons. An antient seal, bearing the impress of the Arms of Biddulph, was lately dug up in the neighbourhood.

The race of ORMUS, however, became allied to that powerful family, and through that connection to LLEWELLYN, the last and gallant *Prince* of WALES, *Felicia*, fourth in descent from the founder of the Biddulphs, having married Robert, youngest son of Simon de Montfort, who, after the discomfiture and death of the Earl, remained privately in England, and changed his name to Wellesborne, while his elder brothers, Simon and Grey, being banished, became the respective founders of the foreign lines of Mountfort, Earl of Bigorre, in France, and then of the Mountfords, of Tuscany, and the Earls of Campo-Bacchi in Naples.

In the 54th HENRY III. 1270, it seems that Thomas de BIDDULPH, with his kinsman James de Audley, attended *Prince* EDWARD in the Crusade to the Holy Land, which he undertook, accompanied by Elinor, afterwards his Queen, when Acon was gallantly rescued from the infidels. There is a tradition to this day in the neighbourhood of *Biddulph*, that certain families, whose lineaments betray their Eastern origin, are descendants of some Saracen followers, who attended their master on his return from this crusade.

ROBERT DE BIDDULPH was, with his kinsman, James de AUDLEY, at the battle of Poictiers, when the French king was taken under EDWARD III.

The Staffordshire vassals of THE FORES-

ren and his descendants, furnished some of those bands of bold yeomen, whose cloth-yard arrows contributed so much to the glory of the English arms.

They formed the right wing of the English army under HENRY V., and particulars are given of a skirmish near Amiens, some days before the battle of Agincourt, when, being charged by the French, they recovered the Standard of Hugh Stafford, Lord Bouchier, and completely routed their assailants.

In the wars between the Houses of York and Lancaster, this Staffordshire kindred adhered to the fortunes of the latter, and fought under the cognizance of the Red Rose. They suffered severely early in this lamentable contest at the battle of *Bloreheath*, A.D. 1459, in their own neighbourhood, at which Lord Audley, who commanded, with most of the gentlemen who gallantly fought in that cause, were slain.

In the reign of HENRY VIII. the family of Biddulph became divided into two branches. The elder line, represented by Sir RICHARD BIDDULPH, knt., who succeeded to the estates, adhered steadily to the principles and faith of their ancestors during all the religious revolutions of that and the succeeding reigns, with many of the ancient families in the northern parts of England.

RICHARD BIDDULPH, of Biddulph, son of William of Biddulph, and the direct descendant of Ormus le Guidon, had two sons,

I. RICHARD (Sir), his heir.
II. Symon, who settled at Elmhurst, embraced the established forms of the Protestant faith, and married Joyce, dau. of Sir Robert Weston, sprung from a common ancestor with the Earls of Portland. Being the father of a numerous offspring, the hive sent forth its swarms, and, as has been often the case in the cadets of ancient houses, some of them devoting themselves to the higher branches of commerce, laid the foundations of future opulence, and became the parent stocks of flourishing branches, destined to carry on, and maintain the family name, when, after many generations, the elder line should become gradually extinct. Symon was father of another

Symon Biddulph, esq. of Elmhurst, whose son,

SYMON BIDDULPH, esq.* of Elmhurst, *d.* in 1632, leaving by Joyce, his wife, dau. of Richard Floyer, esq., of Uttoxeter, several sons and daughters, of whom,

1. MICHAEL, of Elmhurst, *m.* Elizabeth, dau. of Sir W. Skeffington, bart. of Fisherwick, and had issue,
   - MICHAEL, of Elmhurst, who *d. s. p.* in 1666.
   - THEOPHILUS, of Westcombe, in Kent, who was created a BARONET in 1664.† (See BURKE's Peerage & Baronetage.)
2. GEORGE, a merchant in London, died unm.
3. ANTHONY, founder of the lines of Polesworth, LEDBURY, AMROTH CASTLE, &c. which see.
4. John, } one of
5. Humphrey, } these gentlemen entered into the service of the East India Company, and was of those enterprizing men who laid the foundation of its splendid empire. He was agent to the company at Surat in 1616.
6. William, in holy orders: this gentleman seems likewise to have been no way deficient in spirit and talents. He was Chaplain to the English Factory, at Aleppo, in the reign of JAMES I. Of his travels there is a most curious account in "the Collection of Voyages from the library of the Earl of Oxford."‡

* A house near Lichfield, since taken down, of which a print is given in Plot, who dedicates it to "the worshipful, the generous, the much honoured gentleman, Michael Biddulph, esq. of Elmhurst."

† We may here mention an anecdote relative to the Baronet's line—that Farquhar, who wrote his "Beaux Stratagem," at Litchfield, took the character of his *Lady Bountiful* from Lady Biddulph, then residing at the Palace there, as he did his *Boniface* from the Landlord of the George, and *Cherry*, from his daughter.

‡ It is entitled "The Preacher's Travels," and purports to be, "The ten years' travels of four Englishmen and a Preacher, into Africa, Asia, Troy, Bithynia, Thracia, the Black Sea, Syria, Cilicia, Pisidia, Mesopotamia, Damascus, Canaan, Galilee, Samaria, Judæa, Palæstina, Jerusalem, Jericho, and to the Red Sea, and divers other places, very useful to travellers, and no less delightful to all persons who take pleasure to

The eldest son,

SIR RICHARD BIDDULPH, knt. succeeded to the family estates, *temp.* HENRY VIII. He *m.* Petronilla, dau. of Sir Robert Aston, of an ancient family, seated in the counties of Stafford and Chester, and had a son and successor,

RICHARD BIDDULPH, of Biddulph, who wedded Margaret, dau. and co-heir of Sir John Salwey, by Margaret, his wife, dau. of Hugh Erdeswick, (see vol. i. p. 153,) and was succeeded by his son,

FRANCIS BIDDULPH, esq. of Biddulph, who *m.* Isabel, dau. of Sir Thomas Giffard, of Chillington, and had a son RICHARD, his heir. The reign of ELIZABETH was distinguished by the noble mansions which the representatives of the ancient families erected on their domains, in the style which is called the "Tudor architecture." The house which Francis Biddulph built at Biddulph, appears, from the noble ruins still extant, to have all the best features of this style.† The son and successor,

RICHARD BIDDULPH, esq. of Biddulph, born in 1559, married Ann, daughter of — Draycott, esq. of Paynsley, and had issue,

JOHN, his heir.

Mary, *m.* to Christopher Clough, esq. of Mindtoun, Salop.

Frances, *m.* to Marmaduke Holdby, esq. of Shakelton, county of York.

Anne, *m.* to Thomas Worthington, of Lancashire.

The son and heir,

JOHN BIDDULPH, esq. of Biddulph, lived in the troubled times of the *first* CHARLES, when both branches of the family, the Catholic and the Protestant, espoused with zeal the royal cause, and suffered severely for their devotion. John Biddulph, of Biddulph, contributed men and money, with the other Catholics of Staffordshire, to the formation of the king's first army; that which fought at Edgehill. Biddulph-Hall was soon after garrisoned, and made a strong and important post in keeping up the communications with Chester, &c. A younger brother of the family was one of the gentlemen of Staffordshire, who seized, and kept the Close of Litchfield, until it was retaken by the Parliamentary forces under Lord Brook, who, during the siege took possession of, and occupied as quarters, the house of Mr. Michael Biddulph, of Elmhurst, then M.P. for the city. In the subsequent fight at Hopton Heath, this "Captain Biddulph" fell at the head of his troop, gallantly seconding the charge of the Earl of Northampton, with whose family the Biddulphs were now, or shortly after connected, by the marriage of Mary, daughter of Francis Biddulph, esq. of Biddulph, with George Compton, esq. of Brambletye-house. Biddulph-hall, as it was one of the first of the posts garrisoned for the king, was one of the last to surrender. We find a garrison there even after the disastrous battle of Marston Moor; and early in 1645, the king, in person, visited all those quarters, in his way to Chester, shortly before his last fight at Naseby, after which Biddulph-Hall was plundered and laid in ruins, except the

---

hear of the manners, government, religion, and customs, of foreign and heathen countries." The Editor describes Mr. William Biddulph, as "Preacher to the Company of English Merchants residing in Aleppo," and testifies to his "learning, sound judgment, and veracity, and, as not having delivered every thing that was told for a truth, but examined every particular with judgment and reason."

In one of his letters "he relateth his travels from Aleppo to Jerusalem, by the Sea of Galilee, or Tiberias, and the Lake of Gennesareth, and so through the whole land of Canaan, which way was never travelled by any Englishman before. And this journey," he quaintly observes, in conclusion, "may be called Jacob's journey, because all the whole way which they travelled thither, is the way which Jacob travelled from Bethel to Beersheba, to his uncle Laban's house, at Padanaran, in Mesopotamia."

He appears to have been at Jerusalem at Easter, 1611.

His admonition to his "loving countrymen, that either shall hereafter serve in the wars of Hungary, against the Turks, or trade in those places, utterly to detest the Turkish religion, is very characteristic and becoming his sacred profession. He compares heathenism and mahometanism to *glass*,—"touch not glass, for though it be bright, yet it is brittle; it cannot endure the hammer;" and christianism to *gold*; "do you melt it, or do you rub it, or do you beat it, it shineth still more orient."

† Its date A.D. 1558, appears on the arched entrance which, opening in the southern front, is enriched with pilasters and other ornaments, well carved and modelled in the Italian style, then blended (by the encouragement given to Italian architects) with the features of English architecture, which, borrowed both from the ecclesiastical and castellated style, mixed with a revival of Roman forms. The pilasters and ornaments are renewed on the second story, accompanying a gallery, or balcony, over the gate, surmounted by a sort of battlemented pyramid, while the principal apartments on this side end in two noble bays, or oriels, also carried up to the same height. On the other side are similar bays, of noble proportions, and on the north rises a lofty tower, ending in a dome, which is vaulted with stone, moulded into the shape of scales, in a singular, but most effective manner. The whole is of beautiful grey stone, and does credit to the spirit and magnificence of the founder, who little thought that an edifice, calculated to be the residence of his family for ages, would, within less than a century, fall a sacrifice to democratic and puritanical violence.

tower and exterior walls, within less than a century, and in the life-time of the grandson of its munificent founder; and "Biddulph" ceased, after five centuries, to be the seat and residence of the race of ORMUS.

Captain Biddulph *m.* Mary, daughter of Thomas Eyre, esq. of Hassop, and had issue,

I. FRANCIS, his heir.
II. John, or, Thomas, who was groom of the chamber to JAMES II. and, with the Duke of Berwick, was the only attendant of the unfortunate Prince when he stepped into the boat at Sheerness, and severed himself for ever from the British soil and crown.

I. Prudence, *m.* to John Crompton, esq. of Milnwich, county of Stafford.
II. Dorothy, *m.* to Thomas Lane. The Biddulphs were also connected by another intermarriage with the royalist family of the Lanes. Jane Lane, who assisted in the escape of CHARLES II. being Aunt to Jane, wife of Symon Biddulph, esq. of Frankton and Birbury, to whom she bequeathed a splendid sapphire jewel, presented to her by the Queen of Bohemia, which, with a noble picture by Vandyke, of Charles and his Queen, (both now in possession of the Warwickshire family,) and a baronetcy conferred on Sir Theophilus Biddulph, in 1664, were the memorials of the distinguished loyalty of the Protestant branch of this family during those disastrous times.

John Biddulph died in 1642, and was succeeded by his son,

FRANCIS BIDDULPH, esq. of Biddulph, *b.* 7th of April, 1619, who *m.* Margaret, dau. of George Preston, esq. of Holker, and had issue,

I. RICHARD, his heir.
II. John.
III. Henry, died in 1683, *s. p.*

I. Mary, *m.* to George Compton, esq. of Brambletye, county of Sussex.
II. Margaret, } died unm.
III. Anne, }

The eldest son and successor,

RICHARD BIDDULPH, esq. of Biddulph, aged 19, on the 7th of April, 1663, wedded Ann, dau. of Sir Henry Goring, and heiress to her brother Sir Wm. Goring, bart., and had issue,

I. JOHN, his heir.
II. Francis, buried at Burton, 1749.
III. Richard.

I. Elizabeth, married to Charles, Lord Dormer.
II. Ann, *m.* to Anthony Wright, esq. of Whealside, Essex.

Mr. Biddulph died before 1679, was buried at Burton, and succeeded by his son,

JOHN BIDDULPH, esq. of Biddulph and Burton, who *m.* Mary, daughter of Charles Arundel, esq. and had issue,

I. RICHARD.
II. CHARLES.

He died in May, 1720, aged 45, was buried at Burt, and succeeded in the representation of the family by his elder son,

RICHARD BIDDULPH, esq. of Boderton, who died unmarried, in 1767, aged 60, and was succeeded by his brother,

CHARLES BIDDULPH, esq. of Biddulph and Burton, who *m.* 1st. Elizabeth, dau. of Sir Henry Bedingfeld, bart. of Oxburgh, and, 2dly, Frances-Appollonia, dau. of George Brownlow Doughty, esq. of Snarford Hall, Lincolnshire, and widow of Henry Wells, esq. By the first lady, only, who died in 1763, he had issue, viz.

I. JOHN, his heir.
II. Charles, *d.* unm. 1821.
III. Thomas, *m.* in France, Miss Faucart, but *d. s. p.* in 1789.

I. Mary.

Mr. Biddulph died 17th May, 1784, and was succeeded by his eldest son, the present JOHN BIDDULPH, esq. of Biddulph and Burton.

*Arms*—Vert, an eagle displayed arg.
*Crests*—1st, a lion rampant, ppr. 2nd, a wolf sejant, arg. wounded on the shoulder, ppr.
*Motto*—Sublimiora petamus.
*Estates*—Biddulph Hall estates in Staffordshire; Burton Park and Brambletye House, in Sussex.
*Seat*—Burton Park, Sussex.

# BIDDULPH, OF LEDBURY.

BIDDULPH, JOHN, esq. of Ledbury, in the county of Hereford, *b.* in March, 1768, *m.* 9th September, 1797, Miss Augusta Roberts, and has, with six daughters, four sons, viz.

I. ROBERT, M. P. for the borough of Hereford, and a magistrate and deputy lieutenant of the county.
II. John.
III. Francis-Thomas.
IV. Ormus.

Mr. Biddulph succeeded to his paternal estates upon the demise of his mother in 1818. He is a magistrate and deputy lieutenant for Herefordshire, and served the office of sheriff in 1820-1.

## Lineage.

ANTHONY BIDDULPH, esq. baptized at Stowe in 1584, younger son of Symon Biddulph, of Elmhurst, and the direct descendant of the family seated at Biddulph (see page 283), wedded Elizabeth, daughter of Robert Palmer, esq. alderman of London, and was father of

MICHAEL BIDDULPH, esq. who *m.* Frances, daughter of Sir William Kingston, bart. and had a son and successor,

ROBERT BIDDULPH, esq. who *m.* Mary, daughter of Sir William Cullen, bart. of East Sheen, and dying in 1670, was succeeded by his son,

ANTHONY BIDDULPH, esq. who first settled at Ledbury, in the county of Hereford. He married Constance, daughter and co-heir of Francis Hall, esq. and had three sons, viz.

I. ROBERT, his heir.
II. Francis, who married thrice. By his first and second wife he had two daughters; Constance, *m.* to the Rev. Thomas Salwey, LL.D. (see vol. i. p. 154), and Anne, *m.* to Benjamin Baugh, esq. of Ludlow. By the third, Margaret, widow of Reginald Pindar, esq. of Kempley, in the county of Gloucester, and daughter and heir of William Lygon, esq. of Madresfield, in Worcestershire, representative of Richard, last Lord Beauchamp of Powick, which title, extinct *temp.* HENRY VI. has been revived in favour of her descendants by Mr. Pindar, since raised to the earldom of Beauchamp, he had a son,

THOMAS, in holy orders, who *m.* first, Martha, daughter and co-heir of the Rev. John Tregenna, representative of the ancient family of Tregenna Castle, in Cornwall, and had one son,

THE REV. THOMAS TREGENNA BIDDULPH, A.M. born at Worcester, minister of St. James's, Bristol, who married Rachel, daughter of Zachary Shrapnel, esq. of Bradford, Wilts, and sister of Major-General Henry Shrapnel, R. A. and had issue,

1. THOMAS-SHRAPNEL, of Amroth Castle, in the county of Pembroke, in holy orders, prebendary of Brecon, a magistrate for the counties of Carmarthen and Pembroke, *m.* Charlotte, daughter of the Rev. James Stillingfleet, prebendary of Worcester, by Elizabeth, his wife, daughter of William Hale, esq. of King's Walden, Herts, and has issue,

FRANCIS-JOHN.
Michael-Anthony.
Thomas - Edward - Stillingfleet.
Margaret-Anne.
Frances - Augusta - Charlotte.

2. Zachariah-Henry, B.D. late fellow of Magdalen College, Oxford, vicar of Shoreham, in Sus-

sex, and of Backwell, in Somersetshire.

3. Theophilus, late of Oxford University, *m.* Catherine, daughter of John Lindon, esq.

1. Rachel-Lydia, *m.* to the Rev. Charles Henning.

2. Henrietta, *m.* to William Pinchard, esq.

The Rev. Thomas Biddulph wedded, secondly, Sarah, daughter of Chauncey Townsend, esq. and had two daughters,

Frances-Phipps, *m.* to James Townsend, esq. commander R. N.

Charlotte-Louisa, *m.* to George Vizard, esq.

III. Michael, a bencher of Lincoln's Inn, *d. s. p.* in 1758.

Anthony Biddulph died in 1717, and was succeeded by his son,

ROBERT BIDDULPH, esq. of Ledbury, who married Anne, daughter of Benjamin Jolliffe, esq. of Cofton Hall, in the county of Worcester, by Mary, his wife, sister of Sir William Jolliffe, bart. (see vol. i. p. 517), and had three sons,

I. MICHAEL, his heir.

II. Benjamin, in holy orders, who left one son,

Benjamin, of Burghill, in Herefordshire.

III. Francis, banker, of Charing Cross, *d. s. p.*

The eldest son,

MICHAEL BIDDULPH, esq. of Ledbury and Cofton Hall, wedded Penelope, eldest daughter of John Dandridge, esq. of Balden's Green, Malvern, Worcestershire, and had issue,

I. ROBERT, who *m.* Charlotte, eldest daughter and co-heir of Richard Myddelton, esq. of Chirk Castle, in Denbighshire, M.P. for the county of Hereford, and died in 1814, leaving two sons and one daughter, viz.

1. ROBERT MYDDELTON-BIDDULPH, esq. of Chirk Castle, late M.P. for Denbighshire.

2. Thomas, an officer in the Guards.

1. Charlotte.

II. JOHN.

I. Penelope, widow of Adam Gordon, esq. of Denmark Hill, Surrey.

II. Mary-Anne, widow of Robert Phillipps, esq. of Longworth, Herefordshire.

III. Anne, widow of David Gordon, esq. of Abergeldie, in Aberdeenshire.

IV. Harriet, *m.* to Thomas Woodyatt, esq. R. N. of Holly Mount, Worcestershire.

Mr. Biddulph died 6th December, 1800, and was succeeded at Ledbury by his second son, the present JOHN BIDDULPH, esq. of Ledbury.

*Arms, Crest,* and *Motto*—see Biddulph, of Biddulph.

*Estates* and *Seats*—The different branches of the Biddulph family are thus seated:—

1. STAFFORDSHIRE: Biddulph Hall estates. SUSSEX: Burton Park, and Brambletye House. } John Biddulph, esq. of Biddulph.

2. WARWICKSHIRE: the estates of Sir Theophilus Biddulph, bart.

3. HEREFORDSHIRE: the estates and seats of John Biddulph, esq. of Ledbury, and of Benjamin Biddulph, esq. of Burghill.

4. NORTH WALES: the seat and estates of Robert Myddelton-Biddulph, esq. of Chirk Castle.

5. SOUTH WALES: 1. The possessions in Caermarthen and Pembrokeshire of John Biddulph, jun. esq. of Llangennick, and of Francis-Thomas Biddulph, esq. bankers. 2. Estates and collieries in Pembrokeshire, of the Rev. Thomas-Shrapnel Biddulph, of Amroth Castle.

## ORMSBY, OF WILLOWBROOK.

**ORMSBY, MARY-JANE**, of Porkington, in the county of Salop, and of Willowbrook, in the county of Sligo, *b.* in the parish of St. Marylebone, Middlesex, *m.* 11th January, 1815, William Gore, esq. (for family of GORE, see vol. i: p. 82), and has had issue,

JOHN RALPH ORMSBY-GORE, *b.* at Porkington, 3rd June, 1816.
William-Richard, *b.* 3rd March, 1819.
Owen-Arthur, *b.* 3rd October, 1820.

Mio-Fanny, *d.* 24th August, 1834.
Harriet-Selina.

Mrs. Ormsby-Gore inherited the estates upon the demise of her father, 24th August, 1804.

### Lineage.

The traditional history states, that Henry Ormsby settled in Ireland during the reign of ELIZABETH, and was the common ancestor of the several branches of the family that were seated in the counties of Roscommon, Sligo, and Mayo; that the said Henry was of the Lincolnshire Ormsbys, and by his first wife, Susanna Kelke, whom he brought with him from England, had three sons, Anthony, ancestor of the Rathlec branch; Edward, of the Tobbervaddy; and Malley, from whom descended the Ormsbys of Cloghan. The said Henry is stated to have wedded, secondly, Elizabeth Newman, the widow of — Crompton, by whom he had also three sons, John, from whom the Moryvilla branch; Philip, of Annagh; and Thomas, of Comyn, in Sligo.

— ORMSBY, esq. married, and had two sons,

I. ———, of whom presently.

II. Thomas, of Comyn, in the county of Sligo, who *m.* Ena Hara, or Owen, daughter of Teige Hare, and left, at his decease in 1662,

1. Anthony, of Comyn, whose will is dated in 1672. He *m.* before 1662, Jane, daughter of Henry Crofton, esq. of Moate, and had issue.
2. Christopher, of Ballanemore, in the county of Mayo, whose will, dated in 1687, was proved in 1696.
3. Henry, who *m.* Catherine, dau. of Captain Lewis Jones, and had Robert, Lewis, and Christopher.
4. Thomas, who was father of three sons, Theophilus, Frederick, and Jeremiah.
5. Francis, *m.* and had issue.
6. Edward.
7. Roger.

1. Una, *m.* to Roger Johnes.
2. Rose, *m.* to Philip Cox.

The elder son,

— ORMSBY, esq. is proved to have been the brother of Thomas Ormsby, of Comyn, by the will of Christopher Ormsby, of Ballanemore, in which Philip Ormsby, of Annagh, is described as the cousin-german of the testator. He was father of

PHILIP ORMSBY, esq. of Annagh, in the county of Sligo, some time a cornet in the army, who espoused Mary, daughter of George Crofton, esq. of Moate, in the county of Roscommon, and had issue,

I. WILLIAM, his heir.
II. Henry, living in 1693.

I. Hannah.
II. Mary, *m.* to the Rev. William Auchenleek.
III. Anne.

The will of Philip Ormsby (in which he desires to be buried in the church of Killaspigborne) bears date 18th January, 1693, and was proved at Dublin, 26th May, 1694. His elder son and successor,

WILLIAM ORMSBY, esq. of Willy Brooke, in the county of Sligo, a colonel in the army, *b.* 14th December, 1656, wedded, before 1693, Mary, daughter of Sir Francis Gore, of Artarman, and had,

I. FRANCIS, his heir.

I. Dorcas, *m.* first, to Francis, son of Francis King, esq. of Knocklough; and secondly, to Edward Jackson, esq.

II. Isabella, *m.* first, in 1714, to Thomas Irwin, esq. of the Tanragoe family; and secondly, to William Boswell, esq.

Mr. Ormsby, whose will is dated 26th December, 1737, and proved at Dublin 13th August, 1739, died in 1738, and was succeeded by his son,

FRANCIS ORMSBY, esq. of Willybrooke, who *m.* in 1716, Mary, eldest daughter of John French, esq. of French Park, in the county of Roscommon, and had issue,

I. WILLIAM, his heir.

II. Philip, a captain in the army, died *s. p.*

III. Francis, in holy orders, died issueless before 1771.

IV. John, } both *d. s. p.*
V. Arthur, }

I. Anne, *d.* unm.

II. Mary, *m.* to Samuel Beckett, esq. and had a daughter Mary Beckett.

III. Sarah, who wedded, in 1758, John Morgan, esq. of Monksfield, in the county of Galway, and had an only child,

SARAH MORGAN, *m.* to Michael Burke, esq. of Ballydugan, in the county of Galway, M.P. for Athenry, and died 11th October, 1813, leaving issue,

1. WILLIAM MALACHY BURKE, of Ballydugan, barrister-at-law, *m.* Anna-Maria, only dau. of John Blake, esq. of Windfield, and has five sons and three daughters, viz. MICHAEL, John, William, Thomas, Edmund, Mary, Sarah, and Caroline.
2. John Burke, in holy orders, rector of Oranmore, married Mary-Anne, sister of Arthur Guinness, esq. of Beaumont, near Dublin, and has issue.
3. Michael Burke, ex-collector of excise.
4. Thomas Burke, of Belvedere Place, Dublin, *m.* Louisa, relict of Thomas Burke, esq. of Spring Garden, and daughter of Dominick Daly, esq.
5. Henry Burke, in holy orders, *m.* Frances Julia, only daughter of Val. Blake, esq. of Lebinch, in Mayo, and has issue.
6. Dennis Burke.

1. Sarah Burke.
2. Mabel Burke, *m.* in the Ambassador's chapel, at Paris, in 1832, to the Rev. James Temple Mausell, and has one son.

Mr. Ormsby *d.* 20th May, 1751, aged about fifty, and was succeeded by his son,

WILLIAM ORMSBY, esq. of Willowbrook, who represented the county of Sligo in parliament. He *m.* Hannah, daughter of Owen Wynne, esq. of Hazlewood, and sister of the Right Hon. Owen Wynne, and by that lady, who died in 1798, he had one son and three daughters,

I. OWEN, his heir.

I. Maria-Susanna, of Sackville Street, Dublin, *d.* unm. 9th January, 1827, aged eighty-one.

II. Jane, *d.* unm. in 1802.

III. Lucy, also *d.* unm.

Mr. Ormsby died at Bruges, in 1781, aged sixty-three, and was succeeded by his only son,

OWEN ORMSBY, esq. of Willowbrook, *b.* at Hazlewood, in April, 1749, who *m.* Margaret, eldest daughter, and eventually heiress, of William Owen, esq. of Porkington, in Shropshire, (see vol. i. p. 84), and dying 24th August, 1804, left an only child and heiress, Mary Jane Ormsby, now MRS. ORMSBY-GORE, of Porkington, in Salop, and of Willowbrook, in the county of Sligo.

*Arms*—Gu. a bend between six cross crosslets fitchee or.

*Crest*—A dexter arm, embowed, in armour, ppr. charged with a rose gu. holding in the hand a man's leg, also in armour, couped at the thigh.

*Estates*—In the counties of Salop, Carnarvon, Merioneth, Montgomery, Denbigh, Sligo, Mayo, &c.

*Seats*—Willowbrook, in the county of Sligo, and Porkington, in Salop.

# EYRE, OF WILTSHIRE.

EYRE, HENRY-SAMUEL, esq. of St. John's Wood, in the county of Middlesex, a Colonel in the Army, succeeded his father, and is male representative of the ancient Wiltshire family of Eyre.

## Lineage.

The old Wiltshire family of Eyre enjoyed, for several centuries, the highest distinction within its native county, and was of consideration in the state,—most of its chiefs having had seats in parliament, and two of them, learned in the law—upon the bench—one as lord-chief-justice of the Common Pleas; a branch, too, which emigrated to Ireland, attained the peerage of that kingdom.

HUMPHREY LE HEYR, of Bromham, in Wilts, married Gilycia, and was father of

NICHOLAS LE HEYR, whose son,

GALFRIDUS LE HEYR, of Bromham, had three sons,

I. GALFRIDUS LE EYR, of Bromham, in the time of EDWARD II. His immediate descendants, the EYRES of BROMHAM, continued to the 17th century. (Visitation of Wilts, 1623.)
II. Stephen le Eyre, living in the time of EDWARD II.
III. JOHN LE EYRE.

The youngest son,

JOHN LE EYRE, of Wedhampton, Wiltshire, *m.* Eleanor, dau. and heir of John Crooke, of Erchefonte, in the same county, and was father of

SIMON EYRE, of Wedhampton, who was succeeded by his son,

THOMAS EYRE, of Wedhampton and Northcombe, both in the county of Wilts, whose son and successor,

WILLIAM EYRE, of Wedhampton, *m.* Juliana Cockerell, and had two sons, WILLIAM, who was chosen prior of Christchurch, Hants, in 1502, and died in 1520, and

JOHN EYRE, of Wedhampton and Northcombe. This gentleman *m.* first, Margaret, dau. of John Button, of Alton, in Wilts; and secondly, Jane, dau. of John Cusse, esq. of Broughton Giffard. By the first wife he had issue,

I. JOHN, of Wedhampton, M.P. for the county of Wilts in 1563, married Alice, daughter and co-heir of Stephen Payne, of Motcombe, in the same shire, and had (with two dau. Mary, who *d. s. p.* and Edith, the wife of Nicholas Bacon, esq. of Whiteparish) two sons, the elder,

JOHN, of Wedhampton and Chalfield, M.P. for New Sarum in 1571, *m.* Anne, eldest dau. and co-heir of Thomas Tropenell, esq. of Chalfield, Wilts, and had (with four daughters, Elizabeth, wife of John Bowshire, of Cothil Alford, in Wilts; Mary, of Burdett, of Sunning; Margaret, of Quinton; and Susanna, of Scrope, of Castlecombe) a son and heir,

SIR WILLIAM EYRE, knt. of Chalfield, M.P. for Wilts in 1597, who *m.* first, Anne, dau. of Sir Edward Baynton, of Bromham, and had three sons, viz.

JOHN (Sir), his heir.
Edward, *d. s. p.*
William (Sir), of Neston, Wilts.

He wedded, 2dly, Elizabeth, dau. of John Jackman, of London, and by her had two other sons, Henry and Robert, who left issue; and three daughters, viz. Anne, the wife of John Long, of Wraxhall, esq.; Lucy, and Olive. He was *s.* by his eldest son,

SIR JOHN EYRE, of Chalfield, M.P. for Calne in 1625, and for Chippenham in 1628. Sir John *d. s. p.* in August, 1639. His brother,

SIR WILLIAM EYRE, M.P. *d.* in 1663, and was *s.* by his son,

WILLIAM EYRE, esq. of Neston, *b.* in 1618, *m.* Anne, dau. of Charles Dauntsey, esq. of Baynton, in Wilts, and left an only son,

WILLIAM EYRE, esq. of Neston, whose dau. and heir, JANE, *m.* Sir John Hanham, bart.

By his second wife (Jane Cusse) John Eyre, esq. had issue,

ROBERT EYRE, esq. M.P. for New Sarum in 1557, and mayor of that city in 1559, *m.* Joan, widow of George Turney, of the same place, and had a son,

THOMAS EYRE, esq. of New Sarum, who held lands in Winbourne, county of Dorset, 21st of ELIZABETH, *m.* Elizabeth, dau. of John Rogers, esq. of Poole, and had issue,

I. ROBERT, his heir.
II. GILES, of Brickworth, in Wiltshire, from whom the family of the extinct LORD EYRE, of Ireland, (see EYRE, of BRICKWORTH, in conclusion).
III. Christopher, born in 1578, founder of EYRE'S HOSPITAL, in Sarum, *m.* Hesther, dau. of George Smythes, of London, (who remarried Sir Francis Wortley, bart.) and *d. s. p.* 5th January, 1624.
IV. Thomas, *b.* in 1580, mayor of Sarum in 1610, ancestor of the Eyres of Box, who merged in the Eyres of Botley Grange.
V. William, *b.* in 1585, barrister-at-law, bequeathed his estate of Bonhams to his great-nephew, Sir Samuel Eyre, and *d.* November, 1646.
VI. John.
I. Elizabeth, *m.* to Gilbert Tooker, esq. of Madington, Wilts.
II. Catherine, *m.* to Thomas Hooper, esq. of Boveridge.
III. Rebecca, *m.* to John Love, esq. of Basing.
IV. Anne, married to John Swaine, of Gunvill, in Dorsetshire.

Thomas Eyre died in 1628, was buried at St. Thomas's, Sarum, on the 10th Sept. in that year, and was *s.* by his eldest son,

ROBERT EYRE, esq. of Chilhampton and Sarum, born in 1569, barrister-at-law, who *m.* Anne, dau. of the Right Rev. John Still, bishop of Bath and Wells, (by Jane, dau. of Sir John Horner, of Cloford), and dying in August, 1638, left (with two daughters, Blanche, *m.* to Thomas Pelham, of Compton Valence, and Catherine, to Charles Chauncey, of Herts) a son and successor,

ROBERT EYRE, esq. of New Sarum and Chilhampton, *b.* in 1610, *m.* Anne, dau. of Sam. Aldersey, esq. of London, descended from the family of Aldersey, of Aldersey, in Cheshire, and had issue,

SAMUEL (Sir), his heir.
Margaret, *m.* to T. Hassell, esq. of London.
Anne, *m.* to Wm. Stear, esq. of London.
Mary, *m.* to William Hitchcock, esq. lord of the manor of Cowsfield, Wilts.

He *d.* in March, 1654, and was *s.* by his son,

SIR SAMUEL EYRE, knt. of Newhouse and Chilhampton, baptized 26th December, 1633, who inherited the estate of Bonhams from his great-uncle, William Eyre, and purchased Newhouse from his cousin, William Eyre, in 1660. Sir Samuel was a lawyer of eminence, and one of the puisne judges of the King's Bench *temp.* WILLIAM III. He *m.* Martha, third dau. and co-heiress of Francis Lucy, esq. (fifth son of Sir Thomas Lucy, of Charlecote), by Elizabeth, dau. and heiress of Bevill Molesworth, esq. of Hoddesdon, Herts, and acquired thereby the estate of Brightwalton, Berks. By her he had issue,

I. ROBERT (Sir), his heir.
II. Francis, D.D. canon of Sarum, *m.* Ann, dau. of Alex. Hyde, D.D. bishop of Sarum, and *d. s. p.* 28th October, 1738, aged sixty-eight.
III. Henry-Samuel, of Saint John's Wood, Middlesex, *d. s. p.* 1754, bequeathing his estates to his nephew, Walpole Eyre.
IV. KINGSMILL, treasurer of Chelsea College, *m.* Susanna, daughter of — Atkinson, esq. and widow of Samuel Keylway, esq. by whom he had,
    1. SAMUEL, of whom hereafter, as heir under the will of his cousin, ROBERT EYRE, esq. of Newhouse.
    2. WALPOLE, of Burnham, Bucks, in whose heir the male line of the family continues: of this gentleman in the sequel.
    3. Elizabeth, married to Polydore, fourth son of John Plumptre, esq. of Nottingham.
I. Martha, married to Sir D. Bulkeley, of Burgate, Hants.
II. Lucy, married to William Crey, esq. of Horningsham, Wilts, whose granddaughter, Elizabeth, dau. of Edmund Abbott, esq. *m.* J. Wyche, esq. of Sarum.

Sir Samuel *d.* 12th September, 1698, and was succeeded by his eldest son,

THE RIGHT HON. SIR ROBERT EYRE, knt. P.C. of Newhouse, *b.* in 1666, recorder of Salisbury in 1696, M.P. for that city in 1700, chancellor to the Prince of Wales (GEORGE II.), and eventually lord-chief-justice of the court of Common Pleas. He *m.* Elizabeth, dau. of Edward Rudge, esq. of Warley Place, Essex, and had three sons and a daughter, viz.

I. ROBERT, his successor.
II. Samuel, D.D. *d. s. p.* Dec. 2, 1742.
III. Edward, Comptroller of Chelsea College, *d. s. p.* June 29, 1750.

I. Elizabeth, married to Richard Lee, esq. of Winslade, in Devonshire.

Chief-justice Eyre *d.* Dec. 28, 1735, was buried at St. Thomas's Sarum, and succeeded by his eldest son,

ROBERT EYRE, esq. of New House, one of the Commissioners of Excise, who married Mary, daughter of Edward Fellowes, esq. of Shottesham, and had an only son, ROBERT, who *d.* in his ninth year, Feb. 7, 1734. Mr. Eyre *d.* in Dec. 1752, bequeathing his estates, after the decease of his widow, to whom he left a life interest, to his cousin Samuel, son of his uncle Kingsmill Eyre: that lady *d.* 24th October, 1762, when

SAMUEL EYRE, esq. inherited, and became "of New House." He married Stewart, daughter of John Russell, esq. Consul-General at Lisbon, and Envoy to the Barbary Powers, and had two daughters, viz.

I. SUSANNAH-HARRIET, married to William, son of Admiral John Purvis, of Darsham, in Suffolk, M.P. for Aldborough, which William assumed the surname of EYRE. (Refer to PURVIS, OF DARSHAM.) His eldest daughter and co-heiress, HARRIET EYRE, *m.* George Matcham, esq. D.C.L. of Sweetlands, in Surrey, eldest son of George Matcham, esq. of Ashfold, by Catharine, his wife, youngest sister of Lord Nelson, and had issue.
II. Charlotte-Louisa, *m.* to Alexander Popham, esq. of Bagborough, in the county of Somerset, and had issue.

Mr. Eyre, who represented New Sarum in parliament, died in December, 1794, and was buried at Exmouth on the 2nd of January, 1795, when his estates passed to his elder daughter, and the representation of the family devolved on his brother,

WALPOLE EYRE, esq. of Burnham, Bucks, who *m.* November, 1767, Miss Sarah Johnson, and had three sons, viz.

HENRY-SAMUEL, his successor.
John-Thomas, *m.* Harriet-Margaret, dau. of — Ainslie, esq. and had issue, Walpole-George; George-John, and Henrietta.
Walpole, *m.* Elizabeth, dau. of —— Johnson, esq. and had Henry-Samuel, Frederick-Edwin, Elizabeth-Annabella, Alathea-Sarah-Henrietta, and Emma-Harriet.

Mr. Eyre *d.* and was *s.* by his eldest son, the present HENRY-SAMUEL EYRE, esq. of Saint John's Wood.

### Branch of Brickworth, from whence the Eyres of Ireland.

GILES EYRE, esq. of Brickworth, baptized 27th Feb. 1572, second son of Thomas Eyre, of New Sarum, was sheriff of Wilts, 1640. He *m.* Jane, dau. of Ambrose Snelgrove, of Redlynch, Wilts, and had issue,

I. GILES, his heir.
II. Ambrose, purchased Newhouse in 1633, and *d.* in 1649. He *m.* Frances, widow of William Tooker, and had two sons and one daughter, viz.
   William, *b.* in 1638, who sold Newhouse to Sir Samuel Eyre in 1660.
   Ambrose, father of William, of the Middle Temple 1677.
   Jane.
III. John, a colonel in the army, who accompanied General Ludlow into Ireland, and having made several large purchases of land in the counties of Galway, Tipperary, and King's County, established himself at Eyre Court Castle, in the first named shire. On the restoration of CHARLES II. he was chosen M.P. for the county, and by a patent, dated 1662, obtained a grant of the manor of Eyre Court, with power to empark eight hundred acres. He *m.* Mary, daughter of Philip Bygoe, esq. high sheriff of the King's County, in 1662, and dying 1685, left two sons,
   1. JOHN, of Eyre Court Castle, who wedded Margery, daughter of Sir George Preston, of Craigmillar, in Midlothian, niece of the Duchess of Ormonde, and had (with two daughters, Mary, *m.* in 1679, to George Evans, esq. of Caherass, and Elizabeth, the wife of Richard Trench, esq. of Garbally) two sons,
      GEORGE, of Eyrecourt Castle, who succeeded his father in 1709. He *m.* Barbara, dau. of Lord Coningsby, but dying *s. p. m.** in 1711, the estates passed to his brother,
      JOHN, of Eyrecourt Castle, who *m.* Rose, daughter of Lord Howth, and *d.* in 1741, leaving a son and successor,
      JOHN EYRE, esq. of Eyrecourt Castle, who wedded Jane Waller, of Castle Waller, in the county of Limerick, and dying in 1745 without issue (his only child, John, had predeceased him in 1743) was succeeded by his brother,

* His daughter Frances married William Jackson, esq. of Coleraine.

THE VERY REV. GILES EYRE, dean of Killaloe, who m. the dau. of Sir Richard Cox, and d. in 1757, leaving issue,

JOHN, his heir.

Richard, m. Anchoretta, dau. of John Eyre, esq. of Eyreville, and dying in 1780, left four sons,

GILES, successor to his uncle.

John, killed at Margueritta.

Richard, in holy orders.

Samuel.

Robert.

The Dean's eldest son,

JOHN EYRE, esq. of Eyrecourt Castle, was elevated to the Irish peerage in 1768, as BARON EYRE, of Eyrecourt.* His lordship m. Eleanor, daughter of James Staunton, esq. of Galway, and d. in 1792, leaving an only child,

Mary, m. to the Hon. Francis Caulfeild, and their daughter, Eleanor Caulfeild, m. the Hon. William Howard.

Lord Eyre was s. at Eyrecourt by his nephew,

GILES EYRE, esq. of Eyrecourt Castle, colonel of the Galway militia, who m. first, Miss Daly, of Raford; and secondly, Miss Walsh, dau. of John Walsh, esq. of Walsh Park, in Tipperary. He d. in 1829, leaving, with a younger son, Giles, and a dau. m. to Col. Disney, of the Hon. East India Company, a successor,

JOHN EYRE, esq. of Eyrecourt Castle, who wedded, in 1820, Mary, daughter of William Armit, esq. of Dublin, and has issue.

2. Samuel, a colonel in the army at Limerick in 1690, and M.P. for the town of Galway in 1715. He m. first, Jane, daughter of Edward Eyre, esq. of Galway, (son of Edward Eyre, esq. of Galway, M. P. ancestor of Hedges Eyre, esq. of Macroom, in Cork) and had a son,

JOHN, who m. Mary, daughter of Thomas Wellington, esq. and was progenitor of the present

THOMAS STRATFORD EYRE, esq. of Eyreville, in the county of Galway.

Colonel Samuel Eyre wedded, secondly, Ann, sixth daughter of Robert Stratford, esq. of Baltinglass, in the county of Wicklow, M.P. and had issue,

Stratford, governor of Galway, and vice-admiral of Munster, who d. s. p.

Thomas, a colonel in the army, M.P. and master of the Ordnance in Ireland, also d. s. p. in 1772.

Ann, m. in 1717, to Robert, only son of Richard Powell, esq. of New Garden, in the county of Limerick, and was great-grandmother of Eyre Burton Powell, esq.

Mary, m. to Thomas Croasdale, esq.

IV. Henry, bencher of Lincoln's Inn, b. in 1625, recorder and M.P. for New Sarum, d. in 1678.

V. William, in holy orders, rector of St. Edmonds, Sarum, author of "Vindiciæ Justificationis," &c.

VI. Edward, baptized 23rd Jan. 1626, settled in Galway, m. Jane, daughter of Sir William Maynard, bart. Visc. Wicklow, and Baron Maynard, from whom descends HEDGES EYRE, esq. of Macroom Castle.

VI. Thomas, M.P. for Wilts in 1658.

The eldest son,

GILES EYRE, esq. M. P. of Brickworth, in the county of Wilts, m. Anne, dau. of Sir Richard Norton, bart. of Rotherfield, and d. in 1685, being succeeded by his son,

SIR GILES EYRE, of Brickworth, recorder of Salisbury, one of the judges of the Court of King's Bench, who wedded, first, Dorothy, daughter of John Ryves, esq. of Ranston, and secondly, Christabella, baroness of Glasford, in Scotland. By the second he had several children; by the first three sons,

I. GILES, his heir.

II. John, b. in 1665, a bencher of Lincoln's Inn, and M.P. d. in 1715, aged fifty.

III. Henry, of the Mid. Temple, barrister at law. d. in 1704, aged thirty-eight.

The eldest son,

GILES EYRE, esq. of Brickworth, born in 1664, died in 1728, leaving two sons, GILES, his heir, and John, of Landford, in Wilts, b. in 1693, who m. Jane, daughter of Philip Buckland, esq. of Standlynch, and had issue, HENRY, successor to his uncle, JOHN,

* Cumberland, the dramatist, whose father was bishop of Clonfert during Lord Eyre's lifetime, gives in his memoirs a curious account of a visit he paid to his lordship's castle.

of Landford; and Jane, the wife of the Rev. Joseph Simpson, D. D. The elder son of Giles, another

GILES EYRE, esq. of Brickworth, *b.* 30th March, 1693, dying unmarried, 1750, the estates passed to his nephew,

HENRY EYRE, esq. of Brickworth, who *d. s. p.* in 1799. His brother,

JOHN EYRE, esq. of Landford, *b.* in 1722, wedded Elizabeth, daughter of Giles Eyre, esq. of Botley Grange, in Hampshire, serjeant-at-law, and had issue,

I. JOHN-MAURICE, his heir.
II. Henry, M.A. rector of Landford and Brickworth, who died in 1798, aged forty-three, leaving by his first wife, Sarah, who died in 1785, a son HENRY, of Botley Grange; and by his second, Frances, daughter of the Rev. Roger Pettiward, D. D. of Putney, two sons and two daughters, George-Pettiward, R.N.; Charles; Frances, *m.* to Capt. Thomas Bussell, and Caroline, *m.* to — Terry, esq. of Bath.
I. Jane, *m.* to Samuel Orr, esq.
II. Ann, *m.* to the Rev. Thomas Rivett.

Mr. Eyre *d.* 10th Sept. 1799, and was *s.* by his son,

JOHN MAURICE EYRE, esq. of Landford House, and Brickworth, *b.* in 1753, who *m.* Frances, daughter of the Rev. Edward Foyle, youngest son of Edward Foyle, esq. and *d.* 7th September, 1815, leaving an only dau. and heiress,

FRANCES-ELIZABETH EYRE, who wedded, 21st February, 1821, THOMAS BOLTON, esq. now Earl Nelson, and has issue.

*Arms*—Arg. on a chev. sa. three quatrefoils or.

*Crest*—On a cap of maintenance a booted leg.*

*Motto*—Virtus sola invicta.

*Town Residence*—Bryanston Square.

* In the early legends of the family, the crest of the booted leg is said to have been introduced by the chivalrous ancestor, whose loss of limb at Ascalon afforded protection to his gallant chief, RICHARD *Cœur de Lion*. This story is probably as veritable as

"Near Ascalon's towers John of Horiston slept."

# FRASER, OF LOVAT.

FRASER, THOMAS-ALEXANDER, of Lovat, in Inverness-shire, and of Strichen, in the county of Aberdeen, *m.* 6th August, 1823, the Hon. Charlotte-Georgina Jerningham, eldest daughter of George, present Lord Stafford, and has issue,

I. SIMON, Master of Lovat, *b.* 21st Dec. 1828.
II. Alexander-Edward, *b.* 13th January, 1831.
III. George-Stafford-Edward, *b.* 17th February, 1834.
I. Amelia-Charlotte.
II. Frances-Georgina.
III. Charlotte-Henrietta.

Lovat succeeded his father in 1803.

## Lineage.

The *clan* FRASER, of which LOVAT is the chief, are of Norman descent. The name of FRISELL, their original designation, occurs in the roll of Battle Abbey, and establishes their advent under the standard of the CONQUEROR.

From East Lothian, their earliest resting place in Scotland, the Frasers diverged into Tweeddale in the twelfth and thirteenth centuries, and subsequently into the shires of Inverness and Aberdeen. Oliver Fraser, the chief of the clan, built and gave his name to Oliver Castle, which continued in after times their principal feudal hold.

In the reigns of ALEXANDER, the second of the name, and his son, ALEXANDER, the third, we trace

SIR GILBERT FRASER, of Oliver Castle exercising the office of sheriff of Traquair or Tweeddale. He was father of three sons,

I. SIMON (Sir), who succeeded to the sheriffdom, and who was one of the most eminent characters of his day. His name occurs repeatedly among the "barones regni Scotiæ" assembled to regulate the succession to the Scottish crown. He was designed in the records of the time *pater*, to distinguish him from his son and successor,

SIR SIMON FRASER, styled *filius*, and not inaptly commemorated as "the flower of chivalrie." He was the friend and faithful associate of WILLIAM WALLACE, and with that illustrious patriot excepted from the conditions* granted by their haughty conqueror to the Scots after the fatal battle of Falkirk. He subsequently joined the standard of BRUCE, and was at the battle of Methven; where, after thrice rescuing his chief, he was himself made prisoner. From this likewise fatal field he was conveyed to London, and there put to death under circumstances of extreme barbarity on the 8th September, 1306. Sir Simon Fraser leaving no male issue, his two daughters divided his extensive estates between them: the elder married the ancestor of the noble family of Yester or Tweeddale; the younger, the progenitor of the Lords Fleming and Earls of Wigton.

II. ANDREW (Sir), of Caithness.

III. WILLIAM, Bishop of St. Andrew's, and Chancellor.

The direct male line of the principal south country family of Fraser, after being the most conspicuous surname in Peebleshire, during the Scoto-Saxon period, from 1097 to 1306, having thus expired in the person of the gallant Sir Simon, the male representation of the clan devolved of course upon the next male heir, in the person of his uncle,

SIR ANDREW FRASER, who independently of the figure which he made in history, claims special attention as the first of the name who established an interest for himself and his descendants in the northern parts of Scotland; more particularly in the shire of Inverness, where they have flourished ever since. He courted, won, and wed an heiress of Caithness, a district, then and for many centuries afterwards, comprehended within the sheriffdom of Inverness. By this lady Sir Andrew left four sons, viz.

I. SIMON, his successor.

II. ALEXANDER (Sir), chamberlain of Scotland, who, with his "brother Simon," fought at the battle of Inverary in the year 1308, and was rewarded by Bruce with the hand of his sister, the *Princess* MARY. After an eminent career, Sir Alexander fell in the disastrous surprise (as it may be most appropriately termed) of the Scots upon Dupplin Moor in August, 1332. His line terminated in a female. DAVID II. in the twenty-sixth year of his reign, confirms a charter by William Keith and Margaret Fraser, his wife, "*neptis et hæres bonæ memoriæ quondam Domini Alexandri Fraser** *milit.*"

III. Andrew.

IV. James.

The eldest son,

SIMON FRASER, who is on all hands admitted to be the immediate male ancestor of the noble family of LOVAT, styled in the Highlands "the descendants of Simson or Simon," like his father formed an honourable matrimonial connection with a lady of Inverness-shire, having espoused Margaret, one of the heiresses of the earldom of Caithness. Simon Fraser is mentioned in record from his appearance with his brother in support of Bruce, from 1308 down to 1333, when he closed a life of renown at the battle of Hallidon Hill. He was *s.* by his eldest son,

SIMON FRASER, who dying unmarried was *s.* by his brother,

HUGH FRASER, who is the first of the fa-

* "All resources but their own courage had failed them; that last resource had failed them now. They hastened to conciliate the favour of the conqueror. Previous to this, Bruce had surrendered. They stipulated for their lives, liberties, and estates; reserving for Edward the power of inflicting fines as he should see fit. From these conditions were excepted Wishart, Bishop of Glasgow; the Stewart; Sir John Soulis; David de Graham; Alexander de Lindsay; SIMON FRASER; Thomas Bois; and WALLACE. As for William Wallace, it is agreed that he shall render himself up at the will and mercy of our sovereign lord the king."—*Lord Hailes.*

* This Sir Alexander Fraser is often erroneously confounded with an Alexander Fraser of "Cowie and Durris," the undoubted male ancestor of the Frasers of Philorth (now Lords Saltoun), which family, it cannot be disputed, derives from William, son of Alexander Fraser, who flourished during the early part of the fourteenth century, and succeeded to his father in the estates of Cowie and Durris; but in the document which proves the fact, he has no knightly designation, a title which record establishes Sir Alexander, the chamberlain, to have borne from 1308; to this circumstance may be added the failure of the male line of the chamberlain before 1355, and the impracticability of showing that he ever held the estate of Collie or Cowie. Moreover, Alexander Fraser, the ancestor of the house of Philorth, was dead long before the chamberlain commenced his career, for there is explicit proof by Ragman's Roll, that on the 7th July, 1296, "William Fraser, the son of the *late* Alexander Fraser," swore fealty to EDWARD I. at Farnel, Forfarshire, contiguous to the quarter of Scotland where the family estates were situated. Thus the chamberlain and Alexander of Cowie were obviously different individuals.

mily designed in legal writings "of Ard and of Lovet," lands which still remain in the possession of his descendants. Under this title he figures in the year 1367. The precise period when the Frasers of Lovat came to the peerage is not ascertained: there is no patent of the honour; and, indeed, prior to the reign of JAMES VI. patents having reference to dignities alone were unknown; but there are strong reasons for believing that the chiefs of the clan sate as parliamentary barons in the reign of JAMES I. And it is certain that since the time of Hugh or Hutcheon Frisel, "Lord of the Lovet," (who is so styled in his marriage articles with the Lord Fenton's sister, 3rd March, 1416, confirmed by the sovereign in September, 1431,) the family has ranked amongst the Scottish nobility, for in the decreet of ranking given out by *King* JAMES VI. (5th March, 1606,) establishing the order of precedence of the various nobles, there is an entry of this very deed as the Lord Lovat's proof of creation and precedency as a lord of parliament, and the king assigns him a place between the Lords Oliphant and Ogilvy. Hugh, first Lord Lovat, died in 1440, and was interred at Beauly, leaving by Janet Fenton, his wife,

HUGH FRASER, second Lord Lovat, who *m.* a sister of David of the Wemyss, Lord of that Ilk, and died in 1450, at an early age, when he was *s.* by his son,

HUGH FRASER, third Lord Lovat. This nobleman espoused the Lady Margaret Lyon, daughter of the Earl of Glammis, who bore him four sons and three daughters. The second daughter married Sir Kenneth Mackenzie, eighth Laird of Kintail, and from that alliance descend the numerous race of the Mackenzies. This Hugh occurs for the first time in record in 1471, and then by the style of "Hugh, Lord Fraser.* An indenture is entered into, 3rd March, 1472, between this nobleman and the town of Nairn, whereby the latter becomes bound to his lordship, in leal and true manrent and service, and he undertakes to be a good lord, maintainer, protector, and defender in all their rightful causes and quarrels. He was *s.* at his decease by his son,

THOMAS FRASER, fourth Lord Lovat, who was served heir to his father, 22nd May, 1501. His lordship wedded, first, Janet, daughter of Sir Alexander Gordon, of Achindown and Midmor; by this lady he had three sons. He married, secondly, Janet, daughter of Andrew, third Lord Gray, and relict of Alexander Blair, of Bathyock, and by her had three other sons and two daughters; one of the latter died unmarried; Janet, the other, became the wife of John Crichton, of Ruthven. From this nobleman's sons sprang many of the most respectable branches of the clan. His lordship, who had numerous grants of land from the crown, was *s.* at his decease by his son,

HUGH FRASER, fifth Lord Lovat, who, in the year 1539, resigned his castle, lands, and baronies into *King* JAMES the Fifth's own hands at Linlithgow, and obtained from that prince a charter, uniting and erecting the various lands and baronies so resigned into one free and entire barony, to be called in all time coming, the barony of Lovat, in favour of himself and the heirs male of his body lawfully begotten, whom failing, to his lawful and nearest heirs male whatsoever, bearing the arms, crest, and surname of Fraser, in fee and heritage and free barony for ever. The charter is dated 26th March, 1539. This lord fell in the bloody battle fought by his clan with the Macdonalds at Lochlochy, 15th July, 1544. The Frasers stript to their shirts, whence the combat is called that of *Blaranlein.* Their chief, his eldest son, and eighty gentlemen of the Frasers were killed; and, if tradition may be credited, every one of them left his wife pregnant of a male child.

His lordship *m.* first, Anne, daughter of Grant of Grant, and had an only son, he who fell with himself in battle. He espoused secondly, Janet, daughter of Ross of Balnagowan, and by her had two sons and two daughters, viz.

- ALEXANDER, his heir.
- Andrew or William, of Struy.
- Ann, *m.* first, to Macleod of Macleod, and secondly to Bain of Tulloch.
- Catherine, *m.* to Rose of Kilravock.

He was *s.* by his son,

ALEXANDER FRASER, sixth Lord Lovat, who espoused Janet, daughter of Campbell of Calder, and had, with one daughter, the wife of Fraser of Dalcross, three sons, namely,

- HUGH, his successor.
- THOMAS, of Knockie and Strichen; of whom at the conclusion, as immediate ancestor of the *present* FRASER OF LOVAT.
- James, ancestor of the Frasers of Ardochy, represented by GENERAL HASTINGS FRASER.

His lordship died in December, 1557, and his eldest son,

HUGH FRASER, inherited as seventh Lord Lovat. This nobleman married Elizabeth, daughter of the Earl of Athol, and had issue,

---

* When the family was first raised to the peerage, the title was simply LORD FRASER, as demonstrative of the chief's being *the* Fraser, or head of the clan.

SIMON, his heir.

Margaret, *m.* to James Cumming, of Altyre.

Anne, *m.* to Hector Munro, of Fowlis.

He was *s.* by his son,

SIMON FRASER, eighth Lord Lovat, who *m.* first, Catherine, daughter of M'Kenzie, of Kintail, by whom he had a son, HUGH, his successor. He wedded, secondly, Jean, daughter of James, Lord Doun, and had

Simon (Sir), of Inverallochy.

James (Sir), of Brea.

Anne, died young.

Margaret, *m.* first, to Arbuthnot of Arbuthnot; and secondly, to Sir James Haldane, of Gleneagles.

His lordship was *s.* by his eldest son,

HUGH FRASER, ninth Lord Lovat, who espoused Isabel, daughter of Sir John Wemyss, of Wemyss, and had issue,

SIMON, Master of Lovat, who *d.* unm. in 1640.

HUGH, Master of Lovat after the decease of his elder brother, *m.* Lady Anne Leslie, eldest daughter of Alexander, Earl of Leven, by whom (who wedded, secondly, Sir Ralph Delaval) he left at his decease, in 1643, a son,

HUGH, who succeeded his grandfather as tenth lord.

THOMAS, of Beaufort, who inherited as eleventh lord.

Anne, *m.* in 1639, to John, thirteenth Earl of Sutherland (his lordship's second wife), but died issueless.

Mary, *m.* to David Ross, of Balnagowan.

Catherine, *m.* first, to Sir John Sinclair, of Dunbeath; secondly, to Robert, first Viscount Arbuthnot; and thirdly, to Andrew, third Lord Fraser.

His lordship *d.* in 1646, and was *s.* by his grandson,

HUGH FRASER, tenth Lord Lovat, *b.* in 1643, *m.* in 1659, when at college, Anne, second daughter of Sir John M'Kenzie, bart. of Turbat, and had one son and three daughters, viz.

HUGH, his heir.

Anne, *b.* in 1661, *m.* to Patrick, second Lord Kinnard, and was mother of the Patrick, third lord.

Isabel, *m.* to Alexander Macdonald, of Glengarry.

Margaret, *m.* to Colonel Andrew Munro.

This nobleman *d.* in 1672, and was *s.* by his son,

HUGH FRASER, eleventh Lord Lovat, who married the Lady Amelia Murray, only daughter of John, first Marquess of Atholl, and had four daughters, viz.

I. AMELIA, *m.* to Alexander M'Kenzie, son of Roderick M'Kenzie, of Prestonhall, one of the senators of the College of Justice, as Lord Prestonhall, which Alexander assumed the surname of FRASER, and was designated "of Fraserdale," and by him had a son,

HUGH FRASER, who was styled by his parents *Master of Lovat*, but his pretensions were eventually set aside by the heir male.

II. Anne, *m.* first, to Norman Macleod, of Macleod; secondly, to Peter Fotheringham, of Powrie; and thirdly, to John, second Lord Cromartie.

III. Catherine, *m.* to Sir William Murray, bart. of Auchtertyre.

IV. Margaret, *d.* unm.

His lordship died at Perth, 4th September, 1696, and thus leaving no male issue, the title and estates reverted to his great uncle,

THOMAS FRASER, of Beaufort, as twelfth LORD LOVAT. He had *m.* a dau. of M'Leod of M'Leod, by whom he had several children; and, as his claim was incontestible, his then eldest surviving son, Captain SIMON FRASER, assumed the designation of "*Master of Lovat.*" But the Earl of Tullibardine, eldest son of the Marquess of Atholl, and Secretary of State, conceived the design of having his niece, AMELIA, eldest daughter of the deceased Lord Lovat, declared heiress to her father, and married to one of his own sons. This project was subsequently in part given up; the family of Atholl resolving on uniting her to Mr. Fraser, the Lord of Saltoun's son. Young Simon, of Beaufort, fancied the lady himself, but his suit miscarrying, he conceived the idea of forcing her mother, the Dowager Lady Lovat, (who held a considerable portion of the estate in right of her jointure) to espouse him; and, after a series of adventrues, revolting to humanity, got possession of her person. Such unparalleled proceedings excited the utmost vigilance of the government. Troops were despatched against Simon, and the Clan Fraser, with orders to exterminate them without mercy. Simon was tried in his absence, and outlawed for treason and rape. His father escaped to the Isle of Skye, where he died in May, 1698-9. The delinquent, himself, was forced to fly into France, where his restless spirit was for a while doomed to inactivity, in the Bastile. His withdrawal enabled the family of Atholl to complete their plans for the total ruin of his house; and to adjudge his honours and estates; which were settled by entail on the heirs of AMELIA FRASER's marriage with young

Prestonhall, who, as stated, under the eleventh Lord, had assumed the name and designation of "Fraser, of Fraserdale." The Rebellion of 1715, changing, however, the face of affairs,

SIMON FRASER, Lord Lovat, as he was styled, re-appeared in his native country, on behalf of government, and was highly instrumental in quelling the insurrection. He regained his title and paternal estates, and eventually terminated a varied career on Tower-hill, in April 1747. In 1740, he signed the association to join CHARLES-EDWARD, from whom he accepted the commission of Lieutenant-General, and General of the Highlands, with a patent, creating him DUKE OF FRASER. On the breaking out of the rebellion, five years afterwards, 1745, he sent his eldest son and his clansmen to join the standard of the Chevalier, but remained at home himself; when all was over he was taken into custody, 1746, conveyed to London, and put upon his trial for high treason, before the House of Lords, on the 7th of March, 1747, convicted on the 10th of the same month, and decapitated on Tower-hill, the 9th of April following, in the 80th year of his age. The proceedings against his lordship began in Westminster Hall, on Monday, the 9th of May, and continued on the 10th, 11th, 13th, 16th, 18th, and 19th days of the same month, when the doom of a traitor was pronounced upon him. His lordship called no witnesses, but spoke at considerable length in defence, making a great merit of his exertions, in 1715, and grievous complaints for the disbanding of his company. From the moment of his condemnation, the unhappy nobleman behaved with dignified composure. When the warrant came down for his execution, he cheerfully exclaimed, "God's will be done!" and, taking the messenger by the hand, drank his health, and thanked him kindly for the favour, as he called it, assuring him he would not change places with any prince in Europe. His last care was to write a letter to his son, replete with the tenderest sentiments. When the hour of execution approached, he conversed in a cheerful and easy tone with those about him, saying, he died "as a Highland chieftain should die—not in his bed." On mounting the steps of the scaffold, the vast crowd extorted an expression of surprise: "God save us! what a bustle there is about taking off an old grey head, that cannot get up three steps without two men to support it." He then kneeled down to the block, and his head, at one blow was severed from his body.*

Beside the compulsatory alliance Lord Lovat forced upon the Dowager, Lady Lovat, he entered into two other marriages. First, with Margaret, fourth daughter of Ludovick Grant, of Grant; and, secondly, with Primrose, fifth daughter of John Campbell, of Mamore, and sister of John, fourth Duke of Argyle. He left two sons, SIMON, his heir, and Alexander, who *d.* in 1762, with one daughter, Janet, married to Macpherson, of Clunie. By Primrose, his lordship had an only child, ARCHIBALD CAMPBELL, of whom presently. The eldest son, the gallant

GENERAL SIMON FRASER, was at the University of St. Andrew when the rebellion broke out in 1745, and was sent for from thence by his father, to head the clan in support of the Chevalier, which the Master most unwillingly did. In 1746, he joined CHARLES-EDWARD, with six hundred of his father's vassals, and thenceforward was most zealous in the discharge of his duties. His clan was one of the few who effected a junction with the PRINCE on the morning of the engagement at Culloden, and fresh auxiliaries from the tribe were hastening up at the very moment of that ill-judged action. "It were to no purpose at this period (says Mr. Anderson, in his interesting account of the Frasers) to comment on the rashness of an army, exhausted by a night march, in want of food and repose, and thinned by desertion, giving battle to another superior in numbers, animated with the hope of victory, and complete in *material*. In justice to the brave men who contended under such disadvantages, be it enough to say that, by their gallant demeanour, they shed a partial light among the expiring hopes of an unfortunate race." On that dreadful day, the clan Fraser behaved with their wonted resolution, and were permitted to march off unattacked, their pipes playing and colours flying. The Master of Lovat surrendered himself in 1746, was confined in the castle of Edinburgh until August, 1747, when he proceeded to Glasgow, there to remain during the king's pleasure. In 1750, however, a full and free pardon passed the seals for him, and every act of his future life justified the favour of government. An offer of a regiment in the French service was soon after made to Fraser, but refused: he desired leave to be employed in the British army: raised, in 1757, a regiment of eighteen hundred men, of which he was constituted colonel, 5th of Jan. 1757, went at their head to America, and highly distinguished himself at Louisbourg and Quebec, where the regiment suffered much. He was a brigadier-general in the forces sent to Portugal, in 1762, to defend that kingdom against the

* His lordship had a grotesque and singular appearance, but his portrait by Hogarth, supersedes any description.

Spaniards, and was eventually appointed colonel of the 71st regiment, and lieutenant-general in the army. In 1761 he was chosen member of parliament for the county of Inverness, and was constantly rechosen until his death. He died without issue in 1782, and was succeeded in his estate, (to which he had been restored for his distinguished military services) by his half brother,

COLONEL ARCHIBALD-CAMPBELL FRASER, of Lovat. This gentleman had by his wife, Jane, sister of Sir William Fraser, bart. of Leadclune, five sons, all of whom he survived: and, by his demise, in December, 1815, the male descendants of HUGH, ninth Lord Lovat, becoming extinct, the male representation of the family, as well as the right to its extensive entailed estates, devolved upon the junior descendant of Alexander, sixth Lord, whose line is thus deduced,

THE HON. THOMAS FRASER, second son of the sixth lord, was of Knockie, in Inverness-shire, in 1567, as appears by the original charter of Alexander Lord Lovat, "filio nostro Thomæ Fraser," bearing that date. In 1576 he was retoured tutor at law to Simon, Lord Lovat, and subsequently wedded* Isabel, daughter of Forbes, of Corfurdie, and widow of William Chalmers, of Strichen, by whom (who died 30th Nov. 1611, and was buried at Beauly) he left at his decease 24 Oct. 1612, aged sixty-six, a son and successor,

THOMAS FRASER, who was served heir to his father, in the estate of Strichen, 31st Oct. 1612, infeft in the barony of Strichen, on precept from Chancery 10th of the following November, and had precept of *clare constat* from Simon, Lord Lovat, as heir to his father in the lands of Ballicherinoch, Knockie, &c. on the 10th of December. He *m.* first, Christian, dau. of William Forbes, of Tolquhoun, and secondly, Lady Margaret M'Leod, Lady Cargach, relict of Sir Rory M'Kenzie. He *d.* in March 1645, and was succeeded by his son,

THOMAS FRASER, of Strichen, and Moniack, who *m.* Christian, dau. of John Forbes, of Pitsligo, and left (with a dau. Christian, *m.* to Alexander Burnet of Craigmill) a son and successor,

THOMAS FRASER, of Strichen, who wedded (contract of marriage dated in 1656) Marion, daughter of Robert Irvine, of Fedderat, and was father of

ALEXANDER FRASER, of Strichen, who left, by the Lady Emilia Stewart, his wife, (their marriage contract is dated in July, 1697) second dau. of James, Lord Doune, three sons and one daughter, viz.

- I. JAMES, his heir.
- II. ALEXANDER, successor to his brother.
- III. Thomas.
- I. Marion, *m.* in 1715, to James Craig, advocate, professor of civil law in the college of Edinburgh.

The eldest son,

JAMES FRASER, of Strichen, was served heir in general to his father on 16th April, 1702. He died, however, without issue, and was *s.* by his brother,

ALEXANDER FRASER, of Strichen, retoured heir in 1725, who, adopting the profession of the law, was admitted a lord of session 5th June, 1730, and appointed a lord of justiciary in 1736. He held, likewise, the honourable office of general of the Scottish

---

* Thomas Fraser, of Knockie, was in the active discharge of his duties as tutor to his nephew, Simon Lord Lovat, when the widow of Thomas Fraser, son of Philorth, entreated his assistance against the family of Gordon. The widow, by name Isabel, daughter of Forbes, of Corfurdie, had taken as her first husband William Chalmers, of Strichen. This person's elder brother, George Chalmers, had been long abroad, and there was little chance of his returning. William died in the possession of the estate. His widow sometime after married Thomas Fraser, son of Philorth, who assumed the title of "Strichen." But the old proprietors, unwilling to part with their inheritance, threatened to dispossess him; and their disputes led to several fruitless conferences. The Chalmers, in their necessity, had recourse to Gordon, of Gight. He and Fraser met at Old Deer, in the hopes of effecting a compromise, but the overtures of either party meeting with contempt, Gordon, in a rage, followed after Fraser, and coming behind him at the Bridge of Dee, laid him dead with one blow of his two-handed sword. To avenge her cause, Isabel Forbes, now for the second time a widow, detailed her woes to Thomas Fraser, of Knocky. He listened to her complaints, used all his interest in her behalf, and in spite of the opposition of the Earl of Huntley himself, had Gight, his kinsman, condemned; but ultimately released him on paying 5000 merks as an assythement for the murder. Gight was afterwards killed at the battle of Glenlivat. It was Knockie's turn to play the suitor, and the lady, in gratitude for his services, became again a wife. Her husband, to prevent further disputes, bought up the claims of the family of Chalmers. His next business was to arrange matters with the daughters of his wife's former husband, Thomas Fraser. On his death, which happened 24th December, 1576, his widow enjoyed the life-rent of his estate, the fee being provided to the children of the marriage, as appears by a crown charter, "Thomas Fraser de Strichen et Isabellæ Forbes, ejus conjugi," dated 8th October, 1573, on which seisin passes 5th November, 1573.

mint. Lord Strichen was remarkable for having sat the unusually long period of forty-five years on the bench. At the time of the Douglas cause (1768) he was the oldest Scottish judge, being of no less than twenty-four years longer standing than any of his brethren. *Si liceat ludere* (says a late collector of olden memoirs) he must have been one of the judges who sat on the famous case of Effie Deans, *anno* 1736. In the year of his appointment to a seat in the justiciary court, he travelled the autumn circuit to Inverness, and was met by his kinsman, Simon Lord Lovat, a few miles from the town, attended by a great retinue, eager to honour and congratulate him on his new dignity. His Lordship *m.* in 1731, Ann, Countess of Bute, and dying 15th Feb. 1775, left an only son,

ALEXANDER FRASER, of Strichen, who *m.* in 1764, Jean, only daughter of William Menzies, esq., of the parish of St. Ann's, Jamaica, brother of James Menzies, of Culdares, and had four sons and four daughters, viz.

I. ALEXANDER, his heir.
II. Stewart-Mackenzie.
III. Thomas.
IV. William.

I. Frances, died young.
II. Frances-Jean, also died young.
III. Anne.
IV. James,* *m.* (contract dated 1799) to John Morison, esq. of Auchintoul.

Strichen was *s.* by his eldest son,

ALEXANDER FRASER, of Strichen, captain of the 1st regiment of dragoon guards, who had previously, in 1794, obtained the estate by virtue of his father's disposition thereof. He wedded (marriage contract dated 10th May, 1800) Amelia, daughter of John Leslie, esq. of Balquhain, and dying 28th Apr. 1803, was *s.* by his son, the present

THOMAS-ALEXANDER FRASER, of Lovat and Strichen, the twenty-first chief in succession from Simon Fraser, of Inverness-shire; the rights of both houses of Lovat and Strichen having centred in his person, exactly 227 years from the time when the second son of the sixth Lord Lovat acquired the estate of Strichen. Upon the 3d Nov. 1823, he was served nearest and lawful heir male of the body of Hugh, Lord Fraser, of Lovat, grandfather of Thomas Fraser, of Knockie and Strichen; second, nearest and lawful heir male of Hugh Lord Fraser, of Lovat, grand nephew of Thomas Fraser, of Beaufort, otherwise Thomas Lord Fraser, of Lovat; third, nearest and lawful heir male of Thomas Lord Fraser, of Lovat; third, nearest and lawful heir male of Thomas Fraser, of Beaufort, otherwise styled Thos. Lord Fraser, of Lovat, father of Simon Lord Fraser, of Lovat, and grandfather of the Hon. Archibald Fraser, of Lovat: And having presented a petition to his Majesty to recognise his claim to the dignity of Baron Lovat, the same was remitted to the House of Lords before the Lords' Committee for privileges, of which, Lovat, in June, 1827, terminated the proof of his pedigree.

The case was again argued and heard in June and July, 1831, before the House of Lords.

*Arms*—Quarterly, first and fourth, azure, three cinquefoils, arg., for FRASER; 2d and 3d, three antique crowns, gules, arms of concession (vulgarly said to be for Bisset).

*Crest*—A stag's head erased, or, armed, argent.

*Supporters*—Two stags sejant ppr.

*Motto*—Je suis pret.

*Estates*—In Inverness-shire and Aberdeenshire.

*Seats*—Beaufort Castle, Inverness-shire, Strichen House, Aberdeenshire.

* This name appears strange for a lady, but so it is in the pedigree.

## SILVERTOP, OF MINSTER-ACRES.

SILVERTOP, GEORGE, esq. of Minster-Acres, in the county of Northumberland, *b.* 6th January, 1774-5, succeeded his father in 1801.

Mr. Silvertop is a deputy lieutenant for the county palatine of Durham. He was sheriff of Northumberland in 1831, being the first Roman Catholic nominated to the high office after the repeal of the penal laws.

## Lineage.

The first member of this family on record, is

WILLIAM SILVERTOP, esq. of Stella, in the parish of Ryton, and county of Durham, who m. Miss Galley, and left at his decease (he was drowned in the river Tyne, and buried at Ryton) two sons, namely,

ALBERT, his heir.

William, of Blyth, in Northumberland, whose will is dated 27th March, 1722, and was proved 6th November in the same year. He left a son and heir, Robert.

The elder son,

ALBERT SILVERTOP, esq. of Stella, *b.* in February, 1667, *m.* 23d May, 1703, Mary, daughter of Joseph Dunn, esq. of Bladon, and by her (whose will bears date 20th Oct. 1750, and was proved 11th Oct. 1751) had issue,

GEORGE, his successor.

Joseph, *b.* 21st May, 1706, *m.* Mary, daughter of Henry Whittingham, esq. of Whittingham Hall, in Lancashire, by whom (who *d.* in 1768) he left two daughters, viz.

Elizabeth, *m.* to Joseph Dunn, esq. of Bladon.

Bridget, *d.* unm., will dated 19th April, and proved 13th Nov. 1790.

Albert, of Newcastle-upon-Tyne, died unm., will dated 31st July, 1782, proved 16th April, 1790.

Dorothy, *m.* to James Gibson, esq., of Stagshaw Close, in Northumberland.

Mary.

Hellen.

Anne, *d.* unm. in 1764.

He was *s.* at his decease (will dated 21st June, 1736, proved 27th February, 1738-9) by his eldest son,

GEORGE SILVERTOP, esq. of Minster-Acres, in the county of Northumberland, *b.* 22d February, 1705, who *m.* first, Bridget, daughter of Henry Whittingham, esq. of Whittingham Hall, (sister of his brother's wife) and had one son and two daughters, namely,

JOHN, his heir.

Mary, *m.* in 1754, to Sir Thomas Haggerston, bart., and was grandmother of the present Sir Thomas Haggerston. She *d.* 22d May, 1773.

Winifred, *m.* to John Wright, esq. of Kelvedon, in Essex.

He wedded, secondly, Mrs. Pearson, but had no other issue. In a newspaper of 1785, it is stated that this was the third time the lady went before the altar as a bride. Her three husbands having been a Quaker, a Protestant, and a Catholic, each being twice her own age. At sixteen she married a man of thirty-two; at thirty, one of sixty; and at forty-two, a gentleman of about eighty-four. She died in 1808, in her seventy-sixth year.

Mr. Silvertop was *s.* at his decease by his only son,

JOHN SILVERTOP, esq. of Minster-Acres, *b.* at Stella, in 1748, *m.* in June, 1772, Catherine, daughter of Sir Henry Lawson, bt. of Brough Hall, in the county of York, (by Anastasia, daughter of Thomas Maire, esq. of Lartington Hall) and had four sons and a daughter, viz.

I. GEORGE, his heir.

II. John, *b.* 3d August, 1777, *d.* young.

III. Henry Thomas Maire, *b.* 28th May, 1779, *m.* Eliza, daughter of Thomas Witham, esq. of Headlam, in the county palatine of Durham, and niece and heiress of William Witham, esq. of Cliffe, in the county of York. Mr. Henry Silvertop, in consequence, assumed the surname of "Witham," and is the present HENRY WITHAM, esq. of Lartington Hall, (see vol. ii, p. 5), which estate in Yorkshire he inherited from his mother's maternal family, the MAIRES.*

* The late SIR HENRY LAWSON, younger brother of Mrs. Silvertop, assumed the name of MAIRE on inheriting the property of his maternal uncle, John Maire, esq. of Lartington Hall, who devised it until he (Henry) should succeed (if ever) to the Lawson title and estates. To these he did succeed on the death of his only brother, Sir John Lawson, in 1811, and then relinquished the name and lands of MAIRE to Mrs. Silvertop.—BURKE's *Peerage and Baronetage*.

IV. Charles, *b.* 16th Jan. 1781, sometime a colonel in the Spanish service.

I. Mary.

Mr. Silvertop *d.* in 1801, (will proved 14th January, 1802) and was *s.* by his elder surviving son, GEORGE SILVERTOP, esq. now of Minster-Acres.

*Arms*—Arg., a fesse gu., charged with a plate, between three bomb shells, sa., bursting and inflamed ppr.

*Crest*—A wolf's head erased, arg., langued gu., pierced with a broken spear cruented ppr.

*Estates*—In Northumberland and Durham.

*Seat*—Minster-Acres.

### Family of Maire.

JOHN MAIRE, of the City of Durham, descended from the Cheshire family of Meire, of Meire, wedded the eldest daughter and co-heir of Sir Christopher Moresby, knt. of Moresby, in Cumberland, and had a son,

CHRISTOPHER MAIRE, of Durham, living towards the close of the 16th century, who *m.* Anne or Agnes, sister and co-heir of John Hindmarsh, of Aislaby, and had three sons, viz.

I. THOMAS, of Hutton, in Durham, *m.* Margaret, dau. of James Watson, of Sheraton, in the same county, and dying about the year 1613, left a son,
  THOMAS, residing at Hutton, aged fifty-four, 20th August, 1666.

II. Christopher, *d. s. p.*

III. ROBERT, of whom presently.

The third son,

ROBERT MAIRE, of Hardwick, in Durham, married Grace, daughter and sole heir of Henry Smith, of Durham, and had issue,

I. THOMAS, of Hardwick, *b.* in 1602.

II. John, of Hartbushes, *m.* Margaret, dau. of George Meynell, of Dalton, in Yorkshire, and was father of
  Christopher, of Hartbushes, who *m.* Frances, daughter of — Ingleby, esq. of Laukland, and had issue,
    1. George, of Hartbushes, who sold that estate to George Silvertop, esq. of Minster-acres. He *m.* a daughter of John Hussey, esq. of Marnhull, in Dorsetshire, and dying about 1766-7, left three sons, John, Edward, and George, who all died unm. The two latter were in holy orders of the Church of Rome.
    2. Henry, a Catholic clergyman.
    3. Peter, also a priest.
    4. Christopher, likewise in orders. This gentleman, an eminent mathematician, was employed with father Boscovich in surveying and planning the Pope's estates. He died at Ghent.
    5. William, in holy orders, who resided in York, and was accidently drowned while bathing.
    6. John, died unmarried.

III. William, died issueless.

IV. Andrew, of Barnacre, in Lancashire in 1666, *m.* Isabel, daughter of John Richardson, esq. of Merscough, in the same county, and had three sons and three daughters.

The eldest son,

THOMAS MAIRE, esq. of Hardwick, *b.* in 1602, *m.* first, Frances, daughter and sole heiress of Sampson Trollop, of Waterhouse, second son of John Trollop, esq. of Thornley, and had by her two daughters,

I. Ann.

II. Dorothy, *m.* to John Wytham, esq. of Preston on Skerne, in Durham.

He wedded secondly, in 1644, Eleanor, dau. of Ralph Conyers,* esq. of Layton, and had issue,

I. THOMAS, his heir.

II. Ralph, aged nine in 1666, who *m.* Elizabeth Collingwood, of Elvet, and had an only daughter, Mary, who died unmarried.

I. Margaret, *m.* to Charles Howard, esq. of Sunderland Briggs.

The son and successor,

THOMAS MAIRE, esq. of Hardwick, *b.* in 1650, wedded Margaret, daughter and sole heir of Francis Appleby, esq. of Lartington, in the county of York, and thus acquired that estate. He died in 1685, was buried at Monk Hesleden, and succeeded by his son,

THOMAS MAIRE, esq. of Hardwick, in Durham, and of Lartington, in Yorkshire, *b.* in 1672, who inherited, as joint heir with George Baker, esq. of Elemore, the manor of Layton, from John Conyers, esq. The share held by the Maire family was subsequently disposed of to Mr. Baker, and by

* Cuthbert Conyers, High Sheriff of the Palatinate, second son of Sir William Conyers, acquired the manor of Layton, in marriage with Mary, daughter of Thomas Layton, of Saxhoe, and had, with several younger children, RALPH of Layton, who, engaging in the Northern rebellion, was attainted in 1569, and JOHN, whose daughter, Helen, became, as stated in the text, wife of Thomas Maire, esq. of Hardwick.

him conveyed, together with his own portion, to William Russell, esq. of Brancepeth Castle. Mr. Maire espoused Mary, youngest daughter of Richard Fermor, esq. of Tusmore, in Oxfordshire, and had

I. FRANCIS, of Hardwick, who *m.* Anne, daughter of John Clavering, esq. of Callaly, in Northumberland, but died *s. p.* during the lifetime of his father, 29th July, 1746.
II. THOMAS, successor to his father.
III. Richard, died at Douay in 1722.
IV. William, of Elvet, a Catholic Bishop in partibus infidelium, viz. of Cinna, and Vicar Apostolic in the Northern district. He *d.* in 1769.
V. JOHN, successor to his brother Thomas.

I. Anna-Anastacia, *m.* to Sir Henry Lawson, bart. of Brough, in the county of York, and dying 5th Nov. 1764, left issue,
  1. SIR JOHN LAWSON, baronet, of Brough, who died in 1811, leaving two daughters, Anastacia-Maria, *m.* to Thomas Strickland, esq. of Sizergh, and Elizabeth, *m.* to John Wright, esq. of Kelvedon Hall, Essex.
  2. HENRY LAWSON, heir to his uncle, and eventual inheritor of the MAIRE estates.

  1. Mary Lawson, *b.* 7th August, 1742, a nun of the third order of St. Francis, died at Taunton in 1813.
  2. CATHERINE-LAWSON, *b.* in 1747, *m.* John Silvertop, esq. of Minster Acres. Mrs. Silvertop inherited the Maire estates on the demise of her brother, Sir John Lawson.
II. Mary, a Benedictine Nun at Ghent, in Flanders.
III. Henrietta.

Mr. Maire died 29th July, 1752, aged eighty, and was *s.* by his eldest surviving son,

THOMAS MAIRE, esq. of Lartington, who died unm. 25th December, 1762, and was interred at Romaldkirk, in Yorkshire. The estates then passed to his brother,

JOHN MAIRE, esq. of Lartington and Hardwick, who *m.* first, Margaret, daughter of Charles Lowe, esq. of Old Graves, in Derbyshire, and secondly, Mary, (relict of Thomas Wood, esq. of Brayton), daughter of Henry Bedingfeld, esq. of Coulsey Wood, Suffolk, but dying *s. p.* 30th September, 1771, bequeathed his estate to his nephew,

HENRY LAWSON, esq. *b.* 5th January 1751, who assumed in consequence the surname and arms of MAIRE. Succeeding, however, in 1811, to his own family estates, he resumed his original name, the Maire possessions passing to his sister,

CATHERINE LAWSON, who had married John Silvertop, esq. of Minster Acres, and by whose second son, Lartington, &c. is now enjoyed.

## HUTTON, OF MARSKE.

HUTTON, JOHN, esq. of Marske, in the county of York, *b.* 24th September, 1774, succeeded his father in September, 1782.

Mr. Hutton was sheriff of the county of York in 1825.

### Lineage.

This family is descended from the HUTTONS of *Priest Hutton*, in Lancashire. In the grant of arms to the family, dated 1st May, 1584, the following assertion is made by Glover, the herald. "Ex antiqua Huttonorum familia in Lancastriensi Palatinatu nobilibus satis parentibus oriundus."

MATTHEW HUTTON, of Priest Hutton, married and had two sons, viz.

I. EDMUND, of the county of Lancaster, father of
    ROBERT HUTTON, D. D. prebendary of Durham, and rector of Houghton-le-Spring, in the palatinate, for thirty-four years. This learned divine, whose opinions verged on Puritanism, was

prosecuted in the year 1621, before the High Commission Court, for a sermon preached in the cathedral reflecting on the king, the bishop, and the ceremonies of the church. He *m.* Grace, daughter of Leonard Pilkington, D.D. brother of the Right Rev. James Pilkington, Bishop of Durham, by whom (who *d.* 23rd November, 1633,) he left at his decease one son and four daughters,

1. ROBERT, ancestor of the HUTTONS of Houghton-le-Spring, proprietors of an old hall and good estate there (see conclusion).

1. Eleanor, *m.* in 1611, to Sampson Ewbanke, of Bishopwearmouth.
2. Joane, *b.* in 1600, *m.* to Robert Bowes, esq. of Biddic, next brother of Sir George Bowes, knt. of Bradley.
3. Jane, *m.* to Thomas Wright.
4. Elizabeth, *m.* to —Cowper, of Lincolnshire.

II. MATTHEW.

The younger son,

MATTHEW HUTTON, who had taken holy orders, was made Dean of York in 1567; elected Bishop of Durham 9th June, and consecrated 27th July, 1589; and translated to the archiepiscopal see of York 24th March, 1594. He married thrice, but by his first and second wives, Catherine Fulmesby, niece of Godrick, Bishop of Ely, (married in 1564,) and Beatrice, daughter of Sir Thomas Fincham or Finshaw, knt. (she died in 1582,) he had no issue; by the third, Frances, daughter of Sir Martin Bowes, knt. who died 10th August, 1620, he was father of two sons and three daughters, who lived to maturity, namely,

I. TIMOTHY (Sir), his successor.

II. Thomas (Sir), of Popleton, in the county of York, *m.* Ann, daughter of Sir John Bennet, of Dawley, near Uxbridge, and by her (who died in 1651) had (with a daughter, Elizabeth, *b.* 17th February, 1619, who *m.* first, John Robinson, esq. of Deighton; and secondly, Edward Bowles or Bowes, of York, and died in 1662,) a son and successor at his decease, 26th January, 1620,

Richard, of Popleton, who wedded first, Ursula, daughter of Sir Edmund Sheffield, son of Edmund, first Earl of Mulgrave, but had no surviving issue. He *m.* secondly, the Hon. Dorothy Fairfax, daughter of Ferdinand, Viscount Fairfax, and by her, who died in June, 1687, had

Thomas (Sir), his heir.

Richard,* of Pudsey, in the county of York.

Matthew, D. D. fellow of Brazennose College, Oxford, and rector of Aynhoe, *m.* Elizabeth, daughter of Sir Roger Burgoyn, bart. and died in 1711, leaving two sons, Roger and Thomas.

Charles, *m.* Millicent, daughter of Sir Edward Rodes, but *d. s. p.* His widow wedded Robert Banks, prebendary of York, and vicar of Hull, in 1712.

Dorothy.

The eldest son,

Sir Thomas Hutton, of Popleton, *m.* Anne, daughter of Nicholas Stringer, esq. of Sutton-upon-Lound, Notts, and dying in 1700 left

Thomas, of Pudsey, who died unm.†

Dorothy, *m.* to Joshua Earnshaw, lord mayor of York in 1692.

Anne, *m.* to Francis Taylor, gent. of the city of York.

Elizabeth, *m.* to Thomas Dawson, lord mayor of York in 1703.

Ellen, *d.* unm.

I. Thomasine, *m.* to Sir William Gee, of Bishops' Burton, in Yorkshire.

II. Elizabeth, *m.* to Richard Remington, archdeacon of York.

III. Anne, *m.* to Sir John Calverley, bart. of Littleburne, in the county of Durham.

Archbishop Hutton was no less distinguished by a sound judgment, great learning, and eloquence, at once manly and persuasive, than by an honourable independency of

---

* Richard Hutton married Beatrice, daughter and co-heir of James Pudsey, esq. of Pudsey, and dying in 1700, left issue,

Richard, living in 1712, *m.* Mary, daughter of Richard Thorp.

Dorothy, died in 1707.

Anne, } both died unm.
Beatrice, }

Eleanor, *m.* 30th March, 1712, to Joseph Briggs, of Leeds, merchant.

† His sisters, who became his co-heirs, sold the estate of Popleton to Richard Wilson, esq. of Leeds.

character; unhappily not very general in his time or his profession. That prelate was no sycophant who durst preach before a court on the instability of kingdoms and the change of dynasties, and durst ring in ELIZABETH's ears the funeral knell of a succession. He left behind him a landed estate of £500 per annum, which still remains with his descendants. There is a monument to the archbishop in the cathedral of York. His elder son and heir,

SIR TIMOTHY HUTTON, purchased the estate of Marske in 1598, and from that the family has since been designated. He was sheriff of the county of York in 1605, and then received the honour of knighthood. He *m.* Elizabeth, daughter of Sir George Bowes, of Streatlam, in the palatinate of Durham, knight marshal,* and had issue,

- MATTHEW, his successor.
- Timothy, baptized 22nd September, 1601, a merchant at Leeds, *m.* Margaret, daughter of Sir John Bennet, knt.
- Philip, *m.* Elizabeth, daughter of Thomas Bowes, eighth son of Sir George Bowes, of Streatlam, and had, Matthew, Timothy, Thomas, John, Elizabeth, and Anne.

- Beatrice, *m.* to James Mauleverer, esq. of Arncliffe, in the county of York.
- Frances, *m.* to John Dodsworth, esq. of Thornton-Watlass, in Yorkshire.
- Elizabeth, *m.* to Edward Cliburne, esq. of Cliburne, in Westmoreland.

Sir Timothy *d.* in 1629, was buried in St. Mary's Church, Richmond, where there is a splendid monument to his memory, and succeeded by his eldest son,

MATTHEW HUTTON, esq. of Marske, *b.* 22nd October, 1597, *m.* at Hornby, in the county of York, the seat of the lady's father, 22nd April, 1617, Barbara, eldest daughter of Sir Conyers D'Arcy,† afterwards LORD D'ARCY, and sister of Conyers, first Earl of Holderness, by whom he had two sons and four daughters, viz.

- JOHN, his heir, *b.* 6th September, 1626.
- Timothy, twin with his brother.

- Dorothy, *b.* at Marske, 22nd July, 1620, *m.* to Sir Philip Warwick, knt. who was interred at Marske, 6th August, 1644.
- Barbara, *b.* at Richmond, in Yorkshire, 23rd October, 1630, *m.* at Marske, 16th April, 1655, to Thomas Lyster, esq. of Bawtry.
- Mary, *b.* at Marske, 4th February, 1637, *m.* to Richard Pierse, esq. of Hutton Bonville, in the county of York.
- Elizabeth, *b.* at Richmond, 4th March, 1638.

Mr. Hutton was *s.* at his decease by his elder son,

JOHN HUTTON, esq. of Marske, who *m.* Frances, second daughter of Bryan Stapylton, esq. of Myton, in the county of York (see vol. ii. p. 209), and had issue,

- JOHN, his successor.

- Frances, *m.* to Andrew Wanley, esq. of Iford, in the county of Gloucester.
- Barbara, *b.* in 1655, *d.* in 1695.
- Olyfe, *b.* in 1656, *m.* to Thomas Alcock, esq. of Chatham.
- Elizabeth, *b.* in 1657, *d.* in 1718.
- Henrietta, *b.* in 1660, buried at Marske in 1728.

He was *s.* by his only son,

JOHN HUTTON, esq. of Marske, *b.* 14th July, 1659, *m.* Dorothy, daughter of William Dyke, esq. of Trant, in Sussex, and *d.* in February, 1730-1 (he was buried on the 2nd March following), leaving issue,

- I. JOHN, his heir.
- II. MATTHEW, D.D. Archbishop of Canterbury, *b.* in 1692, *d.* 19th March, 1758. His grace *m.* Mary, daughter of John Lutman, gent. of Petworth, in the county of Sussex, and had two daughters,
  - Dorothy, *m.* to Francis Popham,

* By his second wife, Jane, daughter of Sir John Talbot, knt.

† The male representation of the old and noble family of D'Arcy having devolved upon this gentleman, he presented a petition to *King* CHARLES I. in 1640, setting forth that after the attainder of Thomas, Lord D'Arcy, his great-grandfather, in the 29th of HENRY VIII., Sir George D'Arcy, knt. eldest son of the said Thomas, being restored in blood by *King* EDWARD VI., obtained a grant of the title and dignity of Lord D'Arcy to himself and the heirs male of his body; and that by the death of John, Lord D'Arcy, late of Aston, in Yorkshire, without issue male in the eleventh of his majesty's reign, the title and dignity of Lord D'Arcy was utterly extinct; and praying, that being grandchild and heir male of Sir Arthur D'Arcy, knt. and likewise son and heir of Elizabeth, daughter and co-heir of John, Lord Conyers, lineal heir to Margery, daughter and co-heir to Philip, Lord D'Arcy, son of John, Lord D'Arcy, one of the barons of the realm in the time of HENRY IV., that his Majesty would please to declare, restore, and confirm to him, the said SIR CONYERS D'ARCY, and to the heirs male of his body, the dignity of LORD D'ARCY, with such precedency as the said John, Lord D'Arcy, had, and by right from his ancestors then enjoyed; whereupon his MAJESTY, graciously condescending, did by letters patent, dated at Westminster, 10th August, 1641, restore and confirm to the said Sir Conyers D'Arcy and the heirs male of his body the dignity of BARON D'ARCY.—BURKE's *Extinct and Dormant Peerage.*

esq. of Littlecott, and died without issue (see vol. ii. p. 200).
MARY.
III. Timothy.
IV. Thomas.

I. Elizabeth, *b.* in 1683, *d.* in 1759.
II. Frances, *b.* in 1686, *d.* in 1772.
III. Dorothy.
IV. Barbara.
V. Henrietta, *b.* in 1701, *m.* to John Dodsworth, esq. of Thornton-Watlass, in the county of York, *d.* in 1797.

The eldest son and heir,

JOHN HUTTON, esq. of Marske, *b.* in 1691, married, first, Barbara Barker, of York, and had issue,

JOHN, his successor.
Matthew, *b.* in 1732, *d.* unm. 31st December, 1782.
James, *b.* in 1739, *d.* at Aldborough, in the county of York, on the 2nd March, 1798, and was buried on the 9th of the same month at Masham. He *m.* Mary, daughter of John Hoyle, esq. of Ashgill, in Yorkshire.

Anne, *b.* in 1731, *m.* to George-Wanley Bowes, esq. of Thornton, in the county of York, and had three dau. their father's co-heirs, viz.
Margaret-Wanley Bowes.
Anne Bowes, *m.* to Thomas Thoroton, esq. late lieutenant-colonel of the Coldstream Regiment of Guards.
Elizabeth Bowes, *m.* to the Rev. Robert Croft.
Elizabeth, *m.* Henry Pulleine, esq. of Carleton Hall, in the county of York.

Mr. Hutton wedded, secondly, Elizabeth, daughter of James, Lord D'Arcy, of the kingdom of Ireland, but had no other issue. He *d.* in 1768, and was *s.* by his eldest son,

JOHN HUTTON, esq. of Marske, *b.* 30th September, 1730, *m.* Anne, daughter of Richard Ling, of Appleby, and had four sons, viz.

I. JOHN, his heir.
II. James, a captain in the army, born 24th January, 1776, died at Marske 24th January, 1803.
III. Matthew, a captain in the army, *b.* 31st December, 1777, *d.* 12th December, 1813, buried at Marske.
IV. Timothy, of Clifton Castle, in the county of York, *b.* 16th October, 1779, *m.* 12th December, 1804, Elizabeth, daughter of William Chaytor, esq. of Croft, in the same county (see vol. ii. p. 143).

Mr. Hutton died on the 24th September, 1782, and was *s.* by his eldest son, JOHN HUTTON, esq. now of Marske.

*Arms*—Gu. on a fess between three cushions arg. fringed and tasselled or, as many fleurs-de-lys of the field.

*Crest*—On a cushion gu. placed lozengeways, an open book, the edges gilt, with the words *Odor Vitæ* inscribed.

*Motto*—Spiritus gladius.

*Estates*—In Yorkshire.

*Seat*—Marske, near Richmond, Yorkshire.

## Hutton, of Houghton le Spring.

ROBERT HUTTON, (son and heir of Dr. Hutton, prebendary of Durham, by his wife Grace Pilkington,) born in 1597, wedded in 1619, Elizabeth, daughter of Christopher Fulthorpe, esq. of Tunstall, and had issue,

I. ROBERT, his heir.
II. Robert, of Lynn, in Norfolk, *d. s. p.*
III. Christopher, merchant, of Newcastle-on-Tyne, married Catherine, daughter of Robert Bowes, esq. of Biddic, and died in 1682, leaving two daughters, viz.
Mary, married in 1690, Ralph Robinson, esq. second son of Ralph Robinson, esq. of Herrington.
Catherine, married in 1696 to the Rev. Edward Weddell, Curate of Houghton le Spring.
I. Grace, married to Robert Lascels, esq. of Sowerby.
II. Mary, married to John Mason, of Notts.
III. Frances, married to Captain George Mason.
IV. Anne, married to William Levinge, of Leicestershire.
V. Eleanor, married to John Gore, of Dublin.
VI. Joan, died unmarried.

Robert Hutton died about the year 1643, and was succeeded by his son,

ROBERT HUTTON, esq. of Houghton le Spring, who, in the command of a troop of horse-guards in Cromwell's army, served throughout the whole of the Scottish campaign; and was with Monk at the storming and plunder of Dundee. After the restoration he remained zealously attached to the Puritans; which may probably account for his being buried in his own orchard, where an altar tomb still bears the following inscription: "Hic jacet Robertvs Hvtton Armiger qui obiit, Avg. die nono, 1680. Et moriendo vivit." To this gentleman, the theme of much village tradition, the erection of the family mansion is generally attributed; and, if the same tradition be credited, with the plunder obtained at the sacking of Dundee; but "the building itself," says Mr. Surtees, "affords strong evidence of an earlier date, and may, more probably be ascribed to the Rector of Houghton, the founder of the family, between the years 1589 and 1623." Its external structure is an oblong square, the corresponding sides exactly uniform, and the chief front to the west equally plain with the rest, without façade, or ornamented door-ways. The windows are regular, divided into five, or into three lights, by stone mullions; and the leads are surmounted by a plain pediment. The mansion has undergone little either of repair or alteration; and, as it has been built with a massy solidity, calculated to resist the injuries of time and neglect, it presents, perhaps, at this day, one of the most perfect specimens extant, of the plain durable style of architecture, which distinguished the *Old Hall House*, the residence of the middling gentry in the reign of JAMES, or ELIZABETH.

The choice of Captain Hutton's burial-place is assigned, by tradition, to another cause than puritanical feeling. On the death of his favourite charger, he requested permission, it is stated, from the rector of Houghton, to inter the animal within the church-yard, near to his own intended future place of rest; but, on being refused, buried the horse in his orchard, and determined to repose himself close to the remains of his faithful servant.

Albert Hutton married Elizabeth, daughter of Thomas Shadforth, esq. of Eppleton, in Durham, by Margaret, his wife, daughter of Marmaduke Blakiston, Prebendary of Durham, and left a son and successor,

ROBERT HUTTON, esq. of Houghton le Spring, baptized 3rd February, 1666, who wedded Jane, daughter of John Garshell, gentleman, of Newcastle, and was father of

ROBERT HUTTON, esq. of Houghton le Spring, who *m.* 4th October, 1714, Elizabeth, daughter of the Rev. Sir George Wheeler, knt. Rector of Houghton, and prebendary of Durham, and had issue,

- I. ROBERT, his heir.
- II. George, born in 1722, married in 1753, Elizabeth, daughter of John Coles, of Ditcham, Hants, and had a son,
  - JOHN, successor to his uncle.

- I. Grace, born the 6th of April, 1717, married to John Woodifield, esq. of Yarm, in Yorkshire, and was mother of
  - Mary Woodifield, *m.* to George Bulman, esq.

Mr. Hutton died in 1725, was buried on the 22nd of October in that year, and succeeded by his son,

ROBERT HUTTON, esq. of Houghton le Spring, Barrister-at-law, and Justice of the Peace for the County of Durham, born on the 6th of October, 1715. This gentleman *d. s. p.* in 1764, and was succeeded by his nephew,

The REV. JOHN HUTTON, M.A. of Houghton le Spring, in Durham, and of Tenderden Hole, in Kent, a Magistrate for both Counties. He wedded Sylvestra, daughter of James Monypenny, esq. but *d. s. p.* when this branch became Extinct.

## BANKES, OF KINGSTON HALL.

BANKES, WILLIAM JOHN, esq. M.A. of Kingston Hall, in the county of Dorset, and of Soughton Hall, in Flintshire, succeeded to the former at the decease of his father in 1834, having previously inherited the latter on the demise of his great-uncle, the Right Hon. Sir William Wynne, in 1815.

Mr. Bankes, as lord of Corfe Castle, is lord lieutenant and admiral of the Isle of Purbeck, and lord of the hundred of Robarrow and Hasilor. He was elected, in 1821, M. P. for the University of Cambridge, and for the county of Dorset in 1831.

Mr. Bankes is known in the literary world by his Travels in the East.

## Lineage.

The family of BANKES, now for more than two hundred years one of the most influential in the county of Dorset, is deemed by *Fuller* to have been of antiquity;* its elevation is, however, to be traced to the learned professor of the law.

SIR JOHN BANKES, lord chief justice of the common pleas in the time of CHARLES I. This eminent person, the son of John Bankes,† a merchant, by his wife Elizabeth Hassell, was born towards the close of the sixteenth century, and admitted a commoner of Queen's College, Oxford, in 1604. He retired, however, from the University, without taking a degree, and settled at a very early age in Gray's Inn, by the society of which he was called to the bar, and in a brief period attained the reputation of a sound lawyer and able advocate. After graduating through minor offices, he was appointed attorney-general in 1634, and in that capacity appeared for the Crown in the celebrated cause instituted in the Exchequer against the patriot HAMPDEN for his refusal to pay the arbitrary imposition of ship-money. This cause was argued twelve days in the Exchequer Chamber before the assembled judges of England, and decided in favour of the Crown. Sir John Bankes was soon afterwards (1640) constituted LORD CHIEF JUSTICE OF THE COURT OF COMMON PLEAS. Through the subsequent perils that encompassed his royal master, the chief justice adhered with unshaken fidelity to his cause, and attaching himself personally to the king, followed his majesty to York. In his absence, Corfe Castle, the place of his abode, was invested by the rebels, but gallantly defended by his heroic wife, and not surrendered eventually, until betrayed. The name of this distinguished woman was MARY HAWTREY, only daughter of Robert Hawtrey, esq. of Riselip.

The lord chief justice having joined the king at York in Easter term 1642, Lady Bankes, with her children and family, retired to Corfe Castle, and remained in peace there until May, 1643, when the rebels, commanded by Sir Walter Erle and Sir Thomas Trenchard, and already in possession of all the towns on the sea coast, resolving to make themselves masters of this Castle, attacked it with a body of between two and three hundred horse and foot, but were forced to retire. On the 23rd of the succeeding month, however, Sir Walter Erle, with Captains Sydenham, Jarvis, and Scott, and five or six hundred men, renewed the siege, and brought several pieces of ordnance to bear upon the Castle. They obliged the soldiers by oath to give no quarter in case of a resistance, and endeavoured by all means to corrupt the defendants. To render their approach to the walls more secure, they constructed two engines, one called the *Boar*, the other the *Sow*, framed of boards lined with wool to deaden the shot. When the sow moved forward, the besieged aimed at the legs of the bearers which were not covered, killed one, and compelled the rapid flight of the others. The boar dared not advance. After the loss of much time and ammunition, the Earl of Warwick sent Sir Walter one hundred and fifty manners, besides several cartloads of petards, grenadoes, &c. for an assault; £20 were offered to the first man that would scale the wall, but as this order had no effect, the commanders made the men drunk with strong waters, and thus excited, stormed the castle on all sides. The besiegers divided their forces into two parties; one assaulted the middle ward, defended by Capt. Larrence, and the greater part of the garrison; the other attacked the upper ward, which Lady Bankes, her daughters, women, and five soldiers protected, and, to her eternal honour, bravely saved it; for by rolling over stones and hot embers, they repulsed the assailants, and killed and wounded above one hundred men. Sir Walter Erle, hearing that the king's forces, under the Earl of Caernarvon, were advancing, retired in great haste, to London, and left Sydenham to bring off the ordnance, ammunition, and remainder of the soldiers, who retired into the church, intending to march off in the night; but, just as supper was set on the table, an alarm was given that the royal army approached: whereupon Sydenham quitted his supper, artillery, and ammu-

* The Lord-Chief-Justice's ancestors possessed property at and about Kesurck, in Cumberland.

† Whose father was John Bankes, and his mother Jane Multon.

›n, and took boat for Poole, leaving one dred horses on the shore, which the be-ed made their prize. Thus, after six ks' strict siege, Corfe Castle, the key of setshire, was, by the resolution of Lady kes, and the valour of Capt. Laurence about eighty soldiers, with the loss of two men, preserved. In the years 5 and 1646 it was again blockaded by Parliament forces, and at length be-ed by Lieut.-colonel Pitman, an officer ie garrison. When it was delivered up, Commons ordered Corfe Castle to be n up with gunpowder, and thus that ent and magnificent fabric was reduced heap of ruins, and remains a lasting orial of the destructive wars of the reign ie unhappy Charles.

ir John Bankes *d.* in 1644, universally emed for his integrity as a judge, his de-on as a subject, and admitted by all ies to have been one of the brightest iments of the eventful era in which he l. He was *s.* by his eldest surviving

IR RALPH BANKES, of Corfe Castle, who ived the honour of knighthood in 1660. m. Mary, only daughter and heiress of Bruen, esq. of Athelhampton, and with a daughter Mary, who *d.* unm. an son JOHN, his heir. Sir Ralph erected gston Hall, and dying about the year ), was *s.* by his son,

OHN BANKES, esq. of Kingston Hall, who resented the borough of Corfe Castle in it successive parliaments. He wedded rgaret, daughter of Sir Henry Parker, whom (who *m.* secondly, Thomas Lewis, of London) he had, with other children died issueless, two sons and a daughter,

JOHN, } heirs in succession.
HENRY, }

Mary, *m.* to Sir Thomas Anson, bart.

*d.* in 1714, and was *s.* by his elder son,

OHN BANKES, esq. of Kingston Hall. s gentleman, who represented Corfe tle in parliament, dying issueless, in 2, was *s.* by his brother,

HENRY BANKES, esq. of Kingston Hall, rister-at-law, king's counsel, M.P. for rfe Castle, and one of the commissioners the customs. He *m.* first, Eleanor, ghter of Richard Symonds, esq. of Lon-, and, secondly, Margaret, daughter of Right Rev. JOHN WYNNE, D.D. bishop Bath and Wells, and co-heir of her bro-r, the Right Hon. Sir William Wynne, t. chief judge of the prerogative court d dean of the arches. By the first lady had no issue. By the second he had two s and a daughter, namely,

John, who *d.* young.
HENRY, his heir.
Anne, died in 1778.

Mr. Bankes died in 1776, and was *s.* by his only surviving son,

HENRY BANKES, esq. of Kingston Hall. This gentleman represented Corfe Castle from 1780 to 1826, and the county of Dorset from that time until 1831, when, after a spirited struggle, he was defeated at the general election by the supporters of the great measure of parliamentary reform then pending. Upon that occasion the independent and manly deportment of the staunch and venerable tory (for to that political party Mr. Bankes had always attached himself) extorted commendation from the most determined of his political opponents. Mr. Bankes *m.* in 1784, Frances, daughter of William Woodley, esq. governor of the Leeward Islands, and had issue,

I. HENRY, lost at sea, in the Athenienne man-of-war, in 1806.
II. WILLIAM-JOHN, heir to his father and great uncle.
III. GEORGE, of Studland, in the isle of Purbeck, M.P. for Corfe Castle from 1818 to 1823, and again in 1826, one of the lords of the treasury in 1830, subsequently secretary of the board of control, and cursitor baron, *m.* Georgina-Charlotte, only daughter and heiress of Admiral Edmund-Charles Nugent, and has three sons and five daughters, viz.
    Edmund-George, *b.* 24th April, 1826.
    Henry-Hyde-Nugent, *b.* 11th April, 1828.
    Edward-Dee, *b.* 12th Jan. 1831.
    Georgina-Charlotte-Frances.
    Maria-Margaret.
    Adelaide.
    Augusta-Anne, } twins.
    Octavia-Elizabeth, }
IV. Edward, in holy orders, rector of Corfe Castle, and prebendary of Gloucester and Bristol cathedrals, *m.* in 1820, Lady Frances-Jane-Scott, younger daughter of John, Earl of Eldon, lord chancellor of England, and has issue, John Scott, Eldon-Surtees, and Frances.

I. Anne-Frances, *m.* to Edward, present Earl of Falmouth.
II. Maria-Wynne, *m.* to the late Hon. Thomas Stapleton, son and heir of Lord Le Despencer.

"Mr. Bankes," says a writer in the Gentleman's Magazine, "was an accomplished scholar, intimately acquainted with ancient and modern literature, and of a refined and acknowledged taste in the arts; accomplishments that enabled him peculiarly to grace his duties as one of the most active and zealous trustees of the British Museum, of which he was generally regarded as the organ and advocate in the House of Commons. His public life was marked by firmness in principle, a peculiar disinterestedness and undeviating adherence to conscientiously-formed opinions. He was the author of "The Civil and Constitutional History of Rome, from the Foundation to the Age of Augustus," published in 1818, in two volumes, 8vo. He died 17th Dec. 1834, and was succeeded by his eldest surviving son, the present WILLIAM JOHN BANKES, esq. of Kingston Hall.

*Arms*—Sa. a cross engrailed erm. between four fleurs-de-lys or, quartering Bruen, Martin, Pydel, Wynne, and Jones.

*Crest*—A Moor's head, full faced, couped at the shoulders ppr. on the head a cap of maintenance gu. turned up erm. adorned with a crescent, whence issues a fleur-de-lys.

*Estates*—In the counties of Dorset, Flint, Caernarvon, and Merioneth, with black-lead mines in Boroughdale, in Cumberland.

*Seats*—Kingston Hall, and Soughton Hall.

# PIPER, OF CULLITON.

PIPER, ROBERT-SLOPER, esq. a captain in the corps of Royal Engineers, *b.* 1st March, 1790, *m.* 15th January, 1824, Mary, eldest daughter of Francis Barrow,* esq. of Strood, in Kent, and has an only child, ROBERT WILLIAM, *b.* 6th December, 1824.

Captain Piper, who has been for more than twenty-six years a commissioned officer, served six campaigns under the Duke of Wellington in the Peninsula, France, and Flanders.

## Lineage.

This family, originally of the kingdom of Saxony, derives its descent from Magnus Piper, of Nieustadt, in Holstein, whose ancestors were from Lubec.

JOHN PIPER,* esq. formerly a captain in the 6th regiment of infantry, and late of Culliton House, in the county of Devon, the first of the family who naturalized in

* This gentleman had an elder and only brother, who, dying from the effects of a severe contusion, left two sons,

I. JOHN PIPER, formerly captain in the 102nd regiment.
II. HUGH PIPER, a lieutenant-colonel in the army, and commanding His Majesty's 38th regiment in Bengal.

* The ancestors of FRANCIS BARROW, esq. were, in the time of CHARLES II. the proprietors of the manor of Graveney, in the parishes of Hartlip, Linton, Borden, &c. several portions of which are still held by the surviving descendants. Mr. Barrow married Elizabeth, daughter and heir of Mathew Kirby, esq. of Chatham, and West Farleigh, in Kent, and had issue,

I. Francis, in holy orders, born in 1791, *m.* Ann Maude Boys, and has an only child, Francis.
II. George, born in 1806, *d.* unm.

I. MARY, married, as in the text, to CAPTAIN PIPER.
II. Ann, *d.* unm.
III. Elizabeth, *m.* in 1823, to John Schenick Grant, esq. an officer of engineers in the Hon. East India Company's Service.

land, being destined at an early age for military profession, was sent to Berlin education, and in the year 1757, having pleted his course of study, entered the ssian service as a volunteer. He subently obtained a commission in the lish army. He was present at the bat of Minden, where he was severely nded through both legs, and afterwards ed in the West Indies, participating in apture of Martinique. Hostilities comcing soon after with America, he proed, about the year 1769, to that counwith the 25th regiment, and being apted to the staff, continued to act there 1782. He then returned to England, ed entirely from active life in 1788, and hased the property of Culliton, in Dehire, from Sir John De la Pole, bart. bute, on which he resided until his dee in 1802, in the sixty-second year of ige. He *m.* Frances, second daughter co-heir of Stephen Airault, esq. of iport, Rhode Island, (the only survivrepresentative of a distinguished and opulent Hugunot family, which emied from La Rochelle upon the revocaof the edict of Nantes),* and had issue,

I. JOHN, *b.* in 1783, C.B. late lieutenant-colonel of the 4th, or King's Own, regiment of infantry, who, after having served his country for a period of twenty-five years, in Canada, Holland, Denmark, Flanders, Sweden, Spain, Portugal, France, and the West Indies, fell a sacrifice to the pernicious effects of climate in the thirty-eighth year of his age, in 1821, hastened by exhaustion from the last and almost mortal wound he received, in the vertebræ of the neck, in the neighbourhood of Bayonne, in November, 1813, whilst successfully holding in check, with the 4th and 84th regiments, the utmost efforts of a column of the French army under Marshal Soult, to turn the left flank of the British position at the passage of the Nive. Besides the cross of the Bath, Lieutenant-colonel Piper had the honour to earn five other medals, all of which, commemorative of his services, His Royal Highness, the late commander-in-chief, permitted his family to retain.

II. Samuel-Airault, *b.* in 1787, M.D. surgeon of the 30th regiment, *m.* in 1823, Miss Augusta Adlam. This gentleman entered the army in 1806, and has since that period served several years on the Madras establishment in the East Indies, and three years in the Island of Ceylon.

III. ROBERT-SLOPER, as above.

I. Mary-Ann, *m.* to A. Mackenzie, esq.

II. Anne, *d.* unm.

III. Elizabeth, *m.* in 1813, to William Cox, esq. a retired officer of the 12th regiment of infantry, and has issue.

*Arms*—Quarterly, embattled or and ermine; over all an eagle displayed sa.

*Crest*—A cubit arm encircled with a wreath of laurel ppr. grasping a boar's head erased sa.

*Motto*—Feroci fortior.

*Estates*—In the county of Kent, acquired by marriage.

---

PIERRE AIRAULT, (the ancestor of Mr. Ste- Airault, above mentioned,) a native of rs, in Anjou, was many years advocate to rliament of Paris, master of requests to the of Anjou, and chief magistrate of the cricourt of Angers. He *m.* Anne des Jardins, ied in 1601, aged sixty-eight, leaving a nus family. His eldest son, RENE, changed ligion; and rose to high preferment, being nted provincial attorney of the provinces of ipagne and Lyons at the court of Rome, and of Rheims, Dizon, and Dole. He died in PIERRE, his second son, succeeded his as president and seneschal of Angers, and ellor of the city, appointments continued in mily until the year 1761. He *m.* his couand left several children, amongst whom Pierre, René, and Guyonne: from the se- Stephen Airault claimed to be descended. nne wedded her cousin, Menagen, the king's ate of the Court of Appeals at Angers.

# BURTON, OF SACKETT'S HILL HOUSE.

**BURTON, SIR RICHARD,** knt. of Sackett's Hill House, in the County of Kent, *b.* 23rd November, 1773, *m.* 27th April, 1802, Elizabeth, only daughter of the late Robert Crofts, esq. of Dumpton House, Isle of Thanet, and has had issue,

I. JOHN, *b.* in 1804, *m.* in 1829, Mary Helena, eldest daughter of Captain George Robinson, R. N. and dying in 1833, left one son and one daughter, viz.
 RICHARD, born in 1830.
 Elizabeth-Ann.
II. Richard, *b.* in 1806, Captain 54th Regiment of Foot, died in 1832.
III. Robert, *b.* in 1807, *m.* in 1828, Mary, youngest dau. of the late Rev. Robert Rastall, Rector of Winthorpe, Notts, and has two sons,
 Robert-Heron, *b.* in 1829.
 Richard-Crofts, *b.* in 1833.
IV. Francis, *b.* in 1809.
V. Carr, *b.* in 1811.

I. Frances-Sarah, *m.* in 1831, to Latham Osborn, esq.
II. Honor.

Sir Richard Burton, who received the honour of knighthood in 1831, succeeded his father in 1809.

## Lineage.

The early records having been destroyed during the civil wars of the reign of CHARLES I. the pedigree of this family can authentically be traced only as far back as

JOHN BURTON, son of Arthur Burton, esq. of Killing Hall, near Ripley, in Yorkshire, who was born in the year 1628, and died in 1715. He was father of

JOHN BURTON, esq. *b.* in 1675, who *m.* first, Edith Meager, and secondly, Dorcas, widow of Colonel Howe, and daughter of the Bishop of Peterborough. By both wives he had issue. He died in 1755, and was succeeded by his son,

RICHARD BURTON, esq. *b.* 1718, Colonel in the York Militia, who wedded in 1742, Frances Ward, of Stockholm, and had five sons and one daughter, namely,

I. JOHN, his heir.
II. Richard, *b.* in 1749, and died in 1750.
III. William, *b.* in 1749, *d.* in 1785.
IV. Arthur, *b.* in 1755, and *d.* in 1813.
V. Richard, *b.* in 1761, and *d.* in 1762.
I. Georgina-Elizabeth.

Colonel Burton died in 1792, and was *s.* by his son,

SIR JOHN BURTON, knt. of Wakefield, in the county of York, *b.* in 1744, who *m.* first, in 1770, Honor, dau. of John Harvey-Thursby, esq. of Abington, in Northamptonshire, (the descendant of an ancient family which claims to be of Saxon origin), by Honor, his wife, dau. of Robert Pigot, esq. of Chetwynd, in Salop, and had, to survive infancy, an only son, RICHARD, his heir. He espoused, secondly, Phillippa Irnham Forster, of Buxton Vale, near Alnwick, in Northumberland, and by her had a son, John, *b.* and *d.* in 1801, and a dau. Phillippa-Frances. Sir John *d.* in 1809, and was *s.* by his son, the present Sir RICHARD BURTON, of Sackett's Hill House.

*Arms*—Sa. a chev. erm. between three crowned owls arg.

*Crest*—A beacon ppr.

*Motto*—Vigilans.

*Estates*—Sackett's Hill, Isle of Thanet, Renville near Canterbury, in Kent and Ayr and Calder Navigation, West Riding of Yorkshire.

*Seat*—Sackett's Hill House.

# TOWNSHEND, OF HEM AND TREVALLYN.

TOWNSHEND, JOHN, esq. of Hem and Trevallyn, in the county of Denbigh, n on the 20th of October, 1791, succeeded his father 17th of August, 1826.

## Lineage.

R ROBERT TOWNSHEND, gentleman of Privy Chamber to *King* CHARLES II. the first knight made by his majesty, is return to London in 1660, was the of William Agborough, esq. by Anne, rife, daughter of Edward Wythes, esq. Copgrove, in Yorkshire, which lady ying, secondly, Aurelian Towns-, esq. her son by her first husband ned the surname and arms of Towns-. Sir Robert left at his decease a son successor,

NTHONY TOWNSHEND, esq. of Hem, in county of Denbigh, who married Mary, hter of Sir John Dugdale, son of the rated Sir William Dugdale, Garter at Arms, and was father of

HN TOWNSHEND, esq. of Hem, who led, first, Mary, daughter of Sir Wil- Meredyth, bart. of Henbury, in Che-, by whom he had no issue; and, ndly, Frances, born in 1702, relict of uel Minshull, esq. and daughter and ss of Nathaniel Lee, esq. of Darnhall, ie Palatinate, by whom he had six sons three daughters, viz.

I. JOHN, his heir.

II. Robert, an officer in the 44th regiment, killed with General Braddock, in North America, *anno*. 1756.

III. William, died unmarried.

IV. Edward, of Wincham and Antrobus, by will of Hester Legh, of Adlington, her only son Thomas Legh, esq. having predeceased her, without issue. Edward Townshend, who was born on the 4th of Feb. 1736-7, married first, 1763, Frances, daughter of Thomas Lee, esq. of Coton, by whom he had no child to survive infancy; and, secondly, in 1773, Anne, eldest dau. of the Rev. John Baldwin, of Hoole, by whom he had

Edward-Venables, of Wincham, born on the 31st of August, 1774, who married Cornelia Anne, daughter of Josias Dupre, esq. of Wilton Park, Berks, Governor of Madras, and had issue,

Hester-Lee, married to the Rev. Richard Massie, of Coddington. (See p. 44.)

Wilhelmina-Maria, died unm.

Sidney.

Barbara-Anne, died unm. in 1806.

Arabella.

Harriet-Frances.

V. Thomas, of Wilbrigton Hall, in the county of Stafford, born on the 25th of August, 1738, married, first, Anne, only daughter and heiress of George Mainwaring, esq. of Bromborough, widow of Massie Taylor, esq. and, secondly, Mary, daughter of Henry Hesketh, esq. of Newton, but had no issue.

VI. George-Salisbury, born on the 19th of April, 1742, married Frances, dau. of the Rev. John Brooke, of Blacklands, in Shropshire, and dying on the 29th of September, 1801, left a son,

George Brooke Brigges Townshend, of Houghton, who assumed the surname of Brooke, by sign manual, on the 28th of March, 1797, and was Sheriff of Salop, in 1811. He married Henrietta, daughter of William Massey, esq. of Moreton Hall, in Cheshire, and has issue.

I. Frances,
II. Susan,
III. Anne,
} who all died unmarried.

Mr. Townshend was succeeded at his decease by his eldest son,

JOHN TOWNSHEND, esq. of Hem, in the county of Denbigh, and of Whitby in Cheshire, born on the 3rd of October, 1730, who married, 1760, Anne, daughter of Henry Bennett, esq. of Moston, in the latter county, and had issue,

I. JOHN-STANISLAUS, his heir.

I. Elizabeth,
II. Frances-Anne,
III. Frances-Sarah,
} died unmarried.
IV. Sarah-Susanna, *m.* in 1800, to the Rev. Charles Mainwaring, of Oteley Park, Salop.

Mr. Townshend died 8th April, 1778, was buried at Gresford, and succeeded by his son,

JOHN-STANISLAUS TOWNSHEND, esq. of Hem, and Trevallyn, who married on the 3rd of August, 1790, Dorothea, only child of Thomas Gladwin, esq. a younger son of Henry Gladwin, esq. of Stubbing, in Derbyshire, and had seven sons and three daughters, viz.

I. JOHN, his heir.
II. Thomas-George, died at Calcutta, in 1819.
III. Henry-Dive, Capt. in the Army.
IV. George, settled in New South Wales, married Elizabeth, daughter of E. J. Manning, esq.
V. Salusbury, died young.
VI. Bennett-Vere, in Holy Orders.
VII. Charles, married Mary Anne, dau. of Francis Barker, esq.

I. Dorothea, *m.* to the Rev. George Cunliffe, Vicar of Wrexham, youngest son of Sir Foster Cunliffe, bart. of Acton Park.
II. Anne.
III. Susanna, married to Captain Henry Meredith Mostyn, Royal Navy, of Segrwydd, and Llewesog Lodge, in the county of Denbigh.

Mr. Townshend died on the 17th of Aug. 1826, and was succeeded by his eldest son, the present John Townshend, esq. of Hem, and Trevallyn.

*Arms*—Az. a chev. engrailed between three escallops erm.

*Crest*—A roebuck's head attired, or, gorged with a collar, az. charged with three escallops arg.

*Mottos*—Huic generi incrementa fides: and, as representative of the Lees of Darnhall, Vince malum patientiâ.

*Estates*—Hem and Trevallyn, in the parish of Gresford, and township of Allington, in the county of Denbigh.

*Seat*—Trevallyn, near Wrexham.

## Lee, of Lee and Darnhall.

JOHN LEE, of Lee, son of John Lee, of Lee, by his wife, a daughter of Dutton, of Dutton, was living in the time of EDWARD I. He married Elizabeth, daughter of Sir Thomas Fulleshurst, of Crewe, and had, with six younger sons, and one daughter, Isabel, his successor,

THOMAS LEE, of Lee, in Cheshire, 15 EDWARD II. and 11 EDWARD III. who wedded the daughter of Sir John Aston, knt. and was succeeded by his son,

JOHN LEE, of Lee, living 22nd of EDWARD III. who married Margery, daughter of Henry Hockenhull, and had issue,

I. THOMAS, his heir.
II. John, of Aston, in Staffordshire, *m.* and had issue.
III. William, of Essex, married, and had issue.
IV. Robert, of Aston, married, and had issue.
V. Benedict, who, in the reign of EDWARD IV. became seated at Quarendon, in the county of Bucks. He married Elizabeth, daughter and heir of John Wood, of Warwick, and was father of

RICHARD, of Quarendon, who married Elizabeth, daughter and coheir of William Sanders, of the co. of Oxford, and had issue,

1. ROBERT (Sir), of Burston, Bucks, grandfather of Sir Henry Lee, K. G. *temp.* ELIZABETH.
2. Benedict, of Hulcote, who married Elizabeth, daughter of Robert Cheney, of Chesham Boys, and was great-great-grandfather of Sir Edward Lee, of Quarendon, who was raised to the peerage as *Earl* of LICHFIELD, in 1674. (See BURKE's *Extinct Peerage.*) The estates of the family on the extinction of the male line, passed to Charlotte, VISCOUNTESS DILLON.
3. Roger, of Pickthorn.
4. John, from whom the Lees of Binfield, in Berkshire, derived.

VI. Henry.
VII. Francis.

ldest son,

OMAS LEE, of Lee, who lived in the of RICHARD II. was father, by Wini-his wife, daughter of William Cotton, tton, near Sandbach, of

N LEE, of Lee, 3rd HENRY V. whose

BERT LEE, of Lee, married *temp.* Y VI. Margery, daughter, and co-s of John Wever, of Stanthorn, in Palatinate of Chester, and was suc-d by his son,

HARD LEE, of Lee, 10th EDWARD IV. married, first, Isabella, or Elizabeth, ter of Richard Massey, of Hough, by he had one son, JOHN, his heir, and, lly, Letitia, daughter of Edward , of Bechton, by whom he had two Robert, of Little Corwed, in Suffolk, urence, who died in 1564.

ard Lee was succeeded by his eldest

N LEE, of Lee, living 2 HENRY VII. by Agnes, his wife, daughter of hrey Mainwaring, of Nantwich, of

ERT LEE, of Lee, who married *temp.* VIII. Ellen, daughter and co-of Robert Minshull, of Hulgreve, d, with a daughter, Margery, mar-rst, to Hodgketh, and, secondly, to ce Woodnoth, of Gonsley, a son and or,

IARD LEE, of Lee, living *temp.* ELIZA-who wedded, first, Margery, dau. of d Harwood, of Stonglow, in the of Stafford, and had by her, a dau. ed, the wife of Roger de Madeley. rried, secondly, Alicia, daughter of d Clyve, of Huxley, and left by her nd heir,

RICHARD LEE, knt. of Lee, in 1613, rried Elizabeth, daughter of Copin-Buxall, and had issue,

HENRY, his heir.

Edward.

. Isaac, who married the relict of —— Hawes, merchant, of Hamburgh, and had a son, Isaac.

Katharine, married to Sir Robert Brerewood, one of the Judges of the Court of King's Bench.

——, *m.* to — Lawton, of Gorsty Hill, Cheshire.

hard died at Darnhall, on the 23rd il, 1627, and was succeeded by his

RY LEE, esq. of Lee, aged forty-two, father's death, who sold Lee Hall to ary Delves. He married, first, Elea-ughter of Sir Hugh Calveley, knight, econdly, Mary, daughter of Randle r, esq. of Alderley, by the former of he had, (with other issue, of whom Henry, the eighth son, left issue: and Roger, the tenth, married Mary, daughter of Peter Holford, of Newborough,) a successor,

THOMAS LEE, esq. of Darnhall, who married Elizabeth, daughter of Samuel Aldersey, of London, merchant, and had one son and four daughters, viz.

I. THOMAS, his heir.

I. Mary, married to George, son of George Huxley, of Brindley.

II. Margaret, *m.* to Thomas Aldersey, esq. of Aldersey, and Spurstow.

III. Anne.

IV. Elizabeth, married to Thomas, son of Colonel Robert Venables, of Antrobus.

Mr. Lee *d.* in 1642, and was *s.* by his son,

THOMAS LEE, esq. of Darnhall, aged twenty-six years, in 1663, who served the office of High Sheriff for Cheshire, in 1697. He married Frances, daughter and coheiress of Robert Venables, esq. of Antrobus and Wincham, and by her, who died in June, 1666, had issue,

I. NATHANIEL, his heir.

II. Thomas, born in 1661.

III. Robert, born in 1664, of Wincham, by gift of his father, married Magdalen, daughter and heiress of Richard Ward, esq. of Cotton, and had,

1. Thomas, of Cotton, who married, 15th of October, 1738, Alice, youngest daughter of Roger Comberbach, esq. Recorder of Chester, and had one son, Edward, Quarter-master-general, in Lieutenant-general Warburton's regiment, died at Philadelphi, unmarried, 5th of April, 1759, and one daughter, Frances, married to Edward Townshend, esq. of Wincham.

2. Robert, who married Hester, daughter of Sir William Glegg, of Gayton, and dying in 1720, aged thirty-four, left a daughter,

HESTER, who married Charles Legh, esq. of Adlington, and had one son, Thomas Legh, esq. of Wincham, who *d. s. p.* Surviving her only child, Mrs. Legh devised, by will, the manor of Wincham to EDWARD TOWNSHEND, esq. fourth son of John Townshend, esq. of Hem.

IV. John, of Cotton, in Salop, who married a daughter of —— Wells, of Sandbach, and died in 1738.

I. Elizabeth, *m.* to John Wade, of Gloucestershire.

The eldest son,

NATHANIEL LEE, esq. of Darnhall, baptized at Whitegate, on the 4th of March, 1655, espoused Sydney, daughter of Sir Robert Cotton, knt. of Combermere, and had two sons and two daughters, viz.

I. Thomas, baptized at Whitegate, on the 20th of July, 1692.

II. JOHN, heir.

I. Salisbury, born in 1698, married in 1714, to Robert Davis, esq. of Manley, and had one daughter, Salisbury.

II. FRANCES, born in 1702, married, first, to Samuel Mynshull, esq. and secondly, as already stated, to JOHN TOWNSHEND, esq. of Hem.

Mr. Lee was succeeded by his son,

JOHN LEE, esq. baptized at Whitegate on the 20th of March, 1696-7, who sold Dernhall, to —— Corbett, esq. He married Isabella, daughter of Sir Henry Bunbury, bart. of Stanney, and had, (with other sons who *d. s. p.* two daughters, Elizabeth and Susan, who both died unmarried),

CHARLES LEE, esq. the American General, born in 1731, who died in 1782, *s. p.*

## BOSANQUET, OF FOREST HOUSE.

BOSANQUET, SAMUEL, esq. of the Forest House, Waltham Forest, in the county of Essex, and of Dingestow Court, in the county of Monmouth, *b.* August, 1768, *m.* 19th January, 1798, Lætitia Philippa, the younger of the two daughters (the elder, Camilla, *m.* to Sir Charles Style, bt.) of James Whatman, esq. of Vinters, Kent, by his first wife, Sarah, eldest daughter of Edward Stanley, esq. LL.D. * and has issue,

SAMUEL RICHARD, *b.* April, 1800, *m.* February, 1830, Emily, eldest daughter of George Courthope, esq. of Whiligh, Sussex, and has issue,
Samuel Courthope, and other children.

James Whatman, *b.* January, 1804.

William Henry, *b.* February, 1805.

Edward Stanley, *b.* March, 1806, in holy orders.

Charles John, *b.* May, 1807, lieutenant R. N. *m.* June, 1832, his cousin, Charlotte Eliza, youngest daughter of Jacob Bosanquet, esq. of Broxbournbury, Herts, and has issue,
Henrietta Lætitia Eliza.

Frederick Bernard, *b.* November, 1813.

Eleanor Lætitia.

Camilla.

Georgiana.

Anna Maria.

Mr. Bosanquet, who is a magistrate and deputy lieutenant for the counties of Essex and Monmouth, and served the office of high sheriff of the latter county in 1816, succeeded his father in 1806.

---

* Mr. Stanley was cousin to Edward Stanley, eleventh Earl of Derby; he *m.* 1741, Catherine, daughter of Joseph Fleming, the brother of the Hon. Gilbert Fleming, lieutenant-general of the Carribee Islands, (see vol. ii. p. 38, account of the family of George Stanley Carey, esq.) and had by her (with two daughters) a son, John Fleming Stanley, whose elder daughter, Sarah Sophia, *m.* Sir David Williams, bart. and his second daughter, Lætitia, *m.* Col. Wynne, of Denbighshire.

## Lineage.

is family is descended from FOULCRAND NQUET, OR DE BOZANQUET, whose grand-

RRE, *m.* about 1623, Antoinette Main-, and was father of

RRE, of Lunel, in Languedoc, who had children,

OHN, *b.* 1660, *d.* in England unmarried, aged ninety.

AVID, *b.* 1661, of whom presently.

eter, *d.* in Turkey.

William Columber, a captain of grenadiers, who left issue (in France), a son and a daughter.

Marguerite, *m.* M. Jean Gaussen, of Geneva.

atherine, *m.* M. Grosset.

ouise.

the revocation of the Edict of Nantz, mily became divided; the two elder John and David, sought refuge in nd, where John was subsequently lised, by private act of parliament, in

cond son,

ID BOSANQUET, *m.* 1697, Elizabeth, er of Claude Hayes, esq. and *d.* 1732, issue,

DAVID, *b.* 1699, a merchant in London, and a learned antiquary; many of the most valuable of the Greek medals in the Hunterian Museum were originally collected by him during his travels. He *d.* in 1741, leaving an only child,

Richard, who *d.* unmarried.

SAMUEL, *b.* 1700, of whom presently.

. Claude, *d. s. p.*

. Benjamin, M.D. F.R.S. one of the council of the Royal Society in 1749, *d. s. p.*

Jacob, *m.* in 1748, Elizabeth, dau. of John Hanbury, esq. of Kelmarsh, in the county of Northampton, and had issue,

1. Jacob Bosanquet, esq. of Broxbournbury, in the county of Herts, forty-five years an East India director, he served the office of high sheriff of the county of Herts, in 1803, *m.* in 1790, Henrietta, daughter of Sir George Armytage, bart. and had issue,

George Jacob Bosanquet, esq. of Broxbournbury. This gentleman was his majesty's chargé d'affaires at Madrid from 1828 to 1830; served the office of high-sheriff of Herts in 1833, *m.* his cousin, Cecilia, dau. of William Franks, esq. of Beech Hill, Herts, and widow of Samuel Robert Gaussen, esq. of Brookmans, Herts, and has issue,

Cecilia Jane Wentworth.

Richard Godfrey.

Henrietta Maria, *m.* to her cousin, John Wentworth, esq.

Charlotte Eliza, *m.* to her cousin Charles John Bosanquet, esq.

2. William, a banker in London, *m.* in 1787, Charlotte Elizabeth, daughter of John Ives, esq. and had issue,

William - George - Ives, *m.* Eliza, daughter of Patrick Cumming, esq. and has issue.

Augustus Henry, *m.* Louisa, daughter of David Bevan, esq. of Belmont, Herts, and has issue.

John, *m.* Elizabeth, daughter of Thomas Boileau, esq. (of the family of Boileau, barons of Castlenau, in Languedoc), and has issue.

Samuel, *m.* Sophia, dau. of James Broadwood, esq.

Edwin, in holy orders, *m.* Eliza, daughter of Thomas Terry, esq. of Dummer House, Hants, and has issue.

Charlotte Elizabeth Ives.

Emma, *m.* to the Chevalier de Kantzow, his Swedish majesty's minister at Lisbon.

Sophia, *m.* to her cousin, William John, eldest son of John William Commerell, esq. of Strood, Sussex.

Harriet, *m.* to John Raymond Barker, esq. of Fairford Park, Gloucestershire.

---

e family is supposed to be now extinct in ; the last of its members known to be in that country, the Chevalier de Bozan- Amagre, near Lunel, and of Somierre, *d.* , 1832, *s. p.* He was the younger and other of M. de Bozanquet de Cardet, who April, 1813, leaving an only daughter, *m.* cousin, M. de Chapel, of Alais. They rmerly the possessors of the castle of Feac, mierre, in Languedoc.

3 Henry, of Clanville, in Hants, served the office of high sheriff of that county in 1815; *m.* in 1790, Caroline, dau. of Christopher Anstey, esq. the poet, and had issue,

Henry, *m.* Mary, daughter of William Richards, esq. and has issue.

4. Susannah, *m.* to James Whatman, esq. of Vinters, Kent.
5. Mary, *m.* to John William Commerell, esq. of Strood, Sussex.
6. Elizabeth, *m.* to her cousin Samuel Robert Gaussen, esq. of Brookmans, Herts.

I. Susannah, *b.* 1698, *m.* Charles Van Notten, esq. of Amsterdam, and had a son,

Charles Van Notten, who assumed by royal license the surname and arms of Pole, and was created a baronet on the 28th of July, 1791. (See BURKE'S *Baronetage*).

II. Elianor, *m.* Henry Lannoy Hunter, esq. and had issue,

Henry, of Beech Hill, Berks.

Harriet, *m.* Bernard Brocas, esq. of Beaurepaire, Hants, and Wokefield, Berks. Sir Bernard Brocas (younger son of the Earl of Foix, in France), came into England with WILLIAM *the Conqueror*, and from that prince received the estate of Beaurepaire. The family formerly held the hereditary post of master of the buckhounds, confirmed to them by *King* EDWARD III. and retained by the family till sold in the reign of JAMES I. (*See Account of the Family of Vavasour*, vol. i. p. 52).

Eleanor, *m.* to her cousin, Samuel Bosanquet, esq. of Forest House.

The second son of David Bosanquet,

SAMUEL BOSANQUET, esq. of the Forest House, lord of the manor of Low Hall, in the county of Essex, *m.* in 1733, Mary, daughter and sole heiress of William Dunster, esq. (son of Henry Dunster, esq. and Mary, daughter and sole heiress of Henry Gardiner, esq. M.P. for Ilchester in the 12th of CHARLES II. through whom this family quarter the arms of Gardiner), by Ann, daughter of Sir Peter Vandeput, and had issue,

SAMUEL, his successor, *b.* in 1744.
William, *d.* unm. in 1813.

Anna Maria, *m.* to her cousin, Peter Gaussen, esq.

Mary, *m.* in 1781, to the Rev. John William de la Flechere, the amiable and pious vicar of Madely, *b.* at Nyon, in Switzerland, 1729, buried at Madely, August, 1785.

The eldest son,

SAMUEL BOSANQUET, esq. of Forest House, and also of Dingestow Court, in the county of Monmouth, lieutenant of the Forest of Waltham, a magistrate and deputy-lieut. for Essex, was high-sheriff of that shire in 1770; he *m.* in 1767, his cousin, Eleanor, daughter of Henry Lannoy Hunter, esq. Mr. Bosanquet was governor of the Bank of England in 1792. He presided at Merchant Tailors' Hall in Dec. 1792, at a meeting of the merchants, bankers, and traders, and other inhabitants of London, held for the purpose of declaring their attachment to the Constitution by King, Lords, and Commons, as established at the Revolution of 1688, in opposition to the republican principles of the French Revolution. He *d.* in 1806, leaving issue,

I. SAMUEL, present proprietor.

II. Charles, of Rock, in the county of Northumberland, a magistrate and deputy lieutenant for the counties of Middlesex and Northumberland, served the office of high sheriff of the latter county in 1828. He was colonel of the London and Westminster light horse volunteers; *m.* Charlotte, dau. of Peter Holford, esq. master in Chancery, and had issue,

1. Charles Holford, *d.* unm.
2. Robert William, in holy orders, *m.* Frances, daughter of Colonel Pulleine, of Crakehall, Yorkshire, and has issue,
   Charles Pulleine Bertie.
3. George Henry, in holy orders.
4. John, } *d. s. p.*
5. Henry, } *d. s. p.*
6. Mary Anne.

III. JOHN BERNARD (The Right Hon. Sir). This gentleman was appointed one of the king's serjeants at law in April, 1827; in January, 1830, he was raised to the bench as one of the judges of the Court of Common Pleas; was sworn of the king's privy council in September, 1833; and in April, 1835, was appointed one of the lords commissioners for executing the office of Lord High Chancellor, and for the custody of the Great Seal of the United Kingdom. His lordship is a commissioner of public records. He *m.* in 1804, Mary Anne, eldest dau. of Richard Lewis, esq. of Llantilio Grossenny, in the county of Monmouth.

ms—Quarterly; first and fourth, or, nount vert. a tree ppr. on a chief gu. cent between two mullets ar. for Bo-st; second gu. a buck's head in base, ired or, in the dexter chief corner a of the third for DUNSTER; third, per r and gu. a fess between three hinds, passant, all counter-changed for GARDINER.

*Crest*—A demi lion ramp. couped gu.

*Estates*—Principally in Essex and Monmouthshire.

*Seats*—Dingestow Court, Monmouthshire; Forest House, Essex.

## VERE, OF BLACKWOOD AND CRAIGIE HALL.

RE-HOPE, JAMES-JOSEPH, esq. of Craigie Hall, in the county of Linv, and of Blackwood, in Lanarkshire, *b.* 3rd June, 1785, *m.* 7th September, the Lady Elizabeth Hay, fourth daughter of the late Marquis of Tweeddale, s issue,

WILLIAM-EDWARD, *b.* 5th March, 1824.
Charles-Edward, *b.* 3rd Oct. 1828.
Hannah-Charlotte, } twins.
Sophia-Jane, }
Harriette.
Jane.
Georgina.
Henrietta-Vane.

ope-Vere, who is a deputy lieutenant, succeeded his father in September, 1811.

### Lineage.

surname of VERE is of great antiand in ancient records was variwritten, de Vere, Veyr, Were, and The family had large possessions in the south of Scotland in very early and was known in history more than ndred years ago.

REDUS DE VERE lived in the reign of *King* MALCOLM IV. who succeeded to the crown of Scotland, *anno* 1153, and he is witness to a charter of *King* WILLIAM, who succeeded Malcolm, in 1165. He left issue two sons,

I. WALTER, his heir.
II. David, who is mentioned in a charter hereafter narrated.

WALTER DE VERE, eldest son of Baltred, appears to have been a man of rank and distinction, as well as of landed estate. He made a donation to the monastery of Kelso "(pro salute animæ suæ, &c.) unius bovatæ terræ in territorio suo de Sproustoun in vice comitatu de Roxbugh," which is confirmed by *King* WILLIAM; Hugo Cancellarius Regis, and David de Vere, brother of the said Walter, are witnesses. It has no date, but, as Hugh the chancellor died in 1199, it must have been in or before that year.

Walter was *s.* by his son,

RADULPHUS, or RALPH DE VERE, who is witness in a confirmation by *King* WILLIAM of a donation to the Abbacy of Cambuskenneth, which also wants a date, but must have been in or before 1214, in which year

*King* WILLIAM died. He confirmed his father's donation to the monastery of Kelso, and died in the end of the reign of ALEXANDER II., leaving issue a son,

THOMAS DE VERE, who succeeded him, and is witness in a charter of a donation to the monastery of Kelso, by Henricus de Sto. Claro, *anno* 1266. This Thomas and his father, Radulphus de Vere, are mentioned by the learned antiquary, Sir James Dalrymple, as progenitors of the Weirs of Blackwood. He was *s.* by his son,

RICARDUS DE WERE, who is mentioned in a donation to the monastery of Kelso, *anno* 1294. He left a son and successor,

THOMAS DE WERE, who is witness in a donation to the said monastery of Kelso, *anno* 1316. He was the proprietor of the lands and barony of BLACKWOOD, in the shire of Lanark, of which the abbot and convent of Kelso were superiors. He *d.* in the reign of DAVID BRUCE, leaving a son,

— WERE, whose Christian name is not known. He died in the beginning of the reign of *King* ROBERT III., and left a son,

ROTALDUS WERE, of Blackwood, who succeeded him, and, as heir to his grandfather Thomas, got a charter from Patrick, abbot of Kelso, *dilecto et fideli suo Rotaldo de Were, terrarum de Blackwood et Dermondstone jacen. in barronia de Lesmahagow et vice comitatu de Lanark, &c.*, dated in 1404. This Rotaldus was designed by the title of Blackwood above 360 years ago, and his posterity have uninterruptedly enjoyed it ever since. He died in the reign of *King* JAMES II. leaving issue a son,

THOMAS WERE, of Blackwood, of whom we have nothing remarkable upon record. He was father of

ROBERT VEYR, of Blackwood, who got a charter of confirmation from Robert, abbot of Kelso (as heir to Rotaldus, his grandfather), *dilecto et fideli suo Roberto de Veyr, terras de Rogershall, Brownhill, &c. in dominio de Blackwood et vice comitatu de Lanark*, dated *anno* 1479. He died soon after, leaving a son,

THOMAS WEIR, of Blackwood, who married Ægidia, daughter of John, third Lord Somerville, instructed by a sasine to "Ægidia Somerville, now spouse to Thomas Weir, of Blackwood, of the five merk lands of Broughton, with their pertinents lying in the shire of Peebles; also of the lands of Mossmening, in the barony of Lesmahagow, and shire of Lanark; in lieu of the tocher given with her by her said father, at the time of solemnizing the marriage;" dated 12th October, 1483. This Thomas had sasine of the lands of Burnetland, in the county of Peebles, proceeding upon a precept from *King* JAMES V., dated 10th May, 1524. He got also a charter of the whole lands and barony of Blackwood, Kypside, Rogershall, Mossmening, &c., from Thomas, abbot, of Kelso, superior thereof, dated 31st January, 1526-7. He acquired some other lands in the barony of Lesmahagow, from James Wallace, by his resignation, dated the last day of October, 1530. By the above writs it appears, that this Thomas had vast possessions in lands; and, as patron of St. Mary's church, of Lesmahagow, gave a presentation to Sir George Ker, to be chaplain there, 7th May, 1539. He died in the beginning of the reign of *Queen* Mary, and left a son,

JAMES WEIR, of Blackwood, who, upon his father's resignation, got a charter from Thomas, abbot of Kelso, "to and in favour of James Weir, eldest lawful son and apparent heir of Thomas Weir of Blackwood, and his heirs male, of all and haill the 20 merk land of old extent of Blackwood, the lands of Dorminstoun, Kypside, the ten merk land of Mossmening," &c.; dated 20th May, 1531. There is a precept from James, commendator of Kelso and Melrose, for infefting James Weir, of Blackwood, and Eupham Hamilton, his spouse, in the lands of Kypside, &c. The sasine following thereon is dated 19th February, 1561. Also a charter of alienation from Hugh Wallace, of Cairnhill, *honorabilo viro Jacobo Weir de Blackwood et Euphemie Hamilton ejus sponsæ, terrarum de Blackwood-yards, Kypside, Dormonside, &c.* lying in the barony of Lesmahagow, and shire of Lanark, dated 28th September, 1557, which were confirmed to them by a charter from William, commendator of Kelso, 9th February, 1561. He was proprietor, likewise, of the lands of Powneil, in Lanarkshire, which appears, by the discharge of 1000 merks, as part of the price thereof, *anno* 1564. He lived to a great age, died in the year 1595, and by the Eupham Hamilton had two sons,

I. JAMES, who *m.* Mariotte Ramsay, daughter of George, Lord Dalbousie, and was father of

  GEORGE, successor to his grandfather,

II. William, who is mentioned in a charter narrated in the sequel.

He was *s.* by his grandson,

GEORGE WEIR, of Blackwood, who *m.* first, Margaret, eldest lawful daughter of William Vere, of Stanebyres, which is instructed by a charter from James Weir, of Blackwood, "to and in favour of George Weir, his grandson and apparent heir, son of the deceased James Weir, younger, of Blackwood, and Mariotte Ramsay, his spouse, with consent of George Ramsay, of Dalhousie, &c. to the said George and Margaret, his future spouse, and the heirs-male of their bodies; which, failing to William Weir, second son of the said James, and uncle of the said George, and the heirs-male of his body; which, failing to the heirs-mail and of entail of the said James whatsomever, &c. They, so succeeding, being obliged to carry the name and arms of Weir, of Blackwood; —— of all and haill the 20 merk land of Blackwood, the ten merk land of Mossmening, the two merk land of Nether Blackwood," &c. &c. dated in August, 1594; and the sasine following thereon, in favour of the said George and Margaret, his spouse, is dated 1st December thereafter. All which is confirmed by a charter under the great seal, to George Weir, of Blackwood, his heirs, &c. dated 10th June, 1595. By the said Margaret Vere he had only one daughter,

MARIOTTE, his heir.

He *m.* secondly, Barbara Johnston, but by her he had no issue; and, dying about the year 1646, was *s.* by his only surviving child,

MARIOTTE WEIR, heiress of Blackwood, who married first, Major James Bannatyne, which appears by a charter, granted "to the said Major James Bannatyne, brother german to John Bannatyne, of Corehouse, proceeding upon a contract of marriage between him and the said Mariotte Weir, of the whole lands and barony of Blackwood, &c. to and in favour of them, and the heirs procreate, or to be procreate, betwixt them of this marriage; which, failing, to the heirs whatsomever of the body of the said Major Bannatyne by any other spouse," &c. &c. whoever, so succeeding, being obliged to carry the name and arms of Blackwood; and at the same time reserving the life-rent of all the said lands to George Weir, of Blackwood, and Barbara Johnston, his spouse, &c. &c. The charter is dated the 2nd, and sasine following thereon, the 9th April, 1642. But Major Bannatyne dying soon after, without issue, the said Mariotte married, secondly, William Lowrie, esq. who was thereupon designated tutor of Blackwood, and by him she had a son,

GEORGE, who, in consequence of the settlements of the estate above recited, was designed GEORGE WEIR, of Blackwood, particularly in a charter of several lands, dated 18th August, 1668. There is a sasine of all and haill the lands and barony of Blackwood, &c. in favour of William Lowrie, esq. tutor of Blackwood, and Mariotte Weir, his spouse, daughter and heiress of umquhile George Weir, of Blackwood, in life-rent, and to George Weir, their eldest lawful son, and apparent heir, in fee and heritage, dated 16th March, 1672. Also a resignation from William Lowrie and Mariotte Weir, in favour of the said George Weir, of Blackwood, and the heirs-male of his body; which, failing, to the eldest heir-female, &c. &c. &c. of all and haill the lands of Brown-castle, and others, in the barony of Blackwood, dated 10th July, 1674. He *m.* first, Anne, daughter of George Cleland, of Gartness, esq. by Margaret, his wife, daughter of — Hamilton, of Wishaw, and by her had a son and daughter, viz.

GEORGE (SIR), his heir.

Margaret, who *d.* young.

He *m.* secondly, Helen, daughter of Mr. Robert Bruce, of Broom Hall, progenitor of the Earls of Elgin and Kincardine, by whom he had a second son,

William, advocate, who *m.* Elizabeth, daughter of John Stewart, esq. of Ascog, and had two daughters.

George was *s.* by his eldest son,

SIR GEORGE WEIR, of Blackwood, who was created a baronet by *King* WILLIAM III. 28th November, 1694. He *m.* Catherine, daughter of Sir John Jardine, of Applegirth, by Lady Margaret Douglas, his wife, daughter of James, Earl of Queensbury, and had two sons, and two daughters,

I. WILLIAM (SIR), his heir.

II. GEORGE (SIR), who, upon the death of his brother without issue-male, succeeded to his title, and was third baronet. He was a captain in the Scots Royal regiment of foot, but dying unm. *anno* 1735, the baronetcy became EXTINCT.

I. Margaret, married to William Hamilton, of Dalserf, esq. and had issue.

II. Catherine, *m.* to John Lockhart, of Cleghorn, esq. and had issue.

Sir George *d.* in February 1716, and was *s.* by his eldest son,

SIR WILLIAM WEIR, second baronet of Blackwood, who *m.* Rachael, daughter of James Hamilton, of Pencaitland, one of the senators of the College of Justice, by Catherine Denholm, his wife, a daughter of Westshiells. By her he had one daughter,

CATHERINE, who carried on the line of this family.

He *m.* secondly, Christian, daughter of Sir Philip Anstruther, of Anstruther-field, but had no other issue. Sir William died in 1722, (his widow *m.* John, sixth Earl of Traquair, and was grandmother of the present earl) when the baronetship devolved upon his brother, Sir George, as before observed, and he was succeeded by his only child,

CATHERINE WEIR, who *m.* in 1733, the Hon. CHARLES HOPE, of Craigie Hall, second son of Charles, second Earl of Hopetoun, by Lady Henrietta Johnston, only daughter of William, first Marquis of Annandale, and had four sons and two daughters,

I. Charles, who *d.* young.
II. WILLIAM, heir to his mother.
III. John, a merchant in London, M.P. for the county of West Lothian, who *m.* in 1762, Mary, daughter of Eliab Breton, esq. of Forty Hall, in Middlesex, and had three sons, viz.
Charles, lord president of the Court of Session, *b.* 29th June, 1763, *m.* 1793, Charlotte, 8th daughter of John, Earl of Hopetown, and had issue,
1. John, *b.* in 1794, married, and has issue.
2. Charles, captain R.N. *m.* in 1826, Anne, eldest daughter of Capt. William-Henry Webley Parry, R.N., C.B., of Noyadd Trefawr, and has issue.
3. James, *m.* in 1828, Elizabeth, eldest daughter of the Right Hon. David Boyle, and has two sons and a daughter.
4. William, captain, 7th foot.
1. Elizabeth.
2. Sophia.
3. Charlotte.
4. Jane Melville.
5. Margaret.
6. Anne Williamina, *m.* to Hercules-James Robertson, esq.
7. Louisa-Augusta-Octavia.
John (Sir), lieutenant-general in the army, *m.* first, Margaret, only daughter and heir of Robert Scott, esq. and has by her, who died 19th March, 1813, three daughters,
1. Mary-Ann.
2. Charlotte, *m.* to L. Mackinnon, esq.
3. Margaret-Sophia.
Sir John Hope espoused, secondly, in 1814, Jane Hester, daughter of John Macdougall, esq. and has surviving issue, three sons, John-Thomas, Henry-Philip, Charles-William, and one daughter.
William Johnstone Hope (Sir), vice-admiral, G.C.B. *b.* in 1766, who married twice, and left, by his first wife, Lady Anne Hope Johnstone, eldest daughter of James, third Earl of Hopetoun, with other issue, the present John-James Hope Johnstone, esq. M. P. claimant to the earldom of Annandale.
IV. Charles, died in infancy.
I. Henriet.
II. Rachael, died young.

The heiress of Blackwood died in 1743, and was succeeded by her eldest surviving son,

WILLIAM HOPE-VERE, esq. of Blackwood, an officer in the first regiment of dragoon guards, and for some time muster-master-general of the forces in North Britain. He *m.* Sophia, daughter of Joseph Corrie, esq. of Dumfries, and had surviving issue,
I. JAMES-JOSEPH, his heir.
II. Edward-Hamilton, *b.* in Jan. 1792.
I. Jane Sophia, *m.* in 1813, to the Hon. Edmund Sexton Perry Knox, second son of the Earl of Ranfurly.

Mr. Hope Vere died in September, 1811, and was *s.* by his son, the present JAMES-JOSEPH HOPE-VERE, esq. of Blackwood, and Craigie Hall.

*Arms*—1st and 4th, az. on a chevron between three bezants or, a bay-leaf ppr. for HOPE; 2nd, arg. on a fess. az. three mullets of the first, for Vere, of Blackwood; 3rd, or, an anchor in pale, gu. for FAIRHOLM.

*Crests*—1st, a broken globe surmounted by a rainbow, all ppr. 2nd, a demi-horse rampant arg. bridled and saddled, gu.

*Mottoes*—For HOPE, At spes non tracta: for VERE, Vero nihil verius.

*Estates*—Craigie Hall, in Linlithgowshire, inherited from the Johnstones, of Annandale; and Blackwood, in Lanarkshire, from the Veres.

*Seats*—Craigie Hall, and Blackwood.

## DENNISTOUN, OF DENNISTOUN.

DENNISTOUN, JAMES, esq. of Dennistoun, born in 1803, a Magistrate and Deputy-Lieutenant, and Member of the faculty of Advocates, succeeded his father on the 1st of June, 1834, married in 1835, Isabella-Katharina, eldest daughter of the Honourable James Wolfe Murray, of Cringletie, one of the Senators of the College of Justice in Scotland.

## Lineage.

ie peerage writers, and genealogical ries of Scotland, are agreed, that cient family ranks with the most t in the western districts of that n. Leaving the doubtful authority anan, of Auchmar, who asserts it to unger branch of the proud Earls of , and to have had large possessions Endrick, in 1016, it appears from a of MALCOLM IV. who died in 1165, : Dennistouns held lands on the n Renfrewshire, in that monarch's Here, it would seem, that one ., or DANIEL, probably of Norman on, settled himself, and, calling the DANZIELSTOUN, assumed therefrom ame. After passing through various , this orthography took its present bout the end of the sixteenth cen- Confining our details rigidly to the of authentic documents, we de- genealogy from

UGH DE DANZIELSTOUN, of that Ilk, rished during the fatal wars of the succession, and with other patriotic f his country, accorded a reluctant on to the victorious EDWARD, in He had issue,

N, (Sir) his successor.

NNA, or Janet, who married Sir dam More, of Rowallan, and was other of

ELIZABETH MORE, whose marriage with *King* ROBERT II. became a fruitful ground of controversy among historians. From this union, in 1347, sprang the long line of the STUART monarchs, through whom the Imperial crown has passed to the reigning dynasty. In reference to this circumstance, the proud proverb has been preserved by the Dennistouns, "Kings came of us, not we of kings."

Sir Hugh was succeeded by his son,

SIR JOHN DE DANZIELSTOUN, of that Ilk, who, during the reign of DAVID the Second, was the constant associate in arms of his illustrious father-in-law, the Earl of Wigton, and of the brave Sir Robert Erskine. Through life, himself and his son Sir Robert maintained a devoted loyalty, with a steadiness as exemplary as it was rare, in an age when the haughty nobles of Scotland often sought to extend their individual influence by trampling on the prerogatives of the crown. Offices of high trust were conferred upon him, and the accession of his relation, ROBERT the Second, was followed by new honours, and by grants of many splendid baronies in various counties. He was for many years High Sheriff of Dunbartonshire, and Governor of Dunbarton Castle, the strongest fortress in the kingdom, and was one of the lords of parliament who concurred in the settlement of the crown upon the descendants of his niece Elizabeth More. He married Mary, daughter of Malcolm, first earl of Wigton, who is lineally represented by the heir of this marriage, and had five sons and a daughter, viz.

I. ROBERT, his heir.

II. Walter, (Mr.) a bold and turbulent churchman. On the death of his elder brother, in 1399, he asserted a right to the castle of Dunbarton, as an appendage of his family, and, assembling the numerous vassals of his house, seized and defended the fortress. ROBERT *the Third*, deeming "discretion a victor's better part," offered his rebellious relative the See of St. Andrew's, as a bribe for the surrender of the castle. The terms were accepted, and the bishop was duly inducted; but contumacious to the last, he held out the castle to his death, in 1402.

III. WILLIAM, (Sir) of Colgrain.

IV. Hugh, } who had various grants
V. Malcolm, } of land from ROBERT the Second, and ROBERT the Third.

I. Janet, married to her cousin, Sir Adam More, of Rowallan—ancestor, through the female line, of the Marquess of Hastings. (*See* BURKE'S *Peerage*, COUNTESS OF LOUDOUN.)

The eldest son and heir,

SIR ROBERT DE DANZIELSTOUN, of that Ilk, was one of the youths selected from the chief families in Scotland in 1357, as hostages for the ransom of *King* DAVID the Second; and, in 1370, was commissioner for a treaty of peace with England. Identified with his distinguished father in loyalty and valour, he enjoyed a like portion of royal favour, and succeeded him in the high trusts of Sheriff of the county, and Keeper of the Castle of Dunbarton, which he held to his death. Having no son, his daughters divided his noble baronies of Danzielstoun, Finlaystoun, and Stainly, in Renfrewshire; Kilmaronock, in Lennox; Mauldisley, Law, Kilcadzow, and Trepwood, in Lanarkshire; Glencairn, in Dumfriesshire; Blackburn and Torbain, in Linlithgowshire; and Collington and Redhall, county of Edinburgh. Of these ladies,

I. MARGARET, married Sir William de Cunninghame, of Kilmaurs, and hence sprang the earls of Glencairn.
II. ELIZABETH, married Sir Robert Maxwell, of Calderwood; and from her sprang the baronets of Calderwood and Pollock, and the earls of Farnham.

After the decease of Sir Robert, the male line of the family was carried on by his brother,

SIR WILLIAM DE DANZIELSTOUN, of Colgrain, in the county of Dunbarton, which estate, and that of Camis Eskau, in the same shire, he acquired before 1377, and had several other grants from the crown. From these we learn that he held preferment in the household of ROBERT III. and of that monarch's eldest son, the unfortunate Earl of Carrick, and on his death, in 1393, his widow, the Lady Marjory, had a pension from the king's chamberlain. He seems to have been *s.* by his son,

—— DE DANZIELSTOUN, of Colgrain, who was a minor in 1399, and *d.* before 1450, leaving, by his wife, Margaret, a son and successor,

WILLIAM DE DANZIELSTOUN, of Colgrain, who appears to have left two sons, Robert, the younger, from whom descended the Dennistouns, of Dalnair and Tullichawen, now extinct; and his heir,

CHARLES DANZIELSTOUN, of Colgrain, who *d.* seised in Auchindennan and Cameron, before 1481, and was *s.* by his son,

ROBERT DANZIELSTOUN, of Colgrain, who wedded Elizabeth, daughter of John Napier, of Merchiston, ancestor of the Lords Napier, and had two sons and a daughter, viz. PATRICK, his heir; Andrew, from whom sprang the Dennistouns of Ferrylands and Auchendenanrie, now extinct, and Janet, the wife of John Darleith, of that Ilk. The elder son,

PATRICK DANZIELSTOUN, of Colgrain, *m.* thrice; his first wife was Giles Colquhoun; the second, Giles, daughter of Sempill, of Fulwood; the third, Matilda, daughter of Sir Humphrey Cunninghame, of Glengarnok. His son and heir,

ROBERT DANZIELSTOUN, of Colgrain, associated himself with William, fourth earl of Glencairn, in his machinations and correspondence with HENRY VIII. of England. For this he was attainted; but in 1546 had a remission, under the Great Seal, for all treasons and crimes committed by him, along with the Earl. The same active and turbulent spirit led him afterwards to take part in the raids then frequent amongst the border clans of the Highlands, in which he seems to have been both an actor and a sufferer. His wife was Katharine, dau. of David Semple, of Noblestoun, by Marion, daughter of Sir William Edmonston, of Duntreath. They left, with other issue,

I. ROBERT, heir.
II. JOHN, living in 1560, was father, by his wife, Euphemia Bontyne, of

WALTER DANZIELSTOUN, who, like his predecessor, resided at Colgrain. He *d.* in 1618, leaving, with several younger children,

JOHN DENNISTOUN, who, by Margaret, daughter and eventual heiress of the ancient family of Spreull, of Dalchurne, had two sons,

1. MR. ARCHIBALD.
2. Mr. William, of Ferrylands, episcopal minister of Glassford. This gentleman was deposed at the Revolution for nonconformity.

The elder son,

MR. ARCHIBALD DENNISTOUN, of Dalchurne, was minister of Campsie, and lost his living by his devotion to episcopacy. He *m.* first, Jane, daughter of Humphry Noble, of Farme and Ardardan, and secondly, Katharine, dau. of James Stirling, of Auchyle: by the former he had

1. WILLIAM, of whom in the sequel as heir male of the family, and husband of the HEIRESS OF COLGRAIN.
2. Archibald.

The son and heir,

ROBERT DANZIELSTOUN, of Colgrain, *m.* Margaret, daughter of John Hamilton, of Ferguslie, and among other children, who left no issue, had Elizabeth, the wife of John Colquhoun, of Camstraddan; Catherine *m.* to John Macgregor, of Ardenconnal; and his successor,

JAMES DENNISTOUN, of Colgrain, who, being a person of facile and extravagant disposition, impaired and involved the family ance to a considerable extent. His l heir,

TER DENNISTOUN, of Colgrain, in ence of these involvments, was ob- alienate Auchindennan, Cameron, er portions of the estate. He *m.* rah, daughter of Sir Patrick Hous- Houston, by the Lady Janet Cun- ne; and secondly, Grace, daughter n Brisbane, of Brisbane; by the he had James, who *d.* unm. and an n, his successor,

DENNISTOUN, of Colgrain, who, the wars of the Commonwealth, con- zealous and steady adherent of the use, and ultimately crowned his ex- by the sacrifice of his life. The last the cavaliers in Scotland was made he Earl of Glencairne, who was con- commander-in-chief by CHARLES II. By him the following commission en to Colgrain:—

ereas I, William, Earl of Glen- by vertue of his Ma. commission, npouered to levie horse and foote he kingdom of Scotland for his Ma. ; and I, being weoll assured of the , courage, and guid affectione of ennistoun, of Cogrene, does heirby le and appointe him to levie the n of all the fencible persons within nox, and to reduce them in foot com- and to place officars over them, and nde the foresaid foote, and to bringe to joyne with his Majesties forces foot: for the which this sall be unto sufficiand warrand. Given under l the 20th day of November, 1653.

"GLENCAIRNE."

a short but romantic campaign, the ny thus assembled was disbanded in t autumn, when John Dennistoun cially included in the treaty of sur- and his real and personal estates empted from attainder. This bene- d not long enjoy, but died the ensu- r, after lingering sufferings from a received in the Highland expedition. Jean, daughter of William Semple, ood, and had three daughters, viz.

MARGARET, who succeeded to the es- ates in virtue of an entail made by er father, under condition of marry- ng the HEIR MALE of the family.

Jean.

Janet, *m.* William Semple, of Ful- wood.

he decease of Col. Dennistoun, the presentation devolved upon the elder l heir of Mr. Archibald Dennistoun, hurne, minister of Campsie, (whose have traced),

WILLIAM DENNISTOUN, who, under the settlement of Col. Dennistoun, became the husband of his eldest daughter, MARGARET, *heiress of Colgrain.* Small, however, was the heritage thus re-united to the representation of this ancient house. The embarrassments which had gradually increased during the civil wars, in which the laird was on the losing side, were fatally augmented by the selfish mismanagement during the minority of the heiress: a long life of prudent economy was inadequate to retrieve the estate, and William's patrimony of Dalchurne was entirely lost. In one respect this was fortunate, as it perhaps prevented his taking the active part in politics which his jacobite zeal might in other circumstances have suggested. Of sixteen children, one only survived their parents, viz.

JOHN DENNISTOUN, of Colgrain, who freed the property from debt, and by Jane, heiress of Moses Buchanan, of Glins, had, beside several daughters,

JAMES DENNISTOUN, of Colgrain. This laird *m.* first, Janet, daughter of John Baird, of Craigtoun, and by her left,

I. JAMES, his successor.

I. Jean, *m.* to Andrew Buchanan, of Ardenconnal, and had issue.

He wedded, secondly, Mary, daughter of John Lyon, of Parklee, and had three other children, viz.

II. Robert, *m.* to Anne-Penelope, dau. of Archibald Campbell, of Jura, and had issue.

III. RICHARD, who purchased KELVIN GROVE, in the county of Lanerk,*

* Armorial bearings of DENNISTOUN, of Kelvin Grove.

*Arms*—Arg. on a bend sable, between a unicorn's head, erased gules, horned or, and a cross crosslet fitched of the third, a mullet of the first.

*Crest*—A dexter arm, in pale ppr. clothed gu. holding an antique shield sable, charged with a mullet or.

*Motto*—Adversa virtute repello.

and took his designation from that estate. He *m.* Christian, daughter of James Alston, merchant in Glasgow, heir to the estate of Westerton, in the county of Dunbarton, and left surviving issue,

Richard, } both unm.
William, }

Isabella, *m.* to Colin Campbell, esq. son of Archibald Campbell, esq. of Jura, and has issue.

Mary, *m.* to the late Archibald Buchanan, esq. of Auchintoclie, in the county of Dumbarton, and has issue.

II. MARY, *m.* to John Alston, of Westerton, and has issue.

Colgrain *d.* in 1796, and was *s.* by his eldest son,

JAMES DENISTOUN, of Colgrain. This gentleman was convener of the county of Dumbarton for nearly thirty years; during a great part of the time he held the appointment of vice-lieutenant, and commanded the regiment of local militia of that shire. By Margaret, his first wife, daughter of James Donald, of Geilstoun, he left JAMES, his heir; and by Margaret, his second wife, daughter of Allan Dreghorn, of Blochairn, he left four daughters, co-heirs to their mother's large fortune, viz.

ISABELLA-BRYSON, *m.* to Gabriel Hamilton Dundas, of Westburn and Duddingstoun, and has issue.

JANET-BAIRD, *m.* to Hugh Maclean, of Coll, and has issue.

ELIZABETH-DREGHORN, *m.* 22d Feb. 1815, to Sir Duncan Campbell, bart. of Barcaldine, and has issue.

MARY-LYON, *m.* to Sir William Baillie, bart. of Polkemmet, and has issue.

He was *s.* at his decease, in 1816, by his only son,

JAMES DENNISTOUN, of Dennistoun, who inherited the estates of Colgrain and Camis Eskau; and in 1828, on the production of the most satisfactory evidence of his descent, obtained from the Lord Lyon of Scotland authority to bear the arms and style proper to the baronial house of DE DANZIELSTOUN, *of that Ilk.* He commanded the yeomanry cavalry of Dumbartonshire, and served as a deputy lieutenant. By Mary Ramsay, his wife, daughter of George Oswald, of Auchencruive, he had issue,

I. JAMES, his heir.
II. George.
III. Richard, *d.* in 1829.
IV. Robert.
V. Alexander.

I. Margaret.
II. Isabella.
III. Mary.
IV. Elizabeth.
V. Camilla.
VI. Janet.

Dennistoun *d.* 1st June, 1834, and was *s.* by his eldest son, the present JAMES DENNISTOUN of Dennistoun.

*Arms*—Argent, a bend sable.

*Crest*—A dexter arm in pale ppr., clothed gules holding an antique shield sa. charged with a mullet or.

*Supporters*—On the dexter, a lion rampant gules, armed, and langued az.; on the sinister, an antelope arg. armed az. hooped or.

*Motto*—Adversa virtute repello.

*Estates*—In Dunbartonshire.

*Seat*—Camis-Eskau, in that county.

## BLAND, OF KIPPAX PARK.

BLAND, DAVISON-THOMAS, esq. of Kippax Park, in the county of York, *b.* 15th July, 1783, *m.* 20th January, 1812, Appollonia, second daughter of Charles-Philip, sixteenth Lord Stourton, and sister of the present Lord, by whom he has issue,

THOMAS, *b.* 23d November, 1812.
Edward, *b.* 23d August, 1813.
Henry, *b.* 6th December, 1814.

Mr. Bland succeeded his father 27th April, 1794.

## Lineage.

family of BLAND was anciently seated ...ds Gill, in the county of York, but ...le line of the elder stock failing, the ...ntation devolved upon the descen-...r

...ERT BLAND, of Leeming, in the North ..., a younger son of Bland, of Blands ...This Robert wedded a daughter of ...f Deighton, in the same county, and ...ith two daughters, Margaret and Isa-...n only son, his successor,

...ARD BLAND, of Leeming, who m. ... daughter of Thomas Pole, esq. and ...veral children. He directs by his ...t his body be interred in the parish ... of Bumestin, with his ancestors. He ... at his decease by his eldest son,

...ERT BLAND, of Leeming, who. m. ... daughter of William Pepper, gent. ...s father of

...THOMAS BLAND, knt. who settled at ... Park in the time of ELIZABETH, ...s in the commission of the peace for ...nty of York in the 32d of that reign. ... Elizabeth, daughter and heiress of ...s Eastoft, of Redness, and had issue,

...HOMAS (Sir), his heir.

...argaret, m. to Gilbert Nevile, esq. of Grove, Co. Notts.

...izabeth-Muriel, m. to Arthur Burgh, esq. lord mayor of York.

...n the 26th (was buried in St. George's ..., London, 28th) December, 1612, and ...is son,

...THOMAS BLAND, knt. of Kippax Park, ...ce of the peace 13th JAMES I. He m. ...on. Katherine Savile, eldest daughter ...n, Lord Savile, and sister of Thomas, ...f Sussex, by whom (who wedded, se-...r, Walter Welsh, esq.), he had two ...nd two daughters, viz.

THOMAS (Sir), his successor.

Adam, a major of horse in the royal army, and a devoted adherent to the royal cause in the wars of the Commonwealth. Major Bland was one of the Yorkshire gentlemen who seised the Castle of Pontefract for the king, and so boldly defended it, and he is stated, on good authority, to have been amongst those who made the remarkable sortie from the garrison to Doncaster, when the parliamentary general, Rainsborough, was killed. He m. Katherine, relict of Sir John Girlington, knt.

Katherine, m. to Thomas Harrison, esq. of Dancers' Hill, Herts.

Frances, m. to Mr. John Belton, of Rocliffe.

He was s. by his elder son,

SIR THOMAS BLAND, of Kippax Park, who was created a baronet on the 30th August, 1642, by *King* CHARLES I. for his active zeal and devotion in the royal cause. He. m. Rosamond, daughter of Francis Nevile, esq. of Chevet, in the county of York, and by her (who wedded, secondly, Walter Walsh, esq. of Houghton), had issue,

FRANCIS, his heir.

Adam, who m. ——, daughter of Sir Thomas Barnadiston, and relict of Ashcroft, by whom he had Adam, m. to the daughter of Edward Chetham, of Manchester, and Jane.

Rosamond, m. to Martin Headly, an alderman of Leeds.

Katherine, m. to John Frank, esq. of Pontefract.

Frances.

Dorothy.

Elizabeth, m. to the Rev. Mr. Mitchell.

The baronet died in October, 1657, and was s. by his elder son,

SIR FRANCIS BLAND, bart. of Kippax Park. This gentleman m. Jane, daughter of Sir William Lowther, by whom (who survived him fifty years, dying 7th April, 1713, aged seventy-two), he left, at his decease, 14th November, 1663, aged twenty-one, two sons,

THOMAS, } 3rd and 4th baronets.
JOHN, }

The elder son,

SIR THOMAS BLAND, of Kippax Park, *d.* 14th December, 1667, aged five years, and was s. by his brother,

SIR JOHN BLAND, of Kippax Park, *b.* 2d November, 1663. This gentleman sate in parliament for Appleby, afterwards for

Pontefract, and was member, at the time of his death, for the county of Lancaster. He *m.* 31st March, 1685, Anne, daughter and heiress of Sir Edward Mosley, of Hulm, in Lancashire, and had to survive infancy, one son and four daughters, viz.

I. JOHN, his heir.

I. ANNE, *m.* to Thomas Davison, esq. of Blackiston, in the county palatine of Durham,* and had one surviving son,

THOMAS DAVISON, esq. of Blackiston, baptized 19th June, 1712, who *m.* Martha, daughter of William Hoar, esq. of Limehouse, in the county of Middlesex, by whom (who *d.* in 1795), he left at his decease, 5th April, 1756,

THOMAS DAVISON, of whom presently, as inheritor of the estates of BLAND, and assumer of the name.

John Davison, barrister at law, *d.* unm. and was buried at Norton, in the county of Durham, 18th Nov. 1780.

Martha-Anne Davison, *d. s. p.*
Anne-Catherine Davison, died *s. p.*

Mrs. Davison *d.* 17th May, 1715, at the age of twenty-seven, and her widower re-married Theophila, daughter of Chas. Turner, esq. of Kirkleatham, in the county of York, by whom he left, at his decease, 9th Sept. 1748,

William Davison, in holy orders, rector of Scruton, in the county of York, who *m.* 3rd June, 1750, Catherine, eldest daughter of George Vane, esq. of Long Newton, in the county of Durham, by whom he had, with other issue,

The Rev. Thomas Davison, vicar of Hartburne, in Northumberland, who *m.* Elizabeth, daughter of William Webster, esq. of Stocton-upon-Tees, and had several children.

II. Elizabeth, *d.* at Bath, 3d July, 1709, unm. and aged sixteen.

III. Frances, *d.* 31st August, 1712.

IV. Muriel.

Sir John was *s.* at his decease, by his son,

SIR JOHN BLAND, bart. of Kippax Park, M. P. for Lancashire in 1714. He *m.* Lady Frances Finch, daughter of Heneage, first Earl of Aylesford, and had two sons and two daughters, viz.

JOHN, HUNGERFORD, } 7th and 8th barts.

Anne, Elizabeth, } both *d.* unm.

The baronet was *s.* at his decease, in 1743, by his elder son,

SIR JOHN BLAND, of Kippax Park, who *d.* unm. in France, in 1755, and was *s.* by his brother,

SIR HUNGERFORD BLAND, eighth and last baronet, at whose decease, unm. in 1756, the title became EXTINCT, while the estate passed to his cousin, (devisee of Miss Elizabeth Bland's moiety),

THOMAS DAVISON, esq. *b.* 8th June, 1744-5, who, assuming the additional surname of Bland, became Thomas Davison-Bland, of Kippax Park. He *m.* in 1776, Jane, dau. and co-heir of Godfrey Meynell, esq. of Yeldersley, in the county of Derby, and had issue,

THOMAS, his heir.
Henry-George, *b.* 3d February, 1785, *d.* young.

Harriet, *m.* to John Sullivan Wood, esq. lieut.-col. of the 8th dragoons, and *d.* in 1805, *s. p.*
Martha-Anne.
Frances-Augusta.
Judith-Selina.
Charlotte, *m.* in May, 1815, to the Rev. Theophilus Barnes, rector of Castleford, in the county of York.

Mr. Davison-Bland *d.* 27th April, 1794, and was *s.* by his only surviving son, THOMAS DAVISON-BLAND, esq. now of Kippax Park.

*Arms*—Arg. on a bend sa. three pheons or.

*Crest*—Out of a ducal coronet, a lion's head ppr.

*Estate*—In Yorkshire.

*Seat*—Kippax Park.

* Great grandson of SIR THOMAS DAVISON, knt. of Blackiston, high sheriff of the county palatine of Durham, in 1661, by Alice, his wife, daughter of Sir William Lambton, knt. of Lambton.

# PURVIS, OF DARSHAM.

**PURVIS, CHARLES**, esq. of Darsham, in Suffolk, *b.* there 19th February, 1777, *m.* at Marylebone Church, 12th Feb. 1805, Margaret-Eleanor, daughter and co-heir of John Randall, esq. and has had issue,

i. Charles, *b.* at York, 4th February, 1806, died at Dundalk, in Ireland, 19th May, 1808.
ii. William-Wheatley, born at Dundalk 25th March, 1808, *d.* at Colchester in 1815.
iii. Henry-Tillard, *b.* in London 29th April, 1810, *d.* at Richmond in 1818.
iv. Arthur, born at Brighton 25th April, 1813, in the civil service of the East India Company.
v. Frederick, born at Colchester 14th August, 1815.
vi. George-John, born at Ipswich, 4th July, 1816, in the military service of the East India Company.
vii. Charles-Alexander, born at Darsham 30th August, 1819.

i. Charlotte-Sarah.

This gentleman, who was formerly lieutenant-colonel of the Royal Dragoons, succeeded his father in 1808.

## Lineage.

William Purves, of Abbey Hill, near Edinburgh, living in the beginning of the seventeenth century, was father of

Robert Purves, of Abbey Hill, burgess of Edinburgh, who wedded Anne Douglas, and left at his decease in 1665, with a daughter, Sybilla, a son and successor,

William Purves, of Abbey Hill, who was bred to the Scottish bar. Before the usurpation he held an office in the Court of Session, and was one of the clerks to the committees of parliament; but taking an active part in favour of *King* Charles during the civil wars, suffered severely both in person and estate. For several years he was compelled to conceal himself, and in 1656, when peace was restored under the Protector, he accepted, through necessity, a small office in the Exchequer. In this situation, although he never swerved from his fidelity as a public officer, he availed himself of the opportunity he had of rendering service to the persecuted royalists. After the Restoration, he was appointed solicitor-general for Scotland, knighted, and eventually, in 1665, created a Baronet. Sir William married Marjory, daughter of Robert Fleming, of Restalrig, and had four sons, viz.

i. Alexander (Sir), second baronet, appointed his father's successor as solicitor-general for Scotland. He was grandfather of

Sir William Purves, fourth baronet, who *m.* Lady Anne Hume-Campbell, eldest daughter of Alexander, second Earl of Marchmont, and left a son and successor,

Sir Alexander Purves, fifth baronet, father of the present

Sir William Purves-Hume-Campbell, sixth baronet, who assumed his additional surnames upon inheriting the estates of his maternal family.

ii. John, of Abbey Hill.
iii. James, of Purves Vale, of whom presently.

i. Anne, *m.* to Charles, Earl of Home.
ii. Margery, *m.* to Sir Mungo Stirling, of Glolat.
iii. Rosina, *m.* to Dean, of Woodhouslie.

The third son,

JAMES PURVES, esq. of Purves Vale, died in Scotland, leaving by his wife, a daughter of Pringle of Torsonce, six sons, one of whom is supposed to have been

GEORGE PURVIS, esq. who settled in England, and became a captain in the royal navy. He *m.* at Stepney, 18th September, 1679, Margaret Berry, and by her, who was buried at Darsham 16th March, 1717, had issue,

I. GEORGE, his heir.

II. William, *b.* 8th February, 1689, who *m.* Susan Hedges, and had three daughters, viz.

Susan, *m.* to — Thompson, esq. and *d. s. p.*

Sarah, *m.* in 1731, at Darsham, to George Bogul, and had a daughter, *m.* to — Johnson.

Mary, *m.* to — Gregory, and had a daughter, Sarah.

III. Dakins.

I. Elizabeth, *b.* 25th March, 1683.

II. Betty, *b.* 18th July, 1688, *m.* to Benjamin Taylor, of Theberton, Suffolk.

III. Margaret, *b.* 6th March, 1693-4, *m.* first to Thomas Wye, and secondly to John Smith. She *d.* 28th November, 1761.

Captain Purvis *d.* in 1715, was buried 6th April at Darsham, and succeeded by his son,

GEORGE PURVIS, esq. of Darsham, in Suffolk, *b.* 27th July, 1680, who was comptroller of the navy in 1735, and M.P. for Aldeburgh in 1732 and 1734. He *m.* Elizabeth Allen, and by her, who died at Walthamstow 1st June, 1739, had three sons and one daughter, namely,

I. CHARLES-WAGER, his heir.

II. George, *b.* 25th November, 1718, secretary to the Sick and Wounded Office in 1747, *m.* 15th May, 1742, Mary Oadam, and had issue,

1. Richard, *b.* at Stepney, 26th August, 1743, captain in the royal navy, *m.* 3rd January, 1780, Lucy, daughter of the Rev. John Leman, of Wenhaston, and died at Beccles, in Suffolk, in May, 1802, having had

Richard-Oadam, *b.* 18th February, 1785, lieutenant in the royal navy, died at Port Royal, Jamaica, in 1805.

John-Leman, *b.* 1st March, 1786, lieutenant in the East India Company's service, died at Rangoon 8th March, 1805.

George-Thomas, *b.* 7th November, 1789, died young.

Barrington, *b.* 21st March, 1792, captain in the royal navy, *m.* at Lawshall, 11th September, 1820, Amy-Letitia, eldest daughter of the Rev. Dr. Colvile, rector of Lawshall, and dying in London, 4th April, 1822, left a daughter.

Mary, died an infant.

Lucy-Anna, *m.* first, to Captain Duddingston; secondly, to — Duddingston, esq.; and thirdly, to Captain Kidd.

2. John-Child, admiral in the royal navy, *b.* 13th March, 1746, *m.* first, 11th October, 1784, Catherine Sowers, and by her, who died 3rd February, 1789, had two sons and one daughter,

John-Brett, *b.* 12th August, 1787, captain in the royal navy at eighteen, who *m.* Renira-Charlotte, daughter of George Purvis, esq.

Richard-Fortescue, in holy orders, *b.* 4th January, 1789, *m.* 19th January, 1824, Elizabeth-Helen, daughter of the Rev. Thomas Baker, rector of Rollesby, in Norfolk.

Catharine.

Admiral Purvis wedded, secondly, Miss Mary Garrett; and thirdly, 2nd August, 1804, Elizabeth, daughter of Sir Archibald Dickson, bart. and widow of Lieutenant William Dickson.

3. George, R.N. *m.* at Titchfield, 6th July, 1791, Renira-Charlotte Maitland, and had issue,

George-Thomas-Maitland, *b.* 10th June, 1802, who married and had a daughter.

Renira-Charlotte, *m.* to her cousin Captain John-Brett Purvis.

Emma, died in infancy.

Georgiana, *m.* in 1828, to the Rev. Charles Edward Twyford, rector of Trotton, in Sussex.

1. Mary-Oadam, died unmarried in 1812.

2. Elizabeth, *m.* first, to Benjamin Good, esq.; and secondly, to Andrew Long, esq. and *d. s. p.* in 1772.

3. Lissey-Anna, died young in 1758.

4. Emma, *m.* 1st July, 1789, to Major Richard Thomas Timms.

ı. Harvey, died in the West Indies, 2nd February, 1740.

Martha, *m.* to Thomas Pearse, esq. and had a son, Colonel Thomas Deane Pearse, of the East India Company's service, who *d.* in 1789.

ɛe Purvis died at Islington, 6th March, and was *s.* by his son,

ɪʀʟᴇs-Wᴀɢᴇʀ Pᴜʀᴠɪs, esq. of Dar- rear-admiral in the royal navy, born une, 1715, who *m.* at Queen Square ıl, Westminster, 3rd November, 1741, Godfrey, niece of Dr. Mawson, Bishop y, and by her, who died at Yoxford, December, 1777, had

. Cʜᴀʀʟᴇs, his heir.

ı. Thomas, in holy orders, rector of Melton, in Suffolk, *b.* at Darsham, 29th October, 1750, *m.* in November, 1773, Lætitia-Anne-Philippa, daughter of the Rev. John Leman, of Wenhaston, and dying in 1786 left issue,

Amy-Letitia, *m.* 13th September, 1794, to the Rev. Nathaniel Colvile.

Elizabeth-Maria, *m.* to the Rev. John Ewen, of Reydon, Suffolk.

Anna, *d.* unm. in 1801.

ıı. William, *b.* 1st October, 1757, who *m.* at Bath, 13th April, 1789, Harriet-Susan, daughter and heiress of Samuel Eyre, esq. of Newhouse, Wilts, and assumed in consequence the surname and arms of Eʏʀᴇ. He died at Bath in 1810, leaving four daughters, viz.

Hᴀʀʀɪᴇᴛ Eʏʀᴇ, *b.* at Tiverton, in Somersetshire, *m.* in 1817, to George Matcham, esq. D. C. L.

Eliza-Purvis Eyre, *b.* at Downton, Wilts.

Charlotte-Louisa Eyre, born at Downton, Wilts.

Julia-Purvis Eyre.

ı. Elizabeth, *b.* in London, 10th August, 1746, died the December following.

ıı. Amy, died an infant.

ɪɪɪ. Elizabeth, *m.* to Joseph Battin, esq. and *d.* at Bath in 1820.

ɪᴠ. Henrietta-Maria, *d.* unm. 27th February, 1769.

Admiral Purvis died in Kensington Square, 15th January, 1772, was buried at Darsham, and *s.* by his son,

Cʜᴀʀʟᴇs Pᴜʀᴠɪs, esq. of Darsham, born 1st July, 1743, in the commission of the peace for Suffolk, and high sheriff for that county in 1794. He wedded at St. George the Martyr, 27th January, 1774, Elizabeth, daughter of Edward Holden Cruttenden, esq. and by her, who died at Bath 25th March, 1816, had two sons and two daughters, viz.

ɪ. Cʜᴀʀʟᴇs, his heir.

ɪɪ. Edward, *b.* at Darsham, 21st April, 1786, formerly a military officer, now residing at Reading, Berks. He *m.* 24th July, 1817, Lettice-Elizabeth, daughter and heir of the Rev. John Mulso, of Twywell, in Northamptonshire, and has issue,

1. Edward-Mulso.

1. Caroline-Elizabeth.
2. Jane-Lauretta.
3. Eleanor-Sophia.
4. Amelia.
5. Marcella.
6. Mary.

ɪ. Elizabeth, *m.* 8th July, 1817, to the Rev. Edward Ravenshaw, rector of West Kington, Wilts.

ɪɪ. Sarah-Anne, died at Bath 12th July, 1797.

Mr. Purvis died at Bath 10th December, 1808, was buried at Darsham, and succeeded by his son, the present Cʜᴀʀʟᴇs Pᴜʀᴠɪs, esq. of Darsham.

*Arms*—Az. on a fess arg. between three mascles or, as many cinquefoils of the field.

*Crest*—The sun in splendour, rising from clouds, all ppr.; over it, "Clarior e tenebris."

*Estates*—In the parishes of Yoxford and Westleton, Suffolk.

*Seat*—Darsham House, near Yoxford.

# PARTRIDGE, OF HOCKHAM HALL.

**PARTRIDGE, HENRY-SAMUEL**, esq. of Hockham Hall, in Norfolk, *b.* 22nd June, 1782, *m.* 18th July, 1805, Mary-Frances, daughter of the Venerable Luke Heslop, D.D. rector of Marylebone, London, Archdeacon of Buckinghamshire, and has had issue,

I. HENRY-CHAMPION.
II. Edward-Jacob, *d.* 24th November, 1826.
III. Charles-Francis.
IV. Walter-John.
V. Frederick-Robert.
VI. William-Luke.
VII. George-Anthony.

I. Louisa-Katherine, *m.* 7th August, 1833, to Henry Dover, esq. of Bradenham Hall, in the county of Norfolk, and *d.* 30th August, 1834.
II. Charlotte-Anne, died unmarried, 1825.
III. Sophia-Sarah, *m.* 29th August, 1829, to George Gataker, esq. and has issue.
IV. Eleanor-Dorothea.

Mr. Partridge, who is a magistrate, and deputy-lieutenant for the county of Norfolk, succeeded his father 30th December, 1803.

## Lineage.

HENRY PARTRIDGE, esq. Alderman of London, born in 1604, died 13th December, 1666, (he was buried in Bray church,) leaving, with two daughters, Hannah and Sarah, who both died unmarried, a son,

HENRY PARTRIDGE, esq. who wedded Joanna, daughter and co-heir of Robert Jaques, esq. of Elmestone, in Kent, Alderman of London, and High Sheriff for Kent, by Joanna, his wife, daughter and heiress of William Foy, esq. and left a son,

HENRY PARTRIDGE, esq. born 17th May, 1671, subsequently to his father's decease, which event occurred on the 5th January, preceding, the year in which that gentleman served as High Sheriff for the county of Berks. He married, first, in Aldgate church, London, 21st October, 1701, Elizabeth, only daughter and heiress of Thomas Holder, esq. of Northwold, by whom, who died 17th January, 1703, he had no issue; and, secondly, Martha, eldest daughter of John Wright, merchant, and by her, who died at Croydon, 20th February, 1760, had,

I. HENRY, his heir.
II. Robert, born at Buckenham House, Norfolk, 19th May, 1713, died unmarried, 9th April, 1779, and was buried at St. Margaret's, Lothbury.
III. Joseph, born at Buckenham House, 1st August, 1714, married Miss Heathfield, of Croydon, but died without issue, 21st October, 1788.
IV. John, born at Buckenham House, 17th October, 1719, died 27th February, 1809, in his ninetieth year, and was buried in Croydon church.

I. Catharine, born in St. Paul's, Covent Garden, 13th November, 1708, died an infant.
II. Sarah, born at Colveston House, Norfolk, died in 1712.
III. Sarah, born at Buckenham House, 7th September, 1716, died unmarried in 1790.
IV. Martha, born at Buckenham House, 17th November, 1717, married in 1739, to Mr. Cole, of the Register's Office in Chancery.

Elizabeth, born 30th October, 1721, married in 1750, to the Rev. Samuel Knight.

. Catharine, born 22nd March, 1726, married, in 1751, to William Purcas, esq. Barrister-at-law, one of the Six Clerks in Chancery, and *d.* in 1773, leaving two daughters,

Catharine Purcas, *m.* in August, 1779, to Mr. Sutton Sharpe, of London, and died in 1791, leaving a dau. Catharine Sharpe.

Jane Purcas, *m.* 8th March, 1776, to Robert Partridge, esq.

rtridge died 3rd July, 1733, and was led by his son,

RY PARTRIDGE, esq. of Northwold, folk, and of Lowbrooks, in Berk-vho was born at Colveston House, anuary, 1711. He married, first, at Lynn, 26th July, 1745, Mary, daugh-heiress of Robert Say, merchant, her, who died 28th April, 1748, aged had two sons, and one daughter,

HENRY, his heir.

Robert, *b.* 18th May, 1747, who married 8th, March, 1776, his cousin Jane, daughter of William Purcas, esq. and dying 14th February, 1817, left one son, and three daughters, viz.

Robert, *b.* in 1797, and *d.* 15th April, 1823.

Jane, *m.* in 1806, to the Rev. Henry Say, rector of North Pickenham, and Houghton on the Hill, Norfolk, and had issue,

Mary, *m.* in 1804, to the Rev. Peter Hansell, Minor Canon of the Cathedral of Norwich, and has four sons and three daughters, namely, Peter, Henry (*m.* Miss Brown), Robert, Edward-Halifax; Mary, Jane, and Catharine.

Catharine died in infancy.

Mary, married to Bryan Burrell, esq. of Broom Park, in Northumberland, and died in 1776, leaving issue, William Burrell, esq. of Broom Park, and Henry Burrell, who died unmarried in 1814.

rtridge espoused, secondly, 1751, daughter of Simon Taylor, merchant n, and by her, who died in 1797, had re sons, and another daughter, viz.

. Walter, born in 1757, who died unmarried, at Gibraltar, in December, 1800.

. John, *b.* in 1766, married in 1801, at Bath, Sarah, daughter of Edward Everard, esq. of Lynn, and died at Brighton, 17th May, 1813, leaving issue,

1. Alice, *m.* 1st January, 1834, to Joseph Fry, esq. and has issue.
2. Pleasance.

II. Martha, *m.* in 1786, to Mr. John Vancouver, and *d. s. p.* in 1807.

Mr. Partridge died at Lynn, 4th November, 1793, aged eighty-two, and was *s.* by his eldest son,

HENRY PARTRIDGE, esq. of Northwold and Lowbrooks, born at Lynn, 24th May, 1746, who *m.* in 1781, Katherine, youngest daughter of Samuel Reynardson, esq. of Holywell, in the county of Lincoln, and by her, who died 15th of December, 1819, and was buried at Cromer, had three sons and four daughters, viz.

I. HENRY-SAMUEL, his heir.

II. Charles-Robert, born in 1791, died in 1800.

III. John-Anthony, in holy orders, rector of Malpas, Cheshire, married 18th May, 1826, Louisa-Isabella, youngest daughter of the late Thomas Tyrwhitt Drake, esq. of Shardeloes, in the county of Buckingham, (*See Vol. I. page* 582,) and has issue,

John-Francis, *b.* 29th May, 1827.
Anthony-William, *b.* 1st Dec. 1831.
Isabella-Katherine.
Charlotte-Anne.

I. Katherine-Mary.

II. Sarah-Frances, married 9th Nov. 1815, to Benjamin Wilson, esq. of Sledah Hall, in the county of Wexford, eldest son of Christian Wilson, esq. of Benville, and has issue,

Christian Wilson, born 17th Oct. 1817.
Edward-Benjamin Wilson, born 24th July, 1824.
Henry-John Wilson, born 2nd April, 1827.
Katherine-Fredsweed Wilson.
Frances-Sarah Wilson.
Jemima-Charlotte Wilson.
Sophia-Arabella Wilson.
Louisa-Dorothea Wilson.

III. Charlotte, married 16th April, 1808, to Jocelyn Henry Conner Thomas, esq. son of the Rev. Dr. Thomas, of Everton, in Ireland, and has issue,

Jocelyn-Bartholomew Thomas, *b.* 16th of March, 1809.
Bartholomew-John-William Thomas, *b.* in 1811.
Henry-Samuel Thomas, *b.* 30th November, 1813.
Edward-Rice Thomas, *b.* 8th February, 1817.
Charles-Stanhope Thomas, *b.* 1st December, 1819.
Katherine Thomas, *m.* in 1827, to Major Turton.

Charlotte-Mary Thomas, born at Bruges.
Louisa-Sophia Thomas, born at Hobarts-town.
Anne-Theresa Thomas, born at Hobarts-town.

IV. Sophia, married 11th April, 1808, to John Thruston Mott, esq. of Barningham Hall, in Norfolk, and has issue.

Mr. Partridge died 30th December, 1803, and was succeeded by his son, the present HENRY-SAMUEL PARTRIDGE, esq. of Hockham Hall.

*Arms*—Gu. on a fess cotised or, between three partridges, with wings displayed of the last, three torteaux.

*Crest*—A partridge, as in the arms.

*Motto*—Dum spiro spero.

*Estates*—HOCKHAM, Magna and Parva, in Norfolk, obtained in 1811, by exchange of part of the former family estates at Cranwich, and Northwold, in Norfolk, and Warley Hall, and Mash Hall, in Essex. LOWBROOKS, in Berkshire, parish of Bray, acquired in 1614, with the heiress of Robert Jaques, esq. Impropriate rectory of Methwold, and Southery, in Norfolk: manor of Northwold, and farm, &c. at Whittington hamlet, of Northwold.

*Seat*—Hockham Hall, near Thetford.

## DIXON, OF GLEDHOW.

DIXON, HENRY, esq. of Gledhow, in the county of York, born 19th November, 1794, married on the 24th of December, 1829, Emma-Matilda, niece of Sir Robert Wilmot, of Chaddesden, near Derby. Mr. Dixon succeeded his father in 1825.

### Lineage.

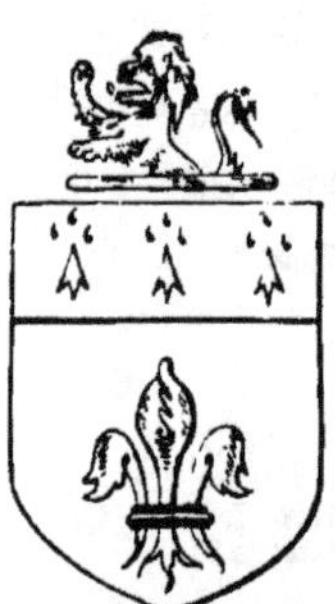

WILLIAM DIXON, of Heaton Royds, filed a bill in 1564, against the then Lord of the Manor of Heaton, and several of the freeholders, for inclosing a considerable part of the Commons within that Manor, which by an order of court, dated the 12th of June, 1566, was ordered to be laid open and enjoyed, in common, as heretofore. He was father of

ABRAHAM DIXON, of Heaton Royds, party to deeds in 1608, 1611, and 1642, whose son,

JOHN DIXON, of Heaton Royds, married in 1611, Mary, daughter of Richard Baylie, of Allerton, and had issue,

I. JEREMIAH, his heir.
II. John, of Bradford, to whom Heaton Royds, Shay, or, Shaw belonged. His daughter married Dr. Firth, of Thornton.
III. William, of Bowling, Captain in Cromwell's army, living in 1664. His son, John, was a party to deeds in 1674, 1676, and 1678.
IV. Abraham.
V. Joshua, who settled at Leeds, where he was living in 1652, and 1674. He married Eleanor, sister of William Dodgson, and aunt of Mr. Alderman John Dodgson, twice mayor of Leeds. By this lady, he left, with two daughters, Hannah, Mrs. Woolfall, and Martha, Mrs. Jackson, two sons, namely,
    1. JEREMIAH, of Leeds, who married Mary, daughter of Alderman John Dodgson, and by her, who died at York 21st January, 1743-4, aged sixty-six, left, at his decease, 16th October, 1721, a son,

JOHN, of whom presently,
2. Joshua, of Leeds, merchant, who died in 1721, aged forty-six, leaving, by Phœbe, his wife, daughter of Simpson, of Simpson's Fold, one son and three daughters, viz.
Joshua, *b.* in 1708, Alderman and Mayor of Leeds in 1765, who *m.* Hannah, daughter of Francis Pitt, of Wakefield, and died in 1775, having had
Jeremiah, A.M. Perpetual Curate of Woolley, a Magistrate and Deputy Lieutenant for the West Riding of Yorkshire, born in 1751; married in 1780, Ann, daughter of Mr. John Gott, of Woodhall, and had, with other issue,
JOSHUA, of Leeds, *b.* in 1784, married in 1808, Susanna, dau. of the Rev. William Shepley, and had issue,
Hannah, married in 1769, to the Rev. Thomas Faber, Vicar of Calverley.
Elizabeth, married, first, to William Denton, esq. of Pledwick, and, secondly, to Thomas Jones, esq. of Leeds.

I. Isabella.
II. Esther.
III. Judith.
IV. Mary, married to John Hull, of Thornton.
V. Martha.

John Dixon, of Heaton Royds, died about the year 1646, and was succeeded by his son,

JEREMIAH DIXON, esq. of Heaton Royds, born in 1612, who died in 1707, leaving, by Martha, his wife, a son and successor,

JEREMIAH DIXON, esq. of Heaton Royds, who died issueless about the year 1725, devising his estate at Heaton Royds, to Joshua, the son of Joshua Dixon, of Leeds, and bequeathing a valuable property, called Birchenlee, near Bradford, for the benefit of the minister, for the time being, of the Presbyterian chapel at that place, in the yard of which he lies buried. The representation of the family passed, at his decease, to his cousin,

JOHN DIXON, of Leeds, Merchant, son of Jeremiah, and great-grandson of John, of Heaton Royds. This gentleman wedded Frances, daughter of Thomas Gower, esq. of Hutton, who was son of Edward Gower, esq. of Hutton, and grandson of Edward Gower, esq. whose elder brother, Sir Thomas Gower, bart. of Stittenham, wedded the heiress of the Levesons, of Trentham, and was direct ancestor of the present Duke of Sutherland. By this lady, Mr. Dixon left, at his demise, on the 4th of February, 1749, aged fifty-four, a son and successor,

JEREMIAH DIXON, esq. F.R.S. who purchased, in 1764, the estate of Gledhow, from the Wilson family, in 1765, the manor of Chapel Allerton, from Mr. Kellingback, and, in 1771, the estates of Lady Dawes and her son. In the years 1766 and 1767, Mr. Dixon made considerable additions to the old mansion at Gledhow, and, during the remainder of his life, continued to ornament it with beautiful plantations. He *m.* Mary, daughter of the Rev. Henry Wickham, Rector of Guiseley, and had issue,

I. JOHN, his heir.
II. Jeremiah, Mayor of Leeds in 1784, married Mary, dau. of John Smeaton, esq. who built the Edystone Lighthouse.
III. Henry, of Brookefarm, near Liverpool, married Catherina-Towneley Plumbe, daughter of Thomas Plumbe, esq. and sister of the present Colonel Plumbe Tempest, of Tong Hall, in Yorkshire, by whom, who died in 1819, he had five sons and three daughters,
1. Henry, Captain in the eighty-first regiment, married Miss Harriet Frazer, of Halifax, in Nova Scotia.
2. Thomas.
3. William, in Holy Orders.
4. George, an Officer in the Army.
5. Edward, Lieutenant R. N.
1. Frances-Elizabeth.
2. Georgiana-Charlotte.
3. Henriana-Annetta.

I. Mary, of Thorp Arch.
II. Frances, married to the Rev. William Shepley, Curate of Horsforth.
III. Annabella, married to Ellis Leckonby Hodgson, esq. of Stapleton Hall.
IV. Charlotte, married to John Grimston, esq. of Neswick.

Mr. Dixon died 7th June, 1782, aged fifty-six, was buried at Leeds, and succeeded by his son,

JOHN DIXON, esq. of Gledhow, born 27th June, 1753, Colonel of the First West

York Militia, who *m.* 13th July, 1784, Lydia, daughter of the Rev. T. Parker, of Astle, in the county of Chester, and had issue,

I. HENRY, his heir.
II. John, Captain in the First Foot, *b.* 13th February, 1799.
III. George, Capt. in the Third Guards, *b.* 5th August, 1801.
IV. Charles, deceased.
I. Lydia.
II. Mary, *m.* to George Stone, esq.
III. Jane, married to Captain Charles Loftus, son of the late General Loftus, (*See Vol. I. page* 213.)
IV. Anne, married to T. Kinnersley, esq. of Clough Hall, Staffordshire.

Colonel Dixon, who was a Magistrate, and Deputy-Lieutenant for the West Riding of Yorkshire, died in 1825, and was succeeded by his son, the present HENRY DIXON, esq. of Gledhow.

*Arms*—Gu. a fleur de lys or, a chief ermine.

*Crest*—A demi lion rampt. arg.

*Estates*—In the counties of York and Chester.

*Seats*—Gledhow, near Leeds, and Astle, near Knutsford.

## BULKELEY, OF STANDLOW.

BULKELEY, HENRY, esq. of Standlow, in the county of Stafford, *b.* 1st of October, 1791, succeeded upon the demise of his father.

### Lineage.

This family deduces from remote antiquity. Its surname, derived from a ridge of mountains in the county Palatine of Chester, was spelt, in the reign of JOHN, and for generations preceding, BULCLOGH (or large mountain.) In the 20th HENRY IV. and in the visitations of EDWARD IV. its designation was Bulclogh, Lord of Bulclogh de Perwycke and de Stanlow; subsequently it was described, as Bulkely, Lord of Bulkeley, in Cheshire, and of the manors of Eaton, Presland, Alprove, Norbury, Wore, and Stanlow, and, in Inquisitions Post Mortem, of later date, of Stoke and Mayfield,

ROBERT BULCLOGH, Lord of Bulclogh, in the time of *King* JOHN, was father of

WILLIAM BULCLOGH, of Bulclogh, who left five sons, viz.

ROBERT, his successor.
Willcock, of Petty Hall, in Cheshire, married Mary, daughter of Henry Venables, Baron of Kinderton, and had an only son,
  Willcock.
Roger, of Orton Madock.
Ralph, of Rudal Heath, died issueless.
David, of Bickerton.

The eldest son,

ROBERT BULCLOGH, of Bulclogh, married a daughter of Thomas Butler, of Warrington, and had (with daughters) Peter, ancestor of the Bulkeleys, of Wore, in Salop, and an elder son, his heir,

WILLIAM BULCLOGH, of Bulclogh, living in 1302, who, marrying twice, had, by his first wife, Maud, daughter of Sir John Davenport, knt. four sons, and, by the second, Alice, daughter of Bryan St. Pierre, a fifth, as follow,

I. WILLIAM, heir and inheritor of Bulclogh, whose line terminated with his grandaughter,
  ALICE BULKELEY, the wife of Thomas Holford, of Holford, in Cheshire.
II. ROBERT, of whom presently,
III. Roger, of Norbury, in Cheshire, whose descendants assumed the surname of Norbury.

[T]homas, married Alice, daughter [an]d co-heir of Matthew Alprahum, [...]d, acquiring thereby that estate, [se]tled there. His only daughter [an]d heiress, Helen, m. Sir Thomas [Ar]derne, of Aldford. "The elder [br]anch of the ARDERNES (says Lysons) [wh]ose chief seat was at Aldford, [wh]ere they had a castle, became [ext]inct in the principal line, by the [dea]th of Walkeline Arderne, in or [ab]out the reign of RICHARD II.

[Ri]chard (the son of the second mar[ria]ge,) had the manor of Prestland, [fro]m which he assumed the surname [of] "Prestland," which his descend[ant]s continued to bear.

[The secon]d son,

[...] BULCLOGH, became of EATON, in [...] and was sheriff of that county in [...] wedded Isabel, daughter of Philip [...] of Malpas, and had (with a daugh[ter ...], wife of Thomas Weaver, esq. of [...]) two sons, viz.

[ROBE]RT, his heir.

[RICH]ARD,* from whom the *Extinct* [BARON]ETS BULKELEY, (*refer to* BURKE'S [*Ex*]*tinct and Dormant Peerage*).

[His] son and heir,

[ROBERT] BULKELEY, esq. of Eaton, who had [th]e office of sheriff of Cheshire, in [his] father being then alive, was [...]

[Sir WI]LLIAM BULKELEY, knt. of Eaton, [Just]ice of Chester in the reign of [...]. who married Margaret, daugh[ter of] Richard Molyneux, of Sephton, [and d]aughter (maternally) of Thomas, [... De]rby, by whom he had issue,

[THO]MAS, of Eaton, who married Eli[zab]eth, daughter of Sir Geoffry War[bur]ton, of Warburton, (*See Vol. II.* [pag]e 2,) and had three sons, and [...] daughters, namely,

[I]. THOMAS, *m.* Eleanor, daughter of Sir William Brereton, and had a son, THOMAS, who *d. s. p.*

2. Robert, whose son, William, died unmarried.
3. William, whose two sons, Robert and Richard, *d. s. p.*
1. Jane, *m.* to Roger Puleston, esq. of Kumbrall.
2. Elizabeth, married to John Probisher, esq. of Chirke, in the county of Flint.

II. Arthur, living 25th HENRY VIII.

III. RALPH.

The youngest son,

RALPH BULKELEY, esq. living in the beginning of the fifteenth century, married the daughter and heiress of Vernon, of Whitcroft, in Cheshire, and of Perwyche, or Parwick, in the county of Derby, and acquired thereby those estates. He was father of,

WILLIAM BULKELEY, esq. an officer under the Lord Audley, and Master of the Wardrobe, who, for his public services, had a confirmation of his estates, by the name of William, *the Hunter*. His son,

RICHARD BULKELEY, esq. of Parwick, acquired the lordship of Stanlowe, in the county of Stafford, by his wife, Joan, dau. and heir of Richard Sherratt, of Cheddleton and Stanlowe. His son and successor,

HUMPHREY BULKELEY, esq. of Standlowe, married Joan, daughter of William Egerton, of Walgrange, and had two sons, William and Thomas: the elder,

WILLIAM BULKELEY, esq. of Standlowe, upon whom his father entailed the estates in the counties of Derby and Stafford, married thrice. By his first wife, Alice Jodrell, he had a son THOMAS. By the second, Margaret, widow of William Bromley, esq. and daughter of Sir William Young, of Kimton, knt. he had William, Rowland, and Alice, wife of Humphrey Hill, of Hawkestone. By the third, a daughter of Husse, of Battlefield, in Salop, he had no issue. He was succeeded by his eldest son,

THOMAS BULKELEY, esq. of Standlow, who married in 1573, Catharine, daughter of Robert Holingshead, esq. of Baddesley, in Cheshire, and had ARTHUR, Alexander, Timothy, and Fortune. The eldest son and heir,

ARTHUR BULKELEY, esq. of Standlow, *b.* in 1563, *m.* in 1582, Joyce, daughter of John Ashenhurst, esq. of Ashenhurst, and was succeeded by his eldest son,

JOHN BULKELEY, esq. of Standlow, *b.* in 1583, who married first, in 1608, Eleanor, daughter of Thomas Benyon, esq. of Marbury, in Cheshire, and had three daughters, Anne, *m.* to John Williamson, of Cholley; Alice, the wife of William Watkis, esq. of Aston; and Mary, wife of Thomas Robins, esq. He wedded secondly, in 1619, Sarah, daughter of Edward Mainwaring, esq. of Whitmore, and had issue,

* [O]f this RICHARD's direct descendants [LAN]CELOT BULKELEY, consecrated ARCH[BISHOP OF D]UBLIN, in 1619. He married Alice, [...] Rowland Bulkeley, esq. of Beaumaris, whose love of lamb remains upon [...] commissioners of government hav[ing issu]ed an order to prohibit the killing of [lamb, owi]ng to the great decay and scarcity of [...], the penalty of 10*s.* for each lamb, to [be paid as] well by the killer as the consumer, [Mrs. Bulke]ley petitioned for license to eat lamb, [on account o]f her great age, and weakness of body: [in conside]ration whereof, her petition was [granted, an]d she had a license, 17th March, 1652, [to kill and] dress so much as should be necessary [for her] use and eating, not to exceed, how[ever, ...] lambs in the whole of that year.

THOMAS, his heir.

Arthur, *b.* in 1622, who purchased an estate in the county of Louth, married Elizabeth, daughter of James Fox, esq. of Manchester, son of Sir Patrick Fox, of Westmeath, and had four daughters, viz.

Eleanor, *m.* to — Palmer, esq.

Elizabeth, *m.* to — Jackson, esq. of the county of Meath.

Sarah, *m.* to — Butler, esq. of the county of Kilkenny.

Margaret, *m.* to Mr. Lamprey, of Dublin, and her son, Arthur Lamprey, was sheriff of Dublin in 1755.

John.

Sarah, *m.* to Thomas Jolley, esq.

Eleanor.

John Bulkeley *d.* in 1665, at the advanced age of eighty-three, and was *s.* by his eldest son,

THOMAS BULKELEY, esq. of Standlow, *b.* 3d February, 1620, who *m.* 19th December, 1646, Alice, daughter of Godfrey Froggatt, esq. of Mathfield, in the county of Stafford, and dying 22d August, 1675, left issue,

JOHN, his heir.

Arthur, *b.* in 1664, *m.* in 1700, Elizabeth, daughter of Henry Lowe, esq. of Whittington, in Derbyshire, and had a son,

ARTHUR, eventual inheritor of Standlow.

He was *s.* by his eldest son,

JOHN BULKELEY, esq. of Standlow. This gentleman *m.* in 1675, Elizabeth, daughter of Sampson Webb, esq. of Aston, in the county of Stafford, and had one son and a daughter, viz.

THOMAS, his heir.

Catherine, *b.* 7th August, 1679, *m.* to Thomas Sleigh, of Boothlow in Staffordshire, and had two daughters,

Elizabeth Sleigh.

Catherine Sleigh, *m.* to Samuel Lanskford, of Leek.

He *d.* in 1696, and was *s.* by his eldest son,

THOMAS BULKELEY, esq. of Standlow, who wedded, 1st May, 1700, Mary, daughter of Richard Wright, esq. of Nantwich, in Cheshire, and had surviving issue,

Elizabeth, *m.* to Mr. Foder, an apothecary, near Congleton.

Anne, *m.* to the Rev. Roger Hughson, who *d.* 9th January, 1747.

This gentleman, on his marriage, entailed his house and some of his lands at Standlow upon his issue male; failure of which, upon his right heirs male. He *d.* 19th May, 1736, and was *s.* under the entail, by his cousin,

ARTHUR BULKELEY, esq. who *m.* 14th September, 1742, Jane, eldest daughter of Roger Newham, gent. of Staveley Forge, in the county of Derby, and had issue,

THOMAS-ASHTON, his heir.

John, *d.* 13th March, 1782, aged thirty-five, unmarried.

Henry, *b.* 13th March, 1760, *d.* 21st July, 1821, unm.

Kitty, *b.* 9th Aug. 1755, *d.* unm. in 1814.

Anne, *b.* 25th January, 1764, *m.* John Wright, gent. and *d. s. p.* 24th Nov. 1832.

He was *s.* at his decease, 25th May, 1771, by his eldest son,

THOMAS ASHTON BULKELEY, esq. of Hill-Top House, in the county of Derby,* who *m.*

---

* The following is a recorded account of this gentleman's baptism:—

On the 12th July, 1744, was christened, at Whittington, near Chesterfield, Thomas Ashton Bulkeley, the following persons, by their representatives standing sponsors,

Edward Downs, esq. of Worth, in Cheshire, the infant's *great-great-great*-great uncle.

Mr. Ashton, Master of Jesus College, Cambridge, and his brother, Mr. Joseph Ashton, of Surrey-street, in the Strand, the infant's *great-great*-great uncles.

Mrs. Elizabeth Wood, of Barnsley, in Yorkshire, the infant's *great-great-great* - great aunt.

Mrs. Jane Wainwright, of Middlewood Hall, in Yorkshire, the infant's *great-great*-grandmother.

Mrs. Dorothy Green, of the same place, the infant's great grandmother.

The infant has a mother, grandmother, great grandmother, and great-great grandmother now living, and Mrs. Wainwright, the great-great grandmother, who is now eighty-nine, although she cannot say, "Rise up, daughter, and go to thy daughter, for thy daughter's daughter has a daughter;" she can say, what is in equal degree to it, "Rise up, daughter, &c. thy daughter's daughter has a son." The infant, by the mother's side, is lineally descended from ROBERT ASHTON, esq. of Bradway, in Derbyshire, and Dorothy, his wife, who were the said Mrs. Wainwrights, Dr. Ashton and Mr. Joseph Ashton's father and mother, and of whom some remarkable circumstances may be related, viz.

That during their whole lives they were eminent for all Christian virtues, that they never had more than twelve children, eight sons and four daughters, who were all nursed by her, and lived to be men and women, that they were as good parents in every respect to all their children, without partiality to any of them, as ever children were blessed with. That they lived in the same house at BRADWAY above fifty years, and they had near twenty in family great part of the time. No person whatever died in the house during the first fifty years, they lived together sixty-four years after their marriage, but it must be owned that they were tied together with a double knot, for being married in Oliver's time, the ceremony was twice performed, once by a justice of the peace, according to the law of that time, and again by a clergyman according to the rites of the Church of England, of which they were both worthy members.

June, 1778, Elizabeth, daughter of Mr. el Yardley, of Horton, in the county of rd, and had issue,

HENRY, his heir.

Elizabeth, *m.* first, to Charles Daintry, esq. of Darleston Green, in Staffordshire, and secondly, to Richard Froggatt, esq. of the Hagg, in Derbyshire, without issue.

Sarah, *m.* first, to Mr. John Birks, of Brampton, in Yorkshire, and has issue,

John Birks, *b.* 5th August, 1815.
Bulkeley-Henry Birks, *b.* 8th June, 1817.
Elizabeth Birks.
Sarah Birks.
Pamela-Prescilla Birks.

She wedded, secondly, Mr. Handcock.

Mr. Bulkeley was succeeded at his decease by his only son, the present HENRY BULKELEY, esq. of Standlow.

*Arms*—Sable, a chevron, between three bulls' heads caboshed arg. armed or.

*Crest*—Out of a ducal coronet a bull's head arg.

*Estates*—In Staffordshire.

*Seat*—Standlow, in that county.

## FFARINGTON, OF SHAWE HALL.

RINGTON, WILLIAM, esq. of Shawe Hall, in the county palatine of Lancaster, *m.* first, in 1791, Sybella-Georgiana, daughter of Edward Wilbraham Bootle, esq. of Lathom, and sister of Lord Skelmersdale, by whom (who *d.* in 1799) he had, with three sons, who all died in youth, three daughters, of which the eldest, Mary-Isabella, *d.* young; Sybella-Georgina, the second, wedded Thomas Scarisbrick, esq. of Scarisbrick, and Frances-Anne, the youngest, *d.* in 1821. He wedded, secondly, in 1803, Hannah, daughter of John Mathews, esq. of Tynemouth, and by that lady, who died in 1833, had issue,

George, who *d.* in 1819.
William-Mathews, *d.* in 1827.
JAMES NOWELL, *b.* in 1813.

Susan-Marie.
Mary-Hannah.

arington succeeded his uncle, Sir William ffarington. He is a deputy-lieut. as high sheriff in 1813 for the county of Lancaster. For several years he was el of the 2nd regiment of Lancaster militia, and served with it in Ireland.

### Lineage.

FFARINGTONS, of ffarington, Wearand Shawe Hall, all in the parish of ad,* and county palatine of Lancaster, at the time of the Conquest, and have preserved an uninterrupted male succession. They resided at ffarington so recently as the time of ELIZABETH, and continued at Wearden† until the close of the 16th century, when they removed to Shawe Hall. Of the mansion of Wearden, a portion re-

* e manor and hundred of LEYLAND was held EDWARD *the Confessor*, and the Men of the which was of the superior order, as well e of Salford, enjoyed the privilege of at- to their own harvest in autumn, instead king's.

† At Werden, a building of early date, the eldest sons of the family resided during their father's lifetime, as we find they continued to do in ELIZABETH's time, when Sir Henry lived at ffarynton, and his son William at Werden.

mains, and the ancient outbuildings are remarkable for retaining still in fine preservation the family arms carved on the ends of their projecting beams of oak.

WARIN BUSSEL, seated at Penwortham, one of the barons under Roger de Poicton, in the time of the CONQUEROR, held, among his ample demesnes, the parish of Leland, and was a considerable benefactor to the Abbey of Evesham, in Worcestershire, to which he gave the Priory of Penwortham. His son,

WARIN BUSSEL, was father of

ROBERT BUSSEL, whose daughter, AVICIA BUSSEL, *m.* in the 14th HENRY III. (1230), JOHN DE FFARINGTON, grandson of W. de Meles, corredor of the church of Leyland, and son of Richard de ffarington, of Hogwic. This

JOHN DE FFARINGTON, and AVIS, his wife, in the 7th EDWARD I. (1279), had a process directed to William Walton to deliver up his lands in Leyland, and John Croft, and Emma, his wife, and W., the son of Adam de Walton, were required to do the like, "which lands, John, the son of W. de Meles, had in free marriage with Alicia, the daughter of Robert Bussel, and which were to descend after the death of John and Avicia, and William, their son, according to the form of donation." From this John de ffarington lineally derived,*

SIR JOHN DE FFARYNGTON, who wedded Margaret Butler, and had four sons, viz.

I. WILLIAM, who *m.* Jane Redmayne.
II. JOHN, of whom presently.
III. Thomas, proposed himself a monk at Glastonbury.
IV. Nicholas, who *m.* Jane Longworthy, and was father of
   Thomas, who left, by Anne Worsley, his wife, two sons, viz.
      Perceval, of Northbroke, whose grand-daughter, Margaret ffarington, *m.* Nicholas Garstang.
      Roger, knight of the shire for the county of Lancashire, 31-34th EDWARD III.

The second son,

JOHN FFARYNTON, *m.* Margaret Anderton, and left a son and successor,

SIR JOHN FFARYNTON, father, by Clarissa, his wife, daughter of — Kighley, of Inskip, of three sons, WILLIAM, his heir; Robert, of Southbrooke, who *m.* and had issue; and Roger, a priest. The eldest son,

WILLIAM DE FFARYNTON, to whom was granted 22nd EDWARD III. (1349), a right of park and free-warren in Leyland and Farmeston, espoused Jennet Dalton, and had issue,

I. WILLIAM (Sir), his heir.
II. Thomas, who *m.* the daughter and heiress of John Southworth, of Little ffarington.
III. Nicholas.

The eldest son and successor,

SIR WILLIAM FFARYNGTON, whose name appears in Froissart's Chronicle, wedded Dorothy, daughter of — Standish, of Duxbury, in the county of Lancaster, and had issue,

I. WILLIAM, *d. s. p.*
II. JOHN.
III. Robert, a priest.
IV. PETER, who *m.* Elizabeth Shakerley, of Shakerley, and had a son Thomas, who *m.* Ann Banister, of Bank, and left, with a daughter Elizabeth, the wife of John Butler, of Kirkland, a son,
   PETER, of Little ffarington, who wedded Alice Huddleston, of Huddleston, and had five daughters, Isabella, wife of Richard Banister, of Banister Hall; Alice, *m.* first, to Skelton, and secondly, to Norreys, of Blackrode; Cecilia, to Thomas Charnock, of Charnock; Elizabeth, to John Cuerden, of Cuerden; and Ann, to John ffarington.

Sir William was *s.* by his son,

JOHN FFARINGTON, who was father, by Alice Houghton, his wife, of

SIR WILLIAM FFARINGTON, who espoused Cecilie Tunstall, and had two sons and one daughter, viz.

I. WILLIAM (Sir), his heir.
II. Henry, who *m.* Cecilie, daughter and heir of Edmund Linguard, of Linguard, and became ancestor of the branch of the family which settled at Chichester, in Sussex, and of which Richard ffarington, sheriff of London in 1609, and Sir Richard ffarington, created a BARONET in 1697, were members.
I. Anne, married to Sir John Bulkley, of Beaumaris.

* The intermediate descent was as follows:

John de ffarynton=Avis
|
John de ffarynton=Maude Banister
|
William de ffarynton=Alice Farendon
|
Sir Wm. de ffaryngton=Alice Trafford
|
Sir John de ffaryngton=Margaret Butler. — Margaret, *m.* to Thomas Latham, of Parbold.

The eldest son,

SIR WILLIAM FFARINGTON, married Cicelie Leyland, and left, at his decease, a son and successor,

SIR WILLIAM FFARINGTON, whose will bears date in 1500, *inquis post mortem* 17 HENRY VIII. He married Alice, dau. of Sir Richard Ashton, knt. of Croston, and had three sons, and four daughters, William, who married Margaret, sister of Sir Robert Hesketh; HENRY (Sir) of whom presently, Laurence, a priest; Isabella, married to Singleton, of Brockhall; Janet, to William Heaton, of Birchley; Catherine, *m.* to John Bendish; and Alice, *m.* to James Anderton, of Werden.

The second son,

SIR HENRY FFARINGTON, to whom several letters among the state papers are addressed, commanding him to inquire into the conduct of certain Catholic priests, who, it was asserted, had aspersed Anna Boleyne, was a commissioner for suppressing the monasteries. He wedded, first, Anne, daughter of Sir Alexander Ratcliffe, by whom he had issue, and, secondly, Dorothy, daughter of Sir —— Okeover, of Okeover, in Staffordshire, by whom he left, at his decease, his will is dated 1549, a son,

WILLIAM FFARINGTON, living in the reign of ELIZABETH. To this gentleman, who then resided at Werden, Laurence Dalton gave the additional crest, and confirmed the arms. He married Jane, daughter of Sir Thomas Talbot, of Bashall, and had three sons, namely,

I. THOMAS (Sir) his heir.
II. William, died *s. p.*
III. Henry, who *m.* Margaret, daughter and heiress of Edward Browster, of Maxfield, and had a son,
    Thomas, who *m.* Anne Worral, and was grandfather of,
        Major-General William Farrington, of Chiselhurst, who wedded the daughter of Sir Edward Battinson, of Sudbury, and had a son, Thomas, commissioner of excise progenitor of the late General Sir Anthony ffarington, and Albinia, married to Robert, Duke of Ancaster.

William ffarington, whose will is dated in 1609, was *s.* by his eldest son,

SIR THOMAS FFARINGTON, who espoused Mabel, daughter and co-heir of George Benson, esq. of Hyndill, in Westmoreland, and had three sons and six daughters, of whom the eldest son was,

WILLIAM FFARINGTON, esq. of Shaw Hall, high sheriff for Lancashire, in 1636. This gentleman, a staunch cavalier, valiantly assisted the Countess of Derby in her gallant defence of Lathom, against the parliamentarians, and, in consequence, had his estate sequestered. His sufferings and services were, however, highly appreciated by his royal master, and the name of his son, William ffarington, appears among those who were to have been rewarded with the knighthood of the royal oak, had that order been established. This noted cavalier married Margaret Worral, and left, at his decease, his will is dated 1657, (with two younger sons, and four daughters, Margaret, the wife of Edward Fleetwood, of Penwortham; Anne, of Clayton, of Clayton, Elizabeth, of Charnocke, of Charnocke; and Alice, of Banister, of Bank) a son and successor,

WILLIAM FFARINGTON, esq. of Shawe Hall, who *m.* the dau. of Edward Fleetwood, esq. of Penwortham, and had issue,

I. HENRY, his heir.
II. GEORGE, successor to his brother.
I. Margery, *m.* to Arthur Ingleby, esq. of Yorkshire.
II. Margaret, *m.* to Alexander Nowell, esq. of Read.
III. Mary, *m.* to William Anderton, esq. of Euxton.

William ffarington, whose will is dated 20th February, 1672, was succeeded by his son,

HENRY FFARINGTON, esq. of Shawe Hall, who wedded Susan, daughter of Degory Wheare, D. D. Master of Gloucester Hall, Professor of History at Oxford, and had issue,

I. Henry, who *m.* Anne, daughter of —— Dicconson, esq. of Wrightington, and appears to have predeceased his father.
II. William, who *m.* Elizabeth, daughter of —— Swetenham, esq. of Somerford Booths, in Cheshire, and seems to have also *d. v. p.*
I. Margaret, *m.* to the Rev. Thomas Armetriding.
II. Agnes.
III. Anne, *m.* to —— Kelsall, esq. an Irish gentleman.

Mr. ffarington, whose will is dated 20th May, 1687, was *s.* by his brother,

GEORGE FFARINGTON, esq. of Shawe Hall, who *m.* Elizabeth, daughter of —— Whitmore, esq. of Thirsington, in Cheshire, and had two sons and two daughters, viz.

I. WILLIAM, his heir.
II. Valentine, *b.* in 1676, *m.* Agnes, dau. of —— Prickett, esq. of Westmoreland, and had, with other issue, who died *s. p.*
    Elizabeth, *m.* to Col. Gardner, of Coleraine, and was mother of the FIRST LORD GARDNER.
    Sarah, *m.* to Nicholas Starkie, esq. of Riddleston.
I. Elizabeth, *b.* in 1672, } both *d. s. p.*
II. Margaret, *b.* in 1680, }

The elder son,

WILLIAM FFARINGTON, esq. of Shawe Hall, *b.* in 1675, was sheriff of Lancashire in 1713. He wedded Elizabeth, daughter of Dr. James Rufine, of Boulogne (who fled from France, owing to the persecution of the Hugonots), and had,

I. GEORGE, his heir.

II. William, rector of Warrington, and vicar of Leigh, who *m.* Hester, dau. and co-heir of —— Gilbody, of Manchester, and dying in 1767, aged sixty-three, left issue,

1. William, who *m.* Ann-Frances, daughter of Captain William Nash, and *d.* in 1803, aged fifty-seven, having had seven sons and one daughter, viz.

   WILLIAM, Captain R. N. *m.* Frances-Anne, daughter of Edmund Green, esq. and has issue, William, Edmund-Francis, Richard-Atherton, and Frances-Anne.

   Henry, George, } both died in the navy.

   Edward-Frazer, died in the army at the capture of Java.

   Robert, Richard, Joseph, } died infants.

   Esther-Frances, *m.* to Leonard Streete Coxe, esq.

2. Joseph, *m.* Susan, dau. of the Rev. Dr. Hammond, prebendary of Norwich, but had no issue.

3. George,

4. Henry, *m.* Mary-Anne, dau. of James Borron, esq. and has issue two sons and five daughters, viz.

   William, *m.* Marianne Haxby.

   Henry, *m.* Elizabeth Woodcock.

   Mary-Anne.

   Elizabeth, married to Captain Fenton.

   Sarah, died *s. p.*

   Harriet, *m.* to Rev. Frederick Norris.

   Frances, *m.* to Charles Parkinson, esq.

5. Richard-Atherton, *m.* Elizabeth Borron, but had no issue.

6. Edward.

7. James.

8. Robert, D.D. rector of Saint George's in the East, London.

III. Henry, *b.* in 1715, *m.* the dau. of —— Peachey, esq. of London.

I. Elizabeth, *b.* in 1702, *m.* to Richard Atherton, esq. of Atherton, and was great-great-grandmother of the present Lord Lilford.

II. Margaret, *m.* to William Bysel, esq. of Seabournes, in Herefordshire, and had two sons, William and Austen, Captains, R.N.

III. Isabella, *b.* in 1711, *m.* to the Rev. John Woodcock, of Staffordshire.

Mr. ffarington was succeeded by his eldest son,

GEORGE FFARINGTON, esq. of Shawe Hall, *b.* in 1696, who *m.* Margaret, daughter, and sole heir of John Bradshaw, esq. of Pennington, and had, with several other sons, who died issueless (one was killed at the battle of Fontenoy,)

I. WILLIAM (Sir), his heir.

II. James, *b.* in 1733, who *m.* first, Jane Ashton, but by her had no child, and, secondly, Mary, daughter of Roger Nowell, esq. of Altham, by whom he had one son, and four daughters, viz.

1. WILLIAM, successor to his uncle.

1. Margaret, *s. p.*

2. Jane, *s. p.*

3. Mary-Isabella, *m.* to George Watkin Kenrick, esq. of Chester, and died in 1829.

4. Charlotte, mar. to Alexander Nowell, esq. M.P. of Underley, in Westmoreland.

I. Margaret, *m.* to James Prior Clayton, esq.

II. Barbara, *m.* to the Rev. T. Mallory, of Mobberley.

III. Isabella, *m.* to Gill. Slater, esq. of Chesterfield and Liverpool.

IV. Mary, *m.* to Isaac Hamon, esq. of Portarlington, in Ireland.

The eldest son,

SIR WILLIAM FFARINGTON, knt. of Shawe Hall, born in 1730, died without issue, and was succeeded by his nephew, the present WILLIAM FFARINGTON, esq. of Shawe Hall.

*Arms*—1st and 4th, arg. a chevron gu. between three leopards' heads sa. 2d and 3d gu. three cinquefoils arg.

*Crests*—The ancient crest was, as described in the old heraldic works, "in som called a Lezard, in som a seawolfe als, a dragone wevre az." (*Page 45, Harl. MSS.* 1987.) This was confirmed, and the present crest given by Lawrence Dalton, Norroy King at Arms in 1560, at which period the name appears spelt with a Y."

*Mottoes—Ancient*, Labor Omnia Vincit; *modern*, Domat Omnia Virtus.

*Estates*—In Lancashire.

*Seat*—Shawe Hall: a large, but irregular mansion, with some spacious rooms, one of seventy feet by thirty-six, ornamented with some choice works of ancient art: amongst other the fine "Noli me tangere," of Titian; a museum of natural history, consecrated chapel, &c.

# HEREFORD, OF SUFTON COURT.

:REFORD, RICHARD, esq. of Sufton Court, in the county of Hereford, *b.* ıly, 1803, *m.* 5th June, 1828, Harriot-Arabella, daughter of the late Capt. Sir ·t Mends, knt. R.N. and has issue,

RICHARD-JAMES, *b.* 1st April, 1833.
Harriot-Mary.

[ereford succeeded his father, 2d February, 1823. He is in the commission of ›ace.

## Lineage.

family of HEREFORD, one of very ıntiquity, derived its surname, accord- an old manuscript, from "the name ity on the borders of the principality ıles, formerly very well fortify'd, and dinary residence of the ancient earls reford. The ancestors of the family here a long while, to secure them- from the incursions of ye people of ›untry, till at last that nation, falling the government of the English, in the f EDWARD, *the first*, and the ancient :ls between the two nations being at l, they came and liv'd in a land (aula) Sufton Hall, or Sufton Castle, under rd Mordiford, three miles from Here- owards the south; and their posterity ı there to this day, and are lords f, as of many other inheritances and situated in the province."

the elder branch were the earls of ›rd, who were likewise high consta- f England. Their line terminated in ses, daughters of Milo de Gloucester, Hereford, the eldest of whom, MAR- married Humphrey de Bohun; and ı, Humphrey de Bohun, became earl reford, and constable of England.

Contemporaneous with those potent feudal lords, there resided in the city of Hereford, in the time of HENRY II. A.D. 1170,

ROGER HEREFORD, "a famous philosopher (says the same manuscript), who published, during the period that Henry of Hereford, and Mabel, his brother, enjoyed the county of Hereford, the books quoted by John Pits.* This Roger," the philosopher, "was born on the borders of Wales, and was probably a student of Cambridge, as most part of his works were, it is reported, preserved a long time there. He was very much esteemed by the great men of his time, as well for his excellent qualities, as for the extraordinariness of his progress in all sorts of learning. He was of a sharp wit; and was so great a lover of the sciences, that if one ask'd him, wch were the things, whereof the desire is never satisfy'd in never so great plenty, he would answer, not as a covetous man, that they were riches, but as a philosopher, that it was learning. He never lost a moment, but always spent in study all the time cou'd be spar'd from his employments, to wch his was obliged to attend. His works were—A Book of Judiciary Astrology, Quoniam Regulas artis Astronomiæ; of the Theory of Planets; Divers Astronomers, according to the different manuscripts of the Public Library at Oxford; a Book of Collections of the Years of Planets; a Book of the setting and rising of Constellations; a Book of the Horizon and the Circle; a Book of Metals."

This eminent man flourished about the year 1170, in the reign of the second HENRY, and sixteen years after the death of Roger,

* John Pits, an Englishman, doctor of divinity at Liverdun, in Lorrain, author of an Historical Account of England, in which, vol. i. p. 237, Roger Hereford's works are (according to the above expression) quoted.

EARL OF HEREFORD, one of the brothers of the heiresses who divided the great estates of these earls; so that he seems to have been born at the close of HENRY the First's time. He left at his decease a son,

HENRY DE HEREFORD, of whom there is an entry in the Pipe Roll, in the eighth of JOHN, *anno* 1201, "that Master Henry of Hereford owes a palfrey, for a fief of the king, to William of Braieuse, for the land of Witton." This appears to have been the first estate in the family. Henry had two sons,

ROGER, his successor.

Thomas, who was sheriff of the county of Hereford, in the 7th of HENRY III.; for in that year we find him receiving an order from the Crown to deliver up, in his official capacity, up to William Canteloup, the city of Pembridge, with every thing thereto belonging, of which the said William was appointed governor during pleasure.

ROGER DE HEREFORD, the elder son, held lands in Breinton, *anno* 1222, under the dean and chapter of Hereford: he left a son and heir,

HENRY DE HEREFORD,* who, being a minor, was placed under the care of Thomas Dansey, in the 7th of Henry III. He was lord of the manors of Sufton and Mordiford, in which he was *s.* at his decease, in 1304, by his son,

JOHN DE HEREFORD, lord of the manors of Sufton and Mordiford, born in 1272, who, by his wife, Matilda, had (with probably other) issue,

HENRY (Sir) his heir.

JOHN, successor to his elder brother.

NICHOLAS, heir to his nephew, THOMAS, the son of John.

By the inquisition made at Hereford, 10th year of EDWARD III. after the decease of this John de Hereford, it appears that, with sundry other lands, he held in quality of immediate feudatory to the king, the land of Mordiford, in the county of Hereford, with the homage of a pair of gilt spurs for all services. He died in the 64th year of his age, and was *s.* by his eldest son,

SIR HENRY DE HEREFORD, of Sufton and Mordiford, who, embracing the profession of arms, distinguished himself in the Scottish wars, and received the honour of knighthood from King EDWARD III. with a general pardon for all offences committed by him against the state. † In 1352, he was present in the parliament held at Westminster, as one of the representatives of the county of Hereford; and the same year he was a second time summoned to the great parliament which was to be held at the same place. He died unmarried, in 1361, and was *s.* by his brother,

JOHN DE HEREFORD, of Sufton and Mordiford, *b.* in 1321, *m.* Margaret, and had an only child, THOMAS, his successor, at his decease, in 1387. (His wife outlived him, and her son,)

THOMAS DE HEREFORD, of Sufton and Mordiford, *b.* 1365, and dying, in 1390, without issue, was *s.* by his uncle,

NICHOLAS DE HEREFORD, of Sufton and Mordiford, *b.* in 1330, *m.* and had two sons, viz.

ROGER, his heir.

John, of Bodenham, married, but his wife's name is unknown.

After the decease of his wife, this gentleman became a priest, and was a D.D. and fellow of Queen's College. Of him the following details are given in the manuscript to which we have before referred:—"Nicholas de Hereford, born in 1330, his father being already old, twenty-six years after his eldest brother Henry, and nine years after his brother John, married a very young woman, and had two children, Roger and John. It appears that he took orders, his wife being dead; and he seems to be, as far as one can conjecture, the same as Nicholas Hereford, Professor of Divinity, and of the Society of Queen's College at Oxford. For the name and surname, and age, and conformity of the time, all agree in proving it. In 1381, Nicholas Hereford and Philip Repingdone, prebendary of Leicester, since chancellour of the University of Oxford, bishop of Lincoln, and cardinal, were accused of heresie, with many other divines of the said University, and of favouring and keeping up Wicliff's doctrine." This affair caused considerable agitation amongst the clergy; and there is a Protestation of Innocence and Submission to the Church, upon vellum, from Hereford and Repingdone, preserved in the Bodleian

---

* Contemporaneous with this Henry, were ELIAS DE HEREFORD, recorder of the Royal Exchequer, and WILLIAM DE HEREFORD, sheriff of London, in the 16th of EDWARD I.

† EDWARD, by the grace of God, King of England, Lord of Ireland, and Duke of Guesenne, to all his Bailiffs and Trustees who shall see these present letters, sends greeting. Know ye, that of our special grace, and that for the good services that Henry of Hereford has done us in the Scotch war, we have granted him the pardon of all manslaughter, felonies, roberies, thefts, and transgressions whatsoever he has committed, in our kingdom, before the 10th of July last, as well to the prejudice of the immunities granted by our father, Edward, heretofore king of England, as by us, for which he was called up, &c....and we grant him our Royal protection.... Witness myself, at Berwick, the 9th of October, in the 9th year of our reign.

brary at Oxford. Mr. Nicholas (as he is ·led) eventually obtained a protection m the Crown against his accusers; was erwards in great favour with the king ENRY IV.), who granted, by charter, o our beloved subject, Mr. Nicholas ereford, treasurer of the cathedral church Hereford, a vessel of wine, to receive ery year for his life, upon our prize, in r town of Bristol, from the hands of our st cupbearer, or his deputy." His friend, pingdone, was also much in favour, being omoted to a bishoprick and a cardinal's t. Nicholas was succeeded at his decease his elder son,

ROGER DE HEREFORD, of Sufton and Mor-ford, *b.* about the year 1364, who *d.* in 26, and was *s.* by his son,

WILLIAM DE HEREFORD, of Sufton and ordiford, *b.* in 1409, who was *s.* by his son,

THOMAS DE HEREFORD, of Sufton, who 23rd July, 1517, leaving, with a dau. ne, *m.* to Foulkes Walwyn, a son and ccessor,

WILLIAM HEREFORD, esq. of Sufton, *b.* in 77, *d.* in 1545, and *s.* by his son,

ROGER HEREFORD, esq. of Sufton, who ed 13th July, 1561, leaving, by Margaret, wife, dau. and heiress of —— Sturmey,

I. JOHN, his heir.

I. Isabella, *m.* to Anthony Kirle, of the county of Hereford.

II. Joan.

III. Dorothy.

IV. Jane.

V. Eleanor.

VI. Mary.

e elder son,

JOHN HEREFORD, of Sufton, *b.* 8th Sept. 58, wedded first, in 1578, Catherine, dau. Richard Lee, of Langley, and had a son, ICHARD, his heir. He *m.* secondly, Eliza-th, daughter of Humphry Archer, esq. of mworth, in Warwickshire, and by her, ho died in 1641, left,

I. Roger, of Priors Court, *m.* 20th Sept. 1620, Penelope, daughter of Robert Kirle, of Walford, near Ross, and had a son, John, *b.* in 1625, who wedded Elizabeth, dau. and heir of Henry Sampson, of Holm Lacy, and had a son, John, of Holm Lacy, in right of his mother.

II. Henry, A.M. } died *s. p.*
III. Townshend, }

IV. Giles.

I. Margaret, *m.* first to Richard Walwyn, of Dormynton, and secondly to Anthony Bucker.

hn Hereford died at Priors Court, 20th ctober, 1619, and was *s.* by his son,

RICHARD HEREFORD, esq. of Sufton, *b.* th May, 1579, who *m.* first, Mary, dau. John Scudamore, esq. of Bellingham, in the county of Hereford, and secondly, Margaret, dau. of William Pershall, esq. of Horsley, in Staffordshire, and had issue,

I. ROGER, his heir.

II. William, who *m.* Elizabeth Booth, of Priors Lee, in Salop, and had two sons and two daughters, namely,

1. John, of Hereford, who married, and left three daughters, his coheirs, Mary, *m.* first, to William Castle, of Reading, and secondly, to Thomas Bayle; Elizabeth, *m.* to Benjamin Hill; and Jane, *m.* to William Higgins, of Kington.

2. Booth, of Hereford, died *s. p.*

1. Elizabeth, *m.* to John Morse, esq. alderman of Hereford.

2. Margery, *m.* first, to —— Goch, and secondly, to —— Carter.

III. Giles.

I. Elizabeth, married to Bridstock Harford, M.D.

II. Margaret, *b.* in 1621, *m.* first, to William Whitington, esq. of Hampton Bishop, and secondly, to Thomas Rodd, esq.

III. Jane, *b.* in 1623, *m.* to John Beale.

Richard Hereford died about the year 1636, and was succeeded by his son,

ROGER HEREFORD, esq. of Sufton, who *m.* Frances, daughter of James Rodd, esq. of Hereford, and by her, who died in 1689, had issue,

I. JAMES, his heir.

II. Francis, *b.* in 1640, an eminent merchant and consul at Dunkirk, who *m.* Frances, dau. of Mr. de Brower, of Newport, and had issue.

III. Roger, of Dunkirk, twice mayor of that town, who *m.* Anthony, dau. of Gaspard Molliene, mayor of Collis, and had issue,

Roger, *b.* at Dunkirk, in 1690.

Ann, *m.* to Peter William le Grand, de Bourgard, master to the king's forests de Creey in Bree.

Frances, *m.* to Mr. Lewis de Chalonne de Courtebourne, chancellor knight of the order of St. Louis.

Mary.

IV. William, *d.* unm.

I. Margery, *m.* in 1665, to Thomas Broad, A.M.

II. Ann.

III. Elizabeth.

The eldest son,

JAMES HEREFORD, esq. of Sufton, bapt. 23rd December, 1634, succeeded his father in 1659. He *m.* thrice, but had issue only by his wife Hester, dau. of Robert Holmes, esq. of Eye, and niece of Sir John Kirle, of Much March, viz.

I. JOHN, his heir.
II. James, *b.* in 1668, *m.* Ann, dau. of Dr. Thomas Green, of Grosley.
I. Elizabeth, *m.* to Wm. Havard, esq.
II. Anne, *b.* in 1670, *m.* to her cousin, the Rev. Francis Broad, A.M. prebendary of Hereford.
III. Hester, died an infant.

Mr. Hereford was buried at Modiford, 4th January, 1693, and succeeded by his son,

JOHN HEREFORD, esq. of Sufton, who espoused the daughter and heiress of Thomas Walwyn, esq. of Huntless, in Herefordshire, and had three sons and one dau. viz. ROGER, his heir; John, who *d.* in 1711; Walwyn, *b.* in 1694; and Frances, *m.* to Richard Poole, esq. of Barry Court. Mr. Hereford served as high sheriff for the county of Hereford in 1700, died on the 4th of May, in that year, and was *s.* by his son,

ROGER HEREFORD, esq. of Sufton, *b.* 7th July, 1687, who *m.* at Cannon Froom, 12th May, 1711, Frances, dau. of Charles Hopton, esq. of London, a younger son of Sir Edward Hopton of Cannon Froom, and had issue,

I. JAMES (Sir), his heir.
II. JOHN, *b.* in 1717, died in 1720.
III. Henry, *b.* in 1725.
IV. Francis, *b.* 1728.

I. Frances, *b.* in 1714, *m.* John Caldicott, esq. of Holmer House, in the county of Hereford, and had a son,
JAMES, who succeeded his uncle, Sir James Hereford, of Sufton.
II. Elizabeth, *b.* in 1716, and *d.* in 1755.
III. Deborah, *b.* in 1722, *d.* in 1743.
IV. Anne, *b.* in 1729, *m.* to —— Baker, esq. of Lugwardine.

Mr. Hereford was *s.* at his decease by his eldest son,

SIR JAMES HEREFORD, knt. of Sufton, *b.* in 1713, who married twice, first, Martha, dau. of — Skinner, and secondly, Frances, dau. of — Hopton, esq. of Cannon Frome, but dying issueless, in 1786, devised his estates, by will, to (the son of his eldest sister) his nephew,

JAMES CALDICOTT, esq. of Holmer House, b. in 1756, who assumed, in consequence, the surname and arms of HEREFORD. He *m.* Mary, dau. of John Scudamore, esq. of Kentchurch Court, in the county of Hereford, and had issue,

I. RICHARD, his heir.
I. Mary.
II. Sarah, *m.* to David Lambe, esq. of Hereford.
III. Frances.
IV. Catharine, *d.* unm. in 1826.
V. Anne, *m.* to John Kelly Tuder, esq. R.N. of Penally, Pembrokeshire.
VI. Lucy.

Mr. Hereford died, in February, 1823, and was succeeded by his son, the present RICHARD HEREFORD, esq. of Sufton.

*Arms*—Gu. three eagles displayed arg.

*Crest*—An eagle displayed.

*Estates*—Sufton and Larport, in the parish of Mordiford, Garlands, in Fownhope, and Holmer House, in the parish of Holmer, all in Herefordshire.

*Seat*—Sufton Court, near Hereford.

## LLOYD, OF ASTON.

LLOYD, WILLIAM, esq. of Aston, in the county of Salop, *b.* in 1780, *m.* in 1805, Louisa, eldest daughter and co-heir of the late Admiral Sir Eliab Harvey, G. C. B. of Rolls Park, in Essex, (see vol. ii.) and has issue,

EDWARD HARVEY.
Richard.
Louisa-Eliza.
Charlotte.

Mr. Lloyd succeeded his father in 1803. He is a magistrate and deputy-lieutenant of Shropshire, and was sheriff in 1810.

## Lineage.

[e] patronymic of this ancient family Rosindale; but, on their settling in [...]s, they adopted, with Welch con[...]ns, the surname of Lloyd; and are [...]imes written Lloyd-Rosindale, and [...]imes Rosindale-Lloyd. The original [...]e of Aston deduced lineally from [...]n Evell, lord of Cynlleth and Moch[...] in the county of Denbigh, the common [...]tor of many families in Salop and [...]igh, of whom, and his descendants, we already treated in detail (Vol. ii. *page* [...]nder Edwards, of *Ness-Strange*.

[...]redith ap Howell, of Oswestry and [...]oed, ninth in descent from Enion Evell, [...]ed Thomasine, dau. and heir of Rich[...]reland, esq. and had (with an elder [R]ichard, and two daughters)

[...]an Lloyd, of Park Promise, who [...]ed Joan, dau. of Richard Stanney, of [...]stry, and was father of

[Ro]bert Lloyd, who *m.* Gwenhwyvar [o]f Wm. Edwards, esq. of Chirk Hall, [...]ighshire, and was succeeded by his son,

[Ro]bert Lloyd, of Aston, who married a [...]ter of Thomas Charlton, esq. of Apley, [...]p, and left a son,

[An]drew Lloyd, esq. of Aston. This [...]man, like his neighbour, Mytton, [...]lston, adopted the cause of the parlia[...] against *King* Charles I. and held a [...]in's commission in the army. Prest[...] in his "Respublica," describes the [...]r of "Captaine Andrewe Lloyde," [...]ton-Abbot, thus: "Argent, in base, a [...]or scroll of three folds, its points curled [...]gent, shaded crimson, lined or; in [...]g, '*Ora at pugna—juvit et jubavit—*[...]a,' in fesse, near the sinister side; a [...] in pale, closed argent, clasped and [...]l or; from the dexter chief angle, [...], blue, and crimson clouds, from which [...]ed arm and hand, grasping a broad[...]l, held as in bend sinister, ppr. hilted [...]inged argent and sable." Capt. Lloyd [M]argaret, dau. of Thomas Powell, esq. [W]hittington Park, and had (with other [...])

- [T]homas, his heir.
- [R]ichard (Sir), chancellor of Durham, and judge of the Admiralty Court. Sir Richard, who died in 1686, was father of
  - Sir Nathanial Lloyd, knt. remembered as a liberal benefactor to the colleges of Trinity Hall and All Souls, Oxford. In the chapel of the former there is a monument to his memory.

[e]lder son,

[Th]omas Lloyd, esq. of Aston, acquired, by marriage with Sarah, dau. and co-heir of Francis Albany, esq. the lordship and estate of Whittington, in Shropshire, and had, *inter alios*,

- Robert, his heir.
- Elizabeth, *m.* to Foulk Lloyd, esq. of Foxhall, in the county of Derby, (*see* family of Rosindale Lloyd in conclusion), and had three sons, viz.
  - John Lloyd, / Thomas Lloyd, } successively "of Aston."
  - Rosindale Lloyd, who *m.* Jane, dau. of Robert Davies, esq. of Llannerch, and died in 1734. He had
    - Thomas, / Rosindale, } both *d.* unm.
    - William (the *Rev.*) who succeeded his uncle in the Aston and other family estates.

Mr. Lloyd *d.* in 1692, and was *s.* by his son,

Robert Lloyd, esq. of Aston, M.P. for the county of Salop, who married Mary, eldest dau. of Sir John Bridgeman, bart. and left a son and heir,

Robert Lloyd, esq. of Aston, who, like his father, represented the county of Salop in parliament. He died unm. 7th June, 1734, when the Aston and other estates devolved upon (the eldest son of his aunt) his cousin,

John Lloyd, esq. of Foxhall, who, dying without issue, in 1741, was *s.* by his brother,

Thomas Lloyd, esq. of Aston, at whose decease, unm. in 1754, the estates passed to his nephew,

*The Rev.* William Lloyd, of Aston. This gentleman *m.* Elizabeth, dau. of William Sneyd, esq. of Bishton, in the county of Stafford, and had an only son and heir,

*The Rev.* John-Robert Lloyd, of Aston, who wedded Martha, fourth dau. of John Shakespeare, esq. of London, and had issue,

- William, his heir.
- Charles-Arthur-Albany, in holy orders, rector of Whittington, in the county of Salop, *m.* Mrs. Hannah Simpson Cowan, and has issue.
- George-Newton-Kynaston, in holy orders, rector of Selattyn, in Salop, *m.* Miss Corrie, and has one son.
- Elizabeth, *m.* to — Curtis, esq. of Ireland, and is deceased.
- Charlotte, *m.* in 1803, to the Hon. Thomas Kenyon, brother of Lord Kenyon, and has issue,

The rev. gentleman *d.* in 1803, and was *s.* by his eldest son, William Lloyd, esq. now of Aston.

### Family of Rosindale-Lloyd.

Henry Rosindale, of Rosindale, near Clithero, in the county of Lancaster, served under Henry de Lacy, earl of Lincoln, who had a grant of the lordship of Denbigh, and who, in the 16th year of Edward the First's reign, granted to the said Henry Rosindale certain lands, parcel of the said lordship, on condition that he and his heirs should serve with a certain number of horsemen, for a period in the said grant specified, in the castle of Denbigh, in all wars that should occur between the King of England and the Prince of Wales, at his own charges and cost. The grandson of this Henry,

William Rosindale adopted the surname of Lloyd, and *m.* Ermine, dau. and heir of Robert Pigott, esq. Fourth in descent from this marriage, was

John Lloyd, of Henllan, who wedded Elizabeth, daughter of Henry Hookes, esq. and had two sons, viz.

I. Hugh, who died in the lifetime of his father, leaving a son,
   Piers, successor to his grandfather.
II. Thomas, father of
   Robert, of Denbigh, father of
      Humphrey Lloyd, the celebrated antiquary and historian. This eminent man was born at Denbigh, but in what house of learning at Oxford he first applied himself to academic studies, Anthony Wood is unable to determine; "sure it is (saith he), that after he had taken the degree of bachelor of arts, which was in 1547, I find him by the name of Humphrey Lloyd to be a commoner in Brazennose College, and in the year 1551 to proceed in arts as a member of that house, at which time, it seems, he studied physic, being then ripe in years; afterwards retiring to his own country he lived mostly within the walls of Denbigh Castle, practised his faculty, and sometimes that of music for diversion sake, being then esteemed a well-bred gentleman. He was a person of great eloquence, an excellent rhetorician, a sound philosopher, a most noted antiquary, and of great skill and knowledge in British affairs." Camden styles him "a learned Briton, for knowledge of antiquities reputed by our countrymen to carry, after a sort, all the credit and renown." Humphrey Lloyd was author of many works illustrative of British history; amongst others, he wrote De Moriâ Druidum insula Antiquati suæ restituta 1568; Chronicon Walliae; and the History of Cambria. He represented his native city some years in parliament, and died about the year 1570, and was buried in the church of Whittington. He *m.* Barbara, daughter of the Hon. George Lumley,* attainted and executed in the 20th of Henry VIII. and was great-great-grandfather of the Rev. Dr. Robert Lloyd, who claimed unsuccessfully the Barony of Lumley in 1723 (see Burke's *Extinct Peerage*).

John Lloyd was *s.* by his grandson,

Piers Lloyd, esq. of Henllan, who married Margaret, daughter of Robert Salusbury, esq. of Lanrwst, and was *s.* by his son,

Foulk Lloyd, esq. who was sheriff of Denbighshire in the years 1555 and 1568. He *m.* Mary, daughter and heir of William Dacre, esq. and had issue,

John Lloyd, esq. whose son,

Foulk Lloyd, esq. was sheriff of Denbighshire in 1593 and 1623. He was father of

Hugh Lloyd, esq. who was sheriff in 1636. His son and heir,

Foulk Lloyd, esq. of Foxhall, near Denbigh, was *s.* by his son,

Hugh Lloyd, esq. of Foxhall, who was sheriff of Denbighshire in 1669. He married Margaret, daughter of William Glynn, esq. of Glynnllivon, in the county of Carnarvon, and was *s.* by his son,

Foulk Lloyd, esq. of Foxhall, who *m.* Elizabeth, daughter of Thomas Lloyd, esq. and thus his descendants became of Aston.

---

* Lumley Lloyd, the eldest dau. of Humphrey Lloyd, the antiquary, *m.* Robert Coytmore, esq. of Coytmore, and was progenitor of
   Bridget Coytmore, of Coytmore, who *m.* Edward Philip Pugh, esq. and had two daughters,
      1. Bridget Pugh, *m.* to Col. Glynne Wynne.
      2. Anna Pugh, *m.* to Henry Hughes, esq.; and their only dau. and heir, Anna Maria, *m.* Colonel Walsham, of Knill.

—The *coat* of LLOYD, *alias* ROSIN-ere quarterly or and azure, two roe-assant, counterchanged of the field; *crest* was a roebuck's head or. But ceding to the estates of the previous of LLOYD of *Aston*, they assumed earing; namely, party per fesse, d argent, a lion rampant, counter-of the field.

—Hwy pery clôd na golud. (In , Longer will fame last than wealth.)

*rs*—The manor and estate of Aston, lordship or manor of Whittington, and the manor of Selattyn, with the right of presentation to the rectories of Whittington and Selattyn, all in the county of Salop.

*Town Residence*—Upper Brook Street, Grosvenor Square.

*Seat*—Aston, in Shropshire. There are several places named Aston, in the county of Salop; but this Aston is usually called Aston Abbot, or Abbot's Aston, the abbot and monks of Haghmond having had considerable possessions there until the dissolution of the monasteries.

## BATEMAN, OF HARTINGTON HALL.

EMAN, RICHARD-THOMAS, esq. of Hartington Hall, in the county of *b.* 9th September, 1794, *m.* 26th May, 1820, Madelene, daughter of Robert hby, esq. of Cliffe, in Warwickshire, by Lucy, his third wife, daughter of Ferrers, esq. of Baddesley, and has issue, HUGH; Richard; Thomas; Willoughby; Elizabeth; and Madeleine.

Bateman succeeded his father, Richard Bateman, esq. in 1821, and his uncle, h Bateman, bart. in 1824.

### Lineage.

ame of BATEMAN occurs so early as of EDWARD III. when WILLIAM N, Bishop of Norwich, and founder ty Hall, in Cambridge, was sent to to lay before the Pope his royal claim to the crown of France. The brother, BARTHOLOMEW BATEMAN, mber of parliament for Norfolk in eenth year of the same reign.

the family of Bateman now imme-nder discussion was settled at Har-before the year 1600, appears by ies in the Herald's College, as well letter of Sir Anthony Bateman, lord f London in 1664, dated in January, 1644, in which, after stating that his father is "just dead at an advanced age," he says, that the deceased had remembered in his will "the poor of Hartington,* where he was born."

ROBERT BATEMAN, of Hartington, in the county of Derby, was father of

WILLIAM BATEMAN, whose son,

RICHARD BATEMAN, of Hartington, living in 1561, *m.* Ellen, daughter of William Topleyes, of Tissington, in Derbyshire, and had two sons,

I. HUGH, his successor.

II. RICHARD, chamberlain of London, and some time one of the representatives in parliament for that city, baptized at Hartington 8th September, 1561, will dated 3rd August, 1641, proved 2nd August, 1645. He *m.* Elizabeth, daughter of John Westrow, esq. of London (she was

* The manor of Hartington was at that time in the crown. It was afterwards granted by JAMES the First to the first Duke of Buckingham, and sold by the trustees of the second duke to the Earl of Devonshire in 1663 for £20,000. It subsequently gave title to the marquisate in the Devonshire family.

living in 1662-3), and had, with other issue,

1. SIR WILLIAM BATEMAN, knt. of London.
2. SIR ANTHONY BATEMAN, lord mayor of London in 1664, *m.* at Charlton, in Kent, 6th January, 1645, Elizabeth, daughter of — Russell, of Cheapside.
3. SIR THOMAS BATEMAN, who was created a baronet in 1664, as Sir Thomas Bateman, "of How Hall," in Norfolk.

In 1666 these gentlemen, who all appear to have been merchants in London, sustained great losses by the dreadful fire of that year in the city, many of their houses were burnt, and their property and papers destroyed. Sir Thomas's house in Coleman Street was so damaged that he left it, and went to reside at Isleworth, and soon afterwards removed to Chelsea, and rented in 1670 a house of Mr. Cheney, who married the Duke of Norfolk's daughter.

The elder son,

HUGH BATEMAN, who was baptized 13th March, 1554, lived in 1601 at Meadow Plock, which he rented of Henry Cavendish, of Tutbury. He *m.* Margaret, daughter of John Sleigh, esq. of Hartington, by whom (who *d.* in 1612) he left at his decease in 1616 (he was buried at Youlgrave, in the county of Derby, 23rd February in that year,) a daughter, Grace, the wife of George Parker, esq. of Park Hall, in Staffordshire, ancestor of the Earls of Macclesfield, and a son, his successor,

RICHARD BATEMAN, esq. of Hartington, baptized there 16th January, 1586, who *m.* 1st May, 1614, Anne, daughter of John Beresford, esq. of Alstonfield, in the county of Derby, and had two sons, Hugh, of Derby, an utter barrister of Gray's Inn, *b.* in 1616, who died in 1682, and

ROBERT BATEMAN, esq. citizen of London, baptized at Hartington 8th September, 1622, who *m.* Anne, daughter of Sir William Thorold, bart. of Marston, and dying in 1658 (his will, dated 14th March, 1658, was proved 24th March following,) left a son and successor,

HUGH BATEMAN, esq. of the parish of All Saints, Derby, who *m.* 24th December, 1683, at Radborne, Mary, daughter of John Taylor, gent. of Derby, and had a son,

HUGH BATEMAN, esq. who inherited the estate of Hartington in 1731. He *m.* Elizabeth, daughter and at length co-heiress of John Osborne, esq. of Derby, by Elizabeth, his wife, daughter and eventual co-heiress of William Sacheverell, esq. lord of the manors of Barton, in Nottinghamshire, and of Morley, in Derbyshire.* By this lady he had a son,

RICHARD, of Derby, baptized at All Saints' Church there 17th January, 1718-19, who *m.* 11th June, 1755, Catherine, daughter of William Fitzherbert, esq. of Tissington, in Derbyshire, and sister of W. Fitzherbert, esq. formerly recorder of Derby and M.P. for that borough. By this lady, who was buried at All Saints' Church 19th February, 1776, he had two sons,

1. HUGH, successor to his grandfather.
2. Richard, a deputy-lieutenant and magistrate for the counties of Derby and Stafford, and high sheriff for the former shire in 1812, who *m.* 12th October, 1792, Elizabeth, only child and sole heiress of the Rev. Thomas Keelinge,† of Uttoxeter, in Staffordshire, and dying 29th March, 1821, left issue,
   - RICHARD-THOMAS, of whom presently.
   - John, *b.* in February, 1800, in holy orders, *m.* Emily, dau. of E. Shewell, esq.
   - James-Alleyne-Sacheverel, *b.* 10th December, 1805, a deputy-lieutenant for Derbyshire.
   - Thomas-Osborne, *b.* 1st March, 1809.
   - Joyce-Osborne, *d.* in 1808.
   - Mary-Elizabeth, *m.* 20th March, 1829, to the Rev. James Hamilton Chichester, of Arlington, in Devonshire, and *d.* in 1830.
   - Eliza-Catherine, died in 1819 unm.

Hugh Bateman died 24th November, 1777, and was *s.* by his grandson,

---

* For Sacheverell of Morley, *see Family of* POLE OF RADBORNE.

† By Mary Savage, his wife, daughter of the Rev. John Savage, of the Rock Savage family. The mother of Mr. Keelinge was Elizabeth Leigh, of Greenhill, Staffordshire, sprung from the Leighs of Stoneleigh. The Savages settled at Steynsby in the reign of HENRY VIII.; having married, it is supposed, the heiress of Steynsby. The elder branch settled about the middle of the fourteenth century at Clifton, afterwards called Rock Savage, in Cheshire, an estate they acquired with the heiress of Daniel.

UGH BATEMAN, esq. of Hartington Hall, 1st March, 1756, who was created a net 15th December, 1806, with re- der on failure of the issue male of his to the heirs male of his daughters. m. 4th February, 1786, Temperance, hter of John Gisborne, esq. of Derby, had two daughters,

I. CATHERINE-JULIANA, who m. in 1815 Edward Dolman Scott, esq. eldest son of Sir Joseph Scott, bart. and had a son,

FRANCIS-EDWARD SCOTT, esq. b. in 1824, who succeeded his maternal grandfather, and is the present BARONET.

II. Amelia-Anne, m. to Sir Alexander Hoed, bart.

Sir Hugh Bateman died in March 1824, and was s. at Hartington by his nephew, the present RICHARD-THOMAS BATEMAN, esq. of Hartington Hall.

*Arms*—Or, three crescents with an estoile of six points above each crescent gu. a canton az.

*Crest*—A crescent and estoile, as in the arms, between two eagles' wings or.

*Estates*—In Derbyshire, &c.

## SHEDDEN, OF PAULERSPURY PARK.

DDEN, GEORGE, esq. of Paulerspury Park, Northamptonshire; of Knockmarlock, in the county of Ayr; and Hardmead, Bucks; m. his cousin Mary, elder daughter and co-heir of William Goodrich, esq. of Spring Hill, in the Isle of Wight, and had by her, who d. in 1827, four sons, and eight daughters, viz.

William George.
Robert John.
Roscow Cole.
Edward Cole.

Catherine Goodrich.
Agatha-Wells Bridger, m. to Robert Hawthorn, esq. and has issue.
Margaret-Bridger-Goodrich, m. to the Rev. James Galloway, and has issue.
Mary George, d. unm. in 1826.
Beatrix.
Louisa.
Lavinia.
Octavia.

Shedden succeeded his father in 1826.

### Lineage.

is is the junior branch of the Scottish y of Shedden, of Roughwood;

BERT SHEDDEN (son of John Shedden, hant in Beith, N. B.) resided sometime merchant in Holland, afterwards settled native place, and acquired property prior to the year 1675.

BERT SHEDDEN, his eldest son, pur- d, in 1690, the estate of Roughwood, in the parish of Beith, also the lands of Milnburn, in Tarbolton, of Coalburn and of Auchingree, in Dalry, all in the county of Ayr. He also acquired the lands of Kerse, in the county of Renfrew in 1685, m. Jean, daughter of John Harvie, of Greenend, and had issue,

I. JOHN, of Roughwood and Milnburn, who s. his father in 1725, m. in 1727,

Jean, daughter of Gavin Ralston, of that Ilk, and at his decease, in 1770, left one daughter and one surviving son,

William Shedden, of Roughwood and Milnburn, resided sometime in Virginia; his property there was confiscated on account of his joining the royal party. After the American Revolution he settled as a merchant in New York, where he died in 1798, leaving

William - Patrick - Ralston-Shedden, lately a merchant at Calcutta. He *m.* in 1822, Frances, dau. of William Browne, esq. of that city, and has since returned to England. He has issue.

Jane Ralston.

Marion, married, in 1761, to John Patrick, of Trearne, by whom she had issue.

II. Robert, of Coalburn, *d.* unm.

III. William.

I. Elizabeth, *m.* to George Brown, esq. of Knockmarlock, and had issue.

The youngest son,

WILLIAM SHEDDEN, of Auchingree and Kerse, *b.* in 1708, *m.* Beatrix, daughter of Robert Dobbie, chamberlain of Giffen, and had two sons and three daughters, viz.

I. ROBERT, his successor.

II. John, was lost at sea off Whitehaven, returning from Ireland in 1776, and left no issue.

I. Anne, *m.* to James Patrick, of Shotts, in the county of Ayr: issue extinct.

II. Jean, *d.* unmarried.

III. Beatrix, *m.* to John Shedden, of Muirston, near Beith, son of Thomas Shedden, of Windy-House, Ayrshire, by whom she had issue,

John Shedden, of Muirston and Windy-House.

Agatha.

Mr. Shedden *d.* in 1751, and was *s.* by his elder son,

ROBERT SHEDDEN, esq. *b.* in 1741, who went to Virginia in 1759, and settled as a merchant at Portsmouth in that colony; having, however, attached himself to the side of loyalty and the mother country on the breaking out of the American rebellion, he was obliged to fly with his family on board Lord Dunmore's fleet, and his property in Virginia was consequently confiscated. He took refuge at Bermuda in 1776, afterwards at New York, while in possession of the British; and on the peace of 1783 he returned to his native country, and established in London a commercial house of the first respectability. Mr. Shedden *m.* in 1767, in Virgina, Agatha-Wells, daughter of John Goodrich, esq. of Nansemond Plantation, a family greatly distinguished for their loyal adherence to the royal cause during the unhappy contest with the mother country. The issue of this marriage was as follows,

I. GEORGE, his successor.

II. Robert, of Brooklands, Hants, and Mary Church, Devon, deputy lieut. and sheriff in 1822, for the county of Southampton, *m.* Millicent, only daughter of Robert Duncan Munro, esq. and has an only child,

Emily, who *m.* in 1827, Henry George Joseph Cary, esq. of Tor Abbey, in the county of Devon, (see vol. ii. p. 33).

III. John, a colonel in the army, of Efford and Eastonton, in Hampshire. Col. Shedden *m.* Sophia, daughter of Matthew Lewis, esq. under-secretary of war, and co-heir, with her sister Fanny Maria Lady Lushington, of M. G. Lewis, esq. M. P. by whom he has three sons and two daughters, viz.

Lewis, captain of the 15th Hussars.

Goodrich, captain of the 8th Hussars.

Lindsay, of the 17th Lancers.

Adelaide, *m.* to Major Joseph Pringle Taylor, and has issue.

Millicent.

IV. William, merchant of London, *m.* Wilhelmina, one of the two daughters of Capt. William Miller, R. N. and left, at his decease, in 1820, an only child,

Robert.

V. Bartlet Bridger, of Aldham Hall, Suffolk, *m.* Mary Shedden, eldest daughter of his uncle, Bartlet Goodrich, esq. of Saling Grove, Essex, and left, at his decease, in 1823, an only daughter and heiress,

Mary Bridger Shedden, who *m.* in 1823, Thomas Barret Lennard, esq. M.P. eldest son of Sir Thos. Barret Lennard, bart. of Bell House, Essex, and has issue.

I. Margaret, *m.* to Edward Allfrey, esq. of Banstead, Surrey, and Roberts Bridge, Sussex, and has issue.

II. Agatha-Beatrix Goodrich.

III. Mary-Elizabeth, *m.* to the Rev. G. S. Griffen Stonestreet, LL.B. of Halton, Hastings, and Stondon Hall, Essex, prebendary of Lincoln, and has issue.

hedden was *s.* at his death, in 1826,* s eldest son, GEORGE SHEDDEN, esq. f Paulerspury Park.

*ms*—As matriculated in the Lyon , az. on a chevron between three grif- eads erased arg.; as many cross ets fitchie gu. on a chief of the second callop shell of the first between two foils of the third.

*Crest*—A hermit ppr. couped below the shoulders, vested russet, his hood pendant at the back.

*Motto*—Fidem meam observabo.

*Estates*—In the counties of Northampton and Buckingham, and in Ayrshire, North Britain.

*Town Residence*—Bedford-square.

*Seat*—Spring Hill Cottage, Isle of Wight.

---

opy of the Inscription on the Monument in the Manor Chapel of Paulerspury Church:—

In the Vault of this Chancel pertaining to the Manor
are deposited the remains of
ROBERT SHEDDEN, Esq.
of Paulerspury Park, (and of Hardmead, Bucks),
Son of William, the youngest son of Robert
Shedden, of Roughwood, (and of Coalburn),
in the county of Ayr, North Britain.
He married Agatha Wells, daughter of John Goodrich, Esq.
of Nansemond Plantation, in the province of Virginia, where he was
residing as a merchant prior to the American Rebellion,
in which contest, adhering to the cause of Loyalty,
his possessions were confiscated,
and his flattering prospects in the Colony sacrificed;
but being blessed with prudence and with energy of Character,
on his return to Great Britain he amply redeemed,
during forty years of activity and perseverance,
the cost of Loyalty and Fidelity.
In the eventful struggles which convulsed Europe
he continued a steady and consistent supporter
of the Constitution and Established Religion,
and was distinguished as a Patron and Guardian of
Patriotic Institutions which befriended
the Widows and Orphans of those who fell in battle,
universally respected for Probity and Liberality as a Merchant,
and pre-eminently
for his judgment and enterprise in Marine Insurance,
Mild, Charitable, and Generous,
beloved by his numerous Family and Descendants,
Devout and Humble,
This Monument will but feebly convey
That general affection and regard
which greeted his Virtues, and cherishes his Memory.
He departed this life the XXIX September,
A. D. MDCCCXXVI,
Ætat. LXXXV.

# SCUDAMORE, OF KENTCHURCH.

SCUDAMORE, JOHN-LUCY, esq. of Kentchurch Court, in the county of Hereford, *b.* 20th February, 1798, *m.* at Norton, in Radnorshire, October, 1822, Sarah Laura, elder daughter of Sir Harford Jones Brydges, bart. of Boultibrooke, and has had issue, a son, born at Florence, 24th November, 1823, who died in infancy, and a daughter, Laura-Adelaide. Mr. Scudamore, who is a captain in the Hereford militia, and a deputy-lieutenant for the county, succeeded his father, April 12, 1805.

## Lineage.

The SCUDAMORES, one of the most eminent families in the West of England, have been established at Kentchurch for many centuries. At an early period it became divided into two distinct families, the Scudamores of Kentchurch, and the Scudamores of Home Lacy,* but the exact period when the branches separated has not been accurately ascertained.

SIR ALAN SCUDAMORE, knt. living 4th of WILLIAM *Rufus*, married Jane, daughter and heir of Sir Alexander Ketchmey, (Catchmay) Lord of Troy, and Bigswear, in Monmouthshire, and left a son and successor,

SIR TITUS SCUDAMORE, Lord of Troy and Bigswear, who wedded Joyce, daughter of Sir Robert Clifford, Lord of Clifford, and had two sons, WILCOCK (Sir), who married Eleanor, daughter and heir of Sir Brian Trowhek, knt. and

JENKIN SCUDAMORE, who wedded Alice, or Agnes, daughter and heir of Sir Robert Ewyas, knt. and had two sons, JOHN (Sir) his heir; and Philip, who was, according to some authorities, ancestor of the Home Lacy branch. The elder son,

SIR JOHN SCUDAMORE, married Jane, dau. of Sir Walter Baskerville, of Erdisley, in the county of Hereford, and was father of

SIR JOHN SCUDAMORE, who *m.* Joyce, dau. and co-heir of Sir Robert Marbery, knt. and left a son and successor,

SIR JENKIN SCUDAMORE, who wedded Alice, daughter and co-heir of Sir Walter Pedwarden, or, Bredwarden, knt. and had two sons, JOHN, (Sir) his heir, and Philip, who, on the authority of most of the ancient pedigrees, was ancestor of the Scudamores of Home Lacy. The elder son,

SIR JOHN SCUDAMORE, knt. of Kentchurch, living in the reigns of EDWARD the Second, and HENRY the Fourth, espoused Elizabeth, daughter and co-heir of the celebrated Owen Glendowr, and left a son and successor,

JOHN SCUDAMORE, of Kentchurch, by some styled a knight. He *m.* Margaret, daughter and heir of Sir Thomas Brytt, and was father of

SIR JOHN SCUDAMORE, knt. of Kentchurch, living 13th EDWARD IV. (1473,) who wedded Joan, daughter of John ap Harry (Parry) of

* SIR JAMES SCUDAMORE, of Home Lacy, in the time of ELIZABETH, is celebrated as "Sir Scudamore," in Spenser's Fairy Queen. He left, at his decease, (with a daughter Mary, the wife of Sir Giles Brydges, of Walton,) a son and successor,

JOHN SCUDAMORE, esq. of Home Lacy, created VISCOUNT SCUDAMORE, of Sligo, in 1628, an honour which expired with his great grandson,

JAMES, third Viscount Scudamore, who *d.* in 1716, leaving an only daughter and heiress,

The HON. FRANCES SCUDAMORE, *b.* in 1711, *m.* first, to Henry Somerset, Duke of Beaufort, and, secondly, to Charles Fitzroy Scudamore, esq. By the latter she left an only child,

FRANCES SCUDAMORE, of Holme Lacy, who wedded Charles, late Duke of Norfolk, but dying issueless in 1820, Holme Lacy passed to the present SIR EDWIN F. SCUDAMORE-STANHOPE, bart. the descendant of Mary Scudamore, wife of Sir Giles Brydges.

ton, in Herefordshire, and had two sons,

I. JAMES, or JOHN, his heir.
II. Richard, of Rowlston, m. Jane, dau. of Richard Monington, esq. of Brinsop, in the county of Hereford, and had a son,
John, of Rolleston, who m. Anne, daughter of Philip Scudamore, esq. of Home Lacy (Pedigree of the Home Lacy family by Cooke, Clar.) According to other accounts, she was called Joyce, but her surname is not given. John Scudamore was father of
PHILIP, of Rowlstone, of whom presently, as continuator of the family, and possessor, *jure uxoris*, of KENTCHURCH.

John's elder son,

[J]AMES SCUDAMORE, (or, according to [H]. MSS, 1545, fol. 42,) JOHN SCUDA[MOR]E, of Kentchurch, married Eleanor, [dau]ghter of Griffith ap Nicholas, of Newton, [C]armarthenshire, by Alice, his wife, dau. [of S]ir Thomas Perrot, of Heraldston, in the [coun]ty of Pembroke, and had, (with a dau. [Cath]erine, wife of Richard Monington, esq. [of W]arnsfield) a son,

[T]HOMAS SCUDAMORE, esq. of Kentchurch, [who] left, by Margaret, his wife, daughter [of M]organ Jenkin ap Philip of Pencoyd, in [Mo]nmouthshire, two sons, JAMES, his heir, [and] Nicholas, ancestor, according to the [H]. MSS. of the Scudamores of Llancillo, [in th]e county of Monmouth. The elder son,

[J]AMES SCUDAMORE, esq. of Kentchurch, [live]d in the reign of HENRY the Seventh. He [m. J]oane, or Sibell, daughter of Sir James [Bas]kerville, knt. of Erdisley, in Hereford[shir]e, (for an account of that ancient family, [see] Vol. I. p. 89,) and had two daughters, [his] co-heirs, of whom Eleanor became the [wife] of Miles ap Harry, esq. of Newcourt,

[JO]AN SCUDAMORE, inheriting Kentchurch, [we]dded her cousin PHILIP SCUDAMORE, esq. [of R]owlstone, and left a son and successor,

[J]OHN SCUDAMORE, esq. of Kentchurch, [who] leases lands in Langua, in 1562, and is [pa]rty to his son's marriage settlement in [157]5. He m. Margaret, or Mary, daugh[ter a]nd co-heir of Sir William, or Sir John [Hu]ard, knt. of Oxfordshire, and had,

I. THOMAS, his heir.
I. Alice, m. to Anthony Elton, esq. of the Hazell, in Herefordshire.
II. Mary, m. to Rees Morgan, esq. of Trillegh, in Llanvihangel, Kilcorney, in Monmouthshire.

[The] son,

[T]HOMAS SCUDAMORE, esq. of Kentchurch, [marr]ied, first, Jane, or Joan, daughter of [Wil]liam Scudamore, esq. of Holm Lacy, [seco]ndly, (marriage settlement dated 1575,) Agnes, dau. and co-heir of Henry White, esq. and, thirdly, Anne, daughter of —— Middlemore, living a widow in 1616. Mr. Scudamore left, at his decease, which occurred previously to the 44th ELIZABETH, with a younger son, Philip, named in the entail of settlement, 42nd of that queen, a successor,

JOHN SCUDAMORE, esq. of Kentchurch, who wedded before 16th March, 1600, as appears by settlement after marriage of that date, Amy, daughter of John Starkey, esq. of Darlie Hall, in the county of Chester, and by her (who m. secondly, Thomas Cavendish, esq.) had eight sons and one daughter, viz.

I. JOHN, his heir.
II. Philip, m. Margery, daughter of Edmund Weaver, alderman of Hereford, and had two sons, Philip and John, and one daughter, Elizabeth, m. to John Hoskyns, esq.
III. Richard, died unm. in 1683.
IV. Ambrose, living in London in 1683, married there a daughter of — Ward, and had issue, John, Samuel, and Amie.
V. Humphrey, named in his father's will, a witness to a deed at Kentchurch in 1637. He m. Magdalen, daughter of Paul Delahay, esq. of Trewin, in Herefordshire, but died *s. p.*
VI. James, died unm.
VII. Jonathan, died unmarried.
VIII. Martin, in holy orders, a posthumous son, m. Frances, daughter of John Scudamore, of Trecella, in the parish of Llangarron, Herefordshire.
I. Mary, m. to Hugh Woodward, esq. of London. Among the Kentchurch writings he appears as a lessee of Howton (a farm and manor now belonging to John Lucy Scudamore, esq. of Kentchurch) for fifty-five years, which expired about 1695.

John Scudamore died 30th March, 1616, aged thirty-seven, and was succeeded by his son,

JOHN SCUDAMORE, esq. of Kentchurch, and Rollstone, who m. Elizabeth, daughter of Sir William Cooke, of Highnam, in the county of Gloucester, and had issue,

I. William, aged fifteen in 1634, m. Rachael, daughter of William Herbert, esq. of Colebrooke, in Monmouthshire, aunt to Sir James Herbert, living in 1683, but predeceased his father, issueless, about the year 1652.
II. JOHN, successor to his father.
III. Thomas, died unm. 9th August, 1647, aged twenty, buried at St. Peter's in the Bayley, Oxford.

IV. Walter of Grosmont, *d.* 26th November, 1682, *s. p.*

V. Robert, } both died issueless.
VI. Ambrose, }

VII. James, entered of Christ Church, Oxford, 1661, aged nineteen, afterwards a student there; drowned at Hereford in July, 1666: he was author of "Homer a la Mode."

I. Radagond, *b.* in 1622, *m.* William Bailey, esq. of Fretherne, in Gloucestershire, and died 15th June, 1702, aged eighty.

II. Dorothy, *m.* to Rowland Prichard, esq. of Compstone, in Monmouthshire; articles before marriage dated March 8, 1659.

III. Elizabeth, *m.* to Thomas Lloyd, esq.

Mr. Scudamore died in 1670, and was *s.* by his son,

JOHN SCUDAMORE, esq. of Kentchurch, aged fifty-eight in 1683, who *m.* Mary, daughter of Andrew Lloyd, esq. of Aston, in Salop, and by her, who died 6th January, 1705, had six sons and three daughters, namely,

I. AMBROSE, aged twenty-three in 1683, who *m.* at Burghill in Herefordshire, 10th April, 1676, Ann, daughter of John Fleet, esq. of Hollow, in the county of Worcester, and dying, *vitâ patris*, in July, 1700, left issue,

1. WILLIAM, heir to his grandfather.
2. Ambrose, *b.* before 1696, a party to the settlement of October, 1701.
3. Robert, *b.* in 1689, also a party to that settlement.
1. Elizabeth, named in the said settlement.

II. Robert, a party (as were his younger brothers, except Andrew) to the settlement of 15th October, 1701: in 1695 he had (with his brother Walter) a lease for life of Howton from his father. He had an only daughter, Mary, baptized at Burghill in 1713-14.

III. John, called in some pedigrees consul at Aleppo.

IV. Walter, described of Rollstone in 1716, buried 16th November, 1737.

V. Richard, of Rowlstone, who was buried there 24th December, 1741, leaving by Joan, his wife, three sons and four daughters, viz.

1. JOHN, successor to his cousin at Kentchurch.
2. Richard, baptized at Rollston 8th April, 1731, named in an entail in his brother John's will, *anno* 1750. He was in the army.
3. Walter, baptized at Rollston 17th January, 1734-5, also named in an entail in his eldest brother's will. He was educated at Oxford, and intended for the church. He *d.* unm. 29th June, 1760.
1. Catharine, *b.* 21st October, 1724, *m.* 14th June, 1755, to Philip Westfaling, esq. of Rudhall, in Herefordshire, but *d. s. p.*
2. Mary, *m.* to Samuel Torriano, of London.
3. Anne, baptized at Rolleston 26th November, 1728, was of Hereford, where she died at an advanced age.
4. Dorothy, baptized at Rollston, 20th January, 1732-3, *m.* to — Frere, of Barbadoes.

VI. Andrew, presumed to be dead in 1701.

I. Elizabeth, *m.* at Kentchurch, 4th March, 1689, to Robert Unett, esq. of Castle Frome, in Herefordshire.

II. Anne.

III. Margaret.

Mr. Scudamore died 28th December, 1704, and was *s.* by his grandson,

WILLIAM SCUDAMORE, esq. of Kentchurch, who *m.* (settlement before marriage 15th October, 1701) Penelope, daughter of Edmund Lechmere, esq. of Hanley Castle, and sister to Nicholas, Lord Lechmere, by whom, who was interred at Kentchurch 24th July, 1730, he had one son and four daughters, viz.

I. John, baptized 2nd September, 1709, buried 4th August, 1713.

I. Mary, baptized at Kentchurch 29th November, 1703, *m.* before 1730, to John Wynde, esq. of St. Laurence Pountney, London: both living with issue in 1746.

II. Penelope, born 9th September, 1710, *m.* before 1736, to Lewis Clive, of Howton Grove, in the county of Hereford, third son of Edward Clive, esq. of Wormbridge. She died 10th July, 1743; he, 14th November, 1753, and both were buried at Wormbridge.

III. Rachel, *b.* 15th May, 1710, died unm. and was buried at Kentchurch, 16th September, 1737.

IV. Lucy, died in infancy.

Mr. Scudamore died in 1741, and, his only son having died before him, was succeeded, by virtue of the remainder in the settlement of 1701, by his cousin,

IN SCUDAMORE, esq. of Kentchurch, el of the Herefordshire Militia, and for the city of Hereford during thirty-'ears. This gentleman, who was bap-at Rollston 30th October, 1727, wedded, daughter and heir of Nicholas Wes-', esq. and had issue,

JOHN, his heir.

. Richard-Philip, b. 30th June, 1752, M. P. for Hereford, after the death of his brother, from 1805 to 1816, died in London, unm. 5th March, 1831.

Mary, m. at Kentchurch, 15th February, 1787, to James Hereford, esq. of Sufton.

Scudamore died 4th July, 1796, and by his elder son,

IN SCUDAMORE, esq. of Kentchurch, colonel in the Duke of Ancaster's ent of Light Dragoons, who was elected for Hereford at the demise of his father, and continued to represent that city until his death. He m. 3rd May, 1797, Lucy, only daughter of James Walwyn, esq. of Longworth, in the county of Hereford, M. P. by Sarah, his wife, eldest daughter of Thomas Phillipps, esq. of Eaton Bishop, in the same shire, and by her, who died in childbirth, 24th February, 1798, left at his decease in London, 12th April, 1805, an only child, the present JOHN-LUCY SCUDAMORE, esq. of Kentchurch.

*Arms*—Quarterly; first and fourth, gu. three stirrups, leathered and buckled or, SCUDAMORE (modern); second and third, or, a cross patee fitchee gu. SCUDAMORE (ancient).

*Crest*—A bear's paw ppr. issuing from a ducal coronet or.

*Motto*—Scuto amoris Divini.

*Estates*—In Herefordshire.

*Seat*—Kentchurch Court.

## NICHOLSON, OF BALLOW.

OLSON-STEELE, WILLIAM-NICHOLSON, esq. of Ballow House, in the county of Down, b. 5th April, 1772, s. his maternal uncle, William Nicholson, esq. of Ballow, on the 5th April, 1798, and in compliance with the testamentary injunction of that gentleman, assumed the additional surname of "Nicholson," m. 27th February, 1807, Isabella, sixth daughter of Jacob Hancock, esq.* of Lisburn, and has issue,

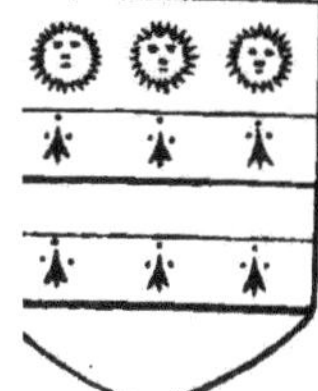

ROBERT, b. 22nd July, 1809.
John, b. 26th October, 1812.
William, b. 21st September, 1817.
James, b. 5th February, 1819.
Charles, b. 21st May, 1828.

Elizabeth, m. 10th December, 1832, to James Rose Cleland, esq. a magistrate and deputy lieutenant for the county of Down, and has a son and daughter,

James-Blackwood Cleland, b. 30th January, 1835.
Agnes-Elizabeth Cleland.

Margaret.
Mary.
Isabella.
Emily.

eele-Nicholson is in the commission of the peace for the county of Down. He led his father on the 23rd March, 1814.

---

his wife, Elizabeth, daughter of Thomas Phelps, of Dublin, and his wife, Sarah Wilcox, ld of Issachar Wilcox, of the same city.

## Lineage.

The family of NICHOLSON, originally from Cumberland, was located in Ireland by

WILLIAM NICHOLSON, *b.* in 1587, who settled at Ballow, in the county of Down, in the beginning of the seventeenth century. He *d.* on the 5th April, 1661, leaving, by his wife, Jannet Brown, who outlived him, and *d.* at the advanced age of eighty, in 1680, a son and successor,

WILLIAM NICHOLSON, esq. of Ballow, who *m.* Miss Eleanor Dunlop, and, dying 3rd January, 1704, was *s.* by his son,

WILLIAM NICHOLSON, esq. of Ballow, *b.* in 1699, who *m.* Mary, dau. of Hugh Whyte, esq. of Ballyree, (by his second wife, Anne, daughter of Alexander Hamilton, esq. of Ballyvernon, and his wife Isabella, eldest daughter of John Blackwood, lineal ancestor of Lord Dufferin). By that lady (who wedded, secondly, Patrick Cleland, of Ballymagee, and *d.* 29th October, 1797, aged eighty-four,) he had issue,

- Hugh, *d.* in minority.
- WILLIAM, heir to his father.
- Robert-Donaldson, *d.* unm. in 1803.
- Susanna, *b.* in 1729, *m.* to Hugh Jackson, esq. of Ballywooley, and had issue.
- MARGARET-MAXWELL, *b.* in 1734, wedded ROBERT-GAWEN STEELE, esq. and had, with other issue,
  - WILLIAM-NICHOLSON STEELE, who inherited the Nicholson property under his uncle William's will.

Mr. Nicholson *d.* 17th June, 1740, and was *s.* by his elder surviving son,

WILLIAM NICHOLSON, esq. of Ballow, who *m.* first, in 1774, Agnes, daughter of John Cleland, esq. of Whitehorn, in Scotland, and relict of William Rose, an officer in the East India Company's military service. He wedded, secondly, Sarah, daughter of — Wells, of Belfast, but had issue by neither. He *d.* 5th April, 1798, and devised his estates to his nephew, William-Nicholson Steele, who assumed the additional surname of Nicholson, and is the present WILLIAM-NICHOLSON STEELE-NICHOLSON, esq. of Ballow.

### Family of Steele.

JOHN STEELE, esq. of Portavoe and Carnalea, *m.* Miss Mary Blackwood, and had issue,

- James, of whom nothing is known.
- JOHN.
- Mary, *m.* to John Crawford, of Holestone, in the county of Antrim.
- Margaret.

The second son,

JOHN STEELE, esq. of Belfast, *m.* 23rd November, 1721, Isabell, daughter of Alex. Hamilton, esq. of Ballyvernon, and by her (who *d.* 15th May, 1739), had eight sons, of whom three survived infancy, viz.

- Hamilton, M. D. and surgeon in the army, *b.* 24th February, 1724-5, died in the Island of Grenada in 1782.
- ROBERT-GAWEN.
- William, *b.* 20th March, 1738-9.

Mr. Steele was *s.* by his elder surviving son,

ROBERT-GAWEN STEELE, esq. born 11th March, 1732-3, who *m.* first, MARGARET-MAXWELL, daughter of WILLIAM NICHOLSON, esq. of Ballow, and had

- Hamilton, *b.* 21st June, 1768, *d.* in 1807.
- WILLIAM-NICHOLSON, his successor.
- Robert, *b.* 22nd March, 1775, *d.* unm. in 1806.
- Mary, *b.* 24th February, 1770, *m.* to Hugh Kearns, esq. and *d.* 9th Feb. 1833, leaving issue.

Mr. Steele wedded, secondly, in May, 1806, Miss Mary Carmichael, but had no other issue. He *d.* 23rd March, 1814, and was *s.* by his elder surviving son, WILLIAM-NICHOLSON STEELE-NICHOLSON, esq. of Ballow, who had previously inherited the Nicholson property, and assumed that surname.

*Arms*—Quarterly; gules, two bars erm. in chief three suns or, for NICHOLSON; 2nd and 3rd, arg. a bend counter-compony or and sable, between two lions' heads, erased gules, on a chief az. three billets or, for STEELE.

*Crests*—From a ducal coronet gu. a lion's head, ermine, for NICHOLSON; a demi-eagle, with wings displayed, holding in its beak a snake ppr. for STEELE.

*Motto*—Deus mihi sol.

*Estates*—In the counties of Down, Donegall, and Antrim.

*Seat*—Ballow House, Downshire.

## TALBOT, OF CASTLE TALBOT.

OT, WILLIAM, esq. of Castle Talbot, in the county of Wexford, *m.* first, Maria-Mary, third daughter of Laurence O'Toole, esq.* and had issue,

MATTHEW-WILLIAM, captain in the 27th Regiment of Foot, now on half pay.
Lawrence, lieutenant R. N. deceased.
Maria-Theresa, *m.* 27th June, 1814, to John, present Earl of Shrewsbury.
Margaret, *m.* to George, only son of George Bryan, esq. of Jenkins Town, in the county of Kilkenny.
Julia, widow of Major Bishopp.

Mr. Talbot espoused, secondly, Anne, daughter of Robert Woodcock, esq. of Killown, and by that lady has had issue, Charles; George, deceased; Anne; and Catherine. He *m.* thirdly, Anne, daughter of John Beauman, esq. of Hyde Park, in the county of Wexford (see vol. ii. p. 602). He succeeded at the decease of his father, and is in the commission of the peace for the county of Wexford.

### Lineage.

is a branch of the noble house of ıbury, springing from SIR JOHN r, of Salwerp, grandson of the re-l Sir Gilbert Talbot, of Grafton, K.G. ommanded the right wing of the vic- army at Bosworth, and was third John, second Earl of Shrewsbury. he decease of Edward, the eighth earl, ', the honors of the house devolved he Grafton line, and GEORGE, of n, became ninth Earl of Shrewsbury. 'andson (son of his third son) of Sir 'albot, of Salwerp,

ICIS TALBOT, esq. obtained from the in 1630 two very extensive territorial in the county of Wexford: the first, ent, comprising seventeen thousand of fine land; the second, ten thousand of good land, all in the best part of inty. He *m.* Anne, daughter of Sir d Synot, of Rosegarland, bart. and son and heir,

TER TALBOT, esq. of Ballinamona, in ounty of Wexford, M.P. for that , who wedded Mary, eldest daughter Thomas Esmond, bart. of Ballynastra, ıd (with Commodore Talbot, of the royal navy, who wedded Miss Plunket, of Castle Plunket, and had an only child, William, of the royal navy, who died issueless), an elder son and heir,

WILLIAM TALBOT, esq. of Ballinamona, afterwards Castle Talbot, high sheriff of the county of Wexford. This gentleman *m.* Anne, eldest daughter of Sir Richard Masterson, of Munniseed House, and had two sons, ROGER, his heir, and Gabriel, in holy orders, chaplain to the King of Portugal. He was *s.* at his decease by his elder son,

ROGER TALBOT, esq. of Castle Talbot, who *m.* first Anne, only child of William Walsh, esq.† of the Walsh Mountains, in the county of Kilkenny, and niece of Sir Dudley Colcough, bart. of Tintern Abbey, M.P. for Wexford, and had an only son,

WILLIAM, his heir,

He wedded, secondly, Jane, only child of George Fitzpatrick, esq. and niece of Edward, first Lord Gowran,‡ and had another son, MATTHEW. Mr. Talbot was *s.* by his elder son,

WILLIAM TALBOT, esq. of Castle Talbot. This gentleman married Maria, only child

---

* scended from the ancient Irish house of O'TOOLE, princes of Hy-Marrag and Hy-Mul, in the of Dublin, so early as the twelfth century.

† e ancient family of Walsh gave a Duchess to the Noble House of Villiers. A younger branch, the Count Walsh de Serent, became settled in France.

‡ is peerage (created in 1715), with the earldom of Upper Ossory, expired at the decease , *second* EARL, without male issue, in 1818.

of Skeffington Smith, esq. of Dama Castle, in the county of Kilkenny and had three daughters, viz.

JANE, *m.* to Edward Masterson, esq. of Castletown.

ELIZABETH, *m.* to Lawrence O'Toole, esq. of Richfield, in the county of Wexford.

MARGARET, *m.* to Michael Sutton, esq. of Summer Hill, in the county of Wexford, and Dama Castle, Kilkenny.

Mr. Talbot dying without male issue, the property acquired by his marriage was divided amongst his daughters, while his paternal estates passed to his half brother,

MATTHEW TALBOT, esq. of Castle Talbot, who *m.* first, Juliana, Countess dowager of Anglesey, widow of Richard Annesley, fifth Earl of Anglesey, and mother of Arthur, first Earl of Mountnorris, by whom (who *d.* in 1776) he had an only son,

WILLIAM, his heir.

He wedded, secondly, in 1782, Jane Countess D'Arcy,* in France, and had issue,

John, deceased.

Matthew-D'Arcy, of Ballina, captain in the King's Own Stafford Regiment, and a magistrate of the county of Wexford.

JOHN-HYACINTH, of Talbot Hall (see Talbot, of Talbot Hall).

James, on the half pay of the Grenadier Guards, and a magistrate of the county of Wexford.

Matilda-Maria, *d.* in 1826.

Catherine, deceased.

Anna-Maria (Countess) chanoinesse of the royal order of Theresa de Baviere.

Mr. Talbot was *s.* by his eldest son, the present WILLIAM TALBOT, esq. of Castle Talbot.

*Arms*—Gu. a lion rampant, within a bordure engr. or.

*Crest*—On a chapeau gu. turned up ermine, a lion statant or, the tail extended.

*Motto*—Prest d'accomplir.

*Estates*—In the county of Wexford.

*Seat*—Castle Talbot, in the county of Wexford.

* This lady was only daughter of JOHN D'ARCY, esq. of Kiltulla, in the county of Galway (see page 146) and was great-granddaughter of the celebrated Duke of Berwick. She married first, in 1776, when but sixteen years of age, her kinsman, Mons. le Comte D'Arcy, general in the service of the King of France, aidecamp du roy, &c. (Refer to his life amongst "Les Hommes Celebres de France," and his Funeral Oration par Mons. le Marquis Condorcet.) Count D'Arcy died on his road to Britanny, to take the command of the army there, of the cholera morbus in 1779, and left his countess a widow at the age of nineteen. The count wrote several valuable works on artillery. He received all the honours of the court, having established by proof his eligibility to mount in the king's carriage, for which it was necessary to prove four hundred years of nobility. These proofs are in the archives of the king's library in Paris.

## TALBOT, OF TALBOT HALL.

TALBOT, JOHN-HYACINTH, esq. of Talbot Hall, in the county of Wexford, *b.* in 1794, *m.* in May, 1822, Anna-Eliza, only daughter and heiress of the late Walter Redmond, esq. of Bally Trent House, in the same county, and by her, who died in 1826, has three daughters, namely,

ANNA-ELIZA-MARY.
JANE.
MATILDA.

Mr. Talbot represents the borough of New Ross in parliament, and is a magistrate and deputy lieutenant for the county of Wexford.

### Lineage.

For descent, arms, &c. see TALBOT, of CASTLE TALBOT.

*Estates*—In the counties of Wexford and Dublin.

*Seats*—Talbot Hall, Bally Trent House, and Bettyville, in the county of Wexford.

# LONGE, OF SPIXWORTH.

LONGE, JOHN, esq. of Spixworth Park, in the county of Norfolk, *b.* 14th July, 1799, *m.* Caroline-Elizabeth, daughter of Francis Warneford, esq. of Warneford Place, in Wiltshire.

Mr. Longe inherited Spixworth at the decease of Katherine, widow of his cousin, Francis Longe, esq. He succeeded his father in 1834, and is in the commission of the peace for Norfolk.

## Lineage.

The parish register of Aswelthorpe mentions one THOMAS LONGE going to the king's host at Nottingham, in the year 1485.

— LONGE, of Hingham, in the county of Norfolk, had two sons, viz.

JOHN, who had by his wife Margery (she died his widow in 1546) two daughters,

CATHERINE, *m.* to Robert Baker.

ISABEL, *m.* to William Bawdewyn.

WILLIAM.

The younger son,

WILLIAM LONGE, of Hingham, died in 1557, leaving, by Catherine, his wife, two sons and a daughter.

JOHN, his heir.

William, of Depeham, who had John, Peter, William, Margaret, Ann, and Amye, all born before 1557.

Catherine, *m.* to John Burrough.

He was *s.* by his elder son,

JOHN LONGE, of Hingham, who had, with Thomas, and three daughters, Catherine, Mary, and Margaret, an elder son, his heir at his decease,

JOHN LONGE, of Hingham, *b.* in 1558, and died in 1622, when he was *s.* by his son,

ROBERT LONGE, esq. of Fowlden, *b.* in 1588, who was sheriff of Norfolk in 1644. He *m.* 25th May, 1614, Elizabeth, daughter of John King, citizen of London, and had issue,

John, who died in 1616, aged twelve years.

ROBERT, his heir.

Henry, who married twice, but *d. s. p.* in November, 1635.

Richard, *d. s. p.* in 1663.

Samuel, *d.* young.

Elizabeth, *b.* in 1615, *m.* to Clement Heigham, esq. of Barrow, in Suffolk.

Margaret, *b.* in 1618, *m.* first, Francis Batchcroft, esq. of Bexwell, and secondly, Gascoine Weld, esq. of Braconash.

Susan, *b.* in March, 1621, *m.* to the Rev. Mr. Longther, and died *s. p.* in 1673.

Mary, *b.* in May, 1626, *m.* to E. Britiffe, esq. of Baconsthorpe.

Sarah, *b.* in March, 1634, *m.* first, to Tobias Frere, esq. of Harleston, and secondly, to — Wogan, esq. She *d.* in February, 1684.

He died 17th September, 1656, and was *s.* by his eldest surviving son,

ROBERT LONGE, esq. of Reymerston, *b.* in January, 1619. This gentleman married four times. His first wife was Anne, dau. and co-heir of Thomas Milner, esq. of Lynn Regis, and by her, who died in May, 1653, had (with two daughters, Prisilla and Elizabeth, who both died young) seven sons, namely,

1. ROBERT, *b.* in August, 1642, inherited Rymerston at the decease of his father in 1688, *m.* first Abigail, daughter and co-heir of William Taylor, esq. of Gayton, and had

THOMAS, his heir, *b.* 3rd September, 1666, and *d. s. p.* in 1720.

WILLIAM, *b.* in November, 1669, and *d.* in 1734.

Anne, *b.* in 1667, *d.* in February, 1714.

He *m.* secondly, Susanah, daughter of — Heigham, esq. of Barrow, and had another daughter, Elizabeth, who *d.* young.

II. Thomas, *b.* in August 1643, *m.* Elizabeth, daughter of — Ingram, esq. and *d. s. p.* in 1709.

III. John.

IV. Charles, of Risby, Suffolk, B.D. *b.* in January, 1645, *m.* Elizabeth, dau. of Roger Pepys, esq. of Impingham, in Cambridgeshire, and had two daughters, Ellen and Elizabeth, who both died young.

V. Henry, *b.* in 1649, } both *d.* young.
VI. William, *b.* in 1652, }

He wedded for his second wife, Elizabeth, daughter of Francis Bacon, of Norwich, one of the Judges of the Court of King's Bench, and by that lady, who *d.* in January, 1659, had another son, the

VII. FRANCIS, of whom presently.

By his third wife, Frances, widow of Edmund Gournay, esq. of West Basham, who died in 1670, he had no issue. By the fourth and last wife, Ellen, daughter and heir of Thomas Gournay, esq. of West Basham, he had two daughters,

I. Anne, *b.* in August 1673, died young.

II. Ellen, *b.* in January 1674, *m.* to Richard Ferrier, esq. of Yarmouth.

He died in December, 1688. His seventh son (the only child of the second marriage)

FRANCIS LONGE, esq. who was recorder of Yarmouth, purchased the estate of Spixworth. He *m.* Susanna, daughter and heir of Tobias Frere, esq. and by her (who died in 1681) had issue to survive youth,

Robert, *b.* in April, 1688, married, but died issueless at Felton Hill, in Staffordshire, in 1736.

FRANCIS.

Elizabeth, *b.* in 1685, *m.* to Thomas Dalton, esq. of St. Edmund's Bury.

Ellen, *b.* in April, 1687, *m.* to Nicholas Larwood, esq. of Norwich.

Susan, *b.* in October, 1790, *m.* to John Reeve, of Norwich, Merchant, and *d. s. p.*

Mr. Longe died in December, 1734. His second son,

FRANCIS LONGE, esq. of Spixworth and Reymerston, *b.* in August 1689, *m.* at Norton, in Suffolk, Elizabeth, daughter of Edward Godfrey, esq. of London, by whom (who *d.* in 1767) he had issue,

I. FRANCIS, his heir.

II. JOHN, in holy orders, rector of Spixworth, and chaplain to the king, *b.* in July, 1731, *m.* Dorothy, daughter of Peter Edwin, esq. by whom (who *d.* in 1810) he left at his decease, in September 1806, with a younger son, Robert, who *m.* Mary, daughter of Thomas Parrant, gent, a son and heir,

JOHN, in holy orders, vicar of Codenham, cum Crowfield, in Suffolk, *b.* in April 1765, *m.* first, Charlotte, dau. of — Browne, esq. of Ipswich, and had

Francis, *b.* in 1798, *d.* in January, 1819.

JOHN, who inherited SPIXWORTH PARK from his cousin, Frances Longe, esq. at the decease of that gentleman's widow, in 1828.

Robert, in holy orders, *b.* 6th November, 1800, *m.* Margaret-Douglass, daughter of the Rev. Charles Davy, rector of Barking, Suffolk, and has issue.

Henry-Browne, in holy orders, *b.* 17th March, 1803.

Charlotte-Dorothy, *m.* to Robert Martin Leake, esq. of Woodhurst, in Surrey.

He wedded secondly, Frances, daughter of Col. Warde, of Salhouse, in Norfolk, but had no other issue.

Francis Longe, *d.* in October, 1735, and was *s.* by his elder son,

FRANCIS LONGE, esq. of Spixworth and Reymerston, *b.* in June, 1726, who served the office of sheriff for Norfolk, in 1752. He *m.* Tabitha, daughter of John Howes, esq. of Morningthorpe, and by her (who died in November, 1760) left at his decease, in February, 1776 (he had a daughter, Susan, *b.* in 1757, who *d.* unm. in 1772) an only son and heir,

FRANCIS LONGE, esq. of Spixworth, *b.* in April, 1748. This gentleman *m.* Katherine, second daughter of Sir George Jackson, bart. and co-heir of her mother, Mary, only child and heir of William Warde, esq. of London, but had no issue. Mr. Longe was sheriff of Norfolk in 1786. He died in July, 1812, devising Spixworth, after the decease of his widow, (he had previously sold Reymerston) to his cousin JOHN, son of the Rev. John Longe, vicar of Codenham, who succeeded on the death of the lady in 1828, and is the present JOHN LONGE, esq. of Spixworth Park.

*Arms*—Gules, a saltier engrailed or, and on a chief or, three cross croslets of the first.

*Crests*—A lion sejant gules, holding a saltier, engrailed or.

*Estates*—In Norfolk and Suffolk.

*Seat*—Spixworth Park, Norfolk.

# PENDARVES, OF PENDARVES.

**NDARVES-WYNNE, EDWARD WILLIAM,** esq. of Pendarves, in the of Cornwall, *m.* at Dawlish, 5th July, 1804, Tryphena, third dau. and now sole ing heiress of the Rev. Browse Trist, of Bowden in Devonshire.

s gentleman, whose patronymic is STACKHOUSE, assumed the additional surname NNE, by sign manual, dated 4th January, 1815; and on the 28th February, in me year, that of PENDARVES, in place of Stackhouse. He has represented all in parliament since 1826.

## Lineage.

Pendarves' of Pendarves are of cen- standing in the parish of Camborne unty of Cornwall, yet few particulars of the family prior to the reign of ETH, when

KANDER PENDARVES, the son of Tho- ndarves, married Alice, dau. of John hrey, esq. of Camborne, and by her, ed in 1640, left a son and successor, IARD PENDARVES, esq. of Pendarves, 600, who *m.* at Camborne, 13th April, Catherine, dau. of William Arundel, Menedarva (see vol. i. p. 514), and ue,

WILLIAM, his heir.

Richard, bapt. 22nd April, 1633, who *m.* Elizabeth, dau. of Thomas Corbett, esq. of London, and had a son, RICHARD.

. THOMAS, bapt. 4th Sept. 1645, *m.* Grace, second daughter of Robert Hoblyn, esq. of Nanswhydden, and dying, 16th March, 1703, left one son and one daughter,

WILLIAM (Sir), successor to his cousin.

GRACE, heiress to her brother.

IV. Benjamin, bapt. 27th Oct. 1649; buried in June, 1652.

V. Alexander, bapt. in February, 1651; buried 30th August, 1655, *s. p.*

I. Catherine, bapt. 12th July, 1638.

II. Anne, bapt. 22nd December, 1639.

III. DORCAS, bapt. at Camborne, 7th December, 1640; *m.* at St. Erme, 11th March, 1674, John Courtenay, esq. (son of Reskimer Courtenay, of Probus, in Cornwall, and grandson of Peter Courtenay, of Lanrake, in Devon), and had an only daughter and heiress,

CATHERINE COURTNEY, who *m.* John Williams, esq. of Trehane, in Cornwall, and by him, who died in 1705, had three daughters and co-heirs, viz.

1. MARY WILLIAMS, *d.* unm.
2. ANNE WILLIAMS, *m.* to John Fortescue, esq. and *d. s. p.*
3. CATHERINE WILLIAMS, *m.* at St. Erme, 31st Oct. 1738, to Rev. William Stackhouse, D. D. rector of St. Erme, and by him, who died 6th Aug. 1771, she had issue,

WILLLIAM STACKHOUSE, of Trehane, in Cornwall, *b.* in 1740; *m.* 1st May, 1770, Mary, dau. of Jonathan Rashleigh, esq. of Menabilly, and had three sons and four daughters, viz.

WILLIAM, vicar of Modbury, in the county of Devon, *m.* Sarah, dau. of William Smith, of Southampton, and has issue.

John, of London, merchant, *m.* Frances, dau. of Thomas Rashleigh, esq. 8th son of Jonathan Rashleigh, esq. of Menabilly, and has issue.

Jonathan.

Catherine, *m.* to the Rev. Hen. Pooley, of Lansallos, in Cornwall.

Mary, *m.* to the Rev. Thomas Carlyon.

Rachel, *m.* to Wm. Rashleigh, esq. of Menabilly, son of Jonath. Rashleigh, M.A.

Sarah.

Susanna.

JOHN STACKHOUSE, of whom presently, as inheritor of PENDARVES.

Mary Stackhouse.

Catherine Stackhouse, *m.* 5th March, 1771, to the Rev. Jonathan Rashleigh, M.A. rector of Wickham, in Hampshire.

IV. Alice, *b.* in 1644, *m.* in 1666, to Reynold Bawden, esq.

Richard Pendarves died in 1674, and was succeeded by his eldest son,

WILLIAM PENDARVES, esq. of Pendarves, bapt. 4th July, 1630, who married at Camborne, 23d May, 1667, Admonition, dau. of Edmond Prideaux, esq. of Padstow, but died without issue, 22nd December, 1683, when he was succeeded by his nephew,

RICHARD PENDARVES, esq. of Pendarves, at whose decease, issueless, 4th June, 1706, aged 21, the estates and representation of the family devolved on his cousin-german,

SIR WILLIAM PENDARVES, of Pendarves, who received the honour of knighthood, and represented the borough of St. Ives in parliament. He *m.* Penelope, dau. of Sydney Godolphin, esq. but dying *s. p.* 12th March, 1726, aged thirty-seven, was succeeded by his sister,

GRACE PENDARVES, of Pendarves, who *m.* first, Robert Coster, esq. and secondly, Samuel Percival, esq. of Clifton. Having no child, she devised her estates to her cousin,

JOHN STACKHOUSE, esq. second son of Dr. Stackhouse, by Catherine Williams, his wife, great-grand-daughter of RICHARD PENDARVES, esq. of Pendarves. Mr. Stackhouse, who was baptized at St. Erme, 15th March, 1741, wedded 21st April, 1773, Susanna, only child and heiress of Edward Acton, esq. of Acton Scot, in Shropshire, by Anne, his wife, dau. and eventually sole heiress of William Gregory, esq. of Woolhope, in Herefordshire,* and had issue,

I. JOHN, *d.* in 1782, aged seven.

II. EDWARD-WILLIAM, successor to his father.

III. Thomas-Pendarves, who inherited the estates of Acton Scott, in Salop, and How Caple, in the county of Hereford, and assumed the surname of ACTON, at the decease of his mother, in 1834. Mr. Stackhouse Acton *m.* 28th January, 1812, Frances, eldest dau. of Thomas Andrew Knight, esq. of Downton Castle.

I. Anne-Gregor, *m.* to the Rev. Thomas Coleman, rector of Church Stretton.

II. Catherine, *m.* in 1831, to the Rev. William Fowler Holt, of Bath.

Mr. Stackhouse died at Bath, 22nd November, 1819, and was succeeded by his son, the present EDWARD WILLIAM WYNNE PENDARVES, esq. of Pendarves.

*Arms.*—Quarterly, first and fourth sa. a falcon between three mullets or, second and third, gu. a chev. between three lions rampt. or; quartering, among many others, Stackhouse, Williams, Courtenay, Abrincis, Avenel, St. Aubyn, Valletort, Beauchamp, Clare, Gifford, M'Murrough, Carminow, Bodrugan, &c. &c. &c.

*Crests*—First, a lion rampt. reguardant or; second, a demi-bear, erm. muzzled, lined, and ringed, or; third, a saltier raguly or.

*Estates*—In Cornwall.

*Town-Residence*—Eaton Place.

*Seat*—Pendarves, Cornwall.

---

* By Susanna, his wife, eldest dau. and co-heir of William Brydges, esq. serjeant-at-law, and sister of Grace Brydges, who *m.* William Wynne, serjeant-at-law, son of Owen Wynne, LL.D. of Gwynfynnyd, warden of the Mint, and died 25th Nov. 1779, aged seventy-nine, leaving issue,

EDWARD WYNNE, of the Middle Temple, who *d. s. p.* 26th December, 1784, aged fifty.

LUTTRELL WYNNE, LL.D. died unm. 29th November, 1814, and was buried in the cloisters of Westminster Abbey. By his will, dated 17th August, 1806, he bequeathed his manors in Cornwall, and all his other estates, wheresoever and whatsoever, to his cousin, EDWARD WILLIAM STACKHOUSE, esq. of Pendarves.

Susanna Wynne, *m.* to Thomas Piercy, esq. captain, R. N. but died without surviving issue, 18th August, 1806. Both are buried in Canterbury cathedral.

# LE HUNTE, OF ARTRAMONT.

LE HUNTE, GEORGE, esq. of Artramont, in the county of Wexford, *b.* 15th June, 1814, succeeded at the decease of his father.

## Lineage.

This family, which was previously of respectability in England, settled in Ireland in the time of the Commonwealth, its founder there being a colonel in the parliament's army, and captain of Cromwell's guard. The first upon record,

JOHN LE HUNTE, was of the county of Suffolk, and married the daughter and heir of John Upwell, in Norfolk. His son,

SIR WARREN LE HUNTE, knt. of Bayton, in Suffolk, was father of

EUSTACE LE HUNTE, esq. of Bayton, who *m.* Elizabeth, dau. and co-heir of Edward Hunt, esq. of Wingham, in Essex, and left a son and heir,

ROBERT LE HUNTE, esq. of Springfield, near Chelmsford, in Essex, whose son and heir,

JOHN LE HUNTE, esq. of Springfield, *m.* Anne, dau. and co-heir of — Rushbrooke, esq. of Rushbrooke, in Suffolk, and was *s.* by his son,

ABEL LE HUNTE, esq. of Springfield, who wedded Mary, dau. of William Clopton, esq. of Kindwell, living in 1413, and left a son and heir,

JOHN LE HUNTE, esq. of Springfield, who *m.* the daughter and heir of Francis Topsfield, esq. of Uldham, in Essex, and was *s.* by his son,

ROBERT LE HUNTE, esq. of Springfield, who wedded Margaret, daughter of John M'Williams, esq. of Stainbourn, in Essex, and left a son and successor,

JOHN LE HUNTE, esq. of Huntshall, in Essex. This gentleman married twice, by his first wife, whose name and family are unknown, he had a son, who succeeded him, and died without issue; by his second wife, likewise unknown, he had another son, who, after the death of the elder, became

WILLIAM LE HUNTE, esq. of Huntshall, who *m.* Agnes, daughter of Sir William Waldgrave, knt. of Smallbridge, in Suffolk, and was *s.* by his son,

WILLIAM LE HUNTE, esq. of Huntshall, who wedded Anne, daughter and co-heir of Roger Fotheringay, esq. and, dying, 9th October, 1551, left a son and heir,

RICHARD LE HUNTE, esq. of Huntshall, in Ashen, in Essex. This gentleman mar. Anne, dau. and heir of Thomas Knighton, esq. of Little Bradley, in Suffolk, and was afterwards of that place. By this lady (who wedded, secondly, Thomas Soams, of Bottley, in Norfolk, who died in 1569,) he had issue,

- JOHN, his heir.
- William.
- Alice, *m.* first, to John Day, afterwards to William Stowe, of Hertfordshire, and, thirdly, to Edward Grimstone, serjeant-at-law.

He was *s.* by his elder son,

JOHN LE HUNTE, esq. of Little Bradley, in the county of Suffolk, and had (with two daughters, Elizabeth, the wife of Robert Hovell, alias Smith, of Ashford, in Suffolk, and Mary, who died *s. p.*) an only son and successor,

SIR GEORGE LE HUNTE, knight, of Little Bradley, who was sheriff of Suffolk in 1610. He *m.* first, Barbara, daughter of Sir Ralph Shelton, of Norfolk, knt. and had three sons and two daughters, born between the years 1603 and 1613. He wedded, secondly, Elizabeth, dau. of Sir John Peyton, bart. of Isleham, and widow of Sir Anthony Irby, of Lincolnshire. By this lady he had two other sons, and five daughters. Sir George died in 1641, and was buried at Little Bradley. His youngest son,

Richard le Hunt, *b.* at Little Bradley, 10th August, 1620, held the rank of colonel in the parliament's army, and was captain of Cromwell's guard, as appears by the following commission,—

"By the right hon. Oliver Cromwell, lieutenant-general of all the forces under the command of his excellency the lord-general Fairfax, and commander-in-chief of all the forces employed by the parliament of England for the service of Ireland.

"*To Colonel Richard Le Hunte, Captaine of my Guard.*

"I do hereby constitute and appoint you captayne of that troop of horse, consistinge of fifty troops, beside officers raised, and to be raised for the service aforesaid, which I have especially made choice of to attend and guard my own person. And you are hereby required and authorized to take the said Troope into your charge, and them duly to exercise in arms, and to do your best care and endeavour to keep them in good order and discipline, commandinge them to obey you as their Captain, and you are to obey and observe orders and commands, as you shall receive from myselfe, and other your superior officers, according to the discipline of warre.

"O. Cromwell.

"Given under my hand and seale, the 2nd day of June, Anno Domini 1649."

Colonel Le Hunte eventually settled at Cashell, in the county of Tipperary, and represented that city in parliament, in 1661. He *m.* Mary, daughter of Thomas Lloyd, esq. of Killiffith, in the county of Pembroke, by whom (who died about the year 1688, her will being dated and proved in the beginning of that year,) he had issue,

- I. George, his heir.
- II. Charles, living in 1687, died before 1702, *m.* a sister of Ambrose Jones, of ——, and left two sons,
  - George, who was of age in 1711.
  - Richard, of Kilmacon, in the county of Kilkenny, will dated in February, 1700.
- III. Thomas, whose second wife was Catherine, sister of John Bligh, first Earl of Darnley. She died *s. p.* in 1772.

- I. Anne, *d.* in 1702.
- II. Jane, *m.* to William Hughes, esq. of Cashell; both living in 1687.
- III. Mary, *m.* to Francis Bolton, esq. of Coudeny, in the county of Tipperary.
- IV. Catherine-Mary, died young.

His will is dated 29th March, 1668, and he was *s.* at his decease by his eldest son,

George le Hunte, esq. a minor at his father's decease, *m.* Alice, dau. and heir of Francis Leger, esq. of Cappagh, in the county of Tipperary, by whom (who remarried, in September, 1698, Robert Stewart, esq. of Castle Rothary, in the county of Wicklow), he had five sons and three daughters, viz.

- I. Richard, M. P. for Eniscorthy, died in June, 1747.
- II. Francis, of Bremanstown, in the county of Dublin, M.D. married the widow Briton, and left an only son,
  - Richard le Hunte, of Astramont, in the county of Wexford, whose will bears date 28th February, 1779.
- III. George.
- IV. William, B.D. vicar of Kidderminster, died in 1746. He had married Miss Richards.
- V. Thomas, barrister-at-law, *m.* in 1735, Alice, only daughter of the Rev. Jerome Ryves, D.D. dean of St. Patrick's, in Dublin, and dying in 1775, left three daughters, his co-heirs, viz.
  - Anne, *m.* in May, 1769, to the Rev. Abraham Lymes, D.D. of Killbreke, in the county of Wicklow, and died 5th May, 1817.
  - Alice, *m.* to Samuel Hayes, esq. of Avendale, in the county of Wicklow, and *d. s. p.* in October, 1815.
  - Jane, *m.* to John Lloyd, esq. of Gloster, in the King's County, M.P. for that county (see vol. ii. page 550), and died in 1824.

- I. Anne, *m.* to Alderman Humphrey French, of the city of Dublin, who served the office of lord mayor.
- II. Elizabeth, *m.* to the Rev. Mr. Buchanan.
- III. Jane, *m.* to George Warburton, esq. of Garryhinch.

Mr. Le Hunte died at Haverfordwest 27th May, 1697. His third son,

George le Hunte, esq. of Ballymartin, in the county of Wexford, *m.* Editha, daughter and heir of — Jones, esq. and was father of

George le Hunte, esq. who became "of Astramont, in the county of Wexford." He wedded Alicia-Maria, daughter of — Corry, esq. and had issue,

- I. Richard, his heir.
- II. William-Augustus, successor to his brother.
- III. George, *b.* in 1776.
- IV. Charles, } *b.* 2nd June, 1788.
- V. Francis, }

- I. Alicia.
- II. Anne, *m.* to S. Purdon, esq.
- III. Editha, *m.* to Sir Henry Meredyth,

art. of Carlandstown, in the county f Meath.

Hunte died at Clifton in 1799, and y his son,

RD LE HUNTE, esq. of Artramont, February, 1769, who espoused Miss , and had one son, Richard, who ninor; and three daughters, Maria, M. Hobson, esq. barrister-at-law; m. to W. Doyle, esq.; and Louisa, of W. Wilson, esq. Mr. Le Hunte ius without male issue, the repre- i of the family devolved on his bro-

IAM-AUGUSTUS LE HUNTE, esq. of nt, *b.* in 1774, who *m.* first, Patty, ighter of Colonel Warburton, of ich, but by her had no issue. He secondly, Miss J. M. Huson, eldest of Lieutenant-colonel Huson, by had a daughter, Alicia; and third-ly, the daughter of the Rev. J. Miller, by whom he had issue,

I. GEORGE, his heir.
II. William-Augustus, *b.* in 1819.
III. Francis, *b.* in 1820.

I. Harriet.
II. Patty-Warburton.
III. Maria.
IV. Mary-Anne, twin with Maria.
V. Editha.

Mr. Le Hunte was *s.* at his decease by his son, the present GEORGE LE HUNTE, esq. of Artramont.

*Arms*—Quarterly; 1st and 4th, a saltier; 2nd and 3rd, a stag's head caboshed.

*Crest*—A lion sejant.

*Motto*—Parcere prostratis.

*Estates*—In Wexford.

*Seat*—Artramont.

## BROCKMAN, OF BEACHBOROUGH.

CKMAN, *the Reverend* WILLIAM, of Beachborough, in the county of 12th August, 1788, *s.* his father on the 28th January, 1832.

Brockman, is in the commission of the peace for East Kent.

### Lineage.

ld Kentish family of BROCKMAN, states the existing house (formerly inherited under the will of James an in 1767, appears upon record so the time of RICHARD II. Amongst nts enrolled in the Tower, of the h year of that monarch's reign, a grant to

BROKEMAN, of the manor of Pirrie, ig to Old Romney and Medley, with other lands in Howting and Crundale, which vested in the crown on the attainder of Sir Robert Belknap. His descendant,

WILLIAM BROKEMAN, esq. of Witham, in Essex, *m.* Elizabeth, daughter and heir of John Fryer, and was *s.* by his son,

JOHN BROKEMAN, esq. of Witham, who *m.* Florence, daughter of John St. Leger,* of Ulcombe, and widow of John Clifford, esq. and had issue,

I. THOMAS, his heir, progenitor of the Brockmans of Witham.
II. HENRY.

He died in 1500, and was succeeded by his elder son, THOMAS, while the second son,

* The family of ST. LEGER, amongst the oldest in Kent, represented that county in parliament in the 20th EDWARD III. The above JOHN ST. LEGER had, beside the daughter, Florence, who married John Brokeman, four sons, viz.

RALPH (Sir), of Ulcombe, constable of Leeds Castle, ancestor of the LORDS DONERAILE, in Ireland.

THOMAS (Sir), sheriff of Surrey and Sussex in the 11th EDWARD IV. *m.* Anne Plantagenet, sister of *King* EDWARD IV. This lady had been previously the wife of Henry

HENRY BROCKMAN, esq. of Newington, became, by purchase from George Fogge, of Braborne, "of Beachborough in Kent," where having rebuilt the mansion, he fixed his abode. He married the daughter and heiress of Thomas Chilton, of the same county, and had two sons and a daughter, viz.

- WILLIAM, his successor.
- JOHN.
- Anne, *m.* to Thomas Broadnax, esq. of Goodmersham, and from this marriage lineally descended
  - Thomas Broadnax, of Goodmersham, who assumed, in 1738, the surname of KNIGHT, and was *s.* by his son,
    - Thomas Knight, who dying *s. p.* devised his estates to his cousin, Edward Austen, who assumed the name of KNIGHT, and is the present Edward Knight, esq. of Goodmersham. (See vol. i.)

He died in 1573, and was *s.* by his elder son,

WILLIAM BROCKMAN, esq. of Beachborough, who *m.* Margaret, eldest daughter of Humphrey Clarke, esq. of Kingsworth, and by her (who *d.* in 1610) left at his decease in 1605 (aged seventy-four), with a daughter, Margaret, the wife of Sir Edward Duke, knt. of Aylesford, a son and successor,

HENRY BROCKMAN, esq. of Beachborough. This gentleman wedded Helen, daughter of Nicholas Sawkins, esq. of Lyming, and had issue,

- WILLIAM (Sir), his heir.
- Zouch, of Cheriton, in 1680, then fifty-nine years of age, *m.* Elizabeth, daughter of Richard Evering, esq. and was *s.* by his son,
  - William, of Cheriton, who died in 1696, and was *s.* by his son,
    - Henry, of Cheriton, who *m.* Elizabeth Randolph, and left at his decease in 1752 (aged sixty-seven) three daughters, viz.
      - Mary, *d.* unm. in 1780.
      - Elizabeth, *m.* to Mr. Knapp.
      - CAROLINE, *m.* to *the Rev.* RALPH DRAKE, of whom in the sequel as inheritor of Beachborough.
- Margaret, *m.* to Valentine Norton, esq. of Fordwich.
- Helen, *m.* to the Rev. John Stroute.
- Elizabeth, *m.* to Robert Curteis, esq.
- Mary.
- Agnes.

He died in 1630, and was *s.* by his elder son,

SIR WILLIAM BROCKMAN, knt. of Beachborough. This gentleman, amongst the most devoted adherents of *King* CHARLES I. distinguished himself by a courageous defence of the town of Maidstone against Fairfax and a considerable body of the parliament's forces. He was appointed in the eighteenth of his majesty's reign, by the king, then in arms at Oxford, sheriff of Kent, but was superseded in his office by the parliament, and Sir John Honeywood constituted sheriff in his stead. The defence of Maidstone occurred in 1648, when Fairfax, with the elite of his division, marched upon that place, at the time garrisoned by probably a thousand royalist horse and foot, under the command of Sir John Mayney. The republican general passing the river at Farleigh Bridge, which had been but feebly guarded, attacked the town with a corps of ten thousand men at least; carrying without difficulty some slight fortifications which were thrown up at the entrance. The assault, about seven o'clock in the evening, became general, and the fighting fierce and sanguinary in every street, which with the houses were lined by the royalists, whose strength had been augmented by Sir William Brockman, who brought in a reinforcement of eight hundred men during the preliminary skirmishing. The resistance of the townsmen was so determined and gallant, that Fairfax had literally to contend for every inch of ground; the conflict had already been prolonged to midnight, when the royalists, overpowered by numbers, were driven into the church-yard, and thence taking shelter in the church, continued to resist with unabated ardour, until eventually reduced to surrender upon conditions securing their personal safety. Few actions displayed more of that chivalric courage and devoted resolve which characterized the adherents of the king during the civil wars than this. Lord Clarendon terms it "a sharp encounter very bravely fought with the general's whole strength." Sir William *m.* at Newington, 28th May, 1616, Anne,

---

Holland, Duke of Exeter, but divorced from him, at her *own suit (see* BURKE'S *Extinct and Dormant Peerage).* By her Sir Thomas left an only daughter and heir,

ANNE ST. LEGER, who wedded Sir George Manners, Lord Ros, and was mother of Thomas Manners, Lord Ros, created EARL OF RUTLAND.

JAMES (Sir), ancestor of the St. Legers, of Devonshire.

BARTHOLOMEW, *m.* Blanch, daughter of Lord Fitzwalter.

ghter and heir of Simon Bunce,* insted, and had issue,
s, his heir.
ha, buried at Newington, in 1687, m.
erine, *d.* unm. in 1633.
gery, *m.* to Sir William Hugeson, Linstead, in the county of Kent, which county her son,
James Hugeson, esq. of Linstead, served the office of sheriff.
, *m.* at Newington, 12th December, 50, to Sir John Boyes, of Bonning-n, in Kent.

am Brockman died in 1654, was t Newington on the 6th December ear, and *s.* by his son,

Brockman, esq. of Beachborough, ucy, daughter of James Young, of merchant, by whom (who died in ried at Newington 22nd June in ,) he had a son and two daughters,

liam, his successor.
e, baptized at Newington 25th January, 1652, *m.* to Sir Miles Cooke, e of the masters in chancery, and ed in 1688.
abeth, died unm. and was interred Newington in 1687.

Mr. Brockman was *s.* by his son,

William Brockman, esq. of Beachborough. This gentleman wedded Anne, elder daughter and co-heir of Richard Glydd, esq.* of Pendhill, in the county of Surrey, and had issue,

William, married, but died in the lifetime of his father issueless.
James, heir to his father.
John, *d.* unm. in 1739.

He died in 1741 at the advanced age of eighty-three, and was *s.* by his son,

James Brockman, esq. of Beachborough, who died unm. in 1767, aged seventy-one, devising his estates to (the great-nephew of his mother) his cousin,

*The Rev.* Ralph Drake, who thus became "of Beachborough," and assumed by act of parliament in 1768 (8th George III.), in compliance with the testamentary injunction of his deceased kinsman, the surname and arms of Brockman. He *m.* Caroline, youngest daughter of Henry Brockman, esq. of Cheriton, and had issue,

I. James, his heir.
II. Julius, in holy orders, rector of Cheriton and vicar of Newington, *b.* about 1770, *m.* in 1793, Harriet, daughter of the Rev. Thomas Locke, of Newcastle, in the county of Limerick, and had ten sons and four daughters, viz.
   Julius-William, *m.* in 1828, at Sheerness, Cornelia, daughter of the Rev. Mr. Ferryman.
   Charles.
   John, *m.* in London, in 1823, Eliza, daughter of General Stevenson.
   Ralph-Thomas.
   William, *m.* in 1827, Frances, daughter of Hugh Hammersley, esq.
   Thomas.
   Henry.
   George.
   Robert.
   James.

   Anne, *m.* at Cheriton, in 1822, to the Rev. Edmund Burke Lewis, of Toddington, in Bedfordshire.

---

* ard Bunce, of Malmesbury, living in ty of Canterbury, *temp.* Henry VIII. a daughter, Catherine, wife of John of Rodmersham, a son,
unce, father of
Bunce, of Ottrinden, who died in 1606, Elizabeth, his wife, daughter of Matner,
son Bunce, his heir, of Linsted and Otden, who *m.* Dorothy, daughter of Win Grimsditch, of Grimsditch, in the nty of Chester, and left an only daughand heir,
Anne Bunce, who became, as stated in the text, wife of Sir William Brockman.
ichard Bunce.
Matthew Bunce.
tephen of Boughton, died in 1634. He *m.* Anne, daughter of Arthur Barnn, and had issue; his eldest daughter Sir John Roberts, of Breaksbourn, in nt, and their daughter, Martha Roberts, ring wedded Edward Gibbon, esq. of estcliffe, near Dover, great grand-uncle the historian, left an only surviving ld,
Jane Gibbon, sole heir of her father, who *m.* John Brydges, esq. barrister-at-law, and brought him Wootton, in the county of Kent. The able antiquary, distinguished writer, and amiable man, Sir Samuel Egerton Brydges, bart. is grandson of this marriage.

* The younger daughter and co-heir of Richard Glydd, Martha Glydd, married Ralph Drake, (descended from the Drakes of Bletchynglie,) and had, with a son, Ralph, and four daughters, a younger son,
John Drake, who *m.* Anne Hayes, and had, with three younger daughters,
Ralph Drake, in holy orders, who inherited the estates of the Brockmans under the will of James Brockman, esq. in 1767.
Anne Drake, *m.* first, to William Smith, gent. of Heyton; and secondly, to the Rev. George Lynch, of Ripple. She died *s. p.* in 1787.

Caroline, *m.* to Captain Boyle Travers, of the Rifle Brigade, son of George Travers, esq. of Belvedere, in the county of Cork.

Harriet, *m.* in 1829, to Thomas du Boulay, esq. of Walthamstow.

Frances, *m.* to the Rev. H. Boucher.

I. Anne, *m.* to William-Thomas Locke, esq. of Newcastle, in the county of Limerick.

II. Elizabeth, *m.* to John Foster, esq. of the Middle Temple.

III. Mary, *m.* to William Honeywood, esq. of Sibeton, M.P. for Kent.

IV. Sarah, *m.* to the Rev. John Backhouse, rector of Upper Deal.

Mr. Drake-Brockman *d.* in November, 1781, aged fifty-seven, was buried at Newington, and *s.* by his elder son,

JAMES DRAKE-BROCKMAN, esq. of Beachborough, who served the office of sheriff of Kent in 1791. He wedded, 7th June, 1786, Catherine-Elizabeth, daughter of the Rev. William Tatton, D.D. prebendary of Canterbury, and had issue,

James, major of the East Kent Militia, who died 14th April, 1829, unm.

WILLIAM, in holy orders, heir to his father after the decease of his elder brother.

Henry-Lynch, died at Elvas, in Portugal, in 1809.

Tatton, in holy orders, curate of Frant, near Tunbridge Wells, *m.* the daughter of Sir Henry Hawley, bart.

Edward, barrister-at-law.

George, captain in the 85th regiment.

Frederick.

Francis-Head.

Charlotte, *m.* to the Rev. Kennett Champain Bayley, rector of Acrise, in Kent, and vicar of Waybridge, Surrey.

Lucy-Anne, *m.* at Newington, 3rd June, 1828, to Robert, son of Charles Frazer, esq. minister plenipotentiary for Hamburgh.

Mr. Brockman died 28th January, 1832, and was *s.* by his eldest surviving son, the *present* REV. WILLIAM DRAKE-BROCKMAN, of Beachborough.

*Arms*—Or, a cross formee fitchee *sa.* on a chief of the second three fleurs-de-lys of the field. (Granted in 1606.)

*Crest*—On a sword erect argent, pummel and hilt or, a stag's head caboshed ppr. attired of the second, the blade through the head and bloody at the point.

*Estates*—In Kent.

*Seat*—Beachborough.

## CORRANCE-WHITE, OF PARHAM HALL.

CORRANCE, MARY, of Parham Hall, in the county of Suffolk, inherited the estates of her cousin, Mrs. Elizabeth Long, under the will of that lady, in 1792, *m.* in 1782, Snowden White, of Nottingham, M.D. by whom, who *d.* in 1797, she has one surviving son and heir,

FREDERICK WHITE, of Loudham Hall, in Suffolk, *m.* at Winborn Minster, 27th September, 1819, Frances-Anne, third daughter of William Woodley, esq. governor of Berbice, and has issue,

FREDERICK-SNOWDEN WHITE, *b.* 17th January, 1722.

Charles-Thomas White, *b.* 7th March, 1823.

Henry-William White, *b.* 30th April, 1828.

George-Edward White, *b.* 9th April, 1830.

Frances-Anne White.

Louisa-Jane White.

### Lineage.

THOMAS URREN, of Stratford upon Avon, in the county of Warwick, was father of

ALLEN URREN, alias CURRANCE, of London, citizen and merchant taylor, who had a grant of arms on the 27th February, 1619. He *m.* Catharine, sister of Richard Bell, of York, and had issue,

JOHN, his heir.

Catherine, *m.* to Sir John Melton, knt. secretary to the council of York.
Anne, }
Lucy, } *

Mr. Currance purchased Wimbish Hall, in Essex, before 1629. He was *s.* at his decease by his son,

JOHN CURRANCE, esq. of Rendlesham. This gentleman purchased Parham Hall, in Suffolk, formerly the property and residence of the lords Willoughby, of Parham, between the years 1680 and 1690. He wedded Margaret, daughter of Sir John Hare, knt. and with two daughters, Elizabeth, who *d.* unm. and Anne, the wife of — Woodnoth, left at his decease about the year 1694 (his will bears date 17th November, 1693, and was proved 7th May following) a son and successor,

JOHN CORRANCE, esq. of Rendlesham, who wedded Elizabeth, daughter of — Vilet, of Oxford, and had issue,

I. CLEMENCE, his heir.
II. John, of Foxton, in Leicestershire, *d.* 19th February, 1740, without legitimate issue.
III. RICHARD, a civilian, residing in London, *m.* a daughter of — Warren, of Newmarket, and had a son,
  JOHN CORRANCE, major in the army, held a captain's commission in the 8th Foot at Culloden, was at the battles of Dettingen and Fontenoy, *m.* Margaret, daughter of — Bantoft, of Hintlesham, and had issue,
    John Corrance, who *d.* at the age of nine.
    MARY CORRANCE, who *m.* SNOWDEN WHITE, M.D.
    SUSANNA CORRANCE, *d.* unm. in 1809.
IV. Edward.
V. Allen, of Wicken, Suffolk, baptized at Parham, 10th June, 1702, *m.* Katherine, dau. of ———, and had
  Allen, in holy orders, rector of Brightwell, in Oxfordshire, died *s. p.*
  Elizabeth, *m.* to the Rev. Mr. Smith, and had a daughter,
    Catherine Smith, who *d.* unm.
I. Elizabeth, *m.* to Francis Lowe, esq. of Brightwell, in the county of Oxford, and had two daughters,
  CATHARINE LOWE, *m.* to William Lowndes, esq. of Brightwell, who assumed the surname of STONE (see p. 258).
  Anne Lowe, *m.* to Thomas Polter, esq.

* One of these ladies *m.* first, — Heals, and secondly, Robert Lane, esq. of Rendlesham.

Mr. Corrance purchased Parham House and estate, formerly the property of Sir John Warren, bart. about 1699. He *d.* in London, 29th April, 1704, was interred at Parham, and *s.* by his eldest son,

CLEMENCE CORRANCE, esq. of Parham, who represented Oxford in parliament from 1708 to 1714. He *m.* 20th October, 1705, Mary, daughter of Sir Robert Davers, bart. and had issue,

I. JOHN, his heir.
II. Robert, in holy orders, *b.* 18th October, 1715, chaplain to Admiral Davers, died, off Carthagena, unm.

I. Henrietta, *d.* in 1744, aged twenty-seven, unm.
II. Mary, *m.* to William Castle, esq. and had, with a daughter, Mary Castle, who *m.* — Clavel, esq. but *d. s. p.* a son,
  William Castle, who *m.* Catherine, daughter of — Frome, esq. and left an only child,
    Catharine Castle, *m.* in 1788, to Edward Bouverie, esq. of De la Pre Abbey, in the county of Northampton (see vol. ii. p. 7).
III. ELIZABETH, *b.* in 1708, *m.* ISRAEL LONG, esq. of Dunston, in the county of Norfolk, and had an only daughter (to survive infancy),
  ELIZABETH LONG, who *d.* unm. in the lifetime of her mother, aged twenty-six.

He *d.* in March, 1724, was buried at Rougham on the 30th of that month, and *s.* by his eldest son,

JOHN CORRANCE, esq. of Rougham, baptized 6th October, 1711, *m.* first, in 1730, Elizabeth, daughter of — Bransby, esq. of Shottisham, in Norfolk, but that lady dying without issue, in October, 1733, he wedded secondly, in May, 1734, Anne, daughter of Robert Chester, esq. of Cokenhatch, in the county of Herts (see vol. ii. p. 17), and by her, who *d.* in 1748, and was buried at Rougham, had an only child, ANNE, baptized 31st January, 1737. Mr. Corrance *d.* in 1742, was interred at Rougham on the 1st June in that year, and succeeded by his infant daughter,

ANNE CORRANCE, at whose decease, in February, 1747 (she was buried at Rougham on the 18th of that month), the estates devolved upon

ELIZABETH LONG, who outlived her only child, and *d.* at the advanced age of eighty-four, 30th December, 1792, bequeathing her property to her cousin, MARY CORRANCE, who had married SNOWDEN WHITE, M.D. and is the present MRS. WHITE, of Parham Hall.

### Family of White.

THOMAS WHITE, esq. of Pirton, in the county of Herts, lord of that manor, an officer in the Parliament's army, *m.* Elizabeth ———, and had, with THOMAS, his heir, and several other children, a younger son,

SAMUEL WHITE, of St. Ives, gent. who *d.* in 1736 (will dated 10th October in that year, and proved on the 30th), leaving, by his first wife,

SNOWDEN, his successor.

Anne, *m.* to — Charnells, esq. of Leicestershire, and *d. s. p.*

And, by the second, Samuel, Thomas, and Hannah, of Derby.

The eldest son,

SNOWDEN WHITE, esq. of Newton Flotman, in the county of Norfolk, *m.* Elizabeth, daughter of Dr. Latham, of Derbyshire, and had issue,

SNOWDEN, his heir.

Mary, } *d.* unm.
Anne, }

Sarah, *m.* to — Wragg, of Derbyshire.

He *d.* about 1773, and was *s.* by his son,

SNOWDEN WHITE, M.D. of Nottingham, who *m.* MARY, elder daughter of MAJOR JOHN CORRANCE, and dying in 1797, left an only son,

FREDERICK WHITE, esq. of Loudham Hall, in Suffolk.

*Arms*—Arg. on a chev. between three wolves' heads erased sa. a wolf's head or for WHITE; arg. on a chev. between three ravens sa. three leopards' faces or, for CORRANCE.

*Crest* — A wolf's head erased sa. for WHITE. A raven holding with his dexter claw an escutcheon sa. charged with a leopard's face or.

*Estates*—In Suffolk, including the estates of Parham Hall, Parham House, and the manor of Parham, with the advowsons of Parham and Hacheston, &c.

*Seat*—Loudham Hall.

## SCOTT, OF HARDEN.

SCOTT, HUGH, esq. of Harden, in the county of Roxburgh, *b.* in 1758; *m.* in 1795, Harriet Bruhl, daughter of Hans Maurice, Count Bruhl, of Martinskirker, in Saxony,* by whom he has issue,

HENRY-FRANCIS, deputy lieutenant in the counties of Berwick and Roxburgh, and member in four parliaments for the latter shire.

William-Hugh, at the English bar, *m.* Eleanor, daughter of the late Archdeacon Baillie Hamilton.

Francis, also at the English bar.

Maria-Amabel.

Elizabeth-Anne.

Anne, *m.* to Charles Baillie, esq.

Mr. Scott succeeded his father in 1793. He is a justice of the peace and deputy lieutenant in the counties of Berwick, Roxburgh, and Selkirk, and was representative in parliament for Berwickshire.

### Lineage.

The family of SCOTT derives from UCHTRED FITZ SCOTT, who flourished at the court of *King* DAVID I. and was ancestor of SIR MICHAEL SCOTT, of Murthockstone, (which territory came to the Scotts with the heiress of Murthockstone, of that Ilk), from whose eldest son sprang, in the female line, the present DUCAL FAMILY OF BUCCLEUCH,

* The *Hon.* ALMERIA CARPENTER, only daughter of George, second Lord Carpenter, espoused, first, Charles, second earl of Egremont, by whom she had George-O'Brien, the present earl, and other children. Her ladyship *m.* secondly, COUNT BRUHL, and by him was mother of Mrs. Scott, of Harden.

and from his second son, the SCOTTS OF SINTON.

WILLIAM SCOTT, first Laird of Harden, was the second son of the Laird of Sinton. He was a fierce and gallant warrior, and was commonly called "Willy with the Boltfoot." He *m.* AKER, dau. of the Laird of Ferniehirst, and was *s.* by his son,

WALTER SCOTT, second Laird of Harden, surnamed "Auld Wat." Of this chief, his illustrious descendant, SIR WALTER SCOTT, thus speaks.* "We may form some idea of the style of life maintained by the border warriors, from the anecdotes, handed down by tradition, concerning Walter Scott of Harden, who flourished towards the middle of the sixteenth century. This ancient laird was a renowned freebooter, and used to ride with a numerous band of followers. The spoil, which they carried off from England, or from their neighbours, was concealed in a deep and impervious glen, on the brink of which the Old Tower of Harden was situated. From thence the cattle were brought out, one by one, as they were wanted, to supply the rude and plentiful table of the laird. When the last bullock was killed and devoured, it was the lady's custom to place on the table a dish, which, on being uncovered, was found to contain a pair of clean spurs; a hint to the riders, that they must shift for their next meal. Upon one occasion, when the village herd was driving out the cattle to pasture, the old laird heard him call loudly to *drive out Harden's cow.* '*Harden's cow!*' echoed the affronted chief, 'Is it come to that pass?" by my faith they shall sune say Harden's *kye* (cows).' Accordingly, he sounded his bugle, mounted his horse, set out with his followers, and returned next day with '*a bow of kye, and a bassen'd* (brindled) *bull.*' On his return with this gallant prey, he passed a very large hay-stack. It occurred to the provident laird, that this would be extremely convenient to fodder his new stock of cattle; but as no means of transporting it occurred, he was fain to take leave of it with this apostrophe, now proverbial: 'By my soul, had ye but four feet, ye should not stand lang there.'" The laird *m.* Mary Scott, celebrated in song by the title of the FLOWER OF YARROW. By their marriage contract, the father-in-law, Philip Scott, of Dryhope, was to find Harden 'in horse meat, and man's meat, at his Tower of Dryhope, for a year and a day; but five barons pledge themselves, that, at the expiry of that period, the son-in-law should remove, without attempting to continue in possession by force! A notary public signed for all the parties to the deed, none of whom could write their names. The original is still in the charter room of the present Mr. Scott, of Harden. By the Flower of Yarrow, the Laird of Harden had, with daughters, four sons, namely,

WILLIAM (Sir), his heir.

Walter, who *m.* a daughter of John Hay, of Haystoun, in Peebles. This gentleman was killed in a fray, at a fishing, by one of the Scotts of Gilmanscleugh; his brothers flew in arms; but the old laird secured them in the dungeon of his Tower, hurried to Edinburgh, stated the crime, and obtained a gift of the land of the offenders from the Crown. He returned to Harden with equal speed, released his sons, and shewed them the charter. "To horse, lads!" cried the savage warrior, "and let us take possession! the lands of Gilmanscleugh are well worth a dead son." The property, thus obtained, continued in the family till the beginning of the last century, when it was sold by John Scott, of Harden, to Anne, Duchess of Buccleuch.

Hugh, from whom the Scotts of Gala.

Francis, ancestor of the Scotts now of Sinton.

Harden wedded, secondly, Margaret, daughter of Edgar, of Wedderlie, and relict of William Spotswood, of that Ilk, by whom he had a daughter, Margaret, *m.* first, to David Pringle, the younger, of Gallasheils, and, secondly, to Sir William Macdougall, of Mackerston. He was *s.* at his decease in 1629, by his eldest son,

SIR WILLIAM SCOTT, third Laird of Harden, who enjoyed, in a high degree, the favour of *King* JAMES VI. This chief being made prisoner by Sir Gideon Murray, of Elibank, in a bloody border feud, was condemned to lose his head, or to marry Agnes, a daughter of his captor, known by the descriptive appellation of "Muckle-mouthed Meg." To the latter alternative he consented, but not before he had ascended the scaffold; he lived with the lady, however, long and happily, and had by her eight children, namely,

I. WILLIAM (Sir), his successor.

II. Gideon (Sir), *m.* Margaret, daughter of Sir Thomas Hamilton, of Preston, and dying in 1672, left issue,

1. WALTER, of Highchester, who wedded, in his fourteenth year, at Wemyss Castle, 9th February, 1659, Mary, COUNTESS OF BUCCLEUCH, then eleven years of age, and one of the greatest heiresses in Scotland. This affair made considerable noise, and became matter of discussion before the provincial Synod of

* Minstrelsy of the Scottish Border.

Fife, upon an accusation against the presbytery for granting a warrant for the marriage without proclamation. The presbytery was however absolved, because the order was grounded upon an act of the general assembly, allowing such marriages in case of necessity, or fear of rape. The countess died in two years afterwards, *s.p.* and Mr. Scott, who had been created (in consequence of the marriage) EARL OF TARRAS *for life*, by patent dated 4th September, 1660; *m.* secondly, 31st December, 1677, Helen, eldest daughter of Thomas Hepburn, of Humbie, by whom his lordship had issue,

1. GIDEON, of Highchester, *b.* 25th October, 1678, and served heir to his father, Lord Tarras, 7th September, 1694. He married, first, the sister of Sir Francis Kinlock, bart. of Gilmerton, but by her had no issue. He espoused, secondly, Lady Mary Drummond, daughter of John, Earl of Melfort, and left at his decease, in 1707, two sons,

   WALTER, who succeeded, in 1710, to the lands of HARDEN.

   JOHN, heir to his brother.

2. WALTER, who inherited HARDEN, at the decease of his nephew in 1734.
3. Thomas, *d.* in France unm.

1. Helen.
2. Agnes.
3. Margaret.

2. Francis, who first adopted the military profession, but afterwards became a churchman, and was high in favour with the Grand Duke of Tuscany, in whose dominions he died.

1. Agnes, *m.* to John Riddel, the younger, of that Ilk.
2. Margaret, *m.* to James Corbet, jun. esq. of Tolcorse.
3. ——, *m.* first, to James Grant, of Dalvey; and, secondly, to Doctor William Rutherford, of Barnhills.

III. WALTER, of Raeburn. *(See that family).*

IV. James, *m.* Agnes, daughter of Sir Walter Riddel, of that Ilk, and from him descended the Scotts of Thirlestane.

V. John, *m.* Agnes, only daughter of Robert Scott, of Harwood, and hence the Scotts of Woll.

I. Elizabeth, *m.* to Andrew Ker, esq. of Greenhead.

II. Margaret, *m.* to Thomas Ker, esq. of Mersington.

III. Janet, *m.* to John, son of Sir John Murray, of Philiphaugh.

The third Laird of Harden espoused, secondly, Margaret, daughter of William Ker, esq. of Linton, but had no other issue. He *d.* in 1665, and was *s.* by his eldest son,

SIR WILLIAM SCOTT, fourth Laird of Harden, who received the honour of knighthood from *King* CHARLES II. immediately after the RESTORATION. He wedded Christian, third daughter of Robert, sixth Lord Boyd, and had two sons and two daughters, viz.

WILLIAM, } heirs in succession.
ROBERT, }

Christian, *m.* to William Ker, of Chatto.

Margaret, *m.* to Sir Patrick Scott, bart. of Ancrum.

This laird was *s.* at his decease by his elder son,

SIR WILLIAM SCOTT, fifth Laird of Harden, who wedded Jean, only daughter of Sir John Nisbet, of Dirleton, Lord President of Session, by whom (who *m.* secondly, Sir William Scott, of Thirlestane) he had no issue. He *d.* in 1707, and was *s.* by his brother,

ROBERT SCOTT, sixth Laird of Harden, at whose decease, issueless, the representation and estates of the family passed to his cousin, (refer to descendants of Sir Gideon Scott, second son of Sir William, third laird),

WALTER SCOTT, of Highchester, who thus became seventh LAIRD OF HARDEN. He *d.* without issue, in 1710, and was *s.* by his brother,

JOHN SCOTT, eighth Laird of Harden, who wedded Lady Jane Erskine, daughter of Alexander, fifth Earl of Kelly, and had two daughters,

ANNE, *m.* to Thomas Sharp, esq. of Houston.

Mary.

Dying without male issue, the estates reverted to his uncle,

WALTER SCOTT, (second son of the EARL OF TARRAS), as ninth Laird of Harden. This gentleman married no less than four wives: first, Agnes, daughter of John Nisbet, esq. of Bewlie, without issue; secondly, Agnes, daughter of William Scott, esq. of Thirlestane, by whom he had a daughter, Christian; thirdly, Anne, only daughter of John Scott, of Gorrenbony, and had two sons and three daughters, namely,

WALTER, his heir.

ıcis, a merchant in India.

ı.

ın, m. to George Brown, esq. of ston.

e.

th wife was Anne, eldest daughter y Ker, esq. of Frogden, without le d. in 1746, and was s. by his

R SCOTT, esq. tenth Laird of Har-. for the county of Roxburgh from 765, when he was appointed re-d cashier of excise in Scotland. ady Diana Hume, daughter of ird Earl of Marchmont, and left cease in January, 1793, an only resent SCOTT, OF HARDEN, twenty-UCHTRED FITZ SCOTT, in the le descent. HARDEN is also en-the name of HEPBURN, as pro-f the estate of Humbie, to which he succeeded as heir of entail of the issue of HELEN HEPBURN, who m. his grand uncle, WALTER SCOTT, EARL OF TARRAS.

*Arms*—Or, two mullets in chief and a crescent in base arg.

*Crest*—A lady richly attired, holding in her right hand the sun and in the left a half moon.

*Supporters*—Two mermaids ppr. holding mirrors.

*Mottoes*—For SCOTT, Reparabit cornua Phœbe: for HEPBURN, Keep.

*Estates*—Mertoun, in Berwickshire; Harden, in Roxburghshire; Oakwood, in Selkirk; Humbie, in East Lothian. The last inherited by the present Mr. Scott, as heir of entail of the "Hepburns of Humbie."

*Town Residence*—John Street, Berkeley Square.

*Seat*—Mertoun, in the county of Berwick.

## SCOTT, OF RAEBURN.

WALTER, esq. of Raeburn, in the shire of Selkirk, espoused, in 1772, Jean, third daughter of Robert Scott, of Sandyknow, by Barbara, his wife, second daughter of Thomas Haliburton, of Newmains, and had issue,

- WILLIAM, m. Susan, eldest daughter of Alexander Horsbrough, esq. of that Ilk, by Violet, his wife, daughter of Thomas Turnbull, and has issue.
- Robert, of Prince of Wales Island, East Indies.
- Hugh, late a captain in the East India Company's Shipping Service, who m. Sarah, only daughter of William Jessop, esq. of Butterby Hall, in the county of Derby.
- Walter, who died unmarried.
- John, major in the 8th Native Bengal Infantry.
- Barbara.

Mr. Scott succeeded to the estates upon the demise of his father.

### Lineage.

ı a branch of the house of HAR-ıortalized by giving birth to the OF WAVERLEY.

ILLIAM SCOTT, third laird of Har-g *temp.* JAMES VI. m. Agnes, dau. ideon Murray, of Elibank, trea-ute of Scotland, had, with other

TON (Sir), ancestor of the present use of HARDEN.

WALTER SCOTT, (third son), who is instructed, by a charter under the great seal, "Domino Willielmo Scott de Harden, militi et Walter Scott suo filio legitimo tertio genito terrarum de Robertown, &c." in Selkirkshire, dated 18th December, 1627. He m. Ann Isobel, daughter of William Macdougall, of Makerston, by Margaret, daughter of Walter Scott, of Harden, and had two sons and two daughters, viz.

WILLIAM, his heir.

Walter, known by the name of *Bearded Watt*, from a vow which he had made to go unshaven until the restoration of the STUARTS. He *m.* Jean, daughter of Campbell of Silvercraigs, by whom he had two sons, Walter and Robert. The younger,

ROBERT SCOTT, was father of

WALTER SCOTT, writer to the Signet, who *m.* Anne, daughter of John Rutherford, M.D. and was father of

SIR WALTER SCOTT, BART. AUTHOR OF THE WAVERVERLEY NOVELS. See BURKE'S *Peerage and Baronetage.*

Isobel, *m.* to Captain Anderson.

Christian, *m.* to James Menzies, fourth son of Alexander Menzies, of Culleralleгs, in the county of Lanark.

It appears, by acts of the privy council, 1665-6, that Raeburn and his wife were infected with Quakerism, and that the laird was in consequence deprived of the education of his children, had part of his estate wrested from him, and was thrown into the prison of Edinburgh, while his wife suffered incarceration in that of Jedburgh. He died soon after the Restoration, and was *s.* by his eldest son,

WILLIAM SCOTT, of Raeburn, a person of considerable erudition, who *m.* Anna, eldest daughter of Sir John Scott, bart. of Ancram, by Elizabeth, his wife, daughter of Francis Scott, of Maugertown, and had,

WALTER, his heir.

Isobel, *m.* in 1711, to John Rutherford, younger of Knowsworth, M.D.

Raeburn died 6th August, 1699 (his widow *m.* secondly, in 1702, John Scott, of Sinton), and was *s.* by his only son,

WALTER SCOTT, of Raeburn, who *m.* 19th November, 1703, Anne, third daughter of Hugh Scott, of Gala, by Isabella, his wife, daughter of Sir Thomas Ker, of Cavers, and had one son, William, and two daughters, Isobel and Anne.

This laird was killed in a duel by one of the Pringles of Crighton, near Selkirk, (in a field still named *Raeburn's Meadow*), on the 3rd October, 1707, at the age of twenty-four. His relict wedded, secondly, Henry Macdougall, of Makerstoun, and thirdly, Home of Eccles.

The only son and successor,

WILLIAM SCOTT, of Raeburn, born in 1704, who *m.* in 1743, Jean Elliott, and left at his decease one daughter, Anne, *m.* to Thomas, second son of Robert Scott, of Sandyknow, and an only son, WALTER SCOTT, esq. of Raeburn.

*Arms*, &c. see SCOTT OF HARDEN.

*Estates*—In Selkirkshire.

*Seat*—Raeburn.

## BETHUNE, OF BALFOUR.

BETHUNE, GILBERT, esq. of Balfour, in the county of Fife, *b.* in 1765, succeeded his brother, in 1798. This gentleman, formerly in the army, and afterwards lieutenant-colonel of the Fifeshire Fencible Corps of Infantry, is a magistrate and deputy-lieutenant for Fifeshire.

### Lineage.

The Scotch historians and genealogists all agree, that the BETUNES of Scotland came originally from France, in some of the later ages; but the cause or period of their advent has not been yet determined with certainty.

Mr. Peter Victor Cayer, author of the Funeral Panegyrick on JAMES BETHUNE, Archbishop of Glasgow, nephew of the seventh laird of Balfour, who died in 1603, tells us that, amongst other considerable gentlemen of quality who came to Scotland in 1449, in the retinue of Mary, princess of Gueldres, then married to JAMES *the Second*, was one Monsieur de BETHUNE, for whom the king conceived a singular partiality, and, to engage him to live in Scotland, gave him in marriage the daughter and sole f the baron of Balfour, in Fife, ve rise to the family of BETHUNE- and the BETHUNES of Scotland.

ndefinite and uncircumstantiated Monsieur de Chesne, author of the y of the House of Bethune, in llustrates, by endeavouring to de- he arms and person of this Mon- Bethune, who had the good fortune he favour of the king, and marry s of Balfour. From a great many ties and conjectures, Monsieur de concludes that it was James (Jaco- Bethune, fourth son of John de lord of Barc, &c. and of Isabella ville, his wife, and younger brother t de Bethune, lord of Barc, &c. eal descendant is the present duke in France.

onjecture of Mr. Cayer, though y plausible, is not founded upon of. None of our ancient histo- ition any of the name of BETHUNE ncess of Gueldre's retinue; and as ur de Chesne's suppositions, though le Bethune lived at the time men- ere is not the least evidence of his g in Scotland.

ran de Moustrelet, a contempo- r, who speaks at large of John de and others of his kindred, makes n of the arrival of Jacotine de Be- r of his ever leaving the Low .

er well disposed Mr. Cayer and de Chesne might be to do justice ouse of BETHUNE-BALFOUR, it is le to conclude that neither of them ciently acquainted with the subject chosen to treat upon. There can ubt that the family of Bethune, Beaton, in which different ways is found to be spelt in various was of considerable note in Scot- ny generations before it became vith that of BALFOUR, and the h that family happened long before cess of Gueldres or Jacotine de were born. Bishop Leslie, and cotch historians, state that the s came from France into Scotland e of *King* MALCOLM *the Third*, who reign 1057, and died 1093. We t now upon what grounds these ts are founded; and at this distance when most of the old family papers r destroyed, we must be contented tever evidence can be now obtained arly transactions. About the period noted, it was customary for gentle- give their writs and securities, in of some of their neighbours, whose were accordingly inserted as wit- all their grants and charters. reign of WILLIAM (who succeeded to the crown in 1165, only seventy-five years after the death of MALCOLM III.) ROBERTUS DE BETHUNE is witness to a charter of Rogerus de Quincey, Earl of Wigton, to Seyerus de Seton, of an annuity out of the Miln and Miln lands of Trauent.

DAVID DE BETVN, and JOANNES DE BETUN, are witnesses to a royal charter by ALEXANDER II. (who began his reign 1214, and *d.* 1249) to the abbey of Aberbrothick "de Terris, in territorio de Kermuir, in the county of Angus." It was in that county the family of the Bethunes was then most considerable. The chief of them was the Laird of Westhall, of whom the rest are descended. Again, in that neighbourhood we find in the beginning of the reign of ALEXANDER III. about 1250, Dominus DAVID DE BETUN and ROBERTUS DE BETUN, are with several other honourable gentlemen, witnesses to a charter of Christiana de Valoines, Lady Panmure, to John Lydell, of the lands of Balbanin, and Panlathine. But a stronger evidence of the high station of the family of BETUNE in those early times, is that both Mr. Prynne and Mr. Rymer mention ROBERT DE BETUNE as swearing fealty to, and being present with EDWARD I. King of England, at the discussion of the pleas for the crown of Scotland, betwixt JOHN BALIOL and ROBERT BRUCE, which is confirmed beyond all doubt, by some of the seals, yet preserved, that are appended to *King* EDWARD's decision, 1292, amongst which is sigillum Roberti de Betune de Scotia, which is a fesse, and on a chief a file of three pendants.

DAVID DE BETUN, (Miles) and ALEXANDER DE BETUN, were at the parliament of Cambus-kenneth, 1314; and, to the act of forfeiture passed in that parliament, is appended one of their seals, which is the same coat of arms that is upon the forementioned seal of Robert de Betune. Alexander, continuing loyal, to the royal family of Bruce, was knighted for his valour, and is mentioned, amongst other great men, by Hector Bruce, as one of the chiefs who were killed in the great battle of Dupplin, 12th August, 1332.

ROBERT DE BETUNE, Familiarius Regis, a younger son of Sir Alexander, *m.* Janet Balfour, daughter of Sir Michael de Balfour, of that ilk, in Fife, who had also a son John de Balfour, but the son dying without issue, Janet became heiress to the Balfour property.* By the heiress of Balfour, Robert left a son,

JOHN BETUNE, who succeeded to the pro-

* There is a charter in the rolls by *King* ROBERT II. ratifying a deed and grant, "Quo Duncanus Comes de Fife, dedit et concessit Johanni Beaton, de totis et integris terris de Balfour et de Newton, et de Calile in vicecomitatu de Fife jacentibus." "Apud Edinburgh, 18 Maii, Anno Regni Nostri septimo."

perty of Balfour, in Fife, on the death, issueless, of his uncle, and was the first laird of Balfour, of the name of Bethune. The Bethune and Balfour properties being united in John Bethune, he quartered the arms of Balfour with those of Bethune. The arms of Bethune, which John bore, were argent, the fesse (common to all the Bethune family), betwixt three maselis, or; those of Balfour were argent a cheveron, sable, charged with an otter's head, erased, of the first; which armorial blazoning, with the motto "Debonnaire," and two otters proper for supporters, the family of BETHUNE of Balfour have preserved ever since. JOHN BETUNE acquired from Duncan M'Duff, Earl of Fife, the lands of Holkettle, the king's charter of confirmation of the Earl of Fife's disposition is still extant; and some time after that earl's death, which happened in 15.., John got, by a charter, from Isabella, Countess of Fife, Earl Duncan's daughter, which is yet preserved, the lands of Sollybicks "pro bono et fideli servitio." He *m.* Katharine Stewart, daughter of the laird of Innermay, whose original sasine of life-rent, *anno* 1386, is still extant, and was *s.* by his son,

JOHN BETUNE, the second laird of Balfour, who *m.* the daughter of Stewart, of Rosaith. There is still existing a service relating to him. This John, it is understood, built the east part of the present house of Balfour. His son,

ARCHIBALD BETUNE, became the third laird. His charter from Duke Murdoch, the governor of Scotland, dated 1421, is yet preserved, wherein he is designed "dilecto nostro consanguineo Archibaldo Betoun," for he was related to the royal family both by his mother Rosaith's daughter, and by his grandmother, daughter of Innermay. Archibald was succeeded by his son,

JOHN BETUNE, the fourth laird of Balfour, who *m.* Katharine Stirling, daughter to the laird of Keir, and got "in tocher" with her the eighth part of the lands of Kennoway, which was the beginning of the Bethune interest in that barony, an interest the family possesses at this day. The papers relating to John Betune are lost, but he is mentioned as witness in several writs of the neighbourhood that may be yet seen. He was *s.* by his son,

JOHN BETUNE, the fifth laird, who, marrying Margary Boswell, daughter to the laird of Balmuto, had by her six sons and five daughters,

I. JOHN, who succeeded him in the estate.

II. David, who was comptroller and the treasurer to *King* JAMES IV. and the founder of the family of BETUNE OF CREICH, which for many generations made a good figure in Scotland. A daughter of this David was MARY BETHUNE, one of the four Maries, (celebrated in an old song,* published in the "Border Minstrelsy," and supposed to be sung by Mary Fleming at the day of her death), who were maids of honour to *Queen* MARY. She *m.* Lord Viscount Stormont.

III. Robert, who was abbot of Coupar, in Angus, and afterwards abbot of Melrose and Glenlus.

IV. Archibald Laird of Pitlochie, and of Kapeldrau, whose line became long since extinct.

V. Andrew, prior of St. Andrews.

VI. James, who was abbot of Dunfermline, Kelwining, and Aberbrothwick, then archbishop of Glasgow, and afterwards archbishop of St. Andrew's, and chancellor of Scotland. James was in high estimation as a wise and good man. He began the new college at St. Andrew's, and executed many useful public works, such as Bridges, &c. the benefit of which is felt at this day. James bore his patrimonial arms of Bethune-Balfour, which are yet to be seen on his public buildings. He died in 1539.

I. Janet, married to Dury of that Ilk.

II. Margaret, *m.* Andrew Sibbald, of Letholme.

III. Grissel, married James Hay, of Fordy.

IV. Elizabeth, *m.* Alexander Reid, provost of Inverness.

JOHN BETUNE, the eldest son, became the sixth Laird, and *m.* Elizabeth Moneypenny, daughter of the Laird of Kinkell, by whom he had six sons, and five daughters,

I. JOHN, who succeeded him.

II. James, who became Laird of Balfarge, and was the father of

JAMES BETUNE, who was archbishop of Glasgow, at the time of the reformation. He was also ambassador of Queen Mary, and after her death, of her son JAMES VI. at the court of France. The archbishop was noted for his great honour and hospitality, and for his piety and worth. Amongst other pious and generous acts, he founded the Scotch College at

* "Yestreen the queen had four Maries,
The night she'll hae but three;
There was Marie Seton, and Marie Beatoun,
And Marie Carmichael, and me."

Paris, and *d.* there, aged eighty-six, in the year 1603.*

DAVID, embraced the profession of ıe church, and had the management f his uncle, the Chancellor Betun's ffairs, in the latter part of the life of ıat prelate. At the death of the hancellor, David succeeded his unle in the abbacy of Aberbrothwick, nd also in the archbishoprick of St. ındrew's. He was likewise bishop f Mirepoix, in France and evenıally Cardinalis St. Stephani, in Ionte Cælio. He was the Pope's egatus natus, and Legatus a latere; nd was twice appointed ambassador › the court of France. Cardinal letun, or Beaton, as the name is freuently spelt, is represented in very ifferent lights according to the feelıgs and views of different historians, nd of the party they embraced. He ossessed great property and influnce; and exerted himself, perhaps ith more zeal than discretion, in serting and maintaining the relion by law established; and the ıthority of the see of Rome. He ved in most troubled times, and as : such periods, especially when region has a share in the ferment, ıen are often excited to extraordiıry and violent measures, a conıiracy was formed against the Carinal, headed by one Norman, Lesy, who, having, with his followers, fected an entrance into the castle f St. Andrews, murdered the prelate ı cold blood. This daring outrage as perpetrated in the year 1545 29th May). The Cardinal had, it asserted, many children. All that now known of his male issue, that Thomas Betune, formerly of lether Tarvet, latterly of Kilconıhar, in Fife, considers his family › be descended from Archibald, the ardinal's second son. The Cardial's eldest daughter was married, ith great pomp and solemnity, to the arl of Crawford. Another daughter, is said, married Scott, Earl of Bucleuch; a third the Earl of Murray; nd a fourth, Murray, of Blackarronie, Peebleshire. The great Duke of Lauderdale used to say, ıat there was more of the Cardinal's lood running in the veins of the cotch nobility, than of any single ıan since his time. The Cardinal's armorial blazon only differed from his paternal coat, in that he took for his crest a crosier, with the motto "Intentio." The ornaments of the Cardinal's Hall, at Rome, were removed from Italy to the family residence of Balfour, in Fife, where they now are to be seen, occupying the entire end of the dining room, and forming a curious specimen of the taste and workmanship of his period. His Eminence feued out the lands of Kelnennie to his nephew, John Betune, of Balfour; and repaired the hall at Balfour, where his coat of arms is exhibited.

IV. Walter, was minister of Balangne,
V. Thomas, died young.
VI. George, was parson of Govan.
VII. James, laird of Melgund, in Angus.

I. Beatrix, *m.* to Moncur, laird of Balumbree.
II. Elizabeth, *m.* to Sir John Wardlaw, of Torrie.
III. Katherine, *m.* to Sir William Graham, of Fintrie.
IV. Janet, *m.* to Hay, of Mountain.
V. Margaret, *m.* to Graham of Claverhouse, afterwards Viscount Dundee.

John Balfour died in 1524, and with his wife, is buried in the Kirk at Mark Inch, where a memorial of their burial exists fixed to a pillar. His son and successor,

JOHN BETUNE, the seventh laird of Balfour, married Christian Stewart, daughter of the Laird of Rosaith, by whom he had two sons and two daughters,

I. JOHN, his heir.
II. Andrew, who was minister of Essie.

I. Katharine, married John Borthwick, Laird of Balhoussie.
II. Janet, *m.* James Gaims, of Leyes.

The elder son,

JOHN BETUNE, the eighth laird, *m.* Agnes Anstruther, daughter of the Laird of Anstruther, by whom he had three sons and four daughters,

I. JOHN, his heir.
II. Robert, successor to his brother.
III. James, a clergyman, in Roxburghshire.

I. Christian, *m.* to Melville, of Cairnbee.
II. Margaret, *m.* to James Row, of Perth, minister, and reformer.
III. Agnes, *m.* to Robert Strong, portioner of Kilrenny, and
IV. Katharine, *m.* to Twedie, of Drumelzier.

The eldest son,

JOHN BETUNE, the ninth laird, *b.* in 1546, wedded Elizabeth Pitcairn, but dying without issue, was succeeded by his brother,

* ...s held the Abbaye de Notre Dame, de ... Porton, and the Prieuré de St. Pierre, ...ise. His epitaph is in the church of St. ...ateran, at Paris. Mem. de Sully, vol. 2.

ROBERT BETUNE, the tenth laird of Balfour, who had by Agnes Trail, his wife, daughter of Trail, of Blebo, four sons and four daughters,

I. DAVID, his heir.
II. James, } both went to France with
III. JOHN, } Colonel Colville, and served under Henry IV. of France.
IV. Alexander, resided at Anstruther. He had a son Alexander, who married a daughter of William M'Dougal, of Garthlands, and got with her the estate of Langermerston, &c. to the value of 10,000*l.*, in those days a large dower.
I. Agnes, *m.* to Hamilton, of Kilbrackmount.
II. Lucretia, *m.* to Balfour, of Torme.
III. Jean, *m.* to Whipps, of Treaton.
IV. Elizabeth, *m.* to Lindesay, of Kirkfother.

The eldest son,

DAVID BETUNE, eleventh laird, *b.* in 1574, *m.* Margaret Wardlaw, daughter of the laird of Torrie, and by her had three sons and three daughters,

I. JOHN, who succeeded him, *b.* 1594.
II. Robert, who *m.* Marian Inglis, of Athenry, Fife, and became first laird of Bandon.
III. Andrew, who became first laird of Castle Blebo, in Fife.
I. Janet, *m.* to Campbell of Keithilk, in Angus.
II. Margaret, *m.* to Sir Henry Wardlaw, of Petrivie.
III. Agnes, *m.* to David Colville, brother to Cleish, and afterwards Lord Colville.

Balfour was *s.* by his eldest son,

JOHN BETUNE, or BETHUNE (as the name was at this period usually written), the twelfth laird, who *m.* Katharine Halyburton, and had six sons and two daughters,

I. JAMES, his heir.
II. DAVID, who *m.* Elizabeth Aytoun, of Finglassie.
III. Robert, who *m.* a daughter of Eliott of Stobs, Roxburghshire, but had no issue.
IV. William, a captain in the army under Charles II. *d.* 1651.
V. Andrew, an advocate.
VI. George, a lieutenant.
I. Agnes, married to Seton, of Latherick.
II. Elizabeth, *m.* to Andrew Bruce, Bishop of Dunkeld, and afterwards of Orkney.

John Bethune was *s.* by his son,

JAMES BETHUNE, the thirteenth laird, *b.* in 1620, who married Anne, daughter of Sir John Moncrief, of that Ilk, by whom he had two sons, John, who died a bachelor during the lifetime of his father, and

DAVID BETHUNE, who was born in 1657, and became fourteenth laird. He *m.* Rachel, daughter of Sir John Hope, of Hopetoun (ancestor of the Earls of Hopetoun), by whom he had two sons and five daughters, viz.

I. JAMES, his heir.
II. Charles, who died at Lisle in 1708.
I. Katharine, who *m.* David Campbell, of Keithilk in Angus, and had a daughter, Rachel, *m.* to John Pitullo, of Balhousie.
II. Anne, *m.* in 1709, to her cousin, DAVID BETHUNE, son of Bethune of Bandon, who, through his wife Anne, obtained, on the death of James, her brother, and fifteenth laird, the property of Balfour.
III. Margaret, died young.
IV. Elizabeth, died in 1715 unm.
V. Helen, *m.* to John Landale.

The elder son,

JAMES BETHUNE, fifteenth laird of Balfour, married Anne Hamilton, daughter of Major-general Hamilton, of Rood House, East Lothian, but had no issue. He succeeded his father in 1709, and in 1715 joined the Stuart party in their attempt to possess the government of the kingdom. Failing in that measure, he escaped to the continent, and died at Rheims, in France, in 1719. At his decease, the property of Balfour would have descended to his niece, Rachel Campbell, daughter to his eldest sister, Katharine, but his cousin, DAVID BETHUNE, son of Bethune of Bandon (who married James's second sister, Anne), having, through the pecuniary aid of his brother, Henry Bethune, of Bandon, induced Rachel, then married to John Patullo, to forego her claims, gained possession of the estate and became

DAVID BETHUNE, sixteenth laird of Balfour. By Anne, his wife, he had two daughters,

ANNE, married to David Bethune, of Kilconquhar, in Fife.

MARY, married to William Congalton, of that Ilk, in East Lothian, and had six sons and three daughters, viz.

CHARLES CONGALTON, who married Anne Elliot, youngest dau. of Sir Gilbert Elliot, bart. of Minto, Roxburghshire, by whom he had two sons and one daughter, viz.

I. WILLIAM CONGALTON, who inherited Balfour.
II. GILBERT CONGALTON, heir to his brother.

1. Eleanor Congalton, who *m.* Colonel John Drinkwater, of Salford, Manchester, and had three sons and four daughters, viz.

JOHN - ELLIOT DRINKWATER.

Charles-Ramsay Drinkwater.

Edward Drinkwater.

Eleanor - Anne Drinkwater, *m.* in 1825, to the Rev. W. T. Hadow, of Streatley, in Bedfordshire.

Mary - Elizabeth Drinkwater.

Harriet - Sophia Drinkwater.

Georgina-Augusta Drinkwater.

David Congalton, died unmarried in India.

Henry Congalton, died unmarried in the army.

Andrew Congalton, a captain in the royal navy, born in 1751, had one son, Charles, who died in 1827.

John Congalton, died unmarried in the East India Company's service.

Hugh Congalton, died unmarried, a lieutenant in the navy.

Janet Congalton, died young.

Anne Congalton, died unmarried in 1815 at Balfour.

Isabella Congalton, died at Balfour in 1830.

Upon David Bethune's becoming possessed of the property of Balfour, he made a new disposition of it, appointing his brother Henry his successor; and after his death, his two daughters, Anne and Mary Bethune, and their heirs general. He *d.* in 1731, (his wife Anne, it is presumed, had died previously), when his brother,

HENRY BETHUNE, *s.* as seventeenth laird. He *m.* Isabella Maxwell, of Edinburgh, but had no children. He *d.* in 1760, aged eighty-one years, and was *s.* by his eldest niece,

ANNE BETHUNE, the wife of David Bethune, of Kilconquhar. This lady dying, however, without issue, in 1785, (her husband David had died in 1781-2), she was *s.* by her grand nephew, (the grandson of her sister Mary),

WILLIAM CONGALTON, who became the nineteenth laird of Balfour, in 1785, and assumed the name of BETHUNE. He died without issue in 1798, and was *s.* by his brother the *present* GILBERT BETHUNE, esq. of Balfour.

*Arms*—Quarterly, 1st and 4th, argent, a fesse between three mascles or, for BETHUNE; 2nd and 3rd, arg. a chevron sable, charged with an otter's head, erased, of the first.

*Crest*—An otter's head erased ppr.

*Supporters*—Two otters ppr.

*Motto*—Debonnaire.

*Estates*—In Fifeshire.

*Seat*—Balfour, in Fifeshire.

## MOSTYN, OF KIDDINGTON.

N-BROWNE, GEORGE, esq. of Kiddington, in the county of Oxford, *b.* at Bath, 7th March, 1804, *m.* in July, 1828, Caroline, dau. of Colonel Arthur Vansittart, of Shottesbroke, in Berkshire, and grandaughter, maternally, of William, late Lord Aucland, by whom he has a son,

GEORGE-CHARLES, *b.* 3rd April, 1830.

Mr. Mostyn succeeded his father on the 11th March, 1821.

## Lineage.

This family derives, through a female descent, from the ancient and honourable house of Brown, Viscounts Montague, it represents a branch of that noble stock, and thus establishes them kindred to the most illustrious names in our history. At the coronation of *King* RICHARD II,

SIR ANTHONY BROWN was amongst those persons of distinction who were made Knights of the Bath. He had two sons, Sir Robert and Sir Stephen: the younger filled the civic chair of London, in 1439, and, during his mayoralty, a scarcity of wheat occurring, he imported large cargoes of rye from Prussia, and distributed them gratuitously amongst the poorer classes of people. The elder son,

SIR ROBERT BROWN, was father of

SIR THOMAS BROWN, who was Treasurer of the Household to *King* HENRY VI. He espoused Eleanor, daughter and co-heir of Sir Thomas Fitz Alan, and niece of John, thirteenth earl of Arundel, by whom he acquired the Castle of Beechworth, in Surrey, which his eldest son, Sir George Brown, inherited. Sir Thomas's third son,

SIR ANTHONY BROWN, was appointed by *King* HENRY VII. in the first year of that monarch's reign, STANDARD-BEARER for the whole realm of England, and elsewhere. He *m.* Lucy, one of the daughters, and co-heirs of Sir John Nevill, created Marquess of Montagu,* and widow of Sir Thomas Fitz Williams, knt. of Aldwarke, in the county of York, and was *s.* at his decease, in 1506, by his only son,

SIR ANTHONY BROWN,† who made a distinguished figure in the reign of HENRY VIII. He was a knight of the garter, standard-bearer to the king, and one of the executors of the will of his royal master. He *m.* first, Alice, daughter of Sir John Gage, of Firle, and, secondly, Elizabeth, second daughter of Gerald, earl of Kildare; by the latter he had no surviving issue. He *d.* in 1548, and was *s.* by his elder son,

SIR ANTHONY BROWN, knt. who was sheriff of Surrey and Sussex, in the last year of *King* EDWARD VI. and was raised to the peerage by *Queen* MARY, as VISCOUNT MONTAGU, on the 2nd of September, 1554. This elevation appears to be preparatory to his mission to the Pope, with Thomas Thurlby, bishop of Ely, by order of parliament, for the purpose of re-uniting the realm of England with the holy see. He was afterwards made a knight of the garter, but, upon the accession of ELIZABETH, his name was left out of the privy council, and he voted, soon after, in his place in parliament, with the Earl of Shrewsbury, against abolishing the Pope's supremacy. Yet he contrived, Camden states, to get into favour with the queen; "ELIZABETH, (says that learned author,) having experienced his loyalty, had great esteem for him, (though he was a stiff Romanist,) and paid him a visit some time before his death; for, she was sensible that his regard for that religion was owing to his cradle and education, and proceeded rather from principle than faction, as some people's did. His lordship's first wife, was the Lady Jane Ratcliffe, daughter of Robert, Earl of Sussex; in his issue, by whom (she died 20th July, 1553), the VISCOUNTY OF MONTAGUE vested, until the year 1797, when the dignity is supposed to have become EXTINCT. (*See* BURKE'S *Extinct Peerage.*) He married, secondly, Margdalen, daughter of William, Lord Dacre, of Gillesland, and had, by that lady, (with three daughters,) two sons, Sir George Brown, of the county of Kent, and

SIR HENRY BROWNE, knight, who purchased, in the year 1613, the manors of Upper and Lower Kiddington,‡ and the

---

* He was third son of Richard Nevill, Earl of Salisbury, K.G. by the Lady Alice Montacute, daughter and heir of Thomas de Montacute, Earl of Salisbury, and, by his wife, the Lady Eleanor Holland, daughter of Thomas Holland, Earl of Kent, and sister and co-heir of Edmund, Earl of Kent: she was grandaughter of JOANE PLANTAGENET, the Fair Maid of Kent, who was daughter of EDMUND, of *Woodstock*, Earl of Kent, second son of *King* EDWARD the First.

† Sir Anthony was the builder of Coudray House, at Medhurst, in Surrey, which remained, until destroyed by fire, on the 24th September, 1793, the most beautiful and genuine model of a magnificent mansion in the reign of HENRY the Eighth.

‡ KIDDINGTON, or, Cuddington, anciently and properly, according to its British etymology, written *Cudenton*, or, the Itre Toun among the woods, is a small village, pleasantly situated on the river Glym, twelve miles from the city of Oxford.

Soon after the CONQUEST, about the year 1130, in the reign of HENRY the First, the Norman family of DE SALCEY, or, SAUCEY, seem to have become proprietors of the manors of Kiddington and Asterley, with other large estates in the neighbourhood. They were a family of high rank and distinction, though unnoticed in history; and were great landed proprietors, not only in this,

manor of Asterley, with the advowson of the church of Kiddington, in the county of Oxford, from the family of Babington. He *m.* first, Anne, daughter of Sir William Catesby, knt. of Ashley Legers, in Northamptonshire, and had two daughters, both nuns at Graveline. He wedded, secondly, Mary, daughter of Sir William Hungate, bart. of Saxton, in Yorkshire, and widow of Sir Marmaduke Grimston, knt. of Holderness, in the same county, by whom he left, at his decease in 1638, a son and heir,

SIR PETER BROWNE, of Kiddington, a distinguished royalist, who died at Oxford in the year 1643 of wounds received at the battle of Naseby. Sir Peter left issue, by Margaret, daughter of Sir Henry Knollys, knt. of Grove Place, in Hampshire, two sons, Henry and Francis; of those, the elder,

HENRY BROWNE, esq. of Kiddington, in consideration of the bravery and devotion so recently evinced by the family in the royal cause, was created a baronet by letters patent of *King* CHARLES II. dated at Brussels, 1st July, 1659. He *m.* Florence, third daughter and co-heir of Sir Charles Somerset, of Troy, in Monmouthshire (made a knight of the Bath at the creation of *Prince* HENRY in 1610), sixth son of Edward, Earl of Worcester, ancestor of the Dukes of Beaufort, and was *s.* by his eldest son,

SIR CHARLES BROWNE, second baronet, of Kiddington. This gentleman married thrice. His first wife was Lady Barbara Lee, widow of Colonel Lee, and youngest daughter of Edward Lee, first Earl of Lichfield;* the second, Mrs. Holman, of Warkworth, near Banbury, daughter of Mr. Wells, a Hampshire gentleman; and the third, Frances Sheldon, sister of William Sheldon, of Beoley, in the county of Worcester, and widow of Henry Fermor, esq. of Tusmore, in the county of Oxford. By the second and third ladies he had no issue, but by the first he left at his decase in 1754 an only daughter and heiress,

BARBARA (BROWNE), of Kiddington, then the wife of Sir Edward Mostyn, bart. of Talacre, whom she married in 1748 (for the family of Mostyn, refer to BURKE's *Peerage and Baronetage*). By him she had two sons, Piers and Charles Mostyn. She wedded, secondly, Edward Gore, esq. of Barrow Court, in Somersetshire, and by that gentleman had several children, of whom, William Gore, the eldest son, on marrying the heiress of the Langton family in 1783, assumed the additional name of Langton (see vol. i. page 145). Lady Mostyn's elder son by her first husband, succeeding his father in 1735, became Sir Piers Mostyn. The younger, in pursuance of the will of his grandfather, assumed the additional surname and arms of "Browne," and inheriting on the death of her ladyship in 1801 the Browne property, became

CHARLES BROWNE-MOSTYN, esq. of Kiddington. He *m.* first, in 1775, Elizabeth, fourth daughter of Henry Witham, esq. of Cliffe (see vol. ii. page 7), by whom he had a son, Edward, who *d.* young, and a daughter, Catherine, who *d.* in 1809. He wedded, secondly, Anne, daughter of — Tucker, esq. and had a son and heir,

CHARLES BROWNE-MOSTYN, esq. of Kiddington, *b.* at Aix, in Provence, in 1780, who married on the 17th May, 1801, Maria, only daughter of George Butler, esq. of Ballyragget, by whom (who *d.* 30th January, 1813,) he left at his decease on the 11th March, 1821, a son, the present GEORGE BROWNE-MOSTYN, esq. of Kiddington.

*Arms*—Quarterly; 1st and 4th, per bend sinister erm. and ermines a lion rampant or, for MOSTYN; 2nd and 3rd, sa. three lions passant between two gemels in bend arg. for BROWNE.

*Crest*—A lion rampant or.

*Estates*—In Oxfordshire.

*Seat*—Kiddington, near Woodstock.

---

but in the counties of Buckingham, Nottingham, York, Derby, Hereford, and Northampton, particularly in the latter, where it is supposed they gave their name to Salcey Forest. In or about the year 1220, SIBEL DE SAUCEY, heiress of the family, wedded Richard de Willescote, or, Williamscote, and thus Kiddington and Asterley became the inheritance of the de Williamscotes, from those it passed, in the reign of HENRY the Sixth, to the family of Babington, a branch of the Babingtons, of Chillwell, in Nottinghamshire, and by them was sold, as in the text, to Sir Henry Browne. There was another branch of the Babington family seated at Dethick, in Derbyshire, of which was Anthony Babington, executed in the reign of ELIZABETH, for conspiring to release MARY, *Queen of Scots.*

* By Lady Charlotte Fitzroy, natural daughter of *King* CHARLES II. by Barbara Villiers, Duchess of Cleveland.

# BROCKHOLES, OF CLAUGHTON.

BROCKHOLES-FITZHERBERT, THOMAS, esq. of Claughton Hall, in the county of Lancaster, *b.* 15th June, 1800, *s.* his father in July, 1817.

## Lineage.

This family, originally of Brockholls, has been seated at Claughton for many centuries.

ROGER BROCKHOLLS, of Brockholls, *temp.* EDWARD II. married Nicholaa, daughter of John de Rigmaden, and had two sons, Adam, his heir, and

JOHN BROCKHOLLS, who had, in patrimony, the lands of Claughton, in Lancashire. He wedded a lady named Margaret, and was *s.* by his son,

ROGER BROCKHOLLS, of Claughton, living in the reign of EDWARD the Third, father of

ROGER BROCKHOLLS, of Claughton, whose wife was named Ellena, but of what family is not recorded. He left a daughter, Agnes, alive in the 8th HENRY V. and a son,

JOHN BROCKHOLLS, of Claughton, who acquired the manor of Heton, Lancashire, in marriage with Catharine, daughter and heiress of William de Heton, by whom he had a numerous issue. The eldest son,

ROGER BROCKHOLLS, of Claughton and Heton, was living in the sixteenth year of HENRY VI. His wife was Margaret, and his son and successor,

THOMAS BROCKHOLES, of Claughton, who died *temp.* EDWARD IV. and was *s.* by his son,

ROGER BROCKHOLES, of Claughton, who *m.* Ellen, daughter of William Chorley, and, dying in the reign of the seventh HENRY, left a son and successor,

JOHN BROCKHOLES, of Claughton, aged fourteen at the decease of his father. He mar. first, Alicia de Brotherton, and, secondly, Ellen, daughter of Hugh Sherborne, of Stonyhurst, and had issue,

- I. CUTHBERT, who *m.* Margaret, daughter of Thomas Rigmaden of Wedacre, but appears to have died issueless during his father's life-time. His widow wedded, secondly, —— Entwistle.
- II. THOMAS, heir to his father.
- I. Mary, *m.* to William Singleton.
- II. Katherine, *m.* to Thomas Kidde.

The only surviving son,

THOMAS BROCKHOLES, *s.* his father at Claughton, 38th HENRY VIII. and *m.* Dorothy, daughter of John Rigmaden, of New Hall; he died 9th ELIZABETH, leaving a daughter, Elizabeth, *b.* in 1562, *m.* John, son and heir of Edward Braddell, of Portfield, and a son and successor,

THOMAS BROCKHOLES, of Claughton, who wedded, first, Janet, daughter of Edward Braddell, of Portfield, and secondly, Dorothy, daughter of Nicholas Leyburn, of Cunswick. By the former he had one son and three daughters, viz.

- I. JOHN, his heir.
- I. Bridget, *m.* to Henry Curwen, of Camerton, in Cumberland.
- II. Jane, *m.* to Robert Male, of Clayton, in Lancashire.
- III. Dorothy, *d.* unmarried.

By the latter he had a second son,

- II. Thomas, of Heaton, who made his will 13th CHARLES I. He *m.* Mary, daughter of Christopher Wright, and had several sons and daughters.

Thomas Brockholes *d.* about the year 1589, and was *s.* by his son,

JOHN BROCKHOLES, esq. of Claughton, who married thrice, first, Isabel, daughter of James Hodgson, of Lancaster; secondly, Elizabeth, daughter of Thomas Cowell, of the same place; and thirdly, Dorothy, dau. of John White, of Garstang. By the first wife he had, with a daughter Dorothy, *m.* to John Green, of Bowers House, a son, THOMAS, his heir: by the second, one son, John, who *m.* Elizabeth, daughter of John Bradell, of Portfield, and a daughter, Eliza-

of Nicholas Fisher, of Kendal; e third, two daughters, Augustine, , the wife of Richard Parkinson, each Hall, in Lancashire. John s *d.* 16th March, 1642, and was *s.* ,

BROCKHOLES, esq. *b.* 7th April, espoused, first, Mary, daughter heir of John Holden, esq.; and Jane Harlin, of Garstang. (This ded, secondly, Gilbert Shuttle- younger brother of Shuttleworth, e.) By his first wife he had issue,

IN, his heir.
omas.
oger.
bell, *m.* to Alexander Osbaldes-, of Sunderland.
ridget, *m.* to Thomas Harris, esq. Fairdock House, Lancashire, and two daughters, the elder became wife of — Parkinson, esq. of tes House, and the younger *m.* omas Whittingham, esq. of Whit- gham, by whom she had issue,
Maria Whittingham, *m.* to Richard Silvertop, esq.
Catherine Whittingham, *m.* first, to J. C. Dalton, esq. of Thurnham Hall; and, secondly, to J. Clavering, esq. of Birmingham.
Mary, died unm.
orothy, *m.* to — Thornbury, esq.
Leyburne.
ne, *m.* to James Walmesley.

son,

ROCKHOLES, esq. of Claughton, *b.* *m.* first, Miss Barcroft, daughter ss of William Barcroft, esq. of in the county of Lancaster, and r,

omas, living in 1733, *d. s. p.*
oger, living in 1733, a Catholic rgyman.
harles, living in 1733, also in or- s of the church of Rome.
WILLIAM, successor to his father.
n, *m.* to Robert Davies, esq. of les, and had a son, who *d.* in 2, aged ninety-two.
ary, *m.* to William Hesketh, esq. the Maynes, in Lancashire, and issue,
. THOMAS HESKETH, successor to his uncle, William Brockholes, at Claughton.
. JOSEPH HESKETH, } heirs in suc-
. JAMES HESKETH, } cession to the Claughton estates.
. Aloysia Hesketh, a nun at Ghent.
. Catharine Hesketh, abbess of the convent at Ghent. At the French revolution the lady abbess returned to England and died at Preston, in Lancashire, aged eighty-three.

He wedded, secondly, in 1716, Mary, eldest daughter and co-heir of Michael Johnson, esq. of Twyzell Hall, in the palatinate of Durham, by Mary his wife, daughter and heir of William Eure, of Elvet, grandson of William Lord Eure. By this lady (who *m.* secondly, in January, 1723-4, Richard Jones, esq. of Caton, in Lancashire *) he had two daughters,

Mary, died in infancy.
Catharine, *b.* in 1718; *m.* in 1738, Charles Howard, of Greystoke, who became tenth duke of Norfolk, and by him was mother of
Charles, eleventh duke of Norfolk, who *d. s. p.* in 1815.
Her grace died in 1784.

Mr. Brockholes *d.* 6th March, 1719, and by his will, dated the 21st of the preceding November, entailed his estates on his fourth son, William, in tail male, with remainder to his grandson, Thomas Hesketh.† At his decease Claughton devolved accordingly on

WILLIAM BROCKHOLES, esq. who *m.* Jane, one of the three daughters and co-heirs of Michael Johnson, esq. of Twyzell, sister of Mary Johnson, his father's second wife, and widow of John Owen, esq. of Osmondscroft. By this lady he left no issue, and was *s.* at his demise by his nephew,

---

* And by him had a son,
MICHAEL JONES, *b.* 23rd November, 1729; *m.* 23rd October, 1773, Mary, daughter of Mathew Smith, esq. and widow of Edward Coyney, esq. of Weston Coyney, in Staffordshire, and died at Lancaster in July, 1801, leaving issue,
1. CHARLES JONES, capt. 1st regiment of Dragoon Guards.
2. Michael Jones, barrister-at-law.
3. Edward Jones, capt. (half pay) 29th regiment of Foot.
4. James Jones, lieut.-col. in the army, knight of the Guelphic order of Hanover, and of the order of CHARLES III. of Spain.
1. Mary Jones, *m.* in April, 1818, to Monsieur Pierre de Sandelin, chevalier de St. Louis, seigneur de Halmes, &c. near St. Omer.
2. Constantia Jones.

† The Hesketh of Maynes were a branch of the Heskeths of Hesketh, and their descent may be found in the Visitations of 1613 and 1664. They maintained for many years a leading position among the gentry of Lancashire, and allied with some of its most eminent families—the Westleys of Mowbrick, the Andertons of Euxton, &c.

THOMAS HESKETH, esq. who assumed, upon inheriting Claughton, the surname and arms of BROCKHOLES. Dying, however, unmarried, he was *s.* by his brother,

JOSEPH HESKETH, esq. of Claughton, who also took the name of BROCKHOLES. He *m.* 8th August, 1768, Constantia, daughter of Basil Fitzherbert, esq. of Swinnerton, in the county of Stafford, but having no issue, he settled by will his estates upon his brother James for life, with remainder to William Fitzherbert, his wife's brother. He died 15th April, 1783, and was succeeded accordingly by his brother,

JAMES HESKETH, esq. of Claughton, who likewise assumed the surname and arms of BROCKHOLES. He died, however, issueless, when the estates passed under the late proprietor's settlement to

WILLIAM FITZHERBERT, esq. (second son of Bazil Fitzherbert, esq. of Swinnerton Park, in the county of Stafford), *b.* 26th October, 1758, who took, upon inheriting, the additional surname and arms of BROCKHOLES. He *m.* 20th June, 1791, Mary, eldest daughter and co-heir of James Windsor Heneage, esq. of Cadeby, in Lincolnshire, by Elizabeth his wife, daughter and heir of John Browne, esq. of Gatcombe, in the Isle of Wight, and had issue,

I. JOSEPH, *b.* 18th September, 1793, *d.* in 1810.
II. William, died young.
III. John-James, died young.
IV. THOMAS, successor to his father.
V. Francis, *b.* in June, 1802.
VI. Charles, *m.* the daughter of Mr. Carruthers, of Liverpool.

I. Mary.
II. Eliza-Constantia, *d.* 24th July, 1814, buried at Hengrave.
III. Frances, died unm. in 1833.
IV. Mary-Ann.

Mr. Fitzherbert-Brockholes *d.* in July, 1817, and was *s.* by his eldest surviving son, the present THOMAS FITZHERBERT-BROCKHOLES, esq. of Claughton.

*Arms*—Quarterly, 1st and 4th, arg. a chev. between three brocks or badgers sa. passant sa. for BROCKHOLES; 2nd, arg. a chief vaire or and gu. over all a bend sa. for FITZHERBERT; 3rd, arg. on a bend sa. three garbs or, for HESKETH.

*Crest*—A brock or badger passant sa.

*Estates*—In Lancashire.

*Seat*—Claughton Hall.

## LEWIS, OF GREENMEADOW.

LEWIS, WYNDHAM, esq. of Greenmeadow, in the county of Glamorgan, *b.* 7th October, 1780; *m.* in December, 1815, Mary-Anne, only daughter of John Evans, esq. of Branceford Peak, Devonshire, by Eleanor his wife, daughter of the Rev. James Viney, rector of Bishopston, Wilts.

Mr. Lewis, who is a barrister-at-law, was elected M. P. for Cardiff in 1820, for Aldburgh in 1827, and for Maidstone in 1835. He is a magistrate, deputy-lieutenant, and major of the Local Militia, in the county of Glamorgan.

### Lineage.

V. Gronsell als Williams

This family traces its descent to the most remote period of British history, and through a line of ancestors, whose names are conspicuous in all the records of the ancient Britons.

Descended from the line of the ancient British princes was TEON, who, at the close of his life, in the fifth century, became a member of the college of St. Illtyd, and was, first, bishop of Caer Loew (now called Gloucester), and afterwards bishop of London, from whence he was driven by the Pagan Saxons. The patrimony of this Teon is presumed to have been in that part of Britain now called Shropshire, as a range of hills in that county are to this day called,

, by the Welsh, *Carneddau Teon*, *e Stone Heaps of Teon:* to the nhabitants they are known by the he Stiperstones Hills.

in descent from Teon was GWAETH- ose father GWLYDDEN, commonly ODDIEN, had married Morfydd, and sole heir to Owain ap Teith- rd of Cardigan, by whom he ac- ge possessions in South Wales.

IVOED was contemporary with Ed- of the Saxons, and was, in con- ith the vassalage of those periods, l, with other Welsh chieftains, by meet him at Chester, to row him, al barge, on the river Dee, in fealty. Gwaethvoed, in answer mmons, said he could not row, e would not, if he could, except save a person's life, whether assal. Edgar sent a second and rious message, which Gwaethvoed em at all to notice, until the mes- ged to know what reply he should the king; when Gwaethvoed, in language, answered thus: "Say *'ear him who fears not death*"— A OFNE ANGAU.) This stern reply, g at once to Edgar the fearless character he had to deal with, tly changed his autocratic decree re of mutual friendship, and going ivoed, gave the chief his hand in his sincerity. Gwaethvoed mar- ydd, one of the daughters and co- vor, king or lord of Gwent, by was father of x Gwerystan ap H, who is stated to have married ghter of Tangno ap Cadvael, lord ry, in North Wales.

R, son of Cedrych, was lord of h, in Morganwg (Glamorgan- d married Myfanwy, daughter of lord of Glamorgan. His son,

AP CEDIVOR, married Gwladys, of Arthen, king or lord of Gwent, he was father of

MEURIG, known in Welsh his- VOR BACH (that is *Ivor Petit* or r), who, though a man of low sta- of high mind and courage: he lest, daughter of Madoc ap Cra- whom he obtained the lordship of dd (St. Kenyth's), in Glamorgan- in the time of HENRY II. disputes between him and William Con- of Gloucester (then lord of Gla- because the earl's predecessor had castle of Cardiff upon some part of dship, besides dispossessing him lands: whereupon Ivor, having his forces together, took the castle by escalade, killing 120 soldiers, ng the earl, his countess, and their son prisoners; these prisoners, with the spoils of the castle, he conveyed to the mountains of Sainghenydd, nor did he release them until he had compensation for the rents of which he had been deprived: it was also agreed further, that Griffith, eldest son of Ivor, should receive in marriage the earl's daughter, in consideration of which Ivor and Griffith should quit claim to the lands on which Cardiff Castle was erected. In one of the feuds so common in those days Ivor was eventually slain, and the valley which was the scene of his last action is still called *Pant Coed Ivor*.

GRIFFITH AP IVOR, by the daughter of William Consul, had, with other issue, a son,

HOWEL MELYN AP GRIFFITH, who *m.* Sarah, daughter of Sir Mayo le Soer, knt. lord of St. Fagan's, and was father of

MADOC AP HOWEL MELYN, of Merthyr, who *m.* Ewerydd, daughter and co-heir of Lewis ap Rys ap Rosser, (descended from Maenyrch), and had a son,

LLEWELYN AP MADOC, of Merthyr, father, by Joan his wife, daughter of Rys ap Grono, lord of Glyn Nedd, of

LLEWELYN VYCHAN AP LLEWELYN, who *m.* Anne, daughter of Evan ap Einion, of Pryscedwyn, and was direct ancestor* of

EDWARD LEWIS, of The Van, who first adopted the family surname. He *m.* Anne, daughter of Sir William Morgan, knt. of Pencoed, and was *s.* by his son,

THOMAS LEWIS, of the Van, who wedded, first, Margaret, daughter of Robert Gamage, esq. of Coety, and widow of Miles Mathew, esq. of Castle Mynych, but by her had no

* The intervening descent follows:

LLEWELYN VYCHAN = Anne, daughter of Evan of Einion

RYS ap Llewelyn Vychan = Margaret, daughter of Thomas Bassett, of St. Hilary

LLEWELYN ANWYL ap Rys = Anne, daughter of Howel Gam ap Cadogan, lord of Penrhôs

RICHARD GWYN ap Lewis Anwyl = Joan, daughter of Evan Trahaern ap Meyrick of Merthyr

1. dau. of Lewis ap Rosser ap Llewelyn = LEWIS ap Richard Gwyn = 2d. Gwladys, dau. and heir of Evan John Philip, of Llanvrynach, and widow of John Walbeoffe

RICHARD, ancestor of the Prichards, of Llancayach

EDWARD LEWIS, of the Van.

Williams. N + Q 2nd XI p185

issue; and, secondly, Catherine, daughter of Sir George Mathew, knt. of Radir, high sheriff for Glamorganshire in 1546. By this lady (who wedded, secondly, Sir Rowland Morgan, knt.) he left a son and successor,

SIR EDWARD LEWIS, knt. of the Van, who *m.* Blanch, daughter of Thomas Morgan, esq. of Machen, and had four sons, viz.

I. EDWARD (Sir), of the Van, who *m.* Anne, daughter of the Earl of Dorset, and widow of Lord Beauchamp, by whom he had a son,

RICHARD LEWIS, of the Van, father of

WILLIAM LEWIS, of the Van, who died in 1661, leaving a son and successor,

THOMAS LEWIS, of the Van, whose only daughter and heiress, ELIZABETH, *m.* Other, third EARL OF PLYMOUTH, who died in 1732.

II. William (Sir), knt.

III. Nicholas.

IV. THOMAS (Sir), of whom presently.

The youngest son,

SIR THOMAS LEWIS, knt. of Llanishen, espoused the daughter of Edmund Thomas, esq. of Wenvoe, and was father of

GABRIEL LEWIS, esq. of Llanishen, sheriff in 1614, who *m.* Elizabeth, daughter of William Carne, esq. of Nash, and left a son and successor,

THOMAS LEWIS, esq. of Llanishen, sheriff in 1629. This gentleman *m.* the daughter of Thomas Johns, of Abergavenny, and was *s.* by his son,

GABRIEL LEWIS, esq. of Llanishen, sheriff in 1662, who *m.* Grace, daughter of Humphrey Wyndham, and was father of

THOMAS LEWIS, esq. of Llanishen, who served the office of sheriff in 1683. He *m.* first, Elizabeth Van, by whom he had a son,

GABRIEL, sheriff in 1715, father of

THOMAS, sheriff in 1745, who left one son, Wyndham, *b.* in 1752, and two daughters, Elizabeth and Blanch.

Thomas Lewis wedded, secondly, Elizabeth Morgan, and had, with a daughter, Grace, a son,

THOMAS LEWIS, esq. who married and had (with another son, William, of Greenmeadow, who died issueless)

THE REV. WYNDHAM LEWIS, who wedded Mary, daughter of Samuel Price, esq. of Park, and Coyty, in the county of Glamorgan, and had the present WYNDHAM LEWIS, esq. M.P. besides three other sons and two daughters, viz. Thomas (who *m.* Dorothy-Augusta Goodrich, and died leaving a son, John, and a daughter, *m.* to — Langley, esq.); Henry (who *m.* Mary Emerson, and has issue); William; Mary-Anne, *m.* to Richard-Rice Williams, esq.; and Catherine, *m.* to Thomas Williams, esq.

*Arms*—Sa. a lion rampant arg.

*Crest*—A lion sejant arg.

*Motto*—Patriæ fidus.

*Estates*—In the counties of Glamorgan, Monmouth, Gloucester, and Somerset.

*Town Residence*—Grosvenor Gate, Park Lane.

*Seat*—Greenmeadow, near Cardiff.

## HUME, OF HUMEWOOD.

HUME, WILLIAM-WENTWORTH-FITZWILLIAM, esq. of Humewood, in the county of Wicklow, *b.* 28th October, 1805; *m.* 8th June, 1829, Margaret-Bruce, eldest daughter of Robert Chaloner, esq. of Gisboro', in Yorkshire, by the Hon. Frances-Laura Dundas, his wife, daughter of the late Lord Dundas,* and has issue,

WILLIAM-HOARE, *b.* 16th February, 1834.

Charlotte-Anna.

Mr. Hume, who is a magistrate and deputy-lieutenant for the county of Wicklow, succeeded his father in November, 1815.

* By his wife, the Lady Charlotte Fitzwilliam.

## Lineage.

Sir Thomas Hume, *dominus de eodem*, the seventh generation of that ancient family in a direct male line, flourished in the reigns of *King* Robert II. and III. He *m.* Nichola Pepdie, heiress of Dunglass, and had two sons, Alexander (Sir), his successor, ancestor to the Earls of Home, and Sir David Hume, from whom descended

Alexander Hume, third Baron of Polworth. This nobleman *m.* first, Margaret, daughter of Robert, second Lord Crichton, of Sanquhar, ancestor of the Earl of Dumfries, and got a charter under the great seal: "Alexandro Hume de Polworth et Margarettæ Crichton ejus sponsæ terrarum de Bregamsheils, etc." dated 26th July, 1511: by her he had three sons, viz.

I. Patrick, his heir.
II. Alexander, of Heugh, *d. s. p.*
III. Gavin.

The third son.

Gavin Hume, afterwards styled "Captain of Tantallon," espoused the cause of *Queen* Mary, and served as lieutenant under James, Earl of Arran, Duke of Chatelherault. Subsequently, an officer in the Gens d'Armes, he took part in the famous battle of St. Quintins in the year 1557, and his military skill and bravery on that occasion are recorded by many French and other historians: Thuonus, (vol. i. lib. xix. p. 658), giving an account of this engagement, says that "the second breach was given to be defended by Hume, the lieutenant of the Earl of Arran:" and that Colgni, in his Commentaries, attributes to him the chief praise of the military skill displayed on the occasion; in page 659 of the same volume, he mentions that Hume with several other Scotch were taken prisoners. Ide Serres also, in his History of France, Lond. 1611, p. 716, makes mention of the capture of Hume at St. Quintins. Gavin *m.* a French lady, and had a son and successor,

Andrew Hume, who returned to Scotland and purchased the estate of the Rhodes, near to the lands of his cousin, the first Sir John Hume, of North Berwick. He *m.* Mosea Seaton, dau. of Seaton, of Barnes, and niece to the Earl of Winton, by whom he had, with a daughter, supposed to have wedded George Hume, of Pinkerton, four sons, viz.

I. Robert, his heir.
II. Thomas, who became the confidential favourite of Sir John Preston, Earl of Desmond, and through the influence of that nobleman's daughter, Elizabeth, Duchess of Ormonde, obtained the hand of Miss French, a great heiress, her grace's ward, in marriage. In consequence of which he settled in Ireland, and after the Restoration acquired large tracts of land in the county of Tipperary, under grant from the Crown, dated in February, 1665. In the same year he was presented with the freedom of the city of Dublin in a silver box, and subsequently had the honour of knighthood from the Duke of Ormond, then lord lieutenant of Ireland. Sir Thomas died at an advanced age, 4th July, 1668, as appears from a registry of his death in the office of Arms, Dublin. He had no issue, and some time before his demise, he induced his nephew, Thomas, the eldest son of his elder brother Robert to come from Scotland, under the promise of making him his sole heir. Dying, however, intestate, a considerable portion of his property devolved upon his widow, Lady Anne Hume, who obtained administration, as appears from an entry in the Prerogative Office in Dublin, dated in August, 1668. Her ladyship afterwards compromised with Thomas, the nephew, for a sum of money, and married for her second husband Captain George Mathews, half brother to the old Duke of Ormond, whereby the lands in Tipperary merged in the Landaff estate. Lady Anne survived Captain Mathews, and died in the beginning of March, 1701. By her last will, which was duly registered and proved the 13th of that month, she bequeathed, after some legacies, all the estate, arrears of rent, and of dower, goods and chattels, to Sir Henry Wemys and Thomas Hume, by the description of Thomas Hume, nephew of

her first husband, and appointed them her executors.

III. John.

IV. William.

Andrew Hume *d.* in 1594 or 1595, and was *s.* by his eldest son,

ROBERT HUME, who *m.* Anne, daughter of Dr. Mitchelson, Laird of Brackness, and grand-daughter of Sir Bruce Semple, of Cathcart, by whom he had a son,

THOMAS HUME, esq. who succeeded his uncle in Ireland, and purchased the estate of Humewood, in the county of Wicklow, which he settled in 1704 on his eldest son; dividing his property in the county of Cavan amongst his younger children. He married, first, Miss Jane Lauder, of the county of Leitrim; and, secondly, Elizabeth Galbraith, widow of Hugh Galbraith, of St. Johnstown, in the county of Fermanagh. By the first only he had issue, viz.

I. WILLIAM, his heir.

II. George, died young.

III. Robert, ancestor of the HUMES of Lisanure Castle, in the county of Cavan, and of Cariga, in Leitrim, and of the Humes of Dublin.

Mr. Hume died in 1718, and was *s.* by his eldest son,

WILLIAM HUME, esq. of Humewood, who *m.* Anna, daughter of John Dennison, esq. of the city of Dublin, and had two sons and four daughters, viz.

I. GEORGE, his heir.

II. Dennison, who died without issue.

I. Isabella.

II. Sarah.

III. Catherine.

IV. Margaret.

He died 26th May, 1752, having previously settled, by deed dated 6th December, 1744, his estate on his eldest son,

GEORGE HUME, esq. of Humewood, who married Anna, daughter of Thomas Butler, esq. of Ballymurtagh, in the county of Wicklow, and had five sons and two daughters, viz.

I. WILLIAM, his heir.

II. George, *d. s. p.*

III. Dennison, *d. s. p.*

IV. John La Touch, who married and left issue.

V. Clement, who also married and left issue.

I. Isabella.

II. Anna, who *m.* Benjamin Wills, esq. of the city of Dublin.

He died August, 1765, and was succeeded by his eldest son,

WILLIAM HUME, esq. of Humewood, who represented the county of Wicklow in two successive parliaments, being returned at the general election in 1789, by a considerable majority over his opponent the Hon. John Stratford, afterwards Earl of Alborough; and at the general election of 1796 without opposition. In command of a yeomanry corps Mr. Hume took an active and zealous part in quelling the late Irish rebellion, and was shot by a party of rebels in the Wicklow mountains 8th of October, 1798. He *m.* Catherine, daughter of Sir Joseph Hoare, bart. M. P. of Annabella, in the county of Cork, and had two sons and four daughters, viz.

I. WILLIAM-HOARE, his heir.

II. Joseph-Samuel, who *m.* Miss Smith, and left issue one son, now settled in America, and three daughters.

I. Catherine, *m.* — Franks, esq. of Carrig, county of Cork.

II. Anne, *m.* Rev. Dominick E. Blake.

III. Jane, *m.* Hon. and Rev. Maurice Mahon.

IV. Grace.

The eldest son,

WILLIAM-HOARE HUME, esq. of Humewood, was elected in 1799, by a large majority, to fill the vacancy (in the representation of the county) occasioned by the death of his father. His opponent was the Hon. Colonel Howard, brother to Lord Wicklow. Mr. Hume thenceforward continued to represent Wicklow in the Irish and Imperial Parliaments until his decease. He wedded Charlotte-Anne, daughter of the late Samuel Dick, esq. of Dublin, and sister to Quintin Dick, esq. M.P. for Maldon, and had issue,

I. WILLIAM-WENTWORTH-FITZWILLIAM, his heir.

II. Quintin-Dick, in holy orders.

III. George-Ponsonby, in the army.

I. Charlotte-Isabella-Forster.

II. Charlotte-Jane.

Mr. Hume died in November, 1815, and was *s.* by his eldest son, WILLIAM-WENTWORTH-FITZWILLIAM HUME, esq. of Humewood.

*Arms*—Quarterly, 1st and 4th, vert. a lion rampant arg.; 2nd and 3rd, arg. three ravens vert.

*Crest*—A lion's head erased arg.

*Motto*—True to the end.

*Estates*—In the county of Wicklow.

*Seat*—Humewood, county of Wicklow.

# WILKINS, OF CLIFTON.

WILKINS, CANN, esq. of Clifton, in the county of Gloucester, *m.* Mary, daughter of Thomas Evans, esq. of Bultloyd, in Glamorganshire, and widow of William Williams, esq. of Pwlly Pant, by whom he has surviving issue,

I. Walter-Thompson.
II. Herbert-William.
III. Robert-Henry.
I. Charlotte-Augusta.

Mr. Wilkins is a magistrate and deputy-lieutenant for the counties of Glamorgan and Somerset.

## Lineage.

Robert de Wintona, or Wincestria, came into Glamorganshire with Robert Fitzhamon: he was lord of the manor of Languian, near Cowbridge, and built a castle there, the ruins of which are still extant; the valley, underneath, is called Pant Wilkyn (Wilkyn's vale) to this day. From Robert lineally descended *

Thomas Wilkyn, who died in 1558. He *m.* Gwenllian, daughter of Jenkin ap Richard, *alias* Gwyn of Lansanon, in Glamorganshire, and had a son,

The Rev. Thomas Wilkyn, rector of Porthkerry, and St. Mary Church, in the county of Glamorgan, who wedded, first, Elizabeth, daughter of Lewis Harry, of Lancadle; and, secondly, Margaret, daughter of Morgan ap James Mathews of Roos. He died in 1623, and was *s.* by his son,

The Rev. Roger Wilkins, A. M. rector of St. Mary Church, who *m.* Blanch, daughter of Christopher Gaynon, of St. Bride's, Monmouthshire, and was *s.* in 1648, by his son,

The Rev. Thomas Wilkins, L.L.B. rector of Llanmaes and St. Mary Church, and prebendary of Llandaff, *m.* Jane, daughter of Thomas Carne, of Nash, by Jane his wife, daughter of Sir Edward Stradling, bart. of St. Donat's Castle, and left at his decease, in 1696, two sons, Thomas, and Roger, who *m.* Elizabeth, daughter of Thomas Lewis, esq. of Llanishen, and had a daughter, Jane.

* The intervening descent is as follows:

Robert de Wintona, who came into Glamorganshire.
|
Nicholas de Wintona.
|
Michael de Wintona.
|
Wilklyne de Wintona.
|
William de Wincestria, cotemporary with Hamon Turberville.
|
William de Wincestria, living *temp.* Edw. I. and Edw. II.
|
John de Wincestria, lord of the manor of Landough, in Glamorganshire.
|
Robert Winchester, lord of Landough.
|
William, of Winchester, *m.* Anne, daughter of Hopkin Vaughan.
|
John, dictus Wilcolina aut Wilkyn, *m.* Gwenllian, daughter of Griffith Gethin, *temp.* Edw. III.
|
John Wilcolyne, or Wilkyn, *temp.* Edward III. and Richard II. *m.* Isabel, daughter of John Raleigh.
|
John Wilkyn *m.* Anne, daughter of Howel Carne, of Nash, in Glamorganshire.
|
Richard Wilkyn *m.* Jennet, daughter of Thomas Madoc, of Llanfair, alive in 1505.
|
Thomas Wilkyn, who *d.* in 1558.

The elder son,

THOMAS WILKINS, prothonotary on the Brecon circuit, *m.* first, Anne, daughter of Richard Cann, esq. brother of Sir Robert Cann, bart. of Compton, in Gloucestershire, and had issue,

I. CANN, his heir.

He married, secondly, Anne, daughter of Meredith Bowen, esq. of Lanwerne, in Breconshire, and had by her,

II. John, prothonotary on the Brecon circuit, *m.* Sibyl, daughter of Walter Jeffreys, esq. of the Priory, in the county of Brecon, and had issue,

1. Thomas, *m.* Elizabeth, daughter of the Rev. William Games, rector of Llandoffy, and had a son, John, who *m.* Anne, daughter of Thomas Williams, esq. of Brecon.
2. Walter, for forty years M. P. for Radnorshire, *m.* Catherine-Augusta, daughter of Samuel Hayward, esq. of Walworth Hall, Gloucestershire, and had a son,

    Walter, of Maeslough Castle, *m.* in 1806, Catharine-Eliza-Marianne, dau. of George, Viscount Hereford, and had one son and three daughters, viz.

    Walter, now M. P. for Radnorshire, *m.* Julia, daughter of the Rev. Richard-John Collinson, rector of Gateshead, and has Walter and Emily.

    Catherine, *m.* to William Vann, esq.

    Mary-Ann, *m.* to William Meyrick, esq.

    Georgiana-Frances, *m.* to Charles Stretton, esq.
3. John, rector of Dissuth and Broynllis, in the commission of the peace for Breconshire.
4. Jeffreys, *m.* Catharine, daughter and co-heir of Rev. Gregory Parry, of Llandevaylog, prebendary of Worcester, and had issue,

    JOHN-PARRY, now of Maesderwen. *See* vol. ii. p. 218.

    Jeffreys, *m.* Hannah Lei, and has issue.

    Walter, of Hay Castle, Breconshire, in holy orders, *m.* — Chiappini, sister of the Dowager Baroness Newborough, and has four sons and two daughters, viz.

    1. Thomas, of the Royal Artillery.
    2. Walter.
    3. Charles.
    4. Henry.
    1. Frances-Maria, *m.* to Spencer Bulkley, third Lord Newborough.
    2. Catharine.

    Richard, *m.* Angelena, daughter of Thomas Green, esq. of Llansantped, late M. P. for Arundel.

    Edward.

    Elizabeth, *m.* to John Jones, esq.

    Catherine, *m.* to Capt. William Murray.
5. William, prothonotary on the Brecon circuit.

1. Anne, *m.* to John Maybery, esq. and had a son, Thomas Maybery, prothonotary on the Brecon circuit, who *m.* Elizabeth, daughter of Richard Davies, canon of St. Davids, and has four sons and six daughters, viz.

    Walter, prothonotary on the Brecon circuit.

    Charles, in holy orders.

    Henry.

    Edward.

    Elizabeth.

    Anne, *m.* to Edward Jones, esq. of Velindree, in Carmarthenshire.

    Frances.

    Mary.

    Martha.

    Catharine.
2. Magdalen, *m.* to Robert Corrie, esq. and had a son, Robert Corrie, in holy orders.
3. Jane, *m.* to Meredith-Herbert James, esq. of the county of Brecon.
4. Johanna, *m.* to George, third son of Cann Wilkins, esq.
5. Elizabeth, *m.* to Samuel Price, esq. of Brecon.
6. Frances.

Thomas Wilkins (the prothonotary) was *s.* by his son,

CANN WILKINS, esq. *b.* 31st October, 1702, who *m.* Mary, daughter of Mrs. Anne Morgan, widow of Thomas Morgan, esq. of St. George's, in the county of Somerset, and had issue,

I. THOMAS, a magistrate for Somersetshire, and high sheriff of that county in 1787, assumed the surname and arms of Morgan. He *m.* first, Elizabeth, daughter of Ebenezer Mussell, esq. by Elizabeth his wife, daughter of Sir John Davie, bart. of Crediton, in Devonshire, and by her had one daughter, Elizabeth, m. to Eli Bates, esq. He wedded, secondly, Mary, daughter of John Thompson, esq. of the city of Waterford, and had a daughter, Mary-Anne, who m. Thomas-Edward Thomas, esq. of Swansea, and has a son, Iltid-Thomas.

II. Richard, vicar of St. George's, m. Cordelia, daughter of the Rev. Conyers Place, of Marnhall, in Dorsetshire, and had a son, Cann, who d. young.

III. George.

The third son,

The Rev. George Wilkins, rector of St. Michael's, Bristol, b. in 1743, m. first, Mary, daughter of John Dinwiddie, esq.; secondly, Johanna, daughter of John Wilkins, esq. of the Priory, in the county of Brecon, by whom he had one daughter, m. to John-Parry Wilkins, esq.; and, thirdly, Anne, daughter of John Thompson, esq. of Waterford, by whom, who died in 1791, he had four sons and one daughter, viz.

I. Cann, his heir.

II. George, late captain 39th regiment, in the commission of the peace for Somersetshire, m. Emma-Juliana, daughter of the late George Robinson, esq. of Bath, and has issue, Frederica-Isabella and George Jean de Winton.

III. Thomas, lieut. R. N. deceased, m. Miss Lynch, and had one daughter, Mary-Anne-Morgan.

IV. William, major in the Light Cavalry on the Bombay establishment.

I. Harriett, m. first, to William Jeffreys, esq. of Swansea; and, secondly, to George Bird, esq. of the same place.

Mr. Wilkins was succeeded at his decease by his eldest son, the present Cann Wilkins, esq. of Clifton.

*Arms*—Or, a wyvern ppr.

*Crest*—A wyvern ppr.

*Motto*—Syn ar,dy Hun: *Anglice*, Beware of thyself.

*Estates*—In Gloucestershire, Glamorganshire, Breconshire, and Radnorshire.

*Residence*—Clifton.

## WATTS, OF HAWKESDALE HALL.

WATTS, JOHN-JAMES, esq. of Hawkesdale Hall, in the county of Cumberland, b. 15th March, 1803; succeeded his father in 1815.

Mr. Watts holds a commission in the Cumberland and Westmoreland Yeomanry Cavalry.

### Lineage.

This family, whose name has, at various times, been differently written "*Wath*," "*Wathes*," "*Wattys*," &c. &c. was of considerable antiquity in the county of Northampton, where it flourished for the greater part of three centuries.

Simon Wathes, [traditionally descended from a French soldier of fortune, who accompanied *King* Stephen into England, A. D. 1135], was father of

John Wathes, who in right of his wife was possessed of a third of the meane lordship of Eston, in the county of Worcester, 20th of Edward III. A. D. 1347. He had issue,

William Wathes, who was father of

Nicholas Wathes, who had two sons,

Simon, his heir.

William, a priest.

The elder,

Simon Wattys, was possessed of his

hereditary property at Eston, in Worcestershire, 7th HENRY VI. A. D. 1428, and by his wife Margery de Stotesbury, of Whitfield, in the county of Northampton, left a son,

RICHARD WATTYS, "Miles," who fought under the banner of York at the battle of Wakefield, where he fell, or died soon after the conflict of his wounds, leaving, by his wife, Isabel Stafford, a son and heir,

THOMAS WATTYS, who was plaintiff in an action at law against William de Stotesbury, William de Lovett, and others, for the recovery of the manor of Whitfield, in the county of Northampton, the last year of the reign of HENRY VI. A. D. 1461. By his wife Alice, heiress to an estate at Beby, in the county of Leicester; he had issue,

I. JOHN, his heir.
II. Richard, who had a son, Richard, and two daughters, Mary, the wife of George Gage, of Raundes, in the county of Northampton, and Joan, the wife of Gervas Astley.
III. Thomas, the father of John, from whom descended the family of Watts, seated in Norfolk.

I. Elizabeth, the wife of Richard Osborne, who received with her in frank marriage the manor of Whitfield.

The eldest son,

JOHN WATTES, of Beby, in the county of Leicester, was party to a deed of surrender of the manor of Mykelham, and other lands, 2nd HENRY VIII. A. D. 1511. He, likewise, by a deed, dated the 6th year of HENRY VIII. A. D. 1514, gave up the manor of Oxendon Parva, and other lands in the county of Northampton, which he had held in trust for George Boyville. He was twice married; by his second wife, whose name has not been preserved, he had issue,

I. John, the father of Thomas Wattes, and Stafford Wattes, of Barleston, in the county of Leicester, who died A. D. 1619, and was buried in St. Martin's Church, in the city of Leicester, leaving issue by his wife, Elizabeth, daughter of Stephen Everard, of Flether, county of Leicester, by Joan, daughter of Thomas Babington, of Rothley Temple, in that county, descended from the house of Dethic, in Derbyshire.
II. Francis, father of
    1. Hugh.
    2. Francis.
    3. Robert.

By his first wife, Magdelaine, daughter and heiress of Thomas Berkeley, of the city of Worcester, John Wattes had a son and heir,

THOMAS WATTES, esq. of Beby, who was aged twenty-four, the 27th HENRY VIII. A. D. 1535. In the 2nd year of ELIZABETH, A. D. 1560, upon the final suppression of the religious houses in England, this Thomas had a grant of the lands and lordship of Blakesley, in the county of Northampton, together with the rectory and advowson of the vicarage, all which had been part and parcel of the possessions of the order of knights-hospitallers of St. John of Jerusalem, of which possessions he levied a fine in the 9th year of the same reign. This gentleman was twice married. By his first wife, the daughter of — Crouch, he had a son and heir, WILLIAM. His second wife was Catharine, daughter of — Sulyard, of the county of Essex. Mr. Watts died the 35th of ELIZABETH, A. D. 1593, aged eighty-two, and was succeeded by his son,

WILLIAM WATTS, esq. of Blakesley. This gentleman added to his patrimonial property of Blakesley the neighbouring lordship, called Zouch's manor, which he purchased of Nicholas Baynton, to whom it had been sold by the Lord de la Zouch. He also acquired by purchase part of the hamlet of "Wodende," within the lordship of Blakesley. Mr. Watts departed this life the 16th of June, A. D. 1614, and was buried in the parish church of Blakesley, where there was a monument with the following quaint epitaph, in Roman capitals:

"An Epitaphe upon the death of that worthie Gentleman, Mr. W. Wattes, of Blaxley, who dyed An. Dom. MDCXIV. XVI of June.

"It is no marble monument must grace
His worthie corps, who lies within this place;
The many graces which did him adorne
In youth, in years, these weaker helpes doe scorne.
Uprighte he was, and zealous in his life;
Kinde to his children, loving to his wife."

This gentleman espoused Mary,* daughter of the famous Lord Chief Justice Sir

* By this match Mr. Watts' posterity are founder's kin to All Soul's College, Oxford, thus: William Chicheley, brother to Archbishop Chicheley, the founder, by his wife Beatrix, daughter of John Barret, had Sir John Chicheley, knt. who espousing Margaret, daughter of William Knollys, had by her a daughter, Agnes Chicheley, the wife of John Tattershall, esq. of Eltham, in the county of Kent, and had issue Margery Tattershall, co-heir to her father, who conveyed the estate of Eltham to her husband, John Roper, esq. of Sawcliff, in the same county [ancestor of the Lords Teynham]. The issue of this marriage, John Roper, esq. of Eltham, attorney-general to HENRY VIII. wedded Jane, daughter and co-heir to Sir John Fineux, chief justice of the King's Bench, and had, *inter alios*, a daughter, Helen, wife of Sir Edward Montagu, of Boughton, knt. father by her of Mary Montagu, the wife of William Watts, esq. of Blakesley, as in the text.

Montagu,* knt. of Boughton, in the f Northampton, [ancestor of the Montagu and Manchester, the earls x, Sandwich, &c.]; by which lady sue,

DWARD, his heir.

Iontagu, barrister-at-law, of Lin-ln's Inn, who espoused Dorothy, ughter of Sir George Paule, of ımbeth, in Surrey, and had issue.

ary, wife of Anthony Palmer, esq. Stoke-Doyley, in the same county.

r son and heir,

D WATTS, esq. of Blakesley, wed-ıbeth, daughter of Sir Ralph Co-knt. of North-Mymms, in the county ord. This gentleman was sum-the heralds in their Visitation of y of Northampton, A.D. 1615, and accordingly to certify his descent. dy above-mentioned he had

ILLIAM.

dward, who was engaged in the yalist Army during the civil war, t by his wife, Elizabeth Rudd, an ly daughter, Mary, who conveyed estate and manor of Blakesley her husband, the Rev. John Petty-. Their only surviving child, aria-Penelope-Watts Pettyfer, es-used William Wight, esq. of Little ord, in the county of Essex, by om she had William, Henry, and izabeth, (the wife of Sir James arrington, of Burton or Burford), of whom died *s. p.* William ight, esq. the last possessor of akesley, dying without issue in 39, bequeathed all his property, will, to his nearest relatives, with mainder to a perfect stranger, with om he was not even personally quainted, merely because he bore same name and arms; into whose ssession accordingly Blakesley, d the other property of the said illiam Wight, passed about the ose of the last century.

CONINGSBY, of whom presently.

Amphilus.

Ralph.

ary.

Elizabeth.

l son,

CONINGSBY WATTS, early embarked in the royal cause, and suffered in consequence both in person and property. By his wife, Barbara, daughter and eventually sole heir of George Danet, esq. of the city of London, he had

I. Montagu, who died young.
II. John, from whom descended a family of the name of Watts, in the county of Leicester, which became extinct at the close of the last century.
III. GEORGE, of whom hereafter.

I. Barbara, wife of George Bentley, esq. of Monmouth.

The third but second surviving son,

GEORGE WATTS, a Turkey merchant in the city of Bristol, having a strong predilection for antiquarian researches, accumulated at great cost and labour many documents concerning his own family. He made himself remarkable by his zeal for a Protestant succession, which brought him into difficulty during the Duke of Monmouth's rebellion. He was the first of his family who bore his coat of arms quartered as at present borne. By his first wife, Mary, daughter of George Dennis, esq. of Bideford, he had a daughter, Mary, who *m.* Andrew Nelthorpe, esq. By his second wife, Miss Anne Harrington, he had

I. Edward, who died an infant.
II. CHARLES.
III. Montagu, who inherited the greater part of his father's fortune, which he lost by embarking in that ruinous scheme, the South Sea Bubble. He *m.* Miss Jane Seymour, and left issue.
IV. William, M. A. a clergyman.

I. Florence, died young.
II. Anne, wife of Captain Frazer.

The eldest son,

CHARLES WATTS, who was an officer in the army, and died abroad in 1745, offended his father and was disinherited. He married Katherine,* daughter of Robert Scrope, esq. (by his wife Katherine Middleton), and had

I. George, } *d.* young.
II. Robert, } *d.* young.
III. William Middleton, } *d.* young.
IV. William.

I. Katherine, *d.* young.

The youngest son,

THE REV. WILLIAM WATTS, A.M. of Queen's College, Oxford, was presented to the rectory of Moresby, in the county of

* Edward Montagu was lineally descended royal blood of Plantagenet; his imme-stor, Sir John Montagu, having married de Monthermer, grand-daughter of Monthermer, Earl of Gloucester, by tagenet, called D'Acre, daughter of *King* I. of England.

* This lady had two brothers, who emigrated to America in the beginning of the last century; since which nothing is known of them; so it is presumed that in her posterity she was their heir.

Cumberland, by Sir James Lowther, bart. A.D. 1754. This gentleman, inheriting from his grandfather a taste for antiquities, made many valuable collections, principally concerning the county of Cumberland, and mainly assisted Joseph Nicolson, esq. of Hawkesdale Hall, in that county, [whose niece he married], in his arduous undertaking of compiling the History of his native county; of which Mr. Watts was for many years an active magistrate. He married Mary, daughter of John Nicolson,* esq. and sister [and in her issue] sole heir of John Nicolson, esq. of Hawkesdale Hall, in Cumberland, and great niece of Dr. William Nicolson,† Bishop of Carlisle, afterwards of Londonderry, and eventually Archbishop of Cashel; by which lady he left issue a daughter, Mary, wife of the Rev. William Brisco, of Langrigg, in the county of Cumberland, [descended from a younger branch of the house of Crofton], whose widow she died, without issue, 1826, and a son,

The Rev. Clement Watts, M.A. of Queen's College, Oxford, who was presented by that college to the vicarage of Holm Cultram, in the county of Cumberland. He was in the commission of the peace for the county, and wedded Mary, daughter of William Benn, esq. of More Row, and only sister of Sir John-Benn Walsh, bart. of Ormthwaite Hall, in the same county, by whom [who survived him till 1818] he had

I. John-Nicolson, his heir.
II. William, who died young.
III. Thomas, who was in the Madras civil service, *m.* Miss Catherine Garling, and died in 1812, without issue.
I. Mary, wife of John Brocklebank,

* Although the family of Watts, of Hawkesdale, descend from the royal house of Plantagenet through other matches, yet the following line from *King* Edward III. is selected as being almost entirely through families of, or connected with the county of Cumberland.

*King* Edward III. by his wife Philippa, of Hainault, had Lionel, of Antwerp, Duke of Clarence, who by his wife Elizabeth, daughter and heir to John de Burgh, Earl of Ulster, left an only daughter, Philippa, wife to Edmond Mortimer, Earl of March. Their daughter, Elizabeth, espoused the famous Harry Hotspur, Lord Percy. Of this illustrious couple was born a daughter, Elizabeth Percy, the wife of John, Lord Clifford, Knight of the Garter, by whom she was mother to Thomas, Lord Clifford, who by his wife Joan, daughter of Thomas, Lord Dacre, of the North, K.G. had issue, *inter alios*, a daughter, Joan de Clifford, wife of Sir Richard Musgrave, of Musgrave and Eden Hall. A daughter of this marriage espoused John Martindale, esq. of Newton, whose grand-daughter conveyed that property in marriage to William Musgrave, esq. of Hayton Castle, the representative of another branch of the famous and knightly family of Musgrave. They had issue, Anne Musgrave, the wife of John Brisco, esq. of Crofton, whose son, William Brisco, esq. by his wife Jane, daughter of William Orpheur, of Plumland, had issue John Brisco, of Crofton, who by Mary, daughter of Sir Thomas Braithwaite, of Barneshead, was father of Mary Brisco, the wife of the Rev. Joseph Nicolson, rector of Plumland and Torpenhow, father by her of William Nicolson, Bishop of Carlisle, and John Nicolson, esq. of Hawkesdale, whose grand-daughter, Mary Nicolson, [viz. daughter of John, his son, and niece of Joseph, of Hawkesdale, historian of the county], married, as in the text, the Rev. William Watts.

† The family of Nicolson were of note in the counties of Cumberland and Westmoreland for the best part of three centuries, and matched with some of the most distinguished houses of those and the neighbouring counties, as with the Curwens, of Poulton, county of Lancaster; the Gilpins, of Kentmere; the Senhouses, of Netherhall; the Scotts, of the Park-broom: the Featherstonhaughs, of Kirkoswald; the Kynnarsleys, of Kendal, [by an heiress of a younger son of the Salkelds, of Whitehall]; the Briscos, of Crofton, &c. &c. They were members of the corporation of Carlisle, and served the office of mayor of that ancient city. The Hawkesdale branch of the family, by the death of the Rev. Clement Nicolson, in 1827, became totally extinct in the male line.

Of one branch, descended from Robert, brother to Joseph Nicolson, of Park-broom, (the grandfather of the Bishop Nicolson), the last representative was the memorable Margery Jackson, so famous in Cumbrian song, the recollection of whose eccentricities yet survives among the aged inhabitants of the city of Carlisle.

Dr. Nicholson, Archbishop of Cashel, who for his transcendent learning, was called the "Star of the North," was born in 1655; and, at the age of fifteen, was admitted of Queen's College, Oxford. In 1679, he was elected Fellow of Queen's College, having first completed his degree of M.A. In 1681, he was collated to a prebendal stall in the cathedral church of Carlisle, and also into the vicarage of Torpenhow, and in the year following to the archdeaconry of Carlisle. In 1696-97 and 99, he published his English Historical Library, and in 1705, his Leges Marchiarum, or Border Laws. In 1702, he was elected Bishop of Carlisle, and in 1715, appointed by the King Lord Almoner. In 1718, he was translated to the see of Londonderry; and, in 1726, he was promoted to the archbishoprick of Cashel, but died suddenly a few days after, and was buried in the cathedral church of Londonderry. He left to the Dean and Chapter of Carlisle many folio vols. of MSS. consisting of copies and extracts from various books, MSS. registers, records, and charters, relating to the diocese of Carlisle. By his wife, Elizabeth, daughter of John Archer, of Oxenholme, in the county of Westmoreland, he had a numerous family.—Vide *Nicolson's Cumberland*, vol. ii.

esq. of Hazleholm, in the county of Cumberland.

The eldest son,

JOHN NICOLSON WATTS, esq. succeeded upon the death of his great-uncle John Nicolson, esq. of Hawkesdale, to that and other estates in the county of Cumberland. Mr. Watts went out to India early in life, in the Company's civil service, on the Madras Establishment, where he died at the early age of thirty-five, and was buried at St. Thomé, A. D. 1815. He had issue by his wife, Ann-Pitt, daughter of James Dodson, esq. [Mrs. Watts died July, 1826].

I. John-Benn, } died young.
II. Henry Brisco, }
III. JOHN JAMES, successor to his father.
IV. Montagu, a lieutenant in the Madras Horse Artillery, b. 5th March, A. D. 1808.
V. Henry, lieutenant in the Madras Engineers, b. 26th January, 1810.

I. Helen Cramer, b. 20th September, 1805; m. in 1826, to Henry Dickinson, esq. of the Madras civil service; and d. 29th May, 1831, leaving an only daughter,
  Helen-Gordon-Dickinson, b. 13th January, 1828.
II. Mary-Anne, b. 1st August, 1811; m. 1830, to Henry Briggs, esq. of the Madras Light Cavalry, [who died 15th March, 1834], and has issue,
  1. Henry Briggs, b. 5th August, 1834.
  1. Eliza Briggs, b. 13th November, 1832.

Mr. Watts was succeeded by his eldest son, the present JOHN-JAMES WATTS, esq. of Hawkesdale Hall.

*Arms*—Quarterly, 1st and 4th, arg. a fess and in chief two cross crosslets, gu. 2nd and 3rd, ermine, on a chief gules, a bezant, between two billets, or.

*Crests*—1st, a dexter-arm, embowed, in armour, ppr. grasping in the gauntlet an amphisbona, (or a snake with a head at each extremity), or, langued gu. 2nd, a lozenge, gu. between two wings, elevated, or.

*Estates*—In the parishes of Dalston, Stanwix, and Irthington, in the county of Cumberland.

*Seat*—Hawkesdale Hall, in Cumberland.

## O'DONOVAN, OF THE COUNTY OF CORK.

O'DONOVAN, *The Rev.* MORGAN, chieftain of the ancient Irish Sept of O'Donovan, rector of Dundurrow, in the diocese of Cork, b. April, 1769; succeeded as chief on the death of his kinsman, Lieutenant-general Richard O'Donovan, of the 6th Dragoons, of Banlaghan, in the county of Cork, in November, 1829; m. November, 1795, Alicia, eldest daughter of William Jones, esq. of the city of Cork, by Elinor Winthrop his wife, and has issue,

MORGAN-WILLIAM, b. August, 1796, barrister-at-law.
William-Jones, b. January, 1799.
Henry-Winthrop, b. December, 1811, A. B.
Melian.
Eleanor.

## Lineage.

This family and sept is one of the most ancient among the aboriginal Irish, and in old times possessed an extensive territory called the Cantred of Hy Dunobhan, situated between the present towns of Bantry, Dunmanway, and Skibbereen, in the south west of the county of Cork, of portions of which the estates of the late and present chieftains consist. Keatinge traces its descent from the oldest branches of his Hibernian genealogy, and places their escutcheon as thirteenth in his armorial table. Mr. Gough, in his edition of Camden's Britannia, following the account given by Smith, the historian of the county of Cork, says, "The Irish antiquarians allow but eight families of royal extraction in Munster, of which they place four in Carbery, which comprehended all the south-west part of this county (Cork), and these were, besides the Mac Cartys, O'Mahon or Mahown, O'Donovan, and O'Driscol. The family of O'Donovan is allowed to be of royal extraction. Their territory in this county went formerly by the name of Clancahill, a part of West Carbery, comprehending the large and mountainous parish of Dromaleague and other tracts, in which parish they had their chief residence at Castle Donovan. This family came hither from a barony in the county of Limerick called Coshma, where they built the famous castle of Crom, which afterwards fell to the Kildare family, and from which the motto 'Crom-a-boo,' still used by that noble house, was taken. The representative of this ancient family has his seat at Banlaghan, in West Carbery." Besides Castle Donovan, he says, the castles of Banduff and of Rahine also belonged to them.

The male line of the family branch of Banlaghan expired on the death of Lieutenant-general Richard O'Donovan in 1829.

DONELL or DANILL, chieftain of the sept, who died about the year 1618, left six sons and one daughter, viz.

- I. DONELL, from whom descended
  - DANIEL O'DONOVAN, of Banlaghan, who *m.* first, Miss Kearny, daughter of Francis Kearny, esq. of Garrettstown, in the county of Cork, but by her had no issue; and, secondly Jane, daughter of Richard Becher, esq. of Hollybrook, by whom he had,
    - RICHARD, of Banlaghan, a lieutenant-general in the army, who *m.* Miss Powell, but had no issue. He died in 1829.
    - John, killed in 1796, in the Maroon war in Jamaica.
    - Jane, died in 1832.
    - Helen, *m.* to John, son of Sir Robert Warren, bart.

  Daniel O'Donovan, by his last will, dated in 1770, devised a remainder in his estates, on failure of the male issue of his two sons, Richard and John, "to his kinsman, Morgan Donovan, esq. of the city of Cork," father of the present chief of the family. He did so in fulfilment of a mutual agreement between him and this Morgan's father, that on the failure of male issue of either branch, the survivor should inherit in order to unite the family estates. The branch of Banlaghan has been allied by marriage with the houses of Tonson, Lords Riversdale, Kearney, Hungerford, Becher, and many other eminent ones in the county of Cork. It also for nearly two centuries frequently represented the borough of Baltimore in the Irish parliament.
- II. TEIGE, of Rahine and Drishane, of whom presently.
- III. Donogh, who left a son, Teige, who wedded his cousin, Honora, dau. of his uncle, Dermod.
- IV. Dermod.
- V. Richard, *m.* left a son, Daniel.
- VI. Murrogh.
- I. Honora.

The second son,

TEIGE, of Rahine and Drishane, *m.* Joane Gaggin, by whom he had issue,

- I. Daniel M'Teige, *d. s. p.*
- II. Murrogh.
- I. Joane.
- II. Ellen.
- III. Eiline.
- IV. Shilie.
- V. Honora, *m.* Dermod Anglin, *d.* in 167—.

He died in 1639, and was ultimately succeeded by his second son,

MURROGH, of Litterlicky, who *m.* Jane Galwey, by whom he had issue,

- I. CORNELIUS, his heir.
- II. Teige.
- III. William, *m.* left two sons, Murrogh and William, both *d. s. p.*
- IV. Bartholomew, V. Richard, VI. Dermod, VII. Murrogh, } of whom we have no account.

He was succeeded by his eldest son,

CORNELIUS DONOVAN, who *m.* in 1684, a daughter of Sir Nicholas Coppinger, knt.

recorder of the city of Cork, by whom he had (with a younger son, Timothy, who settled in Jamaica, *m.* there, and died *s. p.* leaving a widow, who afterwards *m.* Admiral Sir William Burnaby, bart.) his successor,

THE REV. MORGAN DONOVAN, *b.* in 1687, A. B. Oxon. who *m.* in 1733, Mary, daughter of Thomas Ronayne, esq. of Hodnetts Grove, by Miss Kearny, of Garrettstown, and niece of Philip Ronayne, author of a celebrated "Treatise on Algebra,"* and a personal friend of Sir Isaac Newton. By this lady he had issue one son and two daughters, viz.

- I. MORGAN, his heir.
- I. Mary, *m.* to John-Townsend Becher, esq. of Creagh, in the county of Cork, and had issue,
  1. Henry, killed on the day he came of age by the bursting of a gun.
  1. Anne, *m.* Major James Lombard, of Ballygriffin, left issue female.
  2. Mary, *m.* William Wrixon, esq. of Ballygiblin, and was mother of Sir William Wrixon Becher, bart. and other issue.
- II. Anne, *m.* Warden Flood, esq. of Paulstown Castle, county of Kilkenny, M. P. judge of the admiralty in Ireland, and nephew of the Right Hon. Lord Chief Justice Flood, and had issue four sons and a daughter, viz.
  1. Warden Flood, died unm.
  2. Henry Flood, of Paulstown Castle, *m.* Anna-Maria, daughter of Henry Lennon, esq. and has issue two sons and two daughters.
  3. Francis Flood, a major in the army, *d.* unm. in the West Indies.
  4. Donovan Flood, *m.* Miss Vigneau, and left a son and daughter.
  5. Marianne Flood, *m.* Rev. Stewart Hamilton, of Strabane, *d. s. p.*

The only son,

MORGAN DONOVAN, esq. succeeded his father in 1759, and *m.* in 1766, Melian, daughter of Savage French, esq. of Marino, in the county of Cork, by Mary, sister and heiress of Sampson Towgood, esq. barrister-at-law. By this lady, who *d.* in 1813, he had issue,

- I. MORGAN, his heir.
- II. Savage, M. D. *m.* Miss Jagoe, and *d.* 1807, *s. p.*
- III. Philip.
- IV. Sampson-Towgood, *d.* 1809, unm.
- V. Henry-Becher, lieutenant 28th Foot, *d.* 1799, unm. at Minorca.
- I. Mary-Towgood, *m.* 1811, William-Augustus, next brother of Sir Richard Kellett, bart.
- II. Melian, *m.* 1812, Nat. Evanson, esq. of Roaring Water, in the county of Cork, and *d.* 1813, *s. p.*
- III. Anne Becher.

This gentleman deceasing in 1802, was succeeded by his eldest son, the present REV. MORGAN O'DONOVAN, now chieftain of the family.

*Arms*—Argent, issuing from the sinister side of the shield, a cubit dexter arm vested gules, cuffed azure, the hand ppr. grasping an old Irish sword, the blade entwined with a serpent ppr.

*Crest*—On a chapeau gules turned up ermine, an eagle rising ppr.

*Supporters* of the chieftain only—Dexter, a lion ppr.; sinister, a griffin ppr.

*Mottoes*—Adjuvante Deo in hostes; also, Vir super hostem.

*Estates*—Part of the ancient Cantred of Hy Dunobhan, or Clancahill, in West Carbery, county of Cork, held by patent of confirmation from *Queen* ELIZABETH. Also Montpellier, in the south liberties of the city of Cork.

*Seats*—Montpellier, Cork, and Dundurrow Rectory.

* Of this Treatise on Algebra, very popular in its day, there have been several editions printed in London; the first in 1717.

## CALVERT, OF ALBURY HALL.

CALVERT, JOHN, esq. of Albury Hall, in the county of Hertford, succeeded his father in 1804. Mr. Calvert sat in parliament during many years, representing successively the boroughs of Malmsbury, Tamworth, St. Albans, and Huntingdon.

## Lineage.

Felix Calverd, of Little Hadham, in Herts. son of the Rev. Mr. Calverd, minister of Andover, and a descendant of the Calverds of Lancashire, *b.* 18th August, 1596; *m.* Susan or Elizabeth Betts, of Colchester, and had issue,

I. Thomas, his heir.

II. Felix, of Furneux Pelham Hall, bapt. at Great Hadham 15th February, 1623-4; *m.* Joan Day, of Hadham, and was ancestor of the Calverts of Hunsdon.

III. Peter, of Nine Ashes, Herts, who *m.* Honor Bates, of Hertford, and dying in 1675, left (with another son, Peter, an officer in *King* William's army, killed in a duel at Chester, and two daughters, Honor, *m.* to William Calvert, esq. of Furneux Pelham, and Susannah, to Sir Henry-Rigby Jason),

Felix, of Nine Ashes, who *m.* Elizabeth, only child and heir of Joshua White, of London, and left at his decease, in 1713, five sons and four daughters, viz.

1. Richard, of Hall Place, in Bexley, Kent, *m.* 9th December, 1741, Mary, third daughter and co-heiress of Josias Nicolson, esq. of Clapham, and relict of John Verney, eldest son of Ralph, Lord Fermanagh. By this lady (who died in 1789) Mr. Calvert left, at his demise in 1782, two sons, Richard, of Fulmer, in Bucks, and George, of the Coldstream Guards, who both died issueless, with one daughter, Catharine, *m.* to the Rev. Robert Wright, rector of Middle Claydon, who assumed the surname of Verney.
2. Peter, who *m.* in 1723, Honor, daughter of Felix Calvert, esq. of Albury Hall, and dying in 1772, left

   Peter, LL.D. F. R. and A. S. dean of the Arches and judge of the Prerogative Court, *d.* in 1788.

   Mary, *m.* in 1773, to Thomas Calvert, esq. of Albury.

   Frances, *m.* in 1774, to the Hon. Charles Hamilton.

   Ann, died at Bath, unm. in 1819.

   Elizabeth, died in London, unm. in 1801.
3. Felix.
4. William.
5. John, died in 1720.

1. Elizabeth.
2. Susannah, *b.* in 1712, *m.* John Peyton, esq. by whom she was mother of Sir Yelverton Peyton, bart.
3. Mary, *m.* in 1723, to Felix Calvert, esq. of Albury.
4. Anne, died unmarried.

I. Mary, bapt. 12th June, 1622.

II. Susan, buried at Great Hadham 23rd June, 1632.

III. Mary, bapt. 9th May, 1633; *m.* to John or George Cornedge, of London.

IV. Sarah, bapt. 16th June, 1639; *m.* to George Benn.

V. Susan, buried in 1669.

VI. Jane, *m.* 31st March, 1657, to William Feast, and *d.* in 1671.

Felix Calverd *d.* in 1674, and was *s.* by his son,

Thomas Calvert, esq. of London, who *m.* Anne, daughter of William Ambrose, esq. of Reading, in Berkshire, and dying in 1668, left a daughter, Sarah, the wife of Denzel Onslow, and a son,

Felix Calvert, esq. of Albury Hall, Herts, and of Marcham, in Berkshire, who represented Reading in parliament anno 1713. He wedded Mary, daughter of Sir Francis Winnington, baronet, of Stamford Court, in the county of Worcester, and had issue,

I. Felix, his heir.

II. Peter, of Red Lion Square, Middlesex, *d.* in 1782.

ohn, buried in 1739.
eorge, buried 8th September, 1740.
ancis, living in 1736.
'illiam.
sor, *m.* in 1723, to Peter Calvert,

zabeth.
ne.
ane, *m.* to Joseph Hall.
ry, *m.* to Robert Farrington.
t *d.* in 1755, and was *s.* by his

ALVERT, esq. of Albury Hall, who
ruary, 1723, Mary, daughter of
ert, esq. of Nine Ashes, and had

N, his heir.
ix, who *m.* 9th February, 1758,
ecca, daughter of — Bayley, of
sby, in Warwickshire, and by her
o wedded, secondly, Sir Yelver-
Peyton, bart.) left, at his decease
764, a son,
homas, of the East India Company's civil service, who *m.* Miss Ann Philpot, and had two sons and five daughters. Of the latter, the youngest, Elizabeth, *m.* Monsieur de Prejun.
ter, of Hampton Court Palace,
5th July, 1762, Mary, daughter
Dr. Reeves, M.D. and was father
e late
ENERAL SIR HARRY CALVERT, G.C.B. colonel of the 14th Foot, who was created a baronet in 1818. His son, having assumed the surname of VERNEY, is the present SIR HENRY VERNEY, bart.
chard, buried 22nd April, 1743.
omas, of Hutton, in Essex, *m.* 27th May, 1773, Mary, daughter of Peter Calvert, esq. of St. George's, Hanover Square.

I. Mary, under age in 1745.
II. Anne, *m.* to Christopher Anstey, esq. of Trumpington, in Cambridgeshire.
III. Jane, *m.* in 1759, to Thomas Western, esq. of Abingdon Hall, in Cambridgeshire.
IV. Elizabeth, *m.* in 1765, to James Burnett, esq. of Grosvenor Street.

Mr. Calvert *d.* in 1755, and was *s.* by his son,

JOHN CALVERT, esq. of Albury Hall, who sat in parliament successively for the boroughs of Hertford, Tamworth, and Wendover. He *m.* in September, 1757, Elizabeth, daughter of Sir Edward Hulse, and by her, who died in 1807, aged seventy-five, had two sons, viz.

I. JOHN, his heir.
II. Edward, bapt. 27th August, 1759, *m.* first, Mary-Anne, daughter of Peter Blundell, esq. and relict of Edmund Fortescue, esq.; and, secondly, Anne, daughter of Richard Byron, esq. Mr. Edward Calvert *d.* in Wimpole Street, London, 30th November, 1825.

Mr. Calvert died 22nd February, 1804, and was succeeded by his elder son, the present JOHN CALVERT, esq. of Albury.

*Arms*—Paly of six, or and sa. a bend counterchanged.

*Crest*—Out of a ducal coronet or, two pennons, the dexter or, the other sa. the staves gu.

*Estates*—In Herts.

*Seat*—Albury Hall.

## HARTOPP, OF DALBY.

OPP, EDWARD-BOURCHIER, esq. of Dalby House, in the county of
*b.* 14th December, 1809; bapt. at St. George's, Hanover Square; *m.* at
5th February, 1834, Honoria, second daughter of the late Major-general
ent, and has a son,

RGE, *b.* 15th February, 1835; bapt. at Dr. Everard's Chapel, Brighton.

pp, who succeeded his father in 1813, is a magistrate and deputy-lieu-
Leicestershire, and was its high sheriff in 1832.

## Lineage.

The Hall at Little Dalby has been the residence of this branch of the ancient family of Hartopp since the reign of ELIZABETH.

RALPH HARTOPP, living in 1377, married a daughter of Alexander Mayne, and had, with two daughters, Priscilla, *m.* to Oliver Cooke, and Philippa, to George Holles, a son and successor,

ALEXANDER HARTOPP, whose great great grandson,

RICHARD HARTOPP, was father of

THOMAS HARTOPP, who wedded Ellen, daughter of John Allen, and had three sons and one daughter, viz.

I. WILLIAM, his heir.

II. Valentine, of Burton Lazars, in Leicestershire, who died in 1633, leaving by Anne his wife, daughter and heiress of William Goodman, of Goadby, three daughters, Jane, the wife of William Street; Mary, of Nicholas Stringer; and Elizabeth, of George Bale; a son and successor,

SIR WILLIAM HARTOPP, of Burton Lazars, knighted at Ashby-de-la-Zouch in 1617, *m.* Mary, daughter of John Bolt, of Milton Ernest, in Bedfordshire, and dying in 1622, left a son and heir,

SIR THOMAS HARTOPP, of Burton Lazars, *b.* in 1600, who left by Dorothy his first wife, daughter of Sir Thomas Bendish, bart. four sons and two daughters, viz.

1. WILLIAM (Sir), of Rotherby, who *m.* Agnes, daughter of Sir Martin Lister, knt. and had, with several daughters, one of whom *m.* William Talbot, Bishop of Salisbury, two sons, THOMAS and Martin, M.D. The elder,

THOMAS HARTOPP, esq. of Quorndon, a colonel in the army, *d.* in 1727, aged seventy-two, leaving by Anne his wife, daughter of St. John Bennet, esq. three daughters and one son,

CHIVERTON HARTOPP, esq. of Woodhouse and Welby, who *m.* Catharine, daughter of Thomas Mansfield, esq. of West Leake, and dying in 1759, left three daughters,

CATHARINE, *m.* to James - Modyford Heywood, esq.

ELIZABETH, *d.* unm.

MARY, *m.* to Richard, Earl Howe.

2. Edward.

3. Thomas, an alderman of London, *m.* in 1674, Elizabeth, daughter of Sir John Buckworth, and had, with several daughters, one of whom *m.* William Hartopp, esq. of Little Dalby, a son,

Peter, of Walthamstow, a Turkey merchant, living in 1718.

4. John.

1. Dorothy, *m.* to William Hartopp, of Little Dalby.

2. Mary.

III. Richard, of the Middle Temple, *d. s. p.*

I. Joan, *m.* to Octavian Fisher, of Threkingham, in Lincolnshire.

The eldest son,

WILLIAM HARTOPP, esq. who *d.* 2nd September, 1586, left, by Eleanor Adcock his wife, four sons, namely,

I. Thomas, *b.* in 1570, died issueless.

II. EDWARD, of Buckminster and Freathby, created a BARONET in 1619. He *m.* Mary, daughter of Sir Erasmus Dryden, bart. and left, with other issue, a son and successor,

SIR EDWARD HARTOPP, second baronet, *b.* in 1608; *m.* Mary, daughter of Sir John Coke, of Melbourn, in Derbyshire, and was *s.* in 1657-8, by his son,

SIR JOHN HARTOPP, third baronet, *b.* in 1637; *m.* Elizabeth, daughter of Charles Fleetwood, esq.

and left at his decease, in 1722, a son,

SIR JOHN HARTOPP, fourth baronet, *b.* in 1680, who died in 1762, leaving by Sarah his first wife, daughter of Sir Joseph Woolfe, knt. two daughters, his co-heirs, viz.

1. SARAH, *m.* Joseph Hurlock, esq., and their only daughter and heiress Anne, marrying Edmund Bunney, esq. that gentleman assumed the surname of HARTOPP, and was created a BARONET, as SIR EDMUND-CRADOCK HARTOPP, of Freathby, in 1796.
2. ELIZABETH, *m.* to Timothy Dallowe, M.D. but *d. s. p.*

III. Valentine, of Little Dalby, who *m.* Miss Pratt, of Lutterworth, and had five sons and two daughters, viz.

1. Thomas, *b.* in 1600.
2. Edward, *b.* in 1601.
3. Elyam, *b.* in 1603.
4. Richard, *b.* in 1606.
5. William.

1. Mary.
2. Elizabeth.

IV. GEORGE, of whom we have to treat.

The fourth son,

GEORGE HARTOPP, esq. of Little Dalby, *m.* Eleanor, daughter of William Lister, esq. of Rippingate, and by her (who wedded, secondly, William Goodman, gent. of Goadby) had issue,

I. WILLIAM, his heir.

II. Thomas, who was bapt. 1628. This gentleman was very remarkable for his strength and courage, and it is related of him that, being at Antwerp, and seeing a prize fight, wherein the combatants did not acquit themselves to the satisfaction of the spectators, he was so offended thereat, that he got upon the stage, and challenging them, encountered no less than five, one after another, whom he entirely disabled, whereby he gained very great applause; and, being of a comely personage and stature, a lady of quality and fortune, who was present at the fight, fell so much in love with him, that she sent him word, "She was at his service, if he were disposed to marry," and he, embracing the offer, settled at Antwerp, served the king of Spain in his armies, and his son was afterwards a colonel in the emperor's service, and governor of Liere in Brabant, where he is buried in the chapel of Ter Cluyse, under a monument, with the following inscription: "Cy gist Messire Thomas Hartopp, d'ancienne et noble famille d'Engleterre, en son vivant colonel d'un regiment d'infanterie au service de S. M. Imperiale et Catholique, gouverneur de la ville et dependence de Liere. Il y deceda le 20 Juin, 1723, et laissa deux fitz de noble dame Marie Constance Van Hove sa compagne, laquelle fit dresser ce memoire Priez Dieu pour le repos éternel de son ame."

III. George, bapt. 1631, settled in Ireland.

I. Elizabeth, bapt. 1627.

II. Frances, bapt. 1635; *m.* in 1663, to Isaac Ingram.

The eldest son,

WILLIAM HARTOPP, esq. bapt. in 1625; *m.* Dorothy, daughter of Sir Thomas Hartopp, knt. of Burton Lazars, and by her, who died in 1707, aged seventy, had, with many other sons,

WILLIAM, his heir, bapt. in 1654, who *m.* Elizabeth, daughter of Mr. Alderman Thomas Hartopp, of London, and died in 1724. His widow espoused, secondly, John Steward, of Worcestershire, and died in 1726.

SAMUEL, of whom presently.

Dorothy, bapt. in 1652; *m.* in 1674, to Samuel Templer, esq. of Ashley, in Northamptonshire.

Eleanor, bapt. in 1655; *m.* in 1678, to John Kerchevall, esq. of Orston, Notts.

Mary, *b.* in 1666; *m.* in 1684, to Thomas Hayes, gent.

The youngest son,

THE REV. SAMUEL HARTOPP, *b.* in 1665, vicar of Little Dalby; died in 1717, leaving by Elizabeth his wife, who died in 1721, aged forty-seven, two sons and one daughter, viz.

SAMUEL, his heir.

William, *b.* in 1706, vicar of Little Dalby, and rector of Cold Overton; *m.* Dorothy Lambart, and had an only child, Dorothy, who *d.* young. He *d.* himself in 1762.

Elizabeth, *b.* in 1703.

The elder son,

SAMUEL HARTOPP, esq. *b.* in 1700; wedded in 1730, Letitia, daughter of Edward Wigley, esq. of Scraptoft, (for an account of the WIGLEY family, see vol. ii. p. 675), and dying in 1752, left a son and successor,

EDWARD-WILLIAM HARTOPP, esq. *b.* in 1731, high sheriff for Leicestershire in 1763. He *m.* Elizabeth, daughter of Thomas Boothby, esq. of Potters Marston, and by her, who died in 1769, left issue,

I. EDWARD, his heir.
II. Samuel, LL.B. vicar of Little Dalby, and rector of Cold Overton, *m.* Mary, daughter of William Pywell, esq. of Barnwell, in Northamptonshire.
III. Thomas, died young.
I. Elizabeth, *m.* to the Rev. Henry-Ryder Knapp, M.A. Fellow of King's College, Cambridge.
II. Letitia, died in 1775, aged fourteen.
III. Mary, *m.* to George Pywell, esq. of Alexton Hall.
IV. Anne, died young.
V. Martha, died young.

Mr. Hartopp died in 1773, and was *s.* by his son,

EDWARD HARTOPP, esq. of Little Dalby, who assumed the additional surname and arms of WIGLEY. He wedded the Hon. Juliana Evans, daughter of George, Lord Carbery, and by her (who died 20th May, 1807, and is buried at Little Dalby) had issue,

I. EDWARD, his heir.
II. William-Evans, in holy orders, rector of Harby, Leicestershire, who *m.* Eliza-Georgiana, daughter of — Gubbins, esq. and has an only child, Edward-Samuel-Evans.
I. Juliana, died unm.

Mr. Hartopp Wigley died 30th June, 1806, was buried at Little Dalby, and *s.* by his son,

EDWARD HARTOPP, esq. of Little Dalby, who *m.* in 1806, Anna-Eleanora, eldest daughter of Sir Bourchier Wrey, bart. and by her (who wedded, secondly, 9th December, 1816, Sir Lawrence-Vaughan Palk, bart.) had two sons,

I. EDWARD-BOURCHIER, his heir.
II. Robert-Palk, *b.* in October, 1812; bapt. at Tawstock, Devon.

Mr. Hartopp died in 1813, and was *s.* by his elder son, the present EDWARD-BOURCHIER HARTOPP, esq. of Dalby.

*Arms*—Sa. a chev. erm. between three otters arg.

*Crest*—Out of a ducal coronet or, a pelican vulning herself, arg.

*Estates*—In Leicestershire, and in the counties of Limerick and Kerry, Ireland.

*Seat*—Dalby House.

## WRIGHT, OF MOTTRAM ST. ANDREW.

WRIGHT, LAURENCE, esq. of Mottram St. Andrew, in the palatinate of Chester, *b.* at Hams, in Warwickshire, in 1752, *m.* Anne, daughter of John Waterhouse, esq. lieutenant-colonel of the 1st Surrey militia.

Mr. Wright succeeded his father in 1799.

### Lineage.

THOMAS WRIGHT, alias Bickley, of Nantwich, living about the time of HENRY VIII. *m.* Margaret, a daughter of the ancient family of Cotes, of Woodcote, in Shropshire, and had a son and successor,

JOHN WRIGHT, father, by Elizabeth his wife, daughter of — Leeche, of the county of Stafford, of

ROGER WRIGHT, who was living in the reign of EDWARD VI. He wedded Margery, daughter and heiress of Richard Leeche, of Wich Malbank, and had issue,

I. Roger, who *m.* Eleanor, daughter of Robert Minshull, of Hulgreve.
II. William, in holy orders.
III. Edward, who *m.* Eleanor, daughter of Humphrey Minshull, by Alice his

e, daughter and co-heir of Laurence Rope.
Henry, who m. Margery, daughter John Minshull.
ichard, who m. Margaret, daughter of Alexander Elcock, of Stockport, and had six sons and one daughter, viz.

I. Richard, m. Katherine, daughter of Ralph Brayne, of Aston, and had two daughters,
  MARGARET, m. to Ralph Woodnoth.
  ELIZABETH, m. to Hugh Davenport.
II. Jerome, professor of divinity at Oxford.
III. Henry, m. Jane, daughter of John Woodnoth, lord of Shavington, representative of an ancient Anglo-Saxon family.
. Francis, m. Susan, daughter of — Carpenter, of London.
. James.
. Roger.
. Elizabeth, m. to Thomas Mynshull, of Wich Malbank.

HOMAS, of whose line we have to it.
Ralph, who m. Ellen, daughter of lph Bagnald.
John, who m. the daughter of rid Bradley, of Stinton.
eginald, who m. Anne, daughter Roger Wettenhall, of Coppenhall.
atthew, who m. the daughter of Rymer, of St. Albans.

ne, who m. Randulph Crewe, of ch Malbank, and had a son, John we, of Nantwich, who died in 1598, ring two sons, SIR RANDULPH EWE, and SIR THOMAS CREWE. former, a distinguished lawyer, ame chief justice of the Court of g's Bench, and purchasing the nor of Crewe, founded the family ted there, which was ennobled in 6. The latter, also learned in law, wedded the daughter and ress of Reginald Bray, of Stene, became ancestor of JOHN CREWE, ated LORD CREWE, of Stene, in h CHARLES II. The Crewes, of Utton descended from John Crewe, . M.P. for Cheshire, (a younger of the chief justice), obtained the ate of Utkinton in marriage with ry, the daughter and co-heiress of John Done.
ne, m. to J. Mainwaring, esq. of veley.
largaret, m. to R. Crewe, esq.
son,

THOMAS WRIGHT, esq. wedded Ellen, daughter of Robert Sadler, by Margery his wife, daughter and co-heiress of Laurence Frodsham, of Elton, and had a son and successor,

LAURENCE WRIGHT, esq. of Nantwich, who m. Margaret, daughter of Robert Pickering, of Nantwich, and had four sons, viz.

I. LAURENCE, his heir.
II. Roger.
III. Robert, m. Katherine Birch.
IV. Thomas, in holy orders, rector of Wilmslow, who m. the daughter of Francis Hobson, and d. in 1661. During the civil war, Mr. Wright's living and estate were sequestered, and he was regularly besieged in his parsonage-house by Colonel Dukenfield. Tradition, which asserts him to have survived the restoration, and to have been reinstated in his living at a great age, is confirmed by the parish register as follows: "Oct. 1661, the 20th day, about nyne of the clocke in the night, Mr. Thomas Wright, gentleman and parsonn of Wilmeslow, ended his lyfe, and was buried in the tombe on the northe syde of the chancell, the 23rd day of the same month of October, 1661."

The eldest son,

LAURENCE WRIGHT, esq. of Nantwich, espoused at Stockport, 21st March, 1595, Anne, elder daughter (and co-heiress with her sister Catherine, the wife of Henry Bradshaw, esq. of Marple) of Ralph Wynington, of Offerton, by Anne his wife, daughter of George Bowden, of Derbyshire, and thus acquired the Offerton estate, which had been obtained *temp.* EDWARD IV. by Thomas Wynington, in marriage with the heiress of a family bearing the local name. By this lady, Mr. Wright left a son and successor,

LAURENCE WRIGHT, esq. of Offerton, in Cheshire, bapt. at Stockport 17th December, 1598, who m. Margaret, daughter and sole heiress of Robert Robinson, esq. of Mobberley, (of the Robinsons, of Yorkshire), and was s. by his son,

THOMAS WRIGHT, esq. of Offerton and Mobberley, who m. Mary, daughter of John Hignet, of London, and had two sons,

I. LAURENCE, his heir.
II. Henry, of Clifford's Inn, London, who m. Elizabeth, daughter of William Black, esq. of London, and had (with another son, Henry, who d. s. p. in 1725)
  William, who m. 14th February, 1720, Frances-Alicia, daughter of Ralph Wilbraham, esq. of Townsend, but died without sur-

viving issue, 13th December, 1770, leaving Henry-Offley Wright, his kinsman, his heir.

The elder son,

LAURENCE WRIGHT, esq. of Mobberley, *m.* Eleanora, daughter and heiress of the Rev. Samuel Shipton, B.D. rector of Alderley, in Cheshire, and had, with a daughter, Penelope, who died unm. in 1712, a son and successor,

HENRY WRIGHT, esq. of Mobberley, *b.* in 1688, who wedded Purefoy, daughter of Sir Willoughby Aston, bart. of Aston, by Mary his wife, daughter of John Offley, esq. of Madeley, and by her, who died 30th January, 1768, aged seventy-eight, he had issue,

I. Laurence, died young.
II. HENRY-OFFLEY, successor to his father.
I. Eleanor, *m.* to George Lloyd, esq. of Hulme Hall, in Lancashire, and *d.* 2nd May, 1735, in the 22nd year of her age, leaving one son, John Lloyd, *b.* the 18th of the preceding April, father of John-Gamaliel Lloyd, esq. of Welcombe House. (See vol. i. p. 244).
II. Theodosia, *m.* to Sir Wolstan Dixie, bart. of Market Bosworth, and *d.* in 1751, leaving one son, Willoughby, and six daughters, two of whom only married, viz. Eleanor-Frances, who became the wife of George Pochin, esq. of Bourne, (see vol. i. p. 235), and Rosamond, of Clement Kynnersley, esq. of Loxley (see vol. i. p. 168).
III. Mary, died young.

Mr. Wright died 12th October, 1744, was buried at Mobberley, and *s.* by his only surviving son,

THE REV. HENRY-OFFLEY WRIGHT, of Mobberley, who inherited the estates of his cousin, William Wright, esq. in 1770. He *m.* Jane, second daughter and co-heir of Ralph Adderley, esq. of Coton, in Staffordshire, by Lettice his wife, daughter of Thomas Kynnersley, esq. of Loxley Park, (see vol. ii. p. 280), and had by her, who *d.* 19th March, 1779, four sons and two daughters, viz.

I. LAURENCE, his heir.
II. William, in holy orders, Fellow of St. John's College, Cambridge, died unm.
III. Thomas, rector of Market Bosworth, in Leicestershire, who *m.* Mary, daughter of William Dilke, esq. of Maxstoke Castle, in the county of Warwick, and has issue,
   1. Henry, in holy orders, *m.* Mary Catherine, daughter of the Rev. Thomas Adnutt, rector of Croft, and has issue.
   2. Thomas.
   3. William.
   4. Charles.
   5. Francis.
   6. Laurence.
   1. Jane, *m.* to John Blakiston, esq. of Leicestershire.
IV. Henry-Adderley, lieutenant-colonel 25th regiment, *m.* Alice, widow of Major-general Rigby, and daughter of Robert Sclater, esq. of Roefield, in Lancashire.
I. Frances, *m.* to Richard-Parry Price, esq. of Bryn-y-pys, near Wrexham, and has one son.
II. Letitia, *m.* to the Rev. John Watson, M.A. vicar of Prestbury, and *d.* leaving one son and two daughters.

Mr. Wright *d.* 17th June, 1799, aged eighty, was buried at Mobberley, and succeeded by his eldest son, the present LAURENCE WRIGHT, esq. of Mottram St. Andrew.

*Arms*—Sa. a chev. arg. between three bulls' heads cabossed of the second.

*Crest*—Out of a ducal coronet or, a bull's head arg. attired of the first.

*Estates*—In Cheshire.

*Seat*—Mottram St. Andrew.

*Town Residence*—Cadogan Place.

## HARWOOD, OF HAGBOURN AND STREATLEY.

HARWOOD, *The Reverend* THOMAS, D.D., F.S.A., of Lichfield, *b.* 18th May, 1767; educated at Eton and at University College, Oxford; *m.* 7th January, 1793, at Aston, county of Warwick, Maria, daughter of Charles Woodward, esq. and has had by her, who *d.* 21st October, 1829, four sons and six daughters, viz.

I. THOMAS, *b.* 6th January, 1796, *m.* 19th October, 1820, Mary-Anne, daughter of Thomas Hardy, esq. and has issue, Thomas, and three other children.

II. Charles, barrister-at-law, of the Inner Temple, and F.S.A. *m.* 14th January, 1822, Anne, daughter and heiress of Edward Moxam, esq. of Bromyard, county of Hereford.
III. John, captain in the service of the Honorable East India Company, *m.* 26th March, 1828, Olivia Halliday, daughter of John Crooke, esq. eldest son of John Cross Crooke, esq. of Kempshot Park, county of Hants, and *d.* 11th September, 1829, leaving an only son, John, *b.* at Madras, 7th January, 1829.
IV. Edward-Berwick, *m.* 6th September, 1832, Maria-Frances, only daughter of Henry Jadis, esq. of Bryanstone-square, and has a son, Vane-Delaval.

I. Maria, *m.* 27th October, 1817, to William Bayley, esq. and has issue.
II. Harriott-Elizabeth.
III. Anne-Sophia, *m.* 11th June, 1829, to George Cope, esq. and has issue.
IV. Agnes.
V. Sarah.
VI. Louisa-Scudamore, *b.* 1818, *d.* in 1835.

arwood is an author of reputation in county antiquities.

## Lineage.

ıe of Harwood is of Saxon origin, nciently spelt Herward, Horwode, wood. According to Domesday, had lands in the counties of Lin- Varwick previous to the conquest. n of Leofric, Earl of Mercia, and Brune, in Lincolnshire, and the djoining, and was chosen by the ıd nobility, who retired to the Isle er the Conqueror's invasion, to be ıl of their forces. In the Saxon was called "The Mirror of d," and Ingulphus dwells mi- the incidents of his life. Here- the last Earl of Mercia, who Bourne, and was buried in the re. Hume, in speaking of the 's subjugation of the Isle of Ely, ereward alone forced his way, and through the enemy, and still his hostilities by sea against the till at last William, charmed with y, received him into favour, and im to his estate." And Camden t "Horland, in Lincolnshire, was y WILLIAM I. to Joy Talbois, of ose insolence Herward, a hopeful ed Englishman, son of Leofric, une or Bourn, not being able to his own and his family's safety oncerned, having obtained knight- ı Brens, abbot of Peterborough, rsion to the Normans had already elf, made war against him, and g him several overthrows, at last prisoner, and allowed him to ran- ılf, on condition that he himself restored to the king's favour, and die in his allegiance and protection: such was the effect of merit even in an enemy." Camden also states, under the title "Cambridgeshire," A. D. 1071, "many English, unable to bear the Conqueror's oppressions, came hither, under the conduct of the Earl Edwin, of Chester, Morchar, and Siward, and of Egsider, bishop of Durham, ravaged the adjacent country under the command of *Hereward*, an English nobleman, and built here in the marshes a woode castle, called Hereward's Castle in Matthew Paris' time. William having this, besieged the island, made roads of great length in the marshes, built many bridges over the bogs, and erected a castle at a place called Wipberum, on which all but *Hereward*, and his followers, submitted."

In the time of EDWARD I. in the "Nomina Nobilium Equitumque, &c., de Northfolk" Sir Robert Herward is mentioned as bearing the following arms, "d'azure a une fesse gabonne de goules et de vert iij bewtes d'argent." This family continued in the county of Lincoln and in the immediate vicinity of Bourne, for many centuries. One of the last of this line was George Harwood, a merchant, of London, who entered his pedigree in the visitation for Cornhill, in 1634. He was son of William Harwood, of Thurlby, near Bourn, in the county of Lincoln, and was brother of Sir Edward Harwood, knight, of whom Fuller says, "his birth was gentile, and from a root fit to engraft his future education and excellency." Sir Edward was one of the four standing colonels in the low countries in the long war, in support of the King of Bohemia, and was killed at the siege of Mastricht, in 1632. In the visitation of London, in 1634, this George Harwood is recorded as bearing the same arms as were borne by the above Sir Robert Herward, and in the "nomina nobilium, equitumque &c." temp. EDWARD I. Sir Robert Hereward de Cauntebrigeschir is mentioned as bearing "Che' ker de or et d' azure a une bende, de goules iij Egles d'Argent." * Families, of this line, were settled in the counties of Stafford and Oxford, spelling their names Horewode, Whorwood, and Harwood, and bore for their arms "arg. a chevron between three stags' heads caboshed sa." and were of Compton, Sandwell, and Stourton castle, in the former county, and of Holton, in the latter.

Of the Staffordshire family was Sir William Whorwood, knight, Attorney-general to *King* HENRY VIII., whose only daughter and co-heiress by his first wife (a daughter of Edward Grey, esq. of Enville) married Ambrose Dudley, Earl of Warwick, and whose only daughter and co-heiress by his second wife (Margaret, daughter of Lord Chief Baron Brooke) married the eldest son of Sir Robert Throgmorton, knight. The name of Whorwood is extinct in Staffordshire, and the Sandwell estate is now the property and residence of the Earl of Dartmouth, and Stourton Castle, passed by purchase, to the Foleys.—In the 16th of ELIZABETH, William Thomas Harwood, arm, in the 17th of ELIZABETH, William Harwood arm. and in the 16th of James I., Thomas Horwood arm. were sheriffs of Staffordshire.

Willus de Horwode, another descendant of the Herwards, of Lincolnshire, held the Manors of Stevenbury, Preston Candover, Fremantel, and Polhampton, in the county of Hants, and of Bradfield, in the neighbouring county of Berks, in the time of *King* EDWARD III., and the family of Horwode and Harwood continued in possession of these manors for many generations.

There is a family of Harwood (descended from these Horwodes) living in Hampshire, and at this time possessed of estates in the neighbourhood of Preston and Fremantel. And a branch of the Hampshire Herwards (descended from Robertus Hereward, of the counties of Lincoln and Cambridge who, temp. EDWARD I., bore for their arms 'chi' ker d'or et d'azure une bende de gules iij egles d'argent,") resided at Nicholas-Pres, near Whitchurch, county of Salop, temp. HENRY VI., and continued there for six generations, when they returned to Odiam, county of Hants, and they bore, during the whole of the time they were in Shropshire, the ancient coat of Sir Robert Hereward, of Cambridgeshire.†

But the branch of this family, of which we shall have chiefly to treat, settled themselves at a very early period in the county of Berks, bearing the Staffordshire coat, but distinguished by a different colour, the Berkshire branch having the bearings *gules* instead of *sable*.‡ They were of Hagbourne, in that shire, and were settled there

---

* The arms of the Earls of Mercia were an eagle displayed.

† The following is the descent of *Herward of Pres*, county of Salop.

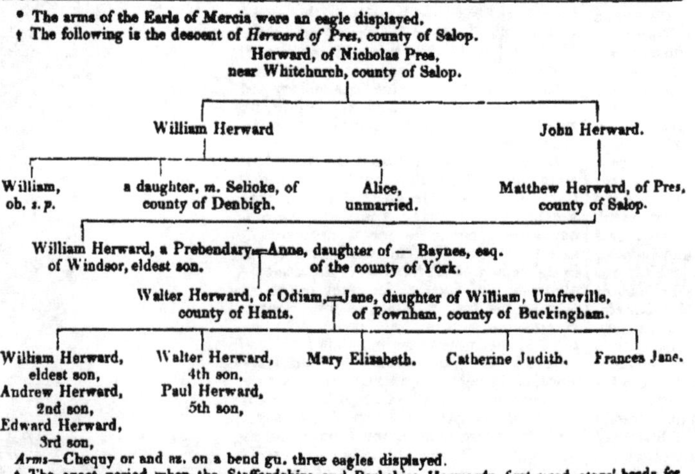


*Arms*—Chequy or and az. on a bend gu. three eagles displayed.

‡ The exact period when the Staffordshire and Berkshire Harwoods first used stags' heads for their armorial bearings, has not been ascertained. Previous to CHARLES I. and II. they used indiscriminately the bearings of eagles' and stags' heads; but since that period they have borne the stags'

four or five hundred years from the time of *King* EDWARD III, if not from an earlier period. About 1314, John Hereward was a juror on an Inquisition touching some land at Chesterton, (juxta Goring), which was decided in favour of the abbot of Oseney.* In 1332, Robert Herward was archdeacon of Taunton, and prebendary of Lincoln; and in 1330, Robert of Ely, and Thomas Harwoode or Whorwode, were sheriffs of London.

William Hereward was Abbot of Cirencester, anno 1346, and *Robertus Hereward* gave by grant, dated in the 19th of *King* EDWARD III., (1345), certain lands in *East Hackbourne*, county of Berks, to the Abbey of Cirencester, to which Abbey the church and rectorial tithes of Hagbourne belonged.† From him descended Johannes Horwode, (whose name was returned amongst the gentry of Berkshire by the commissioners for the preservation of the peace, for the year 1433, 12th HENRY VI.) ancestor of *Harwood*, of Hagbourne, father of

JOHN HARWOOD, the elder, of East Hagbourne,‡ who was buried there, and whose widow afterwards married John Bunce, of Hagbourne.

This John Harwood, the elder, *m.* at Cholsey, county of Berks, in 1560, Joane, daughter of Hadham, of Cholsey, and had issue,

- I. JOHN, of Hagbourne, who, by his wife Eleanor, (who survived him) had issue,
  1. John, of Hagbourne.
  2. Richard.
  3. Henry, *m.* October 8, 1610, at South Stoke, to Elizabeth, dau. of — Lewendon or Loveden.
  1. Eleanor.
- II. RALPH (of whom hereafter).
- III. Robert.
- I. Joan, *d.* January, 1589, unmarried.
- II. A daughter, *m.* John Acre,§ and had issue a son, John.

The second son,

RALPH HARWOOD, of East Hagbourne, *d.* in 1623, and was buried at East Hagbourne: he *m.* a sister of Robert Sayer, esq.‖ and left issue.

- I. JOHN, his heir.
- II. Richard, of East Hagbourne and Goring, county of Oxford, buried at Hagbourne, 19th September, 1679: by his wife Elizabeth, who was buried in 1668, he had issue,
  1. John, *m.* in 1668, Elizabeth, daughter of — Coxhead, who *d.* in 1680, leaving issue, John Harwood, who *m.* in 1725, Ann, daughter of — Parsons and had issue.
  2. Thomas, buried 1728, *m.* 1678, Sarah, daughter of George,¶ or St. George, who *d.* 1688, leaving issue.
- I. Eleanor.**
- II. Mary.**

The eldest son,

JOHN HARWOOD, lived at East Hagbourne and Goring, and *d.* at Hagbourne, intestate

---

heads; and there is a monument in South Stoke Church, near Streatly, to the memory of Lucy Harward (wife of Kemp Harward), who had resided in Gloucestershire, and who was living in the time of *Queen* ANNE, upon which are the same arms as were borne by Robertus Hereward, of Cambridgeshire, *temp.* EDWARD I., namely, "chequey of or and az. on a bend gu. three eagles displayed arg.," and in the Harl. MSS., No. 457, the arms borne by "Samuel Harware or Harward of Stoke and Coventry" were "a bend dannette, between two stags' heads at gaze couped or," but no date is given in this MS.

* In the reign of EDWARD II. (about 1314) an Inquisition was directed by the escheator of Oxfordshire to inquire how the abbey of Oseney had appropriated to its house two virgates of land in Chesterton, nigh adjoining Oseney, by the gift of Bardulf de Chesterton, without the king's license, and contrary to the statute of 7th EDWARD I. and amongst the jury of the neighbouring inhabitants were *John Hereward* and *Richard Alleyn*, who, with the other jurors, made a return under their oaths and seals, that William Abbot, of Oseney, predecessor of the then Abbot, in the 4th year of EDWARD I. had purchased to himself and his successors, two virgotes of land in Chesterton, one from Bardulf, son of Roger Bardulf, before the statute of mortmain. Oseney is near Goring and Streatley.

† Lawrence Horewode was vicar of St. Lawrence, Reading, Anno. 1429.

‡ East Hagbourne and West Hagbourne are the same parish. There was formerly a church at each place, but now the only church is at the chief place, East Hagbourne.

§ Arms of Acre and D'Acre, gules three escallops arg.

‖ Arms of Sayer, "or on a bend gu., three cinquefoils of the field."

¶ Arms of George, arg. on a fess gules between three falcons displayed az. three besants, on each a griffin's head erased sable.

** It is most probable that one of these daughters of Ralph married a Fellowes, of which family there were opulent branches in the neighbourhood of Reading, for a funeral escutcheon was found in the Old House at Hagbourn, formerly the residence of the Harwoods, having the Harwood arms emblazoned (the colour being *gules*) impaling Fellowes. This escutcheon (now preserved) appeared in the opinion of *Townsend*, the late learned Windsor Herald, to have been used about the middle of the seventeenth century.

in 1678. He *m.* Ann, daughter of Thomas Allen, esq.* and had issue,

I. JOHN, his heir.
II. Ralph, a merchant in London, who *d.* 1684, leaving issue by his wife Martha, with two other children, who *d. s. p.* a son,
Ralph, who *d.* issueless, at Tottenham, in 1749.
III. THOMAS, of Streatly, county of Berks, sheriff of Berks in 1695, of whom in the sequel.

I. Anne, *m.* at South Stoke, October 10th, 1664, William Higges, afterwards of Hagbourne.†

The eldest son,

JOHN HARWOOD, of Hagbourne and of London, and afterwards of Crickheath, Salop, *b.* in 1623, *d.* 1682, and buried at Hagbourne.‡ He *m.* Martha,§ daughter of Edward Muckleston, of Pen-y-lan, esq. Recorder of Oswestry, by Mary, daughter and sole heiress of Thomas Corbett, esq.‖ of Merrington, and had issue,

I. JOHN,¶ LL.D., F.R.S., and F.S.A. of Doctors Commons, Commissary of St. Paul's, and official of St. Mary's, Salop, and of Hagbourne and Crickheath, county of Salop, entered at Christ Church, Oxford, 1679, *m.* Anne, *d.* of Samuel Bulteel, esq. of the county of Devon, and had issue,
1. Samuel, who *m.* 19th December, 1741, Mary, second daughter of Walter Gough, esq. of Oldfallings and Perry Hall, county of Stafford,** and left issue,
Samuel, of Crickheath and Kenwick, who *m.* Harriet, dau. of Henry Mitton, esq. of Shipton, by a daughter of †† Sir Henry Edwardes, bart. The male line of this elder branch of the Harwoods became extinct.
2. James, vicar of Dartford, *m.* Rebecca, daughter of Richard Chase, esq. (and sister of the Hon. Mrs. St. John, wife of the Dean of Worcester) and had issue,
1. JAMES, *b.* 1769, of Christ Church, Oxford, *d.* unmarried 24th October, 1783.‡‡
1. Susan, *m.* Rev. William

* The family of Allen is of great antiquity in Berks. It appears from the Roll of Inquisition, post mortem or escheats, that there was in that county a Ric'us Alein and a Rob'tus Alein in the 9th and 12th HENRY IV., and a Waltus Aleyn in 9th EDWARD II. Their arms are "arg. two bars az., surmounted by an anchor in pale, proper."

† Griffiths Higges, S. T. P., of this family, made Dean of Lichfield in 1638, was born at South Stoke, near Streatley, educated at Reading school and St. John's College, Oxford; became Fellow of Merton College and Proctor of that University in 1622. In 1627 he went to the Hague as Chaplain to the Queen of Bohemia. On his return to England he obtained the rich rectory of Cliff, near Dover, he was also chaunter of St. David's, and chaplain to the King. He was at great expense in adorning Lichfield cathedral, and was a man of learning and a benefactor to his college. He suffered much in the rebellion, and retired to the place of his nativity, where he died December 15th, 1659, aged seventy, and was buried in the chancel of that church, in which there is a long Latin inscription to his memory, written by himself. He bequeathed his library to Merton College, in Oxford, but his books having been plundered in the time of the rebellion and lodged in the library at Stafford, the College could never recover them. Part of the inscription is as follows: "Hic jacet Griffinus Higgs, filius secundo Genitus Griffini Higgs, et Saræ Paine, Roberti Paine, de Caversham, in Agro Oxoniensi Baptizatus erat apud Stochium Abbatis in eodem comitatu, in Festo Sanctum Simonis et Judæ Anno salutis humanæ reparatæ 1589. Avum paternum habuit Nicholaum Higgs, *è Familia non Ignobili Higgesianâ*, apud Glocestionenses oriendum."

‡ In which church there is a monument with the following inscription:

"P. M. S.
Hic jacet
Johannes Harwood, de Salop,
Mercator Londinensis,
Johannis Harwood, de Hagbourne,
Filius natu Maximus,
Cui hoc Marmor
suæ
Erga optimum pater-familias
Pietatis monumentum,
Posuit
Johannes filius Primogenitus.
Obiit Londini, Prid. Cal., Oct., 1682,
Æt Suæ 59.§§

§ Not Anne, as mentioned in vol. ii., p. 169.

‖ The Corbets are one of the most distinguished Norman families in England, and of which four or five of the chief branches still hold very large possessions in Shropshire, Cheshire, and Lincolnshire, being all of them descended from the ancient Barons of Cause.

This Thomas Corbett, was of Pontesbury, a younger branch.

¶ He was one of the original founders of the Antiquarian Society, (vide. vol. i. of the Archæologia,) and was, with his connection, the Envoy Hill, and Dr. Whistler, a great friend and correspondent of the celebrated Evelyn.

** This family (of whom was the eminent antiquary) was the eldest branch of Gough, Lord Calthorpe. (See vol. ii.)

†† The heiress of Edwardes, bart. married Viscount Malpas, and was mother of the first Marquis Cholmondeley.

‡‡ The following lines were placed on a white marble tablet against the wall, in the south aisle

§§ The overseers of his will were Sir Adam Ottley, knt. Philip Prince, esq. and Richard Presland.

Eveleigh, rector of Lamberhurst and Aylesford, in Kent.
2. Sarah, *m.* Rev. Henry Bagshaw Harrison, rector of Bugbrooke, Northamptonshire.
1. Anne, *m.* Seth Jermy, esq. and had issue.
II. Thomas, of Tern, near Shrewsbury, *m.* Margaret, daughter of Rowland Hill, esq. of Hawkstone, and relict of Richard Atcherley, esq. of Marton, county of Salop, and by her (who was sister also of the Right Honorable Richard Hill,*) had issue,
1. Thomas Harwood, esq. of Tern, who took the name of HILL, and was father of the first LORD BERWICK,† (*vide. Peerage.*)
2. Rowland, Rector of Thornton, county of Chester, and of Hodnet, county of Salop.
1. Martha, *m.* her cousin Walter Gough, esq. of Oldfallings.
2. Anne, *m.* John Kynaston, esq. of Hordley, county of Salop, M. P. for Shropshire, and had issue.‡
III. Edward, of Chester, *m.* Elizabeth, daughter of Thomas Hayes, by a daughter of Wrottesely Prince, esq.§ and had issue,
1. Edward, in holy orders, rector of Thornton, county of Chester, *m.* Theodosia, daughter of J. Trevisa, esq. of Crocadon, county of Cornwall, who left issue, two sons and a daughter.
2. Samuel, *m.* and left issue.
3. Ralph, *d.* 1767, *s. p.*
4. Simon.

of Christ Church Cathedral, to the memory of this person.

"Jacobus Harwood, A. M.,
Hujusce Ædis Alumnus,
obiit Ulyssip. Oct. XXIV, M.D. CCLXXXIII,
ÆT. XXIV.
Tabis furtivo incursu
Ne, Cœli quidem mutatione compescendæ,
In mortem brevi proreptus;
Quem cum nemo vitæ honestate et morum suavitate,
Pauci studiorum profectu antecesserint
Hocce Cœnotaphio cautum est,
Ne desideratissimi Juvenis Memoria
(Cujus illustre exemplar ex suorum animis nunquam excidet)
Nullo indicio ac monumento
Posteris innotescat."

* The Right Hon. Richard Hill was an eminent statesman in the reign of *King* WILLIAM and the two subsequent reigns, and, refusing the highest honours for himself, received from GEORGE I. a baronetcy for Rowland Hill, his nephew and heir at law, with remainder to Samuel Barbour Hill, of Shenstone, who married the Lady Elizabeth, sister of Philip, the celebrated Earl of Chesterfield, but he died without issue, leaving a sister and heiress, who married Egerton of Tatton. Upon his death, however, the Shenstone and other entailed estates devolved to Noel Hill. The next limitations in remainder of the baronetcy were to his nephews Thomas Harwood and Rowland Harwood.

† This Thomas Harwood (afterwards Hill) was offered an Irish peerage during the Newcastle Administration, which he declined from the most honourable motives.

His first wife was Anne, daughter of Richard Powys, esq. and aunt of Lady Sydney, Lady Dynever, and Lady Courtown, and great aunt of Lady Chatham, and the late Duchess of Buccleugh. By that wife, besides other children who died young, he had two daughters, Margaret, wife of Bennett Sherard, Earl of Harborough (by whom he had Lord Sherard and another child, who died in their infancy), and Anne, who married Robert Burton, esq. of Longner, county of Salop, whose numerous descendants still survive; and from this family are descended the Burton Conynghams of Ireland, now represented by the Marquis Conyngham, the lord chamberlain. Thomas Harwood Hill, married secondly, Susanna Maria, eldest daughter and co-heir with her sister Lucy, Countess of Harborough, of the Hon. William Noel, Justice of the Common Pleas, and uncle of the first Viscount Wentworth, grandson of Lord Lovelace, and the Earl of Cleveland, by whom he had, besides Samuel and Susan who died young, Noel Hill and Maria, married, first, to Sir Bryan Broughton Delves, bart. and, secondly, to Henry Errington, esq. half brother of the Earl of Sefton.

Thomas Harwood Hill was in many parliaments and to a late period in life M. P. for Shrewsbury, which seat he resigned in favour of his son Noel, afterwards member for the county of Salop. Noel Hill, *m.* Anne, daughter of Henry Vernon (by the Lady Henrietta Wentworth, daughter of Thomas, Earl of Strafford, and co-heir with her sisters Lady Anne Conolly and Lady Lucy Howard, to William, Earl of Strafford), whose eldest daughter, the Lady Henrietta, (sister of this Anne), was late Countess of Grosvenor, mother of the Marquis of Westminster.

The patent of peerage for Noel Hill was to have been made out for one of the above titles of Cleveland or Lovelace; the former was abandoned out of compliment to Viscount Wentworth, then living, and the second was actually inserted in the patent, *but afterwards suddenly changed to Berwick.*

‡ John Kynaston (their grandson) was also M. P. for Shropshire, and afterwards took the name of Powell. They both claimed the ancient barony of Powis or Grey, or Charlton de Powis. The grandson was created a baronet with remainder to his brother, the present Sir Edward Kynaston.

§ His mother was a Wrottesley, of Wrottesley. The heiress of Prince married an Astley, whose sole heiress carried their great estates in Shropshire to the Earl of Tankerville.

1. Mary, *m.* Bartholomew Greenwod, esq.
2. Elizabeth, *m.* Edward Burroughs, esq. and *d. s. p.*

I. Mary, who *d.* unmarried.

II. Anne, *m.* George Curtis, esq. eldest son of Sir George Curtis, of Otterden-place, Kent, by Ann, daughter of Sir John Banks, knt. Lord Chief Justice of England, and left issue.*

III. Martha, *m.* Simon Hanmer,† of Kenwick, county of Stafford, esq. and had issue a daughter.

IV. Abigail, *m.* John Congreve, of Congreve and Stretton, county of Stafford, esq. first cousin of the poet Congreve,‡ and had issue.

Having thus detailed the senior branch, we proceed to that of Streatley:

THOMAS HARWOOD, sheriff of Berks in 1695, of Streatley, the third son of John Harwood, of Hagbourne, was brought up in the navy. He was lieutenant of the Henry, in which ship, at the commencement of the Dutch war, he fought in the memorable battle of the 3rd June, 1664. In 1665, he was commander of the Return. He was lieutenant of the Royal Prince, of 100 guns, the heaviest and largest ship of the whole fleet, engaged in the great battle of the 1st, 2nd, and 3rd of June, 1666. On the third day of the battle, while his admiral, Sir George Ayscough, was endeavouring to form a junction with Prince Rupert and his squadron, who was hastening to the assistance of the English fleet, then hard pressed by the Dutch, the Royal Prince struck on a sand called the Galloper, when, after having for a considerable time defended the ship with the utmost bravery against a host of enemies, the admiral was compelled to surrender the ship; and the Dutch being unable to get their conquest off, after having removed the men, set her on fire. He was, with his admiral, imprisoned in the castle of Louvestain. On his return from captivity he was, in 1667, promoted to the command of the Drake. From the time he quitted this ship, which he did soon after, in consequence of peace being concluded with the Dutch, he had no command till the commencement of the second Dutch war, when he was made captain of the St. Andrew, in which ship Sir John Kempthorne hoisted his flag. Captain Harwood served in this station, in the Blue squadron, at the battle of Solebay in 1672, having been one of the commanders who weathered the Dutch towards the conclusion of the engagement, and completed their defeat. Having retired from the navy, he resided on his estate at Streatley, became justice of the peace for Berkshire, and in 1695 served the office (as we have before said) of sheriff of that county. He *m.* Mary, daughter of Admiral Richard Swanley,*

* Their issue was an only daughter Anne, *m.* first, to Thomas Wheeler, esq. eldest son of Sir George Wheeler, D. D., prebendary of Durham, by Grace, daughter of Sir Thomas Higgons, of Hewel, near Odiam, by Bridget, sister of John Granville, Earl of Bath. Granville Wheeler, next brother of Thomas, *m.* Catherine, daughter of Theophilus, Earl of Huntingdon, and left issue. The above Ann, *m.* secondly, Humphrey Walcot, esq. of Sudbury, of the family of Walcot, of Walcot, Salop.

† Descended from a twin brother of the ancestor of Sir Thomas Hanmer, bart.

‡ The arms of Congreve impaling Harwood are still to be seen on an entablature over the door at Stretton Hall, now the property of Edward Monckton, esq.; and there is an old oak on the lawn near the house, under which, it is said, the poet Congreve wrote many scenes of "the Old Batchelor."

* Lysons, in his Environs of London, published in 1795, states, "that there was a tomb in the churchyard of Stepney, county of Middlesex, to the memory of Captain Richard Swanley, late admiral in the Irish Seas, who died 1650."

From Rushworth, Hist. Coll. Vol. V. Ann. 1644, June 4. A petition from several of the gentry of Wales was read, desiring Captain Swanley (who was returned with the fleet into the Downs, and come to London to give an account of his successes) might speedily be sent back, and continue commander in chief among 'em, whereupon it was ordered that the frigates be brought to the Downs to be refitted, and he be commanded into Wales as was desired. The captain being called to the bar, had the thanks of the house for his good services, and a gold chain of £200 value was ordered him, and one of £100 to Captain Smith, his vice-admiral.

The following letters from Admiral Swanley are recorded, and are copied into Fenton's account of Pembrokeshire, Appendix, p. 27.

Copy of a Letter sent to the gentlemen of the county of Pembroke.

"As in duty bound, I have in all fidelity honoured my king, and ever have been a lover of my country: now as I stand engaged, God hath called me to be a servant to both. In discharge of the trust imposed, I am come hither, to desire your sweet compliance with me in the preservation of the gospel in its inherent purity, as also the king's honour with the subjects' liberty, a work that every good Christian ought to be active in, both with the tender of life and fortunes, for which you have the obligation of our Saviour to save you harmless, who saith, 'If any man shall hazard life and fortunes, or what is most dear to him for my sake, shall undoubtedly preserve them," and for your counter-security, you have three kingdoms in the body of parliament engaged. Now why stand you gazing like the timorous Israelites, or the host of the Philistines? Did not a little youth, inspired by the spirit of God, David by name, slay their champion and overthrow that idolatrous host? And shall a jesuitical army, with a malignant party as odious in the

commander of the squadron in the Irish Seas, during the Commonwealth, and had issue,

I. THOMAS, D.D. his heir.

II. Richard, living in 1704.

III. Samuel, living in 1700.

IV. John, died about 1700, on a voyage to Guinea, and had issue by his first wife, Jane, an only son,

Swanley Harwood, *b.* 29th December, 1698, who left issue.

I. Anne, *b.* 1672; *m.* Moses Burley, esq. of Reading, Berks; she *d.* May 20, 1697, leaving issue.

II. Elizabeth, *m.* first, on the 1st August, 1682, Robert Davies, esq. of London, and of Kettlebaston and Preston, county of Suffolk, who died in 1695; secondly, to Humphrey Bent, gent. of London.

III. Mary, *m.* first, — Wild, gent.; secondly, — Silk, gent.

IV. Sarah, *m.* December 17, 1688, John Abery, esq. of Reading, and had issue,

1. Harwood Abery, *b.* 1699; *d.* 1748, *s. p.* He endowed an hospital at Reading.

2. Thomas Abery, who by Elizabeth his wife, had, amongst other children,

Elizabeth, *m.* Thomas Flory, esq. of Reading, and had issue,

Aubery Flory, who died 1790.

Deborah, died 1763, æt. twenty.

A daughter, *m.* Sir James Patey, knt. who had two daughters, one *m.* Admiral Sir Charles Brisbane, K.C.B. and the other *m.* the Rev. Aubery Phelps, rector of Stanwell, county of Middlesex.

1. A daughter, *m.* John Huscroft, esq. of London, and had issue,

John.

Henry.

Thomas Harwood, of Streatley, *d.* 1711-12, having survived his wife, who *d.* in 1702, and was *s.* by his eldest son,

THOMAS HARWOOD, D. D. of Streatley, rector of Littleton, county of Middlesex, where he founded a school for the poor, and built a rectory-house, *b.* in 1664, educated at Eton and University College, Oxford; *m.* September, 1698, Agnes, relict of Admiral Strong,* and daughter of Abraham

sight of God as those cursed Philistines, make you dismayed? No, be comforted, God and the State, have presented for you a more visible means of deliverance in sending this fleet, consisting of twelve warlike ships, with land forces and store of ammunition, whereof the major part is not yet come in, occasioned by foul weather at sea, but upon the first opportunity of wind and weather undoubtedly will arrive. And by God's assistance, I am confident, that, if the gentlemen of this county will join with me in my endeavours, we shall drive that malignant rout who seeks to enslave this nation under the yoke of the antichristian beast, not only out of this county but out of the dominion of Wales. Wherefore I shall desire the gentlemen of this county to give me their resolutions; and if any of them shall not comply, let such look to no favour from me, if it shall please God to give us the victory, but what God's enemies and the destroyers of their country deserve; and let not any man's heart be dismayed, for God hath promised to be with His protecting power, even to the end of the world, to whose protection I commit you all; and expecting your answer, I remain and rest, ever ready to engage my life with you in the defence of this great work.

"RICHARD SWANLEY."

"To the Commander in Chief of the Forces at Pix Hill, under command of the Earl of Carbery.

"Gentlemen,—I understand that you have reported that you have frightened me away with the noise of your guns. Assure yourselves that if I had been acquainted with the channel, as I make no doubt I shall be before I go hence, I had tried which had been the strongest, my ships or your mud walls, and having some other business now in hand, I defer that to a fitter opportunity: I come not to build castles in the air, nor in any hostile manner, to make any division in this country but only for peace, which at this time I am willing to proffer to you; and if you please to send a man or two to treat upon propositions which shall tend to the glory of God, the honour of the king, and the happiness of the subject. If you desire a friendly parly I promise you, upon the faith of a Christian and the word of a commander, that you shall as safely return as come, of which if you doubt, I will send hostages of such quality as you send to me. Thus expecting your answer, till then I remain your loving friend,

"Feb. 2, 1643. RICHARD SWANLEY."

* John Strong, when commodore of a small squadron in the South Seas, is said by Dr. Johnson, in his pamphlet called "Falkland Islands," to have discovered them, and that his MSS. are in the Harl. Coll. in the British Museum. He was presented by *King* JAMES II. with a medal of silver, affixed to a chain now extant, for his meritorious services in recovering a rich Spanish wreck. It is dated 1687. The following is an extract from "Evelyn's Numism," "Christopher, Duke of Albemarle, was the chief promoter of Captain Phipps'† famous scheme of fishing on a Spanish wreck off Hispaniola, by which 300,000

† He was the immediate ancestor of the present Earl of Mulgrave, Lord Lieutenant of Ireland.

Houlditch, esq. a captain in the royal navy, and governor of Cape Coast Castle; she was buried at Littleton, October 21, 1749. They had issue,

- I. THOMAS, his heir.
- II. Richard, *b.* August 14, 1701; *d.* January 29, 1729, *s. p.*
- III. Abraham, *b.* April, 1707, captain of the Orange, East Indiaman, died at Sheperton, July, 1754, *s. p.*
- IV. John, bapt. July 26, 1711; buried at Littleton, 22nd March, 1728, *s. p.*

- I. Dorothy, bapt. July 21, 1703; died unmarried 1740, and was buried in the Bulstrode vault, in the chapel at Hounslow.

Dr. Harwood died 10th November, 1744, aged eighty-one, and was buried in the chancel of Littleton church. He was succeeded in the Streatley estates, by his eldest son,

THOMAS HARWOOD, M.A. of Streatley, rector of Sheperton, Middlesex, *b.* in 1700; educated at Eton, and at University College, Oxford; *m.* at Aldworth, Berks, October 5, 1727, Anne, daughter and co-heiress of Richard Skærmere, esq. of Aldworth, and Compton, Berks, a descendant of the Scudamores, of Holm Lacy, by Elizabeth, daughter and co-heiress of John Whistler, esq. of Aldworth,*; she was buried at Littleton, April 6, 1738. They had issue,

- I. THOMAS, his heir.
- II. John, *b.* at Ashford, 17th May, 1731, of London and Chiswick, *m.* first, Sarah, daughter and co-heiress of John Spateman, esq. of Yoxall, county of Stafford, who died November 9, 1796; secondly, to Anne, daughter of Major Watson, of Worcester, who died 1731, *s. p.* He *d.* July 12, 1812, and by his first wife, had issue,
    - Sarah Harwood, only child, born August 24, 1782; *m.* August 24, 1808, Rev. Henry Penny, M.A. of Kensington, Middlesex, and has issue,
        - 1. Henry-Harwood Penny, *b.* in 1809.
        - 1. Anne.
- III. Richard, IV. Robert, V. Skærmer, } died infants.

- I. Anne Harwood, *b.* May, 1732; *m.* 1754, Edmund Bettesworth, M.A. vicar of Highworth, Wilts, son of Dr. Bettesworth, dean of the Arches and judge of the Prerogative Court of Canterbury, and brother of Dr. John Bettesworth, chancellor of London; she died *s. p.* January 14, 1812, and was buried in the chancel of Lambeth, in the same vault in which Archbishops Tennyson and Cornwallis, and the wife of Bishop Gibson, and the Bettesworth family, were deposited.

Thomas Harwood, M.A. died 4th January, 1752, and was *s.* in the Streatley estate, and in the rectory and other estates at Sheperton, by his eldest son,

THOMAS HARWOOD, B.A. of Streatley, rector of Sheperton, *b.* August 24, 1728; educated at Eton, and at University College, Oxford; *m.* 15th June, 1765, at Sheperton, Anne, daughter and co-heiress of John Brown, esq. of Chertsey, by Elizabeth, dau. of Henry Atfield, esq. of Guildford and Chertsey, by Elizabeth his wife, daughter and co-heiress of Christopher Cresswell, esq. of New Park, in Crandley, Surrey. She died January 27, 1808, and was buried at St. Mary Tavy, near Tavistock. They had issue,

- I. THOMAS, D.D.

- I. Anne-Cresswell, *m.* Charles Lyons, esq. and died in November, 1831, *s. p.*
- II. Elizabeth, *d.* unmarried in 1802.

Thomas Harwood, B.A. sold the estates of Streatley and Sheperton, and *d.* 18th March, 1796, leaving an only son, the present THOMAS HARWOOD, D.D. F.S.A.

*Arms*—Arg. a chevron between three stags' heads caboshed, gules.

*Crest*—On a wreath, a stag's head, caboshed, gules, holding in its mouth an oak bough, proper, acorned, or.

*Residence*—Burntwood and Lichfield.

---

pounds in silver were recovered from the bottom of the sea, where it had been forty-four years. He had £90,000 for his share, and the captain £20,000. In 1687 a medal was struck on this occasion; of this medal there is an engraving in Evelyn's Numismata, (vide the Life of Sir William Phipps by Increase Mathur), "upon occasion of the Spanish wreck, out of which great treasure had been gotten from the bottom of the sea by our bold and ingenious urinators, after it had been submerged for many years, was the following medallion struck, bearing the effigies of both their majesties, inscribed, JACOBUS II. et MARIA, D.G. Mag. Bri. Fran. et Hib. Rex et Regina. Reverse—The ship at anchor which carried the divers and engineers—semper tibi pendeat Hamus Exurge Naufragia reperta, 1687." Commodore Strong was in 1690 commander of their majesties' ship the Welfare. The medal and chain are yet in the possession of the Rev. Dr. Harwood, of Lichfield.

* She was (through the Whistlers, Ayscoughs, and D'Oyley's) descended from Wellesbourne, son of Simon de Montfort, Earl of Leicester, and her descendants claimed to be co-heirs of Frances, only daughter and heir of the late Charles-Fitzroy Scudamore, wife of Charles, eleventh Duke of Norfolk. The arms of Skærmore, in Aldworth Church, are the same as those of the Holm Lacy Scudamores.

# WOLLASTON, OF SHENTON.

**WOLLASTON, FREDERICK-WILLIAM,** esq. of Shenton Hall, in the county of Leicester, *m.* 29th July, 1817, at St. George's, Hanover-square, Lucy, daughter of Sir Henry Strachey, bart. of Sutton Court, in Somersetshire.

Colonel Wollaston, formerly colonel commanding the 22nd light dragoons, and brigadier general in Ireland, *s.* his father in 1801. He is a magistrate and deputy-lieutenant for Leicestershire, and was its high sheriff in 1807.

## Lineage.

"It appears, by a considerable number of very ancient deeds, that this family flourished before and in the reign of EDWARD III. at Wollaston, in Staffordshire, that it took the name from that place; that Henry, John, and William de Wollaston, were at that time lords of that manor; and that in all those old deeds, or most of them, the name is spelt, as this part of the family spell their name now (viz. *Wollaston*), and only they, until very lately, when others, from example, have spelt it in the same manner. In RICHARD II.'s reign they parted with the said manor to the Aston family; and then dispersed into other parts of that county. Some went to Trescot, and some to Perton, in the parish of Tettenhall, Staffordshire, of which last the present family of Shenton in Leicestershire, and of Great Finborough in Suffolk, is descended (as appears by a genealogy now in the hands of William Wollaston, and a gift of loaves of bread every Sunday to the poor of Tettenhall, which is still given by the said William Wollaston as a memorial of their residence there). At that time, it is probable, they left out of their name the *de*, and were no longer called de Wollaston, but Wollaston. They were gentlemen: always lived upon their estates, seemingly with the same disposition and character as at present; contented and without ambition so as to make much noise in the world, or to much enlarge their fortunes, until, in the beginning of *Queen* ELIZABETH's reign, one of the younger sons of the family at Perton was sent up to London, and there, by assiduity, and living to the age of ninety-three, he became very rich. His money he laid out in the purchase of those very estates which are now in the family; first in Staffordshire (the county in which he was born, and his ancestors and relations lived), by purchasing Oncote Hall, &c. in the parish of Eccleshal, where he and his son resided; after, by repurchasing, in the very beginning of the reign of JAMES I. the manor of Wollaston, and the estate there of the Lord Aston, in whose family it had been ever since the reign of RICHARD II."*

THOMAS WOLLASTON, of Perton, in Staffordshire, a person of rank and influence in the reign of HENRY VII. had a grant from the crown of the office of keeper of the outwoods of Lyndridge, which he held until 1523. He left,

I. JOHN, of Perton, whose son,

THOMAS WOLLASTON, of Walshall, in Staffordshire, *b.* in June, 1515, *m.* 13th June, 1541, Joan, daughter of John Ham, gent. and had (with a younger son, George, who died without issue, and three daughters, Agnes, Elizabeth, and Jane) his successor,

* Account of the family written by William Wollaston, esq.

JOHN WOLLASTON, of Walshall, who espoused Susan, daughter and heir of the Rev. Richard Fox, B.D. prebendary of Lichfield, and rector of Witherly, in Leicestershire, second son of Sir Richard Fox, knt. of Herefordshire. By this lady he left, at his decease in 1615, *inter alios*, a son and heir,

THOMAS WOLLASTON, esq. of Walshall, who *m*. Beatrix, only dau. of William Austen, of Pattingham, in Staffordshire, and was father of

JOHN WOLLASTON, esq. of Walshall, *b*. in 1617, who *m*. Blanch, only daughter and heir of John Mayne, esq. of Elmedon, in the county of Warwick, and had two sons and two daughters, viz.

1. THOMAS, aged nineteen in April, 1663.
2. John, *d*. in 1685.

1. Blanche, *m*. to John Pyott, second son of Richard Pyott, esq. of Streathay, in Staffordshire, by Mary his wife, daughter of Sir William Skeffington, of Fisherwick.
2. Beatrice.

II. WILLIAM, of whose line we have to treat.

The second son,

WILLIAM WOLLASTON, of Trescot Grange, in the county of Stafford, *m*. a daughter of John Barnsley, esq. of Trysull, of the Worcestershire family of that name, and left, with other issue, two sons, viz.

I. WILLIAM, of Trescott Grange, who *m*. a daughter of — Jordaine, of Dunsley, and had issue,

Hugh, *b*. in 1553, of Trescott Grange, who *d*. in 1609, leaving two sons, Edward, *b*. in 1597, who sold Trescott Grange, and Richard, whose son, John, was in Spain in 1659.

Elizabeth, *m*. first, to — Smith, and, secondly, to her cousin, Edward Wollaston.

Alice, *m*. to Henry Wollaston.

II. HENRY, of whom we have to treat.

The younger son,

HENRY WOLLASTON, of Perton, in Staffordshire, *m*. a lady named Elliott, and had three sons, viz.

I. Richard, of London, *s. p*.

II. HENRY, of whom presently.

III. Edward, of Perton, who *m*. Elizabeth, daughter of William Wollaston, of Trescott Grange, and had two sons,

JOHN (Sir), alderman and lord mayor of London, well known in the civil wars, *m*. Rebecca, daughter of Edward Green, citizen, but died *s. p*.

Henry, citizen of London, 1669, ancestor of the Wollastons, of Loseby.*

The second son,

HENRY WOLLASTON, alderman of London, died in 1617,† having obtained a grant in the preceding year of the family arms. He *m*. first, Sarah, daughter of William Burgess, of Kippington, in Kent, and had by her two sons and four daughters, viz.

I. WILLIAM, his heir.

II. Thomas, of Abbot's Langley, Herts, and afterwards of Oncott, in the county of Stafford, one of the filazers of Yorkshire, *b*. in 1587. He *m*. first, Philadelphia Vincent, an heiress, by whom he had an only son, who died in infancy; and, secondly, Sabina, daughter of Sir George Old-

---

* RICHARD WOLLASTON, of Wormley, *b*. in 1635, son of Henry mentioned in the text, purchased the manor of Loseby and half that of Wormley. He *d*. in 1691, having had two sons,

I. JOSIAH, *b*. in 1652, who *m*. Elizabeth, sister of Sir Edward Lawrence, of St. Ives, and predeceasing his father in 1689, left, with a daughter, Rebecca, who *d*. in 1690, a son,

ISAAC, *b*. in 1673, of Loseby, *m*. Sarah Lawrence, and dying in 1736, left several children, who died issueless, except

SIR ISAAC WOLLASTON, bart. of Loseby, who *m*. Sarah-Rowland Marche, of the Isle of Wight, and left, with a son, Sir Isaac-Lawrence Wollaston, bart. who *d. s. p*. in 1756, two daughters,

Sarah, who had the St. Ives estate, and those in the Isle of Ely. She married Taylor White, esq. and had issue.

Anne, who had the Loseby estate. She *m*. Sir Thomas Folke, and had issue.

II. John, who inherited the Hertfordshire and Hampshire estates. He *m*. Hannah Horton, and died in 1692, leaving issue,

1. Richard, M.P. for Whitchurch, *m*. Faith, daughter of George Browne, esq. and had several children.
2. John.
3. Jeremiah.
4. Jonathan, *m*. Rebecca Mayo, of Bayfield Place, Herts, and left a son, Israel, who *m*. Sarah, daughter of Daniel Waldo, Hambro' merchant, and *d*. in 1765.

† By his will, bread is still given at Perton and Waltham Abbey.

rich, by whom he left, at his decease in April, 1674, aged eighty-seven, with three daughters, three sons, viz.

1. GEORGE, of Trinity College, Cambridge, who became a Jesuit, and *d. s. p.*
2. Thomas, *b.* in 1633, left issue.
3. William, of Coton Clanford, *b.* 27th October, 1634; *m.* Elizabeth Downs, and by her, who died 24th September, 1707, left, at his decease 10th Mar. 1691-2, six sons and two daughters, viz.
   Henry, of Lichfield, who died at Chester, *s. p.* in 1694.
   WILLIAM, of whom presently as inheritor of SHENTON at the decease of his father's cousin-german, William Wollaston, esq.
   Thomas, of Lichfield, died in 1712.
   John, *d. s. p.* in 1720.
   Edward, *b.* in 1667, *d.* in 1685.
   Joseph, *b.* in 1669, *d.* in 1697.

   Sarah.
   Elizabeth, *b.* in 1674, died in 1692.

I. Frances, *m.* to Robert Jason, of Greenstreet, near Enfield.
II. Judith, *m.* to Sir William Terry, of Newington Green, Middlesex.
III. Sarah, *m.* to Samuel Middlemore, merchant, of London.
IV. Alice, *m.* to Ralph Grey, citizen of London.

The eldest son,

WILLIAM WOLLASTON, esq. *b.* in 1580, of Oncott Hall, in Staffordshire, and afterwards of Shenton, in Leicestershire, was high sheriff of the latter county in 1629, and of the former the next year. He married twice, but had issue only by his second wife, Anne, daughter of Humphrey Whitgrave, of Bridgeford, in Staffordshire, viz. four sons,

I. HENRY, of Finborough Magna, in Suffolk, *b.* in 1618; *m.* Elizabeth, daughter of Thomas Keightley, esq. of Hartingfordbury Park, Herts, but predeceased his father issueless in March, 1662.
II. WILLIAM, heir to his father.
III. Richard, } *d.* in infancy.
IV. John, }

Mr. Wollaston *d.* 10th December, 1666, aged eighty-six, and was *s.* by his only surviving son,

WILLIAM WOLLASTON, esq. of Shenton, a deputy lieutenant of Leicestershire, and sheriff in 1672-3. This gentleman *m.* Elizabeth, daughter and sole heir of Captain Francis Cave, of Ingersby, by Rebecca his wife, daughter of Robert Roper, esq. of Heanor, in the county of Derby, and widow of Sir William Villiers, of Brokesby. By her he had issue,

I. William, } both *d.* young.
II. Henry, }
III. Francis, died of the small-pox in the Temple 28th November, 1684, aged seventeen, buried at Waltham Abbey.

I. Elizabeth, died young.
II. Anne, *m.* to Sir John Chester, bart.
III. Rebecca, *m.* to John Wilkins, esq. of Ravenston.

Mr. Wollaston outliving thus his male issue, devised Shenton, at his decease, 19th August, 1688, aged sixty-five, to his cousin,

WILLIAM WOLLASTON, an eminent writer on ethics and theology, *b.* at Cotton Clanford, in Staffordshire, in 1659. He studied at Sidney College, Cambridge, and having proceeded M.A. in 1681, entered into holy orders. His first settlement was as preceptor at a free school at Birmingham, to which was annexed a small lectureship; and he afterwards became second master in the same school. In 1688 the death of his cousin put him in possession of considerable landed property, when he removed to London, and resided in Charter House Square. His marriage shortly after with a lady of large fortune having rendered him independent, he relinquished all thoughts of rising in the church, and devoted his whole time to literary researches. In 1691 he published "The designs of the Book of Ecclesiastes represented in an English poem," 8vo. but this he would afterwards have suppressed, from a conviction that he had no talents for poetry. He printed in 1722, for private distribution only, a work entitled "The Religion of Nature delineated," which he afterwards revised for more extensive circulation. This treatise, in which the author advances some ingenious speculations concerning the principles of ethical science, notwithstanding the abstruse nature of the subject, attracted the notice of the learned, and procured the writer a distinguished station among the philosophers of the last century. He *m.* in 1689, Catherine, second daughter and co-heir of Nicholas Charlton, esq. of London, and by her, who died in 1720, aged fifty, had issue,

I. CHARLTON, of Charter House Square, *b.* 8th September, 1690, Fellow Commoner of Sidney College, Cambridge, died 6th August, 1729, buried at Finbro'.
II. WILLIAM, of whom presently.
III. Francis, of Charter House Square, *b.* 6th June, 1694; *m.* 19th November, 1728, Mary, eldest daughter of Dr. John-Francis Fauquier, and *d.*

27th December, 1774, having had issue,

1. Francis, of Charter House Squ. LL.B. rector of Chislehurst, of Dereham, and St. Vidas, London, precentor of St. David's, F.R.S. *b.* 23rd November, 1731; *m.* 11th May, 1758, Althea, fifth daughter of John Hyde, esq. and by her, who *d.* 8th June, 1798, left, at his decease, 31st October, 1815,

   Francis-John-Hyde, *b.* 13th April, 1762, archdeacon of Essex, rector of South Weald, prebendary of St. Paul's, Jacksonian professor Univ. Camb. &c. He *m.* 13th August, 1793, Frances Hayles, and dying in 1823, left issue,

   1. Francis-Hayles, *b.* 1st May, 1803, rector of Dereham; *m.* 7th June, 1825, his cousin, Caroline Wollaston.

   1. Frances-Althea, *m.* to the Rev. T. William Trevor, of Caernarvon, has three sons and two daughters.
   2. Althea-Jane, *m.* to the Rev. H. R. Moody, rector of Chartham, Kent, and has issue.

   George-Hyde, of Clapham Common, *b.* 10th July, 1765; *m.* 23rd Oct. 1796, Mary-Ann, daughter of William Luard, esq. of Dorset Street, and by her, who died in 1817, had issue,

   1. George-Luard, *b.* in 1797, and *d.* in 1801.
   2. William-Luard, *b.* in 1799, and *d.* in 1821.
   3. Frederic-Luard, *b.* in 1802; *m.* 17th March, 1834, Diana-Harriet, daughter of John Sperling, esq. of Dynes Hall.
   4. Alexander-Luard, *b.* 14th June, 1804.
   5. Edward-Luard, *b.* 18th December, 1814.

   1. Mary-Ann, *d.* in 1826.
   2. Henrietta.
   3. Charlotte.
   4. Sophia.

   William-Hyde, *b.* 6th August, 1766, M.D. F.R.S.; *d.* 22nd December, 1828.

   Frederick-Hyde, *b.* 12th June, 1770; *d. s. p.* in September, 1809.

   Charles-Hyde, *b.* 22nd November, 1772, M.A. vicar of East Dereham, *m.* Sarah-Willett, daughter of William Ottley, esq. of St. Kitts, and has a son,

   William-Charles, *b.* 19th December, 1795, M.A.; *m.* 9th April, 1817, Charlotte-Jane, daughter of the Rev. Richard Fawcett, vicar of Leeds, and has issue, Charles-Richard, *b.* in 1818; William-Ottley; Charlotte-Maria; Drury-Ottley; and Percy.

   Henry-Hyde, *b.* and *d.* in 1774.

   Henry-Septimus-Hyde, *b.* 14th April, 1776; *m.* first, 23rd December, 1802, Mary-Ann Blankenhagen, who *d.* 25th June, 1805; secondly, 24th June, 1813, Frances Bucannan, who *d.* 26th December, 1827; and, thirdly, Frances Monro. By the first he has one son, 1. Henry-Francis, *b.* in 1803, and one daughter, Caroline, *m.* to her cousin, the Rev. Francis H. Wollaston. By the second, he has surviving issue,

   2. George-Bucannan, *b.* in 1814.
   3. Charles-Bucannan, *b.* in 1816.
   4. Alfred-Bucannan, *b.* in 1818.
   5. Charlton-James-Bucannan, *b.* in 1820.

   1. Elizabeth.

   By his last wife, Mr. Henry Wollaston has one son, William-Monro, *b.* in 1831.

   Mary-Hyde, *m.* in 1803, to the Rev. William Panchen, who *d.* in 1827.

   Althea-Hyde, *m.* in 1784, to Thomas Heberden, canon of Exeter.

   Charlotte-Hyde.

   Katharine-Hyde.

   Henrietta-Hyde.

   Anna-Hyde, *d.* unm. in 1829.

   Louisa-Hyde, *d.* an infant in 1772.

   Amelia-Hyde.

   Sophia-Hyde, *d.* unm. in 1810.

   Louisa-Decima-Hyde, *m.* in 1806, to the Rev. James-

Leonard Jackson, of Dorsetshire.

2. Charlton, *b.* in 1733, M. D. F.R.S. *m.* in 1758, Phillis Byam, and by her (who wedded, secondly, James Frampton, esq. of Moreton, in Dorsetshire, and *d.* in 1829, aged ninety-three) he left at his decease, in 1764,

Charlton-Byam, *b.* in 1765, B.A. of Dorchester, and of the Middle Temple.

Phillis-Byam, *m.* 3rd July, 1781, to Evelyn Shirley, esq. of Eatington, (see vol. i. p. 50).

3. William-Henry, *b.* in 1737, and *d. s. p.* in 1759.

4. George, D. D. of Richmond, Surrey, *b.* in 1738; *m.* Elizabeth, eldest daughter of Charles Palmer, esq. of Thurnscoe Hall, in Yorkshire, bank director, and had one daughter,

Elizabeth-Palmer, *m.* in 1790, to the Rev. James Cowe, vicar of Sunbury.

1. Mary, *m.* in 1760, to William Heberden, M.D. and *d.* in 1813, leaving issue.

2. Catherine, *b.* and *d.* in 1734.

IV. Nicholas, *b.* in 1696; *m.* Anne, daughter of Francis Shipman, and *d.* in 1772, leaving a daughter, Anne, *m.* to Capt. Johnson.

V. John, *b.* in 1699, LL.B. of Cambridge; *d.* in 1720.

VI. Theophilus, *b.* in 1700; *d.* an infant.

VII. Richard, *d.* in 1705.

I. Catherine, *m.* in 1719, to William Pymm, esq. of Nortonbury and Radwell.

II. Bethiah, *b.* in 1697; *d.* in 1726.

III. Anne, *b.* in 1701; *m.* to Samuel Dixon, esq.

IV. Elizabeth, *b.* in 1707, and *d.* in 1723.

William Wollaston, the author of "Religion of Nature," died 29th October, 1724, at Coton Clanford. His second son,

WILLIAM WOLLASTON, esq. of Finbro', in Suffolk, and St. James's Square, *b.* in 1693, M. P. for Ipswich. He *m.* 6th April, 1728, Elizabeth, second daughter of John-Francis Fauquier, esq. and had issue,

I. WILLIAM, his heir.

II. Francis, *b.* in 1732, and *d. s. p.* in 1755, at Bengal.

III. FREDERICK, successor to his brother.

IV. Samuel, *b.* in 1737; *d.* in July, 1798.

V. Robert, *b.* in 1741; *m.* Judith Hatley, but *d. s. p.* in 1774.

I. Elizabeth, *m.* first, in 1753, to the Hon. William-Richard Chetwynd; and, secondly, to Jeffery Thompson, M.D.

II. Catherine, *m.* to the Rev. Edward Boucher.

III. Mary, *m.* to Thomas Mulcaster, esq.

Mr. Wollaston *d.* in 1764, and was *s.* by his son,

WILLIAM WOLLASTON, esq. of Finborough, *b.* in 1730, sometime colonel of the Eastern Battalion of Suffolk Militia, and M. P. for Ipswich. This gentleman *m.* Blanche, sister of Sir Thomas-Hyde Page, but dying at Bath, 9th November, 1797, without issue, was *s.* by his brother,

THE REV. FREDERICK WOLLASTON, *b.* in 1735, LL.D. prebendary of Peterborough, &c. who *m.* first, Mary, daughter of Orbel Ray, esq. and by her, who *d.* in 1758, had an only son, who *d.* an infant. He *m.* secondly, Priscilla, daughter of D. Ottley, esq. of St. Kitts, and by that lady, who *d.* in 1819, had issue,

I. FREDERICK-WILLIAM, his heir.

II. George, lieutenant-colonel of the West Suffolk Militia, and a deputy-lieutenant for that county, died unm. in 1833, buried at Finborough.

III. Charles, rear-admiral R.N. now of Bury St. Edmunds.

IV. Henry-John, rector of Scotter, in Lincolnshire, *m.* at Bury St. Edmunds, 5th July, 1803, Louisa, second daughter of William Symons, esq. and by her, who *d.* in April, 1833, left, at his decease in the October following,

1. Frederick-William, captain in the Enniskillen Dragoons, *b.* 19th June, 1804.

2. Henry-John, rector of Byfield, Northamptonshire, *b.* 4th Aug. 1805.

3. Charles, in the East India Company's cavalry service, *b.* 18th October, 1806.

4. George, *b.* in 1807; *d.* in 1818.

5. William, *b.* in 1810; *d.* in India in 1831.

6. Charlton-James, *b.* in 1811, and *d.* in 1818.

7. Robert-Septimus, *b.* in 1813, and *d.* in 1814.

8. Arthur, *b.* in 1814, and *d.* in 1828.

9. Edward-Ottley, *b.* 11th October, 1820.

10. Thomas-Vernon, *b.* 2nd March, 1822.

1. Louisa, *m.* in 1834, to the Rev.

Henry-Frederick Hutton, rector of Gate Burton, in Lincolnshire.
2. Charlotte-Catherine, *d.* unm. in 1834.
3. Frances-Priscilla.
4. Lucy-Jane.
5. Harriet, *d.* young.

The Rev. Frederick Wollaston *d.* in 1801, and was *s.* by his eldest son, the present COLONEL WOLLASTON, of Shenton.

*Arms*—Arg. three mullets sa. pierced of the field. Quartering the ensigns of CHARLTON.

*Crest*—A demi-griffin, saliant arg. in a mural crown or, holding a mullet sa. pierced salver.

*Motto*—Ne quid falsi.

*Estates*—In the county of Leicester.

*Seat*—Shenton Hall.

## DRINKWATER, OF SALFORD.

DRINKWATER, JOHN, esq. F. S. A. of Salford, in the county of Lancaster, a lieutenant-colonel in the army, and colonel in Middlesex; *b.* 9th June, 1762, *m.* 6th June, 1799, Eleanor, daughter of Charles Congalton, esq. of Congleton, in the shire of Midlothian, and sister of Gilbert (Congalton) Bethune, esq. of Balfour, in Fifeshire, by whom he has had issue,

JOHN-ELLIOT, barrister-at-law, *b.* 12th July, 1801.
Charles-Ramsay, captain in the royal navy, *b.* 27th December, 1802.
Edward, in the admiralty, *b.* 24th March, 1812.

Eleanor-Anne, *m.* 28th June, 1825, to the Rev. W. T. Hadow, of Streatley, and St. Andrews, rector of Haseley, in the county of Warwick, and of Mickleton, *cum* Ebrington, in Gloucestershire, and has issue,

William-Elliot, *b.* in 1826.
Gilbert-Bethune, *b.* in 1832.

Harriet-Sophia.
Julia-Eleanor.
Jessica-Elizabeth.

Mary-Elizabeth.
Harriet-Sophia, *d.* in 1827.
Georgina-Augusta.

### Lineage.

The family of Drinkwater, of which that before us is a branch, appears to have been settled at a remote period in the county of Chester. The name is said by some to be a deviation from DERWENTWATER, but the assertion is unsupported by authority, nor does it seem at all probable; for we find a similar surname in every kingdom of modern Europe, in France, Spain, Italy, and Germany. One part of the family enjoyed considerable property at Bent, and another at Massey Green, in the parish of Warburton, and in the immediate vicinity. In the court rolls of that parish the name of ARNOLD DRINKWATER occurs as early as the reign of HENRY VII., and that of RICHARD DRINKWATER, of Bent, in March, 1587. The antique stone font, (still existing 1835) in Warburton church, bears the inscription of "WILLIAM DRINKWATER, THE KEEPER, 1595."

In 1620,

RICHARD DRINKWATER, son probably of the above mentioned RICHARD, erected a considerable mansion on the family estate at Bent, to which his son,

ARNOLD DRINKWATER, made additions in 1633, part of which, bearing the date of 1659, remained to a very recent period. This Arnold's son,

RICHARD DRINKWATER, *m.* in 1666, ISA-

ughter of Peter Drinkwater, of
reen, in the same parish of War-
d had a numerous progeny, no
fifteen children, from whom des-
DRINKWATERS, whose names ap-
e parochial registers of Warbur-
the earliest time mentioned to the
handsome cenotaph in the church-
Warburton covers the remains of
rinkwater, who is stated to have
cently as 1819. Isabella Drink-
in 1729, her father,

DRINKWATER, of Massey Green,
from a younger branch of the
ily, had, beside that lady, a son

DRINKWATER, esq. of Massey
l Thelwall, both in the county of
This gentleman, *m.* Elizabeth,
of John Leigh, of Outrington, and

IEL DRINKWATER, esq. who fixed
nce at Latchford, near Warring-
married several times, and lived
age; his last wife survived him.
e left two sons and a daughter,

HN, who lived at Wooley Green,
an estate given him by his father.
married and had three sons,

JOHN, who *d.* unmarried.
George, whose descendants removed to Liverpool.
Nathaniel, who entered into the
merchants service. He *m.* and
left issue.

ETER, of whom presently.

ary.

id son,

DRINKWATER was educated for the
became a fellow of Brazennose
Oxford, and was afterwards in-
of two livings in Northampton-
undts and Oundle. He was also
to the Duke of Manchester, and
nuch at Kimbolton. He *m.* Anne
f Higham Ferrers (a descendant of
rated Sir Henry Ireton), and had
JOHN and Peter. At the decease
rinkwater, his widow removed from
ptonshire to Lancashire, and upon
se the family property, which was
ible, was divided between her two
e elder, John, taking the real, and
ger, Peter, the personal.

DRINKWATER, the elder son, *b.* in
at Latchford, *m.* Mary Barton, of
near Northwich, a relation of the
of Belmont, and had issue,

I. PETER, who having an ingenious turn and some knowledge of mechanics, repaired to London, and established himself in business. He *m.* Miss Hawes, and had a large family, but only one daughter, Mary-Anne, survived him.

II. JOHN, of whom presently.

I. Mary-Anne, *m.* to —— Walworth, esq. and *d. s. p.* in 1800.

This John Drinkwater who inherited considerable property in the counties of Chester, Lancaster, and Northampton, wasted the whole of it, and entailed great embarrassments on his family. He *d.* in 1759-60. His second son,

JOHN DRINKWATER, *b.* in 1740, entered the royal navy, and served during the war of 1758-9 in the West Indies, where as surgeon of the Ripon of sixty guns, he was at the capture of Guadaloupe, &c. In 1761, he *m.* first, Elizabeth Andrews, of Salford, in Lancashire, and soon after established his residence in that town, where he lived many years. He wedded, secondly, in 1779, Elizabeth Ford. By the first lady he had issue, viz.

I. JOHN, his heir.

II. Thomas, *b.* in 1765, entered the army, and obtaining the majority of the 62nd foot, distinguished himself in the first campaigns in St. Domingo, in 1793-4. His regiment at length was so reduced by losses as to be sent home to recruit the battalion. They were embarked with a number of sick officers and invalids (returning to England) in an armed freight ship of some force. Approaching the Channel, the ship was warned by the British cruizers of many of the enemies' ships being at sea. With the troops the freight ship had on board, it was decided that she was equal to cope with any opponent of a moderate class; and the military on board were regularly exercised and stationed to make the best defence. Major Drinkwater had, of course, the command of the troops, and had been superintending the exercise of musketry with a party of them stationed in the main top, when a squall came on which obliged them to descend. The major, after remaining in the top to direct his men, was in the act of coming down, when a ratline gave way under him and he was precipitated into the sea, the ship then going at the rate of eight or nine knots an hour. He was an excellent swimmer, and so long as he was seen was observed to bear up manfully. Boats were of course hoisted out and the ship rounded to, in the hope of recovering him, but although the remainder of the day was given to search, Major Drinkwater was never seen afterwards.

III. Samuel-Ireton, drowned, previously to 1785, whilst bathing in the Irwell.

Mr. Drinkwater obtained in 1783 the diploma of M.D., and dying in 1797 was succeeded by his son, the present Colonel JOHN DRINKWATER. This gentleman entered the army in 1777, as an ensign in the royal Manchester volunteers, a corps of 1000 men raised by the town in three months, in support of Government in the American war after the convention of Saratoga. With this regiment he proceeded to Gibraltar, in the summer of 1778, and served with it during the memorable blockade, bombardment, and siege of that garrison.

At the peace of 1783, the 72nd regiment was disbanded, but before that event, Col. Drinkwater purchased a company; on being placed on half-pay, he published a history of the Siege of Gibraltar, which His Majesty GEORGE III. was pleased to receive under his immediate patronage, and, ever afterwards, graciously honoured Colonel Drinkwater by his particular notice. Having completed this work, Colonel Drinkwater paid the regulated price to return on active service, and in 1787 joined the 2nd battalion of the first or royal regiment of foot, then quartered in his old garrison at Gibraltar.

During his second residence at Gibraltar Colonel Drinkwater suggested and carried into effect measures necessary for the establishment of a garrison library, which was followed up with such spirit and good judgment, as very soon to include a numerous and highly valuable collection of literature, on all subjects and in most languages; and which has since become the model for forming similar establishments in many British garrisons, at home and abroad.

Hostilities with revolutionary France taking place in 1793, the royal regiment was detached with other troops to reinforce Toulon, recently occupied by Admiral Lord Hood and the coalesced powers; and General O'Hara being appointed governor of that fortress, the General selected Colonel Drinkwater as his military secretary, and when General O'Hara was taken prisoner, he continued to occupy that situation under General O'Hara's successor, Sir David Dundas.

On the evacuation of Toulon in December, 1793, Colonel Drinkwater was present during the subsequent proceedings against the French troops in Corsica, where Colonel Drinkwater attended General Dundas, until the French were driven from the island.

When General Dundas returned to England, and the command of the army devolved on Lieutenant-General the Hon. Charles Stuart, Colonel Drinkwater continued to fill the situation of military secretary until Corsica was annexed to the British dominions.

Colonel Drinkwater was then appointed secretary of the military department in Corsica, in which capacity he acted until Corsica was given up in October, 1796. From 1793 to 1796, Colonel Drinkwater acted as deputy judge advocate to the army, and for some time as commissary of Musters.

On the evacuation of Corsica, the Viceroy Sir Gilbert Elliot (subsequently created the Earl of Minto), retired with the army to Porto Ferajo, in the Island of Elba, and from thence proceeded on a diplomatic mission to the Courts of Naples and Rome, on which occasion, Colonel Drinkwater attended his Excellency. When Sir Gilbert Elliot returned to Elba, he found Commodore Nelson had been dispatched by Admiral Sir John Jervis to withdraw the British forces from that station, but such a measure not being considered expedient, Commodore Nelson returned to the fleet then off the coast of Portugal, and Sir Gilbert Elliot availed himself of the opportunity to accompany the Commodore to confer with the Admiral on his way to England. Colonel Drinkwater accompanying his Excellency on that occasion, was so fortunate as to be present in the brilliant action between Admiral Sir John Jervis's squadron and the Spanish fleet, off Cape St. Vincent, in February, 1797, the particulars of which (to do honour to his friend Commodore Nelson's distinguished conduct in that engagement) Col. Drinkwater afterwards published, anonymously, under the title of a "Narrative of the Proceedings of the British Fleet, commanded by Admiral Sir John Jervis," on the 14th February, 1797.

Colonel Drinkwater's official situation at Toulon having given him an intimate acquaintance with most of the public transactions on that complicated and embarrassing service, he had been deputed in 1794 by His Majesty's Commissioners Lord Hood and Sir Gilbert Elliot to Leghorn, in order to receive and investigate the numerous claims of the Toulonese, for payment of articles supplied to the coalesced powers at Toulon. On that occasion demands to the extent of nearly £50,000 were received by him; but having discovered in these claims, much imposition and fraud, Colonel Drinkwater took such steps as eventually saved to the British Government the payment of those demands. On Colonel Drinkwater's arrival in England, he was strongly urged to superintend the arrangement and settlement of the public accounts of the general expenditure in Corsica, to which he ultimately assented, and, in consequence, went on half-pay.

On the renewal of hostilities with France in 1803, Colonel Drinkwater deemed it his duty to take charge of the volunteer corps of his parish (Ealing, Middlesex), and he had afterwards the local rank of colonel given him with the command of a brigade, embracing the corps of Kensington, and those of the intermediate parishes between London and Twickenham.

In 1805, Colonel Drinkwater was named with General Sir Hildebrand Oakes, &c. to be a Member of the Parliamentary Commission of Military Enquiry; and on Sir Hildebrand's being appointed Governor of Malta, succeeded that distinguished officer in the chair of the board, which Colonel Drinkwater occupied for upwards of five years. On the change of Administration in 1807, Colonel Drinkwater was offered the situation of Under Secretary of State in the War and Colonial Department, which he thought proper to decline; as he did also the offer of knighthood.

Colonel Drinkwater continued to preside at the Military Board of Enquiry until 1811, when His late Majesty *King* George IV. then Prince Regent, was graciously pleased to select him as a fit person to succeed Sir Willoughby Gordon, in the charge of the Commissariat Department. This, however, was finally entrusted to Mr. J. C. Herries, the private secretary of the then Prime Minister (Mr. Percival), and Colonel Drinkwater was appointed to the patent office of one of the comptrollers of the army accounts.

In 1834 Colonel Drinkwater had completed fifty-seven years of public service in offices of more variety, labour, and responsibility than perhaps it had fallen to the lot of any other officer then in active employ to occupy, and on the 31st of March following the department of the Comptrollers of Army Accounts was abolished, on which occasion the Lords of the Treasury were pleased to record on their official minutes, "that the services of Colonel Drinkwater entitled him from their long continuance, responsibility, and importance, and the constant regard to the public interests with which they have been executed to their most favorable consideration."

When the Comptrollers' Office was abolished, 31st of March, 1835, Colonel Drinkwater was within a few months of completing his seventy-third year.

*Arms*—Party perpale—gules and azure—on a fess wavy arg. three billets of the second between three garbs, or.

*Crest*—Three wheat-ears—two in saltire, one in pale, or, encircled by a ducal coronet.

*Motto*—Labore omnia florent.

*Estates*—in Salford, Lancashire.

*Town Residence*—Fitzroy-sq., London.

*Seat*—Palmer's Lodge, Elstree, Herts.

## PAGET, OF CRANMORE HALL.

PAGET, JOHN-MOORE, esq. of Cranmore Hall, in the county of Somerset, *b.* 17th June, 1791, *m.* 4th October, 1827, Elizabeth-Jane, eldest daughter of the Rev. John Frederick Doveton, rector of Mells cum Leigh, and of Burnet, in the same shire, and vicar of Betchworth, in Surrey, a magistrate and deputy-lieutenant for the former county, and has issue,

I. Arthur-John-Snow, *b.* 16th December, 1830.
II. Richard-Horner-Paget, *b.* 14th March, 1832.

I. Jane-Blanche-Somerville.
II. Margaret-Doveton.

Mr. Paget succeeded his father 21st August, 1825.

## Lineage.

The Rev. JOHN PAGET, born in 1664, stated to have been grandson of the fourth brother of one of the Lords Paget, possessed an estate near Daventry in Northamptonshire, where he resided, until presented by Lord Willoughby de Broke (whose domestic chaplain he was) to the rectory of Pointingdon, Somersetshire, which manor, since restored to the Willoughbys, he purchased of his lordship. Mr. Paget was also rector of Sandford Orcas, in the same county. He *m.* Mary Ruddock of Ansford, a lady of good family, and had two sons and four daughters, viz.

I. JOHN, *b.* 18th February, 1694, *m.* Elizabeth Webb, of Roundhill, in Somersetshire, and *d. s. p.* 11th December, 1765.

II. THOMAS, of whom presently.

I. Mary, died unmarried.

II. Anne, *d.* unmarried.

III. Jane, *d.* unmarried.

IV. Elizabeth, *m.* to the Rev. Elias Bishop, rector of Bassingham, and perpetual curate of Thirlby, Lincolnshire.

Mr. Paget died 20th April, 1745. His second son,

The Rev. THOMAS PAGET, *b.* 11th January, 1703, was fellow of Christchurch College, Oxford, and held successively the livings of St. Mewans, Cornwall; Clifton and Bradford Abbas, Dorset; and Mells cum Leigh in Somersetshire. He *m.* Elizabeth Cobb, of Berkshire, and had five sons and two daughters, viz.

I. THOMAS, *d.* in the East Indies, unmarried.

II. John, *b.* in 1728, vicar of Doulting, in Somersetshire, *m.* first, Ann, daughter of the Rev. Benjamin Millward, rector of Mells and Cloford, by whom he had a daughter,

Anna Aletheia Elizabetha, *m.* to the Rev. William Phelips, of Montacute, in Somersetshire.

He *m.* secondly, Sarah Jefferey, and had by her another daughter,

Sarah Jeffery, *m.* to the Rev. Edward Bradford, rector of Stalbridge, Dorset, and had one son, who died unmarried, and one daughter, Sarah, *m.* to the present Sir William Coles Medlycott, bart., of Venn House.

The Rev. John Paget died in 1782.

III. RICHARD, of whom presently.

IV. William, *b.* 5th November, 1735, *m.* Sarah, daughter and heiress of — Salmon, esq., of Wrington, and dying in September, 1785, left one daughter,

Sarah-Maria, who *m.* the Rev. John Peploe Mosley, rector of Rolleston, in Staffordshire, and was mother of John Edward Mosley, who *m.* Caroline Sophia Paget.

V. Robert, *b.* in 1739, fellow of Magdalen College, Oxford, LL.D., *d.* unmarried 10th August, 1793.

I. Elizabeth, who *m.* Thomas Horner, esq. of Mells Park, in the county of Somerset, and *d.* in 1802, leaving one son, the present Thomas Strangways Horner, esq., and one daughter, Elizabeth-Anne, now Lady Hippisley, of Stoneaston House.

II. Mary, who *m.* Rev. John Bishop, D.D., successively rector of Whatley and Mells-cum Leigh, and vicar of Doulting, and *d. s. p.* 6th January, 1806.

Mr. Paget died 2nd January, 1783. His third son,

RICHARD PAGET, M.D., *b.* 1st December, 1730, was fellow of Magdalen College, Oxford. He *m.* 1st July, 1760, Mary, only surviving daughter and heiress of James Moore, esq. of Chilcompton, in Somersetshire, and had three sons, namely,

I. JOHN, his heir.

II. Richard, *b.* 7th July, 1766, probationer fellow of Magdalen College, Oxford, in holy orders, *d.* unmarried 9th December, 1794.

III. Thomas, *b.* 7th December, 1767, *m.* in 1800 his cousin Mary, youngest daughter of Francis Moore, esq. of Egginton House, Bedfordshire, and *d. s. p.* 10th April, 1813.

Dr. Paget *d.* 8th April, 1803 (his widow

survived until the 2nd November, 1807), and was succeeded by his eldest son,

JOHN PAGET, esq. of Cranmore Hall, in the county of Somerset, *b.* 12th December, 1761, who *m.* in February, 1784, Jane, eldest daughter and coheir of the Rev. Paul George Snow, rector and patron of Clipsham, in Rutlandshire, and prebendary of Wells cathedral, by Mary, his wife, fourth daughter of Edward Willes, Lord Bishop of Bath and Wells, and had issue,

I. JOHN MOORE, his heir.

I. Jane-Elizabeth, *m.* 29th August, 1809, to John Gough, esq. of Perry Hall, in the county of Stafford. (See vol ii. p. 392.)

II. Mary-Anne, *m.* 25th May, 1819, to Francis Hutchinson Synge, esq. second son of Sir Robert Synge, bart.

III. Anne-Mary, twin with Mary-Anne.

IV. Laura-Frances, *m.* 19th May, 1812, to the Rev. William Malet Hoblyn, and has one son and four daughters.

V. Caroline-Sophia, *m.* 21st May, 1824, to John Edward Mosley, esq. and has two daughters.

Mr. Paget died 21st August, 1825, and was succeeded by his only son, the present

JOHN MOORE PAGET, esq. of Cranmore Hall.

*Arms*—Sa. on a cross engrailed between four eagles displayed arg. five lions passant guardant of the field; quartering MOORE, BRADFORD, and SNOW.

*Crest*—A demi-tiger rampt. sa. tufted and maned arg. ducally gorged, or.

*Motto*—Diciendo y haciendo.

*Estates*—The freehold manor of East Cranmore, comprising the entire parish, acquired by Dr. Richard Paget by his marriage with Mary Moore. The Newberry estate in the parish of Kilmersdon also inherited from the Moores, which family appear to have resided there from time immemorial. Other lands in the parishes of Midsomer Norton, Babington, Mells, Cloford and Doulting, all in Somersetshire, and part of the manor of Clipsham, in Rutlandshire.

*Seats*—Cranmore Hall and Newberry House, both in Somersetshire.

## MEREDITH, OF PENTREBYCHAN.

MEREDITH-WARTER, HENRY, esq. of Pentrebychan, in the county of Denbigh, succeeded his uncle, Thomas Meredith, in 1802, and assumed, by royal license in 1824, the surname and arms of MEREDITH. He *m.* in 1821, Elizabeth Lowry, only daughter of the celebrated African traveller, Mungo Park, and has one son, HENRY, and a daughter, Marion.

### Lineage.

This ancient family traces its descent to EUNYDD, usually styled EUNYDD GWERNGWY, a chieftain of North Wales, and head of one of the fifteenth tribes. This Eunydd served with much distinction under David, the son of Owen Gwynedd, Prince of North Wales, in the 12th century, in the wars between the Welsh and English, for which he received considerable grants of land in addition to his patrimonial estate.

MEREDITH AP DAVID, of Alington, was eighth in descent from Eunydd, and father of

ROWLAND MEREDITH, of Alington, who assumed the family surname. He *m.* Elizabeth, daughter of Edward Brereton, of Borasham, and was *s.* by his son,

JOHN MEREDITH, of Alington, who *m.* Catherine, daughter of John ap Iolyn ap Madoc, gent. and had two sons, JOHN and RICHARD. The elder was ancestor of the line of Meredith, of Alington, now extinct, while the younger,

RICHARD MEREDITH, seated at Pentrebychan, founded the family before us. He wedded Jane, daughter and heir of Morgan ap David ap Robert, gent. and had issue,

I. WILLIAM, (Sir) knt. of Stansly, in the county of Denbigh, and of Leeds Abbey, in Kent. This gentleman was treasurer and paymaster of the army in the reign of ELIZABETH, and JAMES I. He *m.* Jane, daughter of Sir Thomas Palmer, of Wingham, and left, with two daughters, Anne, *m.* to Francis, Lord Cottington, and Jane, to Sir Peter Wyche, a son and successor,

WILLIAM, of Stansly, who was created a BARONET in 1622. He *m.* first, Susanna, daughter of — Barker, esq. of London, by whom he had six sons and six daughters; and, secondly, a sister of Sir Henry Goring and relict of Thomas Aynscombe, esq. by whom he had no issue. Of his sons, four died unmarried, the sixth, Roger, a master in Chancery, married Anne, daughter of Sir Brocket Spencer, bart. but *d. s. p.* Of the daughters, the only one married, Elizabeth, who became the wife of Sir Henry Oxenden, bart. Sir William's son and heir,

Sir Richard Meredith, second bart. of Stansly, *m.* Susanna, daughter of Philip Skippen, esq. of Topsham, in Norfolk, and had six sons and five daughters. He was *s.* by his eldest son,

SIR WILLIAM MEREDITH, third bart. of Stansly, at whose decease unmarried the title and estates passed to his next brother,

SIR RICHARD MEREDITH, fourth bart. of Stansly, who also *d.* unmarried in August, 1723, and was *s.* by his only surviving brother,

SIR ROGER MEREDITH, fifth bart. at whose demise *s. p.* in 1738, the BARONETCY expired.

II. HUGH, whose line we are about to detail.

The second son,

HUGH MEREDITH, of Wrexham and Pentrebychan, living *temp.* ELIZABETH, espoused Elizabeth, daughter of John Trott, esq. of Colney Heath, in Middlesex, and was succeeded by his son,

ELLIS MEREDITH, esq. of Pentrebychan, who *m.* Anne, daughter of Roger Myddleton, esq. of Cadwgan, in the county of Denbigh, and had two sons, HUGH and William, and two daughters, Anne and Elizabeth. The elder son,

HUGH MEREDITH, esq. of Pentrebychan, wedded, Mary, daughter of Francis Yardley, esq. of Esbistock and Farndon, and had three sons and two daughters, namely, ELLIS, Hugh, William, Elizabeth, and Mary. He was *s.* by the eldest son,

ELLIS MEREDITH, esq. of Pentrebychan, who *m.* in 1676, Elizabeth, daughter of Hugh Currer, esq. of Kildwick, in Yorkshire, (for an account of the CURRER family see page 95,) and left a son and successor,

THOMAS MEREDITH, esq. of Pentrebychan, barrister-at-law, living towards the close of the seventeenth century, who *m.* Elizabeth, daughter and heiress of Richard Myddleton, esq. of Bodlith, in Denbighshire, and had two sons, the younger Myddelton, and the elder,

THOMAS MEREDITH, esq. of Pentrebychan. This gentleman *m.* Miss Newton, of Heathly, in Lancashire, and had two sons and a daughter, viz.

I. RICHARD, his heir.
II. THOMAS, M.D. successor to his brother.

I. Margaret, *m.* Joseph Warter, esq. of Sibberscott, in Shropshire, and was mother of

HENRY WARTER, who inherited Pentrebychan from his uncle.

The elder son,

RICHARD MEREDITH, esq. of Pentrebychan, dying issueless in 1800, was *s.* by his brother,

THOMAS MEREDITH, M.D. of Pentrebychan, who also died without issue in 1802, and bequeathed his estate to his nephew, Henry Warter, who, having assumed the surname and arms of MEREDITH, is the present HENRY WARTER MEREDITH, esq. of Pentrebychan.

*Arms*—Az. a lion rampt. or.

*Crest*—A lion's head erased or.

*Motto*—HEB DDUW HEB DDIM, A DUW A DIGON. (In English "without God without everything, with God having enough.)

*Estates*—In Denbighshire, Shropshire, and Cheshire.

*Seat*—Pentrebychan Hall, Denbighshire.

# MORE, OF LINLEY.

MORE, ROBERT BRIDGEMAN, esq. of Linley, in Salop, *b.* 29th April, 1788, succeeded his father 12th January, 1818. Mr. More was sheriff of Shropshire, in 1822.

## Lineage.

This is a family of great antiquity, deriving its name from the parish of More, near Bishops Castle.

RICHARD DE MORE, of More, in the parish of More, and county of Salop, living in the beginning of the thirteenth century, was father of

RICHARD DE MORE, of More, who married and had three sons, namely,

- I. ROGER, of More, living in 1294, as appears by a charter of that date, in which Thomas de Montgomery grants to him and his wife the manor of Lydham. Roger wedded Alice, dau. of Adam de Montgomery, and sister and heir of the said Thomas de Montgomery, but died *s. p.*
- II. WILLIAM, of whose line we have to treat.
- III. Richard, a priest.

The second son,

WILLIAM DE MORE, left two sons, Sir Roger de la More, living in 1379, who succeeded his uncle in the More estate, but *d.* issueless, and

WILLIAM DE MORE, father of

WILLIAM DE MORE, of More, in Salop, and of More House, in Corvedale, which he inherited from his uncle Sir Roger. He was living 21 RICHARD II. and left a son,

RICHARD MORE, of More and Larden, living 11 HENRY VI. who *m.* Agnes Hill, and their son,

JOHN MORE, of Larden, who flourished in the reign of HENRY VII. wedded Joyce Aston, and had two sons, WILLIAM, his heir, and Richard, ancestor of the Mores, formerly of Millichope, in Salop. The elder,

WILLIAM MORE, esq. of Larden, in 1491, *m.* Elizabeth, daughter of John Berkeley, and had two sons, viz.

- I. EDWARD, his heir.
- II. Thomas, of Nedham, in Suffolk, whose son,
    - ROBERT, returned into Shropshire and was of Linley; he was buried at the More 20th March, 1603-4, leaving a son,
        - RICHARD, of whom presently.

The elder son,

EDWARD MORE, esq. of Larden, 8 HENRY VIII. *m.* Elizabeth, daughter of Edward Cludde, esq. of Orleton, (for an account of that ancient Saxon family, see vol. i. p. 483), and had three sons, viz.

- I. THOMAS, his heir.
- II. John, clerk of the exchequer, father of Sir Edward More, knt. of Odiham, in Hampshire, who left five sons and two daughters, viz. EDWARD (Sir), of Odiham;* Adrian, *d. s. p.*; John, *d.* unm.; William, left a son; Thomas, *d.* young; Elizabeth, *m.* to Sir Thomas Drew, of Broadhembury, Devon; and Frances, the wife of William, Lord Stourton.
- III. Eustace.

The eldest son,

THOMAS MORE, esq. who succeeded his father at Larden, married, and left at his decease a son and successor,

JASPER MORE, esq. of Larden, who died in 1613, leaving three daughters only (one of whom married Samuel More, the parliamentarian). The More and Larden estates passed to his cousin,

RICHARD MORE, esq. of Linley, who thus reunited the ancient estates of the family, being styled of More, Linley, and Larden;

* Sir Edward's son, Edward More, esq. *m.* Frances, daughter of Sir John Lenthall, but died without surviving issue.

he married a sister of Sir Thomas Harris, of Boreatton, bart.; was sheriff in 1619, and represented the town of Bishop's Castle in the Long or Fatal Parliament of Charles I. The part he took was decidedly anti-monarchial, and he appears early among the most active partizans of the Parliament within the county: but he died 6th December, 1643, before the triumph of his party, and was succeeded by his eldest son,

SAMUEL MORE, esq. of More, Linley, and Larden, then forty-nine years of age, who inherited his father's principles, or perhaps influenced them, and took a leading part in the civil commotions of Shropshire. While yet but an heir-apparent, he was a member of what was called the Committee of Parliament for Shropshire, whose business it was to raise money for the good cause, to seize the property of delinquents, &c., and whose proceedings are forcibly described by Sir Robert Howard (colleague of Richard More, in the representation of Bishop's Castle) in his comedy of 'The Committee.' He had scarcely paid the last rites to his father, when he was called upon to take the command of Hopton Castle, one of the few fortresses in Shropshire which were at that time in the interest of the Parliament; its owner, Mr. Wallop, the heir of the Corbets, as they of the Hoptons, being one of the fiercest of the republican faction. The situation of this castle, in a singularly sequestered valley entirely commanded by the surrounding hills, seemed to render the defence of it hopeless; yet such was the spirit and vigilance, and so great were the resources of Mr. More's military talent, or so low was the art of war at that time, that, with at the most but thirty-one men, he was able to hold out this little fortress for more than a month, against all the forces which the garrison of Ludlow could bring against it, though these were sometimes not fewer than five hundred horse and foot. For this stubborn resistance, however, the men, with the exception of their commander, paid the forfeit of their lives; and though it is impossible, upon such an incident, not to execrate the horrors of civil warfare, and deplore the untimely fate of the gallant little band, yet Mr. More (whose journal of this siege, still preserved, is a most curious document) does not venture to deny that the surrender was wholly unconditional: and it is a known provision of military law, instituted to prevent the unnecessary effusion of human blood, that the defence of a forfeited place with numbers so entirely disproportioned as in the present instance, entitles the captors to punish the garrison with death. Subsequent events crowned with success the party espoused by Colonel More, as he is generally called; and he took a leading part throughout the Interregnum, in the internal regulations of Shropshire, of which he was returned to be one of the four representatives to the parliament, summoned by Cromwell for September, 1656. Usurpers are invariably found to infringe that liberty which they were raised to guard, and the Protector, upon this occasion, adopted the extraordinary expedient of excluding by force, from his House of Commons, all those who were disapproved by him, or who refused to receive a ticket of approbation. Colonel More had the honour to be of this number; and, having witnessed the tyranny of unlawful sway, he was, perhaps, disposed the better to acquiesce in the restoration of the monarchy, which he survived two years. Notwithstanding his civil and military occupations, he found time for letters, and, in 1650, published a translation of "*Mede's Clavis Apocalyptica.*" His first wife, a daughter of his kinsman, Jasper More, brought him three children. By a second marriage he had three sons and four daughters, one of whom, Anne, married Sir John Turton, a puisne judge of the King's Bench; an union recommended, perhaps, by the cognate principles of the two families, for Mr. Turton, the father, was a warm opposer of Charles I. The sons were,

I. RICHARD, his heir.
II. Thomas, M.D. died unmarried in 1697, aged 69.
III. Robert, of Linley, who *m.* Sarah, daughter of John Walcot, of Walcot, in Salop, and had an only son,
 ROBERT, successor to his cousin, Thomas More, of More and Larden.

The eldest son,

RICHARD MORE, esq. of More and Larden, born in 1627, admitted of Gray's-Inn in 1646, and Member of Parliament for Bishop's Castle from 1688 to his death, ten years after; *m.* in 1659, Anne, daughter of Isaac Pennington, whose factious conduct, as a trumpet of sedition, when Lord Mayor of London, in 1643, no reader of our history can forget; by this lady, from whom he was divorced, he had no issue. He married, secondly, Dorcas Owen, and had, with a younger son, Richard, slain in battle in 1709, a successor,

THOMAS MORE, esq. of More and Larden, at whose decease, *s. p.* in 1731, his estates passed to his cousin-German, only son of Robert More, of Linley (third son of Colonel More),

ROBERT MORE, esq. who thus became seated at Linley. He was a person of considerable attainments, and of a character far above the common level. He was born in May, 1703, and in his youth visited many parts of the continent with improvement and profit. In the Parliament of 1727 and 1734, he sate in the House of Commons for Bishop's Castle. In 1754 he was elected member for the town of Shrewsbury; but his name does not occur as ever having spoken in the House of Commons, in which he did not retain his seat after the dissolution of parliament. On retiring into private life, he again embarked for the continent, traversed Sweden and Denmark, having previously explored the interior of Spain, of which country he saw the capabilities, and lamented the destiny. From conversations on these subjects, at the table of Sir Benjamin Neave, the English resident, he attracted the notice of the Spanish ministry, who offered him a guard to protect him from insult in the course of his researches; but this, after some experience of the attendant trouble and expense, he found it expedient to decline. He had, however, the satisfaction of laying the foundation of some of the most valuable improvements introduced into that country previously to the French revolution. The obligations of Spain to Mr. More are distinctly acknowledged by Baron Dillon. Mr. More was an inflexible whig, and was proud of the exploits of his grandfather, the defender of Hopton Castle. His correspondence with a celebrated orator of the last age is said to have been extremely characteristic, and proves that his talents would have shone conspicuously on the stage of the Great World; but he cultivated retirement, and the sententious pregnancy of his works was confined to the narrow scene of local politics.* Mr. More was a fellow of the Royal Society. He *m.* first, in 1750, Miss Wilson, daughter of Robert Wilson, esq. of Shrewsbury, and had by her,

- I. THOMAS, of Larden Hall, who *m.* in 1795, Harriott, daughter of Thomas Mytton, esq. of Shipton, in Salop, by Mary, his wife, daughter of Sir Henry Edwards, bart. and dying in 1804, left issue,
  - ROBERT-HENRY-GAYER MORE, in holy orders, now of Larden Hall, *b.* in 1798.
  - Harriott-Mary, *m.* to her cousin, the Rev. Thomas Frederick More.
- II. ROBERT, of whom presently.

Mr. More married, secondly, Catherine, daughter of Thomas More, esq. of Millechope, which lady died without issue in 1792. He died himself, 5th January, 1780, and was succeeded, at Larden, by his eldest son, Thomas, and at Linley, &c. by his second son,

ROBERT MORE, esq. of More, Linley, and Shelve, who was high sheriff of Salop in 1785. He *m.* 4th August, 1781, Eliza Taylor, of Hadham, Herts, and had issue,

- I. ROBERT-BRIDGEMAN, his heir.
- II. Thomas-Frederick, in holy orders, rector of Loveley, More, and Shelve, *b.* 19th January, 1790, *m.* his cousin, Harriott-Mary, daughter of Thomas More, esq. of Larden, and has had issue,
  1. Robert-Henry, deceased.
  2. Harriott-Louisa.
- III. Henry, an officer in the Peninsula war, *d.* in 1814.

- I. Catherine-Louisa, *m.* 12th February, 1811, Thomas White, M. D. of Glastonbury and Exeter, and has issue,
  1. Robert More White, *b.* 13th December, 1812.
  2. Laura White.
  3. Caroline-Elizabeth White, deceased.
- II. Charlotte, *m.* Arthur Neale, esq. barrister-at-law, of Bellevue, in the county of Stafford, and, dying in 1828, left one son and two daughters, viz.
  1. Arthur-Somery Neale.
  2. Laura-Charlotte Neale.
  3. Cicely-Ann Neale.
- III. Laura-Octavia, deceased.
- IV. Olivia.

Mr. More died 12th January, 1818, and was *s.* by his eldest son, the present ROBERT-BRIDGEMAN MORE, esq. of Linley.

*Arms*—Sa. a swan close ppr. beaked gu. all within a border engrailed arg.

*Crest*—An eagle arg. preying upon a hare sa.

*Estates*—In the parishes of More, Shelve, &c. in the county of Salop.

*Seat*—Linley Hall, Shropshire.

* Blakeway's Sheriffs of Salop.

# HAY-MACDOUGAL, OF MACKERSTON.

MACDOUGAL-HAY, ANNA-MARIA, of Mackerston, in the county of Roxburgh, inherited the estates under an entail, at the decease of her father, 13th April, 1825; *m.* in November, 1819, *Lieutenant-General* Sir Thomas Brisbane, K.C.B.* and has issue,

THOMAS-AUSTRALIA-MACDOUGAL-BRISBANE,
Isabella-Maria Macdougal-Brisbane,
Eleanora-Australia Macdougal-Brisbane.

## Lineage.

The tradition and belief have long prevailed that the MACDOWALS† (for the "MACDOUGALS of MACKERSTON" seem of the same stock, and formerly spelt their surname in the same manner) are descended from the old lords or princes of Galloway, who were almost sovereigns in their own districts, although acknowledging fealty to the crown of Scotland. This impression received countenance from the exact coincidence of their arms *(a lion rampant)* and the christian names of their respective progenitors. Fergus was the first Lord of Galloway, and not long after we hear of Uchtred of Galloway, and Duncan, Earl of Carrick their kinsman, and these are the very Christian names of the earlier Macdowals. But be the tradition as it may, it is now impossible *properly* to connect the latter with the former, and ascertain the particular line of descent.

FERGUS MACDOWILL and DOWGAL MACDOWYL swear fealty to *King* EDWARD III. among the barons of the shire of Dumfries, and there are grants not very long after to persons of the name of Dougal Macdowel.

DUNCAN MACDOWEL was a powerful chief in Galloway and a person of great celebrity about the middle of the fourteenth century. Hostile generally to the Bruces, he inclined towards the English, on Baliol's interest, probably with the view of rendering himself independent in a country which still venerated its ancient line of princes, and ill submitted to foreign domination. In the year 1342 he maintained his fortress of Estholm, on the coast of Galloway, against the Scotch, being furnished by the English king (EDWARD III.) with ships of war and the other requisite means of defence;‡ but in 1353 William Douglas, the knight of Liddlesdale, having at the head of a strong force advanced to that quarter, contrived by dexterous negotiation to detach the chief, and with him the whole of Galloway from the English cause, and eventually to induce them to swear fealty to *King* DAVID II.§

* For the family of BRISBANE, refer to vol. ii. p. 332.

† Occasionally all the Macdowals substituted "Macdougal" for "Macdowal," but the latter is by far the more prevalent, and appears the more correct orthography, and may possibly have been preferred in distinction from the "Macdougals" of the Highlands, who are a perfectly separate race.

‡ Amongst the Rotuli Scotiæ the following orders of EDWARD III. are extant:—10th April, 1342, to dispatch a great ship of war "cum dilecto et fideli nostro Duncano Maydowell ad partes de Galeweye" with merchandize, &c. for his fortalice there: 15th April, same year, to his lieutenant to succour him if besieged; and 1st December, also in that year, commanding victuals to be sent speedily "*ad insulam de Estholm* in Scotia, pro munitione ejusdem, et sustentatione dilecti et fidelis nostri Duncani Maydowell custodis insule predicte."

§ HAILES' ANN. vol. ii. p. 250. Fordun, to whom Lord Hailes refers, says that Douglas brought him "et totam terram Galeweice ad fidem Regis."

This Duncan (or Dowgald as Winton styles him) there is every reason to believe was the progenitor of the "Macdowells of Mackerston," as that family, it is admitted upon all hands, was the only one of the name known to have settled in Roxburghshire, and the English monarch in the year 1353, as well as subsequently to Douglas's expedition, commands* the sheriff of Roxburghshire to seize the lands, tenements, goods, chattels, and so forth of this very Duncan and his wife, which are specifically stated to be situated within that county, and were thus attempted to be wrested from him in consequence of his desertion. This notice of his wife is besides important, as it will be immediately seen that it was by an heiress of the name of Margaret, at that very time that the Macdowals acquired Mackerston. The direct and more immediate ancestor however of the family is

FERGUS MACDOWELL, of Mackerston, who figures after the middle of the fourteenth century, a man of rank and condition, being designed "nobilis vir," and who certainly possessed ample estates in the county of Roxburgh. *King* ROBERT II. confirms, 3d May, 1374, "Fergusio Macdowylle† totam Baroniam de Malcarstone cum pertinentiis infra vicecomitatum de Roxburghe que fuit Margarete Fraser matris ipsius Fergusii et quam ipsa Margarete nobis sursum reddidet," &c. And there is another charter of the same date confirming to him the entire baronies of Yhelthone and Cripton (Clifton) also on the resignation of Margaret Fraser, his mother, and to be held "in liberas integras et disctinctas Baronias faciendo inde servitia delicta et consueta." In this manner Fergus inherited from his mother three separate baronies.‡

This Fergus left two sons, namely Ughtred, (the younger), to whom and his heirs he granted an annual rent of twenty merks "de villa de Malcerstun," which was confirmed by ROBERT II. on the 3rd March, 1384; and the elder, his heir,

SIR DUNGAL MACDOWEL, of Makerston. In an old inventory at Mackerston there is mention of "ane charter be Robert, King of Scotland, to Dougal Macdougall, sone of ye said Fergus of the barronie of Mackerston, dated 24 June, et regni sui 12." It is not practicable to fix the precise date of this charter, owing to the omission by what Robert the grant was made; it was probably, however, by the second of the name, in which event the time would be in 1384. Sir Dungal left a son and heir,

SIR ARCHIBALD MACDOWELL, of Macker-

* Order dated 18th August, 1353. The motive for the seizure is thus assigned:—"Quia Duncanus Macdowaille contra fidelitatem et suamentum nobis per ipsum prestita, Scotis inimicis nostris contra nos jam adhesit," &c.—Rob. Scot.

† This is the first notice of the surname of the Mackerston family.

‡ Two important inferences may be drawn from these deeds, *First*, That the Macdowals of Mackerston had a better right to be considered the eldest, and perhaps, principal stock of the Macdowels, as they were not only originally baronial, and independent, but became distinguished earlier than any of the three families who contended for the chieftainship last century: these were the Macdowels (Macdowals) of Garthland, Logan, and French. The Macdowals of Garthland could not condescend upon any written evidence prior to 1413, when they first appear, only as vassals to the Douglases, from whom at the time they acquired Garthland; and the other two were obliged to resort to proof of no retrospective effect of a much later date. *Second*, That the Macdowels acquired Mackerston, &c. in the person of the father of Fergus—whose surname at least must have been Macdowel—by his marriage with Margaret Frazer, an heiress, who brought the baronies of Mackerston, Yhelthone and Clifton, in Roxburghshire. The Frazers were of old standing in the south, where they first figured before proceeding to the north, and it is in virtue of this alliance that the Macdowals of Mackerston conjoin the "*frais*," the arms of Fraser, with their paternal coat, "the lion of Galloway."

In Robertson's Index, containing entries of many old and authentic charters formerly existing, but now lost, there is one by DAVID II. (who reigned from 1329 to 1371) to MARGARET CORBET, *Lady of Maccraston*, of an annual rent due out of Mackerston forfeited by William Beaton. This proves that Margaret Corbet was, at that time, heiress of Mackerston; and we have an entry previously about a Margaret Corbet, who complains to Robert the Bruce of the murder of Sir Gilbert Frazer, her husband. Combining, therefore, these various circumstances, the existence before the middle of the fourteenth century, of Margaret Corbet, heiress of Mackerston, the marriage then of Margaret Corbet with Sir Gilbert Frazer, and the subsequent appearance of a Margaret Fraser, heiress of Mackerston, we may be led to the ancestry of the latter, who was the mother of Fergus Macdowall, and conclude that she was no other than the child of Sir Gilbert Frazer by Margaret Corbet, of Mackerston, and that she succeeded in her right to the property. Some time after the death of Sir Gilbert Fraser, Margaret Corbet, "Domina de Malkerston," as she is expressly designed in the Rotuli Scotiæ, married Patrick Charteris; and in 1334 EDWARD III. issues an order for restoring both to their estates in terms of certain conditions that had been entered into between Edward Bohun, David, Earl of Athol, and Patrick, relative to the surrender of Lochmaben Castle. The connection of Margaret in this manner through her said husband, with Galloway (that county then comprising great part of Dumfriesshire), and influence of the family of Charteris in that quarter may possibly have led to the marriage of her daughter, Margaret Frazer, with a Macdowell.

ston, who obtained from ROBERT III. (who reigned from 1390 to 1406) a confirmation of the family estates, consisting of the lands of Mackerston, Yetholine and Elistone (Clifton) in Roxburgshire. And on the 17th March, 1430, there is the continuation of a charter (dated 14th November, 1411) by Sir Archibald to Ughtred Macdowel, younger son of Fergus, in which he is designed "Patricio Archibald Macdowel militis," of twenty husband lands in the village of Mackerston, in lieu of the twenty merks of annual rent which are stated to have been granted him "per nobilem virum Ferguisium Macdowell patrem predicti Uchtredi, et dominum Dungallum patrem predicti Archibaldi, dominos quondam de Malcarston." In this charter there are some curious allusions to localities. The limits of the husband lands are defined from the western part of the cemetery of the church of St. Peter of Mackerston towards Abbothill in the southern part of the village. The village of Mackerston was formerly more populous than at present; the monks of Kelso alone had there twelve cottages, each having a tuft and half an acre of land, &c., and they had at the same time a brew-house. On this Chalmers remarks, "Those ancient establishments (the religious houses) raised and maintained a more efficient population than our modern system." Sir Archibald Macdowell aggrandized his family by another baronial alliance, having married Euphemia Gifford, one of the daughters and coheirs of Sir Hew Gifford, of Yester, by whom he left

DUNGALL MACDOWALL, of Mackerston, Yester, &c., to whom and his heirs, Robert Duke of Albany confirms, on the 11th March, 1409, the baronies of Yester, Duncaulan, Morhame, Teline, and Polganie, in the shires of Edinburgh, Forfar, and Perth, upon the resignation of "Euphemia Giffart filie quondam Hugonis Giffart militis unius hæridis ejusdem matris dicti Dougalli," and under reservation of her life rent. Dungall was *s.* by his son,

DUNCAN MACDOWALL, who obtained 11th April, 1441, upon the resignation of his father, "Dungall Macdowall, of Mackersston," (of whom he is designated the eldest son), a royal charter of Yester Duncanlau and Morham, in East Lothian, to him and Elizabeth Hay, his wife, and their heirs. He left, by this lady, a son and successor,

DUNGAL MACDOWELL, sixth laird of Mackerston, Yester, Giffordgate, Teyling, Polgavie, &c. who obtained, 12th August 1463, from his cousin, William Maxwell, of Teyling, (descended of another Gifford, coheiress), his fourth part of the baronies of Yester, Duncanlau, Morham, and Giffordgate, and that in excambion for those portions of the Gifford inheritance, Teyling and Polgavie, which are said in the deed of conveyance to have been the property "quondam Dungalli avi sui." There are various notices of this Dungal or Dougal (which are the same) upon record, and he appears to have had litigations with the Hays of Yester and the Kerrs of Cessford, ancestors of the dukes of Roxburghe, after the middle of the fourteenth century. Sir David Hay, of Yester, pursued him the 20th May, 1474, for maintaining possession of the Castle of Morham, in East Lothian, and it was decided that Dungal should deliver it to Sir William, the Hay of Morham, (evidently Sir William, of Folla), and receive in return the lands of Limplum Barro, and Duncanlau. This arrangement, however, never took place. Dungal's plea may be easily discovered. He was entitled, as a Gifford co-heir, and probably as the second, to the next principal castle and mansion after Yester, and therefore to Moreham,* which, however, it was the interest of the Hays to secure, who accordingly offered him certain lands in exchange for it, and the neighbouring property. Walter Ker, of Coverton, afterwards Cessford, 8th March, 1478, summoned "Dougall Macdowell, of Makarstoun," as a party in a civil suit. Dungal, who was alive in 1498, left at his decease, a son and heir,

ANDREW MACDOWALL, of Mackerston, Yester, Duncanlau, &c. who on the 3rd Feb. 1477, as "son and apparent heir of Dungal Macdowell, of Mackerston," was put in the fee "Baroniarum" of the estates of his family. He *m.* Euphemia Hepburn, daughter of Patrick, then Lord Hailes, but afterwards raised to the dignity of Earl of Bothwell, great grandfather of the notorious James, Earl of Bothwell. This lady he survived; for before the year 1498, he was engaged in another matrimonial affair, which ended untowardly. In that year, Walter Ker, of Cessford, pursues Dongal Macdowel, of Maccarston, "for the payment of a hundred pounds, in ye quhilk Dougall Macdowel was bound, after ye forme of contract of ane indenture maid betwixt him and ye said Walter for non-fulfilling of certaine appunctments after ye forme of ye said indenture." Walter is ordered by the court to prove what costs he had incurred in the matter, "except ye availe of ye marriage of Andro Macdowell, ye son and apperande are to ye said Dougal, quhilk suld haife beine coupleted between him and Elizabeth Ker, eldest daughter to ye said Walter, quhilk sal not be." This is all that has been transmitted of the matter. Andrew had been in possession of the estates as successor to his father, before the 28th May, 1505; for under that date, as laird of Mackerston, he is wit-

* Moreham is contiguous to Yester and was a part indubitably of the old Gifford inheritance.

o a deed upon record. About the close e fifteenth century, it would appear he Macdowels of Mackerston had at- l the height of their grandeur, being proprietors of a great estate, well al- and of baronial rank: but on the 26th 1490, they ceased to possess the baro- n East Lothian, for on that date, An- who, as we have seen, had been put ssession of the fee, alienated these to Patrick, Earl of Bothwell, his father- , who afterwards made them over to ays of Yester.* Andrew Macdowel ued to live down to the 26th August, as appears by a royal charter upon l, but the time of his death has not ascertained. The next heir and chief family, who can be traced, is

OMAS MACDOUGAL, of Mackerston, who hed before and after the middle of the nth century. He is mentioned in the f parliament in 1545. There is every to believe he was the son and heir of w; at least his heir, although it must nitted, that in no legal authority yet is he so designed. Still, however, g militates against the conceived re- ship. He *m.* Janet, daughter and heir lter Scot, of Howfaslet, a distinguished , from whom Lord Napier, the Scots rlstane, and others of note, are des- l, and had three sons and a daughter,

AMES, his heir.
homas.
Richard.
upheme, contracted, in 1561, in mar- riage to Robert Lander, son and heir apparent of Robert Lander, of that ilk.

ade his will at Mackerston, 24th April, wherein he directs his "corps to be l in the queir of Maccerston;" appoints Macdowell, and Thomas Macdowell, sons") executors: and Sir John Ed- one, of that ilk, Gilbert Ker, Andro on and heir of Gilbert Ker, of Prime- ch, &c. their overmen, and enjoins as and Richard to renunce and gif the and of Mackerston "to James, my eld- ne, to remain with the hous," that is, or family of Mackerston. This will onfirmed by the commissaries of Edin- , 27th Feb. 1575. The will contains a nd curious list of his effects and move- as well as of his debts. The only lands d to are those of Mackerston, and nlaw, which latter estate he may have ed with the heiress of Howfaslet, but is no mention of the old family pos- n of Yetholme, Clifton, or the East Lothian properties. He was *s.* by his eldest son,

JAMES MACDOWEL, of Mackerston, who entered into a contract, 10th July, 1572, with Sir John Stuart, of Traequair, relative to the mill of Mackerston, which is witnessed by his brother, Thomas Macdowel. He *d.* before the 20th Feb. 1585, leaving, with a younger son, James, his successor,

THOMAS MACDOWELL, tenth laird of Mackerston, who obtained, 20th February, 1585, a ratification of a tack (there said to have been granted, 23rd Oct. 1583, by Francis, Earl of Bothwell, to "Umquhille James Macdowel, of Mackerston, his airis and assignais, &c." under the description of "Thomas Macdowell, now of Mackairston, sone and aire to ye said Unquhill James Macdougall, his fader." He *m.* Margaret Hume, who survived him. She being declared in a reversion, 24th Nov. 1609, "relict of Umquhill Thomas Macdowell," and dying before 18th December, 1604, left issue,

JAMES, his successor.
WILLIAM (Sir), of whom presently.
Thomas, who, by his wife Prudence, daughter of Henry Fitzwilliam, of Leainton, Lincolnshire, left an only child,
  Barbara, who wedded her cousin, Henry Macdowel, of Mackerston.
George, *d. s. p.*
Robert, of Lintonlaw, who *d.* without issue, 12th July, 1658, when his niece, Barbara, was served heir of *Conquest* in his property.

The eldest son,

JAMES MACDOUGAL, of Mackerston, was served heir in especial of Thomas, his father, 18th Dec. 1604, and on the 23rd October in the same year, was contracted in marriage to Margaret Haitly, eldest daughter of Marion Lumsden, Lady Mellerstain (evidently wife of the Laird of Mellerstain). From any thing yet discovered there was no issue of this marriage, and not very long after, on the 28th January, 1613, the laird desponed the barony of Mackerston and family estate to Sir William Macdowel, his brother-german, and the heirs male of his body; whom failing, to Thomas Macdowel, his brother-german, and the heirs male of his body; and failing, to the younger brothers, George and Robert; upon which conveyance his eldest brother was infeft 4th February, 1613, as

SIR WILLIAM MACDOUGALL, of Mackerston. He *m.* (contract dated 22nd November, 1625) Margaret, daughter of Sir William Scott, of Harden, and dying some time previously to 1657, was *s.* by his son,

HENRY MACDOUGAL, of Mackerston, who *m.* Barbara, daughter and heiress of his

* he Hays thus acquired the whole of Yester, they still continue to enjoy.

uncle, Thomas Macdougal, and left, at his decease, in 1671, with a daughter Barbara, *m.* to William, third Viscount Kilsyth, a son and successor,

THOMAS MACDOUGAL, of Mackerston, who wedded Margaret, eldest daughter of Sir James Innes, bart., of Innes, by Margaret, his wife, daughter of Henry, Lord Ker, eldest son of Robert, first earl of Roxburgh, and left three sons, HENRY, Thomas, and William. The eldest,

HENRY MACDOUGAL, of Mackerston, was served heir in special of his father, 19th May, 1702, and infeft accordingly. He *m.* Ann, daughter of Hugh Scot, of Gala, by Isabel, his wife, daughter of Sir Thomas Ker, of Cavers, and left an only child,

BARBARA MACDOUGAL, of Mackerston, served heir in general to her father, 2d Jan. 1723, and infeft on the 28th June following, in the barony of Mackerston, in terms of the settlement of the estate executed by her father in 1715. This lady wedded Sir George Hay, bart., of Alderstone, who assumed the surname of Macdougall, and had, with a daughter, Ann, *m.* to John Scott, of Gala, a son and successor,

SIR HENRY-HAY MACDOUGALL, baronet, of Mackerston, who *m.* 11th May, 1782, Isabella, daughter of Admiral Sir James Douglas, bart. of Springwood Park, and by her, who died 12th June, 1796, had issue,

- I. GEORGE, who *d.* 15th April, 1795.

- I. ANNA-MARIA, heiress to her father.
- II. Barbara, *d.* unm. at Madeira, 8th July, 1810.
- III. Henrietta.
- IV. Elizabeth.

Sir Henry *d.* 13th April, 1825, and was succeeded in the barony of Mackerston by his eldest daughter, ANNA-MARIA, the present Lady MACDOUGAL-BRISBANE.

*Arms*—Of MACDOUGAL. Az. a lion ramp. arg. crowned with an antique crown, or, armed and langued gu. within a border of the second, charged with six fraisers of the first.

*Crest*—A lion issuing guardant ppr. holding in his dexter paw a cross crosslet, fitchee gu.

*Motto*—Fear God.

*Estates*—In Roxburghshire.

*Seat*—Mackerston.

## Hay, of Alderston.

This family sprang originally from the HAYS of Falla or Limplum, who may be regarded as the eldest collateral branch of the noble house of Tweeddale.

SIR WILLIAM HAY, of Locherwort and Yester, who lived early in the fifteenth century, left, by Alicia Hay his wife, two sons, viz.

- I. DAVID (Sir), who inherited Yester,* and was ancestor of the Lords Hay, of Yester, and of the Earls and Marquesses of Tweeddale.
- II. EDMUND, founder of the branches of Falla and Limplum.

The younger son,

EDMUND HAY, of Falla and Limplum, is frequently to be traced upon record. He had, 12th August, 1429, a grant from Sir David Hay, of Yester, of the lands of Thalek (Falla), in the barony of Oliver Castle and county of Peebles, wherein he is designed "Brother German of Sir David." He had also a charter, 4th February, 1438-9, from Isabella de Forresta or Forrester, with consent of James de Wedeele, her son, of half of the lands of Wandrews (part of Duncanlaw), and another, 15th May, 1439 under the discretion of "Edmund Hay, of Falla," of Kyppling or part of Limplum, and both were confirmed by a royal charter, dated 16th November, 1439. A charter, 23rd February, 1449, by "Alicia Hay, *relict* of the deceased William Hay, of Yester, knt. to God and the altar of Saint Mary, in the collegiate church of St. Bothans or Yester, is witnessed 'Edmundo de Haya de Lim-

* The genealogists of Scotland, Douglas, Wood, and Crawfurd, are manifestly in error regarding the pedigree of the Hays, of Yester. They affirm that Sir William Hay married, *first*, Johanna Gifford, eldest daughter and co-heir of Sir Hew Gifford, of Yester, and by that lady was father of SIR DAVID; and that EDMUND was the offspring of a second marriage with Alicia Hay. And furthermore, they make Sir William himself the son of Sir Thomas Hay, of Locherwort, by Christian, sister of Cardinal Wardlaw. But that they are quite incorrect is evident, from an act of parliament in 1661 narrating various ancient writs, and among others the following: "A confirmation granted be Johanna Hay, SPOUSE, of umquhill SIR THOMAS HAY, of Louchquerant, eldest daughter and one of the airs of umquhill Hew Giffart. Domini de Yester WILLIAM HAY, of *Louchguerwort*, her sonne and air, &c. of certain infeftments, &c. Sasine granted be Johanna Gifford *in her lawful viductis* to Sir Robert Maitland, knt. of the lands of Lettington, conform to the charter granted be the said Hew to the said umquhill Sir Robert Maitland, &c. dated at Haddington, first Decembris, 1399."

Hence, so far from Sir William Hay having espoused Johanna Gifford, she was the wife of a totally different person, and indeed he could not have done so, the lady being his mother; neither did Johanna, as they pretend, predecease her lord of Locherwort to make room for Alicia Hay, for she is now proved to have survived him. Again, not content with marrying Johanna to her son Sir William, instead of Sir Thomas, his father,

plum, *filio meo,'*" and it also bears especial mention of Sir David Hay, of Yester, as the son of Alicia. The name of Edmund's wife was Annabella, according to Father Hay, a distinguished antiquarian and descendant of the family, sister of the aspiring but unfortunate Thomas Boyd, Earl of Arran. "Edmund de la Haye, of Fallow, and Annabell *his wife*, had a grant, 9th December, 1449, of the marriage of William Maxwell, son and heir of the deceased William Maxwell, of Teyling." Edmund left a son and heir,

SIR WILLIAM HAY, of Tallo and Limplum. This laird pursued, 13th October, 1466, Sir David Hay, of Yester, "for withholding from him the lands of Morham, called Boyd's quarter and Limplum," and the lords' auditors of parliament decided that he should possess these lands in terms of the tack made, "be Robert Lord Boyde to umquhile Edmond ye Hay, of Tallo, and his aieris ye farder of ye saide Wilzaume." It may be here observed, that beside Johanna and Euphemia Gifford, who have been noticed, there were two other co-heirs of Gifford, one of whom is stated to have married Robert Boyd, of Kilmarnock, which accounts for the latter having had a quarter of Morham, called "Boyd's Quarter," and an interest in the rest of the Gifford succession, which not being entailed descended at common law to the four daughters, as heirs portioners. The fourth and remaining sister and co-heir married Eustace Maxwell, the marriage of whose son and heir, William, as has been shewn was granted in 1449 to Edmund Hay, of Tallo. Sir William died previously to 16th October, 1479, when Margaret Mowbray "ye spouse of umquhill Sir William ye Hay, of Tallo, knt," pursues Anabile Boid (in all probability his mother-in-law) and Gawan Creichton, for ejecting herself and servants from the lands of Limplum, and eating and destroying her corn and meadows, and obtained a decision in her favour. Sir William Hay was *s.* by his son,

WILLIAM HAY, of Tallo and Limplum, who had been infeft into the latter estate prior to the 23rd October, 1490. His wife was Margaret Cockburn, whom Father Hay states to have been of the Cockburns of Henderland. The next chief of the family,

WILLIAM HAY, of Tallo, was probably the son and heir of that marriage. He figures as head upon record in 1528, when, on the 3rd April in that year, George Hay, of Menziane, brought an action before the official of St. Andrews against "an honourable man, William Hay, the laird of Tallo." This chief wedded Janet Spottiswoode, who, according to Father Hay, was daughter of the Laird of Spottiswoode, and had issue,

JOHN, of Tallo, his successor, whose line it is not requisite to trace further, our object being confined to the descendants of his youngest brother, WILLIAM. It may be interesting however to state that he married Janet Hepburn, and had two sons, JOHN and William; JOHN was the unfortunate person who, allied in blood to the Hepburns and their chief the Earl of Bothwell, was employed by that unprincipled nobleman as a tool in the perpetration of the murder of Darnley, and was the person who lighted the match which caused the explosion. His death in 1568, before that of his father and grandfather, saved the estates from the penalties of his treason, and the succession eventually opened to his younger brother, WILLIAM, who, in 1586, is designed "William Hay, of Lumplum, son and air of umquhill John Hay, of Tallo." Not long after this the principal branch lost their estates, and gradually dwindling away, fell into such obscurity that no trace of them in the male line can be discovered.

Edmund, advocate, who died 12th July, 1589, apparently without issue. His

---

who was her real husband, they have had the cruelty to deprive the former of his genuine parent altogether, and to substitute in her place one Catherine Wardlaw, sister of a cardinal, but whatever lustre the reflected dignity of his eminence might have shed upon the family of Hay, of Yester, this Catherine was not only an utter stranger to them, but there is every reason to believe was a mere nonentity. Both Edmund and his eldest brother David therefore were sprung from their grandmother Johanna, eldest daughter and co-heir of Sir Hew Gifford, of Yester, from the ancient Norman family of that name, which produced the noted magician,† and possessed the baronies of Yester, Morham, and Duncanlaw, in East Lothian and Tayling and Poldame, in the county of Perth and Forfar. It was by means of this alliance that the Hays, of Locherwart and Oliver Castle, acquired part of Yester, and it is not a little remarkable that by the marriage of Sir George Hay Macdougall, bart. (descended of the above Edmund), in the last century, with the heiress of Makdougal, of Makerston, the blood of the two sisters became united, as the latter family were lineal heirs of Euphemia Giffard, younger sister of Johanna, and a co-heir in the same inheritance.

† Every one is acquainted with this chief of the house of Gifford since the appearance of Marmion. Fordun thus speaks of him in noting his death in 1267: "Hugo Gifford, de Yester, moritur cujus castrum vel saltem caveam et dongionem arte demoniscula antiquæ relationes fuerunt fabricatas," &c. vol. ii. p. 105.

will is dated 5th August, 1588. In it he mentions his first wife, Agnes Smith, and constitutes his second wife, Isabel Abernethie, "his onlie executrix." He leaves to William Hay, of Wynden, (his brother), and failing him to Mr. William Hay, son of the latter, the following articles: "ane stand of his best claithing, to wit; ane doublet, ane pair of hois, ane pair of brekes, ane coit, cloik and gowne; to wit, ane furrit gowne of chamlot of silk wyt ye second pece, ye last saltful of silver, and after my wyffis deceis my cupbaird of warmet tree."

WILLIAM.

Margaret, m. to Robert Lyle, of Slampelt (marriage contract dated 7th March, 1540).

The youngest son,

WILLIAM HAY, of Wyndane and Barra, figures with his eldest brother John, of Tallo, in a judicial proceeding, 26th January, 1569. He died 18th January, 1597, leaving issue by his wife, Margaret Hay, daughter of the Laird of Monkton.

I. WILLIAM (Mr.), advocate, his heir.
II. JOHN (Sir), heir to his brother.
III. George, witness to his father's will.

The eldest son and heir,

MR. WILLIAM HAY, of Barra, is designed, in a judicial entry in 1605, "now portioner of Barra," and heir of the late William Hay, "portioner of Barra, his father." The obituary of Robert Boyd, of Trockrig, states that Mr. William Hay de Barro, whom it also makes commissary of Glasgow, died at the beginning of May, 1618, subsequent to which Barra and the male representation appear to have devolved upon his brother,

SIR JOHN HAY, of Barra and Lauds, lord clerk register, who was a lawyer, and man of abilities, and sufficiently distinguished in the turbulent times in which he lived. While very young he was employed by the city of Edinburgh to welcome *King* JAMES I. at the Westport, in the name of the town, which commission he executed in an elegant oration, still preserved in a work called the "Muse's Welcome." He became an ordinary senator of the college of justice, and lord of the council and exchequer: and after the death of Sir John Hamilton, knt. of Magdalens, was preferred (8th January, 1633) to be LORD REGISTER. He had received the honour of knighthood from *King* CHARLES I. 9th March, 1632. He was one of Balmerino's assizers, and things becoming troublesome in 1641, he resigned all his offices into the king's hands. His dismission is signed the 17th July, 1641. He was subsequently accused of treason, sent to the castle of Edinburgh, tried by the estates, and ultimately acquitted. After these events Sir John remained quiet until Montrose came south, when he joined him, and was taken prisoner at the battle of Philiphaugh, when his life was placed in jeopardy, but a bribe to the Earl of Lanark averted the danger. He subsequently sunk into repose and comparative obscurity,* and died at Dudingstone 20th November, 1654. Sir John m. first, 16th May, 1602, Marion Johnston, daughter of a younger son of Johnston, of Kewby, and by that lady, who died in August, 1621, he had issue,

I. HENRY (Sir), b. 8th April, 1603, admitted advocate in 1637, was one of the commissaries of Edinburgh. He m. Helen, daughter of Beaton, of Creich, and had three sons and two daughters.
II. William (Mr.), of Aberlady, b. 9th November, 1604; m. Helen, daughter of Sir John Sinclair, of Stevenson, and had two sons, John and Henry. His line is supposed to be now EXTINCT.
III. John (Mr.), baptized 11th October, 1612.
IV. Alexander (Mr.), bapt. 27th February, 1614.
V. James, bapt. 23rd November, 1617.
VI. David, bapt. 23rd November, 1619.

I. Janet, b. 7th May, 1607; m. to Mr. John Edmonstone.
II. Margaret.
III. Helen, bapt. 23rd October, 1610.
IV. Marion, bapt. 4th February, 1621.

He m. secondly, Rebecca, daughter of Alexander Thomson, of Dudingstone, advocate, and by her, who died 20th October, 1632, had

I. Andrew, a Catholic priest, b. 24th March, and baptized the following day, 1623. Of this Andrew, Father Hay gives a singular account. He says that he was called "Grave Andrew" by CHARLES II. and became "a charitable assistant to my Lady Drummond, relict of the conservator with whom it was thought he was married," and gained so much influence over her that she bequeathed him her whole estate. Andrew Hay, who suffered severely during the spoliation of the Catholics by the mob, eventually retired to the Scotch seminary at Paris, where he lost his sight, and died 20th November, 1702.
II. THOMAS, ancestor of the HAYS, of ALDERSTONE, of whom presently.
III. George, bapt. 29th March, 1629;

* This account of the Lord Register is from Father Hay's Memoirs in the Advocates' Library. Father Hay was his grandson.

*m.* Jean, daughter of Sir Henry Spottiswoode, gentleman of the privy chamber, and was father of

RICHARD, commonly called "Father Hay," an antiquarian of great research, as is proved by his collection in the Advocates' Library. He was born at Edinburgh in 1661, and according to his own expression "thrust" into the Scots college in France, in 1673 or 1674. He quitted France in 1686, for the purpose of establishing a society of Canons Regulars in Scotland, where he remained until the revolution. Returning to France, he was made prior of Essours 11th August, 1692, and of Bernicourt 1st August, 1694.

iv. Patrick.

i. Margaret, bapt. 20th June, 1624; *m.* to John Stewart, of Kettleston, son of Sir Lewis Stewart, knt. of Kirkhill.

ii. Anna, bapt. 2nd November, 1626; *m.* to David Aikenhead.

iii. Rebecca, baptized 20th January, 1629.

second son of the second marriage of John Hay, the lord clerk register,

I. THOMAS HAY, of Hermistone, one of clerks of the privy council and session, also styled of Alderstone, to which he ars to have had a personal right, although it was not feudalized till in the person of John Hay, of Alderstone, his son. Anna, daughter of Sir John Gibson, of Pentland, and had issue,

i. JOHN (Sir), his heir.

ii. Andrew, a captain of dragoons, appears to have died *s. p.*

iii. Alexander, of Huntingdon, sheriff-depute of Haddingtonshire, and died at Edinburgh 28th March, 1745, leaving, with other issue, a son, Thomas, Lord Huntingdon, a lord of session.

iv. Thomas, of Mordington, *m.* Jean Renton, of Lammerton, and *d.* without issue in December, 1752, at an advanced age, having settled his estate on his nephews, George-Hay Macdougal, of Mackerston, and Thomas Hay, of Huntingdon.

v. William, a merchant engaged in the enterprize to Darien; died at Jamaica, leaving a son, William, a minor in 1753.

i. Jean, *m.* to Mark Learmouth, advocate.

ii. Margaret.

Thomas Hay *d.* in 1697, and was *s.* by his son,

SIR JOHN HAY, of Hermeston, who was created a BARONET in 1703. He *m.* Catherine, daughter of Sir George Suttie, bart. of Balgone, and had issue,

i. THOMAS (Sir), his heir.

ii. GEORGE (Sir), successor to his brother.

i. Anna.

ii. Marion.

iii. Catherine.

Sir John *d.* in 1706, and was *s.* by his son,

SIR THOMAS HAY, second bart. of Alderstone, captain of dragoons, who *m.* first, in 1724, Eleanor, daughter of Sir Hew Dalrymple, bart. president of the court of session; secondly, in 1740, Frances, Lady Byron, daughter of William Lord Berkeley, of Stratton; and thirdly, in 1761, Margaret, daughter of John Don, esq. but by none of them had he issue. Dying at Alderstone, 26th November, 1769, Sir Thomas was *s.* by his brother,

SIR GEORGE HAY, third bart. of Alderstone, who wedded, as stated in the MACDOUGALL family, the HEIRESS of that house.

## BLANCHARD, OF GRIMSARGH HALL.

BLANCHARD, JAMES, esq. of Grimsargh Hall, in the county of Lancaster, *b.* December, 1774, *m.* 12th July, 1804, Anne, daughter of Richard Butler, esq. of ington Hall, in the same shire, and has issue,

JOHN, *b.* 22nd September, 1807, captain of the 1st regiment Royal Lancashire militia.

Mr. Blanchard, who *s.* his father 17th March, 1823, is an acting magistrate for ashire.

## Lineage.

George Blanchard, of Alston, landed proprietor and yeoman as were his predecessors for many generations, was father of

Edward Blanchard, of Alston, who *m.* Jane Hothersall, of Hothersall, and had one son and one daughter, viz.

George,

Anne, *m.* to Alexander Gregson, gent. of Salmesbury.

Mr. Blanchard *d.* in 1752, and was *s.* by his son,

George Blanchard, of Alston, *b.* 4th of June, 1742, who *m.* Miss Margaret Smith, of Forton, in Lancashire, and by her, who *d.* in 1776, had issue,

James, his heir.

Elizabeth, *m.* to Evan Richard Gerrard, esq. of Haighton, in Lancashire.

Ann, *m.* to James Sidgreaves, esq. of Goosmargh, Lancashire.

He *d.* 17th March, 1823, and was *s.* by his son, the present James Blanchard, esq. of Grimsargh Hall.

*Arms*—Gu. a chev. or, between in chief two bezants, and in base a griffin's head erased of the second.

*Crest*—On a chapeau, an arm embowed, clad in armour, holding a battle axe.

*Estates*—In Alston and Grimsargh, Lancashire, descended from the late George Blanchard; with property in Preston, Fulwood, Haighton, Whittingham, and Goosnargh, purchased by the present possessor. Estates in Plessington and Blanchard obtained by marriage.

*Seat*—Grimsargh Hall, Lancashire.

# CHADWICK, OF MAVESYN-RIDWARE.

CHADWICK, HUGO-MALVEYSIN, esq., of Mavesyn-Ridware, in the county of Stafford, and of Healey, Lancashire, *b.* 28th November, 1793, *m.* in June, 1826, Eliza-Catherine, youngest daughter of the late Lieutenant-General Chapman, of Tainfield House, Somersetshire, and sister of Sir Stephen Remnant Chapman, K.C.H. Governor of Bermuda, and has two daughters, namely,

Elizabeth-Catherine.
Laura-Isabella-Louisa.

Mr. Chadwick succeeded his father 29th July, 1829.

## Lineage.

The representation and lands of the MALVEYSINS, being now in the family of CHADWICK, we shall commence with that ancient family. "For the origin of the name and family of Malvoisin," says Shaw, in his History of Staffordshire, "we must refer to the puissant host of our Norman conqueror, to the splendid genealogies of the ancient French nobility, and the formidable works of war in remote ages of chivalry and romance. Our old historians inform us, that when a besieging army erected a tower or castle near the place besieged, such castle was called, in French, a *malvoisin*; signifying that it was a *dangerous neighbour* to the enemy, because it threatened to cut him off from all possibility of relief. In the northern but fruitful district of the Isle of France, situate in the confines of the Gastinois, and not very far from the banks of the Seine, some time stood one of these awful bulwarks, from which it is presumed the neighbouring and illustrious Lords of Rosny first assumed the name of Malvoisin; a name standing proudly conspicuous in the ancient French records of feudal grandeur, and which may be traced amongst the nations of Europe, in succeeding ages, by various acts of munificent piety and romantic valour. Of this family was Sampson Mauveisin, Archbishop of Rheims, and the renowned Sir Guy Mauvoisin, who fought under the banner of St. Louis against the Saracens of Egypt; but the head of this house, in the eleventh century, was that venerable chief Raoul Mauvoisin, surnamed Le Barbu, living, in 1080, at the seigniory of Rosny, near the city of Mantes, and ranking amongst the principal seigniors of the county. The names of his sons, *Robert* and *Hugo*, and his grandson, *William*, who fell in battle, may remind us of the same favourite and distinguished names, so familiar in the pedigree of our Anglo-Norman line at Ridware; and it is natural to expect that some individual of this powerful race would, on that memorable day when the Normans invaded England, be ambitious to draw his sword at the call of Duke William, his neighbour, and probably his feudal lord; accordingly, it appears, by the roll of Battle Abbey, that Malvesyn was one of those 'two hundred and sixty knights, famous in the Conqueror's army,' who fought in his cause at Hastings, and by whose means he won the crown of England, the name being thus recorded among the rest of those bold adventurers—

'Danvey et Devesyn,
Malure et Malvesyn.'

Having braved all the dangers, and, therefore, having a right to share the spoils of victory, Malvesyn would be eager to fix his residence on some of the conquered lands; and we are assured, by uniform tradition, that his valour was rewarded with a grant of the lordship of Rideware; which was held, probably by this Norman knight, under the Montgomeries, Norman Earls of Shrewsbury, by the knightly tenure of bearing arms against the Welsh. But there were other lands of which he got possession, seemingly at the same early period, and which were likewise held under the same barony, by the same military service; amongst which was the lordship of Berewicke (*juxta* Allingham), in Shropshire; and as the leading branch of this family gave their name to the seigniory of *Mauvesyn Rosny*, in France, so these two younger branches communicated the same name to their respective lordships of *Mauvesyn Ridware* and *Mauvesyn Berwick*, in England; which became their principal places of abode, and where they long continued to flourish, in the days of our Henrys and the Edwards, a knightly gallant race in the age of gallantry; foremost, like their Norman kindred, in deeds of arms and works of piety. Indeed, these Lords of Rideware and Berewicke may be said to have lived in arms; each stationed near the borders of Wales, and holding his domains under the same Baron Marcher, by the hardy tenure of border service, they would find it no easy task to defend what their common ancestor had won by the sword."

HENRY MALVEYSIN, son probably of the Norman, must have been born in the Conqueror's reign, being of sufficient age in the year 1100 to attest the foundation grant of William Fitzalan to the Abbey of Haghmon, in Shropshire. He is presumed to have been father of

HUGO DE MALVEYSIN, of Rideware, living in the times of HENRY I. and STEPHEN. He died early in the succeeding reign, and was buried, according to tradition, under an arch in the north wall of his manorial church, where his bones, stone coffin, and effigy still remain. He left issue,

I. HUGO, who is supposed to have put on the cowl and to have died a monk.
II. WILLIAM (Sir), his father's heir.
III. Hugo, first parson of Rideware church.

The second son,

SIR WILLIAM MALVEYSIN, Lord of Rideware in the reigns of HENRY II., RICHARD, and JOHN, seems to have had three sons and one daughter, viz.

I. HUGO, of whom nothing is known.

II. HENRY, successor to his father.

III. William, Rector of Rideware Mauveysyn. There is *no proof* that this William was the William Malvoisin, Bishop of Glasgow, translated thence to St. Andrew's, 4th JOHN, holding a council at Perth, to promote a crusade, in the 13th of the same reign, attending a grand council at Rome four years after this, and dying *temp.* HENRY III. after having governed his church with great wisdom and felicity.

I. Sarah, *m.* to Sir William de Kileby, of Kileby, in Leicestershire.

Sir William was succeeded by his son,

SIR HENRY MALVEYSIN, kt., Lord of Rideware, living in the reigns of RICHARD I. JOHN, and HENRY III. who also possessed lands in Great Casterton, in the county of Rutland. He *m.* a lady named Matilda, and, dying before the 42nd of HENRY III, was succeeded by his son,

SIR ROBERT MALVEYSIN, of Rideware-Malveysin and Great Casterton, whom, in the 40th HENRY III. we find recorded by the name of "*Rob'tus de Redware*," amongst those gentry of Staffordshire who were possessed of one knight's fee, or more, but were not created knights; he then compounding, for half a merk, to have respite from knighthood. But though he was not "miles gladio cinctus," an honour which became a burthen to the military tenants, yet, being possessed of an entire knight's fee, he was by hereditary succession a knight by tenure, bound to perform knight's service, by serving, in the wars, well arrayed, and furnished in all points.

As far as it can be judged from deeds, S. D. Sir Robert died before 51 Henry III. in those days when much blood was spilled in Wales, and in the barons' wars. He left a son, Henry, Lord of Rideware-Mavesyn; and, as I take it, a second son, Roger, who had lands in Rideware-Mavesyn in 1291 and 1306; in which he was succeeded by his son William, living in 1337, who had a son John, not named after 1399.

SIR HENRY MALVEYSIN, knt. (the croisader), eldest son and heir of Sir Robert, "fil & here's Roberti Malveisin," lived in the reigns of Henry III. Edward I. and Edward II. and was Lord of Rideware-Mauveysyn; but being under age at his father's death, he and his lands there were, for a time, under the wardship of Sir John Fitz-Alan.

Sir Henry began his career at a turbulent period, when the rebellious barons were up in arms, and when Fitz-Alan, with whom he was bound to serve, fought alternately for Leicester and the King. By the tenure of his lands, also, he must have toiled amongst the mountains of Wales when Llewellyn was subdued. That he was a knight in the reign of Edward I. using three bendlets as his seal of arms, and that he was a knight-croisader, who bore in battle three bendlets on his shield, in the Scottish wars, and in a glorious croisade, is proved by record and by his monumental effigy. His eldest son and heir,

SIR ROBERT MALVEYSIN, knt. (the Forester) "filius p'mogenitus," lived in the reigns of Edward I. II. and III. and was Lord of Rideware-Malveysin and Shipley, having some manorial rights, as well as lands in Great Casterton and Exton, and lands also in Parva Rideware, Colton, Rugeley, Handsacre, and Heynton. By his second wife, a daughter of Sir John de Freford, he had several children, and was succeeded by his third son,

THOMAS MAUVEYSIN, the two elder sons having predeceased their father, *s. p.* This Thomas was Lord of Rideware-Mauveysin in the reign of Edward III. but was not a knight. He was succeeded by his only son and heir,

SIR ROBERT MAUVEYSIN, knt. Lord of Rideware-Mauveysin and Shippeley, who lived in the reigns of Edward III. Richard II. and the beginning of Henry IV. Temp. Richard II. this Robert alienated considerable lands, by deed of gift, to his uncle, Rese Mauveysin, on payment of one red rose annually. It does not appear for what purpose this was done, though the lands of Bragge Casterton are never after mentioned in the Mauveysin Rideware deeds. Sir Robert was thrice appointed sheriff for the county.

"In relating the fatal contest (says Shaw) between Mauveysin and his neighbour Handsacre, it must not be forgot that great animosities are said to have prevailed in former times between the inhabitants of the parts lying north and south of the Trent; but it was in a dispute concerning the privileges of their adjoining royalties that the seeds of discord seem to have been sown; which being encouraged by the fierce manners of a barbarous age, the rancour of party, and the fury of rebellion, was to be terminated only by fire and sword, bloodshed and death. We find that in 5 Richard II. Sir Robert Mauveysin leased to one John Hamond, fisherman, for life, all that part of his fishery in the Trent called Bryggewatir, between Hondsacredom and Oxenholme Pole, at the annual rent of 12*s.* with liberty to use all sorts of nets, except a coddenet. But that this was any annoyance, or gave any umbrage to Handsacre does not appear, though it is likely the fisherman and uiller might disagree; and Robert Mull- of this very mill, the Briggemuln, ap- s afterwards at the Court of Rideware veysin. The middle of the *southern* m, on which this mill and dam were si- d, was and is, by the testimony of the t inhabitants of Mavesyn Ridware, and ancient and accustomed perambula- , the true boundaries of the two parishes royalties; such part, therefore, of the nises, whether mill, dam, or floodgates, ojected beyond the middle of the stream, abut upon the manor of Ridware Mave- But a mill and fishery were in those days necessary appendages of such manors; their privileges in such a situation were y to affect in some degrees the two ad- ng royalties. Accordingly, it appears a dispute arose, which ended in an open are; for in 1 HENRY IV. there was a nt affray, when Malveysin's adherents t and destroyed the mill; Lawrence de leley, one of Handsacre's people, being in the tumult.

at it seems their animosity was mutually med by civil war and the great national e. This affray having happened about ime when Henry of Bolingbroke landed ngland to claim the crown, in whose ne came Malveysin's superior, Fitz- a, earl of Arundel,—it is likely, there- that Sir Robert Malveysin, having d to join HENRY, thought this a favour- moment for attacking Handsacre, who ured the opposite side; and though the r was obliged to give way after the ruin s party, when HENRY IV. mounted the ne, yet he gladly obeyed the first signal volt, confident of success in the cause of spur.

e oldest account we have seen of this ily feud, is one in Latin, in the British eum, from which the following is taken: The river Trent flows with a clear stream, Mavesin-Ridware, so called because on orthern bank is situated the ancient in- tance of the Malveysins. The inhabi- s say that a jealousy subsisting between amilies of Mavesin and Handsacre, it so pened when HENRY IV. had obtained the m of England from RICHARD II. and it rumoured that Percy, earl of Northum- and, was in arms against the King, Man- in had ridden forth, with six or seven of vassals, on the part of King HENRY; it nced also, that Handsacre, who espoused opposite cause, had left home the same with an equal number of attendants, to Percy. These rivals met, and, in- ed with rage, rushed furiously to bat-

Handsacre was slain; and the victorious lveysin, proud of his conquest, marching ward to Shrewsbury, there lost his life, ting valiantly for the King. Thus fell Sir Robert Malveysin, July 22nd, 1403, bleeding in his sovereign's cause, and breath- ing in his last efforts the undaunted spirit of his Norman ancestors. *Thus conquering fell the last representative of an ancient va- liant race*, which first entered England in arms, ranged under the Conqueror's banner; and, after toiling in the paths of glory for more than three centuries, honourably fin- ished its career on the field of victory. His body being conveyed to Maveysin-Ridware, was there interred, in the cemetry of his an- cestors, and over it was erected an altar- tomb in the middle of the chapel, decorated with his effigy, with a suitable inscription, which still remains.

By his wife Johanna, (presumed to be) a daughter of Chetwynd, of Ingestrie, he left two daughters, Elizabeth, aged fourteen years, and Margaret, aged eleven years. The younger became the wife of Sir William Handsacre, knt. (descended from the kings of Scotland), "to whom she brought her purparty, as a recompense for the death of his father, slain by hers." "And what a pic- ture is this of the manners of the age!" Thus joyfully terminated an unhappy feud, in a manner which might have been no less agreeable to the dead than it was to the liv- ing; for Sir Robert might have exclaimed to the vanquished Handsacre:

> "This earth which bears the dead,
> Bears not alive a better gentleman."

And we shall find hereafter that the repre- sentatives of these once rival houses were united by marriage a second time.

ELIZABETH MALVEYSIN, the eldest daugh- ter, espoused first, in 18th RICHARD II. Roger, the son and heir of Sir William de Chetwynd, of Ingestrie, knt. (by Alina St. Paul, his wife); but this Roger died soon after, without issue; when his widow married Sir John Cawarden, knt. of an ancient Che- shire family, and they had, with other issue, a son,

JOHN CAWARDEN, esq. who lived in the reign of HENRY VI. and EDWARD IV. and succeeded to his mother's lands at Mauvey- syn-Rydeware, being also lord of Shipley, and having other lands in Pipe Rideware and Haynton. He married Katharine, the daughter of Sir John Gresley, of Drakelow and Colton, knt. of the Bath, by Mary, his wife, dau. of Sir Thomas Clarell. This lady predeceased her husband, leaving issue, and he wedded secondly Margaret, dau. of Sir William Boteler, knt. by whom he had no children. He died 7th July, fifteenth ED- WARD IV. and was s. by his son,

JOHN CAWARDEN, esq. who was of age in 17th EDWARD IV. He married Elizabeth, dau. of John Massey, esq. of Grafton, in the county of Chester, and they had issue, seven children, viz. Robert, his heir, who is designated "*son of John, son of John, son of Elizabeth Mavesyn,*" two other sons, and four daughters. Dying on the Feast of the Pentecost, 2nd RICHARD III. he was *s.* by his son,

ROBERT CAWARDEN, esq. "*father of Thomas, and grandfather of David.*" He was born in 12 EDWARD IV. and, being a minor at his father's death, became the ward of his mother. He *m.* Eleonora, the daughter of Sir John Bagot, of Blithefield, knt. and had issue several children. The eldest son,

THOMAS CAWARDEN, esq. succeeded his father in Mavesyn-Ridware, and had, in 33 HENRY VIII. a grant of Abbey lands. He *m.* Elizabeth the dau. of Thomas Purefoy, gent. by whom he had three sons, viz.

I. David.
II. Richard, living 1st and 2nd PHILIP and MARY.
III. Thomas (Sir) who was knighted by the king at the memorable siege of Boulogne, in France, in 36th HENRY VIII. This Sir Thomas married Bridget, the eldest daughter and co-heir of Arthur Plantagenet, Viscount Lisle, natural son of King EDWARD IV. by Lady Elizabeth Lucy, and therefore she bore the royal arms, with a due difference.

The eldest son,

DAVID CAWARDEN, esq. of Mavesyn, Ridware, *s.* his father. He married about 2nd Edward VI. Maude, dau. of his kinsman, William Westcote, esq. of Handsacre, (descended, through the female line, from the family of Handsacre), by whom he had issue, with other children,

THOMAS CAWARDEN, esq. of Mauveysin-Ridware, which he held under Queen ELIZABETH, by knight's service, as of her manor of Oswestry. He was allied in blood as well to Sir William Handsacre as to Sir Robert Malveysin, those once rival houses having been united in marriage a second time, in the persons of his father and mother. By Anne, his wife, who *m.* secondly Henry Burwey, gent. he left at his decease, in 1592, four surviving daughters and co-heirs, viz.

I. ELIZABETH, *b.* in 1577, married Gerard Stanley, of Harlaston, and had, with three sons, who all *d. s. p.* one dau. Anne, the wife of William Pargiter, whose descendant, Philip Pargiter, bequeathed, in the year 1773, his property in Maveysyn-Ridware, to the late Mr. Cobb, of Lichfield.
II. MAUD, *b.* in 1578, *m.* to the Rev. John Langton, rector of Mavesyn-Ridware.
III. JOYCE, *b.* in 1579, the wife of JOHN CHADWICKE, esq. of whom presently.
IV. MARY, *b.* in 1588, married to Henry Sewal, esq. mayor of Coventry.

The third daughter,

JOYCE CAWARDEN, *m.* first, in 1594, John Chadwicke, esq. who in her right became possessed of the ancient manor hall, with five parts in the right of the manor of Mavesyn-Ridware, and the whole of the fishery; and secondly, John Birkenhead, gent. of Burton-upon-Trent. By the first husband, the heiress of Mavesyn-Ridware, left, *inter-alios*, a son and successor,

LEWIS CHADWICKE, esq. of Mavesyn-Ridware, *b.* in 1596, who also possessed lands in Lichfield and Stafford, and at Edingale, in Derbyshire. At the breaking out of the civil wars, he took up arms in the service of the Parliament, being lieu.-colonel of horse at the battle of Stafford, in 1642, of which place he became governor, and was president of the Committee of Sequestration there, being one who signed the order for the demolition of the castle. In 1644, he was on the Committee at Stafford, with Basil Fielding, earl of Denbigh, by whom he was appointed governor of Caverswall Castle, and afterwards to the command of the garrison at Biddulph House. We find him at Uxbridge during the treaty for peace, whence Lord Denbigh granted him a pass through his guard to London, on 21st February, the very day preceding that on which the treaty was broken off; after which we hear no more of him in the wars. He was, however, afterwards in possession of St. Lucia, in the West Indies, by purchase, and was commonly styled Governor thereof; having, on the 20th November, 1650, a grant of the whole of the island, from John Hay, earl of Carlisle, to whom it had been given by CHARLES I. Colonel Chadwicke *m.* Mary, dau. and heir of Anthony Bagot, esq. of Colton, (second son of Richard Bagot, of Blithfield, esq.) by Katharine, his wife, dau. and co-heir of Michael Lowe, esq. of Tynemore,* and, dying in 1655, left an only surviving daughter and heiress,

KATHARINE CHADWICKE, of Mavesyn-Ridware, born about the year 1620, who *m.* first JOHN CHADWICKE, esq. of Healey; secondly, in 1670, Jonathan Chadwicke, esq. of Chadwicke; and thirdly, George Halstead, esq. of Manchester, where she *d.* in June, 1697, and was buried in the south aisle of the collegiate church. By her first husband only, Mr. Chadwicke, of Healey, a staunch Parliamentarian, the heiress of Mavesyn-Ridware, had issue, viz. five sons and three daughters,

I. CHARLES, heir.
II. John, bapt. at Ridware, 28th March, 1638, M. A. Emanuel College, Cambridge, Vicar of Darenth, Longfield, and Sutton at Hone, in Kent, *m.* a

* By Margaret Biddulph, his wife.

lady named Mary, and dying, in 1705, left issue,

1. CHARLES, who *d.* unm.
2. Edward, who *d. s. p.*
3. Robert, captain of the Launceston man-of-war, in 1717, *m.* at Mongeham, in Kent, 28th July, 1713, Mary, widow of Captain Wright, R. N. and second dau. and heir of Nordash Raud, esq. of Stone Hall: by this lady he left two daughters, his co-heirs, viz.

MARY, on whom the Mongeham estate was entailed. She *m.* in London, William Morrice, esq. (See family of MORRICE, of BETSHANGER).

URSULA, *m.* to James Fortrage, esq. of Wombwell Hall, in Kent, and *d. s. p.*

1. Mary, *m.* to Mr. Maud.

III. Jordan, of Oldham, *b.* at Nottingham, in 1640, *m.* a dau. of —— Ingham, of Cleggswood, and widow of — Dearden, gent. of Whitfield. By her he left at his decease, in 1728, two sons,

1. John, *b.* in 1689, *m.* Mary Buckley, and had two sons, John, bap. in 1734, who left no male issue; and James, of Saddleworth, who *d. s. p.*
2. Richard, *b.* in 1698, and died in 1754. He *m.* first Mrs. Rachael Gartside, of Oldham, by whom he had an only son, Lewis, who left issue; and secondly to Miss Hopwood, of Rhodes Green, cousin of Robert Hopwood, esq. of Hopwood, but by her had no issue.

IV. Lewis, of Whitworth, *b.* at Nottingham, in 1641, who *m.* a dau. of —— Birch, of Underwood, and had one son, Lewis, A.M. who died unm. and Catherine, *m.* first to —— Kershaw, esq. and secondly to —— Yeomans, gent. of Gloucestershire.

V. Robert, *d.* unm.

I. Catherine, *d.* in 1668, unm.

II. Alice, *b.* in 1648.

III. Mary, *m.* to Robert Illingworth, esq. of Huntsbank, near Manchester.

[th]e eldest son,

[C]HARLES CHADWICK, esq. of Healey and [Rid]ware, bapt. 6th March, 1637, who *m.* [in] 1665, Anne, only daughter of Valence [Sac]heverell, esq. lord of the manors of [Ne]w Hall, in Warwickshire, and of Cal[low], in the county of Derby, by Anne, his [wif]e, daughter of Sir George Devereux, [kt]. of Sheldon Hall, and by her, who died in 1689, had one son and two daughters, viz.

I. CHARLES, his heir.

I. Anne, bapt. at Sutton, 14th October, 1666, and buried in 1684.

II. Catherine, bapt. at Ridware, 29th August, 1672, *m.* in 1698 to Ralph, son of Matthew Floyer, esq. of Hints, in Staffordshire.

Mr. Chadwick died at Sutton, in February, 1697, and was *s.* by his son,

CHARLES CHADWICK, esq. of Healey and Ridware, bapt. 22nd February, 1675, who served the office of high sheriff for Derbyshire in 1709, and for Staffordshire in 1719. He *m.* first, in 1699, Dorothy, daughter of Sir Thomas Dolman, knt. of Shaw House, Berkshire, and had issue,

I. George, who died in infancy in 1702.

II. CHARLES, successor to his father.

I. Mary, died unm. in 1770.

II. Dorothy, *b.* in 1701, who inherited, in 1779, from her brother Charles, the estates of Ridware, New Hall, and Callow. She died unmarried, 30th November, 1784, and was *s.* by her nephew, Charles Chadwick, esq. of Healey.

III. Anne, died young.

Charles Chadwick *m.* secondly, 20th November, 1714, his cousin Mary, daughter of Robert Illingworth, esq. and by her, who died in 1737, had an only son,

I. JOHN, of whom presently.

Mr. Chadwick died on Christmas-day, 1756, aged 82, and was succeeded by his son,

CHARLES CHADWICK, esq. of Ridware, New Hall, and Callow, *b.* at Sutton, 1st February, 1706, who assumed, in compliance with the testamentary injunction of his great uncle, George Sacheverell, esq. the surname and arms of SACHEVERELL. He *m.* in 1741, Anna-Maria, eldest daughter and co-heir of William Brearley, gent. of Handworth, but died without issue 31st July, 1779. His widow surviving succeeded to the large property of her only sister, Jane (who had *m.* first, Captain Clapton, and secondly, Walter Gough, esq. of Perry Hall), and died, 12th January, 1795, aged eighty-five. At the demise of (Mr. Chadwick) Sacheverell, the representation of the family devolved on his half brother,

JOHN CHADWICK, esq. of Healey Hall, *b.* at Ridware, 22nd January, 1720, lieutenant-colonel of the Royal Lancashire Militia, a magistrate for the counties of Lancaster, Stafford and York, and a deputy lieutenant for the first named. On the 1st August, 1791, by grant and exemplification from Sir Isaac Heard, Garter, he assumed the ancient crest of Malveysin, with variations, viz. a talbot's head gu. having the arms of Handsacre on the collar, and pierced through the neck with an arrow; alluding to Handsacre slain by Malveysin, and to Malveysin himself killed at the battle of Shrewsbury. Colonel Chadwick *m.* 24th September, 1743, at Norley, in Cheshire, Susannah, youngest daughter of Robert Holt, esq. of Shevington, descended from the Holts of Grizzlehurst, by Loveday, his wife, daughter of Edward Herle, esq. of Wigan, sprung from the Cornish Herles. By this lady, who died 19th January, 1765, he left, at his decease, 23rd November, 1800, a daughter, Mary, who *d.* unmarried at Manchester, 31st January, 1822, and a son and successor,

CHARLES CHADWICK, esq. of Healey, Ridware, New Hall, and Callow, which three last estates he had inherited from his aunt, Dorothy Chadwick. This gentleman, who was born 2nd October, 1753, *m.* on St. Chad's-day, 1788, at Swillington church, Yorkshire, Frances, only suviving daughter and eventual heiress of Richard Green,* esq. of Leventhorp House, in the county of York, by Frances, his wife, sister of Sir Henry Cavendish, bart. of Doveridge, and granddaughter of James Holt, esq. the last male heir of Stubley and Castleton. Mr. Chadwick, who was a magistrate and deputy-lieutenant for the counties of Lancaster and Stafford, and in the commission of the peace for the West Riding of Yorkshire, died in 1829, and was *s.* by his only son, the present HUGO-MALVEYSIN CHADWICK, esq. of Mavesyn, Ridware, Healey, New Hall, Callow, and Leventhorpe.

*Arms*—Gu. an inescutcheon within an orle of martlets arg. Quartering

| | |
|---|---|
| Kyrkeshagh | Lehtolres |
| Okeden | Heley |
| Butterworth | Bucley |
| Chadwicke | Cawarden |
| Malvoisyn | Bagot |
| Mallory | Blithfield |
| Lowe | Sacheverell |
| Snitterton | Hopwell |
| Statham | Massey |
| Risley | Morley |
| Delalaunde | Crewe |
| Holt | Grisllehurst |
| Sumpter | Brockhole |
| Mancester | Roos |
| Albini | Asheldam |
| Horkesley | Abraham |
| Herle | Arvas |
| Prideaux | Salter |
| Folkeroy | Asheldon |
| Carminow | Trenouth |
| Wolveden | Trewithen |
| Green | |
| Redshaw and Radcliffe. | |

*Crests*—First, a lily arg. stalked and leaved vert. for CHADWICK; second, a talbot's head gu. having the arms of Handsacre (erm. three cronels gu.) on the collar, and pierced through the neck with an arrow.

*Motto*—Stans cum rege.

*Estates*—Mavesyn Ridware, Staffordshire; New Hall, Warwickshire; Callow, Derbyshire; Healy Hall, Lancashire; and Leventhorpe House, Yorkshire.

*Seat*—Mavesyn Ridware, in Staffordshire.

## Family at Chadwick.

**Previous to its alliance with the heiress of Mavesyn Ridware.**

WILLIAM DE CHADWYKE, the first of the name on record, was born probably about the year 1355, as he was living in 1413, being then styled *Senior*, and having a son, William, of age. William de Chadwyke, son of William de Chadwyke, sen. had a grant from Adam de Bamford, in 1413, of certain messuages, lands and tenements, in the vill of Bury; but, though the elder William is expressly styled De Chadwyke, and had this grant in the adjoining manor of Bury, and though it is very *probable* that he was of Chadwyke Hall, still no proof exists to identify him with that family.

The first of the line named in the original deeds still preserved at Healey,

NICHOLAS DE CHADWYK, born in the time of EDWARD III. died, in or before the 23rd HENRY VI. leaving by Maud, his wife, daughter and heir of Thomas de Paris, with whom he acquired lands in Spotland, Honersfeld, and Castleton, two sons, and two daughters, viz.

I. ROBERT, of Chadwyk, successor to his father; appears to have *d. s. p.*
II. JOHN, of whom presently.

I. Isabel, *m.* to William Helde.
II. Maud, *m.* to Geffrey Newam.

The second son,

JOHN DE CHADWYK, died in the lifetime of his elder brother, Robert, in or about the year 1445, leaving three sons, namely,

I. HENRY, of Chadwyk, living 25th March, 1470, ancestor of the CHADWICKS, of Chadwick. JONATHAN CHADWICK, M. D. of Chadwick, aged forty-five, in 1664, *m.* first, Maria, daughter of Thomas Chetham, esq. of Nuthurst, and secondly, in 1670, Catherine, daughter and heiress of Col. Lewis Chadwicke, of Mavesin Ridware, and widow of Lieutenant-colonel John Chadwicke, of Healey Hall. Dr. Chadwick left issue only by his first wife, viz.

* This gentleman was the direct descendant and heir at law of the heiresses of Redshaw, of Ripon and Radcliffe, of Wakefield.

JOHN, M. A. *b.* in 1649, of Chadwick Hall.
JONATHAN, M. A. of Chadwick Hall.
WILLIAM, M.A. of Chadwick Hall.
} who all died issueless.

SARAH, who inherited the estate of Chadwick, after the death of her youngest brother. She *d.* unm. in 1722, having bequeathed, it is stated, her lands to her maternal relative, the Rev. Roger Kay, by whom they were left in charity to the school of Bury.

II. JORDAN, of whom presently.
III. Hugh, living in 1483 and 1492.

second son,

RDAN CHADWYK, who held lands in the ship of Spotland, under Jankyn Holt, e 32nd HENRY VI. *m.* Elianore, daugh- f Christopher Kyrkeshagh, of Hunders- , and by her, who was living 16th June, , had four sons and one daughter viz.

I. JOHN, his heir.
II. Ralph, who had lands in Heley, and was living in 1498.
III. Oliver, who was slain in one of those bloody affrays so frequent in feudal times; in consequence of which a writ of appeal of death was sued, the parties being John, and Jordaune Chadwicke, his next of blood, with John Byron, esq. and all their tenants and servants, against Sir John Trafford, knt. his tenants and servants; whereupon the sum of sixty pounds was deemed to be paid by Trufford to Biron, to be distributed amongst the cousins and friends of the late Oliver Chadwyke, in the parish church of Manchester, on the award of Sir Thomas Stanley, Lord Stanley.
IV. Alan.

I. A daughter, *m.* to John Wolstonholme, of Wolstonholme.

eldest son,

HN CHADWYKE, espoused, in 1483, , eldest daughter and co-heir of Adam len, of Heley, lineally descended from n de Okeden, who *m.* Haurse, the heir homas de Heley. John Chadwyke *d.* 98, leaving, with a younger son, James, est, his successor,

IOMAS CHADWYKE, of Heley, who was ior at the time of his father's decease, nder the guardianship of James Stanclerk. He *m.* about 1512, Catherine, hter of James Bucley, of Bucley, and ssue,

. JOHN, his heir.
I. James, of Castellon.

. Elizabeth, *m.* to Arthur Bently, esq. of Wood House, in Spotland.

Thomas Chadwick died about the year 1556, and was *s.* by his son,

JOHN CHADWYCK, of Healey, who, in 1574, in the musters of soldiers for Lancashire, against the threatened Spanish invasion, was to furnish one long bow, one sheffe arrows, one steel cap, and one bill. He *m.* in 1551, Agnes, daughter of James Heywood, of Heywood, and had issue,

I. ROBERT, his heir.
II. Charles, of Christ College, Cambridge, A.B. 1579; A. M. 1583; senior fellow of Emanuel College at the time of its foundation, in 1585; signed the orders of the college as president, 10th December, 1588; B.D. 1589; instituted rector of Woodham Ferrers, in Essex, 30th January, 1601; D. D. 1607; was chaplain to *Queen* ELIZABETH and to JAMES I. He *d.* unmarried, 4th May, 1627.
III. John, of Christ College, Cambridge, D. D. rector of Darfield, in the West Riding of Yorkshire, *m.* a lady of the Nevill family, but *d. s. p.* in 1631.
IV. Thomas, living in 1620, who *m.* Alice, daughter of Elias Haslam, of Spotland, and had a son, Elias, born in 1621.
V. Jordan, of Christ College, Cambridge, chosen a fellow of Emanuel College, at its foundation in 1585, died before 1614, probably unm.

I. Grace, *m.* in 1586, to Richard Entwisle, esq. of Foxholes.
II. Elizabeth, *m.* to Ralph Holland, of Rochdale.
III. Margaret, *m.* to James Marland, of Marland.
IV. Another daughter, *m.* to Edmund Linney, of Rochdale.

John Chadwyck, dying at Healey at the advanced age of 103, in 1615, was succeeded by his son,

ROBERT CHADWYCKE, esq. of Healey, who rebuilt with stone the old family mansion there. He *m.* in 1581, Alice, daughter of Edward Butterworth, of Belfield, and by her, who *d.* in 1628, had issue,

I. JORDAN, his heir.
II. John, A. M. rector of Standish, in Lancashire, who married, first, Alice, daughter of Richard Turner, of Tawnton, in Essex, and secondly, Elizabeth, daughter of John Ashworth, parson of Warrington. He died in 1646, leaving children by both wives. His eldest son, JOHN, was seated at Tawnton Hall, near Ashton-under-Lyme.
III. Charles, *b.* in 1603, and *d. s. p.* in 1628.

I. Mary, *m.* to Robert Wroe, of Unsworth.

II. Anne, *m.* to Anthony Huxley, parson of Longford, in Derbyshire.
III. Elizabeth, bapt. 9th August, 1590.
IV. Grace, *m.* in 1617, to her cousin, Richard Entwistles, esq. of Foxholes.

Robert Chadwycke *d.* in 1625, and was *s.* by his eldest son,

JORDAN CHADWICKE, esq. of Healey Hall, bapt. at Rochdale, 17th December, 1587, who *m.* in 1616, Elizabeth, daughter and heir of Richard Matthew, gent. of Oldham, in Lancashire, and had issue,

I. JOHN, his heir.
II. Charles, D. D. of Emanuel College, afterwards of Starring, near Rochdale, *m.* and had issue.
III. George, *b.* in 1622, *d.* young.

I. Elizabeth, *m.* to the Rev. William Brooke, of Manchester.

Jordan Chadwicke died in 1634, and was *s.* by his son,

JOHN CHADWICKE, esq. of Healey Hall, who *m.* as already stated, the HEIRESS of MAVESYN RIDWARE.

## JENNEY, OF BREDFIELD.

**JENNEY, EDMUND,** esq. of Bredfield House, in the county of Suffolk, baptized 20th July, 1768; succeeded his father in August, 1801. Mr. Jenney is a justice of the peace and deputy-lieutenant for Suffolk.

### Lineage.

This family, originally of France, assumed its surname from the town of *Guisnes*, near Calais. It probably came into England with the Conqueror; for Bloomfield states that proprietors of the name of DE GISNETO, DE GISNE, or GYNEY, were *soon after* the Conquest possessed of the Manor of Haverland, in Norfolk, and that they held it until the time of HENRY V. From that house it would appear that the one before us branched, and that the name in process of time changed from Gyney to Jenny, the mode in which it has been spelt since the beginning of the fifteenth century at least.

In the 9th of RICHARD II. (1385), Thomas, son of Sir Thomas de Gyney, knt. enfeoffed his Manor of Gislingham, in Suffolk, called Geneys, which he had then lately purchased of John de Weyland—this Manor still bears the name of JENNIES.

EDMUND JENNEY, of Knoddishall, in Suffolk, was father of,

WILLIAM JENNEY, of Knoddishall, and Theberton, who left, by his wife Maud, a son and heir,

JOHN JENNEY, esq. of Knodishall, who was a Burgess of Norwich, in 1452. He *m.* Maud, daughter and heir of John Bokill, of Friston, in Suffolk, by Jane, daughter and heir of John Layston, by Maud, daughter and heir of William Gerrard, and had issue,

WILLIAM, (Sir) his heir.
John, in holy orders, rector of Ufford, in Suffolk, before 1483.
John, who *m.* Elizabeth, daughter and co-heir of Thomas Wetherby, esq. of Intwood, in Norfolk, and became of that place, where he was living in 1461, 1475. He *d.* in 1497, leaving issue.

Anne.
Margaret.

He *d.* 3rd December, 1460, was buried at Knodishall, and *s.* by his eldest son,

SIR WILLIAM JENNEY, knt. of Knodishall, one of the judges of the King's Bench in 1477, who wedded, first, Elizabeth, daughter of Thomas Cawse, esq. and by her, who was living in 1466, had four sons and four daughters, viz.

EDMUND, (Sir) his successor.

Hugh, living in 1473.

Nicholas, of Heringfleet, *m.* Margery, daughter of Roger Bosard, gent. of Delchingham, in Norfolk.

Richard, of Heringfleet.

Margaret, *m.* to Christopher, Lord Willoughby de Eresby, and became a widow in 1498.

Ellenor, *m.* first, to Sir Robert Brewse, knt. and secondly, to Sir Robert Fienes, knt. brother of Richard, Lord Dacre.

Thomasine, a nun, living in 1522.

Catherine, *m.* to John Berney, esq. of Gunton.

The judge *m.* secondly, Eleanor, widow of Robert Ingleys, esq. and daughter of John Sampson, esq.; but by her, who *d.* in 1496, and was buried at Norwich, he had no issue. He *d.* 23rd December, 1483, and was *s.* by his eldest son,

SIR EDMUND JENNEY, knt. of Knodishall. This gentleman *m.* about 1467, Catherine, daughter and heir of Robert Boys, esq.* (by Jane, his wife, daughter and heir of Edward Wychingham, esq.) and had issue,

WILLIAM, *b.* 24th May, 1470, *m.* first, Audrey, daughter of Sir Robert Clere, knt. of Ormsby, in Norfolk, but, by that lady, who *d.* in 1502, had no issue. She wedded, secondly, Elizabeth, daughter of Mr. Alderman Thomas Button, of London, and left at his decease, 28th February, 10th HENRY VIII. a daughter, Elizabeth, and a son,

FRANCIS, heir to his grandfather.

Robert, *b.* in 1484, *d. s. p.* in 1560.

CHRISTOPHER, (Sir) of Cressingham, *b.* in 1486. One of the judges of the Common Pleas, in 1539, *m.* Elizabeth, daughter and co-heir of William Eyre, esq. of Bury St. Edmunds.

John, *b.* in 1488, *m.* in 1512, Anne, widow of William Bocher, esq. of Willoughby, in Suffolk, and left issue.

Jane, *b.* in 1468, *m.* to William Playters, esq. of Sotterley, and *d.* in 1540.

Elizabeth, *b.* in 1471.

Anne, *b.* in 1473, *m.* to Thomas Billingford, gent. of Stoke, in Norfolk.

Rose, *b.* in 1474, *m.* in 1493, to John King, gent. of Shelley.

Thomase, *m.* to William Duke, esq. of Brampton, in Suffolk.

Isabella, *m.* to Richard Littlebury, gent. and living in 1521.

Sir Edmund *d.* in 1522, and was *s.* by his grandson,

FRANCIS JENNEY, esq. of Knodishall. *b.* in 1510. This gentleman married twice, first, Margaret, daughter of Sir Robert Peyton, knt. of Iselham, and, secondly, Mary, daughter of Robert Brograve, esq. of Beckham, in Kent. By the latter he had no issue, but by the former was father of the following numerous family:

ARTHUR, his heir.

Thomas, *b.* in 1536, of Ipswich, whose daughter, Margaret, *m.* William Luckyn, esq. of Great Badow.

Christopher, *b.* in 1537, living at Stonham Parva, in 1589, buried at Theberton, 3rd March, 1609.

William, *b.* in 1545, living in 1589.

Edmund, collector of the customs at Ipswich, *d.* in 1624, aged 75, buried at St. Stephens, Ipswich.

Jane, *b.* in 1532.

Anne, in 1535, *m.* — Smith, and had a son, Maxamilian Smith.

Elizabeth, *b.* in 1540.

Margaret, *b.* in 1541, *m.* to Arthur Vesey, and had a son, Robert Vesey.

Bridget.

Mary, *m.* to Woolmer.

Martha, *m.* to Richard Browne, and had a son, Philip Browne.

He *d.* in 1590, and was succeeded by his eldest son,

ARTHUR JENNEY, esq. of Knodishall, *b.* in 1533, *m.* before 1559, Elye, daughter of George Jernigan, esq. of Somerleyton, in Suffolk, and had issue,

FRANCIS, who *m.* Anne, daughter and co-heir of George Rede, esq. of Thorington, in Suffolk, and by her (who wedded, secondly, William, son of Thomas Jermy, esq. of Brightwell, in the same county), left at his decease, in the lifetime of his father,

ARTHUR, (Sir) successor to his grandfather.

Martha, *m.* 10th October, 1622, to the Rev. Philip Tincke.

George, of London, in 1611, and of Woodbridge, in 1640, *m.* Anne ---

Arthur, of Ipswich, *d. s. p.* in 1640.

Philip.

Edmund, buried 27th July, 1579.

Anne, *m.* to — Vinyard.

Jernegan, *m.* Mr. Wattes, of Aldeby, in Norfolk, and *d. s. p.*

Mr. Jenney died in 1604, was buried at Theberton, 19th March, in that year, and *s.* by his grandson,

SIR ARTHUR JENNEY, knt. of Knodishall,

---

* ROBERT BOYS was son and heir of Roger Boys and of Sybilla his wife, daughter and heir of Robert Illeigh, son and heir of Edmund Illeigh and Alice his wife, daughter and heir of John Plumstead.

who was sheriff of Suffolk in 1645, and of Norfolk in 1654. This gentleman *m.* first, in 1616, Anne, daughter of Sir Robert Barker, and by that lady had, with other issue,

I. ROBERT, (Sir) his heir.
II. George, of Morton, in Norfolk, *b.* in 1630, *m.* and had
  Suckling, who *d. s. p.*
  George, who died in 1749, leaving, by Bridget, his wife, four daughters, his co-heirs, viz.
    1. Mary, *m.* to the Rev. Richard Tapps, of Norwich, and left an only daughter and heiress, who wedded, first, John Chambers, esq. of Norwich, without issue, and secondly, Robert Plumtree, esq. of the same place.
    2. Bridget, } died unmarried.
    3. Sarah, }
    4. Anne, married to Rev. Mr. Greete.
I. Anne, *m.* to John Sadler, of Norwich, gent.
II. Judith, *m.* to Thomas, fourth son of Sir John Rous.
III. Jernegan, *m.* to Wm. Rookwood, esq. of Weston.
IV. Abigail, *m.* to Richard Costivell, esq. of Bolney, Sussex.
V. Mary, *m.* to —— Miller, or Milner.

Sir Arthur wedded, secondly, Catherine, daughter of Sir John Porter, and by her had a son, Thomas, of Campsey Ash, who *d. s. p.* in 1675. He espoused, thirdly, Helen, widow of John Freeman, esq. and daughter of Francis Stonard, esq. of Knowleshill, in Essex, by whom he had two daughters, Susann, who *d. s. p.* and Isabella, who wedded the Rev. John Talbot, of Icklingham. Sir Arthur married, fourthly, Mary, daughter of Thomas Hall, esq. of Godalmin, in Surrey, and by her (who survived him, and remarried William Nicholls, gent.) had a son,

Edmund, *b.* 17th April, 1664.

He died 24th March, 1667-8, aged seventy-five, was buried at Knodishall, and *s.* by his eldest son,

SIR ROBERT JENNEY, knt. of Knodishall, who *m.* in 1640, Elizabeth, daughter of Sir John Offley, knt. of Madeley, in the county of Stafford, and had issue,

OFFLEY, his heir.

EDMUND, of Campsey-Ash, *m.* in 1683, DOROTHY, daughter and co-heir of ROBERT MARRYOTT, esq. of Bredfield, by whom (who wedded, secondly, Thomas Knight, of London, *s. p.*) he left at his decease, 17th February, 1694-5,

  ARTHUR, of Woodbridge, who *m.* in 1711, Mirabella, daughter of Henry Edgar, gent. of Eye, in Suffolk, and widow of Robert Burley, gent. of Wisbech, and dying in 1729,

    EDMUND, of Bredfield, of whom presently, as chief of the family.
    Edgar, *d.* in 1746.
    Arthur, of Rendlesham, in Suffolk, *m.* a daughter of — Langley, and left at his decease in 1742, a son,
      Edmund, of Bungay, who *m.* Elizabeth, daughter of — Denny, of Eye, in Suffolk, and left in 1800, with two daughters, Elizabeth, *m.* to Thomas Crowther, esq. and Marianne, *m.* to Philip Bell, gent. an only surviving son,
        William, *b.* 9th December, 1779, living in 1834, *m.* Caroline Frances, daughter of Major Archibald Stewart, of the Blues, and grand-daugh. maternally of Sir Henry Harpur, of Calke Abbey, and has issue,
          Stewart - William, *b.* 28th Dec. 1816.
          Arthur - Henry, *b.* 31st March, 1819.
          Frances - Caroline, *m.* 25th Sept. 1827, to the Rev. Henry R. Crewe, brother of Sir Geo. Crewe, bart.
          Lucy-Elizabeth.
          Caroline-Maria.
          Georgiana - Selina.

  Catherine, *m.* to Nicholas, son of Arthur Drury, esq. of Fitwood, in Norfolk.

Sir Robert died in 1660, and was *s.* by his eldest son,

OFFLEY JENNEY, esq. of Knodishall, baptized 4th April, 1641, *m.* in 1666, Alethea, eldest daughter of Sir Edward Duke, bart. of Benhall, and by that lady (who wedded, secondly, Ralph Snelling, esq. of Yoxford, and, thirdly, William Foster, esq. of Madesford), left, at his decease in 1670, an only surviving child,

ROBERT JENNEY, esq. of Leisten, baptized 3rd December, 1677, married, at Knodishall, Deborah, daughter of John Braham, esq. of Ash, and had issue,

OFFLEY, *b.* in 1692, *d.* 6th September, 1735, unmarried.

Deborah, *d.* an infant.

Mr. Jenney *d.* in 1741, was buried at Knodishall, on 28th February, in that year, and succeeded in the representation of the family by his cousin,

EDMUND JENNEY, esq. of Bredfield, who *m.* in 1765, Anne, daughter of Philip Broke, esq. of Nacton, by whom, who died 19th October, 1821, aged eighty-four, he had issue,

EDMUND, his heir.

Philip, *d.* unmarried, 13th June, 1819.

Isabella, *b.* 19th December, 1775, and *d.* 4th May, 1779.

Anne, living in 1834, unmarried.

Mr. Jenney died in 1801, was buried at Bredfield, 29th August, in that year, and succeeded by his only surviving son, the present EDMUND JENNEY, esq. of Bredfield.

*Arms*—Erm. a bend gu. cotised or, quartering Bokill; Leiston; Gerrard; Bois; Wichingham; Illey; Plumstead; Falstoff; Holbrooke; Rede; Toley; Marryott; and Bloomfield.

*Crest*—On a glove in fess arg. a hawk or falcon close or, belled of the last.

*Estates*—In the parishes of Bredfield, Hasketon, Boulge, Wetheringset, Stonham, &c. &c., all in Suffolk.

*Seats*—Bredfield House, and Hasketon, near Woodbridge.

## MORE, OF BARNBOROUGH.

MORE, THOMAS-PETER, esq. of Barnborough, in the county of York, *b.* 23rd April, 1794, assumed, by sign manual, 24th June, 1797, upon succeeding to the estates of his grandmother, the surname and arms of MORE, in place of his patronymic METCALFE.

### Lineage.

The Mores of Barnborough derived immediately from

SIR JOHN MORE, knight, born about the year 1440. He was one of the justices of the court of King's Bench in the time of HENRY VIII. whose family is represented as old and respectable, and himself described as "homo civilis, suavis, innocens, mitis, misericors, æquus, et integer; annis quidem gravis, sed corpore plusquam pro ætate vivido." Camden, in his remains, relates a bon mot of the learned judge's, which says more for his wit than his gallantry, and will not, we fear, prepossess the fair sex much in his favour. His lordship is said to have compared a man choosing a wife to one who dipped his hand into a bag, which contained twenty snakes and one eel; *it was twenty to one he caught the eel.* After this, it is not a little surprising to find that he had the resolution to take three dips himself; for we learn that he was thrice married. The maiden name of his first wife was Handcombe, of Holywell, in Bedfordshire. The age of portents was not yet gone by; and Dr. Clement, a famous physician of the time, reported of this lady, that, on the night after her marriage, she saw, in a dream, engraven on her wedding ring, the number and characters of her children, *the face of one shining with superior brightness.* Those children were Jane, married to Richard Stafferton, esq.; Elizabeth, wife of John Rastell, the father of Judge Rastell; and THOMAS, the celebrated Chancellor SIR THOMAS MORE. Of Sir John's other wives, we only know that the christian name of the last was Alice, that she outlived her step-son, and that, being deprived of her possessions in HENRY's fury, a little before her death, she *d.* at Northal, in Herts. The only son of Sir John,

THOMAS MORE, was born at his father's usual residence in Milk-street, London, in 1480, and educated, first, at a school at St. Anthony's, in Threadneedle-street, and afterwards at Oxford, where he soon acquired a considerable proficiency in classical learning. Being destined for the profession of the law, he came to New Inn, in London, whence, after some time, he removed to Lincoln's Inn, of which his father was a member. In his twenty-second year he was returned to the parliament called by HENRY VII. for the purpose of demanding an aid for the marriage of his eldest daughter to the king of Scotland. The Commons, in general, thought the demand exorbitant; but no one had courage to oppose it, till Mr. More set the example, and by his powerful eloquence the motion was rejected. The king was so greatly offended at this opposition, that in revenge, he sent Mr. More's father, on a frivolous pretence, to the Tower, and obliged him to pay £100 for his liberty. After being called to the bar, young More was appointed law reader at Furnival's Inn, which place he held about three years; and he also read a public lecture in the church of St. Lawrence, Old Jewry, upon St. Austin's treatise *De civitate Dei*. At one time he seems to have formed the design of becoming a Franciscan friar; but he was afterwards dissuaded from it, and married Jane, the eldest daughter of John Colt, esq. of Newhall, in Essex. In the year 1508 he was appointed judge of the sheriffs' court, in the city of London, was made a justice of the peace, and attained great eminence at the bar. In 1516, he went to Flanders in the retinue of Bishop Tonstal and Dr. Knight, who were sent by *King* HENRY VIII. to renew the alliance with the Archduke of Austria, afterwards Charles V. On his return to England, Cardinal Wolsey wished to engage Mr. More in the service of the crown, and offered him a pension, which he declined. It was not long, however, before he accepted the place of master of the requests. He was also created a knight, admitted a member of the privy council, and, in 1520, made treasurer of the exchequer. About this time he built a house on the banks of the Thames, at Chelsea, and married a second wife. In the 14th year of Henry VIII. Sir Thomas More was appointed Speaker of the House of Commons, in which capacity he had the courage to oppose Wolsey in his demand of an oppressive subsidy. Soon afterwards, however, he was made chancellor of the duchy of Lancaster, and treated with great familiarity by the king.

In the year 1526, he was sent, with Cardinal Wolsey and others, on a joint embassy to France, and in 1529, with Bishop Tonstal, to Cambray. Notwithstanding his opposition to the measures of the court, he was appointed chancellor in the year following the disgrace of Wolsey; but in 1533, he resigned the seals, probably to avoid the danger of refusing his sanction to the king's divorce. He now retired to his house at Chelsea; dismissed many of his servants; sent his children, with their families, whom he seems to have maintained in his own house, to their respective homes; and spent his time in study and devotion. He was not long, however, permitted to enjoy tranquillity. Though now reduced to a private station, and even to indigence, his opinion of the legality of the king's marriage with Anne Boleyn, was deemed of so much importance, that various attempts were made to procure his approbation, but these proving ineffectual, he was, along with some others, included in a bill of attainder in the House of Lords, for misprision of treason, by encouraging Elizabeth Barton, the Nun of Kent, in her treasonable practices. His innocence in this affair, however, appeared so clearly, that they were obliged to strike his name out of the bill. He was then accused of other crimes, but with the same effect; until, upon refusing to take the oath enjoined by the act of supremacy, he was committed to the Tower; and, after fifteen months' imprisonment, was tried at the bar of the King's Bench for high treason. The proof rested upon the single evidence of Rich, the solicitor-general, whom Sir Thomas, in his defence, sufficiently discredited. The jury, however, brought him in guilty; he was condemned to suffer as a traitor, and was accordingly beheaded on Tower-hill on the 5th July, 1535. His body was first interred in the Tower, but was afterwards begged and obtained by his daughter Margaret, and deposited in the chancel of the church at Chelsea, where a monument, with an inscription written by himself, had been some time before erected, and is still to be seen. The same daughter also procured his head, after it had remained fourteen days upon London bridge, and placed it in a vault belonging to the Roper family, under a chapel adjoining to St. Dunstan's church, in Canterbury.

Sir Thomas More was a man of considerable learning, eminent talents, and inflexible integrity. When only twenty years old, he was so devoted to monkish discipline, that he wore a hair shirt next his skin, frequently fasted, and slept upon a plank. Yet his disposition was cheerful, and he had an affectation of wit, which he could not restrain even upon the most serious occasions. He was the author of various books, chiefly of a polemical nature. His *Utopia* is the only performance that has survived in the esteem the world. Hume says, that of all the iters of that age in England, Sir Thos More seems to come nearest to the iracter of a classic author. His English rks were collected, and published by 'er of *Queen* MARY, in 1557; his Latin Basil, in 1563; and at Louvain, in 1566. ife of Sir Thomas More, by his son-in-', Mr. Roper, of Wellhall, in Kent, was lished by Mr. Hearne, at Oxford, in 6.

Sir Thomas's only son,

OHN MORE, esq. *m.* Anne, daughter and r of Edward Cresacre, esq. of Barnough, in the county of York, by whom o *d.* in 1577) he acquired that estate, and l issue,

- I. THOMAS, his heir.
- II. Augustine, *d.* unmarried.
- III. Edward, buried at Barnborough, 2nd May, 1620, leaving a daughter, Anne.
- IV. Thomas, a Protestant minister; he was dead in 1606, and had left issue, Cyprian, Thomas, and Constantine.
- V. Bartholomew, died young of the plague.

- I. Anne, *m.* 8th September, 1559, to John West, son and heir of George West.

eldest son,

'HOMAS MORE, esq. of Barnborough, *b.* Chelsea, 8th August, 23rd HENRY VIII. Mary, daughter of John Scrope, esq. of mbleton, in the county of Buckingham, had issue,

- I. John, baptized 1557, died before his father, *s. p.*
- II. Thomas, baptized 1565—6, resigned the inheritance, and became a priest.
- III. Henry, baptized 1566-7, also resigned the inheritance, and became a priest.
- IV. CRESACRE, heir.

- I. Anne.
- II. Margaret, *m.* to John Garford.
- III. Mary, *m.* to More, of Bampton, in Oxfordshire.
- IV. Jane, *m.* to Lawrence Povey, of London.
- V. Magdalen, *d.* young.
- VI. Catherine, *m.* to Charles Bird, of Staundon.
- VII. Grace, *m.* to Thomas Greenwood, of Brise Norton.

youngest son,

RESACRE MORE, esq. of Barnborough, More Place, North Mims, baptized 6th , 1572, *m.* Elizabeth, daughter of Tho- Gage, esq. of Firle, and left at his dee, (with two daughters, Helen, born in 3, Lady Abbess at Louvaine, and Bridget, Prioress of the English Benedictine nuns of Our Lady of Hope at Paris), a son and successor,

THOMAS MORE, esq. of More Place, who *m.* Mary, daughter of Sir Basil Brooke, knt. of Madeley, in Salop, and had issue,

- I. WILLIAM, who predeceased his father issueless.
- II. BASIL, heir.
- III. Cresacre, } who appear to have
- IV. Thomas, } *d.* unmarried.
- V. John, had a son, John.

- I. Frances, *m.* to George Shelden, esq. of Beoley.
- II. Mary, living unm. 1697.
- III. Margaret, a nun, *d.* 24th December, 1691.
- IV. Bridget, *m.* to Thomas Gifford, esq.

The eldest surviving son,

BASIL MORE, esq. having sold the More Place estate, was of Barnborough alone. He *m.* Ann, daughter of Sir William Humble, bart. of Thorpe-Underwood, in the county of Northampton, and had, by her (who *d.* in 1694), eight sons and four daughters, viz.

- I. Basil, *b.* 1st May, 1665, *d.* unm. 9th June, 1689.
- II. CRISTOPHER-CRESACRE, heir to his father.
- III. William, of Barnard's Inn, born in 1670, *d.* in 1710.
- IV. Thomas, *b.* in 1671, *d.* in 1696.
- V. John, *d.* unm.
- VI. George, *b.* in 1674, *d.* unm.
- VII. Augustus, *b.* in 1676, *d.* in 1719, leaving a son and daughter.
- VIII. Charles, *b.* in 1683, *d.* in 1715-16.

- I. Bridget, *m.* to John Forcer, esq. of Harbour House, Durham.
- II. Mary, *m.* James Morgan.
- III. Anne, a nun at Louvaine.
- IV. Frances, *m.* to — Goate.

Mr. More *d.* 17th November, 1702, and was *s.* by his son,

CHRISTOPHER-CRESACRE MORE, esq. of Barnborough, born 1st April, 1666, who *m.* Catherine, daughter of Humphrey Wharton, esq. of Westminster, and by her (who *d.* in 1744), had issue,

- I. THOMAS, his heir.

- I. Ann, baptized at North Mims, 9th June, 1689, *m.* to William Binkes, or Binley, of Richmond, in Yorkshire.
- II. Catharine, *b.* in 1691, *d.* unm. at Brussels.
- III. Mary, baptized 8th Sept. 1701, *m.* to Charles Waterton, esq. of Walton.

Mr. More *d.* 25th April, 1729, and was *s.* by his son,

THOMAS MORE, esq. of Barnborough, *b.* 28th February, 1691-2, who *m.* Catharine, daughter of Peter Gifford, esq. of White-Ladies, and had issue,

I. THOMAS, his heir.
II. Christopher, a priest, *d.* at Bath, about 1769.

I. BRIDGET, successor to her brother.
II. Catherine, *d. s. p.* at York, 1784.
III. Mary, *b.* at York, veiled a nun, by the name of Mary-Augustina, in the convent of Augustine Dames, at Bruges, 1753, chosen Prioress of the House, 1766, *d.* there 23rd March, 1807.

Mr. More *d.* 28th August, 1739, and was *s.* by his son,

THOMAS MORE, esq. of Barnborough, a brother of the society of Jesus, and principal of the English Jesuits at the dissolution of the order: he resigned his estate to his sisters, and *d.* at Bath 20th May, 1796.

The eldest of those ladies,

BRIDGET MORE, who possessed the moiety of the Barnborough estates, married, first, Peter Metcalfe, esq. of Glandford Bridge, and had an only son,

THOMAS-PETER METCALFE, of Bath, who *m.* Teresa, daughter of George Throckmorton, esq. son and heir apparent of Sir Robert Throckmorton, baronet, and dying in 1793, left one son and a daughter, viz.

THOMAS-PETER METCALFE, successor to his grandmother.

Teresa-Maria Metcalfe, married to Charles Eyston, esq. of East Hendred. (See vol. i. p. 12.)

Mrs. Metcalfe wedded, secondly, Robert Dalton, esq. of Thurnham, in the county of Lancaster, and had by him one son and two daughters, viz.

William Dalton, *b.* in 1763, who *m.* Louisa, daughter of Frederick Smith, esq. of St. Mary-le-bone, and had issue.

Bridget-Anne, *m.* to Sir James Fitzgerald, bart.

Constantia, *d.* unm.

She (Mrs. Bridget Dalton) *d.* 7th May, 1797, and was *s.* by her grandson, the present THOMAS-PETER (Metcalfe) MORE, esq. of Barnborough.

*Arms*—Or, a chev. engrailed between three more cocks sa.

*Crest*—A moor's head and shoulders, ppr. in his ear a ring or.

*Estates*—In Yorkshire.

*Seat*—Barnborough, Yorkshire.

### Family of Cresacre.

The Cresacres were resident lords of Barnborough, from the thirteenth century until their extinction in the reign of HENRY VIII.

JOHN CRESACRE, lord of Barnborough, 12th and 21st EDWARD I. was father of

THOMAS CRESACRE, of Barnborough, 17th EDWARD III. who *m.* and left a son,

JOHN CRESACRE, of Barnborough, 24th EDWARD III. who *m.* Alice, or Sibil, daughter of Robert Wasteneys, of Headon, and was father of

JOHN CRESACRE, of Barnborough, 20th RICHARD II. who *m.* a daughter of — Cranbull.

Their son,

JAMES CRESACRE, of Barnborough, 21st HENRY VI. wedding Elizabeth, daughter of John Woodrove, left a son,

PERCIVAL CRESACRE, of Barnborough, who espoused Alice, daughter of Thomas Mounteney, and by her (who *d.* in 1450, and was buried at Barnborough) had issue,

I. JOHN, his heir.
II. James, *d.* unmarried.
III. Edward, sub-dean of the cathedral church of York.
IV. Ambrose, living 8th EDWARD IV.

I. Isabel, *m.* first, to John Bosvile, of Ardsley, and secondly, to Henry Langton.

This Percival Cresacre was living as late as 1455, when he was a feoffee of his dau. Isabel Langton, for the foundation of the Bosvile chantry in the church of Cawthorne. The date of his decease has not been ascertained. Respecting the manner of his death there is a romantic tradition, firmly believed at Barnborough, and the figure of the lion couchant at the foot of the oaken statue, is appealed to in confirmation of it; as is also a rubiginous stone in the pavement of the porch. The tradition is, that he was attacked by a wild cat, from one of the little woods of Barnborough, and that there was a running fight, till they reached the porch of the church, where the mortal combat ended in the death of both.

Whatever portion of truth there may be in the story, it is evident that it derives no support from the image of the lion in the monument, or the tincture of the stone in the porch, which is only one of many such found near Barnborough. That some such incident did occur in the family of Cresacre, is rendered, however, in some degree, probable, by the adoption of the cat-a-mountain for their crest, which may be seen over their arms on the tower of the church. On the other hand, it may have been that the accidental adoption of the crest may have laid the foundation of the story.

That the cat was anciently considered as a beast of chase, is evident from many proofs, going back to the age of the CONFESSOR, in one of whose charters, supposing it to be genuine, there is given, with the forest of Chalmer, and Dancing, in Essex,

> Hart and hind, doe and bock,
> Fox and cat, hare and brock.

And again,

> Four greyhounds, and six raches,
> For hare and fox, and wild cates.

The eldest son,

JOHN CRESACRE, of Barnborough, 33rd HENRY VI. *m.* a daughter of Nicholas Wortley, and was *s.* by his son,

JOHN CRESACRE, of Barnborough, 18th EDWARD IV. who *m.* Margaret, daughter of Sir Hugh Hastings, of Fenwick, and was father of

EDWARD CRESACRE, of Barnborough, who *m.* Jane, daughter of Sir Richard Basset, of Fletborough, in Nottinghamshire, and dying in 1512, aged twenty-seven, left an only daughter and heiress,

ANNE CRESACRE, who *m.* JOHN MORE, esq.

# LEGH, OF ADLINGTON.

LEGH, CHARLES-RICHARD-BANASTRE, esq. of Adlington Hall, in the palatinate of Chester, *b.* 4th March, 1821, succeeded his father 25th April, 1829.

## Lineage.

ROBERT DE LEGH, second son of John Legh, of Booths, (see vol. ii. p. 45), by Ellen his wife, dau. and heiress of Thomas de Corona, of Adlington, living *temp.* EDWARD II. wedded Matilda, dau. and heiress of Adam de Norley, and was father of

ROBERT LEGH, of Adlington, who *m.* Matilda, dau. and co-heiress of Sir John de Arderne, knt. of Aldford and Alvanley, representative of one of the most ancient of those knightly families of which the county of Chester may so justly boast, and had two sons, viz.

I. ROBERT (Sir), his heir.
II. Piers (Sir), who *m.* in Nov. 1388, Margaret, only dau. and heiress of Sir Thomas Danyers, knt. of Bradley. and obtained by this alliance a grant of the lands of Hanley, now LYME, in Macclesfield. From his eldest son,
   PETER (Sir), knt.-banneret, who accompanying King HENRY to France, distinguished himself in the wars of that valiant prince, and was slain at AZINCOURT, descended the LEGHS, of Lyme; for an account of whom, refer to vol. ii. p. 686.

The elder son,

SIR ROBERT LEGH, knt. of Adlington, sheriff of Cheshire, 17 and 22 RICHARD II. married Isabella, daughter and heiress of Sir Thomas Belgrave, knt. by Joan, his wife, dau. and heiress of Sir Robert Pulford, and left with a dau. Joanna, *m.* first, to Ralph Davenport, of Davenport; and, secondly, to John Legh, of High Legh, a son and successor,

ROBERT LEGH, of Adlington. It being deemed necessary that this gentleman should give up his claims to the estates of the Pulford family, in favour of Sir Thomas Grosvenor, relinquishment thereof was made with the following unusual ceremonies, devised, probably, from a wish to add to its impressiveness and notoriety.

"On the 24th of April, 1412, Sir Thomas le Grosvenor, knt. Robert, son of Sir Robert Legh, knt. and Henry de Birtheles, counsel of Sir Thomas le Grosvenor, read, in Macklesfield chapel, a series of deeds relating to successive settlements, by the Pulford family, of the manors of Buerton *juxta* Salghton, Claverton, and Pulford, the advowson of Pulford, lands in Middle Aldesey, Crooke Aldesey, and Cawarthyn, the fourth part of the manor of Chollegh, and the eighth part of the manor of Broxton. By these settlements, it appears that the said estates were settled on John, son of Robert de Pulford; remainder for life to Johanna, his mother; remainder to Robert his son, and his wife Isabella; remainder to their issue; remainder, in default of issue, to the right heirs of John.

After the reading of these deeds, it was stated, that Sir Robert Legh, and Isabella his wife, and their son Robert Legh, pretended a right to these estates, under a settlement by Thomas de Belgrave and Joan his wife (daughter of Robert, and sister and heir of Joan de Pulford); and, to settle family differences, that it had been agreed that Sir Thomas Grosvenor should take a solemn oath on the body of Christ, in the presence of twenty-four gentlemen, or as many as he wished.

Accordingly, Robert del Birches, chaplain, whom Robert de Legh had brought with him, celebrated a mass of the Holy Trinity, and consecrated the Host, and after the mass (albo cum amiclo, stolâ, et manipulo indutus) held forth the Host before the altar, whereupon Sir Thomas Grosvenor knelt before him, whilst the settlements were again read by James Holt, counsel of Robert de Legh, and then swore upon the Lord's body, that he believed in the truth of these charters. Immediately after this, Sir Laurence Merbury, knt. sheriff, and fifty-seven of the principal knights and gentlemen of Cheshire, affirmed themselves singly to be witnesses of the oath, all elevating their hands at the same time towards the Host. This first part of the ceremony concluded with Sir Thomas Grosvenor receiving the sacrament, and Robert Legh and Sir Thomas kissing each other, "in affirmationem concordiæ prædictæ." Immediately after this, Robert Legh acknowledged the right of all the said lands to be vested in Sir Thomas Grosvenor and his heirs, and an instrument to that effect was accordingly drawn up by the notary, Roger Salghall, in the presence of several of the clergy, and attested by the seals and signatures of fifty-eight knights and gentlemen. Seldom will the reader find a more goodly group collected together, nor will he easily devise a ceremony which would assort better with the romantic spirit of the time, and which thus turned a dry legal conveyance into an exhibition of chivalrous pageantry. Robert Legh left, at his decease (inq. p. m. 3 Henry V.) by Matilda, his wife, (remarried to William de Honford), four sons and one daughter, viz. ROBERT; James, Rector of Rosthorne, in 1456; William; Peter; and Ellen, the wife of Roger Legh, of Ridge. The eldest son,

ROBERT LEGH, esq. of Adlington, wedded, first, Isabella, daughter of John Savage, of Clifton, by whom he had no issue; and, secondly, Isabella, daughter of Sir William Stanley, knt. of Hooton; by whom he had,

I. ROBERT, his heir.

I. Margaret, *m.* first, to Thomas Mere, of Mere; and, secondly, to Robert Reddish, of Catteral.
II. Margery, *m.* to William Davenport, esq. of Bramall.
III. Isabel, *m.* first, to Laurence Warren, esq. of Poynton; and, secondly, to Sir George Holford, of Holford.
IV. Matilda, *m.* to John Mainwaring, esq. of Peover.
V. Agnes, *m.* to Sir Andrew Brereton, of Brereton.
VI. —— *m.* to —— Pigott, esq. of Chetwynd, Salop.

Robert Legh was *s.* at his decease (inq. p. m. 18 Edward IV.) by his son,

ROBERT LEGH, esq. of Adlington, who *m.* Ellen, dau. of Sir Robert Booth, of Dunham-Massey, and had six sons and five daughters, namely,

I. THOMAS, his heir.
II. Richard, } of whom we have no
III. Randle, } account.
IV. Reginald, of Annesley, in the county of Nottingham, *m.* Mary, dau. of Thomas, brother of Sir Richard Vernon, and had issue.
V. John.
VI. William.

I. Isabel, *m.* to Robert Holt, of Chesham, in Lancashire.
II. Blanche, *m.* to Richard Lancaster, of Rainhill.
III. Margaret, *m.* to Ralph Hide, of Skegby.
IV. Margery, *m.* to John Moor, of Park Hall.
V. Elizabeth, *m.* to Thomas Leversage, of Macclesfield.

The eldest son,

THOMAS LEGH, esq. of Adlington, was returned heir to his father by inquisition, dated 2 HENRY VII. He *m.* Catherine, dau. of Sir John Savage, knt. of Clifton, and had two sons and two daughters, viz.

I. GEORGE, his heir.
II. William.

I. Eleanor, *m.* to Sir Piers Dutton, knt. of Dutton.
II. Elizabeth, *m.* to William Hulton, esq. of Hulton, in Lancashire.

Thomas Legh *d.* in the time of HENRY VIII. and was *s.* by his son,

George Legh, esq. of Adlington, aged twenty-two, in the 11th of Henry VIII. who *m.* Jane, dau. of Peter Larke, citizen of London, relict of George Paulet, brother to the Marquis of Winchester, and dying 21st of the same reign, left, with three daughters, Mary, Elizabeth, and Ellen, a son and successor,

Thomas Legh, esq. of Adlington, *b.* 19th Henry VIII. who *m.* Maria, dau. of Richard Grosvenor, esq. of Eaton, and by her, who wedded, secondly, Sir Richard Egerton, knt. of Ridley, and *d.* in 1599, left a son,

Thomas Legh, esq. of Adlington, who served the office of sheriff of Cheshire, in 1588. He *m.* Sibilla, dau. of Sir Urian Brereton, knt. of Honford, and had, with several other sons, and six daughters, (the eldest of whom, Mary, became the wife of — Glazeor, esq. of Lea, and the second, Margaret, of Henry Arderne, esq. of Arden and Alvanley,) a son and successor.

Sir Urian Legh, knt. of Adlington, aged thirty-five, 44 Elizabeth, who received the honour of knighthood from the Earl of Essex at the siege of Cadiz, and during that expedition is traditionally said to have been engaged in an adventure which gave rise to the well known ballad of "The Spanish Lady's Love." Another gallant knight, Sir John Bolle, however, is asserted in vol. ii. p. 390, to have been the hero of that romantic tradition. A fine original portrait of Sir Urian, in a Spanish dress, is preserved at Bramall, which has been copied for the family at Adlington. He was sheriff of Cheshire in the year of Sir Richard George's Visitation of the county in 1613, and survived until the 3rd of Charles I. when his inquisition was taken. He *m.* Margaret, second daughter of Sir Edmund Trafford, knt. of Trafford, and had three sons and two daughters, viz.

- I. Thomas, his heir.
- II. Urian, a citizen of London.
- III. Henry, *d. s. p.*
- IV. Francis.

- I. Mary, *m.* to Sir H. Leigh, of Cumberland.
- II. Lucy, *m.* to Alexander Rigby, of Chester.

Sir Urian was *s.* by his eldest son,

Thomas Legh, esq. of Adlington, sheriff of Cheshire 5 Charles I. who *m.* Anne, daughter of John Gobert, esq. of Bosworth, in Leicestershire, and by her (who wedded, secondly, Alexander Rigby, one of the barons of the Exchequer; and, thirdly, Sir John Booth, knt. of Woodford) had issue,

- I. Thomas, his heir.
- II. Charles, *m.* Margaret, daughter of Thomas Bagshaw, of Ridge, in Derbyshire.
- III. Peter, *m.* Elizabeth Young, of Salop.
- IV. Henry, of Pyrehill, in the county of Salop.
- V. John, slain in the civil wars.

- I. Penelope, *m.* to William Wright, esq. of Longton.
- II. Mary, *m.* to John Hurleston, esq. of Picton.
- III. Frances, *m.* to Sir John Pershall, of Sugnall, in Staffordshire.
- IV. Anne, *m.* to Peter Davenport, esq. of Bramall.
- V. Mary, *m.* to Alexander Rigby.
- VI. Lucy, *m.* to Robert Ireland, of Albrighton.

Thomas Legh *d.* about the year 1645, and was *s.* by his eldest son,

Thomas Legh, esq. of Adlington, *b.* in 1614, sheriff of Cheshire 9th Charles I. He *m.* Mary, daughter of Thomas Bolles, esq. of Osberton, Notts, by Mary his wife, daughter and co-heir of William Witham, esq. of Leadstone Hall, in Yorkshire, and was *s.* by his eldest son,

Thomas Legh, esq. of Adlington, sheriff of Cheshire 14th Charles II. *b.* in 1643; *m.* Joanna, daughter of Sir John Maynard, serjeant-at-law, one of the commissioners of the great seal, and had

- I. John, his heir.
- II. Robert, of Chorley, *m.* Margaret, daughter of Sir Richard Standish, bart. of Duxbury, and had issue,
  - 1. Thomas, } all *d.* unm.
  - 2. Richard,
  - 3. Henry,
  - 1. Ann, *m.* Richard Crosse, esq. of Crosse Hall, in Lancashire, and had three sons and four daughters, viz.
    - Thomas Crosse, who *m.* Mrs. Pedder, and dying in 1802, left, with three daughters, (Anne, *m.* to James Hilton, esq. of Pennington; Sarah, to Thomas Wilson-France, esq.; and Margaret, to the Rev. James Armetriding) an only son,
      - Richard Crosse, of whom presently as inheritor of Adlington.
    - Legh Crosse, who *m.* Miss Cooper, and *d.* leaving issue.
    - Charles Crosse, *d. s. p.*
    - Frances Crosse, *m.* to — Mawdesley, esq.
    - Elizabeth Crosse, *m.* to Thomas Armetriding.
    - Catherine Crosse, *m.* first, to — Clement; and, secondly, to — Wessell.

2. Margaret, *d.* unm.
3. Frances, *m.* to — Lancaster; and, secondly, to — Oliver, *d. s. p.*
4. Elizabeth, *m.* to William Turner, of Blake Hall, Yorkshire.
5. Mary, *d.* unm.

I. Joanna, *m.* to John Owen, esq. of Upholland, in Lancashire.
II. Ann, *m.* to Thomas Towneley, esq. of Royle, in Lancashire.

The elder son,

JOHN LEGH, esq. of Adlington, *m.* in 1693, the Lady Isabella Robarts, daughter of Bodville, Lord Bodmyn, and sister to the Earl of Radnor, by whom he had one son and two daughters, viz.

I. CHARLES, his heir.
I. Elizabeth, died unm.
II. Lucy-Frances, who *m.* Sir Peter Davenport, knt. and by him, who *d.* in 1746, left an only child,
   ELIZABETH DAVENPORT, of whom presently, as inheritor of Adlington at the decease of her uncle.

Mr. Legh died in 1735, and was *s.* by his only son,

CHARLES LEGH, esq. of Adlington, who espoused Hester, dau. and co-heiress of Robert Lee, esq. of Wincham, in Cheshire, (see that family under Townsend, of Hem), and had an only child,

THOMAS, of Wincham, who married Mary, dau. of Francis Reynolds, esq. of Strangeways, in Lancashire, and died, *vitâ patris*, in 1775, aged forty, without surviving issue.

Mr. Legh *d.* at Buxton, in July, 1781. His only son having predeceased him, Adlington, with its dependencies, passed, under a settlement he had made, to his niece,

ELIZABETH DAVENPORT, who *m.* in 1752, John Rowlls, esq. of Kingston, Receiver-General for Surrey; and by him, who died in 1779, had issue,

I. JOHN ROWLLS, who *m.* Harriet, sister and co-heir of Sir Peter Warburton, bart. of Arley; and, predeceasing his mother, left an only dau. and heir,
   ELIZABETH-HESTER ROWLLS, *m.* to Thomas Delves Broughton, esq. fourth son of Sir Thos. Broughton, bart.
II. William-Peter Rowlls, slain in a duel at Cranford Bridge.
III. Charles-Edward Rowlls, *d.* without issue.

I. Elizabeth Rowlls, *m.* first, to A. Calley, and afterwards to Thomas Haverfield.

Mrs. Rowlls, who assumed the surname of Legh, *d.* in 1806, leaving no surviving male issue; when the Adlington estates devolved, in accordance with the settlement of her predecessor, on her kinsman,

RICHARD CROSSE, esq. of Shaw Hill, near Preston, in Lancashire, who assumed, in consequence, the surname and arms of LEGH. He *m.* in 1787, Anne, only surviving dau. of Robert Parker, esq. of Cuerden Hall, by Anne, his wife, daughter and heiress of Thomas Townley, esq. of Royle, (see vol. i. p. 117), and by her, who *d.* in 1807, had issue,

I. THOMAS, his heir.
II. Richard-Townley.

I. Sarah.
II. Ann-Mary.
III. Jane-Legh.

Mr. (Cross) Legh was *s.* at his decease, by his son,

THOMAS LEGH, esq. of Adlington, *b.* in Sept. 1792, who *m.* Louisa, dau. of George Newnham, esq. of New Timber Place, in Sussex, and by her (who wedded, secondly, 12th May, 1830, the Hon. Thomas Americus Erskine, eldest son of David Montague Lord Erskine), had issue,

I. CHARLES-RICHARD-BANASTRE, his heir.
II. Thomas-Henry-Townley, *b.* in Feb. and *d.* in Sept. 1822.

I. Mary-Anne, *m.* 6th Dec. 1830, to the Hon. and Rev. Augustus Cavendish, fourth son of the late Lord Waterpark.
II. Marcella-Louisa.
III. Emily-Anne.

Mr. Legh *d.* 25th April, 1829, and was *s.* by his only surviving son, the present CHARLES-RICHARD-BANASTRE LEGH, esq. of Adlington.

*Arms*—Az., two bars arg. debruised by a bend componè, or and gu. for difference.

*Crest*—A unicorn's head, couped, arg. armed and maned, or; on the neck, a cross patonce, gu.

*** The Leghs, of Adlington, bore, anciently, "az. within a border arg. three ducal coronets or; in the centre point, a plate;" being the coat of Corona, of Adlington, differenced.

*Estates*—In Cheshire.

*Seat*—Adlington Hall. This mansion lies about a quarter of a mile to the right of the road from Stockport to Macclesfield, about eight miles south of the former place, on the edge of an extensive park, in a low situation. The house is very spacious, and built in a quadrangular form, three sides of which are irregular, and still consist partly of timber and plaster buildings terminating in gables. The principal front on the south side is of brick, two stories high, with projecting wings, and portico in the centre supported by stone columns. In the south-east angle of this front is the domestic chapel of Adlington, fitted up in a handsome and appropriate manner; and in the opposite front, to the north, is the great hall of the mansion, which appears to be of the time of Elizabeth.

A court leet and court baron are held twice in the year for the manor; to the former of which, all tenants and resiants within the manor owe suit and service.

Adlington House was garrisoned for King Charles, in the civil wars, and besieged by the parliamentarians after the raising of the siege of Nantwich. It is noticed, as follows, in Burghall's Diary: "Friday, 14th (Feb. 1645). Adlington House was delivered up, after being besieged a fortnight. A younger son of Mr. Legh's, and a hundred and fifty soldiers, had all fair quarter, and leave to depart, leaving seven hundred arms and fifteen barrels of powder.

## SUCKLING, OF WOODTON HALL.

SUCKLING, *The Reverend* ALFRED-INIGO, LL. B. of Woodton Hall, in the county of Norfolk, *b.* 31st January, 1796, *m.* 31st January, 1816, Lucy-Clementina, eldest daughter of Samuel Clarke, esq. and has issue,

I. ROBERT-ALFRED, R. N. *b.* 18th July, 1818.
II. Maurice-Shelton, *b.* 10th June, 1819.
III. Charles-Richard, *b.* 8th April, 1825.
IV. Henry-Edward, *b.* 7th January, 1827.

I. Lucy.
II. Catherine-Webb.
III. Rosa-Matilda.
IV. Margaret-Anne.
V. Fanny-Jane.
VI. Elizabeth-Cranfield.

This gentleman, formerly of Pembroke College, Cambridge, and now a magistrate for Norfolk, succeeded his uncle, Lieutenant Maurice William Suckling, in 1820, and assumed, in compliance with the testamentary injunction of his maternal grandfather, the surname and arms of SUCKLING, instead of his patronymic, Fox.

### Lineage.

THOMAS SUCKLING, who was admitted in the year 1348 to a messuage, and several acres of land held of the manor of Woodton cum Langhall, in Norfolk, was father of

JOHN SUCKLING, living in 1353, whose grandson, (it is presumed),

PHILIP SUCKLING, possessed the messuage and lands above alluded to, and *d.* in 1430, leaving, by Johanna, his wife, a son and successor,

STEPHEN SUCKLING, living in 1479, whose son,

JOHN SUCKLING, was father of

JOHN SUCKLING, who was appointed trustee to certain church lands in Woodton. He was the first of the family who bore the surname of SUCKLING only, previously they had called themselves SUCKLING alias ESTHAWE. He wedded a lady named Alice, but of what family is not recorded, and, dying about the year 1515, was buried at Woodton, and *s.* by his son,

ROBERT SUCKLING, who *d.* in 1539, and was interred at Norwich. He left three sons, RICHARD, John, and Nicholas: the eldest of whom,

RICHARD SUCKLING, succeeded him. He *m.* Jane, daughter of — Swaney, of the county of York, and had issue, ROBERT, his heir; John; Johanna, *m.* to — Ling, of Norwich; Elizabeth, *m.* to Thomas Rochester; Cicely; and Fanny, the wife of — Markes, of Burford. He died in 1551, was buried at Norwich, and succeeded by his eldest son,

ROBERT SUCKLING, who *m.* first, Elizabeth, daughter of William Barwick, esq. of Westhorpe, by whom he had issue,

i. Edmond, D.D. dean of Norwich, who gave the communion plate to the cathedral of that city. They bear the arms of Suckling, impaling the deanery, with a Latin inscription. By Amie, his wife, he left two daughters, one married to the Rev. Thomas Spendlove, prebendary of Norwich Cathedral, and the other Lucy Suckling, to Thomas Marsham, of Stratton Strawless. (See vol i. p. 418.)

ii. Robert, of Campania.

iii. John (Sir), of whom presently.

i. Anne, *m.* to Thomas Layer, esq. of Norwich.

ii. Mary, *m.* to — Hassel, esq. of London.

iii. Elizabeth, *m.* to Charles Cardinal, esq. of Dedham, in Essex.

iv. Maud, *m.* to Sir Peter Gleane, knt.

Robert Suckling wedded, secondly, Johanna, daughter of William Cardinall, esq. of Bromley, and by her had

i. Charles, of whom hereafter, as successor to the representation of the family, upon the demise of Sir John Suckling, the poet.

ii. Christopher, of Wix, in Essex.

Mr. Suckling served as representative in parliament for the city of Norwich in the years 1570 and 1585. He was a member of the company of Merchant Adventurers, and his arms, impaled with those of that community, are still in the spandrils of the Old Hall at Woodton, which he erected, having purchased the manor and advowson thereof from Sir Christopher Haydon for about £300. He possessed, previously, almost all the *land* in the parish, but, as the manor was only then acquired, Blomfield, the historian of Norfolk, commences with this gentleman, thus accounting for the mistake Nelson's biographers have all committed in saying that "his lordship's maternal ancestors, the Sucklings, have been resident at Woodton for *three* centuries," whereas five would be nearer the truth. Robert Suckling's third son, but eldest to leave male issue,

Sir John Suckling, knt. privy counsellor to James I. *m.* first, Martha, sister to Lionel Cranfield, esq. of Middlesex, and secondly, a daughter of — Reeve, of Bury St. Edmunds, in the county of Suffolk. By the first only he had issue, viz.

i. John (Sir), his heir.

ii. Lionel, died *s. p.*

i. Anne, *m.* to Sir John Davis, of Pangbourne, and *d.* in 1659.

ii. Mary, *d.* unmarried, 1658.

Sir John *d.* in 1627, and was *s.* by his son,

Sir John Suckling, the celebrated poet. This distinguished person early displayed an extraordinary facility of acquiring every branch of education. He spoke Latin at an almost incredibly youthful period, and could write in that language at the age of nine. It is probable that he was taught more languages than one at the same time, and, by practising frequently with men of education who kept company with his father, soon acquired an ease and elegance of address which qualified him for the court as well as for foreign travel. His father is represented as a man of a serious turn and grave manners; the son volatile, good-tempered, and thoughtless, characteristics which he seems to have preserved throughout life. It does not appear that he was sent to either university, yet a perusal of his prose works can leave no doubt that he laid a very solid and extensive foundation for various learning, and studied, not only such authors as were suitable to the vivacity of his disposition, but made himself acquainted with those of a political and religious nature.

After continuing for some years under his father's tutorage, he travelled over the kingdom, and then went to the continent, where, his biographer informs us, "he made an honourable collection of the virtues of each nation, without any tincture of their defects, unless it were a little too much of the French air, which was, indeed, the fault of his complexion, rather than his person." It was about this time, probably in his twentieth year, that he joined the standard of Gustavus Adolphus, and was present at five battles and three sieges, besides minor engagements, within the space of six months.

On his return, he spent his time, and expended his fortune, among the wits of his age, to whom he was recommended, not only by generous and social habits, but by a solid sense in argument and conversation far beyond what might be expected from his years, and the apparent lightness of his disposition. Among his principal associates we find the names of Lord Falkland, Davenant, Ben Jonson, Digby, Carew, Sir Toby Matthews, and the "ever memorable" Hales of Eton, to whom he addresses a lively invitation to come to town. His plays, "Aglaura," "Breunoralt," "The Gobblins," and an unfinished piece, entitled "The sad One," added considerably to his fame, although they have not been able to perpetuate it. The first only was printed in his life-time. All his plays, we are told, were acted with applause, and he spared no expense in costly dresses and decorations.

While thus seemingly devoted to pleasure only, the unfortunate aspect of public affairs roused him to a sense of duty, and induced him to offer his services, and devote his life and fortune, to the cause of royalty. How properly he could contemplate the unjust dispute between the court and the nation appears in his letter to Mr. Germaine (afterwards Lord Albemarle), a composition almost unrivalled in that age for elegance of style and depth of observation. It was, however, too much the practice with those who made voluntary offers of soldiers, to equip them in an expensive and useless manner. Suckling, who was magnificent in all his expenses, was not to be outdone in an article which he had studied more than became a soldier, and which he might suppose would afford unquestionable proof of his attachment to the royal cause; and, having been permitted to raise a troop of horse, consisting of an hundred men, he equipped them so richly, that they are said to have cost him the sum of twelve thousand pounds.

This exposed him to some degree of ridicule, a weapon which the republicans often wielded with successful dexterity, and which, in this instance, was sharpened by the misconduct of his gaudy troopers. It appears, too, that in 1639, the royal army, of which his corps formed a part, was defeated by the Scotch, and that Sir John's men behaved remarkably ill. All this is possible, without any imputation on the courage of their commander; but it afforded his enemies an opportunity of turning the expedition into ridicule with an effect that it is still remembered. The lines in Dr. Percy's collection, by Sir John Mennis, are not the only specimen of the wit of the times at our author's expense.

This unhappy affair is said by Lloyd to have contributed to shorten the poet's days; but Lord Oxford informed Oldys, on the authority of Dean Chetwood, who said he had it from Lord Roscommon, that Sir John Suckling, in his way to France, was robbed of a casket of gold and jewels, by his valet, who gave him poison, and besides, stuck the blade of a penknife into his boot, in such a manner that Sir John was disabled from pursuing the villain, and was wounded incurably in the heel. Dr. Warton, in his note to an Essay on Pope, relates the story somewhat differently: "Sir John Suckling was robbed by his valet-de-chambre; the moment he discovered it, he clapped on his boots in a passionate hurry, and perceived not a large rusty nail that was concealed at the bottom, which pierced his heel, and brought on a mortification." He died May 7th, 1641, in the thirty-second year of his age. That he was on his way to France when he met with the occasion of his death, seems to be confirmed by a ludicrous poem, lately re-printed in the "Censura Literaria," entitled "A Letter sent by Sir John Suckling from France, deploring his sad estate and flight: with a discoverie of the plot and conspiracie, intended by him and his adherents against England. Imprinted at London, 1641." This poem is dated Paris, June 16, 1641, at which time the author probably had not learned that the object of his satire was beyond his reach.

As a poet, he wrote for amusement, and was not stimulated by ambition, or anxious for fame. His pieces were sent loose to the world; and not having been collected until after his death, they are probably less correct than he left them. Many of his verses are as rugged and unharmonious as those of Donne; but his songs and ballads are elegant and graceful. He was particularly happy and original in expressing the feelings of artificial love, disdain, or disappointment. The "Session of the Poets," the "Lines to a Rival," the "Honest Lover," and the "Ballad upon a Wedding," are sufficient to entitle him to the honours of poetry, which the author of the Lives published under the name of Cibber is extremely anxious to wrest from him.

His works have been often reprinted; first in 1646, 8vo.; again, in 1659 and 1676; very correctly, by Tonson, in 1719; and elegantly, but incorrectly, by Davies, in 1770. The edition of Tonson has been followed in the late edition of the "English Poets," with the omission of such pieces as were thought degrading to his memory, and insulting to public decency. But whatever opinion is entertained of Suckling as a poet, it may be doubted whether his prose writings are not calculated to raise a yet higher opinion of his talents. His Letters, with a dash of gallantry more free than modern times will admit, are shrewd in observation, and often elegant in style. That addressed to Mr. Germaine has already been noticed, and his "Account of Religion by Reason" is remarkable for soundness of argument and purity of expression, far exceeding the controversial productions of that age. This piece affords a presumption that he was even now no stranger to those reflections which elevate the human character, and that, if his life had been spared, it would have been probably devoted to more honourable objects than those in which he had employed his youthful days. At Sir John's decease, issueless, in 1641, the representation of the family passed to his uncle,

CHARLES SUCKLING, esq. of Woodton, who *m.* first, Mary, dau. and co-heir of Stephen Drury, esq. of Aylsham, and by her had an only son, ROBERT, his heir; he wedded secondly, Dorothy, dau. of Anthony Drury, esq. of Beesthorpe, and had with other issue, a son, Charles, of Bracondale, who *m.* Maria Aldrich, of Mangreen Hall, and *d.* in 1666.

Mr. Suckling *d.* himself in 1644, and was *s.* by his son,

ROBERT SUCKLING, esq. of Woodton, high sheriff for Norfolk in 1664, who married, first, Anne, third daughter of Sir Thomas Wodehouse, bart. M. P. of Kimberley, by Blanch, his wife, dau. of John, Lord Hunsdon, and had a son, ROBERT, his heir. He *m.* secondly, Margaret, second daughter of Sir William Doyley, bart. of Shottisham, by whom he had,

I. Horatio.
II. William.
I. Elizabeth, *m.* to Abraham Castell, esq. of Yarmouth.

Mr. Suckling *d.* in 1690, and was *s.* by his eldest son,

ROBERT SUCKLING, esq. of Woodton, who *m.* Sarah, daughter of Maurice Shelton, esq. of Shelton, and dying in 1708, left two sons and one daughter, viz.

I. ROBERT, his heir.
II. Maurice, D.D. prebendary of Westminster, who *m.* Anne, elder dau. of Sir Charles Turner, bart. of Warham, by Mary, his wife, sister of the celebrated Sir Robert Walpole, K.G. and and had issue,

MAURICE, capt. R.N. who *m.* Mary Walpole, niece of the first Earl of Orford, but died *s. p.* This gentleman, the early patron of Nelson, fought, on the 21st Oct. 1757, a naval action, off Cape Francois, parallelled only by his nephew's achievements: with three ships, carrying 184 guns, and 1232 men, he defeated a French squadron of much heavier metal, bearing 366 guns and 3440 men. He was subsequently returned to Parliament for Portsmouth, made comptroller of the Navy, and one of the elder brethren of the Trinity House. It is not a little singular that the great action of Trafalgar was fought on the same day of the month, the 21st October, and to the circumstance Nelson alluded at the commencement of that memorable engagement.

William, who also *d.* issueless.

Catherine, who married, 11th May, 1749, the Rev. Edmund Nelson, M. A. rector of Burham Thorpe, in Norfolk, and had issue,

MAURICE NELSON, *d. s. p.* in 1801.

WILLIAM NELSON, late EARL NELSON.

HORATIO NELSON, VISCOUNT NELSON, the hero of TRAFALGAR.

Susannah Nelson, *m.* Thomas Bolton, esq. and their son Thomas is the present EARL NELSON.

Anne Nelson, *d.* unm.

Catherine Nelson, *m.* to Geo. Matcham, esq.

I. Lucy, *m.* to Thomas Stone, esq. of of Bedingham, and *d. s. p.*

Mr. Suckling was *s.* by his elder son,

ROBERT SUCKLING, esq. of Woodton, who wedded Dorothy, daughter of John Berney, esq. and dying in 1734, left issue,

I. DENZIL, who *m.* Hannah Tubby, and left at his demise, in 1744, a son, Robert, who died issueless.
II. Robert, in holy orders, who *d. s. p.*
III. RICHARD, of whom presently.
IV. Horace, in holy orders, who *d.* without issue.
I. Mary, *m.* to Roger Howman, esq.

The third son,

RICHARD SUCKLING, esq. *m.* Ann Kibert, and was father of

ROBERT SUCKLING, esq. of Woodton, capt. in the West Norfolk Militia, who *m.* Susannah Webb, a descendant of Inigo Jones, and had issue,

I. ROBERT-GEORGE, captain, R.A. died issueless, in the West Indies.
II. MAURICE-WILLIAM, his heir.
III. John Thomas, *m.* Mary-Anne, dau. of —— French, esq. of Broome, in Suffolk, and had issue.
I. Anna-Maria, who *m.* at St. Peter's church, Norwich, about 1794, Alexander Fox, esq. and had an only son,

ALFRED-INIGO FOX, successor to his uncle.

II. Emily-Susanna, married to Nicholas Cheesman, esq. of the county of York, and has, with other issue, a son,

Robert Suckling Cheesman.

The entail having been cut off, Captain Suckling settled the estate on his son, MAURICE-WILLIAM, and failure of his issue, on the son of his eldest daughter. He died in 1812, and was *s.* accordingly by

MAURICE-WILLIAM SUCKLING, esq. lieut. R. N. who *m.* first, Catharine, daughter of Framlingham, M. D.; and secondly, Caroline, dau. of — Ramell, esq.; but dying issueless, 1st Dec. 1820, the estates passed under the settlement to his nephew, Alfred Inigo Fox, who, having assumed the surname and arms of SUCKLING, is the present *Rev.* ALFRED INIGO SUCKLING, of Woodton Hall.

*Arms*—Party per pale, gu. and az. three bucks trippant, or, for SUCKLING—quartering arg. a chev. chequy erm. and gu. with two chevronells between three boars' heads couped of the last for Fox.

*Crest*—A stag courant or, with a sprig of honeysuckle in his mouth.

*Motto*—Mora trahit periculum.

*Estates*—Manors and advowsons of Woodton and Langhall, in Norfolk, gradually acquired by purchase, from 1348 to 1650; manor and advowson of Barsham, in Suffolk, purchased by Sir John Suckling, in 1613; manor and advowson of Shipmeadow, Suffolk, purchased a short time previously; with estates in St. Andrews, &c. in same county.

*Seat*—Woodton Hall.

## RAIKES, OF WELTON HOUSE.

RAIKES, ROBERT, esq. of Welton House, in the county of York, *b.* 31st August, 1765, *m.* 4th November, 1789, Anne, only daughter of Thomas Williamson, esq. of Welton House, and has issue,

I. THOMAS, *b.* 6th September, 1790, *m.* first, Elizabeth, daughter and heiress of Thomas Armstrong, esq. of Castle Armstrong, in the King's county, and has,

1. ROBERT, *b.* 18th October 1818.
2. Thomas, *b.* 26th October, 1823.

3. Grace-Louisa.
4. Ann.

He married, secondly, 17th February, 1825, Elizabeth-Frances, eldest daughter of Charles Lutwidge, esq. collector of the customs at the port of Hull, and has by her another son and another daughter, viz.

Charles, *b.* 27th November, 1828.

Elizabeth-Lucy.

II. Robert, *b.* 26th October, 1801, *m.* Eleanor-Catharine, eldest daughter of the late Admiral Puget, and has issue,

1. Robert-William, *b.* 8th November, 1828.
2. Arthur, *b.* 7th April, 1831.
3. Henry-Puget, *b.* 16th September, 1834.

1. Ellen-Anna.
2. Annette-Cecilia.

I. Anne-Louisa, *m.* 3rd November, 1831, to the Reverend Charles Henry Lutwidge, esq. M.A. vicar of Burton Agnes, in the East Riding of Yorkshire, eldest son of Charles Lutwidge, esq. of Hull.

II. Martha, *d.* 24th August, 1797, buried in Barking Church-yard, Essex.

Mr. Raikes, who inherits Welton from his father-in-law, Thomas Williamson, esq. was formerly a magistrate and deputy-lieutenant for the county of Essex, and high-sheriff thereof in 1802.

### Lineage.

WILLIAM RAIKES, esq. *m.* in 1762, Martha Pelly, eldest daughter of Job Mathew, esq. of Essex, and had three sons and three daughters, viz.

I. WILLIAM-MATHEW, *b.* 12th August, 1763, *m.* Elizabeth, only daughter of — Reeve, esq. of Hampstead in the county of Gloucester, but *d. s. p.* 8th April, 1824.

II. ROBERT, now of WELTON HOUSE.

III. JOB-MATHEW, *b.* 12th July, 1767, married Charlotte, eldest daughter of

Charles Bayley, esq. of Jamaica, and *d.* 1st October, 1833, he had three sons and four daughters.

I. Marianne, *m.* to Isaac Currie, esq. Banker, of London, and *d.* 11th July, 1834.

II. Martha, *m.* to the Rev. William Kinleside, vicar of Augmering, Sussex.

III. Charlotte, *m.* to Brice Pearce, esq. of London, and died 3rd August, 1834.

*Arms*—A chev. between three griffins' heads.

*Crest*—A griffin's head.

*Motto*—Honestum præferre utili.

*Estates*—Welton, Brafford's House, South Wold, Wouldby, and several estates at Elloughton, Brafford's, Aldborough, Burstwick, Elstronwick, Drypool, and Willerby, all in the county of York, together with the patronage of the vicarage of Burton Agnes, East Riding.

*Seat*—Welton House, near Cave.

## MACPHERSON, OF CLUNY-MACPHERSON.

MACPHERSON, EWEN, of Cluny-Macpherson, in Inverness-shire, CHIEF of the MACPHERSONS, and lineal descendant, in the male line, of the chiefs of the Clan Chattan, *b.* 24th April, 1804, *m.* 20th December, 1832, Sarah Justina, youngest daughter of the late Henry Davidson, esq. of Tulloch Castle, in the shire of Ross, and has a son,

DUNCAN.

Cluny-Macpherson, a captain on half-pay, 42nd Royal Highlanders, succeeded his father, 1st August, 1817, and is a magistrate and deputy-lieutenant for the county of Inverness.

### Lineage.

GILLICATTAN, head or chief of the clan Chattan, who, on account of his immense stature, rare military genius, and other accomplishments, acquired the designation *Moir*, lived in the reign of *King* MALCOLM *Canmore*, and left a son,

DIARMED or DORMUND, captain of the clan Chattan, who *s.* his father about the year 1090, and was father of

GILLICATTAN, the second of that name, captain of the clan Chattan, who flourished and made a considerable figure in the reign of *King* DAVID I. left two sons,

I. DIARMED,

II. MURIACH,

and was succeeded by the elder,

DIARMED, captain of the clan Chattan, who did not long survive his father, and dying without issue, *anno* 1153, was *s.* by his brother,

MURIACH or MURDOCH, who, being a younger son, was bred to the church, and was parson of Kingousie, then a large and honourable benefice; but, upon the death of his elder brother without issue, he became head of his family, and captain of the clan Chattan. He then obtained a dispensation from the pope, in 1173, and married a daughter of the Thane of Calder, by whom he had five sons,

I. GILLICATTAN, his heir.

II. Ewan, or Eugine, called *Baan*, from the fairness of his complexion. He lived in the reign of ALEXANDER II. and, surnames about this time becoming hereditary, he obtained that of MACPARSON, or son of the Parson. He *m.* and left three sons,

1. KENNETH, of whom presently,

as continuator of the male line upon the demise of his cousin, Dougal Phaol.

2. John, living *temp.* ALEXANDER III. designed of Pitmean. He *m.* and had two sons, from whom descended many families of the name, viz. the MACPHERSONS of Pitmean, Strathmassie, Ferfodoun, Kenlochlagan, Invertromeny, Pitchern, Clune, Pitgowan, Garvamore, Balladmore, Balladbeg, Inneraven, Carnbeg, Craegarnell, &c. &c.

3. Gillies, progenitor of the MACPHERSONS, of Inneressie.

III. Neill, called *Cromb*, from his stooping and round shoulders. "He had," says Douglas, "a rare mechanical genius, applied himself to the business of a smith, and made and contrived several utensils of iron, of very curious workmanship." He is stated to have taken a surname from his trade, and to have been ancestor of the Scottish families of Smith.

IV. Ferquhard, *Gilleriach, the Swift*, from whom sprung the Macgillivrays of Drumnaglash, in Inverness-shire, and those of Pennygoit, in the Isle of Mull.

V. David, *Dow*, or *the Black*, from whom the old Davidsons of Invernahaven are said to be descended.

Muriach *d.* towards the close of the reign of WILLIAM the Lion, and was *s.* by his eldest son,

GILLICATTAN, third of the name, captain of the clan Chattan, whose only son,

DOUGAL PHAOL, or, according to Nisbet, Dougal Daol, succeeded, and was captain of the clan Chattan. He *d.* in the reign of Alexander III. leaving an only daughter,

EVA, who, in 1291 or 1292, became the wife of ANGUS MACINTOSH of that ilk, chieftain of the clan Macintosh, and conveyed to her husband a considerable portion of the clan Chattan estate. See MACINTOSH, of MACINTOSH.

Dougal dying thus, without male issue, the dignity of captain of the clan Chattan has ever since been the subject of contention between the families of Macintosh, of Macintosh, (claiming the honour as representatives, of the *senior* line, through the abovementioned, Eva, the daughter and heiress of DOUGAL), and the Macphersons of Clunie, (founding their pretensions on their unbroken male filiation and representing Ewan, the next brother of Dougal). The Macintoshes obtaining, with EVA, the daughter of DOUGAL, the Lochaber estate, the inhabitants thereof followed the chief of MACINTOSH as their superior and master, who was therefore designed captain of the clan Chattan. The rest of the clan, however, adhering to KENNETH, as the heir male, retired to Badenoch, where they settled, and where they soon acquired large possessions, and have been always styled the clan Macpherson, and likewise captains of the clan Chattan. We venture not an opinion on the merits of the rival houses, but merely give, without note or comment, the pretensions of each. Dougal's cousin-german (the son of his uncle Ewan),

KENNETH MACPHERSON, became, at Dougal's decease, undoubted male representative of the family. He was living in the reign of ALEXANDER III. and *m.* Isabel, daughter of Ferquhard Macintosh, of Macintosh, by whom he had two sons,

I. DUNCAN, his heir.

II. Bean, or Benjamin, ancestor of the MACPHERSONS of BRIN, &c.

The elder son,

DUNCAN MACPHERSON, of Clunie, lived in the reign of Robert Bruce; and, being a man of a noble spirit, a steady loyalist, and particularly known to the king, obtained a commission (as head of his clan) from that great prince to reduce the Cumings, and others his rebel subjects in Badenoch, to obedience, which he performed so effectually, that he got a grant of large territorial tracts; and he had also, for his special services against the Cumings, a hand and dagger added to his armorial bearing, &c.

He was succeeded by his son,

DONALD PHAOL MACPHERSON, of Clunie, called *Donald Moir*.

In the beginning of the reign of ROBERT II. there happened a bloody conflict between the Macphersons and the clan Cameron, at Invernahaven, in Badenoch, where the greatest part of the clan Cameron were killed on the spot; those who survived were taken prisoners, but Donald generously gave them all their liberty.

In this Donald's time the dissentions between the clan Chattan, and the clan Kay, ran so very high, that they took up the attention of the whole court. The king and the Duke of Albany sent the Earls of Crawford and of Murray (then two of the greatest men in the kingdom) to try to settle their differences, and, if possible, to effect a reconciliation, but all to no purpose. It was at last proposed that each clan should choose thirty of their own number to fight in the North Inch of Perth, with their broad-swords only, and thereby put an end to their disputes. The combat was cheerfully agreed to by both parties. They met accordingly on the day appointed: the king and an incredible number of the nobility and gentry being spectators. Prompted by old malice and inveterate hatred, they fought with inexpressible resolution and fury. Twenty-nine of the clan Kay were killed on the spot; the one who remained unhurt, made his escape by swimming over the river Tay, and, it is said, was put to death by his own clan when he came home, for not choosing to die in the field of honour with his companions, rather than save his life by flying.

Of the clan Chattan nineteen were killed in the field, and the other eleven so much wounded that none of them were able to pursue their single antagonist who fled. This happened on the Monday before the feast of St. Michael, anno 1396; and the victory was adjudged in favour of the clan Chattan.

We must here observe, that the family of Clunie contend that the thirty combatants of the clan Chattan were all Macphersons; "because," say they, "their antagonists, the clan Kay, were followers of the Cumings of Badenoch, and envied the Macphersons the possession of their lands, which was the cause of their constant feuds."

The Macintoshes also allege, that these thirty were of their party of the clan Chattan, and all Macintoshes.

Donald Moir *m.* a daughter of Macintosh, of Mammore, in Lochaber, by whom he had two sons,

- I. DONALD-OIG, his heir.
- II. Gillicattan-Beg, or Little Malcolm, of whom the Macphersons of Effich, Breakachie, &c. &c. are descended.

He was succeeded by his eldest son,

DONALD-OIG MACPHERSON, of Clunie, who, in the reign of JAMES I. married a daughter of Gordon of Buckie, and had two sons.

- I. EWAN, or EUGINE, his heir.
- II. Paul, from whom the Macphersons of Dalissour, &c. &c. are descended.

He was *s.* by his eldest son,

EUGINE MACPHERSON, of Clunie, who *d.* in the end of the reign of JAMES III. leaving a son and successor,

DORMUND MACPHERSON, who got a charter under the great seal from *King* JAMES IV. "Dormundo Macpherson, terrarum de Strantheaune, Garnamuch," &c. &c. dated 6th February, 1509. He died in the reign of JAMES V. and was *s.* by his son,

EWAN Macpherson, of Clunie, a man of distinguished merit, and a firm and devoted adherent of the unfortunate *Queen* MARY. He married a daughter of Macintosh, of Stone, by whom he had two sons,

- I. ANDREW, his heir.
- II. John, successor to his brother.

He was succeeded by eldest son,

ANDREW MACPHERSON, of Clunie, &c. who dying soon after his father, without issue, was succeeded by his brother,

JOHN MACPHERSON, of Clunie, who got a charter under the great seal from King JAMES VI. "Johanni Macpherson, villarum et terrarum de Tullich, Elrich, &c. in vice comitatu de Inverness," dated in 1594. In October of the same year, he was with the Earl of Huntly, at the battle of Glenlivet, where the king's troops were defeated under the command of the Earl of Argyle; but he suffered nothing on that account, for Huntly and all his adherents were soon after received into the king's favour.

He married a daughter of Gordon, of Auchanassie, and died about the year 1600, leaving a son,

JOHN MACPHERSON, of Clunie, &c. who succeeded him, and got a charter under the great seal; "Johanni Macpherson, filio Johannis, &c. terrarum de Tullich, Elrick, &c. in Invernesshire," dated 1613. He was succeeded by his son,

EWAN MACPHERSON, of Clunie, who got a charter under the great seal, "Eugenio Macpherson, terrarum et villarum de Tullich, Elrick, &c. &c." dated anno 1623. He married a daughter of Duncan Forbes, of Culloden, by whom he had three sons and one daughter,

- I. DONALD, his heir.
- II. Andrew, successor to his brother.
- III. John, of Nuid, living *temp.* CHARLES I. who *m.* a dau. of Farquharson, of Monaltrie, and had four sons and two daughters, viz.
  1. DONALD, his heir.
  2. William, who *m.* twice, and left a great many descendants; particularly the celebrated JAMES MACPHERSON, the translator of Ossian.
  3. Andrew, ancestor of the Macphersons of Crathy-Croy, &c.
  4. Murdoch, of whom there are no male descendants.

  1. Janet, *m.* to Fraser, of Fouirs; secondly, to Angus Macpherson, of Dalraddie; thirdly, to Grant; fourthly, to Angus Macpherson, of Inneressie; and, fifthly, to — Macqueen. She had issue by all.
  2. Bessie, *m.* to Donald Macpherson, of Phoness, and had issue.

The eldest son of John, of Nuid,

DONALD MACPHERSON, of Nuid, *m.* first, *temp.* CHARLES II. a dau. of Hugh Rose, of Kilravock; and. secondly, a dau. of Gordon, of

Knockspeck. By the former, he left at his decease (with seven daughters, the eldest *m.* to Grant, of Laggan; the second, to Macgregor, of —; the third, to — Macintosh; the fourth, to Robert Macintosh; the fifth, to Ewan Macpherson, of Clunie; the sixth, to John Macpherson, son of Malcolm, of Phoness; and the seventh, to Robert Innes, of Mid-Keith), three sons, WILLIAM, his heir; James, who left issue; and John, ancestor of Macpherson of Cullenlian, Rawliah, &c. The eldest son,

WILLIAM MACPHERSON, of Nuid, living *temp.* JAMES VII. *m.* Isabel, dau. of Lauchlan Macintosh, esq. and had four sons and six daughters, viz.

1. LAUCHLAN, of Nuid, who succeeded to the chieftainship, and became of Clunie, at the decease of his cousin, Duncan. Of this Lauchlan, more hereafter.
2. James, who died unmarried.
3. Andrew, who left issue.
4. William, a writer in Edinburgh, *m.* Jean, daughter of James Adamson, merchant, and had six sons, James, Angus, David, John, Robert, and Norman.

1. Isabel, *m.* to Angus Macpherson, of Killiehuntly.
2. Margaret, *m.* to Macintosh, of Linvulg.
3. Jean, *m.* to Ewan Macpherson, of Pittourie.
4. — *m.* to Macdonald, of Keyltierie.
5. — *m.* to Mackintosh, of Pharr.
6. Mary, *m.* to Donald, son of Malcolm Macpherson, of Brakachie.

I. Marjory, *m.* to John Macpherson, of Inneressie.

Ewan Macpherson *d.* about the year 1640, and was *s.* by his eldest son,

DONALD MACPHERSON, of Clunie, who attached himself to the royal cause, and suffered much in consequence. Dying issueless, he was succeeded by his brother,

ANDREW MACPHERSON, of Clunie, who also inherited, as heir of entail, the estate of Brin. He *m.* a dau. of Gordon, of Erradoul, and, dying in 1666, was *s.* by his son,

EUGENE MACPHERSON, of Clunie, living *temp.* CHARLES II. who *m.* a dau. of Donald Macpherson, of Nuid, and had two sons, Andrew and Duncan. The elder,

ANDREW MACPHERSON, of Clunie, dying unm. was succeeded by his brother,

DUNCAN MACPHERSON, of Clunie, who *m.* first, a dau. of the provost (Rose) of Inverness, and had by her a daughter,

ANNE, *m.* to Sir Duncan Campbell, knt. uncle of John Campbell, esq. of Calder, and had issue.

Clunie wedded, secondly, a dau. of — Gordon, by whom he had one son, who *d.* unm. Duncan dying at an advanced age, in 1722, without surviving male issue, the representation devolved on his cousin (refer to descendants of John, third son of Ewan Macpherson, of Clunie, who died about 1640),

LACHLAN MACPHERSON, of Nuid, who then became of Clunie. He *m.* Jean. dau. of the brave Sir Ewen Cameron, of Locheil, by whom he had seven sons and three daughters,

I. EWEN, his heir.
II. John, major in the 78th regiment of foot, commanded by Simon Frazer, esq. eldest son of Simon, Lord Lovat: tutor and guardian to his nephew, Duncan, of Clunie, during his minority.
III. James, in the army, *d.* unmarried.
IV. Donald, died also unmarried.
V. Lachlan, in the army, married, and had two sons.
VI. Andrew, an officer in the Queen's royal regiment of Highlanders, commanded by General Graham, of Gorthy, married, and had issue.
VII. Alan, died unmarried.

I. Isabel, *m.* to William Macintosh, of Aberarder.
II. Christian, *m.* to Donald Macpherson, of Brakachie.
III. Unah, *m.* to Lewis Macpherson, of Dalraddie.

Lachlan, of Clunie, died anno 17—, and was succeeded by his eldest son,

EWEN MACPHERSON, of Clunie, who *m.* Janet, daughter of Simon, eleventh Lord Frazer, of Lovat, by whom he had a son, DUNCAN, his heir, and a daughter, Margaret, *m.* to Col. D. Macpherson, of Bleaton. He died at Dunkirk, and was *s.* by his only son,

DUNCAN MACPHERSON, of Clunie, *b.* in 1750, lieutenant-colonel third regiment of Guards, who *m.* 12th June, 1798, Catherine, youngest daughter of the late Sir Ewen Cameron, of Fassfern, bart. and had issue,

I. EWEN, his heir.
II. Ewen-Cameron, lieut. 48th regiment Bengal N. Infantry; *d.* 15th April, 1832.
III. Archibald-Frazer, lieut. 43rd regt. Bengal N. Infantry.
IV. John-Cameron, lieutenant 42nd regiment, or Royal Highlanders.

I. Louisa-Campbell.
II. Catherina.
III. Jannetta-Fraser, *m.* in Jan. 1822, to A. T. F. Fraser, esq. of Abertarff,

IV. Maria-Cameron.

Col. Macpherson *d.* 1st Aug. 1817, and was *s.* by his eldest son, the present EWEN MACPHERSON, of Cluny-Macpherson, chieftain of the clan.

*Arms*—Party per fess, or and azure; a lymphad, or galley, with her sails furled up, her oars in action, of the first. In the dexter chief point, a hand couped, grasping a dagger, point upwards, gules (for killing Cuming); and, in the sinister chief point, a cross crosslet fitched, of the last.

*Crest*—A cat sejant, proper.

*Motto*—Touch not a cat but a glove:—*Gaelic.* Na bean do'n chat gun lamhainn.

*Supporters*—Two Highlandmen, with steel helmets on their heads, thighs bare, their shirt tied between them, and round targets on their arms.

*Estates*—In Inverness-shire.

*Seats*—At Clunie, in Badenoch, Inverness-shire.

## PRYSE, OF GOGERDDAN.

PRYSE, PRYSE, esq. of Gogerddan, in the county of Cardigan, and of Buscot Park, Berkshire, succeeded to the Welsh estates on the death of Mrs. Margaret Pryse, (whereupon he assumed the surname and arms of Pryse) in 1798, and to those in Berkshire, upon the demise of his father, *m.* first, in 1798, Harriet, daughter of William, second Lord Ashbrook, and widow of the Hon. and Rev. John Ellis-Agar, which lady dying without issue in 1813, Mr. Pryse wedded, secondly, Jane, daughter of Peter Cavallier, esq. of Gisborough, in Cleveland, by whom he has three sons, viz.

I. PRYSE, *b.* 1st June, 1815.
II. Edward-Lewis, *b.* 27th June, 1817.
III. John-Pugh, *b.* 10th September, 1818.

This gentleman, who has represented the borough of Cardigan in parliament for several years, served the office of high sheriff of Cardiganshire, in 1798.

### Lineage.

GWAETH-VOED, Lord of Cardigan, and Gwynway, descended from Llys Hawdoc, was living at the commencement of the eleventh century. He *m.* Morvydd, daughter and co-heir of Ivor, king of Gwent, and dying in 1057, left a son,

CADIVOR, Lord of Cardigan, who *m.* Joan, daughter of Eluston, prince of Ferley, in 1099, and was father of

IVOR, Lord of Iscoed, who *m.* Lleykey, daughter of Cadivor ap Dinawall, Lord of Castle Howel, in the county of Cardigan, and was *s.* by his son,

GRUFFYDD, of Castle Odwin, whose wife was Agnes, daughter of Robert ap Madawc, of Cedowen. Their son and successor,

IEVAN, of Castle Odwin, and Glyn Aëron, wedded Elliwe, daughter of Meredydd ap Caradoc Vanrach, and left a son and successor,

IEVAN LLOYD, of Glyn Aeron, father, by Angharad, his wife, daughter of Richard ap Eineon, of the celebrated

RHYDDERCH AP IEVAN LLOYD, a poet of the first rank, who lived in the next age after Dafydd ap Gwilym. He was owner of the estate of Gogerthan, in Cardiganshire, and received his education at Oxford. Among other works of his, we have a curious ode in English, which shows the pronunciation of that language in those days, of which, perhaps, no other proof in the world can be brought. Rhydderch *m.* Maud, daughter of Gruffyd Grice, and left a son,

DAVID AP RHYDDERCH, who *m.* Ellen, daughter of Richard ap Owain ap Richard, of Ywch Aeron, and was father of

DAVID LLOYD, whose son, by Gwenllian,

daughter and heir of Meredydd ap Llynn, of Penabery.

Rhys ap David, of Gogerthan, *m.* Catherine, daughter of Rhys ap Davydd Lloyd, of Newton Elyston, and was *s.* by his son,

Richard ap Rhys, or Pryse, of Gogerthan, who wedded Ellen, daughter and co-heir of William ap Jenkin ap Jorweth, and left a son and successor,

John Pryse, of Gogerthan, who *m.* first, Elizabeth, daughter of Sir Thomas Perrot, of Haroldstone, in Pembrokeshire, and had two sons, viz.

I. Richard (Sir), his heir.
II. Thomas, of Glanvraed, *m.* Bridget, daughter and heir of John Gruffydd, esq. by whom he acquired that estate, and had
  1. Thomas, of Glanvraed, who *m.* Elizabeth, daughter of John Parry, esq. of Blaenpant, and was father of
    Thomas, of Ynyscrigog, who *m.* Susan, heir of Sir Richard Pugh, of Dôlyvorthy, in Montgomeryshire, and had two sons, viz.
      Thomas, of Glanvraed, who *m.* Maud, daughter of Lewis Owens, of Penyarth Meirion, and had one son,
        Lewis, who died in 1720, leaving, by Anne, his wife, daughter and heir of John Lloyd, esq. of Aberllyffny, four daughters.*
      Richard, of Ynyscrigog, *m.* Mary, daughter of Richard James, esq. and was father of
        Thomas, of Dôl, in Cardiganshire, who *m.* Mary, widow of John Pryse, esq. of Glanmeryn, and had a son, Richard, who died unm. in 1742.
  2. Walter, of Tunahir, in Montgomeryshire, *m.* Ann, daughter and heir of John Pugh, esq. of Glanmeryn, and had two sons, viz.
    Thomas, of Tunahir, who *m.* Mary, daughter of Evans Montgomery, and was father of
      John, of Glanmeryn, *m.* Mary, daughter of David Lewis, of Dôlhaidd, and had a son,
        Thomas, of whom presently, as inheritor of Gogerthan.
    Richard, who *m.* Elizabeth daughter of Captain Edwards, of Chirches, in Denbighshire, and was father of
      Walter, of Painswick, in Gloucestershire, living in 1743, *m.* first, Mary, daughter and coheiress of John Sewell, of Heany, in Essex, and secondly, Elizabeth, grand-daughter and heiress of Sir William Lewis, of Borden. By the former he left, with two daughters, Mary and Elizabeth, a son,
        Lewis, of whom in the sequel, as inheritor of Gogerthan.
  1. Eldest daughter, *m.* to Sir Walter Lloyd, knt. of Llanvair.
  2. Second daughter, *m.* to Lloyd, of Llanllyr.
  3. Third daughter, *m.* first, to Richard Pughe, of Dôl y fondu, and secondly, to Parry, of Noyadd.
  4. Fourth daughter, *m.* to Thomas Powell, of Llechwedd Dyrus.
  5. Fifth daughter, *m.* first, to Lloyd, of Ynyshir, and secondly, to — Knolls.
  6. Sixth daughter, *m.* to Pugh, of Escairhurois.
  7. Seventh daughter, *m.* to — Bettone, esq.

John Pryse wedded, secondly, Bridget, daughter of James Pryse, of Mynachdy, and had by her, a son,

III. James (Sir), who *d.* in 1642, leaving, by Elizabeth, his wife, daughter of Humphrey Wynn, esq. an only daughter and heiress,
  Bridget Pryse, of Ynysymaengwyn, who *m.* first, Robert Corbet, esq. second son of Sir Vincent Corbet, bart. of Moreton Corbet, and secondly, Sir Walter Lloyd, M. P. of Llanfair Clewedogan. From her first marriage

---

* The daughters and co-heirs of Lewis Pryse, of Glanvraed, were,

I. Mary, *m.* to John Campbell, of Stacpole.
II. Margaret, *m.* to — Corbet.
III. Anna.
IV. Jane, *m.* to Phillips, of Pent y Parke.

descend the present ATHELSTAN CORBET, esq. of Ynysymaengwyn.

John Pryse's eldest son,

SIR RICHARD PRYSE, knt. of Gogerthan, wedded Gwenllian, dau. and sole heir of Thomas Pryse ap Morris ap Owain ap Evan Blaney, of Aberbychan, in Montgomeryshire, and had two sons and five daughters, namely,

I. JOHN (Sir), his heir.
II. William, *d.* unm. at Oxford.

I. Bridget, *m.* to Sir John Lewis, knt. of Abernant Bychan, Cardiganshire.
II. Elizabeth, *m.* to Rowland Pugh, esq. of Mathravern, in Montgomeryshire.
III. Mary, *m.* to Edward Purcell, esq. of Nant y Cryba, Montgomeryshire.
IV. Lettice, *m.* to Thomas Lloyd, esq. of Llanlyr, in Cardiganshire.
V. Katherine, *m.* first, to James Stedman, esq. of Strata Florida, and, secondly, to Sir John Pryse.

Sir Richard Pryse died 6th Feb. 1622, was buried in the church of Llanbadarn Fawr, and succeeded by his son,

SIR JOHN PRYSE, knt. of Gogerthan, and Aberbychan, who *m.* Mary, daughter of Sir Henry Bromley, of Shradon Castle, in Salop, and had two sons and two daughters, viz.

I. RICHARD (Sir), his heir.
II. Thomas, of Gray's Inn, 1622.

I. Elizabeth, *m.* to Francis, son of Walter Vaughan, esq. of Llanelly.
II. Mary, died unmarried.

The elder son,

SIR RICHARD PRYSE, of Gogerthan, who was created a BARONET, 9th August, 1641, *m.* first, Hester, daughter of Sir Hugh Middleton, bart. and, secondly, Mary, daughter of Lord Ruthin, relict of Sir Anthony Vandycke. By the former, he had,

I. RICHARD, } successive baronets.
II. THOMAS, }
III. Carbery, *m.* Hester, daughter of Sir Bulstrode Whitlock, knt. and had one son,
    CARBERY, successor to his uncle, Sir Thomas.

Sir Richard was succeeded, about 1651, by his eldest son,

SIR RICHARD PRYSE, second baronet of Gogerthan; to whom succeeded his brother,

SIR THOMAS PRYSE, third baronet of Gogerthan, at whose decease, without issue, May 1682, the title and estates devolved on his nephew,

SIR CARBERY PRYSE, fourth baronet of Gogerthan, during whose lifetime, *anno* 1690, mines were discovered on the estate at Gogerthan, which, in their time, were not exceeded by any in the kingdom for riches, and obtained the appellation of the Welsh Potosi. By virtue of an act of parliament passed in the 1st of WILLIAM and MARY, Sir Carbery, in the year 1690, took in several partners, and divided his waste into four thousand shares; got Mr. Waller, a miner from the north, to be his agent, at the salary of £200 per annum, and began to work mines on his own land. The Society of Miners Royal, finding them rich, laid claim to them by their patents, the act not being sufficiently clear. Upon this, a lawsuit ensued, in 1692, between Sir Carbery, and Mr. Sheppard on behalf of the company, whereupon the former and his partners, among whom were several noblemen, the Duke of Leeds, the Marquis of Carmarthen, &c. taking advantage of the times, procured, in the year 1693, a most glorious act, which empowered all the subjects of the crown of England to enjoy and work their own mines, in England and Wales, notwithstanding they contained gold and silver, provided the king and those that claimed under him may have the ore, paying the proprietors for it upon the bank within thirty days after it is raised, and before it is removed for lead: lead, nine pounds per ton; copper, ten pounds, &c. On his success, Sir Carbery is said to have rode on horseback (having relays of horses on the road) from London to Escair-hir within forty-eight hours; so that, in so short a time, the happy news was spread among the inhabitants of that part of Wales. Sir Carberry died without issue, about the year 1695, when the baronetcy expired, while the estates eventually passed to his kinsman,

THOMAS PRYSE, esq. of Gogerthan, M.P. for Cardigan, 1743, who married Maria-Charlotte, daughter and heiress of Rowland Pughe, esq. of Mathavern, in Montgomeryshire; and had an only son, John Pugh, who dying issueless, the Gogerthan estates ultimately devolved on his relative,

LEWIS PRYSE, esq. who wedded Margaret, daughter and co-heiress of Edward Ryves, esq. of Woodstock; and had by her, who died 23rd January, 1798, aged 74, one son and one daughter, viz.

LEWIS, who died unmarried, 25th Sept. 1776, aged 25.

Margaret, on whose son the estates eventually devolved.

Mr. Pryse died, 12th March, 1798, aged 62. His only child to leave issue,

MARGARET PRYSE, wedded Edward-Loveden Loveden, esq. of Buscot,* in the county

* The manor of Buscot was possessed by the Stonors, in 1479, and probably at a much earlier period. In 1557, it was purchased of Sir Francis Stonor by Walter Loveden. The first of the Lovedens who resided in Berkshire, came from Crendon, in Bucks, where the family was of consi-

of Berks, and dying, 30th January, 1784, left issue,

PRYSE LOVEDEN, heir.

Margaret Loveden, married to the Rev. Samuel Warneford, D. D. brother of Colonel Warneford, of Warneford Place, Wilts.

Jane Loveden.

Mr. Loveden, surviving his wife, married, secondly, Elizabeth, daughter and sole heiress of John Darker, esq. of Gayton Park, in Northamptonshire, and, thirdly, a daughter of Thomas Linthall, esq. Mr. Loveden's only son having inherited the estates of his maternal ancestors, and having assumed their surname, is the present PRYSE PRYSE, esq. M.P. of Gogerddan and Buscot.

derable antiquity, and settled at Lambourn, having married an heiress of the Erles, of that place. They afterwards removed to Fifield and Buscot. EDWARD LOVEDEN, the last male heir of the family, died unmarried, in 1749. His estates eventually passed to his great-nephew, EDWARD LOVEDEN TOWNSEND, esq. (son of Thomas Townsend, esq. of Cirencester, who died 1st January, 1767, aged 44); and that gentleman assumed, in consequence, the surname and arms of LOVEDEN. He married, as in the text, the heiress of the PRYSES, of Gogerddan.

*Arms*—Or, a lion rampant reguardant, sa. quartering Loveden, gu. a bend between four sinister hands couped, arg.

*Crest*—A lion, as in the arms, holding in his paws a fleur-de-lis.

*Motto*—Duw au bendithio.

*Estates*—Chiefly in Cardiganshire, Pembrokeshire, and Berkshire.

*Seats*—Gogerddan, Cardiganshire, and Buscot Park, Berkshire.

## MARTIN, OF ANSTEY.

MARTIN, WILLIAM, esq. of Anstey, in the county of Leicester, *b.* in 1777, *m.* Ann Wood, daughter of John Richards, esq. (the last of the ancient family of that name, seated at Normanton, on Sour, Notts, a branch of which resided at Ashby-de-la-Zouch, in Leicestershire*) and has had issue,

I. William, *b.* in 1809, died in 1829.
II. ROBERT, M.A. *b.* in 1810, who succeeded his uncle in the possession of the livings of Ratby and Breedon, in Leicestershire. He is also commissary of the peculiar of Groby, and incumbent of Newtown Linford, in the same county. He resides at Anstey Pastures.
III. Charles-Thomas, *b.* in 1812, and *d.* in 1824.
IV. John, *b.* in 1815.
V. Charles-Bosworth, *b.* in 1825.

I. Anne-Elizabeth.

Mr. Martin resides at Stewardshay, in Leicestershire.

### Lineage.

The family of Martyn is of Norman descent, and of considerable antiquity, in the county of Leicester.

In 1221, Robert Martyn was a priest at Ashby Folville; but in early times the family resided at Leicester, and frequently held the highest offices in that ancient and important borough. In the years 1333, 1338, and 1364, John Martyn was mayor of Leicester, and was also (temp. EDWARD III.) returned member of parliament twice for the borough. Shortly afterwards the family

* James Richards, esq. served the office of sheriff for Leicestershire in 1796.

held possessions at Anstey, anciently called Hanstigie, or Anstige, in the county of Leicester, which they have ever since possessed, and where they have resided to the present time.

25th HENRY VI. A. D. 1447, John Martyn held the estate at Anstey, and was witness to a grant of certain lands lying in the fields of Anstey, "in Wolfdale," by John de Leverych, of Leicester, for the repair of the church, bridges, &c. of Anstey, and of which land the family of Martyn, with others, have ever since been the trustees.

He was succeeded by his son, Thomas Martyn, who, about the year 1490, in conjunction with William Haket, (they being the wardens of the chapel of Anstey), gave and demised the "Brereyard" in Anstey aforesaid to the same purposes as the above bequest, of which they were trustees. He left a son, Thomas Martyn, who resided at Anstey, and was the father of Robert Martyn, who married, in 1588, Bridget Marshall. He purchased part of the property of the abbot and convent of St. Mary de Pratis, at Leicester, lying in Anstey, which remained in the Crown till 1st July, 1609, when it was conveyed in fee simple to the above Robert Martyn, and others. He had one brother, Thomas Martyn, who, with others, had a lease of thirty-one years of "Anstey pastures," an extra-parochial liberty, situate near Anstey, from QUEEN ELIZABETH. This estate, formerly parcel of the "Ffrith of Leicestre," and of the ancient duchy of Lancaster, was, after the expiration of the lease, purchased, in the 4th of JAMES I. (from Robert, earl of Salisbury, lord-treasurer of England), by Robert Martyn of Anstey, on payment of a chief rent. In the ancient grant, the boundaries are described as extending "from the middle of y[e] furlonge, by y[e] olde pale beyonde Anstie gate, alias Cowegate, towards Leicestre, followinge y[e] same olde pale of y[e] Ffrith of Leicestre to Groby gate, and from thence eastwarde by ye newe ditche there, in length twoe furlonges and three pearches; from thence towarde y[e] north, unto y[e] poole there called Woodcocke-well, and goinge from y[e] same poole to the midle of the furlonge near Cowegate, where the boundaries aforesaide doe begyne." The present seat of the family is at Anstey Pastures, the old residence, an ancient house in the village of Anstey, being rendered unfit from age.

ROBERT MARTYN, who purchased Anstey Pastures, was the elder brother* of Thomas Martyn, who *d. s. p.* and was buried at Anstey, 1594. By his wife, Bridget, Robert Martyn had issue,

I. THOMAS, *b.* 1591, his heir. He died in 1658.
II. Edward, *b.* 1595, *d.* 1597.
III. Robert, *b.* 1598, *d.* the same year.
IV. George, *b.* 1600, who lived at Leicester, and was mayor of that borough in the year 1655.
V. Robert, *b.* 1612, *d.* 1617.
VI. Robert, *b.* 1623, in holy orders.

I. Anne, *b.* in 1589, married John Land, 1618.
II. Mary, *b.* in 1593.
III. A daughter, *b.* in 1603.

The eldest son,

THOMAS MARTYN, of Anstey, *m.* a lady named Amye, and had issue,

I. THOMAS, *b.* 1620, in the law, *m.* Mabell, and had, with two daughters, Mabell and Margaret, a son, THOMAS, heir to his grandfather; he *d.* before his father, and never came into possession of the estate.
II. William, *b.* 1627, buried at Anstey, 1680, who was twice married, and left one daughter, Grace Martyn.
III. John, who lived at Grobey Hall, in 1680, and left a son, Capt. William Martyn, an officer in the army. He owned and lived in the old manor house at Glenfield, county of Leicester, and spent a considerable estate in law with the then Earl of Stamford, about the manor of Glenfield. He afterwards, however, enjoyed a good income, and left a large family. This branch is now extinct.

I. Joyce, *b.* 1618, *m.* Mr. Sheires, 1640; *m.* secondly, — Storer, *s. p.*

Mr. Martyn, of Anstey, *d.* in 1658, and was *s.* by his grandson,

THOMAS MARTYN, esq. of Anstey, who *m.* Mary, daughter of John Bent. gent. of Stanton, county of Leicester, and had issue,

I. ROBERT, his heir.

II. Amy, *b.* in 1681, *d.* in 1687. On a stone in the south aisle of Anstey church is this inscription:

> Here lieth interred, Amy,
> the daughter of Thomas Martin, Gent.
> She departed this present life April
> XVIII. MDCLXXXVII. aged about five years.
>
> Here also lies her niece, that cry'd
> For Baptism, and then she dyed.

Thomas Martyn *d.* in 1697, and was *s.* by his son,

ROBERT MARTIN, esq. of Anstey, *b.* in 1684, in whose time the *y* in the name was changed to *i*. He *d.* in 1760, aged 84. His wife, Anne, *d.* in 1772, aged 86. It is recorded on their

* He had one sister, Anne, who *m.* John Fletcher.

grave that they lived together in the marriage state sixty years. They had issue,

I. THOMAS, heir.
II. Robert, *b.* in 1717, *d.* young.
III. John, *b.* in 1718, *d.* in 1762.

I. Priscilla, *b.* 1721.
II. Frances, *b.* 1725.

The eldest son,

THOMAS MARTIN, esq. of Anstey, *b.* in 1712, married Hannah, daughter of William Grubb, gent. of Kilby, in Leicestershire, and by her, who *d.* in 1782, had issue,

I. ROBERT, his heir.
II. William, *b.* in 1753, and *d.* 1763.

I. Mary, *b.* in 1756, married to Edward Dudley Hudson, gent. of Narborough, in Leicestershire; buried at Anstey, in 1785.

Mr. Martin *d.* in 1797, aged eighty-five, and was *s.* by his son,

ROBERT MARTIN, esq. of Anstey, *b.* in 1743, who *m.* Miss Ann Hallam, of Barrow, in Leicestershire, and dying in 1805, left issue to survive him,

I. ROBERT, M. A. Fellow of Trinity College, Cambridge, who took the honour of second wrangler in the year 1796. He was vicar of Ratby and Breedon, and commissary of the Peculiar of Groby. He died in 1832.
II. WILLIAM, PRESENT POSSESSOR of the Anstey estate, now resident at Stewardshay, in Leicestershire.

*Arms*—Gu. a chev. arg. between three escallops.

*Crest*—Out of a mural crown vert, a Talbot's head, eared and langued gu. collared of the first.

*Motto*—Sure and steadfast.

*Estates*—At Anstey, and Anstey Pastures, an extra-parochial liberty in the county of Leicester—the first from time immemorial, and the latter since the reign of ELIZABETH.

*Seat*—Anstey Pastures.

## COXWELL, OF ABLINGTON.

COXWELL, *The Reverend* CHARLES, A.M. of Ablington House, in the county of Gloucester, rector of Dowdeswell, *b.* 23rd April, 1771, *m.* 17th June, 1796, Anne, youngest daughter of the Reverend Richard Rogers, of Dowdeswell, and has issue,

I. EDWARD-ROGERS.
II. Richard-Rogers.
III. Charles-Rogers.
IV. William-Rogers.

I. Mary-Rogers.
II. Anne-Rogers.

Mr. Coxwell succeeded his father, the Rev. Charles Coxwell, rector of Barnesley, a magistrate and deputy-lieutenant for the county of Gloucester, in 1829.

### Lineage.

The family of COXWELL has been established in Gloucestershire for many centuries, and resident at Ablington in constant succession since the beginning of the reign of ELIZABETH. Over the doorway of the porch of the mansion is the following inscription engraven on stone in a recess, "PLEADE. THOV. MY. CAVSE. O LORD. BY JHON COXWEL. ANO. DOMENY. 1590." A junior branch (now extinct) formerly was seated at Turkdean, which estate passed by marriage to Sir Montague Nelthorpe, bart.

of Saxby, with Elizabeth, only daughter of Henry Coxwell, esq. who was buried in the chancel of Turkdean Church, in 1718.

Another branch had large possessions in Cirencester, occasioning a street to be called after their family name.

JOHN COXWELL, of Cirencester, in 1516, married Joanna, dau. of — Partridge, esq. of the same place, and had, with other sons and daughters (of the latter Barbara, wedded John Holbeach, of Wilton, in Somersetshire, and Rachael, Edmund Long, of Lyneham, grandson of Sir Henry Long, of Wraxall, and Draycott),

NATHANIEL COXWELL, esq. of Ablington, living in 1633, a magistrate for the county of Gloucester, who married Susanna, daughter of Edward Long, esq. of Monkton, in Wilts, third son of Henry Long, of Whaddon, and left, with a daughter, Anne, the wife of William Horton, of Worcestershire, a son and successor,

EDWARD COXWELL, esq. of Ablington, who was buried in Bibury Church, *anno* 1645. He *m.* the daughter of William Taylor, of Banbury, and was succeeded by his son,

JOHN COXWELL, esq. of Ablington, *b.* in 1622, who wedded in 1650, Anne, daughter of John Long, esq. of Monkton, and by her, who died in 1710, he left, at his decease in 1697, with other issue, a son,

CHARLES COXWELL, esq. of Ablington, *b.* in 1660, who *m.* Eleanor, daughter of Lawrence Head, esq. of Winterbourne, in Berkshire, and was succeeded, at his decease, 15th February, 1701-2, being buried at Bibury, by his son,

JOHN COXWELL, esq. of Ablington, who espoused Mary, daughter of — Westmacott, esq. and had issue, John, who died in Scotland, CHARLES, James, Edward, and Henry. The second, but eldest surviving son,

THE REV. CHARLES COXWELL, of Ablington, succeeded his father in the family estate in 1754. He *m.* 24th April, 1770, Mary, daughter of Joseph Small, esq. of Cirencester, and had issue,

I. CHARLES, his heir.
II. John, deceased.
III. Joseph, commander R.N.
IV. Thomas-Tracy, vicar of Great Marlow, Bucks.
V. Edward, captain Royal Artillery.

I. Mary, *m.* to the Rev. John Hughes, Rector of Tidworth, Wilts.
II. Eleanor, *m.* to William Gaisford.
III. Anne, *m.* to the Reverend Joseph Porter, A.M. rector of St. John's, Bristol.
IV. Elizabeth, *m.* to Richard Estcourt Cresswell, esq. of Pinkney Park, Wilts.

Mr. Coxwell died in 1829, and was *s.* by his eldest son, the present Rev. CHARLES COXWELL, of Ablington.

*Arms*—Arg. a bend wavy between six cocks gu.

*Crest*—A griffin's head.

*Estates*—In Gloucestershire.

*Seat*—Ablington House, near Fairford.

## THISTLETHWAYTE, OF SOUTHWICK PARK.

THISTLETHWAYTE, THOMAS, esq. of Southwick Park, in Hampshire, *b.* 14th September, 1779, married, first, in April, 1803, Miss Guitton, by whom he has issue,

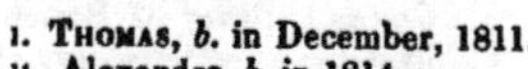

I. THOMAS, *b.* in December, 1811.
II. Alexander, *b.* in 1814.

I. Selina, *m.* to William Garnier, esq. eldest son of the Reverend W. Garnier, of Rookesbury, Hants.
II. Elizabeth.
III. Mary-Anne, *m.* to the Reverend Stephen Butler.
IV. Catharine, *m.* to Sir Francis Collier, R.N.
V. Louisa, *m.* to Edward W. Trafford, esq. son of the late Sigismund Trafford Southwell, esq. of Wroxham Hall, Norfolk.
VI. Matilda.
VII. Caroline.
VIII. Laura.

He wedded, secondly, in 1827, (his first wife died in 1823) Tryphena, daughter of Henry Bathurst, Lord Bishop of Norwich, and great niece to Allen, the celebrated Earl Bathurst, and has issue,

III. Augustus-Frederick, *b.* in July, 1830.
IV. Arthur-Henry, *b.* in July, 1832.

I. Grace.

Mr. Thistlethwayte, who succeeded his father in 1800, is a magistrate and deputy-lieutenant for Hampshire, and was high-sheriff in 1806. In the following year, he was returned to parliament by that county.

## Lineage.

This family, of Saxon origin, first settled in Yorkshire, but removed thence in the time of HENRY VII. to Winterslaw, in the county of Wilts, which property was sold by the present Mr. Thistlethwayte's grandfather to Lord Holland. For centuries, the Thistlethwaytes have ranked amongst the most influential landed proprietors in the South of England, and have allied with the most eminent houses.

ALEXANDER THISTLETHWAYTE, esq. head of the family at the close of the 16th or the early part of the 17th century, *m.* Cecilia, dau. of Sir Anthony Hungerford, of Blackburton, in Oxfordshire, by Sarah, his second wife, dau. and co-heir of John Crowch, of London,* and was succeeded by his son,

ALEXANDER THISTLETHWAYTE, esq. of Winterslaw, who espoused Dorothy, daughter of Sir Edward Penruddock, knt. of Compton Chamberlaine, in Wiltshire, by Mary, his wife, daughter and heiress of George Massey, esq. of Puddington, in the palatinate of Chester. Sir Edward Penruddock was the second son of George Penruddock, standard bearer under the Earl of Pembroke, at the battle of St. Quintins, *temp.* *Queen* MARY, who engaged in single combat a nobleman of France, and gained great honour for his victory over him. Mr. Thistlethwayte was succeeded at his decease by his son,

ALEXANDER THISTLETHWAYTE, esq. of Winterslow, who *m.* Catherine, daughter and heir of Andrew Childecot, esq. of Whiteway, in the Isle of Purbeck, Dorsetshire, and was father of

FRANCIS THISTLETHWAYTE, esq. of Winterslow, who *m.* in 1683, Mary, daughter and co-heir of Major Robert Pelham, of Compton Valence, in Dorsetshire,† and was succeeded by his son,

ALEXANDER THISTLETHWAYTE, esq. of Winterslow, *b.* in 1686, who wedded, in 1717, Mary, daughter of Richard Whithed, esq. of Norman Court, Hants, by his wife,

* In the visitation of Wilts, 1623, the pedigree, as there entered, and testified by William Camden, Clarencieux, differs in some degree from the statement in the text. The following is the descent in the visitation:

Alexander Thistlethwayte, of Winterslowe, in the county of Wilts.

Alexander Thistlethwayte, of Winterslowe, son and heir, *m.* Joanna, daughter of — Moore, of Winterslow.

Alexander Thistlethwayte, of Winterslowe, *m.* Dorothy, daughter of Sir Edward Penruddock.

Alexander, son and heir, Oct. 13, Anno. 1623.

† THOMAS PELHAM, esq. of Buxsted, in Sussex (lineally descended from the valiant John de Pelham, so distinguished in the wars of the martial reign of EDWARD III. and so celebrated as the captor of the French King, at the Battle of Poictiers), died 1st February, 1556, having had by Margaret, his wife, who was buried with him in the choir of Laughton, with two daughters, four sons,

I. JOHN, who *m.* Anne, daughter of Sir Thomas Fynes, knt. but *d. v. p.* issueless.
II. Thomas, *d.* unmarried.
III. WILLIAM, (Sir) ancestor of the DUKE of NEWCASTLE, the EARL of CHICHESTER, and LORD YARBOROUGH.
IV. ANTHONY, seated at Buxsted, who died 22nd November, 1566, leaving by Margaret, his wife, a son,
    HERBERT PELHAM, esq. of Michaelham, in Sussex, who *m.* Elisabeth, second daughter of Thomas, Lord Delawarr, and left *inter alios*, a son,
        THOMAS PELHAM, esq. of Compton Valence, who *m.* Blanch, daughter of Robert Eyre, esq. of Wells, and dying, in 1696, left a son and successor,
            ROBERT PELHAM, esq. of Compton - Valence, whose dau. MARY, married as in the text, FRANCIS THISTLETHWAYTE, esq.

the daughter of Richard Norton, esq. of Southwick, in the same county, and had three sons, of whom

FRANCIS THISTLETHWAYTE, esq. of Norman Court, *b.* in 1719, recovered as heir at law, after his uncle, Mr. Norton's decease, the Southwick estate, which had been bequeathed, in an extraordinary will, to Government, and assumed the surname and arms of WHITHED. This gentleman, the intimate friend of Horace Walpole, was, it is said, to have been created Lord Carnarvon, but his death occurred previous to the intended elevation. Dying without issue, he was succeeded by his brother,

The Reverend THOMAS THISTLETHWAYTE, D.D. of Southwick, *b.* in 1720, who *m.* Selina, daughter of Peter Bathurst, esq. of Clarendon Park, Wilts, by the lady Selina Shirley, his wife, daughter of Robert, first Earl Ferrers, and had issue,

I. ROBERT, his heir.
II. Alexander.

I. Selina, *m.* in 1777, to Philip, fifth Earl of Chesterfield.
II. Eliza, *m.* in 1784, to Arthur Stanhope, esq. of Tilney-street.

Dr. Thistlethwayte was *s.* at his decease by his elder son,

ROBERT THISTLETHWAYTE, esq. of Southwick, who represented Hampshire for more than twenty years in parliament. He wedded Selina, daughter and co-heir (with her sister Eliza, *m.* to Sir John Morshead,) of Sir Thomas Frederick, bart. and niece of Jane, Duchess of Atholl, and had issue,

I. Robert, *d.* unmarried.
II. THOMAS, heir.
III. Alexander, who *m.* six weeks before his death, Eliza-Mary, daughter of Joseph Betteswortb Sherer, esq. which lady wedded, secondly, 28th April, 1820, the late Earl of Huntingdon.
IV. Henry, *d.* unmarried.

I. Selina, *d.* young.
II. Catharine, *d.* young.
III. Eliza.

Mr. Thistlethwayte *d.* in 1800, and was *s.* by his son, the present THOMAS THISTLETHWAYTE, esq. of Southwick.

*Arms*—Or, on a bend az. three pheons of the field.

*Crest*—A demi-lion az. holding a pheon, or.

*Estates*—In Hampshire.

*Seat*—Southwick Park. This seat was formerly a priory of black canons, which became of historical celebrity, from its having been the scene of the marriage of HENRY VI. with MARGARET of Anjou. The priory was originally built at Porchester, by HENRY I. in the year 1133, but was shortly afterwards removed to Southwick, where it continued to flourish till the period of the dissolution. Its privileges were extensive, and in 1235 the canons procured the grant of a market and a fair to be held, but the former has been long disused: they also obtained liberty of free warren in 1321. At the dissolution, the site and demesnes of the priory were granted to JOHN WHITE, esquire of the body to HENRY VIII. This gentleman, who died in 1567, left a son, EDWARD WHITE, esq. of Southwick, high sheriff for Hampshire in 1573, who married Mary, sister and co-heir (with her sister, Honora, Countess of Sussex) of Richard Pounde, esq. of Drayton, and had, with other issue, a son and successor, JOHN WHITE, esq. of Southwick, high sheriff in 1598, whose daughter, HONORA, wedded DANIEL NORTON, son of Sir Richard Norton, knt. of Rotherfield, in Hampshire, the representative of a most ancient and eminent family in that county, and thus the Nortons acquired the Southwick estate. Colonel Daniel Norton was a staunch parliamentarian, and signalized himself in behalf of the Commons during the civil wars. His descendant, Richard Norton, esq. of Southwick, was the last male heir of the family, and bequeathed, by a most extraordinary will, his great landed and personal property to the parliament of Great Britain, in trust for the use "of the poor, hungry, thirsty, naked strangers, sick, wounded, and prisoners, to the end of the world." This singular disposition, however, was set aside, and the estate eventually devolved on the THISTLETHWAYTES. The present Mr. Thistlethwayte pulled down the fine old house of Southwick, and erected, about twenty years ago, a very handsome new mansion, on a more elevated situation. The estate of NORMAN COURT was sold in 1807 to the present Charles Baring Wall, esq. M.P.

# CRESWELL, OF RAVENSTONE.

CRESWELL, ROBERT-GREEN, esq. of Ravenstone, in the counties of Leicester and Derby, *b.* 18th February, 1778, succeeded to the estates in the demise of his father, in 1825.

## Lineage.

THE CRESWELLS have been resident landholders at Ravenstone from a remote period, as their title deeds and family records clearly prove. We shall, however, commence with

ROBERT CRESWELL, who was living at Ravenstone during the time of the civil wars, and purchased property there in 1645 and 1650. He was father of

RICHARD CRESWELL, who *m.* Mary Lawrence, a daughter of an ancient family of that name in Sutton Bonington, county of Nottingham. He *d.* 29th March, 1734, ætat. sixty-five, and was buried at Ravenstone. His son and successor,

ROBERT CRESWELL, *m.* 1725, Catherine, daughter of Matthew White, of Great Appleby, gent. and *d.* 30th June, 1747, aged forty-three, and was buried at Ravenstone. He left issue by his wife, one son and three daughters,

RICHARD, his heir.

Mary, *d.* 1777, } unmarried.
Catherine, *d.* 1797, }
Elizabeth, *m.* Thomas Sperry, and had issue.

RICHARD CRESWELL, the only son, succeeded to the whole of the landed property of his father and mother. He *m.* Elizabeth, daughter of Ambrose Salisbury, by whom he had issue,

ROBERT, his successor.
Richard, who *d.* unm. 29th November, 1830.

Elizabeth, married John Eames, and had issue.
Catherine, married John Miln, and had issue.

Mr. Creswell died 26th June, 1768, and was buried at Ravenstone. His widow died in 1806. The elder son,

ROBERT CRESWELL, esq. on succeeding to the possession of the estates, took down the old house, (the previous residence of the family), and erected the present mansion. He married twice, first, in May, 1777, to Ann, third daughter of Robert Green, esq. of Normanton on the Heath, in the county of Leicester, and Margery, his wife, by whom he had two sons and three daughters,

ROBERT GREEN, his heir.
Richard-Edward, *b.* 1779, *m.* 1810, Alice, daughter of Henry Chapman, gent. by whom he has issue,
1. The Rev. Richard-Henry Creswell, *m.* 1835, Ann, dau. of Valentine Green, esq. of Normanton.
2. Robert.
3. Edward.
1. Mary-Ann.
2. Elizabeth-Martha-Caroline.

Mary-Ann, *m.* William Hall, esq. of Tempe, in the parish of Swepstone, and had issue.
Elizabeth, married the Rev. John Oliver, rector of Swepstone.
Catherine, unmarried.

By his second marriage, Mr. Creswell had one son,

Creswell Creswell.

Mr. Creswell died in February, 1825, was buried at Ravenstone, and *s.* by his son, the present ROBERT GREEN CRESWELL, esq. of Ravenstone.

*Estates*—Counties of Leicester and Derby.
*Seat*—Ravenstone.

# MACLEOD, OF MACLEOD.

**MACLEOD, NORMAN,** esq. of Macleod, *b.* 18th July, 1812; succeeded his father 25th of March, 1835.

## Lineage.

The genealogy of this very eminent Scottish clan cannot be more interestingly commenced than by an extract from a manuscript memoir of his own life by the late General Macleod, to which we shall have, in the details, other occasions to refer.

"My family," says the general, "is derived from the ancient royal stock of Denmark. In those unhappy times when heroism was little better than piracy, and when the Danes first infested and then subdued England, my ancestor was invested with the tributary sovereignty of the Isle of Man. His history, the succession, or the share these princes of Man had in the predatory wars of that rude age, are lost in dark and vague tradition. The first fact which seems clearly ascertained is, that Leod, the son of the King of Man, in the conquest of that island by the English under the Earl of Derby, fled with his followers to the Hebrides. He there probably found his countrymen, and, either by conquest, agreement, or alliance, possessed himself of that part of those isles now called Lewes and Harries. Leod had two sons, Tormod and Torquil. The first married the daughter of a powerful chief in the Isle of Skye; he was a warrior of great prowess. His father gave or left to him Harries, and, by dint of his valour and by marriage, he possessed himself of a large dominion in Skye, which, together with Harries, I, his lineal successor, inherit. Torquil and his posterity possessed Lewis, which, with other acquisitions, they have since lost, and the family is now represented by Macleod of Rasay. From Leod, whose name is held in high traditional veneration, all his descendants and many of his followers have taken the patronymic of MACLEOD. My ancestors, whose family seat has always been at Dunvegan, seem to have lived for some centuries, as might be expected, from men who had gained their lands by their swords, and were placed in islands of no easy access. They had frequent wars and alliances with their neighbours in Skye, by which, it appears, they neither gained nor lost: they frequently attacked or assisted the petty kings in Ireland or the chiefs on the coast of Scotland; but they neither increased nor diminished their own possessions. In the reign of *King* DAVID of Scotland they at last took a charter for their lands, from which time they seem long to have practised the patriarch's life; beloved by their people, unconnected with the government of Scotland, and undisturbed by it."

OLAVE OLOIS,* King of Man and the isles,

* On the demise of his father, GODRED, this prince being no more than ten years of age, his bastard brother, Reginald, was made king by the people, and he, Olave, was allotted the Isle of Lewis, but endeavouring as he advanced in life to recover his patrimony, he was seized by the usurper and delivered to WILLIAM, *King* of Scotland, who detained him a captive for seven years; he was released, however, on the death of WILLIAM, and put into possession of the Isle of Lewis, and being then divorced from his wife by the Pope's legate, on the ground of consanguinity, he married Christina, daughter of Farquhar, Earl of Ross. This led Reginald, the bastard's queen, sister of the repudiated lady, to instigate her own son, Godred Don, to murder Olave: but the plot being discovered, Olave fled to his father-in-law, the Earl of Ross, who furnished him with ships and men, and being likewise assisted by Pol, or Paul, the son of Broke, at the time sheriff of Sky, he surprised Godred (anno 1223) in an island on a fresh water loch in Trotterness, in which there was a chapel and monastery, dedicated to St. Columbus. In 1224, Olave and the Bastard divided Man between them, and he subsequently became sole monarch, having subdued all his foes.

who *d.* in 1237, left by his first wife three sons, HAROLD, REGINALD, and MAGNUS, who all successively enjoyed the kingdom of Mann, which terminated in 1265 by the surrender made of the sovereignty by Magnus, King of Norway, to ALEXANDER III. of Scotland, and, in the same year, Magnus, the last king of Mann, died. Olave, by his third wife, Christina, daughter of Farquhar, Earl of Ross, had three sons, Guin or Gun, of whom the Guns in Sutherland; LEOID, LOYD or LEOD, of whom the clan MACLEOD; and Leaundrish, of whom the clan Leandrish, in Ross.

LEOD, second son of Olave Olgis, or Olaus V. King of Mann and the isles, by the Earl of Ross's daughter, having been fostered in the house of Pol, obtained from him the Heries, from which he (Leod) and his descendants taking their designation, were, in former times, styled of Glenelg and Dunvegan. He married the daughter of Macraild Armine, a Danish knight, and by her acquired the lands of Menginish, Bracadale, Durinish, Lindale, Vaterness and a part of Trotterness, and had two sons—TORMODE, who succeeded him, and Torquhil, ancestor of the Macleods of Lewis,* whose successors were possessed of a great estate when forfeited in the reign of *King* JAMES VI. Both the families had the surname or patronymic of Macleod, but were distinguished by the appellation of Shiel Tormoid, or the descendants of Tormoid, and Shiel Torquhil, or the descendants of Torquhil, and by the designations of "Macleod of Herries," and "Macleod of Lewis." The elder son and heir,

TORMODE MACLEOD, was father of

MALCOLM MACLEOD, known by the name of *Caishrevir*, or Thick-legged, who obtained a charter, before the year 1360, from *King* DAVID Bruce, whereby that prince granted, "Delecto et fideli nostro Malcolmo filio Tormodi Mac Loyd pro homagio et servitio suo duas partes tenementi de Glenelg, viz. Octo davatas et quinque denariatas terræ cum pertinentiis infra vice-comitatum de Inverness faciendo nobis et heredibus nostris prædictus Malcolmus et heredes sui servitium unius navis vigenti et sex Remorum quoties super hoc per nos fuerint requisiti prout facere tenebantur tempore patris nostri." He had three sons, viz.

JOHN, his successor.

Tormod, from whom sprang that branch of the Macleods in Herries which possessed Bernera before Sir Normand Macleod got it from the family as his patrimony.

Murdo, ancestor of the family of Gesto, from whom John Macleod, major in General Gordon's Regiment of Scots, in the service of the united provinces.

The eldest son and heir,

JOHN MACLEOD, was *s.* by his son,

WILLIAM MACLEOD, commonly called *Achlerick*, or formerly a clerk, as he was at first, but the second son and bred to the church. Soon after his accession to the estate he raised a spreath out of that part of Lovat's lands called Aird, in revenge of an injury he had received in that country in his youth, brought the cattle to Skye, and slaughtered them in Hearlosh, in a place from that incident yet called Baniscanigh, or field of Offalls. His property being at one time invaded by enemies, chiefly followers of Macdonald, Lord of the Isles, he came up with the aggressors at Lochsligichan, and, by a stratagem evincing no ordinary military genius, gave them a total overthrow. The plunder of this exploit he divided at a rock, which, from the circumstance, retains to this day the name of Creggan ni feavigh, or Rock of the Spoil. He married a daughter of the Ogilvies, and had two sons, JOHN, his successor, and Tormod, from whom are descended the branches of the Macleods, called the Mac Vieulliams, of whom Borline, &c. and the Macvie alister Roys, of whom Ballimore, St. Kilda, &c. The elder son and heir,

JOHN MACLEOD, who was remarkable for great bodily strength and personal courage, distinguished himself amongst the companions of Donald, Lord of the Isles, at the battle of Haarlaw. He married a daughter of the family of Douglas, and had WILLIAM, his heir, and Tormod, whose male heir was the William of Meidle, mentioned in the destination of the estate made by Sir Rory Macleod, to be hereafter specified, but that branch is now extinct. The elder son,

WILLIAM MACLEOD, *alias* William *Nimbristigh*, or the *Skirmisher*, went by order of *King* JAMES II. to aid John, Earl of Ross, against his bastard son, and was lost in a naval engagement in Cammisveraigor Bloody-bay, in the sound of Mull. He was married to a daughter of Maclean of Lochbuy. In a charter granted on the 28th June, 1449, by John, Earl of Ross, Lord of the Isles, to his brother Hugh, this William and McLeod of Lewis are witnesses, and are named in this order, "Willielmus Macleod de Glenelg et Macleod de Legglies." He was *s.* by his son,

ALEXANDER MACLEOD, known as *Crottach* or humpbacked, who *m.* a daughter of Cameron, of Lochiel, and had three sons and a daughter. The daughter wedded, first, John-Oge-M'Dhoil Ghruamigh, second son of the family of Slate; she espoused, secondly, Allan M'Jain, captain, of Clanka-

* Of the Macleods of Lewis are descended Macleod of Rasay, Macleod of Gensies, Macleod of Cadboll, and John Macleod, esq. the proprietor of a considerable estate in Jamaica.

nald, and from this chief's bad treatment of her arose the feuds between M'Leod and Clankanald; her third husband was M'Donald, of Keppoch. Alexander *Crottach* obtained a charter from *King* JAMES IV. which probably was the first granted to the family of any lands they possessed in the Æbudæ, or the Western Isles, by the kings of Scotland. The charter is dated 15th June, 1498, and it grants and confirms "Dilecto nostro Alexandro Makloyd filio et heredi quondam Willielmi Johannis Makloyd, son de Dunvegan terras quæ vulgariter nuncupantur Ardmianach in Herage de Lewis cum suis pertinen, cum omnibus minutis insulis addictam Ardmianach pertinen:" and of the lands of Duriness, Mengincss, Bracadale, and Lyndale, and Twopenny lands of Trotterness, with the office of bailliary of the whole lands of Trotterness, with the pertinents being within the lordship of the isles, which were held formerly of John, lord of the Isles, and came by his forfeiture to be held of the crown; to be held of the king ward and holding one ship of twenty-six oars, and two ships of sixteen oars, in readiness for the king's service, as well in time of peace as of war, whenever they should be required so to do, and reserving to the king and his successors the airies or nests of falcons within the said bounds. Hugh, Lord Fraser, of Lovat, obtained two decrees of appraising of the barony of Glenelg, against the said Alexander Macleod, on the 13th January, 1532, and 3rd March, 1534, on which he was infeft in virtue of a charter under the great seal, and on the 13th February, 1539, the said Alexander obtained, on Lord Lovat's resignation, a charter of that barony from *King* JAMES V. on which he was infeft in the same year, and thus he was regularly invested in the whole family estate. This laird rebuilt the monastery of Rowadale, in Harris. He was *s.* by his eldest son,

WILLIAM MACLEOD, who was served heir in special to his father, and in virtue of a precept from the chancery was, on the 15th May, 1548, infeft in the whole family estate. By his wife, Anne or Agnes Fraser, daughter of Hugh, fifth Lord Fraser, of Lovat, he had an only daughter, MARY, *m.* first, to Duncan Campbell, of Castleswyne, younger son of Auchinbreck; and, secondly, to M'Niel, of Barra. He was *s.* at his decease, having thus no son, by his next brother,

DONALD MACLEOD, who enjoyed the inheritance but a brief period, being murdered in Kingsborrow, in Trotterness, then a part of the estate. He was *s.* by his brother,

TORMOD MACLEOD, of Macleod, who in July, 1580, was infeft in the whole estate. This laird *m.* first, Giles, daughter of Hector Maclean, of Duart, by whom he had issue,

- I. WILLIAM, } successively heirs.
- II. RODERICK, } successively heirs.
- III. Alexander, of Minginish, from whom Alexander Macleod, of Ferrinnilea, William Macleod, of Ose, and Lieut. Norman Macleod.

- I. Margaret, *m.* to Donald Macdonald, of Slate. The feuds which subsisted between the Macleods and Macdonalds arose from the bad treatment of the lady by her husband.
- II. ——, *m.* first, to Macleod, of Lewis; and, secondly, to Macdonald, of Benbeaila.

Tormod wedded, secondly, a daughter of the Earl of Argyll, and had by her a daughter, Jannet, who became the wife of Maclean, of Coll. Macleod was a man of courage and conduct, and an adherent of the unhappy MARY, of Scotland. He died in March, 1584, and was *s.* by his eldest son,

WILLIAM MACLEOD, of Macleod, who was served heir 31st July, 1585. He *m.* Janet, daughter of Lachlan M'Intosh, of Dunachten, and dying in October, 1590, without issue, was *s.* by his brother,

SIR RODERICK MACLEOD, of Macleod, commonly *Rory more*, or great Roderick, who received the honour of knighthood from *King* JAMES VI. and was infeft in the whole estate as heir to his brother in September, 1596. This laird appears to have been involved in much difficulty, but his address and courage bore him eventually through. An act of parliament having passed, 19th December, 1597, obliging, under pain of forfeiture, all the chieftains and other landholders in the Highlands and Isles, to produce the title-deeds of their estates before the lords of the exchequer, to be considered by them previously to the 25th day of May following, and Sir Roderick refusing compliance, *King* JAMES conferred his whole estate, with the exception of Trotterness, Slate, and Uist, upon James Lord Balmerinock, Sir James Spence, of Wolmerston, and Sir George Hay, of Nether Cliff, afterwards Viscount Duplin, equally between them, on which these gentlemen, taking out a charter under the great seal, were infeft, and Sir George Hay acquired right to Balmerinock's and Wolmerston's shares. At the same time, to augment his embarrassment, Sir Roderick was on bad terms with Sir Roderick M'Kenzie, of Coigach, tutor of Kintail, ancestor of the earls of Cromartie, then a privy councillor and a man of considerable power and influence, who, aware of the fiery disposition of Macleod, affronted him in presence of the council, that he might commit some act which should render him amenable to the law;—the desired effect was produced;—Macleod knocked M'Kenzie immediately down, and thus subjected himself to capital punishment: at this period too his country was invaded by the Macdonalds of Slate, while himself and a large number of his clan were in the island of Mull; and although the invaders were gallantly opposed by Alexander Macleod, of Minginish, with so many of the clan as he could collect together, the Macdonalds, after a bloody skirmish in Cuillen, carried away a spreath; in retaliation, when Sir Roderick returned, he made an inroad into Trotterness, and burned and destroyed the whole country. He had also at this time deadly feuds with the family of Clankanald. He was however long and greatly befriended by the Earl of Argyll, and, on the 7th July, 1606, engaged himself by contract to resign his barony of Glenelg into the king's hands in favour of that nobleman, on his lordship's becoming bound to grant to him (Sir Roderick) and his heirs male a charter of that barony, to be held of Argyll and his heirs by service of ward, marriage, and relief; he subsequently accommodated matters with Sir Roderick M'Kenzie, and entered into bonds of friendship with Macdonald, of Slate, Macdonald, of Clankanald, and Mackinnon; and at length, on the 4th May, 1610, obtained from *King* JAMES a remission. On the 18th July, in the same year, he purchased from Kenneth, Lord Mackenzie, of Kintail, the barony of Vaterness, disposing to Kintail of the Twopenny land of Trotterness, and the office of bailliary of the whole lands of Trotterness. On the 19th of the same month he obtained from George Hay, Viscount Duplin, a disposition of the whole estate, and on these titles, with his own resignation, he acquired from the crown a new charter, dated 4th April, 1611, of Vaterness and his other estates, containing a novodamus taxing the ward, and erecting the whole into a barony, to be called the barony of Dunvegan, in favour of himself and the heirs male of his body, remainder to his brother german, Alexander Macleod, of Mingíness, remainder to William Macleod, *alias* Macwilliam Macleod, of Meidle, the heir male of Tormod, second son of John, sixth laird of Macleod, remainder to his own nearest and lawful heirs male whatsoever; and upon this charter he was infeft 22nd October, 1611. On the 16th September, 1613, he was served heir in special to William Macleod, his uncle, in the lands of Trotterness, Slate, and North Uist, and was infeft in them 11th February, 1614. Those lands he desponed of, in February, 1618, to Sir Donald Macdonald, of Slate. Sir Roderick became a great favourite with *King* JAMES VI. who, on the 18th May, 1610, wrote to him a letter requiring his assistance in an affair to be communicated to him by the Earl of Dunbar, which his majesty says, "he shall not fail to remember, when any occasion fit for your good shall be offered." In 1613 the king conferred the honour of knighthood on him, and in the June of that year he wrote three several letters from Greenwich, recommending Macleod and his affairs, in the strongest terms, to the privy council of Scotland. On the 16th June, 1616, his majesty granted to Sir Roderick a license, under his hand and seal, to come out of Scotland to court whenever he should think convenient, without being liable to any challenge or pursuit for so doing. Sir Roderick died in the beginning of 1626, leaving issue by his wife, Isabella, daughter of Macdonald, of Glengary, five sons and five daughters, viz.

I. JOHN, his successor.

II. Roderick, of Talliskir.*

---

* This gentleman, RODERICK MACLEOD, of Talliskir, on the death of his elder brother, JOHN, who succeeded his father, and became fourteenth laird of Macleod, was appointed tutor to his nephew, RODERICK MACLEOD, the fifteenth laird, John's son and heir, then in minority. On the arrival of Charles II. in Scotland, in 1650, and the issue of his Majesty's proclamation, commanding all his subjects to repair to the Royal Standard with as many men as they could levy, Roderick immediately raised a regiment, seven hundred strong, of his clan and followers, and appointed his brother Normand, of Bérnera, lieutenant-colonel, who cheerfully obeyed the royal summons, and after remaining some time with the king's army, received orders to complete his corps by a levy of three hundred men more. This he accomplished; but being in want of arms, he obtained an order on John Bunkle, then commissary, to supply him. The commissary, however, refused to comply, unless Talliskir would pass his bond for the value, which, rather than prejudice the service, was passed. This bond was afterwards assigned to William M'Culloch, who used utmost diligence upon it against Talliskir, during the Usurpation. These proceedings were at last suspended; and Colonel Macleod relieved from the claim by act of parliament, in 1661. At the head of this regiment, himself and his brother attended the King to the fatal field of Worcester, where almost every man of the corps was either killed, or taken prisoner, and transported to the plantations. The colonel had a narrow escape, and after concealing himself a short time in England, got in disguise to Scotland, where he became active in encouraging a spirit of loyalty among the Highland clans; the best affected of whom met at Glenelg on the 21st April, 1653, and agreed on raising a body of two thousand men for the King's service, and to apprise his Majesty of Great Britain, the King of Denmark, the Princess Royal, and the States of Holland, with their resolution. This mission was entrusted to Lieutenant-Col. Normand Macleod, to be carried to *King* CHARLES, who conveyed in return a most flattering letter from the exiled monarch to his brother

III. Normand, of Berneray.
IV. William, of Stammer.
V. Donald, of Grishernish.

I. Margaret, *m.* to M'Lean, of Duart.
II. Mary, *m.* to -- M'Leon, brother of Duart, and her son succeeded to the estate.
III. Moire, commonly called *Moire Voire*, *m.* to John Musdortich, captain of Clankanald, which marriage terminated the feuds between the two families.
IV. Janet, *m.* to John Macleod, of Rasay.
V. Florence, *m.* to Donald M'Sween.

It is remarkable that this chieftain was a proficient in Latin, had travelled on the Continent, and spoke French with fluency, yet could neither utter nor understand the Scotch or English dialect. His eldest son and heir,

JOHN MACLEOD, of Macleod, surnamed *John More*, from his great size, was infeft in the whole family estate, 9th November, 1626, on a precept from the Chancery, and was subsequently under a decree of the Privy Council of Scotland, compelled to resign his barony of Glenelg in the king's hands, in favour of the Earl of Argyll, (son of the nobleman with whom his father had entered into the contract,) and to take a charter of it, holding of his lordship, paying twenty thousand merks for taxing the ward, marriage and relief, by which tenure it is yet held of the house of Argyll. This laird was a staunch Royalist, and opposed the measures of the Covenanters from the commencement, for which conduct he received a letter of thanks from *King* CHARLES I. dated at Durham 2nd May, 1639. He continued firm in his allegiance, to the hour of his death, which happened in September, 1649. He was remarkable for his goodness and piety, and took so much pains to civilize the country, that he acquired the appellation of Lot in Sodon. He *m.* Sibella,

Talliskir. When, subsequently, the royal cause entirely failed, Colonel Macleod lived privately at home until the Restoration, when the King, in consideration of his faithful services, conferred upon him the honour of knighthood. Sir Roderick *m.* first, a daughter of Donald, first Lord Rae; and secondly, Mary, daughter of M'Kinnon, of that ilk: by the latter he had JOHN, Magnus, who died a youth, and a daughter Isabell, *m.* to Donald M'Lean, of Coll. She *d.* about the year 1675. His son JOHN was *m.* to Janet, only daughter of Alexander Macleod, of Grishernish, and had a son and heir, Donald, who *m.* Christian, daughter of John Macleod, and left issue. John, of Talliskir, lieut.-colonel in the service of the States of Holland; Magnus, an officer in Col. Campbell's regiment of Highlanders; Roderick, professor of philosophy in the king's college of Aberdeen; Normand, captain-lieut. in the regiment of light-armed infantry in America, and one of the superintendants of the Indians. Janet, *m.* to Hugh M'Lean, of Coll; and Isabell, the wife of Hector M'Lean, of Islecomonk.

NORMAND MACLEOD, of Berneray, third son of Sir Roderick, concurred most heartily during his nephew's minority in all the measures adopted by his eldest brother, Sir Roderick, the tutor of Macleod. He was at the battle of Worcester, in the rank of lieut.-colonel of his brother's regiment, and being taken prisoner there, was detained in custody for eighteen months, during which period he was tried for his life on the supposition of being a Welchman, from the affinity, the surnames of Ap Lloyd and Macleod; but being well known to the Scots army, his identity was easily established, when there was an end to the case, and the prisoner remanded. It was then proposed to him to subscribe the oath called the tender, and his liberty was offered to him; but peremptorily refusing, his incarceration was prolonged, and his treatment rendered more severe; but being a man of abilities, address, and enterprise, he at length effected his escape, and joined his friends in the Highlands, attended the council of war already mentioned, and was deputed to convey the result of the proceedings to King CHARLES. He was afterwards active in the many attempts made to re-establish the King's affairs in Scotland, and when General Middleton was no longer able to keep the field, but obliged to retire to the Western Isles, Lieut.-colonel Macleod conducted him to his own house at Berneray, where he remained in security, until provided with means, by his gallant host, to make his escape beyond sea. After the Restoration, he received, with his brother, the honour of knighthood, but got no other reward, except through the Earl of Middleton he obtained the forfeited estate of a certain Highland family, which took place in consequence of a correspondence discovered between its chief and the usurpers. Sir Normand *m.* first, Margaret, only child of John M'Kenzie, of Lochalin, second son of Kenneth, Lord Kintail, by whom he had an only son, JOHN MACLEOD, of Contulich, who wedded Isabella, eldest daughter of Kenneth M'Kenzie, of Scatwell, and had a numerous issue, of whom the eldest son, John Macleod, of Muiravonside, was father of Alexander Macleod, advocate, and Elizabeth, the wife of John Macdonald, of Largie, and the second son, Donald Macleod, of Berners, had, by his first marriage, Norman Macleod, of Unish, and Captain Alexander Macleod, of the Lord Mansfield Indiaman, with several daughters; and by his second marriage, John Macleod. Sir Normand espoused, secondly, Catherine, eldest daughter of Sir James Macdonald, of Slate, by whom he had

William, of Laskindir, father of Alexander, of Laskindir, of Roderick, clerk to the signet; of Margaret, *m.* to Ronald Macdonald, of Clankaland, and Alice, the wife of Roderick M'Neill.

Marion, *m.* to Donald M'Lean, of Colt.
———— *m.* to Alexander Macleod, of Rasay, and afterwards to Angus M'Donell, of Scotherin.

daughter of Kenneth, Lord M'Kenzie, of Kintail, and has issue,

RODERICK, } successive lairds.
JOHN, }

Mary, m. first, to Sir James Macdonald, of Slate, and secondly, to Muir, of Rowallan.

Marion, m. to Donald Macdonald, captain of Clankaland, and was mother of Allan, captain of Clankaland, who fell at Sheriff Muir.

Giles, m. first, to Sir Allan M'Lean, of Duart, and secondly, to Campbell, of Glendaruel.

Sibella, m. to Thomas Fraser, of Beaufort, and was mother of Simon Fraser, the last Lord Lovat, (see p. 297).

Margaret, m. to Sir James Campbell, of Laars.

The eldest son,

RODERICK MACLEOD, fifteenth laird of Macleod, was served heir in special to his father 22nd November, 1655, and on the 24th February in the next year infeft in the whole estate, except the barony of Glenelg, in which he was infeft 19th October, 1677. This chief being under age until the close of the great rebellion, his uncles, Sir Roderick and Sir Normand Macleod, with their clans and followers, having adhered to the royal cause, the estate of Macleod was sequestered, but when all Scotland submitted, the laird at length capitulated, 30th May, 1655, and was admitted by General Monk, to OLIVER'S protection, on his finding security for his peaceable deportment under the penalty of £6000, and paying a fine of £2500; his uncles were, however, so obnoxious, that they were expressly excepted in the capitulation, and were obliged to live ever after in seclusion. He married Margaret, eldest daughter of Sir John M'Kenzie, of Tarbat, but dying in January, 1664, without issue, was s. by his brother,

JOHN MACLEOD, of Macleod, who was served heir on the 11th August, 1664, and infeft in the whole estate held of the crown, on a precept from the chancery, and in Glenelg, on a precept of "clare constat" from the subject superior. He m. Florence, second daughter of Sir James Macdonald, of Slate, and had issue,

I. RODERICK, } successive lairds.
II. NORMAND, }
III. William, who d. a youth, at Glasgow.

I. Isabell, m. to Stuart, of Appin.
II. Janet, m. to Sir James Campbell, of Auchinbreck.

He died in August, 1693, and was s. by his eldest son,

RODERICK MACLEOD, of Macleod, who wedded, in February, 1694, Lady Isabella M'Kenzie, third daughter of Kenneth, Earl of Seaforth, and dying in August, 1699, without issue, was s. by his brother,

NORMAND MACLEOD, of Macleod, who m. in September, 1703, Anne, daughter of Hugh Fraser, eleventh Lord Lovat, and was s. by his posthumous son,

NORMAND MACLEOD, nineteenth Laird of Macleod, who, on the 10th November, 1731, was infeft as heir to his father in the barony of Glenelg, and on the 11th May, 1732, as heir to his grandfather in the remainder of the estate.

Of this gentleman, his grandson, General Macleod, thus speaks: "My grandfather Norman was an only and posthumous son. By the frugality of his ancestors, and the savings of his minority, he found an ancient inheritance in the most prosperous condition. With a body singularly well made, and active, he possessed very lively parts; the circumstance of the times introduced him to the public with great advantage; and till the unfortunate 1745 he was much considered. An attachment to the race of Stuart then prevailed in Scotland, and many of the leading men in England still favoured it. His independent fortune and promising character early obtained him the representation in parliament of Inverness-shire, his native county. The number and fidelity of his clan, and his influence with his neighbours, were known, and there is reason to believe that many allurements were held out to seduce him into engagements which were then considered only dangerous, but not guilty or dishonourable. It would be neither pleasing nor useful to inquire how deeply he was concerned in the preludes to the Rebellion, nor indeed have I been able to learn; it is certain that in the year 1746, he raised a company of his vassals to serve under my father, his only son, in Lord Loudon's regiment, and afterwards appeared, with six hundred of his clan, in defence of the present royal family. From this period he was unfortunate: the Jacobites treated him as an apostate, and the successful party did not reward his loyalty. The former course of his life had been expensive: his temper was convivial and hospitable, and he continued to impair his fortune until his death, in 1772. He was the first of our family who was led, by the change of manners, to leave the patriarchal government of his clan, and to mix in the pursuits and ambition of the world. It was not then common to see the representatives of the Highland tribes endeavouring to raise themselves to eminence in the nation, by the arts of eloquence, or regular military gradation; they were contented with their private opulence, and local dignity; or trusted their rank in the state to the antiquity of their families, or their provincial influence. Had Norman felt, in his youth, the necessity of professional or parliamentary exertions, and had he received a suitable education, he would not have left his family in distress; but the excellence of his parts, and the vigour of his mind would have attained a station more advantageous for the flight of his successors."

The laird married, first, Janet, daughter of Sir Donald Macdonald, of Slate, and had one son, John, his successor. He espoused, secondly, Anne, daughter of William Martin, of Inchfure, and by her had three daughters, Elizabeth, Anne, and Rich-Mary. His only son,

JOHN, *m.* Emilia, only daughter of Brodie, of Brodie, lord Lyon king of arms, and dying 7th January, 1767, left, with five daughters,* an only son,

NORMAN, successor to his grandfather.

Macleod died, as already stated, in 1772, and was succeeded by his grandson,

NORMAN MACLEOD, twentieth laird of Macleod, of whom the most interesting details which can be furnished are those given by himself in the manuscript memoir to which we have already referred.

"I was born on the fourth day of March, 1754, at Brodie House, the seat of my maternal grandfather, Brodie, of Brodie, Lyon king at arms. During my boyhood, my father, with his family, went to reside at Beverley, in Yorkshire, where he died, and was buried in the Minster. I was placed under the care of Mr. George Stuart, one of the professors in the College of Edinburgh; and the abilities, care, and maternal love of my surviving parent, left me no other reason to regret my father than that which nature dictates for a brave, worthy, and so near relation.

"In the year 1771, a strange passion for emigrating to America seized many of the middling and poorer sort of Highlanders. The change of manners in their chieftains, since 1745, produced effects which were evidently the proximate cause of this unnatural dereliction of their own, and appetite for a foreign, country. The laws which deprived the Highlanders of their arms and garb, would certainly have destroyed the feudal military power of the chieftains; but the fond attachment of the people to their patriarchs would have yielded to no laws. They were themselves the destroyers of that pleasing influence. Sucked into the vortex of the nation, and allured to the capitals, they degenerated from patriarchs and chieftains to landlords; and they became as anxious for increase of rent, as the new-made lairds, the *novi homines*, the mercantile purchasers of the lowlands. Many tenants, whose fathers for generations had enjoyed their little spots, were removed for higher bidders; those who agreed at any price for their ancient *lares*—their *patriæ domi*—were forced to pay an increased rent, without being taught any new method to increase their produce. In the Hebrides, especially, this change was not gradual, but sudden; and sudden and baleful were its effects. The people, freed by the laws from the power of the chieftains, and loosened by the chieftains themselves from the bonds of affection, turned their eyes and their hearts to new scenes. America seemed to open its arms to receive every discontented Briton. To those possessed of very small sums of money, it offered large possessions of uncultivated but excellent land, in a preferable climate; to the poor, it held out high wages for labour; to all, it promised property and independence. Many artful emissaries, who had an interest in the transportation or settlement of emigrants, industriously displayed these temptations; and the desire of leaving their country for the new land of promise became furious and epidemic. Like all other popular furies, it infected not only those who had reason to complain of their situation or injuries, but those who were most favoured, and most comfortably settled. In the beginning of 1772, my grandfather, who had always been a most beneficent and beloved chieftain, but whose necessities had lately induced him to raise his rents, became much alarmed by this new spirit, which had reached his clan. Aged and infirm, he was unable to apply the remedy in person; he devolved the task on me; and gave me for an assistant our nearest male relation, Colonel Macleod, of Talisker. The duty imposed on us was difficult: the estate was loaded with debt; incumbered with a numerous issue from himself and my father, and loaded with some jointures; his tenants had lost, in that severe winter, above a third of their cattle, which constituted their substance; their spirits were soured by their losses, and the late augmentations of rent; and their ideas of America were inflamed by the strongest representations, and the example of their neighbouring clans. My friend and I were empowered to grant such deductions in the rents as might seem necessary and reasonable; but we found it terrible to decide between the justice to creditors, the necessities of an ancient family, which we ourselves represented, and the claims and distresses of an impoverished tenantry. To God I owe, and I trust will ever pay, the most fervent thanks, that this terrible task enabled us to lay the foundation of circum-

* One of these ladies, Emilia, *m.* Capt. Gustavus Moore, of Salston, in Ireland.

stances, though then unlooked for, that I hope will prove the means, not only of the rescue, but of the aggrandizement of our family. I was young, and had the warmth of the liberal passions natural to that age; I called the people of the different districts of our estate together; I laid before them the situation of our family—its debts, its burthens, its distress; I acknowledged the hardships under which they laboured; I described and reminded them of the manner in which they and their ancestors had lived with mine; I combated their passion for America, by a real account of the dangers and hardships they might encounter there; I besought them to love their young chieftain, and to renew with him the ancient manners; I promised to live among them; I threw myself upon them; I recalled to their remembrance an ancestor who had also found his estate in ruin, and whose memory was held in the highest veneration; I desired every district to point out some of their oldest and most respected men, to settle with me every claim, and I promised to do every thing for their relief which in reason I could. My worthy relation ably seconded me, and our labour was not in vain. We gave considerable abatements in the rents: few emigrated; and the clan conceived the most lively attachment to me, which they most effectually manifested. When we were engaged in these affairs, my grandfather died, and was buried at St. Andrews. I returned to Hampshire, and easily prevailed with my excellent mother and sisters to repair, in performance of my promise to my clan, to Dunvegan. In my first visit to Skye, Mr. Pennant arrived there; and he has kindly noticed in his Tour the exertions we then made.

"I remained at home with my family and clan till the end of 1774; but I confess that I consider this as the most gloomy period of my life. Educated in a liberal manner, fired with ambition, fond of society, I found myself in confinement in a remote corner of the world, without any hope of extinguishing the debts of my family, or of ever emerging from poverty and obscurity. A long life of painful economy seemed my only method to perform the duty I owed to my ancestors and posterity; and the burthen was so heavy, that only partial relief could be hoped even from that melancholy sacrifice. I had also the torment of seeing my mother and sisters, who were fitted for better scenes, immured with me; and their affectionate patience only added to my sufferings. In 1774, Dr. Samuel Johnson, with his companion, Mr. Boswell, visited our dreary regions: it was my good fortune to be enabled to practise the virtue of hospitality on this occasion. The learned traveller spent a fortnight at Dunvegan, and indeed amply repaid our cares to please him, by the most instructive and entertaining conversation. I procured for him the company of the most learned clergymen and sagacious inhabitants of the Islands, and every other assistance within our power to the inquiries he wished to make."

Thus abruptly terminates General Macleod's own narrative. It has, however, been continued by his son and successor, the late laird; from whose papers it appears, that, wearied with the inactivity, and disgusted with the obscurity of the Isle of Skye, he at length determined upon adopting the profession of arms, and obtained leave to raise an independent company, with the rank of captain. "It was about this time," says his son, "that being thrown from his horse, near Inverness, he was carried to Suddie House, where he first became acquainted with his future wife, who nursed him while confined by the accident. They were soon after married, and embarked for America, but were taken prisoners on the voyage, and very kindly treated by Washington, of whom I have often heard him speak in terms of the greatest affection." Soon after his return to Britain, on the 21st March, 1780, he was advanced to the rank of lieutenant-colonel, having raised a second batallion for the 42nd regiment. This he accompanied to India, and there acquired high reputation in the war against Tippoo Sahib. In a correspondence which took place between the Sultan and General Macleod (at this time he had the command of a division of the Indian army, although but twenty-nine years of age), the following spirited passage occurs in one of the general's despatches: "You, or your interpreter, have said, in your letter to me, that I have lied, or made a mensonge. Permit me to inform you, prince, that this language is not good for you to give, or me to receive; and if I were alone with you in the desert you would not dare to say these words to me. An Englishman scorns to lie; an English general who would dare to lie would be crushed to pieces by the just rage of our magnanimous king. You have said that I lied, or made a mensonge. This is an irreparable affront to an English warrior. I tell you our customs; if you have courage enough to meet me, take a hundred of your bravest men on foot, meet me on the seashore, I will fight you, and a hundred men of mine will fight with yours." Mr. John Norman Macleod continues: "At the time my father got the rank of lieutenant-colonel, and went to India in 1782 or 1783 (I believe the former), Mrs. Macleod (his first wife) went with his mother and children to France, where she died, leaving a son and daughter, He *m.* shortly after, my mother, Sarah, dau. of N. Stackhouse, esq. second in council, at Bombay; she was then in her seventeenth year, and he just thirty. They had been but a short time acquainted, but long enough for a man of his warm passions to form the strongest attachment to her. I know at this moment but little of the public history of my father at that period. From subsequent misfortunes that befel him, my mother has never willingly talked of his career in India; all I know is, that he, a very young lieutenant-colonel in the king's service, commanded the army on the Malabar coast, taking rank according to the regulation of those days of all Company's officers of the same rank, though of older standing; he served with great success, and made a good deal of money, about £100,000; but I believe, although not addicted to play, he suffered himself to comply with the custom of his associates, and lost all, or nearly all of his savings. In consequence of a new order, that Company's officers should hold rank according to the dates of their commissions, my father found himself under the necessity of resigning his command to those who had formerly obeyed him; and remaining in this situation not being consistent with his ideas of military propriety, he returned to England in the year 1789. My mother, with his children, followed him to Britain in 1790; and he was shortly afterwards unanimously returned at the general election for the county of Inverness." We are subsequently told that, owing to some misunderstanding with Henry Dundas, afterwards Lord Melville, he joined the opposition, and became one of the most strenuous opponents of Mr. Pitt's administration. "His military prospects (we continue to quote from his son) were now closed for ever, and from the early age of thirty-five till forty-seven, when he died, was to him a constant scene of disappointment, misfortune, and remorse. His income was far from being competent to his rank in life. I suspect it did not amount to more than two thousand a year; and while he was in America and India, his commissioners had sold large tracts of his estate (Harris and Loch Snizort Side), for less than half their value. As he was the first of the family who parted with his inheritance, he was doubly grieved to find that he had impoverished his heirs, without materially benefiting himself." At the general election which followed the dissolution in 1796, General M'Leod stood a contest against the Paget family for the borough of Milburn Port, and was defeated, at an expense of £15,000; to meet which, he was obliged to dispose of a very large tract of his estate, Vaternish, which brought exactly that sum, although a few years after it sold for £30,000. He subsequently resided at Edinburgh, and in 1801 removed to a small country house he had hired at Newhaven. His health, which had long been declining, now began rapidly to decay. He accepted in this year an invitation from Captain Murray, of the Prince of Wales Excise yacht, to take a trip to Guernsey, in hope that a change of air might be of service; but he hardly arrived there, when his family received an account of his death. By his first wife (Mary Mackenzie, Suddie), General M'Leod had a son, Norman, who died young, and a daughter, Mary, who *m.* Captain Norman Ramsay, and died shortly after. By the second (Sarah Stackhouse) he had surviving issue,

JOHN NORMAN, his successor.

Sarah, *m.* to Robert Pringle, esq. of Stitchell, and both died soon after.

Amelia, *m.* to Sir J. Pringle, bart. of Stitchell.

Anne-Eliza, married 3rd July, 1831, to Spencer Perceval, esq. eldest son of the late Right Hon. Spencer Perceval.

He was *s.* by his eldest son,

JOHN NORMAN MACLEOD, esq. of Macleod, *b.* in 1788, *m.* 16th November, 1809, Anne, daughter of John Stephenson, esq. of the county of Kent, and had issue,

NORMAN, his heir.
John-Leod.

Emily-Sarah.
Anne-Eliza.
Harriette-Maria.
Mary-Lowther.
Elizabeth-Roma.

Macleod died 25th March, 1835, and was *s.* by his elder son, the present "MACLEOD OF MACLEOD."

*Estates*—In Inverness-shire.

*Seat*—Dunvegan Castle, Isle of Skye.

# TWEMLOW, OF PEATSWOOD.

TWEMLOW, THOMAS, esq. of Peatswood, in the county of Stafford, *b.* 3rd July, 1782, *m.* 9th August, 1828, Harriet Frances, youngest daughter of the late Edward Townshend, esq. of Wincham, Cheshire.

Mr. Twemlow succeeded his father 21st February, 1801. He is a magistrate and deputy-lieutenant for the counties of Stafford and Salop, and was sheriff of the former in 1830.

## Lineage.

GEORGE TWEMLOW, of Arclyd, born in 1631, married in 1662, Mary Linguard, grand-daughter and sole heiress of William Linguard, (who purchased an estate in Arclyd, Cheshire, *temp.* JAMES I.) and had, with many other children, a son and successor,

JOHN TWEMLOW, of Arclyd, who *m.* in 1698, Mary, daughter of James Poole, and by her, who was buried at Sandbach, had three sons and two daughters, namely,

- I. GEORGE, his heir.
- II. Joseph, of Etwall, in the county of Derby, rector of Morley, who died *s. p.* in 1775.
- III. William, *d.* young.

- I. Martha.
- II. Elizabeth.

The eldest son,

GEORGE TWEMLOW, esq. of Arclyd, born in 1703, *m.* in 1727, Mary, daughter of Francis Parrott, and had, by her, who died in 1753, aged fifty-two, and was buried at Sandbach, six sons and two daughters, viz.

- I. JOHN, of Arclyd, *b.* 7th January, 1730, *m.* Ann, daughter of James Whalley, and *d.* 27th August, 1789, leaving two sons,
  1. Thomas, of Liverpool, and of Liscard, in Cheshire, who wedded Miss Elizabeth Hamilton, and had issue.
  2. John, who *m.* Sarah, daughter of John Twiss, esq. and has issue.
- II. Francis, *b.* 16th May, 1728, *d.* unm. 25th November, 1766.
- III. George, of the Hill, Sandbach, *b.* 3rd August, 1736, *d.* unmarried, 29th January, 1808.
- IV. THOMAS, of whom presently.
- V. Joseph, *b.* 22nd September, 1742, *m.* Miss Mary Wilson, and *d.* 28th November, 1765, leaving a son, John.
- VI. William, *b.* 25th January, 1745-6, died young.

- I. Ann, *b.* in 1729, died in 1757.
- II. Mary, *b.* in 1733-4, died in 1756.

Mr. Twemlow died in 1778, and was succeeded in the Arclyd estate by his eldest son, John. His fourth son,

THOMAS TWEMLOW, esq. of the Hill, Sandbach, Cheshire, *b.* 18th November, 1738, married, first, 10th November, 1770, Abigail, daughter of John Mare, by whom he had George, Catherine, and Anne. The two first died young. He wedded, secondly, 21st September, 1778, Mary, daughter and co-heiress of the Rev. Joseph Ward, vicar of Prestbury, in the palatinate, and had, by her,

- THOMAS, his heir.
- Francis, of Betley Court, Staffordshire, *m.* 21st June, 1814, at Betley, in Staffordshire, Elizabeth, second dau. of the late Sir Thomas Fletcher, bart. and has issue.

- Ann.
- Mary.

Mr. Twemlow died 21st February, 1801, and was succeeded by his elder son, the present THOMAS TWEMLOW, esq. of Peatswood.

*Arms*—Az. two bars engrailed or, charged with three boars' heads sa.

*Crest*—A parrot perched on the stump of a tree ppr.

*Estates*—In Staffordshire.

*Seat*—Peatswood.

# SWINTON, OF SWINTON.

SWINTON, SAMUEL, esq. of Swinton, in Berwickshire, *b.* 28th August, 1773, *m.* 19th March, 1800, Miss Isabella Routledge, and has issue,

I. GEORGE-MELVILLE, *b.* 24th August, 1815.
II. John-Monckton, *b.* 4th April, 1819.
III. Samuel-Charles-Alston, *b.* 22nd September, 1820.

I. Anne-Elizabeth, *m.* to her cousin, George Swinton, esq. chief secretary to the Government of Bengal.
II. Mary, *m.* in 1822, to James W. Hogg, esq. barrister in Calcutta.
III. Elizabeth Charlotte, *m.* to John Melville, esq. of Upper Harley-street.
IV. Isabella.
V. Jessie-Bebb.

Mr. Swinton served for thirty-four years in India, as a civil servant, holding the highest offices in the gift of Government, and is a magistrate and deputy lieutenant for the county of Berwick.

## Lineage.

This family, originally Saxon, took its surname from the barony of Swinton, in Berwickshire.

EDULF DE SWINTON, of Swinton, who appears to have flourished in the reigns of MACBETH and MALCOLM Canmore, left a son,

LIULPH or LIULF, living in the beginning of *King* EDGAR, (whose reign terminated in 1107,) and was father of

UDARD, sheriff of the county of Berwick *temp.* ALEXANDER I. who was succeeded by

HERNULF or A'LNULF, who obtained a charter from DAVID I. in which the three preceding proprietors of the lands and barony are named "David rex Scotorum, et Henricus suus filius omnibus vicecomitibus suis, cunctisque baronibus Francis et Anglis salutem, sciatis quod dedi et concessi huic meo militi Hernulfo Swinton infeodo, sibi et hæredi suo; cum omnibus hominibus suisque pecuniis tenere bene et libere et honorifice, sicut ullus ex meis baronibus, melius ac liberius tenet, et quicquid ad eam pertinet per easdem consuetudines, per quas Liulfus filius Edulfi, et Udardus filius suus tenuerunt, tenere de Sancto Cuthberto et de me, xl solidos reddente monachis de Dunelmia, sine omnibus aliis servitiis, Testibus, Willielmo filio Duncani et Maduc consule et comite Duncano, et Radulfo Luulel Marmion Marsel, et Waltero filio Alani, et Herberto Camerario, et Adam filio Edwardi, Willielmo de Lindsay, apud Haddingtunian, vale."

Hernulf died in the reign of MALCOLM IV. and was *s.* by

SIR ALAN DE SWINTON, *miles*,—who got a charter of the barony of Swinton from Bertram, prior of Coldingham, superior thereof in the reign of *King* WILLIAM the Lion. He died about the year 1200, and was interred in the church of Swinton, where his name and arms are over a stone image upon his tomb, and was *s.* by

SIR ADAM DE SWINTON, who is mentioned in a donation made by his relic to the monastery of Soltray. Sir Adam died before the year 1229, and was *s.* by

SIR ALAN DE SWINTON, of whom there are many documents in the reign of *King* ALEXANDER II. He was *s.* by

ALAN DE SWINTON, who, in the reign of *King* ALEXANDER III. is mentioned in the Chartulary of Coldingham, as proprietor of the lands and barony of Swinton *anno* 1273. He was *s.* by

HENRY DE SWINTON, cotemporary with whom was

WILLIAM DE SWINTON, probably a son of the family, who in Ragman's roll is designated "Vicaire de l'Eglise de Swinton, *anno* 1296."

HENRY DE SWINTON (Alan's successor) was, with many others of his countrymen, compelled to submit to *King* EDWARD I. of England, when he had overrun Scotland, *anno* 1296. This Henry was *s.* by

HENRY DE SWINTON, who is witness in a charter by Isabella Senescalla, domina de Fife, to Michael Balfour, of an annuity of eight merks sterling out of the lands of Easterferry. He was *s.* by

SIR JOHN SWINTON, a distinguished soldier and statesman, and high in favour with the Second and Third ROBERTS. His military achievements are recorded by the ancient Scottish writers. At the battle of Otterburn, 31st July, 1388, he had a chief command, and to his intrepidity the Scots were indebted for the great victory obtained over the English (although with the loss of Douglas) on that memorable field. It is related of Sir John, that in the wars with the English, he visited the enemy's camp, and gave a general challenge to fight any of their army. He was appointed one of the ambassadors extraordinary by *King* ROBERT III. to negociate a treaty with the court of England, for which they got a safe conduct from *King* RICHARD II. for themselves and sixty knights in their retinue, 4th July, 1392. He was afterwards employed upon another negociation, and obtained a safe conduct from *King* HENRY IV. to go to England, with twenty horsemen in his retinue, 7th July, 1400. The gallant bearing and heroic death of the Lord of Swinton, at the fatal battle of Homildon, have afforded a subject for the poetic genius of Scott, and are the materials on which he founded the drama of "Haledon Hill." Pinkerton thus records Swinton's fall: "The English advanced to the assault, and Henry Percy was about to lead them up the hill, when March caught his bridle, and advised him to advance no farther, but to pour the dreadful shower of English arrows into the enemy. This advice was followed with the usual fortune; for in all ages the bow was the English weapon of victory, and though the Scots, and perhaps the French, were superior in the use of the spear, yet this weapon was useless after the distant bow had decided the combat. ROBERT the Great, sensible of this at the battle of Bannockburn, ordered a prepared detachment of cavalry to rush among the English archers at the commencement, totally to disperse them, and stop the deadly effusion. But Douglas now used no such precaution; and the consequence was, that his people, drawn up on the face of the hill, presented one general mark to the enemy, none of whose arrows descended in vain. The Scots fell without fight and unrevenged, till a spirited knight, Swinton, exclaimed aloud, 'O my brave countrymen! what fascination has seized you to-day, that you stand like deer to be shot, instead of indulging your ancient courage, and meeting your enemies hand to hand? Let those who will, descend with me, that we may gain victory, and life, or fall like men.' This being heard by Adam Gordon, between whom and Swinton there existed a deadly feud, attended with the mutual slaughter of many followers, he instantly fell on his knees before Swinton, begged his pardon, and desired to be dubbed a knight by him whom he must now regard as the wisest and boldest of that order in Britain. The ceremony performed, Swinton and Gordon descended the hill, accompanied by only one hundred men, and a desperate valour led the whole body to death. Had a similar spirit been shewn by the Scottish army, it is probable that the event of that day would have been different." He *m.* first, Margaret, Countess of Douglas and Marr, widow of William, first Earl of Douglas, but by that lady had no issue; and secondly, Lady Margaret Stewart, daughter of *King* ROBERT II. by whom he had a son,

SIR JOHN SWINTON, of that ilk, who succeeded him, a man of singular merit, and a soldier of as undaunted valour. At the battle of Beauge, in France, in 1420, Swinton unhorsed the Duke of Clarence, the English general, brother of *King* HENRY V. whom he distinguished by a coronet set with precious stones, which the duke wore around his helmet, and wounded him so grievously in the face with his lance that he immediately expired.* Sir John afterwards fell at the battle of Vernoil, where the Scots' auxiliaries were commanded by the gallant Earl of Buchan, constable of France, son of Robert, Duke of Albany, governor of Scotland *anno* 1424. Swinton *m.* first, Lady Marjory Dunbar, daughter of George, Earl of March; but she died without issue. He espoused, secondly, his cousin-german, Lady Marjory Stewart, daughter of Robert, Duke of Albany. He was *s.* by his son,

SIR JOHN SWINTON, who, being an infant at his father's death, was left under the care of William de Wedderburn, *scutifer*. Sir John died about the year 1493, leaving (with a daughter, Margaret, who *m.* John Falside, and in her widowhood was prioress of the monastery of Elcho) a son and successor,

SIR JOHN SWINTON, of that ilk, who, *anno* 1475, wedded Katharine Lauder, a daughter of the family of Bass, by whom he had, with other issue, a son,

JOHN SWINTON, of that ilk, who *m.* in 1518, Margaret, daughter of David Hume, of Wedderburn, and had issue,

---

* And Swinton placed the lance in rest
That humbled erst the sparkling crest
Of Clarence's Plantagenet.
*Lay of the Last Minstrel.*

I. JOHN (Sir), his heir.
II. George.

I. Helen.
II. Agnes.
III. Janet, *m.* to John Nicolson, an eminent lawyer, ancestor of the Nicolsons, of Lasswade and Carnock.
IV. Margaret, went into the monastery of Elcho.
V. Katharine.
VI. Elizabeth, *m.* to Matthew Sinclair, of Longformacus.
VII. Isabel.
VIII. Mary.

He died about the year 1549, and was *s.* by his elder son,

SIR JOHN SWINTON, of that ilk, who, in the year 1552, married his cousin, Katharine, daughter of Robert Lauder, of Bass, and dying in 1584, was *s.* by his eldest son,

ROBERT SWINTON, a man of good parts, who was long sheriff of Berwickshire. He *m.* first, Katharine Hay, daughter of William, Lord Yester, by whom he had one son, JOHN, his heir, and a daughter, Katharine, *m.* to Sir Alexander Nisbet, of that ilk. He *m.* secondly, *anno* 1597, Jean Hepburn, sister of Patrick Hepburn, of White Castle, by whom he had two sons and one daughter, viz.

I. ALEXANDER, afterwards Sir Alexander, who carried on the line of the family.
II. Robert.

I. Helen, *m.* in 1628, to John Hepburn, of Smeaton.

Swinton *d.* in 1628, and was *s.* by his son,

JOHN SWINTON, of that ilk, who was served heir in general to the second Sir John Swinton, *suo tritavo*, on 22nd July, 1630. He survived his father only five years, and dying unmarried, in 1633, was *s.* by his brother,

SIR ALEXANDER SWINTON, of that ilk, who had acquired the lands of Hiltoun, but disposed of them upon his succession to the family estate, and was appointed sheriff of Berwick, *anno* 1640. In the year 1620, he married Margaret, daughter of James Home, of Framepath, and Sir Bothans, a cadet of the family of Home, and had issue by her six sons and five daughters,

I. JOHN, his heir.
II. Alexander, Lord Mersington, one of the senators of the college of justice, who *m.* first, ——, by whom he had two sons, who went to England; and, secondly, Katherine Skeen, a daughter of the family of Hallyards, by whom he had two other sons and seven daughters,
   1. Charles, who was colonel of a regiment in the service of the states of Holland, and *m.* Alice Newman, of a good family in England.
   2. James, a captain in the same regiment, who married a lady in Holland. These two brothers were both killed in the French trenches at the battle of Malplaquet.

   1. Mary, *m.* first, to Fletcher, of Aberlady; and after his death to Brigadier James Bruce, of Kennet, (see vol. ii. p. 487).
   2. Elizabeth, *m.* to Sir Alexander Cummin, of Culter.
   3. Janet, *m.* to John Belsches, of Tofts.
   4. Alice, *m.* to her cousin, Swinton, of Laughton.
   5. Helen, *m.* to Colonel Francis Charteris, of Amisfield.
   6. Katherine, married to Laurence Drummond, a brother of Pitkellony.
   7. Beatrix, *m.* to Sir Alexander Brown, of Bassendean.
III. Robert, an officer in the army, killed at the battle of Worcester, on the king's side, attempting to carry off Cromwell's standard which he had seized.
IV. James, who was in the same army at the same battle.
V. George, of Chesters, writer to the signet, who *m.* Eupheme, sister of Brown, of Thornydykes, whose only daughter, Katherine, was *m.* to David Dundas, of Philipston.
VI. David, of Laughton, a merchant in Edinburgh, who *m.* Margaret Broadfoot.

I. Jane, *m.* to Sir James Cockburn, of Ryslaw.
II. Margaret, *m.* to Mark Ker, of Moriston.
III. Katherine, *m.* to Brown, of Thornydykes.
IV. Elizabeth, *m.* to Hepburn, of Beanston.
V. Helen, *m.* to Dr. George Hepburn, of Monkrig.

Sir Alexander died in 1652, and was *s.* by his eldest son,

JOHN SWINTON, of that ilk, who was appointed, in 1649, one of the colonels for Berwickshire, for putting the kingdom in a posture of defence, and is then designed John de Swinton, jun. de Eodem. He was also chosen one of the committee of estates, and appointed one of the commissioners for plantation of kirks, 14th March, that same year.

Cromwell, when in Scotland, carried Swinton a prisoner to England, and had him with him at the battle of Worcester, where he was only a spectator; however, he was forfeited by the convention of estates in absence, and without proof, anno 1651. Oliver afterwards conceiving a great esteem for his captive, made him one of the commissioners for the administration of justice to the people of Scotland, in 1657.

After the restoration of *King* CHARLES II. the old decree of forfeiture against him was confirmed in 1661, and he outed of his estate, which remained under forfeiture till 1690.

He *m.* first, (in 1645), Margaret Stewart, daughter of William, Lord Blantyre, by whom he had three sons and one daughter,

- I. ALEXANDER, his heir.
- II. JOHN, afterwards Sir John, who carried on the line of the family.
- III. Isaac.

- I. Margaret, *m.* to Sir John Riddel, of that ilk.

He *m.* secondly, Francisca Hancock, widow of Arnot Sonmans, a considerable proprietor in the Jerseys, but by her had no issue. He died anno 1679, and was *s.* by his eldest son,

ALEXANDER SWINTON, of that ilk, who survived his father only a few years, and dying unmarried, was succeeded by his brother,

SIR JOHN SWINTON, of that ilk, who resided in Holland during the forfeiture, and was a considerable merchant there. He returned to Britain at the Revolution, and in the year 1690 the decree of forfeiture was rescinded, and the family estate was restored to him, *per modum justitiæ*.

He was a member of the Union Parliament, and was appointed one of the commissioners of equivalent.

He *m.* first, Sarah, daughter of William Welsh, merchant in London, by whom he had many children; but none of them came to maturity, except one daughter, Frances, who married the Rev. Henry Veitch, minister of Swinton.

Sir John *m.* secondly, Anne, daughter of Sir Robert Sinclair, of Longformacus, by Margaret, his wife, daughter of William, Lord Alexander, by Lady Jane Douglas, his wife, daughter of William, first Marquis of Douglas. By her he had four sons and five daughters:

- I. JOHN, his heir.
- II. Robert, merchant in North-Berwick, who *m.* Katherine, daughter of Robert Rutherford, of Farnilee, and left issue.
- III. Francis, doctor of medicine, who *d.* abroad, unmarried.
- IV. William, merchant in North-Berwick.

- I. Jean, *m.* to Dr. John Rutherford.
- II. Margaret.
- III. Johanna, *m.* to Alexander Keith, of Ravelstone.
- IV. Anne, *d.* young.

Sir John *d.* in 1724, and was *s.* by his eldest son,

JOHN SWINTON, of that ilk, advocate. He *m.* Mary, daughter of the Rev. Samuel Semple, minister of the Gospel at Libberton, by Elizabeth, his wife, daughter of Sir Archibald Murray, of Blackbarony; and by her he had six sons and six daughters,

- I. JOHN, his heir, who succeeded to SWINTON.*
- II. SAMUEL, of whom presently.
- III. Robert, who *d.* abroad, in the service of the East India Company.
- IV. Archibald, a captain in the service of the East India Company.
- V. Francis, who *d.* in the service of the said Company.
- V. Pringle, who *d.* in infancy.

- I. Elizabeth.
- II. Anne, married to Robert Hepburn, of Baads, esq.
- III. Jean, died unmarried.
- IV. Mary.
- V. Frances, who *d.* young.
- VI. Katharine.

The second son,

CAPTAIN SAMUEL SWINTON, R. N. wedded Jean Felicité Lefebvre, and was father of Samuel, who having purchased the estate of Swinton from his cousin, Robert Hepburne Swinton, esq. the present head and representative of the family of Swinton of that ilk, is now SWINTON, of Swinton.

*Arms*—Sa. a chev. or, between three boars' heads erased arg.

*Crest*—A boar chained to a tree, and above, on an escrol, *J'espere*.

*Motto*—Je pense.

---

* JOHN SWINTON, of that Ilk. Lord Swinton, one of the senators of the college of justice, *m.* Margaret, daughter of John Mitchelson, esq. of Middleton, and had six sons, 1. John, 2. Samuel, 3. Archibald, 4. Robert, 5. George, 6. William; and seven daughters, 1. Margaret, 2. Mary, 3. Isabella, 4. Elizabeth, 5. Harriot, 6. Catherine, 7. Anne. He *d.* in 1799, and was *s.* by his eldest son,

JOHN SWINTON, of that Ilk, advocate, who *m.* his cousin, Mary-Anne, daughter of Robert Hepburne, esq. of Clerkington, and had, 1. John, 2. Robert-Hepburne; 1. Isabella, 2. Margaret. He *d.* in 1820, and was *s.* by his eldest son, John, who dying unm. in 1829, the line of the family is now carried on by his younger brother,

ROBERT HEPBURNE SWINTON, of that Ilk, *m.* Juliana, daughter of — Hecher, esq. has two sons, 1. John-Edulphus, 2. Robert.

The *supporters* borne by the head of the family are *two boars standing in a compartment, whereon are these words, Je pense.*

# FRYER, OF THE WERGS.

FRYER, RICHARD, esq. of the Wergs, in the county of Stafford, *b.* 11th November, 1771, *m.* 6th August, 1794, Mary, only child of William Fleeming,* esq. and niece and sole heiress of John Fleeming, esq. of the Wergs. By this lady he has surviving issue,

I. WILLIAM-FLEEMING, who inherits the estates at the Wergs, through his mother and under the will of his great uncle John Fleeming, esq.
II. Richard.

I. Elizabeth, *m.* to the Reverend Thomas Walker, A.M. Prebendary of the Collegiate Church of Wolverhampton.
II. Mary, *m.* to Henry Morson, esq. of the county of Kent.
III. Dorothea, *m.* to Stubbs Wightwick, esq. of Great Bloxwich, in Staffordshire.
IV. Susanna, *m.* to Robert Thacker, esq. second son of William Thacker, esq. of Minchall Hall, Staffordshire.

Mr. Fryer, an eminent banker, in Wolverhampton, succeeded his father on attaining the age of twenty-one, having been a minor several years. He is a deputy-lieutenant for the county of Stafford, and was chosen representative of the borough of Wolverhampton in the first reformed parliament, December, 1832.

## Lineage.

RICHARD FRYER, esq. *b.* 22nd July, 1693, son of Richard Fryer, a descendant of the Fryers, of Thornes, near Shenstone, where the old hall, surrounded by a moat, now stands, left a son and successor,

RICHARD FRYER, esq. of Wednesfield, *b.* 26th March, 1719, who married Dorothea, daughter of John Wood, esq. of Wednesbury, Hall, and grand-daughter of — Hope, esq. of Neechells Hall, in the county of Staffordshire, who was a firm adherent of royalty and raised, for the cause of CHARLES II., a troop of horse, which he equipped and clothed at his own expense. By this lady Mr. Fryer left at his decease, (with another son, John, of Wednesfield, and two daughters, Elizabeth, and Mary widow of John Howard, esq. of Chester,) the present RICHARD FRYER, esq. of the Wergs

*Arms*—Or, between two flaunches gu. two billets charged with three oak leaves or.

*Crest*—A tower encircled by a snake, and surmounted of a cock ppr.

*Motto*—Mea fides in sapientia.

*Estates*—In Staffordshire.

*Seats*—The Wergs, and New - Cross House, both in Staffordshire.

---

* The Fleemings have been located at the Wergs upwards of four hundred years, holding their lands by prescription down to the present time, and through the ebbs and flows of succeeding generations have neither increased nor diminished their estate.—It is worthy of remark, as recorded in "Pit's History of Staffordshire," that the timber on the Wergs is equal to (if not the finest) any in the county of Staffordshire. "Amongst a number of well grown trees of various species," says that writer, "I could pick out a few oaks worth thirty guineas each."

*Arms*—Of FLEEMING, arg. a chev. engr. between three crosses patee fitchee sa.

*Crest*—A Cornish chough.

# PENN, OF STOKE PARK.

**PENN, GRANVILLE,** esq. of Stoke Park, in the county of Buckingham, *b.* in New-street, Spring-gardens, 9th December, 1761, *m.* 24th June, 1791, Isabella, eldest daughter of the late General Gordon Forbes,* colonel of the 29th regiment of foot, by Margaret, his wife, eldest daughter of Benjamin Sullivan, esq. of Cork, and has had issue,

I. John-William, *d.* an infant in 1802.
II. GRANVILLE-JOHN, M.A. of Christ Church, Oxford, barrister-at-law, a deputy-lieutenant for the county of Buckingham.
III. Thomas-Gordon, M.A. of Christ Church, Oxford, in holy orders.
IV. William, M.A. of Christ Church, Oxford.
I. Juliana, *d.* young in 1104.
II. Sophia, *m.* to Colonel Sir William Gomon, K.C.B. and *d. s. p.* in 1827.
III. Louisa-Emily.
IV. Isabella-Mary.
V. Henrietta-Adna.

Mr. Penn, who is in the commission of the peace for Bucks, succeeded his brother 21st June, 1834. He is distinguished in the literary world as author of "Observations in Illustration of Virgil's Fourth Eclogue," "Examination of the Primary Argument of the Iliad," the Bioscope," "The Christian Survey," "A Comparative Estimate of the Mineral and Mosaical Geologies," and "Memorials of the Professional Life, and Times of Admiral Sir William Penn."

## Lineage.

WILLIAM PENN, of Minety, in the county of Gloucester, and of Penn's Lodge, in Wiltshire, died in 1591, and lies buried before the altar in the church of Minety; in which parish he inherited a patrimonial estate, long possessed by his ancestors, but which, soon after his death, was alienated to a branch of the family of Pleydell. His son,

WILLIAM PENN, who predeceased his father, married a Gloucestershire lady named Rastall, and left two sons, WILLIAM, whose line is extinct, and

GILES PENN, Captain R.N. who held for some time the office of English consul in the Mediterranean. He *m.* into the family of Gilbert (which came originally from Yorkshire, but was then settled in Somersetshire), and had two sons, GEORGE, envoy to Spain, who died unmarried, and

SIR WILLIAM PENN, *b.* at Bristol in 1621, who adopting the gallant profession of his father, became a distinguished naval officer, Admiral of England, and was one of the commanders at the taking of Jamaica. He was passionately attached from his youth to maritime affairs, and, before he had reached his thirty-second year, had gone through the various promotions of captain, rear-admiral of Ireland, vice-admiral of England, general in the first Dutch war, and commander-in-chief under the Duke of York, in the signal victory over the Dutch in 1665, on which occasion he was knighted. On his return he was sent to parliament by the borough of Weymouth; in 1660 he was made a commissioner of the admiralty and navy, governor of the fort and town of Kinsale, vice-admiral of Munster, and a member of that provincial council. He then took leave of the sea, but still continued his other employments till 1669, when, through bodily infirmities, he withdrew to Wanstead in Essex, and there died in 1670. Although he was thus engaged, both under the parliament and king, he took no part in the civil war, but adhered to the duties of his profession. Beside the reputation of a great and patriotic officer, he acquired credit for having improved the navy in several important departments. He was the author of many little tracts on this subject, some of which are preserved in the British Museum. The monument erected to his memory, by his wife, in Redcliffe church, Bristol, contains

* Of the family of Forbes of Skellater, in Aberdeenshire.

a short account of his life and promotions;* but in Thurloe's State Papers there are minutes of his proceedings in America, not mentioned on the monument, which he delivered to Oliver Cromwell's council in September, 1655. He arrived at Portsmouth in August, and thence wrote to Cromwell, but receiving no answer, he appeared before the council, and was committed to the tower, for leaving his command without permission, to the hazard of the army, but soon after discharged.† Sir William *m.* Margaret, daughter of John Jasper, of Rotterdam, and by her, who died in 1681-2, had issue,

WILLIAM, his heir.

Richard, died young.

Margaret, *m.* to Anthony Lowther, esq. of Mask, in Yorkshire, whose descendant in the second generation, Sir Thomas Lowther, bart. of Holker, married Lady Elizabeth Cavendish, daughter of William, Duke of Devonshire. Their only child, William, dying unmarried in 1756, his estates passed by will to the noble house of Cavendish.

Sir William Penn died in 1670, and was *s.* by his son,

WILLIAM PENN, who was born in the parish of St. Catherine, near the Tower of London, 14th October, 1644. This eminent man entered as a commoner at Christchurch, Oxford, in 1660, and remained at the university two years, where he formed an intimacy with Robert Spencer and John Locke. Though fond at this time of youthful sports, he had given his attention to the preaching of one Thomas Loe, a quaker, and thence imbibed strong religious impressions. He withdrew, with some other students, from the national worship, and held private meetings, where they preached and prayed among themselves. This line of conduct giving great offence to the heads of the college, Mr. Penn, though but sixteen years of age, was fined for non-conformity, and, continuing his religious exercises, was at length expelled the university. On his return home, his father, who was highly incensed, sent him to France, in company with some persons of rank; and he continued abroad a considerable period, returning not only well skilled in the French language, but a polite and accomplished gentleman. He was subsequently entered as a student of law, at Lincoln's Inn, but his sojourn there was of short duration; for in 1666, having been entrusted by his father with the management of a considerable estate in Ireland, he was at Cork, where he met with a person whom he had known at Oxford, who had become a proselyte to quakerism; and he found the principles of his friend so con-

---

* Inscription on Sir William Penn's Monument:

"To the just memory of Sir William Penn, kt. and sometimes
Generall: Borne at Bristoll An. 1621: Son of Captain Giles
Penn, severall yeares Consul for y[e] English in y[e] Mediterranean;
of the Penns of Penn's-lodge in y[e] county of
Wilts, and those Penns of Penn in y[e] county of Bucks; and by
his mother from y[e] Gilberts in y[e] county of Somerset,
Originally from Yorkshire: Addicted from his
Youth to Maritame Affaires; he was made Captain at
the yeares of 21; Rear-Admiral of Ireland at 23; Vice-Admiral
of Ireland at 25; Admiral to the Streights
at 29; Vice-Admiral of England at 31, and General
in the first Dutch Warres at 32. Whence retiring,
in Ao 1655, he was chosen a Parliament man for the
Town of Weymouth in 1660; made a Commissioner of
the Admiralty and Navy; Governor of the Town and Fort
of King-Sail; Vice-Admiral of Munster, and a Member of
that Provincial Counseill; and in Anno 1664, was
chosen great Captain Commander under his
Royal Highnesse in y[t] signall and most
evidently successful fight against the Dutch fleet.

Thus, he took leave of the Sea, his old Element; but
continued still his other employs till 1669; at what
time, through Bodely Infirmities (contracted by y[e]
Care and fatigue of Publique Affaires)
He withdrew,
Prepared and made for his End; and with a gentle and
Even Gale, in much peace, arrived and anchored in his
Last and Best Port, at Wanstead, in y[e] county of Essex,
y[e] 16th Sept. 1670. Being then but 49 and 4 Months old.
To whose Name and merit his surviving Lady
hath erected this remembrance.

† For full and interesting particulars of Sir William Penn, see "The Memorials of his Life" by Mr. Granville Penn.

genial to his enthusiastic feelings, that he immediately adopted them. This step produced an open breach with his father * on his return to England; but he was too zealous a professor to be reclaimed by harsh treatment, and in 1668 he was committed to the Tower for preaching against the Established Church. While in confinement he composed a tract entitled, "No Cross, no Crown; a discourse showing the nature and discipline of the Holy Cross of Christ," which is the most esteemed of his writings. He was no sooner released than he recommenced preaching, and, being in consequence arrested, together with his companion William Mead, was indicted at the Old Bailey Sessions for illegally holding forth, and although acquitted by the verdict of the jury, they were arbitrarily imprisoned in Newgate by order of the court. On obtaining his liberty, Penn visited Holland and Germany as a missionary, but he hastily returned to England, owing to the illness of his father, whom he found on his death-bed, and with whom he effected a reconciliation previous to the old gentleman's decease, which happened shortly after. †

In 1681, *King* Charles II. in consideration of the services of Mr. Penn's father, and several debts due to him from the crown at the period of his demise, granted to William Penn and his heirs the province lying on the west side of the river Delaware, in North America, which thence obtained the name of Pennsylvania. Mr. Penn immediately published a brief account of the province, proposing an easy purchase of land, and good terms of settlement for such as were inclined to remove thither. A great number of purchasers came forward, and formed a company, called, "The Free Society of Traders in Pennsylvania." Shortly after, the enlightened and beneficent proprietor sailed to colonize his newly-acquired territories, with a band of persecuted Quakers, who followed his fortune; and having entered into a treaty with the Indian natives, ‡ founded the city of Philadelphia. He abolished negro slavery in his dominions, and established a code of laws for their internal government, which contributed much to the prosperity of the colony.

On the accession of *King* James II. Penn became a great favourite at court, and was one of the most zealous advisers of the measures for allowing liberty of conscience which then appeared. The Revolution placed the Quakers, in common with other dissenters, under the protection of the laws in the exercise of their religion, and Penn, having witnessed this favourable change in their situation, returned to America, where he was joyfully received, and found the affairs of his settlement in a prosperous condition. After residing in Pennsylvania a few years, he came home to negociate some matters with the British Government, relative to the commerce of the colony, whither he did not again return, dying at his seat at Ruscomb, in Berkshire, in 1718. Beside the tract already mentioned, Penn was the author of "Primitive Christianity revived, in the Faith and Practice of the People called Quakers;" "A brief Account of the Rise and Progress of the Quakers;" "A Treatise on Oaths," &c. &c.

"William Penn, the great legislator of the Quakers," says Father O'Leary, "had the success of a conqueror in establishing and defending his colony, among savage tribes, without ever drawing the sword; the goodness of the most benevolent rulers, in treating his subjects as his own children; and the tenderness of an universal father, who opened his arms to all mankind without distinction of sect or party. In his republic, it was not the religious creed, but personal merit, that entitled every member of society to the protection and *emoluments* of the state." With respect to the settlement, it has been supposed that, during the seventy years while William Penn's principles prevailed, or the Quakers had the principal share in the government, there was no spot on the globe where, number for number, there was so much virtue or so much true happiness as among the inhabitants of Pennylvania; and that, during the time it exhibited (setting aside

* The species of conflict between them cannot easily be described. The father felt great affection for an accomplished and dutiful son, and ardently desired the promotion of his temporal interests, which he feared would be obstructed by the course of life he had embraced. The son was sensible of the duty he owed to his parent, and afflicted in believing that he could not obey him but at the risk of his eternal welfare.

† His last moments are thus recorded by his son:—"My father after (nearly) thirty years employment, with good success, in divers places of eminent trust and honour in his own country, upon a serious reflection not long before his death, spoke to me in this manner: 'Son William, I am weary of the world: I would not live over my days if I could command them with a wish, for the snares of life are greater than the fear of death .... Three things I commend unto you. First, let nothing in this world tempt you to wrong your conscience; so you will keep peace at home, which will be a feast to you in a day of trouble. Secondly, whatever you design to do, lay it justly and time it seasonably, for that gives security and dispatch. Lastly, be not troubled at disappointments; for if they may be recovered, do it; if they can't, trouble is vain."

‡ Penn's friendly and pacific manner of treating the Indians, produced in them an extraordinary love for him and his people; so that they have maintained a perfect amity with the Anglo-Americans in Pennsylvania ever since.

the difficulties of a new colony) a kind of little paradise upon earth. Hence the period from 1682 to 1754, with the same exception, has been denominated the golden age of Pennsylvania. Nor has this name been improperly bestowed upon it, if we examine into facts; for in a constitution where merit only was publicly rewarded, there must have been a constant growth of virtue, and, of course happiness with it. In a constitution, also, where every man had free scope for his exertions, and the power of enjoying the fruits of his own labour, there must have been the constant opportunity of improving his temporal condition.

William Penn *m.* first, Gulielma Maria, daughter of Sir William Springett, and had by her a son,

WILLIAM, to whom his father left his estates in Ireland. This William was father of another WILLIAM PENN, whose daughter, CHRISTIANA, marrying — Gaskill, esq. of Gloucestershire, was mother of

ALEXANDER-FORBES GASKILL, esq. of Shannagarry, in the county of Cork.

He wedded, secondly, Hannah, daughter of Thomas Callowhill, of Bristol, and had by her three sons, viz.

John, who died unm. in 1746, and bequeathed his moiety of the province of Pennsylvania to his brother Thomas.

THOMAS, of whom presently.

Richard, who *m.* Hannah, daughter of Richard Lardner, M.D. and left two sons, John, who *m.* Anne Allen, of Philadelphia, but *d. s. p.* and RICHARD, who *m.* Mary Masters, of the same place, and had issue two sons and two daughters, viz. WILLIAM, Richard, Hannah, and Mary, the wife of Samuel Paynter, esq. of Richmond, Surrey.

William Penn died in 1718, and was interred in the Quakers' burial ground at Jordans, near Beaconsfield. His second son by his second marriage,

THOMAS PENN, esq. of Stoke Pogies, in the county of Buckingham, espoused, in 1751, Lady Juliana Fermor, fourth daughter of Thomas, first Earl of Pomfret, and by her, who was born in 1729, and died in 1801, had issue,

I. William, died an infant in 1753.
II. William, also died in infancy.
III. Thomas, died an infant.
IV. JOHN, heir to his father.
V. GRANVILLE, successor to his brother.

I. Juliana, *m.* to William Baker, esq. of Bayfordbury, Herts, and died leaving a daughter, Sophia-Margaret, relict of the Hon. and Most Rev. William Stuart, D.D. Archbishop of Armagh.
II. Louisa, died young.

Mr. Penn died in 1775, and his demise is thus recorded in the Pennsylvania Gazette. "By the last ships from London we have an account that, on the 21st March last, died the Hon. Thomas Penn, esq. one of the proprietors of this province, and last survivor of all the children of its illustrious founder, William Penn, whose virtues, as well as abilities, he inherited in an eminent degree. He was born 8th March, 1701-2, being a few months younger than our present charter of privileges, which he constantly declared himself desirous of preserving inviolable, as the great fundamental compact by which all ought to be bound. He had the principal direction of the affairs of this government for half a century, and saw such an increase of population, arts, and improvement in it, as during the like period, perhaps, no man before him ever beheld in a country of his own. He rejoiced at the sight; was a kind landlord, and gave a liberal, often a magnificent, encouragement to our various public institutions. The hospital, the college, our different libraries, and religious societies, can witness the truth of this. For he did not confine himself to sect or party; but, as became his station, and the genius of his father's benevolent policy, he professed himself a friend to universal liberty, and extended his bounty to all. In short, the grave, which generally stops the tongue of flattery, should open the mouth of justice. We may be permitted to conclude his character by saying, that he was both a great and a good man." He was interred in his family vault at Stoke Pogeis, and *s.* by his son,

JOHN PENN, esq. of Stoke Pogeis, *b.* 22nd February, 1760, a justice of the peace for Buckinghamshire, and governor of Portland Castle, in the county of Dorset. He died unmarried, 21st June, 1834, the last proprietary and hereditary governor of the heretofore province (now state) of Pennsylvania, and was *s.* by his brother, the present GRANVILLE PENN, esq. of Stoke Park.

*Arms*—Arg. on a fess sa. three bezants of the field.

*Crest*—A demi-lion rampant, collared with the fess of the arms.

*Motto*—Dum clarum rectum teneam.

*Estates*—In the county of Bucks, including the manors of Stoke Poges and Eton. The latter was purchased by the late John Penn, esq.

*Town Residence*—New Street, Spring Gardens.

*Seat*—Stoke Park, Bucks.

# KER-SEYMER, OF HANFORD.

SEYMER-KER, HENRY, esq. of Hanford, in the county of Dorset, succeeded his father in 1834. Mr. Seymer was elected fellow of All Soul's College, Oxford, in 1831.

## Lineage.

This family, resident for several centuries at Hanford, in Dorsetshire, claims a common progenitor with the ducal house of Somerset. In Collins's Peerage, under that dukedom, there is a conjecture as to the descent of the Seymers of Hanford, from Humphrey Seymer, of Even Swindon. The conjecture arose probably from the coincidence of date, similarity of arms, and the spelling of the name. It appears in the early part of the pedigree of the ducal family the termination was ER.

JOHN SEYMER, of Hanford, living in the 22nd EDWARD IV.* *m.* a daughter of William Pulvertopp, and was *s.* by his son,

RICHARD SEYMER, of Hanford, in the 12th HENRY VIII. who wedded Helena, daugh- of — Gaunt, and had a son and heir,

JOHN SEYMER, of Hanford, living in the 31st HENRY VIII. This gentleman *m.* Edith, daughter of William Laver, and was *s.* by his son,

JOHN SEYMER, of Hanford, who *m.* Elizabeth, daughter and heir of Thomas Attwater†, of Todbere, in Dorsetshire, by whom (who wedded, secondly, John Bayly, and thirdly, William Hannam, of Purse Candel) he had issue,

- JOHN, his successor.
- Alice, *m.* to Henry Stephens, of Sherburn.
- Anne, *m.* to Henry Gayne.

He was *s.* by his son,

JOHN SEYMER, esq. of Hanford, who *m.* Agnes, daughter of William Rawles, esq. of Fifehead, in the county of Dorset, and relict of Robert Saunders, esq. and had three sons and six daughters, viz.

- ROBERT (Sir), his heir.
- John, of Stoke Wake, *m.* Anne, daughter of John Fry, of Gunville, and *d.* in 1700.
- Richard.
- Samuel.
- Anne, *m.* to John Squibb, of Winterbourne Whitechurch.
- Elizabeth, *m.* to Laurence Swetenham, of Sherborne.
- Bridget, *m.* to Thomas Young, of Child Ockford.
- Judith, *m.* to John Dolling, of Worth.
- Edith, *m.* to Richard Ryves, of Child, Ockford.
- Johanna, married to Arthur Squibb, of Knowl, in Somersetshire.

He *d.* 12th January, in the 9th *King* JAMES I., and by inquisition taken after the decease of his eldest son, in 1626, he was found to have been seised in demesne as in fee of the manor, site, capital, messuage, farm, rectory, and lands in Hanford, with several fisheries on the river; of one messuage, and twenty-eight acres of land in Todbere, and sixty in Marnhull; one messuage, and two hundred and eight acres of land in Tileshead, Culston, and Edington, in Wilts. He was *s.* by his son,

SIR ROBERT SEYMER, of Hanford, one of

* It is presumed that the family held the estate of Hanford under the abbesses of Tarent, until the dissolution in HENRY VIIIth's time; it has been their constant abode ever since.

† Grandson of WILLIAM ATTWATER, of Tidelishid, by Agnes, his wife, daughter and heiress of John Lymbergh, which William was lineally descended from Roger Attwater, of Coveleston, *temp.* EDWARD III.

the tellers of the exchequer, who received the honour of knighthood at Whitehall 19th February, 1619. This gentleman *m.* in 1603, Johanna, daughter of William Pitt, esq. of Iwern Stepleton, and had Robert, who died before himself, HENRY, his successor, and Penelope-Edith, the wife of Richard King, esq. Sir Robert *d.* in 1624, seised of the premises in Hanford, held of the king in chief, one tenth of a knight's fee: the premises in Todbere, Tileshead, &c. He was likewise seised in demesne as of fee, of a messuage called Lymbergh House, and eighty acres of land in Marnhull and Todbere, and of divers other estates, with the manors and advowsons of Stoke Wake, and Bere Marsh, in Dorsetshire. He was *s.* by his son,

HENRY SEYMER, esq. of Hanford, who *m.* Mary, daughter of Henry Welsted, esq. by whom (who wedded, secondly, John Ryves, of Ranston, esq. whose estate was sequestered in 1645; she *d.* in 1688,) he had Mary, who *m.* in 1656, Thomas Baker, esq. of Shaftesbury, and a son and heir,

ROBERT SEYMER, esq. of Hanford. This gentleman wedded Bridget, daughter of — Phelips, esq. of Montacute, in Somersetshire, and by her (who died in 1721) had issue,

Henry, who *d.* in 1692.
ROBERT, his heir.

Mary, *m.* in 1686, to John Hoskins, esq. of Ibberton.
Catherine, *d.* in 1692.
Anne, *b.* in 1669, *m.* in 1692, to Richard Nutcomb, esq.
Bridget, *b.* in 1676, *d.* an infant.

He *d.* in 1706, and was *s.* by his only surviving son,

ROBERT SEYMER, esq. of Hanford, who *m.* a daughter of — Henly, esq. of Glanvilles Wotton, and had four sons and three daughters, viz.

Robert, *b.* in 1688, *d.* in 1712.
HENRY, *b.* in 1690, his heir.
John, *b.* in 1692, *d.* in 1708.
Edward, *b.* in 1694.

Bridget, *m.* to John Forrester, esq. of Alveston.
Anne, *m.* first, to – Powell, esq. and secondly, to — Bridget, esq.
Mary, *d.* unm.

The eldest surviving son, and eventual heir,

HENRY SEYMER, esq. of Hanford, wedded Anne, eldest daughter of the Most Rev. William Wake, Archbishop of Canterbury, and dying in 1745, left, with a daughter Bridget, *b.* in 1716, who became the wife of — Love, esq. a son and successor,

HENRY SEYMER, esq. of Hanford, born in 1714. This gentleman *m.* Bridget, daughter of Thomas Haysome, esq. of Weymouth, by whom (who died 10th December, 1800,) he had issue,

HENRY, his heir.
Robert-Martin, Thomas, William, Edward, } all *d. s. p.*
George, who *m.* first, Anne, daughter of the Rev. Mr. Sturges, and had a daughter Anne, *m.* to Stephen Terry, esq. of Dummer, Hants. He wedded, secondly, Alicia, daughter of John Gunning, esq. and by that lady had John-Gunning, Alicia-Dorothea, and Catharine-Jane.
Bridget, married in 1774, to Edmund Lambert, esq. of Boyton, in Wilts.
Anne, *m.* in 1781, to the Rev. Charles Birch, rector of Chiselbourne, in Dorsetshire, and a prebendary of Chichester.
Amy, Mary, } died unm.
Catharine,
Etheldreda, *m.* in 1786, to Major William Chester, of the 35th regiment.

This gentleman, from his early years, pursued the study of natural history, and attained a degree of excellence in entomology, conchology, and mineralogy, particularly in the investigation of extraneous fossils. His cabinets of shells were very rich, as he never lost an opportunity of procuring the finest offered for sale; and although residing at so great a distance from the metropolis, he was always able to secure, through his agents in town, any collections brought from abroad. Martin, in his great work on shells, mentions Mr. Seymer's collection with high commendation; and to Mr. Seymer the "Hortus Europæ Americanus" was dedicated. With the naturalists of his time, Edwards, Fothergill, Pennant, Foster, Drury, and Francillon, he maintained an uninterrupted correspondence. The well known Dr. Pulteney, residing no more than five miles distant from him, much of their time was passed together, and the Doctor has frequently declared that some of the happiest hours of his life were spent in Mr. Seymer's society. Although botany was less his study than other parts of the system of nature, yet

Nature he loved; with her he spent his hours,
And stored his garden with her fairest flowers.

He *d.* on the 13th June, 1785, and was *s.* by his eldest son,

HENRY SEYMER, esq. of Hanford, D.C.L. *b.* in 1745, who wedded, 22nd March, 1781, Grizilda, or Grace, daughter of James Ker, esq. of Morriston and Kersfield, in the county of Berwick, by Lucy, daughter of George Pitt, esq. of Strathfieldsay, and had issue,

HENRY, his successor.
George-Augustus, in holy orders, rector of Severn Courtenay, and of Benton Bradstock, in Dorsetshire, *m.* first, Isabella, only daughter of John Bastard, esq. of Blandford; and secondly, Susannah-Elizabeth, fourth daughter of the Rev. Charles Birch, by Anne, second daughter of Henry Seymer, esq. (his grandfather), but has no issue.

Grace-Amelia, *m.* in 1819, to William Morton Pitt, esq. of Kingston House, in Dorsetshire, and has issue,
Louisa, *m.* in January, 1825, to the Rev. John Davis, rector of Melcombe, Horsey, and perpetual curate of Cerne Albas, in the county of Dorset.
Marcia-Lucy, *m.* to Henry Beckford, esq. and *d.* in 1828.
Eliza-Bridget.

Mr. Seymer, who was a fellow of All Souls College, Oxford, and took the degree of D. C. L. died 3rd December, 1800, and was *s.* by his elder son,

HENRY SEYMER, esq. of Hanford, who, in consequence of inheriting the property of his maternal family, at the decease of his aunt, Mary-Louisa Ker, in December, 1829, assumed the additional surname and arms of Ker, by sign manual, in 1830. He was *b.* 22nd January, 1782, and *m.* 27th January, 1807, Harriet, daughter of Peter Beckford, esq. of Stapleton, in Dorsetshire, by the Hon. Louisa Pitt, second daughter of George, first Lord Rivers, of Strathfieldsay, Hants, and had issue,

HENRY, his successor.
Horace-William.
Harriet-Marcia, *m.* 22nd Feb. 1827, to the Rev. James Duff Ward, fifth son of George Ward, esq. of Northwood Park, in the Isle of Wight, and was left a widow, (Mr. Ward *d.* at Rome) in January, 1831, with a son and two daughters.

Mr. Seymer, who was a magistrate and deputy-lieutenant for Dorsetshire, and sheriff in 1810, *d.* in 1834, and was *s.* by his elder son, the present HENRY SEYMER, esq. of Hanford.

*Arms*—Or, two wings conjoined gu. on a chief of the second three martlets arg. quartering KER.

*Crest*—On a chapeau gu. turned up ermine, two wings or.

*Estate*—In Dorsetshire.

*Seat*—Hanford, near Blandford.

## BEWICKE, OF CLOSE HOUSE.

BEWICKE, CALVERLY-BEWICKE, esq. of Close House, in the county of Northumberland, *m.* Elizabeth-Philadelphia, daughter of Thomas Wilkinson, esq. of Coxhoe, in Durham, by Anne, his wife, daughter and co-heir of Robert Spearman, esq. of Oldacres, and has issue,

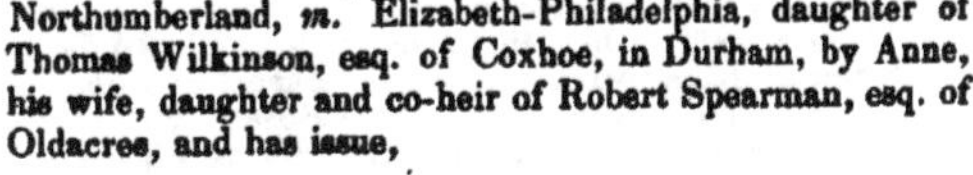

CALVERLY.
Robert-Calverly, *b.* in 1818.
Thomas.
William.

Margaret.
Elizabeth.

This gentleman having inherited the estates of his mother's brother, Colonel CALVERLY BEWICKE, relinquished his patronymic of ANDERSON, and assumed the surname of BEWICKE by sign manual, 16th December, 1815.

## Lineage.

This family anciently possessed lands at Bewicke, in Northumberland, whence it derived its surname; but in the reign of Edward II. the then Bewicke, of Bewicke, confederating with the Scotch, forfeited his patrimonial estate.

Peter Bewicke, who was sheriff of Newcastle in the year 1476, and mayor in 1490, left three sons,

Andrew, his heir.

Peter, sheriff in 1534, who had three daughters,

Mary.

Barbara.

Eliza, *m.* to James Grey, esq. descended from Grey, of Norton, ancestor of Grey, of Backworth.

Thomas, sheriff in 1535.

The eldest son,

Andrew Bewicke, sheriff of Newcastle upon-Tyne, in 1528, and mayor in ten years afterwards, married Margaret, daughter of Cuthbert Hunter, merchant, in the same borough, and by her, (who wedded, secondly, Ralph Jeunison, who served also the office of mayor, for Newcastle,) had two sons, viz.

I. Robert, his successor.

II. Cuthbert, who *m.* 8th May, 1599, Barbara, dau. of Edward Craister, esq. of Craister, by Alice Mitford, his wife, and left a daughter and heiress,

Jane Bewicke, *b.* 1st May, 1600, wedded Edward Stote, esq. who was captain of foot, in the service of *King* Charles I. and *d.* in 1660, (she was buried 6th August, in that year) leaving by him, who died in 1648, one son,

Sir Richard Stote, knt. *b.* 12th April, 1621, sergeant-at-law, of Joemond Hall, in Northumberland, and a justice of the peace for that county, married Margaret Holmes, and dying in December, 1682, left one son and three daughters, viz.

Bertram Stote, *b.* 8th February, 1674, M.P. for Northumberland, *d.* a bachelor, 22nd July, 1707, when his sisters became his co-heirs.

Margaret Stote, *m.* to the Reverend J. Tong, of Denton, Durham, and died in 1734, *s. p.*

Frances Stote, *m.* to the celebrated orator and patriot William Shippen, whom Walpole said was the only man whose price he did not know. He was called "honest Will Shippen." Mrs. Shippen *d. s. p.*

Dorothy Stote, *m.* to the Honorable Dixie Windsor, a younger son of the Earl of Plymouth, and *d.* in 1756, *s. p.*

The elder son and heir,

Robert Bewicke, esq. *b.* 18th October, 1561, *m.* 24th January, 1596, Eleanor, dau. of Alderman William Huntley, of Newcastle, and had issue,

William, *m.* Elizabeth, daughter of Henry Maddison, esq. and by that lady, who wedded, secondly, Thomas Loraine, esq. of Kirkbarle, left at his decease, 22nd February, 1636, his father then living,

Robert, who *d. s. p.*

Eleanor, *m.* to Claudius Fenwick, M.D. of Newcastle.

Thomas.

Jane, *m.* to Thomas Mitford, esq. a younger son of Mitford, of Mitford, and left issue.

This Robert Bewicke was sheriff of Newcastle, in 1615, and mayor in 1628 and 1629. He purchased the manor of Chantrey, and Chapel of Abbey le Close, otherwise Close House, and demesne lands in Houghton, with the whole hamlet of Houghton beside. He was returned a grand-juror for Northumberland, in 1637, and interred in the Chantrey or Chapel of St. Margaret, in St. Nicholas Church, at Newcastle. His second but only surviving son,

Thomas Bewicke, esq. who was of Close House, and Urpeth Lodge, served the office of sheriff for the county palatine of Durham, in 1655, and was a trustee in Cromwell's foundation charter of Durham College. After the restoration, being one of the gentlemen selected for the projected order of the royal oak, his property was returned at £2000. a year. He *m.* Jane, daughter of Sheffield Calverly, esq. a younger son of the house of Calverly, in the county of York, and had issue,

Robert, his heir.

Thomas, *b.* 30th November, 1648, *m.* Eleanor —, and had a son Thomas, who *d.* a bachelor, 27th July, 1700, and a daughter,

Philadelphia, who *m.* Utrick Whitfield, esq. younger son of Matthew Whitfield, esq. of Whitfield, and died without issue.

Joseph, who resided with his eldest brother, and died a bachelor, *b.* 28th July, 1658, and *d.* a bachelor, 1696.

Calverly, *b.* 8th July, 1661, eventual continuator of the family.

Benjamin, *b.* in 1665, *d. s. p.*

Jane, Margaret, } died unmarried.

Barbara, *m.* to Mr. Alderman (William) Ramsay, of Newcastle.

The eldest son and heir,

Robert Bewicke, esq. of Close House, *b.* 9th December, 1643, was high sheriff of Northumberland in 1695, and *d.* a bachelor in 1703. By his achievement in Heddon, on the Wall Church, it appears that he was usually called "Rich Bewicke." His fourth brother,

Calverly Bewicke, became of Close House, and carried on the family. He *m.* Dorothy Izard, and had issue,

I. Robert, his successor.

II. Calverly, of London, merchant, *b.* in 1694, *m.* Alice, daughter of Robert Smith, esq. of London, by whom (who *d.* in 1775) he left at his decease in 1774,

1. Benjamin, of Ormond-street, London, who wedded, first, Elizabeth Smith, but he had no issue. He married, secondly, about 1760, Anne, daughter of John Glesson, esq. of London, and had,

Calverly-John, in holy orders, rector of Allaton, in Leicestershire, *m.* first, Mrs. Vaugh, without issue, and, secondly, Caroline, daughter of Nathaniel Newenham, esq. an alderman of London.

Benjamin *d.* unmarried, about 1787.

Robert, of London, merchant.

Philip, died unmarried, in 1814.

Thomas, of Bungay, in Suffolk, *m.* in 1797, Sarah, dau. of the Reverend Robert Etheridge, of Stanton, in Norfolk, and has, with several daughters, a son,

Calverly-Richard, *b.* in 1798.

Rebecca, *m.* 26th April, 1815, to William Augustus Standert, esq.

2. Calverly, of Clapham, *m.* Jane, daughter of Robert Thornton, esq. of the same place, and died in 1814, having had,

Henry, who *d.* unmarried.

Jane, *m.* to — Blackbury, esq. of Ramsgate.

1. Anne, *m.* to Dr. Philip Young.
2. Sarah, } *d.* unmarried.
3. Dorothy, }
4. Alice, *m.* to Daniel Eyre, esq. of Wiltshire.

I. Dorothy, *m.* to Thomas Lambton, esq. of Hardwicke.

II. Elizabeth.

He died 1st September, 1729, and was *s.* by his elder son,

Robert Bewicke, esq. of Close House, *b.* 14th January, 1689, high sheriff of Northumberland in 1726. This gentleman *m.* in 1724, Jane, daughter of Robert Lynn, esq. of Mainsforth, and heiress through her mother of Joseph Wilson, esq. of Cassop, by whom he had two sons, viz.

Robert, his heir.

Wilson, in holy orders, D.D. rector of Bodenham, in Herefordshire, proprietor of lands at Cassop, in Durham, as heir to his mother, *m.* his cousin, Margaret, daughter of John Orde, esq. of Sedgefield, and died without issue.

Mr. Bewicke was *s.* at his decease by his elder son,

Sir Robert Bewicke, of Close House, *b.* in 1728, who was high sheriff of Northumberland in 1760, when he received the honour of knighthood. He *m.* Mary, daughter of Robert Huish, esq. of Nottingham, and had two sons and six daughters, viz.

I. Calverly, his heir.

II. Robert, who *d.* unm.

I. Jane, *m.* to Sir Paul Joddrell, and had a daughter,

Paulina Joddrell, who *m.* John Seale, esq. of Mount Boone, in Devonshire, M.P. for Dartmouth.

II. Mary, *m.* to Alexander Anderson, esq. of Highgate, and had issue,

John-Robert Anderson, of London, *b.* in 1775; *m.* in 1809, Elizabeth, daughter of Robert Boswell, esq. of Edinburgh, and has issue.

Calverly-Bewicke Anderson, who, on inheriting the estates of his maternal family, at the decease of his uncle, assumed the surname of Bewicke.

Paul Anderson.

Charlotte Anderson.
Mary-Anne Anderson.

III. Anne, *m.* to James Woodmason, esq. of Belcamp, near Dublin, whom she survived, without issue.

IV. Margaret, *m.* to Thomas Bond, esq. of Norton House, Devon, and survived him, without issue.

V. Alicia, *d.* unm.

VI. Dorothy, *m.* to William Lynn, esq. of Clapham.

VII. Eleanor, *m.* to Alexander Anderson, esq.

Sir Robert *d.* in 1771, and was *s.* by his elder son,

CALVERLY BEWICKE, esq. of Close House and Urpeth Lodge, lieutenant-colonel of the Durham militia, and M.P. for Winchelsea, who *m.* first, Deborah, daughter of Thomas Wilkinson, esq. of Brancepeth, in Durham; and, secondly, Margaret, youngest daughter and co-heir of Robert Spearman, esq. of Oldacres, in the same county, but had no issue. Colonel Bewicke served the office of sheriff of Northumberland, and dying in Oct. 1815, was *s.* by his nephew, Calverly-Bewicke Anderson, esq. who, having taken the surname of BEWICKE, in place of his patronymic, is the present CALVERLY-BEWICKE BEWICKE, esq.

*Arms*—Arg. five losenges in fesse gu. each charged with a mullet of the first between three bears' heads erased sa.

*Crest*—A bugle's head erased at the neck, arg. armed, maned, and gorged with a mural crown gu.

*Estates*—In Northumberland and Durham.

*Seat*—Close House, Northumberland, and Urpeth Lodge, Durham.

## DE BURGH, OF WEST DRAYTON.

DE BURGH, HUBERT, esq. of West Drayton, in the county of Middlesex, *b.* 15th November, 1799, *m.* 6th September, 1827, Marianne, sixth daughter of Admiral and Lady Elizabeth Tollemache, and has issue,

HUBERT.
Another son, *b.* 6th September, 1834.

Constance-Selina.

Mr. De Burgh inherited the estates at the decease of his mother, 20th September, 1809. He is a magistrate and deputy-lieutenant for the county of Middlesex, and captain commander of the Uxbridge Yeomanry. He is also one of the co-heirs to the BARONY OF BURG, or BOROUGH OF GAINSBOROUGH (now in abeyance). See BURKE'S *Extinct Peerage.*

### Lineage.

This is a branch, through female descent, of the great family of DE BURGH,* founded in England at the Conquest, and now represented by the noble house of Clanricarde.

* JOHN, EARL OF COMYN AND BARON OF TONSBURGH, in Normandy, descended from CHARLEMAGNE, being general of the forces and governor of the chief towns in the principality, thence assumed the surname of "De Burgh." His eldest son,

HUBERT DE BURGO, died in the lifetime of his father, leaving, by his wife, Arlotta, mother of

THOMAS BURGH, sixth Lord Burgh, or Borough, of Gainsborough, K. G. summoned to parliament from 11th January, 1563, to 24th October, 1597, holding a high rank among the statesmen of the time of ELIZABETH, was accredited, in the 36th year of her Majesty's reign, ambassador to the court of Scotland, and afterwards constituted lord-lieutenant of Ireland, in which government he died, 8th October, 1597. His lordship *m.* Frances, daughter of John Vaughan, esq. of Golden Grove, in the county of Caermarthen, and had issue,

ROBERT, his successor, seventh lord, who died at the early age of eight, when the BARONY OF BURGH fell into *abeyance* between his sisters, as it still continues among their descendants.

Thomas, *d.* before his brother.

ELIZABETH, *m.* first, to George Brooke, son of William, Lord Cobham, which George was executed for high treason, being concerned in "Raleigh's conspiracy," *temp.* JAMES I. and attainted. His son, SIR WILLIAM BROKE, K. B. was restored in blood. Her ladyship *m.* secondly, Francis Read, esq.

FRANCES, of whom presently.

ANNE, *m.* to Sir Drue Drury, whose line is extinct.

KATHERINE, *m.* to Thomas Knivet, esq. and from this marriage descends ROBERT WILSON, esq. recently declared LORD BERNERS. *(See* BURKE'S *Peerage and Baronetage.)*

The third daughter,

*The Honourable* FRANCES BURGH, espoused FRANCIS COPPINGER, esq.* and had issue,

William Coppinger, who *d. s. p.* 27th April, 1738.

Seymour Coppinger, who had three sons and two daughters, but all *d. s. p.*

---

WILLIAM the Conqueror, ROBERT and Odo. The younger, who was bishop of Bayeux, was created Earl of Kent, while the elder,

ROBERT DE BURGO, having taken a prominent part in the battle of Hastings, was rewarded by his half-brother, WILLIAM the Conqueror, with seven hundred and ninety-three manors in England, and the earldom of Cornwall. From his elder grandson, ADELM DE BURGH, the Marquesses of Clanricarde, and the other families of De Burgh, or Burke, derive. His younger grandson was HUBERT DE BURGH, the celebrated earl of Kent, in the time of HENRY III. (BURKE'S *Peerage and Baronetage.)*

* This gentleman was descended from Walter Coppinger, esq. of Buxall, in Suffolk, thus,

Walter Coppinger, esq. of Buxall.

Sir William Coppinger, Lord Mayor of London, died in 1513.

William Coppinger, of Buxall.

John Coppinger = Joan, daughter and co-heir of William Bond, esq. Clerk of the Green Cloth, *temp.* HENRY, VII.

Henry, of Devington, in Kent. = Agnes, dau. of Sir Thomas Jermyn, knt. of Rushbrooke, in Suffolk. | Ralph. | Thomasin. | Elizabeth.

Thomas, of Stoke, in Kent. = Frances, only daughter of Sir Wm. Brooke, Baron Cobham, K. G. by his wife, Dorothy Neville, dau. of Lord Abergavenny. | William. Ambrose. Edmond. Robert. | Henry, rector of Lewisham. | Ralph. John. Edward. | Frances. Elizabeth. | Susan = Sir George Clive, of Harley, in Cheshire.

FRANCIS COPPINGER, who *m.* the *Hon.* FRANCES BURGH, as above. | William Coppinger, eldest son, died without issue.

*Arms of Coppinger*—Or, three bends gu. on a band az. three balls arg.

Henry Coppinger, Edward Coppinger, Drew Coppinger, } all died issueless.
NICHOLAS COPPINGER, of whom presently.
James Coppinger, Frances Coppinger, Katherine Coppinger, } *d. s. p.*
Lettice Coppinger, *m.* to Sir William Hooker.

The sixth son,

NICHOLAS COPPINGER, esq. *m.* Elizabeth Anderson, and dying, in 1686, left a son,

FRANCIS COPPINGER, esq. of Lincoln's Inn, who wedded Miss Jane Garnet, aunt to the Right Rev. John Garnet, bishop of Clogher, and had issue,

JOHN, who married KATHERINE, eldest daughter and co-heir of TIMOTHY FYSH, esq.* of Scarborough in the county of York, and by her, who died 16th April, 1763, left, with other issue, at his decease (before his father) 9th November, 1758,

FYSH, successor to his grandfather.
John, *m.* to Dorothy, only daughter of Joseph Peele, esq.

Frances, *d. s. p.*
Elizabeth, *m.* to Allatson Burgh, esq.

William, Nicholas, Henry, } *d. s. p.*

Mary, *m.* to Peter Pierson, esq.
Susannah, *m.* to David Thomas, esq. of Pwllywrach, in Glamorganshire.

Mr. Coppinger died at the advanced age of eighty-eight, in December, 1759, and was *s.* by his grandson,

FYSH COPPINGER, esq. of West Drayton, in the county of Middlesex, who *m.* Easter, daughter of Cornelius Burgh, esq. of Scarborough, and assumed, by sign manual, in 1790, the surname and arms of "DE BURGH," in consequence of his descent from the *Honourable* FRANCES BURGH, one of the co-heirs to the BARONY OF BURGH, *of Gainsborough.* He had issue,

FYSH DE BURGH, captain in the first regiment of Guards, who died from a fever contracted while on duty in the Tower, 23rd January, 1793, unm.

CATHERINE DE BURGH, who wedded, 22nd May, 1794, JAMES GODFREY LILL, esq. of Gaulstown, in the county of Westmeath, who assumed, in pursuance of the will of his father-in-law, the surname and arms of DE BURGH.

Mr. Fysh de Burgh, sen. was *s.* at his decease by his only daughter,

MRS. CAMTERINE DE BURGH, who, by her husband, James Godfrey (Lill) De Burgh, esq.† had issue,

HUBERT, her heir.
Robert Lill, in holy orders.
Catherine Alicia, *m.* to Charles Tyrwhitt Jones, esq. only brother of Sir Thomas John Tyrwhitt-Jones, bart.

She died, 20th September, 1809, and was *s.* by her elder son, the present HUBERT DE BURGH, esq. of West Drayton.

*Arms*—Az. three fleurs de lys erm.

*Crest*—A dexter arm embowed in armour, couped at the shoulder, gauntlet open, exposing the hand ppr. armed ar. a bugle horn, az. tassels gold.

*Motto*—Nec parvis sisto.

*Estates*—In Middlesex, and in Westmeath, Ireland.

*Seat*—Manor House, West Drayton.

* TIMOTHY FYSH, esq. left three daughters, his co-heirs, viz.
KATHERINE, *m.* as above, to FRANCIS COPPINGER, esq.
ELIZABETH, *m.* to Cornelius Burgh, esq.
ANN, *m.* to Timothy Foord, esq.

† JAMES GODFREY (LILL) DE BURGH, esq. *m.* secondly, in 1811, Eliza, widow of — Hayne, esq. of Ashbourne, in the county of Derby, and by that lady left, at his decease, 7th March, 1832, two sons, James-Godfrey and Hubert-Lill.

## FARNHAM, OF QUORNDON HOUSE.

FARNHAM, EDWARD-BASIL, esq. of Quorndon House, in the county of Leicester, *b.* 19th April, 1799, succeeded his father in 1835. Mr. Farnham is a deputy-lieutenant for Leicestershire.

## Lineage.

By deeds without dates there appear to have been two Lords of QUERNDON prior to the reign of EDWARD I. viz.

ROBERT FARNHAM, and SIR ROBERT FARNHAM, knt. The son and heir of the latter,

SIR JOHN FARNHAM, of Querndon, in the county of Leicester, lived under the sceptre of the *first* EDWARD, and was father of

SIR ROBERT FARNHAM, knight, living in 1346, who left a son and heir,

JOHN FARNHAM, esq. who founded a chantry in 1393, and marrying Margaret, the daughter and heir of — Billington, had two sons, viz.

I. ROBERT, living in 1440, *m.* Katherine, daughter of John Jeke, esq. of Wikington, in the county of Stafford. The line of this gentleman terminated in the five daughters and co-heirs of Edward Farnham, esq. of Quorndon, who *d.* in 1680, viz.
   - MARY, married to Francis Caulfeild, esq.
   - PHILIPPA, *m.* to Edward Prior, esq.
   - SARAH, married to Benjamin Farnham, esq.
   - PHŒBY, *d.* unm. in 1766.
   - MERCY, married to Edward Sculthorpe, esq.

II. THOMAS.

The younger son,

THOMAS FARNHAM, esq. living at the Nether Hall, in 1438, married a daughter of — Hersey, of Grove, in Notts, and was *s.* by his son,

JOHN FARNHAM, esq. of Nether Hall, who *m.* a daughter of — Strelley, and left a son and heir,

THOMAS FARNHAM, esq. of Nether Hall, who *d.* in 1508, leaving, by his wife, Miss Kniveton, of Derbyshire, a son and successor,

WILLIAM FARNHAM, esq. of Nether Hall. This gentleman married a daughter of Sir George Nevill, knt. by Barbara, his wife, sister of Sir John Hersey (refer to vol. ii. page 6), and had, with other issue,

- JOHN, his heir.
- Thomas, of Stoughton, one of the tellers of the Exchequer in the reigns of EDWARD VI. and *Queen* MARY, *m.* Helen, daughter of Roger Chaloner, esq. and *d.* in 1562, leaving an only daughter and heiress, KATHERINE, who *m.* Sir Thomas Beaumont, knt. of Stoughton, and *d.* in 1614. His widow wedded Francis Saunders, esq. of Welford.
- MATTHEW, successor to his elder brother.
- Walter, *d.* in 1587.
- Margaret, *m.* to Bartholomew Wollock, esq. of Scotland.

He died in 1548, and was *s.* by his eldest son,

JOHN FARNHAM, esq. of the Nether Hall, living there in 1567, *m.* Dorothy, daughter of — Walwyn, esq. and had an only daughter and heir, Dorothy, the wife of Sir George Wright, knt. Mr. Farnham, who was one of the gentlemen pensioners to *Queen* ELIZABETH, died in 1587, at the advanced age of eighty, and was *s.* in the Nether Hall by his brother,

MATTHEW FARNHAM, esq. who wedded Laurentia, daughter of Richard Barret, esq. of Medbourn, Leicestershire, and had, with a daughter, Margaret, *m.* to Richard Dawes, gent. of Stapleton, in the county of Leicester, a son and successor,

HUMPHREY FARNHAM, esq. of the Nether Hall, who *m.* Elizabeth, only daughter of William Digby, esq. of Welby, and had issue,

- WILLIAM, *b.* in 1587, *d.* unmarried, 8th February, 1624-5.
- HENRY, died unmarried, buried 31st May, 1626.
- THOMAS, heir, after his two elder brothers.
- Margaret, living in 1653, *m.* to Thomas Aldersey, esq. of Brangate, in Kent, and had an only son,
   - Farnham Aldersey, of Maidstone, who *d.* 4th October, 1691, leaving a son.
- Elizabeth, *b.* in 1595.
- Dorothy, *b.* in 1596.
- Jane, *b.* in 1598.

He died about the year 1620, and after the decease of the two elder sons, the third son,

THOMAS FARNHAM, esq. became of Nether Hall. He wedded Frances, daughter of Sir Thomas Waldron, knt. of Charley, in Leicestershire, and, dying in August, 1666, left two sons and four daughters, viz.

HENRY, his heir.
Thomas d. unmarried.
Frances, b. in 1630, married to Clifton Rhodes, esq. of Stocton, Notts.
Margaret, bapt. 6th July, 1635, m. to Richard Wilson, esq. of Knight Thorpe, in Leicestershire.
Dorothy, m. to Henry Waldron, esq. of Farnham Castle, in the county of Cavan.
Elizabeth, m. to the Rev. Nicholas Hall, rector of Loughborough.

The elder son and heir,

HENRY FARNHAM, esq. of Nether Hall, a captain in the army, m. in 1660, Martha, daughter of Thomas Mousley, gent. of the county of Stafford, and had issue,

THOMAS, b. in 1665, left at his decease, a widow, Margaret, who d. in 1738.
Henry, b. in 1667.
John, b. in 1669.
BENJAMIN.
William, b. in 1675.
George, bapt. 27th October, 1683.

Frances, b. in 1661.
Martha, b. in 1663, d. unmarried.
Sarah, b. in 1673, m. first, to Sir — Gething, and secondly, to Mr. Boyle.
Mary, b. in 1677.
Anne, b. in 1679, m. to William Stephens, esq. of Quorndon.

The fourth son,

BENJAMIN FARNHAM, esq. m. in 1703, SARAH, one of the daughters and co-heirs of Edward Farnham, esq. of Quorndon, and dying in 1747, aged seventy-seven, was s. by his son,

EDWARD FARNHAM, esq. of Quorndon, b. 16th March, 1704, who m. 3rd March, 1725, Easter Lake, of Canterbury, and by her (who was buried 1st May, 1767) had,

I. JOHN, b. 20th April, 1757, d. v. p. in 1741.
II. WILLIAM, heir.
III. Edward-Bestere, b. in 1740, and d. in 1741.
IV. THOMAS, successor to his brother William.
V. EDWARD, successor to his brother Thomas.

I. Esther, m. to John Willows, esq. and d. in 1794.
II. Anne, m. to Noah Bolaine, esq. of Canterbury.
III. Sarah, m. first, to Sir Charles Halford, bart. and secondly to Basil, Earl of Denbigh.

Mr. Farnham d. 3rd June, 1775, and was s. by his son,

THE REV. WILLIAM FARNHAM, b. in 1738, who died issueless, and was succeeded by his brother,

THOMAS FARNHAM, Capt. R.N. of Quorndon House, b. 30th October, 1743, at whose decease, unmarried, 2nd December, 1793, the estates and representation of the family devolved on his brother,

EDWARD FARNHAM, esq. of Quorndon House, b. in 1753, who served the office of sheriff of Leicestershire in 1817, m. in 1795, Harriet, youngest daughter and co-heir of the Rev. Dr. Rhudde, chaplain in ordinary to his late Majesty, and had issue,

I. EDWARD-BASIL, his heir.

I. Sarah-Anne.
II. Mary-Eliza.

Mr. Farnham died in 1835, and was s. by his son, the present EDWARD-BASIL FARNHAM, esq. of Quorndon House.

*Arms*—Quarterly or, and az. in the two first quarters a crescent counterchanged.

*Crest*—An eagle, or, wings close, preying on a rabbit arg.

*Estates*—In the counties of Leicester and Surrey.

*Seat*—Quorndon House, in Leicestershire.

## SAYER, OF PETT.

SAYER, GEORGE-EDWARD, esq. of Pett, in Kent, b. 2nd February, 1795, a magistrate and deputy-lieutenant for that county, succeeded his father in May, 1814.

## Lineage.

The SAYERS were settled at a very early period in the county of Essex, where we find William and John Sayer, of Birch, in the reign of EDWARD II., William Sayer, of Coppeford, who *d.* in 1348, and Matthew Sayer, who held lands in Aldham, in 1411. They subsequently became resident in Colchester, and filled the highest offices in that corporation.

JOHN SAYRE, alderman thereof, died in 1509, leaving a son and successor,

JOHN SAYRE, who *d.* in 1563. He was father of

GEORGE SAYER, alderman and one of the bailiffs of Colchester, who purchased *temp.* ELIZABETH, from William, Marquis of Northampton, the estate of Bourchiers Hall, in the county of Essex. He *m.* first, Agnes, daughter and co-heir of Thomas Wesden, or Westden, of Lincolnshire, and had, by her, with three daughters, three sons, viz.

William, who *d.* without issue.

Richard, who married twice, but had only one son, who died young, and a daughter, who survived him.

GEORGE, of whose line we have to treat.

Mr. Alderman Sayer wedded, secondly, Frances, daughter of Thomas Sammon, but by her had no issue. He *d.* 19th May, 1577, possessed of the manors, Bourchers Hall, Copford, Odwell, &c. &c.

His youngest son,

GEORGE SAYER, esq. *m.* Rose, daughter of William Cardinal, esq. of Great Bromley, and had issue,

GEORGE (Sir), his heir.

Thomas, seated at Bowton, in Suffolk.

Mary, *m.* to John Prettyman, of Suffolk.

Frances, *m.* to Robert Browne, of Colchester.

George Sayer *d.* 3d July, 1596, and was *s.* by his elder son,

SIR GEORGE SAYER, of Bourcher's Hall, aged thirty at his father's decease, who received the honour of knighthood 4th June, 1607. He *m.* Dorothy, daughter of Sir John Higham, of Barrow Hall, Suffolk, and had issue,

I. JOHN, his heir.

II. Higham, who was buried 1st March, 1658.

III. Francis.

IV. Richard.

I. Ann.

II. Susan.

Sir George *d.* 7th March, 1630, (his widow surviving until 1651), and was *s.* by his son,

JOHN SAYER, esq. of Bourcher's Hall, M. P. for Colchester in 1645, *b.* in 1589, who was a very active committee-man during the Commonwealth. He *m.* Esther, daughter of Robert Honywood, esq. of Mark's Hall, in Essex, and had two sons and one daughter, viz.

I. GEORGE, of Bourcher's Hall, knighted in 1640, who *d.* 11th July, 1650, leaving, by Jane, his wife, a posthumous daughter,

ESTHER, *b.* in September, 1650, who became his sole heir, and *m.* the learned Sir John Marsham, bart. of Caxton, Kent.

II. JOHN (Sir), of whom presently.

I. Dorothy, *m.* to John Barnaby, esq. of Colchester.

John Sayer *d.* in 1658, and was buried at Aldham, in Essex. His second son,

SIR JOHN SAYER, knt. page to the Prince of Orange, and colonel of foot, married Katherine, daughter of John Van Hossen Van Piershill, of Zealand, and had five sons, GEORGE, Robert, John, Charles, and Adolphus. Sir John *d.* 4th September, 1667, was buried at St. Margaret's, Westminster, and *s.* by his eldest son,

GEORGE SAYER, esq. vice-chamberlain to *Queen* CATHERINE, consort to CHARLES II., and also to *Queen* MARY, who made him sub-governor, and gentleman of the bedchamber to William, Duke of Gloucester. He *m.* Frances, daughter and heiress of Sir Philip Honywood, of Petts, in Kent, and dying in May, 1718, aged sixty-three, left a son and successor,

GEORGE SAYER, esq. of Petts, who married Mary Godfrey, and had, with two daughters, Mary and Catherine, who both *d.* unm. a son,

GEORGE SAYER, esq. of Petts, who married Mary, daughter of John Greenhill, esq. and had two sons, and three daughters, viz.

- I. GEORGE, his heir.
- II. John, a major in the army, who *m.* Charlotte, daughter of Charles Van, esq. of Llanwern, in Monmouthshire, and has a son,
  - The Rev. JOHN SAYER, vicar of Arlingham, Gloucestershire, who *m.* Miss Eliza Hodges, and has one son, John, and one daughter, Mary-Elizabeth.

- I. Mary, died unm. in April, 1829.
- II. Catherine, *m.* to the Rev. William Gregory, second son of Dr. John Gregory, of Edinburgh.
- III. Frances, *d.* unm. 3d March, 1829.

Mr. Sayer was *s.* by his elder son,

The Rev. GEORGE SAYER, LL.B. of Pett, rector of Egglescliffe, in Durham, who *m.* in 1786, Catherine, only daughter of James Wakeley, esq. and had issue,

- I. GEORGE-EDWARD, his heir.

- I. Mary, *m.* to Henry Egerton, esq. of Lincoln's Inn, barrister-at-law.
- II. Catherine.
- III. Charlotte.
- IV. Selina.
- V. Jane.

Mr. Sayer *d.* in May, 1814, and was *s.* by his son, the present GEORGE-EDWARD SAYER, esq. of Pett.

*Arms*—Gu. a chev. arg. between three peewits ppr.

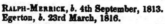

*Crest*—A dexter arm, in armour, embowed ppr. garnished or, the hand grasping a griffin's head erased or.

*Estates*—In Kent: in the reign of HENRY VIII. William Warham alienated the manor of Pett to Robert Atwater, whose youngest daughter and co-heir, Mary, conveyed it, together with other estates in Lenham, and elsewhere, in the neighbourhood, to her husband, ROBERT HONYWOOD, esq. a descendant of the Honywoods, of Honewood, in Postling, Kent, where they resided at the time of the CONQUEST. The estate of Pett continued with the family of Honywood, until conveyed by the heiress of Sir Philip Honywood to George Sayer, esq.

*Seat*—Pett, in the parish of Charing, Kent.

## LEEKE, OF LONGFORD HALL.

LEEKE, THOMAS, esq. of Longford Hall, in the county of Salop, barrister-at-law, *b.* 21st November, 1788, *m.* first, 13th November, 1812, Louisa, youngest daughter of the late Brigadier General Robert Shawe, a distinguished officer, descended from an ancient family in the county of Galway, and by her, who died 16th April, 1816, had two sons and one daughter, viz.

RALPH-MERRICK, *b.* 4th September, 1813.
Egerton, *b.* 23rd March, 1816.

Charlotte.

Mr. Leeke married, secondly, 21st January, 1822, Anna-Shawe, only daughter of the late Honorable Matthew Plunkett, brother to the 10th Lord Louth. He succeeded his father in the representation of the family and as high steward of the corporation of Newport, 30th September, 1829, and is a magistrate for the counties of Salop and Stafford.

## Lineage.

This family has, for several centuries, been of importance in the county of Salop. The immediate ancestor of the present line,

RALPH LEEKE, of Ludlow, was living in 1334. His seal is represented in a pedigree of the family, which is attested by Sir William Segar, as bearing his shield of arms, the same as now used with the legend, "SIGILL. RADI LEEKE ARMIGERI." The contract for the marriage of his son,

RALPH LEEKE, with the daughter of Philip de Middleton, ancestor of the Myddeltons, of Chirk Castle, bears date in 1334. Fourth in descent from this Ralph, was

RICHARD LEEKE, who *m.* in 1539, Alice Ottley, of Pitchford, and was great grandfather of

RALPH LEEKE, who *m.* and had three sons, viz.

- I. THOMAS, who attained great eminence in the profession of the law, and was appointed a baron of the Exchequer, 25th November, 1642. On the 6th December, 1644, a commission of the peace for the county of Salop was renewed, in order to place him therein. It has not been ascertained whether this commission proceeded from the authority of the king, or from that of the parliament; but as Shropshire was still chiefly in the obedience of CHARLES, it seems most probable that the baron espoused the royal party, especially as he is said to have lost upwards of £7000 in the civil wars. After the fall of the monarchy, however, he submitted, in common with Sir Matthew Hale, and others, to the ruling powers. He was in office in 1654, and probably continued so until the Restoration, when he was not re-appointed. He died without issue, in 1662, having on the 1st February, in that year, devised an estate at Trevanney, in the county of Montgomery, to trustees (Sir John Weld the younger, Sir Richard Oateley, Samuel Baldwin, esq. of the Inner Temple, Thomas Jones, esq. of Shrewsbury, John Stanier, esq. of Shropshire, and Richard Jenkins, esq. of Eaton) for he erection and maintenance of a free grammar school at High Ercal, of which the present Thomas Leeke, esq. of Longford, is a trustee and visiter.
- II. WILLIAM, of whose line we have to treat.
- III. Humphrey.

The second son,

WILLIAM LEEKE, continued the line of the family. His fourth descendant,

THOMAS LEEKE, esq. of the Vineyard, near Wellington, *m.* Elizabeth Henshaw, and had four sons, viz.

- I. Thomas, who *d.* in India.
- II. RALPH, of whom presently.
- III. Egerton, who resided on his patrimonial estate at the Vineyard, and *m.* Sarah Henshaw.
- IV. Stephen, an eminent solicitor in Chester, where he realized a considerable fortune.

The second son,

RALPH LEEKE, esq. at the age of sixteen, embarked as cadet in the Hon. East India Company's service, for the presidency of Bengal, from which, through the patronage of his relation, Mr. Cartier, then governor of Calcutta, he was transferred to the civil service, and resided for a considerable time as collector in the province of Typerah, where he realized a large fortune. Returning to England in 1786, he purchased, the following year, from the Earl of Shrewsbury, the manors and estates of Longford* and Church Aston, in Shropshire, and erected upon the former an elegant mansion, of white stone, after the design of Bonomi, the architect, where he resided for the remaining forty years of his life. He *m.* 13th December, 1787, Honoria Frances, only daughter of Walter Harvey Thursby, esq. (younger brother of John Harvey Thursby, esq. of Abington Abbey, Northamptonshire) by Dorothy, his wife, eldest daughter of the late Rev. William Pigott, rector of Edgemond,† and had issue,

- I. THOMAS, his heir.
- II. Ralph Harvey, rector of Longford, *b.* 4th October, 1794.

- I. Augusta.
- II. Caroline, *m.* 7th September, 1824, to the Hon. and Rev. William Nevill, second son of the Earl of Abergavenny, and has issue.
- III. Emily-Frances-Anne.

Mr. Leeke, who was the friend and cotemporary of Sir Hugh Inglis, Warren Hastings, Sir T. Metcalfe, Lord Teignmouth, &c.

---

* The beautiful residence, Longford Hall, was recently destroyed by fire.

† By Dorothy, his wife, daughter of John Cotes, esq. of Woodcote, who *m.* Lady Dorothy Shirley, daughter of the Earl of Ferrars.

served the office of high sheriff of Salop, in 1796, and acted for several years as a magistrate and deputy-lieutenant for that county.* He was also a munificent patron of various improvements in the town of Newport, and high steward of that corporation. He *d.* at Longford Hall, 30th September, 1829, and was *s.* in the representation of the family by his elder son, the present THOMAS LEEKE, esq. By will, he devised the estates and manors of Longford and Aston to trustees, who are to pay three-fifths of the rental to his widow. At her demise, Thomas Leeke, the eldest son, becomes tenant for life, with remainder to his eldest son in tail.

*Arms*—Arg. on a chief gu. a fleur de lys or. Over all a bend engrailed az.

*Crest*—A leg couped at the thigh, charged with two fleurs de lys.

*Motto*—Agendo gnaviter.

*Estates*—In Salop.

*Seat*—Longford Hall.

* At the time of Napoleon's threatened invasion, Mr. Leeke raised a corps of infantry, consisting of three hundred and twenty men, which obtained a high state of discipline under his command as lieutenant-colonel.

## BEDINGFELD, OF DITCHINGHAM.

BEDINGFELD, JOHN-JAMES, esq. of Ditchingham Hall, in the county of Norfolk, *b.* 14th February, 1773, *m.* 1st January, 1800, Sarah, daughter and co-heir of Paul Piersy, esq. of Fairhill, in the county of Cork, and has had issue,

I. JOHN LONGUEVILLE, *b.* 19th October, 1800, *m.* 21st July, 1829, Mary, second daughter of John, Lord Henniker, and has

PHILIP, *b.* 25th April, 1830.
John, *b.* 19th August, 1831.

Mary-Henniker.
Sarah-Sophia.

II. Philip, *b.* 14th November, 1803, captain 37th native infantry, Madras.

III. William, *b.* 31st December, 1805, lost his life while serving as a midshipman R. N.

IV. James, *b.* 19th September, 1809, rector of Bedingfeld, in Suffolk.

I. Lucinda-Caroline, *m.* 19th October, 1824, to Reverend John Robert Hopper, rector of Wells, in Norfolk, and has issue.

Mr. Bedingfeld, who succeeded his father in 1797, is a magistrate for the counties of Norfolk and Suffolk, and a deputy-lieutenant for the former.

### Lineage.

The family of BEDINGFELD is one (as Camden says) of undoubted antiquity, deriving its name from a town in Suffolk, and deducing its lineage from the era of the Conquest, through an uninterrupted line of distinguished ancestors. From OGENUS DE PUGIS, alias LONGUEVILLE, a Norman knight, and fellow-soldier of Duke William, lineally descended

JAMES BEDINGFELD, (second son of Sir Peter, and brother of Sir Thomas Bedingfeld, ancestor of the Oburgh family), who was living in 1350. He *m.* Alice, daughter and heir of Peter de Fleming, by whom he acquired Fleming's Hall and Manor, and had, with a daughter, Margaret, the wife of Thomas Appleyard, of Dunston, in Norfolk, a son and successor,

WILLIAM BEDINGFELD, living *temp.* HENRY VI. who wedded Mary, daughter of Thomas Playters, of Sotterly, in Suffolk, and had two sons, JOHN, his heir; William, a clerk, 22 EDWARD IV. and a daughter, Catharine, *m.* to John Winter. The elder son,

JOHN BEDINGFELD, living *temp.* EDWARD IV. married Alice, daughter of Walter Stonham, and was father of

THOMAS BEDINGFELD, of Bedingfeld, *temp.* HENRY VII. and VIII. who *m.* Joan, dau. of Roger Busarde, of Ditchingham, and thus obtained that estate. By her, he left (with a younger son, Thomas, Rector of Alderton, in Suffolk, and a daughter, Alice, a nun) his successor,

PHILIP BEDINGFELD, of Ditchingham, who *m.* Anne, daughter and heiress of Richard Yaxley, of Yaxley, by Alice, his wife, daughter and heiress of Stratton, and had issue,

- I. THOMAS, his heir.
- II. Robert, said to be solicitor-general to *Queen* ELIZABETH. He *m.* thrice; first, Elizabeth, daughter of Sir John Heydon, knt. of Baconsthorpe, which lady died without issue; and, secondly, Mary, daughter of Sir Henry D'Oyley, of Shottisham, by whom he had one son and one daughter, viz.
  - Henry, who *m.* Mary, daughter of Thomas Darcy, esq. and had one son, Philip (Sir), who *m.* Frances, daughter of Sir Henry Peyton, and two daughters, Mary and Margaret, the wife of Robert Morse, of Shirston.
  - Philippa, *m.* to John Heigham, son of Sir Clement Heigham.

  Robert Bedingfeld, *m.* thirdly, Anne, daughter of John Appleyard, esq.
- III. Richard, who died *s. p.*
- IV. Edmund, who *m.* — Browne, of Walsoken, and had a son, William, whose daughter, Elizabeth, *m.* Thomas Garey.
- V. Henry, who *m.* — Walsingham, and had a son, Edmund, who *m.* Anne, daughter of Henry Curtis of Huntingfield, in Suffolk, and four daughters; Philippa, *m.* to Thomas Darcy; Catharine, *m.* first, to John Winter, and, secondly, to — Beaupré, of Outwell; Elizabeth, *m.* first, to — Tibbenham, of Earsham, and, secondly, to Thomas Cod; and Margaret, *m.* to Edward Thoresby, of Bocking, in Essex.

The eldest son,

THOMAS BEDINGFELD, of Ditchingham, wedded Mary, daughter of William Methwold, of Langford, in Norfolk, and by her, who died in 1605, had issue,

- I. THOMAS, his heir.
- II. Richard, died *s. p.*

- I. Frances, *m.* to Robert Crisp.
- II. Anne, *m.* to — Symonds, of Suffield.
- III. Philippa.
- IV. Susan, *m.* to — Moulins, of London.

The elder son, and successor,

THOMAS BEDINGFELD, of Ditchingham, *b.* in 1553, who *m.* Dorothy, daughter of John Southwell, of Darsham, in Suffolk, and had,

- I. PHILIP, his heir.
- II. Thomas (Sir), knt, sergeant-at-law, and one of the judges. He was seated at Darsham, and marrying Mary, daughter of Charles Hoskins, esq. of Ockstead, in Surrey, had issue,
  1. Thomas, who died *v. p.* in 1658, leaving, by Hannah, his wife, daughter of Philip Bacon, esq. of Woolverston, in Suffolk, (who *m.* secondly, Sir Philip Parker, bart.) one son and two daughters, viz.
     - Thomas, who was murdered at Norwich, by Mr. Berney, in 1684, for which that gentleman was executed.

     - Elizabeth, *m.* to William H. De Grey, esq. of Merton, and their grand-daughter, Anne De Grey, wedded Colonel Erasmus Earle, of Heydon.
     - Philippa, *m.* to Sir John Rous, bart. of Henham, and had issue.

  1. Mary, *m.* to Sir John Knevett, K.B. of Ashwelthorpe.
  2. Dorothy, *m.* to Sir W. Catlyn.
- III. Robert, D.D. Rector of Newton, in the Isle of Ely, who *m.* Anne, dau. of Edmund Thoresby, esq. and dying in 1651, left issue,
  1. Edmund, Rector of Bishop's Cleve, in Gloucestershire, who *m.* first, Mary, daughter of Chetwind, of Staffordshire, and, secondly, Catherine Norwood, of Gloucestershire. By the latter he had two sons, viz.
     - Philip, of Broomsthorpe, Norfolk, who *m.* Elizabeth, dau. of John Hare, and had two sons and two daughters; Edmund, Philip, Catherine, and Susanna, *m.* to John Davis, esq. of Watlington, in Norfolk.
     - Henry, who *m.* Theodosia, daughter of Gerard Cater, of London.
  2. Robert.

3. Anthony.
1. Mary, *m.* to Sir Henry Bedingfeld, the lord chief-justice.

IV. John, of Halesworth, *m.* Joyce, daughter of Edmund Morgan, esq. of Lambeth, in Surrey, and had,
1. Edmund who *m.* Mary, daughter and co-heir of John Shawbury, esq. and relict of Thomas Newce, esq. of Rainthorp Hall.
2. Thomas, M.D. who *m.* Mary, daughter of John Weston, esq. and had issue.
3. John, who *m.* Martha, daughter of Sir Francis Williamson, and was father of a daughter, Penelope, *m.* to Dr. Lewis Atterbury, brother of the Bishop of Rochester.
4. Henry (Sir), lord chief justice, *m.* his cousin, and *d.* in 1688.
5. Robert (Sir), lord mayor of London, who *m.* first, Elizabeth Harvey, and, secondly, Anne, daughter of William Strode, esq. of Kent, widow of William Reynardson, merchant.
6. Anthony, who married and had issue.
7. Philip.

V. Anthony, an alderman of London.

Thomas Bedingfeld died in 1636, and was succeeded by his eldest son,

PHILIP BEDINGFELD, esq. of Ditchingham, who *m.* Anne, daughter of Edward Bacon, esq. of Shrubland Hall, in Suffolk, son of the lord keeper, and had issue,

I. Thomas, *b.* in 1618, and *d. s. p.* in 1661.
II. PHILIP, his heir.
III. Edward,
IV. John,
V. Robert,
VI. Francis,
VII. Anthony,
VIII. James,

} who all appear to have died *s. p.*

I. Dorothy, *m.* to Francis Bacon, esq. of Norwich, son of Judge Bacon. and was mother of Dorothy Bacon, who *m.* Robert Davy, esq. of Ditchingham, and had a son, Robert Davy, who *m.* Elizabeth, daughter of Philip Bedingfeld, esq. of Ditchingham.
II. Helena, died unmarried.
III. Anne, *m.* to John Sicklemore, esq. of Ipswich.
IV. Mary, *m.* to William Jermy, esq. and their daughter Elizabeth wedding Francis Barker, esq. of Sibton, had a son, Francis Barker, who *m.* Cecilia, daughter of Thomas Bloss, esq. of Belstead, and left a daughter, Elizabeth, *m.* to Thomas Lynch, esq.
V. Elizabeth.

The eldest surviving son,

PHILIP BEDINGFELD, esq. of Ditchingham, *b.* in 1620, *m.* Ursula daughter of Sir John Potts, of Manington, in Norfolk, and had (with other issue, of whom Charles wedded Agnita, daughter and co-heir of Sir William Cook, bart. of Broom Hall, and had several children) a son and successor,

PHILIP BEDINGFELD, esq. of Ditchingham, who *m.* Elizabeth, daughter and co-heir of William Strode, esq. of Coventry, and had issue,

I. JOHN, his heir.
II. JAMES, successor to his brother.
III. Strode, to whom Sir George Strode, his uncle, gave his estate, 1710. He *d. s. p.*
IV. Philip.
V. Charles.
VI. Thomas, who *m.* Arabella, daughter of the Rev. Charles Buchanan, rector of Ditchingham, and had one son and three daughters.

I. Catharine.
II. Elizabeth, *m.* to Robert Davy, esq. of Ditchingham.
III. Mary.

The eldest son,

THE REV. JOHN BEDINGFELD, L.L.B. of Ditchingham, who built the present mansion there, *m.* Catherine, daughter of Clere Garneys, esq. of Hedenham, but dying *s. p.* in 1729, was *s.* by his brother,

JAMES BEDINGFELD, esq. of Ditchingham, who *m.* Mary, daughter of Francis Maskull, gent. of London, and left, with a younger son, James, and three daughters, Elizabeth, Anne, and Mary, a successor,

PHILIP BEDINGFELD, esq. of Ditchingham, *b.* 31st May, 1716, who married, first, Mary, daughter of Sir Edmund Bacon, bart. of Gillingham, and had, by her, three sons and two daughters, viz.

I. PHILIP, his heir.
II. BACON, successor to his brother.
III. James, who *m.* Miss Pierson, but *d. s. p.*
IV. John.

I. Mary, *m.* to Brampton Gurdon, esq. of Dilingham and Letton.
II. Ann, *m.* to William Leigh, esq. of Rushall, Staffordshire.

Mr. Bedingfeld wedded, secondly, Mrs. Forster, daughter of — Spendlove, esq. of Norwich, and had further issue,

I. Francis-Philip, *b.* in 1763, who *m.* Catharine, daughter of Thomas Havers, esq. of Thelton, in Norfolk, and had three sons, Francis, Thomas, and Richard, and two daughters, Catharine and Mary.
II. Elizabeth, *m.* first, to Capt. Addison, and secondly, to the Rev. E. Forster.

Mr. Bedingfeld died in 1791, and was *s.* by his son,

PHILIP BEDINGFELD, esq. of Ditchingham, who *m.* Henrietta-Priscilla, daughter of Robert Hemby, esq. of Ipswich, but dying without issue, shortly after his father, in September, 1791, the estate devolved on his brother,

REV. BACON BEDINGFELD, of Ditchingham, *b.* 16th May, 1746, who *m.* 19th June, 1770, Susannah, dau. of Donatus O'Brien, esq. of Blatherwycke Park, in Northamptonshire, and had by her, who *d.* 9th May, 1812,

I. Philip-Bacon, who died *s. p.*
II. JOHN-JAMES, his heir.

I. Susanna-Harriot, *m.* first, to John Talbot, brother to the late Earl of Shrewsbury, and secondly, to Hon. Henry Roper Curzon, eldest son of Lord Teynham.
II. Lucy-Eleanor.
III. Caroline-Elizabeth, widow of Joseph Mortimer, esq. of Wiltshire.
IV. Matilda-Stafford-Sophia, widow of Donatus O'Brien, esq. of Tixover.

Mr. Bedingfeld died 13th July, 1797, and was *s.* by his son, the present JOHN-JAMES BEDINGFELD, esq. of Ditchingham.

*Arms*—Erm. an eagle displayed, gu. armed or.

*Crest*—A demi-eagle gu.

*Motto*—Aquila non capit muscas—or Despicio terrena.

*Estates*—Bedingfeld, in Suffolk, held since the Conquest; and Ditchingham and Hederham, in Norfolk, acquired *temp.* HENRY VII.

*Seat*—Ditchingham Hall.

## PHILIPPS, OF DALE CASTLE.

PHILIPPS-LLOYD, JOHN-PHILIPPS-ALLEN, esq. of Dale Castle, in the county of Pembroke, and of Foes-y-bleiddiad, Cardiganshire, *b.* 26th January, 1802, *m.* 9th December, 1823, Charlotte-Caroline, youngest daughter of Captain Bartlet, of the royal engineers, and has surviving issue,

I. JOHN-ALLEN, *b.* 24th September, 1824.
II. Frederick-Augustus-Spry, *b.* 15th October, 1833.

I. Charlotte-Maria-Carleton.
II. Elizabeth-Mary.

This gentleman, whose patronymic is LLOYD, assumed the surname of PHILIPPS, upon the demise of Lord Milford, under the will of James Philipps, esq. of Penty Park, brother of Mary-Lloyd, his great-great-grandmother. He is in the commission of the peace for the counties of Cardigan and Pembroke, major in the royal Cardigan militia, and a deputy-lieutenant for the former shire, as well as for the town and county of Haverford-west.

### Lineage.

The paternal line of this ancient family is that of LLOYD, and its early history ascends to the most remote period of the authentic British annals.

RHODRI MAWR, (or Roderick the Great), lord paramount of Wales, and sovereign of the Isle of Man, was slain in a battle with the Saxons, in the Isle of Anglesey, in the year 877. He had, with other children, a son,

TUDWAL, called Tudwal *gloff*, or *the lame*, having been wounded in the knee, in the battle fought against the Saxons and Danes, near Conway, and which is recorded in Welsh history as "*Dial Rodri*," or the "*Revenge of Roderick;*" it was fought in the year 878; and the Saxons and Danes being defeated, the death of Roderick was assumed to be avenged, and thus the event became recorded with the above appellation.

The arms borne by TUDWAL GLOFF were, * *azure, a wolf saliant argent, langued and armed gules.* Eighth in descent from Tudwal gloff was,

CEDIVIR, the son of Dinawal. He served under Prince Rhys, usually styled "The Lord Rhys," of South Wales, and distinguished himself on various occasions. In the eleventh year of the reign of HENRY II. Cedivir, at the head of a detachment of the forces of Prince Rhys, took, by escalade, the castle of Cardigan, then held by the Earl of Clare and a body of Flemings for the English monarch. For this service he was rewarded by the grant of various extensive tracts of land in Cardiganshire, the gift of Prince Rhys, who also bestowed upon him his daughter in marriage; and his descendants have, to the present day, ranked among the principal landed proprietors and gentry of Cardiganshire.

Lineally descended from Cedivor ap Dinawal is the family of whom we are about to treat, as also many others in Cardiganshire, Caermarthenshire, and Pembrokeshire. For the bravery displayed by him in the assault and taking of Cardigan castle, Cedivor received from Prince Rhys a grant of the following arms: "Sa. a spear's head arg. imbrued gu. between three scaling ladders of the second (2 and 1); on a chief of the third, a castle triple-towered ppr." Of the numerous descendants of Cedivor who retained their patrimonial estates in Cardiganshire was,

MEREDITH, father of

MORGAN AP MEREDITH, who *m.* Margaret, daughter of Evan ap Griffith ap Rys, of Cayo, and was *s.* by his son,

DAVID LLOYD AP MORGAN, who was of Foes-y-Bleiddiad. He wedded Mary, daughter of Rys ap David Llwyd, of Gogerddan, and had a son,

OLIVER LLOYD, of Foes-y-bleiddiad, father, by Gwenllian, his wife, daughter of Rydderch ap David ap Llewelyn ap Cadwgan, of

DAVID LLOYD, of Foes-y-bleiddiad, living in 1613, who *m.* Gwladys, daughter of Richard Herbert, esq. of Pencelli, and was *s.* by his son,

OLIVER LLOYD, of Foes-y-bleiddiad. This gentleman, living about the middle of the seventeenth century, espoused Jane, daughter of John Lloyd, of Llanllŷr, in the county of Cardigan, and had a son and successor,

JOHN LLOYD, esq. of Foes-y-bleiddiad, barrister at law, who *m.* Elizabeth, daughter and co-heir of Thomas Lloyd, esq. of Wernvylig and Llanllŷr, in Cardiganshire, and was father of

* This is now the crest of the *Lloyd* family of Foes-y-bleiddiad.

DAVID LLOYD, of Foes-y-bleiddiad, whose son, by Sage, his wife, daughter of John Lloyd, esq. of Cilywynne,

JOHN LLOYD, esq. of Foes-y-bleiddiad, wedded Mary, daughter of James Philipps, esq. of Pentypark, in the county of Pembroke, and sister of James Philipps, esq. of Penty Park, whose only child, Mary, *m.* Sir Richard Philipps, bart. created Lord Milford, and *d. s. p.* Mr. Lloyd was *s.* by his son,

JAMES LLOYD, esq. of Foes-y-bleiddiad, who *m.* 4th June, 1750, Anna Maria, only child and heir of Richard Lloyd, esq. of Mabws and Ystradteilo, in Cardiganshire, by his wife, the daughter and heir of Edward Games, of Tregaer, descended from Sir David Gam, and had issue,

I. JOHN, his heir.
II. Richard, *b.* in 1755, *d.* in 1777.
III. James-Philipps, *b.* in 1762, a colonel in the army, married, and had issue.
IV. Vaughan, *b.* in 1764, *d.* in 1772.

I. Letitia-Maria, *b.* in 1751, *m.* to Admiral Thomas, of Llanvaughan.
II. Janetta-Margaretta, *d.* unmarried.
III. Anna-Louisa, *d.* unmarried.
IV. Elizabeth, *b.* in 1760, *d.* unmarried.

Mr. Lloyd *d.* 6th June, 1800, and was *s.* by his eldest son,

JOHN LLOYD, esq. of Foes-y-bleiddiad and Mabws, *b.* in 1753, who was high sheriff for the county of Cardigan, in 1803. He *m.* 8th July, 1776, Elinor, daughter and heiress of John Allen, esq. of Dale Castle, in Pembrokeshire, and had issue,

I. JOHN-ALLEN, captain in the Coldstream Guards, *b.* 22nd March, 1777, *m.* in 1801, Elizabeth, daughter of Col. Bisshopp, of Storrington, in Sussex, uncle to the late Lord Delazouche, and predeceasing his father, in October, 1805, left issue,
    I. JOHN-PHILIPPS-ALLEN, heir to his grandfather.
    II. Harry-James, lieut. 53rd regt. *b.* 7th October, 1803.
    III. Richard Cecil, lieut. 3rd regt. *b.* 19th June, 1805.
II. James-David, *b.* 22nd October, 1786, *m.* in 1828, Frances, daughter of the Rev. T. Levett, and *d.* in April, 1832, without issue.

I. Anna-Maria-Elinor, died 24th April, 1834, unmarried.
II. Mary-Justina-Martha, married to Sir Geo. Cooper, chief judge at Madras.
III. Jane-Louisa.
IV. Caroline-Amelia, married in 1819, to Bowen R. Robertson, esq. lieut. R.N.

Mr. Lloyd *d.* in 1820, and was *s.* by his grandson, the present JOHN-PHILIPPS-ALLEN LLOYD-PHILIPPS, esq. of Dale Castle.

*Arms*—Arg. a lion rampant sa. ducally gorged and chained or.

*Crest*—A lion, as in the arms.

*Motto*—Ducit amor patriæ.

*Estates*—In the counties of Pembroke, Carnarvon, &c.

*Seat*—Dale Castle, Pembrokeshire.

## TIGHE, OF WOODSTOCK.

TIGHE, WILLIAM-FREDERICK-FOWNES, esq. of Woodstock, in the county of Kilkenny, *b.* 17th March, 1794, *m.* 18th April, 1825, Lady Louisa-Maddelena Lennox, fifth daughter of Charles, fourth Duke of Richmond, and had an only daughter, Charlotte-Frances, who died an infant in 1827. Mr. Tighe succeeded his father in 1816; he is a magistrate and deputy-lieutenant for the county of Kilkenny, and was sheriff in 1823.

### Lineage.

The name of TIGH, TEIGH, or, as now written, TIGHE, was assumed from a village in Rutlandshire, the earliest abode of the family, whence, however, it departed at a remote period, and settled at Carlby, in the county of Lincoln, where Leicester Tigh, the last of the English line, was residing *temp.* CHARLES II. In the previous reign, and before the rebellion of 1641,

RICHARD TIGH (son of William Tigh), went over to Ireland and settled there. He was sheriff of Dublin in 1649, colonel of the Dublin Militia, mayor of Dublin in 1651, 1652, and 1655, and member for the same city in Cromwell's Union Parliament in 1656. He acquired considerable estates in the counties of Carlow, Dublin, and Westmeath, during the time of two CHARLESES, and marrying Mary, daughter of Newman Rooke, esq. of London, left surviving issue,

WILLIAM, his heir.

Anne, *m.* first, to Theophilus Sandford, ancestor of Lord Mount Sandford; secondly, to John Preston, great grandson of Jenico Preston, third Viscount Gormanston, and thirdly, to Oliver Lambart, third son of Charles, first Earl of Cavan.

Rebecca, *m.* to Hugh Leeson, esq. ancestor of the Earls of Miltown.

Mary, *m.* in 1670 to Francis Wheeler, ancestor of Sir Jonah-Denny Wheeler Cuffe, bart. of Lyrath, in the county of Kilkenny.

Richard Tighe was *s.* by his youngest and only surviving son,

WILLIAM TIGHE, esq. *b.* in 1657, who *m.* Anne, daughter of Christopher Lovat, esq. and by her (who wedded, secondly, Thomas Coote, one of the Judges of the King's Bench, ancestor of the Earls of Bellamont of the second creation) had one son and one daughter, viz.

RICHARD, his heir.

Mary, *m.* first, in 1694, to Captain Alexander Stewart, second son of William, first Viscount Mountjoy, by whom she had an only daughter, Anne, who espoused first, Luke Gardiner, esq. ancestor of the late Earl of Blessington, and secondly, the Rev. John Hodder.

Mr. Tighe died in 1679, and was *s.* by his only son,

THE RIGHT HON. RICHARD TIGHE, who was sworn of the Privy Council, *temp.* GEORGE I. and sat in parliament for Belturbet in 1703, for Newtown in 1715, and for Augher in 1727. He married Barbara, daughter and heiress of Christian Borr, esq. of Drynogh, in the county of Wexford, by his wife, an heiress of the family of Hore in the same county, and had, beside daughters, a son and successor,

WILLIAM TIGHE, esq. of Rossana, in the county of Wicklow, keeper of the records in Birmingham Tower, M.P. for Clonmines in 1733, and for Wicklow in 1761. This gentleman *m.* first, in March, 1736, Lady

Mary Bligh, eldest daughter of John, first Earl of Darnley, by Lady Theodosia Hyde, Baroness Clifton, his wife, daughter and heir of Edward, Earl of Clarendon, and had three sons and one daughter, namely,

- I. WILLIAM, his successor.
- II. Edward, M.P. for Belturbet in 1763, and for Wicklow in 1790, *m.* Miss Jones, daughter of — Jones, esq. of the county of Westmeath, and left one son,
  - George-William, who *m.* Margaret, widow of Stephen, second Earl of Mountcashel, and daughter of Robert, Earl of Kingstown.
- III. Richard-William, M.P. for Wicklow in 1768, *m.* Sarah, daughter of S. Richards, esq. of the county of Wexford, and had, with other issue, who died young, two surviving sons, Edward, who *m.* Lucy, daughter of — King, esq. and Robert.
- I. Theodosia, *m.* to the Rev. William Blackford, and had one son, John Blackford, esq. of Altidore, in the county of Wicklow, and one daughter, Mary Blackford, the wife of her cousin, Henry Tighe, esq.

Mr. Tighe *m.* secondly, the widow of Captain Theaker, of Wicklow, by whom he had a son, Thomas, who married and had issue, and a daughter, Barbara. He *d.* in 1766, and was *s.* by his son,

WILLIAM TIGHE, esq. of Rossana, M.P. for Athboy in 1761, and subsequently for Wicklow, who *m.* in 1765, Sarah, only child of the Right Hon. Sir William Fownes, bart. of Woodstock, in the county of Kilkenny, by Lady Elizabeth Ponsonby, dau. of Brabazon, Earl of Bessborough, and had issue,

- I. WILLIAM, his heir.
- II. Henry, M.P. for Inistioge, *m.* his first cousin, Mary Blackford* who *d.* in 1805, without issue.
- III. John-Edward, unmarried.
- I. Elizabeth, *m.* to the Rev. Thomas Kelly, of Kellyville, in the Queen's county.
- II. Marianne-Caroline, *m.* to Charles Hamilton, esq. of Hamwood, in the county of Meath.

Mr. Tighe died in 1782, and was *s.* by his eldest son,

WILLIAM TIGHE, esq. of Woodstock, in the county of Kilkenny, member for the borough of Wicklow in the Irish, and for the county in the Imperial, Parliament. This gentleman, as patron of the boroughs of Wicklow and Inistioge, returned four members to parliament, and was, at the time of the union, one of the most influential commoners in Ireland. He *m.* in 1793, Marianne, daughter and co-heiress of Daniel Gahan, esq. of Coolquil, in the county of Tipperary, M.P. for Fethard (by his second wife, Hannah Bunbury), and eventually co-heiress of her uncle, Matthew Bunbury, esq. of Kilfeacle, in the county of Tipperary. By this lady, who still survives, he had issue,

- I. WILLIAM-FREDERICK-FOWNES, his heir.
- II. Daniel, of Rossana, in the county of Wicklow, *m.* in 1825, Frances, third daughter of the late Hon. Sir Edward Crofton, bart. by Lady Charlotte Stewart, his wife, daughter of John, seventh Earl of Galloway, and has issue,
  1. Frederick-Edward, *b.* in June, 1826.
  2. James-Stuart, born in March, 1831.
  1. Marianne-Frances.
  2. Louisa-Elizabeth.
  3. Theresa-Augusta.
  4. Georgiana-Harriet.
- I. Hannah, *m.* in 1818, to Lord Patrick-James-Herbert Chrichton Stuart, only brother of the present Marquis of Bute, and has issue.

Mr. Tighe died in 1816, and was *s.* by his eldest son, the present WILLIAM-FREDERICK-FOWNES TIGHE, esq. of Woodstock.

*Arms*—Party per chev. embattled arg. and sa. five cross crosslets in chief, four in base counterchanged.

*Crest*—A wolf's head erased ppr. with a collar arg. charged with a cross crosslet sa.

*Motto*—Summum nec metuam diem nec optem.

*Estates*—The family estates are principally situated in the counties of Kilkenny, Westmeath, Carlow, Wicklow, Tipperary, and Dublin.

*Seat*—Woodstock, Inistioge.

### Family of Fownes.

Sir WILLIAM FOWNES was appointed, 14th March, 1698, with Henry Lord Shelburne, ranger or gamekeeper, or master of the game, ranger of Phœnix Park, and of all the parks, forests, chases, and woods in Ireland; he was Sheriff of Dublin in 1697, and Lord Mayor in 1708, and was created a baronet of Ireland, 26th October, 1724; he died 3rd of April, 1735, and was buried at Saint Andrew's, Dublin, having had issue,

KENDRICK, who *d.* in the lifetime of his father, 13th October, 1717, leaving by his wife, Elizabeth, daughter

* This lady, distinguished for beauty and talent, was the highly gifted author of PSYCHE.

and heir of Stephen Sweete, esq. of the city of Kilkenny, commonly called Colonel Sweete, an only son,

WILLIAM, successor to his grandfather.

Mrs. Fownes remarried with Edward Cooke, esq. of Castletown, in the county of Kilkenny.

Elizabeth, *m.* to Robert Cope, esq. of Loughgall, in the county of Armagh, who *d.* 4th December, 1748.

He was *s.* by his grandson,

SIR WILLIAM FOWNES, of Woodstock, second baronet, member of the privy council and parliament of Ireland, who married, in 1739, Lady Elizabeth Ponsonby, daughter of Brabazon, Earl of Bessborough, and had an only daughter,

SARAH FOWNES, *b.* in August, 1743, *m.* 23rd May, 1765, to WILLIAM TIGHE, esq. of Rossana, in the county of Wicklow. At Sir William Fownes's decease the baronetcy became extinct, while his estates passed to his daughter, Mrs. Tighe.

# CLOUGH, OF PLAS-CLOUGH.

CLOUGH, RICHARD-BUTLER, esq. of Plâs-Clough, in the county of Denbigh, and of Minydon, in Carnarvonshire, *b.* 22nd December, 1781, a magistrate and deputy-lieutenant for the former county, and formerly a captain in the Royal Denbigh Militia.

## Lineage.

This family, as its name and arms* imply, is of Norman origin, and deduces from the Lords of Rohan, in the dukedom. Its first settlement in England appears by an ancient deed from Whalley Cartulary, bearing date in 1315 to have been in the northern counties. In Wales, the first settler on record was,

RICHARD CLOUGH, commonly called HEN, or the old, from having lived during the reigns of HENRY VII. and VIII. of EDWARD VI. and of the Queens MARY and ELIZABETH. In the Harl. MSS. fol. 1971, entitled, N. Wales Ped. it is stated that he married in the time of HENRY VIII. and settled on Lleweni Green, near Denbigh. He had five sons and one daughter, namely,

I. THOMAS, *m.* a daughter of — Dutton, of Dunham, in Cheshire, and had issue.
II. William, } *d. s. p.*
III. Humphrey, } *d. s. p.*
IV. Hugh, of Grove House, Denbighshire, *d. s. p.*
V. RICHARD (Sir).

I. Anne, *m.* to Griffith Shaw, of Denbigh.

The fifth son,

SIR RICHARD CLOUGH, knt. became an eminent merchant, and was partner of the celebrated Sir Thomas Gresham, who, at Sir Richard's suggestion, erected the Royal Exchange. Sir Richard built, in the year 1567, on his paternal estate, the mansion of Plâs Clough, which is still in the possession of his lineal descendants. By his first wife he had a son and heir, RICHARD, and by the second, who was daughter and heir

* CLOUGH, according to Dr. Johnson, and other lexicographers, is a Norman word signifying a valley between high hills, and the mascles in the first quartering of the shield are peculiar to the duchy of Rohan, and borne by the lords thereof, and their descendants, as stated by Colombriere, author of La Science Heraldique. He says, "I am of opinion that the Lords of Rohan, who I believe are the first that bore these figures on their arms, though descended from the ancient kings or princes of Bretagne, assumed them, because, in the most ancient viscounty of Rohan, afterwards erected into a duchy, there are abundance of small flints, which, being cut in two, this figure appears on the inside of them; the carp, too, which are found in the fish-ponds, exhibit a similar mark on their scales. These circumstances, so very peculiar to the country, and at the same time so extraordinary, the ancient lords adopted the figures for their arms, and transmitted them to their posterity, giving them the name of mascles, from the Latin word, mascula, whence some of the house have taken for their motto, 'Sine maculâ macla'—a mascle without a spot."

of Robert Tudor, of Bernin, and great-grand-daughter of Owen Tudor, by Queen Katherine of France, widow of HENRY V. of England (this lady he espoused with the consent of *Queen* ELIZABETH, who was her guardian), he had two daughters,

I. MARY, *m.* to William Wynn, esq. of Melai, in the county of Denbigh, to whom Sir Richard gave Maynan Abbey, in Carnarvonshire, now in possession of her descendant, Spencer, third Baron Newborough.

II. KATHERINE, *m.* to Roger Salusbury, D.C.L. of Jesus College, Oxford, younger son of Sir John Salusbury, knt. of Lleweni, to whom Sir Richard gave the curious mansion of Bachegraig, which he had erected in the Dutch style of architecture, near Denbigh, and which afterwards descended, by inheritance, through many generations of that family, to Hester-Lynch Salusbury, the celebrated Mrs. Piozzi, the friend and correspondent of Johnson, who left it from her grandson and heir, Captain Mostyn, R.N. to the present Sir John Piozzi Salusbury, of Brynbella, knt.

Sir Richard was knighted, and obtained arms of augmentation on his return from a pilgrimage to Jerusalem. He died at Antwerp in 1570, and his remains were interred there, with the exception of the right hand and heart, which he desired might be transmitted to his native parish of Denbigh in a silver urn, to be deposited on the coffin of the last possessor of his property. He was *s.* by his son,

RICHARD CLOUGH, esq. of Plâs Clough, who wedded a daughter of — Drihurst, of Denbigh, and was *s.* by his son,

WILLIAM CLOUGH, esq. of Plâs Clough. This gentleman *m.* Mary, daughter of John Vaughan, esq. of Groes, in Denbighshire, and dying in 1685, was *s.* by his only son,

JOHN CLOUGH, esq. of Plâs Clough, who wedded Susannah, daughter and heir of Owen Smith, esq. of Carnarvon, and left a son and successor,

HUGH CLOUGH, esq. of Plâs Clough, *b.* in 1679, *m.* Anne, eldest daughter of Thomas Williams, esq. of Halkin Hall, in the county of Flint, and had issue,

HUGH, his successor.

Susan, *m.* first to — Robinson, esq. of Watcroft, and secondly, to the Rev. T. Ince, of Christleton.

Anne, *m.* to Edward Pryce, esq. of Bodvach, whose only daughter and heir,

ANNE PRYCE, *m.* Bell Lloyd, esq. and was mother of Sir Edward Pryce Lloyd, created in 1831 LORD MOSTYN. (*See* BURKE'S *Peerage and Baronetage.*)

The son and heir,

HUGH CLOUGH, esq. of Plâs Clough, *b.* in 1709, served the office of high sheriff for Denbighshire. He *m.* Catherine, daughter and heir of Henry Powell, esq. of Glanywern, in the county of Denbigh, by his wife *Margaret, daughter of Richard Williams, esq. of Llangefni, in Anglesea, and had, with other issue,

I. Hugh, *b.* in 1746, fellow of King's College, Cambridge. An account of the death of this gifted young man is given by his early friend HAYLEY, in the memoirs of that author.

II. RICHARD, heir to his father.

III. Thomas, *b.* in 1756, M.A. rector of Denbigh and canon of St. Asaph, *m.* Dorothea, eldest daughter of John Lloyd, esq. and at her brother's death heir to Havodûnas, in Denbighshire. By this lady, who *d.* in 1814, he left at his decease, in the same year,

Thomas-Hugh, *m.* Caroline, dau. of R. Price, esq. of Rhiwlas, county of Merioneth.

Howel-Powel, married Barbara, daughter of — Westrop, esq. of Limerick.

Dorothea-Catherine, *m.* to the Rev. Richard Howard, D.D. canon of Bangor, and rector of Denbigh.

Eliza, *m.* Charles-Gethin Kenrick, esq.

Mary-Anne.

IV. Roger, *b.* in 1759, sometime of Bathafern Park, county of Denbigh, which he bought when he sold Warminghurst Park to the Duke of Norfolk: canon of St. Asaph, and rector of Lansannon, in Denbighshire, married Anne-Jemima, eldest daughter and co-heir of James Butler, esq. of Warminghurst Park, in the county of Sussex, and had issue by her, who *d.* in 1812,

1. Roger Butler, in holy orders, *b.* in 1782, M.A. Vicar of Corwen, *m.* Amelia-Maria, dau. of R. Price, esq. of Rhiwlas, in the county of Merioneth, and *d.* in 1830, having had two daughters,

Amelia-Jemima, *m.* to Walter-Powel Jones, esq. of Cefn Rûg, and has issue.

Catherine-Elina, *d.* in 1827.

2. James Butler, *b.* in 1784, *m.* Anne, daughter of I. Perfect,

* From this lady, by a previous marriage, descended the families of Williams of Tyfry, in Anglesea, now merged in that of Sir John Williams, bart. of Bostlewyddan, in Flintshire, of Wynn of Maesneuadd, Merionethshire, and of Admiral Lloyd, of Tregauan, in Anglesea.

esq. of Pontefract, and has three sons and one daughter.

3. Henry Butler, *b.* in 1789, Captain in 17th Native Infantry, *d.* at Calcutta in 1823.
4. Charles Butler, *b.* in 1793, M.A. rector of Llanferras, in Denbighshire, and vicar of Mold, Flintshire, *m.* Margaret Sydney, daughter of Edward Jones, esq. of Weprè Hall, in the latter county.
5. Frederick Butler, *b.* in 1795, recorder of Ruthin, *m.* Elizabeth Butler, daughter of the Rev. George Marshall, of Horsham, in Sussex, and *d.* in 1826, leaving a daughter.
6. Alfred Butler, born in 1796, S.T.B. Fellow of Jesus College, Oxford, 1817.
1. Ann-Jemima.
2. Catherine.
3. Martha-Matilda.
4. Anna-Maria.

I. Margaret, *b.* in 1742, married John Foulkes, esq. (descended from Marchudd ap Cynan, founder of one of the fifteen tribes of Wales) and had three sons, viz. 1. John-Powel Foulkes, lieutenant-colonel of the royal Denbigh militia, *m.* Caroline, second daughter and co-heir of Robert Jocelyn, esq. of Stanstedbury, Herts; 2. Hugh, deceased; 3. Henry, D. D. Principal of Jesus College, Oxford, *m.* in 1817, Mary, dau. of J. Houghton, esq. of Wavertree; and six daughters, viz. 1. Catherine, *m.* to Col. Jones; 2. Margaret; 3. Diana, deceased; 4. Mary-Ann; 5. Patty-Jemima, *m.* to the Rev. Mascie D. Taylor, of Lymm Hall, Cheshire; and 6. Louisa-Matilda, deceased.

Hugh Clough was *s.* by his son,

RICHARD CLOUGH, esq. of Plâs Clough and Glanywern, *b.* in 1753, who *m.* Patty, second daughter and co-heir of James Butler, esq. of Warminghurst Park, in Sussex, and had issue,

I. RICHARD-BUTLER, his heir.
II. Hugh-Powel, *b.* in 1783, and *d.* at Gibraltar in 1805.
III. James-Henry, *b.* in 1784, *m.* first, Harriett, second daughter of Joseph Parr, esq. of Firgrove, in Lancashire, and had, by her, one daughter,
    Harriett-Ellen, *m.* to John Williams, eldest son of the Rev. T. Ellis, M.A. treasurer of Bangor, of Bodanw, in Merionethshire, and Glasfryn, in the county of Carnarvon, and has issue.

He wedded secondly, Anne, daughter of — Stone, esq. of Rolleston Park, in Stafford.

Mr. Clough, who served the office of sheriff for Denbighshire in 1782, died in 1784, and was succeeded by his eldest son, the present RICHARD-BUTLER CLOUGH, esq. of Plâs Clough.

*Arms*—Quarterly, 1st, az. a greyhound's head couped arg. between three mascles of the last for CLOUGH; 2nd, or, a lion passant az. crowned, on a chief, the red cross between four cross crosslets gu. and on each side a sword arg. handled or, Augmentation coat given to Sir RICHARD CLOUGH; 3rd, party per chev. or, and sa. three panthers' heads erased counterchanged for SMITH; 4th, arg. a chev. sa. between three boars' heads of the second for POWELL; 5th, party per pale or and az. on a chief gu. three leopards' heads erased or, for CALDECOTT; 6th, az. three covered cups or, for BUTLER.

*Crests*—A demi-lion rampant az. holding in the dexter paw a sword arg. handled or, for CLOUGH. A bent arm az. holding a covered cup or, for BUTLER.

*Motto*—Sine maculâ macla.

*Estates*—In the counties of Denbigh and Carnarvon.

*Seats*—Plâs Clough and Minydon.

## Family of Butler.

JAMES BUTLER, esq. of Amberley Castle, in Sussex, M. P. for Arundel in 1678 and 1681 (descended from the House of Ormonde), wedded Grace, third daughter and co-heir* of Richard Caldecot, esq. by Grace, his wife, daughter of William Boyes, esq. of Hawkhurst, in Kent, and had, by her, who died in 1734, aged eighty-six, with several other children, Katherine, the wife of Sir Thomas Blount, bart. of Tittenhanger, and a son,

JAMES BUTLER, esq. of Warminghurst Park, in Sussex, M.P. for that county, who *m.* Elizabeth, daughter of Sir Charles Cæsar, knt. of Bennington, Herts, and relict of Sir Richard Bennet, bart. By this lady, who died in 1727, aged forty-eight, Mr. Butler left, at his decease in 1741, a son and successor,

JOHN BUTLER, esq. of Warminghurst Park, M.P. for Sussex, who *m.* Katherine,

---

* With her sisters, Cordelia, married to Henry Shelley, esq. of Lewes, and Elizabeth, the wife of Apsley Newton, esq. of Southover, in Sussex.

daughter of John Morgan, esq. of Tredegar, lord-lieutenant of the counties of Monmouth and Brecon, and, dying in 1675, was *s.* by his son,

JAMES BUTLER, esq. of Warminghurst Park, who *m.* Martha, daughter of the Rev. Thomas Dolben, rector of Stoke Pogeis, Bucks, and died in 1775, leaving two daughters and co-heirs, viz.

ANN-JEMIMA *m.* to the Rev. ROGER CLOUGH, canon of St. Asaph.

PATTY, *m.* to RICHARD CLOUGH, esq.

# SHUTTLEWORTH, OF LANCASHIRE AND DURHAM.

SHUTTLEWORTH, *The Rev.* PHILIP-NICHOLAS, D.D. Warden of New College, Oxford, *b.* at Kirkham, 9th February, 1782, and baptized there on the 2nd March following, *m.* at Hambleden, Bucks, in 1823, Emma-Martha, daughter of George Welch, esq. of High Leck, in Westmorland, and has issue,

I. PHILIP-UGHTRED, *b.* in August, 1826.

I. Frances-Emma. II. Agnes-Emma. III. Helen-Mary.

## Lineage.

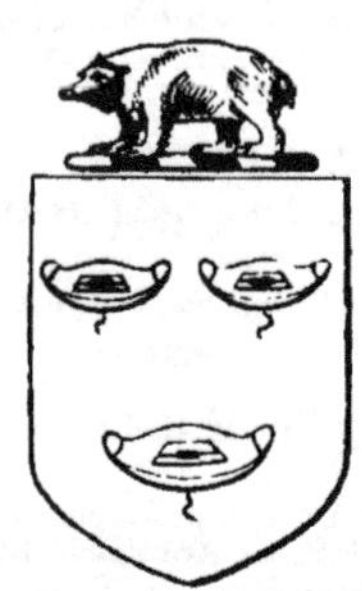

The origin of the family of SHUTTLEWORTH, and its settlement at Gawthorp, in the county of Lancaster, appears to have arisen from the intermarriage of HENRY SHUTTLEWORTH with AGNES, daughter and heiress of WILLIAM DE HACKING,—their son, UGHTRED SHUTTLEWORTH, being the first of Gawthorp. The proof of the fact was extracted, by Christopher Townley, from the old court rolls at Clitheroe, which are now lost:

"Halmot apud Brunlay, 12. RICH. II. Joh. de Eves sursam red. 25½ acres de Rodlaund, in Villa Ightenhull, ad usum Ughtred de Shutlleworth."

HUGH SHUTTLEWORTH was father of

LAWRENCE SHUTTLEWORTH, of Gawthorp, living in 1464, who *m.* Elizabeth, daughter of Richard Worsley, of Mearley, and was *s.* by his son,

NICHOLAS SHUTTLEWORTH, of Gawthorp, who wedded Helen, daughter of Christopher Parker, of Radholm Park, and left a son and heir,

HUGH SHUTTLEWORTH, of Gawthorp, who *d.* in December, 1596, and was buried at Padiham, on the 26th of that month, leaving, by his wife, Anne, daughter of Thomas Grimshaw, esq. of Clayton, three sons and a daughter, viz.

I. RICHARD (Sir), his heir.

II. LAWRENCE, in holy orders, successor to his elder brother.

III. Thomas, who *m.* Anne, daughter of Richard Lever, esq. and by her (who died in 1637, aged sixty-eight) left at his decease, before his brother,

1. RICHARD, heir to his uncle, Lawrence.
2. Nicholas.
3. Ughtred, of Gray's Inn, barrister-at-law.
4. Anne.
5. Hellen, *m.* to Sir Ralph Assheton, bart.
6. Elizabeth, *m.* to Sir Matthew Whitfield, of Whitfield.

I. Helen, *m.* to C. Nowell, of Little Mearley.

The eldest son and heir,

SIR RICHARD SHUTTLEWORTH, knight, of Gawthorp, was serjeant-at-law, and chief justice of Chester, in the 31st of ELIZABETH. This gentleman commenced the erection of Gawthorp hall, a beautiful specimen of Gothic architecture, which was completed by his successor. He *m.* Mary, widow of Robert Barton, esq. of Smethells, but died without issue, about the year 1600, when the estate passed to his brother,

THE REV. LAWRENCE SHUTTLEWORTH,

B.D. rector of Witchford, in Warwickshire, who finished the erection of Gawthorp hall. He died *s. p.* in 1607 or 1608, and was *s.* by his nephew,

RICHARD SHUTTLEWORTH, esq. of Gawthorp, who *m.* Fleetwood, daughter and heir of R. Barton, esq. of Barton, and had issue,

I. RICHARD, who *m.* Jane, or Joan, dau. of Mr. Kirk, citizen of London, and died in the lifetime of his father, *anno* 1648, leaving two sons and a daughter, viz.
  1. RICHARD (Sir), heir to his grandfather.
  2. NICHOLAS, of whom presently, as founder of the branch before us.
  1. Fleetwood, living, unmarried, in 1664.

II. Nicholas.
III. Ughtred, who *m.* Jane, daughter of Radcliff Asshton, esq. of Cuerdale.
IV. Barton.
V. John.
VI. Edward.
VII. William, captain in the Parliament's army, slain at Lancaster.

I. Margaret, *m.* to Nicholas Towneley, esq. of Royle.
II. Anne, *m.* first, to — Asshton, of Cuerdale, and secondly, to R. Towneley, esq. of Barnside and Carr.

In the Oliverian times, when rank and property were compelled to sail with the current, this Richard Shuttleworth, of Gawthorp, and John Starkie, esq. of Huntroyde, were two leading magistrates for the hundred of Blackburn, and their names as hymeneal priests, according to the prevalent usage of the period, frequently occur in the parish registers of the neighbouring churches. Mr. Shuttleworth *d.* in June, 1669, at the advanced age of eighty-two, and was *s.* by his elder grandson, SIR RICHARD SHUTTLEWORTH,* knt. of Gawthorp, while the younger,

NICHOLAS SHUTTLEWORTH, esq. became of Forcet, in the county of York, and of the city of Durham. He *m.* at St. Oswalds, Durham, 28th September, 1671, Elizabeth, elder daughter and co-heir of Thomas Moor, of Berwick upon Tweed, gent. and had issue,

I. RICHARD, of Durham, living in 1705, when he was nominated one of the executors to the will of his brother Nicholas. He died soon after, unmarried.
II. Thomas, bapt. at St. Oswalds, 27th December, 1674.
III. NICHOLAS.

I. Fleetwood, *m.* to Sir Henry Belasyse, knt. of Brancepeth Castle, in the county of Durham, lieutenant-general of the British forces in Flanders, and governor of Berwick upon Tweed (his second wife), by whom (who *d.* 16th December, 1717) she left at her decease, 26th February, 1732, an only son,
  WILLIAM BELASYSE, esq. of Brancepeth Castle, who *m.* Bridget, only daughter and heir of Rupert Billingsley, esq. and dying 11th

---

* SIR RICHARD SHUTTLEWORTH, of Gawthorp, *b.* in 1644; *m.* Margaret, daughter of John Tempest, esq. of Old Durham, and dying in July, 1687, was buried at Padiham. "The opulence of the Shuttleworth family, (says Dr. Whitaker), and at the same time the convenience of paper currency, appear from the following entry in the accounts of an agent at Gawthorp, in 1677: '13th December, item, for rundlets to carry money into Forcet;' this was another beautiful seat of the Shuttleworths." Sir Richard was *s.* by his son,

RICHARD SHUTTLEWORTH, esq. of Gawthorp, M.P. who died in December, 1748, leaving by his wife, another Miss Tempest of Old Durham, a son and successor,

JAMES SHUTTLEWORTH, esq. of Gawthorp. This gentleman wedded Mary, daughter and heiress of Robert Holden, esq. of Aston, in the county of Derby, and had issue,

I. ROBERT, his heir.
II. James, of Aston, *d. s. p.*
III. William.
IV. Charles, who took the name of HOLDEN; married, and has issue.

I. Mary, *m.* first, to Sir Charles Turner, bart. and secondly, to Sir Thomas Gascoigne.
II. Elizabeth, *m.* to Francis Hurt, esq. of Alderwasley.

Mr. Shuttleworth dying in 1773, aged fifty-eight, was succeeded by his son,

ROBERT SHUTTLEWORTH, esq. of Gawthorp, who *m.* Anne, daughter of General Desaguliers, and had issue,

JAMES, of Barton, who *m.* twice, and had issue.
ROBERT, who *s.* at Gawthorpe.
Anne, *m.* first, Richard Streetfeild, esq. and secondly, to — Prime, esq.
Emma, *m.* James West, esq.
Elizabeth.
Catherine, married to Richard Hurt, esq. of Wirksworth.

Mr. Shuttleworth *d.* in 1816, and devised Gawthorp and his other estates in Whalley, to his second son,

ROBERT SHUTTLEWORTH, esq. of Gawthorp, *b.* in 1784. This gentleman, by profession a barrister, was chairman of the quarter sessions at Preston. He *m.* in 1816, Janet, eldest daughter of Sir John Marjoribanks, bart. of Lees, in the county of Berwick, by whom (who re-married in 1825, Frederick North, esq. of Rougham, in Norfolk) he left at his decease, 6th March, 1818, an only daughter and heiress,

JANET SHUTTLEWORTH, of Gawthorp Hall, in the county of Lancaster.

February, 1769, left an only dau. and heiress,

BRIDGET BELASYSE, who died unm. 5th April, 1774, aged thirty-eight, leaving the whole of her fortune to the family of Belasyse, Lord Fauconberg.

II. Elizabeth, bapt. at St. Oswalds, 10th February, 1673.

The third son,

NICHOLAS SHUTTLEWORTH, of the city of Durham, and of Elvet, in Durham, gent. baptized at St. Oswalds, 1st July, 1678; *m.* Lucy, one of the daughters of the Rev. Francis Blackeston, rector of Whitburne, in Durham, and by her (who wedded, secondly, Thomas Philipson) had, with a dau. Elizabeth, the wife of — Darnall, of Newcastle upon Tyne, a posthumous son, (he died in 1705, and was buried at St. Oswalds 13th September in that year).

NICHOLAS SHUTTLEWORTH, esq. of the city of Durham, *b.* 2nd, and bapt. at St. Oswalds 8th May, 1706, who *m.* 25th September, 1729, Elizabeth, eldest daughter of Humphrey March, and sister and heir of Humphrey March, of Foxton, in the county of Durham, and had issue,

I. RICHARD, his heir.
II. Nicholas, bapt. at St. Oswalds, 5th August, 1734, *d.* unmarried in 1750, on his passage to Bombay.
III. HUMPHREY, in holy orders.

I. Anne, bapt. at St. Oswalds, 8th September, 1730; *m.* John Smith, M.D. of the city of Durham.
II. Elizabeth, bapt. 25th December, 1732; *d.* unm. in 1790.

He *d.* in 1770, was buried at St. Oswalds, 18th September in that year, and *s.* by his eldest son,

RICHARD SHUTTLEWORTH, esq. bapt. at St. Oswalds, 21st Sept. 1731, and dying unmarried 26th August, 1797, will dated 9th January, 1794, was *s.* by his brother,

THE REV. HUMPHREY SHUTTLEWORTH, vicar of Preston and Kirkham, in the county of Lancaster, *b.* in the city of Durham 29th January, 1736; who wedded at Preston, 28th February, 1774, Anna, only child (by his second wife, Margaret, daughter of Edward Rigby, esq. of Middleton) of Philip Houghton, esq. third son of Sir Charles Houghton, bart. of Houghton Tower, and had issue,

Richard-Henry, of Gray's Inn, *b.* 4th July, 1780; married, but died *s. p.*
PHILIP-NICHOLAS.

Mary-Elizabeth, living unm. in 1835.
Caroline, *d.* in October, 1827, unm.
Frances-Anne, *d.* in 1816, unm.

The Rev. Humphrey Shuttleworth died in 1812, and was buried at Kirkham. His only surviving son is the present REV. PHILIP-NICHOLAS SHUTTLEWORTH, D.D. warden of New College.

*Arms*—Arg. three weavers' shuttles sa. topped and furnished with quills of yarn, the threads pendent or.

*Crest*—A bear passant arg.

## SOTHERON, OF KIRKLINGTON.

SOTHERON, FRANK, esq. of Kirklington, in the county of Nottingham, admiral of the blue, *m.* at Darrington, about the year 1809, Caroline-Matilda, daughter of Captain Barker, by whom he had an only child,

Lucy-Sarah, *m.* to Thomas Sutton Bucknall Estcourt, esq. of New Park, in Wiltshire, late M. P. for Marlborough.

His first wife dying 29th May, 1812, the admiral wedded, secondly, at Hampton, in Middlesex, 13th November, 1813, Jane, eldest daughter of Wilson Gale, esq. of Conishead Priory, in Lancashire, who assumed the surname of Braddyll, upon the demise of his cousin, Thomas Braddyll, esq.

## Lineage.

The Sotherons have been most respectably settled on their own estates at Holm, in Spaldingmore, in the East Riding, and Hook, in the West Riding of the county of York, for more than two centuries.

WILLIAM SOTHERON, esq. sometime of Pontefract, *m.* Lucy, daughter of Edward Thompson, esq. of Marston, in Yorkshire, and co-heir of her brother Tyndall Thompson, esq. and was *s.* by his son,

WILLIAM SOTHERON, esq. of Darrington, who espoused Sarah, only surviving child and heir of Samuel Savile, esq. of Thrybergh, and had issue,

I. FRANK, his heir.
II. William, a major in the army, M.P. for Pontefract in several parliaments, who *m.* Sarah Shipley, daughter of Thomas Barker, esq. of Potter Newton, near Leeds, but *d. s. p.* in 1806.
III. Savile, of Trinity College, Cambridge, *d.* unm. in 1782, buried in South Audley Chapel.

I. Lucy, died unm. in 1820, buried at Haddon-on-the-Wall, near Newcastle.
II. Elizabeth, *m.* to Robert Sinclair, esq. recorder of York, and *d. s. p.*
III. Mary-Catherine, *d.* unm. about 1831, buried at Darrington.
IV. Henrietta, *m.* to the Rev. William Dealtry, of Wigginton, in Yorkshire.

Mr. Sotheron was *s.* at his decease, by his eldest son, the present ADMIRAL SOTHERON, of Kirklington.

*Arms*—Gu. on a bend indented between six cross crosslets arg. three eaglets displayed sa. Quartering Thompson, Tyndal, Reresby, Deincourt, Savile, Thornhill, Frank, and Lonsdale.

*Crest*—An eagle, with two heads displayed party per pale arg. and gu. the wings semmée of cross crosslets counterchanged; murally crowned, beaked and membered, or.

*Estates*—In the counties of York and Nottingham.

*Seat*—Kirklington, Notts.

### Family of Savile.

The SAVILES emigrated from the province of Anjou, in France, and were resident, antecedently to the year 1300, in the county of York, where we find Sir John Savile seated at Savile Hall, at a very remote period.

JOHN SAVILE, esq. of Methley, in Yorkshire, (son of Sir John Savile, baron of the Exchequer, by Elizabeth, his second wife, daughter of Thomas Wentworth, esq. of North Elmsall), who inherited the estates in 1633, and was the direct descendant of Sir John Savile, of Savile Hall, whom we have just alluded to, *m.* first, Mary, daughter of John Robinson, esq. of Ryther, in Yorkshire, and secondly, Margaret, daughter of Sir Henry Garraway, knt. lord mayor of London. By the latter he had issue,

JOHN, his successor.

Margaret, *m.* to Sir William Ingleby, bart. of Ripley.
Elizabeth, *m.* to Leonard Wastell, esq.
Catharine, *m.* first, to Sir William Cholmondeley, bart. of Whitby, and secondly, to Sir Nicholas Stroud.
Anne, } who appear to have *d.* unm.
Mary, }
Dorothy, *m.* to John Clavering, esq. of Newcastle, son and heir of Sir James Clavering.

The son and heir,

JOHN SAVILE, esq. of Methley, *b.* in 1644, added to his paternal inheritance, by the purchase of the estate of THRIBERGH, from Sir William Reresby, bart.* He married Sarah, daughter of Peter Tryon, esq. of Bulwick, in the county of Northampton, and had issue,

I. JOHN, who predeceased his father in 1711, leaving, by Mary, his wife, daughter and co-heir of Sir John Bankes, knt. of Aylesford, in Kent, two sons and a daughter, viz.

* This SIR WILLIAM RERESBY afforded a melancholy contrast to the high reputation of his distinguished father, Sir John Reresby. "In 1705," says Hunter, "he had sold Thribergh, and the estates which were connected with it. He was alive in 1727, when Wotton's account of the baronets was published. In that work he is said "to be reduced to a low condition. Brooke was

JOHN, drowned 8th May, 1713, at which time he was on the point of marriage with Miss Jane Fenay, the heiress of the house of Fenay, of Fenay. "He was lost" (we extract from a contemporary manuscript) "in a draw-well in the court of the White Bear, at Wakefield. It was left uncovered, and he walked into it on a dark night. There were several gentlemen at the inn, one of whom, Mr. Watson, of Bolton-upon-Dearne, swung down by the rope in the hope of saving Mr. Savile. Both got into the bucket, but while they were ascending, the rope broke, and they were drowned."

Henry, of Methley, *d.* unmarried in 1723.

ELIZABETH, heiress of Thrybergh, who wedded the Hon. John Finch, second son of Heneage, Earl of Aylesford, and dying in 1767, left a son, SAVILE FINCH, esq. of Thrybergh, M. P. for Malton, who had no issue, and having full power over the estates, left them to his wife, Judith, daughter of John Fullerton, esq. That lady resided, for twenty years after her husband's decease, at Thrybergh, and dying in 1803, bequeathed her possessions to her own family, the Fullertons.

II. CHARLES, of Methley, ancestor of Lord Mexborough.

III. James, of Nortgate-street, in Wakefield, who *m.* Dorothy, or Anne Oxley, and dying *v. p.* before 1712, left an only daughter and heiress, Sarah, *m.* to the Rev. Joseph Leech, vicar of Adwick-le-Street.

IV. SAMUEL, of whom presently.

I. Sarah, *m.* to Sir Thomas Slingsby, bart.

The fourth son,

SAMUEL SAVILE, of Thrybergh, was lord of the manors of Darrington, Redness, Swinflete, Brinsworth, and Denaby, all in the county of York. He *m.* Elizabeth, daughter and co-heir of Robert Frank, esq. of Pontefract, and by her (who *m.* secondly, John Hoare, esq. and was mother of Catherine, wife of Bacon Frank, esq.) had an only daughter and heiress,

SARAH SAVILE, *m.* to WILLIAM SOTHERON, esq.

---

informed that he was tapster of the Fleet Prison. This is not improbable, for his tastes and habits appear to have been of the lowest order. I have seen one sad evidence. He died in great obscurity, a melancholy instance how low pursuits and base pleasures may sully the noblest name, and waste an estate gathered with labour, and preserved by care in a race of distinguished ancestors. Gaming was amongst his follies; and particularly that lowest specimen of the folly, the fights of game cocks. The tradition at Thrybergh is (for his name is not quite forgotten) that the estate of Deanaby was staked and lost on a single main."

## TRAPPES, OF NIDD.

TRAPPES, FRANCIS-MICHAEL, esq. of Nidd, in the county of York, *m.* 4th December, 1788, Elizabeth, daughter of James Lomax, esq. of Clayton Hall, in Lancashire, and has surviving issue,

I. FRANCIS, *b.* 28th January, 1790.
II. Robert, *b.* 30th April, 1793.
III. Michael, *b.* 23rd April, 1797.
IV. Henry, *b.* 20th June, 1805.
V. Roger-Mitton, *b.* 7th June, 1807.
VI. Richard, *b.* 15th November, 1808.

I. Elizabeth.
II. Anne-Dorothy.

Mr. Trappes succeeded his father in 1803.

## Lineage.

STEPHEN TRAPPES, citizen of London, *temp.* EDWARD IV. was born at Theydon Boys, in Essex, and died in the 1st of HENRY VII. leaving, by Elena, his wife, a son and daughter, Reginald and Elizabeth, both living in 1485. Stephen's brother,

THOMAS TRAPPES, of Theydon Boys, in Essex, living in 1485, was father of

THOMAS TRAPPES, of Theydon Boys, who was succeeded by his son,

ROBERT TRAPPES, citizen and goldsmith of London, who was buried in St. Leonard's, Foster Lane, in 1560. He married twice. By his first wife, he had three sons and one daughter, viz.

- I. NICHOLAS, of London, who *m.* Mary, daughter of Thomas Calton, of the same city, and died in 1544, leaving two daughters, his co-heirs,
  - ALICE, unmarried at her father's decease.
  - MARY, also unmarried in 1544; subsequently the wife of Lord Giles Poulet, third son of the Marquis of Winchester.
- II. George, who left three sons and two daughters.
- III. William, of whom nothing is known.

- I. Philippa, *m.* to Sir George Gifford, knt. of Middle Cleydon, Bucks.

By his second wife, Joan, daughter of Richard Cryspe, of Northampton, founder of several fellowships and scholarships in Caius College, Cambridge. Robert Trappes had two sons and one daughter, viz.

- IV. Robert, of London, who *m.* Dorothy, daughter of Robert Brown, of London, and by her (who wedded, secondly, William Atkinson) left at his decease, in 1576,
  1. Robert, of London, whose will was proved 23rd November, 1587. He *m.* Katharine Tracy, and by her (who *m.* secondly, Sir John Billingsley, knt.) he had an only son, Robert, who died *s. p.* before 1634.
  2. Rowland, high sheriff of the counties of Surrey and Sussex, died without issue. Will dated in 1594.
  3. Roger, of Cheam, in Surrey, living in 1616, had an only child, Roger.
  4. Robert-Brown, of Rainworth, in Essex, died unmarried.
  5. Giles, of London, living in 1630, *m.* Elizabeth Vernon, and had, with a son, Robert, of Edmonton, who died unmarried, four daughters, his eventual co-heirs, namely, Dorothy, Frances, Katherine, the wife of Robert Tristand, and Elizabeth, of William Newdigate, esq.
  6. William, of London, who died in 1630, leaving issue,
  7. Andrew, living in 1616.
  8. Richard, *d. s. p.* before 1634.

  1. Dorothy, *m.* to Ralph Atkinson, gent.
- V. FRANCIS, of whom presently.

- II. Joyce, *m.* first, to — Saxye, and, secondly, to — Frankland. This lady, who died without surviving issue, in 1586, was foundress of a fellowship in Brazennose College, Oxford, a benefactress to Lincoln College, in the same university, and to Caius and Emanuel Colleges, Cambridge.

The second son of the second marriage of Robert Trappes,

FRANCIS TRAPPES, esq. of London, whose will was proved 21st March, 1576, married, first, Frances Baude, of Lincolnshire, by whom he had two daughters, Joan and Frances; and, secondly, Ann, only child and heiress of Robert Byrnand, esq. of Knaresborough, by Anne, his wife, daughter of Richard Norton, esq. of Norton Conyers.* By the heiress of Byrnand, who wedded, secondly, William Blount, esq. of London, and, thirdly, Sir John Egerton, of Egerton, in Cheshire, Francis Trappes had issue,

- I. FRANCIS (Sir), his heir.
- II. Robert, of Brockham, in Surrey, living in 1619, *m.* Eleanor, daughter of Edward Fleet, of London, merchant, and had issue.
- III. Henry, a posthumous son, living in 1619.

- I. Mary, *m.* to Richard Cooper, esq. of Kippington, in Kent.
- II. Ursula, *m.* to Lewis Bowde, esq. of Lincoln's Inn, barrister-at-law.

The eldest son (adopting his mother's name) was

---

* This Richard Norton married Susan, daughter of Richard Neville, Lord Lartimer, and lineal descendant, through her grandmother, Jane Bourchier, of the Lady Anne Plantagenet, daughter of Thomas, of Woodstock, and granddaughter of King EDWARD III.

Sir Francis Trappes Byrnand, of Harrogate and Nidd, in the county of York, who was knighted at Windsor, in July, 1603. He *m.* Mary, third daughter, and eventually co-heir (with her sister, Anne, the wife of Sir William Wentworth, of Wentworth Woodhouse) of Richard Atkinson, esq. of Stowel, in Gloucestershire, and had,

- I. Robert, his heir.
- II. Henry.
- III. Francis.
- IV. John.

- I. Ann, *m.* in London, 21st February, 1641, to Sir George Radcliffe, knt. of Overthorpe, attorney-general to *King* Charles I. and dying, in 1659, was buried in Westminster Abbey.
- II. Elizabeth, } who all appear to have died unmarried.
- III. Joyce, }
- IV. Frances, }
- V. Mary, *m.* to Charles Towneley, esq. of Towneley, in Lancashire, who was slain at Marston Moor, in 1643.
- VI. Margaret. died unmarried, 16th October, 1701, aged eighty-three.
- VII. Clara, sometime of Pontefract, died unmarried.
- VIII. Ursula, } both living unmarried, 9th May, 1687.
- IX. Lucy, }

Sir Francis died in February, 1642, was interred in St. Martin's, Coney Street, York, and succeeded by his son,

Robert Trappes-Byrnand, esq. of Nidd and Harrowgate, aged twenty, in December, 1619, who *m.* Elizabeth, daughter of Stephen Taylor, and left, with three daughters, Mary, *m.* to Francis Armytage, esq.* of South Kirby, Anne, to Francis Radcliffe, esq. of Sheffield Manor, and Elizabeth, to William Armytage, esq.* of Killing Hall), a son and successor,

Francis Trappes-Byrnand, esq. of Nidd, who *m.* at York, Jane,† fourth daughter of Michael Warton, esq. of Beverley, by Catherine, his wife, daughter and co-heir of Christopher Maltby, esq. of Maltby, and had issue,

- I. Francis, his heir.
- II. Michael, at Doway College, and under age, in 1678.
- III. Henry, of London, living there in 1723.
- IV. William, living 5th February, 1677.
- V. Christopher, *m.* at Tadcaster, Elizabeth, daughter and heir of William Hargraves, esq. of Carlton, in Craven, by Mary, his wife, daughter of John Tempest, esq. of Broughton, and had,
  1. Francis, of whom presently.
  2. Christopher, died unmarried.
  3. Hugh, died unmarried.
  4. Henry, died unmarried, in 1788, aged eighty.

  1. Elizabeth, *m.* to James Towgood, of Skipton, in Craven.
  2. Anne, died unmarried.
  3. Jane, died unmarried.
  4. Catherine, *m.* to George Feather, of Habendin.
  5. Lucy, *m.* to Thomas Hill, of Manchester.
  6. Mary, *m.* to William Wilson, of Carlton.
- VI. Ralph, named in the will of his father, 1677.

- I. Mary, under age in 1678. Executor to her father's will.
- II. Katherine, living 27th July, 1676.
- III. Jane, under age in 1677.

Mr. Trappes-Byrnand died in 1678, and was succeeded by his son,

Francis Trappes Byrnand, esq. of Nidd, who *m.* in 1683, Elizabeth, sister and coheir of Ralph Appleby, esq. of Linton, in Yorkshire, and had by her, who died in the convent at Liege, in 1724, four sons and five daughters, viz.

- I. Francis, his heir.
- II. John, *b.* 27th January, 1691, died unmarried.
- III. Thomas, *b.* 21st March, 1692, died unmarried, 1723.
- IV. Ambrose, *b.* 4th November, 1696.

- I. Katherine, *m.* to Hugh Anderton, esq. of Euxton, in Lancashire.
- II. Elizabeth, died unmarried.
- III. Margaret, *b.* in 1697, *m.* to George Craythorne, esq. of Ness, in Yorkshire.
- IV. Jane, died unmarried.
- V. Anne, died unmarried.

Mr. Trappes-Byrnand died in 1710, and was *s.* by his son,

Francis Trappes, esq. of Nidd, who died unmarried, in December, 1761, and was buried on the 10th of that month, at Nidd. His cousin,

Francis Trappes, esq. of Carlton, continued the line of the family. This gentleman married Miss Grace Joy, and dying, 10th October, 1786, aged eighty-eight, left a daughter, Elizabeth, the wife of W. Calvert, esq. and a son and successor,

Francis Trappes, esq. of Nidd, who *m.*

* These gentlemen were sons of Sir Francis Armytage, bart. of Kirklees.

† This lady's brother, Michael Warton, esq. of Beverley, born in 1614, *m.* Susan, daughter of John Poulett, esq. of Hinton St. George, in the county of Somerset, and was father of Elizabeth Warton, who *m.* Charles Pelham, esq. of Brocklesby, and had a daughter, Elizabeth Pelham, the wife of John Stringer, esq. of Sutton-upon-Sound, and mother of Anne, Countess Fitzwilliam.

in August, 1762, Margaret, youngest daughter and coheir of William Witham, esq.* of Preston-upon-Tees, and had issue,

I. FRANCIS-MICHAEL, his heir.
II. John, captain 2nd regiment of foot, *b.* 24th June, 1770, died, unmarried, 22nd December, 1809, in his passage from Jamaica.
III. William, *b.* 29th February, 1773.
IV. Charles, a major in the army, born 29th October, 1776, died, at the Cape of Good Hope, in 1827, leaving issue.
V. James.
VI. Thomas, born 10th August, 1780, R. N.
VII. William, died young.

I. Margaret, *m.* at Nidd, 7th March, 1791, to William Tunstall, esq. of Baltimore.
II. Dorothy, died, unmarried, in 1803. buried at Nidd.
III. Anne, died in 1787.
IV. Mary-Isabel, *m.* at Bath, in August, 1809, to Thomas Tunstall, esq. of Preston-upon-Skerne.

Mr. Trappes died 14th August, 1803, and was *s.* by his eldest son, the present FRANCIS-MICHAEL TRAPPES, esq.

*Arms*—Arg. three caltraps sa.
*Crest*—A man's head, couped at the shoulders, on the head a steel cap, garnished with a plume of feathers, all ppr.
*Estates*—In Yorkshire.
*Seat*—Nidd.

* Mr. Witham's daughters and co-heirs were:
ANNE, *m.* to Michael Tunstall, esq. of Durham.
CATHERINE, a nun at Sion House, Lisbon, died about 1795.
DOROTHY, *m.* to Thomas Langdale, esq. of London.
MARGARET, *m.* to FRANCIS TRAPPES, esq.

## GATACRE, OF GATACRE.

GATACRE, EDWARD, esq. of Gatacre, in the county of Salop, *b.* 16th April, 1768, *m.* first, in 1805, Annabella, eldest daughter and co-heir of the late Robert Lloyd, esq. of Swan Hill, and by her, who died 17th February, 1817, has had issue,

EDWARD-LLOYD.
Richard, who died young.

Annabella-Jane.

He *m.* secondly, in 1826, Harriet-Constantia, eldest daughter of the late Richard Jenkins, esq. of Bicton.

Colonel Gatacre, who succeeded his father 21st August, 1821, is colonel of the Shropshire militia, and a magistrate and deputy-lieutenant for that county.

### Lineage.

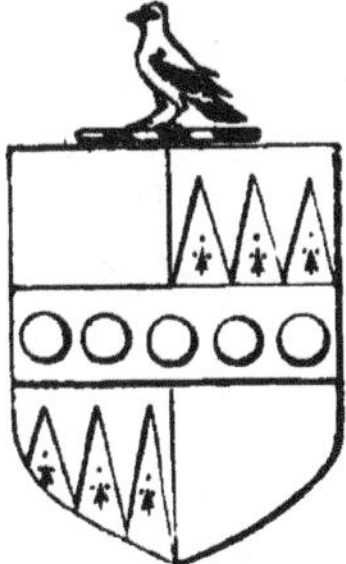

It appears that in the reign of HENRY III, STEPHEN DE GATACRE possessed the manors of Gatacre and Sutton, with lands in Claverley, which he held of the king by military service, and which had been obtained by his ancestor, by grant from EDWARD the Confessor. He *d.* after the year 1229, having had two sons,

THOMAS, who predeceased his father, leaving, by Alice his wife, two sons, ROBERT and WILLIAM.
Reginald, living *temp.* EDWARD I. whose son, Bertram, alive in 1293, was father of Osbert, who had two sons, William, in holy orders, of Claverley, living in 1324, and Simon.

He was *s.* by his grandson,

ROBERT DE GATACRE, lord of Gatacre, at whose decease, unmarried, the estates and representation of the family devolved on his brother,

WILLIAM DE GATACRE, lord of Gatacre in 1293 and 1313, who left (with another child, Avis, who possessed lands in the parish of Claverley in 1314) a son and heir,

GALFRY DE GATACRE, lord of Gatacre in 1314 and 1319, whose son,

THOMAS DE GATACRE, of Gatacre, living *temp.* EDWARD II. *m.* Joan, daughter of Richard de Leigh, of Leigh and Park Hall, in the county of Stafford, and dying in 1367, was *s.* by his son,

THOMAS DE GATACRE, of Gatacre, *temp.* RICHARD II. who *m.* a lady named Alice, but of what family is not recorded, and by her, who was living a widow in 1410, left two sons. The elder,

WILLIAM DE GATACRE, of Gatacre in 1398, dying unm. was *s.* by his brother,

JOHN DE GATACRE, of Gatacre, who flourished in the reigns of HENRY IV., V. and VI. He wedded Joice, daughter of JOHN BURLEY, esq. of Bomcroft Castle, sheriff of Shropshire in 1409, *(see end of this article)* and had issue,

- I. JOHN, his heir.
- II. Humphrey, esquire of the body to HENRY VI. living in 1509, *m.* Eleanor, daughter and heir of Richard Blyke, esq. of Astley, in Salop, and had a daughter,
  - Joice, *m.* to Thomas Eynes, or Keynes, of Church Stretton.
- III. Richard, living in 1448.

- I. Isabel, possessed of lands in Claverley.

The eldest son,

JOHN GATACRE, esq. of Gatacre, sat in parliament for Bridgenorth 12th EDWARD IV. He *m.* Jane, daughter of Nicholas Yonge, esq. of Caynton, in Salop, and was father of

JOHN GATACRE, esq. of Gatacre, who *m.* first, Eleanor, daughter of John Acton, esq. of Aldenham, but by her had no issue; and, secondly, Elizabeth, daughter of Sir Adam Bostock, knt. of Bostock, in Cheshire, by whom (her will was proved in 1501) he had two sons, ROBERT and Arthur, and one daughter, Christabel, *m.* to John Lyster, esq. of Rowton Castle, (see vol. ii). He died in 1499, and was *s.* by his elder son,

ROBERT GATACRE, esq. of Gatacre, in 1500, who *m.* Joan, second daughter of John Hoord, of Bridgenorth, and had issue, WILLIAM, his heir; Richard; Francis; Mary, *m.* to John Wolryche, esq. of Dudmaston; Margery, to William Middlemore, esq. of Worcestershire; and Jane, to John Whitton, esq. of Whitton Court. Mr. Gatacre *d.* in 1509, and was *s.* by his eldest son,

WILLIAM GATACRE, esq. of Gatacre, who *m.* Helen, daughter of William Mytton, esq. of Shrewsbury, and had issue,

- I. Humphrey, died young.
- II. FRANCIS, his heir.
- III. Thomas, in holy orders, rector of St. Edmunds, Lombard Street, London, a learned and eminent divine: from him descends the present THOMAS GATAKER, esq. of Mildenhall. (See vol. i. p. 589).
- IV. George.
- V. John, of Swinnerton, *d. s. p.*

- I. Dorothy, *m.* to Sir Robert Brooke, knt. of Madeley Court, chief justice of the Common Pleas.
- II. Barbara, *m.* to James Barker, esq. of Gloucestershire.
- III. Catherine, *m.* to Richard Kettleby.
- IV. Alice, *m.* to Simon Mucklowe, of Howden.
- V. Elizabeth, *m.* to Robert Pigott, of Chetwynd.

Mr. Gatacre *d.* 20th December, 1577, was buried at Claverley, and *s.* by his eldest son,

FRANCIS GATACRE, esq. of Gatacre, who *m.* Elizabeth second daughter and co-heir of Humphrey Swinnerton, esq. of Swinnerton, in Staffordshire, and had two sons and three daughters, viz.

- I. WILLIAM, his heir.
- II. Thomas, of Shipley, who died in 1648, leaving a daughter, Jane.

- I. Margaret, *m.* to Edward Morgan, esq. of Northfield, Worcestershire.
- II. Elizabeth, *m.* to Andrew Vyse, esq. of Standon, in Staffordshire.
- III. Dorothy, *m.* to Thomas Skrymshire, esq. of Johnstone, in Staffordshire.

Francis Gatacre *d.* 19th June, 1590, and was *s.* by his elder son,

WILLIAM GATACRE, esq. of Gatacre, who *m.* Anne, daughter and heir of Jerome Corbet, esq. one of the council in the marches of Wales, and had eight sons and one dau. viz.

- I. JOHN, his heir.
- II. William, *d.* in 1653.
- III. Francis, *d.* in 1611.
- IV. Ambrose, *b.* in 1610, living at Shiffnall.
- V. Jerome, of Willey, *d.* in 1669.
- VI. Edward, *d.* in 1645.
- VII. Augustine, *d.* young.
- VIII. George, of Cannock, in Staffordshire.

- I. Elizabeth.

William Gatacre *d.* in 1615, and was *s.* by his son,

JOHN GATACRE, esq. of Gatacre, who *m.* Mary, daughter of William Polwhele, esq. of Polwhele, and by her, who died in 1667, had issue,

i. THOMAS, his heir.
ii. William, of Shipley.
iii. Jerome, *b.* in 1658.

i. Penelope, died an infant.
ii. Margaret-Frances, *d.* in 1685.
iii. Catharine, living in 1669.
iv. Anne, *m.* prior to 1667.

John Gatacre died in 1667, was buried at Claverley, and *s.* by his son,

THOMAS GATACRE, esq. of Gatacre, *b.* in 1641, who *m.* Sarah, daughter of Sir Walter Acton, bart. of Aldenham, and had issue,

i. THOMAS, his heir.
ii. EDWARD, successor to his brother.
iii. George, died unm. in 1739.
iv. Jerome, died unm. in 1740.

i. Sarah.
ii Mary.
iii. Catharine, *m.* in 1735, to William Eaves, of Claverley.
iv. Frances, died in 1731.
v. Elizabeth, *m.* in 1739, to Elias Deane, gent. of Farmcote.
vi. Jane, *m.* in 1718, to William Hall, of Stourbridge.

Thomas Gatacre died in 1707, was buried at Claverley, and *s.* by his son,

THOMAS GATACRE, esq. of Gatacre, *b.* in 1676, who was killed by a fall from his horse in 1734. He died unm. and was *s.* by his brother,

EDWARD GATACRE, esq. of Gatacre, *b.* in 1680, who *m.* 3rd October, 1734, Margaret, eldest daughter of Benjamin Yate, gent. of Ludstone, and dying in 1747, left, with a daughter, Sarah, who died unm. 24th July, 1787, a son and successor,

EDWARD GATACRE, esq. of Gatacre, *b.* 11th September, 1735, who *m.* in 1767, Mary Pitchford, of the family of Pitchford, of Pitchford, and dying 21st August, 1821, was succeeded by his only child, the present EDWARD GATACRE, esq. of Gatacre.

*Arms*---Quarterly gu. and erm. on the second and third three piles of the first, on a fesse az. five bezants.

*Crest*---A raven ppr.

*Estate*---Gatacre, parish of Claverley, Salop, by grant from EDWARD the Confessor.

*Seat*---Gatacre.

## Family of Burley.

The Burleys, who formerly wrote themselves Boerley, derived the name from Burley, in Herefordshire, which they held under their superior lords, the Mortimers, and made a considerable figure for several generations. Walter Burley, one of the first fellows of Merton College, was a younger son or grandson of Sir Simon de Burlega, knight, who appears a subscribing witness to a deed of Ralph de Mortimer, who died in 1247. In an age when learned men prided themselves upon abstruseness and subtilty, Walter Burley obtained the honourable appellation of the *plain* and the *perspicuous Doctor*—qualities which eminently fitted him for the instruction of youth, and procured for him the important office of preceptor to the Prince of Wales, afterwards EDWARD III. wherein he conducted himself so meritoriously, that the King selected him to superintend the education of his son, the Black Prince. This probably enabled him to introduce at court his relation, another Sir Simon de Burley, esteemed one of the most accomplished men of his age, and as such appointed governor of the young prince, afterwards *King* RICHARD II. Sir Simon de Burley, and his two brothers, Sir Richard and Sir John, "men of worth and valour," are mentioned amongst the officers despatched by the Black Prince in 1366 to escort Don Pedro the cruel, the deposed King of Castile, from his asylum at Corrunna to Bordeaux. He is also mentioned, on the same authority, as one of the gallant cavaliers who volunteered their services to accompany Sir Thomas Felton on his adventurous exploit to gain intelligence in the enemies' quarters, which terminated in the death or captivity of them all. Sir Simon must have been of the number of those made prisoners on this occasion, so characteristic of the chivalrous spirit of the age. He was a younger son, and therefore what the historian, Knighton, says, that his patrimony did not exceed twenty marks, may possibly have been true, as the family estates were enjoyed by his elder brother; but, by the favour of his sovereign, wealth and honours were lavishly poured upon him. In the first year of RICHARD II. being already a knight, he was appointed keeper of Windsor castle for life. In the next year, Laustephan castle was confirmed to him. In 1380, Simon de Burley, chamberlain, was one of the King's commissioners to treat with the German Princes. In 1382, when he is styled Under-Chamberlain of the King, he was constituted master of the falcons, and keeper of the royal mews at Charing, with a fee of elevenpence a day, and received grants of the manor of Parrock, in Kent, and castle Emlyn, in Kermerdin; next year, of Leyborne castle, in Kent, late Juliana's de Leyborne; and the year after, that of liberties at his castle of Lennalx, in Herefordshire. In 1385, he was one of the executors of Joan, Princess of Wales, the King's mother. In 1386, he had a grant of Castle Frome, in the same county, forfeited by the felony of Lady Deveros. He was also warden of the Cinque Ports, constable of Dover castle, privy counsellor, knight banneret, and knight of the garter.

In so turbulent a reign as that in which Sir Simon de Burley flourished, he could not be neutral, or hope to escape uninjured. Walsingham represents him and Richard Styry as two of those who prejudiced the King against the Earl of Arundel, but Walsingham writes with a manifest leaning to the "Opposition." On the other hand, Carte, the perpetual advocate of the legitimate Sovereign, represents him as a victim to his affection for the King, and attachment to the constitution.

The *truth* seems to be, that the King was weak, with a strong desire for despotic power; his uncles, imperious and factious. Amongst them all, Sir Simon was brought to the block, May 5th, 1388; and in the same year, the Archbishop of Canterbury had a grant of the parks of Langley and Elmham, in Kent, which accrued to the Crown by virtue of his attainder. The judgment against him was reversed in the following reign—a fair presumption, says Mr. Hallam, of its injustice. Sir Simon's brother, John, was also a knight of the garter, and, besides his eldest son, William, who was seated at Burley, had two other sons, Richard, an eminent man in his day, K.G. marshall of the field, and privy counsellor to John of Gaunt, whom he accompanied into Spain, and died there the same year his uncle was beheaded; and Sir Roger, father of John Burley, of Bromcroft Castle, sheriff of Salop in 1409, whose daughter, JOYCE, became the wife of JOHN de GATACRE, of Gatacre.

His son, William Burley, of Bromcroft, sheriff, in 1426, M.P. for Salop, and speaker of the House of Commons, left two daughters, his heirs,

Joan, *m.* first, to Sir Philip Chetwynd, of Ingestre, and secondly, to Sir Thomas Lyttleton, the celebrated author of the "Tenures."

Elizabeth, *m.* to Thomas Trussel, of Billesley, in Warwickshire.

## GRESLEY, OF NETHER-SEALE.

GRESLEY, WILLIAM-NIGEL, esq. of Nether-Seale Hall, in the county of Leicester, *b.* in March, 1806, *m.* in March, 1831, Georgina-Anne, second daughter of the late George Reid, esq. of the Island of Jamaica, and has issue,

I. THOMAS, *b.* 17th January, 1832.
II. Nigel, *b.* in August, 1834.

I. Louisa-Mary.

Mr. Gresley succeeded his father in October, 1829.

### Lineage.

This family, which is a branch of that seated at Drakelow, in Derbyshire, and now represented by SIR ROGER GRESLEY, bart. derives from NIGELL, younger son of Roger de Toena, standard-bearer of Normandy, who arrived in England with an elder brother, Robert, in the train of Duke WILLIAM; and at the time of the survey, held extensive possessions in the counties of Derby and Stafford, of which *Grasele* or GRESLEY in the former, where he fixed his abode, was one. From this gallant soldier, through a long line of distinguished individuals (*see* BURKE's *Peerage and Baronetage*), lineally descended

SIR GEORGE GRESLEY, knt. of Drakelow, who was created a BARONET in 1611. He *m.* Susanna, daughter of Sir Humphrey Ferrars, of Tamworth Castle, and had (with two daughters, Elizabeth, who died unmarried, and Dorothy, *m.* first, to Robert Milward, esq. and secondly, to Edward Wilmot, D.D.), a son,

THOMAS GRESLEY, esq. who *m.* in 1622, Bridget, daughter of Sir Thomas Burdet, bart. of Foremark, and dying in the lifetime of his father, December, 1642, left issue,

- I. THOMAS, his heir.
- II. George, *m.* in 1669, Jane, daughter of Thomas Nelson, esq. and died *s. p.*
- I. Frances, *m.* to John Whitehall, esq. of Pipe Ridware.
- II. Bridget, *m.* to Thomas Brome, esq.
- III. Katherine, *m.* to Richard Dyott, esq. of Lichfield.
- IV. Elizabeth, *m.* to Philip Trafford, esq. of Swithamley.
- V. Mary, *m.* to the Rev. John Harpur, of Little Over.

The eldest son,

SIR THOMAS GRESLEY, of Drakelow, succeeded his grandfather as second baronet, and marrying Frances, daughter and co-heir of Gilbert Morewood, of London and of Nether Seale, in the county of Leicester, regained the old family estate of Nether Seale, which had been alienated by his progenitor. By this lady he had issue,

- I. WILLIAM (Sir), third baronet of Drakelow, ancestor of the present SIR ROGER GRESLEY, bart. of Drakelow.
- II. THOMAS, of whom presently.
- III. Charles, of Dunstal, in Staffordshire, *m.* in 1695, Anne, daughter and co-heir of John Bott, esq. by Elizabeth Wolferstan, his wife (see vol. i. p. 188), and had three daughters, Elizabeth, *m.* first, to Thomas Bott, and secondly, to S. Beardsley, gent.; Frances, died unmar. and Anne, *m.* to Edward Mathew, gent. of Coventry.
- I. Frances, *m.* to William Inge, esq. of Thorpe Constantine. (See vol. i. p. 323.)
- II. Elizabeth, *d.* unmarried.
- III. Dorothy, *m.* to Thomas Ward.
- IV. Mary, *m.* to D. Watson, esq.
- V. Grace, *m.* to Robert Roby, esq. of Castle Donnington.
- VI. Anne, *d.* unmarried.
- VII. Katherine, } all *d.* unmarried.
- VIII. Lettice, }
- IX. Isabella, }
- X. Sarah, *m.* to Paul Belladon, esq. of Stapenhill.

Sir Thomas's second son,

THOMAS GRESLEY, esq. became seated at Nether Seale, in Leicestershire. He *m.* Elizabeth, daughter of John Lee, gent. of Ladyhole, in the county of Derby, and heir to her brother William, by whom, who *d.* in 1732, he had issue,

- I. LEE, his heir.
- II. JOHN, successor to his brother.
- III. James, in holy orders.
- IV. Robert, bapt. 6th October, 1717.
- I. Elizabeth.

The eldest son,

LEE GRESLEY, esq. of Nether Seale, barrister-at-law, dying unmarried, was *s.* by his brother,

JOHN GRESLEY, esq. of Nether Seale, who married first, Dorothy, daughter of John Wilcockson, of Wirksworth, in Derbyshire, and by her had issue,

- I. THOMAS, his heir.
- II. John, fellow of Emanuel College, and rector of Auler, in Somersetshire, died unmarried in 1795, aged fifty-eight.
- I. Elizabeth, *m.* to Samuel Ball, of Tamworth.

Mr. Gresley wedded, secondly, Mary Bradley, relict of Mr. Toplis, and had further issue,

- III. Charles, } who both *d. s. p.*
- IV. James, }
- V. William, of Tamworth and Liverpool, *m.* first, Anne, only daughter of the Rev. Richard Watkins, rector of Clifton Camville, and secondly, Mary, only daughter of — Annington, esq. of Twickenham, but died *s. p.* in 1797.
- VI. Robert, *d.* leaving issue.
- VII. Walsingham, *d.* unmarried.

The eldest son and successor,

THE REV. THOMAS GRESLEY, D.D. patron and rector of Seale, *m.* first, Elizabeth, daughter of William Vincent, esq. and by that lady, who died in 1769, had issue,

- I. WILLIAM, his heir.
- II. Thomas, rector of Hinton, and vicar of Polesworth.
- III. Richard, of Stowe House, Staffordshire, barrister-at-law, *b.* 9th August, 1766, *m.* first, in 1800, Caroline, youngest daughter of the late Andrew Grote, esq. of Blackheath, and by her, who died 1st October, 1817, had
  1. William, in holy orders, *b.* 16th March, 1801.
  2. Richard-Newcombe, of the Middle Temple, *b.* 30th June, 1804.
  3. Francis, in the Hon. East India Company's Military Service, *b.* 5th May, 1807.
  4. Andrew, *b.* 22nd January, 1814.

1. Caroline.
2. Elizabeth.

Mr. Richard Gresley wedded, secondly, 5th December, 1820, Mary, widow of Robert Drummond, esq. of Megginch Castle, in the county of Perth, and daughter of the Rev. Joseph Phillimore, rector of Orton on the Hill.

I. Elizabeth, *d.* 28th Nov. 1792, aged twenty-nine.
II. Mary.

Dr. Gresley wedded, secondly, Elizabeth Wilkes, relict of William Pycroft, esq. of Over Seale, but had no other surviving issue. He *d.* 18th April, 1785, and was *s.* by his son,

THE REV. WILLIAM GRESLEY, B.A. of Nether Seale, patron and rector of Seale, who *m.* first, 5th May, 1798, Louisa-Jane, daughter of Sir Nigel Gresley, bart. of Drakelow, and had issue,

I. WILLIAM-NIGEL, his heir.

I. Louisa-Elizabeth, *m.* in July, 1826, to the Rev. Spencer Madan, vicar of Bath Easton, and canon residentiary of Lichfield Cathedral.

He *m.* secondly, 29th August, 1811, Mary, daughter of Thomas Thorpe, esq. of Over Seale, in Leicestershire, and had

II. John-Morewood.
III. Charles.
II. Frances-Mary.
III. Harriet.
IV. Maria.

Mr. Gresley died 3rd October, 1829, and was *s.* by his eldest son, the present WILLIAM NIGEL GRESLEY, esq. of Nether Seale.

*Arms*—Vaire ermine and gu.

*Crest*—A lion passant ermine, armed, langued, and collared gu.

*Estates*—In Leicestershire.

*Seat*—Nether Seale Hall.

## FREWEN-TURNER, OF COLD-OVERTON.

TURNER-FREWEN, THOMAS, esq. of Cold-Overton, in the county of Leicester, *b.* 26th August, 1811, *m.* 4th October, 1832, Anne, youngest child of W. Wilson Carus Wilson, esq. of Casterton Hall, in Westmoreland, and has a daughter,

Mary.

Mr. Frewen-Turner succeeded his father 1st February, 1829, and is knight of the shire for Leicester.

### Lineage.

The Frewens, a family of considerable antiquity, were seated, at a very remote period, in the county of Worcester: in 1473, we find Richard Frewen, one of the bailiffs of Worcester, and another Richard Frewen, prior of Great Malvern. A third Richard Frewen and his wife are represented in stained glass in one of the abbey windows, and were great benefactors to the monastery. In the church at Hanley Castle there is, likewise, a monument to Richard Frewen, who was buried in 1584, and his son, Francis, in 1606.

The immediate ancestor of the present family of the Frewens,

JOHN FREWEN, came out of Worcestershire, where he was born about the year 1560: he settled at Northiam, in Sussex, of which place he was rector more than fifty years: he was a puritan, and author of several works against the Catholics. He *d.* in 1628, leaving, with other issue,

I. ACCEPTED, who was born in Kent, educated in the free school at Canterbury, became a student, and soon after, about the beginning of 1604, in his sixteenth year, a demy of

Magdalen College; where, making great proficiency in logic and philosophy, he was elected probat, fellow of that house, about St. Mary Magdalen's day, *anno* 1612, being then master of arts. At that time he entered into the sacred function, and became a frequent preacher, being puritanically inclined. In 1622, he attended in the court of *Prince* CHARLES, while he was in Spain courting the infanta; and, in 1625, he was made chaplain in ordinary to the king. In 1626, he was elected president of his college, and in the next year proceeded in divinity. In 1628 and 1629, he executed the office of vice-chancellor of the university of Oxford; and, on the 13th September, 1631, being then, or about that time, prebendary of Canterbury, was installed dean of Gloucester, upon the removal of Dr. George Warburton thence to the deanery of Wells. In 1638 and 1639, upon the solicitations of Dr. Laud, archbishop of Canterbury and chancellor of this university, Dr. Frewen again served the office of vice-chancellor; and, on the 17th of August, 1643, he was chosen by his majesty to succeed Dr. Wright in the see of Lichfield and Coventry; but the times being then much disturbed, he was not consecrated until the next year, when the solemnity was performed in the chapel of Magdalen College by the archbishop of York, and the bishops of Worcester, Oxford, Salisbury, and Peterborough. This preferment being then however but little better than titular, the hierarchy having been about that time silenced, he retired to London, and lived there, and elsewhere, among his relations for several years. At length, after the restoration of *King* CHARLES II. he was elected to the see of York on the 22nd September, translated 4th October, and enthronized in the person of Tob. Wickham, prebendary of that church on the 11th of the same month, *anno* 1660. The see of Lichfield being also vacant for about a year, in expectation that Mr. Richard Baxter would take it, (for the king intended it for him conditionally he would conform), Dr. Frewen had the benefit of that too, all the fines for renewing, and for the filling up lives, to his very great profit, beside what he got from York. At length Mr. Baxter, the coryphæus of the presbyterian party, refusing it, lest he, in a high manner, should displease the brethren, it was offered to Dr. Richard Baylie, president of St. John's College, and dean of Sarum, who had been a very great sufferer for the king's cause; but he refusing it, because Dr. Frewen had skimmed it, it was conferred on Dr. John Hacket, of Cambridge. Dr. Frewen, who was accounted a general scholar, and a good orator, but hath nothing extant, only a Latin oration, with certain verses on the death of Prince Henry (for his Moral Philosophy Lectures are not yet made public), died at his manor of Bishops Thorp, near York, on the 28th of March, in sixteen hundred sixty and four, and was buried on the third day of May following, under the great east window of the cathedral church of St. Peter, in York.

It is related of Dr. Accepted Frewen, that, when chaplain to the Earl of Bristol, ambassador at the Spanish court, he was introduced to Prince Charles, who had arrived at Madrid to visit the infanta, and that he preached a sermon before his royal highness, from the text 1 Kings, xiii. 21st verse, which is still extant, and which is said to have had such an effect on the prince that he broke off the intended match.

II. Thankfull, secretary to the Lord Keeper Coventry, *d.* unm. 30th November, 1656.

III. John, who succeeded his father in the rectory of Northiam, where he died in 1658, leaving issue. "The Rev. Thankfull Frewen, one of his grandsons," says Nicholls' History of Leicestershire, "was rector of Northiam above fifty-six years, and died 9th September, 1749. Of this branch of the Frewen family was Charles Frewen, esq. of Clewer, near Windsor, only son of Charles Frewen, esq. deputy clerk of the crown, and Brunswick herald. He was *b.* 23rd January, 1733, and *d.* without issue, 12th October, 1791. Of the same branch also was Edward Frewen, D.D. of St. John's College, Cambridge."

IV. STEPHEN, of whom presently.

I. Mary, *m.* to John Bigg.

The fourth son,

STEPHEN FREWEN, esq. *b.* in 1600, was a merchant and alderman of London, where he realized a considerable fortune. He *m.* Catherine, daughter and heiress of George Scott, esq. of Conghurst, in Kent, from whom he inherited large property in that county. Mr. Alderman Frewen subsequently purchased extensive estates in Sussex, and died at his seat, Brickwall House, in 1679, leaving an only son,

THOMAS FREWEN, esq. of Brickwall House, M.P. for the borough of Rye, *b.* in 1630, who *m.* Judith, daughter and heiress of John Wolferstone, esq. by whom he acquired estates at Putney, in Surrey, and had a son, EDWARD (Sir), his heir. He wedded, secondly, Bridget, daughter of Sir Thomas Layton, of Brafferton Hall and Sigston Castle, in the county of York, by whom (who eventually became heiress to her brother, Sir Thomas Layton) he had two sons and one daughter, viz.

- LAYTON, who inherited his mother's estates in Yorkshire. He was father of
  - LAYTON, successor to his cousin, Thomas Frewen, esq.
- John, M.A. rector of Sidbury, in Devon, *m.* Rachel, youngest daughter of Richard Stevens, esq. of Culham, Berks, and had issue,
  - THOMAS, successor to his cousin, Layton.
  - John, M.A. rector of Tortworth, Gloucestershire, *b.* in 1712, left a daughter, Selina.
  - Bridget, *b.* in 1704, died unm.
  - Rachel, *m.* to Simon Knight, esq. of Rugby.
  - Mary, *m.* to the Rev. Stanley Burrough, M.A. rector of Tapcote.
- Mary, *m.* to Henry Turner, esq. of Cold Overton, in Leicestershire, serjeant-at-law.

Mr. Frewen espoused, thirdly, Jane, Lady Wymondesold, relict of Sir Daws Wymondesold, and daughter of Sir Robert Croke, of Haynam, in Gloucestershire. He *d.* in 1702, and was *s.* by his son,

SIR EDWARD FREWEN, of Brickwall House, M.P. for Rye, who received the honour of knighthood at the coronation of *King* JAMES II. He *m.* Selina, daughter of John Godschall, of East Sheen, in Surrey, and by her, who died in 1714, left at his decease, in 1723, aged sixty-two, with a daughter, Selina, *m.* to John Turner, esq. of Cold Overton, a son and heir,

THOMAS FREWEN, esq. of Brickwall House, M.P. for Rye, *b.* in 1688, who *m.* Martha, only daughter of Henry Turner, esq. of Cold Overton, and by her, who died in 1752, left at his decease, in 1738, a son and successor,

THOMAS FREWEN, esq. of Brickwall House, *b.* in 1716, at whose decease, unm. in 1766, his estates in Kent and Sussex devolved on his cousin,

LAYTON FREWEN, esq. of Brickwall House and Brafferton Hall, who assumed the surname and arms of TURNER on succeeding to the Leicestershire property of his cousin, John Turner, esq. of Cold Overton. He died without issue, in 1777, was buried at Brafferton, in Yorkshire, and *s.* by his cousin-german,

THE REV. THOMAS FREWEN, rector of Sapcote, in Leicestershire, who took in consequence the name of TURNER. This gentleman, *b.* in 1708, died at Cold Overton Hall in 1791, and was *s.* by his son,

JOHN FREWEN-TURNER, esq. of Cold Overton, M.P. for Athlone, *b.* in 1755, high sheriff for Leicestershire in 1791, who married, and had issue,

- THOMAS, his heir.
- Charles-Hay.
- John.
- Selina.

Mr. Frewen Turner died in 1829, was buried at Cold Overton, and *s.* by his son, the present THOMAS FREWEN-TURNER, esq. of Cold Overton.

*Arms*—Quarterly, 1st and 4th, erm. on a cross sa. five millrinds arg. for TURNER; 2d and 3d, erm. four barrulets az. a demi-lion passant in chief of the second.

*Estates*—In Leicestershire, Sussex, &c.

*Seats*—Cold Overton Hall, Leicestershire, and Brickwall House, Sussex.

### Family of Turner.

HENRY TURNER, of Cold Overton, inherited the Leicestershire estates from his father, who had realized a large fortune in trade, and purchased the property from the St. Johns. Mr. Turner married, as already stated, Mary Frewen, and had, with a daughter, Martha, the wife of Thomas Frewen, esq. a son,

JOHN TURNER, esq. of Cold Overton, who wedded his cousin, Selina, daughter of Sir Edward Frewen, knt. and dying without issue, devised his estates to his cousin, Layton Frewen, esq. of Brafferton.

# DEVENISH-MEARES, OF MEARES COURT.

**MEARES-DEVENISH, WILLIAM**, esq. of Meares Court, in the county of Westmeath, *b.* in 1758, *m.* 21st September, 1791, Deborah, daughter of Joseph Coghlan, esq. of Kilumney, in the county of Cork, and has issue,

JOHN, who *m.* in 1831, Maria, daughter of Charles Kelly, esq. of Charleville, in Westmeath.
Matthew, in holy orders, *m.* in 1821, Augusta, daughter of the late Charles Devenish, esq. of Dublin.

Catherine, *m.* in 1813, to the Rev. Frederick A. Potter, rector of Rathconrath.
Mary-Anne.

This gentleman, whose patronymic is DEVENISH, succeeded to Meares Court upon the demise of his aunt, Mrs. Gouldsbury, in 1811, and assumed in consequence the additional surname and arms of MEARES. He is a magistrate for the county of Westmeath.

## Lineage.

The MEARES, of Meares Court, came from Corsby, in Wiltshire, where the family had been settled from the year 1341. The name, originally DELAMARE, became, in process of time, Le Meares, and MEARES. The *Le* was first omitted by LEWIS, whose eldest son, *b.* at Corsby, married Mary Rochford, of Killbryde (of the Rochford family, of which was the Earl of Belvedere), and was grandfather of

LEWIS MEARES, esq. *b.* at Corsby, in 1625, who acquired, about the year 1647, the estate of Meares Court, where his descendants have since constantly resided. He *m.* in Dublin, *anno* 1648, Mary Palmer, and had, with other issue, a son and successor,

LEWIS MEARES, esq. *b.* in Dublin, in 1651, who wedded, 27th January, 1678, Elizabeth, daughter of Capt. John Jones, second son of Dr. Henry Jones, Lord Bishop of Meath, and had several sons and daughters. His eldest son,

LEWIS MEARES, esq. of Meares Court, in the county of Westmeath, *b.* there 7th August, 1682, *m.* 17th December, 1705, Catherine, eldest daughter of John Wakeley, esq. of Ballyburley, in the King's County, and was *s.* by his son,

JOHN MEARES, esq. of Meares Court, *b.* 28th May, 1709, who married in November, 1729, Sarah, daughter of Arthur Magan, esq. of Togherstown, in Westmeath, and had, with six daughters, one son,

JOHN MEARES, esq. of Meares Court, *b.* 4th June, 1742, who *m.* 30th May, 1771, Mary, second daughter of — Vandeleur, esq. of Kilrush, in the county of Clare, and *d.* without issue, 9th October, 1790, when his sisters became his co-heirs. The eldest of those ladies,

CATHERINE MEARES, espoused John Devenish esq. of Portlik, in Westmeath, and had eight sons and five daughters. The third son, William, inherited Meares Court, in 1811 (after the demise of the six sisters of the late John Meares, esq.), and having assumed the surname of MEARES, is the present WILLIAM DEVENISH MEARES, esq. of Meares Court.

*Arms*—Arg. a ship with three masts, sails furled, shrouded sa.

*Crest*—A king-fisher ppr.

*Motto*—Omnia providentiæ committo.

*Estates*—In Westmeath, Ireland.

*Town Residence*—Gardiner Street, Dublin.

*Seat*—Meares Court, in the county of Westmeath.

# O'NEILL, OF BUNOWEN CASTLE.

**O'NEILL, AUGUSTUS-JOHN,** esq. of Bunowen Castle, in the county of Galway, a magistrate for that county, and late member in parliament for the borough of Kingston-upon-Hull, *b.* 22nd June, 1792, succeeded to the estates on the death of his father, 8th April, 1830, *m.* January, 1829, Elizabeth, daughter of Robert Bellamy, of Sandford, esq. and has issue,

CHARLES-JOHN-MAITLAND, *b.* 20th December, 1830.

Charlotte-Augusta-Elizabeth.

## Lineage.

NIAL the Great, called Nial of the Nine Hostages, monarch of Ireland in the latter part of the fourth century, had eight sons; the four elder were princes in Ulster, and were called, from their great ancestor, the Northern Hii Nials; the four younger were chieftains in Leinster, and were called the Southern Hii Nials. From the time of Nial to the accession of Brian the Great, in 1002, the throne of Ireland was exclusively possessed by the descendants of Nial. Ergan, his eldest son, was progenitor of the house of O'Neill, so distinguished in the history of Ireland, which continued in enjoyment of the principality of Ulster until the reign of JAMES I. Henry VIII. induced Conn, the then prince, to surrender his name of O'Neill, and created him, in lieu thereof, Earl of Tyrone. His grandson, Hugh, resumed that princely title, and, as the O'Neill, carried on a successful war against the English crown during the entire reign of *Queen* ELIZABETH. The principal line of this branch of the Niall family became extinct in the time of CHARLES I. Connel, the second son of Nial the Great, was ancestor of the O'Donnels, who were, under the O'Neills, chieftains of Tyrconnel, until JAMES I. made Rorie, the then chieftain, Earl of Tyrconnel. He was afterwards attainted and fled to Spain, where he was created Condé of Tyrconnel, by PHILIP III. He and his descendants enjoyed the highest rank in that kingdom until the family became extinct, about the year 1693. FIACHA, the fifth son of Nial the Great, was ancestor of the M'Geoghegans, who were heads of the Southern Hii Nials, and chieftains of Moycashell, or Kinelagh, a district now comprising the western part of the county of Westmeath, and many adjoining lands. Geraldus Cambrensis states, that the M'Geoghegans were princes of Moycashell, on the invasion of the English in the time of HENRY II. Their vicinity to the pale brought them into constant collision with the English authorities in Ireland, and they are frequently proclaimed as the king's Irish enemies, and frequently summoned to his assistance as his friends. The M'Geoghegans are included in most of the royal writs for military aid, or of credence to officers; and in that of 9th EDWARD III. the then M'Geoghegan is ranked amongst the chief of the Irish who were requested to join the king in an expedition against Scotland. O'Neill, of Ulster, O'Conor, of Connaught, O'Malaghlan, of Meath, and eight other native princes, are named with M'Geoghegan in this writ.

In the time of HENRY VIII.

ROSSE M'GROGHEGAN, the then M'Geoghegan, and chieftain of Kinelagh, or Moycashell, entered into a treaty with Lord Leonard Grey, Viscount Graney, the king's deputy in Ireland, by which, as chieftain of his nation and territory, he agreed to bear allegiance to the King of England, to serve him against all his enemies, and to aid him with certain forces when called upon. This treaty bears date 28th November, 29th HENRY VIII. Rosse was *s.* by his son,

CONNOR, the M'Geoghegan and chieftain of Moycashell. He had two legitimate sons,

I. CONLAGH, his successor.

II. HUGH, who became heir to his brother,

and an illegitimate son, called

Rosse M'Geoghegan.

On the death of Connor, the territory was divided; Conlagh succeeded to Moycashell, and Hugh obtained Castletown. Conlagh had no issue, and surrendered his estates to Queen Elizabeth, on condition that she would re-grant them, with a limitation, in default of male issue to himself, to his nephew, Niel, the son of the illegitimate Rosse. This re-grant passed, and

HUGH was thereby deprived of his inheritance. On the death of his brother, however, he became chief of his nation and head of his branch of the family of Nial the great. He *m.* Ellinor, daughter of Walter Tirrel, of Clunmeagh, in Westmeath, and dying 10th June, 1622, left issue by her, besides other children,

ARTHUR, his successor, the last M'Geoghegan and chieftain of the family. During the civil war, he rendered himself conspicuous for his zeal and fidelity in the cause of CHARLES I. for which, on the reduction of Ireland by Cromwell, he was deprived of all his estates, the inheritance of his ancestors for so many centuries, which were granted to adventurers of the Cromwellian party, to whom they were confirmed on the restoration. His wife, during the war, saved some soldiers of Cromwell's army, who had been defeated in an engagement with her husband's troops, from the fury of her own people; and, in gratitude for this service, a grant was made to her of the Bunowen estate, in the county of Galway, which had been taken from the O'Flaherties; and thus were the M'Geoghegans transplanted from Westmeath into Connaught. Arthur married Julia, called in Irish, Giles, daughter of James M'Coghlan, of the Hill, in the King's County, esq. by whom he had

I. HUGH, who died during the war, leaving a son, Edward, who died *s. p.*
II. EDWARD, to whom, and to the heirs male of whose body, the Bunowen estate was limited, upon the death of Julia.

Arthur was killed in battle, and was *s.* by his son,

EDWARD GEOGHEGAN, esq. of Bunowen, who *m.* Margaret, daughter of James Dillon, esq. of Ballymoloy, in Westmeath, by whom he had,

CHARLES GEOGHEGAN, esq. of Bunowen Castle, who, by Mary, daughter of Valentine Blake, esq. of Drum, in the county of Galway, had a son,

EDWARD GEOGHEGAN, esq. of Bunowen, who intermarried with Cecilia, daughter of Richard Blake, esq. of Ardfry, in the county of Galway. Mr. Blake was descended from Richard Blake, speaker of the Supreme Council of Kilkenny from 1642 to 1651, and, by his son, was grandfather of Joseph, first Lord Wallscourt, and by his daughter, of the Countesses of Kerry and Louth, and the Viscountess Kingsland. Edward Geoghegan *d.* 9th September, 1765, leaving issue,

RICHARD GEOGHEGAN, esq. of Bunowen, a gentleman celebrated for his literary attainments, and as the first person who devoted himself to the reclamation of the waste lands in the remote districts of Connemarra. Mr. Geoghegan *m.* Mary-Anne, daughter of John Bodkin, esq. of Auna, in the county of Galway, and had,

I. JOHN DAVID, his successor.
II. Connolly, an officer in foreign service, who died *s. p.*

Richard died in July, 1800, and was *s.* by his son,

JOHN DAVID GEOGHEGAN, esq. of Bunowen Castle, *b.* 4th December, 1750. Mr. Geoghegan was member in the Irish Parliament until 1799, and was one of the delegates of the celebrated Irish volunteers. From the time of the extinction of the senior branch of the O'Neills, in the reign of CHARLES I. it had been the anxious desire of the successive representatives of the M'Geoghegan family, as the undoubted heads of the Southern Hii Nials, and the descendants of Fiacha, son of the great Niall, to assume the family name of O'Neill; but the attainders and forfeitures against them, and the persecutions which they, in common with the greater portion of the ancient nobility and gentry of Ireland, suffered for so many generations, rendered any attempt to effectuate their desire as fruitless as it would have been dangerous. Times, however, changed: Mr. Geoghegan held a high and confidential office under the Crown, that of accountant-general of the Court of Exchequer, and had been the chosen representative of the people; he was, therefore, no longer debarred from making the application; he accordingly petitioned *King* GEORGE III.; and his majesty being satisfied, as he states in his privy-seal letter, dated at Whitehall, February 13, 1808, that Mr. Geoghegan was paternally descended from Nial, of the nine hostages, granted him his royal license and authority to take and use the surname of O'Neill. Mr. Geoghegan, who thus became O'Neill, married Gertrude, daughter and co-heir of Robert Fetherstone, esq. of White Rock House, in the county of Longford, and had surviving issue,

I. AUGUSTUS-JOHN, his heir.
II. Charles-Fetherstone, *b.* December, 1802.

I. Gertrude, married to Thomas Fleetwood Walker, esq. of Elm Hall, in the county of Kildare, by whom she had one son and one daughter.

Mr. O'Neill died 8th April, 1830, and was *s.* by his elder son, AUGUSTUS JOHN O'NEILL, esq. now of Bunowen.

*Estates*—In Galway.
*Seat*—Bunowen Castle.

# COLLINS, OF HATCH BEAUCHAMP.

COLLINS, HENRY-POWELL, esq. of Hatch Court, in the county of Somerset, *b.* in 1776, captain of the 4th dragoon guards, *m.* at Deanlizard, in Dorsetshire, 4th June, 1800, Dorothea, daughter of Sir John Lethbridge, bart. of Sandhill Park, and had an only child,

DOROTHEA-JACINTHA, born at Harnish House, near Chippenham, Wilts, *m.* at Hatch Beauchamp, in 1822, to William Gore Langton, esq. eldest son of Colonel Gore Langton, of Newton Park, M.P. for Somersetshire, and dying 26th March, 1827, left an only son.

Captain Collins, who *s.* his brother, in 1807, is a magistrate and deputy-lieutenant for Somersetshire, was high sheriff of that county in 1827, and M.P. for Taunton in 1818.

## Lineage.

JOHN COLLINS, esq. of Hatch Court in the county of Somerset, a magistrate, deputy-lieutenant, and high sheriff for that shire, married at St. Mary-le-bone, London, 25th November, 1769, Jane, daughter of — Langford, esq. of the county of Hertford, and by her, who died at Belmont, 18th February, 1808, had issue,

I. JOHN-RAW, his heir.

II. HENRY-POWELL, successor to his brother.

III. Bonner, of Belmont, in Somersetshire, captain of the Ilminster yeomanry cavalry, *b.* in 1779, *m.* at Lyme-Regis, in Dorsetshire, 1st January, 1805, Sarah-Susannah, daughter of the Rev. Mr. Cove of Teinmouth, in Devon, and by her, who died 14th October, 1820, has three daughters.

I. Jane, *m.* at Henlade, 17th June, 1797, to Richard Henry Tolson, esq. of Woodland Lodge, Somersetshire, major in the 2nd life guards, and dying 30th December, 1807, left an only child, Jane Dinness Tolson, *m.* to Richard Harcourt Symons, esq. of Fairfield Lodge, Dorsetshire, second son of the late Thomas Symons, esq. of the Mynde Park, Herefordshire, and has issue.

II. Ann, *m.* at Bath, in 1799, to John Allen Cooper, esq. lieutenant 1st life guards, and had issue,

John Cooper, *b.* in 1801, lieutenant in the East Indies.

Augustus Cooper, *b.* in 1804, lieutenant R.N.

Charles Cooper, *b.* in 1808, lieutenant Bengal army.

Frederick Cooper, *b.* in 1810.

Henry Cooper, *d.* in 1831.

Ann Maria Cooper, *m.* in 1832, to Charles Baynton, esq. captain in the army.

Sophia Cooper, *m.* in 1832, to Lawrence Baynton, esq.

Mr. Collins died in 1792, was buried at Ilminster, and succeeded by his eldest son,

JOHN-RAW COLLINS, esq. of Hatch Court, *b.* in 1775, major of the Somerset fencible cavalry, a magistrate, deputy-lieutenant, and high sheriff for that county. He *m.* at Southampton, in 1796, Jemima, daughter of Francis Coleman, esq. of Sidmouth, and had an only child,

Jemima-Jane, *m.* to — Harvey, esq. of Langley Park, Bucks, and *d.* in 1827, leaving issue.

Major Collins *d.* in 1807, and was *s.* by his brother, the present HENRY-POWELL COLLINS, esq. of Hatch Beauchamp.

*Arms*—Gu. a crescent erm. between eight martlets arg.

*Crest*—A demi griffin or, armed gu.

*Motto*—Frangas non flectas.

*Estates*—In Somersetshire.

*Seat*—Hatch Court.

# POYNTZ, OF COWDRAY PARK.

**POYNTZ, WILLIAM-STEPHEN**, esq. of Cowdray Park, in Sussex, and of Midgham House, in the county of Berks, *b.* 20th January, 1770, *m.* 1st September, 1794, Hon. Elizabeth Mary Browne, sister and heir of Samuel, sixth Viscount Montague, and has issue,

- I. WILLIAM-MONTAGUE-BROWNE.
- II. Courtenay-John-Browne.

- I. Frances-Selina, *m.* to Lord Clinton.
- II. Elizabeth-Frances, *m.* to Hon. Frederick Spencer, R.N.
- III. Isabella, *m.* to the Marquess of Exeter.

Mr. Poyntz, who is a magistrate and deputy-lieutenant for the counties of Sussex and Hantz, succeeded his father in 1809.

## Lineage.

This family, and that of Clifford, spring from a common ancestor,

DROGO FITZ-PONS, who accompanied WILLIAM the *Conqueror* into England. He had two sons, Richard, of Clifford Castle, in Herefordshire, ancestor of the Earls of Cumberland, the Lords Clifford, of Chudleigh, &c. and

OSBERT FITZ-PONS, who was sheriff of Gloucester, 5th Stephen. He was great grandfather of

HUGH POYNTZ, Lord of Dodington, in Gloucestershire, who *m.* Julian, daughter of Hugh Bardolph, and one of the five nieces and heirs of Robert Bardolph; and left a son and successor,

HUGH POYNTZ, who, joining the revolted barons, had his lands in the counties of Somerset, Dorset, and Gloucester, seized by the crown in the 17th of JOHN, while he was himself imprisoned in the castle of Bristol. He *m.* Heloise, sister and co-heir of William Mallet, Baron of Cary Mallet, in the county of Somerset, and was *s.* by his son,

NICHOLAS POYNTZ, Lord of Carry Mallet, who, residing in Gloucestershire, had military summons from the crown to march against the Welsh in the 41st and 42nd HENRY III. but afterwards joined the other barons who took up arms against the king. He died in the 1st EDWARD I. and was *s.* by his son (by Elizabeth, his wife, daughter of William de la Zouch),

SIR HUGH POYNTZ, knt. who, being engaged in the wars of Wales, Gascony, and Scotland, was summoned to parliament as a BARON in 1295. His lordship wedded Margaret, daughter of Sir William Paveley, and, dying in 1307, was succeeded by his son,

NICHOLAS POYNTZ, second baron, summoned to parliament from 1309 to 1311. He *m.* first, Elizabeth, daughter of Eudo de Zouche, and had, by her, one son,

> HUGH, third baron, K.B. whose son, Sir NICHOLAS POYNTZ, fourth baron, *m.* Alianore, daughter of Sir John Erleigh, knt. and had two daughters, between whom the barony of POYNTZ fell into abeyance at his lordship's decease. The elder, Amicia, married John Barry, and the younger, Margaret, John Newborough.

Lord Poyntz espoused, secondly, Matilda, daughter and heir of Sir John Acton, of Iron Acton, in the county of Gloucester, by whom he left a son,

SIR JOHN POYNTZ, of Iron Acton, lord of that manor in right of his mother. He served the office of sheriff of Gloucestershire in 1363, and, marrying Elizabeth, daughter and co-heir of Sir Philip Clanvowe, had a son,

ROBERT POYNTZ, of Iron Acton, who succeeded his father in 1377, and was sheriff of Gloucestershire, 20th RICHARD II. He *m.* Catherine, daughter and co-heir of Thomas Fitz-Nichol, of the Berkeley family, and, dying 17th Henry VI. was *s.* by his son,

Nicholas Poyntz, of Iron Acton, who *m.* first, Elizabeth, daughter of Sir Edward Mill, of Harscomb, in Gloucestershire, and secondly, Elizabeth, daughter of Henry Hussey, of Harting, in Sussex. By the latter he had a daughter, Jane, *m.* to William Dodington, of Woodlands, in Wiltshire, and by the former, three sons, namely,

I. John, his heir.
II. Henry, who *m.* Eleanor, daughter and heir of William Bawdwin, of Northokenden, in Essex, and was ancestor of the family of Poyntz, seated in that county.*
III. Humphrey, died *s. p.*

Nicholas died in 1449, and was *s.* by his eldest son,

John Poyntz, of Iron Acton, who died in 1507, leaving by Alice, his wife, daughter of — Cox, of Skrynvrayth, in Monmouthshire, a son and successor,

Robert Poyntz, of Iron Acton, who was high sheriff of Gloucestershire in 1491, 1494, and 1500. He married Margaret, natural daughter of Anthony Wideville, Earl of Rivers, and had issue,

I. Anthony (Sir), of Iron Acton, high sheriff for Gloucestershire in 1522 and 1557, who *m.* Elizabeth, daughter and co-heir of Sir William Huddersfield, of Shillingford, in Devon, and dying 26th Henry VIII. was *s.* by his son,

Sir Nicholas Poyntz, of Iron Acton, sheriff in 1538 and 1544, who wedded Jane, daughter of Thomas Lord Berkeley, and left at his decease, 4 Phil. and Mary, a son and successor,

Sir Nicholas Poyntz, of Iron Acton, sheriff in 1569, who was made a Knight of the Bath at the coronation of Elizabeth. He *m.* first, Anne, daughter of Ralph Verney, of Penley, Bucks, and secondly, Margaret, daughter of Edward, third Earl of Derby. By the former he had a son,

Sir John Poyntz, knt. of Iron Acton, sheriff in 1591, who *m.* first, Ursula, daughter of Sir John Sydenham, of Brampton, in Somersetshire, and secondly, Elizabeth, daughter and heir of Alexander Sydenham. By the latter he had a son, Nicholas, knighted at the coronation of Charles II. and by the former, a successor,

Sir Robert Poyntz, of Iron Acton, likewise knighted at *King* Charles's coronation. This gentleman wrote a treatise in vindication of monarchy, and, dying in 1665, was buried with his ancestors in Acton church. He had two wives. By the first, Frances, daughter and co-heir of G. Gibbon, of Rohenden, in Kent, he had an only daughter, and by the second, Cicely Smyth, a son,

Sir John Poyntz, of Iron Acton, who wedded Anne, daughter of Robert Cæsar, esq. of Wellings, Herts, but, dying issueless in 1680, left his estate to his widow, from whom it was purchased by William Player, esq. after having continued with the ancestors of Sir John Poyntz for nearly six hundred years. Iron Acton passed from Mr. Player to Sir Samuel Astry, from him to Simon Harcourt, esq. then to Sir Philip Parker, and from him to Walter Long, esq. of South Wraxall.

---

* Henry Poyntz, by Eleanor Bawdwin, his wife, left, with two daughters, Agnes, *m.* to William Copdo, and Margaret, to John Fuller, a son and successor,

John Poyntz, esq. of Northokendon, in Essex, married Eleanor, daughter and co-heir of Sir John Dancote, and had one son, John, and two daughters, Matilda, *m.* to John Barrett, esq. of Alveley, and Margaret, to John de Bures, gent. His son and heir,

John Poyntz, esq. of Northokenden, wedded Maud, daughter and co-heir of William Perte, of Alveley, and was succeeded by his son,

William Poyntz, esq. of Northokenden, who *m.* Elizabeth, sister of Sir John Shaa, Lord Mayor of London, and dying in 1500, left a son and successor,

John Poyntz, esq. of Northokenden, who *m.* Anne, sister and heir of Isaac Sibley, of Bucks, but, dying issueless in 1558, was succeeded by his brother,

Thomas Poyntz, esq. of Northokenden, who, at the time of his decease, 5th May, 1562, was possessed of extensive estates in the county of Essex, which he held of the queen in free soccage by fealty. He *m.* Anne, daughter and co-heir of John Calva, esq. a German, and had, with other issue, a daughter, Susanna, wife of Sir Richard Saltonstall, and a son,

Sir Gabriel Poyntz, knt. of Northokenden, born in 1538, high sheriff of Essex in 1577 and 1589. He *m.* Etheldred, daughter of Peter Cutts, esq. of Arkesden, and widow of Ralph Latham, and dying in 1607, left an only daughter and heiress,

Catharine Poyntz, who conveyed the estate of Northokenden to her husband, Sir John Morice, knt. of Chipping Ongar, and it remained with their male descendants until the demise of Richard Poyntz, alias Morice, esq. in 1643, when it passed to the Lyttelton family.

II. JOHN, of whose line we have to treat.

III. Francis (Sir), died unmarried 18th HENRY VIII.

The second son,

JOHN POYNTZ, esq. wedded Catherine, daughter of Sir Matthew Browne, knt. of Beechworth Castle, in Surrey, living in 1530. (The descendants of this lady, as will be shown hereafter, upon the several demises of Ambrose, heir of Sir A. Browne, bart. who *d. v. p.* issueless, and Margaret, the wife of William Fenwick, in 1726, became the representatives of the elder branch of the family of Browne.) By her he left two sons,

I. MATTHEW, of Alderley, 42nd ELIZABETH, who *m.* Winefred, daughter and co-heir of Henry Wild, of Camberwell, in Surrey, and had, with several other children, one of whom Joan, married Robert Hale, of Alderley, a son and successor,

NICHOLAS, of Alderley, who married Anne, daughter of Maurice Berkeley, of Bruton, and had issue.

II. WILLIAM.

The second son,

WILLIAM POYNTZ, esq. was seated at Reygate, in the county of Surrey. He *m.* Elizabeth, daughter and co-heir of Thomas Newdigate, esq. of Newdigate, in the same shire, and left a son and successor,

JOHN POYNTZ, esq. of Reygate, who married Anne, daughter of John Sydenham, of Nympsfield, in the county of Gloucester, and was succeeded at his decease, in 1598, by his son,

NEWDIGATE POYNTZ, esq. who *d.* in 1643, leaving, by Sarah, his wife, daughter of Newdigate Foxley, esq. of Harringworth, in the county of Northampton, a son and successor,

WILLIAM POYNTZ, esq. of London, who married Jane, daughter of Joseph Morteage, of the same city, and had four sons, William, treasurer of the Excise, (who *m.* Mary, daughter of John Aston, esq. and left an only daughter, Anne, living in 1727, died unmarried); STEPHEN, of Midgeham; Deane, who died *s. p.*; and Joseph. The second son,

The Right Hon. STEPHEN POYNTZ, of Midgham, in Berkshire, was ambassador to the king of Sweden, and plenipotentiary at Soissons, in 1728. He *m.* Anna-Maria, daughter of Lewis Mordaunt, esq. grandson of John, Earl of Peterborough, and had issue,

WILLIAM, his heir.

Charles, D.D. prebendary of Durham, *d. s. p.*

Margaret-Georgina, *m.* to George, Earl Spencer, and *d.* in 1814, leaving one son, George-John, late Earl Spencer, and two daughters, Georgiana, Duchess of Devonshire, and Henrietta-Frances, Countess of Bessborough.

Louisa, *d.* young.

Mr. Poyntz was *s.* by his elder son,

WILLIAM POYNTZ, esq. of Midgham, who espoused, in 1762, Isabella, daughter of Kelland Courtenay, esq. of Panisford, Devon, and had issue,

WILLIAM-STEPHEN, his heir.

Mordaunt-Montagu, *d.* young.

Georgiana, *m.* to Lord John Townshend.

Louisa-Charlotte, *m.* to the Hon. and Rev. George Bridgeman.

Isabella-Henrietta, *m.* to Edmund, Earl of Cork and Orrery.

Carolina-Amelia, *m.* to the Hon. Sir Courtenay Boyle.

Mr. Poyntz *d.* in 1809, and was *s.* by his son, the present WILLIAM-STEPHEN POYNTZ, esq. of Midgham and Cowdray.

*Arms*—Barry of eight gu. and or. It appears from the roll of the siege of Karlaveroc, in 1300, that there had been a controversy between Fitz-Alan and Poyntz respecting their each bearing barry of eight:—

Le Beau Brian Fitz-Aleyne,
De courtoisey et de honneur pleyn,
I vi ov' banniere barrée,
De or et de gu. bein parèe,
Dont le chalenge estoit le poins
Par entre lui et Hue Points,
Ki portoit cel ni plus ni moins,
Dont mervielle avoint meinte et meins.

The Poyntz family quarter Clanvowe, Acton, Fitz-Nichol, Wydeville, Scales, Luxembourg, De Beaulx, Redvers, Beauchamp, Browne, and Courteney.

*Crest*—A cubit arm, erect, the fist clenched, pp. vested arg.

*Estates*—In Sussex and Berkshire.

*Seats*—Midgham House, Berks, and Cowdray Park, Sussex.

### Family of Browne.

SIR ANTHONY BROWNE, created a knight of the Bath at the coronation of RICHARD II., married, and had two sons, Sir Richard, his heir, and Sir Stephen, lord mayor of London in 1439. The elder

SIR ROBERT BROWNE, living *temp.* HENRY V., was father of

SIR THOMAS BROWNE, treasurer of the household to HENRY VI. and sheriff of Kent in 1444 and 1460. He *m.* Eleanor, daughter and sole heir of Sir Thomas Fitz-Alan, of

Beechworth Castle, brother of John, Earl of Arundel, and had issue,

I. GEORGE (Sir), his heir.

II. William, whose son removed to Tavistock. This line is extinct.

III. Robert (Sir), knt. *m.* Mary, daughter of Sir William Mallet, knt. and had an only daughter and heiress, Eleanor, wife, first, of Sir Thomas Fogge, and secondly, of Sir William Kempe.

IV. Anthony (Sir), standard-bearer of England, esquire of the body, governor of Queenboro' Castle, and constable of the castle of Calais. From this eminent person derive the LORDS MONTAGU, the heiress of which distinguished family, the Hon. ELIZABETH MARY BROWN, wedded WILLIAM STEPHEN POYNTZ. (See BURKE's *Extinct Peerage*).

I. Catherine, *m.* to Humphrey Sackville, of Buckhurst.

Sir Thomas was *s.* by his eldest son,

SIR GEORGE BROWNE, knt. of Beechworth Castle, sheriff of Kent in 1481, who espousing the cause of the Earl of Richmond, was included in the proclamation for apprehending the Duke of Buckingham and his associates, and being soon after taken, suffered decapitation in London *anno* 1483. He *m.* Elizabeth, daughter of Sir William Paston, and widow of Richard Lord Poynings, and was *s.* by his son,

SIR MATTHEW BROWNE, knt. of Beechworth Castle, sheriff of Surrey in 1496, living in 1530, who *m.* Fridiswide, daughter of Sir Richard Guilford, K.G. of Hempsted, in Kent, and had issue,

HENRY, who predeceased his father, leaving, by Catharine, his second wife, daughter of Sir William Shelley, of Michelgrove, a son,

THOMAS, successor to his grandfather.

Jane, *m.* to Sir Edward Bray. (See page 245.)

Catherine, *m.* to JOHN POYNTZ, esq. of Alderley, sheriff of Surrey 14th and 26th ELIZABETH, and from this marriage lineally descends the present WILLIAM STEPHEN POYNTZ, esq. of Cowdray.

Sir Matthew was *s.* by his grandson,

SIR THOMAS BROWNE, knt.* of Beechworth Castle, who *m.* Mabell, dau. and heir of Sir William Fitz-Williams, and had, with two daughters, Elizabeth, the wife of Robert Honywood, of Kent, and Jane, of Sir Oliff Leigh, of Addington, in Surrey, a son and successor,

SIR MATTHEW BROWNE, of Beechworth Castle, who *m.* Jane, daughter of Sir Thomas Vincent, of Stoke Dabernon, and dying in the *first* of JAMES I. was *s.* by his son,

SIR AMBROSE BROWNE, of Beechworth Castle, created a baronet in 1727, who *m.* Elizabeth, dau. of William Adam, esq. of Saffron Waldon, and *d.* in 1661, leaving issue, two sons, ADAM, his heir; and Ambrose, who predeceased his father unm., with two daughters, the elder *m.* to George Browne, esq. of Buckland, and the younger to — Jevon, esq. The surviving son,

SIR ADAM BROWNE, second baronet, of Beechworth, M.P. for Surrey, married Philippa, daughter of Sir John Cooper, bart. of Winbourn St. Giles, in Dorsetshire, and *d.* 3rd November, 1690, having had one son, Ambrose, who predeceased him unm. in 1688, and an only daughter and heiress,

MARGARET BROWNE, of Beechworth, who *m.* in 1691, William Fenwick, esq. high sheriff of Surrey in 1705, and *d.* issueless in 1726. Shortly after her decease, the estate of Beechworth was sold to Abraham Tucker, esq. and eventually descended to Sir Henry Paulet St. John Mildmay, who, in 1798, disposed of the mansion, manor, &c. to Henry Peters, esq. At the death of Mrs. Fenwick the representation of the family is stated to have devolved on the descendants of CATHARINE BROWNE, who wedded JOHN POYNTZ, esq.

* He *m.* secondly, Helen Harding, and was father, by her, of Richard Browne, esq. of Shingleton, in Kent.

# LEIGH, OF BARDON.

LEIGH, ROBERT, esq. of Taunton, *b.* in 1773, late captain 1st Somerset militia, and a deputy-lieutenant for that county.

## Lineage.

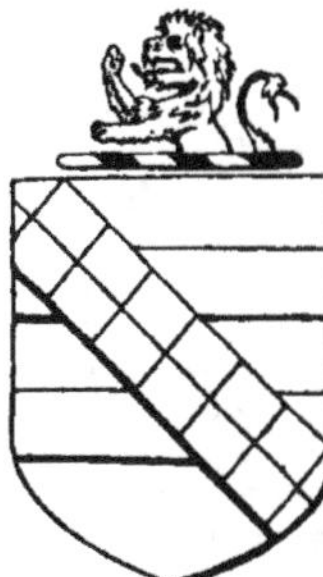

This is a branch of an ancient Devonshire family, Walter de Lega having, as appears by Sir William Pole's collections towards a description of Devon, held lands therein in the reign of HENRY II. Lysons, in the sixth volume of his Magna Britannia, in his account of families extinct since 1620, or removed out of the county, states, that "Leigh, of Ridge, in Bishop's Morchard, married the heiress of Ridge. Ten descents are described in the visitation of 1620, when there was male issue."

ROBERT LEIGH, a scion of the Leighs of Ridge, removed out of Devonshire, and settled at Bardon, in Somersetshire, *anno* 1595. His great grandson,

ROBERT LEIGH, of Bardon, married in 1674, Margaret, daughter of John Collard, of Spaxton, in the county of Somerset, a gentleman of good estate, to whom arms had been granted for his loyalty, after the restoration in 1666. Their eldest son,

ROBERT LEIGH, esq. of Bardon, married Elizabeth Treble, of Taunton, and was father of

WILLIAM LEIGH, esq. who wedded Rebecca Sanders, of Yeovil, whose mother was Susanna Dampier, of the Bruton family, and a relative of the celebrated navigator; by her he had issue,

I. William, lieutenant 4th reg. foot, *d.* unmarried.
II. ROBERT, of whom presently.

I. Rebecca, *m.* to George Beadon, of Oakford, Devonshire, brother of the late Bishop of Bath and Wells, and had issue.
II. Elizabeth, *m.* to Peter Gaye, esq. of Newton Bushell, Devonshire, and had issue.
III. Susanna, *d.* unmarried.
IV. Ann, *m.* to William Marshall, of London, Merchant, and *d. s. p.*

The second but eldest surviving son,

ROBERT LEIGH, esq. of Bardon, *m.* in 1770, Maria Bourget, a native of Berlin, and had five sons and one daughter, viz.

I. ROBERT, his heir.
II. William, now of Bardon, having purchased the estate from his elder brother, *m.* Frances-Wilson, eldest daughter of Thomas Oliver, esq. of London, and has two sons and five daughters. Robert, the elder son, wedded in 1828, Charlotte, third dau. of the late Samuel Cox, esq. of Beaminster, in Dorset.
III. Henry-James, of Taunton, who *m.* Miss Anne Whitmash Waters, of Blandford, in Dorsetshire.
IV. Frederick, who *m.* Anna Kennaway, of Exeter, niece of Sir John Kennaway, bart.
V. John, in holy orders, *d.* unmarried.

I. Mary, *m.* to the Rev. Robert Tripp.
II. Anne, *m.* first, to Montague Bere Baker Bere, esq. of Morebath, in Devon, secondly, to John Burgess, Karslake, esq. of the same county, and thirdly, to Richard C. Camper, esq. of Exeter.

Mr. Leigh *d.* in 1798, and was *s.* by his eldest son, the present ROBERT LEIGH, esq.

*Arms.*—Arg. two bars az. a bend compone or and gu.

*Crest*—A demi lion rampt. armed and langued gu.

*Motto*—Legibus antiquis.

*Estates*—In Somersetshire.

# MAULEVERER, OF ARNCLIFFE HALL.

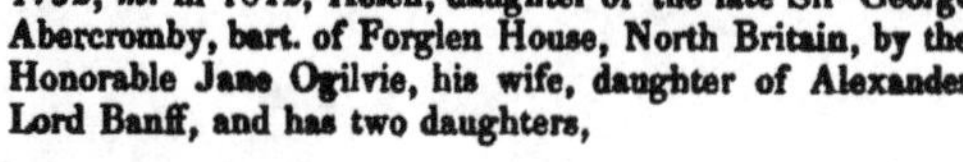

**MAULEVERER, WILLIAM,** esq. of Arncliffe Hall, in the county of York, *b.* in 1792, *m.* in 1812, Helen, daughter of the late Sir George Abercromby, bart. of Forglen House, North Britain, by the Honorable Jane Ogilvie, his wife, daughter of Alexander Lord Banff, and has two daughters,

JANE.
GEORGINA-HELEN.

This gentleman having succeeded, at the decease of his aunt, Miss Mary Mauleverer, in 1833, to the Mauleverer estates, changed, by act of Parliament, his patronymic "GOWAN" for the surname of "MAULEVERER."

Mr. Mauleverer is a magistrate and deputy-lieutenant for the North Riding. On the passing of the Reform Bill, he stood for the borough of South Shields, and although the defeated candidate, was chaired by the inhabitants and presented with a diamond ring, as a mark of their esteem and regret. In this year (1835) a subscription has been raised by some of his neighbours to present him with a piece of plate, for his exertions at the recent election for the North Riding.

## Lineage.

The name of this family in ancient writings is called MALUS-LEPORARIUS (*Mallevorer*), the bad hare-hunter, and tradition says, that a gentleman of Yorkshire, being to let slip a brace of greyhounds, to run for a considerable wager, so held them in swing that they were more likely to strangle themselves than kill the hare, when the designation was fixed upon the unskilful sportsman, and transmitted to his posterity. But Peter le Neve, Norroy, supposes it to be *Malus-operarius*, or the bad-worker; because that in Domesday Book is found, (title Essex, page 94) "terra Adami, filii Durandi de Malis operibus, in French Malouverer, which is easily varied to Mauleverer.

SIR RICHARD MAULEVERER, knt. came into England with the CONQUEROR, and was constituted master or ranger of the forests, chases, and parks, north of Trent. He was father of

SIR JOHN MAULEVERER, knt. who *m.* Bendreda, daughter of Sir Henry Hurst, knt. and had issue,

- NICHOLAS, his heir.
- John or Thomas, *m.* Cassandra, daughter of — Bridguile.
- Robert, *m.* Dionisia, daughter of Sir George Pierpoint, knt.

Sir John was *s.* by his son,

NICHOLAS MAULEVERER, who espoused Alice, daughter of Sir Thomas Grosvenor, knt. and had issue,

- ROBERT (Sir), his heir.

- Anne, *m.* to Sir Richard Yorke, knt.
- Mary, *m.* to Mr. Clapham.
- Margaret, *m.* to Mr. Strangwayes.
- Julian, *m.* to — Dove, of Utkinton.

The only son and heir,

SIR ROBERT MAULEVERER, was knighted, and, marrying Amisia, daughter of Sir John Trussell, left issue,

- JOHN, his heir.
- Richard, who *m.* (according to Thoresby) Frances Dyneley.
- Thomas, who *m.* Jane, daughter of Gerard Salvin, of North Duffield.

- Mary, *m.* to John Dyneley, esq.
- Anne, *m.* to Sir Gerard Salvin, of North Duffield, high sheriff of Yorkshire, and sometime escheator for the king, south of Trent. From this marriage descend the SALVINS of CROXDALE,

NEWBIGGIN, SUNDERLAND BRIDGE, &c. (See vol. i. p. 535).

Sir Robert was *s.* by his eldest son,

JOHN MAULEVERER, esq. living in the early part of the reign of EDWARD I. who *m.* Dorothy, daughter of Sir Ninian Markinfield, knt. and had three sons and two daughters, viz.

JOHN, his heir.
Richard, who *m.* a daughter of Sir John Sturley, knt. and was ancestor of the MAULEVERERS of Bramsley.
Thomas, who died issueless.

Isabel, *m.* to Sir Thomas Pigott, or Sir Thomas Bygod.
Jane, *m.* first, to Sir George Grey; and, secondly, to Sir George Penbruge, or Sir George Tray.

The eldest son,

JOHN MAULEVERER, wedded Margaret, daughter of Sir Hugh Norton, and had issue,

HENRY, his heir.
John.
Thomas, who *m.* Catherine, daughter of Robert Mennil.

Margaret, *m.* to John Crathorne.

John Mauleverer was *s.* by his eldest son,

HENRY MAULEVERER, whose son and successor, by Margaret his wife, daughter of Sir Thomas Lowther, knt.

SIR WILLIAM MAULEVERER, espoused Mary, daughter of Sir Richard Hansard, and left, with two daughters, Margaret, *m.* to Sir Richard Conyers, and Anne, *m.* to Henry Widdrington, a son,

THOMAS MAULEVERER, who *m.* Ellen, dau. of Sir Thomas Tempest, knt. and had (with a younger son, Robert, who *m.* a daughter of Sir Hugh Willoughby, of Wollaton, and a daughter, Jane, the wife of John Hopton, of Ormley) his successor,

SIR WILLIAM MAULEVERER, knt. who *m.* Anne, daughter of Sir John Neville, of Liversage, and had

WILLIAM (Sir), his heir.
John, *m.* Mary, daughter of John Musgrave.
Richard, *m.* a daughter of Thomas Clifford.

Margaret, *m.* to John Musgrave.
Ann, *m.* to John Vavasor, of Weston, and was ancestor to the VAVASOURS of that place. This Ann released to John, her son, all right in the manor of Weston, *anno* 1400.

Sir William was *s.* by his eldest son, another

SIR WILLIAM MAULEVERER, knt. who *m.* Mary, daughter of Sir Ralph Bygod, knt. of Settrington, and had issue,

WILLIAM (Sir), his heir.
John, *m.* Mary, daughter of John Aske, esq.
Mary, *m.* to John Vavasour, esq. of Hazlewood.
Anne.

The elder son,

SIR WILLIAM MAULEVERER, *m.* Isabel, daughter of Sir Henry Oughtred, knt. and left a daughter, Jane, the wife of William Skargill, and a son,

WILLIAM MAULEVERER, esq. of Potter Newton, who *m.* Catherine, daughter of Sir Ralph Bossvill, knt. of Erdsley, and was father of

ROBERT MAULEVERER, esq. who *m.* Elizabeth, daughter and heir of John Barlow, esq. and thus acquired the lordship of Wothersome, in Yorkshire. His son and heir,

SIR WILLIAM MAULEVERER, knt. of Wothersome, living 3rd EDWARD IV. wedded Joan, daughter and co-heir of Sir John Colville,* of Arncliffe, in the county of York, and had a son and successor,

EDMUND MAULEVERER, esq. of Arncliffe, who *m.* Elenor Vavasour, and had three sons, by the eldest of whom,

SIR WILLIAM MAULEVERER, knt. he was succeeded. This gentleman espoused; Jane, daughter of Sir John Conyers, of Sockburn, and had four sons and two daughters,

I. JAMES, who *m.* Anne, daughter and co-heir of Ralph Wycliff, of Wycliff, and left three daughters,
   Jane, *m.* to Richard Aldburgh, esq. of Aldburgh.
   Anne, *m.* to Thomas Gower, esq. of Stitnam, *d. s. p.*
   Catherine, *m.* to William Conyers, esq. of Marske.
II. ROBERT, of whom presently.
III. William, died *s. p.*
IV. Henry, a priest.

I. Anne, *m.* to J. Rowcliffe, esq.
II. Catherine, *m.* to William Wombwell, esq. of Wombwell.

---

* Philip Colville, grandson of another Philip Colville = Ingalis dau. and heir of Robert Ingram, esq. of Arncliffe
|
William Colville
|
Robert Colville
|
Robert Colville, who *m.* Elizabeth, daughter and heir of Sir John Conyers
|
William Colville, who *m.* a daughter of John, Lord Fauconberg.
|
Sir James Colville, who *m.* a daughter of John, Lord D'Arcy
|
Joan = Sir William Mauleverer. — The other *m.* Sir John Wandsworth, knt.

Sir William's second son,

ROBERT MAULEVERER, esq. (buried at Leeds in 1443) *m.* Alice, daughter of Sir Thomas Markinfield, knt. and had a son,

SIR EDMUND MAULEVERER, knt. of Arncliffe, who *m.* Mary, daughter of Sir Christopher Danby, and left, with three daughters, Martha, the wife of Ralph Gower, esq. of Stitnam, Catherine, who *d.* unmarried, and Alice, the wife of Anthony Garforth, a son,

WILLIAM MAULEVERER, esq. of Arncliffe, living towards the close of the sixteenth century, who left, by Elenor his wife, daughter of Richard Aldburgh, esq. of Aldburgh, five sons and six daughters, all of whom appear to have died unmarried, excepting two daughters, Alice, who became the wife of Richard Tempest, esq. of Tong Hall (see vol. i. p. 291), Martha, who wedded H. Blakiston, esq. and one son, his heir,

JAMES MAULEVERER, esq. of Arncliffe, who *m.* Beatrice, daughter of Sir Timothy Hutton, knt. of Marske, (see vol. ii), and had, with other issue who *d. s. p.*

TIMOTHY, his heir.

Elizabeth, *m.* to John Blakiston, esq.

Elenor, *m.* to Anthony Nowell.

Beatrice, *m.* to George Wright, esq. of Bolton on Swale.

The son and successor,

TIMOTHY MAULEVERER, esq. of Arncliffe, *m.* Elizabeth, daughter of George Metcalfe, esq. of North Allerton, and was *s.* by his son,

TIMOTHY MAULEVERER, esq. of Arncliffe, who was governor of the poor knights at Windsor in 1694. He *m.* Elizabeth, daughter of James Bellingham, esq. of Levens, in Westmoreland, and had, with other issue, a son and successor,

TIMOTHY MAULEVERER, esq. of Arncliffe, who *m.* Jane, daughter of Thomas Hodgkinson, esq. of Preston, a co-heir, and was *s.* by his son,

TIMOTHY MAULEVERER, esq. of Arncliffe, who *m.* Sarah Pawson, daughter and co-heir of John Wilberforce, esq. of Gainsborough, in Lincolnshire, and had issue,

Jane, *m.* to Robert Lindsey, esq. of Lavighry, in the county of Tyrone.

Sarah, *m.* to J. Arthur Worsop, esq. of Alverly Grange, in Yorkshire.

ANNE, *m.* in 1780, to CLOTWORTHY GOWAN, esq.

Frances.

Mary.

Mr. Mauleverer died in 1784. His third daughter,

ANNE MAULEVERER, who *m.* Col. Clotworthy Gowan, (son of the Rev. Clotworthy Gowan, rector of Invern, in the county of Derry), had issue,

I. WILLIAM GOWAN, who succeeded his aunt, Mary Mauleverer, at Arncliffe, in 1833, and assuming, in consequence, by act of parliament, the surname of MAULEVERER, is the present WILLIAM MAULEVERER, esq. of Arncliffe.

II. Clotworthy Gowan, a civil servant at Bengal, and Persian secretary to Sir A. Wellesley. He is deceased.

III. George Gowan, judge in the Madras civil service.

I. Jane Gowan, *m.* to the Hon. Colonel Butler, and died in 1834.

II. Mary Gowan, *m.* to Thomas C. Roberts, esq.

*Arms*—Sa. three greyhounds courant, in pale arg.

*Crest*—A maplebranch arising out of the trunk of a tree.

*Motto*—En Dieu ma foy.

*Estates*—In Yorkshire.

*Seat*—Arncliffe Hall.

## BLACKSTONE, OF CASTLE PRIORY.

BLACKSTONE, WILLIAM-SEYMOUR, esq. of Castle Priory, in the county of Berks, *b.* 30th October, 1809, M.P. for Wallingford. Mr. Blackstone is a magistrate for Berkshire and Oxfordshire, and a deputy-lieutenant for the former.

## Lineage.

CHARLES BLACKSTONE, esq. of Cheapside, London, married, in 1718, Mary, eldest daughter of Lovelace Bigg, esq. of Chilton Follyatt, in Wilts, by Dorothy, his wife, eldest dau. of William Wither, esq. of Manydown, (see vol. ii. p. 401), and had issue,

I. Henry, fellow of New College, Oxford, and subsequently vicar of Adderbury, in the county of Oxford, *m.* Jane-Dymock, daughter of John Brereton, esq. of Winchester, and *d.* in 1776, leaving two daughters.

II. Charles, fellow of Winchester College, *m.* Sarah, daughter of the Rev. Edmund Cooke, and left issue,

Charles, vicar of Andover, *m.* in 1792, Margaret, daughter of Lovelace Bigg-Wither, esq. of Manydown, and had issue Frederick, in holy orders, and Margaret.

III. WILLIAM (Sir).

The third son,

SIR WILLIAM BLACKSTONE, the learned and popular commentator on the constitution and laws of England, was born in 1723, and at about the age of seven commenced his education in the Charter-house, on the foundation of which he was admitted in 1735. In this seminary he applied himself to every branch of useful education, with the same assiduity which accompanied his studies through after-life. His talents and industry rendered him the favourite of his masters, who encouraged and assisted him with the utmost attention, so that at fifteen he was at the head of the school, and, although so young, was thought well qualified to be removed to the university. He was accordingly entered a commoner at Pembroke College, in Oxford, on the 30th of November, 1738, and was the next day matriculated. At this time he was elected to one of the Charter-house exhibitions, by the governors, to commence from the Michaelmas preceding; but was permitted to continue a scholar there till after the 12th of December, being the anniversary commemoration of the founder, to give him an opportunity of speaking the customary oration, which he had prepared, and which did him great credit. About this time, also, he obtained Mr. Benson's gold prize-medal of Milton, for verses on that illustrious poet. Thus, before he quitted school, did his genius begin to appear, and to receive public marks of approbation and reward; and so well pleased were the Society of Pembroke College with their young pupil, that, in February following, they unanimously elected him to one of Lady Holford's exhibitions for Charter-house scholars in that house. At the university he prosecuted his studies with unremitting ardour; and although the classics, and particularly the Greek and Roman poets, were his favourites, they did not entirely engross his attention; logic, mathematics, and the other sciences, were not neglected. From the first of these, studied rationally, and abstracted from the jargon of the schools, he laid the foundation of that close method of reasoning for which he was so remarkable; and from the mathematics, he not only acquired the habit of accustoming his mind to a close investigation of every subject that occurred to him, till he arrived at the degree of demonstration of which the nature of it would admit, but he converted that dry study, as it is usually esteemed, into an amusement, by pursuing the branch of it which relates to architecture. This science he was peculiarly fond of, and made himself so far master of it, that, at the early age of twenty, he compiled a treatise, entitled Elements of Architecture, intended for his own use only, and not for publication, but which was esteemed, by those judges who have perused it, in no respect unworthy of his maturer judgment.

Having determined to embrace the profession of the law, he entered himself of the Middle Temple; and, in 1744, he quitted Oxford, and those classical pursuits which were so congenial to his taste. This transition to studies of a less pleasing nature, he very feelingly commemorated in an elegant poem, entitled, The Lawyer's Farewell to his Muse, which was afterwards printed in the fourth volume of Dodsley's Collection, and which is allowed to display a very early maturity of taste and judgment. He now applied himself with great assiduity to the study of his profession, dividing his residence between the Temple and the University, a place to which he always retained his youthful attachment. He had been elected a fellow of All Souls College in 1743, and on the 28th of November, 1746, he was called to the bar. As he was very deficient in elocution, and possessed none of the popular talents of an advocate, his progress in the profession was extremely slow; and being without any avocations of business, the active turn of his mind displayed itself in the office of bursar, or steward, of All Souls. In this situation he is said to have merited great praise for his skill and diligence in arranging the records, and improving the revenues, of the College, and in expediting the necessary measures for completing the magnificent structure of the Codrington library. In 1749, he was appointed, through the interest of a relation, recorder of Wallingford, in Berkshire; and in the following year, probably with a view to more constant residence at Oxford, he took the degree of doctor of laws. Having now attended the courts of law at Westminster for seven years, without success, he determined to quit the practice of his profession, and retire to his fellowship at Oxford. The system of education in the English universities supplying no provision for teaching the laws and constitution of the country, Dr. Blackstone undertook to remedy this defect, by a course of lectures on that important subject; and the manner in which he executed the task has conferred a lasting distinction on Oxford. His first course was delivered in 1753, and was repeated for a series of years, with increasing effect and reputation. These lectures doubtless suggested to Mr. Viner the idea of founding, by his will, a liberal establishment in the university of Oxford for the study of the common law; and Dr. Blackstone was, with great propriety, chosen the first Vinerian professor. The reputation which he had acquired by his lectures induced him, in the year 1759, to return to the Temple, and resume his attendance at Westminster-hall; and he now advanced with great rapidity in the career of his profession. In 1761, he was chosen member of Parliament for Hindon, and received a patent of procedure to rank as King's counsel, having previously declined the office of chief justice of Ireland. On the establishment of the Queen's household, in 1763, he was appointed solicitor-general to her majesty.

The first volume of his Commentaries on the Laws of England was published at Oxford, in 4to. in the year 1765, and the other three volumes followed soon afterwards. This work, to which he is indebted for the permanence of his reputation, comprehends the substance of his academical prelections, and is by far the most elegant and popular book on the municipal laws of England which has yet appeared. Before the publication of Blackstone's Commentaries the study was generally considered as extremely repulsive, but he has treated it with a degree of elegance and interest which may recommend it to every inquisitive reader.

On the resignation of Mr. Dunning, in 1770, he was offered the situation of solicitor-general, which naturally leads to the highest offices of the law; and on his declining it, he was appointed one of the justices of the Court of Common Pleas. In this honourable and tranquil station he continued till the time of his death, which happened in consequence of a dropsy, on the 14th of February, 1780. His health, which had been considerably impaired by the labours of his early years, by an unfortunate aversion from exercise, and perhaps by some habits of excess, had been declining for some time, but it had begun seriously to fail towards the latter end of the preceding year.

The private character of Blackstone seems to have been highly estimable for mildness, benevolence, and every social and domestic virtue. A love of business, and useful employment, was one of the ruling passions of his life; and the leisure which he employed during his latter years was devoted to schemes of social improvement in the neighbourhood where he resided, or to great public undertakings.

Sir William Blackstone married Sarah, eldest daughter of James Clitheroe, esq. of Boston House, in the county of Middlesex, and had issue,

- I. HENRY, *b.* in 1763, *d.* without issue, in 1826.
- II. JAMES, of whom presently.
- III. William, *d.* unmarried, in 1814.
- IV. Charles, fellow of Winchester College, and rector of Worting, in Hampshire, *d.* unmarried, in 1835.
- I. Sarah, *m.* to the Rev. Thomas Rennel, D.D. dean of Winchester, and *d.* in 1830, having had
  1. Thomas Rennell, prebendary of Sarum, and vicar of Kennington, *d. s. p.* in 1824.
  2. William Blackstone Rennell, in holy orders, fellow of King's College, Cambridge.
  3. Chares-John Rennell, barrister-at-law.
  4. Sarah Rennell, *m.* to the Right Rev. William, Bishop of Barbadoes.
  5. Elizabeth.
- II. Mary, *m.* to the Rev. William Cole, L.L.D. prebendary of Westminster, *d. s. p.* in 1830.

III. Philippa, m. in 1790, to Harry Lee, fellow of Winchester College, and has issue,

1. Harry Lee, fellow of Winchester College.
2. William-Blackstone Lee, fellow of New College, Oxford.

Sir William died 4th February, 1780. His second son,

JAMES BLACKSTONE, esq. of the Middle Temple, barrister-at-law, b. in 1764, m. in 1804, Elizabeth Hamank, dau. of Richard Jenkyns, esq. of Cornwall, and had issue,

WILLIAM-SEYMOUR, his heir.
Elizabeth, m. to the Rev. William-Watson-James-Augustus Langford, and has issue.
Jane-Martha.

Mr. Blackstone died 7th July, 1830, and was s. by his son, the present WILLIAM-SEYMOUR BLACKSTONE, esq. of Castle Priory, Wallingford.

*Arms*—Arg. two bars gu. in chief three cocks of the second.

*Crest*—A cock or.

*Estates*—In the counties of Oxford and Berks.

*Seat*—Castle Priory, Wallingford.

# LAMBERT, OF CARNAGH.

LAMBERT, HENRY, esq. of Carnagh, in the county of Wexford, b. in September, 1786, succeeded his father in July, 1808. Mr. Lambert is a magistrate and deputy-lieutenant for Wexford, and has represented that county in parliament.

## Lineage.

PATRICK LAMBERT, esq. of Carnagh, head [o]f the family in the early part of the eigh[t]eenth century, married Catherine White, [a]cquired with her estates in the county of [K]ilkenny, and had two sons and a daughter. [T]he elder son,

JAMES LAMBERT, esq. of Carnagh, dying [a]t Bath, without issue, in 1757, was suc[c]eeded by his brother,

HENRY LAMBERT, esq. of Carnagh, who [w]edded Margaret Fitzimon, of the House of [G]lancullen, in the county of Dublin, and had [th]ree sons and two daughters. The eldest [s]on,

PATRICK LAMBERT, esq. of Carnagh, m. in 1781, Mary-Anne, eldest daughter of George Lattin, esq. of Morrestown Lattin, in Kildare, and had issue,

HENRY, his heir.
Ambrose, who resides on his estate in the county of Kilkenny, m. in December, 1823, Eliza, daughter of John Snow, esq. and niece of Thomas Wyse, esq. of the Manor in the county of Waterford.

Catherine, married in 1811, to Gerald Aylmer, esq. head of the ancient house of Lyons, in Kildare, and brother to the late Countess of Kenmare.
Margaret.
Letitia.
Jane.

Mr. Lambert died in July, 1808, and was succeeded by his elder son, the present HENRY LAMBERT, esq. of Carnagh.

*Arms*—Quarterly, 1st and 4th vert. a lamb arg.; 2nd and 3rd erm. an eagle displayed gu.

*Crest*—A sagittary gu. and arg. charged with a trefoil vert. the bow and arrow or.

*Motto*—Deus providebit.

*Estates*—In the co. of Wexford.

*Seat*—Carnagh.

# DOD, OF EDGE.

DOD, CHARLOTTE, of Edge Hall, in the county of Chester, succeeded her father in 1829.

## Lineage.

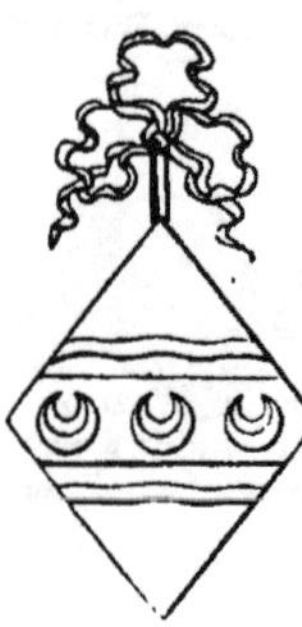

Hova, son of Cadwgan Dot, the founder of this family, about the time of Henry II. settled at Edge, in Cheshire, in consequence of his marriage with the daughter and heiress of the Lord of Edge, with whom he had a fourth of the manor. The name of the proprietor whose daughter Hova married does not appear, but it is probable that he was the son of Edwin, a Saxon thane, who was allowed, after the Norman conquest, to retain possession of his lands at Edge, in Cheshire. "Presuming this descent," says Ormerod, "it is impossible to overlook the following particulars:—Dot, the Saxon lord of sixteen manors, either exclusively, or of a considerable proportion thereof, was joint Lord of Cholmondeley, Hampton, Groppenhall, and two-thirds of Bickerton, with this very Edwin. Dot was ejected from all his manors, and the circumstance of the heiress of the relics of Edwin's lands matching herself with a man who bore the name of one so closely connected with her apparent ancestor (prefixing thereto the addition of a name derived from the land to which that friend of her ancestor would be most likely to fly for shelter), seems to make this marriage the result of old family friendship and alliance, and to lead to a deduction of Cadwgan Dot, from the Dot of Domesday. A descent in the male line from a Saxon, noticed in that record, would be unique in the county of Chester." The Dod pedigree entered, by Baron Dod, in the visitation of 1613, gives four descents after Cadwgan, and again commences with Hova Dod, after which it proceeds in a clear descent.

The last named

Hova Dod, had two sons; the younger, John of Smith's Pentrey, in Broxton, married Margery, daughter of Hugh le Byrd, of Broxton, and the elder,

Thomas Dod, of Edge, *temp.* Edward III. wedded Mabell, daughter of David Mere, and had two sons, namely,

> Thomas, his heir.
>
> John, of Farndon, living *temp.* Richard II. who *m.* Johanna, daughter and heiress of John Warren, of Ightfield, in Shropshire, and was ancestor of the Dods of Cloverley, now represented by John-Whitehall Dod, esq. of Cloverley. (See vol. i. p. 297.)

The elder son,

Thomas Dod, of Edge, *m.* Mary, or Matilda, daughter of David Bird, of Broxton, and left a son and successor,

David Dod, of Edge, who espoused Cecilia, daughter and co-heiress of William de Bickerton, and was father of

Sir Anthony Dod, of Edge, one of the heroes of Agincourt, knighted by King Henry on that memorable field. He died on his return homewards, and was interred in the cathedral of Canterbury. His son and heir,

David Dod, of Edge, was one of the Cheshire gentlemen who signed the supplication to Henry VI. respecting the liberties of the palatinate. He *m.* first, a daughter of the ancient family of Downes, of Shrigley, and, secondly, a daughter of Piers Stanley, of Ewlowe. By the former, he left at his decease a son and successor,

Stephen Dod, of Edge, omitted in the visitation and in the pedigrees by Sir Richard St. George. He was living 24th Henry VI. and married Beatrix, daughter and heiress of Thomas Willaston, of Willaston, in the county of Salop, by whom he had a son,

DAVID DOD, of Edge, living in the 3rd and 14th EDWARD IV. who *m.* Anne, daughter of Hugh Massey, esq. of Coddington, in Cheshire, and had two sons, namely,

JOHN, his heir.

David, who founded the family of Dod, of Shocklach, which gave a dignitary to the cathedral of Chester, in THOMAS DOD, who was possessed of the family estate, and was archdeacon of Richmond, dean of Rippon, and rector of Astbury and Malpas. Of the Shocklach line, was also JOHN DOD, the decalogist, uncle to Dr. Dod, whom we have just mentioned. This eminent man, who was born in 1547, associating much with Drs. Fulke, Chaderton, and Whitaker, imbibed the principles and strictness for which they were famous, and conceived an early dislike to some of the ceremonies or discipline of the church, but to which we are not told. After taking orders, he first preached a weekly lecture at Ely, until invited by Sir Anthony Cope to be minister of Hanwell in Oxfordshire, in 1577, where he became a constant and diligent preacher, and highly popular. Nor was his hospitality less conspicuous, as he kept an open table on Sundays and Wednesdays, lecture days, generally entertaining on these occasions from eight to twelve persons at dinner. At Hanwell he remained twenty years, in the course of which he married, and had a large family; but, owing to his non-conformity in some points, he was suspended by Dr. Bridges, Bishop of Oxford. After this he preached for some time at Fenny-Compton, in Warwickshire, and from thence was called to Cannons Ashby, in Northamptonshire, where he was patronised by Sir Erasmus Dryden; and here again he was silenced, in consequence of a complaint made by Bishop Neale to *King* JAMES, who commanded Archbishop Abbott to pronounce that sentence. During this suspension of his public services, he appears to have written his Commentary on the Decalogue and Proverbs, which he published in conjunction with one Robert Cleaver, probably another silenced puritan, of whom we can find no account. At length, by the interest of the family of Knightley, of Northamptonshire, after the death of *King* JAMES, he was presented in 1624 to the living of Fawesley, in that county. Here he recommended himself as before, not more by his earnest and affectionate services in the pulpit, than by his charity and hospitality, and particularly by his frequent visits and advice, which last he delivered in a manner peculiarly striking. A great many of his sayings became almost proverbial, and remained so for above a century, being, as may yet be remembered, frequently printed in a small tract and suspended in every cottage. At the breaking out of the rebellion he was a considerable sufferer, his house being plundered, as the house of a puritan, although he was a decided enemy to the proceedings of the republicans. When they were about to abolish the order of bishops, &c. Dr. Browning sent to Mr. Dod for his opinion, who answered, "that he had been scandalised with the proud and tyrannical practices of the Marian bishops; but now, after more than sixty years' experience of many protestant bishops, who had been worthy preachers, learned and orthodox writers, great champions for the protestant cause, he wished all his friends not to be any impediment to them, and exhorted all men not to take up arms against the king, which was his doctrine, he said, upon the fifth commandment, and he would never depart from it." He died in August, 1645, at the very advanced age of ninety-seven, and was buried at Fawsley. Fuller says, "with him the old puritan seemed to expire, and in his grave to be interred. Humble, meek, patient, as in his censures of, so in his alms to others." The celebrated Dr. Wilkins was his grandson.

The elder son,

JOHN DOD, esq. of Edge, married Emma, daughter and heiress of Humphrey Brereton, third son of Bartholomew Brereton, of Grafton, and had two sons and two daughters, viz.

I. DAVID, his heir.
II. Richard.

I. Ellen, *m.* to Henry Typper, of Gloucester.
II. Magdalen, *m.* to Richard Ball.

He died *temp.* HENRY VII. and by inq. post mortem, dated 21st of that reign, was found to have held in demesne as of fee tail, two messuages, lands, and two mills, in Great and Little Edge, from the king in soccage, by the render of xx*d* for all secular services and demands, as of a third of the barony of Malpas, lately belonging to Sir Thomas Cokesey, knt. His son and successor,

DAVID DOD, esq. of Edge, wedded Katherine, daughter of Nicholas Manley, esq. of Poulton, and had issue,

I. RANDLE, his heir.
II. John, whose son, Randle, married at Malpas 25th September, 1781, his cousin Margaret, daughter of Randle Dod, esq. of Edge, but died without male issue.
III. David, buried at Malpas 19th Mar. 1589, *s. p.*
IV. Francis, who *m.* Mary, daughter and co-heiress of George Dalton, esq. of London, and had, with several other children, one of whom was prebendary of Chester, a son,

SIR EDWARD DOD, of whom presently, as successor to his cousin Randle.

V. Bartholomew, of London, married Elizabeth, daughter and co-heiress of George Dalton, and had issue.
VI. Roger.
VII. Philip, of London, who *m.* Elizabeth, daughter of John Van Hole, of Antwerp, and had issue.
VIII. William, of Chester, who *m.* Elizabeth, daughter of William Hockenhull, of Prenton, and had issue.

I. Elizabeth, *m.* to George Bird, esq. of Broxton.
II. Anne, *m.* to William Streley, esq. of Streley.
III. Jane, *m.* to Thomas Caldecote, esq. of Caldecote.
IV. Catherine, *m.* to — Goode.
V. Mary, *m.* to John Grosvenor, esq. of Belleau Hill, *s. p.*
VI. Grace, *m.* to John Moyle, esq. of Chester.

The eldest son,

RANDLE DOD, esq. of Edge, wedded, first, Elizabeth, daughter and heiress of Thomas Horton, esq. of Toternhoe, in Bedfordshire, and secondly, Anne, daughter of Randle Brereton, esq. of Malpas; by the former he had issue,

I. URIAN, his heir.

I. Anne, *m.* to Hugh Massey, esq. of Broxton.
II. Jane, *m.* to — Wren, esq. of Kent.
III. Margaret, *m.* to Randle Dod, esq.
IV. Elizabeth, *m.* in 1584, to Ralph Yeardley, esq. of Caldecote.
V. Katherine, *m.* to John Golborne, esq. of Overton.
VI. Alice.

Randle Dod *d.* 11th May, 18 ELIZABETH, and was *s.* by his only son,

URIAN DOD, esq. of Edge, who *d.* without issue, 18th July, 22 ELIZABETH, seized of the manor of Edge, with lands in Barton and Willaston, and was *s.* by his cousin,

SIR EDWARD DOD, baron of the exchequer of Chester, who then became "of Edge." He *m.* Margaret, daughter and eventual heiress of Roger Mainwaring, esq. of Nantwich, and had three sons and three daughters, viz.

I. THOMAS, his heir.
II. John, baptized 5th November, 1617, died in infancy.
III. Edward, bapt. 1st January, 1628, a captain in Lord Cholmondeley's regiment, buried in Chester cathedral, 27th February, 1643.

I. Margaret, *b.* in 1603, } both *d.* young.
II. Mary, }
III. Elizabeth, bapt. 1616, *m.* to Hugh Maurice, esq. of the Farme, in Salop.

Sir Edward Dod *d.* 25th November, 1649, and was *s.* by his son,

THOMAS DOD, esq. of Edge, bapt. at Malpas, 7th Sept. 1604, who *m.* Anne, daughter of Edward Holland, esq. of Denton, in Lancashire, and by her (who died in 1680) had

I. RANDLE, his heir.
II. Thomas, of Ormskirk, baptized at Malpas, 19th July, 1633, presented his nephew, William Dod, to the rectory of Malpas, 8th July, 1680.
III. William, baptized in 1654.

I. Anne, *m.* to William Gamull, esq. of Crabwall, Cheshire.
II. Jane, *m.* to the Rev. Henry Crewe.
III. Dorothy, *m.* to William Doley, of London.
IV. Mary, *m.* to — Brown, and died in 1678.

Thomas Dod *d.* 1st January, 1653-4, and was *s.* by his son,

RANDLE DOD, esq. of Edge, born in 1633, who *m.* first, Barbara, daughter and coheiress of William Morgell, esq. of Gray's Inn, and secondly, Hester, daughter of William Essington, of London, merchant. By the former he had issue,

I. RANDLE, his heir.
II. William, successor to his brother.

I. Barbara, *b.* in 1654, who bequeathed her estates of Childer Thorton and Boughton to the minor canons of Chester cathedral, by will dated in 1703.
II. Anne, *b.* in 1655, *d.* in 1666.
III. Elizabeth, married in 1685, to John Leigh, esq. of Eden Hall, in Cumberland.

Mr. Dod *d.* in 1679, and was *s.* by his elder son,

RANDLE DOD, esq. of Edge, *b.* 16th Nov. 1656, at whose decease *s. p.* in 1686, the estates and representation of the family devolved on his brother,

THE REV. WILLIAM DOD, Rector of the Lower Mediety of Malpas, who then became "of Edge." He *m.* Elizabeth, daughter of — Entwistle, esq. of Foxholes, in Lancashire, and by her (who died in 1700) had issue,

- WILLIAM, FRANCIS, THOMAS, } successive heirs.
- Randulph, *b.* in 1690, *d. s. p.* in 1772.
- John, *b.* in 1692, died issueless.
- Richard, *b.* in 1693, Edward, *b.* in 1697, Benjamin, *b.* in 1698, Robert, *b.* in 1699, } all *d. s. p.*

- Anne, *m.* in 1734, to William Dimmock, esq.

- Dorothy, *d.* in infancy.
- Mary, bapt. 14th May, 1696.
- Elizabeth, *b.* in 1689, *m.* to the Rev. John Taylor, Rector of Malpas.

Mr. Dod *d.* in 1716, and was *s.* by his eldest son,

WILLIAM DOD, esq. of Edge, *b.* April, 1686, who was high sheriff of Cheshire in 1735. Dying issueless, in 1739, he was *s.* by his next brother,

FRANCIS DOD, esq. of Edge, who also died *s. p.* 20th April, 1752, and was *s.* by his brother,

THOMAS DOD, esq. of Edge, baptized 5th July, 1688, who *m.* at Chester cathedral, 28th June, 1748, Rebecca, daughter of — Crewe, esq. of Crewe, near Farndon, and of Holt, in the county of Denbigh, and by her (who *d.* 26th June, 1778) had two sons and two daughters, viz.

- THOMAS-CREWE, his heir.
- William, bapt. at Malpas in 1757.

- Rebecca, *m.* to William Mostyn Owen, esq. of Woodhouse, in Salop.
- Anne-Sobieski, *m.* to Robert Watkin Wynne, esq. of Plas Newyd, and Gaithmailio, in Denbighshire.

Mr. Dod *d.* 30th December, 1759, and was *s.* by his son,

THOMAS-CREWE DOD, esq. of Edge, bapt. at Malpas, 11th July, 1754, who *m.* 20th September, 1786, Anne, fourth daughter of Ralph Sneyd, esq. of Keel, in the county of Stafford, and had issue,

- Thomas, *b.* in 1794, *d.* young.
- John-Anthony, *b.* in 1798, *d.* unmarried in 1821, in India.

- CHARLOTTE, heiress to her father.
- Anne.
- Harriet, *d.* young.
- Frances-Rosamond, *m.* to the Rev. P. Parker.
- Soby-Rebecca, *m.* to H. R. Sneyd, esq.

Mr. Dod *d.* in 1827, and was *s.* by his eldest daughter, the present MISS DOD, of Edge.

*Arms*—Arg. on a fesse gu. between two cotises wavy sa. three crescents or.

*Crest*—A serpent vert, issuing from and piercing a garb or.

*Motto*—In copia cautus.

*Estates*—In the county of Chester, &c.

*Seat*—Edge Hall. Near one extremity of the Dod estate in Edge, in a place called the Hall Heys, are vestiges of a mansion, which was most probably the earliest residence of the family. The present seat is of considerable antiquity, but has been so repeatedly altered in various styles, that no date can be inferred from its architecture. This house has also been moated, and stands very low, the ground sloping to it in almost every direction; at the back is a parklike enclosure, ascending gently to a terrace, on the summit of a rocky eminence well planted with trees, through the interstices of which the eye commands the higher Broxton and Bickerton hills behind, and in front, the Clwydian range, with loftier mountains above them, seen over the broad vale of Chester. On the right the estuaries appear in the distance, and on the left is a boundless continuation of the magnificent vale below, broken in some places by the Montgomeryshire hills, and completely losing itself in the vista.

# RICHARDS, OF CAERYNWCH.

**RICHARDS, RICHARD,** esq. of Caerynwch, in the county of Merioneth, *b.* 22nd September, 1787, *m.* in 1814, Harriet, daughter, of Jonathan Dennett, esq. of Lincoln's Inn, and has issue,

RICHARD-MEREDYDD.

Emily-Katharine.
Williama-Frances.
Anna-Maria-Harriett.

Mr. Richards succeeded his father in 1823. He is accountant-general of the Court of Exchequer, and a deputy-lieutenant for Merionethshire.

## Lineage.

The estate of Caerynwch has been possessed by the maternal ancestors of Mr. Richards for many centuries.

JOHN HUMPHREYS, gent. living in 1700, married Grace, daughter and heir of Robert Vaughan, of Caerynwch, by whom he acquired that estate, and had a son and successor,

JOHN HUMPHREYS, esq. of Caerynwch, who wedded (marriage settlement dated in 1717) Margaret Vaughan, heiress of Castellmock, in the county of Montgomery, and was *s.* by his son,

ROBERT-VAUGHAN HUMPHREYS, esq. of Caerynwch, who served the office of sheriff for Merionethshire in 1760. He *m.* Jane, daughter of Humphrey Meredith, esq. of Pengwern, in the county of Carnarvon, relict of Owen Lloyd, of Tythin Agnas, and left an only daughter and heiress,

CATHERINE HUMPHREYS, of Caerynwch, who wedded 30th September, 1785.

SIR RICHARD RICHARDS, son of Thomas Richards, esq. of Coed, and Catherine his wife, sister of the Rev. Mr. Parry, warden of Ruthin. This gentleman, *b.* in 1752, adopting the legal profession, rose to eminence, and obtained great practice at the bar. In 1813, he was appointed chief justice of Chester; in 1814, one of the barons of the exchequer; and, in 1817, chief baron upon the demise of Sir A. Thompson. "In the whole circle of his profession," says a writer in the Gentleman's Magazine, "no man stood higher in private estimation or public respect than Sir Richard Richards. His peculiar urbanity and benevolence, which pervaded every action of his life, gained for him the affectionate attachment of all who had the happiness to share his acquaintance: his whole time was spent, when free from the cares of his judicial duties, in the exercise of philanthropy, and the offices of social life. As a lawyer and a judge, his decisions, particularly in exchequer cases, were sound, and built upon the firm basis of deep penetration. He fully enjoyed the friendship and confidence of the lord chancellor, for whom on several occasions he presided, under special commission, as speaker of the House of Lords." By Catherine, the heiress, of Caerynwch, Sir Richard had issue,

- RICHARD, his heir.
- William-Parry, who *m.* Frances, youngest daughter and co-heir of J. Dennett, esq. of London.
- Robert-Vaughan, who *m.* Jane, daughter of Matthew Chalie, esq.
- Thomas-Watkin, rector of Puttenham, Surrey, and of Seighford, Staffordshire, who *m.* Miss Marianne Pope.
- Griffith.
- Charles.
- Henry.
- Jane, *m.* to the Rev. Temple Frere, rector of Roydon, Norfolk.
- Catherine, died unm. in 1825.

Sir Richard *d.* 11th November, 1823, (Lady Richards survived until 1825), and was *s.* by his son, the present RICHARD RICHARDS, esq. of Caerynwch.

*Estates*—In Merionethshire.

*Town Residence*—Bedford Square.

*Seat*—Caerynwch.

# BURROUGHES, OF BURLINGHAM.

BURROUGHES, HENRY-NEGUS, esq. of Burlingham Hall, Norfolk, *b.* 8th February, 1791, *m.* 25th August, 1818, Jane Sarah, daughter of the Reverend Dixon Hoste, rector of Tittesshall, Cum Godwick, and sister of Sir William Hoste, bart. and has issue,

JAMES-BURKIN, *b.* 10th November, 1819.
Henry-Negus, *b.* 21st November, 1821.
William, *b.* 18th September, 1827.

Jane.
Mary.

Mr. Burroughes was high sheriff for Norfolk in 1817.

## Lineage.

The family of Burroughes, of old standing in Norfolk, has been extensive land owners in that and the neighbouring county of Suffolk.

JEREMIAH BURROUGHES, esq. wedded Diana, sister and co-heir of James Burkin, esq. of Burlingham, in the county of Norfolk, and had a son and successor,

JEREMIAH BURROUGHES, esq. who *m.* Diana, daughter and heiress of R. Randall, esq. of Wymondham, in Norfolk, and had three sons, viz.

I. JAMES, his heir.
II. Randall, who *m.* Elizabeth-Maria, daughter and sole heiress of William Ellis, esq. of Kiddall Hall, in the county of York, and was grandfather of the present
  Rev. ELLIS BURROUGHES, of Long Stratton. (See that family, p. 554.)
III. Thomas, who died at an early age, leaving one son and one daughter,
  Thomas, who *m.* Mary, daughter and heiress of the Rev. R. Masters, of Cambridgeshire.
  Elizabeth, *m.* to T. Norgate, M.D. of Ashfield, in Suffolk.

The eldest son,

JAMES-BURKIN BURROUGHES, esq. of Burlingham Hall, *b.* 16th March, 1760, *m.* in 1789, Christabel, daughter and heiress of Henry Negus, esq. of Hoveton Hall, in Norfolk, and had issue,

HENRY-NEGUS, his heir.
Jeremiah, in holy orders, who *m.* in 1828, Pleasance, daughter of the late Sir Thomas Preston, bart. by Jane, his wife, youngest daughter of Thomas Bagge, esq. of King's Lynn.
William.

Mary, *m.* to Lieutenant-colonel Sir George-Charles Hoste, brother of the late Sir William Hoste, bart.

Mr. Burroughes *d.* 30th November, 1803, and was *s.* by his eldest son, HENRY-NEGUS BURROUGHES, esq. of Burlingham.

*Arms*—Arg. two chevrons between three chaplets vert, quartering NEGUS and BURKIN.

*Crest*—A griffin's head erased arg. charged with two chevrons vert.

*Motto*—Animo et fide.

*Estates*—Burlingham North, St. Peter, on which the residence stands: Burlingham North, St. Andrew, Burlingham South, St. Edmunds, Blofield, Hemlington, and Panxworth, in Norfolk. The manorial rights of the foregoing parishes, with the exception of Panxworth, are in the possession of the present H. N. BURROUGHES, esq.

*Seat*—Burlingham Hall.

# BURROUGHES, OF LONG STRATTON.

**BURROUGHES,** *The Reverend* **ELLIS, of the Manor House, Long Stratton, Norfolk,** *b.* **17th January, 1797,** *m.* **16th September, 1823, Elizabeth-Phillips, eldest daughter of Lieutenant-general Sir Francis Wilder, late M.P. for Arundel, and has**

- I. ELLIS.
- II. Randall-Robert.

- I. Frances-Sarah.

Mr. Burroughes, who succeeded his father in December, 1831, is a magistrate and deputy-lieutenant for Norfolk.

## Lineage.

That branch of the family of BURROUGHES, representing that of ELLIS, of Kiddall, we shall detail the latter until it merge in the former.

The ELLISES came originally, with WILLIAM of Normandy, into England; but no ancient documents, prior to the reign of RICHARD I. exist. In the reign of the chivalrous monarch,

ARCHIBALD ELLYS appears to have distinguished himself in Palestine, and to have received grants of manors and lands from the King.

THOMAS ELLIS, or ELYS, living about 1400, married Anne, daughter of Walter, or William Calverley, of Calverley, in Yorkshire, and had, with a daughter, Ellen, *m.* to Michael Fawkes, esq. of Farneley, a son,

WILLIAM ELLIS, of Kiddall, who married Joanna, daughter of William Percheyhay, esq. of Ryton, had issue, HENRY, William, who married Alice, daughter of Mr. Vavasour on the Wolds, and Anne, *m.* J. Moor, esq. of Austrorp. The elder son,

HENRY ELLIS, of Kidhall, living *temp.* EDWARD IV. married Anne, daughter of John Gascoigne, esq. of Lazingcroft, and had a son,

JOHN-GASCOIGNE ELLIS, of Kidhall, who married, about the middle of the sixteenth century, Mary, daughter of Martin Anne, esq. of Frickley, and had issue, JOHN, Nicholas, Martin, Henry, Robert, Richard, Francis, Thomas, Gervais, Anne, married to Thomas Barley, of Ecclesfield, Frances, and Mary, *m.* to Bryan Babthorp, of Babthorp.

JOHN ELLIS, of Kidhall, son and heir, *m.* Elizabeth, daughter of William-Peter Plompton, esq. and had, with a daughter, Mary, *m.* first, to Sir Anthony Chester, bart. of Chichley, co. Bucks, and secondly, to Samuel Lodington, esq. three sons, WILLIAM, Henry, and Charles, all slain in the service of *King* CHARLES I. as was John, their father. The eldest son,

WILLIAM ELLIS, esq. of Kidhall, *m.* Mary, daughter of — Austen, esq. of London, and was *s.* by his son,

WILLIAM ELLIS, esq. of Kidhall, who *m.* Anne, daughter of Thomas Colepepper, esq. of Perton, co. Hants, and was *s.* at his decease (he was slain at the siege of Charlemont, in Ireland) by his son,

WILLIAM ELLIS, esq. of Kidhall, married Mary, daughter of Sir William Lowther, of Swillington, who *d.* in 1687, and aunt of the first Earl of Lonsdale. By this lady he had issue,

- I. WILLIAM, his heir.
- II. John.
- III. Henry, from whom sprang WELBORE ELLIS, successively Bishop of Kildare and Meath, who *m.* Diana, daughter of Sir John Briscoe, of Amberly Castle, in Sussex, and had one son and one daughter, viz.
  - WELBORE, *b.* in 1713, secretary of state in Ireland, who was raised to the peerage in 1794 as BARON MENDIP, of Mendip, in Somersetshire, with remainder to the male issue of his sister. His lordship married first, Elizabeth, daughter of the Hon. Sir William Stanhope, K. B. and secondly, Anne, sister and heir of the Right Hon. Hans Stanley, Governor of the Isle of Wight, but *d. s. p.* in 1802.
  - Anne, *m.* first, to Henry Agar, esq. M.P. by whom she was grandmother of HENRY-Welbore-Agar-Ellis, VISCOUNT CLIFDEN.

and secondly, to George Dunbar, esq.

I. Mary.
II. Jane, *m.* to the Rev. Mr. Mosley, rector of Roleston.

The eldest son and successor,

WILLIAM ELLIS, esq. of Kidhall, *m.* Mary, daughter of Dutton Scaman, esq. of Westminster, and had issue, JOHN, William, Henry, Charles, Mary, Annabell, and Catherine-Mildred, and was succeeded by the eldest,

JOHN ELLIS, of Kidhall, who married a daughter of J. Butterfield, esq. of Leeds, and had two sons, William, and Charles, of whom the elder,

WILLIAM ELLIS, esq. of Kidhall, married Elizabeth, daughter and heiress of T. Bourn, of Mattingley, co. Hants, and had issue an only daughter and heiress,

ELIZABETH-MARIA ELLIS, who *m.* RANDALL BURROUGHES, esq. of Long Stratton, in Norfolk, and had issue,

I. ELLIS BURROUGHES, his heir.

I. Elizabeth-Maria Burroughes, *m.* to the Rev. J. Ward, D.D.
II. Diana Burroughes, *m.* to the Rev. W. Walford, A.M.

Mr. Burroughes was *s.* at his decease by his only son,

THE REV. ELLIS BURROUGHES, of Long Stratton, who espoused, in 1795, Sarah-Nasmyth, only daughter of Robert Marsh, esq. and had issue,

I. ELLIS, his heir.
II. Walter.
III. Randall-Ellis.

He died in 1831, and was *s.* by his eldest son, the present Rev. ELLIS BURROUGHES, of Long Stratton.

*Arms*—Arg. two chevrons between three chaplets vert. quartering ELLIS or, on a plain cross sa. five crescents arg.

*Crest*—A griffin's head erased arg. charged with two chevrons vert.

*Motto*—Animo et fide: the Ellis motto is, "Huic habeo non tibi."

*Estates*—At Long Stratton, Wacton, and Pulham, Norfolk, and Kiddall (or Kidhall), in Yorkshire. The present Rev. Ellis Burroughes is lord of the manors of Stratton Hall, Wilhams, and Reezes, in Norfolk.

*Seat*—Long Stratton.

## CHAMPNEYS, OF OSTENHANGER.

CHAMPNEYS, *The Rev.* HENRY-WILLIAM, of Ostenhanger, in Kent, rector of Badsworth, in the county of York, *b.* at Portsmouth, 26th May, 1770, *m.* 3rd May, 1796, Lucy, eldest daughter of the Reverend Geoffrey Hornby, rector of Winwick, by Lucy, his wife, second daughter of James, Lord Stanley, and has had issue,

I. HENRY-WILLIAM-JUSTINIAN, *b.* in 1798, died at Paris, in 1819.
II. THOMAS-PHIPPS-AMYAN, *b.* in 1808.
III. Edward-Geoffrey-John, *b.* in 1813, in the East India Company's service.
IV. Maximilian-Hugh-Stanley, *b.* in 1816.
V. Charles-James-Hornby, *b.* in 1817.

I. Lucy-Henrietta.
II. Frances-Susanna.
III. Louisa-Charlotte-Margaret.
IV. Emily-Catharine, *m.* in 1825, to Adam Hodgson, esq. of Liverpool.
V. Mary-Sophia.

This gentleman; whose patronymic is BURT, assumed the surname and arms of CHAMPNEYS, by sign manual 10th November, 1778.

## Lineage.

The family of CHAMPNEYS came into England with the CONQUEROR, and its name is to be found inscribed on the roll of Battle Abbey.*

SIR AMYAN CHAMPNEYS, knt. living *temp.* HENRY II. was father of another

SIR AMYAN CHAMPNEYS, knt. who *m.* Anne, daughter of Reginald Courtenay, progenitor of the Earls of Devon, and had a son and successor,

SIR JOHN CHAMPNEYS, who *m.* a daughter of Sir Richard Turberville, knt. and was direct ancestor of†

SIR JOHN CHAMPNEYS, knt. who was Lord Mayor of London in 1534. He purchased Hall Place, in Kent, and marrying Meriel, daughter of John Barrett, esq. of Belhouse, in Essex, left, with other issue, a son,

JUSTINIAN CHAMPNEYS, esq. of Hall Place, Bexley, high sheriff for Kent in 1582, who *m.* first, Helen, daughter and heir of Thomas Halle, of London, and granddaughter of Roger Halle, by Margaret, his wife, eldest daughter and co-heir of Sir Thomas Mirfine, and by her, who died in 1565, had a son, JUSTINIAN, his heir. He wedded, secondly, Theodora, daughter and heir of John Blundell, esq. of Steeple Barton, and had, by her,

- Richard, of Hall Place, and afterwards of Woolwich, who *m.* Bridget, daughter of Robert Rolfe, esq. of Hadleigh, in Suffolk, and died in 1653. His daughter and eventual heiress,
  - CATHARINE, wedded Edwin Sandys, esq. of Northborne Court, in Kent, a parliamentary colonel, slain at the battle of Worcester. The grandson of this marriage, SIR RICHARD SANDYS, bart. of Northborne, *m.* Mary, daughter and co-heir of Sir Francis Rolle, and dying in 1726, left two daughters,
    - PRISCILLA SANDYS, *m.* Henry Sandys, esq. of Downe Hall, in Kent, and had issue.
    - ANNE SANDYS, *m.* to Charles Pyott, esq. of St. Martins, in Canterbury, and died in 1753, leaving an only dau. and heir.
- Meriel, *m.* first, to Sir Richard Swann, knt. of Southfleet, in Kent, and secondly, to Edward Rolt, esq. of Perton Hall, in the county of Bedford.
- Theodora, *m.* to John Keys, esq.
- Elizabeth, *d.* in 1576.

Justinian Champneys *d.* in 1596, and was *s.* by his son,

JUSTINIAN CHAMPNEYS, esq. of Gray's Inn and of Wrotham, who *m.* at Little Chart, in 1602, Sarah, daughter of John Darell, esq. of Cale Hill, by Anne his wife, daughter and co-heir of Robert Horne, Bishop of Winchester, and had issue,

- RICHARD, his heir.
- Robert, living at St. Lucar, in Spain, in 1641, and married to a Spanish lady.
- James, bapt. at Wrotham, 17th April, 1616.
- Henry, bapt. at Wrotham, living in 1645.
- John, rector of Digswell, Herts, *m.* in 1635, Martha, daughter of Sir Alexander Cave, knt. of Bragrave, in Northamptonshire, and dying in 1645, left

---

* The Champney's, of Orchardleigh, the senior branch of the family are now represented by Sir THOMAS S. MOSTYN-CHAMPNEYS, bart.

† The intervening descent was as follows:

Sir John Champneys, who *m.* the daughter of Turberville.
|
Sir Hugh Champneys, who *m.* Maud, daughter and heir of Sir John Avenell, knt. son of Sir Geoffry.
|
Sir John Champneys, who *m.* Anne, daughter of Thomas Waryes, esq.
|
Ralph Champneys, who *m.* Alma Torts, of the county of Devon.
|
John Champneys, esq. who *m.* Beatrice, dau. of Sir John Cheverell.
|
Richard Champneys, esq. who *m.* a daughter of Williamscotte, of Gloucester.
|
Richard Champneys, esq. who *m.* Mary Stackpole.
|
Sir John Champneys, knt. who *m.* Elizabeth, daughter of Sir Hugh Bytton.
|
John Champneys, esq. *temp.* HENRY VI. who *m.* Johanna, daughter of Sir Humphrey Aylworth, esq. of Aylworth, in Gloucestershire.
|
Robert or John Champneys, esq. of Chew Magna, in the county of Somerset.
|
Sir John Champneys.

Justinian, of Gray's Inn, barrister at-law, *b.* in 1637, *d.* unmarried, at Boxley Abbey, in Kent, 1712-13.

Mary, *m.* to — Hewitt, esq.

Ann, died in 1615.

Elizabeth, *m.* to the Rev. Mr. Male, of Vange, in Essex.

Mr. Champneys died in 1622, and was *s.* by his son,

RICHARD CHAMPNEYS, esq. of Biddenden, in Kent, bapt. at Wrotham, 7th June, 1608, who *m.* at East Sutton, Martha Bishop, and dying in 1670, left, with a daughter, Martha, *m.* to Richard Butcher, esq. of Wye, a son and successor,

JUSTINIAN CHAMPNEYS, esq. barrister-at-law, of Ostenhanger, in Kent, bapt. at Biddenden, January, 1669-70, who *m.* in 1695, Sarah, daughter of Andrew Hughes, esq. of Ringleton, in the same county, and by her, who *d.* in 1728, had issue,

JUSTINIAN, his heir.

WILLIAM, successor to his brother.

Henry, of Vinters, Boxley, in Kent, died unm. 26th August, 1781.

Richard, died an infant.

Sarah, *m.* to the Rev. Stringer Belcher, rector of Ulcomb, and had four daughters, Catherine, *m.* in 1746, to Benjamin-Neale Baily, esq. of Silverspring, in the county of Wexford; Judith, *d.* unmarried; Elizabeth, *d.* unmarried; and Sarah, the wife of the Rev. Joseph Butler, D.D. who took the name of MILNER.

Mr. Champneys *d.* in 1754, and was *s.* by his eldest son,

JUSTINIAN CHAMPNEYS, esq. of Vinters, *b.* in 1696, who *m.* Elizabeth, daughter of John Marriott, esq. of Sturston Hall, Suffolk, and dying *s. p.* in 1758, the representation of the family devolved on his next brother,

WILLIAM CHAMPNEYS, esq. of Vinters, one of his Majesty's commissioners of the revenue in Ireland, usher of the black rod, &c. born at Cale Hill, in 1699, who *m.* at Bradford, Wilts, in July, 1740, Hannah, daughter of John Trigge, esq. of Newnham, in Gloucestershire, and, dying in 1766, left an only daughter and heiress,

HARRIET CHAMPNEYS, bapt. at Boxley, 23rd February, 1744-5, who *m.* at St. Alphage, Canterbury, 15th December, 1767, John Byrte, esq. of Boley Hill, Rochester, whose name was changed to BURT, by a misspelling in His Majesty's commission. Mr. Byrte, who was born 20th January, 1734, was son of Joseph Byrte, esq. of Fordingbridge, in Hampshire, descended from an ancient family seated at Candlemarsh, in the county of Dorset. By the heiress of Champneys he left issue,

I. HENRY-WILLIAM BURT, who assumed the surname and arms of CHAMPNEYS, and is the present Rev. HENRY-WILLIAM CHAMPNEYS, of Ostenhanger.

II. Thomas-Charles Burt, *b.* 23rd October, 1773; *m.* at Ashford, in 1800, Catherine, daughter of George Jemmett, esq. by Mary his wife, daughter of Edward Curteis, esq. of Tenterden, and has surviving issue,

John, *b.* in June, 1807.

Frances-Ann.

Eleanor.

I. Harriet Burt, died unmarried, 23rd December, 1799.

II. Frances, died in infancy.

*Arms*—Per pale arg. and sa. within a bordure engrailed, counterchanged a lion rampant gu.

*Crest*—A demi-moor side faced, habited or, cuffs, cape, and ornaments on the shoulders gu. wreathed about the temples of the two last: holding in the dexter hand a gold ring, with a sapphire stone set therein.

*Estates*—In Kent.

*Seat*—Ostenhanger, Kent.

## GARTH, OF MORDEN.

GARTH, ELIZABETH, of Morden, in Surrey, *m.* in 1775, WILLIAM LOWNDES, esq. of Brightwell, in the county of Oxford, who subsequently assumed the additional surname of STONE, and by him, who *d.* in 1830, had several children, (SEE *page* 259) of whom the second son,

RICHARD, in holy orders, is her heir. He *m.* Mary, daughter of — Douglas, esq. of Worcester, and has issue.

Mrs. (Garth) Lowndes-Stone, inherited the estate at the decease of her elder sister, Mrs. Clara Meyrick, without male issue, in 1827.

## Lineage.

The family of GARTH was first settled at Morden about the year 1500.

EDWARD GARTH, esq. one of the six clerks of the Court of Chancery, left a son,

RICHARD GARTH, esq. of Morden, living in 1564, who *m.* first, Elizabeth, daughter of — Dixon, and had by her,

- ROBERT, who *m.* Elizabeth, daughter of Sir Benjamin Tichborne, and *d.* 25th April, 1613.
- GEORGE, of whom presently.
- Thomas, who *m.* a daughter of — Sampson, of London.
- Lazarus, *d. s. p.*

- Jane, *m.* to Sir John Savile, one of the Barons of the Exchequer, *temp.* JAMES I. and had one son, Sir Henry Savile, of Methley, bart. who *d. s. p.* in 1633, and two daughters, Elizabeth, *m.* to Sir John Jackson, knt. of Hickleton, and Jane, to Sir Henry Goodrich, of Ribston.

He married, secondly, Jane, daughter of — Busher, esq. of Lincolnshire, by whom he had a son, Alexander, of Ravensbury, in Mitcham, 1623, who married Alice, daughter of the Rev. Richard Ward, rector of Bedington, and had issue. Richard Garth's second son,

GEORGE GARTH, esq. of Morden, married Jane, daughter of Anthony Duffield, esq. and by her who died in 1609, aged forty, had several children, by the eldest of whom,

RICHARD GARTH, esq. of Morden, he was succeeded at his decease, 19th April, 1627. This gentleman wedded Dorothy Styles, and dying 23rd November, 1639, aged forty-four, left a son,

GEORGE GARTH, esq. of Morden, who *m.* in 1646, Anne, eldest daughter of Sir John Carleton, bart. of Brightwell and Holcomb, Oxfordshire, by Anne, his wife, relict of Sir John Cotton, knt. and daughter of Sir R. Houghton, of Houghton Tower, in Lancashire. By this lady, who was co-heir of her brother Sir George Carleton, he had issue,

- I. George, who *d.* an infant.
- II. RICHARD, his heir.

- I. Dorothy, who *d.* in 1693, } all unm.
- II. Anne, who *d.* in 1671, } all unm.
- III. Catharine, who *d.* in 1688, } all unm.

Mr. Garth's first wife died in 1655, and was buried at Morden, where a monument is erected to her memory. He *m.* secondly, Jane, daughter of Sir Humphrey Bennett, and had by her a son, Henry, who died young, and a daughter, Elizabeth, *m.* to — Gardiner, esq. He died in 1676, was interred under a monument at Morden, and succeeded by his son,

RICHARD GARTH, esq. of Morden, *b.* in 1651, who *m.* Miss Catharine Stone, and dying in 1700, was buried at Morden, and succeeded by his son,

RICHARD GARTH, esq. *b.* in 1682, who *m.* Elizabeth, daughter of William Emerson, and was succeeded at his decease 10th January, 1727, by his only son,

RICHARD GARTH, esq. of Morden, *b.* in 1714, who wedded Mary, daughter of Peter Leheup, esq. of the parish of St. GEORGE'S, Hanover-square, by Clara, his wife, daughter of William Lowndes, esq. of Winslow, in Buckinghamshire, and by her, who *d.* 19th January, 1780, aged forty-seven, left three daughters, namely,

- CLARA, his heir, *m.* in 1774, to Owen Putland Meyrick, esq. of Bodorgan.
- ELIZABETH, *m.* to William Lowndes Stone, esq. Of this lady presently, as inheritor of the estates from her sister.
- MARY, *m.* to Sir John Frederick, bart. *d.* in 1794, leaving issue.

Mr. Garth dying without male children in 1787, devised his estates at Morden to his eldest daughter for life, with remainder to her second son, and on failure of her male issue, to his younger daughters, with a similar reversion. Accordingly at Mr. Garth's decease, his eldest daughter,

CLARA GARTH, then married to Owen Putland Meyrick, esq. of Bordorgan, became proprietor of Morden, but leaving at her decease in 1827, daughters only, viz. Clara, *m.* to Augustus Elliott Fuller esq. and Lucy, to — Hartman, esq. she was succeeded by her next sister, ELIZABETH LOWNDES STONE, the present possessor of the estates.

*Arms*—Or, two lions passant in pale between three cross crosslets fitchee sa.

*Estates*—At Morden, Merton, and Mitcham, in Surrey.

*Seat*—Morden.

## HALFORD, OF PADDOCK HOUSE.

HALFORD, RICHARD, esq. of Paddock House, in Kent, *b.* in 1766, *m.* first, Sarah, daughter of Robert Tournay Bargrave, esq. of Eastry Court, and had by her an only son,

ROBERT-BARGRAVE, who *d.* at the age of twenty.

Mr. Halford wedded, secondly, Charlotte,* relict of George Denne, esq. late of Chislett Court, in the same county, but has no issue.

### Lineage.

The HALFORDS of Kent derive either from the son or brother of Sir Richard Halford, the first baronet of Wistow, but, owing to the loss of some family documents at the time of the revolution, the precise fact cannot now be ascertained. The house of Halford, one of great antiquity, was, originally seated in Warwickshire, at a place called Halford, where one branch of the family continued to reside until a century and a half ago. Dugdale, in his history of that county, mentions a Robert de Halford, of Halford, who held half a knight's fee under the Earl of Warwick, *temp.* HENRY III. The senior branch, the Halfords, of Wistow, maintained for several generations a leading position in the county of Leicester, until the decease of Sir Charles Halford, in 1780, when Wistow passed, under his will to his widow, who bequeathed the estate to her nephew, Dr. VAUGHAN who was subsequently created a BARONET, and assuming in 1815 the surname of Halford, is the present SIR HENRY HALFORD.

RICHARD HALFORD, esq. son of the Rev. Richard Halford, who held the living of Lyminge, in Kent, a scion of the Wistow family, married Mary Creed, niece of Sir James Creed, M.P. for the city of Canterbury, about the year 1760, and left, with two daughters, Mary and Sarah, a son,

RICHARD HALFORD, esq. of Canterbury, who wedded in 1775, Elizabeth, only daughter of Thomas Staines, esq. grandfather of Sir Thomas Staines, K.C.B. of the Isle of Thanet, and had issue,

RICHARD, his heir.

George, major in the 59th regiment of infantry, who distinguished himself in several engagements, and was abroad under the Duke of Wellington, in all his campaigns, until sent to join the first battalion of his regiment at Calcutta, where he *d.* unmarried in 1826.

Mr. Halford was succeeded by his elder son, the present RICHARD HALFORD, esq. of Paddock.

*Arms*—Arg. a greyhound passant sa. on a chief az. three fleurs-de-lis or.

*Crest*—A demi greyhound, sa. collared or.

*Motto*—Virtus in actione consistit.

*Estates*—Wingmore Court and Alkham, in Kent.

*Seat*—The Paddock House, near Canterbury.

* This lady has a daughter by her first husband.

## DRUMMOND, OF CADLANDS.

DRUMMOND, ANDREW-ROBERT, esq. of Cadlands, in the county of Hants, *b.* in 1794, *m.* 7th March, 1822, Lady Elizabeth-Frederica Manners, daughter of John-Henry, present Duke of Rutland, and has issue,

I. ANDREW-JOHN, *b.* 13th May, 1823.
II. Edgar-Atheling, *b.* 21st August, 1825.
III. Alfred-Manners, *b.* 28th August, 1829.
IV. Another son, *b.* 4th June, 1833.

I. Annabella-Mary-Elizabeth.
II. Frederica-Mary-Adeliza.

Mr. Drummond succeeded his father in 1833.

### Lineage.

The family of DRUMMOND derives, according to Scotch genealogists, from MAURICE, an Hungarian, who accompanied Edgar-Atheling, and his sister Margaret, into Scotland, where he was appointed by MALCOLM III. Seneschal or Steward, of Lennox.

The Drummonds of Cadlands spring immediately from a younger son of the noble house of STRATHALLAN, which itself descended from a scion of the Lords Drummond.

WILLIAM DRUMMOND, 4th Viscount Strathallan, elder brother of Andrew Drummond, ancestor of the Drummonds of Stanmore, having personally espoused the fortunes of the CHEVALIER in 1745, was slain at the battle of Culloden, and his name included in the bill of attainder passed the following year. His lordship wedded the Hon. Margaret Murray, daughter of William, Lord Nairne, and had issue,

JAMES, attainted with his father. His line is EXTINCT.

WILLIAM, whose son, James-Andrew, was restored to the ancient honours of his family by act of parliament in 1824, and is the present VISCOUNT STRATHALLAN. (See BURKE's *Peerage*.)

ROBERT, of whom presently.

Henry, of the Grange, in Hampshire, *m.* in 1761, Elizabeth, daughter of the Honorable Charles Compton, and *d.* in 1795, leaving one son,

Henry, who *m.* in 1786, Anne, dau. of Henry, Viscount Melville, and by her, who wedded, secondly, James Strange, esq. had three sons and one daughter, viz.

Henry, of Albany Park, Surrey, *b.* in 1786, *m.* in 1807, Henrietta, dau. of Robert, ninth Earl of Kinnoul, and has issue, Malcolm, Arthur, Louisa, and Adelaide.

Robert, R. N. *b.* in 1789, died in 1811.

Spencer-Rodney, in holy orders, *m.* 6th May, 1817, Caroline, daughter of Montagu Montagu, esq. and has a dau. Caroline-Anne.

Elizabeth, *m.* in 1815, to John Portal, esq. of Freefolk, Hants.

The third son,

ROBERT DRUMMOND, *b.* in 1729, an eminent banker, of London, was seated at Cadlands, in Hampshire. He *m.* in 1753, Winifred, daughter of William Thompson, esq. of Ipston, in Oxfordshire, and granddaughter of Sir Berkeley Lucy, bart. by whom he had issue,

I. ANDREW-BERKELEY, his heir.
II. Charles, banker, of London, *b.* in 1759, *m.* in 1789, Frances-Dorothy, daughter of the Reverend Edward Lockwood, of Portman-square, and dying in 1823, left issue,
1. Charles, *b.* in 1790, *m.* in 1819, Mary-Dulcibella, daughter of William, first Lord Auckland, and has five sons, Robert, Charles, Maurice, Walter, and Morton; and three daughters, Theresa-Charlotte, Eleanor-Mary, and Mary-Dulcibella.
2. Edward, *b.* 30th March, 1792.
3. Berkeley, lieutenant-colonel in the army, *b.* 27th March, 1796, *m.* 5th April, 1832, Maria, dau. of William Arthur Crosbie, esq.
4. Arthur, in holy orders, *b.* 20th August, 1797, *m.* 13th May, 1830, Margaretta-Maria, second dau. of Sir Thomas Maryon Wilson, bart.

1. Charlotte-Matilda.
2. Anne-Elizabeth.

III. Henry-Roger, in holy orders, *m.* Susan, daughter of William Wells, esq. of Bickley, in Kent, and died in 1806, leaving issue,
1. Andrew.
2. Henry-Andrew, married in 1819, Maria, daughter of Captain William James Turquand, R.N. and has issue.

1. Katherine, *m.* to the Reverend George Randolph.

IV. Richard, an officer in the 19th dragoons, died unmarried in Dalmatia, 1796.
V. Edward, colonel of the 60th foot.

I. Charlotte-Teresa, *m.* to Peregrine-Edward Towneley, esq. of Towneley, in Lancashire. (See vol. 2, p. 262.)

Mr. Drummond died in 1804, and was *s.* by his eldest son,

ANDREW BERKELEY DRUMMOND, esq. of Cadlands, *b.* in 1755, who *m.* in 1781, Lady Mary Percival, daughter of John, second Earl of Egmont, and had two sons and two daughters, viz.

I. ANDREW-ROBERT, his heir.
II. William-Charles, a lieutenant-col. in the army, *b.* 4th July, 1796.

I. Mary, *m.* in 1830, to the Reverend Francis Fulford.
II. Catherine-Isabella, *m.* in 1826, to the Reverend Henry Perceval, son of the Right Hon. Spencer Perceval, and nephew to Lord Arden.

Mr. Drummond *d.* in December, 1833, and was succeeded by his son, the present ANDREW-ROBERT DRUMMOND, esq. of Cadlands.

*Arms*—Quarterly, 1st and 4th or, three bars wavy gu. 2nd and 3rd or, a lion's head, erased, within a double tressure flory, counterflory, gu.

*Crest*—A goshawk, wings expanded, ppr.

*Estates*—In Hampshire, &c.

*Seat*—Cadlands, Hants.

## DRUMMOND, OF STANMORE.

DRUMMOND, GEORGE-HARLEY, esq. of Stanmore, in Middlesex, *b.* in 1783, *m.* in 1801, Margaret, daughter of Alexander Munro, esq. of Glasgow, and has issue,

GEORGE, *b.* in 1802, *m.* in 1831, Marianne, daughter of Henry Berkeley Portman, esq. of Bryanston, in Dorsetshire, (see vol i. p. 63) and has issue.

Henry-Dundas, in the army, *b.* in 1812.
Margaret.

Mr. Drummond succeeded his father in 1789, and has represented the county of Kincardine in parliament.

## Lineage.

Andrew Drummond, esq. (brother of William, 4th Viscount Strathallan,) founder of the well known banking-house of Drummond and Co. purchased the estate of Stanmore, in Middlesex, in 1729, and died in 1769, aged eighty-two, leaving, by Strachan, his wife, a daughter, Isabel, *m.* to Captain Peters, and a son,

John Drummond, esq. of Stanmore, in Middlesex, M.P. for Thetford, who married in 1744, Charlotte, daughter of Lord William Beauclerk, son of Charles, 1st Duke of St. Albans, and had issue,

I. George, his heir.
II. John, banker of London, *b.* in 1766, *m.* first, in 1789, Hester, sister of Thomas Cholmondeley, Lord Delamere, and had one son and two daughters, viz.
    1. John, born in 1791, married Georgiana-Augusta, daughter of Admiral Sir Eliab Harvey, G.C.B. of Rolls Park, Essex, and has several sons and daughters.
    1. Charlotte, *m.* in 1823, to Robert Hibbert, esq.
    2. Harriet-Anne.

    Mr. John Drummond wedded, secondly, in 1806, Barbara, daughter of Charles Chester, esq. of Chicheley, Bucks, and had by her, two sons and a daughter, viz.
    2. Spencer, *b.* 12th October, 1808.
    3. Heneage, *b.* in 1810.
    3. Frances-Elizabeth-Barbara.

I. Charlottee, *m.* in 1769, to her cousin Reverend Henry Beauclerk.
II. Jane-Diana, *m.* in 1776, to Richard Bethel Cox, esq.

Mr. Drummond *d.* in 1774, and was *s.* by his elder son,

George Drummond, esq. of Stanmore, *b.* in 1758, who *m.* in 1779 Martha, daughter of the Right Hon. Thomas Harley, and had issue,

I. George-Harley, his heir.
II. Andrew-Mortimer, *b.* in 1786, *m.* in 1808, Lady Emily-Charlotte-Percy, daughter of Algernon, Earl of Beverley, and has,
    1. Mortimer-Percy, *b.* 7th September, 1816.

    1. Emily-Susan.
    2. Eleanor-Charlotte.
    3. Julia-Frances.
    4. Cecil-Elizabeth.
    5. Agnes-Priscilla.
    6. Susan-Charlotte.
    7. Marian.

I. Henrietta-Maria, *m.* in 1803, to Vice Admiral Sir Charles Hamilton, bart.

Mr. Drummond died in 1789, and was succeeded by his son, the present George Harley Drummond, esq. of Stanmore.

*Arms and Crest*—See Drummond, of Cadlands.

*Estates*—In Middlesex, and in Scotland.

*Seat*—Stanmore.

# RODES, OF BARLBOROUGH.

RODES-REASTON, *The Reverend* CORNELIUS-HEATHCOTE, M.A. of Barlborough, in the county of Derby, *b.* 3rd March, 1792, *m.* at St. George's, Hanover-square, 18th June, 1825, Anna-Maria-Harriet, youngest daughter of William Gossip, esq. of Hatfield House, in Yorkshire.

This gentleman, whose patronymic is Reaston, assumed by sign manual, 20th April, 1825, the additional surname and arms of Rodes, upon succeeding to the estates of his uncle, Cornelius Heathcote Rodes, esq.

## Lineage.

The first settler in England of this family, on genealogical record, is "GERARD DE RODES, a feudal baron, the capital seat of whose barony was Horn Castle, in Lincolnshire: he lived in the reigns of HENRY II., RICHARD I., JOHN, and HENRY III., from all of whom he received great favours; and by *King* JOHN was sent embassador to foreign parts 29th March, in the 9th year of his reign."

It is probable that Gerard de Rodes was one of the family of the Counts d'Armagnac and Rodes, or Rhodes, mentioned by Froissart, vol. x. p. 354, who came over with HENRY II. and Margaret his mother, from Normandy; but as these Counts seem designated by the first title, D'Armagnac, it is equally, and perhaps more probable, that *his* ancestor was a De Rhodes, hereditary knight* of Flanders, mentioned in Froissart, (vol. i. p. 121, and elsewhere), among the nobility of Flanders, who came over with the Earl of Flanders and Tofti, Harold's brother, to assist WILLIAM the Conqueror.

As we find in Camden that the barony of Horn Castle was a soke, or seigniory of thirteen lordships, Gerard de Rodes was consequently a greater baron; and as embassador he attained a still higher rank; his absence in that capacity will account for his name not occurring on the Roll of Magna Charta: there is no genealogical account of the extinction of the baronial title; but we find in Camden that the barony itself was given by RICHARD II. to the Bishop of Carlysle and his successors.†

From GERARD DE RODES lineally descended

WILLIAM DE RHODES, (the son of Thomas, of Thorp, juxta Rotheram, in Yorkshire), who *m.* Anne, daughter and heiress of John Cachehorse, of Stavely Woodthorpe, in Derbyshire, and had a son and successor,

JOHN RODES, of Stavely Woodthorpe, whose son,

JOHN RODES, or RHODES, of Stavely Woodthorpe, was father of

ROBERT RODES, of Stavely Woodthorpe, who *m.* Elizabeth, daughter of — Wasse, and had

JOHN RODES, of Stavely Woodthorpe, high sheriff for Derbyshire in 1591, who left, by his first wife, Attelina, daughter of Thomas Hewit, of Wallis, or Wales, in Yorkshire, a son and successor,

FRANCIS RODES, of Stavely Woodthorpe, one of the justices of the Common Pleas in the time of ELIZABETH. This gentleman built Barlborough Hall in 1583, but died at his residence at Stavely Woodthorpe a few years after its completion. He *m.* first Elizabeth, daughter of Brian Sandford, esq. of Thorp Salvine, in Yorkshire, and had, with daughters, two sons,

I. JOHN, his heir, *b.* 1562.
II. Peter, of Hickleton.

The judge *m.* secondly, Mary, daughter of Francis Charlton, esq. of Appley, in Shropshire, by whom he had, with other issue, a son,

GODFREY (Sir), of Great Houghton, knighted at Havering, 13th July, 1615, who married four wives, and left, with other issue, a daughter, Elizabeth, the third wife and widow of the ill-fated Earl of Strafford, and a son and successor,

SIR EDWARD RODES, knt. of Great Houghton,‡ from whom descended

---

* Flanders was at that period generally in alliance with England. We find in Froissart a Sir John de Rhodes, among other knights, coming over to Yorkshire to serve in EDWARD's army against Bruce, vol. i. p. 40. We, however, see subsequently, p. 125, the same knight, or his descendants, Sir John de Rhodes, laying down his life for his legitimate sovereign in the island of Ladsant, against a low usurper supported by the English.—*Hume.*

† Camden's Britannia, Lincolnshire, p. 418.

‡ Of Sir Edward Rhodes, of Great Houghton, the following account is extracted from "Hunter's History of Doncaster."

"Notwithstanding the near connection which subsisted between Sir Edward Rhodes and the

William Rodes, esq. of Great Houghton, the last male heir of this branch of the family, who died unmarried in 1740, leaving his two sisters, his co-heirs, viz. Mary, who *d.* unm. and Martha, who wedded Hans Busk, esq. of Leeds, and had, with other children, who died issueless, a daughter, Rachael Busk, the wife of Richard Slater Milnes, esq. M.P. of Fryston.

Judge Rodes's eldest son,

Sir John Rodes, knighted at the Tower, 15th March, 1603, high sheriff of Derbyshire 36 Elizabeth, sold Stavely Woodthorpe, now attached to Bolsover, the Duke of Portland's, and resided at Barlborough: he had three wives; the first was Anne, daughter of George Benson, of Westmoreland, by whom he had no issue; the second, Dorothy, daughter of George Savile, esq. of Wakefield, in Yorkshire, grandson of Sir John Savile, of Thornhill, by whom he had one son, John Rhodes, of Horbury, supposed, from presumptive evidence, to have been ancestor of the Devonshire family of Rhodes (see Rhodes, of Bellair); and the third was Frances, daughter of Marmaduke Constable, of Holderness, by whom he left, at his decease in 1639, with other children, who appear to have died unmarried, two daughters, Lennox, *m.* to Sir Marmaduke Langdale, first Lord Langdale, and Catherine, the wife of Sir George Hotham, and a son and successor,

Sir Francis Rodes, of Barlborough, in Derbyshire, knighted at Whitehall, 9th August, 1641, and created a baronet the 14th of the same month, who *m.* Elizabeth, daughter and sole heiress of Sir George Lassells, knt. of Sturton and Gateford, Notts. and by her, (who wedded, secondly, Allan Lockhart, and died in 1666,) had with several daughters, five sons, viz.

- I. Lassells, died during his father's lifetime, in infancy.
- II. Francis, heir.
- III. Peter, a divine, slain at Winfield Manor.
- IV. Clifton, who *m.* first, Lettice, fourth daughter of Sir Gervase Clifton, of Clifton, by the Lady Frances Clifford his wife, daughter of the Right Hon. Francis, Earl of Cumberland, and, secondly, Elizabeth, daughter of John Skrimshire, of Cottgrave, by whom he had a son John.*
- V. John, of Sturton, who *m.* Elizabeth, daughter of Simon Jessop, esq. and had, with two other sons, who married in America, a successor,
  - John, who *m.* Mary, daughter of William Tigh, of London, son of Tigh, of Carlby, in Lincolnshire, and had issue.

---

Earl of Strafford, there was a wide difference in the political views of each. Few persons entered more eagerly into the objects contemplated by the parliament, when affairs were advancing to a crisis; and it was for the most part to Sir Edward Rhodes, and his two friends the Hothams, that the scheme for maintaining the peace of Yorkshire, arranged by the two great parties at Rothwell before the war began, was frustrated: his zeal might be quickened by personal injury; for in the beginning of September, 1642, an attack was made on his house at Great Houghton, by a party of royalists under the command of Captain Grey, when, according to the diurnals of the time, all the outhouses were burnt, his goods' plundered to the amount of £600, his lady uncivilly treated, some of his servants wounded, and one slain. One of the stipulations at the treaty of Rothwell was that reparation should be made to Sir Edward Rodes for the injury done him."

"Of all the gentry of Yorkshire," says Clarendon, "there were only two dissenters, on the parliament side, to that engagement of neutrality, young Hotham and Sir Edward Rodes who, although of better quality, was not so much known or considered as the other; but they quickly found seconds enough when the parliament refused to ratify the treaty, and declared it to be injurious to the common cause."—*History of the Rebellion.*

His name is not prominent in the history of the military affairs of the time; he served under Cromwell at the battle of Preston, and was sent in pursuit of the Duke of Hamilton: he had a colonel's commission from Cromwell in 1654, and was one of his privy council: it would seem that he was much in Scotland[1] during the protectorate, for he was returned member to one of Cromwell's parliaments for the shire of Perth, at the same time that his son was returned for Linlithgow, Stirling, and Clackmannan. At the restoration he was allowed to retire quietly to his house at Great Houghton, where he was living at Sir William Dugdale's visitation, but died soon after.

* This John is stated in a pedigree drawn up by Robert Dale, Blanch Lion, in 1695, to have been *cast away at sea*. There appears however to be considerable doubt as to the fact, which most probably refers to John, of Horbury, the brother of the first bart.

[1] It would appear, from the following quotations of Sir Walter Scott from Old Ballads, that the family had a seat either in Scotland, or somewhere on the borders nearer than Horncastle, Lincolnshire.

"The house of the Rhodes on the hill."
*Old Ballad.*

The Gordon then his bugle blew,
And said, "Awa, awa,
The house of Rhodes is all on fire,
I hold it time to 'ga."

Sir Francis was *s.* at his decease in 1645 by his eldest son,

SIR FRANCIS RODES, second baronet, of Barlborough, who *m.* Anne, daughter of Sir Gervase Clifton, bart. of Clifton, by the Lady Frances Clifford, his wife, daughter of Francis, Earl of Cumberland, and had, with a daughter, Jane, *m.* to Captain Hussey, a son and successor,

SIR FRANCIS RODES, third baronet, of Barlborough, sheriff of Notts. in 1671, who *m.* Martha, daughter of William Thornton, esq. of Grantham, and had issue,

I. JOHN (Sir), his heir.

I. Frances, who *m.* Gilbert Heathcote, esq. M.D. of Cutthorp, in Derbyshire, and had a son and two daughters, viz.

Cornelius Heathcote, M.D. who *m.* Elizabeth Middlebrooke, of Thorn, in Yorkshire, and had issue,

GILBERT HEATHCOTE, of whom presently, as successor to his great uncle, SIR JOHN RODES.

John Heathcote, who died at the age of twenty-eight, leaving, by Milicent Saterthwaite, his wife, two sons and two daughters, viz.

1. CORNELIUS, successor to his uncle.
2. John, died unm.

1. Elizabeth, who *m.* the Rev. Philip Acklom Reaston, rector of Barlborough, and *d.* in 1821, leaving a son,

CORNELIUS - HEATHCOTE REASTON, who inherited Barlborough from his uncle, and is the present proprietor.

2. Mary, *m.* first, to — Miers; and, secondly, to Capt. Massey.

Martha, *m.* to Benjamin Bartlett, esq. of Bradford.

Elizabeth, *m.* to Peter Acklom, esq. of Hornsey.

II. Anne, *m.* to William Thornton, of Bloxham.

Sir Francis Rodes died in 1675, and was *s.* by his son,

SIR JOHN RODES, fourth baronet, of Barlborough, who died unm. in 1743, and was *s.* by his grand-nephew,

CORNELIUS HEATHCOTE, esq. who then became of Barlborough, and assumed the surname and arms of RODES. He died unmarried, in 1768, when the estates passed to his nephew,

CORNELIUS HEATHCOTE, esq. of Barlborough, who also took the name of RODES. Dying unm. 6th March, 1825, aged seventy, he was succeeded by his nephew, the Rev. CORNELIUS - HEATHCOTE REASTON, who, adopting the surname of RODES, is the present Rev. CORNELIUS-HEATHCOTE-REASTON RODES, of Barlborough.

*Arms*—Quarterly, 1st and 4th arg. a lion passant guardant in bend gu. between two acorns az. within as many cotises ermines. 2nd and 3rd, arg. on a chev. gu. between three rudders az. as many cinquefoils of the field.

*Crests*—1st, a cubit arm erect, grasping an oak branch, all ppr. 2nd, a demi-lion rampant arg. collared or, sustaining a rudder az. and a banner gu. charged with a cinquefoil arg.

*Estates*—In the parishes of Barlborough, Elmton, and Brampton, in Derbyshire.

*Seat*—Barlborough Hall. "This seat," says Pilkington, "is a handsome mansion of the age of *Queen* ELIZABETH, having been built in her reign by Francis Rodes, one of the justices of the Common Pleas. The principal front of this house retains its original appearance, having projecting bows terminating in octagonal embattled turrets, and large transom windows: the inside has been modernized; but in one of the lower rooms, taken out of the great chamber, is a very magnificent stone chimney-piece, enriched with fluted Doric pillars, supporting statues of Justice and Religion, and coats of arms and various articles in bas-relief: in the upper part are the arms of Rodes, with these inscriptions, "Francis Rodes serviens suæ Reginæ ad legem Anno Domini 1584, ætatis suæ 50." In the lower part are two shields of the arms of Rodes with different empalements, the one supported by a judge on the dexter, and a lady on the sinister side, inscribed Elizabeth Sandford; the other with similar supporters inscribed Franciscus Rodes, Maria Charlton; at the bottom is this inscription, Constitutus Justiciarius in Banco Communi 30 ELIZ. On the sides are other inscriptions, more particularly describing the wives and their issues: the buff coat and sword of Sir Francis Rodes, worn in the time of CHARLES I. are preserved in this house; they are engraved in Grose's Ancient Armour, plate xxxix."

# RHODES, OF BELLAIR AND SHAPWICK.

**RHODES, GEORGE AMBROSE,** esq. of Bellair and Shapwick, both in the county of Devon, Fellow of Gonville and Caius College, Cambridge, and a Doctor of Medicine; inherited the estates at the decease of his cousin, Ambrose Andrew Rhodes, esq. one of the gentlemen of the privy chamber to his Majesty *King* GEORGE III. in November, 1800.*

## Lineage.

JOHN RHODES, of Horbury, the eldest son of Sir John Rhodes, knt. of Barlborough, is supposed to have been the first † settler in Devonshire, where, by the professional industry, talent, and integrity of his posterity, one of them, in the person of Ambrose Rhodes, esq. of Buckland House, Buckland, Toussaint, was restored to that rank in society from which his progenitor had been displaced.

John, of Horbury, is so designated in Wotton, and in the pedigree ‡ at the herald's college, where it is added, "that he was disinherited." This exact coincidence with the family tradition, together with an oral communication § between one of the Barlborough family and the grandfather of the present Mr. Rhodes in 1755, appears to identify John Rhodes, of Horbury, with John Rhodes, the first settler at Modbury, in Devon, whose marriage to Blanche Hamlyn, in 1610, is on the Modbury register. As none of the name occur again on the register, until 1663, this omission also corresponds with another part of the family tradition, as will appear hereafter.

We are thus enabled, by tradition, confirmed by correspondence of name, time, and place; by the credibility of witnesses; by presumptive and collateral evidence; and an examination of cotemporary public records, to follow the fortunes, and trace the family history of this gentleman and his descendants, for two generations without having had access to any other ¶ account of him but the two brief notices above mentioned.

Following those guides, it will appear

* Mr. Rhodes, in right of his mother, is representative of the family of Sleech, of Sussex, now extinct in name, and, through his maternal grandmother has become, by the recent death of John Burridge Cholwich, esq. of Faringdon House, and Cholwich Town, the lineal representative of that ancient Saxon family. He is descended both paternally and maternally from the Earls of Devon and the Plantagenets.

† None of the name of Rhodes were, previously to 1610, to be found in Devonshire, nor indeed, at the present period, is there another family of the name in any of the three western counties.

‡ Recently examined, 1834.

§ The result of this interview, as communicated by Mrs. Bridget Hartwell, a near relative of the present proprietor, who was at it, was briefly as follows: "That the armorial bearings[1] of the parties were found, on comparison, to be similar; that the first settler at Modbury was *the eldest son of a knight*, who, finding himself *disinherited by his father*, sailed from *Yorkshire* to Germany; and returning shortly after, was shipwrecked in Bigbury Bay; landed at Marlborough, and purchased property at Modbury."

¶ We find him, however, alluded to in Betham's Baronetage, Art. *Milnes*, "Sir John Rodes, whose *second son*, Francis, was created a baronet, 1641."

[1] Confirmed to Ambrose Rhodes, esq. of Buckland, in 1726, on his marriage, with those of Andrew: arms of Rhodes empaling Andrew.

that John Rhodes, being educated by his maternal grandfather, Mr. Savile, of Wakefield, and commercially established at Horbury,* a manufacturing town in the parish of Wakefield, on finding, when he came of age, that his younger brother was heir elect to his father's domain, freighted a ship for Germany, with a view to a commercial speculation, and also to visit some relatives in Saxony, and to fix his residence there; and that, returning shortly after, either repentant, or in the course of traffic, he was, by stress of weather, driven into Bigbury Bay, on the south coast of Devon; that his vessel was saved by the precautions of the then Sir Philip Courtenay,† lord of the manors adjacent; that he landed near a small town called Marlborough, and dated a letter to his friends from that place, giving an account of his disaster; but not receiving any answer, (as it subsequently appeared from a misapprehension, they knowing only one Marlborough inland), he purchased property ‡ at Modbury, and married there; and shortly after his marriage returned§ with his wife to Germany, where a son was born to him, who was named Ambrose, after his relative, Ambrosius Rhodius, ¶ a celebrated professor of astronomy at Wittenberg, which name has been cherished by his descendants for six subsequent generations.

Ambrose Rhodes, the son of John Rhodes and Blanche Hamlyn, was educated at the University of Wittenberg, and took the degree of doctor of medicine. He married, according to the date on an old piece of plate, a wedding present, in 1638. His wife was, traditionally, one of the daughters of Ambrosius Rhodius, his godfather. He practised at Christiana, in Norway, and was professor of natural philosophy at the college there; but, according to Moreri (Supplement), interfering imprudently in political affairs, he was confined in the fortress of Wardehuis, in 1660, and died a year or two after in imprisonment. He wrote "De Astrorum Inflexu," 1642, "De Transmutatione Animarum Pythagoreâ," and sundry medical treatises.

His son and successor,

Ambrose Rhodes, *b.* 1640, having received a medical education at Christiana, came, after the death of his father, under such unfortunate circumstances, to England, and took possession of the small patrimonial property at Modbury, in Devon, to which he made some additions, and practised as a physician in that town until the time of his death, in 1689. He married first, 1663,

* This place is written Harbury in Wotton, but Horbury is evidently designed, there being no such place as Harbury in Yorkshire.

† See Polwhele's History of Devon, Notes on Marlborough and West Allington.

‡ The property, house, and land, is found rated, on some old parish books, to his grandson, in 1665, under the name of Dr. Rhodes, whose arms, on an old deed, show a foreign impression.

§ Probably having disposed of his cargo saved, and re-shipping another from Modbury, then a commercial town.

¶ The following account of Ambrosius Rhodius[1] or De Rhodes, is taken from Freberi Theatrum virorum illustrium, and Aikin's Biography. "He was born at Kemberg, a town near Wittenberg, in Saxony, in 1577; his father was Ambrose Rhodes,[2] consul at that place; his mother, the daughter of Matthew Winckell, the superior of its church. After a previous classical education, he was sent to Wittenberg, where, with a studentship given to him by the elector, he was instructed in the sciences of mathematics and medicine. Shortly after, by the recommendation of Melchier Justel, he went to Prague to assist Tycho Braye in his observations; he there obtained the friendship of the celebrated Kepler.

On his return to Wittenberg, after a tour through Moravia and Syria, he gave lectures in mathematics, and was elected mathematical professor in 1609, with a stipend from the Elector of Saxony; and became doctor of medicine in 1610. In 1612 he married Catherine, daughter of John Tanger, his predecessor in office, and had a large family. He brought water, at his own expense, into the city of Wittenberg, which water was called the Aqua Rhodia. After attaining other university honours and preferments, he died of apoplexy, at the age of fifty-six, in 1633. He wrote on the Comet, in 1618; on Twilight; on the use of Learning in a Republic. The following anagram was added to his epitaph, by Augustus Bucknerus.

"Io Musis das robur."

It will appear, from the above anagram, that this celebrated man was also a poet, or critic. Being also classed by Freherus among the archiatres, or

[1] It was usual in those days for learned men at the foreign universities, to Latinize their names.

[2] We have no means at present of ascertaining of what nation this gentleman was consul, (probably in a mercantile capacity), nor his affinity to the Barlborough family, whether direct or collateral, as a descendant of the knights of Flanders; an identity of name, time, and place, together with other contingencies, suggest a connection with the history of Ambrose, called the good Earl of Warwick, elder brother of the Earl of Leicester, who, at the probable time of his birth, in 1552, was serving in the Spanish armies in the low countries; and subsequently patronised commerce, and was said to have speculated in the woollen trade, which was not thought at that period beneath the dignity of a nobleman. In the time of Froissart, that branch of commerce was of such importance, that we see a delegate of the staple sent to Flanders, with the arbitration of peace or war.

Elizabeth Baker, who died in the following year, and secondly, in 1667, Juliana, daughter of Thomas Prestwood, esq. of Whitford and Baterford, by whom he had

AMBROSE, of whom presently.

Alice, who m. Richard Collins, esq. merchant, of Modbury, and had an only daughter, Phillis, m. to —— Hurrel,‡ esq. whose daughter, Phillis, m. to Thomas Froude, esq. of Edmesson, in the parish of Modbury, was mother of the present Venerable Archdeacon Froude, of Edmesson.

The only son,

AMBROSE RHODES, followed his father's profession, and purchased sundry estates in Little Modbury, together with the great tithes, all which have descended to the present family. He m. in 1703, Elizabeth, daughter of George Prestwood, esq. of Whitford and Baterford, mentioned as follows, in Prince's Worthies of Devon: "George Prestwood, esq. who was sheriff of the county in 1692, whose ancestor, several generations back, transplanted himself from Worcestershire, where the present gentleman possesses still a fair paternal estate." Risdon, also, speaking of Baterford, says, "William Gibbs, of Fenton, sold the same to Thomas Prestwood, of Exon (great grandfather of George, the above), who deriveth his descent from Worcestershire, and is allied to antient houses* in this county." Mr. Rhodes had issue,

AMBROSE, his heir.

George, who was educated at Eton and Oxford for a physician, but was recalled, without graduating at the university, to assist his father in his practice, which was very extensive. He is mentioned in the memoirs of Bampfylde More Carew, rather in his sporting than medical capacity. He followed for some years his own hounds, and his profession, with equal spirit and success; but shortly after his father's death, who bequeathed him the largest share of his pro-

physicians to kings, and being a privy counsellor of the Elector, and professor more than twenty years, he ranked, by German law, as a nobleman, and was a member of the Upper Diet. Family tradition has always spoken of him as also an astrologer, and practiser of legerdemain, which is highly probable, as astrology was in those days almost invariably connected with astronomy; and he, no doubt, caught his conjuring propensities from Tycho Braye, who is said by Cox,[1] in his Memoirs, to have entertained JAMES I. who visited him at Prague, with various feats of jugglery.[2] Much matter of curious investigation is afforded by the connexion in those days of the abstruse sciences with magic, of astronomy with prophecy, the fate of nations and of princes, which has been turned to a poor account by some late writers on these subjects.—*Tour in Denmark, &c.*

‡ Of Totness, descendant of Hurrels, of Woodleigh.

[1] Tour in Denmark, &c.

[2] There is now at Bellair a picture, or copy of a picture, of Ambrosius Rhodius, worked in worsted, habited as a knight, performing tricks of legerdemain before knights and ladies. Underneath the picture we find the initials C. T. 1740. The initials are those of Lady Charity Treby, wife of the Hon. Sir George Treby, secretary at war, of Plympton House, a near relative and neighbour of Mr. Rhodes, of Buckland; this web was probably, therefore, her workmanship. (*See Descent of Prestwood.*) The combination in this picture of characters so little apparently congruous, would seem a playful performance of the lady above mentioned, if biography did not inform us that not only Tycho Braye, but Cornelius Agrippa, was philosopher, knight, and conjurer.

* In the time of Risdon, Prestwoood was allied to Courtenay, Strode, Champernown, Martyn, Clifford, Fortescue, Hele; subsequently became allied to Osborne, Duke of Leeds, Treby, Molesworth, Parker, Drewe, Kelly, Drake, and Churchill.

WILLIAM STRODE, of Newenham, *temp.* Queen ELIZABETH, m. Elizabeth, only daughter and heiress of Sir Philip Courtenay, and grand-daughter of Philip Courtenay, of Molland, who was great-grandson of Hugh Courtenay, earl of Devon, by Elizabeth Bohun, his wife, grand-daughter of EDWARD I. Besides other issue, William Strode left two daughters,

1. ELIZABETH STRODE, who m. Walter Hele, of Lewston, and dying in 1632, left a son,

SAMPSON HELE, who wedded Johanna Glanville, and had one son and one daughter, viz.

SAMPSON HELE, whose grandson, Roger Hele, of Halwell, m. Juliana, daughter of Thomas Prestwood, and left two daughters,

Juliana, m. first, to Peregrine, third Duke of Leeds, and secondly, to Lord Portmore.

Charity, m. to Sir Geo. Treby, M.P. of Plympton House.

Susan Hele, who m. Thomas Isaacke, esq. of Polshoe, and was grandmother of Frances Isaacke, who m. WILLIAM CHOLWICH, esq. of Oldston, and their great-grandson,

JOHN CHOLWICH, esq. of Faringdon House, m. Philippa Hornbrooke, and had a son and daughter, viz.

John, whose son, John Burridge Colwich, esq. d. s. p. in 1835.

Mary, m. to the Rev. John Sleech; and their dau. Elizabeth, marrying the Rev. GEORGE RHODES, was mother of the present GEORGE AMBROSE RHODES, esq. of Bellair.

perty, he gave up his medical pursuits, and lived as a private gentleman. He *m.* in 1740, Elizabeth, dau. of the Rev. Archdeacon Baker, vicar of Modbury, and sister of Sir George Baker, bart. physician to GEORGE III. and dying in 1772, aged sixty-nine, left issue,

I. George, *b.* in 1743, of Exeter College, Oxford, vicar of Colyton Shute, and Monckton, in Devon, who *m.* Elizabeth, daughter of the Rev. JOHN SLEECH, Archdeacon of Cornwall, and had,

1. GEORGE-AMBROSE, of whom presently as successor to his cousin and present representative of the family.
2. John, who died young.
3. Ambrose-William, in holy orders, late of Worcester College, Oxford, *d.* 1818.
4. Charles-Sleech,* Captain of the Royal Engineers, killed at the storming and capture of St. Sebastian, 31st August, 1813.
5. John-Henry, Capt. R. N. who married Barbara, only daughter and heir of Charles Clay, esq. of Ryllin, near St. Asaph, N. Wales.
6. Baker, drowned while young.
7. Edward-Duncan, B.D. rector of Ermington, Devon.

1. Elizabeth-Maria.
2. Susannah Loveday.
3. Frances-Bridget, died in 1832.
4. Mary-Sleech, *d.* in 1828.
5. Charlotte-Anna, married to John-Gustavus Ferriman, esq. of Rhodeville, near Cheltenham.

---

II. MARIA STRODE, who *m.* Thomas Prestwood, esq. of Whitford and Baterford, son of Thomas Prestwood, esq. of Exon, and grandson of Reginald Prestwood, of Worcestershire, and had a son,

GEORGE PRESTWOOD, who *m.* Juliana, daughter of Nicholas Martyn, descended from Martyn, of Kemeys, Dartington, &c. and had, with a daughter, Susan, the wife of William Martyn, recorder of Exeter, a son,

THOMAS PRESTWOOD, who left one son and one daughter, viz.

I. GEORGE PRESTWOOD, of Baterford, sheriff in 1692, who married Mary Isaacke, of Polshoe, sister of Francis Cholwich, and had issue,

1. THOMAS, of Baterford, who *m.* Honora Fowel, and left a son, Thomas, who *m.* Anne, daughter of Sir William Drake, of Ash, but *d. s. p.* and a daughter, Juliana, the wife of Roger Hele, esq. of Halwell.

2. Mary, who *m.* William Huckmore, esq. of Buckland Baron, and had two daughters,

Mary, *m.* Solomon Andrew, esq. of Lyme Regis, and was mother of Sarah Andrew, the wife of AMBROSE RHODES, esq. of Buckland.

Honora, married Sir Davidge Gould, (whose sister wedded Gen. Fielding, father of Henry Fielding), and was grandmother of Honora Gould, *m.* to the Earl of Cavan.

3. Elizabeth, *m.* to Ambrose Rhodes, esq. of Modbury, and was great-grandmother of the present GEORGE AMBROSE RHODES, esq. of Bellair.

II. Juliana Prestwood, married to Ambrose Rhodes, esq. of Modbury.

* The account of his death, received from his friend, the late Lieutenant-colonel Piper, of the 4th regiment of Infantry, who was at the siege, is inscribed on a monument erected to Captain Rhodes, in Heavitree church, together with a fraternal tribute to his memory. "Whilst leading the storming party to the breach, his right arm was shattered to pieces by a musket ball; notwithstanding which, he mounted the breach, waved his hat, and fell, pierced by eleven balls."

"If ever honour, courtesy and truth,
Deck'd the fair forehead of ingenuous youth,
If wisdom, stamp'd on manhood's early pride,
And inborn courage, ah! too nobly tried!
If snatch'd untimely from this nether sphere,
Accomplish'd worth might ever claim a tear;
Such tribute, O lamented shade! is thine;
O, formed alike in camps or courts to shine,
The chieftain's mirror, and the soldier's friend.
Pure was thy life, and glorious was its end:
Sons of Iberia, scatter round his tomb
Such flowers as soonest fade and earliest bloom;
Cull the first fragrance of the opening year;
New plant thy vine and nurse thine olive there.
For in thy deadliest breach he foremost stood,
And seal'd thy country's freedom with his blood:
Yes, I had hoped, when hush'd the voice of strife,
To walk with him, what yet remain'd of life;—
Just as we thought to greet him, he was gone;—
Father of heav'n and earth, thy will be done."

6. Sarah-Baker, *m.* to the Rev. Henry Wolcombe, vicar of Pillaton, Cornwall, second brother of John-Morth Wolcombe, esq. of Ashbury, Devon.
7. Catherine-Philippa, died aged sixteen.

II. Ambrose-George, lost at sea.
III. Hele, died in infancy.
IV. William, went to India in a mercantile capacity, and *d.* there.
V. Thomas, of the Navy Office, died aged seventeen.
VI. George-Hele,* *b.* in 1756, formerly of Oriel College, Oxford, died in 1826. He was an accomplished scholar and gentleman.

I. Bridget, *m.* to Broderick Hartwell, esq. of Bellair, near Plymouth, elder brother of the late Sir Francis Hartwell, bart.
II. Prestwood, *m.* to Mr. Paulin, merchant of London.
III. Honora, *m.* to the Rev. Mr. Woldridge, vicar of Maker, near Plymouth, and had a daughter, Honora, the wife of General Barclay, of the Royal Marines, by whom she had one son, John-Fletcher Barclay, late lieutenant-colonel of a regiment of Infantry, and a daughter, Honora, *m.* to the Rev. Forester Leighton, son of Sir Edward Leighton, bart. of Loton Park, Salop.

Ambrose† Rhodes died in 1739, aged seventy-one, and was *s.* by his son,

AMBROSE RHODES, esq. of Buckland House, Buckland Toussaint, who married in 1726, Sarah Andrew, sole daughter and heiress of Solomon Andrew, esq. of Lyme Regis, Dorset. This lady is supposed to have been the original from which Fielding drew his portrait‡ of Sophia Western. Henry Fielding, the son of General Fielding, and Miss Gould, daughter of Judge Gould, of Sharpham§ Park, Somerset, and grandson of the Earl of Denbigh, had probably been in the habits of intimacy with his cousin, Miss Andrew, from their earliest years. At his return from his studies at Leyden, when he was one-and-twenty, their acquaintance seems to have been renewed, after her father's death, at the residence of one of her guardians and uncles, Andrew Tucker, esq. of Lyme Regis; and the attentions of Mr. Fielding were so marked and assiduous,‖ that it was thought prudent to remove the young lady to the residence and care of another of her guardians and near relatives, Ambrose Rhodes, esq. of Modbury, to whose eldest son, then an Oxonian, she was shortly¶ afterwards married. Mr. Rhodes resided for thirty years at Buckland House, Buckland Toussaint. He is the same gentleman mentioned in the Memoirs of Bampfylde More Carew as having been imposed on by that hero in two different disguises, at his seat near Kingsbridge, and a third time, in the same day, at Modbury. Upon the sale of Buckland by his relative, Mr. Southcot, he purchased, and resided at, Bellair. By Sarah, his wife, Mr. Rhodes had a daughter, Mary, who *d.* aged twenty-four, and a son,

AMBROSE-ANDREW RHODES, esq. of Bellair, who succeeded his father in 1777, and became possessed of considerable landed property in the parish of Modbury, together with the great tithes; also, in right of his mother, of divers estates and manors in Devon, Dorset, and Somersetshire. He was appointed gentleman of the privy chamber to His Majesty GEORGE III. in 1786, and dying unmarried in 1800, was *s.* by his cousin, the present GEORGE-AMBROSE RHODES, esq. of Bellair.

* The family of Hele was at one time so influential, that Prince records an assize where the sheriff and grand jury were all Heles.

† Died 1739, æt. 71. The exact coincidence of the date of the decease of Ambrose Rhodes and his progenitor, Sir John Rhodes, in two following centuries, the latter of whom disinherited, the former of whom established an eldest son, is worthy of remark; as also, that Sir John Rhodes, last baronet, the third representative of the second son of Sir John Rhodes, knt. died about this time, 1743, childless, whilst the third representative, or great-grandson of the eldest son, left a fair and flourishing progeny.

‡ A portrait of this lady, by Downman, taken at an advanced age, is at Bellair, also portraits of some of the personages above mentioned, by Sir Godfrey Kneller, Hudson, and Sir Joshua Reynolds.

§ Fielding is reported to have subsequently composed part of his Tom Jones in the Tennis Court at Sharpham, in the intervals of the games. Pliny the younger found hunting favourable to composition: Addison, the stimulus of wine; Fielding, that of tennis.

‖ It is reported that he made an unsuccessful attempt at abduction.

¶ The marriage of this gentleman seems a quicker step than he was at that time accustomed to, if we may judge from the following epitaph made for him, when at Oxford, he having inherited somewhat of a German phlegmatic temperament, and always walking very slow.

"Here lies old Rhodes, quite out of breath;
He walk'd too slow, to outwalk Death."

He was, however, a gentleman of by no means inactive benevolence; and although he bore no resemblance to Fielding's character of Squire

*Arms*—Arg. a lion passant guardant gu. between two acorns, in bend, azure, cottised ermines. Quartering, Sleech, Andrew, and Cholwich.

*Crest*—A hand holding an oak branch all ppr.

*Motto*—Cœlum non animum.

*Estates*—Shapwick,* Axminster, Aish, Stoke Gabriel, Modbury, with the great tithes, and at Walham Green, Middlesex.

*Seats*—Bellair, Heavitree, and Wodehouse Rhodorick,† Up Lyme.

### Family of Sleech.

Of the remote ‡ origin of this family, now extinct in name, nothing is at present accurately known; they were formerly settled in Kent at Eton Bridge, and in Sussex about Little Hampton, bearing for arms, as appears in Camden's Register, "checkers, or and gules; a canton sinister, argent." Of those in Sussex, Captain Richard Sleech, the last male, had a grandson by a daughter,

EDWARD SLEECH, esq. of the Kent branch, who first settled at Windsor about 1660-70, and *m.* Anne Saunders, by whom (who remarried after his death, in 1681, the Rev. John Newborough, master of Eton college) he had a daughter, Lucy, married to the Rev. Stephen Weston, fellow of Eton, and afterwards Bishop of Exeter; and

The Rev. RICHARD SLEECH, fellow of Eton, prebendary of Windsor, and rector of Hichham and Farnham, who *m.* Elizabeth, daughter of the Rev. Mr. Upman, fellow of Eton, and had issue,

I. STEPHEN, who was provost of Eton, canon of Windsor, and chaplain to GEORGE II.; he died unmarried.

II. JOHN, rector of Faringdon and vicar of Sidbury, Devon, canon of Exeter, prebendary of Gloucester, and archdeacon of Cornwall. He was the schoolfellow, at Eton, and esteemed friend through life, of the first Lord Camden. He *m.* Mary, daughter of JOHN CHOLWICH, esq. of Faringdon House, in Devon, and had seven children, four of whom died young; a fifth, the Rev. Charles Sleech, died at the age of twenty-one, unmarried; a daughter, Maria, *m.* the Rev. Richard Brereton, of Wotton House, Gloucestershire, and died *s. p.*; and another, ELIZABETH, married the Rev. GEORGE RHODES. Archdeacon Sleech *d.* in 1788; his memory and many virtues still live in the breasts of surviving friends and relatives; among the former the Rev. Mr. Polwhele, the historian of Devon, has paid to them a poetical tribute, of which the following lines are characteristic and appropriate:

Sweet is the balmy sigh, when sorrow grieves
 For friendship torn from all the hopes of earth;
But doubly precious is the sigh that heaves
 O'er the pale ashes of distinguish'd worth.
Lamented Sleech, such excellence was thine,
 Through many a path of varying life display'd,
Whether we view the dignified divine,
 Or trace thy virtues to the private shade.
Whilst kindred minds thy youthful traits engage,
 Thy light-unfolding § bloom let others trace;
I only knew thy venerable age
 Where mildly beamed the patriarch and the saint;

---

Western (who is said to have been a caricature of one of the former proprietors of Montacute, Somersetshire), yet the following incident is characteristic of the journey to London of the country squire in those days, and may remind us of Squire Western and Mrs. Honour:—"Shortly after Mr. Rhodes's arrival in London, one of his men servants, walking out into the street, lost his way; and the housekeeper, in great trouble, suggested his being cried. Robin, however, a lad of more than Devonian acuteness, in his perplexity, saw a razor-grinder passing by, and gave the man a shilling to add his name to his cry. Razors to grind!—Squire Rhodes's man Robin, &c. It so happened that the razor-grinder passed near the house where Mr. R. resided, and where the housekeeper was at the door, on the look-out for Robin. On hearing the above cry, she exclaimed, in great joy, "Here's our Robin cried, sure enough; and here he is himself," &c.

* "The manor of Shapwick, within the manor of Axminster, was purchased, for Newenham Abbey, of Reginald de Shapwick, by Reginald de Mohun."—*Cartulary of Newenham Abbey.*

† *Ροδω ορτιος οικος* "the house of the Rhodes on the hill."—*Old Ballad.* This estate, (adjacent to Shapwick), an occasional residence, unrivalled perhaps in natural beauties, was purchased thirty years since, and adorned by the present proprietor.

‡ Traditionally from Germany: the name is very uncommon; and only one occurrence of it suggests itself in Sleech Wood, in the parish of Up Lyme, Devon, belonging to — Henley, esq. The tenure would probably explain the appellation; if held under the college of Eton, it evidently was so called after one of the Sleeches, provosts and masters of that college and school: an additional coincidence, apparently a casual one, is worthy of remark; Sleech Wood, a very fine and extensive one, in the back ground of the old residence of the Henleys, forms a beautiful feature in the prospect from Rhode, the seat of Sir John Talbot, and from Wodehouse, that of Mr. Rhodes, situated on two parallel hills. Rhode was called after Rhode Horn, a promontory adjacent; both were part of the Drake property of Ash.

§ This line is graphically descriptive of a portrait by Hudson, now at Bellair, taken at an early period of life. The above lines are extracted from a manuscript poem in a family collection.

Ah! first I knew thee, when thy liberal charge,*
With all the spirit of thy Camden glow'd;
And fraught with a benevolence too large
For narrow souls, in fine expansion flow'd.

His successor in the archdeaconry of Cornwall, the Rev. Mr. Moore, late vicar of Heavitree, in his first visitation charge, highly eulogized his style and character.

III. Edward, clerk of the exchequer, who *m.* Elizabeth Bishop, of London, and had one daughter, Anna, who died unmarried, and was succeeded in her landed property at Walham Green, Middlesex, by G. A. RHODES, esq.

IV. Henry, fellow of Eton, who *m.* Miss Younge, and had issue, Elizabeth, *m.* to the Rev. Thomas Dampier, dean of Rochester and bishop of Ely, and Fanny, who died unm.

I. Anne, *m.* to the Rev. Charles Hawtrey, subdean and canon of Exeter, and had four sons and five daughters, of whom the eldest, Stephen, barrister, was recorder of Exeter; and Anne, *m.* the Rev. John Marshall, of Exeter.

II. Elizabeth, *m.* to the Rev. Dr. Harris, fellow of Eton.

III. Mary, *d.* unm.

IV. Lucy, *d.* unm.

V. Catherine, *m.* to the Rev. William Cook, D.D. first master, and fellow of Eton, and afterwards provost of King's College, Cambridge, and dean of Ely, who had issue, Anne, *m.* to Benjamin Way, esq. of Denham House, Bucks; Catherine, *m.* to the Rev. Dr. Hallifax, Bishop of St. Asaph; Frances, who *d.* unm. in 1835; Mary; Susan, *m.* to Treby-Hele Hayes, esq. of Dallamore, Devon; Charlotte, *m.* to Pierce-Joseph Taylor, esq. of Ogwell House, Devon; and Edward, late under secretary of state for the foreign department, who *m.* — Georges, and *d. s. p.*

The minor ramifications of the above branches are very numerous, fair, and flourishing.

* At his first visitation, Cornwall, charge to the clergy.

## POWELL, OF BRANDLESOME HALL.

POWELL, HENRY-FOLLIOTT, esq. of Brandlesome Hall, in Lancashire, a captain in the Ceylon rifle regiment, *b.* at Okeover Hall, in the county of Stafford, 21st January, 1803; *m.* at the residence of the sitting magistrate at Kaits Jaffna district, in the island of Ceylon, 1st October, 1830, Catherine-Vassal, second daughter of the late George Burleigh, esq. some time on the medical staff of that island, and has issue,

I. HENRY-COTTRELL,* *b.* at St. Peter's, Columbo, 5th July, 1831.

I. Frances-Catherine.*
II. Ellen-Eliza.*

Captain Powell succeeded his father in 1834.

* These three registered in Trinity District church, Mary-le-bone, county of Middlesex, July, 1835.

## Lineage.

This family derives its descent, paternally, from Rhys ap Tudor, king of South Wales; as would appear from the arms allowed (with the filial difference of the *third* son of the *fifth* house) by the heralds, at their visitation of London, *anno* 1634, to the posterity of

WALTER POWELL, who was seated, in the reign of *Queen* ELIZABETH, at Bucknell, in Salop, and, by a daughter and co-heir of the family of Skull, of Much-Cowarne, in Herefordshire, had issue two sons, THOMAS and Richard.

THOMAS POWELL, gent. the elder, also of Bucknell, died in 1611-12. He *m.* Mary, daughter of John Walcot, esq. of Walcot, county of Salop, by Mary, daughter of Sir Peter Newton, knt. and had issue by her (who was lineally descended from Sir John Walcot, seated at Walcot in the 6th year of RICHARD II.) two sons, JOHN and Humphrey, and a daughter, Anne.

JOHN POWELL, the elder son and heir, having raised a considerable fortune as one of the company of merchant-adventurers of London, acquired the estate of Stanedge, or Stanage Park, in Radnorshire, by purchase, in the reign of CHARLES I. He *m.* in 1623, his first wife, Jane, daughter of Thomas Docwra, esq. of Puttridge, in Hitchin, Herts. sometime high sheriff of that county, by whom, who died at Hamburgh, he had Samuel Powell, his heir. By his second wife, Elizabeth, daughter of — Walmsley, of London, merchant, he had a son, James, and a daughter, Rachael.

SAMUEL POWELL, esq. of Stanedge, elder son and heir, was born at Hamburgh, and an act passed for his naturalization in 1628. Having succeeded to the patrimonial estate he died there in 1686, and had issue, by Elizabeth, his wife, who survived him, and whose will was proved in 1698, several children, viz.

- I. SAMUEL, of Stanedge.
- II. Littleton, of Ludlow, one of the six clerks in Chancery, who died in 1714.
- III. Charles, who was living in 1696.
- IV. Edward, buried at Brampton Brian, in the county of Hereford, in 1669.
- V. Walter, died an infant in 1670.

- I. Elizabeth, who *m.* the Rev. Robert Adams, of Wilcot, county of Salop.
- II. Anne, wife first of — Thornes, and secondly, of George Bold, esq. of Shelvock, in the county of Salop.
- III. Margaret, who married Thomas Greaves, gent.

He was *s.* by his eldest son,

SAMUEL POWELL, esq. of Stanedge, who *d.* in September, 1700, and was buried at Presteign, having had issue, by the Honourable Elizabeth Folliott, his wife, third dau. of Thomas, and sister and co-heir of Henry, Lord Folliott, of the kingdom of Ireland (which Elizabeth married, secondly, the Rev. Thomas Jones, of Combe, in the county of Flint, and of Goodrich, co. of Hereford), two sons and an only daughter, viz.

- I. FOLLIOTT, of Stanedge.
- II. SAMUEL, of Liverpool, and afterwards of Stanedge.

- I. Elizabeth, who *m.* Richard Knight, esq. of Ludlow, and Bringwood, co. of Salop, and had a daughter, Elizabeth Knight, who wedded Thomas Johnes, esq. and was mother of Thomas Johnes, esq. M.P. of Hafod.

FOLLIOTT POWELL, esq. of Stanedge, the elder son and heir, was baptized at Brampton Brian, 31st July, 1691, and served the office of high sheriff of Radnorshire in 1725. He died 7th June, 1737, and was buried at Bucknell aforesaid, having had issue, by Constance, his wife, three sons and three daughters, viz.

- I. Folliott,
- II. Samuel,
- III. John,

who all died young.

- I. Constance, eldest daughter and co-heir, *m.* Edmund Cox, esq. a captain in the Queen's Dragoon Guards, and died without issue.
- II. Anne, second daughter and co-heir, married Richard Ward, esq. and *d.* in 1809, at the age of ninety-two, leaving issue.
- III. Sarah, third and youngest daughter and co-heir, married Thomas Cooke, surgeon of the Queen's Dragoon Guards.

SAMUEL POWELL, esq. some time of Liverpool, afterwards of Stanedge, brother and heir male of Folliott Powell, was baptized at Brampton Brian, 5th January, 1694, and died 17th April, 1745, and was buried at St. Nicholas' church, Liverpool, having had issue, by Elizabeth, his wife, daughter of the Rev. Richard Richmond, rector of Walton and Sephton, near Liverpool (who died 18th December, 1781, aged eighty-one, and lies buried near her husband), five sons and as many daughters, viz.

- I. RICHARD, of Stanedge.

II. Folliott, a merchant at Manchester, who died unm. 29th November, 1791, aged fifty-seven, and was buried at St. Nicholas aforesaid.
III. Samuel, who died an infant.
IV. Samuel, of Liverpool, died without issue, in April, 1820, aged eighty, and was also buried at St. Nicholas.
V. John, sometime in the R. N. died without issue, 15th January, 1789, aged forty-four, and lies buried at the same place.

I. Elizabeth, who *m.* Matthew Stronge, of Fairview and Liverpool, merchant, by whom she had issue the Rev. Sir James Stronge, created a baronet in 1803. She died in 1793, and was also buried at St. Nicholas.
II. Mary, who *m.* William Higginson, of Whitechurch and Liverpool, and *d.* without issue in 1808, aged eighty-four.
III. Sarah, who *m.* Ralph Robinson, of Liverpool, and died in 1793, without issue.
IV. Rebecca, who *m.* Alexander Duff, esq. of Mayer, co. of Banff, a captain in the army. She died in 1775, leaving issue.
V. Anne, who died at the age of nine.

RICHARD POWELL, esq. of Stanedge, the eldest son and heir, alienated that estate to Richard Knight, esq. and died at Eaton Norris, co. of Lancaster, in July, 1794, and was buried in St. John's, Manchester, having had issue, by Elizabeth, his wife, only surviving daughter of John Cottrell, esq. of Scarborough, and sister of John Cottrell, esq. of Lincoln's Inn, one of the sworn clerks in Chancery (who died 3rd June, 1822, aged eighty-eight), three sons and four daughters, viz.

I. SAMUEL, of whom hereafter.
II. John, born 26th September, 1763, and died 31st October, 1788, without issue.
III. John-Folliott, sometime of Sandy-Brook, in the co. of Derby, and afterwards of Leamington, in Warwickshire, who married in 1801, Frances, eldest daughter of Charles Armett, esq. of the Low, in Cheshire, and Toft, in the co. of Stafford, niece to Sir Joseph Scott, bart. of Great Barr, by whom he had ten sons and three daughters, viz.
   1. Richard-Charles.
   2. John-Folliott.
   3. William.
   4. Edward-Armett.
   5. Cæsar-Cottrell.
   6. Scott.
   7. Arthur.
   8. Charles-Thomas.
   9. Francis-Charles.
   10. Harrison.

   1. Frances, who *m.* the Rev. Peyton Blakiston, brother to Sir Matthew Blakiston, bart.
   2. Mary.
   3. Elizabeth-Anne.

I. Anne, }
II. Mary, } who died infants.
III. Anna-Maria, }
IV. Harriott, who *m.* Holland Watson, esq. of Stockport, in the commission of the peace for the counties of Chester and Lancaster. She *d.* in March, 1819, leaving issue three sons and seven daughters.

The eldest son,

SAMUEL POWELL, esq. of Hammerton Hall, near Boroughbridge, in the county of York, and of Brandlesome Hall, in Lancashire, born 28th January, 1760, married at Walcot church, Bath, 24th February, 1796, Frances, eldest daughter of Henry Richmond,* of Bath, M. D. some time fellow of Trinity College, Cambridge, by Catherine, his wife, eldest daughter of John Atherton, esq. of Walton Hall, and died 16th June, 1834, and was buried in the chancel of St. James's church, Dover, having had issue,

I. John-Cottrell, M.A. of Lincoln's Inn, and of Jesus College, Cambridge, *b.* at Puddington Hall, co. Chester, 18th January, 1798, baptized at Great Neston in the same county. His death, on the 10th June, 1834, was attended by most afflictive circumstances. He was struck from his horse, run over, and killed by one of His Majesty's carriages returning, filled with servants, from Ascot races. He was unmarried, and his remains were interred in the new cemetery at Kelsal Green, com. Middlesex.
II. HENRY-FOLLIOTT, heir to his father.
III. Samuel-Hopper, in holy orders, M.A. *b.* at Okeover Hall aforesaid, 4th March, 1805, sometime of Trinity College, Cambridge. He *m.* at Long Parish, near Andover, 11th October, 1832, Louisa-Burnaby, eldest daughter of Pitt-Burnaby Greene, esq. a captain in the Royal Navy, by whom he has a daughter, Amelia.
IV. Richmond, M.A. in holy orders, late of Trinity College, Cambridge, born at Okeover Hall, 3rd March, 1801, curate of Boxgrove, near Chichester.

* Dr. Richmond was eldest son of the Rev. Legh Richmond, rector of Stockport, by Mary, his wife, eldest daughter of Henry Legh, esq. of High Legh, in Cheshire.

v. Robert-Legh, student and scholar of Pembroke College, Cambridge. He was born at Carlton House, Notts, 21st June, 1811, *d.* unmarried, 15th April, 1834, and was buried in Kensal Green cemetery.

vi. William-Wellington *b.* at Carlton House aforesaid, 18th August, 1813, sometime a midshipman in the Royal Navy, now, 1835, lieutenant in the 9th regiment of Infantry at Mauritius, and under orders for Bengal.

vii. Thomas-Folliott, born at Leighton Hall, Lancashire, 24th March, 1817, baptized at Warton, in that county.

i. Catherine, *b.* at Puddington Hall aforesaid, married at Trinity district church, St. Marylebone, 21st April, 1829, to Commander (now Captain) William-Burnaby Greene, R. N.

ii. Elizabeth, born at Puddington Hall, married at Trinity church aforesaid, 23rd January, 1829, to Lieutenant John Wainwright, R. N. and has issue,

John-Wroughton, *b.* 9th December, 1829.

Frances-Emily.

Harriet-Forbes.

iii. Frances-Anne, born at Okeover Hall.

*Arms*—Gules, a lion rampant or, within a bordure engrailed of the last, differenced by a mullet within an annulet gold.

Through the noble house of Folliott, this family is entitled to numerous quarterings; but those usually borne by them are,

*Skull*—Gules, a bend between six lions' heads erased argent.

*Folliott*—Argent, a lion rampant purpure, ducally crowned or, double queued.

*Crest*—A lion's head erased argent, gorged with a collar flory counterflory gules.

*Motto*—Anima in amicis una.

*Estates*—In Lancashire, Derbyshire, and Yorkshire.

*Town Residence*—32, Upper Harley-street.

*Seat*—Brandlesome Hall, near Bury, in the county of Lancaster.

## LATTIN, OF MORRISTOWN LATTIN.

LATTIN, PATRICK, esq. of Morristown Lattin, in the county of Kildare, *b.* 12th April, 1761, *m.* in 1792, Elizabeth, daughter and heiress of Robert Snow, esq. of Drumdowny, in the county of Kilkenny, and has an only daughter,

PAULINA, *m.* in 1817, to Alexander Mansfield, esq. of Yeomanstown, in the county of Kildare.

Mr. Lattin succeeded his father in 1773.

### Lineage.

The family of LATTIN claims descent from that of ESTOUTEVILLE, in Normandy, of which was

WILLIAM DE STUTEVILLE, who obtained a cardinal's hat in 1439 from *Pope* EUGENIUS IV. The Stutevilles, subsequently to the Conquest, were barons of Lydesdale Castle, in Cumberland, and in feudal times were men of great power, as well through their warlike habits, as their vast territorial possessions. Their estates lay in the counties of Rutland, Cumberland, Lincoln, and Warwick. Of the Warwickshire lands, those at Monk's Kirby were eventually granted by John de Stuteville to the monks of Pipwell, in North Hants. Camden, in his Remains, establishes that surnames were first adopted for distinction sake, and descended to the eldest son only, the others deriving their appellations from the lands allotted as their patrimony. It is at least probable, therefore, that Walter de Latton (who appears, from unquestionable records, to have been at a very early era in North Wilts) assumed his from his residence, retaining still his paternal (the Stuteville) arms. From the Lattins of Lattin diverged several branches, seated in various parts of England, and enjoying high respectability,—the Lattins of Upton, in Berks; of Esher, in Surrey, &c. &c.; as well as the family which obtaining from King JOHN considerable grants of land in IRELAND, settled there, and became seated at Morristown Lattin, in Kildare.

WILLIAM LATTIN, esq. of Morristown Lattin, chief of the Irish branch at the commencement of the seventeenth century, sat in parliament for the borough of Naas, (in 1621), and founded in that town an asylum for the support of four poor women, which has been endowed and kept up, agreeably to the intention of the founder, by the family, to the present time. This William Lattin was direct ancestor of

WILLIAM LATTIN, esq. of Morrestown Lattin, who wedded a daughter of — Caddell, and was father of

PATRICK LATTIN, esq. of Morrestown Lattin, who *m.* Jane,* daughter of William Alcock, esq. of Clough, in the county of Waterford, and had two sons and five daughters, namely,

I. JOHN, who left no issue.
II. GEORGE, successor to his father.

I. Jane, *m.* in 1719, to Alexander Eustace, esq. of Cradoxtown, in the county of Kildare, and had by him, who *d.* in 1752, one son Colonel William Eustace, who *d.* unmarried, and two daughters, Mary, *m.* to Sir Duke Giffard, bart. of Castle Jordan, and Anne, to John Caulfeild, esq.
II. Begnot, *m.* to — Fitzgerald, esq. of Baltiroran, in Meath, great grandfather of the present Sir Percy Nugent, bart. of Donore.
III. The third daughter, *m.* — Kennedy, esq. but died without male issue.
IV. The fourth daughter *m.* — Fitzgerald, esq.
V. Elizabeth who *m.* James Archbold, esq. of Eadestown, in the county of Kildare, (younger son of Richard Archbold, esq. by Mary, his wife, coheiress and great-grandaughter of Nicholas Ball, esq. Alderman and Lord Mayor of Dublin) and was mother of Jane Archbold, who wedded in 1765, John O'Reilly, esq. and had a son, the present JAMES ARCHBOLD O'REILLY, esq. of Boyne Lodge, in Meath, who *m.* Cecilia, sister of Christopher Drake, esq. of Roristown, in the same county, and has issue.

Mr. Lattin was succeeded at his decease by his son,

GEORGE LATTIN, esq. of Morristown Lattin, who *m.* Miss Catherine O'Ferrall, of Ballyna, in the county of Kildare, aunt to the present Richard More O'Ferrall, esq. M.P. and had issue,

I. PATRICK, his heir.
II. Ambrose, *d.* in the Austrian service, in 1789.

I. Mary, *m.* to Patrick Lambert, esq. of Carnagh, in the county of Wexford.
II. Jane, *m.* to Major Fitzgerald, of Snowhaven, in the county of Kilkenny.
III. Anne, *m.* to President Marquis de la Vie, of Bourdeaux.
IV. Begnet, *m.* to James Lambert, esq. of Bantry Lodge, Wexford.
V. Eleanor.
VI. Frances.

Mr. Lattin *d.* in 1773, and was *s.* by his son, the present PATRICK LATTIN, esq. of Morristown Lattin.

*Arms*—Party per fesse; in chief per pale arg. and sa. a saltier engrailed ermines and erm. Counterchanged; in base within a border three crescents.

*Crest*—An eagle's claw, with a crescent gu.

*Estates*—In the county of Kildare, held under grant from *King* JOHN. The family formerly possessed extensive estates in the counties of Wicklow, Kilkenny, and Tipperary.

*Residence*—Chaussee d'Antin, Paris.

*Seat*—Morristown Lattin, in the county of Kildare.

* Her sister married Michael Moore, esq. of Drogheda, and has several daughters, of whom, Mary married Gerald Aylmer, esq. of Lyons; Eleanor, Sir Patrick Bellew, bart.; another, John Coppinger, esq. of Ballyvolane, in the county of Cork, by whom she was mother of Mariana, Duchess of Norfolk, (see vol. ii. page 328,) and a fourth, Christian, wedded Lord Cahir.

# PORTER, OF ALFARTHING.

PORTER, HARRIET-MARY, *m.* to Michael Semper, esq. of the Island of Montserrat, and of the county of Galway. This lady, in conjunction with her three sisters, succeeded to the representation of the ancient family of PORTER, on the demise of her brother, in 1829.

## Lineage.

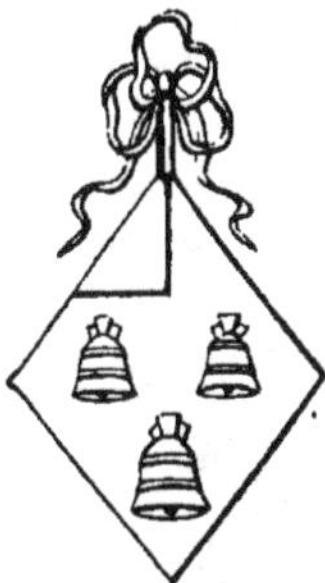

ROBERT PORTER, of Effington, had five sons,

- I. WILLIAM (Sir), living *temp.* HENRY V. *d. s. p.*
- II. ROBERT, of whom presently.
- III. John, of Markham, Notts.
- IV. Henry, a monk at Peterborough.
- V. Stephen, who became seated in Sussex.

The second son,

ROBERT PORTER, had two sons and two daughters, viz.

- THOMAS, whose only daughter and heiress, Agnes, wedded John Underhill, of Hunningham.
- WILLIAM, of whom presently.
- Katherine, *m.* to Edmond Compton, of Compton.
- Margaret, *m.* to William Clopton, of Clopton.

The second son,

WILLIAM PORTER, was father of

RICHARD PORTER, who *m.* the sister of Sir William Lattymer, knt. and left John, who died without issue, and

WILLIAM PORTER, serjeant-at-arms to HENRY VII. who made his will in 1513, upon leaving England for the wars. He married Margaret, daughter of John Gifford, of Twiford, in Buckinghamshire, and had two sons, Edmond (whose granddaughter and heiress Angelica, married Edmond Porter, her cousin), and

ANTHONY PORTER, who married the dau. of — Stradling, and had a son and successor,

EDMOND PORTER, who wedded his cousin, Angelica, daughter of Gyles Porter, of Mickleton, by Donna Juanna de Figueroa, of Montsalet, his wife, and had two sons and two daughters,

- ENDYMION, his heir.
- Giles, died at Oxford, in the service of CHARLES I. He was unmarried.
- Mary, second wife of William Canning, esq. of Foxcote, in Warwickshire.
- Jane, *m.* to — Bartelet.

The elder son,

ENDYMION PORTER, esq. was groom of the bed-chamber to *King* CHARLES I. from whom he obtained a grant of the Wandsworth estate. Of this celebrated courtier, one of the handsomest men of his time, many particulars may be found in Clarendon and Rapin's Histories, and in Evelyn's Memoirs. There exist several portraits of him by Vandyck, but especially a family piece of himself, his wife, and three of his sons, which is esteemed one of that painter's finest productions. He *m.* Olive, daughter* of John,

* JOHN, first LORD BUTLER, of Bramfield, *m.* Elizabeth, sister of George Villiers, Duke of Buckingham, and had, with five sons, all of whom predeceased him, unm.

- WILLIAM, second Lord, who *d.* in 1647, when the barony expired, and his sisters became his co-heirs.
- AUBREY, *m.* first, to Sir Francis Anderson, and, secondly, to Francis Leigh, Earl of Chichester.
- HELEN, *m.* to Sir John Drake, knt.
- JANE, *m.* first, to James Lee, Earl of Marlborough, and, secondly, to Major General Ashburham.
- OLIVE, *m.* to ENDYMION PORTER, esq.
- MARY, *m.* to Edward, Lord Howard, of Escrick.
- ANNE, *m.* first, to Mountjoy Blount, Earl of Newport, and, secondly, to Thomas Weston, Earl of Portland. (BURKE's *Extinct and Dormant Peerage.*)

first Lord Butler, of Bramfield, and co-heir of her brother William, second Lord, and had five sons,

GEORGE, his heir.

Charles, killed in the war against the Scotch, in 1640.

Philip, *d.* unmarried.

Thomas, who *m.* first, Lady Anne Blount, daughter and co-heir of Mountjoy, Earl of Newport, and, secondly, Anne, daughter of William Canning, esq. of Foxcote.

James, Vice Chamberlain to JAMES II. aged sixty-one in 1698. He married Ann, daughter of John Daniell, esq. of Acton, in Suffolk, and relict of Sir Henry Audeley.

Endymion Porter *d.* in 1649, aged sixty-five,† and was succeeded by his son,

GEORGE PORTER, esq. groom of the bed-chamber to CHARLES II. who married Lady Diana Covert, widow of Thomas Covert, esq. of Slaugham, in Sussex, and dau. of George Goring, first Earl of Norwich, (she was co-heir of her brother Charles, second Earl,) by whom he had issue,

GEORGE, his heir.

Endymion, *d.* unmarried, aged about twenty-three.

Aubrey, aged about thirty-six in 1699, who *m.* Kesia, daughter of Sir Thomas Harvey, knt. of Ickworth, in Suffolk, and had a son, Thomas, who *d.* at Vienna, unmarried.

Mary, married Philip Smythe, fourth Viscount Strangford, and had with a son Endymion, fifth Viscount, two daughters, Catherine, *m.* to Henry, 8th Lord Teynham, and Olivia, *m.* to John Darell, esq. of Cale-hill.

Olivia, } living in 1699.
Diana, }

Isabella, *m.* to Edward Bedell, esq. of Woodrising, in Norfolk.

Anne, *m.* to Thomas Coundon, esq. of Willerby.

George Porter *d.* 11th December, 1683, aged sixty-three, and was succeeded by his son,

GEORGE PORTER, esq. Vice Chamberlain to her Majesty KATHARINE, Dowager *Queen* of CHARLES II. He *m.* Mary, only surviving daughter and heir of John Mawson, esq. and had issue,

JOHN, his heir.

James, living in 1752.

Endymion, *b.* in 1701, who *m.* Mary, daughter of Bryan Maguire, esq. of Kilkenny, and had an only daughter, Catherine-Theresa, the wife of Thomas Wadding, esq.

Eleanor, *d.* in 1751, unmarried.

Katharine, living in 1752, unmarried.

Diana, *d.* unmarried.

George Porter *d.* in 1711, and was succeeded by his son,

JOHN PORTER, esq. of the Manor of Alfarthing, in the parish of Wandsworth, county of Surrey, *b.* in 1696, who *m.* Catherine, eldest daughter of Lieutenant General Richard Sutton, of Scofton, in Nottinghamshire, and had issue,

JOHN, his heir.

Mary, *m.* to the Hon. Thomas Arundell, of Wardour.

Catherine.

Frances.

Eleanore, who *m.* Pierce Walsh, esq. of the county of Waterford, and had issue,

PIERCE WALSH, successor to his uncle, John Porter, esq.

Mary Walsh, died in 1829.

Constantia Walsh.

Catherine Walsh, died unm.

Mr. Porter, who was living in 1752, was succeeded by his only son,

JOHN PORTER, esq. of the Manor of Alfarthing, who *m.* Mary, eldest daughter of Cosmo Nevill, esq. of Holt, in the county of Leicester, and his wife, Lady Mary Nevill, but dying without issue, was succeeded by his nephew,

PIERCE WALSH, esq. who assumed, on inheriting the estates, the surname and arms of PORTER. He *m.* Harriet-Hope, daughter of the late Rev. Richard Scrope, D.D. of Castlecombe, Wilts, by Anne, his wife, sister to the late Edmund Lambert, esq. of Boyton House, and had issue,

PIERCE, his heir.

HARRIET-MARY, *m.* to Michael Semper, esq. of the Island of Montserrat.

FRANCES-GEORGINA, *m.* to Mons. Leonard Pieraggi, of Corsica, and has a son, Endymion-Leonard Pieraggi.

ELEONORA, *m.* to John Pigott, esq. of the Queen's county, and has a son, John Pigott.

MARY.

Mr. Walsh Porter *d.* in 1809, and was succeeded by his only son,

PIERCE WALSH PORTER, esq. of the Manor of Alfarthing, at whose decease unmarried, in 1829, the representation of the family devolved on his four sisters, as co-heirs.

*Arms*—Sa. three bells arg. a canton erm.

† His will bears date 26th March, 1639. The executors were his wife Olive and the Earls of Worcester and Newcastle.

# MOSLEY, OF BURNASTON HOUSE.

MOSLEY, ASHTON-NICHOLAS-EVERY, esq. of Burnaston House, in the county of Derby, *b.* 21st November, 1792, *m.* at Kippax, in Yorkshire, 14th February, 1820, Mary-Theresa, only child and heiress of the late William Stables, esq. of Hemsworth, in the latter county, and has issue, (all baptized at Etwall.)

ASHTON, *b.* 5th February, 1821.
Arthur, *b.* 6th May, 1822.
Godfrey-Goodman, *b.* 8th June, 1826.
Rowland, *b.* 19th Marhc, 1830.

Mr. Mosley succeeded his father in 1830. He is a magistrate and deputy-lieutenant for the county of Derby, and served as high sheriff in 1835.

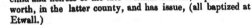

## Lineage.

EDWARD MOSLEY, esq. of Houghend, in the county of Lancaster, (descended from Oswald, second son of Ernald de Moseley, Lord of Moseley, *temp.* King JOHN,) married Margaret, daughter of Alexander Elcock, of Hilgate, in Cheshire, and had three sons, viz.

I. OSWALD, of Garratt Hall.
II. NICHOLAS (Sir), knt. lord mayor of London in 1599, who *d.* in 1612, leaving two sons, ROWLAND, and Edward. The younger was knighted, and made attorney-general of the duchy of Lancaster. The elder,
ROWLAND, *m.* first, Anne, daughter of Humphrey Houghton, of Manchester, by whom he had a daughter, Margaret, the wife of William Whitmore, esq. He wedded, secondly, Anne, daughter and co-heir of Richard Sutton, esq. of Sutton, and left, with another daughter, Anne, a son and successor,
EDWARD (Sir), created a baronet in 1640, who *m.* Mary, daughter of Sir Gervase Cutler, knt. of Stainborough, and had by her one son and two daughters, viz.
EDWARD (Sir), second baronet, who *d. s. p.* in 1656.
Mary, *m.* to Joseph Maynard, esq. whose daughters and co-heirs were Elizabeth, the wife of Sir Henry Hobart, bt. and Mary, of Henry, Earl of Stamford.
Anne, *d.* unm.
III. ANTHONY, of Ancoats.

The third son,

ANTHONY MOSLEY, esq. of Ancoats, in Lancashire, *m.* Alice, daughter of Richard Webster, of Manchester, and had a son and successor,

OSWALD MOSLEY, esq. of Ancoats, who wedded Anne, daughter and co-heir of Ralph Lowe, esq. of Mile-end, in Cheshire, descended from the family of Alderwasley, and had five sons and three daughters, viz.

I. NICHOLAS, of Ancoats, whose son, Oswald, of Ancoats and Rolleston, was created a BARONET in 1720, but the title expired with his (the first baronet's) son, the Rev. Sir JOHN MOSLEY, in 1779.
II. EDWARD (Sir), of Hulme, whose daughter Anne *m.* Sir John Bland, of Kippax.
III. OSWALD, of whom presently.
IV. Samuel.
V. Francis, Rector of Wimslow, father of Francis, Rector of Rolleston, and of two daughters, Anne, *m.* to Richard Whitworth, esq. whose son was created Lord Whitworth; and Catherine, *m.* to John Hooper, esq.

I. Anne, *m.* to Humphrey Booth, esq. of Salford.
II. Margaret, *m.* to John Anger, esq.
III. Mary, *m.* to John Crowther, citizen of London.

The second son,

OSWALD MOSLEY, esq. was great grandfather of

JOHN PARKER MOSLEY, esq. who inherited the estates of his cousin, Sir John Mosley, in 1779, and was created a BARONET 24th March, 1781. He *m.* Elizabeth, daughter of James Bayley, esq. of Manchester, and had issue,

I. OSWALD, whose son is the present Sir OSWALD MOSLEY, bart. of Ancoats. (See BURKE'S *Peerage* and *Baronetage.*)
II. John-Peploe, in holy orders, married Sarah-Maria, daughter of William Paget, esq. and has issue.
III. ASHTON-NICHOLAS, of whom presently.

I. Anne, *m.* to Robert Fielden, esq.
II. Elizabeth, married to the Reverend Streynsham Master, D.D. of Croston, grandson of Sir Streynsham Master, knt. of Codnor Castle, and had issue.
III. Frances-Mary, *m.* to George Smith, esq. brother to Lord Carrington.
IV. Penelope, *m.* to Sir Henry Every, bart.

The second son,

ASHTON-NICHOLAS MOSLEY, esq. of Park Hill, in Derbyshire, *b.* 31st March, 1768, an acting magistrate and deputy-lieutenant for the counties of Derby and Stafford, married, 10th August, 1790, Mary, daughter of Edward Morley, esq. of Horsley, relict first of William Elliot, esq. of Derby, secondly, of Joseph Bird, gent. of Loughborough, and, thirdly, of Sir Edward Every, bart. of Egginton. By this lady, who *d.* 9th February, 1826, Mr. Mosley had issue,

ASHTON-NICHOLAS-EVERY, his heir.
Emma-Penelope, *m.* at Egginton, 21st December, 1824, to the Reverend Francis Ward Spilsbury, of Wellington, in Derbyshire, and has two sons and one daughter.

Mr. Mosley *d.* in 1830, and was succeeded by his only son, the present ASHTON-NICHOLAS-EVERY MOSLEY, esq. of Burwaston House.

*Arms*—Quarterly, 1st and 4th, sa. a chev. between three battle-axes, arg. 2nd and 3rd or, a fesse between three eaglets displayed, sa.

*Crest*—An eagle displayed erm.

*Motto*—Mos legem regit.

*Estates*—In Derbyshire, &c.

*Seat*—Burwaston House.

## DAWSON, OF CASTLE-DAWSON.

DAWSON, *The Right Honourable* GEORGE-ROBERT, of Castle-Dawson, in the county of Londonderry, *b.* 24th December, 1790, *m.* 8th January, 1816, Mary, daughter of Sir Robert Peel, bart. of Drayton Manor, in Staffordshire, and has issue,

ROBERT-PEEL, *b.* 2nd June, 1818.
George-Beresford, *b.* 18th June, 1819.
Henry, *b.* 27th January, 1821.
Francis-Alexander, *b.* 26th April, 1823.
Frederick, *b.* 11th July, 1824.

This gentleman, who succeeded his father 7th December, 1823, represented the county of Londonderry in parliament from 1815 to 1830, and subsequently the borough of Harwich. He was appointed Under Secretary of State for the Home Department in January, 1823; Secretary to the Treasury in January, 1828; sworn a Privy Councillor in November, 1830; and made Secretary to the Admiralty in December, 1834, which office he resigned in 1835.

## Lineage.

This family of DAWSON was established in Ireland in 1611, by CHRISTOPHER DAWSON, esq.* of Acorn Bank, in Westmoreland. He first was father of

THOMAS DAWSON, who purchased the lands at Castle-Dawson, in the county of Londonderry, in the eighth year of CHARLES *the First's* reign, 1633, from George and Dudley Philips. His son and successor,

THOMAS DAWSON, commissary of the musters of the army in Ireland, *d.* in 1683, and was succeeded by his son,

THOMAS DAWSON, esq. of Castle-Dawson, member in Parliament for the borough of Antrim, *m.* Arabella Upton, of Castle-Upton, in the county of Antrim, and dying in 1695, was succeeded by his brother,

JOSHUA DAWSON, esq. of Castle-Dawson, M. P. for the borough of Wicklow, and chief secretary of state for Ireland to the Lords Justices, in 1710. He died 1727, leaving, with other issue, two sons and a daughter, namely,

- ARTHUR, his heir.
- William, who *m.* Sarah Newcomen, widow of Colonel Dawson, of the county of Tipperary, and had issue,
  - ARTHUR, successor to his uncle.
  - Sarah, *m.* to Thomas Newenham, esq. of Coolmere, in the county of Cork.
- Mary, *m.* to the Hon. Henry Hamilton, M. P.

The elder son,

ARTHUR DAWSON, esq. of Castle-Dawson, who represented for a considerable time the county of Londonderry in parliament, was constituted one of the Barons of the Exchequer 1742. He *m.* Jane Oriel, of Shane's Castle, and dying in 1775, was succeeded by his nephew,

ARTHUR DAWSON, esq. of Castle Dawson, born 1745, many years member of parliament for the boroughs of Middleton and Banagher, who *m.* in 1775, Catherine, daughter of George Paul and Lady Araminta Monck, and had issue,

- GEORGE-ROBERT, his heir.
- Henry-Richard, dean of St. Patricks, Dublin, who *m.* Frances Heseltine.
- Araminta.
- Maria, *m.* to Henry Kemmis, esq. of Dublin.
- Louisa.
- Isabella, *m.* to Richard Cane, esq. of Dublin.

Mr. Dawson *d.* 6th December, 1822, and was *s.* by his son, the present GEORGE-ROBERT DAWSON, esq. of Castle-Dawson.

*Arms*—Az. on a bend or, three martlets gu.

*Crest*—An estoile of six points or.

*Motto*—Toujours propice.

*Estates*—In the counties of Londonderry and Cavan, and in the city of Dublin.

*Town Residence* — Upper Grosvenor-street, London.

*Seat* —Castle-Dawson, county Londonderry.

---

* This Christopher Dawson was thus descended:

John Dawson, *m.* Beatrice, dau. of John Lord Vesey, the first of his family that came into Westmorland, anno Domini, 1170.

|

Sir Christopher.

|

Sir John.

|

Sir Thomas Dawson, living anno Domini, 1280.

|

Christopher Dawson, *m.* Mary, daughter of Sir William Beckett, who came of the line of Sir Gilbert Beckett.

|

Richard Dawson.

|

Sir Robert Dawson, *m.* the daughter of Sir John Hall, of Houtington, in Kent.

|

Christopher Dawson, *m.* Esther, daughter of Sir Edward Marshall, of Soerby, in Cumberland.

|

John Dawson, *m.* Elizabeth, daughter of Sir John Browne.

|

Thomas Dawson, *m.* Martha Harrison, daughter of Sir Henry Harrison, of Yorkshire.

|

John Dawson, *m.* Marianne, daughter of Sir John Savage, of Rock Hall.

|

Christopher Dawson.

|

Thomas Dawson, whose son CHRISTOPHER settled in Ireland.

## JENYNS, OF BOTTISHAM HALL.

JENYNS, *The Reverend* GEORGE LEONARD, of Bottisham Hall, in the county of Cambridge, *b.* 19th June, 1763, *m.* 1788, Mary, daughter of the late Dr. Heberden, and has had issue,

Soame, *b.* in 1789, and *d.* in 1803.
GEORGE, *b.* in 1795, *m.* Maria-Jane, daughter of Sir James Gambier, knt. and has surviving issue,

George-Gambier, *b.* in 1822.
Soame-Gambier, *b.* in 1826.
Charles-Fitzgerald-Gambier, *b.* in 1827.
Jemima-Maria-Hicks.
Isabel-Charlotte.

Charles, *b.* 15th August, 1798, *m.* Marianne, only daughter of Samuel Vachell, esq.
Leonard, *b.* 25th May, 1800.
Mary.
Harriet, *m.* to the Reverend John Stephen Henslow, Professor of Botany, at Cambridge.
Elizabeth.

Mr. Jenyns succeeded his cousin, SOAME JENYNS, who died *s.p.* in 1787, under the will of that eminent person, after the decease of his widow, to whom he left a life interest in the estates.

### Lineage.

In the year 1563,
Sir William St. Loe, knt. released all his right in the Manor of Churchill, in Somersetshire, to RALPH JENNYNS,* of Islington, in Middlesex, whose descendant, Richard Jenyns, sold it to John Churchill, esq. of Lincoln's Inn.

SIR JOHN JENYNS, knighted in 1603, the representative of Ralph, married, first, Anne, daughter of Sir William Brounker, and had, by her, one son,

JOHN (Sir), who was made K.B. at the creation of Charles, Prince of Wales, served as sheriff of Herts in 1626, and was M.P. for St. Albans. He *m.* Alice, third daughter of Sir Richard Spencer, and had several children, of whom

RICHARD, of Sandridge, in Herts, *d.* in 1744, leaving by his wife, Frances, daughter and co-heir of Sir Gifford Thornhurst, bart. three daughters,

1. FRANCES, *m.* Richard, Duke of Tyrconnel. Of the beauty and character of the "Belle Jenyns" a contemporary thus speaks: "She had the fairest and brightest complexion that ever was seen; her hair a most beauteous flaxen, her countenance extremely animated, though, generally, persons so exquisitely fair have an insipidity; her whole person was fine, particularly her neck and bosom. The charms of her person, and the unaffected sprightliness of her wit, gained her the general admiration of the whole court; in these fascinating qualities she had there (Charles's court) other competitors; but scarcely one, except Miss Jenyns, maintained throughout the cha-

* On a blue stone in the floor of the church at Churchill, are the portraitures in brass of a man and woman, and the following inscription:
"Here lyeth Ralph Jenyns, esquier, which dyed the x day of Apryll, in the year of our Lorde God, MCCCCCLXXII, and was buryed the XVII day of the same moneth, leaving behynd him Joane, his wyffe, and having by her VIII chyldren, that is to wite fyve sonnes and three doughters."

racter of unblemished chastity."* After the death of the duke, whose sincere attachment to his unfortunate sovereign has never been disputed, the duchess was permitted to erect a house (still standing) in King-street, Dublin, as a nunnery for poor Clares, and in this obscure retirement, burying all the attractions and graces which once so adorned the court of England, she died at the age of ninety-two, and was interred in St. Patrick's cathedral, 9th March, 1730.

2. Barbara, *m.* to Edward Griffith, esq.
3. SARAH, became the celebrated DUCHESS OF MARLBOROUGH.

Sir John Jenyns wedded, secondly, Dorothy, widow of John Latch, esq. and daughter of Thomas Bulbeck,† by Ursula, daughter of Robert Gray, and had with a daughter, Elizabeth, who died unmarried, a son,

THOMAS JENYNS, esq. of Hayes, in Middlesex, *b.* in 1609, who *m.* Veare, daughter of Sir James Palmer, and by her, who died in 1644, left at his decease, in 1650, with other children, who *d. s. p.* a son and successor,

ROGER JENYNS, esq. of Hayes, who *m.* Sarah, daughter of Joseph Latch, esq. and had issue,

I. JOHN, who died in 1715, leaving by Jane, his wife, daughter of James Clitherow, esq. *inter alios*, a son,
    ROGER, who *m.* Miss Harvey, and was father of
        JOHN-HARVEY, who espoused Miss E. Chappelow, and *d.* in 1789, leaving, with a dau. Charlotte-Elizabeth, *m.* to the Rev. J. Vachell,‡ a son,
            GEORGE - LEONARD, of

---

* Of the Duchess of Tyrconnell we have a most interesting account in Mrs. Jameson's "Beauties of the Court of CHARLES II." "Last came," says that accomplished writer, "the heroine of our last memoir, the fair, the elegant, the fascinating Frances Jennings; she who moved through the glittering court 'in unblenched majesty,' who robbed the men of their hearts, the women of their lovers, and never lost herself. The very model of an intellectual coquette; perhaps a little too wilful, a little too wary for a perfect woman; but in the flush and bloom of early youth, and in the dangerous situation in which she was now placed, the first of these qualities was only an additional charm, the last a necessary safeguard. As to hearts, and such things, to bring them to Charles's court was mere work of supererogation; it was like trading to the south sea islands with diamonds and ingots of gold, where glass beads and tinfoil bear just the same value and answered just as well. Frances Jennings was the eldest of the three daughters, co-heirs of Richard Jennings, esq. of Sandridge, near St. Albans. If we may give any credit whatever to the ondits of that time, the mother of Miss Jennings was more remarkable for her beauty than her discretion. Of the two other daughters, Barbara became the wife of Mr. Griffiths, a man of large fortune, and of her we hear no more. Sarah, who was younger than Frances by twelve or fourteen years, became the famous Duchess of Marlborough.

"Miss Jennings was about sixteen when she was appointed Maid of Honour to the Duchess of York. She had no sooner made her appearance in the court circle, than she was at once proclaimed 'Oltre le belle, bella!' Over Miss Hamilton and Miss Stuart she had the advantage of youth and novelty, and over the others every advantage of mind and person. Her form was that of a young Aurora, newly descended to the earth; she never moved without discovering some new charm, or developing some new grace. Her eyes and hair were light, and her complexion transcendently fair; but the rich profusion of her long tresses, the animated bloom upon her cheek, and the varying expression of her countenance and smile, left her nothing of that fadeur which often accompanies exceeding fairness of complexion. Her mouth, as Hamilton tells us, was not perhaps the smallest, but was certainly the loveliest in the world. But nature, in forming this exquisite chef d'œuvre, had in mercy to mankind left part of her handy-work imperfect. Some critics declared that the tip of her nose was not 'de la dernière délicatesse,' that her hands and arms were not quite worthy of the small foot and delicate ankle; and it was admitted that her eyes were not quite as perfect as her mouth. To her external attractions, Miss Jennings added what was rarely met with in the court of Charles, all the witchery of mind and all the dignity of virtue. Her conversation and deportment were alike irresistible, from a just and delightful mixture of softness and sprightliness. A little petulance and caprice of temper; a little heedlessness of manner; a good deal of her sex's pride; yet more vanity; a quickness of imagination, which sometimes hurried her to the verge of an imprudence, and a natural acuteness and readiness of wit which as often extricated her;—

"Yielding by nature, stubborn but for fame."

† Third son of John Bulbeck and Elizabeth Wake.

‡ The issue of the marriage of Charlotte Elizabeth Jenyns and the Rev. J. Vachell are two sons and two daughters, viz.

I. George-Harvey Vachell, *b.* in 1798, *m.* in 1834, Cecilia-Catherine, daughter of the Rev. Thomas Lawton.
II. Harvey Vachell, *b.* in 1805.
I. Mary-Anne Vachell.
II. Charlotte Vachell, *m.* in 1822, to Archdeacon Philpot.

whom presently, as inheritor of the estates of Soame Jenyns, esq.

II. Roger (Sir), of whom presently.
III. Thomas, *d.* unmarried.

I. Sarah, *d.* in infancy.

Roger Jenyns *d.* in 1693. His second son,

Sir Roger Jenyns, knt. born in 1663, purchased the estate of Bottisham, in the county of Cambridge, and became an active magistrate of that shire. He married first, Martha, widow of John Mingay, by whom, who died in 1701, he had two sons and a daughter, Roger, Veare, and Sarah. He wedded, secondly, Elizabeth, daughter of Sir Peter Soame, of Heyden, in Essex, and by her, who *d.* in 1723, left at his decease in 1740, a son and successor,

Soame Jenyns, esq. of Bottisham Hall, *b.* in 1704. This eminent person was chosen in 1742 one of the representatives for the county of Cambridge, from which time he sat in parliament until the year 1780, representing, during these thirty-eight years, either the county or the borough of Cambridge, excepting four years only, when on the call of a new parliament, in the year 1754, he was returned for the borough of Dunwich. He began his political career by supporting the declining influence of Sir Robert Walpole, and obtained from that minister, the situation of a Lord of the Board of Trade, which he retained until its abolition in 1780. As a country gentleman, Mr. Jenyns appeared to greater advantage than as a politician, ably and impartially fulfilling the magisterial duties, and exercising the rights of hospitality in his neighbourhood. It is, however, as an author and wit that his reputation stands on the highest ground. In 1757, appeared his well-known "Free Enquiry into the Nature and Origin of Evil;" in 1776, his celebrated "View of the internal Evidences of the Christian Religion;" and in 1782, his "Disquisitions on various Subjects;" which are marked with his usual wit and shrewd observation. His last production was "Thoughts on Parliamentary Reform," which he wholly opposed. Soame Jenyns's works have been published in four volumes, 12mo. with a life by Cole. He *m.* first, Mary, only daughter of Colonel Soame, of Dereham, in Norfolk, and secondly, Elizabeth, daughter of Henry Grey, esq. of Hackney, but *d. s.p.* 18th December, 1787.

"In private life," says Mr. Cole, "he was a man of great mildness, gentleness, and sweetness of temper. His earnest desire was, as far as possible, never to offend any person." This is confirmed by the Reverend Mr. Cole, of Milton, who is not remarkable for the lenity of his opinions respecting his contemporaries. "Mr. Jenyns was a man of lively fancy and pleasant turn of wit, very sparkling in conversation, and full of merry conceits and agreeable drollery, which was heightened by his inarticulate manner of speaking through his broken teeth, and all this mixed with the utmost humanity and good-nature, having hardly ever heard him severe upon any one, and by no means satirical in his mirth and good-humour."

Mr. Cumberland, in his memoirs of his own life, gives us some characteristic traits of Mr. Jenyns, which correspond with the above: "A disagreement about a name or a date will mar the best story that was ever put together. Sir Joshua Reynolds luckily could not hear an interrupter of this sort. Johnson would not hear, or if he heard him would not heed him. Soame Jenyns heard him, heeded him, set him right, and took up his tale where he had left it, without any diminution of its humour, adding only a few more twists to his snuff-box, a few more taps upon the lid of it, with a preparatory grunt or two, the invariable forerunners of the amenity that was at the heels of them. He was the man who bore his part in all societies with the most even temper and undisturbed hilarity of all the good companions whom I ever knew. He came into your house at the very moment you had put upon your card: he dressed himself, to do your party honour, in all the colours of the jay; his lace indeed had long since lost its lustre, but his coat had faithfully retained its cut since the days when gentlemen wore embroidered figured velvets with short sleeves, boot cuffs, and buckram skirts. As nature cast him in the exact mould of an ill-made pair of stiff stays, he followed her so close in the fashion of his coat, that it was doubted if he did not wear them: because he had a protuberant wen just under his pole, he wore a wig, that did not cover above half his head. His eyes were protruded like the eyes of the lobster, who wears them at the end of his feelers, and yet there was room between one of these and his nose for another wen that added nothing to his beauty: yet I heard this good man very innocently remark, when Gibbon published his history, 'that he wondered any body so ugly could write a book.'

"Such was the exterior of a man, who was the charm of the circle, and gave a zest to every company he came into. His pleasantry was of a sort peculiar to himself, it harmonized with every thing, it was like the bread to our dinner, you did not perhaps make it the whole, or principal part of your meal, but it was an admirable and wholesome auxiliary to your other viands. Soame Jenyns told you no long stories, engrossed not much of your attention, and was not angry with those that did. His thoughts were original, and were apt to have a very whimsical affinity to the paradox in them.

He wrote verses upon dancing, and prose upon the origin of evil; yet he was a very indifferent metaphysician, and a worse dancer. Ill nature and personality, with the single exception of his lines upon Johnson, I never heard fall from his lips; those lines I have forgotten, though I believe I was the first person to whom he recited them; they were very bad, but he had been told that Johnson ridiculed his metaphysics, and some of us had just then been making extempore epitaphs upon each other. Though his wit was harmless, the general cast of it was ironical; there was a terseness in his repartees that had a play of words as well as of thought; as when speaking of the difference between laying out money upon lands or purchasing into the funds, he said, 'one was principal without interest, and the other interest without principal.' Certain it is, he had a brevity of expression that never hung upon the ear, and you felt the point in the very moment he made the push."

Dying issueless, Mr. Jenyns devised his estates, after the demise of his widow, to his cousin, the Reverend GEORGE LEONARD JENYNS, their present possessor.

*Arms*—Az. a chev. between three griffins' heads erased arg. on a chief or, a lion passant gu. between two torteaux.

*Crest*—A leopard's head erased and guard. gu. bezantée, holding in the mouth a cross, formée fitchée arg.

*Estates*—Situated principally at Bottisham, Ditton, and Horningsey, in the county of Cambridge, and at Upwell, in Norfolk.

*Seat*—Bottisham Hall.

## JENNINGS, OF HARTWELL.

JENNINGS, ROBERT-JOHN, esq. *b.* 27th September, 1794, *m.* at Paris, in November, 1819, Maria-Anna-Assunta Marinelli, of Perugia, in Italy, by whom he had an only child,

AUGUSTUS-GEORGE-SIDNEY-ROBERT, *b.* in Paris, 20th January, 1821, and baptized in the chapel of the English Embassy there; the sponsors being Prince Augustus of Prussia, the Earl of Buckinghamshire, and the Hon. Mrs. Grieve.

### Lineage.

THOMAS JENNINGS, esq. of Curteen Hall, Hartwell, in the county of Northampton, was reputed the illegitimate son of the unfortunate Duke of Monmouth, by a daughter of Sir John Jennings, whose family had been long attached to the court of *King* CHARLES. Mr. Jennings married Miss Chamberlayne, a lady of ancient descent and large fortune, by whom he had a very numerous issue, who subsequently intermarried with the families of Lister, Gibbes, Hippesly, the Husseys of Scotney Castle, and the Bracebridges. Among others,

WILLIAM JENNINGS, who became lieutenant colonel of the 62nd regiment, and commanded for some time at Carrickfergus. There he distinguished himself on the landing of the French, in February, 1761, and had the honour to receive a vote of thanks from the Irish Parliament, and also a silver cup,* appropriately inscribed, from the town of Belfast. Colonel Jennings married Miss Tyndall, and died *s. p.* His brother,

ROBERT JENNINGS, was appointed by his godfather, Sir Robert Walpole, deputy-auditor of the Exchequer, at that time a very

* This cup is still in the possession of the representative of the family.

honourable and lucrative office. He *m.* Miss Ford, and by her had twelve children,

I. FRANK, who *d.* young.
II. Thomas, captain in Lord Loudon's regiment, and *d.* young, unmarried.
III. ROBERT, of whom hereafter.
IV. John, captain 30th regiment, *d.* young, unmarried.

I. Mary, *m.* to W. Pearce, esq.
II. Grace, who wedded Robert Collys Vernon, esq. and had several sons and daughters; of the latter, one is married to Colonel Cross, C.B. of the 36th regiment.
III. Catharine, } *d.* unmarried.
IV. Elizabeth, }
V. Anne, who *m.* her cousin, Charles Gibbes, esq.
VI. Martha, espoused, first, George Cuming, esq. chief at Cuddelore, in the East Indies, and, secondly, Lieutenant Colonel Kenny.
VII. Frances, *m.* her cousin Captain Anthony Gibbes, R. N.
VIII. Lucy, wedded John Inge, esq. of the Inges of Leicestershire and Warwickshire.

The third son,

ROBERT JENNINGS, esq. became representative of the family on the death of his elder brothers, and succeeded his father in the Exchequer, which office he held until his death in September, 1805. His long services were rewarded by pensions granted to his widow and son, by *King* GEORGE III. Mr. Jennings *m.* Miss Wheeler, of a Bedfordshire family, by whom he had six children, of these only two survived their infancy.

ROBERT-JOHN, the present representative, who *m.* in 1819, an Italian lady, Mad. Marinelli. She being a Roman Catholic, and also a subject of His Holiness, this marriage was celebrated by a special Bull of the Pope, and likewise in the chapel of the British Ambassador, at Paris.
Harriet, *m.* to John White, esq. of Eastborne, and of Yalding, in Kent.

*Arms*—Erminois, three pole-axes erect, azure, on a chief gules, as many bendlets argent.*

*Crest*—A demy dragon erminois, the wings elevated and erased gules, holding a pole-axe, as in the arms.

*Motto*—Il buon tempo verra.

*Town Residence*—Baker-street, Portman-square.

* These arms were granted by the Herald's College, by a patent dated 24th December, 1760, to Robert Jennings, and the descendants of his father Thomas, (in consequence of some family litigation) in lieu of those they had previously borne.

## STEWARD, OF NOTTINGTON HOUSE.

STEWARD, RICHARD-AUGUSTUS-TUCKER, esq. of Nottington House, in the county of Dorset, *b.* 1st February, 1773, *m.* 12th March, 1823, Louisa-Henrietta, only daughter of Edward Morgan, esq. of Golden Grove, in Flintshire, and has issue,

RICHARD-OLIVER-FRANCIS, *b.* 18th December, 1823.
Frederick-Gordon, *b.* 26th January, 1826.
Edwin-Ashley, *b.* 31st October, 1831.

Augusta-Caroline.
Louisa-Charlotte.

This gentleman, who formerly sat in parliament for Weymouth, is a magistrate and deputy-lieutenant for Dorsetshire, and lieutenant-colonel of the county militia.

## Lineage.

This family, of Scotch origin, emigrated to St. Helena early in the eighteenth century, and subsequently settled at Weymouth.

GABRIEL STEWARD, esq. married Rebecca, daughter and co-heir of Richard Tucker, esq. by Sarah, his wife, daughter of George Gollop, esq. of Berwick, ninth son of Thomas Gollop, esq. high sheriff of Dorsetshire, 27 CHARLES II. (see vol. i. p. 601,) and had issue,

- GABRIEL TUCKER.
- RICHARD-AUGUSTUS, the present Colonel STEWARD.
- Edward-Tucker, rector of Wem, in Salop.
- John-Charles-Tucker, late of the 3rd regiment of guards, captain on half-pay, a widower.
- Rebecca.
- Sarah-Dorothea, *m.* to Lieut. Colonel Browne.
- Maria, *m.* to Captain Baylis Wardell, of the 10th hussars.

Mr. Steward's second son is the present Colonel STEWARD, of Nottington House.

*Arms*—Or, a fesse chequy az. and arg. surmounted of a bend gu. within a bordure of the last.

*Crest*—A pelican vulning ppr.

*Estates*—Badipole, Broadway, Wyke, Weymouth, and Island of Portland, since the years 1600, 1700, and 1800.

*Seat*—Nottington House, Dorsetshire.

# CARLEILL, OF SEWERBY.

CARLEILL, WILLIAM, esq. of Sewerby, in the county of York, baptized at Eyam, in Derbyshire, 8th April, 1768, *m.* 18th June, 1788, Eleanor, daughter of William Greene, esq. of York, and by her, who died 14th June, 1818, has had issue,

- Randolph, *b.* at Brosterfield, 17th October, 1794, buried at Longstone, 20th September, 1814.
- Katharine, *b.* at Edinburgh, and baptized at Eyam.
- Alicia-Maria, *d.* young, buried at Eyam.
- Eleanor, buried at Longstone, 10th December, 1814.
- Martha, *b.* at Burr House, buried at Longstone, 17th August, 1830.
- Anne, *b.* at Brosterfield.
- Elizabeth, *b.* at Longstone.
- Maria, *b.* at Longstone.

Major Carleill, who succeeded his father in 1800, was appointed in 1797, a deputy-lieutenant for the county of Derby, and obtained, in 1803, the command of the South High Peak volunteers, with the rank of major.

## Lineage.

"The surname of CARLEILL or CARLISLE," says Mr. Nicholas Carlisle, in his interesting account of the family, "which is of great antiquity, is evidently local, and was unquestionably assumed from the city of Carlisle. Prior to the Conquest the barony of Carlisle, on which the city of Carlisle is erected, and the Manor of Cumwhinton in the parish of Wetheral, belonged to HILDRED, thence styled Hildredus de Carliell, a cognomen which descended to his posterity, who were successively knights till the invasion of

Scotland by EDWARD I. when Sir William de Carliell, then chief of the family, sold most of his lands in England, and removing into Scotland, seated himself at Kinmount.

The following descent of the CARLEILLS, of Sewerby, is deduced from the parish registers of Bridlington, which commence in 1564, from a visitation of the county of York, taken at Kelham, in 1665, by William Dugdale, and from Hopkinson's manuscripts.

JOHN CARLEILL, of Sewerby, who *d.* 20th January, 1578-9, must have been a person of considerable importance from the large possessions which he left to his son, and his ancestors had, doubtless, been long established at Sewerby, though the previous pedigree cannot be traced. He had issue,

- I. TRISTRAM, his heir.

- I. Anne, *m.* at Bridlington, 28th August, 1576, to Robert Hunter, esq. of Thornton.
- II. Margaret, *m.* 6th October, 1582, to Matthew Martin, esq.
- III. Grace, *m.* 12th November, 1583, to Thomas Peacock, esq.
- IV. Katherine, *m.* 3rd February, 1584-5, to William Strycland, esq.

The only son and successor,

TRISTRAM CARLEILL, esq. of Sewerby, *m.* first, Mary Readshaw, and secondly, Catherine, daughter of Randolph Rode, of Cheshire, by the latter of whom, who *d.* in 1635, he had issue,

- I. RANDOLPH, his heir.
- II. Robert, baptized at Bridlington, 9th July, 1592, a merchant at Kingston-upon-Hull, *m.* Elizabeth, daughter of Gilbert Crowther, esq. of Eland, in Halifax, and was father of two sons and two daughters. The elder of the latter,
  - Dorothy, was the second wife of Thomas Fairfax, esq. of Menston, eldest son of the Hon. Col. Charles Fairfax. She *d.* in 1728, aged ninety, and was buried in the old church at Leeds, where a handsome monument is erected to her memory.
- III. John, *d.* unmarried before 1659.

- I. Anne, *m.* in 1606, to Richard Burgess, merchant of Hull.
- II. Catherine, *m.* to Richard Milner, esq. of Sutton, in Holderness.
- III. Jane, *m.* first, to — Grimston, esq. and, secondly, to Walter Hawksworth, esq. of Godmundham, in Yorkshire.

Tristram Carliell *d.* in 1618, and by an inquisition taken at Agnes Burton, in the county of York, 24th May, 1620, appears to have *d.* seized of the Manor of Sewerby, and of the chapel of Buckton, late parcel of the possessions of the dissolved monastery of Bridlington. He was succeeded by his eldest son,

RANDOLPH CARLIELL, esq. of Sewerby, who had two wives: the first, Frances Legard, *d. s. p.*; by the second, Elizabeth, daughter of Richard Knowsley, of North Burton, in Yorkshire, he had a numerous issue, viz.

- I. ROBERT, his heir.
- II. John, baptized at Bridlington, 4th December, 1630, *m.* Jane Hardy, of Hilston, in Holderness, and had sons and daughters.
- III. Thomas, *d.* unmarried in 1660.

- I. Elizabeth, *m.* first, to Sir Theodore Herring, of York, and, secondly, to Henry Beale, esq. of Knottingley; but there seems to be some contradiction in Dugdale's statement, for in the same visitation, taken at Barnesley, 15th September, 1665, he says, that Henry Beale, of Woodhouse, in the parish of Drax, *m.* Elizabeth, eldest daughter of Randolph Carliell, of Sewerby, "widow of Samuel Heron, Clk."
- II. Mary, *m.* in 1656, to the Reverend James Fisher. It was to this gentleman, the ejected vicar of Sheffield, in 1662, that the formation of the first society of Dissenters in that town is owing. He was a man of great piety and worth, and suffered great afflictions by fines and imprisonment from the violent spirit of the times.
- III. Hannah, *m.* in 1660, to Timothy Preston, of Bridlington.
- IV. Dorothy, *m.* in 1664, to Robert Carleil, merchant of Kingston-upon-Hull.
- V. Amie, *m.* in 1672, to Gregory Creyke, esq. of Marton, in Sewerby, one of the most ancient families in the East Riding, now represented by Colonel CREYKE.
- VI. Susannah.
- VII. Ruth.

Randolph Carliell *d.* in 1659, was buried in the south choir in Bridlington Church, and *s.* by his son,

ROBERT CARLEIL, esq. of Sewerby, baptized at Bridlington, 28th January, 1622-3, who *m.* Anne, daughter and co-heir of Henry Vickerman, of Fraysthorpe, in Yorkshire, and by her, who *d.* in 1696, had two sons and ten daughters, viz.

- I. HENRY, his heir.
- II. Timothy, baptized 6th January, 1667-8, *m.* and had issue.

- I. Elizabeth, *b.* in 1658, of Beningborough.

II. Christian, of Beverley, bapt. 21st July, 1662.
III. Mary, *b.* in 1663, *m.* to Thomas Bayles.
IV. Alathea, baptized 13th June, 1664, *m.* to Thomas Buck, esq. of Carnaby.
V. Amie, *b.* in 1670, *d.* in 1702.
VI. Catherine, baptized 25th June, 1674.
VII. Frances, *b.* 1676, *m.* to — Boulton.
VIII. Ruth, *m.* in 1697, to Robert Grimstone.
IX. Jane, baptized 3rd September, 1678.
X. Dorothy, *m.* to the Rev. William Withers, rector of Thrybergh. One of the sons of this marriage, the Rev. William Withers, M.A. rector of Tankersley, *m.* Miss Buck, of the family of Bury St. Edmunds, and *d.* in 1771, leaving two sons, one of whom was a Physician at York, and the other Recorder of that city.

Robert Carleil *d.* in 1685, and was *s.* by his son,

HENRY CARLEILL, esq. of Sewerby, baptized at Bridlington, 7th December, 1665, who wedded 14th May, 1691, Elizabeth, second daughter of William Smithson, esq. of Malton, in Yorkshire, of the Smithsons, of Stanwick, eventually Earls and Dukes of Northumberland, and had four sons and a daughter. The eldest of the former,

HENRY CARLEILL, esq. of Sewerby, baptized at Bridlington, 15th March, 1691-2, dying *s. p.* was succeeded by his brother,

ROBERT CARLEILL, esq. of Sewerby, who also *d.* issueless in 1729, when the representation of the family devolved on his brother,

WILLIAM CARLEILL, esq. of Bridlington, and afterwards of Ecclesfield Hall, near Sheffield, baptized 13th August, 1695, who *m.* 8th June, 1731, Catharine, eldest daughter of John Greame, esq. of Sewerby, (*see* vol. ii. p. 590,) and, secondly, Elizabeth, daughter of William Greene, esq. of Thundercliffe Grange, grandson of Robert Greene, esq. of Thundercliffe, who compounded for his estates after the civil wars. By his first wife, who *d.* in 1732, Mr. Carleill left at his decease, 30th December, 1779, an only son,

RANDOLPH CARLEILL, esq. of Brosterfield, a deputy-lieutenant for Derbyshire, baptized at Bridlington, 28th May, 1732, who inherited that portion of the Sewerby estate which still remained in the family. This gentleman, who was a captain in the 13th regiment of foot, was engaged in active foreign service for more than twenty years. He *m.* in 1766, Eleanor, daughter of Smithson Greene, esq. of Thundercliffe Grange, by Eleanor, his wife, daughter and heir of Francis Morton, esq. of Brosterfield, in Derbyshire, and dying in December, 1800, was buried in the church of Eyam, and succeeded by his only surviving child, the present WILLIAM CARLEILL, esq.

### Family of Greene.

Thundercliffe was a Grange of the Cistertian Abbey, and Kirkstead, in Lincolnshire, which had forges and other considerable property in the parish of Ecclesfield, and the adjoining one of Rotherham, of the gift of De Busli and De Lovetot. In the general confirmation made by *King* JOHN to the monks of that house the forges of Tunnocliffe, with the appurtenances are mentioned. In the 36 HENRY III. the Abbot of Kirkstead had free warren granted in these lands. At the dissolution, Thomas Rokeby, descended from the great family of the same name in the North Riding of Yorkshire, obtained possession of the estate, which was conveyed by his only dau. and heir to Henry Wombwell, esq. grandson of Thomas Wombwell, esq. of Wombwell. Their son and successor,

NICHOLAS WOMBWELL, esq. of Thundercliffe Grange, who *d.* in 1571, *m.* Isabel, daughter of Thomas Wentworth, esq. of Wentworth Woodhouse, and had two sons, Thomas and Nicholas; the younger, living at Tickhill in 1585, *m.* Elizabeth, widow of Nicholas Mauleverer, esq. of Letwell. The elder,

THOMAS WOMBWELL, esq. of Thundercliffe Grange, rebuilt or enlarged the old Grange, for in the hall were his arms, impaling those of Arthington, and the initials T. W. A. W. 1575. He *m.* Isabel, daughter of Richard Arthington, esq. of Arthington, and dying in 1592, left five surviving daughters his co-heirs, viz.

BARBARA, *m.* in 1577, to Nicholas Shiercliffe, esq. of Ecclesfield Hall.
ISABEL, *m.* in 1584-5, to Frances Stringer, esq. of Sharlston, in Yorkshire.
MARGARET, *m.* in 1584, to Nicholas Wordsworth.
JULIANA.
ELIZABETH, *m.* in 1585, to Nicholas Mauleverer, esq.

The eldest daughter,

BARBARA, the wife of Nicholas Shiercliffe, esq. left a daughter and eventual heiress,

ANNE SHIERCLIFFE, who wedded 28th August, 1604, JAMES GREENE, esq. (son of Thomas Greene, of Cawthorne, in Yorkshire, to whom Richard St. George Norroy granted arms in 1612,) and had several children, of whom Anne Greene, *m.* — Metcalfe, and

ROBERT GREENE, esq. *b.* in 1613, succeeded his mother at Thundercliffe Grange. He *m.* Alice, daughter of Edward Fawcet, of Rufford, and had with other issue,

WILLIAM, his heir.

Matthew, who *m.* Catherine, daughter of Thomas Herdson, of Badsworth, and had an only child, Samuel, who *d.* an infant.

Alice, *m.* to Francis Kellam, of Pontefract.

Sarah, *m.* to Edward Wingfield, esq. of Billingley.

Mary, *m.* to John Wise, esq. of Colton, in Yorkshire.

Isabel, *m.* to Samuel Sanderson, esq. of Firbeck, in Yorkshire.

Mr. Greene *d.* in 1683, and was *s.* by his son,

WILLIAM GREENE, esq. of Thundercliffe Grange, aged about thirty-seven in May, 1674, who *m.* in 1662, Mary, daughter of Nicholas Stone, of Norton, merchant, and had a son and successor,

WILLIAM GREENE, esq. of Thundercliffe Grange, *b.* about 1662, who *m.* twice; by his first wife, Frances, he left a daughter, Frances, *m.* to — Rosil, and by his second, Alice Smithson, three sons and a dau. viz.

SMITHSON, his heir.

Charles, Lancaster Herald in 1729, *d.* in 1742, unmarried.

Henry, of Hague Hall, Yorkshire, left an only daughter, wife of James Allott.

Elizabeth, second wife of William Carleill, esq. of Ecclesfield.

The eldest son,

SMITHSON GREENE, esq. of Thundercliffe Grange, *b.* in 1696, wedded Eleanor, daughter and heir of Francis Morton, esq. of Brosterfield, and dying in 1756, left, *inter alios*, a daughter ELEANOR, *m.* to RANDOLPH CARLEILL, esq. and a son and successor,

WILLIAM GREENE, M. D. of Thundercliffe Grange, who sold the estate to Mr. Hugh Mellor, of Ecclesfield, from whose brother and successor, Thomas Mellor, it was purchased by Thomas, third Earl of Effingham.

*Arms*—Arg. on a chev. sa. between three Cornish choughs ppr. beaked and legged gu. as many mullets of six points or.

*Crest*—A moor's head in profile, couped at the shoulders ppr.

*Estates*—In Yorkshire, partly inherited from the present possessor's father, partly obtained by marriage.

*Seat*—Longstone Hall, Derbyshire.

## MAINWARING, OF WHITMORE.

MAINWARING, SARAH, of Whitmore Hall, in the county of Stafford, succeeded to the estates on the demise of her uncle, Edward Mainwaring, esq. in 1825.

### Lineage.

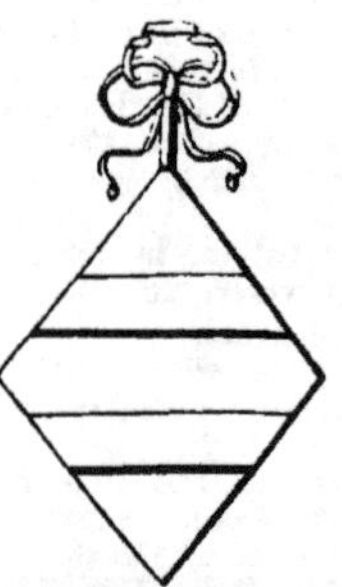

The family of Mesnilwaren, or Mainwaring, was founded by Ranulphus, who accompanied William the Conqueror from Normandy, and received the grant of fifteen lordships in Cheshire, including Peure (now Over Peover). He was succeeded by his son, Richard de Mesnilwaren, whose great grandson, Sir Raufe Manwaringe, knt. was justice of Chester, (*temp.* RICHARD I.) Sir Raufe married Amicia, daughter of Hugh Kyvelioc, Earl Palatine of Cheshire, and was father of Roger Manwaringe, of Warmincham, who gave unto his younger son, William, (*temp.* HENRY III.) the estate of Over Peover, which became, from that period, the chief seat of the family.* Sir John

* See article "Mainwaring," in BURKE's *Peerage and Baronetage*, and also the memoir of Sir William Mainwaring, knt. of West Chester, in the "Biographical Mirror," published by S. and E. Harding, Pall-Mall, in 1795.

Manwaringe, knt. the ninth lineal descendant from the aforesaid William, succeeded to his inheritance in 1495, and died aged forty-five, in 1515; he married Katherine, sister of William Honford, of Honford, in Cheshire, and had issue thirteen sons and two daughters.* Edward, the ninth son,† married Alice,‡ granddaughter and heiress of Humphrey de Boghey, or Bohun, of Whitmore; by this marriage Edward came into possession of the manors of Whitmore, Biddulph, Annesley, and Buckenhall, the two first of which remain in the name of Mainwaring, at the present day.

EDWARD MANWARINGE,§ of Whitmore, had issue, by Alice de Boghey, his wife,

I. EDWARD, his heir.

I. Anne, *m.* to Thomas Rosse, gent.

II. Jane, *d.* in infancy.

The son and successor,

EDWARD MANWARINGE, of Whitmore, *m.* Jane, daughter of Mathew Cradock, of Stafford, gent. and had issue,

I. EDWARD, his heir, born in 1577.

II. John, a merchant, *d.* beyond sea, without issue.

III. Randulph, or Randle, born in 1588, a colonel in the army (*temp.* CHARLES I.) in the cause of the king. He *m.* Eliza, daughter of Humphrey Haws, of London, by whom he had issue. George, his youngest son, was father of James Mainwaring, Mayor of Chester, in 1708, from whom are descended the Mainwarings, of Bromborough Court, in Cheshire. Elizabeth, a daughter of Randle Mainwaring, was *m.* to William Floyer, esq. of Floiers Hayes, in Devonshire.

I. Mary, wife of John Brett, esq. of Domesdale, in Staffordshire.

II. Elizabeth, *m.* to Thomas Jolley, esq. of Leeke, in Staffordshire.

III. Jane, wife of Francis Marten, citizen of London.

IV. Alice, wife of John Baddeley, gent. of Holeditch.

V. Anne, *m.* first, to William Fallows, gent. of Fallows, in Cheshire, afterwards to Hugh Maire, of Norbury, in Staffordshire.

VI. Katherine, *m.* to Thomas Hunt, gent. of Congton.

VII. Dorothy, wife of James Trevis, gent. of Treverton, in Cheshire.

VIII. Frances, *d.* in infancy.

IX. Sarah, *m.* first, to John Buckley, gent. of Stanton, in Staffordshire, and, secondly, to — Baddeley, of Chesterton, aforesaid.

His father dying in 1604,

EDWARD MAINWARINGE,|| a pious and much esteemed gentleman, succeeded to the estate. The manor-house at Whitmore was garrisoned by him, in the civil war, on the side of the parliament, whose cause he joined, in consequence of the king's supposed determination to re-establish the Papal authority in this country. In 1646 he was appointed sheriff for the county of Stafford, and *d.* the following year. He *m.* Sarah,¶ dau. and co-heiress of John Stone, esq. of London, and had issue,

I. EDWARD, born in 1603.

II. John, D.D. Rector of Stoke upon Trent, *m.* first, Susanna, daughter of Walter Pigott, esq. of Chetwind, in

---

* See the account of Over Peover, in "Ormerod's History of Cheshire.

† Of the eight elder brothers of Edward Mainwaring, of Whitmore, seven died without issue, previous to the end of the year 1557, when Philip, the eldest survivor, succeeded to the Peover estate, whose last lineal descendant, Sir Harry Mainwaring, bart. of Over Peover, died unmarried in 1726, leaving his estates by will to his half brother, Thomas Wetenhal, who thereupon assumed the name and arms of Mainwaring. The Mainwarings, of Whitmore, therefore, are now, by the termination of the Peover line, the *senior branch of the family*. Robert, the third surviving son of Sir John Mainwaring, and younger brother of Edward Mainwaring, of Whitmore, was the founder of the Mainwarings, of Martin Sands, in Cheshire.

‡ Her father, Robert de Boghey, died in 1519, during his father's life time.

§ Over the sepulchre of this gentleman, in Whitmore church, a marble monument was erected in the year 1580, on which the following inscription is engraven, in very old English characters:

"Here lyeth the bodies of Edwarde Manwaringe, of Whitmore, in the countie of Stafford, esquire, a younger sonne of Sir John Manwaringe, of Pevor and Badyley, in the countie of Chester, kt: also his wyffe right heir of Whitmore, Bedulph, Andeslay and Baggenall, wiche Edwarde Manwaringe deceased the daye of ......... in the yere of y' Lord, ano M°D°lxvi, on whose soule God have mercy amen.

. . . . . . . . . . .
. . . . . the roade free;
Into thye handes
Oure soules wee geve unto thee.
quod E·E·M.; ano. dmi. 1580."

|| See the life of Master John Ball, of Brazennose College, Oxford, afterwards minister at Whitmore, in Clarke's "Generall Martyrologie," published by T. Underhill, and J. Rothwell, St. Paul's Church-yard, in 1651.

¶ In the parish register of Whitmore there is entered the following curious panegyric of this lady:

"Sarah Mainwaring, virtutis exemplum et ornamentum, sexûs gloria et eclipsis, ex assiduâ pietate in Deum, profusâ liberalitate in pauperes, spectatâ probitate in omnes, ab omnibus imitanda pariter et admiranda, Vidua Edvardi Mainwaring, Armigeri, maximo omnium luctu necnon et damno, sepulchro conditur, July — anno Domini 1648."

the county of Salop. He had a second wife, Anne, daughter of — Gregson, of Turnditch, esq.

I. Jane, *m.* in 1625, to James Abney, esq. of Measham Hall, in the county of Derby, M.P. for Leicester.

His son and heir,

EDWARD MAINWARING, sheriff for Staffordshire, in 1660, *d.* in the seventy-second year of his age. He *m.* Anne, daughter of George Lomax, esq. of Clifton, in the county of Nottingham, and great-granddaughter of Oliver Lomax, esq. of Bury, in Lancashire, and had issue,

I. EDWARD, his heir, born in 1635.
II. John, *d.* when a few weeks old.
III. Philip, born in 1638, drowned in his tenth year.
IV. George, *b.* in 1644, *d.* unm. in 1691.
V. John, of London, *b.* 1645, *m.* and had several children.
VI. Thomas, *d.* without issue, aged forty.

I. Jane.
II. Sarah.
III. Elizabeth.
IV. Anne, *m.* to John Hockenhall, a gentleman of Cheshire.
V. Mary.

The eldest son,

EDWARD MAINWARING, succeeded to his father's estates in 1694, and *d.* in 1704. He married twice. By his first wife, Elizabeth Heneage,* he had ten children, seven of whom died infants, the others were Briget, who was *m.* to — Key, of Islington, in the county of Middlesex, Anne, wife of — Taylor, a divine, and Elizabeth, who *d.* unmarried. In 1679, five years after the death of his wife Elizabeth, Edward Mainwaring *m.* secondly, Bridget, daughter of Sir Thomas Trollop, bart. of Casewick, in the county of Lincoln, and by her had issue,

I. EDWARD, his heir.

I. Mary, *d.* unmarried.
II. Bridget, *m.* to George Davenport, esq. of Calveley, in Cheshire.

His son and successor,

EDWARD MAINWARING, of Whitmore Hall, *b.* in 1681, *m.* Jemima, second daughter of Edmund Pye, of Faringdon, in Berkshire, M.D. by Anne, his wife, daughter of Lord Crewe, of Stene, and had issue,

I. EDWARD, his heir, *b.* in 1709.
II. Henry, rector of Etwell, in Derbyshire, *m.* in 1735, Mary-Elizabeth, sole daughter of John Vaughan, esq. of Caergay, county Merioneth.
III. Thomas, *b.* in 1712, *m.* his first cousin, Frances, eldest daughter of Henry Pye, esq. of Faringdon, and *d.* in 1776, issueless.
IV. Charles, *b.* in 1713, } all *d.* unm.
V. John, *b.* in 1715, } all *d.* unm.
VI. Robert, *b.* in 1716, } all *d.* unm.
VII. James, *b.* in 1718, } all *d.* unm.
VIII. Benjamin, *b.* in 1719, *m.* two wives, and had issue by both.

I. Jemima, *m.* to Richard Nash, esq. of Warburton, in Sussex.

Being left a widower by the death of his first wife in 1721, Edward Mainwaring, married secondly, Martha, eldest dau. and co-heiress of William Lloyd, esq. of Halghton, in the county of Flint, and relict of Sir Thomas Mainwaring, of Baddiley, bart. in Cheshire, but by her had no issue.

His eldest son,

EDWARD MAINWARING, inherited, together with the possessions, the principles of his protestant ancestors, and signalized himself by his great zeal in repelling the invasion of CHARLES-EDWARD, in 1745, against whom he marched to Derby, at the head of his tenantry. He was sheriff for Staffordshire in the year 1768. His wife, Sarah, whom he married in 1735, was a daughter of William Bunbury, esq. of London, attorney-general for the county of Chester, second son of Sir Henry Bunbury, bart. of Bunbury and Stanney, in Cheshire. They had issue,

I. EDWARD, *b.* in 1736.
II. William, of London, *b.* in 1737, who *d.* in the seventy-sixth year of his age. He *m.* Frances, youngest daughter of Richard Stone, of London, banker, (elder brother of the Archbishop of Armagh of that name) by whom he had issue,
    1. Edward, *b.* in 1772, a cornet in the 13th regiment of dragoons, who *d.* unmarried, of a yellow fever, in the West Indies, at the early age of twenty-four.
    2. William, *b.* in 1776, in the civil service of the East India Company, *d.* unmarried, at Madras, in 1811.
    3. Henry, of the royal navy, *b.* in 1779, shot in an engagement with a French frigate, in which, though he was only eighteen years of age, his conduct gave so much satisfaction, as to call forth a public eulogium from his commanding officer, Hardy, (then captain of the Boston frigate).
    4. Rowland-Eyton, *b.* in 1780, a cadet in the service of the East India Company, he was present at the capture of Seringapatam, in 1799: *d.* unmarried.

* This lady was the daughter of Thomas Heneage, esq. of Battersea, in the county of Surrey, and of his wife, the lady Liddell, widow of Sir Thomas Liddell, knt. of Ravensworth Castle, in the county of Durham.

5. Charles, *b.* in 1787, *d.* unmarried in 1832.

1. SARAH, of whom presently.
2. Frances, *d.* in infancy.
3. Anne, *m.* in 1803, to Joseph Sladen, esq. of Doctors Commons, and of Lee, in the county of Kent, *d.* in her thirty-third year, leaving issue.
4. Charlotte, *d.* in infancy.
5. Janet, *m.* in 1803, to Michael Russell, esq. of London, and has issue.
6. Julia.

III. Richard, *d.* an infant.

IV. Rowland, of Four Oaks, in the county of Warwick, a field officer, *b.* in 1745, *d.* in 1815. He had two wives, Elizabeth, his first wife, (dau. of Thomas Mills, of Barlaston, in the county of Stafford,) *d.* without issue. By his second, Jane, daughter of Captain Latham, R.N. he had,

1. Edward-Henry, a lieutenant in the army, who *d.* unmarried in the West Indies.
2. Rowland, of Bath, post-captain R. N. *b.* in 1783. This gentleman, who is now heir apparent to Whitmore,(by the recent death of his cousin, Charles Mainwaring, the first in the entail,) has had two wives. He *m.* first, Sophia-Henrietta, only daughter of Captain Duff, of the army, and by her had issue,

   Rowland, *d.* in India, aged sixteen, midshipman R. N.
   Edward-Pillew.
   Gordon.
   Charles.
   William.
   George.

   Sophia-Henrietta.

   His second wife, Mary-Anne, daughter of — Clarke, esq. *d.* in 1834, leaving an only child,

   Mary-Anne.

   Captain Mainwaring was a midshipman in H. M. S. Majestic, at the battle of the Nile, and assisted likewise at the blockade of Copenhagen.
3. Thomas, *b.* in 1784, in the civil service of the East India Company, Bengal Presidency, *m.* in the East Indies, Sophia Walker, by whom he has issue.
4. George, in the civil service of the East India Company, Bengal Presidency, *m.* in India, Isabella Byers, by whom he had issue.

1. Charlotte-Margaretta, wife (now widow) of Charles Smith, esq. of Northampton, and had issue a son and daughters.
2. Elizabeth, *m.* to the Rev. William Wilkieson, of Woodbury, in Bedfordshire, and has issue.
3. Susanna-Jane, *m.* to Henry Bell, esq. of Newbiggen House, in the county of Northumberland, and has issue.

V. James Eyton, *b.* in 1750, of Magdalen College, Cambridge, and vicar of Ellaston, in the county of Stafford, *d.* in 1808. He *m.* twice: first, Anna, only child of Thomas Vawdrey, esq. of Middlewich, in the county of Chester, by whom he had issue,

1. James, in holy orders, of Emmanuel College, Cambridge, and of Biddenhall, in Cheshire.

1. Anna-Maria.
2. Frances.

Mr. James Eyton Mainwaring *m.* secondly, Anne, daughter of — Bridge, esq. of Chester, who is still living.

I. Martha-Susanna, }
II. Julia, } *d.* unmarried.
III. Charlotte, }

The eldest son,

EDWARD MAINWARING, of Trinity College, Cambridge, and of Whitmore Hall, *s.* his father in 1795. He *m.* Anne, eldest daughter of Sir Philip-Touchet Chetwode, bart. of Oakley Hall, in Staffordshire, and widow of Robert Davison, esq. of the Brand, in the county of Salop, but *d.* without issue in 1825, bequeathing his property to

SARAH MAINWARING, the present proprietress, as eldest surviving child of William, his younger brother.

*Arms*—Argent, two bars gules.

*Crest*—Out of a ducal coronet or, an ass's head in a hempen halter ppr.

*Motto*—Devant si je puis.

*Estates*—In the counties of Stafford and Lancaster.

*Seat*—Whitmore Hall.

# BRODIE, OF BRODIE.

**BRODIE, WILLIAM,** esq. of Brodie, in Morayshire, *b.* 2nd July, 1799, succeeded his grandfather 17th January, 1824, and is lord-lieutenant of Nairnshire.

## Lineage.

This surname, a local one, was taken from a hollow, in Gaelic, *Brothie*, situated near Dyke, in the province of Moray. The old writings of the family were mostly carried away or destroyed, when Lord Leurs Gordon, afterwards (third) Marquis of Huntly, burnt Brodie House, in 1645. It can however be traced very far back, and of old it held the rank of Thane, which seems equivalent to that of Baron.

MALCOLM, was Thane of Brodie, *temp. King* ALEXANDER III. who *d.* 1285, and had a son,

MICHAEL, Thane of Brodie and Dyke, who had a charter from King Robert Bruce, as his father's heir, in 1311, he is mentioned in the evidents of the Priory of Urquhart.

JOHN DE BROTHIE, in 1376, in attendance on the Earl of Mar, lieutenant of the North, is mentioned in the Chartulary of Moray, 11th October, 1380.

THOMAS DE BROTHIE, also appears in the Chartulary of Moray, with his elder and younger sons, in a negotiation regarding the vicarage of Dyke, 4th December, 1386. He had two sons,

I. John.
II. Alexander, vicar of Dyke.

JOHN DE BROTHIE was heir apparent in the above transaction, 4th December, 1386.

RICHARD DE BROTHIE and his wife were buried 16th September, 1446, in the churchyard at Dyke, where the tombstone yet remains.

ALEXANDER BROTHIE, of that ilk, having been chief of the jury who served William Sutherland, heir to Duffus, was summoned before the lords of council to answer for his verdict, 26th January, 1484. He *d.* 1491.

JOHN, THANE of BROYD, repeatedly occurs in the Chartulary of Moray, as an arbiter, 10th April, ult. April, and 21st May, 1492, and from him the succession of the family is distinctly proved. He assisted the Mackenzies against the Macdonalds at the battle of Blair-na-park, and *d.* before 1511, leaving two sons,

I. Alexander.
II. John.

The elder,

ALEXANDER BRODIE, of Brodie, had a charter from William Hay, of Lochloy, to himself and Janet Douglas, his spouse, to which his brother John is a witness, 7th May, 1511. He was one of the jury who served Elizabeth, Countess of Sutherland, heir to her brother, 3rd October, 1514. He died before 1540, leaving a son,

THOMAS BRODIE, of Brodie, who binds his lands to the mill of Grange-green, belonging to Alexander Prior, of Pluscarden, 17th March, 1540. He had a gift from the Queen Regent of the Nonentries of the lands, since the decease of John Brodie, of that ilk, his guid sir, and of Umquhile Alexander Brodie, of that ilk, his father, 6th June, 1545. He had a charter under the great seal 23rd March, 1547, to himself and Agnes Schaw, his spouse, and *d.* before 1550.

ALEXANDER BRODIE, of Brodie, his son and heir, was denounced a rebel for not submitting to the law, his feud with Alexander Cummying, of Alter, 14th November, 1550. He was first married before 1553, to Marjory, daughter of Robert Dunbar, of Durres, a branch of the hereditary sheriffs of Moray, and they had a charter from Patrick, bishop of Moray, 31st October, 1566, which was confirmed under the great seal, 22nd April, 1577. She died before 1569, leaving a son, David. He obtained a decreet of suspension against his said father-in-law, 4th July, 1573, regarding the multures of the lands of Brodie and Dyke, astricted to the Mill of Grangegreen, by the deceased, Thomas Brodie, of that ilk, his father. He married, secondly, (contract 15th March, 1569,) Margaret, widow of Dunbar, of Benagefield, and eldest daughter of John Hay, of Lochloy. They had a charter, 27th January, 1570, and there was an attempt made by her relations to disinherit David, in favor of her son, George, as appears by a charter of the whole estate, from Alexander Hay, director of the Chancery, 4th March, 1576. In his will, made 28th June, 1583, he leaves his eldest son, David, to the care of his mother's brother, David Dunbar, of Grangehill. He mentions his wife, Margaret Hay, and his children, George, Henry, John, Alexander, Thomas, Andrew, Marjory, Elspeth, Janet, Catherine, and Margaret. He *d.* in August following, and his widow married, thirdly, Mr. William Douglas, thesaurer of Moray, made her will and died 14th February, 1609.

DAVID BRODIE, of Brodie, on his father's death lost no time in making out the succession. He had letters of regression under the seal, 23rd November, 1583, and secured the interest of the Hays for five months after his father's death, 23rd January, 1583-4. He was contracted to Janet, the youngest sister of his stepmother, daughter of John Hay, of Lochloy, and Park, heir male of the baronial family of Tullybody, Fouch, the Forest of Boyne, &c. Her mother, Janet, was daughter of William Sutherland, of Duffus, descended from the Earls of Sutherland, and ancestor to Lord Duffus. The charter to himself and Janet Hay, his future spouse of the above date, was confirmed 8th February, 1583-4. He had a charter from his brother George, of the dominical lands of Brodie, 29th May, 1596, and his estate was erected into the Barony of Brodie, 22nd July, 1597. His wife made her will and *d.* on the 17th June, 1607, and according to the diary of his grandson, he was born in 1553, and *d.* in May, 1626, aged seventy-four. They had six sons and one daughter, Janet, who are all mentioned in the history of Moray, and who all had issue.

- I. DAVID, his heir.
- II. Alexander, of Lethin.
- III. John, minister of Auldern and dean of Moray.
- IV. Joseph, minister of Keith, afterwards of Forres.
- V. Francis, of Milton and Inverlochtie.
- VI. William, of Coltfield.

DAVID BRODIE, of Brodie, was served heir of his father David, 26th October, 1626, and had sasine, 24th June, 1627. He also had a sasine as heir to his grandfather, Alexander, 6th June, 1632, and he *d.* 22nd September, same year. According to his son's diary he was born in 1586, and was aged forty-six when he died. He married before 1616, Katherine, daughter of Mr. Thomas Dunbar, of Grange, dean of Moray, by Grizel Crichton, his wife, sister to the admirable Crichton, daughter of Mr. Robert Crichton, of Elliock and Cluny, advocate to Queen Mary, by Elizabeth Stewart, sister to Lord Doun. She survived David (and *m.* secondly, Alexander Dunbar, of Westfield, sheriff of Moray, who was then a minor, according to a settlement, but of age 5th July, 1638, and he *d.* without issue, in 1646). They had three sons and one daughter,

- I. ALEXANDER, his heir.
- II. Joseph, of Aslisk, *m.* first, Christian Baillie, of Jerviswood, by whom he had an only daughter, Katherine, wife of James Dunbar, of Bothe; and, secondly, (contract 13th December, 1664,) Isabel, widow of William Downie, writer in Edinburgh, eldest daughter of George Dundas, of Duddingson, by Katherine, his wife, sister of Sir James Monypenny, knt. of Pitmilly. He made his will 24th September, 1680, and was dead before 16th February, 1682, when it was confirmed. His widow was dead before the 8th May, 1694, when her son George was served heir to her. They had issue,
  1. David, served heir to his father 25th February, 1682, but *d. s. p.* before 20th November, 1683, when his brother George was returned his heir.
  2. GEORGE, of whom presently as successor to BRODIE.
  3. James, of Whitehill, who *m.* 1698, a sister of his brother George's wife, his cousin Margaret, sixth daughter and co-heir of James Brodie, of Brodie, and had a son,
     - JAMES, of Spynie, who wedded Emilia Brodie and had issue,
       - JAMES, of whom in the sequel as inheritor of BRODIE, upon the demise of his cousin Alexander in 1759.
       - George, a colonel in the army, *b.* 2nd August, 1745, *d.* 12th January, 1812.
       - Alexander, who made a large fortune at Madras, and bought Arnhall, in Kincardineshire. He was born 3rd March, 1748, *m.* 16th August, 1793, Elizabeth-Margaret, daughter of the Honorable James Wemyss, of Wemyss Castle, by Lady Elizabeth Sutherland, dau. of William, seventeenth Earl of Sutherland, and *d.* 15th January, 1812, leaving an only daughter and heiress, Elizabeth, *m.* 11th December, 1813, to George,

fifth Duke of Gordon, G.C.B.

Margaret, *b.* 20th August, 1743, *d.* 3rd of March, 1820.

Elizabeth, *b.* 25th September, 1746, *m.* to Mr. Ketchen.

Janet, *b.* 16th July, 1749, *m.* to Mr. Calder, and *d.* 1829.

Isabella, *b.* 5th September, 1751, *d.* 7th August, 1834.

1. Anna, 2. Maria, 3. Janet, } All mentioned in a bond of provision by their fathers. Janet afterwards *m.* 25th April, 1699, to James Sutherland, of Kinsteary.

III. William.

I. Elizabeth, who *m.* 6th June, 1634, Colin Campbell, second son of Sir John Campbell, of Calder, and was ancestor of the Earl of Cawdor.

The eldest son,

ALEXANDER BRODIE, of Brodie, styled Lord Brodie as a senator of the College of Justice, was born 25th July, 1617, was sent into England in 1628, and returned in 1632, when he succeeded and was served heir to his father David, 19th May, 1636, being of age by dispensation of the Lords of Council. He wrote the famous diary which gives a very full and curious account of his life, and shows him to have been a man of piety and talent. He represented the county of Elgin in the parliaments of 1643, and following years of CHARLES I. and, from the many parliamentary committees of which he was a member, appears to have been greatly in the confidence of the estates. He accompanied George Winram, Lord Libberton, to Holland, in March, 1649, and was appointed an ordinary Lord of Session, on 22nd June, that year. He accepted the situation and gave his oath *de fideli administratione* in presence of parliament, on the 23rd July, but did not take his seat on the bench till the 1st November, 1649. He shortly afterwards proceeded to Breda, to treat with CHARLES II. as to the conditions of his return to Scotland. He was a member of the various committees of estates appointed to rule the country during the intervals of parliament, and was elected Commissary General to the army, in October, 1650. Lord Brodie was one of those cited to London, by Cromwell, in June, 1653, to treat of a union between the two kingdoms, but according to the words of his own diary, "resolved and determined in the strength of the Lord, to eschew and avoid employment under Cromwell." He accordingly resisted all the requests made to him, to accept of office as a commissioner for the administration of justice, until after the death of the Protector; but shortly after that event, took his seat on the 3rd December, 1658. He was fined 4,800*l.* Scots, after the restoration, although the monies disbursed by him at Breda had not been yet repaid. He *m.* 28th October, 1635, Elizabeth Innes, widow of John Urquhart, of Craigston, tutor of Cromarty, who *d.* 30th November, 1634, daughter of Sir Robert Innes, bart. of Innes, by Lady Grizel Stewart, daughter of James, the bonny Earl of Moray, and grandaughter of the regent; she *d.* 12th August, 1640, leaving only two children,

I. JAMES, heir to his father.

I. Grizel, who *m.* 7th September, 1654, Sir Robert Dunbar, knt. of Grangehill.

Lord Brodie *d.* in 1679; his diary was published in 1740. His son and successor,

JAMES BRODIE, of Brodie, *b.* 15th September, 1637, succeeded in 1679 and was served heir to his father, 7th October, 1680. His father contracted him 16th July, 1659, to Lady Mary Ker, sister of Robert, first Marquis of Lothian, daughter of William, third Earl of Lothian, by Ann Ker, Countess of Lothian, eldest daughter and heiress of Robert, second Earl of Lothian, by Lady Annabella Campbell, sister of the Marquis of Argyll. Lord Brodie records the event thus, "28th July, My son was married with Lady Mary Ker, and on the 31st July, 1659, she did subscribe her covenant to and with God, and became his, and gave herself up to him." The Laird of Brodie was fined 24,000*l.* in 1685. He made his will 25th September, 1704, and *d.* in March, 1708, leaving his wife surviving. He had no son, but nine daughters, viz.

I. ANNE, *m.* 2nd October, 1679, to William, twelfth Lord Forbes, who *d.* in 1716; she had 20,000 marks tocher.

II. KATHERINE, *m.* to her cousin-german, Robert Dunbar, of Grangehill, and was dead before 1701, when her husband was married again.

III. ELIZABETH, *m.* to Alexander Cuming, of Altyre.

IV. GRIZEL, *m.* 12th November, 1685, to Robert Dunbar, of Dunphail, who was dead in 1717.

V. Emilia, *m.* 16th December, 1692, to her father's cousin-german and successor GEORGE BRODIE, of Asliesk, afterwards of Brodie, and carried on the family.

VI. MARGARET, 8th November, 1698, *m.* to her father's cousin-german JAMES BRODIE, of Whitehill, brother of the preceding.

VII. VERE, *m.* to Joseph Brodie, of Muirhouse, and was dead in 1693, when he *m.* again.

VIII. Lilias, *m.* first, to Mr. Patrick Cuming, chirurgeon, at Inverness, secondly, 16th August, 1708, to Robert Chivez, of Muirtown.

IX. Henrietta, *d.* unmarried.

Of these, Emilia, Margaret, Lilias, Ann, Elizabeth, and Grizel, are mentioned as all daughters and heirs of line and executors to the deceased James Brodie, of that ilk, in a decreet at Edinburgh, 1st February, 1717. He was succeeded by his cousin,

GEORGE BRODIE (son of Joseph Brodie, of Aslisk, and grandson of David Brodie, of Brodie), who succeeded his brother David in Aslisk, in 1683, and his cousin-german and father-in-law, James, in the Barony of Brodie, in 1708. He had a charter as heir to his said cousin in the estate of Penick, 14th August, 1696. He *m.* (contract 16th December, 1692,) Emilia, fifth daughter and co-heir of James Brodie, of Brodie, by Lady Mary Ker, and died before 6th January, 1716, leaving by her, who survived, three sons,

I. JAMES, his heir.

II. ALEXANDER, who *s.* his brother.

III. Joseph.*

I. Henrietta, *m.* 9th April, 1714, John Sinclair, of Ulbster, in Caithness, grandfather by her to the present Right Honorable Baronet of that name.

II. Ann, *m.* George Monro, of Novar, in Ross-shire.

JAMES BRODIE, of Brodie, the eldest son and heir, *d.* young, in 1720, and was succeeded by his brother,

ALEXANDER BRODIE, of Brodie, who was born 17th August, 1697, appointed Lord Lyon, of Scotland, in 1727, and *d.* in 1754. By his wife, Mary Sleigh, *b.* 3rd October, 1704, and *m.* to him 3rd September, 1724, he had only one son, ALEXANDER, his heir, and one daughter, Emilia, *b.* 30th April, 1730, who *m.* John, son and heir of Normand Macleod, of Macleod (see p. 482). The only son,

ALEXANDER BRODIE, of Brodie, *b.* 29th May, 1741, succeeded his father in 1754, *d.* unmarried in 1759, and was succeeded by his second cousin,

JAMES BRODIE, of Brodie, son of James Brodie, of Spynie, and grandson of James Brodie, of Whitehill, brother of George Brodie, of Brodie. This gentleman, lord-lieutenant of the county of Nairn, was born 31st August, 1744, and married 6th March, 1768, to Lady Margaret Duff, youngest daughter of William, first Earl of Fife, by Jean, daughter of Sir James Grant, bart. of Grant. The lady was burnt to death at Brodie House, 24th April, 1786, and he died 17th January, 1824, leaving two sons and three daughters,

I. JAMES, who was in the civil service of the East India Company, at Madras, where he was drowned in his father's lifetime, leaving, by Ann, his wife, daughter of Colonel Story, who wedded, secondly, Lieutenant-general Sir Thomas Bowser, K.C.B. two sons and five daughters, viz.

1. WILLIAM, successor to his grandfather.

2. George, in the Madras cavalry, *d.* in 1826.

1. Margaret, died unmarried, in 1826.

2. Jane, *m.* 10th June, 1823, to Francis Whitworth Russell, esq. of the Bengal civil service, third son of the Right Hon. Sir Henry Russell, bart. Lord Chief Justice of India, by Ann Barbara, his wife, sister and co-heir of Charles, Earl of Whitworth, and has issue.

3. Charlotte, *m.* in 1822, to Edward Humphrey Woodcock, esq. of the Madras civil service, and has issue.

4. Isabella, *m.* in 1821, to Archbald Erskine Patullo, esq. captain in the Madras cavalry, who *d.* leaving issue.

5. Louisa, *m.* in 1825, to Hugh Calveley Cotton, esq. captain Madras engineers, and has issue.

II. William-Douglass, consul in Spain, who *d.* at Madras, 14th August, 1826.

I. Jane-Ann-Catherine.

II. Margaret, married Lieutenant-colonel Colquhoun Grant, of the 54th. They both *d.* in India, leaving one son.

III. Charlotte, *m.* Colonel Keith Macalister, who left her a widow with one son.

James Brodie, of Brodie, *d.* 17th January, 1824, and was *s.* by his grandson, the present WILLIAM BRODIE, of Brodie.

*Arms*—Arg. a chev. gu. between three mullets az.

*Crest*—A right hand holding a bunch of arrows all ppr.

*Supporters*—Two savages wreathed about the head and middle with laurel, each holding a club resting against his shoulder.

*Estates*—In the counties of Moray and Nairn, acquired by the family previously to the reign of ROBERT BRUCE, who confirmed them by charter in 1311. The estate, which still reaches almost from Nairn to Forres, was formerly still more extensive and valuable. The Witches' Mount is on the property, not far from the west gate.

*Seat*—Brodie.

* The three brothers are all mentioned in their sister Henrietta's marriage contract, and the two younger are in their grandfather's will, in 1704.

## BATEMAN, OF MIDDLETON HALL.

BATEMAN, THOMAS, esq. of Middleton by Youlgrave, in the county of Derby, *b.* 27th September, baptized at Hartington, 28th September, 1760, *m.* 13th April, 1786, Rebekah, daughter and co-heir of Arthur Clegg, of Manchester, merchant, and by her (who *d.* in 1797) had issue,

I. WILLIAM, F.A.S. *b.* at Manchester, 25th July, 1787, *m.* 19th June, 1820, Mary, daughter of James Crompton, of Brightmet, in Lancashire, and dying 11th June, 1835, left an only child,

THOMAS, *b.* at Rowsley, 8th November, 1821, and baptized at Youlgrave, 31st January, 1822.

II. Thomas, *b.* at Manchester, 17th January, 1792, *d.* at Everton, near Liverpool, 22nd April, 1810.

I. Rebekah, *m.* 17th September, 1816, to Samuel Hope, esq. of Liverpool, and has issue.

Mr. Bateman succeeded his father in 1774, and was high sheriff of Derbyshire in 1823.

### Lineage.

WILLIAM BATEMAN, of South Winfield, in Derbyshire, held lands there under John de Heriz in 1298 (inq. post mort.) and William Bateman, of Hertyndon, appears on a jury held there 4 RICHARD II.

RICHARD BATEMAN, of Hertyngton, in the county of Derby, is witness to a deed dated Thursday next after the feast of the blessed Virgin, 32 HENRY VI. by which John Hopkinson, of Bondsale, and Agnes, his wife, convey all their lands in Hertyngton to John de la Poole, esq. His son and heir is presumed to have been

JOHN BATEMAN, of Hertyngton, sen. yeoman, who purchased lands in the fields of Hertyngton from Richard Hyll, of Sutton on the Hill, who by deed poll, dated the feast of St. Paul, 25th January, 1486, releases and quit claims to him of all his right, &c. He *d.* in 1525, and was *s.* by his son,

RICHARD BATEMAN, of Hertyngton, yeoman, presented at the manor court, 20th March, 17 HENRY VIII. as son and next heir of John, deceased, and of full age, which John died seised of a messuage and lands in Hertyngton, and also lands purchased of Hyll, that is to say, in Moncliff, and other places. At a court held 17th July, 4 EDWARD VI. he made surrender of lands in Hertyngton to the use of his son and heir,

RICHARD BATEMAN, of Hertyngton, yeoman, witness to his sister Grace's release to her mother, Elizabeth, 13th February, 18 ELIZABETH. He was father of

RICHARD BATEMAN, the younger, of Hertyngton, who was admitted at a court held 20th June, 30 ELIZABETH to a messuage and lands in Hertyngton, upon surrender of his father. He was dead before 1599, leaving issue,

I. JOHN, his heir, who died in 1600, *s. p.*

II. THOMAS, of whom presently.

III. William, of Hartington, *m.* 25th September, 1616, Helen, daughter of William Baslow, of Yolgrave, and had issue, John, Richard, Thomas, Robert, and William.

The second son,

THOMAS BATEMAN, of Hertyngton, at a court held 25th June, 43 ELIZABETH, claimed a messuage and lands which his brother John had died seised of, and seisin was delivered to him accordingly. He *d.* in 1648, leaving by Jane, his first wife, a son and successor,

RICHARD BATEMAN, of Hertyngton, admitted at a court held 4th April, 1650, as son and heir of Thomas, deceased. He *m.* in 1633, Anne Mason, relict of Robert Harrison, of Hertynton, and had several children. He died in 1671 (Presentment made of his death 14th October, in that year, that he died seised of a messuage and lands, and that Thomas is his son and heir, subject to the dower of Anne, his widow), and was succeeded by his son,

THOMAS BATEMAN, of Hartington, baptized there 2nd August, 1646. He *m.* first, 6th August, 1672, Guarterick, daughter of — Cokaine, and by her, who *d.* in 1677, had a son, RICHARD, and two daughters, Mary, *d.* young, and Elizabeth, the wife of Ralph Sterndale. He wedded, secondly, 22nd June, 1683, Mary, daughter of James Sleigh, and by her, who *d.* in 1723, had four daughters,

- Mary, *d.* 1691, in youth.
- Sarah, baptized 1684, *m.* 30th May, 1710, to the Rev. Thomas Johnson, vicar of Hartington, and *d.* there 23rd January, 1750, leaving issue.
- Katherine, baptized 1686, *m.* 4th September, 1711, to Thomas Fern, of Heathcott, and *d.* 1752, leaving issue.
- Anne, baptized 1689, *m.* first, 21st April, 1710, to Samuel Milward, of Hartington, and, secondly, in 1713, to Robert Alsope, of the same place.

Thomas Bateman died in 1713 (his will was dated 21st March, in the preceding year), and was succeeded by his son,

RICHARD BATEMAN, gent. of Hartington, baptized there 4th April, 1677, who *m.* first, 8th March, 1702, Dorothy, daughter of James Sleigh, and had by her, who died in 1704, an only child, Thomas, who *d.* in infancy. He *m.* secondly, 1st August, 1713, Sarah, daughter of William Gould, of Crowdicote, in Hartington, and by her (who was buried 10th July, 1772) had issue,

- I. RICHARD, his heir.
- II. William, *d.* young in 1737.

- I. Guarterick, *m.* 1st Aug. 1736, to William Edensor, of Hartington, and had issue.
- II. Mary, *m.* 28th April, 1735, to Samuel Sleigh, of Hartington, and had issue.
- III. Sarah, *m.* 27th May, 1760, to Mark Robinson, of York, merchant, and *d. s. p.*
- IV. Hannah, *m.* to Joshua Ellis, of Leek, in Staffordshire, and *d. s. p.*
- V. Elizabeth, *m.* 24th June, 1748, to her cousin, Ralph Sterndale, and had issue.
- VI. Dorothy, *d.* in 1752, unmarried.
- VII. Anne, *d.* unm. in 1777, will dated in that year.

Mr. Bateman *d.* in 1761 (his will, bearing date 20th October, 1759, was proved 17th June, 1761), and was *s.* by his son,

RICHARD BATEMAN, esq. of Hartington, baptized there 14th December, 1727, who *m.* 2nd February, 1758, Elizabeth, daughter of Ralph Leek, esq. of The Heath House, Chadleton, in Staffordshire, and by her, who *d.* in 1784, had issue,

- I. THOMAS, his heir.
- II. Richard, baptized at Hartington, 11th May, 1763, married twice, but *d. s. p.* in 1808: his widow *m.* 2nd November, 1810, John Stringer.
- III. William, of Manchester, merchant, baptized at Hartington, 16th January, 1774, *m.* 10th October, 1799, Mary, daughter of Samuel Swire, merchant, by Isabella, his wife, daughter and co-heir of Richard Bent, of Manchester, and of Isabel, his wife, dau. and co-heir of Thorpe, of Hopton, in Yorkshire (see vol. ii. p. 343). Mr. William Bateman died at Ardwick, 14th July, 1817, leaving issue,
  - Henry, of Trinity College, Cambridge, M. A. *b.* 5th October, 1801.
  - Thomas, *b.* 6th April, 1803.
  - William, *b.* 13th July, 1806, *d.* 10th January, 1818.
  - Samuel, *b.* 4th October, 1810.
  - Frederick, *b.* in 1815, *d.* in 1818.

  - Mary, *m.* in 1832, to William Kay, M. D. of Cheltenham.
  - Elizabeth.
  - Isabella-Anne.

- I. Elizabeth, *d.* young.
- II. Nancey, *m.* first, in 1790, to Nathan Sutton, of Leek, and, secondly, to John Gibson, of Tattershall, in Lincolnshire, merchant.

Mr. Bateman *d.* in 1774, and was succeeded by his son, the present THOMAS BATEMAN, esq. who sold, in 1801, to Hugh Bateman, esq. and others, the lands which had descended to him from his ancestor, John Bateman, and purchasing estates in the counties of Lancaster, Chester, and Derby, seated himself at Middleton, in the last named shire.

*Arms*—Or, three crescents, each surmounted by an estoile gu.

*Crest*—A crescent and estoile as in the arms, between two eagles' wings or.

*Estates*—In Lancashire, Cheshire, and Derby.

*Seat*—Middleton Hall, Derbyshire.

# MAITLAND, OF HOLLYWICH.

MAITLAND, FREDERICK, esq. of Hollywich, in Sussex, *b.* 3rd September, 1763, a general officer in the army, *m.* 11th November, 1790, Catherine Worsam, daughter of John Prettejohn, esq. of the Island of Barbadoes, and has had issue,

I. Frederick, *b.* in 1791, *d.* at Bath, in 1804.
II. JOHN-MADAN, formerly a captain in the grenadier guards, *b.* 12th August, 1793, *m.* first, 24th October, 1822, Ellinor-Jane, heiress of the late Gilbert Ansley, esq. by whom, who *d.* in 1823, he has an only daughter, Ellinor-Jane-Susan. He wedded, secondly, 21st July, 1829, Harriett Rawlins, eldest daughter of the Reverend Joseph Pratt.
III. Alexander, *b.* in 1797, *d.* in 1804.
IV. Frederick-Thomas, *b.* 18th September, 1807, captain 24th regiment.

I. Charlotte, *m.* 18th April, 1820, to Captain Thomas Garth, R.N. of Haines-Hill, Berkshire, and has issue.
II. Harriet, *m.* 8th September, 1827, to Donald Maclean, esq. M.P.
III. Frederica-Louisa, *d.* at East-Bourne, 24th August, 1822.

General Maitland is colonel of the 58th regiment, member of the Board of General Officers, and a commissioner of the Royal Military College.

## Lineage.

This is a branch of the noble house of Lauderdale.

GENERAL the HON. SIR ALEXANDER MAITLAND, colonel of the 49th regiment, a younger son of Charles, sixth Earl of Lauderdale, *m.* in 1754, Penelope, daughter of Colonel Martin Madan, and had issue,

I. James-Martin, *d.* unm. aged about nineteen.
II. Alexander-Charles, who *m.* 30th April, 1786, Helen, daughter and heiress of Alexander-Gibson Wright, esq. and assuming the surname and arms of GIBSON, is the present SIR ALEXANDER CHARLES MAITLAND GIBSON, bart. of Clifton-Hall and Kersey. (See BURKE'S *Peerage and Baronetage.*)
III. William, mate of the Earl of Dartmouth, E. I. S. drowned by the wreck of that vessel, on the coast of Madagascar, in 1782. He lost his life by his exertion to save some female passengers.
IV. Augustus, killed on the 6th October, 1799, being then in command of the 3rd battalion of the 1st regiment of the foot guards in Holland.
V. FREDERICK, the present GENERAL MAITLAND, of Hollywich.

I. Penelope-Judith, *m.* 19th October, 1802, to the Reverend Thomas Cope Marsham, who died 11th December, 1817.
II. Charlotte.

*Arms*—Or, a lion rampant dechaussé, within a double tressure flory-counterflory gu.

*Crest*—A lion sejant, affronté, gu. ducally crowned, holding in the dexter paw a sword ppr. pommel and hilt or, in the sinister a fleur-de-lis az.

*Motto*—Consilio et animis.

*Estates*—In Sussex and Kent.

*Town Residence*—24, Berkeley-square.

*Seat*—Hollywich.

# SWINNERTON, OF BUTTERTON.

SWINNERTON, THOMAS, esq. of Butterton, in the county of Stafford, barrister-at-law of the Inner Temple, and recorder of Stafford, *m.* 27th April, 1793, Mary, daughter and heir of Charles Milborne, esq. of Wonaston and of the Priory of Abergavenny, by Lady Martha Harley, his wife, daughter of Edward, third Earl of Oxford, and by her, who died in Wimpole Street, London, May, 1795, has issue,

MARTHA, twin with Mary, *m.* 28th December, 1820, to her cousin, William Bagot, esq. nephew of the first Lord Bagot.

MARY, *m.* to Sir William Pilkington, bart. of Chevet, in Yorkshire, and has issue.

ELIZABETH, *m.* to Charles Kemeys-Tynte, esq. M.P. eldest son of Charles Kemeys-Tynte, esq. of Halswell, and has issue.

Mr. Swinnerton, who succeeded his father 12th October, 1790, is in the commission of the peace, and was high sheriff of Staffordshire in 1795.

## Lineage.

This family (one of great antiquity in the county of Stafford) derived its surname from the lordship of Swynnerton, and was, at a very early period, of knightly and baronial degree.

JOHN DE SWINNERTON, Lord of Swinnerton,* was twice sheriff of Staffordshire. He was father of

SIR THOMAS SWINNERTON, knt. of Swinnerton, who *m.* Matilda, daughter of Sir Robert de Holland, and had two sons, namely,

I. ROGER (Sir), knt. who, in the 34 EDWARD I. had a charter for free-warren in all his demesne lands in his manor of Swinnerton, as also for keeping a market there on Wednesday every week, and a fair yearly upon the festival of our Lady's assumption; and in the 4 EDWARD II. was in the wars in Scotland. In 11 EDWARD II. he was governor of the town of Stafford, and in three years after of the strong castle of Hardelagh, in Wales. In the 15th of the same reign he had the custody of Eccleshall Castle (during the vacancy of the bishoprick of Lichfield and Coventry, whereunto it belonged), and was in some years after constituted constable of the Tower of London. In the 2 EDWARD III. being then a banneret, he had an assignation out of the Exchequer of £145. 13*s.* 8*d.* as well for his wages of war in that expedition made into Scotland as for his services in attending *Queen* ISABEL. In the 9 EDWARD III. he was again in the Scottish wars, and in two years subsequently had summons to parliament among the barons of the realm. He *m.* Johanna, daughter of Sir Robert de Hastange, and dying in 1338, left two sons, ROGER, his heir, and Robert, aged fifteen at the death of his father. The elder,

SIR ROGER DE SWINNERTON, knt. of Swinnerton, left by Matilda, his wife, a son and successor,

* Erdeswick, in his Survey of Staffordshire, says that 20 Conquerour, Comes Alanus held Swinnerton of Robert de Stafford, and that this Alain is ancestor of the Swinnertons. Holinshed, in his Chronicle, states that whilst the Conqueror held siege before York, he advanced at the request of his Queen Maud, his nephew Alane, Earl of Britain, with the gift of all those lands that some time belonged to Earl Edwine, and calls him a man of stout stomach, and one that would defend what was given him. In Tailleur's Chronicle of Normandie in the catalogue of the noblemen that came into England with the Conqueror, this Alain is called Alain Fergant, Earl of Britaine.

SIR THOMAS DE SWINNERTON, knt. of Swinnerton, who *m.* Matilda, daughter of Sir Robert Holland, knt. and was father of

SIR ROBERT DE SWINNERTON, knt. of Swinnerton, who *m.* Elizabeth, daughter and heir of Sir Nicholas Beke, knt. by Joan, his wife, daughter of Ralph, Earl of Stafford, and had an only daughter, Matilda, *m.* first, to John Savage, and secondly, to Richard Peshall.

II. JOHN (Sir), of whose line we have to treat.

The second son,

SIR JOHN DE SWINNERTON, knt. who died 14 EDWARD III. A.D. 1340, married Anne, daughter of Philip de Montgomery, the seneschal, and had issue,

I. JOHN, seneschal of Cannock 16 EDWARD III. *d.* in 1380, leaving by Christiana, his wife, three sons, namely, ROBERT, his heir; John,* sheriff of Stafford in 1392; and Thomas, of Repingdon, in Derbyshire, who *d.* in 1429. The eldest son,

ROBERT DE SWINNERTON, married Johanna, daughter of Thomas de la Pipe, and dying in 1410 was succeeded by his son,

HUMPHREY DE SWINNERTON, sheriff of Staffordshire in 1450, who *m.* Matilda, daughter of Henry Appleby, and died in 1478, leaving, with other issue,† a son and successor,

THOMAS SWINNERTON, of Swinnerton, who *m.* Margaret, daughter of Robert de Tranhem, and was succeeded by his eldest son,

HUMPHREY SWINNERTON, of Swinnerton, who *m.* Margaret, daughter of Sir Thomas Aston, knt. and was father of

SIR THOMAS SWINNERTON, knt. of Swinnerton, who *m.* Alice, daughter of — Harcourt, or else of Robert Stanley, of Yorkshire, and dying in 1530 left a son,

HUMPHREY SWINNERTON, of Swinnerton, who died in 1562, leaving by Cassandra, his wife, dau. of Sir John Gifford, knt. two daughters, his co-heirs, viz.

MARGARET, *m.* to Henry Vernon, esq. of Sudbury, and conveyed to her husband the estate of Hilton, in Staffordshire.

ELIZABETH, *m.* first, in 1562, to William, fourth son of Anthony Fitzherbert, of Norbury, the celebrated judge of the reign of HENRY VIII. and thus conveyed the manor of Swinnerton to the FITZHERBERTS, by whom it is still possessed (see vol. i. p. 80). She wedded, secondly, Francis Gatacre, esq. of Gatacre, and had issue by both marriages.

II. THOMAS.

The second son,

THOMAS SWINNERTON, was of Butterton, in the county of Stafford. He *m.* Matilda, widow of Sir John Latimer, knt. and left a son and successor,

JOHN SWINNERTON, of Butterton, living in 1384, father of

ROGER SWINNERTON, of Butterton, living in 1438, whose son,

THOMAS SWINNERTON, of Butterton, living 11 EDWARD IV. married Margaret, sister and heir of Hugh Clayton, and left a son and successor,

WILLIAM SWINNERTON, of Butterton, to whom succeeded his son,

THOMAS SWINNERTON, of Butterton. This Thomas, by Ellen, his wife, who *m.* secondly, William Rowley, had, besides William his eldest son, Hugh, John, Grace (*m.* to Morris), and Johanna, as may appear by his will, dated 14th June, 1552, by which, *inter alia*, he orders his body to be buried at Madeley, and leaves the ward and marriage of his son William to Randall Leigh, gent. The said son and successor,

WILLIAM SWINNERTON, esq. of Butterton.

---

* This John de Swinnerton married a lady named Juliana, and had a son, John, who died during his father's lifetime, leaving by Clementia, his wife, daughter of John Mallorie, two sons, John, who died in 1431, and Thomas, of Hilton, who *d.* in 1449, leaving two daughters, ANNE, *m.* to John Milton, esq. and ALICE, to Richard Beauford, forester of Cannock.

† The younger children were JOHN SWINNERTON, of Eccleshall, in Staffordshire, and

ROBERT SWINNERTON, esq. who married a lady named Johanna, but of what family is not recorded, and had a son,

RALPH SWINNERTON, esq. of Oswestry, in the county of Salop, father of

THOMAS SWINNERTON, of London, whose son,

SIR JOHN SWINNERTON, was sheriff of London in 1602, and lord mayor of London in 1612. He *m.* Thomazin Buckfold, and had, with other issue,

THOMAS SWINNERTON, esq. of Stanway Hall, Essex, who *m.* Johanna, daughter of Thomas Symond, of London, and left an only daughter and heiress,

THOMASINE SWINNERTON, who *m.* William Dyer, esq. of Tottenham, in Middlesex, created a BARONET in 1678, and was great-great-grandmother of the present SIR THOMAS RICHARD SWINNERTON DYER, bart.

was living in 1584, and left at his decease a son and successor,

THOMAS SWINNERTON, esq. of Butterton, who *m.* Mary, daughter of Hugh Hollines, esq. of Moseley, and had issue,

I. WILLIAM, his heir.
II. Thomas, *b.* and buried in 1600.
III. Hugh, who *m.* Fortune Walker, of Dilvern, in Staffordshire, and had three sons, Edward, of Offleyhey, who *m.* Elizabeth, daughter of John Mayden; Thomas, who *d.* 15th February, 1725, leaving issue; and John, of Shutlane, who *m.* Anne Thornycroft.

I. Dorothy, *m.* to Venables of Keel.
II. Idith.
III. Anne, *m.* to Thomas Landor, esq. of Beech, in Staffordshire.

Thomas Swinnerton died in 1634, and was succeeded by his eldest son,

WILLIAM SWINNERTON, esq. of Butterton, who *m.* Jane, daughter of Michael Nicholl, of Fenton, in Staffordshire, and had four sons and four daughters, viz.

I. THOMAS, his heir.
II. James, of Coventry, who *m.* Anne, daughter of Clarke of Darlaston, near Prees, in Shropshire, and left at his decease an only surviving child, Anne, *m.* to — Hillyard.
III. Michael, of Leek, in Staffordshire, who *m.* Sarah, daughter of John Falkner, and had a daughter, Christian.
IV. Edward, baptized 27th March, 1631.

I. Margaret, *m.* to John Hunt, of Stoke, in Staffordshire.
II. Mary, baptized in October, 1623, buried 24th June, 1630.
III. Edith, baptized 28th February, 1635.
IV. Dorothy, baptized 13th January, 1638, *d.* in 1639.

The eldest son,

THOMAS SWINNERTON, esq. of Butterton, espoused Elizabeth, daughter of Thomas Bentley, of Whitehurst, in Staffordshire, and had issue,

I. WILLIAM, his heir.
II. Thomas, baptized 10th August, 1650, *m.* Sarah, daughter of — Ilsley, esq. of High Hall Hill, in Staffordshire.
III. Michael, baptized and buried in July, 1653.
IV. Samuel, *d. s. p.* in 1685.

I. Maria, baptized 30th March, 1658, *d.* in 1671.

The eldest son,

WILLIAM SWINNERTON, esq. of Butterton, baptized 20th October, 1647, married Eliza, daughter of James Bayley, esq. of Madeley, in Staffordshire, and by her, who *d.* 6th August, 1710, aged fifty-five, had issue,

I. THOMAS, his heir.
II. John, baptized 13th January, 1693, *m.* twice: by his first wife, Hannah, daughter of John Edwardes, esq. of Langleyford, in Durham, he had no issue; but by his second wife he had a son,
    John, who married and left issue,
        John, in holy orders, chaplain to the Bishop of Lichfield, and rector of Wybunbury, in Cheshire, *m.* a daughter of — Hinkes, of Stone, but *d. s. p.*
        Anne, died unmarried.
        Mary, living unmarried in 1835.

I. Eliza, *m.* to Richard Beech, esq. of Newhouse.
II. Jane, *m.* to Thomas Whitehurst, esq. of Hanchurch.
III. Mary, *d.* unmarried in 1724.

Mr. Swinnerton died in 1724, and was *s.* by his son,

THOMAS SWINNERTON, esq. of Butterton, baptized 13th February, 1677, who *m.* 26th December, 1712, Mary, only daughter of William Abnet, esq. of Burston Hall, in Sandon, Staffordshire, and had, with two daughters, Eliza, who died unmarried, and Mary, the wife of — Vaughan, esq. of London, a son and successor,

WILLIAM SWINNERTON, esq. of Butterton, born 5th and baptized 13th October, 1717, of the Inner Temple barrister-at-law, vice-chancellor of the Duchy of Lancaster, and recorder of Stafford and Newcastle. He *m.* first, Margaret, only daughter and heir of Blest Colclough, esq. of Eccleshall, in Staffordshire, younger brother of Cæsar Colclough, esq. of Delph House, in Cheadle, and had issue,

I. Blest-Colclough, died in infancy.
II. THOMAS, his heir.

I. Margaret, died unmarried in 1795, buried at Trentham.
II. Elizabeth, died unmarried in 1827, buried at Trentham.
III. Anne, *m.* in 1773, to the Rev. Walter Bagot, rector of Blythfield and Lea, brother of William, first Lord Bagot, and had, with other issue, a son,
    William Bagot, who *m.* 28th December, 1820, Martha, eldest daughter of the present Thomas Swinnerton, esq. of Butterton.

Mr. Swinnerton married, secondly, the relict of — Crewe, esq. of Crewe Hall, M.P. for Cheshire, but by her had no issue. He *d.* 12th October, 1790, was buried at Trentham, and succeeded by his only son, the present THOMAS SWINNERTON, esq. of Butterton.

*Arms*—Arg. a cross forme flory sa.

*Crest*—A boar passant sa. upon a hill vert.

*Motto*—Avauncez et archez bien. This motto was granted in the Holy Wars as a reward for most extraordinary courage shewn by an ancestor of the family in killing a Turk on the field of battle.

*Estates*—In Staffordshire.

*Seat*—Butterton Hall.

## ESDAILE, OF COTHELSTONE HOUSE.

ESDAILE, EDWARD-JEFFRIES, esq. of Cothelstone-House, in the county of Somerset, *b.* 6th April, 1785, *m.* 10th April, 1809, Eliza, only child of Clement Drake, esq.* of Taunton, and has issue,

EDWARD-JEFFRIES, *b.* 28th June, 1813.
William-Clement-Drake, *b.* 14th January, 1820.

Emily-Frances.
Eliza-Drake.

Mr. Esdaile, who is in the commission of the peace for Somersetshire, served the office of sheriff for that county in 1825.

### Lineage.

At the revocation of the edict of Nantes, the ancestor of this family, descended from an honourable house, then represented by the Baron d'Estaile, being a protestant, fled from France, and his property being confiscated in consequence, he lived and died in obscurity in England.

D'ESTAILE, since anglicized into ESDAILE, his son gained a competency by commercial pursuits, and was father of

SIR JAMES ESDAILE, who became an opulent citizen of London, and filled the civic chair in 1778. He *m.* first, Mary Jennings, and by her had one son and two daughters, viz.

I. PETER, who resided at Great Gaines, in Essex, a seat given to him by his father. He married Miss Frances Humphries, and *d.* without issue.

I. Louisa, *m.* to Sir Benjamin Hammet, M.P. for Taunton, and had three sons and three daughters, viz.

John Hammet, who *m.* Miss Woodford, only daughter of Sir Ralph Woodford.

Francis Hammet.

James-Esdaile Hammet, *m.* Miss Emma Foster.

Eliza Hammet, *m.* to Robert Walpole, esq.

Anne Hammet, *m.* to — Rogers, esq.

II. A daughter, *m.* first to the late well-known Bond Hopkins, esq. and secondly, to Captain Burdett.

* The head of this branch of the Drakes is F. H. N. Drake, esq. of Colliton House, Devonshire.

Sir James wedded, secondly, Miss Mary Mayor, by whom he had,

I. James, who *m.* Miss Hadfield, and had,

1. James, who *m.* Amelia Kennedy, and has had four sons and two daughters, viz. James, who died unmarried, John, Edward, Peter, Amelia, and Anne.
2. John, *d.* unm.
3. Peter, *d.* unm.
4. Joseph, who *m.* Elizabeth Garratt, and has one daughter.
5. Benjamin, who *m.* Charlotte Williams.

1. Elizabeth, *m.* to Robert Burkitt Wyatt, esq. and has six sons and two daughters.
2. Susannah, *d.* unm.

II. Joseph, formerly lieutenant to the Band of Gentlemen Pensioners, *m.* Miss Penelope Wilkinson, and has one son, in holy orders.

III. William, of whom presently.

IV. John, who *m.* Mary, youngest sister of Frances Humphries, the wife of his eldest brother, and has one dau.

Mary, *m.* to George Stubbs, esq. and had one son, who *d.* unmarried, and three daughters.

The third son of James's second marriage,

WILLIAM ESDAILE, esq. an eminent banker in the city of London, *m.* Elizabeth, only child of Edward Jeffries, esq. and had two sons and four daughters, viz.

I. EDWARD JEFFRIES, his heir.
II. Henry.

I. Mary, *m.* to Dr. Richardson, and has one son.
II. Louisa, *m.* to Robert Werter, esq. and has three sons and five daughters.
III. Emma.
IV. Caroline, *m.* to Rees-Goring-Thomas, esq. of Llanon, in Carmarthenshire. (See vol. i. p. 628.)

The elder son having inherited the estates of his maternal grandfather, Edward Jeffries, esq. is the present EDWARD-JEFFRIES ESDAILE, esq. of Cothelstone-House.

*Arms*—Gu. a lion's head erased between three mullets or.

*Crest*—A demi lion rampant, holding a mullet in his paws.

*Estates*—In Somersetshire.

*Seat*—Cothelstone House, Taunton.

## PARES, OF HOPWELL.

PARES, THOMAS, esq. of Hopwell Hall, in the county of Derby, and of Kirby Frith, in the county of Leicester, *b.* 30th October, 1790, *m.* 19th May, 1821, Octavia, daughter of Edward Longdon Mackmurdo, esq. of Clapton, in Middlesex, and, beside two sons who died in infancy, has issue,

I. THOMAS HENRY, *b.* 8th February, 1830.
II. John, *b.* 11th May, 1833.

I. Agnes.
II. Octavia.
III. Anna-Mary.

Mr. Pares succeeded his uncle, as proprietor of Kirby Frith, in 1824, and his father, in Hopwell Hall, in 1833. He is a magistrate for the counties of Derby and Leicester, M.A. of the University of Cambridge, and was M.P. for Leicester, from June, 1818, to June, 1826.

## Lineage.

This family was settled at Leicester *temp.* ELIZABETH, and in the charter of that sovereign JOHN PARE is mentioned, as a then member of the Corporation.

JOHN PARES, *b.* 1635, was Mayor of Leicester, 1695, and *d.* September, 1712, leaving issue, by Mary, his wife, who *d.* 1728, aged 91,

I. JOHN.
II. THOMAS.

JOHN PARES, the eldest son, was Mayor of Leicester, 1714. He *m.* Mary Orme, of Shopnall Hall, in Staffordshire, and died December, 1739, leaving an only child, Mary, who *m.* Samuel Miles, of Leicester. His brother,

THOMAS PARES, married four times, and by the second wife, Dorothy, daughter of — Wilford, had issue,

I. THOMAS, his heir.

I. Mary, who *m.* Thomas Rickards, of Leicester.

THOMAS PARES, the only son of Thomas Pares and his wife Dorothy, was born 14th November, 1716. He *m.* Ann Norton, second cousin to Harry, fourth Earl of Stamford, and grandaughter of George Ashby, of Quenby Hall, M.P. for Leicestershire, and by her had issue,

I. THOMAS, } of whom hereafter.
II. JOHN, }
III. William, LL.B. rector of Narborough, in the county of Leicester, who *m.* Elizabeth, daughter of — Cumberland, and died in 1809, *s. p.*

I. Mary, died at Cheltenham, unm. in October, 1823.
II. Ann, *m.* John Dod, esq. of Cloverly, in the county of Salop, (see vol. i. p. 298.)
III. Dorothy, *d.* young.

Mr. Pares having acquired the Hopwell Hall estate by purchase, about 1780, died there in May, 1805, at the advanced age of eighty-eight, and was buried in the family vault at Ockbrook, of which church he was patron, and lay impropriator.

His eldest son,

THOMAS PARES, born 28th May, 1746, was a fellow of the Society of Antiquarians, and dying at Hopwell Hall, unmarried, 24th October, 1824, was succeeded in the family estates by his next and only surviving brother,

JOHN PARES, born the 15th August, 1749. This gentleman served the office of high-sheriff for Leicestershire, in 1802, upon which occasion, in token of their respect for his character, the gentlemen of the county and town attired themselves in uniform, and accompanied him in his attendance upon the judges. He *m.* Agnes, daughter and co-heiress of Adam Lightbody, esq. of Liverpool, by his wife, Elizabeth Tylston, descended from the ancient family of Tylston, of Cheshire, and by her, who *d.* 31st August, 1812, had issue, beside several children, who *d.* in early age, as follows,

I. THOMAS.
II. John-Tylston, *m.* Mary, daughter of Edwyn Andrew Burnaby, esq. of Baggrave Hall, Leicestershire, and *d.* November, 1831, aged thirty-four years, leaving issue,
    1. Thomas-John.

    1. Agnes-Tylston.
    2. Mary-Tylston.

I. Elizabeth.
II. Anne, *m.* Thomas Paget, esq. M.P. for Leicestershire.
III. Agnes, *m.* the Rev. Edward Thomas Vaughan, M.A. brother to Sir Henry Halford, bart. and to Mr. Justice Vaughan.
IV. Mary.
V. Dorothea.
VI. Hannah, *m.* the Rev. John Jones, M.A. of St. Andrews, Liverpool.
VII. Katharine, *m.* Robert Bickersteth, esq. of Liverpool.

Mr. Pares *d.* 16th June, 1833, and was *s.* by his eldest and only surviving son, the present THOMAS PARES, esq.

*Arms*—Sable, a chevron argent, with a crosslet of the second in the dexter chief.

*Crest*—A demi gryphon or.

*Motto*—PARES cum PARIBUS.

*Estates*—At Hopwell, Ockbrook, and Weston-upon-Trent, Derbyshire; Kirby Frith, Glenfield, and Cotes Deville, Leicestershire.

*Seats*—Hopwell Hall, Derbyshire, and Kirby-Frith House, Leicestershire.

# PERSHOUSE, OF PENN.

PERSHOUSE, WILLIAM-BRADNEY, esq. of Penn Hall, in the county of Stafford, *b.* 18th June, 1785, succeeded his father in 1789, *m.* Alice, daughter of Thomas Titterton, of Wolverhampton, and has an only child,

Alice, *m.* to Thomas Shaw-Hellier, esq. of the Woodhouse, in Staffordshire, and has a daughter, born in 1835.

## Lineage.

ADAM PERSHOUSE, gent. of West Hampton, left by Anne, his wife, three sons and a daughter, viz.

I. JOHN, of age in 1653, who married and had issue,
   ADAM, *d.* in 1706, *s. p.*
   Catherine, *m.* to Matthew Bradney.
   Anne, *m.* to Hugh Granger.
   Mary, *m.* to John Granger.
   Elizabeth, *m.* to Thomas Brett.
II. WILLIAM, of whom presently.
III. Adam.

I. Catherine, *m.* to Nicholas Pershouse.

The second son,

WILLIAM PERSHOUSE, esq. of West Hampton, *m.* (settlement in 1653,) Joyce, dau. of John Stokes, by Mary, his wife, of Oldfalows, in the parish of Bushbury, in the county of Stafford, and was dead in 1699, leaving, with a daughter, Joyce, the wife of William Bayley, a son,

JOHN PERSHOUSE, of Wolverhampton, whose will bears date in 1723. He *m.* (settlement dated 1699,) Mary, daughter of Thomas Jorden, gent. of Aldridge, in Staffordshire, and left a son and successor,

WILLIAM PERSHOUSE, of Wolverhampton, who *m.* Elizabeth, daughter of William Gilbert, of Coventry, and by her, who died in 1770, had issue,

JOHN, of Wolverhampton, who *m.* Betty, daughter of — Cleg, of Manchester, merchant, and dying about the year 1772, left two sons,
   John, of Manchester, *b.* at Wolverhampton, 29th December, 1769.
   James, *b.* at Wolverhampton, 2nd March, 1771.
WILLIAM, of whom presently.
Mary, *b.* in 1740, *d.* unmarried, in April, 1796.
Elizabeth, living, unmarried, at Penn, in 1793.

The second son,

WILLIAM PERSHOUSE, esq. of Wolverhampton, *m.* Ellen, youngest daughter and co-heir of THOMAS BRADNEY, esq. of Penn, in the county of Stafford, and had two sons, WILLIAM-BRADNEY, his heir, and Thomas Bradney, *b.* 18th November, 1788, who *d.* in infancy. Mr. Pershouse *d.* in London, 30th July, 1789, aged thirty-nine, was buried at Penn, and succeeded by his son, the present WILLIAM-BRADNEY PERSHOUSE, esq. of Penn.

### Family of Bradney.

JOHN BRADNEY, gent. of London, who *d.* in 1705, aged about sixty, and was buried at St. Giles's in the fields, *m.* a daughter of — Dyson, of Enfield, in Staffordshire, and by her, who *d.* at Aickleton, in Salop, about the year, 1690, left an only child,

WILLIAM BRADNEY, esq. *b.* at Aickleton, 21st December, 1680, who *m.* Esther, dau. of John Meredith, esq. of Wamborn, in Staffordshire, and dying at Wolverhampton, 3rd May, 1732, was succeeded by his son,

THOMAS BRADNEY, esq. of Penn, in the county of Stafford, a justice of the peace, and high sheriff of that shire, in 1752. This gentleman, who was born at Wolverhampton, 17th July, 1710, *m.* first, Mary, daughter of William Bradley, esq. of Cleobury Mortimer, Salop, which lady died without surviving issue, 30th September, 1742; secondly, Anna Maria, (who also died *s. p.* in

1750,) daughter of Francis Rock, esq. of Newnham, in Worcestershire, and, thirdly, Mary, one of the daughters of John Hoare, esq. of London, second son of Sir Richard Hoare, knt. Lord Mayor of London, and M.P. for that city, by Elizabeth, his wife, daughter and heir of Robert Hookes,* esq. of Conway, in the county of Caernarvon.

*Arms*—Or, on a pile az. a buck's head caboshed of the field.

*Crest*—A greyhound sejant arg. collared sa. resting the dexter paw on a mullet of the first.

*Estates*—In Staffordshire.

*Seat*—Penn Hall, near Wolverhampton.

* Few families can boast a more ancient descent than that of Hookes. So far back as the time of Henry III. we find John Hookes, residing at Hookes, in the county of Lancaster, and his descendants continued seated at Conway until the decease in 1701, of Robert Hookes, whose only daughter and heiress, Elizabeth, married, as stated in the text, John Hoare, esq. During their residence at Conway, the Hookeses intermarried with several of the most distinguished families in the principality, including those of Conway, of Botraven; Rixton, of Conway; Puleston, of Berse; Conway, of Brynyryne, &c. &c. and through their alliance with the Pulestons, lineally descended from Edward I. King of England.

## CALLAGHAN, OF CORK.

CALLAGHAN, DANIEL, esq. of Lotabeg, in the vicinity of Cork, now, for the third time, M.P. for that city. Mr. Callaghan, who was born 7th June, 1786, succeeded his father in April, 1824.

### Lineage.

Daniel Callaghan, esq. one of the most enterprising and successful merchants of Ireland, *b.* in 1760, espoused in 1782, Miss Mary Barry, of Donnalee, and dying in April, 1824, left by that lady, who survives, six sons and three daughters, viz.

- I. John, who *m.* Miss Gosset, of the Island of Jersey, niece of the late Dr. Gosset, of bibliographical celebrity, by whom he has two sons and one daughter.
- II. Daniel, M.P. in three successive parliaments for his native city, as stated above.
- III. Gerard, M.P. for Dundalk, in 1818, and subsequently for Cork, married Miss Clarke, daughter of J. Calvert Clarke, esq. of Teddington, Middlesex, and died 26th February, 1833, leaving issue.
- IV. Patrick.
- V. Richard, a barrister.
- VI. George, late of the 15th dragoons.

- I. Catherine, espoused James Roche, esq. of Aghada, county Cork.
- II. Anne.
- III. Mary.

*Arms*—Az. in base a mount vert, on the sinister a hurst of oak trees, therefrom issuant a wolf passant ppr.

*Crest*—A naked arm holding a sword, with a snake entwined.

*Motto*—Fidus et audax.

*Estates*—In the county of Cork.

*Seat*—Lotabeg.

## STEPHENS, OF TREGENNA.

**STEPHENS, SAMUEL-WALLIS,** esq. of Tregenna Castle, in the county of Cornwall, succeeded his father in 1834.

### Lineage.

This family has possessed estates in Cornwall for four centuries at least. In the reign of EDWARD IV. John Stephyn settled as a merchant in the borough of St. Ives, and acquired considerable possessions there, still enjoyed by his descendants. At a subsequent period, John Stephens, of St Ives, in common with others holding a certain quantity of land, was summoned to the coronation of CHARLES I. there to receive knighthood, and pay the fees, but like many situated so remotely from the capital, he preferred to transmit the fine for refusal, amounting to 16*l.* which was levied to recruit the exhausted treasury. The original receipt for the sum, signed by the treasurer Godolphin, is still preserved in the family.

JOHN STEPHENS, esq. who purchased the ancient manor of Killigrew, in the county of Cornwall, and died in 1764, was the lineal descendant of John Stephyn, the first settled at St. Ives. He married Mary, eldest dau. of Samuel Phillips, esq. of Pendrea, in the county of Cornwall, and had several sons and daughters, who all died young, with the exception of a daughter Anne, and a son,

SAMUEL STEPHENS, esq. M.P. for St. Ives, first returned in 1752, who wedded in June, 1762, Anne, only child and heiress of Richard Seaborne, esq. of the county of Hereford, and dying in March, 1794, was succeeded by his son,

SAMUEL STEPHENS, esq. of Tregenna Castle, a magistrate and deputy-lieutenant for Cornwall, and high sheriff of that county in 1805. In 1806 he was first returned to parliament by St. Ives, and continued to represent that borough for several years. He *m.* 29th November, 1796, Betty, only child and heiress of Captain Wallis, of Tremaine, the celebrated circumnavigator, by Betty, his wife, daughter and co-heir of John Hearle, esq. of Penryn, and had issue,

I. SAMUEL-WALLIS, his heir.
II. John-Augustus.
III. Francis-Hearle, a cavalry officer.
IV. Henry-Lewis, of Oriel College, Oxford.
V. Ferdinand-Thomas.

I. Sarah-Maria, *m.* 6th March, 1827, to the Reverend Charles-William Davy.

Mr. Stephens died in 1834, and was succeeded by his eldest son, the present SAMUEL-WALLIS STEPHENS, esq. of Tregenna Castle.

*Arms*—(Granted *temp.* HENRY VIII. to Henry Stephens, the direct ancestor of the present family,) per pale gu. and vert. a fess indented arg. goutée de sang between three eagles displayed or.

*Crest*—A lion rampant, arg. goutée de sang.

*Motto*—Virtutis amore.

*Estates*—In the counties of Cornwall and Devon.

*Seat*—Tregenna Castle, St. Ives.

# GORDON, OF CULVENNAN.

**GORDON, JAMES**, esq. of Culvennan, in the county of Wigton, lieutenant-colonel commandant of the Kirkcudbrightshire yeomanry cavalry, and a deputy-lieutenant; born 2nd December, 1771; succeeded his father, Sir Alexander Gordon, 21st October, 1830, *m.* 17th September, 1816, Janet, eldest daughter and co-heir of Johnstone Hannay, of Balcary, esq. but has no issue.

## Lineage.

This is a branch of the noble house of Kenmure and Lochinvar, which traces its descent from Richard de Gordoun, in 1120, and from the valiant Sir Adam de Gordoun, one of the "Scots wham Bruce hath aften led."

The Culvennan tree can be surpassed by few in the country; it exhibits descent in many ways from the sovereign of the realm, including Duncan I. and Robert Bruce, as well as from the flower of chivalry and of nobility in England, Scotland, and Ireland.

SIR JOHN GORDON, OF LOCHINVAR, who *d.* in 1517, (for details of whom see Viscount Kenmure, in BURKE'S *Peerage*,) left two sons, Sir Robert, his successor, and William. His estate of Craichlaw, in the county of Wigton, he settled on his second son,

WILLIAM GORDON, OF CRAICHLAW, who *d.* in 1545, and was *s.* by his son,

WILLIAM GORDON, OF CRAICHLAW. This gentleman died in 1570, and was succeeded by his son,

JOHN GORDON, OF CRAICHLAW, whose name we find attached to the bond by the Scottish nobility, for the establishment of James VI. on the Scottish throne. He died in 1580, and was *s.* by his son,

WILLIAM GORDON, OF CRAICHLAW. This gentleman purchased the estate of Culvennan, and dying in 1636, was *s.* therein by his son,

ALEXANDER GORDON, OF CULVENNAN, who died in 1679, and was *s.* by his son,

WILLIAM GORDON, OF CULVENNAN, an enthusiastic presbyterian, suffering, with his kinsman Sir Alexander Gordon, of Earlston, bart. and others of the Scottish nobility and gentry, every species of persecution, their estates forfeited, and their mansions converted into barracks for the soldiery. Mr. Gordon's estates were however restored to him by act of parliament, after the revolution, and dying in 1703, he was *s.* by his son,

WILLIAM GORDON, OF CULVENNAN, to whom succeeded,

SIR ALEXANDER GORDON, OF CULVENNAN, lieutenant-colonel of the Kirkcudbrightshire local militia, and successively sheriff of the counties of Wigton and Kirkcudbright. Sir Alexander's pride in his great ancestor Sir Adam, induced him to visit Dumbarton Castle, for the purpose of seeing the sword of Sir Adam's companion in arms, the patriot WALLACE. Finding it neglected and almost as he thought forgotten, he represented the case to the Duke of Wellington, then at the head of the ordnance department. The consequence was, he received a letter of thanks for his suggestions, the sword which made "tyrants fall at every blow" was sent to the Tower, and when properly mounted and furnished, returned to Dumbarton Castle, where it now forms a most interesting object to visitors. Sir Alexander, who was knighted in 1800, *m.* 17th July, 1769, Grace, only sister of Sir John Dalrymple Hay, of Glenluce, bart. and had, with other children who died young,

I. JAMES, the present representative of the family.

II. David, a captain in the army, born 26th March, 1774, *m.* 2nd September, 1797, Agnes, eldest daughter of William Heyslop, of Lochend, and died 1st November, 1829, leaving issue,

1. William Gordon, of Ernmynzie, *b.* 17th August, 1800, *m.* 17th August, 1825, his cousin-german Agnes-Marion, daughter of John Heyslop, of Lochend, by whom he has three sons, David-Alexander, John-Heyslop, and James.
2. Alexander, *b.* 5th May, 1802, *m.* in 1826, Miss Sarah Cox, but has no issue.
3. James, *b.* 31st January, 1818, in the naval service of the East India Company.

1. Jean.
2. Grace, *b.* 28th May, 1807, *m.* in 1828, Charles Potter, esq. of Darwen, and has issue, John Gerald, and Agnes.
3. Isabella, *b.* 9th March, 1809, *m.* in 1833, James-Richard Clark, esq. but died without issue.

I. Isabella, *b.* 6th October, 1779, unm.

Sir Alexander died 21st October, 1830, at the advanced age of eighty-three.

*Arms*---Azure, a bezant, between three boars' heads erased or, langued gules.

*Crest*---A dexter naked arm, issuing out of a cloud and grasping a flaming sword proper.

*Motto*---Dread God.

*Seat*---Greenlaw House, Kirkcudbrightshire.

## ROLLAND, OF AUCHMITHIE.

ROLLAND, ROBERT, esq. of Auchmithie, in the county of Forfar, a deputy-lieutenant for that shire, and admitted on the Roll of Freeholders in 1831.

### Lineage.

The Rollands representing the Craignytie branch of the ancient clan FARQUHARSON (see vol. ii. p. 98), we shall proceed with details of the latter until it merges in the former.

JOHN FARQUHARSON, of Craignytie, was fourth son of Finla Mor, fifth chief, who was slain at the battle of Pinkie, bearing the royal standard, in 1547. He married, first, a daughter of Forbes, of Towie, and, secondly, a daughter of Farquharson, of Keillor, and left a son and successor,

WILLIAM FARQUHARSON, of Craignytie, who married a daughter of Patrick Ogilvie, and had three sons, namely,

I. WILLIAM, his heir.
II. James, who *m.* a dau. of Guthrie, of Kinblethmont, and was killed in Glenisla, by a party of Lochaber men. He left a son,
   David, of Pitlochrie, who married a dau. of the Rev. Mr. Nevoy, of Glenisla, and was father of
      JAMES, of whom presently, as successor to his granduncle.
III. Alexander, who was killed by Donald Robertson.

The eldest son,

WILLIAM FARQUHARSON, of Craignytie, *m.* Betsy Campbell, but dying without issue, the e tes and representation of this branch of the Farquharsons devolved on his grand-nephew,

JAMES FARQUHARSON, of Craignytie, who married Jean, eldest daughter and co-heiress of Patrick Guthrie, of Auchmithie,* by his

---

* GIDEON GUTHRIE, of Halkerton, in Forfar Restermet, married Lady Torsappie, 1620, had a son,

PATRICK GUTHRIE, of Auchmithie, who married, first, Matilda Ouchterlony, of Cairney, secondly, Janet Reid, by the latter he left no issue, by the former two daughters, co-heiresses,

I. JEAN, *m.* to JAMES FARQUHARSON, of Craignytie.
II. JANET, *m.* to Major William Scrymgeour,

wife, Matilda Ouchterlony, of Cairney, and had an only son and successor,

DAVID FARQUHARSON, of Kinneris, who married a daughter of Neavy, of Hilton, of Guthrie, and was succeeded by his son,

WILLIAM FARQUHARSON, of Kinneris, and Auchmithie, who married, first, a daughter of Turnbull, of Strickathro, and, secondly, a daughter of Erskine, of Kirkbuddo, and had issue,

JOHN, a captain of artillery, died on his passage to India.

Robert, who served as a junior officer in various engagements,† under Admiral Sir Edward Hawke, and died at Port Royal, 21st October, 1762.

AGNES.

The only daughter and eventual heiress,

AGNES FARQUHARSON, born in 1725, wedded John Rolland, esq. of Newton, and Burnton, a magistrate in Arbroath, son of John Rolland, by Margaret Greig, his wife, and descended from Robert Rolland, a younger son of the family of Disblair.‡ By this gentleman, who was born in May, 1716, and died in 1807, the heiress of Auchmithie had issue,

I. ROBERT, the heir, born June 1753.

II. James, twin with Robert, died in childhood.

III. George, died unm.

IV. Patrick, late of Newton, who m. Jane Thom,§ 27th August, 1794, and has issue,

1. Patrick.
2. Alexander, died in Jamaica.
3. George, died at Calcutta.
4. James-Henderson.

1. Agnes.
2. Christiana.
3. Jane.
4. Gray-Watson.
5. Margaret-Turner.

I. Hannah, died in infancy.

The eldest son,

ROBERT ROLLAND, esq. of Auchmithie, b. 1753, m. Gray, daughter of James Watson, esq. of Shillhill, and first cousin of Sir David Scott, bart. of Sitwell Park, and had issue,

I. JOHN, his heir.

II. James, died on board Hon. East India Company's ship Thomas Grenville, on a voyage to China.

III. ROBERT, successor to his brother.

I. Ann.

II. Louisa.

The eldest son,

JOHN ROLLAND, esq. of Auchmithie, born 4th April, 1795, captain in the 3rd regiment of foot, previously served at Madras as lieutenant 22nd dragoons, and also in the 3rd dragoon guards. He died while acting as commandant at Macquarie Harbour, Van Dieman's Land, and leaving no issue, was succeeded by his brother, the present ROBERT ROLLAND, esq. of Auchmithie.

*Arms*—A fesse chequy sa. and or, between two ships, sails furled chief, and a lion rampant in base.

*Crest*—A lymphad, her sails furled and oars in action.

*Motto*—Sustentatus Providentiâ.

*Estates*—In Forfarshire.

*Seat*—Auchmithie.

---

of Dudhope, and had a daughter Margaret, who m. Sir Æneas Macpherson, of Inneressie; her daughter Mary, m. Sir John Maclean, fourth baronet of Morven, who joined Lord Dundee at the battle of Killiekrankie, and fought at the head of his clan at Sherrifmuir.

The following extract minute from the parish records of St. Vigeans, bears reference to the above mentioned Janet Reid, "The minister presents two silver cups of 17oz weight *dedicat be* Janet Reid, relict of Patrick Guthrie, of Auchmithie, and that for the service of Jesus Christ in *this* kirk of St. Vigeans. The session appoints the registration of foresaid pious act *in futuram rei memoriam*. 27th July, 1667." These communion cups are still in use.

† One of his letters describes the action off Brest, which Smollet considers as one of the most perilous and important actions that ever happened in any war between the two nations.

‡ The name of Rolland is of very ancient date in the north of Scotland. Thomas Rolland appears in a jury at Elgin *anno* 1398; but the immediate ancestor of the Disblair family was William Rolland, descended in the female line from the first Earls of Athol. He m. Betsy Ancrel, granddaughter of Crawford of Lochnorris. His grandson, John Rolland, had a daughter, Catharine, who wedded, in 1610, the celebrated Dr. William Guild, principal of King's College, Aberdeen. She founded several bursaries in Marischal College, and the deed of mortification is recorded in the Town Book, Aberdeen. After the death of her husband, she made a mortification to supply a certain annual sum, which was directed to be given, "in all time coming," as a support to any of the family of Rolland who might become reduced in circumstances. James Rolland was served heir to Catherine, his aunt, 1661.

§ Her brother Walter Thom, author of Sketches on Political Economy, &c. married Margaret, sister of John Turner, of Turner Hall, Aberdeenshire.

# WOODHOUSE, OF WOMBURNE WOODHOUSE.

**WOODHOUSE, WILLIAM-HERBERT,** esq. of Eastville, in Lincolnshire, born in 1815, baptized at St. Mary-la-Bonne, Middlesex, *s.* his grandfather in 1833.

## Lineage.

The earliest ancestor of this ancient family on record

William Cocus de Womburn, was engaged in the Crusades *anno* 1193, under the lion-hearted Richard, and thence the arms borne by his descendants were assumed. From him lineally sprung*

Benedict Wodehouse, living 20th Henry VIII. who married, first, in 1554, Catharine, widow of John Foxall, and, secondly, 6th Elizabeth, Elizabeth, widow of William Keeling. By the former he left at his decease, in 1586, three sons and two daughters, viz.

- Benedict, of Womburn, who died 17th Elizabeth, leaving a son, Thomas.
- Walter, of whom presently.
- Thomas, 6th Elizabeth.
- Margaret, *m.* to — Simonds.
- Alice, *m.* to Nicholas Archbald.

The second son,

Walter Wodehouse, died in 1610, leaving by Joan, his wife, daughter of — Hopkyns, of Wednesbury, with two daughters, Margery, the wife of Richard Langley, and Elizabeth, of John Robins, jun. a son and successor,

Francis Woodhouse, who married Eleanor, daughter of — Grosvenor, and had three sons, John, Walter, and Francis. The eldest son,

John Woodhouse, wedded Maria, dau. of John Huntbach, and had five sons, viz.

1. Edward, of Woodhouse, who died in 1688, leaving by Elizabeth, his wife, daughter of John Gough, esq. of Oldfallings, (see vol. ii. p. 393,) three sons, John, Edward, and Francis, who all died without issue. The estate at Womburn Wodehouse passed to the Huntbachs, then to the Hel-

* The intervening descent follows:

William Cocus de Womburn, The Crusader.
|
Nicholas Cocus, *temp.* Henry III.
|
William de Bosco de Womburn, *temp.* Edward I. *m.* Sibella, daughter of Walter, Lord of Bradley.
|
Walter de la Wodehouse.
|
Thomas de la Wodehouse, 11th and 14th Edward II.
|
William de la Wodehouse, *temp.* Edward II. *m.* Matilda.
|
Radulphus atte Wodehouse.
|
Radulphus atte Wodehouse.
|
John de Wodehouse.
|
Thomas Wodehouse de Wodehouse, 2nd Richard II. 11th Henry IV. 17th Henry VI.
|
John Wodehouse, 20th Henry VI. 19th Edward IV.
|
Stephen Wodehouse de Wodehouse, 15th Henry VII. *m.* Alice, dau. and heir of John Wilmyns.
|
John Wodehouse, 13th Henry VIII. died 1523, *m.* Margaret, 15th Henry VII.
|
Stephen Wodehouse de Wodehouse, married Margaret. — Walter Wodehouse de Womburn, 1523.
|
Benedict, as in the text. — William, 18th Henry VIII. — Joan, *d. v. p.* 18th Henry VIII. — Elizabeth, 18th Henry VIII.

liers, by the female line, and is now possessed, under the will of Sir Samuel Hellier, by the Rev. Hellier-Shaw.

II. Francis.
III. JOHN, of whom presently.
IV. Walter.
V. Jonathan.

The third son,

JOHN WOODHOUSE, born in 1627, was in one of our universities preparing for holy orders, when he took his part in the schism of the Presbyterians, which preceded the civil wars, and separated himself from his family. Endowed with considerable merit, learning, and ability, he opened an academy at Sheriff Hales, Shropshire, for the education of young men, whose principles excluded them from the Universities. Many of his scholars became able speakers, and prominent actors in both houses of Parliament, in particular Harley, Earl of Oxford. His latter years Mr. Woodhouse passed in London, and was an eminent preacher at Salters' Hall. He married the daughter and heiress of Major Hubbard, of Rearesby Hall, in Leicestershire, and dying in 1701, left three sons, namely,

I. WILLIAM, who succeeded to his mother's estate at Rearesby, in Leicestershire, which is now in the possession of JOHN WOODHOUSE SIMPSON, esq. only son of the heiress of this branch of the family.
II. George, died unm.
III. JOHN.

The youngest son,

JOHN WOODHOUSE, esq. born in 1677, m. Hannah Sully, and dying in 1733, left, with three daughters, Anne, who died in 1783, Elizabeth, m. to --- Ward, esq. and Hannah, m. to --- Close, esq. a son and successor,

WILLIAM WOODHOUSE, esq. born in 1710, who m. Mary Mompesson, grandaughter and heiress of William Chappel, esq. and by her who died in 1802, had issue,

I. JOHN-CHAPPEL, his heir.

I. Hannah, } twins, who died young.
II. Margaret, }
III. Elizabeth, who died in 1817.
IV. Mary, died young.
V. Anne, m. to William Holbach, esq. of Farnborough, in the county of Warwick, (see vol. i. p. 661.)

Mr. Woodhouse died in 1755, and was succeeded by his son,

*The very Reverend* JOHN-CHAPPEL WOODHOUSE, D.D. Dean of Lichfield, *b.* in 1749. This eminent divine was educated at Christ Church, Oxford, and upon taking holy orders was presented by the late Duke of Sutherland, then Marquis of Stafford, to the living of Donnington, in the county of Salop. In 1805 he published "Woodhouse's Annotations on the Apocalypse," which he re-edited at the request of the Rev. Dr. Van-Mildert, Regius Professor of Divinity at Oxford, now Bishop of Durham. The following testimony to the excellence of the work may be seen in a copy of the book preserved in the library of Haitlebury Castle, which Hurd, Bishop of Worcester, bequeathed to his successors in the see, and is thus written in his lordship's own hand-writing: "This is the best book of its kind that I have seen; it owes its superiority chiefly to two things, 1. The author's understanding for the most parts the Apocalyptic symbols in a *spiritual*, not a *literal* sense. 2. To the care he has taken to fix the precise import of those symbols, from the use made of them by the old prophetical and other writers of the Old and New Testament. Still many difficulties remain, and will remain, to the time of the end. R. W. 15th March, 1806." Dr. Woodhouse was appointed to the Deanery of Lichfield, in 1807, where he resided during the remainder of his life. He was a great benefactor to the cathedral, and presented it with the painted window in the north transept. He died sincerely lamented 17th November, 1833. He m. Mercy Peate, a co-heiress, and by her, who died in 1826, had issue,

CHAPPEL, born in 1780, who m. Amelia, daughter of Sir Charles Oakeley, bart. and dying in 1815, was buried in St. James's Church, Westminster, leaving issue,

John-Chappel, *b.* in 1814, died in 1821.

WILLIAM-HERBERT, successor to his grandfather.

Ellen-Jane, m. first, to the Rev. William Robinson, Rector of Swinnerton, and by him, who died in 1812, had two daughters, who both died young.* She m. secondly, Hugh Dyke Acland, esq. who died in 1834, leaving a son, Hugh-Woodhouse Acland. She wedded, thirdly, in 1835, Richard Hinckley, esq.

Mary-Anne.

Dean Woodhouse was succeeded at his decease by his grandson, the present WILLIAM-HERBERT-WOODHOUSE, esq.

*Arms*—Semée of cross-crosslets, a plain cross arg.

*Crest*---On a coronet a cross-crosslet.

*Motto*---In hoc signo.

*Estates*---Eastville, East Ten, and Stickney, all in Lincolnshire.

---

* These two children are the subject of the beautiful and celebrated monument by Chantrey, in Lichfield Cathedral.

# MONEY, OF MUCH MARCLE.

MONEY KYRLE, JAMES, esq. of Much Marcle, in Herefordshire, of Whetham, in Wiltshire, and of Pitsford, in Northamptonshire, colonel in the army, and a justice of the peace for Herefordshire, *m.* 27th December, 1811, Caroline-Anne, eldest daughter of Robert Taylor, esq. of Gloucester Place, Portman Square.

Colonel Money, who succeeded his father in 1808, assumed, by royal warrant, dated April 26th, 1809, the surname of Kyrle, in addition to his patronymic, together with the arms of that family.

## Lineage.

The Moneys having inherited the representation of various highly distinguished divisions of the ancient families of KYRLE, ERNLE, WASHBOURNE, and STOUGHTON, we shall proceed with details of those descents, until each merges in the immediate line of MONEY.

In the oldest writings relative to the KYRLES, the name is variously written *Crul*, *Crull*, and *Crulle;* afterwards *Cryll*, and sometimes *Curl*,* until at last it was universally spelt KYRLE. The first of the family on record,

ROBERT CRUL, of Altone, or Old Town, near Ross, resided in 1295 at Homme, now Hom Green, in the same neighbourhood. From his son,

WILLIAM CRUL, of the Hulle, or Hill, in Herefordshire, whose name occurs first in 1318, and finally in 1339, descended

WALTER KYRLE, of the Hill, living in 1489, who *m.* and had two sons,

I. WALTER, of the Hill, whose only dau. and heiress, Alice, wedded Christopher Clarke, esq. and was represented by the late Mrs. Jane Clarke, whose devisee is the present KINGSMILL EVANS, esq. of the Hill, (see vol. ii. p. 242).

II. JAMES, of whose descendants we are about to treat.

This

JAMES KYRLE,† inherited Walford Court,‡ and was father of

THOMAS KYRLE, living about the year 1500, who *m.* Johan, daughter and heir of Hugh Abrahall, esq. by Alice, his wife, dau. of John Rudhall, esq. of Rudhall, and had, with four daughters (one of whom, Bridget, *m.* Roger Pye, esq. of Mynde, see vol. i. p. 350), nine sons,

I. WALTER, of Walford Court, who *m.* Joan, daughter of Richard Warncombe, esq. and had, with several other sons, who *d. s. p.* a son and successor,

ROBERT KYRLE, esq. of Walford Court, high sheriff of Herefordshire, who *m.* Jane, daughter of E. Evans, alias Bithell, esq. and had with four daughters, (one of whom, Penelope, married Roger Hereford, esq. of Priors Court,) two sons, namely,

1. JAMES, his heir.
2. Walter, of Ross, barrister-

* A Sir Walter Curl, of Soberton in Hants, was created a baronet in 1678, but the title soon after expired.

† There were many families in various parts of England, in the middle of the sixteenth century, possessing names and arms, each nearly approaching those of Kyrle, who were probably connected with this family.

‡ Walford Court, or Manor House, still exists. From a battery here Captain Kyrle is reported by tradition to have bombarded Goodrich Castle, which, from the relative position of the two places, is not improbable. The estate passed, as hereafter shewn, from the Kyrles to the Gwillyms, and was sold by them to John Clarke, esq. of the Hill, about the year 1727. It is now, under the will of the late Mrs. Clarke, the property of K. Evans, esq.

at-law, and justice of the peace, *m.* Alice, dau. and sole heir of John Mallett, of Berkeley, in the county of Gloucester, and dying in February, 1650, left two sons, viz.

JOHN, "The Man of Ross," born at the Whitehouse Dymock, in May, 1637, *d.* at Ross, *s. p.* 7th November, 1724.*

Walter, living in 1683.

Robert Kyrle was *s.* by his elder son,

JAMES KYRLE, esq. of Walford Court, justice of the peace and high sheriff for Herefordshire. He *m.* Anne,† daughter of Robert Waller, esq. of Beaconsfield, in Bucks, by Anne, his wife, sister of JOHN HAMPDEN, the patriot, and by her, who *d.* 19th September, 1642, had, with four daughters, seven sons, viz.

1. ROBERT, his heir.
2. James, } all *d. s. p.*
3. John, } all *d. s. p.*
4. William, } all *d. s. p.*
5. Richard, (Sir). knt. of the kingdom of Ireland, living in 1683, married two wives, and had issue by both.
6. Edward, *d.* unm.
7. Thomas, *m.* in Ireland, and had a son, Vandervort, who was devisee of "THE MAN OF ROSS."

James Kyrle died 1st February, 1646, and was succeeded by his eldest son,

ROBERT KYRLE, esq. of Walford Court. Inheriting the republican principles of his mother's connections, he was a distinguished military officer under CROMWELL, holding the commission of captain of troopers, and is styled "a stoney hearted Rebell," in the narrative of the plundering of Master Swift's‡ house at Goodrich. He married, first, Mildred, daughter of Sir William Maxey, of Bradwell Hall, Essex, and secondly, Elizabeth, daughter of John Brayn, gent. of Little Dean, in Gloucestershire. By the latter, who *d.* 5th September, 1668, he had issue,

1. James, aged sixteen in 1683, *d.* before June, 1689.

1. Mary, *m.* to — Yates, of Bristol.
2. Elizabeth, *m.* to William Gwillym,§ esq. of Langston, in Herefordshire, and died 12th December, 1714, leaving a son, Robert.

Robert Kyrle *d.* in 1669, aged fifty-one, and was buried in the family chapel in Walford Church, on the 2nd October, in that year.

* The character of this amiable man is so well delineated by general description, that to dwell here on his merits would be superfluous. Suffice it to say that many a tradition of Ross and its vicinity still bears ample testimony to the truth of Pope's beautiful encomium, and that the memory of "The Man of Ross" is still and ever will be warmly cherished among the scenes of his benevolence. Of his ancestry is here, for the first time, presented a full account: of his heirs, we would add that Vandervort Kyrle, his devisee, had two sons and a daughter, Robert, Walter, and Elizabeth. After the death of their father, the property was bequeathed to Robert, the elder son, and his heirs male; he failing issue, it was to have reverted to Walter, the second son, and his heirs male; Walter dying without male issue, then to Elizabeth the daughter (afterwards Mrs. Weale), and her heirs, *male or female:* but, from a flaw in the will, Robert Kyrle cut off the entail and devised it to his wife and daughter, whose descendants now enjoy the same. The Man of Ross is buried in the chancel of Ross Church, where a handsome monument was erected in 1776, by Lieut. Col. James Money, in consequence of a bequest of £200 for that purpose by Constantia, Lady Dupplin, of whom the colonel was executor, and thus the reproach of Pope,

"And what! no monument, inscription, stone!"

is deservedly done away. Lady Dupplin, in her will, styles Mr. Kyrle her "cousen," and desires that when the monument was erected, "the character of him by the late Mr. Pope, collected, as her Executors should think proper, from his writings, should be inscribed thereon by way of epitaph." This, however, being left wholly to the discretion of the executors, was not done; and the inscription is simply—

"This
Monument
was erected
in memory of
MR. JOHN KYRLE,
commonly called
THE MAN OF ROSS.

† Sister of the poet Waller.

‡ This narrative is entitled "Master Swift, Parson of Goodrich, Herefordshire, his wife and tenne children most inhumanely dealt with by Captain Kyrle, a stoney hearted Rebell;" and is found in a scarce and curious work, "England's Complaint against the Sectaries." "Master Swift" was grandfather to the celebrated Dean Swift.

§ Of the same family was the celebrated Herald Gwillym.

II. William, of Blayson, whose only daughter and heiress, Joan, *m.* John Aylway.
III. Charles, who *m.* Joane, daughter of William Pigot, esq. and had issue.
IV. THOMAS, ancestor of the KYRLES, of Much Marcle.
V. Hugh, *d.* in London, unm.
VI. John, *d. s.p.*
VII. James, who *m.* a daughter of — Morgan of Newent.
VIII. Richard, in holy orders, afterwards Sir Richard, vicar of Walford; upon the resignation of which, he became vicar of Much Marcle and Foy. This Sir Richard drew up a pedigree of his family from its earliest establishment in Herefordshire to the year 1602, on which document the present account is founded.
IX. Anthony, a justice of the peace, whose daughter, Sarah, became the wife of William Scudamore, esq. of Bellingham.

The fourth son,

THOMAS KYRLE, esq. Lord of the manor of Much Marcle,* in the county of Hereford, in the commission of the peace for that shire, and for Worcestershire, *m.* Frances, daughter and heir of John Knotsford, esq. of Malvern, and left a son and successor,

JOHN KYRLE, esq. of Much Marcle, justice of the peace, and twice high sheriff for Herefordshire, who was created a BARONET 17th May, 1627. He *m.* Sybill, daughter and heir of Philip Scudamore, esq. and had issue

I. FRANCIS, high sheriff of Herefordshire, who *m.* Hester, daughter of Sir Paul Tracy, bart. of Stanway, in the county of Gloucester, and dying *v. p.* in 1649, left
  1. JOHN, successor to his grandfather.
  2. Richard, *d. s. p.*
  3. Giles, *d. s. p.*
  1. Elizabeth, *m.* to Robert Holmes, esq. of Netherton, in Gloucestershire.
  2. Dorothy, *m.* first, to John Abraball, esq. and secondly, to Sir Bennet Hoskyns.
  3. Anne, *m.* to — Lechmere, esq. of Fownhope.
  4. Hester, *m.* to — Prior, of Pillith, in Radnorshire.
II. Thomas, of Gray's Inn, *d. s. p.*
I. Joane, *m.* to John Nourse, esq.
II. Sibill, *m.* to Thomas Capell, of How Capell, in Herefordshire.

Sir John Kyrle,† *d.* in 1650, and was *s.* at his decease by his grandson,

SIR JOHN KYRLE, bart. of Much Marcle, who *m.* 16th December, 1647, Rebecca Vincent, and by her, who wedded, secondly, John Booth, esq. of Letton, had issue,

I. VINCENTIA, of whom presently.
II. HESTER, *m.* to William Wintour, esq. of Dymock.
III. ELIZABETH, *m.* to John Midlebrooke, esq.
IV. SYBILL, *m.* to Giles Wintour, esq. younger brother of William Wintour, esq. of Dymock.

Sir John Kyrle, who was one of the knights of the shire for Hereford, at the period of his decease, *d.* 4th January, 1679-80, aged sixty, and was succeeded by his eldest dau. and coheir,

VINCENTIA KYRLE, born 2nd October, 1651, who married‡ at Much Marcle, 6th December, 1674, Sir John Ernle, knt. of Burytown, in the county of Wilts, son of Sir John

* The manor of Marcle Magna, or Much Marcle, anciently formed part of the possessions of the Mortimers, Earls of March; some of whom inhabited a castle there, and are interred in the parish church. Having reverted to the crown, it was purchased in the reign of Elizabeth, with the Park, Royalties, &c. by Matthew Smith, esq. of the Middle Temple, and resold by him soon after to Thomas Kyrle, esq.

† Sir John, in 1628, founded a chapel adjoining the church of Much Marcle, wherein, during his lifetime, he erected a monument in memory of himself and his wife. The effigies of the Baronet and the Lady Sibyll are beautifully executed, and being quite fresh and perfect, present an excellent specimen of the state of the arts at the commencement of the 17th century.

‡ Extract from the parish register: "Sir John Ernle, of Berryton, in the county of Wilts, and Mrs. Vincentia Kyrle, the eldest Daughter of the worshipfull John Kyrle, of Homhouse, Bart. were married by licence, Dec. the 6th, 1674." A letter from Sir John Kyrle to Sir John Ernle, the original of which is still extant, thus concisely communicates this marriage:

"Deere Sir John,
This paper nor indeede my Constitution at present, having been upp very late, or early, will not suffice to aske pardon enouf for my longe Silence—But to y[e] matter—Your Sonne was yesterday married, being Sunday y[e] 6[th] Instant, and I hope to his owne, as well as yours and my Content—w[ch] I pray God Continue.—This is all you Can have at present from
Y[o] faythfull loving Brother
and very humble servaunt
John Kyrle.

Dec. y[e] 7[th], —74.
They both present their humble Dutys to you and my Lady, and their respects unto y[e] rest of y[e] ffamiley."

Addressed
"To Sir John Ernle, at his house in Winchester Streete, neere the Afrycan House, London, these presents."

Ernle, knt. Chancellor of the Exchequer, (see Ernle, of Ernle and Whetham) and had one son and one daughter, viz.

JOHN KYRLE ERNLE, the heir.

HESTER ERNLE, born at Fawley, in Herefordshire, 8th February, 1675-6, *m.* WILLIAM WASHBOURNE, esq. son and heir apparent of William Washbourne, esq. of Pytchley, in Northamptonshire, (see Washbourne, of Washbourne and Pytchley,) and left, besides several other children who all died without issue, a daughter,

ELIZABETH WASHBOURNE, who married in 1723, FRANCIS MONEY, esq. of Wellingborough, and died 2nd March, 1726, leaving an only son,

JAMES MONEY, esq. of whom presently.

Vincentia, Lady Ernle, was succeeded at her decease by her son,

JOHN KYRLE ERNLE, esq. of Whetham and Much Marcle, baptized at the latter place, 10th May, 1683, who espoused (marriage settlement dated 10th March, 1704,) Constantia, only daughter of Sir Thomas Rolt, knt. of Saccomb, Herts, and dying in October, 1725, left by her (who was buried in the Bayntun vault at Bromham, Wilts, 14th November, 1755) an only surviving daughter and heiress,

CONSTANTIA ERNLE, who *m.* in 1741, Thomas, Viscount Dupplin, afterwards Earl of Kinnoul, and had an only child, Thomas John Ernle Hay, *b.* 12th August, 1742, who died 14th October, 1743. The countess herself died in 1753, and was interred at Calne, on the 7th July. Leaving no issue, she settled her estates upon the next heir, and sole representative of her ancestors, the son of her first cousin, Elizabeth,

JAMES MONEY, esq. of Pitsford, Northamptonshire, lieutenant-colonel in the army, who was baptized at Wellingborough, 25th September, 1724. He *m.* Eugenia, daughter and sole heiress of George Stoughton, esq. of St. John's, Warwick, (see Stoughton, of Stoughton and St. John's,) and by her, who *d.* in June, 1788, and was buried at Warwick, he left at his decease, 14th June, 1785, an only surviving son and successor,

WILLIAM MONEY, esq. of Much Marcle, *b.* 23rd February, 1748, who *m.* Mary, daughter of William Webster, esq. of Stockton on Tees, in the county of Durham, by Mary, his wife, daughter of Rowland Burdon, esq. of Stockton, (See vol. i. p. 360,) and by her, who *d.* 20th June, 1813, aged 69, had issue,

I. JAMES, his heir.

II. William, of Whetham House, in holy orders, rector of Yatesbury, Wilts, and a justice of the peace for that county, *m.* 16th July, 1805, Emma, daughter of Richard Down, esq. of Halliwick Manor House, Middlesex, and has issue,

1. WILLIAM.
2. Edward-Kyrle.
3. John-Ernle.
4. James-Stoughton.
5. George-Washbourne.
6. Richard-Walter.
7. Charles-Septimus.

1. Emma.

III. George, late Master in Equity, Accountant General, and Keeper of the Records in the Supreme Court of Judicature, Calcutta, *m.* 21st January, 1817, Pulcherie, daughter of Henrie, Marquis de Bourbel,* and sister of Harold, the present marquis, and has issue,

1. William-Bayley.
2. George-Henrie.
3. Alonzo.
4. Edward.
5. James-Aurelian.

1. Mary-Frances-Vincentia, who *d.* an infant, 21st February, 1820.

IV. Kyrle-Ernle, in holy orders, vicar of Much Marcle, prebendary of Hereford, and a justice of the peace for the county of Hereford, *m.* 16th January, 1806, Mary-Thomasina, dau. of Dominick Ffrench,† esq. and has issue,

1. James-Harley, *d.* an infant 21st December, 1808.
2. Kyrle-Ernle-Aubrey.
3. Rowland-William-Taylor.
4. James-Rodney, *d.* an infant 25th November, 1821.

1. Mary-Ernle, *m.* 16th September, 1830, Oswald, son of Thomas Grimston, esq. of Grimston, Yorkshire (see p. 72).
2. Ellenor, *m.* 3rd July, 1827, the Rev. Richard Coke Wilmot, son

* The Bourbels of Montpinçon, in Normandy, rank among the most ancient families of the French noblesse. They were created Baron in the year 936, and Count and Marquis by letters patent *temp.* Henry III.; and together with their titles and honours were naturalized in England at the end of the last century.

† The family of Ffrench derives its origin from Sir Maximilian de Ffrench, an early Norman warrior, whose descendant, Sir Theophilus Ffrench, accompanied his kinsman, WILLIAM THE CONQUEROR, to England, and afterwards settled in Ireland. Numerous branches of the house of Ffrench eventually established themselves in several parts of that kingdom; one of which branches is at present represented by the Right Hon. Charles Baron Ffrench, of Castle Ffrench, in the county of Galway.

of Sir Robert Wilmot, bart. of Chaddesden, Derbyshire.
3. Eugenia-Jane.
4. Caroline - Chatfield, *d.* 25th March, 1831.
5. Vincentia.

v. Rowland, post captain R. N. and companion of the military order of the Bath, *m.* 13th September, 1805, Maria, daughter of William Money, esq. of Walthamstow, Essex, and has issue,
1. Rowland.
2. Ernle-Kyrle.
3. William-Taylor.
4. David-Inglis.
5. George-James-Gambier, *d.* an infant 20th May, 1829.
1. Maria-Rowlanda, *m.* 8th April, 1830, the Rev. Samuel-James Gambier.
2. Amelia-Mary.
3. Mary-Martha, *d.* an infant 30th January, 1817.
4. Angelica-Mary.
5. Emma-Martha.
6. Eva-Maria.

vi. John, commander in the East India Company's Maritime Service, *d.* unm. 6th August, 1825.

i. Hester.
ii. Mary, *d.* in childhood.
iii. Eugenia, *m.* 8th June, 1797, the late William-Taylor Money, esq. of Walthamstow, Essex, knight of the Hanoverian Guelphic Order, and his Britannic Majesty's consul at Venice and Milan, and has issue.
iv. Susannah, *m.* 17th July, 1800, the Rev. Robert Chatfield, D.C.L. vicar of Chatteris, Cambridgeshire, and has issue,
v. Dorothea.
vi. Alice, *d.* unm. 27th October, 1802.
vii. Vincentia, *d.* unm. 1st April, 1816.

William Money, esq. *d.* 6th November, 1808, was buried at Much Marcle, and succeeded by his eldest son, the present Col. JAMES KYRLE MONEY.

*Arms*—Vert, a chev. between three fleur-de-lys or; quartering among many others,

| | |
|---|---|
| Kyrle | Hussey |
| Abrahall | Washbourne |
| Knotsford | Zouch |
| Scudamore | Corbet |
| Ernle | Blount |
| Wroughton | Wysham |
| Best | Walshe |
| Malwyn | Poher |
| Haydock | Thyne |
| Finnamore | Stoughton |
| D'Awtrey | Jones |
| Scardeville | Thorold. |

*Crest*—On a mount vert, a hedge-hog or.

*Motto*—Nil moror ictus.

*Estates*—In the counties of Hereford, Wilts, and Northampton.

*Seats*—Hom House, Herefordshire, Whetham House, Wiltshire, and Pitsford, Northamptonshire.

## Ernle, of Ernle and Whetham.

This family derives its name from the village of EARNLEY, or ERNLE, in Sussex, so called from the Saxon words "Earn," and "Lege," *the place or habitation of eagles;* in allusion to which, three eagles were borne on the shield of Ernle.

In the reign of HENRY III., RICHARD DE ERNLE was seated at Ernle. His second son, John de Ernle, knight of the shire for Sussex, in 1331, *m.* Isabel, daughter and heir of his uncle, William de Ernle, widow of Falco Paulin, and acquired with her in dower the manor of Ernle, together with a large mansion house, moated and castellated, vestiges of which are still to be traced near the church of Ernle.

SIR HENRY ERNLE, knt. lineal descendant and representative of this John, lived in the middle of the fifteenth century, and had a son and successor,

JOHN ERNLE, of Ernle, who *m.* Margaret, daughter of Nicholas Morley, a scion of the house of Morley, of Morley, in Lancashire, by his wife, one of the daughters and coheirs of Sir John Walleys, knt. and was *s.* by his son,

SIR JOHN ERNLE, knt. of Ernle, chief justice of the Court of King's Bench. He *m.* Anne, daughter and heir of Sir John D'Awtrey, of Southampton, and dying in 1536, left a son and successor,

WILLIAM ERNLE, esq. of Cackham* and Ernle, representative in parliament for Chichester, in 1542. He *m.* Bridget, daughter of— Spring, of Lavenham, and by her, (who

* "Cackham Manor Place, situated in the parish of West Wittering, was the occasional residence of the Bishops of Chichester, from the thirteenth to the sixteenth century, when it was transferred to William Ernle, and inhabited by his descendants. It was a spacious mansion, calculated to receive the episcopal retinue, with a hall, chapel, and large apartments. Bishop Sherburne greatly frequented it, and induced by the singularly magnificent sea view, bounded by the Isle of Wight, erected a lofty tower of brick, hexagonal, with labelled windows, whence the commanding prospect might be seen with greatest advantage. The tower is still standing. Of the refectory no traces are left, and of the chapel only a single perforated wall."—*Dallaway's Western-Sussex*, vol. i. p. 14.

wedded secondly, Sir Henry Hussey,) left at his decease in 1545,* a son and successor,

RICHARD ERNLE, esq. of Ernle, who *d.* in 1577, leaving by Elizabeth, his wife, with other issue,

I. RICHARD, of Ernle and Cackham, whose line eventually merged in Elizabeth, *m.* to Edward Higgons, of Bury, commissioner for the Parliament, in 1643.

II. JOHN.

The second son,

JOHN ERNLE, esq. *m.* Jane, daughter and heir of Symon Best, by Agnes, his wife, daughter and heir of John Malwyn, esq. of Echilhampton, Wilts, and was *s.* by his eldest son,

JOHN ERNLE, esq. who *m.* Anne, daughter of Constantine Darell, esq. of Collingbourne, in Wiltshire (see page 148), and left an eldest son and successor,

JOHN ERNLE, esq. of Bourton Manor House, parish of Bishops Cannings, Wilts. By his wife, Lucy, together with other issue,† he was father of

JOHN ERNLE, esq. of Bourton, who *m.* Mary, daughter of William Hyde, esq. of Denchworth, in Berkshire, and dying in 1571, was *s.* by his eldest‡ son,

MICHAEL ERNLE, esq. of Bourton, who served the office of high sheriff for that county in the 22 ELIZABETH. He *m.* first, Mary, only daughter and heir of Roger Finnamore, esq. of Whetham,§ in the parish of Calne, Wilts, and by her had two sons and two daughters, namely,

JOHN, (Sir) his heir.
Richard.

Mary, *m.* to William Blacker, esq. of New Sarum.
Cecilia, *m.* to William Daniel, esq.

He wedded, secondly, Susan, eldest daughter and co-heir of Sir Walter Hungerford,‖ knt. of Farley Castle, Somersetshire, eldest son of Walter, Lord Hungerford, and by her, who *m.* secondly, Sir Cary Reynolds, knt. was father of

EDWARD, of Echilhampton, in the county of Wilts, baptized at Calne, 4th December, 1587, ancestor of the Ernles of Maddington, to whom a baronetcy was granted 2nd February, 1660-1, and who are now represented by MRS. JANE FRANCES DRAX, of Charborough Park, in Dorsetshire; of the Ernles of Brimslade Park, represented by SIR FRANCIS BURDETT, bart.; and of the Ernles of Conock, merged in the family of WARRINER.

Michael Ernle was succeeded at his decease by his eldest son,

SIR JOHN ERNLE, knt. of Whetham, bapt. at Calne, 1st May, 1561, who *m.* (settlement dated 8th November, 1593), Margaret, dau. and co-heir of Thomas Haydock, esq. of Burytoun, in Wiltshire, and by her, who *d.* in 1646, had, with several younger sons¶ and daughters,

I. JOHN, his heir.

II. Michael, (Sir) Governor of Shrews-

---

* He is buried in the church at West Wittering, Sussex, where an ancient monument of Caen stone remains to his memory.—*Dallaway.*

† Among whom was William Ernle, to whose memory a very curious monument, bearing date 1587, is erected in All Canning's Church, Wilts, on which is inscribed the scriptural passage, "Wheresoever a dead carkas is, even thither will the egles resorte"—in reference to the arms of Ernle.

‡ From a younger son, Thomas, who was buried in Westbury Church, Wilts, 3rd September, 1595, descended the ERNLES of BREMBRIDGE.

§ The Finnamores traced their descent from the year 1300, and had long enjoyed the estate of Whetham. The mansion, which was built apparently about the end of the sixteenth century, was originally a remarkably large and handsome edifice, and was surrounded with ornamental grounds of the most curious and costly description. A royal visit was paid at Whetham in the time of John Kyrle Ernle, by ANNE, and a highly wrought ebony cabinet is still preserved here, said to have been presented by her Majesty on that occasion. The state bed was till latterly in existence, and in a part of the house, now pulled down, tradition pointed to a dark and secret recess, called "King Charles's Hole," as one of the places of concealment sought by CHARLES during the Civil War. The visit of ANNE is thus alluded to in a letter to J. K. Ernle from his sister, which is still extant: "I heare you are much talked of in Town for yr extorordinerry wise management in entertaining the Queen. I am happy in haveing soe prudent a brother." Dated 15 Nov. 1703.

‖ SIR WALTER HUNGERFORD *m.* Anne, daughter of Sir William Dormer, knt. and had issue,

EDWARD, who *d.* young.

SUSAN, *m.* to MICHAEL ERNLE, esq.
LUCY, *m.* to Sir John St. John, of Lydiard Tregoze, and from this marriage descend the Viscounts Bolingbroke and St. John (see BURKE's *Peerage*).
JANE, *m.* to Sir John Kerne, knt. of Glamorganshire.
} co-heirs.

—BURKE's *Extinct and Dormant Peerage.*

¶ Among these was Thomas Ernle, rector of Everleigh, Wilts. He was ejected in Cromwell's time from his benefice, and (according to the account of the injured party) *a tinker*, or "*Œrarius*," put in his place. In the parish register the rector thus commemorates the subsequent expulsion of his substitute:

"Exit Tinker. Let all men henceforth know
A Thorne was planted, wher a Vine should grow:
Downe went Saint Paul, Apollo, and Cephas,
Ffor silver Trumpets here was sounding Brasse."

bury Castle, slain in 1645.* The death of this gallant knight is thus described by Clarendon: "Whilst the king's commissioners entertained some hope that this loss (of Weymouth) might have the more disposed the Parliament to a just peace, they received advertisement of a much greater loss sustained by the king, and which was more like to exalt the other side. Colonels Langham and Mitton, two very active officers in the parliament service, about Shropshire and North Wales, by correspondence with some townsmen, and some soldiers in the garrison of Shrewsbury, from whence too many of that garrison were unhappily drawn out two or three days before on some expedition, seized upon that town in the night, and by the same treachery likewise, entered the castle where Sir Michael Earnly, the Governor, had been long sick, and rising upon the alarm out of his bed, was killed in his shirt: whilst he behaved himself as well as was possible, and refused quarter, which did not shorten his life many days, he being even at the point of death of a consumption, which kept him from performing all those offices of vigilance he was accustomed to, being a gallant gentleman, who understood the duty of a soldier by long experience and diligent observation." Burghah's *Journal* also mentions a Sir Michael Ernle, "Captain of the Queen's Troop," who was taken prisoner at Rowton Heath, near Chester, "with a scarf which the Queen," (the beautiful Henrietta-Maria,) "gave him from about her neck, for his colours."

Sir John was buried 4th February, 1648, and succeeded by his eldest son,

JOHN ERNLE, esq. of Whetham, baptized at Calne, 18th January, 1598, m. (settlement dated 21st May, 1616,) Philadelphia, daughter of Arthur Hopton, esq. and dying in 1685, left, with two daughters, a son and successor,

SIR JOHN ERNLE, knt. of Whetham, Chancellor of the Exchequer, and a Member of the Privy Council, *temp.* CHARLES II. and JAMES II. The adherence of the Ernles to the cause of the Stewarts is testified by the circumstance of Sir John's name occurring in the list of those who were to have been invested, at the Restoration, with the order of the *Royal Oak*, (see vol. i. p. 692,) as well as by the grant of the baronetcy, at the same period, to the Echilhampton branch. He m. (settlement dated 1st March, 1646,) first, Susan, eldest daughter of John Howe, esq. of Compton, in Gloucestershire, by whom he had, with other issue,

JOHN, (Sir) his heir.

Philadelphia, m. to John Potenger, esq. of Bingham Melcomb, in Dorsetshire, now represented by Binghams, of Melcomb.

He m. secondly (settlement dated 17th September, 1672), Elizabeth, Lady Seymour, widow of Charles, Lord Seymour, and mother of Charles, sixth Duke of Somerset, by whom he had two daughters, Elizabeth, m. to John Dodson, esq. and Catharine, m. to Ralph Palmer, esq. of the Middle Temple. Sir John d. in 1697, and was buried at Calne. His elder son,

SIR JOHN ERNLE, knt. of Burytown, who d. 25th October, 1686,† m. VINCENTIA, eldest daughter and co-heir of SIR JOHN KYRLE, bart. of Much Marcle, and (as already shewn) is now represented by JAMES KYRLE MONEY, esq.

*Arms of Ernle*—Arg. on a bend sa. three eagles displayed or.

## Washbourne, of Washbourne and Pytchley.

The Washbournes, of Washbourne, were generation after generation of knightly degree, previously to the reign of EDWARD III., and ranked in point of descent with the most ancient families in the kingdom. Shortly after the Conquest, they derived their name from Wasseborne, or Washbourne, in Worcestershire,‡ and at a very early period, quartered the arms of Zouch, Corbet, Wysham, Walshe and Blount, as also those of the Earl of Warwick's second son.§ About the time of EDWARD III. JOHN WASHBOURNE, of Washbourne, (the grandson of Sir Roger Washbourne, who was himself the grandson of another Sir Roger Washbourne, with whom the pedigree ‖ in the visitations commences) married two wives: by the first, Joan, daughter and heir of Sir John Musard, knt. he had an only daughter, ISOLDE, who became the wife of John Salwey, of Kanke, (see vol i. p. 152) and by the

* See *Kimber's Baronetage*, 1771.

† A gold ring was lately dug up at Hall Court, Herefordshire, in the inside of which is engraved, "Sir John Ernle ob. 25 Oct. -86," which proves the date of his death, previously unknown, owing to an hiatus in the Marcle register.

‡ *Nash's Worcestershire*, vol. ii. p. 233.

§ At a later period they also quartered the arms of the Duke of Ormonde, Earl of Derby, &c.

‖ The pedigree is fully given in the Visit. of Worcestershire, by Robert Cooke, Clarencieux, 1569.

second, Margaret, daughter and heir of John Poher, or Power,* a son, NORMAN WASHBOURNE, who retired to his mother's estate in Wichenford, where his descendants continued to reside for several generations, enjoying the highest respectability, and intermarrying with the houses of Kynaston, Mytton, Stapysse, Tracy, Lygon, &c. The direct male line of the family eventually expired with WILLIAM WASHBOURNE, esq. of Wichenford, in Worcestershire, and of Pytchley, in the county of Northampton, the lineal descendant of Norman Washbourne, of Wichenford, and consequently the full male representative of the Washbournes, of Washbourne. He married HESTER, daughter of Sir JOHN ERNLE, knt. of Whetham, and his only child, who left issue, married Francis Money, esq. The Washbournes are consequently (as already shown) now represented by the MONEY family.

*Arms of Washbourne*—Arg. on a fess between six martlets gu. three cinquefoils of the field.

### Stoughton, of Stoughton, and St. John's.

This family derived its name from STOCHE, or STOKE, in Surrey, and TUN, the Saxon word for "enclosure." In the time of STEPHEN,† GODWIN DE STOCTUN resided at Stoctun, and in the 3rd of EDWARD III. HENRY DE STOCTUN had royal license to empark there 160 acres of land. In the early part of the sixteenth century, the family became divided into two branches. The elder division continued at Stoughton, and obtained a baronetcy, 29th Jan. 1660-1, which in 1691 became extinct on the death of Sir Laurence Stoughton, of Stoughton.‡ The younger branch, seating itself at St. John's, Warwick, a large and ancient mansion, originally the Hospital of St. John the Baptist,§ remained there for a series of years, maintaining a leading position in the county, until the male line expired with GEORGE STOUGHTON, esq. of St. John's, who left an elder daughter and heiress, EUGENIA, who *m.* JAMES MONEY, esq. and thus the representation of the Stoughtons, of St. Johns, has merged in the MONEYS.

*Arms of Stoughton*—Az. a cross engrailed erm.

* The Pohers came into England with the Conqueror, and John Le Poher is said, 43 EDWARD III. and 8 RICHARD II. to have held of the bishop half the manor of Wichenford, and was styled Lord of the Manor.—*Nash*, vol. ii. p. 458.

† A pedigree of the Stoughtons in the College of Arms, mentioned by Gwillym, places him here "Tempore Conquestoris."

‡ The mansion, called Stoughton Place, was situated on a delightful eminence near the middle of the manor. On the death of the last baronet, it was pulled down: the site is now a ploughed field of about six acres, with part of the ancient moats remaining, and is known by the name of the "Stoughton Gardens." In the church of Stoke, at the east end of the north aisle, is the Stoughton Chapel. There are many ancient monuments to the family, with quaint and interesting inscriptions.—*Manning's Surrey.*

§ The Hospital of St. John was founded temp. Henry II. by William, Earl of Warwick, for the reception of the houseless poor, and wandering stranger. It had, however, ceased to exist even prior to the general dissolution.—*Feild's Hist. of Warwick*, p. 55.

## VERNON-GRAHAM, OF HILTON PARK.

GRAHAM-VERNON, HENRY-CHARLES-EDWARD, esq. of Hilton Park, in the county of Stafford, succeeded his father in 1814, *m.* Maria, third daughter of George Cooke, esq. of Harefield Park, Middlesex, and by her, who died about 1827, and is buried at Geneva, has issue,

HENRY-CHARLES, who *m.* in 1828, Catherine, second daughter of R. Williams, esq. of Cardiff, in Glamorganshire, and has surviving issue,

Henry.

Maria.

Catherine.

William-Frederick, an officer in the army.

George-Augustus, also in the army.

Emma-Penelope.

## Lineage.

This is a branch of the noble family of Vernon, which assumed its surname from the town of Vernon, in Normandy, and was established in England by one of the companions in arms of the Conqueror.

Henry Vernon, esq. of Houndshill, *b.* in 1616, *m.* Muriel, daughter and heir of Sir George Vernon, of Haslington, one of the Judges of the Court of Common Pleas, and had issue,

- I. George, his heir, of Sudbury, *b.* in 1635, grandfather of George Vernon, esq. of Sudbury, who assumed, in 1728, the additional surname and arms of Venables, and was created in 1672, Lord Vernon, Baron of Kinderton, in the county Palatine of Chester.
- II. Edward, *b.* in 1636.
- III. Henry, of whom presently.

The third son,

Henry Vernon, esq. of Hilton, in the county of Stafford, *b.* in June, 1637, wedded Margaret, daughter of William Ladkins, esq. of Helledon, in Northamptonshire, and by her, who *d.* in 1699, had,

- I. Henry, his heir.
- II. Edward, of London, merchant.
- III. George, killed abroad.
- IV. Thomas, of London, *d.* unmarried, 4th April, 1742, aged seventy.

The eldest son,

Henry Vernon, esq. of Hilton, *m.* Penelope, second dau. and co-heir of Robert Phillips, esq. of Newton, in Warwickshire, and by her, who *d.* 25th January, 1726, and lies buried with her husband at Sharshil, had five sons and two daughters, namely,

- I. Henry, his heir.
- II. Thomas-Phillips, *b.* 20th November, 1719.
- III. John, *b.* 20th January, 1720, *d. s.p.*
- IV. Edward, *b.* in 1723.
- V. Richard, *b.* 18th June, 1725, married Evelyn, daughter of John Leveson, Earl Gower, and widow of John Fitzpatrick, Earl of Upper-Ossory.

- I. Penelope, *b.* 6th June, 1722, *m.* to Sir William Duckenfield Daniel, bart. of Over Tabley, in Cheshire.
- II. Elizabeth, *b.* 17th January, 1724, *d.* young.

Mr. Vernon was succeeded at his decease by his eldest son,

Henry Vernon, esq. of Hilton Park, *b.* 13th September, 1718, who *m.* in 1743, Lady Henrietta Wentworth, youngest daughter of Thomas, Earl of Strafford, and had issue,

- I. Henry, his heir.
- II. William.
- III. Leveson.

- I. Henrietta, *m.* first to Richard, Earl Grosvenor, and, secondly, to General George Porter, M.P. Her ladyship *d.* in 1828.
- II. Anne, *m.* to Lord Berwick.
- III. Lucy.
- IV. Caroline, maid of honour to Charlotte, Queen Consort of George III.
- V. Jane.

The eldest son.

Henry Vernon, esq. of Hilton Park, *m.* first, Penelope, daughter and co-heir of — Graham, esq. of Armagh, by whom he had twins, a daughter who died shortly after her birth, and a son,

Henry-Charles-Edward, his heir.

He wedded, secondly, Margaret, daughter of Thomas Fisher, esq. of Acton, and by her had two sons,

Frederick-William-Thomas, who inheriting Wentworth Castle, and other estates of his grandfather, the Earl of Strafford, assumed the surname of Wentworth, and is the present Frederick-William-Thomas-Vernon Wentworth, esq. of Wentworth Castle, (see vol. ii. p. 81.)

George, *d.* young.

Mr. Vernon *d.* in 1814, and was succeeded by his eldest son, the present Henry-Charles-Edward Vernon-Graham, esq. of Hilton Park.

*Arms*—Arg. a fret sa.

*Crest*—A boar's head erased sa. ducally gorged or.

*Estates*—In Staffordshire.

*Seat*—Hilton Park, in the same county.

# PRICKETT, OF OCTON LODGE.

PRICKETT, ROBERT, esq. of Octon Lodge, in the county of York, *m.* 17th July, 1798, Anne, daughter and sole heir of Samuel Salt, esq. of Tottenham, in Middlesex.

## Lineage.

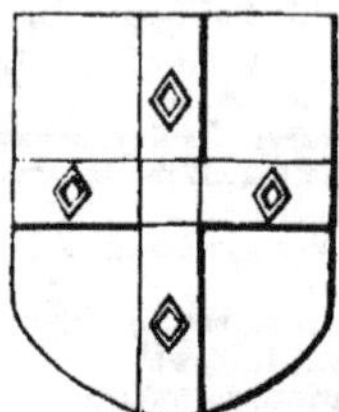

ROBERT PRICKETT, of Everingham, in the county of York, son of Marmaduke Prickett, sprung from Prickett of Natland, in Westmoreland, *m.* Margaret, daughter of Hugh Hindsley, of Woodhouse, in the parish of Sutton, and dying in the time of ELIZABETH, left a son,

MARMADUKE PRICKETT, of Allerthope, in Yorkshire, who *m.* Barbara, daughter of John Bew, of the city of York, and by her, who died in 1664, and was buried at Pocklington, had issue,

I. JOSIAS, his heir.
II. Robert, of Wressle Castle, Yorkshire, *m.* Mary, daughter of Marmaduke, first Lord Langdale, and dying in 1701, left two daughters, viz.
   Barbara, aged nine years 7th September, 1665, *m.* at St. Michael Spurriergate, York, 13th December, 1679, to Richard Lowther, esq. of Maulsmeaburn, in Westmoreland.
   Lenox, aged eight years 7th September, 1665, buried at Pocklington 17th November, 1673.
III. George, of York, serjeant-at-law; admitted of Gray's Inn, London, 15th June, 1656; chosen recorder of York 16th November, 1688; resigned 12th February, 1700; buried at St. Martin's, Coney Street, York; *m.* in 1665, Rebecca, daugh. of Leonard Thompson, some time lord mayor of the city of York, and had
   1. George, buried at St. Michael Spurriergate 11th December, 1673.
   2. Leonard, baptized 1667, buried 1673.
   3. Marmaduke, chosen recorder of the city of York 26th February, 1700; baptized at St. Michael, Coney Street, 7th June, 1670; *d.* 3rd March, 1712.
   4. Robert, baptized at St. Michael Spurriergate 1681, *d.* an infant.
   5. George, some time of the city of London, merchant, *b.* in 1687, *m.* Dorothy, daughter of Francis Langley, of York, and left an only surviving child,
      Marmaduke, M.D. of Trinity College, Cambridge, *d.* at Hull, unm. 1753.
   1. Frances, *m.* in 1699, to William Stainforth, esq. of Simonburn, in Northumberland.
   2. Barbara, died an infant.
   3. Mary, *b.* in 1676.
   4. Lenox, *b.* in 1681.
   5. Tabitha, *b.* in 1682, *m.* in 1719, to William Baynes, esq. of Kilburn, in Yorkshire.

Marmaduke Prickett died in 1652, was buried at Pocklington, and *s.* by his son,

JOSIAS PRICKETT, of Allerthorpe, aged thirty-nine 7th September, 1665, who *m.* at Lund, 14th June, 1660, Mary, daughter of Sir Thomas Remington, knt. of Lund, in the county of York, and had issue,

I. Marmaduke, baptized at Allerthorpe 14th June, 1662.
II Josias, baptized at Allerthorpe 5th March, 1666. He *d.* unm. in 1703.
III. THOMAS, of whom presently.
I. Hannah, baptized in 1669.
II. Rosamund, baptized in 1671.

The third son,

*The Rev.* THOMAS PRICKETT, vicar of Kilham, bapt. at Allerthorpe 17th August, 1668, *m.* Lucy Baines, of Ripon, in Yorkshire, and by her (who *d.* in 1739) had issue,

I. MARMADUKE, of Kilham, baptized there 12th March, 1699, *m.* Anne, daughter of Robert Simpson, of Kilham, and by her, who died 28th January, 1789, aged seventy-eight, left at his decease in 1765,
   1. MARMADUKE, of Bridlington, baptized at Kilham in 1733, *m.* 3rd December, 1763, Frances, only child of the Rev. William Buck, vicar of Church Fenton, in Yorkshire, and dying 21st October, 1809, left issue,

Marmaduke, of Bridlington, *b.* 11th February, 1766, *m.* 14th June, 1803, his cousin, Elizabeth, daughter of Paul Prickett, esq. and has issue,

Marmaduke, M. A. of Trinity College, Cambridge, in holy orders, *b.* 1st July, 1804.

Paul, *b.* 12th July, 1806, *d.* unm. in 1835.

Robert, *b.* 11th November, 1808.

Thomas, *b.* 24th January, 1814.

Anne, *m.* 16th May, 1833, to Adam Washington, esq. of Lincoln's Inn, barrister-at-law, and has issue.

Sarah.

Arthur, *m.* 10th September, 1810, Miss Jane Porter, of Driffield, and died 25th November, 1829, leaving an only son, Arthur, *b.* in 1811.

Dorothy-Anne, *m.* to William Reynolds, esq. of Whitby, in Yorkshire.

Diana, *m.* 27th April, 1812, to Isaac Wilson, of Hull.

Sophia, *d.* unm. in 1832.

2. Thomas, of York, captain in the 36th Foot, and some time governor of Fort William, in Kingston, Jamaica, baptized at Kilham 4th March, 1740-1, *m.* Sarah, only child of Hale Wyvill, esq. of the city of York, and *d. s. p.* February, 1832.
3. George, baptized 17th June, 1744, *d.* unm.
4. Josiah, of Hull, baptized at Kilham 18th January, 1746-7, *m.* 25th February, 1772, Sarah, daughter of William Hudson, esq. of Brigg, in Lincolnshire, and died 27th March, 1831, having had issue,

Marmaduke-Thomas, of Hull, *b.* 23rd October, 1774, *m.* 7th September, 1812, Anastasia, daughter of the Rev. John Armitstead, of Cranage Hall, in Cheshire, and has Josiah-John, George, Thomas, Catherine, Anastasia, and Frances.

George.

William.

Sarah-Anne, died young.

1. Mary, died unm.
2. Anne, *m.* to John Wallis, of York, and had issue.
3. Elizabeth, *m.* to Thomas Swann, of York.

II. Barnabas, of whom presently.

III. Robert, *b.* 4th May, 1703.

IV. George, died in infancy.

I. Elizabeth, buried in 1706.

II. Tabitha.

The Rev. Thomas Prickett *d.* 17th March, 1741-2. His second son,

Barnabas Prickett, esq. of Aubrough, in Holderness, baptized at Kilham 8th July, 1701, *m.* 18th September, 1722, Elizabeth, daughter of Thomas Harrison, esq. of Hunmanby, and left at his decease, with two daughters, Mary, *m.* to Thomas Whitfield, of Hull, and Catherine, a son,

Paul Prickett, esq. of London, who *m.* Sarah, only child of Robert Hunt, esq. of Send, in Surrey, and by her, who *d.* in 1826, had issue,

I. Robert, his heir.

I. Sarah, *m.* to Rowland Richardson, esq. of Streatham, in Surrey, and has issue. Mr. Richardson *d.* in May, 1806.

II. Anne.

III. Clare.

IV. Elizabeth, *m.* to her cousin, Marmaduke Prickett, esq. of Bridlington, and has issue.

Mr. Prickett *d.* 27th March, 1810, aged eighty-one, was buried at Woking, in Surrey, and *s.* by his son, the present Robert Prickett, esq. of Octon Lodge.

*Arms*—Or, on a cross az. quarter-pierced of the field, four mascles of the first.

*Estates*—In Yorkshire.

*Town Residence*—Harley Street.

*Seat*—Octon Lodge, near Sledmere.

## BROOKE, OF MERE.

BROOKE, PETER-LANGFORD, esq. of Mere, in the county palatine of Chester, *b.* 23rd April, 1793, *m.* 1st July, 1818, Elizabeth Sophia, eldest daughter of Vice-Admiral Sir Charles Rowley, K.C.B. and is a widower without issue.

Mr. Brooke, who succeeded his father 21st December, 1815, was formerly lieutenant-colonel of the first regiment of Cheshire yeomanry. He is a magistrate and deputy-lieutenant for that county, and served the office of sheriff in 1824-5.

## Lineage.

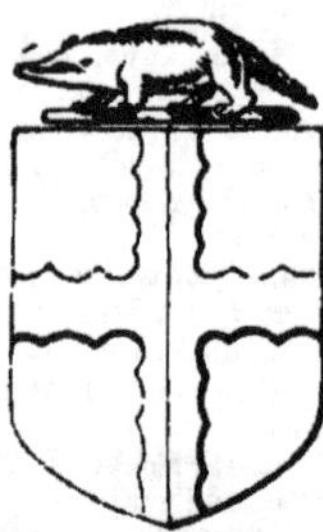

This is a branch of the very ancient family of BROOKE, of Norton.

THOMAS BROOKE, esq. of Norton, sheriff of Cheshire, in 1578 and 1592, (son of Richard Brooke, esq. of Norton, who was a younger son of Thomas Brooke, of Leighton,) married, first, Anne, daughter of Henry Lord Audley, and had by her,

I. RICHARD (Sir), knt. of Norton, ancestor of the present SIR RICHARD BROOKE, bart.
II. George, drowned in Warrington water.

I. Christian, married to Richard Starky, esq. of Stretton.
II. Eleanor, married to John Brooke, esq. of Buckland, in Staffordshire.
III. Margaret, *m.* to — Warburton.

He wedded, secondly, Elizabeth, sister of Thomas Merbury, esq. of Merbury, and by that lady had three sons and six daughters, viz.

I. William.
II. Thomas.
III. Valentine.

I. Townshend, *m.* to Thomas Legh, esq. of East Hall, in High Legh.
II. Elizabeth, *m.* to George Spurstow, esq. of Spurstow, in Cheshire.
III. Dorothy, *m.* to William Barnston, esq. of Churton.
IV. Frances, *m.* to George Legh, esq. of Barton, in Lancashire.
V. Anne, *m.* to Richard Merbury, esq. of Walton, in Cheshire.
VI. Clare, *m.* to Theophilus Legh, esq. of Grange, in Lancashire.

He espoused, thirdly, Eleanor Gerard, by whom he had, (with two daughters, Alice, *m.* to Thomas Birch, esq. of Birch, in Lancashire, and Elinour, to the Reverend William Assheton, rector of Middleton,) a son,

SIR PETER BROOKE, who purchased, in 1652, from John Mere, esq. the manor of Mere, and established himself there. He received the honour of knighthood in 1660, was M.P. for Cheshire, 8 CHARLES II. and high sheriff of that county in 1669. He married, first, Alice, daughter and heiress of Richard Hulse, esq. of Kenilworth; secondly, Frances, daughter of Sir Nicholas Trot, of Quickshot, Herts, widow of William Merbury, esq. of Merbury; and, thirdly, Mabell, daughter of William ffarington, esq. of Werden, widow of Richard Clayton, esq. of Crooke. Sir Peter's two last wives died *s. p.* but by his first he had two sons, viz.

THOMAS, his heir.
Richard, living in 1684, who *m.* Margaret, daughter and heiress of Robert Charnock, esq. of Charnock, in Lancashire, and was ancestor of the BROOKES, of ASTLEY, in that county.

Sir Peter, who rebuilt and beautified the Hall of Mere, was succeeded at his decease by his son,

THOMAS BROOKE, esq. of Mere, who married two wives; by the second, who was a daughter of Grimsdich, of Grimsdich, he had no issue, but, by the first, Margaret, daughter and heiress of Henry Brereton, esq. of Eccleston, (marriage covenant dated 23rd September, 1662,) he had, with two daughters, one of whom married a gentleman named Allen, his son and successor,

PETER BROOKE, esq. of Mere, who married Elizabeth, daughter and co-heiress of Peter Venables, esq. of Over-street, and left (with two daughters, Margaret, and Elizabeth the wife of Thomas Ravenscroft, esq. of Pickhill, in Flintshire,) a son and successor,

PETER BROOKE, esq. of Mere, high sheriff of Cheshire in 1728, who married Frances, only daughter and heiress of Francis Holinshead, esq. of Wheelock, by Felicia, his wife, daughter of William Lawton, esq. of Lawton, and by her, (who *d.* 23rd May, 1777, aged seventy-nine, and was buried at Rosthorne,) had issue,

PETER, his heir.
John, died, unmarried, 29th March, 1780, aged forty-nine, and was buried at Rosthorne.

Felicia, *m.* to George Heron, esq. purchaser of the Manor of Daresbury.
Elizabeth, *m.* to the Rev. Thomas Patten, D.D. rector of Childrey, in Berkshire (see p. 82).
Frances, died unm.

Mr. Brooke died 31st December, 1764, aged

sixty-nine, was buried at Rosthorne, and *s.* by his son,

PETER BROOKE, esq. of Mere, high sheriff of Cheshire in 1706, who *m.* first, Anne-Meriel, daughter of Fleetwood Legh, esq. of Lyme, by Meriel, his wife, daughter and heiress of Sir Francis Leicester, bart. of Tabley, which lady dying issueless in 1740, aged twenty-one, he wedded, secondly, Elizabeth, daughter and heiress of Jonas Langford, esq. of Antigua, and by her, (who died 15th December, 1809, aged seventy-five,) had issue,

JONAS-LANGFORD, his heir.
THOMAS-LANGFORD, successor to his brother.

Elizabeth, *m.* to Randle Ford, esq. barrister-at-law.
Frances, *m.* to Thomas Oliver, esq.
Jane, *m.* first, to William Hulton, esq. of Hulton Park, and, secondly, to William Tyrell Boyce, esq.

Mr. Brooke died 4th January, 1783, aged sixty, was buried at Rosthorne, and *s.* by his son,

JONAS LANGFORD BROOKE, esq. of Mere, who *d.* unmarried at Milan, eighteen months after his father, and was *s.* by his brother,

THOMAS LANGFORD BROOKE, esq. of Mere, who *m.* Maria, daughter of the Reverend Sir Thomas Broughton, bart. of Broughton and Doddington, and had issue,

I. PETER-LANGFORD, his heir.
II. Thomas-Langford, *m.* in 1817, Eliza, daughter of John W. Clough, esq. of Oxton House, Yorkshire.
III. William-Henry-Langford.
IV. Jonas-Langford.

I. Maria-Elizabeth, widow of Meyrick Bankes, esq. late of Winstanley Hall, Lancashire.
II. Jemima, *m.* to Colonel Sir Jeremiah Dickson, K.C.B.

Mr. Brooke *d.* 21st December, 1815, and was *s.* by his eldest son, the present PETER-LANGFORD BROOKE, esq. of Mere.

*Arms*—Or, a cross engrailed party per pale gu. and sa. quarterly with LANGFORD.

*Crest*—A badger passant ppr.

*Motto*—Vis unita fortior.

*Estates*—In Cheshire.

*Seat*—Mere Hall.

## CORBET, OF SUNDORNE.

CORBET, ANDREW-WILLIAM, esq. of Sundorne Castle, in the county of Salop, *b.* 22nd September, 1801, *m.* 14th June, 1823, Mary-Emma, daughter of John Hill, esq. and sister of Sir Rowland Hill, bart. of Hawkestone. Mr. Corbett succeeded his father 19th May, 1817.

### Lineage.

This is a principal branch of the great Norman family, whose ancestor, ROGER CORBET, accompanied WILLIAM I. to the Conquest of England, and of whose earlier descendants an account is given at page 189 of the second volume of this work, in treating of Corbett, of Elsham.

It is there stated that Roger Corbet, the companion of the Conqueror, held twenty-four manors in Shropshire, and one in Montgomeryshire, under his kinsman Roger de Montgomery, Earl of Shrewsbury. His extensive possessions comprised, in the above manors, that of Worthen, and his descendants, in the line of which we are now about to treat, continued to possess a considerable estate at Leigh, in the manor of Worthen, down to the eighteenth century.

WILLIAM CORBET, the eldest son of Roger, was seated at Wattlesborough. His second son,

SIR ROBERT CORBET, knt. had for his inheritance the castle and estates of Caus, with a large portion of his father's domains. He was father of

ROBERT CORBET, also of Caus Castle, who accompanied RICHARD I. to the siege of Acre, and then bore for arms (according to an old roll, which, in 1563, was in the possession of Hugh Fitzwilliam, esq. of Sprotsburgh, an eminent antiquary,) the two ravens, as now borne by all his descendants.

In 1223,

THOMAS CORBET, son of the last-named Robert, made an agreement with *King* HENRY II. to pay 100*l.* (a sum equal to about 3000*l.* of modern currency,) for his relief, according to the feudal tenures of that period, for the lands descended to him from his father. This Thomas Corbet was sheriff of Shropshire in 1249; in 1270 he was a donor to the abbey of Shrewsbury, and in 1272 he founded the chapel of St. Margaret, in Caus. He married Isabel, sister and coheir of Reginald de Valletort, Baron of Trematon Castle, in Cornwall, and widow of Alan de Dunstanville, by whom he had issue, Peter, his only son, and two daughters, Alice, married to Robert de Stafford, Baron of Stafford, and Emme, wife of Sir Brian de Brampton, of Brampton Brian.* He died in 1274, and was *s.* by his son,

PETER CORBET, who, it appears, was "a mighty hunter," for, in the ninth year of *King* EDWARD I. he obtained letters patent from the sovereign, authorizing him to take wolves in all the royal forests in various counties, a proof of the falsehood of the common belief that our island is indebted to the exertions of *King* EDGAR for the extirpation of that savage beast of prey. This Peter Corbet, of Caus, had summons to Parliament, as one of the barons of the realm, from the 22nd of EDWARD I. to his death in 1300. By Alice, his wife, he had three sons, Thomas, Peter, and John. THOMAS CORBET, the eldest son, married Joan, daughter of Alan Plukenet, and died in the lifetime of his father, without issue.

PETER CORBET, the second son, succeeding his father in the estates of his family, joined with Harry de la Pomeroy, in petitioning Parliament for the domains of the Valletort family, to which estates they were now become the heirs; but, as *King* EDWARD II. had himself been found, by inquisition, to be heir to the Earl of Cornwall, the grantee of "Roger de Vauter," the last of the Valletorts who possessed the estates, the petitioners did not find favour in their suit. This Peter Corbet had also summons to Parliament, as Baron Corbet, of Caus, until his death on the 26th May, 1322. He died without issue, and the line of his family was continued by the youngest of the three brothers,

JOHN CORBET, who, by one inquisition, was found to succeed his brother in the Barony of Caus, being then forty-two years of age, and, as soon as EDWARD II. mounted the throne, in 1327, he and Pomeroy revived the suit respecting the Valletort estates, but without success: indeed, John Corbet appears, owing to some circumstances at this distant date not to be ascertained, to have been deprived of a large portion of his family inheritance, for the demesne of Caus, with other estates, became the possessions of the heirs of his aunts Stafford and Brampton. The estates of *Leigh*, otherwise "*Leighton in Walcheria*," being on the confines of Powis Land, in the Marches of Wales, with the chief bailiwick of all his forest, had, however, been granted to John, by Peter, his father, and Peter, brother of John, also granted to Roger, his nephew (son of John), the forestership which his father previously held. In the Leigh estate, John Corbet was *s.* by his son,

ROGER CORBET, who, by the name of Roger Corbet, of "Legh juxta Caus," was returned as one of the knights of the shire for the county of Salop, in the seventeenth year of EDWARD II. his father being then living. This Roger Corbet was *s.* at Leigh by his son,

ROGER CORBET, who appears to have received the honour of knighthood, for in the inquisition taken on his death in the nineteenth year of RICHARD II. 1396, he is styled "Sir Roger Corbet," of Leigh, and the title "knight," is there added. His son,

PETER CORBET, esq. of Leigh, was father of

THOMAS CORBET, esq. of Leigh, sheriff of Shropshire in the year 1427, whose son,

THOMAS CORBET, esq. succeeded to the Leigh estate, and was father of

ROGER CORBET, esq. of Leigh, who, by his wife, Maria, had issue,

THOMAS CORBET, esq. of Leigh. He *s.*

---

* Alice's great grandson,

EDMUND DE STAFFORD, was summoned to parliament as a BARON in 1299, and from him descended in the male line the *extinct* DUKES OF BUCKINGHAM, and in the female the house of Jerningham, now enjoying a barony of Stafford, conferred by CHARLES I. in 1640 on Sir William Howard and his wife, MARY STAFFORD.

Emme's great-grand-daughters, co-heirs of their father, Sir Bryan de Brampton, were

MARGARET DE BRAMPTON, wife of Robert Harley, ancestor of the Earls of Oxford.

ELIZABETH DE BRAMPTON, wife of Edmund de Cornwall.

—BURKE'S *Extinct Peerage.*

Jane, daughter of Sir John Burleigh, knt. of Bromscroft, county of Salop, and their son,

PETER CORBET, esq. of Leigh, married Elizabeth, daughter of Sir William Brereton, knt. of Malpas. By this lady he had issue,

THOMAS CORBET, esq. of Leigh, who m. Jane, daughter of Sir Roger Kynaston, knt. of Middle, and their son,

JOHN CORBET, esq. of Leigh, was sheriff of Shropshire in 1526, and in that year he became an honorary member of the Draper's Company in Shrewsbury, on whose books his admission is thus recorded: "8 June, 18 Hen. VIII. 1526, John Corbet, squyer, and lord of Ly, ys become a broder of the fraternyte, and hath graunted to pay the company yerly a buk of season, and a galon of wyn at his entre." The Company of Drapers is the most wealthy, and was always the most powerful of the ancient corporate guilds in Shrewsbury, and the present commander-in-chief, Lord Hill, is now an honorary member of this guild. John Corbet, esq. was thrice married, first, to Joyce, sister of Sir John Packington, knt. secondly, to Margaret, daughter of Sir Thomas Blount, knt. and, lastly, to Agnes, daughter of William Booth, esq. of Dunham. By his second wife he left issue,

WILLIAM CORBET, esq. of Leigh, who m. Alice, daughter of Thomas Lacon, esq. of Willey, county of Salop, and was s. by his son,

THOMAS CORBET, esq. of Leigh, who married Elinor, daughter of Thomas Williams, esq. of Willaston, in Shropshire, and left a son and successor,

WILLIAM CORBET, esq. of Leigh, father, by Anne, his wife, daughter of Sir William Pelham, knt. of

PELHAM CORBET, esq. of Leigh and Adbright Hussey, in the county of Salop, who wedded Anne, daughter of Sir Andrew Corbet, knt. of Moreton Corbet, and was s. by his son,

ROBERT CORBET, esq. of Leigh and Adbright Hussey, b. in 1629, an officer of the royalist forces, under the Lord Newport. This gentleman removed from Leigh, and resided at Adbright Hussey. He m. Elizabeth, daughter of Roger Kynaston, esq. of Hordley, and dying in May, 1689, was s. by his son,

ROGER CORBET, esq. of Adbright Hussey, and Leigh, b. in 1672, who married Elizabeth, dau. of Sir Francis Edwardes, bart. and was s. by his son,

ANDREW CORBET, esq. of Adbright Hussey, who inherited, in 1740, by the devise of his kinsman, Corbet Kynaston, esq. the Sundorne and other extensive estates in Shropshire. Dying s.p. 15th April, 1741, aged thirty-two, he was s. by his brother,

JOHN CORBET, esq. of Sundorne, Adbright Hussey, &c. who sold the ancient patrimony of Leigh. He m. first, Frances, daughter of Robert Pigott, esq. of Chetwynd, by Frances, his wife, dau. of the Hon. William Ward, and, secondly, Barbara-Letitia, daughter of John Mytton, esq. of Halston. By the latter he had issue,

JOHN, his heir.
Andrew, a lieutenant-col. in the army.
Mary-Elizabeth, m. to Sir John Kynaston Powell, bart. whom she survives, and is now resident in Shrewsbury.

Mr. Corbet died in 1759, and was s. by his son,

JOHN CORBET, esq. of Sundorne, M.P. for Shrewsbury, from 1774 to 1780, and high-sheriff of Salop in 1793. He m. first, Emma-Elizabeth, daughter of Sir Charlton Leighton, bart. and by her, who died 19th September, 1797, had one son and one daughter, viz.

John-Kynaston, died 22nd April, 1806, aged fifteen.
Emma, m. to Sir Richard Puleston, bart. 19th February, 1800.

He wedded, secondly, Anne,* second daughter of the Rev. William Pigott, of Edgmond, in Salop (see page 193), and had issue,

ANDREW-WILLIAM, his heir.
Dryden-Robert.
Vincent.
Kynaston.
Annabella.

Mr. Corbet died 19th May, 1817, aged sixty-five, and was s. by his eldest surviving son, the present ANDREW-WILLIAM CORBET, esq. of Sundorne Castle.

*Arms*—Or, two ravens in pale ppr.

*Crest*—An elephant-and-castle ppr.

*Motto*—Deus pascit corvos.

*Estates*—Sundorne, Adbright Hussey, Uffington, Houghmond, Demesne, &c. &c. in the county of Salop.

*Seat*—Sundorne Castle, near Shrewsbury.

---

* This lady is great grandaughter of Robert Pigott, esq. of Chetwynd Park, by Frances, his wife, daughter of the Hon. William Ward, of Willingsworth, son of Humble, first Lord Ward, of Birmingham, and of the Baroness Dudley; and lineally descended from *King* HENRY VII. through his youngest daughter, Mary, widow of Louis XII. King of France, remarried to Charles Branden, Duke of Suffolk.

# ADAMS, OF HOLYLAND,

**ADAMS, JOHN,** esq. of Holyland, in Pembrokeshire, married 24th July, 1828, Anne, eldest daughter of the late Henry Gibbons, esq. of Oswestry, and has issue,

JOHN-ALEXANDER-PHILIPPS, born 10th January, 1831.
Henry, born in September, 1835.
Augusta-Mary.

Mr. Adams succeeded to the estates on the demise of his father.

## Lineage.

This is a very ancient Pembrokeshire family. The first recorded ancestor,

NICHOLAS ADAMS, or ADAMES, was of Buckspool, about the year 1370. His son and successor,

JOHN ADAMS, marrying Ellen, one of the co-heiresses of David de Paterchurch, became seated at Paterchurch, where his descendants continued to reside. He was father of

WILLIAM ADAMS, of Paterchurch, who *m.* Alice, daughter of Sir William Herbert, knt. Steward of Pembroke, and had, with a dau. Catharine, *m.* to David Bassett, of Gellyswick, a son and successor,

WILLIAM ADAMS, esq. of Paterchurch, who married Maude, daughter of Sir William Perrott, knt. and had two sons, namely,

JOHN, his heir.
Thomas, of Lyfeston, or Loveston, who *m.* Elizabeth, daughter and co-heir of Thomas Watkins, esq. of Henllan, and had issue,
John, who *m.* first, Mary Powell, and secondly, Anne, daughter of John ap David, ap Gwylim, ap Rhys, esq. By the former he left one son and three daughters, namely,
1. Thomas, who *m.* Elizabeth, daughter of Mr. Alderman George Carne, of Haverfordwest.
1. Margaret, *m.* to Thomas Lloyd, esq. of Killykeithed.
2. Elizabeth, married to John Adams, esq.
3. Lucy.
By his second wife John Adams had,
1. John, living in 1591.
1. Anne.
2. Elizabeth.
3. Catherine.
4. Penelope.
5. Mary.

The elder son of William Adams,

JOHN ADAMS, esq. of Paterchurch, represented the Borough of Pembroke in parliament, 33 HENRY VIII. He *m.* Catherine, daughter of Thomas ap David Goch ap Meredyth ap Madoc, Lord of Stapylton, and left a son and successor,

HENRY ADAMS, esq. of Paterchurch, who sat in parliament for Pembroke, in the 1st and 7th EDWARD VI. and 1st MARY, and was high sheriff of the county. He *m.* Anne, daughter of Richard Wogan, esq. of Boulston, by Maud, his wife, daughter of Sir Thomas Philipps, knt. and had issue,

I. JOHN, who *m.* Dorothy, daughter of Francis Laugharne, esq. and had a daughter Anne, the wife of Richard Phillipps, esq. of Rishmoor.
II. NICHOLAS, of whom presently.
III. David.
IV. William, died *s.p.*
V. Thomas, who *m.* Mary Powell, dau. of Sir William ap John.

I. Anne, *m.* James ap Rhys, 1613.
II. Catherine.

III. Frances, *m.* to Francis Laugharne, esq. in 1608.
IV. Maud, *m.* to Henry Stephen, esq.
V. Jane, *m.* to Richard Peny, esq.

The second son,

NICHOLAS ADAMS, esq. M.P. for Pembroke, 31 ELIZABETH, wedded Elizabeth, daughter of Morgan Powell, esq. and had, with other issue, a son and successor,

WILLIAM ADAMS, esq. of Paterchurch, who *m.* Frances Marsh, of the Isle of Wight, and was *s.* by his son,

NICHOLAS ADAMS, esq. of Paterchurch, who *m.* first, Frances, daughter of Rhys Bowen, esq. of Upton Castle, by whom he had one child, Rhys, and secondly, Hester, daughter of Sir Roger Lort, knt. of Stackpool Court, by whom he left a son,

ROGER ADAMS, esq. who *m.* Jane, daughter of — Skyrme, esq. of Lawhadden, and was father of

WILLIAM ADAMS, esq. of Holyland, in Pembrokeshire, who *m.* Philippa, daughter of Charles Philipps, esq. of Haythog, by Philippa, his second wife, daughter of Rowland Laugharne, esq. of St. Brides, and had issue,

I. WILLIAM, his heir.
II. John.
III. John-Philipps, a major in the army.
IV. Roger.

I. Philippa, who *m.* Bulkeley Philipps, esq. of Abercover, in the county of Carmarthen, and left an only dau.
   MARY-PHILIPPA-ARTEMISIA PHILIPPS, who *m.* James Child, esq. of Bigelly, in Pembrokeshire, and had an only child,
      MARY-PHILIPPA-ARTEMISIA CHILD, who wedded John Grant, esq. of Nolton, and had a son,
         RICHARD-BULKELEY-PHILIPPS GRANT, who, having assumed the surname of Philipps, and being created a baronet, is the present Sir Richard-Bulkeley-Philipps Philipps, of Picton Castle.

II. Dorothy.
III. Anne-Laugharne.
IV. Anne.
V. Elizabeth, twin with Roger.
VI. Mary, *m.* to Griffith Meare, esq.
VII. Jane.

Mr. Adams was succeeded at his decease by his eldest son,

WILLIAM ADAMS, esq. of Holyland, who *m.* Anne, second daughter of Joseph Rickson, esq. and had issue,

I. JOHN-PHILIPPS, his heir.
II. Joseph, major in the army, who *m.* Elizabeth, daughter of John Campbell, esq. of Stackpool Court, and was father of
   Lieutenant-General Alexander Adams, who *m.* Frances-Louisa, daughter of the Reverend William Holcombe, canon of St. David's.
III. Roger.

I. Anne, *m.* first, to the Reverend William Thomas, and, secondly, to Matthew Campbell, esq. son of J. H. Campbell, esq. of Bangeston, Lion King at Arms.

The eldest son,

JOHN PHILIPPS ADAMS, esq. of Holyland, a deputy-lieutenant for Pembrokeshire, *m.* Charlotte, daughter of William Corbet, esq. of Darnhall, in Cheshire (see. p. 191), and left two sons, JOHN and William. The elder,

JOHN ADAMS, esq. of Holyland, *m.* Sophia, daughter of the Venerable Archdeacon Holcombe, and left, with a daughter, Augusta, married to Vaughan Lloyd, esq. lieutenant R.N. a son and successor, the present JOHN ADAMS, esq. of Holyland.

*Arms*—Quarterly 1st and 4th arg. a cross gu. thereon five mullets or (DE PATERCHURCH) 2nd and 3rd sa, a martlet arg. (the ancient arms of ADAMS).
*Crest*—A martlet arg.
*Estates*—In Pembrokeshire.
*Seat*—Holyland, near Pembroke.

## MEYRICK, OF BODORGAN.

MEYRICK-FULLER, OWEN-JOHN-AUGUSTUS, esq. of Bodorgan, in Anglesey, *b.* 13th July, 1804. This gentleman, whose patronymic is FULLER, succeeded to the estates of his maternal grandfather, and assumed in consequence, by royal license, the surname and arms of MEYRICK. He is a deputy-lieutenant, and was high-sheriff for the county of Anglesey in 1827.

## Lineage.

In lineal descent from MRIEN, Lord of Rheged, was

CADAVAL YNAD, judge of the Court of Powis, who lived in the reign of JOHN, *King* of England, and was an especial favorite of Llewelyn, Prince of Wales. There is a tradition that this Cadaval gave notice of the approach of an English army in the night time, by running from mountain to mountain with a ragged staff fired, and that the Prince of Powys, in recompense, granted him the firebrands in his arms. He *m.* Rhyangen, or Arianwen, daughter and heir of Jerwerth ap Trahaern, Lord of the district of Cydywain, and had two sons, namely,

SAMUEL, his heir.
Hywel ap Cadaval, who *m.* Annes, dau. of Grufydd ap Einiawn ddistain and had an only daughter and heiress,
Gwenllian, *m.* to Dolphin ap Rhywallon.

The elder son,

SAMUEL AP CADAVAL, Lord of Cydywain, *m.* Eigu, daughter and co-heir of Madoc ap Cadwallon ap Madoc ap Idnerth, Lord of Maclenydd, and left a son and successor,

MADOC AP SAMUEL, who sold Cydywain to his brother-in-law, Rotpert ap Llywarch. He *m.* Eva, daughter of Meredydd Vychan ap Meredydd, and was succeeded by his son,

TUDUR AP MADOC, who *m.* Nest, daughter and heir of Tudur ap Llewelyn ap Cadwallon ap Hywel ap Owain Gwynedd, Prince of North Wales, and was father of

JERWERTH AP TUDUR, who *m.* Agnes Wen, daughter and sole-heir of Robin Vychan ap Robin gôch, of Caergybi, in Anglesea, and had three sons, namely, DAVID, his heir, Cadwgan ap Jerwerth, of Bettws y Wyriol gôch, and Gronw ap Jerwerth, of Caernarvon Mercht.

The eldest son,

DAVYDD AP JERWERTH, of Caergybi, or Holyhead, *m.* Sioned, daughter of David ap Jerwerth gôch, of Llechwedd Issa, and had two sons, the younger, Rhys ap Davydd, *m.* Sionedd, daughter of John Bwld, of Rhiwarthen; the elder,

EINIAWN SAIS AP DAVID, Usher of the Palace at Sheen, *temp.* HENRY V. and HENRY VI. acquired the appellation of *Sais* by serving with the English in the wars of the former monarch, from whom he had an augmentation to his arms: viz. sa. on a chev. arg. between three staves raguly or, fired ppr. a fleur-de-lys gu. between two choughs respecting each other ppr. He wedded Eva, daughter and heiress of Meredydd ap Cadwgan, of BODORGAN, descended from Llywarch Bran, chief of one of the fifteen tribes of North Wales, and had issue,

HEYLIN, his heir.
Rhys ap Einiawn, of Llechwedd issa.
Sion ap Einiawn, of Caergybi.
Jockyn ap Einiawn, *m.* Jane, daughter of Rhys ap Meredydd Vychan, and had issue.

The eldest son,

HEYLIN ap EINIAWN, esq. of Bôdorgan, was living 4 EDWARD IV. (1465) as appears by a deed of that date still preserved at Bôdorgan. He *m.* Angharad, daughter of Hywel ap Ithel ap Tudur, esq. and had (with a daughter, Alson, *m.* to Jenkin ap Sienkin ap Fifion, of Plâs Côch) a son and successor,

LLEWELYN AP HEYLIN, esq. of Bôdorgan, who *m.* Angharad, daughter of Gwilym ap Grufydd ap Davydd, esq. descended from Owain Gwynedd, and had issue,

I. GRUFYDD AP LLEWELYN, of Llangadwalader, *m.* Sioned, dau. of Gronwy ap Tydyr, esq. and had issue.
II. Edmund, parson of Eglwyseg.
III. MEURIC, of whom presently.
IV. Gylym, who married and had four sons. The eldest had a natural son, named Richard Meyric, *b.* in 1544.
V. David.
VI. Resiart.

I. Sioned, *m.* to Thomas ap Davydd, of Bôdwinau, and had issue.

The third son,

MEURIC AP LLEWELYN, of Bôdorgan, was esquire of the body to HENRY VIII. He *m.* Margaret, daughter of Rowland ap Hywel, esq. of Caer Ceiliog, and had seven sons and three daughters, namely,

I. RICHARD, his heir.
II. Rowland, Bishop of Bangor (see MEYRICK, of Goodrich Court).

iii. William, *d. s. p.*
iv. Owain, *d. s. p.*
v. John, first a captain in the navy, and subsequently a clergyman, married Sage, daughter of James ap Grufyd ap Hywel, and had issue.
vi. Reynallt, rector of Llanllechyd, in 1561, *m.* Elizabeth, daughter of Richard Pryse, esq. of Gogerddan, in the county of Cardigan, and had issue.
vii. Edmund, LL.D. Archdeacon of Bangor, who *m.* three wives, and had issue. His will is dated 23rd October, 1605.

i. Alice, *m.* to Thomas Bulkeley, of Beaumaris.
ii. Agnes, *m.* first, to Thomas Mathias, and, secondly, to Philip Yonge.
iii. Sioned, *m.* to David Thomas.

Meuric ap Llewelyn (whose will bears date 30th November, 1538,) was succeeded at his decease by his eldest son,

Richard Meyrick, esq. of Bôdorgan, who *m.* Jane, daughter of Llewelyn ap Rhys, esq. and had a son and successor,

Richard Meyrick, esq. of Bôdorgan, father by Margaret, his wife, daughter of Rys Wyn, esq. of

Richard Meyrick, esq. of Bôdorgan, in 1594. This gentleman wedded Jane, dau. of John Wyn, esq. and was succeeded by his son,

Richard Meyrick, esq. of Bôdorgan, who *m.* Jane, daughter of Owen Wood, esq. of Rhôsmor, and left a son,

William Meyrick, esq. of Bôdorgan, who *m.* Jane, daughter of William Bold, esq. of Tre'rddol, and their son,

Owen Meyrick, esq. of Bôdorgan, represented the county of Anglesey in parliament in 1715. He *m.* Ann, daughter of Piers Lloyd, esq. of Lligwy, and was father of

Owen Meyrick, esq. of Bôdorgan, M.P. for Anglesey in 1766. He *m.* Miss Hester Putland, of London, and was succeeded by his son,

Owen Putland Meyrick, esq. of Bôdorgan, who *m.* in 1774, Clara, eldest daughter and heiress of Richard Garth, esq. of Morden, in Surrey, (see page 558) and was *s.* at his decease by his grandson, the present Owen-John-Augustus Fuller-Meyrick, esq. of Bôdorgan, who is the eldest son of Augustus Eliott Fuller,* esq. of Rose Hill, Sussex, by Clara, his wife, eldest daughter and co-heiress of Owen Putland Meyrick, esq.

*Arms*—Sa. on a chev. arg. between three brands erect, raguly or, inflamed ppr. a fleur-de-lys gu. between two Cornish choughs respecting each other, also ppr. Quarterly with Fuller.

*Crest*—A tower arg. thereon upon a mount vert a Cornish chough ppr. holding in the dexter claw a fleur-de-lys gu.

*Motto*—Heb Dduw heb ddim Dduw a digon.

*Estates*—In Anglesey.

*Seat*—Bôdorgan.

* See family of Fuller.

## MEYRICK, OF GOODRICH COURT.

**MEYRICK, SIR SAMUEL-RUSH,** knt. of Goodrich Court, in the county of Hereford, Doctor of Laws of the University of Oxford, Fellow of the Society of Antiquaries, Advocate in the Ecclesiastical and Admiralty Courts, and Knight Companion of the Royal Hanoverian Guelphic Order, born 26th August, 1783, married 3rd October, 1803, Mary, daughter and co-heiress of James Parry, of Llwyn Hywel, in the county of Cardigan, brother of Thomas Parry, esq. of Llidiade, and has one son,

Llewelyn, born 27th June, 1804, LL.B. of the University of Oxford, F.S.A. &c. succeeded to the property of his grandfather, John Meyrick, esq. of Peterborough House, which estate he joined with his grandmother in selling, in 1807.

Sir Samuel, who is a magistrate and deputy-lieutenant for the county of Hereford, served the office of high sheriff for that shire in 1834.

## Lineage.

This is a branch of the ancient family of MEYRICK, of Bôdorgan.

The *Right Reverend* ROWLAND MEYRICK, second son of Meuric ap Llewelyn, of Bôdorgan, esquire of the body to HENRY VII. VIII.) was Bishop of Bangor in 1559, and one of the Council of the Marches of Wales. He married in 1554, Catherine, daughter of Owen Barrett, esq. of Gellyswick, in the county of Pembroke, and by her (who died in 1598), had issue,

- I. GELLY, (Sir) his heir.
- II. Francis, (Sir) knt. of Monkton, in Pembrokeshire, ancestor of the MEYRICKS, of Bush, in Pembrokeshire. His son, Sir John Meyrick, of Monkton, M.P. was serjeant-major-general to the parliament's army, commanded by the Earl of Essex, and member for Newcastle-under-Lyne, in the Long Parliament. He *m.* first, Alice, daughter of Sir Edward Fitton, of Gawsworth, and, secondly, Jane, dau. of William Meredith, esq. of Wrexham, widow of Sir Peter Wyche, knt.
- III. Henry, in holy orders, who *m.* Jane, daughter of Rhys Bowen, esq. of Upton, in Pembrokeshire.
- IV. John, of Pembroke, whose will bears date 1634.

- I. Catherine, *m.* to Richard Mortimer, esq.
- II. Jane, *m.* two husbands, John Toy, esq. of Caermarthen, and John Herbert, esq.

The Bishop of Bangor died in 1563, and was *s.* by his son,

SIR GELLY MEYRICK, who was knighted at Cadiz, in 1596, and through the influence of Robert, Earl of Essex, obtained from *Queen* ELIZABETH, a grant of Wigmore Castle, in Herefordshire, together with a dozen surrounding manors. Having, however, assisted Essex, in what was called his rebellion, Sir Gelly was attainted and executed in 1600, when his estates became vested in the crown, and were bestowed upon Mr. Harley, of Brampton Brian. He married Elizabeth, daughter of Ievan Lewis, esq. of Gladestry, in Radnorshire, and widow of John Gwynne, esq. of Llanelwedd, in the county of Brecon, and by her, who died in 1625, had issue,

ROWLAND, his heir.

Margaret, *m.* to John Vaughan, Earl of Carberry, and had issue.

Sir Gelly's only son,

ROWLAND MEYRICK, esq. of Gladestry, was, with his sister, the Countess of Carberry, restored in blood by act of parliament, on the accession of JAMES I. and acted as a justice of the peace in 1620. He *m.* Elizabeth, daughter and co-heir of Thomas Blundeville, esq. of Newton Flotman, in the county of Norfolk, and had issue,

Blundeville, bapt. at Newton Flotman, in 1610.

GELLY, his heir.

Rowland, baptized at Newton Flotman, in 1613, buried there, 11th June, 1615.

Francis, baptized at Newton Flotman, 2nd February, 1614, buried there 13th December, 1615.

Margaret, baptized at Newton Flotman, 2nd July, 1617, married to — Norris, esq.

Rowland Meyrick was *s.* by his son,

GELLY MEYRICK, esq. of Gladestry, mentioned in his grandmother's will. He was captain in his uncle's regiment, 1645, and was succeeded at his decease by his eldest son,

JAMES MEYRICK, esq. of Herefordshire, mentioned in the will of his sister-in-law, *anno* 1660. He was father of

JAMES MEYRICK, esq. of Covenhope, in the county of Hereford, whose will is dated at Hereford, in 1719. He *m.* Elizabeth, daughter of John Edwards, esq. of Rorrington, in Shropshire, and had two sons, JAMES, his heir, and John, who *m.* Elizabeth, dau. of — Palmer, of Shobdon, and died at Lucton, in 1720. The elder son,

JAMES MEYRICK, esq. of Eyton Court and Lucton, in Herefordshire, a captain in the army, died in 1749, leaving, by Elizabeth, his wife, who was buried in Eyton church, in 1761, a daughter, Margaret, the wife of — Simmons, and two sons, of whom the elder,

JAMES MEYRICK, esq. baptized at Lucton, in 1718, married two wives, by the first, Mary-Ann Whigges, he had two sons and two daughters, viz.

- I. JAMES, of Wimbledon, Surrey, F.R.S. and S.A. esquire of the Bath, in 1788, and a deputy-lieutenant, and justice of the peace. He *m.* Anne, daughter of Benjamin Whitelock, esq. but died in 1818, *s. p.*
- II. JOHN, of whom presently.

- I. Elizabeth, *m.* to James Trotter, esq. of Horton Place, Surrey, and died in 1819.
- II. Mary, married to Samuel Waring,

esq. of Ludlow, Salop, and died in 1804.

By his second wife, Martha, he had three other sons and two daughters,

I. Thomas, a general officer in the army, who *m.* Elizabeth, natural daughter and heiress of Admiral Lord Keppel, and by her, who died in 1828, left at his decease in 1830, a son, the present

WILLIAM-HENRY MEYRICK, esq. lieutenant-colonel 3rd regiment of foot-guards, born in 1790, *m.* 24th February, 1823, Lady Laura Vane, third dau. of the Duke of Cleveland, and has a son, Augustus-William-Henry, and other children.

II. George, a lieutenant-general in the army.

III. William, of Red Lion Square, London.

I. Caroline, *m.* to John Lee, esq. of Retford.

II. Martha-Sillard, *d.* unm.

Mr. Meyrick died in 1778, and was buried at St. Margaret, Westminster. His second son,

JOHN MEYRICK, esq. of Great George Street, Westminster, and of Peterborough House, Middlesex, F.S.A. was a magistrate and deputy-lieutenant for that county, and colonel of the Fulham Volunteer Light Infantry. He *m.* Hannah, daughter and co-heiress of Samuel Rush, esq. of Ford House, in Hertfordshire, and of Chislehurst, in Kent, and by her, who died 28th September, 1832, left, at his decease in 1805, (he was buried at Fulham,) an only surviving child, the present SIR SAMUEL RUSH MEYRICK, of Goodrich Court.

*Arms*—Az. a fess wavy arg. charged with another invecked erminois between three mullets or, pierced of the field.

*Crest*—A castle per pale arg. and erminois.

*Motto*—Stemmata quid faciunt.

*Estates*—The freeholds in Herefordshire, lying in the vale of Wigmore, which had been hereditary in the family, were sold by James Meyrick, esq. who died in 1778. Peterborough House, bought by the late John Meyrick, esq. was pulled down and a new house erected, in 1795, which, with the ground, was sold to Major Scott Waring. GOODRICH COURT, (the present property of the family,) the architecture of which is of the time of EDWARD II. was built by Sir Samuel, after the design of Edward Blore, in 1828, in a most beautiful situation, on the tour of the Wye. Besides the numerous works of art and antiquity it contains, it is justly celebrated for the most instructive collection of armour in the world. Sir Samuel succeeded to the estate of Samuel Rush, esq. at Chislehurst, Kent, which, in conjunction with his mother, he sold in 1809, and inherited, upon that lady's demise in 1832, freehold at Little Hampton, Sussex.

*Town Residence*—20, Upper Cadogan Place.

*Seat*—Goodrich Court, Herefordshire.

## LLOYD, OF FERNEY HALL.

LLOYD, EVAN, esq. of Ferney Hall, in the county of Salop, a lieutenant-general in the army, and lieutenant-colonel 17th lancers, born in 1768, married, first, Maria, daughter of Benjamin Burton, esq. of Burton Hall, and relict of Michael Cox, esq. of Castletown, but had no issue; and secondly, in 1814, Alicia, Dowager Lady Trimlestown,* daughter of Lieutenant-General Eustace, by whom he has one son and two daughters,

EVAN-HERBERT, born at Turvey House, near Dublin.

Alicia-Mary.
Louis-Anne.

General Lloyd succeeded to the representation of the family upon the demise of his father.

* Relict (his second wife) of Nicholas, fourteenth Lord Trimlestown.

## Lineage.

This family lineally descends from ELYSTAN GLODRYDD, a powerful British chieftain, who derived his name *Elystan*, (or Athelstan) from the Saxon King ATHELSTAN, who was his godfather. The appellation of *Glodrydd* (or the illustrious) was bestowed upon him, not so much for his rank or possessions (which were very extensive, including nearly all the lands between the rivers Severn and Wye) as for his liberality and praiseworthy acts. Elystan died in the early part of the eleventh century, and his eldest son, CADWGAN, Lord of Builth and Radnor, was the ancestor of numerous families, still extant, in the counties of Brecon, Radnor, and Montgomery, as also of many others scattered throughout the principality.

Twelfth in descent from Cadwgan was THOMAS LLOYD ap MEREDITH, the first of his line who adopted the surname of Lloyd. He was a firm and zealous partisan of HENRY VII. and was one of those who led a body of his countrymen to the battle of Bosworth. After Henry obtained the throne, he appointed Thomas Lloyd his lieutenant of the county of Brecon, and bestowed upon him other and more substantial marks of favour.

JOHN LLOYD, of Portherwys, a younger son of Thomas Lloyd, was an esquire of the body to *Queen* ELIZABETH. From Rees Lloyd, the eldest son, descended the Lloyds of Aberanell, in the county of Brecon, of which family was

EVAN LLOYD, esq. who left, by his wife, a lady named Jones, a son and successor,

EVAN LLOYD, esq. who was seated at Cefndyrrys, which beautiful residence on the Wye, now called Welfield House, was sold by the present General Lloyd to his uncle, David Thomas, esq. Evan Lloyd *m.* Miss Thomas, of Llwynturrid, in the county of Brecon, and had issue,

- EVAN, his heir.
- Henry, resident at Ludlow.
- William-James, deceased.
- Thomas, Prebendary of Hereford, who died, leaving two daughters, Anne, *m.* to Thomas Dax, esq. of Bedford Place, London, and Mary, widow of — Pearce, esq.
- Mary, *m.* to — Poppleton, esq. of Warwickshire, and is deceased.
- Elizabeth, *m.* to Thomas Harris, esq. of the Moor in Herefordshire.

Mr. Lloyd was *s.* at his decease by his eldest son, the present Lieutenant-General LLOYD.

*Arms*—Quarterly 1st and 4th, gu. a lion rampant reguardant or; 2nd and 3rd, az. three boars' heads couped sa.

*Crest*—The head and neck of a griffin, issuing from a ducal coronet ppr.

*Motto*—Gwell angeu Na Cywilydd.

*Seat*—Ferney Hall, near Ludlow.

# CREIGHTON, OF CRUM CASTLE.

CREIGHTON, JOHN, esq. of Crum Castle, in the county of Fermanagh, born in 1802, succeeded his father 10th May, 1833, and is a magistrate and deputy-lieutenant for the counties of Fermanagh and Donegal, for both of which he has served the office of sheriff, for the former in 1831, for the latter in 1833.

## Lineage.

The Honorable JOHN CREIGHTON, second son of John, first Earl of Erne, was a lieutenant-colonel in the army, and Governor of Hurst Castle. He *m.* in 1797, Jane, dau. of Colonel Walter Weldon, of the Queen's County, and had issue,

I. JOHN, his heir.
II. Henry, a military officer, *b.* in 1804.
III. Samuel, *b.* in 1811.

I. Jane, *m.* in 1820, to Robert Fowler, esq. son of the Bishop of Ossory.
II. Catherine, *m.* in 1825, to the Rev. Francis Saunderson, of Castle Saunderson.
III. Helen.
IV. Charlotte.
V. Mary.

Colonel Creighton died 10th May, 1833, and was succeeded by his eldest son, the present JOHN CREIGHTON, esq.

*Arms*—Arg. a lion rampant az.

*Crest*—A wyvern's head, couped at the neck vert, vomiting flames ppr.

*Seat*—Crum Castle, rebuilt in 1833.

# HERRICK, OF BEAUMANOR.

HERRICK, WILLIAM, esq. of Beaumanor, in the county of Leicester, born in 1794, succeeded his uncle 18th February, 1832. Mr. Herrick is a barrister-at-law, and M.A. of University College, Oxford.

## Lineage.

"There is a tradition," says Dean Swift,* "that the most ancient family of the ERICKS derive their lineage from ERICK, *the Forester*, a great commander, who raised an army to oppose the invasion of WILLIAM the Conqueror, by whom he was vanquished; but afterwards employed to command that Prince's forces, and in his old age retired to his house in Leicestershire, where his family hath continued ever since." Though the earliest ancestor of the family is only recorded by tradition, we learn from ancient writings of unquestionable authority, that the EYRICKS were seated at a very remote period, at Great Stretton, in Leicestershire, in that respectable line of life, so justly the pride of an Englishman, free tenants of their own lands, two virgates of which they held under the Abbey of Leicester, on the payment of an annual quit rent to the King of a pound of pepper. These virgates had been given to the Abbey by Ralph Friday, Lord of Wibtoft, and were successively held by Roger

* The Dean's father married Mrs. Abigail Erick, of Leicestershire, descended from this family.

Torr, Sir Ralph Neville, Alan and Henry Eyryk, and Robert Eyryk, the son of Alan.

Henry Eyryk (the above named) was grandfather of

Robert Eyryk, of Stretton, who by Joanna, his wife, had three sons, viz.

William, (Sir) his heir.

Robert, known by the name of Robert de Stretton, who entering into holy orders, obtained the degree of LL.D. was appointed chaplain to Edward the Black Prince, and eventually consecrated Bishop of Lichfield. His lordship died in 1385.

John, of Stretton.

From the eldest son,

Sir William Eyrik, knt. of Stretton, descended,

Robert Eyrick, of Houghton on the Hill, living about 1450, who left by Agnes, his wife, two sons, Robert, who died *s.p.* and

Thomas Eyrick, of Houghton, who settled at Leicester, and is the first of the name that appears in the corporation books, where he is mentioned as a member of that body, in 1511. He died about six years after, leaving two sons and a daughter, namely,

Nicholas, who was Mayor of Leicester in 1552. He married and had issue.

John, of whom presently.

Elizabeth, mentioned in her father's will, which bears date in 1517.

The second son,

John Eyrick, or Heyrick, of Leicester, *b.* in 1513, was twice mayor of that corporation, in 1559 and 1572. He *m.* Mary, dau. of John Bond, esq. of Wardend, in Warwickshire, and by her, who died 8th December, 1611, aged ninety-seven, had issue,

I. Robert, who was thrice Mayor of Leicester, and representative of the Borough in parliament. He died in 1618, leaving a numerous family. He is now represented by the Reverend Samuel Heyrick, rector of Brampton, in Northamptonshire.

II. Nicholas, of London, who *m.* in 1582, Julian, daughter of William Stone, esq. of Segenhoe, in Bedfordshire, and dying in 1592, left issue,

1. William, *b.* in 1585, *d. s. p.*
2. Thomas, *b.* in 1588, who *m.* and has issue. He is presumed to have been grandfather of Thomas Heyrick, curate of Harborough, who published some sermons and poems.
3. Nicholas, of London, merchant, living in 1664, aged seventy-five, *m.* Susanna, daughter of William Salter, and had issue.
4. Robert, *b.* in 1591, a poet of considerable merit. This distinguished person, who received his education at St. John's College, Cambridge, entering into holy orders, and obtaining the patronage of the Earl of Exeter, was presented by Charles I. to the vicarage of Dean Prior, in Devonshire, 1st October, 1629, and soon afterwards acquired the reputation of a wit and a poet. During the prevalence of the Parliamentary influence, he was ejected from his living and resided in London until the Restoration, when he regained his vicarage. The period of his decease has not been ascertained. His literary efforts are comprised in a scarce volume, entitled, "*Hesperides," or the Works both Humane and Divine, of Robert Herrick, esq. London,* 1648." 8vo. To this volume was appended his "*Noble Numbers or his Pious Pieces*," in which, says Wood, "he sings the birth of Christ, and sighs for his Saviours sufferings on the cross." These two books made him much admired in the time they were published, and especially by the generous and boon loyalists, who commiserated his sufferings." In 1810, Dr. Nott, of Bristol, published a selection from the "Hesperides," which may probably contribute to revive the memory of Herrick as a poet, who certainly in vigour of fancy, feeling, and ease of versification, is entitled to a superior rank among the bards of the age in which he lived.
5. William, *b.* in 1593.

1. Mercie. 2. Anne.

III. Thomas, died in 1623, *s. p.*

IV. John, Alderman of Leicester, died 1613, leaving issue.

V. William, (Sir) of whom presently.

I. Ursula, *b.* in 1532, *m.* to Laurence Hawes.

II. Agnes, *m.* to William Davie.

III. Mary, *m.* to Sir Thomas Bennet, Lord Mayor of London in 1603.

IV. Elizabeth, *m.* to John Stanford, esq. Recorder of Leicester.

V. Helen, *m.* to --- Holden, esq.

VI. Christiana, *m.* to George Brookes, esq.

VII. Alice, *m.* to --- Hinde.

The fifth son,

Sir William Heyricke, who was born at Leicester about the year 1557, removing to London, in 1574, to reside with his brother Nicholas, then an eminent banker in Cheapside, attached himself to the court, and for a considerable time "resided constantly there." He was a man of great abilities and address; remarkably handsome, as appears by a small picture still preserved of him in his younger days; was high in the confidence of *Queen* ELIZABETH, as well as of *King* JAMES, and by honourable service to both, acquired large property. In the reign of the former sovereign he was despatched on an embassy to the Ottoman Porte, and on his return rewarded with a lucrative appointment in the Exchequer. In 1594-5, he purchased from the agents of Robert, Earl of Essex, that nobleman's estate and interest at Beaumanor, and soon after selecting that delightful spot for his residence, bought in all the different outstanding leases, and, in 1598, obtained from *Queen* ELIZABETH, by letters patent under the great seal, a grant of the manor of Beaumanor. In 1601, he was returned to parliament by the borough of Leicester, but retired upon the demise of her majesty. In 1605 he received the honour of knighthood, was appointed a teller of the Exchequer, and chosen alderman of Farringdon Without; from the civic office he was excused however, on agreeing to pay a fine of 300*l*. Shortly after, Sir William was a second time elected M.P. for Leicester, and for many years devoted his time and abilities to the promotion of the interests of his constituents. During the civil wars he suffered severely, and his fortune was much impaired in that calamitous season. He died 2nd March, 1652-3, and was buried on the 8th in St. Martin's Church, at Leicester, where against the north wall of the choir his gravestone still remains. His picture at Beaumanor exhibits him with a picked beard, a large ruff, and in a white satin doublet, which he used on Christmas day, attending *Queen* ELIZABETH. He wears a sword, and over his dress hangs loosely a large black cloak. His plaited ruffles are closely turned back over his sleeves. In one hand are his gloves, the other, elevated to his breast, holds the stump and tassells of his ruff. On one side, within a wreath, is the motto "Sola supereminet virtus." On the other, "Anno Dom. 1628, ætatis suæ 66." Lady Herrick is dressed in a close black gown richly ornamented with lace and fine ruffles turned up close over the sleeves; a watch in one hand, in the other a prayer book, and at her side a feathered fan. This portrait is dated "July 27th, 1632, ætatis suæ fifty-four."

> "Art may hir outsid thus present to view,
> How faire within no art or tongue can show."

By this lady, (whose christian name was Joan, and who was daughter of Richard May, esq. of London, and sister of Sir Humphrey May, Chancellor of the Duchy of Lancaster,) Sir William Herrick had issue,

I. WILLIAM, his heir.
II. Robert, *b.* in 1598, *d. s.p.*
III. Richard, *b.* in 1600, who *d.* Warden of Manchester, in 1667. He was entered a commoner of St. John's College, Oxford, in 1617, where he took the degree of Bachelor of Arts, in 1619; of M.A. in 1622, and was admitted to a fellowship of All Souls in 1624-5, on the especial recommendation of *King* JAMES. By Helen, his first wife, daughter of Thomas Corbet, esq. of Sprauston, in Norfolk, he had issue, a son, Thomas, *b.* in 1622, and two daughters, Mary, *m.* to John Johnson, of Manchester, and Elizabeth, to the Reverend Richard Holbrook, of Salford. By his second wife, Anna-Maria Hall, of London, widow, dau. of Mr. Erasmus Bretton, he had a son, John, who *d.* young, and a daughter, Helena, *m.* to Thomas Radcliff, esq.
IV. Thomas, *b.* in 1602.
V. Henry, *b.* in 1604.
VI. Roger, Fellow of All Souls.
VII. John, *b.* in 1612 (see HERRICK of Shippool).

I. Elizabeth, *b.* in 1603.
II. Mary, *d.* unm. aged twenty.
III. Martha, *m.* in 1634, to John Holmstead, esq. of Lynn, Norfolk.
IV. Dorothy, *m.* in 1628, to Reverend James Lancashire.
V. Elizabeth, *m.* in 1633, to Beaumont Pight, esq.

Sir William (who was aged ninety-six at his decease) was *s.* by his son,

WILLIAM HERRICK, esq. of Beaumanor, *b.* in 1597, who was appointed in 1633, by *King* CHARLES I. to repair the Castle of Leicester, and place it in a proper state of defence. He *m.* in 1623, Elizabeth, daughter of Humphrey Fox, esq. of London, and dying in 1671, left an only son and successor,

WILLIAM HERRICK, esq. of Beaumanor, *b.* in 1624, who *m.* first, in July, 1649, Anne, eldest daughter of William Bainbrigge, esq. of Lockington, in the county of Leicester, by Elizabeth, his wife, daughter of Gervas Pigott, esq. of Thrumpton, Notts, and had by her, who *d.* in 1655, three sons and one daughter, viz.

I. WILLIAM, his heir.
II. John, of the Outwoods, in the parish of Loughborough, *m.* Mary, daughter of Beaumont Pight, esq. of Denton, in Lincolnshire, and *d.* in 1724.
III. Benjamin, M.D. *b.* 1656, died in 1720, leaving a son, William Bainbrigge, who died in 1733, and a dau.

I. Elizabeth, *m.* to John Levesley, esq. of Belton, in Leicestershire.

He married, secondly, in 1657, Frances,

daughter of William Milward, esq. of Chilcote, in Derbyshire, (son and heir of Sir Thomas Milward, the Judge,) and had by her,

I. Thomas, who *d.* in 1692, aged twenty.

I. Frances, *d.* young, 1664.
II. Mary, *m.* to William Lucas, esq.
III. Christiana, *m.* to Clifton Thompson, esq.

Mr. Herrick died in 1693, and was *s.* by his eldest son,

WILLIAM HERRICK, esq. of Beaumanor, *b.* in 1650, who married Dorothy, daughter of James Wootton, esq. of Weston, in Derbyshire, and by her, who *d.* in 1749, aged one hundred, had issue,

I. WILLIAM, his heir.
II. John, *b.* in 1691, *m.* in 1715, Elizabeth, daughter of Samuel Marshall, esq. of Burton on the Woulds, and dying in 1760, left two sons and two daughters, all deceased.
III. Thomas, of Leicester, *b.* in 1693, *m.* first, in 1720, Martha, dau. of Thomas Noble, esq. M.P. secondly, in 1724, Katharine, daughter of Robert Bakewell, esq. of Swebston, and, thirdly, Elizabeth, daughter of James Winstanley, esq. M.P. of Braunston. He *d.* 10th December, 1766, leaving by his second wife, one son and one dau. viz.

William, of Knighton, who *m.* in 1766, Sarah daughter of Philip Bamford, esq. of Bamford, in Lancashire.

Katherine, *m.* to Richard Dyott, esq. of Freeford Hall, Staffordshire.

I. Elizabeth, *b.* in 1684, *m.* to Robert Bunny, gent.
II. Anne, *b.* in 1687, *d.* in 1759, unm.

Mr. Herrick died in 1705, and was *s.* by his eldest son,

WILLIAM HERRICK, esq. of Beaumanor, *b.* in 1689, who married in 1740, Lucy, daughter of John Gage,* esq. of Bentley Park, Sussex, and by her, who died 25th March, 1778, had to survive infancy, three sons and one daughter, viz.

I. WILLIAM, his heir.
II. John, *b.* 9th November, 1749, sometime of the Middle Temple, London, *d.* unm. 14th May, 1819.
III. Thomas-Bainbrigge, of Gray's Inn, *b.* 23rd November, 1754, married 15th August, 1793, Mary, only daughter of James Perry, esq. of Erdesley Park, in the county of Hereford, and died 24th September, 1824, leaving issue,

WILLIAM, successor to his uncle.
Mary-Anne.
Lucy.

I. Lucy, *m.* in March, 1768, to Richard Gildart, esq. of Norton Hall, in the county of Stafford, and had issue.

Mr. Herrick, who was high sheriff of Leicestershire in 1753, died 27th September, 1773, and was buried in Woodhouse Chapel, where an elegant marble monument is erected with an inscription, thus commencing,

Near this place lie the remains
of
William Herrick, esq. of Beaumanor Park,
whose ancestors were seated in this county
in the eleventh century.

His eldest son and successor,

* The Gages, of Bentley, were a junior branch of the ancient family of that name, seated at Firle, in Sussex.

SIR JOHN GAGE, of Firle, K.G. Chancellor of the Duchy of Lancaster, Constable of the Tower of London, Comptroller of the Household to HENRY VIII. and subsequently Lord Chamberlain to *Queen* MARY, married Philippa, daughter of Sir Richard Guildford, K.G. and had several sons and daughters, of the former, the eldest, Sir EDWARD GAGE, knt. succeeded to Firle, and was ancestor of the present Lord Gage, while the second,

JAMES GAGE, esq. became seated at Bentley, in Sussex, and married three wives. By the first he had three sons, viz.

EDWARD, of Bentley, who married Margaret, daughter of William Shelley, esq. of Michel-grove, and died leaving six daughters his co-heirs.
James, *d. s.p.*
JOHN.

The third son,

JOHN GAGE, esq. of Wormley, Herts, married Eleanor, widow of Sir Thomas Baskerville, knt. and daughter of Richard Habingdon, esq. and left a son,

EDWARD GAGE, esq. of Wormley, and afterwards of Bentley, who married Clara, daughter of William Bindloss, esq. of Essex, and was father of

WILLIAM GAGE, esq. of Bentley, who died in 1653, and was buried at Firle, leaving, with two daughters, Clare and Katherine, a son,

THOMAS GAGE, esq. of Bentley, who married Juliana, daughter and co-heir of Robert Cæsar, esq. of Willian, Herts, by Johanna, his wife, daughter of Sir William Lovelace, of Lovelace (see vol. ii. p. 19), and dying 1682, left, with other children, who died unmarried, two daughters, Anne, married to John Payne, esq. and Henrietta-Maria, to — Curson, esq. and a son and successor,

JOHN GAGE, esq. of Bentley, who married in 1701, Lucy, daughter and heir of John Mayo, esq. by Mary, his wife, daughter and co-heir of George Clarke, esq. of Hackney, and dying at Seville, in Spain, 22nd October, 1731, left issue,

I. THOMAS, *d.* unm. in 1742.
II. CHARLES-CÆSAR, *d. s. p.* 1764.
III. JOHN, A.M. rector of West Bridgeford, Notts, *d.* unm. 1770.

I. LUCY, married (as in the text) to WILLIAM HERRICK, esq. of Beaumanor.

WILLIAM HERRICK, esq. of Beaumanor Park, *b.* 14th December, 1745, served as sheriff for Leicestershire in 1786. He *m.* in 1789, Miss Sarah Stokes, of Woodhouse, and dying without issue, 18th February, 1832, (his wife predeceased him, 29th August, 1823,) was succeeded by his nephew, the present WILLIAM HERRICK, esq. of Beaumanor Park.

*Arms*—Arg. a fess vairé or and gu.

*Crest*—A bull's head couped arg. horned and eared sa. gorged with a chaplet of roses ppr.

*Motto*—Virtus omnia nobilitat.

*Estates*—In Leicestershire.

*Seat*—Beaumanor Park.

## HERRICK, OF SHIPPOOL.

HERRICK, WILLIAM-HENRY, esq. of Shippool, in the county of Cork, captain R.N. born 13th February, 1784, *m.* 8th September, 1814, Mary, only daughter of Robert De la Cour, esq. and has issue,

I. THOMAS-BOUSFIELD, *b.* 25th February, 1819.
II. William-Henry, *b.* 9th February, 1824.
III. Benjamin-Bousfield, *b.* 18th February, 1826.
IV. James-Hugh, *b.* 13th December, 1830.

I. Mary-De-la-Cour.
II. Anne-Harriet.
III. Louisa-Josephine Pettitot.
IV. Georgiana-Henrietta.

Captain Herrick *s.* his father in October, 1796, and has been in the commission of the peace since 1816.

### Lineage.

From the exact coincidence of name, arms, and dates, there can exist but little doubt that this is a junior branch of the HERRICKS of Beaumanor, in Leicestershire.

JOHN HERRICK, esq. born in 1612, was probably the seventh son of the celebrated Sir William Herrick, of Beaumanor, as Sir William had a son, named John, who was born in that very year. John Herrick married twice, and died 8th August, 1689, leaving, by the first wife, a son GERSHOM, and by the second, two sons and a daughter, viz. John, Francis, and Mary. To his second son, John, he bequeathed an estate in the barony of Ibane, which is still possessed by his descendants, who reside at Bellmont, in the county of Cork. To his eldest son,

GERSHOM HERRICK, born in 1665, he devised his estate of Shippool. This gentleman *m.* in 1693, Susanna, only child and heiress of Swithen Smart, esq. by Frances, his wife, eldest daughter of Edward Riggs, esq. of Riggsdale, in the county of Cork, and left a son and successor,

EDWARD HERRICK, esq. of Shippool, born in 1694, who wedded Elizabeth, daughter of Caleb Falkener, esq. of the city of Cork, and had six sons and two daughters. The second son, Edward, Lieutenant R.N. was killed on board "the Dorsetshire," in Sir Edward Hawke's action, 20th September, 1759. The eldest son,

FALKENER HERRICK, esq. of Shippool, *b.* in 1729, *m.* in June, 1753, Sarah, eldest dau. of Thomas Bousfield, esq. of Cork, and had issue,

THOMAS-BOUSFIELD, his heir.
Jane, married to the Reverend Ambrose Hickey.
Elizabeth, *d.* unm. aged thirty-six.

Mr. Herrick was succeeded at his decease by his son,

THOMAS-BOUSFIELD HERRICK, esq. of Shippool, born in 1754, who married in 1783, Anne, only daughter of Henry Moore, esq. of Frankfort House, in the county of Cork, and by her (who wedded, secondly, in 1798, Daniel Cudmore, esq. of the county of Limerick,) had issue,

I. WILLIAM-HENRY, his heir.
II. Henry-Moore, captain in the 45th regiment, killed at the storming of Badajos, unmarried.
III. Edward, lieutenant R.N.
I. Ann, *m.* in January, 1818, to Richard Plummer Davies, esq. captain R.N.

Mr. Herrick died in 1796, and was *s.* by his eldest son, the present WILLIAM-HENRY HERRICK, esq. of Shippool.

*Arms, Crest,* and *Motto*—See Herrick of Beaumanor.

*Estates*—In the county of Cork.

*Seat*—Shippool, near Innishannon.

# FREEMAN, OF GAINES.

FREEMAN, JOHN, esq. of Gaines, in the county of Hereford, *b.* 29th August, 1802, *m.* 16th May, 1826, Constantia, second daughter of the Venerable Richard Francis Onslow, archdeacon of Worcester, and has one son,

JOHN-ARTHUR.

Mr. Freeman, who succeeded his father 22nd October, 1831, is a magistrate for the counties of Hereford and Worcester, and a deputy-lieutenant for the former shire, of which he was high sheriff in 1832.

## Lineage.

BELLINGHAM FREEMAN, esq. son of Francis Freeman, of Suckley, acquired about the year 1683 the Gaines estate, situated in the parish of Whitbourne, Herefordshire, in marriage with Elizabeth, daughter of Richard Gower, esq. of Suckley. He left at his decease a son and successor,

JOHN FREEMAN, esq. of Gaines, who *m.* in 1727, Abigail Jones, of the Orchards, in the county of Hereford, and had issue,

- I. JOHN, his heir.
- II. Thomas.

- I. Betty, *m.* to John Barneby, esq. of Brockhampton.
- II. Anne, *m.* to John Lilly, esq. of the city of Worcester.
- III. Abigail, *m.* to John Freeman, esq. of Letton.

Mr. Freeman died in August, 1764, and was succeeded by his son,

JOHN FREEMAN, esq. of Gaines, who *m.* 30th April, 1761, Miss Anne Harris, and had two sons and a daughter, namely,

- I. JOHN, his heir.
- II. Thomas-Harris, *b.* in 1771, *m.* Mary, daughter of Richard Chambers, esq. of Whitbourne Court, in the county of Hereford.

- I. Theodosia.

Mr. Freeman died in September, 1801, and was *s.* by his son,

JOHN FREEMAN, esq. of Gaines, who *m.* 9th October, 1798, Mary, eldest daughter of James Dansie, esq. of London, and had issue,

- I. JOHN, his heir.

- I. Abigail-Mary, *m.* to Charles Sidebottom, esq. barrister-at-law.
- II. Anne, *m.* to the Rev. Henry Francis Sidebottom.
- III. Elizabeth.
- IV. Mary, *m.* to Fleming St. John, esq. youngest son of the Rev. St. Andrew St. John, prebendary of Worcester.

Mr. Freeman *d.* 22nd October, 1831, and was *s.* by his son, the present JOHN FREEMAN, esq. of Gaines.

*Arms*—Gu. three lozenges arg.

*Crest*—A demi lion rampant, holding a lozenge in his paws.

*Estates*—In Herefordshire.

*Seat*—Gaines.

# HEYCOCK, OF EAST NORTON.

**HEYCOCK, JOHN-HIPPISLEY**, esq. of East Norton, in Leicestershire, *b.* 3rd February, 1793, baptized at Somerby, *m.* 18th May, 1819, Martha, only child of Thomas Lewin, esq. of Thrussington Grange, in the same county, and has four sons and three daughters,* viz.

JOHN, *b.* 5th March, 1822.
Henry, *b.* 6th April, 1825.
Charles, *b.* 11th October, 1827.
Thomas, *b.* 1st June, 1831.

Mary.
Susanna.
Emma.

Mr. Heycock succeeded his father in 1823.

## Lineage.

*The Rev.* JOSEPH HEYCOCK, of Mortimer, in Berkshire, married and had two sons, Joseph, of Reading, who died unmarried, leaving his estate to his brother, and

NICHOLAS HEYCOCK, esq. of Tilton, in Leicestershire, *b.* at Mortimer about the year 1672. He *m.* at Saddington, in 1710, Mary, daughter of — Palmer, esq. of Saddington, in Leicestershire, and had issue,

JOHN, his heir.

Mary, *b.* in 1711, *m.* Edward Muxloe, esq. of Pickwell, in Leicestershire, and had a son,

Edward Muxloe, esq. of Pickwell, high sheriff of Leicestershire, who *m.* Mary-Anne, sister of the Rev. John Hopkinson, rector of Market Overton, in the county of Rutland, and had an only daughter and heiress,

Mary-Anne Muxloe, *m.* to John Wingfield, esq. of Tickencote (see vol. ii. p. 476).

Catherine, *b.* in 1715, *m.* to John Dawson, esq. and had one son, who died unmarried.

Nicholas Heycock *d.* about 1761, was buried at Tilton, and succeeded by his son,

JOHN HEYCOCK, esq. of Norton, in the county of Leicester, *b.* in 1713, baptized at Tilton-on-the-Hill. This gentleman *m.* first, in 1744, Mary, second daughter and co-heir of Benjamin Clarke, esq. of Hardingstone, in Northamptonshire, and by her (who died about 1752, and was buried at Norton,) had issue,

JOSEPH, *b.* in 1748, *m.* Mary Black, of the county of Northampton, and had two sons, Nicholas and John, who both died unmarried.

Mary, *b.* in 1745, *m.* to Richard Raworth, esq. of Owston, and left one son.

Elizabeth, *b.* in 1746, *m.* to John Smith, esq. of Uppingham, in Rutlandshire, and *d. s. p.*

He wedded, secondly, in 1755, Elizabeth, daughter of — Brown, esq. of Skeffington, in Leicestershire, and had by her (who died in 1758, and was buried at Norton,) a daughter, Dorothy, *b.* in 1756, the wife of Henry Hensman, esq. of Pitchley, Northamptonshire, and a son,

JOHN HEYCOCK, esq. of Owston, *b.* at Norton in 1758, and there baptized. He *m.* in 1790, Susanna, second daughter of Tobias Hippisley, esq. of Hambleton, high sheriff of Rutlandshire in 1800, and by her (who died in 1816, and was buried at Owston,) had issue,

I. JOHN-HIPPISLEY, his heir.

II. Charles, in holy orders, rector of Withcot, and minister of Owston, in Leicestershire, *b.* in October, 1794, baptized at Somerby, *m.* Catherine, only daughter of — Bizail, esq. and

---

* All baptized at Norton, in Leicestershire.

niece of the Rev. William Bissil, of Wissendine, in Rutlandshire, and has two daughters, viz.

Catherine.
Susanna.

III. Thomas, of Owston, *b.* in September, 1796, baptized at Owston.

IV. William, of New York, United States of America.

V. Henry, of Beeston Boyd, near Leeds.

VI. Edwin, of Beeston Boyd, near Leeds, *m.* Mary, daughter of — Cockshot, and has surviving issue one son and one daughter.

VII. Frederick, of Byford, in Herefordshire.

VIII. Alfred, died aged about sixteen, and was buried at Owston.

I. Susanna, *d.* unm. in 1810, buried at Owston.

II. Elizabeth, *m.* to Rowland Maurice Fawcett, M.D.

III. Emma, *m.* to Ayscough Smith, esq. of Leesthorpe Hall, in the county of Leicester, and has issue.

Mr. Heycock died in 1823, was buried at Owston, and succeeded by his eldest son, the present JOHN-HIPPISLEY HEYCOCK, esq. of Norton.

*Arms*—Or, a cross sa. in the first quarter a fleur-de-lys.
*Estates*—In Leicestershire.
*Seat*—East Norton.

## ROSS, OF CRAIGIE AND INNERNETHIE.

ROSS, SIR PATRICK, major-general in the army, a knight commander of the order of St. Michael and St. George and of the Royal Hanoverian Guelphic order, and late governor of Antigua, Montserrat, and Barbuda: married 14th April, 1805, Amelia, youngest daughter of General William Sydenham, of the ancient family of that name and place, in the county of Devon, and has issue,

I. PATRICK-WILLIAM-SYDENHAM, *b.* 22nd November, 1821.
II. Charles-Douglas, *b.* 1st December, 1822, died 3rd March, 1824.
III. Charles-Douglas, *b.* 6th August, 1825.

I. Amelia, married to Major S. Holmes, K. H. military secretary at Malta, and has issue two sons and two daughters.
II. Clara-Susanna, *m.* to Rowland-Edward-Louis-Charles Williams, esq. of Weston Grove, Surrey, and Claremont, Antigua, descended from the ancient family of Williams, of Penrhyn, in the county of Carmarthen, and has issue two surviving sons.
III. Mary-Ann.
IV. Georgina-Fanny.

### Lineage.

We have no certain record how or from whom this family had its beginning; but that it was great and flourishing in the time of *Kings* ROBERT and DAVID BRUCE, admits of not the slightest doubt.* In the latter of these reigns a daughter of the family was married to Sir John Drummond of Concraig, predecessor of the Earls of Perth, and Drummond of Balloch, afterwards married another daughter of Ross of Craigie, who was mother of John Drummond, Laird of Milnab, as in the genealogical history of the family of Perth, written

* Nisbett's Heraldry, vol. i. p. 416. Vol. ii. Appendix, p. 24.

by William Drummond, Viscount of Strathallan.

The family of Ross continued eminent till about the middle of the reign of *King* James VI. (I. of England), when it began to decline, and was entirely ruined, and its estates carried off by many creditors in the beginning of the reign of *King* Charles I. John Ross, Laird of Craigie, was a principal favourite with *King* James V. (*Knox's History*) and was taken prisoner by the English at Solway Moss; he is also mentioned in Baker's Chronicle, by an easy mistake, John Ross, Lord of Grey, instead of Laird of Craigie. The Rosses of Craigie had a great estate near the town of Perth, and had intermarriages with several honourable families in that country, as Drummond of Coneraig, Drummond of Balloch, Murray of Balvaird (now Viscount Stormont), Seton of Lathrisk, Ogilvy of Inchmartin, and many others. They were hereditary governors of the Spey Castle, in Perth,* which office continued in the family till the Reformation, when the keys of the fortress were surrendered under a protestation, to the provost and council, by John Ross of Craigie. Among the records of the city is one, dated the 30th June, 1461, in which Robert the Rosse of Craigie is one of the witnesses to a warrant, remitting a fine imposed upon the provost and magistrates of Perth, for the destruction of the houses of Dupline and Aberdalgie; and there is another remission, by warrant under the great seal, dated 5th February, 1526, to the town of Perth, for having burnt the Castle of Craigie. The town of Perth was one of the strongest fortifications in the kingdom, surrounded with castles, the residences of powerful barons, who were often at war with one another, and with the magistrates of Perth. Ruthven, now Huntingtower, was the seat and fortress of the Ruthvens, Aberdalgie and Dupline of the Oliphants, Craigie of the Rosses, Kinfauns of the Charteris, Gascon Hall and Fingash of the Bruces, &c. &c.

From the Craigie line descended

Patrick Ross,† of Innernethie, whose great-grandfather, Patrick Ross, sheriff-clerk of Perth, the grandson of Alexander Ross, second son to the Laird of Craigie, purchased these lands. The branch of Innernethie has always carried the arms of Craigie, as appears from their seals, and over the funeral monument of the above Patrick Ross, in the Grey Friars of Perth. They are allied in this and the preceding generations, since their descent from the house of Craigie, with the families of Norie of Noristoun, in Monteith, Moncrief of Easton Moncrief, Clark of Pittencher, Lindsay of Eveluek, Seton of Lathrisk, Lindsay of Kilspindie, Pitcairn of Pitlons, Osborn of Peppermill, Sinclair of Balgraigie, Douglas of Strathendrie, Balfour of Denmiln, &c.

Patrick Ross of Innernethie married, in 1734, Susanna Douglas, of Strathendrie, in the county of Fife, a branch of the Earls of Morton, and had, with other issue, a second son,

Patrick Ross, a general officer in the army, who married, in 1777, Mary Clara Maule, descended from the family of Panmure, and had issue,

I. Patrick, the present representative of the families of Craigie and Innernethie.
II. John, lieutenant R. N. and is deceased.
III. George-Adam, lieutenant R. N. deceased.
IV. Charles-Robert, East India Company's civil service, deceased.
V. Archibald, lieutenant-colonel in the army, married Margaret, daughter of John Sparkes, esq. died of wounds received in Spain, and left issue five sons and two daughters.
VI. Frederick-James, late lieutenant Royal Dragoons, married Elizabeth, second daughter of P. N. Roberts, esq. and has issue two sons and two daughters.

I. Susanna, married to Colonel Broadhead.

*Arms*—Or, a fesse cheque arg. and sa. between three water-budgets of the second.

*Crest*—A lion's head erased ppr.

*Motto*—Per aspera virtus.

*Residence*—Fitzwilliam House, Richmond, Surrey.

* Cant's History of Perth, notes.

† Nisbett's Heraldry.

# WYNNE, OF GARTHEWIN.

WYNNE, ROBERT-WILLIAM, esq. of Garthewin, in the county of Denbigh, married Letitia, daughter of the late Reverend John Fleming Stanley, and became a widower, without issue, 24th June, 1831. Mr. Wynne was formerly lieutenant-colonel of the Royal Denbighshire Militia, and is a magistrate and deputy-lieutenant for the county of Denbigh.

## Lineage.

This family claims descent from MARCHUDD, a chieftain of North Wales, who served under Prince RODERIC the Great, in the ninth century, and who stands as the head of one of the fifteen tribes of North Wales. Thirteenth in lineal descent from MARCHUDD, was GRONWY LLWYD, who was instrumental in obtaining for EDWARD I. the sovereignty of Wales, and was rewarded for his services by that monarch. The arms borne by his ancestor Marchudd, were "Gu. a saracen's head erased at the neck arg. environed about the temples with a wreath or and arg." but Gronwy Llwyd bore "Gu. three boars' heads in pale, erased arg." and these arms are borne by all his descendants.

Eleventh in descent from Gronwy Llwyd was JOHN WYNNE, esq. of Melau, who married Dorothy, daughter of Hugh Gwyn Griffith, esq. of Berthddû, and had, with other issue, two sons, William and Robert. The elder, William, was a colonel in the service of *King* CHARLES I. and being slain in an attack made upon the Parliamentary garrison at Wem, in the county of Salop, was buried at St. Chad's Church, Shrewsbury, on the 27th October, 1643.* The younger,

ROBERT WYNNE, esq. was an officer in the same service, and assisted at the engagement at Wem; he survived the restoration, and having married Margaret, only daughter and heiress of Robert Price, esq. of Garthewin, founded the branch of the Wynne family, of which we are about to treat. He died 14th April, 1682, leaving, (with three younger sons and three daughters, viz. William, John, Hugh, Dorothy, Katherine, and Margaret,) a son,

*The Reverend* ROBERT WYNNE, A.M. Rector of Llaneistyn and Llanddeiniolen, and a canon of Bangor Cathedral, who *m.* Catherine, daughter of Richard Madryn, esq. of Llannerchfawr, and dying 25th January, 1679, aged forty-three, left issue,

I. ROBERT, his heir.
II. Richard, in the law.
III. William, A.M. *d. s. p.*
IV. Owen, M.D.
V. John, citizen of London.

I. Catherine.
II. Sarah, *m.* to the Rev. Peter Williams, vicar of Mold.

The eldest son,

*The Reverend* ROBERT WYNNE, D.D. of Garthewin, was chancellor of St. Asaph. He married, first, Margaret, daughter and heir of Hugh Lloyd Rosindale, esq. of Segrwyd, and relict of William Wynne, esq. of Melau, and, secondly, Margaret, daughter of John Owen, esq. of Penrhôs, and widow of Owen Bold, of Llangwyfen. By his first wife, Dr. Wynne, left at his decease, 26th June, 1743, a son and successor,

ROBERT WYNNE, esq. of Garthewin, barrister-at-law, who married, first, Diana, dau. of — Gosling, esq. of London, and had, by her who died in 1747, one son and two daughters, namely,

ROBERT, his heir.

Diana, *m.* to Owen Holland, esq. of Conway, and died *s. p.*

Elizabeth, died 18th October, 1758, aged seventeen.

Mr. Wynne, wedded, secondly, Elizabeth,

* John Wynne, the eldest son of Col. Wynne, continued the line of Melau.

daughter of Thomas Eyton, esq. of Leeswood, in Flintshire, but by her had no issue. He died 11th September, 1771, aged seventy-three, and was *s.* by his son,

ROBERT WYNNE, esq. of Garthewin, who espoused Elizabeth, daughter and sole heir of William Dymock, esq. of Acton, and by her, who died 29th December, 1816, in her seventy-fifth year, he left at his decease, 25th July, 1798, aged sixty, a son and successor, the present ROBERT WILLIAM WYNNE, esq. of Garthewin.

*Arms*—Gu. three boars' heads erased in pale arg.

*Crest*—A stag trippant.

*Estates*—Principally in the counties of Denbigh and Caernarvon, also in Shropshire, &c.

*Seat*—Garthewin, near Abergele.

## PHELIPS, OF BRIGGINS PARK.

PHELIPS, CHARLES, esq. of Briggins Park, in the county of Hertford, *m.* 15th June, 1820, Caroline Elizabeth, second daughter of James Taylor, esq. of Wimpole Street, London, and has issue,

I. CHARLES-JAMES, *b.* 18th March, 1821.
II. Edward Blathwayt, *b.* 12th April, 1822.
III. George-Blackmore, *b.* 1st July, 1824.
IV. William-Douglas, *b.* 27th March, 1827.
V. Henry-Plantagenet-Prescott, *b.* 4th February, 1831.
VI. Alfred-Plomer-Ward, *b.* 26th September, 1832.

I. Frances-Emma.
II. Caroline-Mary.

Mr. Phelips succeeded his maternal uncle, Thomas Blackmore, esq. in May, 1824, and was high sheriff of Herts in 1829. He is a magistrate for the counties of Herts and Essex, and a deputy lieutenant of the former.

### Lineage.

"The family of Phelips," says Collinson, "migrated into Somersetshire from Wales, where they were long anciently established, about the time of EDWARD I. and were for many years resident at Barrington, a few miles distant from Montacute. A branch of the family settled at Corf-Mullen, in Dorset, having received a grant of that manor from HENRY VIII. and represented the boroughs of Poole and Wareham in several parliaments."*

In the reign of ELIZABETH,

SIR EDWARD PHELIPS, knt. the queen's serjeant, third son of Sir Thomas Phelips, of Barrington, seated himself at Montacute, and erected there the present noble mansion. He was subsequently Master of the Rolls, Chancellor to Henry, Prince of Wales, and Speaker of the House of Commons. He *m.* Elizabeth Newdigate, of Newdigate, and was succeeded by his son,

SIR ROBERT PHELIPS, knt. of Montacute, who *m.* Bridget, daughter of Sir Thomas Gorge, knt. by Ellen, his wife, Marchioness of Northampton, and dying in 1638, left, with other issue, a son and successor,

COLONEL SIR EDWARD PHELIPS, knt. of Montacute, living in 1663, who married, and had issue,

I. Robert, who *d. v. p.*

* WILLIAM PHELIPS, esq. the last male heir of the Dorsetshire branch dying without issue in 1747, the estate of Corfe Mullen devolved on his niece, JANE (daughter of his second brother, Edward Phelips, esq. of Winbourne), which lady married the Rev. Sir James Hanham, bart. and was mother of the present Sir James Hanham, bart.

The seat of the Phelips's in Dorsetshire was an ancient mansion, pleasantly situated near the river and not far from the chapel, at the east end of the village. In an old window in the hall were the arms of Phelips: arg. a chev. between three roses seeded and leaved ppr.

II. EDWARD, his heir.
III. Thomas, *d. s. p.*
IV. George, left issue.
V. Richard, *d. s. p.*
VI. John, who *d.* in 1701, leaving a son, EDWARD, of whom presently.
VII. A son.
VIII. Roger.

I. Bridget, *m.* to Robert Seymer, esq. of Hanford, in Dorsetshire.

The eldest surviving son,

EDWARD PHELIPS, esq. of Montacute, in 1685, left three daughters, Anne, first wife of her cousin, Edward Phelips, esq., Elizabeth, second wife of the same gentleman, and Edith, *m.* to Carew Hervey Mildmay, esq. of Shawford. At the decease of Edward Phelips the estate devolved on his nephew and son-in-law,

EDWARD PHELIPS, esq. of Montacute, *b.* in 1768, who *m.* first, Anne, eldest daughter, secondly, Elizabeth, second daughter of his predecessor, and had issue by both; by the first, one son and two daughters, viz.

Edward, *b.* in 1704, *d. s. p.*

Anne, *m.* to John Horner, esq. of Mells.
Bridget, *m.* to Sir Gerard Napier.

By the second, three sons and one daughter, of whom the eldest,

EDWARD PHELIPS, esq. *b.* in 1725, left by Maria, his wife, whom he married in 1747, three sons and four daughters, viz.

I. EDWARD, of Montacute, *b.* in 1753, *m.* in 1784, Miss Lockyer, and *d. s. p.*
II. William, in holy orders, *b.* in 1755, *m.* in 1781, Anna-Aletheia-Elizabetha, daughter of the Rev. John Paget, vicar of Doulting in Somersetshire (see p. 424), and had issue,
   1. JOHN, of Montacute, who *m.* in 1816, his first cousin, Mary-Ann, daughter of the Rev. Charles Phelips, and died in 1834, leaving an only surviving daughter, MARY. "The representative of an ancient and honourable family (says a writer in the Gentleman's Magazine), Mr. Phelips, by the excellence of his many public and private virtues fully repaid to society the value of the adventitious claim which is uniformly conceded to a dignified line of ancestry. Having for many years presided as chairman of the criminal court of quarter sessions in his native county, he had by the integrity of his principles and the mildness of his judgment, advanced its judicial character to a degree of estimation rarely acquired under such circumstances."
   2. William, who *m.* Miss Messiter, and died in 1833, leaving
      William.
      Richard.
      Elizabeth.
   3. Edward.
   4. Robert, who *m.* his cousin, Maria, dau. of William Harbyn, esq. of Newton, near Yeovil.
   5. Thomas.
   6. Charles-Henry.
   7. Richard-Colston.

   1. Anna.
   2. Mary, *m.* to the Rev. H. Hoskins.
   3. Sarah.
III. John, *d.* unm.
IV. CHARLES, of whom presently.

I. Maria, *b.* in 1749, *d.* an infant.
II. Elizabeth, *m.* first, to John Clarke, esq. and, secondly, to Peter Bluett, esq.
III. Maria, *m.* to John Old Goodford, esq. of Yeovil (see page 147).
IV. Rhoda, *m.* to Wyndham Harbin, esq. of Newton, near Yeovil.

The fourth son,

THE REV. CHARLES PHELIPS, who *d.* in 1834, married, 6th February, 1792, Mary, daughter of Thomas Blackmore, esq. of Briggins Park, in Herts, by Mary, his wife, sister of John Old Goodford, esq. and by her (who *d.* in 1818) had (with another son, Edward, lieutenant 13th Light Dragoons, killed at the battle of Waterloo, 15th June, 1815, and a daughter, Mary-Anne, *m.* to her first cousin, John Phelips, esq. of Montacute), the present CHARLES PHELIPS, esq. of Briggins Park.

*Arms*—Arg. a chev. gu. between three roses ppr.

*Crest*—A square beacon or chest on two wheels, or, filled with fire ppr.

*Motto*—Pro aris et focis.

*Estates*—In the counties of Herts, Kent, and Essex.

*Seat*—Briggins Park, Herts.

# WELMAN, OF POUNDSFORD PARK.

WELMAN, CHARLES-NOEL, esq. of Poundsford Park, in the county of Somerset, *b.* 4th December, 1814, *m.* 1st May, 1835, Anne Eliza, eldest daughter of C. H. Bolton, esq. eldest son of the late Cornelius Bolton, esq. of Faithlake, in the county of Waterford. Mr. Welman succeeded his father 28th January, 1829.

## Lineage.

The descent of the Welman family cannot authentically be traced further back than the sixteenth century, at the close of which and at the beginning of the seventeenth there were several persons of the name residing in the county of Somerset, all in some degree related. The chief branch resided at Ilchester, and from it the present family of Poundsford Park derives. The first ancestor on record left seven children, viz.

- I. TRISTRAM, his heir.
- II. William, who married and settled at Cudworth. He died in 1653.
- III. Nicholas, who died in February, 1664.
- IV. Edward, who *m.* and settled at Ilminster. He *d.* in July, 1672.
- V. Thomas, who being educated for the church, and having graduated at Oxford, obtained from — Northcot, esq. the living of Luppet, but was thence ejected for non-conformity in 1662. He *m.* and left several children at his decease in 1685, aged eighty.

- I. Elizabeth, *d.* unmarried.
- II. Juliana, *m.* and had issue.

The eldest son,

TRISTRAM WELMAN, removed to Taunton, in Somersetshire, where he died in July, 1650, leaving, with other issue, a son and successor,

SIMON WELMAN, esq. who continued to reside at Taunton, where he possessed considerable property, and was one of the burgesses of that town. He married, and had issue,

- I. ISAAC, his heir.
- II. Simon, who at first was educated for the church, but afterwards, owing to the circumstances of the times, applied himself to the study of medicine, and became an eminent physician in London, where he realized by his profession a considerable fortune. In 1686 he obtained the degree of doctor of medicine, and in 1689 was admitted one of the licentiates of the college of physicians. He *m.* Miss Smith, and had one son, who died young. Dying without surviving issue in 1707, Dr. Welman bequeathed all his estates and property to his brother Isaac, and according to his request was buried in the church of Battersea, Surrey. A portrait of him is still preserved in the hall at Poundsford Park.

- I. Margaret, *m.* to John Satchel, esq. and had issue.
- II. Katharine, *m.* to John Laugdon, esq. and has issue.
- III. Mary, died unm.
- IV. Grace, *m.* to John Gold, esq. and had issue.

Simon Welman died in 1670, and was succeeded by his eldest son,

ISAAC WELMAN, esq. who first resided at Upcott, near Taunton, but subsequently, in 1708, removed to Poundsford Park: in two years after he served the office of high sheriff for Somersetshire. He *m.* first, Miss Babb, and had by her two daughters, viz.

- I. Mary, *m.* to William Buncombe, esq. of Trull, near Taunton, and *d. s. p.* in 1718.
- II. Elizabeth, died unm. at Poundsford Lodge, in 1755, aged seventy-eight.

Mr. Welman wedded, secondly, Miss Prudence Bennet, and by her, who survived a widow until 1729, had issue,

I. SIMON, his heir.

II. Isaac, died unm. at Poundsford Park, in 1709, aged twenty-four.

III. Thomas, *b.* in 1693, who settled at Poundsford Lodge, a property which had been purchased with that of the Park by his uncle, Dr. Simon Welman, and served as high sheriff for Somersetshire in 1733. He *m.* in 1731, Mary, daughter of Benjamin Hawkins, esq. of Exeter, and by her (who died in 1760) left at his decease 6th November, 1757, an only daughter, who wedded William Hawker, esq. nephew of the Rev. M. Towgood, and dying in 1769, aged thirty-six, left issue.

I. Prudence, *m.* to John Whyatt, esq. of Bishopshull, and *d.* in 1761, *s. p.*

II. Hannah, *m.* to the Rev. Farnham Haskol, a non-conforming minister at Bishopshull, and died in 1746, leaving a daughter, *m.* to the Rev. Peard Jillard.

Mr. Welman died in 1715, aged sixty-nine, was buried in a vault at Pitminster Church, and succeeded by his eldest son,

SIMON WELMAN, esq. born in December, 1683, who was appointed in 1715 a deputy lieutenant for Somersetshire, and lieutenant-colonel of the Taunton Yellow Regiment of Militia, of which Sir William Pynsent was colonel. He *m.* in 1709, Elizabeth, daughter of Benjamin Hawkins, merchant of Exeter, and by her, who *d.* at Yard House, in 1764, aged eighty-one, had issue,

I. ISAAC, his heir.

II. Simon, who never married, but always resided, after his brother's marriage, with his sister, Mrs. Halliday, at Yard House, where he died 12th September, 1799, aged eighty-three. His death is thus recorded in the Sherborne paper: "A few days since died at Yard House, Taunton, aged eighty-three, Simon Welman, esq. universally lamented; for to the greatest mildness and lovingness of temper he joined those amiable virtues, which while they endeared him to his relations, commanded the love and esteem of all. In private life his character was unblemished, and as a true christian, he was uniform in discharging the duties of religion."

I. Mary, *m.* to John Halliday, esq. of Yard House, and died in 1792, leaving issue (see vol. ii. p. 130).

II. Elizabeth, died unm. at the age of sixteen, in 1727.

Mr. Welman, who resided at Cutliffe, survived his father but a few months, and never removed to Poundsford Park. He *d.* in 1716, and was *s.* by his son,

ISAAC WELMAN, esq. of Poundsford Park, *b.* in February, 1710, who *m.* in 1737, Jane, only daughter of Robert Tristram, esq. merchant, of Barnstaple, and granddaughter of the Rev. John Hanmer, and had by her (who died at Bath, 4th March, 1775) two sons and three daughters, viz.

I. ISAAC, died young, in 1754.

II. THOMAS, his heir.

I. Jane, *d.* unm. 25th February, 1821, aged eighty-two.

II. Elizabeth, *m.* in July, 1769, to John Meech, esq. of Bridehead, and *d. s. p.*

III. Rebecca, *d.* unmarried, 6th September, 1831, aged eighty-three.

Mr. Welman, who was in the commission of the peace, died 9th February, 1782, and was succeeded by his only surviving son,

THOMAS WELMAN, esq. of Poundsford Park, *b.* 14th June, 1746, who *m.* first, in 1785, Elizabeth, daughter and co-heiress of John Lock, esq. of Hawleigh, a distant relation of the celebrated John Lock, and had by her, who *d.* in March, 1788, aged twenty-one, one son and one daughter, viz.

I. Isaac, died in infancy.

I. Elizabeth, *m.* in 1809, to Charles Noel Noel, esq. eldest son of Sir Gerard Noel, bart. Mr. Charles Noel succeeded in 1823 to the barony of Barham, upon the demise of his mother, but Mrs. Noel did not survive to enjoy the title, as she died in 1811 *s. p.*

Mr. Welman wedded, secondly, in January, 1813, the Hon. Charlotte Noel, daughter of Sir Gerard Noel, by Diana, his wife, Baroness Barham, and dying 28th January, 1829, aged eighty-three, left by her an only child, the present CHARLES-NOEL WELMAN, esq. of Poundsford Park.

*Arms*—Arg. on a bend gu. between two pomes, three mullets or.

*Crest*—A demi-lion rampant arg. holding a mullet between his paws or, langued gu.

*Motto*—Dei providentia Juvat.

*Estates*—In Somersetshire and Dorsetshire.

*Seat*—Poundsford Park, near Taunton.

# BENCE, OF THORINGTON HALL.

BENCE, HENRY-BENCE, esq. of Thorington Hall, Suffolk, lieutenant-colonel in the East Suffolk militia, *b.* 12th March, 1788, *m.* 5th May, 1815, Elizabeth-Susanna, daughter and co-heiress of Nicholas Starkie, esq. of Riddlesden Hall, in the county of York, and has had issue,

HENRY-ALEXANDER-STARKIE, *b.* 15th May, 1816.
Edward-Robert-Starkie, *b.* 27th August, 1823.
Thomas-Starkie, *b.* 1st October, 1824.

Marianne-Katherine, *d.* in 1833.

Colonel Bence, who succeeded his father in September, 1824, is a magistrate for the counties of Suffolk and Norfolk, and a deputy-lieutenant of the former.

## Lineage.

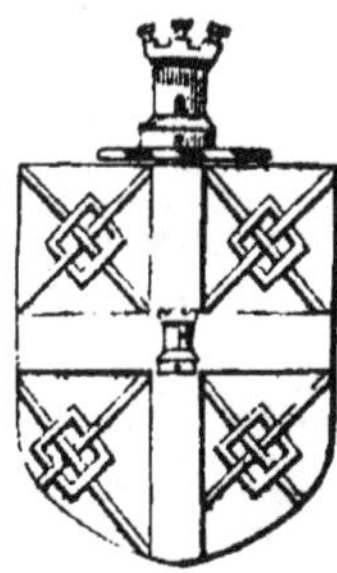

EDMUND BENCE, of Aldeburgh, in Suffolk, died before 1587, as appears by the will of his son Robert, leaving issue,

I. THOMAS, citizen of London, buried there 16th May, 1590.
II. EDMUND, of Aldeburgh, some time bailiff of that town, buried there 11th March, 1597, leaving issue.
III. ROBERT, of Aldeburgh, *m.* in 1574, Anne Willett, and *d.* in 1587, leaving a son, Edmund, of Aldeburgh.
IV. JOHN.

I. Rose, *m.* to — Richards.

The youngest son,

JOHN BENCE, of Aldeburgh, married Joan, probably daughter of William Wignall, as her son William calls William Wignall his grandfather in 1606, and by her, who *d.* in 1586, had issue,

I. ALEXANDER.
II. Robert, of Harwich, in Essex, merchant, whose will, dated 26th May, 1611, was proved 8th June following. He married two wives, and had by the first, a widow named Bridget Coverdall, whom he married in 1575, two daughters, Jane, *m.* to Robert Wheatley, citizen of London, and Margaret, to Henry Marsh, and a son,

John, of Orford, in Suffolk, baptized at Aldeburgh, 28th September, 1578, *d.* about 1619, leaving a son and daughter, Robert and Mary.

III. William, of Aldeburgh, merchant, one of the burgesses of that town in 1588 and 1592, *m.* in 1575, Mary, daughter of — Blome, and relict of — Wright, and *d.* in 1602, leaving issue.

I. Mary, baptized at Aldeburgh 5th May, 1560, *m.* first, to William Hales, and secondly, to James Palmer.
II. Joan, *m.* at Aldeburgh 28th August, 1574, to Arthur Michelson.

John Bence, whose will bears date in 1576, died the following year, and was *s.* by his son,

ALEXANDER BENCE, of Aldeburgh, merchant, *b.* in 1547, six times bailiff of that borough. He *m.* 2nd September, 1571, Mary, daughter of Thomas Squire, and had issue,

I. Thomas, baptized in 1574, desired by his will to be buried in the churchyard of St. Peter, at Aldeburgh.
II. JOHN, of whom presently.
III. Alexander, not twenty-one in 1610, M.P. for the borough of Aldeburgh in 1640, and for the county of Suffolk in 1654. He *m.* two wives, and had issue by the first,

Alexander (Sir), of Dublin, will

dated 16th December, 1675, proved 20th July, 1676.

John, of London, alderman thereof, and M.P. for Aldeburgh in 1658, 1661, 1679, 1681, and 1685. He *m.* twice, and had by his first wife, Judith, daughter of Peter Andrews, of London, an only daughter and heir,

RACHEL, *m.* to Vere Fane, Earl of Westmoreland.

Anne, living in 1648.

Elizabeth, *m.* to John Upton, by whom she had a daughter, Elizabeth Farrington, who was living in 1675, as appears by the will of Sir Alexander Bence.

IV. Squier, of Aldeburgh, baptized in 1597, bailiff three times and burgess in parliament twice, *d.* in 1648, and was buried at Aldeburgh.

V. Robert, of London, baptized in 1584, buried at St. Bennett's, Gracechurch Street, London, 20th March, 1655, in which year his will was dated. He left several sons and daughters.

I. Rose, *m.* to Thomas Johnson.

II. Mary, *m.* to John Base, of Benhall, in Suffolk.

Alexander Bence *d.* 27th January, 1612, and was buried at Aldeburgh. His son,

JOHN BENCE, esq. of Aldeburgh and Benhall, in Suffolk, baptized in 1581, was four times bailiff of Aldeburgh. He *m.* twice, and by his first wife, Mary, daughter of Edmund French, gent. of Kelsall, in Suffolk, had issue,

I. JOHN, of Ringsfield, in Suffolk, high sheriff for Suffolk in 1665. He *m.* Ann, daughter of Christopher Layer, of Norwich, and *d. s. p.* His will, dated 22nd January, 1680, was proved at Norwich 14th April, 1681.

II. EDMUND, of whom presently.

III. Alexander, living in 1635.

I. Mary, *m.* to — Barkley.

II. Elizabeth, *m.* to William Smith, of Parkfield.

John Bence *d.* 2nd July, 1635, and was buried at Aldeburgh. His second son,

EDMUND BENCE, esq. of Benhall, married Mary, daughter of Sir Francis Gallop, knt. and by her (who was buried at Benhall 15th May, 1717,) had issue,

I. JOHN, *b.* in 1670, of Haveningham Hall, in Suffolk, *m.* Catherine, daughter and heir of Sir Thomas Glemham, knt. of Glemham, and granddaughter of the famous Sir Thomas Glemham, knt. governor of Carlisle. By this lady he left an only daughter and heiress,

MARY, *m.* Sir William Barker, bart. of Grimstone Hall, in Suffolk, M.P. and dying before 1727, left a son,

SIR JOHN BARKER, bart. of Sproughton, *b.* in 1724, who *m.* in 1740, Alice, only daughter and heiress of Sir Comport Fytch, of Eltham, and by her, who wedded, secondly, Philip Brooke, esq. had a son and successor,

SIR JOHN FYTCH BARKER, of Sproughton, who *d. s. p.* in 1766.

II. ALEXANDER, of Thorington Hall, baptized at Benhall 20th February, 1671, high sheriff for Suffolk in 1733 and 1742, *m.* Christian, daughter of Sir Anthony Deane, knt. of London, and dying in 1759, left an only daughter to survive him,

ANN, of Thorington Hall, *b.* in 1714, *m.* in 1762, to George Golding, esq. by whom, who *d.* in 1803, she had no issue. Mrs. Golding died in 1794, and was succeeded at Thorington by her first cousin, the REV. BENCE SPARROW.

III. Edward, *d.* young.

IV. ROBERT, of Henstead, baptized in 1675, of whom presently.

V. Edmund.

VI. William, *b.* in 1678, *d.* young.

VII. Thomas, A.M. rector of Kelsall and Carlton, in Suffolk, *b.* in 1679, *m.* Margaret, daughter and heir of Robert Barker, esq. of Bradfield, in that county, and dying in 1757, left two daughters and co-heirs, namely,

Catherine, *b.* in 1708, *m.* in 1747, Gabriel Trusson, esq. of Kalsale, and dying in 1785 left a son, Thomas, and a daughter, Catherine, the wife of Anthony Collett, esq. of Walton, in Suffolk.

Bridget, *b.* in 1709, *m.* in 1756, Thomas Bigsby, M.D. of Saxmundham.

I. Mary, *d.* unmarried in 1765.

II. Abigail, *d.* unmarried in 1750.

Mr. Bence died 5th May, 1702, aged eighty-three, and was buried at Benhall. His fourth son,

ROBERT BENCE, esq. of Henstead, *b.* at Benhall in 1675, *m.* Mary, daughter and heir of the Rev. Laurence Echard, of Henstead, and dying in 1745, left, with a son, Lawrence, who *d.* unmarried in 1746, two daughters. The younger, Mary, *d.* unmarried in 1792; the elder,

ANN BENCE, *b.* in 1707, married at Henstead 16th December, 1740, Robert Sparrow, esq. of Worlingham and Kettleborough, in Suffolk, and by him, who *d.* in 1764, had issue,

ROBERT SPARROW, esq. of Worlingham Hall, who married twice, and had by his first wife, Mary, daughter and heir of Sir John Barnard, bart. of Brampton Park, one son and one daughter, viz.

ROBERT BERNARD SPARROW, esq. of Worlingham Hall, baptized in 1773, who *m.* 14th May, 1797, Lady Olivia Acheson, daughter of Arthur, first Earl of Gosford, and *d.* a general officer in the West Indies in 1805, leaving a daughter and heiress,

MILICENT, *m.* in 1822, to George, Viscount Mandeville.

Mary Sparrow, *m.* to Archibald, present Earl of Gosford.

BENCE SPARROW, of whom we are about to treat.

The second son,

*The Rev.* BENCE SPARROW, rector of Beccles, in Suffolk, inheriting the Thorington estate, assumed by sign manual 2nd May, 1804, the surname and arms of BENCE. He *m.* 16th May, 1786, Harriet, daughter and heir of William Elmy, esq. of Beccles, and had issue,

HENRY-BENCE, his heir.

Anne-Maria, *m.* in 1809, to the Rev. L. R. Brown, rector of Kelsale.

Matilda, *m.* in 1811, to Colonel Jones, of the 5th Dragoon Guards.

Mr. Bence died in September, 1824, and was *s.* by his son, the present HENRY-BENCE BENCE, esq. of Thorington Hall.

*Arms*—Arg. on a cross between four frets gu. a castle of the first.

*Crest*—A castle triple towered.

*Motto*—Virtus castellum meum.

*Estates*—Thoringdon, in Suffolk; Frenchwood, Lancashire; Riddlesden Hall, Yorkshire; and Barnton, Cheshire.

*Town Residence*—Park Lane.

*Seat*—Thorington Hall, Suffolk.

## Starkie, of Frenchwood.

JOHN STARKIE, esq. who served as sheriff of Lancashire in 1656, was the direct descendant in the male line of Geoffry Starky, of Barthington or Barnton, apparently the same with Geoffry, son of Richard Starkie, of Stretton, living about the time of EDWARD I. He *m.* Alice, daughter of Alexander Norres, esq. of Tonge, and had, with other issue,

I. JOHN, *b.* in 1638, *m.* Ann, daughter of William Hulton, esq. of Hulton, and had two sons and two daughters viz.

PIERS, of Barnton and Huntroyd, *d. s. p.* in 1760, aged seventy-four.

John, in the Exchequer, *d. s. p.*

Alice, *m.* to the Hon. Hor. Townshend.

Mary, *m.* to Peter Worthington, gent.

II. NICHOLAS.

The second son,

NICHOLAS STARKIE, esq. married Elizabeth, daughter of Colonel Gunter, of Wiltshire, and had five sons, namely,

I. EDMUND, barrister-at-law, and M.P. for Preston, *d. s. p.*

II. Nicholas, who *m.* Sarah, daughter and co-heir of Valentine ffarington, M.D. of Preston, and had

Nicholas, *d. s. p.*

LE GENDRE, of Huntroyde, married Frances, daughter of Walter Hawksworth, esq. of Hawksworth, in Yorkshire, and had issue.

Betty, *m.* to William Dixon, esq. of Sutton.

III. John, rector of Halneker, Sussex, *d. s. p.*

IV. Thomas, of Preston, *m.* a daughter of George Bulkeley, esq. of Charterhouse Square, and *d. s. p.*

V. WILLIAM.

The youngest son,

WILLIAM STARKIE, esq. of Manchester, married Mary, daughter of Thomas Foxley, of the same place, and left, with three other sons and one daughter,

THOMAS STARKIE, esq. of Frenchwood, who *m.* Catherine, daughter of Edward Downes, esq. of Shrigley, in Cheshire, and was *s.* by his son,

NICHOLAS STARKIE, esq. of Frenchwood, in Lancashire, and of Riddlesdon Hall, Yorkshire, whose daughter and co-heir, Elizabeth-Susannah, *m.* (as already shewn) in 1815, HERNY-BENCE BENCE, esq. of Thorington Hall, Suffolk.

*Arms of Starkie*—Arg. a bend sa. between six storks of the second.

# BUCHANAN, OF ARDINCONNAL.

BUCHANAN, ANDREW, esq. of Ardinconnal, in the county of Dumbarton, deputy-lieutenant, and in the commission of the peace for the counties of Dumbarton and Lanark, in which latter county he possessed the estate of Auchingray, and other lands, *b.* 12th July, 1745, *m.* 3rd July, 1769, Jane, eldest daughter of James Dennistoun, of Colgrain and Dennistoun, or that ilk, and has had issue,

I. ARCHIBALD, of Auchintorlie, in the county of Dumbarton, and Hillington, in the county of Renfrew. To the estate of Auchintorlie, as will afterwards appear, he succeeded on the death of his uncle, George Buchanan, of Auchintorlie, a deputy-lieutenant, and in the commission of the peace for the counties of Dumbarton, Renfrew, and Lanark. He possessed the lands of Toward Castle, in Argyleshire, and made considerable additions to his patrimonial estates, and commanded for many years during the French revolutionary war, a troop of Yeoman cavalry. He *m.* Mary, second daughter of Richard Dennistoun, of Kelvingrove, in the county of Lanark, and *d.* 16th December, 1832, leaving issue,

1. ANDREW, now of Auchintorlie.
2. Richard Dennistoun.

1. Christiana. 2. Jane. 3. Mary 4. Isabella. 5. Gorgina. 6. Archina, all minors.

II. James, of Ardinconnal, which estate he purchased in 1811, from his father, who retained the life rent of the House of Ardinconnal and a considerable part of the estate. He also purchased superiorities of considerable value, in the counties of Dumbarton, Stirling, Caithness, and Renfrew. He is a deputy-lieutenant and in the commission of the peace for the counties of Dumbarton, Lanark, and Caithness. He sold, anno 1827, his interest in the estate of Ardinconnal, having previously settled the life-rent of Blairvadock House and adjoining grounds on his lady. He *m.* Lady Janet Sinclair, eldest daughter of James, twelfth Earl of Caithness, and has issue,

1. ANDREW, attached to H. B. M. embassy to the United States of America.

1. Helen-John-Sinclair, *m.* to William Wootton Abney, esq. of Measham Hall, in the county of Leicester (see vol. i. p. 572).
2. Jane-Dennistoun, *m.* to William Tritton, esq. residing at Inveresk House, Mid-Lothian.
3. Jane-Campbell, *m.* to Richard Fox, esq. of Curragh O'Bridgen, in the county Cavan, and grandson of Barry, third Baron, and first Earl of Farnham.
4. Charlotte Macgregor Murray, *m.* to Charles Henry Forbes, of Kingairloch, in the county of Argyle.
5. Matilda-Frances-Harriet, a minor.

I. Jesse, *m.* to James Monteith, esq. of Craighead, Lanarkshire.

II. Martha, *m.* to George Yuille, esq. of Cardross Park, in the county of Dumbarton, second son of George Yuille, of Darleith, in the same county, to which estate his son succeeded, as heir of entail, on the death of his uncle.

## Lineage.

This is a branch of the ancient and distinguished families of Buchanan, of Buchanan, or that ilk, and of Buchanan, of Lenny, now representative of that house, and chief of the clan Buchanan.

Anselan O'Kyan, the reputed progenitor of the surname, and the first Laird of Buchanan, was Prince of South-Munster, but having been driven from his possessions by the Danes, in an attempt to free his country from their bondage, removed from Ireland into Scotland about the year 1016, and for important services rendered to *King* MALCOLM II. was rewarded with the estate of Buchanan, and other lands of considerable value. As was customary at that period, he assumed the name or designation which attached to his possessions.

JOHN BUCHANAN, eldest son of Sir Walter Buchanan, eleventh Laird of Buchanan, married the heiress of Lenny,* as appears by a charter of *King* ROBERT III. in the year 1363, in favour of John De Buchanan, and Janet De Leny, of the barony of Pitwhonidy, but dying before his father, his son John, on the death of his grandfather, became the twelfth Laird of Buchanan.

This John, Laird of Buchanan and Lenny, who flourished upwards of 400 years ago, and was common ancestor of the great George Buchanan and this family,† had three sons,

I. ALEXANDER, (Sir) who, in 1421, killed the Duke of Clarence, at the battle of Beaugé, and was himself slain at the battle of Verneuil, 1424, unm.‡
II. Walter, (Sir) who succeeded to the estate of Buchanan.
III. JOHN, of whose line we have to treat.

The third son,

JOHN BUCHANAN, during his father's lifetime designed of Ballachondachy, *s.* after his father's death, to the estate of Lenny, and was father of

ANDREW BUCHANAN, as appears by a charter, *penes* Buchanan De Lenny, granted by James II. in the year 1458, in favour of the said Andrew Buchanan, of Lenny, of the barony of Pitwhonidy and other lands.

Andrew, of Lenny, had five sons,

I. JOHN, who succeeded him.
II. Archibald.
III. WALTER.
IV. George.
V. Gilbert.

The third son,

WALTER BUCHANAN, was the first cadet of the family of Lenny. He possessed Mochastel, in the parish of Callender, and was *s.* by his son,

ANDREW BUCHANAN, father of

PATRICK BUCHANAN, whose son,

ALEXANDER BUCHANAN, had two sons, JOHN, his successor at Mochastel, and

WALTER BUCHANAN, of Glenny, whose grandson, Captain James Buchanan, succeeded to the estate of Glenny, but dying in France without issue, his uncle, the second son of Walter, of Glenny,

ALEXANDER BUCHANAN, became heir to his nephew, the Laird of Glenny. He had two sons, Andrew and George. The elder,

ANDREW BUCHANAN, purchased Gartacharan from Lord Napier. He had two sons, ALEXANDER, his successor, and

GEORGE BUCHANAN, a magistrate and merchant in Glasgow, who had four sons and one daughter, viz.

I. GEORGE, a merchant, who with his brothers Andrew, Niel, and Archibald, were the original promoters of the Buchanan Society, in that city,

---

* As no genealogical account of the family of Lenny has yet been published, further than appears in the history of the Buchanans, it may be here remarked, having been there omitted, that Gillispie *Moir* De Lany, first of Buchanan, of Lenny, is mentioned in a charter, A. D. 1227, as having obtained his lands from *King* CULENUS, about 960. It is also mentioned in a genealogical account of the family, composed early in the sixteenth century, and which has been likewise omitted, that "Robert Maccan" was killed in the thirteenth century, in England, having been sent thither on a special mission by the king: and that "John Macandra" was killed at the head of his followers by the English, at the battle of Pinkey, in the year 1547, when gallantly endeavouring to turn the fortune of the day. In the martial, urban, and political achievements of the progenitors of this family, reference must be had to the genealogical accounts of the families of Buchanan, of Buchanan, and of Lenny.

† John, of Buchanan and Leny.

Sir Walter, of Buchanan. — Patrick. — Walter. Thomas. — (Thomas:) Robert. Thomas. — (Thomas:) Patrick Alexander. George, ob. 28th Sept. 1582. In the immediate ensuing age his skull was exhumed and was shown for many years in the college of Edinburgh, being remarkable for its exceeding thinness. For a biographical sketch of this distinguished person, refer to BUCHANAN, of Ardoch.

John, of Lenny. — Andrew. — Walter. — Andrew. — Patrick. — Alexander. — Walter. — Alexander. — Andrew. — George. — Archibald. — Andrew, of Ardinconnal.

‡ In pages 171 and 298 of the Buchanan history, honorable mention is made of Sir Alexander Buchanan, grandson and heir apparent of Sir Walter, the eleventh Laird of Buchanan, whose heroic achievements in the wars in France, especially at the battle of Beaugé, 22nd March, 1421, when he had the honour to kill, in single combat, the Duke of Clarence, brother to HENRY V. of England, procured the grant of the double or royal tressure, floured and counterfloured, with fleurs-de-lis to surround the lion in the arms, and of the ducal cap wreathed with laurel, in place of the old crest, with motto, "audaces juvo" for the crest, and for the arms "clarior hinc honos."

now one of the most flourishing benevolent institutions in the west of Scotland.* He was twice married; secondly, to a dau. of Sir John Forbes, bart. of Foveran, Aberdeenshire, and had four sons and four daughters, but his male line is now extinct.

II. Andrew, of Drumpellier, in the county of Lanark, who had two sons and five daughters. The elder son, JAMES, *m.* Margaret Hamilton, granddaughter of the Earl of Haddington, and sister of the Countesses of Morton and Selkirk and of Lady Halket, of Pitferran. By this lady he had, with a son, who *d.* unm. several daughters, of whom Helen married Admiral Sir George Home, bart. The Drumpellier branch of the Buchanan family is now represented by the descendant of Andrew's second son, ROBERT CARRICK BUCHANAN, esq. of Drumpellier.

III. ARCHIBALD, of Auchintorlie, in the county of Dumbarton.

IV. Neil, of Hillington, in the county of Renfrew, M.P. for the Glasgow district of Burghs, whose male line is now extinct. He left one son and three daughters; of the latter, Ann, the eldest, *m.* Oswald, Bishop of Raphoe, and Marion, the third, became the wife of Oliphant of Rossie, in Perthshire, postmaster-general for Scotland.

I. Mary, *m.* to George Buchanan, of Auchintoshan, in the county of Dumbarton.

The third son,

ARCHIBALD BUCHANAN, esq. purchased Auchintorlie and other lands, in Dumbartonshire, from his brother Andrew, as also the lands of Hillington, in Renfrewshire, upon the death of his brother Niel. He married Martha, daughter of Peter Murdoch, esq. of Glasgow, Lord Provost or chief magistrate of that city, by whom he had issue,

I. PETER, } successively of Auchintorlie.
II. GEORGE, }

III. ANDREW, of Ardinconnal, and heir of destination of Auchintorlie, of whom above.

I. Mary, *m.* Alexander Spiers, of Elderslie, county of Renfrew.

The eldest son and heir,

PETER BUCHANAN, esq. of Auchintorlie, *m.* Miss Catherine Macpherson, who after his death, wedded Sir Ewen Cameron, bart. of Fassifern, in the county of Inverness. Dying *s. p.* Mr. Buchanan was *s.* by his brother,

GEORGE BUCHANAN, esq. of Auchintorlie, who was twice married but had no issue. He left the family estates of Auchintorlie and others in the county of Dumbarton, and Hillington, in the county of Renfrew, as before mentioned, to his nephew ARCHIBALD, eldest son of his brother Andrew of Ardinconnal, having the consent thereto of his brother, the heir of destination. Andrew of Auchintorlie, eldest son of Archibald, a minor, as before mentioned, now represents the family, and is resident at Auchintorlie House, Dumbartonshire.

*Arms*—Quarterly, as in p. 257 and 258 of the History of the Buchanans; 1st and 4th, or, a lion rampant, sable, armed and langued gules, within a double tressure, flowered and counterflowered, with fleurs-de-lis of the second, for BUCHANAN. 2nd and 3rd, sable, a cheveron between two bears' heads erased in chief, and another in base, arg. muzzled gules. On the chief point of the chevron, a cinquefoil of the 1st, for Lenny. This quartering however was omitted last matriculation at the Lord Lion's office.

*Crest*—A hand couped, holding a duke's coronet with two laurel branches wreathed under it.

*Motto*—Clarior hinc honos.

*Estates*—In Dumbartonshire.

*Seat*—Ardinconnal House.

* This society, new in principle, was founded in the year 1725, for the support of the poor of the clan. The surname of Buchanan was very general in the West of Scotland, particularly in the counties of Stirling and Dumbarton. In the former, the lands of Buchanan are situated, from which the family name was acquired. They are now the property of the Duke of Montrose, and Buchanan House is his Grace's residence, in Scotland. This society was established for the sole purpose of giving endowments to individuals of the clan residing in Scotland, in indigent circumstances, and of assisting boys of promising genius in the prosecution of their studies at the Universities or otherwise. From unexampled good management, it has progressively advanced till it has become one of the principal charities in the west of Scotland. The entry money paid by members has never been higher than five guineas, from which small sums and a few very trifling donations, there has accumulated a fund of £800. a year, enabling the directors to distribute not less than £500. per annum among the poor of the clan, and in the education of youth.

# GIBSON, OF QUERNMORE PARK.

GIBSON, JOHN, of Quernmore Park, in the county of Lancaster, a minor; succeeded to the family estates on the death of his father, in 1832.

## Lineage.

The surname of Gibson is of great antiquity both in England and Scotland. In both kingdoms it is met with at a period not long subsequent to the Norman Conquest; and in both, but especially in the latter, have been many eminent men of the name. In Scotland are families of the name which ranked amongst the free barons, or lesser nobility, of that kingdom more than five hundred years ago; and no less than five Scotch families of Gibson, or rather branches of one and the same ancient and wide-spreading house, have been raised to the baronetage of Scotland. In 1628, upwards of two hundred years ago, Sir Alexander Gibson, of Durie, knight, was created a baronet; and not long subsequently the Gibsons of Pentland and the Gibsons of Kierhill had the like dignity conferred upon them; and in modern times the Gibsons of Clifton Hall and the Gibsons of Riccarton have been raised to similar rank. The baronetcy of the Kierhill branch has become extinct, that of the Pentland branch has merged in that of the Gibsons of Durie, and upon the death, without issue, of Sir Robert Gibson, the eighth baronet of Durie, the baronetcy, or rather the two baronetcies of that branch devolved upon the Gibsons of Skyrling, a younger branch of the Gibsons of Pentland. The Gibsons of Skyrling, representing the noble family of Carmichael of Carmichael, *extinct* Earls of Hyndford, have, in compliance with the will of the last Earl of Hyndford, assumed the surname of Carmichael in addition to their own; and the present Sir James Gibson-Carmichael, baronet, of Skyrling, is the representative of the Carmichael family, and also of the Durie and Pentland branches of the Gibson family. The baronetcies of the Clifton Hall and Riccarton branches are existing ones and Sir Charles Maitland Gibson, and Sir James Gibson-Craig are the present baronets of these branches: the latter gentleman representing the ancient family of the Craigs, of Riccarton, has assumed the surname of Craig in addition to his own. The Gibsons of Scotland have married either into, or into distinguished branches of, the noble families of Cranstoun, Murray, Fleming, Hamilton, Hay, Seton, Somerville, Primrose, Carmichael, Maitland and Dundas (into some of them twice or oftener), and into many other ancient and distinguished families of that kingdom. Playfair, in his account of the Scotch family of Gibson (see his "British Family Antiquity"), says, they were "possessed of high antiquity; were free barons at a very early period; were ancient land owners of great importance in the country and of great service to the state, and had produced several able statesmen as well as individuals remarkable for their learning and patriotism:" and in another place he continues, "throughout the pages of Scottish History we frequently find members of the Gibson family employed in the most important negociations, and entrusted with some of the highest offices in the state:" Sir Robert Douglas's account of the family, in his Scotch Baronage, is very similar to that given by Playfair, and proves the ancient consequence and importance of the family. We have given this brief account of this ancient and wide-spreading northern race, by reason that the Lancashire family of the same name (the subject of the present article) is traditionally descended from it; and circumstances exist which corroborate the tradition. The Lancashire Gibsons have been settled in that county nearly two centuries and a half, (since the time of JAMES I.), and during the greatest part of that time have possessed considerable property in the county. They have at different periods been high sheriffs, and are allied to several ancient and distinguished families. They were formerly Lords of Yelland, in Lancashire, but the Yelland and other extensive estates which they once held of the value of three thousand pounds a year or upwards have been alienated. The Yelland branch of the family terminated in females on the death, unmarried, of GEORGE GIBSON, esq. of Yelland hall. Upon his decease his Yelland and other estates devolved upon SARAH GIBSON and ANNE GIBSON. These ladies were the daughters and eventually co-heirs of ROBERT GIBSON, esq. by Sarah, daughter of the Very Reverend Dean William Coxe, D.D. Mr. Gibson was a barrister-at-law, and recorder of Lancaster. He died suddenly, when on the northern circuit, in the prime of life. He was a very learned and able lawyer, and at the time of his death was rising rapidly in his profession; and had he lived, would, there is little doubt, have attained great eminence in it. Of his two daughters, and eventually co-heirs, Anne *m.* William Wickham, esq. of Yorkshire, (of the family of the celebrated William, of Wickham, and ancestor of the Right Honourable William Wickham, who was secretary for Ireland during a part of Mr. Pitt's administration), and the other, Sarah, *d.* unmarried. She died seized of estates in the parishes and townships of Yelland, Lancaster, Dalton, Furness, Plain-Furness, Stenton, Adgarley, Muchland, Skerton, Nether-Skerton, and Scotforth, all in the county of Lancaster, and Preston-Patrick, and Mansergh, in the county of Westmorland, all of which went, under her will, to the Gibsons of Myerscough, in the county of Lancaster. This lady's munificence and benevolence of disposition rendered her worthy of the handsome fortune she possessed, and procured for her universal respect and esteem. The Gibsons of Myerscough, to whom she left her landed property, and of whom we have to treat, spring from

CHARLES GIBSON, a younger son of Edmond Gibson, of Roos-court, in the parish of Dalton, in the county of Lancaster, where he possessed a good estate. Mr. Charles Gibson settled at Preston in the profession of the law, and acquired a fortune with the highest reputation for integrity and honour. He purchased the Myerscough estate, on which he settled previous to his death. He married Frances, daughter of Ralph Assheton, esq. of Laylam, in the county of Lancaster, and great grand-daughter of Sir Ralph Assheton, knt. chief of the ancient and eminent knightly family of the Asshetons, (afterwards baronets), of Assheton-under-lyne, and Middleton, in the county of Lancaster; the principal branch of which terminated, on the death of Sir Ralph Assheton, bart. in two co-heiresses; one of whom married an ancestor of the Earls of Wilton, and the other, an ancestor of the Lords Suffield. Mr. Gibson had issue by his wife,

- I. ROBERT, his heir.
- II. Ralph-Assheton, who *d.* young.
- III. JOHN, M.A. in holy orders, rector of Romaldkirk, in the county of York, and successor to his brother.
- I. Elizabeth, *d.* an infant.
- II. Mary, *m.* William Parke, esq. of Whitbeck-hall, of a very respectable Cumberland family, allied to the Hudlestons of Hutton-John, Stanleys of Ponsonby, &c.

ROBERT GIBSON, esq. of Myerscough, *s.* as heir. He served the office of high sheriff for Lancashire and was a magistrate for the county. He died, unmarried, at an advanced age. Previous to his death, the estates of the elder branch of the family had come by will to his younger brother,

THE REV. JOHN GIBSON, M.A. rector of Romaldkirk, in the county of York. This gentleman *m.* Anne, daughter and eventually sole heiress (who had a considerable fortune) of William Philip Fulford, esq. a merchant in London, and a near branch of the ancient and eminent knightly family of the Fulfords, of Fulford, in the county of Devon; one of whom, Sir Baldwin Fulford, was a distinguished commander in the wars between the houses of York and Lancaster. Mr. Gibson was a gentleman of considerable erudition, and extensive acquirements in various branches of literature. Though he came into possession of a large property on the extinction of the elder branch of his family, yet he continued to reside on his rectory, and to do the duties of it up to the time of his decease. He died at the rectory house of Romaldkirk, and his remains were interred (as were those of his wife, who survived him only a month) in the family vault in Lancaster church. He had issue,

- I. CHARLES, who *s.* as heir, and who afterwards *s.* to the Myerscough property.
- II. Robert, L.L.B. in holy orders, rector of Fifield, in the county of Essex. He *m.* Charlotte, one of the daughters and co-heirs of William Bullock, esq. of Shelly House, in Essex; of the ancient family of the Bullocks of Faulkburn hall, in that county; being first cousin of Colonel Bullock, who represented the county in parliament nearly half a century.* Mrs. Gibson's family being related to the Tylney family, and next in the entail of the Tylney estates, her husband was presented by Lady Katherine Tylney Long, out of regard for his wife's family, to the valuable living

* For an account of the Bullocks of Faulkburn, see vol. ii. p. 621.

of Fifield. The issue of the marriage were

1. William.
2. Charles.
3. Robert, M.A. in holy orders.
4. Henry, M.A. in holy orders, succeeded his father as rector of Fifield.
5. Edward.

I. Frances, *m.* the Rev. Roger Jacson, M.A. rector (and patron) of the valuable living of Bebington, in the county of Chester.
II. Jane, *m.* her cousin, Charles Parke, esq. a major in the army.
III. Sarah, *d.* unmarried.

CHARLES GIBSON, esq. of Quernmore Park and Myerscough House, eldest son of the Rev. John Gibson, and Anne Fulford, succeeded as heir both to the estates of his own and the elder branch of the family. He *m.* Charlotte,* daughter of Edward Wilson, esq. of Dallam tower, in Westmorland (who for many years represented the county in parliament), by Dorothy, one of three daughters and co-heiresses of Sir William Fleming, bart. of Rydal Hall, in the same county;† a family of great eminence and distinction ever since the Conquest, and descended from Sir Michael le Fleming, knt. who was a near kinsman of William the Conqueror, and one of the commanders of the victorious army at the battle of Hastings. Mr. Gibson served the office of high sheriff for the county of Lancaster, was a deputy lieutenant, in the commission of the peace, and colonel commandant of the Lancaster regiment of volunteers. He was a skilful and spirited agriculturist, and was for many years president of the Lancaster Agricultural Society. He had issue,

I. CHARLES, his heir.
II. John, of Gray's Inn.
III. Edward, a lieutenant in the rifle brigade, *d.* at an early age, *m.* Mary, daughter of William Croker, esq. of the city of Dublin, and grand daughter of John Croker, esq. of Ballinaguard, in the county of Limerick, (see Croker, vol. i. p. 340), and left issue.
IV. Robert, M.A. in holy orders, vicar of Bolton le Sands, in the county of Lancaster, *m.* Ellen, daughter and heir of Christopher Smaley, esq. of Holywell, in Flintshire, and has issue.

I. Charlotte, *m.* George Jacson, esq. of Barton Lodge, in the county of Lancaster; of the family of the Jacsons of Bebington, in the county of Chester; one of considerable antiquity, and allied to the Fitzherberts of Somersal (a branch of the Fitzherberts of Norbury and Swinnerton, see vol. i. p. 78); to the Shalcrosses, formerly of Shalcross, in the county of Derby; Ardens of Arden, in Cheshire; Athertons of Walton (a branch of the Athertons of Atherton, now represented by Lord Lilford); Boothbys (baronets) of Ashburn, and other distinguished families.
II. Sarah, *d.* an infant.
III. Dorothy, *m.* John Wilson, esq. of the Howe, near Windermere Lake, in the county of Westmorland; a captain in the royal navy, and only son and heir of Sir John Wilson, knt. one of the judges of his majesty's court of Common Pleas, and for some time one of the lords commissioners of the great seal. Sir John's Widow (who was a daughter of Mr. sergeant Adair, of the ancient and eminent Scotch family of Adair), *m.* secondly, Admiral Sir John Colpoys, G.C.B.

Mr. Gibson having survived his first wife, *m.* secondly, Isabella Elizabeth, eldest daughter of Sir John Thomas Stanley, bart. of Alderley, in the county of Chester (descended from a younger son of Thomas Lord Stanley, ancestor of the Stanleys Earls of Derby) but by this lady, who survived her husband, he had no issue. He was *s.* by his eldest son,

CHARLES GIBSON, esq. of Quernmore Park and Myerscough House, who served the office of high sheriff for the county of Lancaster, was a deputy lieutenant, and in the commission of the peace. He *m.* Jane-Elizabeth, only daughter of the Rev. John Alexander Hunter,* of Harwick, in the

* Mrs. Gibson's only married sister was the wife of the celebrated bishop of Llandaff (bishop Watson) a man alike distinguished for learning, liberality, integrity and independance of principle; and her eldest brother married the greatest heiress in the kingdom, Miss Egerton of Tatton, (of the family of the Dukes of Bridgewater), but his lady having died without leaving surviving issue, the very large estates of her family went to an ancestor of the present Mr. Egerton of Tatton.

† Of the other daughters and co-heiresses of Sir William Fleming, one married Sir Peter Leicester, bart. of Tabley, ancestor of Lord de Tabley, and the other married Thomas Parker, esq. of Browsholme, in the county of York.

* This gentleman who was heir to a good estate, and married to a lady with a very considerable one, actuated by higher and purer motives than those "pertaining to the things of this world," entered into holy orders, and up to the time of his death performed the duties of a small curacy. He was a branch of a very ancient Scotch family, being descended from a younger son, (by a daughter of Graham, of Fintry, see Graham, of Fintry, p. 120) of Hunter, of Polmood,

county of Lincoln, by Henrietta, only dau. and heiress of Thomas Saule, esq. of Lancaster, by Jane Easter, daughter and eventually sole heir of John Haydock, esq. of Pheasantford (or Easingford) in Lancashire, a family of great antiquity in the county. Mr. Gibson *d.* in 1832, leaving his wife surviving. He had issue,

I. Charles, who died young.
II. JOHN, who succeeded as heir, a minor, and is the present JOHN GIBSON, esq. of QUERNMORE.
III. Wilton.
IV. Edmond.
V. John-Hadock.*
VI. Robert.
VII. George.

I. Jane.
II. Henrietta-Charlotte.
III. Elizabeth.

Of the same family with the Gibsons of Quernmore Park are the Gibsons of Barfield, in the county of Cumberland, noticed amongst the gentry of that county in Lysons' History of Cumberland. Of this branch was the Rev. Edmond Gibson,† who married the widow of Major Warburton (of a branch, settled in Ireland, of the eminent Cheshire family of the Warburtons, baronets, of Warburton and Arley), and daughter of Andrew Hudleston, esq. of Hutton John, in the county of Cumberland (a branch of the very ancient and once powerful baronial family of the Hudlestons, of Millom Castle in that county),‡ by Dorothy,§ daughter of Daniel Fleming, esq. of Skirwith, in Cumberland, ancestor of the Flemings, baronets, of Rydal Hall, in the county of Westmorland. Mr. Gibson had issue by his wife,

EDMOND GIBSON, of Barfield, who married his cousin Isabella, daughter of Wilfred Hudleston, esq. of Hutton John, by Joyce, daughter of Thomas Curwen, esq. of Workington, in Cumberland, of the ancient and eminent knightly family of the Curwens of Workington Hall, who are lineally descended in the male line from Ivo de Taileboys, brother of the Earl of Anjou, ancestor of the Plantagenet Kings of England.‖ Mr. Gibson married, secondly, Isabella, widow of — Littledale (of the family of Sir Joseph Littledale, one of the judges of his majesty's Court of King's Bench), and sister of Robert Waters, esq. of Linethwaite, in Cumberland, who served the office of high sheriff for the county. Mr. Gibson had issue by his first wife one son and two daughters, and by his second wife two sons and one daughter. He was succeeded by his only son by his first wife,

ROBERT GIBSON, esq. of Barfield, who for many years was in the commission of the peace for the county of Cumberland. He lived to the patriarchal age of one hundred years within a few months, and at the time of his death was supposed to be the oldest military officer in his majesty's service, having, about eighty years before, entered the army as a cornet in the first regiment of Dragoon Guards. He married Mary, only child of the Reverend Thomas Adderley or Atherley (the name being indiscriminately so written), of the ancient family of the Adderleys, formerly of Adderley (a lordship and parish in Shropshire), and said to be descended from a younger son (who seated

---

in the county of Peebles, "chief," says the family history, "of the name of Hunter, and as ancient as any in Scotland;" but now extinct in the principal branch, (see Hunter, of Hunterston, vol. ii. p. 500). Mr. Hunter's more immediate ancestor was Dr. Alexander Hunter, who about a century ago settled in England as a physician, and had considerable practice. Dr. Hunter was well known for his literary and scientific pursuits, and acquired considerable fame by his Georgical Essays, and as the annotator of Evelyn's Sylva. He married one of the three daughters and co-heiresses (who amongst them inherited a large property) of William Dealtry, esq. of Gainsborough, in the county of Lincoln, who was the elder branch of the Dealtrys of Lofthouse Hall, in the county of York (see Dealtry, of Lofthouse Hall, vol. i. p. 252). Of Mr. Dealtry's other co-heirs one married the Archbishop of Dublin (father of the present Countess of Kilkenny and the Bishop of Ossory) and the other married Godfrey Meynell, esq. of Langley, in the county of Derby.

* Named after his maternal ancestors, who in ancient times were of great note in the county of Lancaster. On the death of Sir Richard Haydock, knt. of Haydock, the elder branch of the Haydocks terminated in an heiress, who married, first, Sir Piers Legh, of Lyme, in the county of Chester, knight banneret (who died of the wounds he had received in the battle of Azincourt) and, secondly, Sir Richard Molyneux, knt. ancestor of the Earls of Sefton.

† Of this name, though it does not appear that he was of the same family, was that eminent scholar and divine, Edmond Gibson, D. D. Bishop of London.

‡ For some account of the Hudlestons of Millom Castle, see vol. ii. page 582, under the head of "Hudleston of Sawston," a younger branch of the family. The Millom Castle family terminated in an heiress, who married Sir Hedworth Williamson, bart. of Whitburn, in the county of Durham, ancestor of the present Sir Hedworth Williamson, bart. one of the representatives in parliament for that county. Upon the extinction in the male line of the Hudlestons of Millom Castle, the Hudlestons of Hutton John became, and are now, the head of the Hudleston family.

§ From a sister of this lady descends Lord Brougham and Vaux.

‖ For an account of the eminent family of the Curwens of Workington, see vol. i. page 577.

himself at Adderley, and from thence assumed the name,) of the eminent baronial family of the Gresleys; a family which, in common with the Cliffords, formerly Earls of Cumberland, and some others, claims lineal descent in the male line from Rollo, Duke of Normandy, ancestor of William the Conqueror. Mr. Gibson had issue by his wife,

Edmond Gibson-Atherley, esq. who by royal license assumed his mother's surname. He married Jane, daughter of George Edward Stanley, esq. of Ponsonby Hall,* in the county of Cumberland (a branch of the Stanleys, Earls of Derby), and sister of Edward Stanley, esq. of Ponsonby Hall (one of the representatives in parliament for that county), and by her has issue an only daughter.

*Arms of Gibson of Quernmore Park*—1st and 4th, az. three storks rising, ppr. for Gibson; 2nd and 3rd, gu. a chev. arg. for Fulford.

*Crests*—First, a stork rising, in its beak an olive branch (though the crest has been generally borne by the family without the olive branch), and second, out of a ducal coronet a lion's gamb grasping a club spiked.

*Estates*—In Quernmore, Lancaster, and Caton, in the county of Lancaster, and Preston-Patrick, in the county of Westmorland.

*Seat*—Quernmore Park, four miles from Lancaster, a large handsome mansion, built of white polished freestone, and situate in a spacious, well wooded park. It was built by the grandfather of the present possessor, upon part of the Quernmore estate, purchased from Lord Clifford, and commands rich and extensive views of the vale of the Lune.

* For an account of the Stanleys of Ponsonby, see vol. i. page 95.

## YARBURGH, OF HESLINGTON.

YARBURGH, NICHOLAS-EDMUND, esq. of Heslington Hall, in the East Riding of the county of York, *b.* in February, 1771, a deputy-lieutenant for that Riding, and major in the third regiment of provisional militia, succeeded his brother, 28th October, 1825.

### Lineage.

The family of Yarburgh is one of great antiquity, and can trace an authenticated male succession from the time of the Norman Conquest. At that period Eustacius de Yarburgh was Lord of Yarburgh, in the county of Lincoln, which manor, together with the patronage of the living, still remains vested in his lineal representative, the present Major Yarburgh, of Heslington. For many successive centuries, the Yarburghs were chiefly settled in various parts of Lincolnshire, but more than two hundred years ago, they removed their residence to Snaith Hall, in the West Riding of the county of York, and subsequently, Snaith Hall being destroyed, to Heslington Hall, near York, an ancient mansion built in the reign of Elizabeth, and acquired in marriage with a co-heiress of the Hesketh, of Heslington, a junior branch of the Lancashire Heskeths.

Eustacius de Yarburgh, Lord of the manor of Yarborough, or Yarburgh, in the county of Lincoln, A. D. 1066, married and had a son,

Robert de Yarburgh, who wedded the daughter of Sir Lambert Manby, and was father of

Lambert de Yarburgh, whose son, by his wife, the daughter of Arthur Ormsby, esq. was

Sir John de Yarburgh, knt. who married Ursula, daughter of Sir Ralph Humberston, knt. and had a son and successor,

Ralph de Yarburgh, living *temp.* King Stephen, who married Ann, daughter of Sir William Staine, and was succeeded by his son,

Robert de Yarburgh, who wedded a daughter of Sir John Bussam, and was father of

William de Yarburgh, who *m.* Beatrix,

daughter of Sir Geoffrey Auke, knt. and left a son and successor,

RICHARD DE YARBURGH, who flourished in the reign of RICHARD II. He married Cassandra, daughter of Sir Richard Maplethorpe, and was *s.* by his son,

ROBERT DE YARBURGH, who *m.* Isabel, daughter of Sir John Ewrby, knt. by Katherine, his wife, dau. and co-heiress of Barnard Mussenden, esq.* and was *s.* by his son,

WILLIAM DE YARBURGH, who married a daughter of Thomas Anguine, esq. and was father of

RICHARD DE YARBURGH, Lord of the manors of Yarburgh and Kelsterne, in the county of Lincoln. This gentleman espoused Joan, daughter and heiress of John Atwell, esq. of Legbourne, in the same shire, descended in the female line from Philip, Baron de Kyme,‡ and was succeeded at his decease by his son,

WILLIAM DE YARBURGH, Lord of Yarburgh, &c. who *m.* Isabel, daughter and heir of Sir John Billing, by Margaret, his wife, daughter and heiress of Sir John Teyes, and left a son and successor,

RICHARD DE YARBURGH, of Yarburgh, father, by Elizabeth, his wife, dau. of Thomas Moyne, esq. of

CHARLES YARBURGH, esq. of Yarburgh, Lord of the manors of Yarburgh, Kelsterne, and Legbourne, all in the county of Lincoln. He *m.* first, Agnes, daughter of Sir John Skipwith, and had by her a son,

RICHARD, who *m.* Margaret, daughter of Thomas Portington, esq. and had a son,

CHARLES, of Yarburgh and Kelsterne, *m.* Elizabeth, daughter of Humphrey Littlebury, esq. of Hagworthingham, in Lincolnshire, and was father of

WILLIAM, who married Eleanor, daughter of Thomas Clifford, esq. and had a son,

HENRY, *b.* in 1591, *d. s. p.*

Charles Yarburgh wedded, secondly, Elizabeth, daughter of Martin Newcomyn, esq. by Mary, his wife, daughter of Sir Brian Sandford, knt. and had by her,

EDMUND, of whom presently.

Christopher, married the daughter and heiress of John Mitchell, afterwards Copeland.

Brian.

Ursula, *m.* to Thomas Wall, esq.

Margaret, *m.* to John Dyan, esq.

Bridget, *m.* to — Radley, esq.

Jane, *m.* to Nicholas Thorncock, esq.

The eldest son of the second marriage,

EDMUND YARBURGH, esq. of Lincoln, was buried in the cathedral of that city, where a monument was erected to his memory, bearing date 1590. He *m.* Margaret, daughter of Sir Vincent Grantham, knt. and had issue, (with another son Charles, of Willoughby, Notts, who *m.* Barbara, daughter of William Whalley, esq. and a daughter, Faith.)

FRANCIS YARBURGH, esq. of Northampton, sergeant-at-law *anno* 37th ELIZABETH. This learned person married, first, Elizabeth, daughter of Robert Farmour, esq. and had by her, a son,

Robert, who *m.* Mary, daughter of Sir Gervais Elwith, knt. and had a daughter, Mary, *m.* to — Saville, esq. of Lincolnshire, and *d. s. p.*

Mr. Sergeant Yarburgh espoused, secondly, Frances, daughter of Leonard Wray, esq. of Ardwick-le-Street, in the county of York. brother of Chief Justice, Sir Christopher Wray, and had by her another son,

EDMUND YARBURGH, esq. of Balne Hall, in Yorkshire, treasurer of lame soldiers in the West Riding of that county, with Sir G. Cutler, of Stainburgh. He *m.* Sarah, dau. and co-heiress of Thomas Wormeley, esq. of Casworth and Hatfield, in Yorkshire, by Thomasine, his wife, daughter and heiress of Nicholas Waller, esq. and had issue,

I. NICHOLAS (Sir), his heir.

II. Thomas, sergeant-at-law, of Campsall, in Yorkshire, *m.* first, Anne, daughter of Thomas Ellis, esq. of

---

* Giles Bruce, Lord of Buckingham, *m.* Jane, daughter and co-heiress of Stephen Mortagne, Baron of Windsor.
|
Maude Bruce, *m.* William Frome.
|
John Frome, *m.*
|
Katherine, *m.* Barnard Mussenden, esq.

‡ Philip Baron de Kyme.
|
Bridget, who *m.* Sir Thomas Atwell, knt.
|
Thomas Atwell, *m.* Ursula, daughter of Sir William Leche, knt.
|
James Atwell, *m.* a daughter of Sir Thomas Bussam, knt.
|
Ralph Atwell, *m.* Sebastian Pigot.
|
John Atwell, *m.* Julian, daughter of Hammond of Upton, esq. of Wainflete.
|
Hammond or Thomas Atwell, *m.* Grace, daughter John O'Keover, esq.
|
John Atwell, *m.* Johanna, daughter and sole heiress of John Legbourne.
|
John Atwell, of Legbourne, *m.* Johanna, daughter and sole heiress of Roger, son of Richard Adrissen, by Agnes, his wife, dau. of Sir John Gaunt.
|
JOAN ATWELL, *m.* RICHARD DE YARBURGH.

Nott-hill, son of Sir Thomas Ellis, of Lincolnshire; and, secondly, Mary, only daughter and heir of Edmund Watson, esq. of Hage Hall, Yorkshire. Mr. Sergeant Thomas Yarburgh, died in 1697, aged seventy-three, leaving, by his second wife, (who wedded, secondly, Henry Currer, esq. of Kildwick, in Yorkshire,) five sons, viz.

1. THOMAS, of Campsmount, who m. Johanna, daughter of Tobias, Harvey, esq. of Womersley, and dying 1st September, 1772, aged eighty-five, left four daughters,
   MARY, JOANNA, ANN, ELIZABETH, who all dying unmarried, left by will the estate of Campsmount (which they inherited from their father) to their relative, by the female side, the late GEORGE COOKE, esq. of Street-thorpe, near Doncaster, on condition that he and his heirs should thenceforth take the name of YARBURGH or YARBOROUGH.
2. Edmund, barrister-at-law and bencher of Gray's Inn, d. unmarried 25th February, 1764, aged seventy-six, and was buried at St. George's, Queen Square, London.
3. Henry, LL.D. rector of Tewing, Herts, and prebendary of York, d. unmarried 28th November, 1774, aged eighty-three.
4. Nicholas, d. unmarried.
5. Francis, D.D. principal of Brazennose College, Oxford, and rector of Aynho, d. unmarried at Bath in 1770.

III. Edmund, of Doncaster, M.D. aged forty, 14th September, 1665, m. Anne, daughter of Thomas Stanhope, esq. of Stalfold, third son of Sir John Stanhope, and had a son, Thomas.

I. Frances, married, first, to Sir John Reresby, bart. of Thribergh; and secondly, to James Moyser, esq.

Edmund Yarburgh d. 6th May, 1631, and was s. by his eldest son,

SIR NICHOLAS YARBURGH, knt. of Snayth Hall, Yorkshire, justice of the peace for the West Riding, and in the commission of array for CHARLES I. He m. Faith, daughter of John Dawney, esq. of Cowick, son of Sir Thomas Dawney, and by her, who d. in 1657, and was buried at Snaith, 24th September, had six sons and two daughters,

I. THOMAS (Sir), his heir.
II. Nicholas, d. unm. 23rd October, 1670.
III. Richard, of London, merchant, anno 1666.
IV. John.
V. Edmund, buried in Trinity Church, York, 8th October, 1694.
VI. Christopher.

I. Elizabeth, m. to Henry Layton, esq. of Rawdon, near Leeds.
II. Faith, m. to Marmaduke Constable, esq. of Wassand, in the East Riding of Yorkshire.

Sir Nicholas died in August, 1655, was interred at Snaith, and succeeded by his eldest son,

SIR THOMAS YARBURGH, knt. of Balne Hall and Snaith, aged twenty-seven, in 1666, high sheriff for Yorkshire, in 1676, and M.P. for Pontefract. This gentleman m. Henrietta-Maria, eldest daughter and co-heir of Colonel Thomas Blague,* of Hollinger, in Suffolk, governor of Wallingford,

* The family of BLAGUE was originally seated in the county of Kent.

ROBERT BLAGUE, Baron of the Exchequer, 19 HENRY VI. m. first, Katherine, daughter and heir of Thomas Browne, esq. of Sussex, and secondly, Acelye, daughter of Sir John Brooke, knt. Lord Cobham, by the latter of whom he left a son,

SIR GEORGE BLAGUE, knt. who wedded Dorothy, daughter of William Badbye, and by her, who m. secondly, Sir Ambrose Jermin, left with two daughters, Judith, the wife of Sir Robert Jermin, of Rushbrooke and Hester, of Charles Legrice, esq. of Brockdish, a son and successor,

HENRY BLAGUE, esq. of Hollinger, in Suffolk, who espoused Hester, daughter of Sir Ambrose Jermin, and had a daughter, Dorothy, m. to Thomas Butler, gent. and a son,

AMBROSE BLAGUE, esq. of Hollinger, or Horringer, who m. twice, and had issue by both wives. His eldest son and successor,

COLONEL THOMAS BLAGUE, of Horringer, Governor of Wallingford Castle, Groom of the Bed-chamber to *Kings* CHARLES I. and II., m. Mary, daughter of Sir Roger North, by Elizabeth, his first wife, daughter and co-heir of Sir John Gilbert, knt. of Great Tinborow, in Suffolk, and had issue, four daughters, his co-heirs. The youngest, MARGARET, so often mentioned in Evelyn's Memoirs, as a most amiable and accomplished woman, m. Sydney Godolphin, the celebrated Earl of Godolphin, and HENRIETTA-MARIA, the eldest, became as mentioned in the text, wife of Sir THOMAS YARBURGH, knt. of Snaith. Of the latter, "*La Blage aux blondes paupieres*," who previously to her marriage, was Maid of Honour to Anne, Duchess of York, figures as one of the heroines of the "Memoires de Grammont," and is thus mentioned by that writer: "Henriette-Marie, fille du Colonel Blague de la Province de Suffolk, epousa le Chevalier Thomas Yarburgh de Snaith, en Yorkshire. Elle etoit sœur de la femme de Sydney Comte de Godolphin; et dans le Masque de Calypso qu'on presenta à la cour, Mademoiselle Blague y joua un role. V. les poemes de Dryden, tom 2, p. 44, aux notes."

Groom of the Bedchamber to *Kings* CHARLES I. and II. by Mary, his wife, daughter of Sir Dudley North, and had issue,

I. JAMES, his heir.
II. Thomas.
III. Blague.
IV. Richard.
V. Charles.

I. Henrietta-Maria, maid of honour to *Queens* CATHERINE and MARY, *m.* to Sir Marmaduke Wyvile, bart. and *d.* in 1722.
II. Margaret, *m.* to Mr. Cutting.
III. Faith.
IV. Rosamund, *m.* to Nicholas Polexfin, esq.
V. Alice, who was introduced at court by her maternal aunt, the wife of the Lord Treasurer Godolphin, and afterwards became Maid of Honour to *Queen* ANNE. Miss Alice Yarburgh never married, and died at Windsor, 12th March, 1786, aged ninety-seven.

Sir Thomas was succeeded at his decease by his eldest son,

JAMES YARBURGH, esq. of Snaith Hall, godson to *King* JAMES II. and one of His Majesty's pages of honour. This gentleman entered the army and attained the rank of lieutenant-colonel in the guards. He *m.* Ann, daughter and co-heir of Thomas Hesketh, esq. of Heslington, representative of a younger branch of the ancient Lancashire family of the same name, by Mary, his wife, daughter of Sir Walter Bethell, of Alne, in Yorkshire, and grandaughter of Sir Henry Slingsby, bart. By the co-heiress of Heslington, (who *d.* in April, 1718,) Colonel Yarburgh had issue,

I. THOMAS, his heir.
II. HENRY, successor to his brother Thomas.
III. James, *d.* unm. in 1740.
IV. HESKETH, who inherited from his brother Henry.
V. CHARLES, successor to his brother Hesketh.
VI. Edward, } both *d.* young.
VII. Nicholas, }

I. Henrietta-Maria, *m.* to Sir John Vanburgh, knt. Clarencieux, King at arms and Comptroller of His Majesty's works, and *d.* in 1776, aged eighty-five, having had one son, an ensign in the guards, who *d.* from wounds received in the battle near Tournay, in 1745.
II. Anne.
III. Rose.

Colonel Yarburgh, who was Lord of the Manors of Yarburgh, Snaith, Cowick, and part of Heslington, died in 1728, and was *s.* by his eldest son,

THOMAS YARBURGH, esq. of Heslington and Snaith, baptized at York, 16th February, 1696, who *m.* Anne, daughter of the Reverend Thomas Thwaits, but by her, who *d.* 27th March, 1753, leaving no issue, he was succeeded, at his decease in 1741, by his brother,

HENRY YARBURGH, esq. of Heslington and Snaith, at whose demise, also without children, the estates and representation of the family devolved on his brother,

HESKETH YARBURGH, esq. of Heslington and Snaith, who *d.* unmarried, at Heslington, in 1754, and was *s.* by his brother,

CHARLES YARBURGH, esq. of Heslington and Snaith, in the county of York, and of Yarburgh, in Lincolnshire. He *m.* first, Mary Griffin, of Wirksworth, in the county of Derby, descended from the Lowes, of Alderwasley, and the Wigleys, of Wigwal, and by her, who died 26th November, 1757, aged forty, had issue,

I. HENRY, his heir.
II. James, *d.* young.

I. Mary, *m.* to the Rev. William Coates, A.M. brother to General Coates, and *d. s. p.* 29th April, 1835, aged eighty-four.

Mr. Yarburgh wedded, secondly, Sarah Griffin, of Wirksworth, and had by her,

I. Charles, baptized 19th October, 1763, entered the navy in 1779, on board the Britannia, and afterwards served in the Hero, which sailed for the East Indies, where he *d.* in 1781.
II. NICHOLAS EDMUND, successor to his brother HENRY.

I. Judith, } both *d.* unm.
II. Rosamund, }
III. Sarah, *m.* 1st August, 1782, to John Greame, esq. nephew of the late John Greame, esq. of Sewerby House, in the East Riding of the county of York, and died 21st October, 1785, leaving one son, YARBURGH, and a daughter, Alicia-Maria, (see vol. ii. p. 590).
IV. Faith, died 31st December, 1782, aged eighteen, unm.
V. Henrietta-Maria, died 11th July, 1788, unm.

Mr. Yarburgh died 13th August, 1789, aged seventy-three, and was *s.* by his son,

HENRY YARBURGH, esq. of Heslington, formerly captain in the 20th Light Dragoons. This gentleman *m.* Anne, daughter of E. Agar, esq. of Canterbury, which lady *d. s. p.* 14th February, 1817. Mr. Yarburgh *d.* himself 28th October, 1825, aged seventy-seven, and was *s.* by his brother, the present NICHOLAS-EDMUND YARBURGH, esq. of Heslington.

*Arms*—Per pale arg. and az. a chev. between three chaplets, all counterchanged. Quartering Atwell, Billing, Wormley, Blague, and Hesketh.

*Crest*—A falcon close or, belled of the last, preying on a duck, ppr.

*Motto*—Non est sine pulvere palma.

*Estates*—The Manors of Yarburgh, in Lincolnshire, and of Heslington, Snaith, &c. in Yorkshire, with property in those respective townships, as also at Balne, Pollington, and elsewhere, chiefly in the East and West Ridings, and likewise the patronage of the several livings of Yarburgh, and of Snaith, Rawcliffe, Whitgift, and Armin, in Yorkshire.

*Seat*—Heslington Hall, near York.

## SCOTT, OF STOURBRIDGE AND GREAT BARR.

SCOTT, ROBERT, esq. of Stourbridge, in Worcestershire, and Great Barr, in Staffordshire, born in York, 15th July, 1803, *m.* 17th February, 1830, Sarah, sole daughter and heiress of John Scott, esq. of Stourbridge and Great Barr, upon which occasion he dropped his paternal surname of Wellbeloved, and assumed, by royal sign-manual, the name and arms of Scott only. He succeeded his father-in-law, 3rd January, 1832. Mr. Scott has issue,

- JOHN-CHARLES-ADDYES, born at Stourbridge, 29th December, 1830.
- Sarah-Emma.
- Mary-Lætitia.
- Elizabeth-Anne.

This gentleman is the youngest son of the Reverend Charles Wellbeloved, of York. He is a barrister-at-law, of the Middle Temple, and on the Oxford circuit, a magistrate for the counties of Worcester and Stafford and a deputy lieutenant of the former shire.

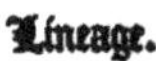

## Lineage.

The first of this family who settled at Stourbridge was

JOHN SCOTT, originally of Chaddesley-Corbet, in the county of Worcester. He removed to Stourbridge about the middle of the seventeenth century, and left issue,

- WILLIAM, his successor.
- Susannah, who *m.* Richard Hall.

His son and successor,

WILLIAM SCOTT, of Stourbridge, married Joanna Potter, of Kidderminster, and died in 1695, leaving issue,

- Joseph, who died *s. p.*
- John, who *m.* and had two sons, William and John, both of whom died *s. p.*
- WILLIAM, who continued the line at Stourbridge.
- Elizabeth, *m.* to Henry Moor, of Leeds.
- Anne, *m.* to Edward Badger, of Stourbridge.

On the death of the two eldest sons, Joseph and John, and of the two sons of the latter, the line at Stourbridge was continued by the third son,

WILLIAM SCOTT, of Stourbridge. He *m.* in 1683, Elizabeth, daughter of the Rev. William Fincher,* vicar of Wednesbury, Staffordshire, and had issue,

- JOHN, who succeeded his father.
- WILLIAM, who *s.* his elder brother.
- Elizabeth, *m.* to Paul White, and *d.* 1738.
- Catharine, *d.* unmarried, 1746.
- Mary, *d.* unmarried, 1720.

Mr. Scott *d.* in 1712, and was succeeded by his eldest son,

JOHN SCOTT, of Stourbridge, who *d.* un-

* The elder of the two daughters of the Rev. W. Fincher married William Ryland, the great-grandfather of Samuel Ryland, esq. formerly of the Laurels, near Birmingham, now of the Priory, near Warwick, who served the office of high sheriff of the county of Worcester, 1822.

married in 1763, aged about sixty-four, and was succeeded by his brother,

WILLIAM SCOTT, of Stourbridge, who m. in 1720, Joanna,* daughter of William Hunt, of Stratford-on-Avon, and dying in 1766, at the age of sixty-six, left issue,

WILLIAM, who succeeded his father.
Thomas, d. early, unmarried.
John, m. 1758, Elizabeth, daughter of William Kettle, of Evesham, d. 23rd September, 1788, aged fifty-seven, leaving issue,
WILLIAM, who succeeded his uncle.
JOHN, of whom hereafter as the first Scott, of Stourbridge and Great Barr.
James, d. an infant.
James, in holy orders, of Cradley, Worcestershire, who was born 4th March, 1768, and died 19th December, 1829.
Sarah, m. Samuel Skey, esq.†
Elizabeth, m. Samuel Bate, and died without issue.
Joanna, m. Samuel Ray, and died without issue.

Mr. Scott was succeeded by his eldest son,

WILLIAM SCOTT, esq. of Stourbridge, who m. in 1771, Anne, daughter and only surviving child of the Rev. John Tonckes, of Birmingham, by Mary, his wife, daughter of John Addyes, esq. of Great Barr, in the county of Stafford, and Moor Hall, in the county of Warwick.‡ Upon the death of

---

* Hannah, daughter of Mary Hunt, by the Rev. John Higgs, and first cousin of Joanna Scott, m. 8th August, 1732, the Rev. John Alexander, sixth Earl of Stirling *de jure*, the grandfather of Alexander Humphrys Alexander, claiming to be ninth Earl of Stirling. Mary Hunt, niece to Joanna Scott, m. John Taylor, of Birmingham, the founder of the family of Taylor, of Mosely Hall, in the county of Worcester.

† Of Spring Grove, in the county of Worcester, and had issue,

I. Samuel, the father of Arthur Skey, esq. now of Spring Grove.

I. Sarah, m. John Taylor, esq. of Moseley Hall, in the county of Worcester, whose daughter, Joanna, m. Sir Thomas Winnington, bart.] of Stanford Court, in the county of Worcester.

II. Joanna, m. Richard Soley, esq. of Sandbourne, in the county of Worcester.

‡ **Family of Addyes.**

This family has been long settled at Great Barr, in the county of Stafford.

SIR DEGORY ADDIS, knt. m. Anne, daughter of Thomas Pewtrell, esq. and d. 27th February, 1521.

From him descended

THOMAS ADDYES, who settled at Great Barr in the sixteenth century, and by his wife, Ann, left issue,

THOMAS, his successor.
William, d. without issue.
John, of Perry Barr, m. Mary —, and left issue,
Thomas, d. without issue.
Mary, d. unmarried.
Ann, m. — Wilson, and d. without issue.
Mary, d. unmarried.

Thomas Addyes was succeeded by his eldest son,

THOMAS ADDYES, who m. Mary Greenshawe, of Knowle, in the county of Warwick, and had issue,

THOMAS, his successor, who d. unmarried.
Nicholas, d. without issue.
JOHN, who succeeded to the estates at Great Barr, upon the death of his brother.
Joseph, d. without issue.
Richard, d. without issue.
Ann, m. — Evett, and d. without issue.
Mary, m. — Dolphin, and had issue,
Nicholas, m. — Hopkins.
William, m. and had issue.
Frances.

Upon the death of Thomas Addyes and of his elder sons, Thomas and Nicholas, the third son,

JOHN ADDYES, succeeded to the property at Great Barr. He m. Mary Hopkins, of Moor Hall, in the county of Warwick, and through her became possessed of a considerable estate there. He had issue,

Thomas, his successor.
Mary, m. the Rev. John Tonckes, and had issue,
Ann, m. William Scott, of Stourbridge, in the county of Worcester, esq.
Ann, m. Richard Scott, esq. of Little Aston, in the county of Warwick, of the family of Scott, of Barr Hall, in the county of Stafford, and had an only daughter,
Mary, m. Andrew Hacket, esq. (son of St. Andrew Hacket, Knight, and grandson of Dr. Hacket, the first Bishop of the united diocese of Lichfield and Coventry), and had issue,
John Addyes, to whom the Moor Hall estate was devised by his godfather Addyes, and is now the residence of the Hacket family. He m. Mary, sister of Sir Joseph Scott, bart. of Barr Hall, and daughter of William Scott, esq. of Barr Hall, by Mary Whitby.
Andrew, m. first, a daughter of Lord Leigh, of Stoneleigh, and left issue; and, secondly, Elizabeth Benyon, of Northamptonshire.
Richard, d. without issue.

John Addyes was succeeded by his eldest son,

THOMAS ADDYES, esq. who m. Ann Hopkins, and had issue,

John, d. young, and without issue.
Mary, d. 3rd April, 1786, unmarried.

Thomas Addyes was succeeded in his Staffordshire, and part of his Warwickshire estates, by his only surviving child, Mary Addyes, the Moor Hall estate having gone over to the descendants of Ann Addyes, by Richard Scott, as above stated. Miss Mary Addyes bequeathed all her estates to her first cousin, Ann, the wife of William Scott, of Stourbridge, in whose family they remain.

Mary Addyes, unm. 3rd April, 1786 (who was sole daughter and heiress of Thomas Addyes, esq. of Great Barr), she bequeathed her estates to her first cousin, the said Anne, wife of William Scott, esq. who having survived her husband, bequeathed the same unto the three nephews of her husband, William, John, and James, leaving the property at Great Barr to the second nephew, John, who thereupon became of Stourbridge and Great Barr. Mrs. Scott *d.* 8th January, 1813, aged eighty-two, and her husband, William Scott, esq. died December, 1792, aged seventy-one. He was succeeded by his eldest nephew,

WILLIAM SCOTT, esq. of Stourbridge, *b.* 12th March, 1760, who *m.* in 1795, Alicia Pynock, and *d. s. p.* 5th December, 1834. His next brother,

JOHN SCOTT, esq. was born 10th January, 1763. He married, October, 1795, Sarah, eldest surviving daughter of John Kettle, esq. of Birmingham.* This gentleman, being in possession of considerable property at Stourbridge, inherited, as before stated, the Staffordshire estates at Great Barr on the death of the widow of his uncle William, 8th January, 1813, and is thus to be considered as the founder of the family of *Scott of Stourbridge and Great Barr*. In the year 1830 he served the office of high sheriff for the county of Worcester. He was also a magistrate and deputy-lieutenant for that county. He died 3rd January, 1832, leaving issue, SARAH, his sole daughter and heiress, married 17th February, 1830, to Robert, youngest son of the Rev. Charles Wellbeloved, of York, who is the present ROBERT SCOTT, esq. of Stourbridge and Great Barr.

*Arms*—Arg. on a mount of bullrushes in base ppr. a bull passant sa. a chief pean billety or, with a canton of the last.

*Crest*—A stag couchant ppr. the dexter paw resting on a billet or, charged on the shoulder with a cross crosslet of the last.

*Motto*—Nunquam libertas gratior.

*Estates*—In Worcestershire, Staffordshire, and Warwickshire.

*Seat*—The Red House, Great Barr, Staffordshire.

* The late John Kettle, esq. of Birmingham, left issue one son, the present John Kettle, esq. of Birmingham, and two daughters, Sarah, as stated in the text, married to John Scott, esq.; and Mary, married to the Rev. John Kentish, of Birmingham and St. Albans, one of the pastors of the New Meeting-house, Birmingham, and sole representative of the family of Kentish of St. Albans.

### Family of Wellbeloved.

The first of this family on record is JOHN WELLBELOVED, of Cobham, Surrey, who, by his wife Mary, left a son,

CHARLES WELLBELOVED, born 3rd February, 1713, at Cobham. This gentleman was four times married, but left issue only by his first wife, Mary, daughter of John Parkins. He died at Mortlake 4th June, 1782, and was succeeded by his only son,

JOHN WELLBELOVED, who was born 23rd July, 1742. By his wife, Elizabeth, he left an only son,

*The Rev.* CHARLES WELLBELOVED, now of York. This gentleman is minister of St. Saviourgate Chapel in York, and principal and theological professor in the Manchester College, in that city. In the literary world he is well known as a theologian and antiquary. He was born in London 6th April, 1769, and married 1st July, 1793, Anne, daughter of John Kinder, esq. of Stoke Newington, in the county of Middlesex. This lady was great-great-granddaughter of Sir Francis Wingate, knt. by the Lady Anne Annesley, daughter of Arthur Annesley, first Earl of Anglesey. By her grandmother she was also descended from the Cornwalls, who derived from Richard, Earl of Cornwall, King of the Romans, who was son of *King* JOHN. Her mother also was cousin-german to Dr. Aikin and Mrs. Barbauld, and nearly connected with several noble families. By this lady Mr. Wellbeloved has had issue,

I. Charles, born 13th June, 1794, married, 4th September, 1834, Mary, daughter of Thomas Read, esq. of Scarborough, and has issue,
   Charles-Henry, born in Leeds 23rd October, 1835.
II. John, twin with his sister Eliza, died at Homburg 8th October, 1819, aged twenty-one.
III. Henry, twin with his sister Harriet, died an infant 29th April, 1800.
IV. Robert, twin with his sister Emma, the present ROBERT SCOTT, esq. of Stourbridge and Great Barr.

I. Lætitia, married 13th August, 1821, to the Rev. John Kenrick, M.A. classical professor in the Manchester College, York. This gentleman's erudition as a classical and general scholar is well known. His writings in connection with theology and the classics are numerous. He is descended from an old and highly respectable family long seated at Wynn Hall, in the county of Denbigh.
II. Anne.
III. Eliza, died an infant 20th April, 1799.

IV. Harriet, married, 16th July, 1827, to the Rev. John-Reynell Wreford, formerly one of the pastors of the new meeting-house in Birmingham, in conjunction with the Rev. John Kentish, before mentioned in the note. This gentleman is a cadet of the family of Wreford of Cleavangar, in the county of Devon, which is also a branch of the Wrefords of Clannaborough, in the same county; both which estates have belonged to the family for nearly two centuries. By his mother, Mary Reynell (who was twenty-first in lineal descent from Richard Reynell, governor of the castles of Exeter and Launceston, 2 RICHARD I. 1191), Mr. Wreford is descended from the family of the Reynells, who for four centuries were seated at Ogwell House, in the county of Devon, and the present representative of which family is Major-general Sir Thomas Reynell, bart. K.C.B. The issue of Mr. and Mrs. Wreford are

Charles-Reynell Wreford, born at Edgbaston, near Birmingham, 16th August, 1828.

John-Kenrick Wreford, born at Edgbaston, near Birmingham, 4th February, 1833.

V. Emma, m. 27th December, 1831, to the Hon. Mr. Justice James Carter, one of the judges of his majesty's Supreme Court of Judicature in New Brunswick, North America. Mr. Carter is a member of the family of Carter of Portsmouth, nephew of the late Sir John Carter, whose only son, John Bonham-Carter, esq. is the present representative of Portsmouth in parliament.

# DRINKWATER, OF SHREWSBURY.

DRINKWATER, RICHARD, esq. of Shrewsbury, *b.* 19th April, 1785, *m.* 12th October, 1815, Miss Elizabeth Clarke, of Wroxeter, in the county of Salop, and has issue,

I. RICHARD-PRATCHET.
II. Arnold.
III. James-Pratchet.
IV. Charles-Henry.
V. Frederick-John.

I. Elizabeth Jane.
II. Mary.
III. Emma.
IV. Margaret-Anne.

Mr. Drinkwater, who possesses considerable freehold property in Shrewsbury,* together with an estate in Denbighshire, served the office of mayor of Shrewsbury in 1834, 1835.

## Lineage.

This is the elder line of the family of Drinkwater of Bent, noticed at page 420. The Bent estate having been alienated, the branch before us embarked in commercial pursuits.

ARNOLD DRINKWATER, esq. of Bent, in Cheshire, who died about 1620, left by his wife, Jane Gleave, of Heatley, a son and successor,

RICHARD DRINKWATER, esq. of Bent, who *m.* first, Margaret Fryth, of Dunham; and secondly, Ellen Fryth, of Banton. By the former he left at his decease 8th October, 1651, a son,

* Mr. Drinkwater gave the site on which the new church dedicated to St. George in Shrewsbury is erected.

ARNOLD DRINKWATER, esq. of Bent, *b.* in 1618, who *m.* Elizabeth Powell, of Ruabon, in Denbigh, and dying in 1671 was buried at Warburton. His son and successor,

RICHARD DRINKWATER, esq. of Bent, wedded 29th December, 1666, Isabella, daughter of Peter Drinkwater, of Massey Green, and sister of Peter Drinkwater, ancestor of the present COLONEL DRINKWATER, of Salford. By this lady he left at his decease 30th May, 1729, aged eighty-two, a son,

ARNOLD DRINKWATER, esq. born in August, 1679, who *m.* first, in 1701, Elizabeth, daughter of William Kay, of Hale, but that lady died issueless. He *m.* secondly, in 1706, Margaret, daughter of John Coppock, of Ringway, and by her, who died 10th May, 1746, was father of

RICHARD DRINKWATER, *b.* 19th December, 1718, who *m.* 23rd December, 1747, Elizabeth, daughter of John Chantler, of Mollington, and had issue,

ARNOLD, of Shrewsbury, merchant, *b.* 31st July, 1750, *d.* unmarried 30th August, 1819, and was interred in the ancient burying-place of his family at Warburton, in Cheshire.

RICHARD.

Margaret.

Elizabeth.

The second son,

RICHARD DRINKWATER, of Shrewsbury, merchant, *b.* 19th February, 1755, married 26th July, 1780, Jane Pratchet, of Hodnet, in Salop, and dying 4th March, 1825, left an only surviving child, the present RICHARD DRINKWATER, esq. of Shrewsbury.

*Arms*—Party per pale gu. and az. on a fess wavy arg. three billets of the second, between three garbs or: these are the arms now borne by all the branches of the family. The ancient coat, often quartered with the above, was, Arg. two bars gu. a canton of the second, charged with a cinquefoil or.

*Crest*—Three wheat ears, two in saltire, one in pale or, encircled by a ducal coronet ppr.

*Estates*—In the counties of Salop and Denbigh.

*Residence*—St. George's Place, Shrewsbury.

# DRINKWATER, OF IRWELL.

DRINKWATER, THOMAS, esq. of Irwell House, in the county of Lancaster, *b.* 5th May, 1775, *m.* 9th August, 1813, Sarah, fourth surviving daughter of Nathan Hyde, esq. of Ardwick, and has issue,

I. Fanny.
II. Ellen.
III. Margaret.
IV. Julia.

Mr. Drinkwater succeeded his father 15th November, 1801, and is in the commission of the peace for Lancashire.

## Lineage.

This is another branch of the ancient family of Drinkwater, and became seated at Irwell about the middle of the last century, at which period

PETER DRINKWATER, esq. son of Thomas Drinkwater, of Whalley, purchased the estate. He *m.* 14th May, 1771, Margaret Bolton, of Preston, and had issue,

I. THOMAS, his heir.
II. John, of Sherborne, in the county of Warwick, who *m.* Ellen, sixth surviving daughter of Nathan Hyde, esq. of Ardwick, in Lancashire, and has one daughter,
   Sophia.

I. Margaret, *m.* to John Pemberton Heywood, esq. of Wakefield, barrister-at-law.
II. Eliza, *m.* to Colonel D'Aguilar, deputy-adjutant-general, Dublin.

Mr. Drinkwater died 15th November, 1801, and was succeeded by his son, the present THOMAS DRINKWATER, esq. of Irwell.

*Arms* and *Crest* — See *Drinkwater, of Shrewsbury*.

*Motto*—Ne quid nimis.

*Estates*—In Lancashire.

*Seat*—Irwell House.

## FROME, OF PUNCKNOLL.

FROME, *The Reverend* GEORGE-CLUTTERBUCK, A. M. lord of the manor of Puncknoll, in the county of Dorset, *b.* in 1779, *m.* 15th November, 1823, Mary-Sophia, third daughter of Edmund Morton Pleydell, esq. of Whatcombe House, by Elizabetha-Margaretta, his wife, daughter of William Richards, esq. of Smedmore House, and has two daughters, viz.

Mary-Sophia.
Elizabeth-Arundell.

Mr. Frome succeeded his father 9th April, 1833.

### Lineage.

The family of Frome is of great antiquity in the counties of Dorset and Wilts, and was seated at a very early period at Woodlands, in the former shire, an estate which was acquired by the marriage of William Frome with the only daughter of John de Brewosa, son of Sir Giles de Brewosa, lord of Knolton and Woodlands, who died 33 EDWARD I. In the reign of RICHARD II. JOHN FROME was knight of the shire in three parliaments, and in the time of HENRY IV. the sheriffalty of the county was served by JOHN FROME. The direct line of Woodlands terminated with the co-heiresses of William Frome, one of whom brought that manor to her husband, William Filiol, whose grandson, SIR WILLIAM FILIOL, died 19 HENRY VIII. leaving a son, William, who died under age, and two daughters, Anne, *m.* first, to Sir Edward Willoughby, of Middleton, and, secondly, to Lord St. John, and Katharine, the wife of Edward, Duke of Somerset.

GEORGE FROME, esq. of the county of Wilts, sprung from a scion of the Dorsetshire family, marrying Susanna, daughter of George Pitt, esq. and had two sons, GEORGE, and William, D.D. prebendary of Sarum. The elder,

THE REV. GEORGE FROME, rector of Tollard Regis, in the county of Wilts, married Arundell, daughter of William Clutterbuck, esq. of Puncknoll House, in Dorsetshire, by Mary, his wife, eldest daughter of Thomas Chaffin, esq.* of Chettle, and Anne, his wife, daughter of Colonel John Penruddock, of Compton Chamberlain, who was beheaded in 1655. Mr. Clutterbuck, who came out of Devonshire, was a sea officer in the reigns of WILLIAM III. and *Queen* ANNE,

---

* The Chafins came originally from Wiltshire, and appear in the visitations of that county. They were originally seated at Folke, in Dorsetshire, but removed to Chettle about the year 1600.

BAMFIELD CHAFIN, esq. of Chettle, son of Thomas Chafin, esq. of Folke, died at Exeter, 8th July, 1644, during the civil wars, and was buried in the cathedral there. He *m.* Mary, daughter of William Muschamp, esq. of Roehampton, and was father of

THOMAS CHAFIN, esq. of Chettle, who compounded and paid for levying money for the king's forces £900. He married twice, and left issue by his first wife, Elizabeth, third daughter of Sir Thomas Trenchard, a son and successor,

THOMAS CHAFIN, esq. of Chettle, who commanded at the battle of Sedgmore a troop of horse raised in Dorsetshire against the Duke of Monmouth. He *m.* Anne, daughter of Colonel John Penruddock, of Compton Chamberlain, and left, with other issue, a son, GEORGE, of Chettle, M.P. for Dorsetshire, and several daughters, of whom Bridget, marrying Thomas Haysome, esq. of Weymouth, was mother of Bridget Haysome, the wife of Henry Seymer, esq. of Hanford, and MARY, marrying, as in the text, WILLIAM CLUTTERBUCK, esq. of Puncknoll, left a daughter, ARUNDELL, the wife of the REV. GEORGE FROME.

and purchased the manor and advowson of Puncknoll from Sir Charles Napier, bart. who *d.* in 1743.

Mr. Frome was *s.* at his decease by his son,

THE REV. GEORGE FROME, rector of Puncknoll and Litton Cheney, who died without issue, 10th January, 1824, aged seventy-nine, and was *s.* by his brother,

THE REV. ROBERT FROME, LL.B. rector of Folke and Minterne Magna, in Dorsetshire, and of Goathill, in Somersetshire, who *m.* Jane, second daughter of the Rev. Duke Butler, LL.B. rector of Okeford Fitzpaine, by Mary, his wife, second daughter of Raufe Freke, esq. of Hannington, in Wiltshire, and died 9th April, 1833, aged eighty-eight, leaving surviving issue, one daughter, Arundell-Mary, and one son, the present Rev. GEORGE-CLUTTERBUCK FROME, of Puncknoll.

*Arms*—Quarterly, 1st and 4th, arg. a fess between three griffins rampant, for FROME; 2nd and 3rd, az. a lion rampant arg. in chief three escallops of the second for CLUTTERBUCK.

*Crest*—A cross-crosslet az. between two wings arg.

*Estates*—In Dorsetshire.

*Seat*—Puncknoll.

# MYTTON, OF SHIPTON.

MYTTON, THOMAS, esq. of Shipton Hall, in the county of Salop, *b.* 11th February, 1789, succeeded to the Shipton estate upon the demise of his grandmother, in 1830.

## Lineage.

The MYTTONS of Shipton are a scion of the very ancient Shropshire house of MYTTON (see vol. ii. p. 517), and immediately derive from

THOMAS MYTTON, who was of Ryton, in the parish of Condover, in the early part of the sixteenth century. He married a lady named Joan, and left at his decease (his will bears date 7th April, 1557,) a son and successor,

RICHARD MYTTON, esq. who *m.* Elizabeth, daughter of Richard Lutwyche, and was father of

EDWARD MYTTON, of Shipton, in the county of Salop, who died 4th June, 1620, and was interred at Shipton. He *m.* first, Eleanor, daughter of Robert Wigfall, of Worcester and of Sutton, in the county of Stafford, and, secondly, Eleanor, relict of Christopher Dighton. By the former he left a son,

HENRY MYTTON, esq. of Shipton, who married two wives, but had issue only by the first, Mary, daughter of Christopher Dighton, esq. of St. Helen's, Worcester. He died 17th September, 1663, was interred at Shipton, and succeeded by his son,

HENRY MYTTON, esq. of Shipton, who *m.* Elizabeth, daughter of Thomas Powys, esq. of Snitton, and relict of Richard Hunt, esq. of Milson, and was succeeded at his decease, in May, 1688 by his son,

THOMAS MYTTON, esq. of Shipton, who *m.* Martha, daughter of Bonham Amies, esq. of Stottesden, Shropshire, and had two sons,

HENRY, his heir.

Thomas, of Cleobury North, *m.* Ann, daughter and co-heir of Michael Henshaw, esq. of Leek, in Staffordshire, and died 3rd July, 1762, leaving a son,

Thomas, of Cleobury North, *b.* 1st September, 1739, who *m.* Mary, daughter of George Goodwin, esq. of Coalbrookdale, and was succeeded at his decease, 2nd December, 1829, by his son, the present

HENRY-GEORGE MYTTON, esq. of Cleobury North, in the county of Salop.

Mr. Mytton died 6th May, 1752, and was *s.* by his son,

HENRY MYTTON, esq. of Shipton, who *m.* Martha, daughter of Walter Gough, esq. of Perry Hall, and of Oldfallings, in the county of Stafford (see vol. ii. p. 396), and had issue,

I. THOMAS, his heir.
II. Henry, died *s. p.*

I. Martha, II. Elizabeth, III. Amy, } who all died unm.
IV. Harriet, *m.* to Samuel Harwood, esq. of Crickheath (see page 410).

Mr. Mytton died 3rd October, 1757, and was succeeded by his son,

THOMAS MYTTON, esq. of Shipton, *b.* 5th March, 1736, who *m.* Mary, third daughter of Sir Henry Edwardes, bart. and by her had issue,

I. Henry-Edwardes, II. Thomas, III. Francis-Snell, IV. Walter Gough, V. Richard, } who all *d. s. p.*
VI. Benjamin, in holy orders, of Pembroke College, Oxford, *m.* Miss Eleanor Russell, and dying at Shipton, 1st November, 1789, left one son,

THOMAS, of whom presently.

I. Eleanor-Martha, *m.* to John Gough, esq. of Perry Hall (see vol. ii. p. 397).
II. Mary-Elizabeth, *m.* to Samuel Holland, esq. of Tenbury.
III. Margaret, *m.* to Thomas More, esq. of Larden, in Shropshire.
IV. Ann.

Mr. Mytton *d.* in July, 1787, and the Shipton estate was enjoyed by his widow until her decease in 1830, when it devolved on her grandson, the present THOMAS MYTTON, esq. of Shipton.

*Arms*—Per pale az. and gu. an eagle displayed with two heads or, all within a border engrailed of the last.

*Crest*—A bull's head erased bezanté.

*Estates*—In Shropshire.

*Seat*—Shipton Hall, near Much Wenlock.

## PARKER, OF WOODTHORPE.

PARKER, HUGH, esq. of Woodthorpe, in the county of Derby, succeeded his father, 6th January, 1794, *m.* Mary daughter of Samuel Walker, esq. of Masborough (see vol. ii. p. 289), and has issue,

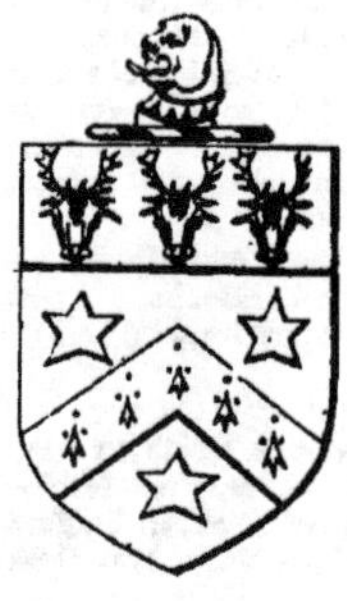

I. JOHN, barrister-at-law, M. P. for Sheffield.
II. Samuel.
III. Hugh, a military officer.

I. Mary.
II. Harriet, *m.* to Edward Valentine Steade, esq. only son of Benjamin Broughton Steade, esq. of Beauchief Abbey, in Derbyshire.
III. Sarah.
IV. Alice-Elizabeth.
V. Margaret-Caroline.

Mr. Parker is a magistrate and deputy lieutenant for the West Riding of Yorkshire.

## Lineage.

The family of **Parker** resided at a remote period on the borders of the counties of Derby and York. Thomas le Parker, of Bulwel, having settled there in the reign of **Richard II.** in consequence of his marriage with Elizabeth, daughter and heir of Adam de Gotham, of the Lees, near Norton. John, sixth in descent from Thomas, dying without male issue, his daughter and heir, Anne, married — Barker, who resided at the Hall in 1667. Thus the main branch of the family became extinct. From a younger son descended Thomas, first Earl of Macclesfield, and from the same family the **Parkers** of Little Norton appear to have branched about the time of **Elizabeth**.

**John Parker**, of Little Norton, in Derbyshire, living in **Elizabeth**'s reign, was father of

**John Parker**, esq. of Little Norton and Jordenthorpe, baptized 4th September, 1575, who *m.* 24th August, 1601, Dionysia, daughter of Thomas Bright, esq. of Bradway, sister of Stephen Bright, esq. of Carbrook, and aunt of Sir John Bright, bart. By this lady, who died in 1604, he had two daughters,

Elizabeth, baptized 20th October, 1602.
Ann, baptized 29th August, 1604.

He *m.* secondly, 2nd July, 1605, Jane, dau. of James Bate, of Jordenthorpe, and, by her, had three sons and two daughters, viz.

John, his heir.
Thomas, baptized 31st March, 1609.
William, baptized 23rd July, 1614.

Jane.
Elizabeth.

The eldest son,

**John Parker**, esq. of Little Norton, baptized 12th August, 1607, *m.* 9th July, 1632, Elizabeth, daughter of Geoffery Roberts, esq. of Dronfield, by Gertrude, his wife, daughter of Rowland Morewood, esq. of The Oakes, in Bradfield, and had, with other issue, a son,

**Rowland Parker**, esq. of Little Norton and Jordenthorp, baptized 8th January, 1640-1, who left by Elizabeth, his wife (she was buried 6th April, 1692), three sons and a daughter, viz. John, Samuel, baptized 15th November, 1666, Philip, baptized 9th May, 1672, and Sarah, baptized 18th November, 1668-9. The eldest son,

**John Parker**, esq. of Norton, baptized 18th August, 1664, *m.* Mary, daughter of William Staniforth, esq. of Mosborough Hall, in Derbyshire, and was father of

**John Parker**, esq. of Graystones, in the parish of Sheffield and Woodthorpe, in the parish of Handsworth, *b.* in 1700, a few months before his father's death. He *m.* Mary, daughter of Samuel Staniforth, of Mosborough Hall, in Derbyshire, and had issue,

I. John, his heir.

I. Sarah, *m.* to George Woodhead, esq. of High Field, near Sheffield.
II. Mary, *m.* to the Rev. Rowland Hodgson, rector of Rawmarsh.

Mr. Parker *d.* 15th April, 1779, was buried at Norton, and succeeded by his son,

**John Parker**, esq. of Woodthorpe, barrister-at-law, who *m.* Alice, daughter of Hugh Marshall, esq. of Horsforth, near Leeds, and had issue,

I. John, baptized at Woodthorpe, in February, 1769, *d.* 10th May, 1773.
II. Hugh, heir to his father.
III. George, of Streetthorpe, *m.* Diana-Elizabeth, daughter of George Cooke Yarborough, esq. of Campsmount and Streetthorpe, and has had

George, a military officer.
Henry-Yarborough, also in the army.

Georgiana, *d.* young.

I. Harriet, *m.* to John Ellison, esq. of Thorne, third son of Richard Ellison, esq. of Sudbrook, near Lincoln.
II. Maria, *m.* in 1793, to Richard Swallow, esq. of New Hall, near Sheffield.

Mr. Parker *d.* 6th January, 1794, was buried at Handsworth, and succeeded by his son, the present **Hugh Parker**, esq. of Woodthorpe.

*Arms*—A chev. pean between three mullets sa. on a chief, az. three bucks' heads caboshed or.

*Crest*—A talbot's head couped arg. ears and tongue gu. gorged with a collar ermines.

*Seat*—Woodthorpe.

# OWSLEY, OF SKEFFINGTON.

. OWSLEY, WILLIAM-POYNTZ-MASON, esq. of Skeffington, in Leicestershire, *b.* 17th August, 1812, *m.* Henrietta-Jane, eldest daughter of the Rev. Richard Farrer, M.A. rector of Ashley, in the county of Northampton, and has had issue,

Anna-Henrietta, died in infancy, in 1833, and was buried at Skeffington.
CAROLINE-LOUISA.

Mr. Owsley succeeded his father.

## Lineage.

THE REV. JOHN OWSLEY, rector of Glooson, in Leicestershire, who was buried there 27th December, 1687, married, in 1659, Dorothy Poyntz, and by her, who died 2nd August, 1705, had to survive infancy six sons and three daughters, viz.

NEWDIGATE, his heir, of Leytonstone, in Essex, *b.* in 1660. This gentleman, who was paymaster-general in *Queen* ANNE's reign, *m.* Miss E. Yates, and had issue,

1. Newdigate, *d.* unm.
2. John, *d.* unm. before 20th December, 1754.
3. Charles, who was educated at Cambridge, and resided at Leytonstone. He *d.* unm. his will bearing date October, 1730.
4. Thomas, *d.* unm.

1. Mary, *m.* to David Lewis, esq. gentleman of the bedchamber to GEORGE II.
2. Sarah,
3. Elizabeth,
4. Dorothea,
5. Jane, } all *d.* unm.

Thomas, who married in Jamaica, and died there.

John, William, } who both died at college.

Poyntz, *b.* 11th April, 1667, *m.* Mary David, of Galby, in Leicestershire, and dying at Glooston, 1st December, 1731, left two daughters, namely,

Dorothea, baptized 5th May, 1701. *d.* unm. 28th July, 1787, aged eighty-six, and was buried at Glooston.

Elizabeth, *m.* first, to — Watts, esq. and, secondly, to Jonathan Spriggs.

Charles, *b.* 3rd September, 1669, captain in the army, *d.* unmarried.

EDITH, of whom presently.
Mary, *b.* 1st November, 1671, *d.* unm.
Dorothea, *b.* 23rd December, 1673, *m.* to — Delgarner.

The eldest daughter,

EDITH OWSLEY, *b.* 14th December, 1662, wedded her first cousin, the REV. WILLIAM OWSLEY, M.A. rector of Glooston, and by him, who *d.* 15th September, 1733, aged seventy-one, she left at her decease, 2nd August, 1714, two sons. The younger, William, married a lady named Heath,* while the elder,

THE REV. JOHN OWSLEY, rector of Glooston, *m.* Elizabeth Howe, and dying in 1743, aged fifty-two, left a son and successor,

JOHN OWSLEY, *b.* in October, 1717, who *m.* Miss Ann Foxton, and by her, who died at Hallaton, 7th August, 1765, aged seventy-eight, had issue,

I. JOHN, his heir.
II. William, died in infancy.
III. Charles, *b.* 5th June, 1756, *m.* Sarah Stafford, and *d.* at Hallaton, *s.p.* 5th January, 1799.

* William Owsley had, by this lady a son, STEPHEN OWSLEY, who had a daughter, Mary.

I. Elizabeth, died an infant.
II. Mary, died unm. 15th September, 1828, and buried in St. Margaret's Chancel, at Leicester.
III. Dorothea, *m.* John Fenwick, and *d.* 26th January, 1820, leaving issue.

Mr. Owsley died at Hallaton, 24th November, 1808, and was *s.* by his son,

THE REV. JOHN OWSLEY, A.B. rector of St. Giles's Blaston, *b.* 29th May, 1742, who *m.* Catharine-Mason Read, and by her, who *d.* 7th May, 1813, aged twenty-three, left an only surviving son, the present WILLIAM POYNTZ MASON OWSLEY, esq. of Skeffington.

*Arms*—Or, a chev. sa. between three holly leaves vert, on a chief of the second a lion passant between two fleurs-de-lys, arg.

*Crest*—A lion rampant holding a holly branch in his paw.

*Estates*—In the county of Leicester.

*Seat*—Skeffington.

# IRTON, OF IRTON.

IRTON, SAMUEL, esq. of Irton, in Cumberland, *b.* 29th September, 1796, *m.* 25th July, 1825, Eleanor, second daughter of Joseph Tiffin Senhouse, esq. of Calder Abbey (see vol. i. p. 216). Mr. Irton, who succeeded his father 2nd November, 1820, is in the commission of the peace for Cumberland, and represents the western division of that county in parliament.

## Lineage.

The Irtons have been seated at Irton in the county of Cumberland from a period antecedent to the CONQUEST, and have since that period been in a direct line successive lords thereof. The first of the family mentioned by Mr. Warburton, Somerset herald, is

BARTRAM D'YRTON, who lived in the beginning of HENRY I.; and Richard is mentioned soon after the CONQUEST, as appears by a deed of gift in the exchequer of lands given to the abbey at York, by Andrew de Morwick, to which Bartram was an evidence. He was succeeded by

ADAM D'YRTON, of Yrton, who was one of the knights of St. John of Jerusalem, and attending Godfrey, of Boulogne, and the other christian princes to the Holy Land, was at the siege of Jerusalem. During the war he slew a Saracen general, and is said to have severed at one blow the infidel's head from his body. He *m.* Joan Stutville, and was father of

HUGH D'YRTON, who married Gertrude Tiliol, of an ancient and eminent family, which possessed Scaleby castle and a large estate on the borders, and was succeeded by his son,

EDMUND D'YRTON, who joined the crusade under RICHARD I. and participated in all that monarch's wars. He lost his life in the journey to Jerusalem, and left by his wife, the daughter of Edmund Dudley, of Yanwick, in Westmorland, a son and successor,

STEPHEN D'YRTON, who married Jane Dacre (who was surety to HENRY III. for her brother, Thomas Dacre, for his safe keeping of the castle of Bridgenorth, in Salop, against the incursions of the Welsh), and had two sons, namely,

ROGER, his heir.
Randolph, who was bred a priest at Rouen, in Normandy. On his return to England he was made prior of Gisburn, in Yorkshire, and being a man of great learning and piety, was constituted by *King* EDWARD I. in 1280, bishop of Carlisle, being likewise appointed one of the commissioners to treat of a marriage between Margaret, Princess of Scotland, and *King* EDWARD's son, as appears by

an ancient parchment roll in the tower of London.

The elder son,

ROGER D'YRTON, *m.* and had a son and successor,

WILLIAM D'YRTON, who *m.* Grace Hanmer, of Shropshire, a near relative of the Hanmers, of Hanmer, in Flintshire, and was *s.* by his son,

ROGER D'YRTON, living in 1292, who *m.* Susan, daughter of Sir Alexander Basinthwaite, and sister of Sir Alexander Basinthwaite, who was slain at the battle of Dunbar, in 1296. By this lady, Roger d'Yrton acquired the manors of Basinthwaite, Loweswater, Unthank, and divers other lands of considerable value, and had a son and heir,

ADAM D'YRTON, who wedded Elizabeth, sole heiress of Sir John Copeland, and obtained with her the manors of Berker, Berkby, and Senton. He left two sons, of whom, the younger, Alexander, *m.* a lady of the family of Odingsels, and settled at Wolverly, in Warwickshire. The elder,

RICHARD D'YRTON, *m.* Margaret, daughter of John Broughton, of Broughton, in Staffordshire, and was father of

CHRISTOPHER IRTON, of Irton, who *m.* Margaret, daughter of Richard Redman, of Herwood castle, and was succeeded by his son,

NICHOLAS IRTON, of Irton, who *m.* a dau. of William Dykes, of Wardell, in Cumberland, and was *s.* by his son,

JOHN IRTON, esq. of Irton, living *temp.* EDWARD IV. who *m.* Anne, daughter of Sir Thomas Lamplugh, knt. by Eleanor, his wife, daughter of Sir Henry Fenwick, of Fenwick (see p. 161), and had, with another son, Joseph (who left two daughters, Elizabeth, *m.* to William Armorer, esq.; and Mary, *m.* to John Skelton, esq. of Armathwaite Castle), a son,

WILLIAM IRTON, esq. of Irton, who was appointed in 1493 general to the Duke of Gloucester, and (as appears by an old grant in the family) his deputy lieutenant. He *m.* a daughter of the ancient house of Fleming of Rydall, and was *s.* by his son,

THOMAS IRTON, OF IRTON, who received the honour of knighthood from the Earl of Surrey, at Floddenfield, and was slain in a skirmish at Kilso, with the Scotch. He *d. s. p.* and was *s.* in 1503 by his brother,

RICHARD IRTON, of Irton, and served as sheriff for Cumberland 22 HENRY VIII. He wedded Anne, daughter of Sir William Middleton, knt. of Stokeld Park, and left a son and heir,

CHRISTOPHER IRTON, esq. of Irton, who *m.* in 1543 Elizabeth, daughter of Sir William Mallory, knt. of Studley park, and was *s.* by his son,

JOHN IRTON, esq. of Irton, who *m.* in 1577, Anne, daughter of Richard Kirby, esq. of Kirby, by Mary, his wife, daughter of Sir Roger Bellingham, and was father of

JOHN IRTON, esq. of Irton, who *m.* in 1638, Anne, sister of Sir Harry Ponsonby, ancestor to the Earls of Bessborough, and left a son and successor,

JOHN IRTON, esq. of Irton, who *m.* in 1658, Elizabeth, daughter of Musgrave, of Meatrig, younger brother of Sir William Musgrave, knt. of Crookdale, and was *s.* by his son,

GEORGE IRTON, esq. of Irton, who *m.* Eliza, daughter of Thomas Lamplugh, esq. of Lamplugh, and was *s.* by his son,

GEORGE IRTON, esq. of Irton, high sheriff of Cumberland in 1753, who *m.* in 1696 Elizabeth, daughter of David Poole, esq. of Knotingley and Syke House, in the county of York, and had two sons and five daughters. He was *s.* by the eldest,

SAMUEL IRTON, esq. of Irton, who *m.* Frances, only daughter and heiress of Robert Tubman, esq. of Cockermouth, and had three sons, with as many daughters.

The eldest surviving son,

EDMUND LAMPLUGH IRTON, esq. of Irton, *m.* first, Miss Hodgson, of Hawkshead, and secondly, 2nd August, 1787, Harriet, daughter of John Hayne, esq. of Ashbourn Green, in the county of Derby. By the latter he had issue,

- SAMUEL, his heir.
- Richard, captain in the rifle brigade, *m.* Sarah, daughter of Joseph Sabine, esq.
- Anne, *m.* to Joseph Gunson, esq. of Ingwell.
- Frances.

Mr. Irton *d.* 2nd November, 1820, and was *s.* by his son, the present SAMUEL IRTON, esq. of Irton, M. P. for West Cumberland.

*Arms*—Arg. a fesse sa. in chief three mullets gu.

*Crest*—A Saracen's head.

*Motto*—Semper constans et fidelis.

*Estates*—In Cumberland.

*Seat*—Irton Hall, situated on the river Irt.

# MAYNARD, OF HARLSEY HALL.

MAYNARD, JOHN-CHARLES, esq. of Harlsey Hall, in the county of York, *b.* 11th January, 1788, *m.* at Brotton 10th June, 1813, Catherine-Grace, only daughter and heiress of John Easterby, esq. of Skiningrove, in the same shire, and had issue,

I. ANTHONY-LAX, *b.* 22nd November, 1814.
II. John-Easterby.
III. Francis-Cresswell.
IV. Edmund-Gilling.
V. Thomas-Burton.
VI. Charles-Septimus.

I. Grace-Elizabeth.
II. Catherine-Jane.
III. Frances-Dorothea.
IV. Emma-Oceana.

Mr. Maynard succeeded his uncle, Anthony Lax Maynard, esq. of Chesterfield and of Harlsey Hall, 3rd July, 1825.

## Lineage.

JOHN MAYNARD, of Kirklevington, in the county of York, married and had one son and one daughter, viz.

THOMAS, of Yarm, in Yorkshire, who *m.* a lady named Bowes, and had a daughter,

Thomasin, who *m.* William Cooper, and was mother of

Margaret Cooper, *m.* to David Jefferson, esq. of Yarm, and *d. s. p.*

JANE.

The daughter,

JANE MAYNARD, married George Burton, esq. and was mother of

MARY BURTON, who wedded John Jefferson, esq. of Elton, in the county of Durham, and had, with a son, DAVID, of Yarm, who *m.* Margaret, daughter of William Cooper, and *d. s. p.*, a daughter,

SARAH JEFFERSON, who *m.* 5th May, 1741, John Lax, esq. of Eryholme, in Yorkshire, and by him, who *d.* 10th December, 1783, had,

I. ANTHONY, her heir.

II. John, *b.* 13th November, 1744, who *m.* at Topcliffe, in Yorkshire, 22nd May, 1786, Elizabeth, daughter of Edmund Gilling, esq. of Marton-le-Moor, and dying 29th July, 1826, left issue,

JOHN-CHARLES, successor to his uncle.

David-Jefferson, fellow of Catherine Hall College, Cambridge, *b.* 18th July, 1789, *d.* unmarried 29th July, 1823.

Anthony-Lax, *b.* 21st July, 1791.

Edmund-Gilling, of Chesterfield, a magistrate and deputy-lieutenant for the county of Derby, *b.* 27th May, 1793, *m.* 22nd May, 1826, Elizabeth, eldest daughter of the late Robert Waller, esq. of Chesterfield, and has issue,

Anthony-Jefferson, baptized at Chesterfield.

Elizabeth, baptized at Chesterfield.

Thomas-Burton, lieutenant in the navy, *b.* 18th May, 1795, *m.* Henrietta, daughter of Dr. Chisholm, and has a son,

Anthony-Edmund.

III. Thomas, *d.* a bachelor in the East Indies, aged twenty.

I. Mary, *m.* to — Lambert, gent. of Newcastle, and died leaving issue.

II. Dorothy, died unm. and was buried at Eryholme.

III. Sarah, *m.* to Robert Charge, esq. of Lowfield, in Yorkshire.

IV. Jane, *m.* to William Taylerson, esq. of Stokesley.

V. Elizabeth, *m.* to George Wood, esq.

VI. Esther, *m.* to Bernard Lucas, esq. of Hasland, in Derbyshire.

Mrs. Lax, who assumed for herself and her

issue, by sign manual, 24th September, 1784, the surname and arms of MAYNARD, died 18th April, 1812, and was succeeded by her eldest son,

ANTHONY LAX-MAYNARD, esq. of Chesterfield, in Derbyshire, and of Harlsey Hall, in the county of York, a deputy-lieutenant for the former, who *m.* Dorothy, youngest daughter of the Rev. Ralph Heathcote, late rector of Morton, in Derbyshire, and vicar of Sileby, in Leicestershire, but dying without issue 3rd July, 1825, was succeeded by his nephew, the present JOHN-CHARLES MAYNARD, esq. of Harlsey Hall.

*Arms*—Quarterly; 1st and 4th arg. on a chevron vert, between three sinister hands couped gu. five ermine spots or, for MAYNARD. 2nd and 3rd, barry of six erminois, on a chief az. three catherine wheels or, for LAX.

*Crests*—For MAYNARD, a stag trippant or, gorged with a collar invected arg. fimbriated sa. For LAX, a mount vert, thereon a catherine wheel as in the arms.

*Motto*—Manus justa nardus.

*Estates*—In Yorkshire.

*Seats*—Harlsey Hall and Skiningrove, Yorkshire.

# WALWYN, OF LONGWORTH.

WALWYN, JAMES, esq. *b.* in 1768, succeeded his father, John Walwyn, esq. M. P.

## Lineage.

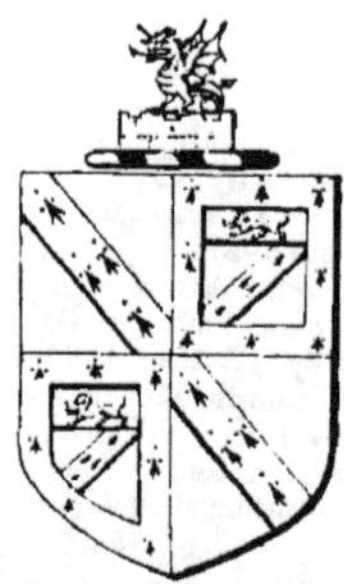

The Welsh genealogists, according to their custom, have carried the antiquity of the WALWYN family very high, deriving the descent of Sir Philip ap David, Lord of Walwayne's Castle, in Pembrokeshire, from Gualgnain, sister's son to *King* ARTHUR, the British hero, and therein they have been followed by William of Malmesbury, Robert of Gloucester, Camden, and several others. "Tunc (anno 1086) in Provinciâ Wallarum quæ Ros vocatur inventum est sepulchrum Walweni, qui fuit haud deneger Arturis ex Sorore Nepos, regnavitque in ea parte Britanniæ quæ adhuc Walwertha vocatur. Miles virtute nominatissimus, sed a Fratre et Nepote Hengristii Regno pulsus," &c. Camden also mentions the same person, as may be seen under the name of Waldwin, which he says "some have interpreted out of the German tongue, which signifies a conqueror, but we now use Gawen instead of Walwyn; but if Walwin was a Britan, and King Arthur's nephew, as William of Malmesbury noteth, when he speaketh of his gyant-like bones found in Wales, I refer the signification to the Britans." The name is composed of two British words, GWAL, which signifies a *wall*, and GWYNNE or WYNNE, *white;* to which the family crest, a wyvern upon an embattled wall or tower argent, refers. It is also local, and the ruins of Walwyn Castle, or the castle with white walls, are yet, or lately were, to be seen in Pembrokeshire, where it gives name to a parish near Haverfordwest.

In the manuscripts of Doctor Blount, of the city of Hereford, we find under the article of Marcle Magna, "These Walwayns are of ancient descent from Gwallain, or Walwayn Castle, in Pembrokeshire, of which family was Sir Philip Walwayn, who being engaged in *King* WILLIAM *Rufus's* time, under Bernard de Newmarch, the Norman, in the conquest of Brecknockshire,* had

* The twelve knights who came into Wales at the conquest of Brecknockshire, in the train of Bernard de Newmarch, were,

Sir Reginald Awbrey, of Abercunricks and Slough.
Sir Peter Gunter, of Gunterstone.
Sir Humphrey ffrergill, of Crickhowell.
Sir Miles Piegard, of Iscbargrog.
Sir John Waldebieffe, of Lanhanffosg.
Sir Humphrey Sollers, of Tredustan.
Sir Richard de Boyes, of Treboyes.
Sir Walter Havard, of Pontwillim.
Sir Hugh Surdnan, of Aberiskir.
Sir John Skull, of Bolgood and Cray.
Sir Philip Walwin, of the Hay.
Sir Richard Paglin, of Peytyns.

certain lands assigned to him at the Hay, in that county, which are at this day called Walwyn's Rents, of which thus Leland: "One showed me in the town of Hay (*temp.* HENRY VIII.) the ruines of a gentelman's place (I think his name was Elias), caulled Waulwine, by whose meanes Prince Lluellin was soddenli taken at Buelth Castle, and there beheaded, and his hidde sent to the king."

SIR PHILIP DE WALWYNNE, in consequence of the new territory assigned him at the Hay, quitted his ancient possessions, and took up his abode there; but being desirous of preserving the remembrance of the seat of his ancestors, assumed it as his surname, after the Norman custom. He was father of

JOHN AP PHILIP DE WALWAYNE, of the Hay, who inherited in 14 HENRY I. and was *s.* in 6 STEPHEN by

SIR JOHN DE WALWAYNE, father of

THOMAS DE WALWAYNE, who married the daughter of Leonard Hackluyt, of Marcle Magna, one of whose family bought the estate of Longeford, which was afterwards disposed of, but which his descendants by the female side repurchased. This marriage appears to have given the first establishment to the family in Herefordshire, and must have occurred, in all probability, early in RICHARD the First's reign. "By a French indenture, dated 7 RICHARD I. 1196, Thomas Fitznichol, knt. steward of Nichol de Stafford, did set to Thomas Walwayne, of Magna Marcley all the manor of Marcle which belonged to Monsr. N. De Stafford, for 18 marks *per ann.* except Halewode." The grandson of this Thomas,

SIR ELY OR HELIAS WALWAYNE, was the knight by whose activity and courage Lluellin, the bravest and last Prince of Wales, was taken and beheaded. "Being sent with a detachment by Sir Edmund Mortimer, he passed over a ford of the river Wye, fell upon Lluellin's troops and put them to flight, in consequence of which that prince was taken and slain." Sir Ely married Maud, daughter and heir of Sir Philip de Grandour, knt. the representative of a very ancient family, and had two sons,

RICHARD, his heir.

John, a clerk, who was one of the king's council and treasurer of the Exchequer 12 EDWARD II. a trust which he discharged with singular credit, as was attested by the king himself.

Sir Ely died in 1286, and was buried at the Hay, being the last of the family who resided at that place. His elder son and successor,

RICHARD WALWAYNE, OR WALEWEYNE, represented the county of Hereford in nine parliaments of the reign of EDWARD III. and served as high sheriff during seven successive years from 1336 to 1342. He *m.* Joan, daughter and heir of Walter de Helyon, of Helyon or Hellins, in Marcle Magna, by whom he acquired that estate, where he fixed his residence, and had a son and successor,

THOMAS WALWAYN, who was sheriff of Herefordshire in 1389 and 1392, and was appointed, in the ensuing year, inspector of the ports of London.* His name also appears as a witness to a deed between Thomas Tyler de Webbeley, Richard Nasch, and others, for release of lands in Longeford, Lugwardyn, and Hampton. He *m.* Catherine, daughter and heir of Sir John Grendon, knt. of Clearwell, in Gloucestershire, and was succeeded by his son,

RICHARD WALWAYN, who *m.* Catherine, daughter and heir of Ralph Bromwich, and was father of

THOMAS WALWAYN, esq. knight of the shire for Hereford in the 1, 5 and 6 of HENRY IV. who purchased the estate of Hagley, near Stourbridge, in Worcestershire, now in the possession of the Lyttleton family. "In the year 1411, 13 HENRY IV." says Nash, "Henry de Haggeley sold the manor and advowson of Haggeley, together with Cowbatch, to Thomas Walwyn, esq. who soon after alienated it to Jane Beauchamp, Lady Bergavenny." From that lady he soon after purchased the manor of Longford, which appears by her release to William Walwayn, his son (to whom he bequeathed that estate), to which her own seal is affixed. He *m.* Isabella, said to be a daughter of the ancient family of Baskerville, and had issue,

I. RICHARD, of Hellins, who *m.* Clementia, daughter and heir of Stephen Write, and acquired with her two parts of the manor of Sutton Frene, which had been purchased from Sir John Talbot, of Swaunton. In 8 HENRY V. this Richard Walwayn conveyed two parts of his manor of Marcley Audeley, or Great Marcley, in trust. He had, beside, the manors of Marden, King's Pawn, Billynsland Ruwarden, in Gloucestershire, Aylton, &c. and one hundred pounds in money for his inheritance. He was *s.* at his decease by his son,

THOMAS WALWAYN, esq. who *m.* Alice, daughter of Sir Leonard Hackluit, knt. and was direct ancestor of

THOMAS WALWAYN, esq. of Hellins, who *m.* Ann, dau.

* Rex concessit Thomæ Walwyn armigero suo officium scrutatoris in Portu Civit. Lond de consensu Consilii sui (*Turr. Lond. per Breve de private sigillo* 18 RICHARD II.)

of Sir Simon Milbourne, and was father of

Sir Richard Walwayn, knt. who *m.* Dorothy, daughter of Sir Thomas Laiton, knt. and was *s.* by his son,

Richard Walwayn, esq. of Hellins, 26 Elizabeth, who *m.* Catherine, dau. of George Parry, of Poston, and had a son and successor,

Ely Walwayn, esq. of Hellins, 40 Elizabeth, who *m.* Anne, daughter of Edward, second son of Sir Anthony Cooke, knt. of Gydy Hall, Essex, and was father of

Fulco Walwayn, esq. of Hellins, who *m.* Margaret, daughter of Sir Walter Pye, knt. and had issue,

John, his heir.

Brydget, married to — Dobyns, esq. and *d.* in 1698.

Frances, *d.* unm. in 1708, aged seventy-seven, and was buried in Hereford Cathedral. She was the last of the name of this branch of the family.

The son and successor,

John Walwayn, esq. of Hellins, living in 1686, wedded Mary, daughter of — Winnington, esq. and left at his decease, two daughters, his coheirs,

Margaret, *m.* to J. Noble, esq.

Frances, *m.* to John Shepherd, esq. and conveyed the estate of Dormington to her husband. She *d.* in 1705.

II. William, of whom presently.

III. Malcolm, who had lands in Ledbury, Eastnor, Catly and Farly, and is mentioned as knight of the shire by the name of Galveyn, in the parliament held at Reading, *temp.* Henry VI. He was likewise returned in the list of gentry the 12th of that king's reign.

I. Joan, *m.* to Hugh Folliot.

The second son,

William Walwayn, esq. took possession of the estate at Longford, according to the will of his father, during whose lifetime he served as sheriff for Herefordshire, in 1409, and of Gloucestershire the following year. He *m.* Jane, or Joan, daughter of Sir Robert Whytteney, knt. as appears by a power of attorney in their joint names to John Bayley and Philip Longeford, to take possession for them of the manors and estates of Longeford, Avenbury, and Butterley. He left two sons, William, who died unmarried, and

John Walwayn, esq. of Longeford, to which, and other estates, a person the name of Weldon having disputed the validity of his title, the affair was referred to the arbitration of four gentlemen of the county, Henry Oldecastell, Thomas Bromewicke, Thomas Fitzherry and Thomas Walweyne, probably of Stoke, and decided in favour of John Walwayne. He married Agnes, dau. and co-heir of Simon Milborne, and had nine sons and three daughters, of whom,

John, the eldest son, was his heir.

Thomas, the second son, succeeded his brother.

Fulco, the fifth son, living *temp.* Henry VIII. left a son,

Thomas, of Old Court, who *m.* Elizabeth, daughter of — Vaughan, and had six sons and two daughters, viz.

1. Thomas.
2. Alexander, of Old Court, who *m.* Ursula, daughter of John Scudamore, esq. of Hom Lacy, and had a numerous family.
3. Richard, who *m.* Margaret, daughter of John Hereford, esq. of Sufton, (see p. 345).
4. Nicholas.
5. Giles.
6. Edward.

1. Ursula, *m.* to — Bullock.
2. Elizabeth-Ann.

George, the eighth son, *m.* Ann, dau. of Simon Beaumont, esq. of Oxfordshire, and had,

Edward, of Southam, who *m.* Christiana, daughter of John Stratford, of Gloucestershire, and had issue.

Simon, *d. s. p.*

Bridget, *m.* to John Wheeler, esq.

Edward, the ninth son, *m.* Brina, dau. of — Bridges, of Hall Court, and had

John, of Coddington, 1669, *m.* Jocosa, daughter of John Rudhall, esq. of Rudhall.

Ann, *m.* to William Stratford, of Gloucestershire.

Elizabeth, *m.* to James Myntridge.

The eldest son,

JOHN WALWEYN, esq. of Longford, dying without issue, was succeeded by his brother,

THOMAS WALWEYN, esq. of Longford, who *m.* Eleanor, daughter and heir of John Vaughan, esq. and had two sons and one daughter, namely,

NICHOLAS, his heir.
John, who *d.* unmarried.

Eleanor, *m.* in 1560, to John Harper, esq.

The elder son and heir,

NICHOLAS WALWEYN, esq. of Longford, wedded Eleanor, daughter of John Lingen, esq. of Sutton, in Herefordshire, and had three sons, THOMAS, John and William, with four daughters, Sibilla, *m.* to Damory; Ann, *m.* to — Hewy; Joan; and Elizabeth, *m.* to Vaughan. Nicholas died in 1558, and was *s.* by his eldest son,

THOMAS WALWYN, esq. of Longford, who *m.* a daughter of Sir John ap Rees, and had issue, NICHOLAS, his heir; Thomas, *b.* in 1563; Richard; and Elizabeth. Mr. Walwyn died in 1580, and was *s.* by his son,

NICHOLAS WALWYN, esq. of Longford, *b.* in 1561, who was sheriff 25 ELIZABETH. He *m.* first, Margaret, daughter of — Price, esq. of Wistaston, and by her, who *d.* in 1610, had issue,

THOMAS, of Longford, who *m.* Milborough, daughter of Pryor, of Woolhope, and *d.* in 1658, leaving a son,
NICHOLAS, of Longford, *b.* in 1609, who married twice, and died in 1685, leaving issue.
RICHARD, of whom presently.
Giles, *d.* in 1618.

Nicholas Walwyn *m.* secondly, Mary, dau. of F. Braco, esq. of Rossedge, by whom he had issue, and *d.* in 1642: his second son,

RICHARD WALWYN, esq. of Ross, in the county of Hereford, *m.* Mary, daughter of John Berington, esq. of Cowarn Court, in the same shire, and had two sons,

JOHN, of Ross, twin with his brother James, *m.* Bridget, daughter of Thomas Brayne, esq. and *d.* in 1708, leaving Nicholas, who *d. s. p.* and Esther, *m.* to — Lovel.
JAMES, of whose line we have to treat.

The second son,

JAMES WALWYN, esq. of Longford, *m.* Ann, only daughter and heir of Sir William Bowyer, and by her, who died in 1691, left at his decease, in 1705, an only surviving son,

JAMES WALWYN, esq. of Longford, or Longworth, sheriff of Herefordshire in 1723, and M. P. for Hereford in 1732. He *m.* Anne, only daughter and heir of Richard Tayler, esq. and had issue,

RICHARD, who predeceased his father in 1750, leaving by Mary, his wife, dau. of the Rev. William Floyer, one son and four daughters, viz.
1. JAMES, successor to his grandfather.
1. Anne, *m.* to the Rev. Robert Foley.
2. Mary.
3. Susanna.
4. Martha.

Anne, *m.* to Morgan Graves, esq. of Mickleton, in Gloucestershire.
Mary, *d.* in 1729.
Martha, *d.* in 1734.

Mr. Walwyn *d.* in 1766, and was *s.* by his grandson,

JAMES WALWYN, esq. of Longworth, who was sheriff of Herefordshire in 1784, and M. P. for the city of Herefordshire in 1785-1790 and 1796. He *m.* Sarah, daughter of Thomas Phillipps, esq. of Eaton, and had issue,

JAMES, his heir.
Richard, *b.* in 1771, *m.* Caroline, third daughter of the Hon. and Rev. Henry Roper, son of the 8th Lord Teynham, and *d.* in 1822, leaving a son,
RICHARD-HENRY, *b.* 8th November, 1804.

Lucy, *m.* in 1797, to John Scudamore, esq. of Kentchurch, M. P. (see page 357).

Mr. Walwyn was succeeded by his eldest son, JAMES WALWYN, esq.

*Arms*—Quarterly; 1st and 4th, gu. a bend erm. WALWYN ancient; 2nd and 3rd, gu. a bend ermine in sinister: on a chief a talbot passant or, within a border of the second.

Quartering with many others,

| | |
|---|---|
| Hackluit, | Rees, of Wales, |
| Grandour, | Le Gros, |
| Hellins, | Solars, |
| Grendon, | Brugge, |
| Bromwich, | Pichard, |
| Milborne, | Sapie, |
| Eynsford, | Breynton, |
| Furnival, | Streaton, |
| Verdon, | Hergest, |
| Lovetot, | Blacket, |
| Baskerville, | Eynsworth, |
| Montgomery, | Vaughan, |
| Fitzwarine, | Bowyer, &c. &c. |

*Crest*—On an embattled wall, or upper part of a tower arg. masoned sa. a wyvern with wings expanded vert, scaled or, pierced through the head with a javelin, ppr.

*Mottoes*—Non deficit alter; and Drwy Rynwedd Gwaed.

# LANDOR, OF IPSLEY COURT.

LANDOR, WALTER-SAVAGE, esq. of Ipsley Court, in the county of Warwick, and of Lanthony Abbey, in Monmouthshire, *b.* in January, 1775, *m.* in May, 1811, Julia Thuillier, of Bath, a lady of Swiss extraction, and has

ARNOLD-SAVAGE.
Walter-Savage.
Charles-Savage.

Julia-Elizabeth-Savage.

This gentleman is known in the world of letters as the author of "Imaginary Conversations of Literary Men and Statesmen" and several other productions. He has long resided in Italy, chiefly on his estate at Fiescoli, near Florence.

## Lineage.

The Landors descend from the De la Laundes, a knightly race of Norman origin, who for a long period enjoyed large estates in the county of Lincoln, comprising the manors of Wispinton, Ywurdeby, and many others. They had also considerable possessions in Leicestershire, in which county is a village called Launde to this day: great part, however, of the Leicestershire estates passed, as Camden notices, by an heiress to the Berkeleys of Wymondham. In the middle ages, when lands could not be disposed of by will, vast estates were frequently conveyed by heiresses into the families of strangers: thus in the reign of EDWARD III. Sybilla, daughter of Sir John de la Launde, carried large estates in Warwickshire to her husband, Roger de Aston, progenitor of the Astons of Tixall; and Goditha, her sister, another daughter of Sir John, brought all her father's lands in Derbyshire, in marriage, to Sir Richard de Stathum (*Tower Rolls*, 51 EDWARD III.) The family of De la Launde continued to flourish in great opulence and esteem until the wars of the Roses; when, after having fought on the side of *King* HENRY, they were stripped of all their possessions by the victorious EDWARD, and never again restored to their former importance. This circumstance is recorded by one of the rolls in the Tower (15 EDWARD IV.), which states that "the king granted to Richard, Duke of Gloucester, in special tail, namely, to his heirs male all the manors and hereditaments (in several counties) which lately belonged to John, Earl of Oxford, and all the manors in the county of Lincoln and other counties which belonged to DE LA LAUNDE, Miles, (to be held) by the accustomed services." Upon the death of this Richard, Duke of Gloucester (then RICHARD III.) these estates were of course forfeited to HENRY VII. but the employer of Empson and Dudley has never been accused of one act of generosity or justice, and it is probable that a very small portion (if any) of the patrimony of the house of De la Launde was ever rescued from the rapacious grasp of the monarch.

In the reigns of HENRY VII. and HENRY VIII., when money becoming more abundant, the race of merchants grew into importance, and began a rivalry with the landed proprietors, it became the custom to drop the preposition which used to precede the name, and distinguished the man of birth, who was generally recognized by the place of his residence. In accordance with this custom, the family now before us, which had been settled in Staffordshire on the wreck of their fortunes, were designated indifferently LAUNDE and LAUNDER. In the reign of CHARLES I., JOHN LAUNDER, of Rugeley, was a captain in the royal army, while Michael Noble, the representative of an old Staffordshire family, which afterwards merged in those of LANDOR and COTTON, was the friend of Cromwell, and member for Lichfield during the long parliament. In the reign of CHARLES II. the name began to be spelt as it now appears, and under WILLIAM and MARY, WALTER LANDOR, esq. of Rugeley, was high sheriff for Staffordshire. The head of the family at the close of the seventeenth century,

ROBERT LANDOR, esq. of Rugeley, in Staffordshire, *b.* 6th June, 1680, *m.* Elizabeth, only daughter and heiress of the Rev. John Taylor, rector of Cotton, and dying 15th May, 1711, left a son and successor,

ROBERT LANDOR, esq. of Rugeley, who *m.* 4th May, 1732, Mary, daughter and coheir of Walter Noble, esq. of Longdon, in the county of Stafford, and by her, who died in 1798, left at his decease 23rd March, 1781, a son and successor,

WALTER LANDOR, esq. who *m.* first, in May, 1760, Mary, only child of Richard Wright, esq. of Warwick, and had by her an only daughter, Maria, *m.* to her cousin, Humphrey Arden, esq. He *m.* secondly, Elizabeth, one of the four daughters and co-heirs of Charles Savage, esq. of Tachbrook, in Warwickshire, and had by her

WALTER-SAVAGE, his heir.
Charles-Savage, in holy orders, rector of Cotton, in Staffordshire, *m.* in January, 1812, Catherine, only child of — Wilson, esq. of Marston Montgomery, Derbyshire, and has, with three daughters, one son,
 Charles-Wilson.
Henry-Eyres.
Robert-Eyres, in holy orders, rector of Birlingham, in Worcestershire.

Elizabeth-Savage.
Mary-Anne, *d.* unm.
Ellen.

The eldest son and heir is the present WALTER-SAVAGE LANDOR, esq. of Ipsley Court.

*Arms*—Arg. two bends gu. each surmounted with a cotice dancette or.

*Crest*—A dexter arm gu. banded with two cotices or, holding in the hand a fleur-de-lys arg.

*Estates*—Chiefly in the counties of Warwick and Monmouth.

*Seats*—Ipsley Court, in Warwickshire; and Lanthony Abbey, Monmouthshire.

# BENTLEY, OF BIRCH HOUSE.

BENTLEY, JOHN, esq. of Birch House, in the county of Lancaster, *b.* 11th April, 1797, succeeded his father, the late John Bentley, esq. 21st June, 1821, and is a magistrate for Lancashire.

## Lineage.

The Bentleys are an old Lancashire family, and their residence was for some centuries at Bentley Hall, near Bury.

JOHN BENTLEY, living about the middle of the 18th century, son of another John Bentley, esq. married Mary, daughter of — Craven, esq and had six children, JOHN, Richard, Thomas, Sarah, Mary and Lydia. The eldest son,

JOHN BENTLEY, esq. of Birch House, *m.* in 1793, Ellen, daughter of Richard Lomax, esq. of Harwood, near Bolton, aunt of the present Robert Lomax, esq. of Harwood, a magistrate for Lancashire, and dying 11th April, 1797, left an only surviving child, the present JOHN BENTLEY, esq. of Birch House.

*Arms*—On a bend sa. three wolves passant.

*Crest*—A wolf rampant ducally collared.

*Motto*—Benigno numine.

*Estates*—Farnworth, Manchester and Heaton Norris, in Lancashire, and in the neighbourhood of Stockport, Cheshire, acquired by purchase.

*Town Residence*—The Crescent, Salford, near Manchester.

*Seat*—Birch House, near Bolton

# PARKER, OF BROWSHOLME.

**PARKER, EDWARD**, esq. of Browsholme and Newton, both in the county of York, *b.* 18th July, 1786, *m.* 4th July, 1816, Ellen, only child of Ambrose William Barcroft, esq. of Noyna, in Lancashire, the last male heir of the Barcrofts of Barcroft, and has had issue,

AMBROSE-BARCROFT, an officer in the 64th regiment of Foot.
Thomas-Goulbourn, who takes the Browsholme Hall, and Alkincoats estates, under his uncle's will.
Edward.
Robert-John.
William-Barcroft, who died 1st December, 1830.
James-William, who died in September, 1832.
Septimus-Barcroft.

Elizabeth-Agatha.
Ellen-Barcroft.
Barbara-Phœbe.
Mary-Martha, *d.* 20th December, 1833.

Mr. Parker succeeded his brother, 22nd April, 1832.

## Lineage.

EDMUND PARKER, younger son of Parker of Horrockford, *anno* 19 HENRY VIII. *m.* Jennet, daughter and heir of — Redmaine, by Elizabeth, his wife, daughter and heir of Robert Parker, of Browsholme, in the forest of Bolland, Yorkshire, and had, with two daughters, Jenet, the wife of Thomas Sherborne, esq. of Ribleton, and Elizabeth, of Leonard Holme, of Grosenary, a son and successor,

ROBERT PARKER, esq. of Browsholme, living in 1591, who *m.* Elizabeth, daughter of Edmund Chadderton, of Nuthurst, father of William Chadderton, Lord Bishop of Lincoln, and had issue,

I. EDMUND, drowned at Cambridge, unmarried.
II. THOMAS, heir.
III. Roger, D.D. fourteen years precentor of Lincoln, elected dean thereof 29th November, 1613, and *d.* 29th August, 1629, aged seventy-one. His wife, Alice, daughter of — Pont, survived, and erected a monument to her husband's memory in the cathedral of Lincoln.
IV. William, of Blisland and Warligon, in Cornwall, D.D. archdeacon of Cornwall, living in 1620, *m.* Joan, daughter of — Panchard, of Wiltshire, and had two sons; the younger, William, rector of Stoark, in Cornwall, died unmarried; the elder,

James, *b.* in 1590, *m.* at Saltash 31st December, 1616, Katherine, eldest daughter of Sir — Buller, and left at his decease in 1680 a numerous family. One of his daughters,

Alice, *m.* in 1641, George Smith, of Warligon, and had two daughters, of whom

Mary, *m.* John Anstis, of Duloe, and was mother of JOHN ANSTIS, garter king at arms.

The eldest surviving son,

THOMAS PARKER, esq. of Browsholme, bow bearer of the forest of Bolland, in the Duchy of Lancaster, espoused Bridget, daughter and co-heir of James Tempest, of Rayne, in Craven, son of Leonard, third son of Roger Tempest, of Broughton, and had by her, who died in 1610, with numerous other children,* a son and successor,

* Of the daughters,

I. JENET, *m.* in August, 1612, Richard Carrier, of Wirksworth, some time fellow of St. John's College, Cambridge, and had a son, Robert Carrier, whose daughter,

JENET CARRIER, *m.* Sir Thomas Parker, Earl of Macclesfield.

II. ELIZABETH, *m.* James Carrier, of Helpston, for her second husband, and had a daughter, Bridget, who *m.* William Parker, esq. and was mother of GEORGE PARKER, esq. of Park Hill, in the county of Stafford.

EDWARD PARKER, esq. of Browsholme, *b.* 3rd August, 1602, who *m.* 28th January, 1629, Mary, daughter of Richard Sunderland, esq. of High Sunderland, in Yorkshire, by Mary, his wife, sixth daughter of Sir Richard Saltonstall, knt. lord mayor of London, and had by her, who *d.* 16th January, 1673, five sons and one daughter, viz.

THOMAS, his heir.

Robert, of Carlton, in Craven, and of Marley Hall, baptized at Waddington 23rd June, 1633, *m.* Jane, daughter of William Rookes, esq. of Roydes Hall (see p. 63), and *d. s. p.*

Edward, of Gray's Inn barrister-at-law, baptized at Waddington 1st May, 1636, *m.* a daughter of Boteler of Kirkland, in Lancashire.

Richard, baptized at Waddington 14th November, 1637.

Roger, baptized at Waddington 20th January, 1638, *m.* and had issue.

Mary, *b.* 17th May, 1641, *m.* to Thomas Heber, esq. of Holling Hall, Yorkshire.

Edward Parker† *d.* in 1667, was buried at Waddington, and succeeded by his son,

THOMAS PARKER, esq. of Browsholme, baptized at Waddington 1st May, 1631, who *m.* Margaret, fifth daughter of Radcliffe Ashton, esq. of Cuerdale, in Lancashire, brother of Sir Ralph Ashton, bart. of Whalley, and had issue,

I. EDWARD, of Browsholme, justice of the peace for Yorkshire, *b.* 1st January, 1658, *d.* 11th July, 1721, *m.* first, Catherine, daughter and heir of Henry Bouche, esq. of Ingleton Hall, and had by her a son,

THOMAS, of Browsholme, baptized at Waddington 17th October, 1689, *d. s. p.* in 1728, leaving his estates at Ingleton, &c. to his half brother John.

Mr. Edward Parker wedded, secondly, Jane, daughter of John Parker, esq. of Extwistle, in Lancashire (see vol. i. p. 116), and had by her several sons and daughters. The eldest son,

JOHN PARKER, esq. *b.* 11th June, 1695, succeeded his half brother at Browsholme, &c. and was bowbearer of the forest of Bolland. He *m.* Elizabeth, daughter of Henry Southouse, esq. of Manaden, in Essex, and dying 28th March, 1754, left, with an only daughter, Elizabeth, *m.* to her cousin, Robert Parker, esq. of Alkincoats, a son and successor,

EDWARD PARKER, esq. of Browsholme, bowbearer of the forest of Bolland, *b.* in 1730, *m.* at Lancaster in 1750, Barbara, daughter and co-heir of Sir William Fleming, bart. of Rydall Hall, in Westmoreland, and dying 22nd December, 1794, left an only son,

JOHN PARKER, esq. of Browsholme, bowbearer of the forest of Bolland, some time fellow commoner of Christ College, Cambridge, and M.P. for Clithero. He *m.* in 1778, Beatrix, daughter of Thomas Lister, esq. of Gisburne Park, and left at his decease in 1797, eight sons, viz.

THOMAS-LISTER, his heir.

Edward, *b.* 3rd November, 1780, *m.* in 1813, Isabella, daughter of the Rev. J. Strode, of Hatfield, Herts, and has issue.

John-Fleming, M.A. in holy orders, *b.* in 1782.

Charles-Robert, *b.* in 1783.

Henry, *b.* in 1784, *m.* in May, 1808, Anne, daughter of John Maclean, esq. of Galway, and has issue.

William, *b.* in 1785, vicar of Waddington.

Septimus, *b.* in 1788, *d.* in 1792.

---

† The following letters of protection, one from a notorious sequestrator, the other from a gallant royalist, show the state of the country during the civil wars.

"For the Col^s and Lieu. Col^s within Craven these.

"Noble Gentlemen, I could desire to move you in the behalfe of Mr. Edward Parker, of Broosome, that you would be pleased to take notice of his house, and give orders to the officers and souldiers of your regiments, that they plunder not, nor violently take away, any his goods, without your privities; for truly the proness of souldiers sometimes to comit some insolencies w^tout comand from their supiors is the cause of my writing at this time; hoping hereby, through your care, to prevent a future evill, in all thankfullness I shall acknowledge (besides the great obligation you putt on Mr. Parker) myself to bee

"Your much obliged

"RIC. SHUTTLEWORTH.

"Gawthorp, 13 Feby. 1644."

"These are to intreat all officers and souldiers of the Scottish armie, and to require all officers and souldiers of the English armie under my comaund, that they forbeare to take or trouble the pson of Edward Parker, of Brousholme, Esquire, or to plunder his goods, or anie other hurt or damage to doe unto him in his estate.

"THO. TYLDESLEY.

"This 8th day of August, Anno Dom. 1648."

Octavus, *b.* and *d.* in 1790.

The eldest son,

THOMAS-LISTER PARKER, esq. of Browsholme, bowbearer of the forest of Bolland, *b.* 27th September, 1779, is the present head of the family. In 1820 he sold to his cousin, Thomas Parker, esq. of Alkincoats, the mansion and estate of Browsholme.

II. ROBERT.

Thomas Parker, whose will bears date 7th July, 1695, was succeeded at his decease by his eldest son, Edward. His second son,

ROBERT PARKER, esq. born in 1662, purchased the estate of Alkincoats. He *m.* a daughter of Whitaker of Symerstone, and had three sons, viz.

THOMAS, his heir.

Robert, of London, who *m.* twice, and had issue.

Edward, died at Alkincoats.

Mr. Parker *d.* 10th November, 1714, and was *s.* by his eldest son,

THOMAS PARKER, esq. of Alkincoats, in the commission of the peace for the county of Lancaster, who *m.* Alice, widow of John Lonsdale, esq. of High Righley, and only child and heiress of John Blakey, esq. of Lanehead, the last descendant of the Blakeys of Blakey. By this lady he left at his decease a son and successor,

ROBERT PARKER, esq. of Alkincoats, formerly of Emanuel College, Cambridge, who *m.* his cousin Elizabeth, only daughter of John Parker, esq. of Browsholme, in Yorkshire, mentioned in her father's will 1753, and had issue,

THOMAS, his heir.

Robert, died unm. in 1805.

John-Toulson, who *m.* 19th July, 1804, Esther-Arthur, daughter of John Arthur Worsop, esq. of Howden, in Yorkshire, and had issue.

The eldest son,

THOMAS PARKER, esq. of Alkincoats, a magistrate and deputy-lieutenant for Lancashire, *m.* 4th May, 1778, Betty, only child and heiress of Edward Parker, esq. of Newton Hall, by Elizabeth, his wife, daughter and heiress of John Goulbourne, esq. of Manchester, and by her, who *d.* 8th November, 1808, had issue,

THOMAS, his heir.

EDWARD, successor to his brother.

Robert, lieutenant in the 76th regiment, *d.* unm. at Walcheren 2nd September, 1809.

John, *m.* Miss Ann Edmondson, of Coates Hall, Yorkshire, and *d.* 4th January, 1830.

Elizabeth, *m.* to Capt. Atherton.

Ellen, *d.* in December, 1800, aged ten.

Mr. Parker *d.* 27th April, 1819, and was *s.* by his son,

THOMAS PARKER, esq. of Alkincoats and Newton Hall, formerly captain in the Royal Horse Guards Blue, a magistrate for Lancashire and the West Riding of Yorkshire, and a deputy-lieutenant of the former, who purchased in 1820 from his cousin, Thomas-Lister Parker, esq. the estate of Browsholme. He *m.* Mary, daughter of William Molyneaux, esq. of Liverpool, but dying without issue 22nd April, 1832, was succeeded by his brother, the present EDWARD PARKER, esq. of Browsholme and Newton Hall.

*Arms*—Vert, a chev. between three stags heads caboshed or.

*Crest*—A stag trippant ppr.

*Motto*—Non fluctu nec flatu movetur.

*Estates*—Browsholme, Alkincoats, Newton, &c. &c.

*Seat*—Browsholme Hall, Yorkshire; a large house of red stone, with a centre, two wings, and a small façade in front, of that species which was peculiar to the reigns of ELIZABETH and JAMES I.

That the office of bowbearer was held by the family as early as 1591 appears from the following warrant, now remaining among their papers:—

"After my hartie comendacons. These shal be to will and require you to delyver, or cause to be delyved, to my verie good Lord, Will'm bushop of Chester, or to y[e] bearer hereof in his name, my fee stagge of this season to be had w[th]in her Maj[ties] forrest of Bowland; and this my lre shal be your sufficient warr't and discharge. Great Bartholomewes, this XXVIth of June, 1591.

"ANT' MILDWAYE.

"To y[e] M[r] of her Ma[ties] game within the forrest of Bowland; and to his deputie or Deputes there."

The fee stag appears to have been due to Sir Anthony Mildway as chancellor of the duchy.

# MACALESTER, OF LOUP AND KENNOX.

MACALESTER-SOMERVILLE, CHARLES, esq. of Kennox, in Ayrshire, *b.* 13th January, 1765, *m.* 28th March, 1792, Janet, daughter and heiress of William Somerville, esq. of Kennox, by Lilias, his wife, daughter and co-heir of Gabriel Porterfield, esq. of Hapland, and has

CHARLES, *m.* in 1828, Mary-Brabazon-Adeline, only child of the late Edward Lyon, esq. of Dublin, formerly an officer in the royal navy, by Anna-Catherine, his wife, daughter of George Frederick Wynstanley, esq. of Philipsburg, and has issue,

Charles.
Edward.

Anna-Catherine.
Janet.
Mary.

James.

Williamina.
Jane.

This gentleman, who is lieutenant-colonel-commandant of the 1st regiment of Ayrshire Local Militia, and a deputy-lieutenant, and justice of the peace, succeeded his father in 1796. His designation, as chief of the clan, is "The Macalester;" but, by the entail of the Kennox estate, the heir who succeeds to it is obliged to take the name and bear the arms of Somerville.

## Lineage.

The Macalesters of Loup are descended, according to some authorities, from Alexander, second son of Dovenaldus, filius Reginaldi, filius Somerledi, Thane of Argyll, who acquired the Western Isles by his marriage with Effrica, daughter of Olavus the Swarthy, King of Man, and granddaughter of Harald Harfager, King of Denmark, and is probably the same Alexander de Ergadia, one of the Scottish nobles who, in 1284, became bound to receive Margaret of Norway as their sovereign. Other pedigrees, however, deduce the Macalesters from Alexander, third son of John, Lord of the Isles, by his second wife, the Princess Margaret, daughter of ROBERT II. King of Scotland; and Buchanan, in his work upon Surnames, mentions the Loup family as the earliest branch of the Macdonalds. For centuries the Macalesters have maintained a leading position in the North, and the "Laird of Lowip" occurs in the "Roll of Landlordis and Baillies in the Hielands," published by authority of parliament *temp.* JAMES VI. *anno* 1587.

ALEXANDER MACALESTER, of Loup, chief of the clan at the close of the seventeenth century, married a daughter of Sir Robert Montgomerie, bart. of Skelmorlie, in Ayrshire, and had, with other issue, two sons,

GODFREY, his heir.

Duncan, who settled in Holland, where he married, in 1717, Johanna, daughter of Arnold Luchetemaker, burggraaf at Meurs, and his eldest son,

ROBERT, attained the rank of general in the Dutch service, and was commandant of the Scots Brigade. His descendants are still settled in Holland.

The eldest son,

GODFREY MACALESTER, of Loup, married Grace, daughter of Sir James Campbell, bart. of Auchinbreck, in Argyllshire, and had two sons, Hector, who *d. s. p.* and

CHARLES MACALESTER, of Loup, who *m.* a daughter of Lamont of Lamont, in Argyllshire, and had two sons, namely,

ANGUS, his heir.

Archibald, who for many years commanded the 35th regiment. He *m.* an English lady, and died a lieutenant-general, leaving a large family. His eldest son until recently was lieutenant-colonel of the Ceylon Rifle Regiment.

Macalester was succeeded by his elder son,

ANGUS MACALESTER, of Loup, who wedded, in 1764, his cousin Jane,* widow of John Dun, esq. daughter of John Macdonald, esq. of Ardnacross (brother to Macdonald of Kingsburgh, in Skye), by Grace, his wife, daughter of Godfrey Macalester, of Loup, and had issue,

CHARLES, his heir.

Joanna, *m.* to John Macalester, of Balinakill, in Argylleshire, and had three sons and two daughters: the eldest son is the present

ANGUS MACALESTER, of Balinakill.

Grace, *m.* to Alexander Alexander, of Carlung, in Ayrshire, late major of the 4th regiment of foot, and has two daughters and one son,

Archibald Alexander.

Macalester died in 1796, and was *s.* by his son, the present

CHARLES SOMERVILLE MACALESTER, of Loup and Kennox.

*Arms*—Quarterly: 1st, arg. a lion rampant gu. 2nd, or, an armed arm couped at the elbow fessways, the hand towards the dexter holding a cross crosslet fitchee gu. 4th, arg. a lymphad or ancient galley, sails furled and oars in action, sa. 3rd, vert, a fish radiant in fess arg.

*Crest*—A dexter arm in armour couped holding a dagger.

*Motto*—Per mare per terras.

*Estates*—Loup, in Argylleshire, and Ardpatrick House, the family mansion are part of the district of Kyntyre, which was bestowed by John, Lord of the Isles, on his second son, ALEXTER, or Alexander, ancestor of the Macalesters of Loup, and of the Alexanders of Menstril, afterwards Earls of Stirling. Ardpatrick was sold about thirty years since to Walter Campbell, esq. of Islay, and Loup soon afterwards passed by sale into the possession of another family of the name of Macalester, unconnected with the present. Since then Kennox has been the family seat.

*Seat*—Kennox.

* Jane Macdonald married John Dun in 1753, and had by him one son,

JOHN DUN-STEWART, *b.* in 1754, who *m.* first, a lady from Newfoundland; secondly, Miss Vans, daughter of Vans of Barnbarroch, by whom he had a son, Alexander Vans Dun; and thirdly, the daughter and heiress of Stewart of Tonderghie, in Wigtonshire, by whom he left, at his decease in 1821, a son, Major Hugh Dun-Stewart, and a daughter.

## Somerville, of Kennox.

The first Somerville of Kennox, in Lanarkshire, was a younger son of Sir William Somerville, bart. of Cambusnethan, in that county; he married a daughter of Inglis of Ingliston, and was succeeded by his son,

WILLIAM SOMERVILLE, of Kennox, who *m.* first, a daughter of Sir — Vere, of Blackwood, which lady *d.* without issue, and, secondly, a daughter of Sir Archibald Fleming, bart. of Ferme, by a daughter of Archibald Stewart, of Scotstoun, who was son to Sir Archibald Stewart, bart. of Blackball, by Margaret, daughter to Bryce Blair of that ilk. Mrs. Somerville's grandmother, Lady Fleming, was daughter to Colquhoun of Luss, and her great-grandmother, daughter to Stirling of Keir, in Stirlingshire. William Somerville was succeeded by his son,

JAMES SOMERVILLE, of Kennox, who disposed of that property, and purchased the barony of Bollingshaw, in Ayrshire, where he built a family residence, which he called Kennox, after his paternal inheritance; he married Janet,† eldest daughter and heiress of Alexander Montgomerie, of Assloss, in Ayrshire, by the only daughter of Alexander Montgomerie, of Kirktonholme, in Lanarkshire; her grandmother by the mother's side was daughter to Corbett of Tollcross, near Glasgow, and her great-grandmother daughter to John Hamilton, of Boghall; her grandmother by the father's side was daughter to William Wallace, of Skewalton, in Ayrshire, her great-grandmother daughter to Kincaid of Auchinreach, and her great-great-grandmother Dorothea, daughter to Robert, third Lord Sempill.

WILLIAM SOMERVILLE, of Kennox, succeeded his father in the year 1743. He *m.* Lilias, youngest daughter of Gabriel Porter-

† Her father, Alexander Montgomerie, of Assloss, was third son to George Montgomerie, of Broomlands, the direct representative of the Honorable William Montgomerie, fourth son to Hugh, first Earl of Eglinton. Montgomerie had four daughters,

I. JANET, above mentioned, who succeeded him in Assloss, which she afterwards disposed of.

II. Margaret, *m.* Forbes of Watertoun, in Aberdeenshire.

III. Penelope, *m.* Sir David Cunningham, bart. of Corsehill.

IV. Anne, *m.* Moir of Leckie, in Stirlingshire, was left the estate of Kirktonholme by the will of her uncle, Sir Walter Montgomerie, knt. and dying without issue, bequeathed it to her youngest sister's son, Captain Alexander Cunningham, of Corsehill, and it is now possessed by his son, Sir James Montgomerie Cunningham, bart. of Corsehill and Kirktonholme.

field, of Hapland,* in Ayrshire (Cadet of Porterfield of that ilk), by Elizabeth, dau. of William Cunninghame, of Craigends, in Renfrewshire, and his lady, Christian, dau. of Sir James Colqhoun, of Luss. Mr. Somerville *d.* in 1796, and was succeeded by his daughter,

JANET SOMERVILLE, the present proprietrix, who inherited from her mother in 1805, having previously married, in 1792, CHARLES MACALESTER, of Loup, in Argyllshire, chief of the clan, as mentioned in the account of that family.

* The last Porterfield of Hapland was killed by a fall from his horse about the year 1768, when his estate was divided among his three sisters as coheiresses; the eldest, Johanna, *m.* Thomas Trotter, of Mortonhall, in Mid-Lothian, the second, Margaret, *m.* John Hamilton, of Barr, in Renfrewshire, and the third, Lilias, *m.* Mr. Somerville.

## CROMPTON, OF MILFORD HOUSE.

CROMPTON, JOHN BELL, esq. of Milford House, in the county of Derby, *b.* 12th January, 1785, *m.* 8th September, 1810, Jane, third daughter of Edward Sacheverell Sitwell, esq. of Stainsby, and had a daughter,

JANE, *m.* 3rd July, 1834, to Lorenzo Kirkpatrick Hall, esq. nephew of J. K. Hall, esq. of Holly Bush, in Staffordshire, and died 28th January, 1835.

Mr. Crompton, who succeeded his father 20th May, 1834, is a magistrate and deputy lieutenant for the county of Derby.

### Lineage.

The first of this family who settled in Derbyshire was

*The Rev.* JOHN CROMPTON, M. A. of Emanuel College, Cambridge, born in 1611, of religious parents at Brightmet, a hamlet in the parish of Bolton, Lancashire. On his return from college, he was appointed lecturer to Dr. Wilmot, at All Hallows, in Derby, and acquired much respect as well for his piety as by his arduous exertions during a raging pestilence, which so desolated that town that grass literally grew in the market place. From Derby he removed to Brailsford, a sequestered living, five miles distant, where he gave the fifth of the whole profits to Mr. Greaves, his sequestered predecessor. He was a firm adherent of royalty, and during *King* CHARLES's exile was narrowly watched, though not molested, by those who were then in authority. On the rising of Sir George Booth, in Lancashire, and Colonel White, at Nottingham, to promote the king's return, Mr. Crompton proceeded, with his neighbours, to assist at Derby, but the project failing, he suffered for a period, several soldiers having been quartered in his house. At the Restoration he was obliged to give up his living to Mr. Edward Love, and removed to Arnold, a small vicarage near Nottingham, which the act of Uniformity soon after dispossessed him of. He died deeply regretted at Mapperley, 9th January, 1668-9, leaving issue. Of his sons, Samuel, a dissenting minister at Doncaster, *d.* in 1734, aged eighty-three, and another,

ABRAHAM CROMPTON, settled at Derby, where he was living in 1713. He died in 1734, leaving by Elizabeth, his wife, who died in 1690, three sons and a daughter, viz.

- SAMUEL.
- Abraham, of Chorley, in Lancashire.
- John, also of Chorley.
- Elizabeth, *m.* first, to Henry Coape, esq. of Duffield, and, secondly, to Samuel Hacker, esq.

The eldest son,

SAMUEL CROMPTON, esq. of Derby, an eminent banker, *m.* 3rd April, 1710, Anne, daughter of William Rodes, esq. of Long Houghton Hall, in the county of York, and had by her, who died 16th May, 1724, three sons and one daughter, viz.

SAMUEL, his heir.

John, of Derby.

Joshua, of Derby, who *m.* in 1758, the daughter and heiress of the Rev. Thomas Colthurst, presbyterian minister at Chester, and had issue,

Thomas, *d. s. p.* aged twenty-two.

Peter, M.D. of Liverpool, *m.* Mary, daughter of John Crompton, esq. of Chorley, and had issue.

Rebecca, buried at Duffield, 15 March, 1788, aged sixty-seven.

Mr. Crompton died in 1757, and was succeeded by his eldest son,

SAMUEL CROMPTON, esq. mayor of Derby, in 1758 and 1767, and in 1768 high sheriff of the county, for which he was during many years receiver-general. He *m.* at Osmaston, 8th May, 1744, Elizabeth, only daughter of Samuel Fox, esq. and by her, who died 29th April, 1789, aged seventy-one, had four sons and one daughter, viz.

I. SAMUEL, mayor of Derby in 1782 and 1788, who purchased from the co-heirs of Roger Gee, esq. of Bishop Burton, the estate of Woodend, in the county of York, where he afterwards resided. He *m.* in 1783, Sarah, daughter of Samuel Fox, esq. of Derby, and dying in 1810, left issue,

SAMUEL, of Woodend, M.P. *b.* in July, 1785, *m.* at Kippax, November, 1829, Isabella-Sophia, daughter of the Hon. and Rev. Archibald-Hamilton Cathcart, and has issue.

Sarah-Elizabeth, *m.* 22nd May, 1827, to Major Edward-Charles Winyates, of the Artillery, and *d.* 28th April, 1828.

II. JOHN, of whom presently.

III. Joshua, of York, who *m.* in 1786, Anne-Maria, daughter and co-heir of William Rookes, esq. of Roydes Hall, by Ann, his wife, sister and heiress of Robert Stansfield, esq. of Esholt, and had, with other issue (for whom see page 62), the present

WILLIAM-ROOKES CROMPTON-STANSFIELD, esq. of Esholt Hall, in the county of York, refer to page 59.

IV. Gilbert, also of York, *b.* in 1755, who *m.* Eliza, daughter of the Rev. George Johnson, rector of Loftus, in the North Riding of Yorkshire, and vicar of Norton, in the county of Durham, and had issue,

Samuel-Gilbert, in holy orders, *m.* Miss Down, and has issue.

George, captain 40th regiment, *d.* in the West Indies, January, 1815.

Robert, a naval officer.

William, lieutenant in the army.

Anne.

I. Elizabeth.

The second son,

JOHN CROMPTON, esq. of the Lilies, in the parish of Duffield, Derbyshire, served the office of mayor of Derby five times from 1792 to 1826, and during his mayoralty in 1810 was high sheriff of the county. He acted for a long time as receiver-general, and as a justice of the peace. He *m.* in 1784, Eliza, only daughter of Archibald Bell, esq. of Manchester, and by her, who died in March, 1807, and was buried at St. Werburgh's, Derby, had issue,

I. JOHN BELL, his heir.

II. Gilbert, of Durant Hall, Chesterfield, a magistrate and deputy lieutenant for the county of Derby, who *m.* in 1817, Deborah-Catharine, dau. of the Rev. George Bossley, vicar of Chesterfield, and has surviving issue, three sons and two daughters, all baptized at Chesterfield, viz.

John-Gilbert.

George.

Charles-William.

Deborah-Sarah.

Mary-Anne.

I. Elizabeth, *m.* in December, 1810, to Thomas Kirkpatrick Hall, esq. of Holly Bush, in Staffordshire.

II. Sarah-Maria, *m.* in October, 1827, to the Rev. Charles Robert Hope.

Mr. Crompton died in 1834, was buried at St. Werburgh's, in Derby, and was succeeded by his elder son, the present JOHN BELL CROMPTON, esq. of Milford House.

*Arms*—Vert, on a bend arg. double cotised erm. between two covered cups, or, a lion passant gu. on a chief az. three pheons or.

*Crest*—A demi-horse rampant, vulned in the breast by an arrow, or, shafted and feathered arg.

*Estates*—In the counties of Derby and Leicester.

*Seat*—Milford House.

# WOOD, OF HOLLIN HALL.

WOOD, HENRY-RICHARD, esq. of Hollin Hall, in the county of York, *b.* 1st February, 1786, *m.* 13th July, 1810, Anne-Eliza, fifth daughter of John Erkersall, esq. of Claverton House, near Bath, and has surviving issue,

FREDERICK-HENRY.
Boynton.
Richard-John.
Maria-Frances.

Mr. Wood, who is in the commission of the peace for the liberty of Ripon, succeeded his father 8th December, 1815.

## Lineage.

This family is descended from

GILES WOOD, of Pickering, in the county of York, living about the year 1500. He was father of

RICHARD WOOD, who married Izabel, daughter of Hugh Hilton, esq. of Slingsby, near Malton, and from him sprang

ANTHONY WOOD, of Copmanthorpe, in the ainsty of York, who married Agnes, daughter of Lawrence Trotter, esq. of the county of Durham, and was father of

JOHN WOOD, who married Dorothy, daughter of Sir Michael Wentworth, knt. of Woolley, by whom he had a family of eight children. The third son,

JOHN WOOD, was an alderman of the city of York. He married, and had a son and successor,

CHARLES WOOD, esq. who married Margaret, daughter of Henry Harrison, esq. and was father of

JOHN WOOD, esq. who was born in York in the year 1682. He married, in 1706, Frances Ingram, relict of Arthur Ingram, esq. of Barnaby, in the county of York, brother to Lord Viscount Irwin, and one of the daughters and co-heiresses of Dr. Nicholson, of the county of Durham. Mr. Wood died in 1757, and was buried in the family vault at Copmanthorpe, near York, leaving a son,

RICHARD WOOD, esq. born, in 1712, who married in 1745, Elizabeth, second daughter of Hutton Perkins, esq. of Mill Hill, in Middlesex, and had,

RICHARD, his heir.
Charles-Boynton.
Elizabeth.
Christiana-Frances.

The eldest son,

RICHARD WOOD, esq. of Hollin Hall, *m.* 3rd May, 1774, Delia, only daughter of John Schaak, esq. of Askham Bryan, near York, and had issue,

I. HENRY-RICHARD, his heir.
II. John, deceased.
III. Charles-Thomas, deceased.
IV. Richard, deceased.

I. Eliza.
II. Delia-Maria, *m.* to Hugh Blaydes, esq. of Ranby Hall, Notts.
III. Louisa-Frances.
IV. Emma-Juliana.

Mr. Wood *d.* 8th December, 1815, and was succeeded by his eldest son, the present HENRY-RICHARD WOOD, esq. of Hollin Hall.

*Arms*—Az. three woodmen ppr. each armed with a club over the right shoulder and a shield in front arg. crossed gu. head and waist encircled with a wreath vert, all standing on a ground ppr.

*Crest*—An oak tree ppr. charged with acorns or.

*Motto*—Pro patriâ.

*Estates*—At Copmanthorpe, near York; and at Hollin Hall, near Ripon. The former is the original family estate: the latter, to which they have transferred their residence, came to the Woods by purchase in or about the year 1719.

*Seat*—Hollin Hall, near Ripon.

## CHILD, OF BIGELLY HOUSE.

CHILD, JAMES-MARK, esq. of Bigelly House, in the county of Pembroke, *b.* 14th February, 1793, *m.* first, 29th May, 1816, Elizabeth, daughter and co-heiress of Richard Stedman Davies, esq. of Maesgwynne, in Carmarthenshire, and of Llangamarch, in Brecon, which lady *d.* 9th May, 1822, without issue. He *m.* secondly, 9th October, 1824, Emma-Elizabeth-Townshend, second daughter of Hugh Webb Bowen, esq. of Camrose House, and Lambston Hall, in Pembrokeshire, by Emma, his wife, daughter of Thomas Ince, esq. of Christelton, in Cheshire, and has by her an only son,

JAMES-MARK-PHILIPPS, *b.* 26th September, 1825.

This gentleman, who succeeded his father, 14th February, 1815, is senior captain in the Royal Pembroke regiment of Militia Rifle Corps, and a deputy lieutenant and magistrate for the counties of Carmarthen and Pembroke. Mr. Child claims, as heir male, the viscountcy of Castlemaine, and has taken the opinion of several eminent lawyers on the subject.

### Lineage.

JOHN CHILD, esq. stated to be the son of one of the sons of Lord Castlemaine, married Anne, third daughter of Richard Jordan, esq. of Pembrokeshire, and was father of

JAMES CHILD, esq. who *m.* 22nd March, 1721, the daughter of Thomas Langharne, esq. of Bigelly, in Pembrokeshire, and had a son and successor,

JAMES CHILD, esq. of Bigelly, who *m.* Margaret, daughter of the Rev. Theophilus Rhys, of the county of Carmarthen, and had four sons and two daughters, viz.

- JAMES, his heir.
- Charles, who died in the West Indies.
- William, who died young in the army.
- John, who died in infancy.

- Ann.
- Elizabeth, *m.* to Hugh Webb Bowen, esq. of Camrose.

Mr. Child was succeeded at his decease by his eldest son,

JAMES CHILD, esq. of Bigelly, who *m.* first, Maria-Philippa-Artemesia, daughter of Bulkeley Philipps, esq. of Pembroke, and niece of Sir John Philipps, bart. of Picton Castle, by whom he had an only daughter,

- MARIA-PHILIPPA-ARTEMESIA, *m.* to John Grant, esq. eldest son of the Rev. Moses Grant, rector of Nolton, Pembrokeshire, and was mother of the present SIR RICHARD BULKELEY PHILIPPS PHILIPPS, bart.

Mr. Child wedded, secondly, Sarah, third daughter of Mark Davis, esq. of North Wraxall, in Wiltshire, and of Bristol, a West India merchant, by whom he left at his decease 14th February, 1815, an only son, the present JAMES-MARK CHILD, esq. of Bigelly.

*Arms*—Gu. a chev. erm. between three eagles close.

*Crest*—An eagle with wings expanded arg. having its neck enveloped with a snake, its tail waved over his back, all ppr.

*Motto*—Imitari quam invidere.

*Estates*—In Pembrokeshire, &c.

*Seats*—Bigelly House and Bonville's Court.

# SCROPE, OF CASTLE COMBE.

SCROPE, WILLIAM, esq. of Castle Combe, Wilts, and of Cockerington, in Lincolnshire, *b.* in 1772, *m.* in 1793, Emma, sole daughter and heiress of Charles Long, esq. of Grittleton, in the county of Wilts, second son of Sir Robert Long, bart. of Draycot, M.P. for Wilts, by Emma, daughter and heiress of Richard, Earl Tylney, and has issue,

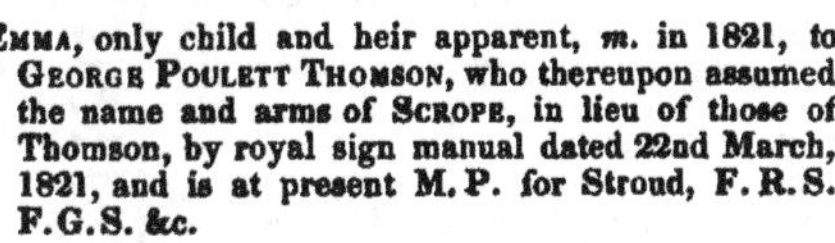

EMMA, only child and heir apparent, *m.* in 1821, to GEORGE POULETT THOMSON, who thereupon assumed the name and arms of SCROPE, in lieu of those of Thomson, by royal sign manual dated 22nd March, 1821, and is at present M.P. for Stroud, F.R.S. F.G.S. &c.

Mr. Scrope inherited the Wiltshire estates on the death of his father in 1787, and those of North and South Cockerington, &c. in Lincolnshire, in 1795, at the decease without issue of Mrs. Peart Scrope, only child of Mary, Countess of Deloraine, sister and heiress to Frederick Scrope, esq. of Cockerington, in virtue of the entail created in the will of the said Frederick Scrope, who died in 1780 *s. p.* the last of that branch of the Scrope family, which had settled in Lincolnshire at the close of the sixteenth century.

## Lineage.

The Scropes of Castle Combe descend in the direct male line from Sir Richard Le Scrope, knt. first BARON SCROPE OF BOLTON, lord high treasurer and chancellor to both *Kings* EDWARD III. and RICHARD II. We were therefore wrong on a former occasion in describing the Scropes of Danby as the only remaining branch of this ancient and eminent family.

Among the numerous baronial families which formerly possessed great influence in England, that of LE SCROPE or SCROPE stands conspicuous. Though some of their titles are now dormant, and others extinct, few persons were more distinguished in the fourteenth, fifteenth, and sixteenth centuries; and Shakespeare has given immortality to no less than three individuals of that name.* The house of Scrope was ennobled in two branches, SCROPE OF BOLTON and SCROPE OF MASHAM AND UPSAL, and its members shared the glory of all the great victories of the middle ages. An unbroken male descent from the Conquest, if not from the time of EDWARD THE CONFESSOR, and the emphatic declaration of the Earl of Arundel, given in 1386 as a witness in the celebrated controversy between Sir Richard Scrope and Sir Robert Grosvenor for the right of bearing the coat, AZURE, A BEND OR, as well as of numerous other deponents in that cause, that the representative of this family "was descended from noble and generous blood of gentry and ancient ancestry, who had always preserved their name and estate in dignity and honour,"† as well as their alliances and property, sufficiently attest their antiquity and importance; whilst the mere enumeration of the dignities which they attained between the reigns of EDWARD II. and CHARLES I. proves the high rank they enjoyed. In this period of three hundred years, the house of Scrope produced two earls and twenty barons, one chancellor, four treasurers, and two chief justices of England, one archbishop and two bishops, five knights of the Garter, and numerous bannerets, the highest military order in the days of chivalry.

RICHARD SCRUPE held various manors in Worcestershire, Herefordshire, and Shrop-

* See the plays of Richard II. Henry IV. and Henry V.

† See the depositions in Sir Harris Nicolas's splendid work on the Scrope and Grosvenor Controversy, p. 164.

shire, in the time of EDWARD THE CONFESSOR, as appears on the authority of Domesday Book, at the compilation of which they were possessed by his son,

OSBORN FITZ-RICHARD, or FITZ-SCROP, who in 1067, whilst WILLIAM THE CONQUEROR and the greater part of his nobles were in Normandy, assisted the castellan of Hereford in subduing the rebel Edric. It was most probably his son or grandson,

HUGH LE SCROPE, who is recorded as owing services to Gilbert de Gant, Earl of Lincoln, in 1149, for certain lands given to the Priory of Bridlington, in Yorkshire. His son,

ROBERT LE SCROPE, likewise granted lands to the same priory. He left issue two sons, Philip and Simon.

PHILIP LE SCROPE was employed in the 6 RICH. I. 1195, to render an account to the king of the revenues of the Archbishop of York. He left only two daughters, Alice and Maud, who both died without issue, and were succeeded in their inheritance by their uncle,

SIMON LE SCROPE, of Flotmanby, in the county of York. He was buried in the church at Wenslay, and was succeeded by his son,

HENRY LE SCROPE, who gave divers lands in Flotmanby, in the reign of *King* JOHN, to the Priory of Bridlington, the Abbey of St. Mary of Rivaulx, and other religious communities. He *m.* Julian, daughter of Roger Brune, of Thornton, and left a son,

WILLIAM LE SCROPE, living 39 HEN. III. 1254, who, as well as his father, was buried with his ancestors at Wenslay. His eldest son,

RICHARD LE SCROPE, who served against the Welsh in 1263, was succeeded by his brother,

SIR WILLIAM LE SCROPE, who possessed lands in Bolton, in Yorkshire, for which he obtained a grant of free warren in the 24 EDWARD I. 1296. Several deponents in the Scrope and Grosvenor Controversy report him to have been celebrated for his conduct in the field, and "the best knight of the whole country at jousts and tournaments." He left issue,

I. HENRY LE SCROPE, his heir.
II. Geoffry le Scrope, of Masham, knight banneret, and chief justice to both EDWARD II. and EDWARD III.; with the latter of whom he also served in a military capacity throughout his French and Scotch wars. He was likewise celebrated for his achievements in the lists of tournaments, and many interesting anecdotes are given concerning him by the deponents in the Scrope and Grosvenor Controversy. He was the progenitor of the line of the LORDS SCROPE OF MASHAM. (See BURKE'S *Extinct Peerage*).

SIR HENRY LE SCROPE, eldest son of Sir William le Scrope, became a judge of the Court of King's Bench in the 2 EDWARD II. He was a trier of petitions in the parliament which met at Lincoln in the 9 EDWARD II. 1316, and in the following year was made CHIEF JUSTICE OF HIS COURT, which high judicial office he filled for seven years. He was summoned to parliament throughout the greater part of the reign of EDWARD II. and was employed in various situations of high trust. On the accession of EDWARD III. he was re-appointed chief justice of the King's Bench, and subsequently made *chief baron of the Exchequer*. He obtained charters of free warren for his manors of Bolton and others in Yorkshire; and for his large benefactions was considered the founder of the wealthy Abbey of St. Agatha of Richmond. He died in 1336, and left issue by his wife, Margaret, daughter of Lord Roos,

I. WILLIAM LE SCROPE.
II. Stephen le Scrope, who *d. s. p.*
III. RICHARD LE SCROPE, who became heir to his brother William.

SIR WILLIAM LE SCROPE accompanied *King* EDWARD III. in several of his French and Scotch expeditions. He was at the battle of Vironfoss, in Picardy, in 1339, at the siege of Tournay in 1340, and at that of Vannes in 1342. He died of a wound received at the siege of Morlaix in 1344, and was buried in the Abbey of St. Agatha. He was succeeded by his brother,

SIR RICHARD SCROPE, first BARON SCROPE OF BOLTON, *b.* in 1328. This gallant soldier was knighted by EDWARD III. at the battle of Durham, where the Scotch were defeated, in 1346, and was present at the siege of Calais in the same year. Without attempting to follow this nobleman through all his martial exploits, which, however, stand recorded by their eye-witnesses, the several royal, noble, and knightly deponents in the celebrated controversy sustained by him with Sir Richard Grosvenor, for the right of bearing his family coat of arms, it is enough to say, that between 1346 and 1385, a period of forty years, there was scarcely a battle of note in England, France, Spain, or Scotland, where the English forces were engaged, in which Scrope did not gain honour. But as a *statesman* he was still more distinguished. He was lord high treasurer to EDWARD III. and twice lord chancellor of England in the reign of RICHARD II. by both which sovereigns he was intrusted with many other employments of honour and confidence. Walsingham states him to have been remarkable for his extraordinary wisdom and integrity, and records his firmness in refusing to put the great seal as chancellor to the profuse grants made by RICHARD II. to his favourites. When RICHARD, incensed at this, sent messenger after messenger to Scrope, "desiring him forthwith to return the great seal, he refused to deliver it to any other person than to the king himself." Lord Scrope was summoned to parliament continuously during the reigns of EDWARD III. and RICHARD II. and was a trier of petitions on many occasions. In 1385 he challenged the right of Sir Robert Grosvenor to bear the arms "Azure, a bend or;" and the memorable suit, instituted for the decision of this heraldic controversy, lasted upwards of four years, and was at length decided in his favour, Scrope having established by the evidence of a vast number of deponents, consisting of the most distinguished men of the day, from John of Gaunt, the king's uncle, to Chaucer the poet, who was then a squire at arms, that "his ancestors had continually borne the contested coat from the Conquest." Lord Scrope built the stately castle of Bolton, in Richmondshire, and died full of honours at the age of seventy-three, in the 4 HENRY IV. 1403. His name is among those of the peers who assented to the deposition of RICHARD II.; but his heir apparent, the Earl of Wilts, sacrificed his life in the service of that unfortunate sovereign; and his younger son, Sir Stephen Scrope, adhered to the dethroned monarch with admirable fidelity. Lord Scrope *m.* Blanch, daughter of Sir William de la Pole, by whom he had four sons,

I. SIR WILLIAM SCROPE, K.G. created EARL OF WILTSHIRE, and appointed *treasurer of England*, in the reign of RICHARD II., by which sovereign he was greatly esteemed, and employed in numerous important services. He purchased the *sovereignty of the Isle of Man* from the Earl of Salisbury; and in 1394, when the truce was confirmed with France, "*Guilliam* LE SCROP" is recorded to have assented to it "*pour le seigneurie de Man*," as one of the "allies" of the King of England. He is the person of whom Shakespeare makes the Lord Roos to say,

> "The Earl of Wiltshire hath the realm in farm." RICH. II. act 2, sc. 1.

On the invasion of Lancaster, the Earl of Wilts defended the castle of Bristol for the king, but was taken by the usurper's troops, and beheaded in 1399, in the lifetime of his father.

II. ROGER, second LORD SCROPE OF BOLTON, who succeeded his father in the title and estates, and was the continuator of the family of SCROPES, BARONS OF BOLTON.*

III. STEPHEN (Sir), of whom we have to treat.

The third son,

SIR STEPHEN SCROPE, Lord of Bentley, in the county of York, and of Castle Combe, in Wilts, was the lineal ancestor of the present owner of Castle Combe. This eminent person appears to have inherited much of the talent, valour, and integrity of his father, and to have almost equally distinguished himself both in a civil and military capacity. By RICHARD II. he was appointed lord justice of Ireland, and by HENRY IV. was made governor of Roxburgh Castle in 1400. In the next year he returned to Ireland as lord deputy to Thomas of Lancaster,

---

* The direct line of the LORDS SCROPE, BARONS OF BOLTON, terminated in the person of SIR EMANUEL SCROPE, eleventh baron, lord president of the king's council, 1619, and created Earl of Sunderland by Charles I. who dying *s. p. l.* the barony became extinct, or at least has remained unclaimed to the present day, though said to be vested in Charles Jones, esq. late captain in the 1st regt. Dragoon Guards (see BURKE's *Extinct and Dormant Peerage*). The immense estates of the Earl of Sunderland were divided between his three natural daughters, of whom the eldest,

I. Mary, *m.* Charles Powlett, sixth Marquis of Winchester, created first Duke of Bolton, from whom the estate of Bolton Castle and Bolton Hall has descended to the present William Orde Powlett, Baron Bolton (see *Peerage*).

II. *Lady* Annabella, *m.* John Grubham Howe, esq. She obtained the royal license June, 1663, to bear the title as if she had been legitimate. From her the present Earl Howe inherits his title and the estate of Langer, Notts.

III. Elizabeth, *m.* Thomas Savage, third Earl of Rivers, ancestor of the Earls of Rivers and Rochfort (see *Peerage*).

The Scropes of Spennithorne, Danby, and Cockerington (qu. vid.) branched off from the line of the Lords Scropes of Bolton, in the reign of HENRY VIII. through

JOHN SCROPE, esq. of Spennithorne, in the county of York, and of Hambledon, in the county of Bucks, second son of Sir Henry Scrope, sixth Baron Scrope of Bolton. He *m.* Phillis, daughter of Ralph Rokeby, esq. of Rokeby, in the county of York, and had, with other issue,

HENRY (afterwards of Spennithorne and Danby), who *m.* Margaret, daughter and heiress of Simon Conyers, of Danby (see pedigree of Scroope, of Danby).

RALPH (of Hambledon, Bucks), who *m.* Elizabeth, daughter of William Lord Windsor, and relict of Sir George Pawlett, knt. and had by her a son,

SIR ADRIAN SCROPE, knt. who settled at Cockerington, in the county of Lincoln, and was progenitor of the Scropes of Cockerington.

the king's son, and died at Tristrel Dermot in that country in 1408. He was faithful to his sovereign and benefactor, RICHARD II. to the last, and accompanying him to Conway Castle upon Lancaster's invasion, was present at the conference there between that usurper and the king, bearing the sword of state. He was likewise with *King* RICHARD on occasion of that melancholy scene in the castle of Flint, which is described with so much pathos by Shakespeare, and scarcely less so by contemporary historians. Shakespeare represents Percy as informing the Duke of Lancaster of the king's concealment in Flint Castle,

> "And with him Lord Aumerle, Lord Salisbury, *Sir Stephen Scroop*, besides a clergyman of holy reverence."
>
> RICH. II. act 2, sc. 4.

Sir Stephen Scrope married Milicent, daughter and co-heir of ROBERT, LORD TIPTOFT or TIBETOT, whose wardship, together with that of her two sisters, had been granted by EDWARD III. to his father, Lord Scrope of Bolton. By his marriage with this lady he obtained the manors and lordships of *Castle Combe*, in the county of Wilts, and Oxendon, in Gloucestershire, which had been held by his father, Sir Richard Scrope, from the year 1388, in right of his wards, and had descended to the Tiptofts from the BARONS BADLESMERE, whose representatives they were. Sir Stephen Scrope dying in 1408, was *s.* by his only son,

STEPHEN SCROPE, esq. of Castle Combe, who did not, however, enter into possession of his maternal estates until after the death of Lady Scrope's second husband, the celebrated SIR JOHN FASTOLF, K.G. by whom they were enjoyed (by the courtesy of England) for nearly fifty years. At length, at his death in 1460, Stephen Scrope, who was still alive, but at an advanced age, succeeded to the estates, and possessed them till his death in the year 1472. He was married to Jane, daughter of Sir John Bingham, knt. by whom he had one son,

SIR JOHN SCROPE of Castle Combe, knt. who, on his father's death, succeeded to the Wiltshire and Gloucestershire estates. He was high sheriff of Wilts in the 7th year of Henry VIII. and married, first, Isabel, daughter of John Newburgh, esq. by whom he had no issue, and secondly, Margaret, daughter of Sir John Wrottesley, of Wrottesley, in the county of Stafford, by whom he had

- RICHARD, his heir.
- Anthony, *d.* inf.
- Anne, *m.* to Heury Viner, of Castle Combe.
- Dorothy.

Sir John Scrope died in 1516, and was succeeded by his eldest son,

RICHARD SCROPE, esq. of Castle Combe, then but twelve years of age. This gentleman resided at Castle Combe all his life, and served the office of high sheriff of Wilts both in the last year of the reign of HENRY VIII. and the first of EDWARD VI. 1545-6, and in these reigns, as well as that of ELIZABETH, was frequently employed in the collection of the royal subsidies, aids, and benevolences. He twice paid a fine to discharge him from being made a knight of the Bath. He *m.* first, Mary, daughter of William Ludlow, of Hill Deverill, Wilts, by whom he had,

- Richard, who died in *v. p.* 1560.
- GEORGE, who succeeded his father.
- Edward, who *d. s. p.* 1568.
- Margaret, *m.* to Anthony Stokes, esq. of Stanshaw, in the county of Gloucester, *d.* 1571.
- Susannah, *m.* to John Snell, esq. of Kington St. Michaels, in the county of Wilts, *d.* 1570.
- Anne, *m.* to Thomas Harford, of Castle Combe, *d.* 1588.

Richard Scrope took for his second wife Alice, daughter of John Palmer, esq. by whom he had no issue, and dying in 1572, was *s.* by his eldest surviving son,

GEORGE SCROPE, esq. of Castle Combe, who *m.* Susannah, daughter of John Eyre, esq. of Woodhampton, in the county of Wilts, and had by her,

- JOHN, his heir.
- William, *b.* 1577, *d. s. p.*
- Elizabeth, *m.* to William Walsh, of the county of Gloucester.
- Mary, *d. s. p.*

Richard Scrope died in 1604, and was *s.* by his eldest son,

JOHN SCROPE, esq. of Castle Combe, who *m.* Jane, daughter of John Brune, esq. of Rowner, in the county of Southampton, and Athelhampton, Dorset, by whom he had

- JOHN, who *m.* first, in 1625, Mary, daughter of John Hungerford, esq. of Cadnam, in Wiltshire, and by that lady had an only daughter, MARY, in giving birth to whom her mother died. He wedded, secondly, Helena, eldest daughter and co-heir of Sir Theobald Gorges, knt. of Ashley, also in Wilts, by Helen, relict of Thomas Parr, Marquess of Northampton, and had by that lady,
  - JOHN, *b.* in 1643, successor to his grandfather.
  - Gorges, *d.* unm.

  John Scrope died in 1645, a month only before his father.
- Elizabeth, *b.* 1598, *m.* William Hodges, esq. of Clifton, in the county of Gloucester.
- Mary, *d.* unmarried.

Frances, *m.* to Thomas Higgs, of Hoxton, in the county of Gloucester.
Anne, *b.* 1616, *m.* to Thomas Codrington, clerk, of Keynsham, in the co. of Somerset.
Susannah, *b.* 1618, married to Edward Flower, of London.

Mr. Scrope *d.* in 1645, and was *s.* by his grandson,

JOHN SCROPE, esq. of Castle Combe, third of the name in succession, who married on coming of age, in 1662, Anna, daughter of Charles Gore, esq. of Alderton, in the county of Wilts, and sister to the celebrated heraldic antiquary, Thomas Gore, and had by her

John, *b.* 1663, *d.* same year.
CHARLES, *b.* 2nd April, 1665, *m.* Agnes, daughter of Robert Codrington, esq. (who *d.* December, 1721), by whom he had issue, with others who *d. s. p.*
 GORGES, *b.* 3rd December, 1700, heir to his grandfather.
 Charles Scrope, esq. died 1st February, 1713, in the lifetime of his father.
Stephen, who *d.* unm.
John, *b.* 1667, *d. s. p.* 1732.

Anne, *b.* 1669, *d.* unm. 1735.
Lydia, *b.* 1670.

This lady dying in 1675, he espoused, secondly, Jane, daughter of William Nelson, esq. of Chaddleworth, in the county of Berks, and had

William, *b.* 1678, who *d.* inf.
RICHARD, *b.* in 1681, who *m.* Frances, daughter of Abraham Wright, esq. of London, and had issue,
 JOHN, D.D. vicar of Kington St. Michael's, and rector of Castle Combe, of whom presently as inheritor of Castle Combe.
 William, *d.* unm.
 RICHARD, successor to his elder brother.
 Charles, *d.* in infancy.

 Frances, *b.* 23rd April, 1724.
 Elizabeth, Anne, Agnes, Rachel, } *d.* unmarried.
 Richard *d.* in September, 1738.

He *d.* in February, 1714, and was *s.* by his grandson,

GORGES SCROPE, esq. of Castle Combe, then fourteen years of age. He *m.* Mary, daughter of — Hobbes, esq. and dying *s. p.* December, 1744, the estate of Castle Combe was held in virtue of his will by his widow, for the term of her life. On her decease in 1774, it reverted to

*The Rev.* JOHN SCROPE, D.D. (eldest son of Richard Scrope and Frances Wright), a distinguished divine and author of several works on divinity, who *d. s. p.* in 1777, and was *s.* by his brother,

*The Rev.* RICHARD SCROPE, D.D. who *m.* Anne, daughter of Edmund Lambert, of Boyton, esq. in the county of Wilts, and had

John, *d.* 1778, unm.
WILLIAM, present proprietor.

Harriett, *b.* 1770 (*d.* 1819) *m.* Walsh Porter, esq. of Wandsworth, in the county of Surrey, and had issue,
 Pierce Walsh Porter, *d.* unm. 1826.
 Endymion, *d.* inf.

 Harriett, *m.* to Michael Semper, esq. of Montserrat.
 Frances, *m.* to Sig. Le Pieraggi, of Corte (Corsica).
 Eleanor, *m.* to Robert Piggott, esq.
 Mary, living unm.

Dr. Scrope died 1787, and was *s.* by his only surviving son, the present WILLIAM SCROPE, esq. of Castle Combe and Cockerington.

*Arms*—Azure, a bend or.

Quarterings:

Tiptoft, Badlesmere, } both which baronies are in abeyance in this family (See BURKE's *Dormant Peerage.*)

| | |
|---|---|
| Chaworth, | Longespee, |
| Clare, | D'Evereux, |
| Gifford, | Ridlesford, |
| St. Hilary, | Gorges, |
| Consul, | Russell of Dirham, |
| Fitzhamon, | Moreville of Wraxall. |
| Marshal, | Newmarch, |
| Strongbow, | Oldhall, |
| Mac Morough, | Engloese. |
| Fitzmaurice, | |

*Crest*—Out of a ducal coronet, a plume of ostrich feathers. This crest was first assumed by the sons of Sir Richard Scrope, first Lord Scrope of Bolton, who as well as his ancestors, and the branch of Scropes, Barons of Masham, bore for a crest a *crab* issuing out of a ducal coronet.

*Motto*—Non hæc sed me.

*Estates*—The lordship and advowson of Castle Combe, and others in Wilts, the manors of N. and S. Cockerington, Alvingham, Somercotes, and others, in Lincolnshire.

*Seats*—Castle Combe, Wilts, and Cockerington Hall, near Louth, Lincolnshire.

# HORNBY, OF DALTON HALL.

HORNBY, EDMUND, esq. of Dalton Hall, in Westmoreland, *b.* 16th June, 1773, *m.* 23rd August, 1796, Lady Charlotte Stanley, daughter of Edward, twelfth Earl of Derby, and has one son,

EDMUND-GEORGE, late M.P. for Warrington, *m.* 30th January, 1827, Sarah, daughter of Thomas Yates, esq. of Irwell House, in Lancashire, first cousin to Sir Robert Peel, and has

Elizabeth-Sarah.
Lucy-Francesca.

Mr. Hornby, who succeeded his father 31st July, 1812, is a magistrate and deputy lieutenant, and was high sheriff for Lancashire in 1828.

## Lineage.

EDMUND HORNBY, esq. (son of Geoffrey Hornby, esq.) *b.* in October, 1728, married Margaret, second daughter of John Winckley, esq. and dying 29th September, 1766, was interred at Poulton at the south side of the altar, where a monument was erected to his memory by his son,

*The Rev.* GEOFFREY HORNBY, rector of Winwick, in Lancashire, who *m.* 25th April, 1772, Lucy, daughter of James, Lord Stanley, and sister of Edward, twelfth Earl of Derby, and by her, who *d.* in February, 1833, had

EDMUND, his heir.
James-John, in holy orders, rector of Winwick, *m.* first, Esther, youngest daughter and co-heir of Robert Vernon Atherton, esq. of Atherton, by Harriet, his wife, daughter and co-heir of Peter Legh, esq. of Lyme (see vol. ii. p. 688); and secondly, Katherine, daughter of — Boyle, esq.
Geoffrey, in holy orders, rector of Bury, Lancashire, *m.* the Hon. Georgiana Byng, sister of the late Lord Torrington, and has issue.
Phipps, captain in the royal navy, and commissioner of the hospital, &c. at Plymouth, *m.* Maria, daughter of General Burgoyne, and has issue.
George, in holy orders.
Charles, lieutenant-colonel in the Scots Fusileer Guards.
Lucy, *m.* to the Rev. H. W. Champneys, rector of Badsworth.
Charlotte, *m.* 30th June, 1798, to Edward, Lord Stanley, now Earl of Derby, and *d.* in 1817.
Georgiana.
Frances-Susannah.
Louisa.
Henrietta.

Mr. Hornby *d.* 31st July, 1812, and was *s.* by his eldest son, the present EDMUND HORNBY, esq. of Dalton Hall.

*Arms*—Or, a chev. between three bugle horns sa.

*Crest*—A bugle horn.

*Estates*—In Lancashire and Westmoreland.

*Seat*—Dalton Hall, near Burton.

# MILLER, OF RADWAY.

**MILLER, FIENNES-SANDERSON**, esq. of Radway, in the county of Warwick, a lieutenant-colonel in the army, and companion of the Bath, *b.* in 1783, *m.* in 1819, Georgiana-Sibella, fifth daughter of the Rev. Philip Story, of Lockington Hall, in Leicestershire, and has issue,

I. FIENNES-SANDERSON.
II. William-Sanderson.
III. Philip-Francis.
IV. Frederic.

I. Georgiana-Sibella.
II. Harriet-Martha.
III. Jane-Anne.

Colonel Miller, who is a magistrate and deputy-lieutenant for Warwickshire, succeeded his father in 1817. He was severely wounded at the Battle of Waterloo, whilst commanding the Enniskillen Dragoons.

Rambles round Edgehill

## Lineage.

The estate of Radway was purchased by the Miller family in 1712.

SANDERSON MILLER, esq. who married Mary Welchman, left one daughter and a son, his successor,

SANDERSON MILLER, esq. of Radway, who married Susanna, only daughter of Edward Trotman, esq. of Shelswell, in Oxfordshire, by Mary, his wife, daughter of Sir Thomas Filmer,* and had issue,

FIENNES-SANDERSON, his heir.
Charles-Sanderson, who *m.* Charlotte, third daughter of Captain Joseph Mead, R.N.

Susanna-Maria, *m.* to Walter Ruding, esq.
Mary, *m.* to the Rev. Thomas Chambers.
Hester, *m.* to her cousin, Fiennes Trotman, esq. of Shelswell and Siston.
Anna, *m.* to Francis Litchfield, esq.

The elder son and heir,

FIENNES-SANDERSON MILLER, esq. of Radway, married, in 1782, Henrietta, second daughter of Joseph Mead, esq. captain in the royal navy, and had

FIENNES-SANDERSON, his heir.
Edward, A.M. in holy orders, vicar of Radway and Ratley, in the county of Warwick, *m.* in 1824, Charlotte, second daughter of the Rev. C. S. Miller, vicar of Harlow, in Essex.

Mr. Miller died in 1817, and was *s.* by his son, the present FIENNES-SANDERSON MILLER, esq. of Radway.

*Arms*—Az. four mascles in cross or.

*Crest*—A demi-lion rampant az. with a mascle between his paws or.

*Estates*—In Warwickshire.

*Seat*—Radway.

* By Susanna, his wife, eldest sister and coheir of Laurence, fifth Viscount Say and Sele.

# LENIGAN, OF CASTLE FOGARTY.

LENIGAN, JAMES, esq. of Castle Fogarty, in the county of Tipperary, *m.* Ellen-Frances, daughter of John Evans, esq. and sister of William Evans, esq. late M. P. for Leominster, by whom he has two daughters, namely,

SARAH-ELLEN-HENRIETTA.
PENELOPE-ELIZABETH-MARIE.

Mr. Lenigan succeeded his father in 1825. He is a magistrate for the county of Tipperary.

## Lineage.

The ancient family of FOGARTY, now represented by the LENIGANS of Castle Fogarty, was of importance in Ireland antecedently to the descent of the English in the reign of Henry II. "That part of Ossory," says Gough, in his continuation of Camden, "which appertains to the county of Tipperary, has in the north the ancient Cantred of Eile ni Bhogartagh, containing the present baronies of Eliogarty and Kilnelongarty; the chiefs of which were the O'FOGARTYS, some of which still remain with considerable landed properties in their paternal country."

The chief of the Sept in 1583,

CONOHER NA SURY O'FOGARTA,* of Munroe, in the county of Tipperary, was father of

DONOUGH O'FOGARTY, who was slain in battle at Lateragh, his father then living, 26th November, 1583, and was the Donogh who married Ellen Purcell, of the ancient baronial family of Loghmoe, and lies buried in the Abbey of Holy Cross, to which he was a considerable benefactor. He was *s.* by his son,

DONALD O'FOGARTY, of Munroe, surnamed *Grany*, or the Ill-favored, whose son and heir,

* *Anglice*—CORNELIUS O'FOGARTY *of the Suir.*

DONOUGH O'FOGARTY, of Inchy O'Fogarty, Fishmoyne, and Bally Fogarty (now CASTLE FOGARTY) left two sons, viz.

- ROGER, his successor.
- William, of Fishmoyne, physician to his majesty *King* CHARLES II. who, under the charge of being concerned in the Meal Tub plot, was imprisoned in the Tower, and died there *s. p.* in 1665. This is the gentleman described in the Act of Settlement as Ensign William Fogarty, and who under that act is included amongst those exempted from confiscation. His will bears date in 1606.

The elder son and heir,

ROGER O'FOGARTY, of Inchy O'Fogarty, *m.* a daughter of Cashuy, and was *s.* by his son,

TEIGE, or TIMOTHY O'FOGARTY, of Bally Fogarty, &c. who *m.* Margaret, daughter of Burke, of Barrycurry (of the family of Lord Brittas), and had issue,

- CORNELIUS, his heir.
- Thomas, *m.* Anne, daughter of James Magrath, esq. of Derrymore, and had a son, Magrath Fogerty, who was father of Thomas Fogerty, and grandfather of Magrath Fogerty, esq. of Ballinlonty, and of Philip Fogerty, esq. barrister-at-law.
- John.
- Dyonisius, a priest.
- Malachy, doctor of the Sorbonne, and prefect of the College of Lombard in Paris, *anno* 1705.

The eldest son and heir,

CORNELIUS FOGARTY, esq. of Castle Fogarty, *b.* 14th May, 1661, captain in the army of *King* JAMES II. *m.* in 1696, Mary, daughter of Michael Kearney, esq. of Milestoun, in the county of Tipperary, and dying in 1730, was *s.* by his son,

TEIGE, or TIMOTHY FOGARTY, esq. of Castle Fogarty, who *d. s. p.* at the age of fifty, in 1747, and was *s.* by his brother,

THOMAS FOGARTY, esq. of Castle Fogarty, who wedded Christian, daughter and eventual heir of James Meyler, esq. of Sally-mount, in the county of Kildare, and had issue,

- JAMES, his heir.
- Thomas, captain in the regiment of Uttonia, in the Spanish service, died unm. in 1781.
- ELIZABETH, *m.* to WILLIAM LANIGAN, esq. of Zoar, in the county of Kilkenny, and by him, who *d.* 23rd November, 1768, left an only son,
  - THOMAS LENIGAN.

Mr. Fogarty died in 1758, and was *s.* by his elder son,

JAMES FOGARTY, esq. of Castle Fogarty, who having conformed to the Established Church, served the office of high sheriff for the county of Tipperary in 1783. He died unm. in 1788, when his sister, ELIZABETH LANIGAN, became his heir, and the estates passed through her to her only son,

THOMAS LENIGAN, esq. who thus became "of Castle Fogarty" (see family of LANIGAN, at foot). This gentleman *m.* first, in 1794, Peniel, daughter of Edmund Armstrong, esq. of Buncraggy, in the county of Clare (by his wife, Hannah, sister of Robert Henry Westropp, esq.) and had issue,

- JAMES, his successor.
- Edmund.
- Anna, *m.* to John Dennis Ryan, esq. lieutenant 13th Dragoons, second surviving son of the late George Ryan, esq. of Inch, in the county of Tipperary, and has four sons and four daughters, viz.
  - George-Adolphus Ryan.
  - Lionel-Thomas Ryan.
  - John-Vivian Ryan.
  - Valentine Ryan.
  - Penelope-Maria Ryan.
  - Annette-Elizabeth Ryan.
  - Emma-Henrietta Ryan.
  - Marian Ryan.
- Elizabeth.
- Henrietta.

Mr. Lenigan wedded, secondly, Clarinda, daughter of John O'Reilly, esq. of Mount Street, in the city of Dublin, and had by that lady two other daughters, viz.

- Mary, a nun.
- Rosetta.

He died 2nd August, 1825, and was *s.* by his elder son, JAMES LENIGAN, esq. now of Castle Fogarty.

## Family of Lanigan.

The name of LANIGAN, or LENIGAN, formerly LANGADEEN, or LLANAGHAN, is Welsh, the family having been originally of Llanaghan, in the county of Brecon, to which place it gave its designation. It has been settled, however, from an early period in Ireland.

WILLIAM LANIGAN, the first upon record, was father of

JOHN LANIGAN, whose son,

WILLIAM LANIGAN, *m.* first, Miss Grace, of Kilkenny, by whom he had issue, and, secondly, Mary, daughter of Charles Gore, esq. of Goreyhiggen, sixth son of Sir Paul Gore, bart. by whom he had two sons and a daughter, namely,

- VALENTINE, who conformed to the Established religion, and was *s.* by his eldest son,
  - WILLIAM, who *m.* Rebecca, daughter of Henry Briscoe, esq. and was *s.* by his eldest son,
    - JOHN, who assumed the surname of STAUNARD, in consequence of inheriting a property under the will of an English gentleman of that name, not a relation. He was *s.* by his son,
      - JOHN STAUNARD, esq. of Grange, whose son is JOHN STAUNARD, esq. now of Grange.
- GEORGE, of whom presently.
- Catharine, *m.* to John Maher, esq.

The second son,

GEORGE LANIGAN, esq. of Zoar, in the county of Kilkenny, *m.* Mabell, third dau. of Edmond Shee, esq. of Cloran, in Tipperary (by his wife, Catherine,* daughter of O'Dwyer of Dundrum), and had issue,

- WILLIAM, his successor.
- Redmond.
- Catherine, *m.* to Edward Kavanagh, esq. of Ross.
- Margaret.

Mr. Lanigan was *s.* by his elder son,

WILLIAM LANIGAN, esq. of Zoar, who, as above stated, *m.* ELIZABETH FOGARTY, only daughter of Thomas Fogarty, esq. and heiress of her brother, JAMES FOGARTY, esq. of CASTLE FOGARTY.

*Arms*—Quarterly; 1st, az. on a pallet arg. three trefoils in pale vert, between two lions rampant, or, each between three fleurs-de-lys, two and one arg. for LENIGAN. 2nd, az. in chief, two lions rampant, supporting a garb, all or, in the dexter base, a crescent, and in the sinister an Irish harp or, stringed arg. for FOGARTY, *ancient*. 3rd, vert, a fess arg. between three garbs, two and one, or, for FOGARTY, *modern*.

*Estates*—In the Barony of Eliogarty, in the county of Tipperary, possessed by the family of Fogarty before the time of STRONGBOW.

*Seat*—Castle Fogarty.

* This lady's sister, Margaret, *m.* Sir John Morres, bart. of Knockagh.

# WYBERGH, OF CLIFTON HALL.

WYBERGH, WILLIAM, esq. of Clifton Hall, in the county of Westmoreland, *b.* 24th July, 1787, succeeded his father 10th September, 1827. Mr. Wybergh is in the commission of the peace for the counties of Cumberland and Westmoreland.

## Lineage.

This is a very ancient family, and has possessed the Clifton estate in an unbroken male descent since the time of EDWARD III. in the 38th of whose reign,

WILLIAM DE WYBERGH, of St. Bees, married Eleanor, only daughter and heiress of Gilbert de Engayne, of Clifton Hall, in Westmoreland, and thus acquired that manor and lands, which had been granted by Sir Hugh de Morville to Gilbert Engaine and his heir about the time of HENRY II. The son and heir of this marriage,

THOMAS DE WYBERGH, of Clifton Hall, wedded a daughter of Lowther of Haulton, in Northumberland, and was father of

THOMAS WYBERGH, of Clifton Hall, who, in the 17 EDWARD IV. on his son William's marriage, settled on the issue of that alliance a tenement in Clifton, then in the possession of Thomas Raper, one acre of land in Clifton called *Drengage* acre, and one parcel of demesne land there. He *m.* a daughter of Sandford of Howgill Castle, in Westmoreland, and dying 19 HENRY VII. left a son and successor,

WILLIAM WYBERGH, of Clifton Hall, living 5 HENRY VIII. who *m.* Margaret, daughter of John Wharton, of Kirkby Thore, in Westmoreland, and was *s.* by his son,

THOMAS WYBERGH, of Clifton Hall, living 18 HENRY VIII. father, by Elizabeth, his wife, daughter of Geoffrey Lancaster, of Crake Trees, of

THOMAS WYBERGH, esq. of Clifton Hall, who *m.* Anne, daughter of Sir Hugh Lowther, knt. of Lowther, by Dorothy, his wife, daughter of Henry, Lord Clifford, and had issue,

- I. THOMAS, his heir.
- II. Richard.
- III. Geoffrey.
- IV. Gerrard.

- I. Ann, *m.* to Cresswell, of Cresswell, in Northumberland.
- II. Elizabeth.

The eldest son,

THOMAS WYBERGH, esq. of Clifton Hall, espoused in October, 1586, Anne, the Dowager Dacre of St. Bees, sister or niece of the celebrated Archbishop Grindall, and dying in 1623 left two sons, THOMAS and Edmund. The younger died in 1661; the elder,

THOMAS WYBERGH, esq. of Clifton Hall, *m.* Matilda, daughter of Christopher Irton, esq. of Irton, in Cumberland, and by her, who died in 1663, had issue,

- I. THOMAS, his heir.
- II. Richard, *b.* in 1629, *d.* in 1648.
- III. Christopher, *b.* in 1630.
- IV. William, *b.* in 1631.
- V. Redman, *b.* in 1633.
- VI. John, *b.* in 1637, and *d.* in 1710.
- VII. Anthony, *b.* in 1638, who *m.* in 1664, Agnes, daughter of Thomas Brougham, esq. of Scales Hall.

- I. Ann, *b.* in 1626.
- II. Eleanor, *b.* in 1627, *m.* first, in 1645, to Sir John Nisbet, of West Nisbet, in Scotland; and secondly, to Swinton of Elbroke, one of the lords of session, by whom she had several children.

Thomas Wybergh *d.* in 1646, and was *s.* by his eldest son,

THOMAS WYBERGH, esq. of Clifton Hall, *b.* in 1628, who suffered severely during the civil wars, and was in the list of delinquents (as they were styled), whose estates were ordered to be sold by an ordinance of CROMWELL's parliament in 1652. The manor of Clifton was mortgaged to Sir John Lowther, and never afterwards redeemed, but the hall and demesne still remain with the Wyberghs. Mr. Wybergh *m.* in 1657, Mary, daughter of Thomas Salkeld, esq. of

Brayton, in Cumberland, and was succeeded by his son,

THOMAS WYBERGH, esq. of Clifton Hall, *b.* in 1663, who *m.* in 1683, Mary, second daughter of Lancelot Simpson, esq. of Penrith, and had by her (who died in 1749, aged eighty-four,) three sons and three daughters, viz.

I. THOMAS, his heir.
II. Robert, *b.* in 1690, *d.* in 1728.
III. William, *b.* in 1702.

I. Mary, *b.* in 1686, *m.* in 1711, to Philip Thirlwell, esq. of Temnon, in the parish of Denton.
II. Elizabeth, *d.* an infant in 1687.
III. Isabella, *b.* in 1689, *m.* in 1716, to Henry Morton, esq. of Bewcastle.

Mr. Wybergh, during the rising of 1715, was taken prisoner by the insurgents, and was exchanged for Allen Ascough, esq.

The following is a copy of the paper he delivered upon that occasion to the Earl of Derwentwater:

"Whereas I, Thomas Wybergh, being a prisoner under the Hon. Gen. Forster, have leave given to me to go to Carlisle, in Cumberland, upon parole, to get Allen Ascough, esq. released, he being now a prisoner there. I therefore, the said Thomas Wybergh, do hereby solemnly promise and declare in my conscience upon the faith of a Christian, that in case I shall not get the said Mr. Ascough released and exchanged for me, that I will within the space of 20 days return to the said General Forster's army, and continue his prisoner during his pleasure.

"Witness my hand at Preston, this 10th day of Nov. 1715."

Mr. Wybergh *d.* in 1738, and was *s.* by his son,

THOMAS WYBERGH, esq. of Clifton Hall, *b.* in 1685, who *m.* in 1713, Mary, only child of Christopher Hilton, esq. of Burton and Ormside, in Westmoreland, and by her, who *d.* in 1759, had issue,

I. WILLIAM, his heir.
II. Cyprian, *b.* in 1716, *d.* in 1726.
III. Thomas, *b.* in 1718, *d.* in 1726.
IV. Hilton-Christopher, *b.* in 1720, *d.* in 1747. He was a lieutenant in the royal navy, and was blown up in the Dartmouth man of war while engaging the Glorioso, a Spanish ship of greater force, off Cape St. Vincent.
V. John, *b.* in 1721, *d.* in 1726.

I. Mary, *b.* in 1713, *d.* in 1728.
II. Abigail, *b.* in 1715, *d.* in 1717.
III. Eleanor, *b.* in 1723, *m.* in 1757, to Captain Anthony Sharp, of Penrith.
IV. Elizabeth, *b.* in 1724, *d.* in 1740.
V. Dorothy, *b.* in 1728, *d.* in 1730.
VI. Susanna, *b.* in 1729, *d.* in 1738.
VII. Mary, *b.* in 1730, *m.* to J. Beatty, esq. of London.
VIII. Ann, *b.* in 1731, *m.* in 1751, to William Shaw, esq. of Appleby.
IX. Barbara, *b.* in 1732, *m.* to W. Docker, esq. of Penrith.
X. Matilda, *b.* in 1734, *m.* to Peter Brougham, esq. of Penrith, major in the East India Company's service, son of Thomas Brougham, who was the eldest son of Dudley Brougham, who died in 1736, and was descended from Christopher Brougham, who married in 1527 a daughter of Dudley of Yanweth, and was an ancestor of Lord Brougham and Vaux.
XI. Catharine, *b.* in 1735, *d.* in 1738.
XII. Frances, *b.* in 1736.
XIII. Isabel, *b.* in 1738, *m.* to William Bateman, esq. of Penrith.
XIV. Margaret, *b.* in 1740.

During the lifetime of this Thomas Wybergh Clifton Hall was plundered on the 17th and 18th December, 1745, by the insurgents, insomuch that the family is supposed to have sustained more loss than any in the country.

The following orders were sent to Clifton Hall by the rebel army.

"Penrith, Nov. 8, 1745.

"These are ordering you, Squire Waybridge, of Cliftoun, to send immediately to the Town House, one thousand stone of hay, fifty bushels of oats, and six carts of straw, for the use of his Royal Highness the Prince of Wales' army, under the pain of military execution.

"W. COMRIE, Comm.

"To Squire Waybridge or any of his Doers."

A similar order on the 17th December, 1745, for 600 stone of hay, 200 bushels of oats, and 8 carts of straw, for the use of Prince Charles' army.

Mr. Wybergh *d.* in 1753, and was *s.* by his eldest son,

WILLIAM WYBERGH, esq. of Clifton Hall, *b.* in 1726, who *m.* in 1754, Mary, youngest daughter of Thomas Crakeplace, esq. of Brigham, in Cumberland, and by her, who died in 1758, left at his decease in 1757 (with a daughter, Margaret, who *m.* in 1786, Rev. Peter How, rector of Workington, and *d.* in 1831), a son and successor,

THOMAS WYBERGH, esq. of Clifton Hall, *b.* in 1757, who *m.* in 1786, Isabella, eldest daughter of John Hartley, esq. of Whitehaven, and had issue,

I. WILLIAM, his heir.
II. Thomas, *b.* in 1788, who assumed the surname of Lawson on the death of his uncle, Sir Wilfrid Lawson, bart. of Brayton, in 1806. He *d.* himself in 1812.
III. John, *b.* in 1789.

IV. Charles, *b.* in 1791, *d.* in 1792.
V. Milham, *b.* in 1792, *d.* in 1793.
VI. Peter, *b.* in 1794, married Jane, daughter of the late A. Tod, esq. of Drygrange, in Roxburghshire, and has issue,
1. William.
2. Archibald.
1. Eliza-Caroline.
2. Annabella.

VII. Wilfrid, *b.* in 1795, who took the name of Lawson on the death of his brother in 1812, and was created a BARONET in 1832. (See BURKE'S *Peerage and Baronetage.*)
VIII. Christopher-Hilton, vicar of Isell and Bromfield, in Cumberland, *b.* in 1799, *m.* Anna-Maria, daughter of the Rev. F. Minshull, and grand-daughter of Dr. Goodenough, late Bishop of Carlisle, and has issue,
1. Thomas.
2. Francis.
3. Christopher.
1. Isabella.
2. Harriet.

IX. James, *b.* in 1802.
I. Elizabeth.
II. Mary.
III. Annabella, *d.* in 1822.

Mr. Wybergh died in 1827, and was *s.* by his eldest son, the present WILLIAM WYBERGH, esq. of Clifton Hall.

*Arms*—Or, three bars, and in chief three estoiles sa.; quartering ENGAYNE, gu. and a fess indented between six cross crosslets or; and HILTON, sa. three annulets in base, two and one, and two saltiers in chief arg.

*Crest*—A griffin's head erased or.

*Motto*—Hominem te esse memento.

*Estates*—In Cumberland and Westmoreland.

*Seat*—Clifton Hall.

## Family of Hilton.

Soon after the time of HENRY VIII. the manor of Burton, in Westmoreland, came into the family of HILTON, probably in marriage with the heiress of BURTON, whose arms were *arg. a bend wavy sa.* During the reigns of the early Plantagenets, the Hiltons occur frequently in the public records, and at various periods represented the borough of Appleby in parliament. A very imperfect pedigree certified at Dugdale's Visitation in 1664, commences with

CHRISTOPHER HILTON, esq. of Burton, living *temp.* EDWARD IV. who *m.* Margaret, daughter of Thomas Marshall, of Kirk Oswald, and was father of

RICHARD* HILTON, esq. of Burton, who *m.* Isabel, daughter of John Barton, esq. of Ormeshead, and was succeeded by his son,

ANDREW HILTON, esq. of Burton, who wedded Alice, daughter of John Aglionby, of Carlisle, and had issue,

JOHN, his heir.
Winifred, *m.* to Leonard Musgrave, of Johnby, in Cumberland.
Julian, *m.* first, to an Irish nobleman; and secondly, to a sea captain.

The son and successor,

JOHN HILTON, esq. of Burton, married Mary, daughter and co-heir of — Saxton, esq. of Byham Hall, in Essex, and had three sons, CYPRIAN, his heir; George, who *m.* Jane, daughter and co-heir of Fletcher of Dovenby; and John, who *d.* unmarried. He *d.* himself in 1630, and was *s.* by his son,

CYPRIAN HILTON, esq. of Burton, who *m.* Frances, daughter of Sir Christopher Pickering, of Ormeshead, by whom he acquired that manor, and had issue,

CHRISTOPHER, his heir.
John, of Stanemore, who *m.* Isabel, daughter of John Farer, of Warcop Tower.
Andrew, who *d. s. p.*
Mary, *m.* to William Farer, of Warcop Tower.

Cyprian Hilton died in 1649, and was *s.* by his son,

CHRISTOPHER HILTON, esq. of Burton and Ormeshead, aged thirty-six at the visitation above alluded to. He *m.* Barbara, daughter of Thomas Brathwaite, esq. of Warcop, and had a son and successor,

CYPRIAN HILTON, esq. of Burton and Ormeshead, who *m.* Abigail, only child of Hugh Wharton, esq. of a younger branch of the Whartons of Wharton Hall, and had nine children, Christopher, George, Hugh, John,† Margaret, Barbara, Elizabeth, Mary, and Abigail. He died in 1693, and was *s.* by his eldest son,

CHRISTOPHER HILTON, esq. of Burton, who *m.* Mary, daughter of John Pattenson, esq. of Penrith, and left at his decease an only daughter and heiress,

MARY HILTON, *m.* to THOMAS WYBERGH, esq. of Clifton Hall.

---

* Called in Sir Daniel Fleming's pedigree of the family THOMAS, and there stated to have married Anne Wharton, of Kirkby Thore. His father in the same document is named ROBERT, and married to a Hartley.

† This John had several sons, who died young, and seven daughters, the eldest of whom, MARY, married Daniel Robinson, esq. high sheriff of Westmoreland.

# INDEX

## TO THE THIRD VOLUME.

*** The capital letters refer to families—the small, to individuals.

END OF VOL. III.

C. Whittingham, Tooks Court, Chancery Lane.

CPSIA information can be obtained
at www.ICGtesting.com
Printed in the USA
BVHW062156170419
545790BV00008B/357/P

9 781297 499913